UNIX® AND LINUX® SYSTEM ADMINISTRATION HANDBOOK

FOURTH EDITION

UNIX® AND LINUX® SYSTEM ADMINISTRATION HANDBOOK

FOURTH EDITION

Evi Nemeth
Garth Snyder
Trent R. Hein
Ben Whaley

with Terry Morreale, Ned McClain,
Ron Jachim, David Schweikert, and Tobi Oetiker

Upper Saddle River, NJ • Boston • Indianapolis • San Francisco
New York • Toronto • Montreal • London • Munich • Paris • Madrid
Capetown • Sydney • Tokyo • Singapore • Mexico City

The publisher offers excellent discounts on this book when ordered in quantity for bulk purchases or special sales, which may include electronic versions and/or custom covers and content particular to your business, training goals, marketing focus, and branding interests. For more information, please contact:

U.S. Corporate and Government Sales
(800) 382-3419
corpsales@pearsontechgroup.com

For sales outside the United States, please contact International Sales (international@pearson.com).

Visit us on the Web: informit.com/ph

Library of Congress Cataloging-in-Publication Data

UNIX and Linux system administration handbook / Evi Nemeth ... [et al.].
—4th ed.
p. cm.
Rev. ed of: Unix system administration handbook, 3rd ed., 2001.
Includes index.
ISBN 978-0-13-148005-6 (pbk. : alk. paper)
1. Operating systems (Computers) 2. UNIX (Computer file) 3. Linux.
I. Nemeth, Evi. II. Unix system administration handbook.
QA76.76.O63N45 2010
005.4'32—dc22

2010018773

ISBN-13: 978-0-13-148005-6
ISBN-10: 0-13-148005-7

Text printed in the United States on recycled paper at Edwards Brothers Malloy in Ann Arbor, Michigan.

Fifth printing, April 2012

Table of Contents

Chapter 3 Booting and Shutting Down 77

Chapter 4 Access Control and Rootly Powers 103

CHAPTER 12 SOFTWARE INSTALLATION AND MANAGEMENT 362

SECTION TWO: NETWORKING

Chapter 28 Green IT 1097

Chapter 29 Performance Analysis 1112

CHAPTER 31 SERIAL DEVICES AND TERMINALS 1162

CHAPTER 32 MANAGEMENT, POLICY, AND POLITICS 1183

Foreword

Twenty-seven years ago, in 1983, I wrote what may have been the first system administrator's guide for the UNIX operating system. I'd been hired as a contractor to write documentation at a UNIX workstation company called Massachusetts Computer Company (MASSCOMP for short). When I finished the graphics programming manuals I'd been hired to write, I was casting around for something else to do there. "When any of us have system problems, we go to Tom Teixeira," I said. "What are our customers going to do?"

The answer was quick: "Uh, oh! We really need a manual." I was soon rehired to extract as much information as I could from Tom Teixeira's head and put it onto paper.

That book covered the basics: the root account, account addition, permission management, backup and restore, a bit about networking with UUCP, and so on. It was oriented toward System V, one of the two dominant flavors of UNIX at the time (the other being Berkeley UNIX).

All things considered, I did a pretty good job of extracting information from Tom and other members of the then rare caste of elite system administrators. But there was no question in my mind that when the *UNIX System Administration Handbook* (USAH) came out in 1989, the bible of the field had arrived—captured not by an amanuensis, but direct from the keyboards of the masters.

By then, O'Reilly had become a publisher. Recognizing that many of my technical writing customers were adopting UNIX, I had begun retaining the rights to the manuals I wrote so that I could resell them to other companies. In late 1985, we introduced our first books that were sold to the public rather than licensed to companies. We focused first on small books about individual topics such as **vi**,

sed and **awk**, **termcap** and **terminfo**, and the UUCP networking system. We called them "Nutshell Handbooks" because we wanted to capture everything "in a nutshell."

We didn't really know anything about publishing. Our books had no spines (they were stapled), indexes, or ISBNs. We sold them by mail order, not through bookstores. But bit by bit, we learned. And eventually, we came into competition with the existing world of computer book publishers.

General UNIX administration was an obvious subject for us, but we didn't tackle it till years later. Why not? I am a big believer in filling unmet needs, not competing for the sake of it. And it was so clear that there was already a book on the topic that was not just good but GREAT! I could imagine neither the need to compete with such a comprehensive book nor the possibility of success in doing so.

Eventually, as our business matured and we entered the retail computer book market, we realized that competition can actually help grow the market. People see one book, and it's an outlier. They see more than one, and, to quote Arlo Guthrie, "they may think it's a movement." Besides, in that first edition of *USAH,* the authors had a clear bias toward BSD-based systems, and we thought there was room for a book with more of a System V bias.

In 1991, we published our own comprehensive book on UNIX system administration, Æleen Frisch's *Essential System Administration.*

As an author, editor, and publisher, I never paid much attention to the competition—except in a few cases. This is one of those cases. The *UNIX System Administration Handbook* is one of the few books we ever measured ourselves against. Could we be as good? Could we be better? Like the NBA duels of Magic Johnson and Larry Bird, the competition brought out the best in us.

Uh, oh again! Fourth edition? Æleen had better get back to work! :-)

Tim O'Reilly
June 2010

Preface

When we were writing the first edition of this book in the mid-1980s, we were eager to compare our manuscript with other books about system administration. To our delight, we could find only three. These days, you have your choice of hundreds. Here are the features that distinguish our book:

- We take a hands-on approach. You already have plenty of manuals; our purpose is to summarize our collective perspective on system administration and to recommend approaches that stand the test of time. This book contains numerous war stories and a wealth of pragmatic advice.
- This is not a book about how to run UNIX or Linux at home, in your garage, or on your PDA. We describe the management of production environments such as businesses, government offices, and universities.
- We cover networking in detail. It is the most difficult aspect of system administration and the area in which we think we can be of most help.
- We cover the major variants of UNIX and Linux.

The Organization of This Book

This book is divided into three large chunks: Basic Administration, Networking, and Bunch o' Stuff.

Basic Administration presents a broad overview of UNIX and Linux from a system administrator's perspective. The chapters in this section cover most of the facts and techniques needed to run a stand-alone system.

The Networking section describes the protocols used on UNIX systems and the techniques used to set up, extend, and maintain networks and Internet-facing servers. High-level network software is also covered here. Among the featured topics are the Domain Name System, the Network File System, electronic mail, and network management.

Bunch o' Stuff includes a variety of supplemental information. Some chapters discuss optional features such as those that support server virtualization. Others give advice on topics ranging from eco-friendly computing to the politics of running a system administration group.

Each chapter is followed by a set of practice exercises. Items are marked with our estimate of the effort required to complete them, where "effort" is an indicator of both the difficulty of the task and the time required. There are four levels:

no stars	Easy, should be straightforward
★	Harder or longer, may require lab work
★★	Hardest or longest, requires lab work and digging
★★★★★	Semester-long projects (only in a few chapters)

Some of the exercises require root or **sudo** access to the system; others require the permission of the local sysadmin group. Both requirements are mentioned in the text of the exercise.

Our contributors

We're delighted that Ned McClain, David Schweikert, and Tobi Oetiker were able to join us once again as contributing authors. With this edition, we also welcome Terry Morreale and Ron Jachim as new contributors. These contributors' deep knowledge of a variety of areas has greatly enriched the content of this book.

Contact information

Please send suggestions, comments, and bug reports to ulsah@book.admin.com. We do answer mail, but please be patient; it is sometimes a few days before one of us is able to respond. Because of the volume of email that this alias receives, we regret that we are unable to answer technical questions.

To view a copy of our current bug list and other late-breaking information, visit our web site, admin.com.

We hope you enjoy this book, and we wish you the best of luck with your adventures in system administration!

Evi Nemeth
Garth Snyder
Trent R. Hein
Ben Whaley

June 2010

Acknowledgments

Many people contributed to this project, bestowing everything from technical reviews and suggested exercises to overall moral support. The following folks deserve special thanks for hanging in there with us:

Ron Aitchison	Peter Haag	Jeremy C. Reed
Eric Allman	Bryan Helvey	Andy Rudoff
Clay Baenziger	Matthijs Mekking	Michael Sinatra
Adam Boggs	Randall Munroe	Paul Vixie
Tom Christiansen	Eric Osterweil	Wouter Wijngaards
Dan Foster	Phil Pennock	
Steve Gaede	William Putnam	

Our editor at Prentice Hall, Mark Taub, deserves not only our thanks but also an award for dealing patiently with flaky authors and a supporting cast that sometimes seemed to run to thousands of contributors.

We've had outstanding technical reviewers. Two in particular, Jonathan Corbet and Pat Parseghian, deserve special mention not only for their diplomatic and detailed comments but also for their willingness to stick with us over the course of multiple editions.

Mary Lou Nohr once again did an exceptional job as copy editor. She is a car crushing plant and botanical garden rolled into one.

This edition's awesome cartoons and cover were conceived and executed by Lisa Haney. Her portfolio is on-line at lisahaney.com.

Linda Grigoleit, Terry Hoffman, and John Sullivan helped us negotiate the IBM network and obtain equipment for evaluation.

Thanks also to Applied Trust (appliedtrust.com), which contributed laboratory space and a variety of logistical support.

Finally, we were unable to reach an agreement that would allow us to publicly acknowledge one of our distinguished contributing authors. His contributions and support throughout the project were nonetheless appreciated, and we send him this palindrome for his collection: "A man, a plan, a canoe, pasta, Hero's rajahs, a coloratura, maps, snipe, percale, macaroni, a gag, a banana bag, a tan, a tag, a banana bag again (or a camel), a crepe, pins, Spam, a rut, a Rolo, cash, a jar, sore hats, a peon, a canal—Panama!"

SECTION ONE

BASIC ADMINISTRATION

1 Where to Start

An awful lot of UNIX and Linux information is available these days, so we've designed this book to occupy a specific niche in the ecosystem of man pages, blogs, magazines, books, and other reference materials that address the needs of system administrators.

First, it's an orientation guide. It reviews the major administrative systems, identifies the different pieces of each, and explains how they work together. In the many cases where you must choose between various implementations of a concept, we describe the advantages and drawbacks of the major players.

Second, it's a quick-reference handbook that summarizes what you need to know to perform common tasks on a variety of common UNIX and Linux systems. For example, the **ps** command, which shows the status of running processes, supports more than 80 command-line options on Linux systems. But a few combinations of options satisfy 99% of a system administrator's needs; see them on page 130.

Finally, this book focuses on the administration of enterprise servers and networks. That is, *serious* system administration. It's easy to set up a single desktop system; harder to keep a virtualized network running smoothly in the face of load spikes, disk failures, and intentional attacks. We describe techniques and rules of thumb that help networks recover from adversity, and we help you choose solutions that scale as your site grows in size, complexity, and heterogeneity.

We don't claim to do all of this with perfect objectivity, but we think we've made our biases fairly clear throughout the text. One of the interesting things about system administration is that reasonable people can have dramatically different notions of what constitute the most appropriate policies and procedures. We offer our subjective opinions to you as raw data. You'll have to decide for yourself how much to accept and to what extent our comments apply to your environment.

1.1 Essential duties of the system administrator

See Chapter 2 for more information about scripting.

The Wikipedia page for "system administrator" includes a nice discussion of the tasks that system administration is generally thought to include. This page currently draws a rather sharp distinction between administration and software development, but in our experience, professional administrators spend much of their time writing scripts. That doesn't make system administrators developers per se, but it does mean that they need many of the same analytical and architectural skills.

The sections below summarize some of the main tasks that administrators are expected to perform. These duties need not necessarily be carried out by a single person, and at many sites the work is distributed among a team. However, at least one person must understand all the components and make sure that every task is being done correctly.

Account provisioning

See Chapter 7 for more information about adding new users.

The system administrator adds accounts for new users, removes the accounts of users that are no longer active, and handles all the account-related issues that come up in between (e.g., forgotten passwords). The process of adding and removing users can be automated, but certain administrative decisions (where to put a user's home directory, which machines to create the account on, etc.) must still be made before a new user can be added.

When a user should no longer have access to the system, the user's account must be disabled. All the files owned by the account should be backed up and then disposed of so that the system does not accumulate unwanted baggage over time.

Adding and removing hardware

See Chapters 8, 13, and 26 for more information about these topics.

When new hardware is purchased or when hardware is moved from one machine to another, the system must be configured to recognize and use that hardware. Hardware-support chores can range from the simple task of adding a printer to the more complex job of adding a disk array.

Now that virtualization has arrived in the enterprise computing sphere, hardware configuration can be more complicated than ever. Devices may need installation at several layers of the virtualization stack, and the system administrator may need to formulate policies that allow the hardware to be shared securely and fairly.

Performing backups

See Chapter 10 for more information about backups.

Performing backups is perhaps the most important job of the system administrator, and it is also the job that is most often ignored or sloppily done. Backups are time consuming and boring, but they are absolutely necessary. Backups can be automated and delegated to an underling, but it is still the system administrator's job to make sure that backups are executed correctly and on schedule (and that the resulting media can actually be used to restore files).

Installing and upgrading software

See Chapter 12 for more information about software management.

When new software is acquired, it must be installed and tested, often under several operating systems and on several types of hardware. Once the software is working correctly, users must be informed of its availability and location. As patches and security updates are released, they must be incorporated smoothly into the local environment.

Local software and administrative scripts should be properly packaged and managed in a fashion that's compatible with the native upgrade procedures used on systems at your site. As this software evolves, new releases should be staged for testing before being deployed to the entire site.

Monitoring the system

Large installations require vigilant supervision. Don't expect users to report problems to you unless the issues are severe. Working around a problem is usually faster than taking the time to document and report it, so users often follow the path of least resistance.

Regularly ensure that email and web services are working correctly, watch log files for early signs of trouble, make sure that local networks are properly connected, and keep an eye on the availability of system resources such as disk space. All of these chores are excellent opportunities for automation, and a variety of off-the-shelf monitoring systems can help sysadmins with this task.

Troubleshooting

System failures are inevitable. It is the administrator's job to play mechanic by diagnosing problems and calling in experts if needed. Finding the problem is often harder than fixing it.

Maintaining local documentation

See page 1200 for suggestions regarding documentation.

As a system is changed to suit an organization's needs, it begins to differ from the plain-vanilla system described by the documentation. Since the system administrator is responsible for making these customizations, it's also the sysadmin's duty to document the changes. This chore includes documenting where cables are run and how they are constructed, keeping maintenance records for all hardware, recording the status of backups, and documenting local procedures and policies.

Vigilantly monitoring security

See Chapter 22 for more information about security.

The system administrator must implement a security policy and periodically check to be sure that the security of the system has not been violated. On low-security systems, this chore might involve only a few basic checks for unauthorized access. On a high-security system, it can include an elaborate network of traps and auditing programs.

Fire fighting

Although helping users with their various problems is rarely included in a system administrator's job description, it claims a significant portion of most administrators' workdays. System administrators are bombarded with problems ranging from "It worked yesterday and now it doesn't! What did you change?" to "I spilled coffee on my keyboard! Should I pour water on it to wash it out?"

In most cases, your response to these issues affects your perceived value as an administrator far more than does any actual technical skill you might possess. You can either howl at the injustice of it all, or you can delight in the fact that a single well-handled trouble ticket scores as many brownie points as five hours of midnight debugging. You pick!

1.2 Suggested background

We assume in this book that you have a certain amount of Linux or UNIX experience. In particular, you should have a general concept of how the system looks and feels from the user's perspective since we don't review this material. Several good books can get you up to speed; see the reading list on page 27.

Even in these days of Compiz-powered 3D desktops, the GUI tools for system administration on UNIX and Linux systems remain fairly simplified in comparison with the richness of the underlying software. In the real world, we still administer by editing configuration files and writing scripts, so you'll need to be comfortable with both a command-line shell and a text editor.

Your editor can be a GUI tool like **gedit** or a command-line tool such as **vi** or **emacs**. Word processors such as Microsoft Word and OpenOffice Writer are quite different from text editors and are nearly useless for administrative tasks. Command-line tools have an edge because they can run over simple SSH connections and on ailing systems that won't boot; there's no need for a window system. They are also much faster for the quick little edits that administrators often make.

We recommend learning **vi** (now seen most commonly in its rewritten form, **vim**), which is standard on all UNIX and Linux systems. Although it may appear a bit pallid when compared with glitzier offerings such as **emacs**, it is powerful and complete. GNU's **nano** is a simple and low-impact "starter editor" that has on-screen prompts. Be wary of nonstandard editors, though; if you become addicted to one, you may soon tire of dragging it along with you to install on every new system.

One of the mainstays of administration (and a theme that runs throughout this book) is the use of scripts to automate administrative tasks. To be an effective administrator, you must be able to read and modify Perl and **bash/sh** scripts.

See Chapter 2 for more information about scripting.

For new scripting projects, we recommend Perl or Python. As a programming language, Perl is admittedly a bit strange. However, it does include many features that are indispensable for administrators. The O'Reilly book *Programming Perl* by Larry Wall et al. is the standard text; it's also a model of good technical writing. A full citation is given on page 27.

Many administrators prefer Python to Perl, and we know of sites that are making a concerted effort to convert. Python is a more elegant language, and Python scripts are generally more readable and easier to maintain. (As Amazon's Steve Yegge said, "The Python community has long been the refuge for folks who finally took the red pill and woke up from the Perl Matrix.") A useful set of links that compare Python to other scripting languages (including Perl) can be found at python.org/doc/Comparisons.html.

Ruby is an up-and-coming language that maintains many of the strengths of Perl while avoiding some of Perl's syntactic pitfalls and adding modern object-oriented features. It doesn't yet have a strong tradition as a scripting language for system administrators, but that will likely change over the next few years.

We also suggest that you learn **expect**, which is not a programming language so much as a front end for driving interactive programs. It's an efficient glue technology that can replace some complex scripting. **expect** is easy to learn.

Chapter 2, *Scripting and the Shell*, summarizes the most important things to know about scripting for **bash**, Perl, and Python. It also reviews regular expressions (text matching patterns) and some shell idioms that are useful for sysadmins.

1.3 Friction between UNIX and Linux

See the section starting on page 1264 for more of the history of UNIX and Linux.

Because they are similar, this book covers both UNIX and Linux systems. Unfortunately, mentioning UNIX and Linux together in the same sentence can sometimes be like stepping into a political minefield, or perhaps blundering into a large patch of quicksand. But since the relationship between UNIX and Linux seems to engender some confusion as well as animosity, it's hard to avoid staking out a position. Here is our perspective and our short version of the facts.

Linux is a reimplementation and elaboration of the UNIX kernel. It conforms to the POSIX standard, runs on several hardware platforms, and is compatible with most existing UNIX software. It differs from many—but not all—variants of UNIX in that it is free, open source, and cooperatively developed. Linux includes technical advances that did not exist in UNIX, so it is more than just a UNIX clone. At the same time, traditional UNIX vendors have continued to refine their systems, so there are certainly areas in which commercial UNIX systems are superior to Linux.

Whatever the relative merits of the systems, Linux is a legally, developmentally, and historically distinct entity that cannot properly be referred to as "UNIX" or as a "version of UNIX." To do so is to slight the work and innovation of the Linux community. At the same time, it's somewhat misleading to insist that Linux is "not UNIX." If your creation walks like a duck and quacks like a duck, you may have invented a duck.

Schisms exist even within the Linux camp. It has been argued, with some justification, that referring to Linux distributions simply as "Linux" fails to acknowledge the work that went into the software that runs outside the kernel (which in fact constitutes the vast majority of software on an average system). Unfortunately, the most commonly suggested alternative, GNU/Linux, has its own political baggage and has been officially endorsed only by the Debian distribution. The Wikipedia entry for "GNU/Linux naming controversy" outlines the arguments on both sides.[1] Interestingly, the use of open source software is now predominant even on most UNIX systems, but no one seems to be pushing for a GNU/UNIX designation just yet.[2]

Linux software is UNIX software. Thanks largely to the GNU Project, most of the important software that gives UNIX systems their value has been developed under some form of open source model.[3] The same code runs on Linux and non-Linux systems. The Apache web server, for example, doesn't much care whether it's running on Linux or Solaris. From the standpoint of applications and most administrative software, Linux is simply one of the best-supported and most widely available varieties of UNIX.

It's also worth noting that Linux is not the only free UNIX-like operating system in the world. OpenSolaris is free and open source, although its exact licensing terms have earned suspicious looks from some open source purists. FreeBSD, NetBSD, and OpenBSD—all offshoots of the Berkeley Software Distribution from UC Berkeley—have ardent followers of their own. These OSes are generally comparable to Linux in their features and reliability, although they enjoy somewhat less support from third-party software vendors.

1. Since Wikipedia contains Linux information and must therefore refer to Linux frequently, the debate has particular relevance to Wikipedia itself. The discussion page for the Wikipedia article is also well worth reading.
2. After all, "GNU's not UNIX!"
3. Several of our technical reviewers protested that we seem to be crediting GNU with the creation of most of the world's free software. We are not! However, GNU has certainly done more than any other group to promote the *idea* of free software as a social enterprise and to structure ongoing debate about licensing terms and interactions between free and nonfree software.

UNIX and Linux systems have both been used in production environments for many years, and they both work well.[4] At this point, the choice between them has more to do with packaging, support, and institutional inertia than any real difference in quality or modernity.

In this book, comments about "Linux" generally apply to Linux distributions but not to traditional UNIX variants. The meaning of "UNIX" is a bit more fluid, as we occasionally apply it to attributes shared by all UNIX derivatives, including Linux (e.g., "UNIX file permissions"). To avoid ambiguity, we usually say "UNIX and Linux" when we mean both.

1.4 Linux distributions

All Linux distributions share the same kernel lineage, but the ancillary materials that go along with that kernel can vary quite a bit. Distributions vary in their focus, support, and popularity. There continue to be hundreds of independent Linux distributions, but our sense is that distributions based on the Debian, Red Hat, and SUSE lineages will continue to predominate in production environments over the next five years.

The differences among Linux distributions are not cosmically significant. In fact, it is something of a mystery why there are so many different distributions, each claiming "easy installation" and "a massive software library" as its distinguishing features. It's hard to avoid the conclusion that people just like to make new Linux distributions.

Many smaller distributions are surprisingly competitive in terms of fit and finish. All major distributions, including the second tier, include a relatively painless installation procedure, a well-tuned desktop environment, and some form of package management. Most distributions also allow you to boot from the distribution DVD, which can be handy for debugging and is also a nice way to take a quick look at a new distribution you are considering.

Since our focus in this book is the management of large-scale installations, we're partial to distributions such as Red Hat Enterprise Linux that take into account the management of networks of machines. Some distributions are designed with production environments in mind, and others are not. The extra crumbs of assistance that the production-oriented systems toss out can make a significant difference in ease of administration.

When you adopt a distribution, you are making an investment in a particular vendor's way of doing things. Instead of looking only at the features of the installed software, it's wise to consider how your organization and that vendor are going to work with each other in the years to come.

4. We consider a "production" environment to be one that an organization relies on to accomplish real work (as opposed to testing, research, or development).

Some important questions to ask are

- Is this distribution going to be around in five years?
- Is this distribution going to stay on top of the latest security patches?
- Is this distribution going to release updated software promptly?
- If I have problems, will the vendor talk to me?

Viewed in this light, some of the more interesting, offbeat distributions don't sound quite so appealing. But don't count them out: E*Trade, for example, runs on Gentoo Linux.

The most viable distributions are not necessarily the most corporate. For example, we expect Debian Linux (OK, OK, Debian GNU/Linux!) to remain viable for a long time despite the fact that Debian is not a company, doesn't sell anything, and offers no formal, on-demand support. Debian itself isn't one of the most widely used distributions, but it benefits from a committed group of contributors and from the enormous popularity of the Ubuntu distribution, which is based on it.

Table 1.1 lists some of the most popular mainstream distributions.

Table 1.1 Most popular general-purpose Linux distributions

Distribution	Web site	Comments
CentOS	centos.org	Free analog of Red Hat Enterprise
Debian	debian.org	Closest to GNU
Fedora	fedoraproject.org	De-corporatized Red Hat Linux
Gentoo	gentoo.org	Compile-it-yourself, optimized
Linux Mint	linuxmint.com	Ubuntu-based, elegant apps
Mandriva	mandriva.com	Long history, "easy to try"
openSUSE	opensuse.org	Free analog of SUSE Linux Enterprise
Oracle Enterprise Linux	oracle.com	Oracle-supported version of RHEL
PCLinuxOS	pclinuxos.com	Fork of Mandriva, KDE-oriented
Red Flag	redflag-linux.com	Chinese distro, similar to Red Hat
Red Hat Enterprise	redhat.com	Reliable, slow-changing, commercial
Slackware	slackware.com	Grizzled, long-surviving distro
SUSE Linux Enterprise	novell.com/linux	Strong in Europe, multilingual
Ubuntu	ubuntu.com	Cleaned-up version of Debian

A comprehensive list of distributions, including many non-English distributions, can be found at linux.org/dist, lwn.net/Distributions, or distrowatch.com.

1.5 Example systems used in this book

We have chosen three popular Linux distributions and three UNIX variants as our examples to discuss throughout this book: Ubuntu Linux, openSUSE, Red Hat Enterprise Linux, Solaris, HP-UX, and AIX. These systems are representative of the overall marketplace and account collectively for an overwhelming majority of the installations in use at large sites today.

Information in this book generally applies to all of our example systems unless a specific attribution is given. Details particular to one system are marked with the vendor's logo:

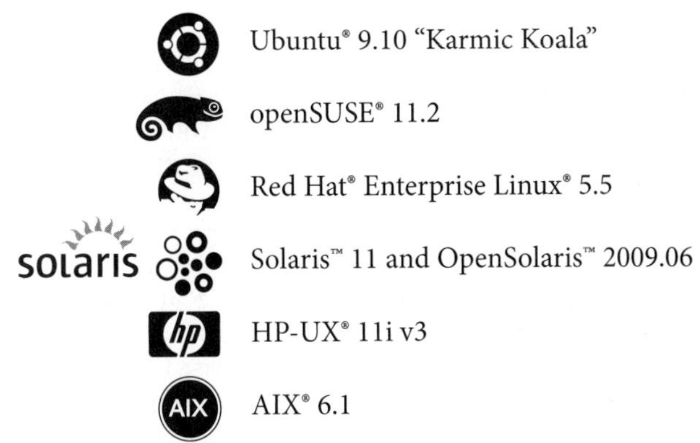

Ubuntu® 9.10 "Karmic Koala"
openSUSE® 11.2
Red Hat® Enterprise Linux® 5.5
solaris
Solaris™ 11 and OpenSolaris™ 2009.06
hp
HP-UX® 11i v3
AIX
AIX® 6.1

These logos are used with the kind permission of their respective owners. However, the vendors have not reviewed or endorsed the contents of this book. The paragraphs below provide a bit more detail about each of these example systems.

Example Linux distributions

Information that's specific to Linux but not to any particular distribution is marked with the Tux penguin logo shown at left.

The Ubuntu distributions maintain an ideological commitment to community development and open access, so there's never any question about which parts of the distribution are free or redistributable. Ubuntu currently enjoys philanthropic funding from South African entrepreneur Mark Shuttleworth.

Ubuntu is based on the Debian distribution and uses Debian's packaging system. It comes in two main forms, a Desktop Edition and a Server Edition. They are essentially similar, but the Server Edition kernel comes pretuned for server use and does not install a GUI or GUI applications such as OpenOffice.

SUSE, now part of Novell, has taken the path of Red Hat and forked into two related distributions: one (openSUSE) that contains only free software; and another (SUSE Linux Enterprise) that costs money, includes a formal support path, and offers a few extra trinkets. Nothing in this book is specific to one SUSE distribution or the other, so we simply refer to them collectively as "SUSE."

Red Hat has been a dominant force in the Linux world for most of the last decade, and its distributions are widely used in North America. In 2003, the original Red Hat Linux distribution was split into a production-centered line called Red Hat Enterprise Linux (which we refer to as RHEL or Red Hat in this book) and a community-based development project called Fedora. The split was motivated by a variety of technical, economic, logistic, and legal reasons.

The distributions were initially similar, but Fedora has made some significant changes over the last five years and the two systems aren't currently synchronized in any meaningful way. RHEL offers great support and stability but is effectively impossible to use without paying licensing fees to Red Hat.

The CentOS Project (centos.org) collects source code that Red Hat is obliged to release under various licensing agreements (most notably, the GNU Public License) and assembles it into a complete distribution that is eerily similar to Red Hat Enterprise Linux, but free of charge. The distribution lacks Red Hat's branding and a few proprietary tools, but is in other respects equivalent. CentOS aspires to full binary and bug-for-bug compatibility with RHEL.

CentOS is an excellent choice for sites that want to deploy a production-oriented distribution without paying tithes to Red Hat. A hybrid approach is also feasible: front-line servers can run Red Hat Enterprise Linux and avail themselves of Red Hat's excellent support, while desktops run CentOS. This arrangement covers the important bases in terms of risk and support while also minimizing cost and administrative complexity.

Example UNIX distributions

Solaris is a System V derivative with many extensions from the company formerly known as Sun Microsystems, now part of Oracle.[5] Sun UNIX (as it was called in the mid-80s) was originally the progeny of Berkeley UNIX, but a (now historic) corporate partnership between Sun and AT&T forced a change of code base. Solaris runs on a variety of hardware platforms, most notably Intel x86 and SPARC.

In Sun's hands, Solaris was free to download and use. However, Oracle has changed this policy, and current downloads are labeled as 90-day free trial editions. The existence of OpenSolaris, an explicitly free and open source version of Solaris, complicates the picture as well. At this point (mid-2010), Oracle's exact plans for Solaris and OpenSolaris remain unclear.

The release of Solaris 11 is expected some time this year, and every indication so far is that it will hew closely to OpenSolaris. In this book, the composite system we refer to as "Solaris" is based on production Solaris 10 and OpenSolaris releases, adjusted with guidance from our network of deep-cover spies within Oracle. In a few cases, we note specifics for Solaris 10 or OpenSolaris.

HP-UX is based on System V and is tied to Hewlett-Packard's hardware platforms. It's closer to the ancestral source tree than either Solaris or AIX, but HP has kept pace with developments in the OS world and has added a variety of its own enhancements. Now that HP has begun supporting Linux as well, the future of HP-UX is somewhat less clear.

5. See page 1264 for some background on BSD, System V, and the general history of UNIX.

IBM's AIX started as a variant of Berkeley's 4.2BSD, but as of version 4 in 1994, most parts of the system migrated to System V. At this point, AIX has drifted rather far from both origins.

In general, we have the impression that AIX has enjoyed less cross-pollination from other systems than most UNIX variants. It also seems to have fallen under the Svengali-like influence of some of IBM's mainframe and AS/400 operating systems, from which it inherits conventions such as the Object Data Manager (see page 432), the use of configuration commands rather than configuration files, and the SMIT administrative interface. Over time, one might charitably say, it has grown to be more and more like itself.

IBM has been pursuing an interestingly OS-agnostic approach to marketing its hardware for most of the last decade. IBM continues to develop and promote AIX, but it's also engaged in partnerships with Red Hat and Novell to ensure that their respective Linux distributions run smoothly on IBM hardware. It will be interesting to see how this approach plays out in the years ahead.

1.6 System-specific administration tools

Modern systems include a variety of visually oriented tools and control panels (such as SUSE's YaST2 and IBM's SMIT) that help you configure or administer selected aspects of the system. These tools are useful, especially for novice administrators, but they also tend to be relatively incomplete reflections of the underlying software. They make many administrative tasks easier, but most fall short of being authoritative.

In this book, we cover the underlying mechanisms that the visual tools manipulate rather than the tools themselves, for several reasons. For one, the visual tools tend to be proprietary (or at least, system-specific). They introduce variation into processes that may actually be quite consistent among systems at a lower level. Second, we believe that it's important for administrators to have an accurate understanding of how their systems work. When the system breaks, the visual tools are often not helpful in tracking down and fixing problems. Finally, manual configuration is often faster, more flexible, more reliable, and easier to script.

1.7 Notation and typographical conventions

In this book, filenames, commands, and literal arguments to commands are shown in boldface. Placeholders (e.g., command arguments that should not be taken literally) are in italics. For example, in the command

cp *file directory*

you're supposed to replace *file* and *directory* with the names of an actual file and an actual directory.

Excerpts from configuration files and terminal sessions are shown in a fixed-width font.[6] Sometimes, we annotate sessions with italic text. For example:

```
$ grep Bob /pub/phonelist                # Look up Bob's phone number
Bob Knowles 555-2834
Bob Smith 555-2311
```

Outside of these specific cases, we have tried to keep special fonts and formatting conventions to a minimum as long as we could do so without compromising intelligibility. For example, we often talk about entities such as the daemon group or the printer anchor-lw with no special formatting at all.

We use the same conventions as the manual pages for command syntax:

- Anything between square brackets ("[" and "]") is optional.
- Anything followed by an ellipsis ("…") can be repeated.
- Curly braces ("{" and "}") mean that you should select one of the items separated by vertical bars ("|").

For example, the specification

bork [**-x**] { **on** | **off** } *filename* …

would match any of the following commands:

bork on /etc/passwd
bork -x off /etc/passwd /etc/smartd.conf
bork off /usr/lib/tmac

We use shell-style globbing characters for pattern matching:

- A star (*) matches zero or more characters.
- A question mark (?) matches one character.
- A tilde or "twiddle" (~) means the home directory of the current user.[7]
- ~*user* means the home directory of *user*.

For example, we might refer to the startup script directories **/etc/rc0.d**, **/etc/rc1.d**, and so on with the shorthand pattern **/etc/rc*.d**.

Text within quotation marks often has a precise technical meaning. In these cases, we ignore the normal rules of U.S. English and put punctuation outside the quotes so that there can be no confusion about what's included and what's not.

1.8 Units

Metric prefixes such as kilo-, mega-, and giga- are defined as powers of 10: one megabuck is 1,000,000 dollars. However, computer types have long poached these prefixes and used them to refer to powers of 2. For example, one "megabyte" of

6. It's not really a fixed-width font, but it looks like one. We liked it better than the real fixed-width fonts that we tried. That's why the columns in some examples may not all line up perfectly.
7. Solaris 10's default shell for root is the original Bourne shell, which (rather surprisingly) does not understand ~ or ~*user* notation.

memory is really 2^{20} or 1,048,576 bytes. The stolen units have even made their way into formal standards such as the JEDEC Solid State Technology Association's Standard 100B.01, which recognizes the prefixes as denoting powers of 2 (albeit with some misgivings).

In an attempt to restore clarity, the International Electrotechnical Commission has defined a set of numeric prefixes (kibi-, mebi-, gibi-, and so on, abbreviated Ki, Mi, and Gi) based explicitly on powers of 2. Those units are always unambiguous, but they are just starting to be widely used. The original kilo-series prefixes are still used in both senses.

Context helps with decoding. RAM is always denominated in powers of 2, but network bandwidth is always a power of 10. Storage space is usually quoted in power-of-10 units, but block and page sizes are in fact powers of 2.

In this book, we use IEC units for powers of 2, metric units for powers of 10, and metric units for rough values and cases in which the exact basis is unclear, undocumented, or impossible to determine. In command output and in excerpts from configuration files, we leave the original values and unit designators. We abbreviate bit as b and byte as B. Table 1.2 shows some examples.

Table 1.2 Unit decoding examples

Example	Meaning
56 kb/s serial line	A serial line that transmits 56,000 bits per second
1kB file	A file that contains 1,000 bytes
4KiB SSD pages	SSD pages that contain 4,096 bytes
8KB of memory	Not used in this book; see note below
100MB file size limit	Nominally 10^8 bytes; in context, ambiguous
100MB disk partition	Nominally 10^8 bytes; in context, probably 99,999,744 bytes[a]
1GiB of RAM	Exactly 1,073,741,824 bytes of memory[b]
1 Gb/s Ethernet	A network that transmits 1,000,000,000 bits per second
1TB hard disk	A hard disk that stores 1,000,000,000,000 bytes

a. That is, 10^8 rounded down to the nearest whole multiple of the disk's 512-byte block size
b. But according to Microsoft, still not enough memory to run the 64-bit version of Windows 7

The abbreviation K, as in "8KB of RAM!", is not part of any standard. It's a computerese adaptation of the metric abbreviation k, for kilo-, and originally meant 1,024 as opposed to 1,000. But since the abbreviations for the larger metric prefixes are already uppercase, the analogy doesn't scale. Later, people became confused about the distinction and started using K for factors of 1,000, too.

The Ubuntu Linux distribution is making a valiant attempt to bring rationality and consistency to this issue; see wiki.ubuntu.com/UnitsPolicy for some additional details.

1.9 MAN PAGES AND OTHER ON-LINE DOCUMENTATION

The manual pages, usually called "man pages" because they are read with the **man** command, constitute the traditional "on-line" documentation. (Of course, these days all the documentation is on-line in some form or another.) Man pages are typically installed with the system. Program-specific man pages come along for the ride when you install new software packages.

Man pages are concise descriptions of individual commands, drivers, file formats, or library routines. They do not address more general topics such as "How do I install a new device?" or "Why is this system so damn slow?" For those questions, consult your vendor's administration guides (see page 18) or, for Linux systems, the documents available from the Linux Documentation Project.

Organization of the man pages

All systems divide the man pages into sections, but there are minor variations in the way some sections are defined. The basic schema used by our example systems is shown in Table 1.3.

Table 1.3 Sections of the man pages

Linux	Solaris	HP-UX	AIX	Contents
1	1	1	1	User-level commands and applications
2	2	2	2	System calls and kernel error codes
3	3	3	3	Library calls
4	7	7	4	Device drivers and network protocols
5	4	4	5	Standard file formats
6	6	–	6	Games and demonstrations
7	5	5	7	Miscellaneous files and documents
8	1m	1m	8	System administration commands
9	9	–	–	Obscure kernel specs and interfaces
–	–	9	–	HP-UX general information

Some sections may be further subdivided. For example, Solaris's section 3c contains man pages about the system's standard C library. There is also considerable variation in the exact distribution of pages; some systems leave section 8 empty and lump the system administration commands into section 1. A lot of systems have discontinued games and demos, leaving nothing in section 6. Many systems have a section of the manuals called "l" (lowercase L) for local man pages.

The exact structure of the sections isn't important for most topics because **man** finds the appropriate page wherever it is stored. You only need to be aware of the section definitions when a topic with the same name appears in multiple sections. For example, **passwd** is both a command and a configuration file, so it has entries in both section 1 and section 4 or 5.

man: read man pages

man *title* formats a specific manual page and sends it to your terminal through **more**, **less**, or whatever program is specified in your PAGER environment variable. *title* is usually a command, device, filename, or name of a library routine. The sections of the manual are searched in roughly numeric order, although sections that describe commands (sections 1, 8, and 6) are usually searched first.

The form **man** *section title* gets you a man page from a particular section. Thus, on most systems, **man sync** gets you the man page for the **sync** command, and **man 2 sync** gets you the man page for the **sync** system call.

Under Solaris, you must preface the section number with the **-s** flag, for example, **man -s 2 sync**.

man -k *keyword* or **apropos** *keyword* prints a list of man pages that have *keyword* in their one-line synopses. For example:

```
$ man -k translate
objcopy (1)         - copy and translate object files
dcgettext (3)       - translate message
tr (1)              - translate or delete characters
snmptranslate (1) - translate SNMP OID values into more useful information
tr (1p)             - translate characters
...
```

The keywords database can become out of date. If you add additional man pages to your system, you may need to rebuild this file with **mandb** (Ubuntu, SUSE), **makewhatis** (Red Hat), or **catman -w** (Solaris, HP-UX, AIX).

Storage of man pages

nroff input for man pages is usually kept in directories under **/usr/share/man**. Linux systems compress them with **gzip** to save space. (The **man** command knows how to uncompress them on the fly.) The **man** command maintains a cache of formatted pages in **/var/cache/man** or **/usr/share/man** if the appropriate directories are writable, but this is a security risk. Most systems preformat the man pages once at installation time (see **catman**) or not at all.

Solaris understands man pages formatted with SGML in addition to the traditional **nroff**. The SGML pages have their own section directories underneath **/usr/share/man**.

The **man** command can search several man page repositories to find the manual pages you request. On Linux systems, you can find out the current default search path with the **manpath** command. This path (from Ubuntu) is typical:

```
ubuntu$ manpath
/usr/local/man:/usr/local/share/man:/usr/share/man
```

If necessary, you can set your MANPATH environment variable to override the default path:

```
export MANPATH=/home/share/localman:/usr/share/man
```

Some systems let you set a custom system-wide default search path for man pages, which can be useful if you need to maintain a parallel tree of man pages such as those generated by OpenPKG. If you want to distribute local documentation in the form of man pages, however, it is simpler to use your system's standard packaging mechanism and to put man pages in the standard man directories. See Chapter 12, *Software Installation and Management*, for more details.

GNU Texinfo

Linux systems include a sort of supplemental on-line man page system called Texinfo. It was invented long ago by the GNU folks in reaction to the fact that the **nroff** command to format man pages was proprietary to AT&T. These days we have GNU's own **groff** to do this job for us and the **nroff** issue is no longer important, but Texinfo still lumbers along like a zombie in search of human brains.

Although the use of Texinfo seems to be gradually fading, a few GNU packages persist in documenting themselves with Texinfo files rather than man pages. You can pipe the output of the Texinfo reader, **info**, through **less** to evade **info**'s built-in navigation system.

Fortunately, packages that are documented with Texinfo usually install man page stubs that tell you to use the **info** command to read about those particular packages. You can safely stick to the **man** command for doing manual searches and delve into **info** land only when instructed to do so. **info info** initiates you into the dark mysteries of Texinfo.

1.10 Other authoritative documentation

Man pages are just a small part of the official documentation. Most of the rest, unfortunately, is scattered about on the web.

System-specific guides

Major vendors have their own dedicated documentation projects, and many continue to produce useful book-length manuals. These days the manuals are usually found on-line rather than in the form of printed books. The extent and quality of the documentation vary widely, but most vendors produce at least an administration guide and an installation guide. Table 1.4 shows where to look for each of our example systems.

The standout in this crowd is IBM, which produces a raft of full-length books on a variety of administration topics. You can buy them as books, but they're also available for free as downloads. The downside to IBM's completeness is that many of the documents seem to lag a version or two behind the current release of AIX.

Table 1.4 Where to find OS vendors' proprietary documentation

System	URL	Comments
Ubuntu	help.ubuntu.com	Mostly user-oriented; see "server guide"
SUSE	novell.com/documentation	Admin stuff is in "reference guide"
RHEL	redhat.com/docs	Mostly documents Red Hat extensions
Solaris	docs.sun.com	Extensive catalog of materials
HP-UX	docs.hp.com	Books, white papers, and tech guides
AIX	www.redbooks.ibm.com	Numerous real books in PDF format
	ibm.com/support	Support gateway to notes, FAQs, etc.

Red Hat is the unfortunate laggard in the documentation race. Most of its documents relate to its proprietary value-added systems rather than to Linux administration generally.

Package-specific documentation

Most of the important software packages in the UNIX and Linux world are maintained by individuals or by third parties such as the Internet Systems Consortium and the Apache Software Foundation. These groups write their own documentation. The quality runs the gamut from embarrassing to spectacular, but jewels such as *Version Control with Subversion* from svnbook.red-bean.com make the hunt worthwhile.

UNIX vendors and Linux distributors always include the appropriate man pages in their packages. Unfortunately, they tend to skimp on other documentation, mostly because there really isn't a standard place to put it (check **/usr/share/doc**). It's often useful to check the original source of the software to see if additional materials are available.

Supplemental documents include white papers (technical reports), design rationales, and book- or pamphlet-length treatments of particular topics. These supplemental materials are not limited to describing just one command, so they can adopt a tutorial or procedural approach. Many pieces of software have both a man page and an article. For example, the man page for **vi** tells you about the command-line arguments that **vi** understands, but you have to go to the in-depth treatment to learn how to actually edit a file.

Books

The best resources for system administrators in the printed realm (aside from this book :-)) are the O'Reilly series of books. The series began with *UNIX in a Nutshell* over 20 years ago and now includes a separate volume on just about every important UNIX and Linux subsystem and command. The series also includes books on the Internet, Windows, and other non-UNIX topics. All the books are reasonably priced, timely, and focused.

Tim O'Reilly has become quite interested in the open source movement and runs a conference, OSCON, on this topic as well as conferences on other trendy techie topics. OSCON occurs twice yearly, once in the United States and once in Europe. See oreilly.com for more information.

RFCs and other Internet documents

The Request for Comments document series describes the protocols and procedures used on the Internet. Most of these documents are relatively detailed and technical, but some are written as overviews. They are absolutely authoritative, and many are quite useful for system administrators. See page 449 for a more complete description of these documents.

The Linux Documentation Project

Linux systems have another major source of reference information: the Linux Documentation Project at tldp.org. This site hosts a huge array of user-contributed documentation ranging from FAQs to full-length guides. The LDP also centralizes efforts to translate Linux-related documents into additional languages.

Unfortunately, many of the LDP documents are not well maintained. Since Linux-years are a lot like dog-years in their relation to real time, untended documents are apt to go out of date quickly. Always check the time stamp on a HOWTO or guide and weigh its credibility accordingly.

1.11 Other sources of information

The sources discussed in the previous section are generally the most reliable, but they're hardly the last word in UNIX and Linux documentation. Countless blogs, discussion forums, and news feeds are available on the Internet.

It should go without saying, but Google is a system administrator's best friend. Unless you're looking up the details of a specific command or file format, Google should be the first resource you consult for any sysadmin question. Make it a habit; if nothing else, you'll avoid the delay and humiliation of having your questions in an on-line forum answered with a link to Google.[8] *When stuck, Google.*

We can't enumerate every useful collection of UNIX and Linux information on the Internet, but a few of the most significant ones are shown in Table 1.5.

Another fun and useful resource is Bruce Hamilton's "Rosetta Stone" page at bhami.com/rosetta.html. It contains pointers to the commands and tools used for various system administration tasks on many different operating systems.

If you're a Linux site, don't be shy about accessing general UNIX resources. Most information is directly applicable to Linux.

8. Or worse yet, a link to Google through lmgtfy.com

Table 1.5 Sysadmin resources on the web

Web site	Description
blogs.sun.com	Great collection of technical articles, many Solaris-related
cpan.org	Authoritative collection of Perl modules
freshmeat.net	Large index of Linux and UNIX software
kernel.org	Official Linux kernel site
linux.com	Linux forum, good for new users[a]
linux.org	General Linux information clearing house
linux.slashdot.org	Linux-specific arm of tech news giant Slashdot
linuxhq.com	Compilation of kernel-related info and patches
lwn.net	Linux and open source news service
lxer.com	Linux news aggregator
rootvg.net	AIX-oriented site with lots of links and good forums
securityfocus.com	General computer security info
serverfault.com	Collaboratively edited database of sysadmin questions
ServerFiles.com	Directory of network admin software and hardware
slashdot.org	Tech news in a variety of categories
solariscentral.org	Open blog with Solaris-related news and articles
sun.com/bigadmin	Sun-specific aggregation site for admin info
sunhelp.org	Very nice collection of Sun-related material
ugu.com	UNIX Guru Universe – all things sysadmin

a. This site is now run by the Linux Foundation.

1.12 Ways to find and install software

Chapter 12, *Software Installation and Management*, addresses software provisioning in detail. But for the impatient, here's a quick primer on how to find out what's installed on your system and how to obtain and install new software.

Modern operating systems divide their contents into packages that can be installed independently of one another. The default installation includes a range of starter packages that you can expand according to your needs.

Add-on software is often provided in the form of precompiled packages as well, although the degree to which this is a mainstream approach varies widely among systems. Most software is developed by independent groups that release the software in the form of source code. Package repositories then pick up the source code, compile it appropriately for the conventions in use on the systems they serve, and package the resulting binaries. It's usually easier to install a system-specific binary package than to fetch and compile the original source code. However, packagers are sometimes a release or two behind the current version.

The fact that two systems use the same package format doesn't necessarily mean that packages for the two systems are interchangeable. Red Hat and SUSE both use RPM, for example, but their filesystem layouts are somewhat different. It's best to use packages designed for your particular system if they are available.

Major Linux distributions provide excellent package management systems that include tools for accessing and searching Internet software repositories. Distributors aggressively maintain these repositories on behalf of the community, so there is rarely a need for Linux administrators to step outside the bounds of their systems' default package manager. Life is good.

UNIX systems show more ambivalence about package management. Solaris, HP-UX, and AIX all provide packaging software that works at the level of individual machines. However, the vendors of these systems don't maintain repositories of open source software, so the user communities are mostly left to fend for themselves.[9] Unfortunately, one of the main pieces of glue that holds a packaging universe together is a way for packages to reliably refer to other packages in order to express dependency or compatibility information. Without some central coordination, the whole ecosystem can quickly fall apart.

In the real world, results have varied. Solaris has an add-on system (**pkgutil** from blastwave.org) that provides for easy software installation from an Internet repository, much like the native systems found on Linux distributions. HP-UX has a nice Internet repository in the form of the HP-UX Porting and Archiving Centre at hpux.connect.org.uk, but packages must be manually and individually downloaded. At the more dismal end of the spectrum, the availability of prepackaged software for AIX is somewhat scattershot.

Administrators without access to prepackaged binaries must install software the old-fashioned way: by downloading a **tar** archive of the source code and manually configuring, compiling, and installing it. Depending on the software and the operating system, this process can range from trivial to nightmarish.

In this book, we generally assume that optional software is already installed rather than torturing you with boilerplate instructions for installing every package. If there's a potential for confusion, we sometimes mention the exact names of the packages needed to complete a particular project. For the most part, however, we don't repeat installation instructions since they tend to be similar from one package to the next.

Determining whether software has already been installed

For a variety of reasons, it can be a bit tricky to determine which software package contains the component you actually need. Rather than starting at the package level, it's easier to use the shell's **which** command to find out if a relevant binary is already in your search path. For example, the following command reveals that the GNU C compiler has already been installed on this machine:

```
aix$ which gcc
/opt/pware/bin/gcc
```

9. OpenSolaris does offer a Linux-quality package management system and Internet repository. This feature does not exist in Solaris 10, but it's likely to be featured in Solaris 11.

If **which** can't find the command you're looking for, try **whereis**; it searches a broader range of system directories and is independent of your shell's search path.

Another alternative is the incredibly useful **locate** command, which consults a precompiled index of the filesystem to locate filenames that match a particular pattern. **locate** is part of the GNU **findutils** package, which is included by default on most Linux systems but must be installed by hand on UNIX.

locate is not specific to commands or packages but can find any type of file. For example, if you weren't sure where to find the **signal.h** include file, you could try

```
ubuntu$ locate signal.h
/usr/include/signal.h
/usr/include/asm/signal.h
/usr/include/asm-generic/signal.h
/usr/include/linux/signal.h
...
```

locate's database is updated periodically by the **updatedb** command, which runs out of **cron**. Therefore, the results of a **locate** don't always reflect recent changes to the filesystem.

See Chapter 12 for more information about package management.

If you know the name of the package you're looking for, you can also use your system's packaging utilities to check directly for the package's presence. For example, on a Red Hat or SUSE system, the following command checks for the presence (and installed version) of the Python scripting language:

```
redhat$ rpm -q python
python-2.4.3-21.el5
```

Adding new software

If you do need to install additional software, you first need to determine the canonical name of the relevant software package. For example, you'd need to translate "I want to install **locate**" to "I need to install the **findutils** package," or translate "I need **named**" to "I have to install BIND." A variety of system-specific indexes on the web can help with this, but Google is usually just as effective. For example, a search for "locate command" takes you directly to several relevant discussions. If you're on a UNIX system, throw in the name of the operating system as well.

Once you know the name of the relevant software, you can download and install it. The complete installation is usually a single command on Linux systems and on Solaris systems that have **pkgutil** installed. For HP-UX and AIX you'll have to download either a prebuilt binary package or the project's original source code. If the latter, try to locate the project's official web page through Google and download the source code from one of the project's mirrors.

The following examples show the installation of the **wget** command on each of our example systems. It's a nifty GNU utility that turns HTTP and FTP downloads into atomic commands—very useful for scripting. **wget** is installed by default on each of our example Linux systems, but the commands shown below can be used for both initial installation and later updates.

Ubuntu uses APT, the Debian Advanced Package Tool:

```
ubuntu# apt-get install wget
Reading package lists... Done
Building dependency tree
Reading state information... Done
wget is already the newest version.
0 upgraded, 0 newly installed, 0 to remove and 0 not upgraded.
```

The SUSE version is

```
suse# yast --install wget
<runs in a terminal-based UI>
```

The Red Hat version is

```
redhat# yum install wget
Loaded plugins: fastestmirror
...
Parsing package install arguments
Package wget-1.10.2-7.el5.i386 is already installed and latest version
Nothing to do
```

On a Solaris system with **pkutil** already installed (see blastwave.org for instructions on setting this up)

```
solaris# /opt/csw/bin/pkgutil --install wget
<multiple pages of output as seven packages are installed>
```

For HP-UX, we found an appropriate binary package on hpux.connect.org.uk and downloaded it to the **/tmp** directory. The commands to unpack and install it were

```
hpux# gunzip /tmp/wget-1.11.4-hppa-11.31.depot.gz
hpux# swinstall -s /tmp/wget-1.11.4-hppa-11.31.depot wget
======= 05/27/09 13:01:31 EDT  BEGIN swinstall SESSION
    (non-interactive) (jobid=hpux11-0030)

    * Session started for user "root@hpux11".

    * Beginning Selection
    * Target connection succeeded for "hpux11:/".
    * Source:          /tmp/wget-1.11.4-hppa-11.31.depot
    * Targets:         hpux11:/
    * Software selections:
        wget.wget-RUN,r=1.11.4,a=HP-UX_B./800
    * Selection succeeded.
    * Beginning Analysis and Execution
    ...
    * Analysis and Execution succeeded.
    ...
```

The package depot on the **swinstall** command line must be specified as a full path starting with /; otherwise, **swinstall** tries to find the file on the network. The **wget** at the end tells **swinstall** which package to install from within the depot file.

Unfortunately, the installation is not really as easy as it first appears. The installed version of **wget** won't actually run because several of the libraries on which it depends have not been installed:

```
hpux$ wget http://samba.org/samba/docs/Samba3-HOWTO.pdf
/usr/lib/dld.sl: Can't open shared library: /usr/local/lib/libcrypto.sl
/usr/lib/dld.sl: No such file or directory
[HP ARIES32]: Core file for 32 bit PA-RISC application
[HP ARIES32]: /usr/local/bin/wget saved to /tmp/core.wget.
```

swinstall does have some dependency management built in, but its abilities unfortunately do not extend to Internet repositories. You'll have to read the fine print and install all the appropriate prerequisite packages (in this case, six more) to make things right.

Building software from source code

There is in fact at least one binary **wget** package available for AIX in RPM format. A Google search for "aix wget rpm" should turn up some good leads. After downloading, the installation command would be a simple

```
aix# rpm --install wget-1.11.4-1.aix5.1.ppc.rpm
```

But just for illustration, let's build the AIX version of **wget** from the original source code.

Our first chore is to find the code, but that's easy: the first Google result for "wget" takes us right to the project page at GNU, and the source tarball is just a link away. After downloading the current version into the **/tmp** directory, we unpack, configure, build, and install it:

```
aix# cd /tmp; gunzip wget-1.11.4.tar.gz
aix# tar xfp wget-1.11.4.tar
aix# cd wget-1.11.4
aix# ./configure --disable-ssl --disable-nls     # See comments below
configure: configuring for GNU Wget 1.11.4
checking build system type... rs6000-ibm-aix
...
config.status: creating src/config.h
config.status: executing default commands
generating po/POTFILES from ./po/POTFILES.in
creating po/Makefile
aix# make
<several pages of compilation output>
aix# make install
<about a page of output>
```

This **configure/make/make install** sequence is common to the majority of UNIX and Linux software and works on all systems as long as you have the development environment and any package-specific prerequisites installed. However, it's always a good idea to check the package's **INSTALL** or **README** file for specifics.

In this case, the **--disable-ssl** and **--disable-nls** options to **configure** omit some **wget** features that depend on other libraries that haven't been installed. In real life, you'd probably want to install the prerequisites. Use **configure --help** to see all the configuration options. Another useful **configure** option is **--prefix=***directory*, which lets you put the software somewhere other than **/usr/local**.

1.13 System administration under duress

System administrators wear many hats. In the real world, they are often people with other jobs who have been asked to look after a few computers on the side. If this is your situation, tread carefully and be aware of how this scenario tends to play out over the long term.

The more experienced you become at system management, the more the user community comes to depend on you. Networks invariably grow, and administrative work tends to accumulate over time as your administration system becomes more sophisticated and you add additional layers. You will soon find that you are the only person in your organization who knows how to perform a variety of important tasks.

Once coworkers come to think of you as the local system administrator, it is difficult to extricate yourself from this role. That is not necessarily a bad thing, but we know several people who have changed jobs to escape it. Since many administrative tasks are intangible, you may also find that you're expected to be both a full-time administrator and a full-time engineer, writer, or analyst.

There is a common tendency for unwilling administrators to fend off requests by adopting a surly attitude and providing poor service.[10] This approach usually backfires; it makes you look bad and creates additional problems.

Instead, consider keeping detailed records of the time you spend on system administration. Your goal should be to keep the work at a manageable level and to assemble evidence that you can use when you ask to be relieved of administrative duties. In most organizations, you will need to lobby the management from six months to a year to get yourself replaced, so plan ahead.

On the other hand, you may find that you enjoy system administration and that you prefer it to real work. Employment prospects remain good. Unfortunately, your political problems will probably intensify. See Chapter 32, *Management, Policy, and Politics*, for a preview of the delights in store.

10. A tendency lovingly and sadistically documented in Simon Travaglia's Bastard Operator from Hell stories; see bofh.ntk.net for the archive. (Look under BOFH.)

1.14 Recommended Reading

ROBBINS, ARNOLD. *UNIX in a Nutshell (4th Edition).* Sebastopol, CA: O'Reilly Media, 2008.

SIEVER, ELLEN, AARON WEBER, AND STEPHEN FIGGINS. *Linux in a Nutshell (5th Edition).* Sebastopol, CA: O'Reilly Media, 2006.

GANCARZ, MIKE. *Linux and the Unix Philosophy.* Boston: Digital Press, 2003.

SALUS, PETER H. *The Daemon, the GNU & the Penguin: How Free and Open Software is Changing the World.* Reed Media Services, 2008.

This fascinating history of the open source movement by UNIX's best-known historian is also available at groklaw.com under the Creative Commons license. The URL for the book itself is quite long; look for a current link at groklaw.com or try this compressed equivalent: tinyurl.com/d6u7j.

RAYMOND, ERIC S. *The Cathedral & The Bazaar: Musings on Linux and Open Source by an Accidental Revolutionary.* Sebastopol, CA: O'Reilly Media, 2001.

System administration

LIMONCELLI, THOMAS A., CHRISTINA J. HOGAN, AND STRATA R. CHALUP. *The Practice of System and Network Administration (Second Edition).* Reading, MA: Addison-Wesley, 2008.

This is a good book with particularly strong coverage of the policy and procedural aspects of system administration. The authors maintain a system administration blog at everythingsysadmin.com.

FRISCH, ÆLEEN. *Essential System Administration (3rd Edition).* Sebastopol, CA: O'Reilly Media, 2002.

This is a classic all-around guide to UNIX system administration that is sadly somewhat out of date. We hope a new version is in the works!

Essential tools

ROBBINS, ARNOLD, ELBERT HANNAH, AND LINDA LAMB. *Learning the vi and Vim Editors.* Sebastopol, CA: O'Reilly Media, 2008.

POWERS, SHELLY, JERRY PEEK, TIM O'REILLY, AND MIKE LOUKIDES. *UNIX Power Tools (3rd Edition).* Sebastopol, CA: O'Reilly Media, 2003.

MICHAEL, RANDAL K. *Mastering UNIX Shell Scripting: BASH, Bourne, and Korn Shell Scripting for Programmers, System Administrators, and UNIX Gurus.* Indianapolis, IN: Wiley Publishing, Inc., 2008.

ROBBINS, ARNOLD AND NELSON H. F. BEEBE. *Classic Shell Scripting.* Sebastopol, CA: O'Reilly Media, 2005.

WALL, LARRY, TOM CHRISTIANSEN, AND JON ORWANT. *Programming Perl (3rd Edition).* Cambridge, MA: O'Reilly Media, 2000.

Christiansen, Tom, and Nathan Torkington. *Perl Cookbook (2nd Edition).* Sebastopol, CA: O'Reilly Media, 2003.

Blank-Edelman, David N. *Automating System Administration with Perl (2nd Edition).* Sebastopol, CA: O'Reilly Media, 2009.

Pilgrim, Mark. *Dive Into Python.* Berkeley, CA: Apress, 2004.

This book is also available for free on the web at diveintopython.org.

Flanagan, David, and Yukihiro Matsumoto. *The Ruby Programming Language.* Sebastopol, CA: O'Reilly Media, 2008.

This book, optimistically subtitled *Everything You Need to Know,* is unfortunately a bit on the dry side. However, it covers the Ruby 1.9 release and includes a wealth of detail that only the language designer is really in a position to know. Best for those who already have a working knowledge of Perl or Python.

1.15 Exercises

E1.1 What command would you use to read about the terminal driver, **tty** (*not* the **tty** command)? How would you read a local **tty** man page that was kept in **/usr/local/share/man**?

E1.2 Does a system-wide config file control the behavior of the **man** command at your site? What lines would you add to this file if you wanted to store local material in **/doc/man**? What directory structure would you have to use in **/doc/man** to make it a full citizen of the man page hierarchy?

★ E1.3 What is the current status of Linux kernel development? What are the hot issues? Who are the key players? How is the project managed?

★ E1.4 Research several UNIX and Linux systems and recommend an operating system for each of the following applications. Explain your choices.

a) A single user working in a home office
b) A university computer science lab
c) A corporate web server
d) A server cluster that runs the database for a shipping company

★ E1.5 Suppose you discover that a certain feature of Apache **httpd** does not appear to work as documented on Ubuntu.

a) What should you do before reporting the bug?
b) If you decide that the bug is real, whom should you notify and how?
c) What information must be included to make the bug report useful?

★★ E1.6 Linux has made dramatic inroads into production environments. Is UNIX doomed? Why or why not?

2 Scripting and the Shell

Good system administrators write scripts. Scripts standardize and automate the performance of administrative chores and free up admins' time for more important and more interesting tasks. In a sense, scripts are also a kind of low-rent documentation in that they act as an authoritative outline of the steps needed to complete a particular task.

In terms of complexity, administrative scripts run the gamut from simple ones that encapsulate a few static commands to major software projects that manage host configurations and administrative data for an entire site. In this book we're primarily interested in the smaller, day-to-day scripting projects that sysadmins normally encounter, so we don't talk much about the support functions (e.g., bug tracking and design review) that are needed for larger projects.

Administrative scripts should emphasize programmer efficiency and code clarity rather than computational efficiency. This is not an excuse to be sloppy, but simply a recognition that it rarely matters whether a script runs in half a second or two seconds. Optimization can have an amazingly low return on investment, even for scripts that run regularly out of **cron**.

For a long time, the standard language for administrative scripts was the one defined by the shell. Most systems' default shell is **bash** (the "Bourne-again" shell), but **sh** (the original Bourne shell) and **ksh** (the Korn shell) are used on a few UNIX systems. Shell scripts are typically used for light tasks such as automating a sequence of commands or assembling several filters to process data.

The shell is always available, so shell scripts are relatively portable and have few dependencies other than the commands they invoke. Whether or not you choose the shell, the shell may choose you: most environments include a hefty complement of existing **sh** scripts, and those scripts frequently need to be read, understood, and tweaked by administrators.

For more sophisticated scripts, it's advisable to jump to a real programming language such as Perl or Python, both of which are well suited for administrative work. These languages incorporate a couple of decades' worth of language design advancements relative to the shell, and their text processing facilities (invaluable to administrators) are so powerful that **sh** can only weep and cower in shame.

The main drawback to Perl and Python is that their environments can be a bit fussy to set up, especially when you start to use third-party libraries that have compiled components. The shell skirts this particular issue by having no module structure and no third-party libraries.

This chapter takes a quick look at **bash**, Perl, and Python as languages for scripting, along with regular expressions as a general technology.

2.1 Shell basics

Before we take up shell scripting, let's review some of the basic features and syntax of the shell. The material in this section applies to all major shells in the **sh** lineage (including **bash** and **ksh**, but not **csh** or **tcsh**), regardless of the exact platform you are using. Try out the forms you're not familiar with, and experiment!

Command editing

We've watched way too many people edit command lines with the arrow keys. You wouldn't do that in your text editor, right?

If you like **emacs**, all the basic **emacs** commands are available to you when you're editing history. <Control-E> goes to the end of the line and <Control-A> to the beginning. <Control-P> steps backward through recently executed commands and recalls them for editing. <Control-R> searches incrementally through your history to find old commands.

If you like **vi**, put your shell's command-line editing into **vi** mode like this:

```
$ set -o vi
```

As in **vi**, editing is modal; however, you start in input mode. Type <Esc> to leave input mode and "i" to reenter it. In edit mode, "w" takes you forward a word, "fX" finds the next X in the line, and so on. You can walk through past command history entries with <Esc> k. Want **emacs** editing mode back again?

```
$ set -o emacs
```

Pipes and redirection

Every process has at least three communication channels available to it: "standard input" (STDIN), "standard output" (STDOUT), and "standard error" (STDERR). The kernel sets up these channels on the process's behalf, so the process itself doesn't necessarily know where they lead. They might connect to a terminal window, a file, a network connection, or a channel belonging to another process, to name a few possibilities.

UNIX has a unified I/O model in which each channel is named with a small integer called a file descriptor. The exact number assigned to a channel is not usually significant, but STDIN, STDOUT, and STDERR are guaranteed to correspond to file descriptors 0, 1, and 2, so it's safe to refer to these channels by number. In the context of an interactive terminal window, STDIN normally reads from the keyboard and both STDOUT and STDERR write their output to the screen.

Most commands accept their input from STDIN and write their output to STDOUT. They write error messages to STDERR. This convention lets you string commands together like building blocks to create composite pipelines.

The shell interprets the symbols <, >, and >> as instructions to reroute a command's input or output to or from a file. A < symbol connects the command's STDIN to the contents of an existing file. The > and >> symbols redirect STDOUT; > replaces the file's existing contents, and >> appends to them. For example, the command

```
$ echo "This is a test message." > /tmp/mymessage
```

stores a single line in the file **/tmp/mymessage**, creating the file if necessary. The command below emails the contents of that file to user johndoe.

```
$ mail -s "Mail test" johndoe < /tmp/mymessage
```

To redirect both STDOUT and STDERR to the same place, use the >**&** symbol. To redirect STDERR only, use **2**>.

The **find** command illustrates why you might want to handle STDOUT and STDERR separately because it tends to produce output on both channels, especially when run as an unprivileged user. For example, a command such as

```
$ find / -name core
```

usually results in so many "permission denied" error messages that genuine hits get lost in the clutter. To discard all the error messages, you can use

```
$ find / -name core 2> /dev/null
```

In this version, only real matches (where the user has read permission on the parent directory) come to the terminal window. To save the list of matching paths to a file, try

```
$ find / -name core > /tmp/corefiles 2> /dev/null
```

This command line sends matching paths to **/tmp/corefiles**, discards errors, and sends nothing to the terminal window.

To connect the STDOUT of one command to the STDIN of another, use the | symbol, commonly known as a pipe. Some examples:

```
$ ps -ef | grep httpd
$ cut -d: -f7 < /etc/passwd | sort -u
```

The first example runs **ps** to generate a list of processes and pipes it through the **grep** command to select lines that contain the word **httpd**. The output of **grep** is not redirected, so the matching lines come to the terminal window.

The **cut** command in the second example picks out the path to each user's shell from **/etc/passwd**. The list of shells is then sent through **sort -u** to produce a sorted list of unique values.

To execute a second command only if its precursor completes successfully, you can separate the commands with an **&&** symbol. For example,

```
$ lpr /tmp/t2 && rm /tmp/t2
```

removes **/tmp/t2** if and only if it is successfully queued for printing. Here, the success of the **lpr** command is defined as its yielding an exit code of zero, so the use of a symbol that suggests "logical AND" for this purpose may be confusing if you're used to short-circuit evaluation in other programming languages. Don't think about it too much; just accept it as a shell idiom.

Conversely, the || symbol executes the following command only if the preceding command fails (produces a nonzero exit status).

In a script, you can use a backslash to break a command onto multiple lines, helping to distinguish the error-handling code from the rest of the command pipeline:

```
cp --preserve --recursive /etc/* /spare/backup \
    || echo "Did NOT make backup"
```

For the converse effect—multiple commands combined onto one line—you can use a semicolon as a statement separator.

Variables and quoting

Variable names are unmarked in assignments but prefixed with a dollar sign when their values are referenced. For example:

```
$ etcdir='/etc'
$ echo $etcdir
/etc
```

Do not put spaces around the = symbol or the shell will mistake your variable name for a command name.

When referencing a variable, you can surround its name with curly braces to clarify to the parser and to human readers where the variable name stops and other text begins; for example, **${etcdir}** instead of just **$etcdir**. The braces are not normally required, but they can be useful when you want to expand variables inside double-quoted strings. Often, you'll want the contents of a variable to be followed by literal letters or punctuation. For example,

```
$ echo "Saved ${rev}th version of mdadm.conf."
Saved 8th version of mdadm.conf.
```

There's no standard convention for the naming of shell variables, but all-caps names typically suggest environment variables or variables read from global configuration files. More often than not, local variables are all-lowercase with components separated by underscores. Variable names are case sensitive.

Environment variables are automatically imported into **bash**'s variable namespace, so they can be set and read with the standard syntax. Use **export** *varname* to promote a shell variable to an environment variable. Commands for environment variables that you want to set up at login time should be included in your **~/.profile** or **~/.bash_profile** file. Other environment variables, such as PWD for the current working directory, are maintained automatically by the shell.

The shell treats strings enclosed in single and double quotes similarly, except that double-quoted strings are subject to globbing (the expansion of filename-matching metacharacters such as * and ?) and variable expansion. For example:

```
$ mylang="Pennsylvania Dutch"
$ echo "I speak ${mylang}."
I speak Pennsylvania Dutch.
$ echo 'I speak ${mylang}.'
I speak ${mylang}.
```

Back quotes, also known as back-ticks, are treated similarly to double quotes, but they have the additional effect of executing the contents of the string as a shell command and replacing the string with the command's output. For example,

```
$ echo "There are `wc -l < /etc/passwd` lines in the passwd file."
There are 28 lines in the passwd file.
```

Common filter commands

Any well-behaved command that reads STDIN and writes STDOUT can be used as a filter (that is, a component of a pipeline) to process data. In this section we briefly review some of the more widely used filter commands (including some used in passing above), but the list is practically endless. Filter commands are so team oriented that it's sometimes hard to show their use in isolation.

Most filter commands accept one or more filenames on the command line. Only if you fail to specify a file do they read their standard input.

cut: separate lines into fields

The **cut** command prints selected portions of its input lines. It's most commonly used to extract delimited fields, as in the example on page 32, but it can return segments defined by column boundaries as well. The default delimiter is <Tab>, but you can change delimiters with the **-d** option. The **-f** options specifies which fields to include in the output.

For an example of the use of **cut**, see the section on **uniq**, below.

sort: sort lines

sort sorts its input lines. Simple, right? Well, maybe not—there are a few potential subtleties regarding the exact parts of each line that are sorted (the "keys") and the collation order to be imposed. Table 2.1 shows a few of the more common options, but check the man page for others.

Table 2.1 sort options

Opt	Meaning
-b	Ignore leading whitespace
-f	Case insensitive sorting
-k	Specify the columns that form the sort key
-n	Compare fields as integer numbers
-r	Reverse sort order
-t	Set field separator (the default is whitespace)
-u	Output unique records only

The commands below illustrate the difference between numeric and dictionary sorting, which is the default. Both commands use the **-t:** and **-k3,3** options to sort the **/etc/group** file by its third colon-separated field, the group ID. The first sorts numerically and the second alphabetically.

```
$ sort -t: -k3,3 -n /etc/group[1]
root:x:0:
bin:x:1:daemon
daemon:x:2:
...

$ sort -t: -k3,3 /etc/group
root:x:0:
bin:x:1:daemon
users:x:100:
...
```

1. **sort** accepts the key specification **-k3** (rather than **-k3,3**), but it probably doesn't do what you expect. Without the terminating field number, the sort key continues to the end of the line.

***uniq**: print unique lines*

uniq is similar in spirit to **sort -u**, but it has some useful options that **sort** does not emulate: **-c** to count the number of instances of each line, **-d** to show only duplicated lines, and **-u** to show only nonduplicated lines. The input must be presorted, usually by being run through **sort**.

For example, the command below shows that 20 users have **/bin/bash** as their login shell and that 12 have **/bin/false**. (The latter are either pseudo-users or users whose accounts have been disabled.)

```
$ cut -d: -f7 /etc/passwd | sort | uniq -c
   20 /bin/bash
   12 /bin/false
```

***wc**: count lines, words, and characters*

Counting the number of lines, words, and characters in a file is another common operation, and the **wc** (word count) command is a convenient way of doing this. Run without options, it displays all three counts:

```
$ wc /etc/passwd
 32  77 2003 /etc/passwd
```

In the context of scripting, it is more common to supply a **-l**, **-w**, or **-c** option to make **wc**'s output consist of a single number. This form is most commonly seen inside backquotes so that the result can be saved or acted upon.

***tee**: copy input to two places*

A command pipeline is typically linear, but it's often helpful to tap into the data stream and send a copy to a file or to the terminal window. You can do this with the **tee** command, which sends its standard input both to standard out and to a file that you specify on the command line. Think of it as a tee fixture in plumbing.

The device **/dev/tty** is a synonym for the current terminal. For example,

```
$ find / -name core | tee /dev/tty | wc -l
```

prints both the pathnames of files named **core** and a count of the number of **core** files that were found.

A common idiom is to terminate a pipeline that will take a long time to run with a **tee** command so that output goes both to a file and to the terminal window for inspection. You can preview the initial results to make sure everything is working as you expected, then leave while the command runs, knowing that the results will be saved.

head and tail: read the beginning or end of a file

Reviewing lines from the beginning or end of a file is a common administrative operation. These commands display ten lines by default, but you can include a command-line option to specify how many lines you want to see.

For interactive use, **head** is more or less obsoleted by the **less** command, which paginates files for display. But **head** still finds plenty of use within scripts.

tail also has a nifty **-f** option that's particularly useful for sysadmins. Instead of exiting immediately after printing the requested number of lines, **tail -f** waits for new lines to be added to the end of the file and prints them as they appear— great for monitoring log files. Be aware, however, that the program writing the file may be buffering its output. Even if lines are being added at regular intervals from a logical perspective, they may only become visible in chunks of 1KiB or 4KiB.[2]

Type <Control-C> to stop monitoring.

grep: search text

grep searches its input text and prints the lines that match a given pattern. Its name is based on the **g/*regular-expression*/p** command from the old **ed** editor that came with the earliest versions of UNIX (and still does).

"Regular expressions" are text-matching patterns written in a standard and well-characterized pattern matching language. They're a universal standard used by most programs that do pattern matching, although there are minor variations among implementations. The odd name stems from regular expressions' sordid origins in theory-of-computation studies. We discuss regular expression syntax in more detail starting on page 48.

Like most filters, **grep** has many options, including **-c** to print a count of matching lines, **-i** to ignore case when matching, and **-v** to print nonmatching (rather than matching) lines. Another useful option is **-l** (lowercase L), which makes **grep** print only the names of matching files rather than printing each line that matches. For example, the command

```
$ sudo grep -l mdadm /var/log/*
/var/log/auth.log
/var/log/syslog.0
```

shows that log entries from **mdadm** have appeared in two different log files.

grep is traditionally a fairly basic regular expression engine, but some versions permit the selection of other dialects. For example, **grep -p** on Linux selects Perl-style expressions, though the man page warns darkly that they are "highly experimental." If you need full power, just use Perl or Python.

2. See *Units* on page 14 for an introduction to these units.

2.2 BASH SCRIPTING

bash is great for simple scripts that automate things y
the command line. Your command-line skills carry o
vice versa, which helps you extract maximum value f
invest in **bash**. But once a **bash** script gets above a hu
features that **bash** doesn't have, it's time to move on to

bash comments start with a hash mark (#) and contin
on the command line, you can break a single logical line onto multiple physical lines by escaping the newline with a backslash. You can also put more than one statement on a line by separating the statements with semicolons.

A **bash** script may consist of nothing but a series of command lines. For example, the following **helloworld** script simply does an **echo**.

```
#!/bin/bash
echo "Hello, world!"
```

The first line is known as the "shebang" statement and declares the text file to be a script for interpretation by **/bin/bash**. The kernel looks for this syntax when deciding how to execute the file. From the perspective of the shell spawned to execute the script, the shebang line is just a comment. If **bash** were in a different location, you would need to adjust this line.

To prepare the file for running, just turn on its execute bit (see page 156).

```
$ chmod +x helloworld
$ ./helloworld[3]
Hello, world!
```

You can also invoke the shell as an interpreter directly:

```
$ bash helloworld
Hello, world!
$ source helloworld
Hello, world!
```

The first command runs **helloworld** in a new instance of **bash**, and the second makes your existing login shell read and execute the contents of the file. The latter option is useful when the script sets up environment variables or makes other customizations that apply only to the current shell. It's commonly used in scripting to incorporate the contents of a configuration file written as a series of **bash** variable assignments.[4]

3. If your shell understands the command **helloworld** without the ./ prefix, that means the current directory (.) is in your search path. This is bad because it gives other users the opportunity to lay traps for you in the hope that you'll try to execute certain commands while **cd**'ed to a directory on which they have write access.
4. The "dot" command is a synonym for **source**, e.g., **. helloworld**.

per-

If you come from the Windows world, you may be accustomed to a file's extension indicating what type of file it is and whether it can be executed. In UNIX and Linux, the file permission bits indicate whether a file can be executed, and if so, by whom. If you wish, you can give your bash scripts a **.sh** suffix to remind you what they are, but you'll then have to type out the **.sh** when you run the command, since UNIX doesn't treat extensions specially.

From commands to scripts

Before we jump into **bash**'s scripting features, a note about methodology. Most people write **bash** scripts the same way they write Perl or Python scripts: with a text editor. However, it's more productive to think of your regular shell command prompt as an interactive script development environment.

For example, suppose you have log files named with the suffixes **.log** and **.LOG** scattered throughout a directory hierarchy and that you want to change them all to the uppercase form. First, let's see if we can find all the files.

```
$ find . -name '*log'
.do-not-touch/important.log
admin.com-log/
foo.log
genius/spew.log
leather_flog
...
```

Oops, it looks like we need to include the dot in our pattern and to leave out directories as well. Type <Control-P> to recall the command and then modify it.

```
$ find . -type f -name '*.log'
.do-not-touch/important.log
foo.log
genius/spew.log
...
```

OK, this looks better. That **.do-not-touch** directory looks dangerous, though; we probably shouldn't mess around in there.

```
$ find . -type f -name '*.log' | grep -v .do-not-touch
foo.log
genius/spew.log
...
```

All right, that's the exact list of files that need renaming. Let's try generating some new names.

```
$ find . -type f -name '*.log' | grep -v .do-not-touch | while read fname
> do
> echo mv $fname ${fname/.log/.LOG/}
> done
mv foo.log foo.LOG
mv genius/spew.log genius/spew.LOG
...
```

Yup, those are the commands we want to run to perform the renaming. So how do we do it for real? We could recall the command and edit out the **echo**, which would make **bash** execute the **mv** commands instead of just printing them. However, piping the commands to a separate instance of **bash** is less error-prone and requires less editing of the previous command.

When we type <Control-P>, we find that **bash** has thoughtfully collapsed our mini-script into a single line. To this condensed command line we simply add a pipe that sends the output to **bash -x**.

```
$ find . -type f -name '*.log' | grep -v .do-not-touch | while read fname; do
    echo mv $fname ${fname/.log/.LOG/}; done | bash -x
+ mv foo.log foo.LOG
+ mv genius/spew.log genius/spew.LOG
...
```

The **-x** option to **bash** prints each command before executing it.

We've now completed the actual renaming, but we'd still like to save this script so that we can use it again. **bash**'s built-in command **fc** is a lot like <Control-P>, but instead of returning the last command to the command line, it transfers the command to your editor of choice. Add a shebang line and usage comment, write the file to a plausible location (**~/bin** or **/usr/local/bin**, perhaps), make the file executable, and you have a script.

To summarize this approach:

- Develop the script (or script component) as a pipeline, one step at a time, entirely on the command line.
- Send output to standard output and check to be sure it looks right.
- At each step, use the shell's command history to recall pipelines and the shell's editing features to tweak them.
- Until the output looks right, you haven't actually done anything, so there's nothing to undo if the command is incorrect.
- Once the output is correct, execute the actual commands and verify that they worked as you intended.
- Use **fc** to capture your work, then clean it up and save it.

In the example above, we printed command lines and then piped them to a subshell for execution. This technique isn't universally applicable, but it's often helpful. Alternatively, you can capture output by redirecting it to a file. No matter what, wait until you see the right stuff in the preview before doing anything that's potentially destructive.

Input and output

The **echo** command is crude but easy. For more control over your output, use **printf**. It is a bit less convenient because you must explicitly put newlines where you want them (use "\n"), but it gives you the option to use tabs and enhanced number formatting in your the output. Compare the output from the following two commands.

```
$ echo "\taa\tbb\tcc\n"
\taa\tbb\tcc\n
$ printf "\taa\tbb\tcc\n"
	aa	bb	cc
```

Some systems have OS-level **echo** and **printf** commands, usually in **/bin** and **/usr/bin**, respectively. Although the commands and the shell built-ins are similar, they may diverge subtly in their specifics, especially in the case of **printf**. Either adhere to **bash**'s syntax or call the external **printf** with a full pathname.

You can use the **read** command to prompt for input. Here's an example:

```
#!/bin/bash

echo -n "Enter your name: "
read user_name

if [ -n "$user_name" ]; then
    echo "Hello $user_name!"
    exit 0
else
    echo "You did not tell me your name!"
    exit 1
fi
```

The **-n** in the **echo** command suppresses the usual newline, but you could also have used **printf** here. We cover the if statement's syntax shortly, but its effect should be obvious here. The -n in the if statement evaluates to true if its string argument is not null. Here's what the script looks like when run:

```
$ sh readexample
Enter your name: Ron
Hello Ron!
```

Command-line arguments and functions

Command-line arguments to a script become variables whose names are numbers. $1 is the first command-line argument, $2 is the second, and so on. $0 is the name by which the script was invoked. That could be something strange such as **../bin/example.sh**, so it's not a fixed value.

The variable $# contains the number of command-line arguments that were supplied, and the variable $* contains all the arguments at once. Neither of these variables includes or counts $0.

If you call a script without arguments or with inappropriate arguments, the script should print a short usage message to remind you how to use it. The example script below accepts two arguments, validates that the arguments are both directories, and displays them. If the arguments are invalid, the script prints a usage message and exits with a nonzero return code. If the caller of the script checks the return code, it will know that this script failed to execute correctly.

```
#!/bin/bash

function show_usage {
    echo "Usage: $0 source_dir dest_dir"
    exit 1
}

# Main program starts here

if [ $# -ne 2 ]; then
    show_usage
else # There are two arguments
    if [ -d $1 ]; then
        source_dir=$1
    else
        echo 'Invalid source directory'
        show_usage
    fi
    if [ -d $2 ]; then
        dest_dir=$2
    else
        echo 'Invalid destination directory'
        show_usage
    fi
fi

printf "Source directory is ${source_dir}\n"
printf "Destination directory is ${dest_dir}\n"
```

We created a separate show_usage function to print the usage message. If the script were later updated to accept additional arguments, the usage message would only have to be changed in one place.[5]

```
$ mkdir aaa bbb
$ sh showusage aaa bbb
Source directory is aaa
Destination directory is bbb
$ sh showusage foo bar
Invalid source directory
Usage: showusage source_dir dest_dir
```

5. Note that the error messages and usage message go to standard output. Shouldn't they go to standard error instead? That would in fact be more correct, but since this script isn't intended for use as a filter, the distinction is less important.

Arguments to **bash** functions are treated much like command-line arguments. The first argument becomes $1, and so on. As you can see in the example above, $0 remains the name of the script.

To make the previous example a bit more robust, we could make the show_usage routine accept an error code as an argument. That would allow a more definitive code to be returned for each different type of failure. The next code excerpt shows how that might look.

```
function show_usage {
    echo "Usage: $0 source_dir dest_dir"
    if [ $# -eq 0 ]; then
        exit 99 # Exit with arbitrary nonzero return code
    else
        exit $1
    fi
}
```

In this version of the routine, the argument is optional. Within a function, $# tells you how many arguments were passed in. The script exits with code 99 if no more-specific code is provided. But a specific value, for example,

```
show_usage 5
```

makes the script exit with that code after printing the usage message. (The shell variable $? contains the exit status of the last command executed, whether used inside a script or at the command line.)

The analogy between functions and commands is strong in **bash**. You can define useful functions in your **~/.bash_profile** file and then use them on the command line as if they were commands. For example, if your site has standardized on network port 7988 for the SSH protocol (a form of "security through obscurity"), you might define

```
function ssh {
    /usr/bin/ssh -p 7988 $*
}
```

in your **~/.bash_profile** to make sure **ssh** is always run with the option **-p 7988**.

Like many shells, bash has an **alias** mechanism that can reproduce this limited example even more concisely, but functions are more general and more powerful. Forget aliases and use functions.

Variable scope

Variables are global within a script, but functions can create their own local variables with a local declaration. Consider the following code.

```
#!/bin/bash

function localizer {
    echo "==> In function localizer, a starts as '$a'"
    local a
    echo "==> After local declaration, a is '$a'"
    a="localizer version"
    echo "==> Leaving localizer, a is '$a'"
}

a="test"
echo "Before calling localizer, a is '$a'"
localizer
echo "After calling localizer, a is '$a'"
```

The log below demonstrates that the local version of $a within the localizer function shadows the global variable $a. The global $a is visible within localizer until the local declaration is encountered; local is in fact a command that creates the local variable at the point when it's executed.

```
$ sh scopetest.sh
Before calling localizer, a is 'test'
==> In function localizer, a starts as 'test'
==> After local declaration, a is ''
==> Leaving localizer, a is 'localizer version'
After calling localizer, a is 'test'
```

Control flow

We've seen several if-then and if-then-else forms in this chapter already; they do exactly what you'd expect. The terminator for an if statement is fi. To chain your if clauses, you can use the elif keyword to mean "else if." For example:

```
if [ $base -eq 1 ] && [ $dm -eq 1 ]; then
    installDMBase
elif [ $base -ne 1 ] && [ $dm -eq 1 ]; then
    installBase
elif [ $base -eq 1 ] && [ $dm -ne 1 ]; then
    installDM
else
    echo '==> Installing nothing'
fi
```

Both the peculiar [] syntax for comparisons and the command-line optionlike names of the integer comparison operators (e.g., -eq) are inherited from the original Bourne shell's channeling of **/bin/test**. The brackets are actually a shorthand way of invoking **test** and are not a syntactic requirement of the if statement.[6]

6. In reality, these operations are now built into the shell and do not actually run **/bin/test**.

Table 2.2 shows the **bash** comparison operators for numbers and strings. **bash** uses textual operators for numbers and symbolic operators for strings, exactly the opposite of Perl.

Table 2.2 Elementary bash comparison operators

String	Numeric	True if
x = y	x -eq y	x is equal to y
x != y	x -ne y	x is not equal to y
x < y[a]	x -lt y	x is less than y
–	x -le y	x is less than or equal to y
x > y[a]	x -gt y	x is greater than y
–	x -ge y	x is greater than or equal to y
-n x	–	x is not null
-z x	–	x is null

a. Must be backslash-escaped or double bracketed to prevent interpretation as an input or output redirection character.

bash shines in its options for evaluating the properties of files (again, courtesy of its **/bin/test** legacy). Table 2.3 shows a few of **bash**'s many file-testing and file-comparison operators.

Table 2.3 bash file evaluation operators

Operator	True if
-d *file*	*file* exists and is a directory
-e *file*	*file* exists
-f *file*	*file* exists and is a regular file
-r *file*	You have read permission on *file*
-s *file*	*file* exists and is not empty
-w *file*	You have write permission on *file*
file1 -nt *file2*	*file1* is newer than *file2*
file1 -ot *file2*	*file1* is older than *file2*

Although the elif form is useful, a case selection is often a better choice for clarity. Its syntax is shown below in a sample routine that centralizes logging for a script. Of particular note are the closing parenthesis after each condition and the two semicolons that follow the statement block to be executed when a condition is met. The case statement ends with esac.

```
# The log level is set in the global variable LOG_LEVEL. The choices
# are, from most to least severe, Error, Warning, Info, and Debug.

function logMsg {
    message_level=$1
    message_itself=$2
```

```
        if [ $message_level -le $LOG_LEVEL ]; then
            case $message_level in
                0) message_level_text="Error" ;;
                1) message_level_text="Warning" ;;
                2) message_level_text="Info" ;;
                3) message_level_text="Debug" ;;
                *) message_level_text="Other"
            esac
            echo "${message_level_text}: $message_itself"
        fi
    }
```

This routine illustrates the common "log level" paradigm used by many administrative applications. The code of the script generates messages at many different levels of detail, but only the ones that pass a globally set threshold, $LOG_LEVEL, are actually logged or acted upon. To clarify the importance of each message, the message text is preceded by a label that denotes its associated log level.

Loops

bash's for...in construct makes it easy to take some action for a group of values or files, especially when combined with filename globbing (the expansion of simple pattern-matching characters such as * and ? to form filenames or lists of filenames). The *.sh pattern in the for loop below returns a list of matching filenames in the current directory. The for statement then iterates through that list, assigning each filename in turn to the variable script.

```
#!/bin/bash

suffix=BACKUP--`date +%Y%m%d-%H%M`

for script in *.sh; do
    newname="$script.$suffix"
    echo "Copying $script to $newname..."
    cp $script $newname
done
```

The output looks like this:

```
$ sh forexample
Copying rhel.sh to rhel.sh.BACKUP--20091210-1708...
Copying sles.sh to sles.sh.BACKUP--20091210-1708...
...
```

The filename expansion is not magic in this context; it works exactly as it does on the command line. Which is to say, the expansion happens first and the line is then processed by the interpreter in its expanded form.[7] You could just as well have entered the filenames statically, as in the line

```
for script in rhel.sh sles.sh; do
```

7. More accurately, the filename expansion is just a little bit magic in that it does maintain a notion of the atomicity of each filename. Filenames that contain spaces will go through the for loop in a single pass.

In fact, any whitespace-separated list of things, including the contents of a variable, works as a target of for...in.

bash also has the more familiar for loop from traditional programming languages in which you specify starting, increment, and termination clauses. For example:

```
for (( i=0 ; i < $CPU_COUNT ; i++ )); do
    CPU_LIST="$CPU_LIST $i"
done
```

The next example illustrates **bash**'s while loop, which is useful for processing command-line arguments and for reading the lines of a file.

```
#!/bin/bash

exec 0<$1
counter=1
while read line; do
    echo "$counter: $line"
    $((counter++))
done
```

Here's what the output looks like:

```
ubuntu$ sh whileexample /etc/passwd
1: root:x:0:0:Superuser:/root:/bin/bash
2: bin:x:1:1:bin:/bin:/bin/bash
3: daemon:x:2:2:Daemon:/sbin:/bin/bash
...
```

This scriptlet has a couple of interesting features. The exec statement redefines the script's standard input to come from whatever file is named by the first command-line argument.[8] The file must exist or the script generates an error.

The read statement within the while clause is in fact a shell built-in, but it acts like an external command. You can put external commands in a while clause as well; in that form, the while loop terminates when the external command returns a nonzero exit status.

The $((counter++)) expression is an odd duck, indeed. The $((...)) notation forces numeric evaluation. It also makes optional the use of $ to mark variable names. The ++ is the familiar postincrement operator from C and other languages. It returns the value of the variable to which it's attached, but has the side effect of incrementing that variable's value as well.

The $((...)) shenanigans work in the context of double quotes, so the body of the loop could be collapsed down to one line.

8. Depending on the invocation, exec can also have the more familiar meaning "stop this script and transfer control to another script or expression." It's yet another shell oddity that both functions are accessed through the same statement.

```
while read line; do
    echo "$((counter++)): $line"
done
```


Arrays and arithmetic

Sophisticated data structures and calculations aren't **bash**'s forte. But it does at least offer arrays and arithmetic.

All **bash** variables are string valued, so **bash** does not distinguish between the number 1 and the character string "1" in assignments. The difference lies in how the variables are used. The following code illustrates the distinction:

```
#!/bin/bash

a=1
b=$((2))

c=$a+$b
d=$(($a+$b))

echo "$a + $b = $c \t(plus sign as string literal)"
echo "$a + $b = $d \t(plus sign as arithmetic addition)"
```

This script produces the output

```
1 + 2 = 1+2  (plus sign as string literal)
1 + 2 = 3    (plus sign as arithmetic addition)
```

Note that the plus sign in the assignment to $c does not even act as a concatenation operator for strings. It's just a literal character. That line is equivalent to

```
c="$a+$b"
```

To force numeric evaluation, you enclose an expression in $((...)), as shown with the assignment to $d above. But even this precaution does not result in $d receiving a numeric value; the value is still stored as the string "3".

bash has the usual assortment of arithmetic, logical, and relational operators; see the man page for details.

Arrays in **bash** are a bit strange, and they're not often used. Nevertheless, they're available if you need them. Literal arrays are delimited by parentheses, and the elements are separated by whitespace. You can use quoting to include literal spaces in an element.

```
example=(aa 'bb cc' dd)
```

Use ${*array_name*[*subscript*]} to access individual elements. Subscripting begins at zero. The subscripts * and @ refer to the array as a whole, and the special forms ${#*array_name*[*]} and ${#*array_name*[@]} yield the number of elements in the array. Don't misremember these as the more logical-seeming ${#*array_name*}; that is in fact the length of the array's first element (equivalent to ${#*array_name*[0]}).

You might think that $example[1] would be an unambiguous reference to the second element of the array, but **bash** parses this string as $example (a shorthand reference to $example[0]) plus the literal string [1]. Always include the curly braces when referring to array variables—no exceptions.

Here's a quick script that illustrates some of the features and pitfalls of array management in **bash**:

```
#!/bin/bash

example=(aa 'bb cc' dd)
example[3]=ee

echo "example[@] = ${example[@]}"
echo "example array contains ${#example[@]} elements"

for elt in "${example[@]}"; do
    echo "  Element = $elt"
done
```

Its output is

```
$ sh arrays
example[@] = aa bb cc dd ee
example array contains 4 elements
    Element = aa
    Element = bb cc
    Element = dd
    Element = ee
```

This example seems straightforward, but only because we've constructed it to be well behaved. Pitfalls await the unwary. For example, replacing the for line with

```
for elt in ${example[@]}; do
```

(without quotes around the array expression) also works fine, but instead of four array elements it yields five: aa, bb, cc, dd, and ee.

The underlying issue is that all **bash** variables are still essentially strings, so the illusion of arrays is wobbly at best. Subtleties regarding when and how strings are separated into elements abound. You can use Perl or Python, or google for Mendel Cooper's *Advanced Bash-Scripting Guide* to investigate the nuances.

2.3 Regular expressions

Regular expressions are supported by most modern languages, though some take them more to heart than others. They're also used by UNIX commands such as **grep** and **vi**. They are so common that the name is usually shortened to "regex." Entire books have been written about how to harness their power, and they have been the subject of numerous doctoral dissertations.

The filename matching and expansion performed by the shell when it interprets command lines such as **wc -l *.pl** *is not* a form of regex matching. It's a different system called "shell globbing," and it uses a different and simpler syntax.

Regular expressions are powerful, but they cannot recognize all possible grammars. Their most notable weakness is that they cannot recognize nested delimiters. For example, it's not possible to write a regular expression that recognizes valid arithmetic expressions when parentheses are allowed for grouping.

Regular expressions reached the apex of their power and perfection in Perl. In fact, Perl's pattern matching features are so elaborate that it's not really accurate to call them an implementation of regular expressions. Perl patterns can match nested delimiters, recognize palindromes, and match an arbitrary string of As followed by the same number of Bs—all feats beyond the reach of regular expressions. However, Perl can process vanilla regular expressions as well.

Perl's pattern matching language remains the industry benchmark, and it has been widely adopted by other languages and tools. Philip Hazel's PCRE (Perl-compatible regular expression) library makes it relatively easy for developers to incorporate the language into their own projects.

Regular expressions are not themselves a scripting language, but they're so useful that they merit featured coverage in any discussion of scripting; hence, this section.[9] Here, we discuss them in their basic form with a few of Perl's refinements.

The matching process

Code that evaluates a regular expression attempts to match a single given text string to a single given pattern. The "text string" to match can be very long and can contain embedded newlines. It's often convenient to use a regex to match the contents of an entire file or HTML document.

For the matcher to declare success, the entire search pattern must match a contiguous section of the search text. However, the pattern can match at any position. After a successful match, the evaluator returns the text of the match along with a list of matches for any specially delimited subsections of the pattern.

Literal characters

In general, characters in a regular expression match themselves. So the pattern

```
I am the walrus
```

matches the string "I am the walrus" and that string only. Since it can match anywhere in the search text, the pattern can be successfully matched to the string "I am the egg man. I am the walrus. Koo koo ka-choo!" However, the actual match is limited to the "I am the walrus" portion. Matching is case sensitive.

9. Perl guru Tom Christiansen commented, "I don't know what a 'scripting language' is, but I agree that regular expressions are neither procedural nor functional languages. Rather, they are a logic-based or declarative language, a class of languages that also includes Prolog and Makefiles. And BNFs. One might also call them rule-based languages. I prefer to call them declarative languages myself."

Special characters

Table 2.4 shows the meanings of some common special symbols that can appear in regular expressions. These are just the basics—there are many, many more.

Table 2.4 Special characters in regular expressions (common ones)

Symbol	What it matches or does
.	Matches any character
[*chars*]	Matches any character from a given set
[^*chars*]	Matches any character not in a given set
^	Matches the beginning of a line
$	Matches the end of a line
\w	Matches any "word" character (same as [A-Za-z0-9_])
\s	Matches any whitespace character (same as [\f\t\n\r])[a]
\d	Matches any digit (same as [0-9])
|	Matches either the element to its left or the one to its right
(*expr*)	Limits scope, groups elements, allows matches to be captured
?	Allows zero or one match of the preceding element
*	Allows zero, one, or many matches of the preceding element
+	Allows one or more matches of the preceding element
{*n*}	Matches exactly *n* instances of the preceding element
{*min*,}	Matches at least *min* instances (note the comma)
{*min*,*max*}	Matches any number of instances from *min* to *max*

a. That is, a space, a form feed, a tab, a newline, or a return

Many special constructs, such as + and |, affect the matching of the "thing" to their left or right. In general, a "thing" is a single character, a subpattern enclosed in parentheses, or a character class enclosed in square brackets. For the | character, however, thingness extends indefinitely to both left and right. If you want to limit the scope of the vertical bar, enclose the bar and both things in their own set of parentheses. For example,

```
I am the (walrus|egg man)\.
```

matches either "I am the walrus." or "I am the egg man.". This example also demonstrates escaping of special characters (here, the dot). The pattern

```
(I am the (walrus|egg man)\. ?){1,2}
```

matches any of the following:

- I am the walrus.
- I am the egg man.
- I am the walrus. I am the egg man.
- I am the egg man. I am the walrus.

Unfortunately, it also matches "I am the egg man. I am the egg man.". (What kind of sense does that make?) More importantly, it also matches "I am the walrus. I am the egg man. I am the walrus.", even though the number of repetitions is explicitly capped at two. That's because the pattern need not match the entire search text. Here, the regex matches two sentences and terminates, declaring success. It simply doesn't care that another repetition is available.

It is a common error to confuse the regular expression metacharacter * (the zero-or-more quantifier) with the shell's * globbing character. The regex version of the star needs something to modify; otherwise, it won't do what you expect. Use .* if any sequence of characters (including no characters at all) is an acceptable match.

Example regular expressions

In the United States, postal ("zip") codes have either five digits or five digits followed by a dash and four more digits. To match a regular zip code, you must match a five-digit number. The following regular expression fits the bill:

```
^\d{5}$
```

The ^ and $ match the beginning and end of the search text but do not actually correspond to characters in the text; they are "zero-width assertions." These characters ensure that only texts consisting of exactly five digits match the regular expression—the regex will not match five digits within a larger string. The \d escape matches a digit, and the quantifier {5} says that there must be exactly five digit matches.

To accommodate either a five-digit zip code or an extended zip+4, add an optional dash and four additional digits:

```
^\d{5}(-\d{4})?$
```

The parentheses group the dash and extra digits together so that they are considered one optional unit. For example, the regex won't match a five-digit zip code followed by a dash. If the dash is present, the four-digit extension must be present as well or there is no match.

A classic demonstration of regex matching is the following expression,

```
M[ou]'?am+[ae]r ([AEae]l[- ])?[GKQ]h?[aeu]+([dtz][dhz]?){1,2}af[iy]
```

which matches most of the variant spellings of the name of Libyan head of state Moammar Gadhafi, including

- Muammar al-Kaddafi (BBC)
- Moammar Gadhafi (Associated Press)
- Muammar al-Qadhafi (Al-Jazeera)
- Mu'ammar Al-Qadhafi (U.S. Department of State)

Do you see how each of these would match the pattern?

This regular expression also illustrates how quickly the limits of legibility can be reached. Many regex systems (including Perl's) support an x option that ignores literal whitespace in the pattern and enables comments, allowing the pattern to be spaced out and split over multiple lines. You can then use whitespace to separate logical groups and clarify relationships, just as you would in a procedural language. For example:

```
M [ou] '? a m+ [ae] r    # First name: Mu'ammar, Moamar, etc.
\s                       # Whitespace; can't use a literal space here
(                        # Group for optional last name prefix
  [AEae] l               #    Al, El, al, or el
  [-\s]                  #    Followed by dash or space
)?
[GKQ] h? [aeu]+          # Initial syllable of last name: Kha, Qua, etc.
(                        # Group for consonants at start of 2nd syllable
  [dtz] [dhz]?           #    dd, dh, etc.
){1,2}                   # Group might occur twice, as in Quadhdhafi
af [iy]
```

This helps a little bit, but it's still pretty easy to torture later readers of your code. So be kind: if you can, use hierarchical matching and multiple small matches instead of trying to cover every possible situation in one large regular expression.

Captures

When a match succeeds, every set of parentheses becomes a "capture group" that records the actual text that it matched. The exact manner in which these pieces are made available to you depends on the implementation and context. In Perl, you can access the results as a list or as a sequence of numbered variables.

Since parentheses can nest, how do you know which match is which? Easy—the matches arrive in the same order as the opening parentheses. There are as many captures as there are opening parentheses, regardless of the role (or lack of role) that each parenthesized group played in the actual matching. When a parenthesized group is not used (e.g., `Mu(')?ammar` when matched against "Muammar"), its corresponding capture is empty.

If a group is matched more than once, only the contents of the last match are returned. For example, with the pattern

```
(I am the (walrus|egg man)\. ?){1,2}
```

matching the text

```
I am the egg man. I am the walrus.
```

there are two results, one for each set of parentheses:

```
I am the walrus.
walrus
```

Note that both capture groups actually matched twice. However, only the last text to match each set of parentheses is actually captured.

Greediness, laziness, and catastrophic backtracking

Regular expressions match from left to right. Each component of the pattern matches the longest possible string before yielding to the next component, a characteristic known as greediness.

If the regex evaluator reaches a state from which a match cannot be completed, it unwinds a bit of the candidate match and makes one of the greedy atoms give up some of its text. For example, consider the regex a*aa being matched against the input text "aaaaaa".

At first, the regex evaluator assigns the entire input to the a* portion of the regex, because the a* is greedy. When there are no more a's to match, the evaluator goes on to try to match the next part of the regex. But oops, it's an a, and there is no more input text that can match an a; time to backtrack. The a* has to give up one of the a's it has matched.

Now the evaluator can match a*a, but it still cannot match the last a in the pattern. So it backtracks again and takes away a second a from the a*. Now the second and third a's in the pattern both have a's to pair with, and the match is complete.

This simple example illustrates some important general points. First, greedy matching plus backtracking makes it expensive to match apparently simple patterns such as <img.*></tr> when processing entire files.[10] The .* portion starts by matching everything from the first <img to the end of the input, and only through repeated backtracking does it contract to fit the local tags.

Furthermore, the ></tr> that this pattern binds to is the *last possible* valid match in the input, which is probably not what you want. More likely, you meant to match an <img> followed by a </tr> tag. A better way to write this pattern is <img[^>]*></tr>, which allows the initial wild-card match to expand only to the end of the current tag because it cannot cross a right-angle-bracket boundary.

You can also use lazy (as opposed to greedy) wild card operators: *? instead of *, and +? instead of +. These versions match as few characters of the input as they can. If that fails, they match more. In many situations, these operators are more efficient and closer to what you want than the greedy versions.

Note, however, that they can produce different matches than the greedy operators; the difference is more than just one of implementation. In our HTML example, the lazy pattern would be <img.*?></tr>. But even here, the .*? could eventually

10. Although this section shows HTML excerpts as examples of text to be matched, regular expressions are not really the right tool for this job. Our external reviewers were uniformly aghast. Perl and Python both have excellent add-ons that parse HTML documents the proper way. You can then access the portions you're interested in with XPath selectors. See the Wikipedia page for XPath and the respective languages' module repositories for details.

grow to include unwanted >'s because the next tag after an <img> might not be a </tr>. Again, probably not what you want.

Patterns with multiple wild-card sections can cause exponential behavior in the regex evaluator, especially if portions of the text can match several of the wild-card expressions and especially if the search text does not in fact match the pattern. This situation is not as unusual as it might sound, especially when pattern matching with HTML. Very often, you'll want to match certain tags followed by other tags, possibly separated by even more tags, a recipe that may require the regex evaluator to try many possible combinations.

Regex guru Jan Goyvaerts calls this phenomenon "catastrophic backtracking" and writes about it in his blog; see regular-expressions.info/catastrophic.html for details and some good solutions.

A couple of take-home points from all this:

- If you can do pattern matching line-by-line rather than file-at-a-time, there is much less risk of poor performance.
- Even though regex notation makes greedy operators the default, they probably shouldn't be. Use lazy operators.
- All instances of .* are inherently suspicious and should be scrutinized.

2.4 Perl programming

Perl, created by Larry Wall, was the first of the truly great scripting languages. It offers vastly more power than **bash**, and well-written Perl code is quite easy to read. On the other hand, Perl does not impose much stylistic discipline on developers, so Perl code written without regard for readability can be cryptic. Perl has been accused of being a write-only language.

Here we describe Perl 5, the version that has been standard for the last decade. Perl 6 is a major revision that's still in development. See perl6.org for details.

Either Perl or Python (discussed starting on page 66) is a better choice for system administration work than traditional programming languages such as C, C++, C#, and Java. They can do more, in fewer lines of code, with less painful debugging, and without the hassle of compilation.

Language choice usually comes down to personal preference or to standards forced upon you by an employer. Both Perl and Python offer libraries of community-written modules and language extensions. Perl has been around longer, so its offerings extend further into the long tail of possibilities. For common system administration tasks, however, the support libraries are roughly equivalent.

Perl's catch phrase is that "there's more than one way to do it." So keep in mind that there are other ways of doing most of what you read in this section.

Perl statements are separated by semicolons.[11] Comments start with a hash mark (#) and continue to the end of the line. Blocks of statements are enclosed in curly braces. Here's a simple "hello, world!" program:

```
#!/usr/bin/perl
print "Hello, world!\n";
```

As with **bash** programs, you must either **chmod +x** the executable file or invoke the Perl interpreter directly.

```
$ chmod +x helloworld
$ ./helloworld
Hello, world!
```

Lines in a Perl script are not shell commands; they're Perl code. Unlike **bash**, which lets you assemble a series of commands and call it a script, Perl does not look outside itself unless you tell it to. That said, Perl provides many of the same conventions as **bash**, such as the use of back-ticks to capture the output from a command.

Variables and arrays

Perl has three fundamental data types: scalars (that is, unitary values such as numbers and strings), arrays, and hashes. Hashes are also known as associative arrays. The type of a variable is always obvious because it's built into the variable name: scalar variables start with $, array variables start with @, and hash variables start with %.

In Perl, the terms "list" and "array" are often used interchangeably, but it's perhaps more accurate to say that a list is a series of values and an array is a variable that can hold such a list. The individual elements of an array are scalars, so like ordinary scalar variables, their names begin with $. Array subscripting begins at zero, and the index of the highest element in array @a is $#a. Add 1 to that to get the array's size.

The array @ARGV contains the script's command-line arguments. You can refer to it just like any other array.

The following script demonstrates the use of arrays:

```
#!/usr/bin/perl

@items = ("socks", "shoes", "shorts");
printf "There are %d articles of clothing.\n", $#items + 1;
print "Put on ${items[2]} first, then ", join(" and ", @items[0,1]), ".\n";
```

The output:

```
$ perl clothes
There are 3 articles of clothing.
Put on shorts first, then socks and shoes.
```

11. Since semicolons are separators and not terminators, the last one in a block is optional.

There's a lot to see in just these few lines. At the risk of blurring our laser-like focus, we include several common idioms in each of our Perl examples. We explain the tricky parts in the text following each example. If you read the examples carefully (don't be a wimp, they're short!), you'll have a working knowledge of the most common Perl forms by the end of this chapter.

Array and string literals

In this example, notice first that (...) creates a literal list. Individual elements of the list are strings, and they're separated by commas. Once the list has been created, it is assigned to the variable @items.

Perl does not strictly require that all strings be quoted. In this particular case, the initial assignment of @items works just as well without the quotes.

```
@items = (socks, shoes, shorts);
```

Perl calls these unquoted strings "barewords," and they're an interpretation of last resort. If something doesn't make sense in any other way, Perl tries to interpret it as a string. In a few limited circumstances, this makes sense and keeps the code clean. However, this is probably not one of those cases. Even if you prefer to quote strings consistently, be prepared to decode other people's quoteless code.

The more Perly way to initialize this array is with the qw (quote words) operator. It is in fact a form of string quotation, and like most quoted entities in Perl, you can choose your own delimiters. The form

```
@items = qw(socks shoes shorts);
```

is the most traditional, but it's a bit misleading since the part after the qw is no longer a list. It is in fact a string to be split at whitespace to form a list. The version

```
@items = qw[socks shoes shorts];
```

works, too, and is perhaps a bit truer to the spirit of what's going on. Note that the commas are gone since their function has been subsumed by qw.

Function calls

Both **print** and **printf** accept an arbitrary number of arguments, and the arguments are separated by commas. But then there's that join(...) thing that looks like some kind of function call; how is it different from **print** and **printf**?

In fact, it's not; **print**, **printf**, and **join** are all plain-vanilla functions. Perl allows you to omit the parentheses in function calls when this does not cause ambiguity, so both forms are common. In the **print** line above, the parenthesized form distinguishes the arguments to **join** from those that go to **print**.

We can tell that the expression @items[0,1] must evaluate to some kind of list since it starts with @. This is in fact an "array slice" or subarray, and the 0,1 subscript lists the indexes of the elements to be included in the slice. Perl accepts a range of values here, too, as in the equivalent expression @items[0..1]. A single numeric subscript would be acceptable here as well: @items[0] is a list containing one scalar, the string "socks". In this case, it's equivalent to the literal ("socks").

Arrays are automatically expanded in function calls, so in the expression

```
join(" and ", @items[0,1])
```

join receives three string arguments: " and ", "socks", and "shoes". It concatenates its second and subsequent arguments, inserting a copy of the first argument between each pair. The result is "socks and shoes".

Type conversions in expressions

In the **printf** line, $#items + 1 evaluates to the number 3. As it happens, $#items is a numeric value, but that's not why the expression is evaluated arithmetically; "2" + 1 works just as well. The magic is in the + operator, which always implies arithmetic. It converts its arguments to numbers and produces a numeric result. Similarly, the dot operator (.), which concatenates strings, converts its operands as needed: "2" . (12 ** 2) yields "2144".

String expansions and disambiguation of variable references

As in **bash**, double-quoted strings are subject to variable expansion. Also as in **bash**, you can surround variable names with curly braces to disambiguate them if necessary, as with ${items[2]}. (Here, the braces are used only for illustration; they are not needed.) The $ clues you in that the expression is going to evaluate to a scalar. @items is the array, but any individual element is itself a scalar, and the naming conventions reflect this fact.

Hashes

A hash (also known as an associative array) represents a set of key/value pairs. You can think of a hash as an array whose subscripts (keys) are arbitrary scalar values; they do not have to be numbers. But in practice, numbers and strings are the usual keys.

Hash variables have % as their first character (e.g., %myhash), but as in the case of arrays, individual values are scalar and so begin with a $. Subscripting is indicated with curly braces rather than square brackets, e.g., $myhash{'ron'}.

Hashes are an important tool for system administrators. Nearly every script you write will use them. In the code below, we read in the contents of a file, parse it according to the rules for **/etc/passwd**, and build a hash of the entries called %names_by_uid. The value of each entry in the hash is the username associated with that UID.

```
#!/usr/bin/perl

while ($_ = <>) {
    ($name, $pw, $uid, $gid, $gecos, $path, $sh) = split /:/;
    $names_by_uid{$uid} = $name;
}
```

```
%uids_by_name = reverse %names_by_uid;

print "\$names_by_uid{0} is $names_by_uid{0}\n";
print "\$uids_by_name{'root'} is $uids_by_name{'root'}\n";
```

As in the previous script example, we've packed a couple of new ideas into these lines. Before we go over each of these nuances, here's the output of the script:

```
$ perl hashexample /etc/passwd
$names_by_uid{0} is root
$uids_by_name{'root'} is 0
```

The while ($_ = <>) reads input one line at a time and assigns it to the variable named $_; the value of the entire assignment statement is the value of the right-hand side, just as in C. When you reach the end of the input, the <> returns a false value and the loop terminates.

To interpret <>, Perl checks the command line to see if you named any files there. If you did, it opens each file in sequence and runs the file's contents through the loop. If you didn't name any files on the command line, Perl takes the input to the loop from standard input.

Within the loop, a series of variables receive the values returned by split, a function that chops up its input string by using the regular expression passed to it as the field separator. Here, the regex is delimited by slashes; this is just another form of quoting, one that's specialized for regular expressions but similar to the interpretation of double quotes. We could just as easily have written split ':' or split ":".

The string that split is to divide at colons is never explicitly specified. When split's second argument is missing, Perl assumes you want to split the value of $_. Clean! Truth be told, even the pattern is optional; the default is to split at whitespace but ignore any leading whitespace.

But wait, there's more. Even the original *assignment* of $_, back at the top of the loop, is unnecessary. If you simply say

```
while (<>) {
```

Perl automatically stores each line in $_. You can process lines without ever making an explicit reference to the variable in which they're stored. Using $_ as a default operand is common, and Perl allows it more or less wherever it makes sense.

In the multiple assignment that captures the contents of each **passwd** field,

```
    ($name, $pw, $uid, $gid, $gecos, $path, $sh) = split /:/;
```

the presence of a list on the left hand side creates a "list context" for split that tells it to return a list of all fields as its result. If the assignment were to a scalar variable, for example,

```
$n_fields = split /:/;
```

split would run in "scalar context" and return only the number of fields that it found. Functions you write can distinguish between scalar and list contexts, too, by using the wantarray function. It returns a true value in list context, a false value in scalar context, and an undefined value in void context.

The line

```
%uids_by_name = reverse %names_by_uid;
```

has some hidden depths, too. A hash in list context (here, as an argument to the reverse function) evaluates to a list of the form (key1, value1, key2, value2, ...). The reverse function reverses the order of the list, yielding (valueN, keyN, ..., value1, key1). Finally, the assignment to the hash variable %uids_by_name converts this list as if it were (key1, value1, ...), thereby producing a permuted index.

References and autovivification

These are advanced topics, but we'd be remiss if we didn't at least mention them. Here's the executive summary. Arrays and hashes can only hold scalar values, but you will often want to store other arrays and hashes within them. For example, returning to our previous example of parsing the **/etc/passwd** file, you might want to store *all* the fields of each **passwd** line in a hash indexed by UID.

You can't store arrays and hashes, but you can store *references* (that is, pointers) to arrays and hashes, which are themselves scalars. To create a reference to an array or hash, you precede the variable name with a backslash (e.g., \@array) or use reference-to-array or reference-to-hash literal syntax. For example, our passwd-parsing loop would become something like this:

```
while (<>) {
    $array_ref = [ split /:/ ];
    $passwd_by_uid{$array_ref->[2]} = $array_ref;
}
```

The square brackets return a reference to an array containing the results of the split. The notation $array_ref->[2] refers to the UID field, the third member of the array referenced by $array_ref.

$array_ref[2] won't work here because we haven't defined an @array_ref array; $array_ref and @array_ref are different variables. Furthermore, you won't receive an error message if you mistakenly use $array_ref[2] here because @array_ref is a perfectly legitimate name for an array; you just haven't assigned it any values.

This lack of warnings may seem like a problem, but it's arguably one of Perl's nicest features, a feature known as "autovivification." Because variable names and referencing syntax always make clear the structure of the data you are trying to access, you need never create any intermediate data structures by hand. Simply make an assignment at the lowest possible level, and the intervening structures materialize automatically. For example, you can create a hash of references to arrays whose contents are references to hashes with a single assignment.

Regular expressions in Perl

You use regular expressions in Perl by "binding" strings to regex operations with the =~ operator. For example, the line

```
if ($text =~ m/ab+c/) {
```

checks to see whether the string stored in $text matches the regular expression ab+c. To operate on the default string, $_, you can simply omit the variable name and binding operator. In fact, you can omit the m, too, since the operation defaults to matching:

```
if (/ab+c/) {
```

Substitutions work similarly:

```
$text =~ s/etc\./and so on/g;        # Substitute text in $text, OR
s/etc\./and so on/g;                 # Apply to $_
```

We sneaked in a g option to replace all instances of "etc." with "and so on", rather than just replacing the first instance. Other common options are i to ignore case, s to make dot (.) match newlines, and m to make the ^ and $ tokens match at the beginning and end of individual lines rather than only at the beginning and end of the search text.

A couple of additional points are illustrated in the following script:

```
#!/usr/bin/perl

$names = "huey dewey louie";
$regex = '(\w+)\s+(\w+)\s+(\w+)';

if ($names =~ m/$regex/) {
    print "1st name is $1.\n2nd name is $2.\n3rd name is $3.\n";
    $names =~ s/$regex/\2 \1/;
    print "New names are \"${names}\".\n";
} else {
    print qq{"$names" did not match "$regex".\n};
}
```

The output:

```
$ perl testregex
1st name is huey.
2nd name is dewey.
3rd name is louie.
New names are "dewey huey".
```

This example shows that variables expand in // quoting, so the regular expression need not be a fixed string. qq is another name for the double-quote operator.

After a match or substitution, the contents of the variables $1, $2, and so on correspond to the text matched by the contents of the capturing parentheses in the regular expression. The contents of these variables are also available during the replacement itself, in which context they are referred to as \1, \2, etc.

Input and output

When you open a file for reading or writing, you define a "filehandle" to identify the channel. In the example below, INFILE is the filehandle for **/etc/passwd** and OUTFILE is the filehandle associated with **/tmp/passwd**. The while loop condition is <INFILE>, which is similar to the <> we have seen before but specific to a particular filehandle. It reads lines from the filehandle INFILE until the end of file, at which time the while loop ends. Each line is placed in the variable $_.

```
#!/usr/bin/perl

open(INFILE, "</etc/passwd") or die "Couldn't open /etc/passwd";
open(OUTFILE, ">/tmp/passwd") or die "Couldn't open /tmp/passwd";

while (<INFILE>) {
    ($name, $pw, $uid, $gid, $gecos, $path, $sh) = split /:/;
    print OUTFILE "$uid\t$name\n";
}
```

open returns a true value if the file is successfully opened, short-circuiting (rendering unnecessary) the evaluation of the die clauses. Perl's or operator is similar to || (which Perl also has), but at lower precedence. or is a generally a better choice when you want to emphasize that everything on the left will be fully evaluated before Perl turns its attention to the consequences of failure.

Perl's syntax for specifying how you want to use each file (read? write? append?) mirrors that of the shell. You can also use "filenames" such as "/bin/df|" to open pipes to and from shell commands.

Control flow

The example below is a Perl version of our earlier **bash** script that validated its command-line arguments. You might want to refer to the **bash** version on page 41 for comparison. Note that Perl's if construct has no then keyword or terminating word, just a block of statements enclosed in curly braces.

You can also add a postfix if clause (or its negated version, unless) to an individual statement to make that statement's execution conditional.

```
#!/usr/bin/perl

sub show_usage {
    print shift, "\n" if scalar(@_);
    print "Usage: $0 source_dir dest_dir\n";
    exit scalar(@_) ? shift : 1;
}
if (@ARGV != 2) {
    show_usage;
} else { # There are two arguments
    ($source_dir, $dest_dir) = @ARGV;
    show_usage "Invalid source directory" unless -d $source_dir;
    -d $dest_dir or show_usage "Invalid destination directory";
}
```

Here, the two lines that use Perl's unary -d operator to validate the directory-ness of $source_dir and $dest_dir are equivalent. The second form (with -d at the start of the line) has the advantage of putting the actual assertion at the beginning of the line, where it's most noticeable. However, the use of or to mean "otherwise" is a bit tortured; some readers of the code may find it confusing.

Evaluating an array variable in scalar context (specified by the scalar operator in this example) returns the number of elements in the array. This is 1 more than the value of $#array; as always in Perl, there's more than one way to do it.

Perl functions receive their arguments in the array named @_. It's common practice to access them with the shift operator, which removes the first element of the argument array and returns its value.

This version of the show_usage function accepts an optional error message to be printed. If you provide an error message, you can also provide a specific exit code. The trinary ?: operator evaluates its first argument; if the result is true, the result of the entire expression is the second argument; otherwise, the third.

As in **bash**, Perl has a dedicated "else if" condition, but its keyword is elsif rather than elif. (For you who use both languages, these fun, minute differences either keep you mentally nimble or drive you insane.)

As Table 2.5 shows, Perl's comparison operators are the opposite of **bash**'s; strings use textual operators, and numbers use traditional algebraic notation. Compare with Table 2.2 on page 44.

Table 2.5 Elementary Perl comparison operators

String	Numeric	True if
x eq y	x = y	x is equal to y
x ne y	x != y	x is not equal to y
x lt y	x < y	x is less than y
x le y	x <= y	x is less than or equal to y
x gt y	x > y	x is greater than y
x ge y	x >= y	x is greater than or equal to y

In Perl, you get all the file-testing operators shown in Table 2.3 on page 44 except for the -nt and -ot operators, which are available in **bash** only.

Like **bash**, Perl has two types of for loops. The more common form iterates through an explicit list of arguments. For example, the code below iterates through a list of animals, printing one per line.

```
@animals = qw(lions tigers bears);
foreach $animal (@animals) {
    print "$animal \n" ;
}
```

The more traditional C-style for loop is also available:

```
for ($counter=1; $counter <= 10; $counter++) {
    printf "$counter ";
}
```

We've shown these with the traditional for and foreach labels, but those are in fact the same keyword in Perl and you can use whichever form you prefer.

Versions of Perl before 5.10 (2007) have no explicit case or switch statement, but there are several ways to accomplish the same thing. In addition to the obvious-but-clunky option of cascading if statements, another possibility is to use a for statement to set the value of $_ and provide a context from which last can escape:

```
for ($ARGV[0]) {

    m/^websphere/   && do { print "Install for websphere\n"; last; };
    m/^tomcat/      && do { print "Install for tomcat\n" ; last; };
    m/^geronimo/    && do { print "Install for geronimo\n"; last; };

    print "Invalid option supplied.\n"; exit 1;
}
```

The regular expressions are compared with the argument stored in $_. Unsuccessful matches short-circuit the && and fall through to the next test case. Once a regex matches, its corresponding do block is executed. The last statements escape from the for block immediately.

Accepting and validating input

The script below combines many of the Perl constructs we've reviewed over the last few pages, including a subroutine, some postfix if statements, and a for loop. The program itself is merely a wrapper around the main function get_string, a generic input validation routine. This routine prompts for a string, removes any trailing newline, and verifies that the string is not null. Null strings cause the prompt to be repeated up to three times, after which the script gives up.

```
#!/usr/bin/perl

$maxatt = 3; # Maximum tries to supply valid input

sub get_string {
    my ($prompt, $response) = shift;
    # Try to read input up to $maxatt times
    for (my $attempts = 0; $attempts < $maxatt; $attempts++) {
        print "Please try again.\n" if $attempts;
        print "$prompt: ";
        $response = readline(*STDIN);
        chomp($response);
        return $response if $response;
    }
    die "Too many failed input attempts";
}
```

```
# Get names with get_string and convert to uppercase
$fname = uc get_string "First name";
$lname = uc get_string "Last name";
printf "Whole name: $fname $lname\n";
```

The output:

```
$ perl validate
First name: John Ball
Last name: Park
Whole name: JOHN BALL PARK
```

The get_string function and the for loop both illustrate the use of the my operator to create variables of local scope. By default, all variables are global in Perl.

The list of local variables for get_string is initialized with a single scalar drawn from the routine's argument array. Variables in the initialization list that have no corresponding value (here, $response) remain undefined.

The *STDIN passed to the readline function is a "typeglob," a festering wart of language design. It's best not to inquire too deeply into what it really means, lest one's head explode. The short explanation is that Perl filehandles are not first-class data types, so you must generally put a star in front of their names to pass them as arguments to functions.

In the assignments for $fname and $lname, the uc (convert to uppercase) and get_string functions are both called without parentheses. Since there is no possibility of ambiguity given the single argument, this works fine.

Perl as a filter

You can use Perl without a script by putting isolated expressions on the command line. This is a great way to do quick text transformations and one that largely obsoletes older filter programs such as **sed**, **awk**, and **tr**.

Use the **-pe** command-line option to loop through STDIN, run a simple expression on each line, and print the result. For example, the command

```
ubuntu$ perl -pe 's#/bin/sh$#/bin/bash#' /etc/passwd
root:x:0:0:root:/root:/bin/bash
daemon:x:1:1:daemon:/usr/sbin:/bin/bash
...
```

replaces **/bin/sh** at the end of lines in **/etc/passwd** with **/bin/bash**, emitting the transformed **passwd** file to STDOUT. You may be more accustomed to seeing the text substitution operator with slashes as delimiters (e.g., **s/foo/bar/**), but Perl allows any character. Here, the search text and replacement text both contain slashes, so it's simpler to use # as the delimiter. If you use paired delimiters, you must use four of them instead of the normal three, e.g., **s(foo)(bar)**.

Perl's **-a** option turns on autosplit mode, which separates input lines into fields that are stored in the array named @F. Whitespace is the default field separator, but you can set another separator pattern with the **-F** option.

Autosplit is handy to use in conjunction with **-p** or its nonautoprinting variant, **-n**. For example, the commands below use **perl -ane** to slice and dice the output from two variations of **df**. The third line then runs **join** to combine the two sets of fields on the Filesystem field, producing a composite table that includes fields drawn from both versions of the **df** output.

```
suse$ df -h | perl -ane 'print join("\t", @F[0..4]), "\n"' > tmp1
suse$ df -i | perl -ane 'print join("\t", @F[0,1,4]), "\n"' > tmp2
suse$ join tmp1 tmp2
Filesystem   Size   Used   Avail   Use%  Inodes   IUse%
/dev/hda3    3.0G   1.9G   931M    68%   393216   27%
udev         126M   172K   126M    1%    32086    2%
/dev/hda1    92M    26M    61M     30%   24096    1%
/dev/hda6    479M   8.1M   446M    2%    126976   1%
...
```

A script version with no temporary files would look something like this:

```
#!/usr/bin/perl

for (split(/\n/, `df -h`)) {
    @F = split;
    $h_part{$F[0]} = [ @F[0..4] ];
}

for (split(/\n/, `df -i`) {
    @F = split;
    print join("\t", @{$h_part{$F[0]}}, $F[1], $F[4]), "\n";
}
```

The truly intrepid can use **-i** in conjunction with **-pe** to edit files in place; Perl reads the files in, presents their lines for editing, and saves the results out to the original files. You can supply a pattern to **-i** that tells Perl how to back up the original version of each file. For example, **-i.bak** backs up **passwd** as **passwd.bak**. Beware—if you don't supply a backup pattern, you don't get backups at all. Note that there's no space between the **-i** and the suffix.

Add-on modules for Perl

CPAN, the Comprehensive Perl Archive Network at cpan.org, is the warehouse for user-contributed Perl libraries. Installation of new modules is greatly facilitated by the **cpan** command, which acts much like a **yum** or APT package manager dedicated to Perl modules. If you're on a Linux system, check to see if your distribution packages the module you're looking for as a standard feature—it's much easier to install the system-level package once and then let the system take care of updating itself over time.

On systems that don't have a **cpan** command, try running **perl -MCPAN -e shell** as an alternate route to the same feature:

```
$ sudo perl -MCPAN -e shell

cpan shell -- CPAN exploration and modules installation (v1.9205)
ReadLine support available (maybe install Bundle::CPAN or Bundle::CPANxxl?)

cpan[1]> install Class::Date
CPAN: Storable loaded ok (v2.18)
CPAN: LWP::UserAgent loaded ok (v5.819)
CPAN: Time::HiRes loaded ok (v1.9711)
... several more pages of status updates ...
```

It's possible for users to install Perl modules in their home directories for personal use, but the process isn't necessarily straightforward. We recommend a liberal policy regarding system-wide installation of third-party modules from CPAN; the community provides a central point of distribution, the code is open to inspection, and module contributors are identified by name. Perl modules are no more dangerous than any other open source software.

Many Perl modules use components written in C for better performance. Installation involves compiling these segments, so you need a complete development environment including the C compiler and a full set of libraries.

As with most languages, the most common error found in Perl programs is the reimplementation of features that are already provided by community-written modules.[12] Get in the habit of visiting CPAN as the first step in tackling any Perl problem. It saves development and debugging time.

2.5 Python scripting

As projects become larger and more complex, the benefits of object-oriented design and implementation become clearer. Perl missed the OO boat by about five years, and although it paddled furiously to keep up, Perl's version of object-oriented programming still feels a bit hackish.

This section describes Python 2. Python 3 is in the works and is likely to be released during the lifetime of this book. But unlike Perl 6, it appears likely to be a relatively incremental update.

Engineers with a strong OO background usually like Python and Ruby, both scripting languages with a pronounced OO inflection. Python seems to be well onto the downhill side of the adoption curve at this point, so it's a relatively easy sale for management. Several operating systems, including OpenSolaris, are

12. Tom Christiansen commented, "That wouldn't be my own first choice, but it is a good one. My nominee for the most common error in programs is that they are usually never rewritten. When you take English composition, you are often asked to turn in an initial draft and then a final revision, separately. This process is just as important in programming. You've heard the adage 'Never ship the prototype.' Well, that's what's happening: people hack things out and never rewrite them for clarity and efficiency."

making major investments in Python scriptability. Ruby, by contrast, is still primarily associated with web development and is rarely used for general scripting.

Python was created by Guido van Rossum. It's easier to code and more readable than Perl. Python offers a simple-to-understand syntax that is easy to follow even if you didn't develop the code. If you're tired of remembering which comparison operators to use, you'll appreciate Python's unified approach. Python also offers additional data types that some system administrators find useful.

If Python is not already on your system, check your vendor's or distributor's list of available packages. It's an extremely common package and should be universally available. Failing that, you can get Python source code from python.org. That is also a central location for finding add-in modules developed by others.

For a more thorough introduction to Python than we can give here, Mark Pilgrim's *Dive Into Python* is a great place to start. It's available for reading or for download (without charge) at diveintopython.org, or as a printed book from Apress. A complete citation can be found on page 75.

Python quick start

As usual, we start with a quick "Hello, world!" script. As it happens, Python's "Hello, world!" is almost identical to Perl's.

```
#!/usr/bin/python
print "Hello, world!"
```

To get it running, set the execute bit or invoke the **python** interpreter directly:

```
$ chmod +x helloworld
$ ./helloworld
Hello, world!
```

This one-liner fails to illustrate Python's most scandalous break with tradition, namely, that indentation is logically significant. Python does not use braces, brackets, or begin and end to delineate blocks. Statements at the same level of indentation automatically form blocks. The exact indentation style (spaces or tabs, depth of indentation) does not matter. Python blocking is best shown by example, so here's an if-then-else statement:

```
#!/usr/bin/python

import sys

a = sys.argv[1]

if a == "1":
    print 'a is one'
    print 'This is still the then clause of the if statement.'
else:
    print 'a is', a
    print 'This is still the else clause of the if statement.'

print 'This is after the if statement.'
```

The third line imports the sys module, which contains the argv array. The then and else clauses both have two lines, each indented to the same level. The final print statement is outside the context of the if statement. As in Perl, Python's print statement accepts an arbitrary number of arguments. But unlike Perl, Python inserts a space between each pair of arguments and supplies a newline automatically. You can suppress the newline by including an extra comma at the end of the print line; the null argument tells print not to output the newline character.

Colons at the end of a line are normally a clue that the line introduces and is associated with an indented block that follows it.

```
$ python blockexample 1
a is one
This is still the then clause of the if statement.
This is after the if statement.

$ python blockexample 2
a is 2
This is still the else clause of the if statement.
This is after the if statement.
```

Python's indentation convention gives you less flexibility in the formatting of code, but it has the advantage of making code written by different people look the same, and it means that there is no need to sprinkle your code with pesky semicolons just to terminate statements.

Comments are introduced with a hash mark (#) and last until the end of the line, just as in **bash** and Perl.

You can split long lines by backslashing the end of line breaks. When you do this, only the indentation of the first line is significant. You can indent the continuation lines however you like. Lines with unbalanced parentheses, square brackets, or curly braces automatically signal continuation even in the absence of backslashes, but you can include the backslashes if doing so clarifies the structure of the code.

Some cut and paste operations convert tabs to spaces, and unless you know what you're looking for, this can drive you nuts. The golden rule is never to mix tabs and spaces; use one or the other for indentation. A lot of software makes the traditional assumption that tabs should fall at 8-space intervals, which is really too much indentation for readable code. Most in the Python community seem to prefer spaces and 4-character indentation.

However you decide to attack the indentation problem, most editors have options that can help save your sanity, either by outlawing tabs in favor of spaces or by displaying spaces and tabs differently. As a last resort, you can translate tabs to spaces with the **expand** command or use **perl -pe** to replace tabs with a more easily seen character string.

Objects, strings, numbers, lists, dictionaries, tuples, and files

All data types in Python are objects, and this gives them more power and flexibility than they have in Perl.

In Python, lists are enclosed in square brackets instead of parentheses. Arrays index from zero, which is one of the few concepts that doesn't change among the three scripting languages covered in this chapter.

New with Python are "tuples," which are essentially immutable lists. Tuples are faster than arrays and are helpful for representing data that should in fact be unmodifiable. The syntax for tuples is the same as for lists, except that the delimiters are parentheses instead of square brackets. Because (thing) looks like a simple algebraic expression, tuples that contain only a single element need an extra comma to disambiguate them: (thing,).

Here's some basic variable and data type wrangling in Python:

```
#!/usr/bin/python

name = 'Gwen'
rating = 10
characters = [ 'SpongeBob', 'Patrick', 'Squidward' ]
elements = ( 'lithium', 'carbon', 'boron' )

print "name:\t%s\nrating:\t%d" % (name, rating)
print "characters:\t%s" % characters
print "elements:\t%s" % (elements, )
```

This example produces the following output:

```
$ python objects
name:         Gwen
rating:       10
characters:   ['SpongeBob', 'Patrick', 'Squidward']
elements:     ('lithium', 'carbon', 'boron')
```

Variables in Python are not syntactically marked or declared by type, but the objects to which they refer do have an underlying type. In most cases, Python does not automatically convert types for you, but individual functions or operators may do so. For example, you cannot concatenate a string and a number (with the + operator) without explicitly converting the number to its string representation. However, formatting operators and statements do coerce everything to string form. Every object has a string representation.

The string formatting operator % is a lot like the sprintf function from C or Perl, but it can be used anywhere a string can appear. It's a binary operator that takes the string on its left and the values to be inserted on its right. If there is more than one value to insert, the values must be presented as a tuple.

A Python dictionary is the same thing as a Perl hash; that is, a list of key/value pairs. Dictionary literals are enclosed in curly braces, with each key/value pair being separated by a colon.

```
#!/usr/bin/python

ordinal = { 1 : 'first', 2 : 'second', 3 : 'third' }
print "The ordinal array contains", ordinal
print "The ordinal of 1 is", ordinal[1]
```

In use, Python dictionaries are a lot like arrays, except that the subscripts (keys) can be objects other than integers.

```
$ python dictionary
The ordinal array contains {1: 'first', 2: 'second', 3: 'third'}
The ordinal of 1 is first
```

Python handles open files as objects with associated methods. True to its name, the readline method reads a single line, so the example below reads and prints two lines from the **/etc/passwd** file.

```
#!/usr/bin/python

f = open('/etc/passwd', 'r')
print f.readline(),
print f.readline(),
f.close()
```

```
$ python fileio
at:x:25:25:Batch jobs daemon:/var/spool/atjobs:/bin/true
bin:x:1:1:bin:/bin:/bin/true
```

The trailing commas are in the print statements to suppress newlines because each line already includes a newline character as it is read from the original file.

Input validation example

The scriptlet below is the Python version of our by-now-familiar input validator. It demonstrates the use of subroutines and command-line arguments along with a couple of other Pythonisms.

```
#!/usr/bin/python

import sys
import os

def show_usage(message, code = 1):
    print message
    print "%s: source_dir dest_dir" % sys.argv[0]
    sys.exit(code)
```

```
if len(sys.argv) != 3:
    show_usage("2 arguments required; you supplied %d" % (len(sys.argv) - 1))
elif not os.path.isdir(sys.argv[1]):
    show_usage("Invalid source directory")
elif not os.path.isdir(sys.argv[2]):
    show_usage("Invalid destination directory")

source, dest = sys.argv[1:3]

print "Source Directory is", source
print "Destination Directory is", dest
```

In addition to importing the sys module, we also import the os module to gain access to the os.path.isdir routine. Note that import doesn't shortcut your access to any symbols defined by modules; you must use fully qualified names that start with the module name.

The definition of the show_usage routine supplies a default value for the exit code in case the caller does not specify this argument explicitly. Since all data types are objects, function arguments are passed by reference.

The sys.argv array contains the script name in the 0 position, so its length is 1 greater than the number of command-line arguments that were actually supplied. The form sys.argv[1:3] is an array slice. Curiously, slices do not include the element at the far end of the specified range, so this slice includes only sys.argv[1] and sys.argv[2]. You could simply say sys.argv[1:] to include the second and subsequent arguments.

Like both **bash** and Perl, Python has a dedicated "else if" condition; the keyword is elif. There is no explicit case or switch statement.

The parallel assignment of the source and dest variables is a bit different from the Perl version in that the variables themselves are not in a list. Python allows parallel assignments in either form.

Python uses the same comparison operators for numeric and string values. The "not equal" comparison operator is !=, but there is no unary ! operator; use not for this. The Boolean operators and and or are also spelled out.

Loops

The fragment below uses a for...in construct to iterate through the range 1 to 10.

```
for counter in range(1, 10):
    print counter,
```

As with the array slice in the previous example, the right endpoint of the range is not actually included. The output includes only the numbers 1 through 9:

```
1 2 3 4 5 6 7 8 9
```

This is Python's only type of for loop, but it's a powerhouse. Python's for has several features that distinguish it from for in other languages:

- There is nothing special about numeric ranges. Any object can support Python's iteration model, and most common objects do. You can iterate through a string (by character), a list, a file (by character, line, or block), an array slice, etc.
- Iterators can yield multiple values, and you can have multiple loop variables. The assignment at the top of each iteration acts just like Python's regular multiple assignments.
- Both for and while loops can have else clauses at the end. The else clause is executed only if the loop terminates normally, as opposed to exiting through a break statement. This feature may initially seem counterintuitive, but it handles certain use cases quite elegantly.

The example script below accepts a regular expression on the command line and matches it against a list of Snow White's dwarves and the colors of their dwarf suits. The first match is printed with the portions that match the regex surrounded by underscores.

```
#!/usr/bin/python

import sys
import re

suits = { 'Bashful':'red', 'Sneezy':'green', 'Doc':'blue', 'Dopey':'orange',
    'Grumpy':'yellow', 'Happy':'taupe', 'Sleepy':'puce' }
pattern = re.compile("(%s)" % sys.argv[1])

for dwarf, color in suits.items():
    if pattern.search(dwarf) or pattern.search(color):
        print "%s's dwarf suit is %s." % \
            (pattern.sub(r"_\1_", dwarf), pattern.sub(r"_\1_", color))
        break
else:
    print "No dwarves or dwarf suits matched the pattern."
```

Here's some sample output:

```
$ python dwarfsearch '[aeiou]{2}'
Sn_ee_zy's dwarf suit is gr_ee_n.

$ python dwarfsearch go
No dwarves or dwarf suits matched the pattern.
```

The assignment to suits demonstrates Python's syntax for encoding literal dictionaries. The suits.items() method is an iterator for key/value pairs—note that we're extracting both a dwarf and a suit color on each iteration. If you only wanted to iterate through the keys, you could just say for dwarf in suits.

Python implements regular expression handling through its `re` module. No regex features are built into the language itself, so regex-wrangling with Python is a bit clunkier than with Perl. Here, the regex `pattern` is initially compiled from the first command-line argument surrounded by parentheses to form a capture group. Strings are then tested and modified with the `search` and `sub` methods of the regex object. You can also call `re.search` et al. directly as functions, supplying the regex to use as the first argument. The `\1` in the substitution string is a back-reference to the contents of the first capture group.

2.6 Scripting best practices

Although the code fragments in this chapter contain few comments and seldom print usage messages, that's only because we've skeletonized each example to make specific points. Real scripts should behave better. There are whole books on best practices for coding, but here are a few basic guidelines:

- When run with inappropriate arguments, scripts should print a usage message and exit. For extra credit, implement **--help** this way, too.
- Validate inputs and sanity-check derived values. Before doing an **rm -rf** on a calculated path, for example, you might have the script double-check that the path conforms to the pattern you expect. You may find your scripting language's "taint" feature helpful.
- Return an appropriate exit code: zero for success and nonzero for failure. Don't feel compelled to give every failure mode a unique exit code, however; consider what callers will actually want to know.
- Use appropriate naming conventions for variables, scripts, and routines. Conform to the conventions of the language, the rest of your site's code base, and most importantly, the other variables and functions defined in the current project. Use mixed case or underscores to make long names readable.[13]
- Use variable names that reflect the values they store, but keep them short. `number_of_lines_of_input` is way too long; try `n_lines`.
- Consider developing a style guide so that you and your colleagues can write code according to the same conventions. A guide makes it easier for you to read other people's code and for them to read yours.
- Start every script with a comment block that tells what the script does and what parameters it takes. Include your name and the date. If the script requires nonstandard tools, libraries, or modules to be installed on the system, list those as well.

13. The naming of the scripts themselves is important, too. In this context, dashes are more common than underscores for simulating spaces, as in **system-config-printer**.

- Comment at the level you yourself will find helpful when you return to the script after a month or two. Some useful points to comment on are the following: choices of algorithm, reasons for not doing things in a more obvious way, unusual paths through the code, anything that was a stumbling block during development. Don't clutter code with useless comments; assume intelligence and language proficiency on the part of the reader.

- Code comments work best at the granularity of blocks or functions. Comments that describe the function of a variable should appear with the variable's declaration or first use.

- It's OK to run scripts as root, but avoid making them setuid; it's tricky to make setuid scripts completely secure. Use **sudo** to implement appropriate access control policies instead.

- With **bash**, use **-x** to echo commands before they are executed and **-n** to check commands for syntax without executing them.

- Perl's **-w** option warns you about suspicious behaviors such as variables used before their values are set. You can include this option on a script's shebang line or turn it on in the program's text with `use warnings`.

- In Python, you are in debug mode unless you explicitly turn it off with a **-0** argument on the command line. That means you can test the special `__debug__` variable before printing diagnostic output.

Tom Christiansen suggests the following five Golden Rules for producing useful error messages:

- Error messages should go to STDERR, not STDOUT.
- Include the name of the program that's issuing the error.
- State what function or operation failed.
- If a system call fails, include the **perror** string ($! in Perl).
- Exit with some code other than 0.

Perl makes it easy to follow all five rules:

```
die "can't open $filename: $!";
```

2.7 Recommended Reading

Brooks, Frederick P., Jr. *The Mythical Man-Month: Essays on Software Engineering*. Reading, MA: Addison-Wesley, 1995.

Shell basics and bash scripting

Albing, Carl, JP Vossen, and Cameron Newham. *Bash Cookbook*. Sebastopol, CA: O'Reilly Media, 2007.

Kernighan, Brian W., and Rob Pike. *The UNIX Programming Environment.* Englewood Cliffs, NJ: Prentice-Hall, 1984.

Newham, Cameron, and Bill Rosenblatt. *Learning the bash Shell (3rd Edition)*, Sebastopol, CA: O'Reilly Media, 2005.

Powers, Shelley, Jerry Peek, Tim O'Reilly, and Mike Loukides. *Unix Power Tools, (3rd Edition)*, Sebastopol, CA: O'Reilly Media, 2002.

Regular expressions

Friedl, Jeffrey. *Mastering Regular Expressions (3rd Edition)*, Sebastopol, CA: O'Reilly Media, 2006.

Goyvaerts, Jan, and Steven Levithan. *Regular Expressions Cookbook.* Sebastopol, CA: O'Reilly Media, 2009.

Perl scripting

Wall, Larry, Tom Christiansen, and Jon Orwant. *Programming Perl (3rd Edition)*, Sebastopol, CA: O'Reilly Media, 2000.

Schwartz, Randal L., Tom Phoenix, and brian d foy. *Learning Perl (5th Edition)*, Sebastopol, CA: O'Reilly Media, 2008.

Blank-Edelman, David. *Automating System Administration with Perl*, Sebastopol, CA: O'Reilly Media, 2009.

Christiansen, Tom, and Nathan Torkington. *Perl Cookbook (2nd Edition).* Sebastopol, CA: O'Reilly Media, 2003.

Python scripting

Beazley, David M. *Python Essential Reference (4th Edition)*, Reading, MA: Addison-Wesley, 2009.

Gift, Noah, and Jeremy M. Jones. *Python for Unix and Linux System Administrators*, Sebastopol, CA: O'Reilly Media, 2008.

Martelli, Alex, Anna Martelli Ravenscroft, and David Ascher. *Python Cookbook (2nd Edition)*, Sebastopol, CA: O'Reilly Media, 2005.

Pilgrim, Mark. *Dive Into Python.* Berkeley, CA: Apress, 2004. This book is also available for free on the web at diveintopython.org.

2.8 Exercises

E2.1 UNIX allows spaces in filenames. How do you find files whose names contain embedded spaces? How do you delete them? Do **bash**, Perl, and Python handle spaces in filenames gracefully, or do you need to take special precautions? Outline appropriate rules of thumb for scripting.

E2.2 Write a simple **bash** script (or pair of scripts) to back up and restore your system.

E2.3 Using regular expressions, write a Perl or Python script to parse a date in the form produced by the **date** command (e.g., Tue Oct 20 18:09:33 PDT 2009) and determine whether it is valid (e.g., no February 30th, valid time zone, etc.). Is there an off-the-shelf library or module that lets you do this in one line? If so, explain how to install it and recode your script to use it.

E2.4 Write a script that enumerates the system's users and groups from **/etc/passwd** and **/etc/group** (or their network database equivalents). For each user, print the user's UID and the groups of which the user is a member.

E2.5 Refine the get_string example on page 63 to accept only integers. It should accept three parameters: the prompt string, a lower limit on the acceptable integers, and an upper limit on the acceptable integers.

E2.6 Find an undocumented script that's used in your environment. Read it and make sure you understand its function. Add comments and write a man page for the script.

★ E2.7 Write a script that displays a one-screen summary of status data related to one of the following categories: CPU, memory, disk, or network. The script should leverage OS commands and files to build an easy-to-understand dashboard that includes as much information as possible.

★ E2.8 Build a menu-driven interface that makes it easy to select command-line options for **top**, **sar**, or the performance analysis tool of your choice.

★ E2.9 Write a script to test a server's network connectivity and the upstream services on which it depends (e.g., DNS, file service, LDAP or other directory service). Have it send you email or a text message if problems are discovered.

3 Booting and Shutting Down

Like most things UNIX, system startup and shutdown have matured into carefully engineered processes that accommodate many possible contingencies. As administrators, we negotiate the intricacies of the boot process to prevent and troubleshoot problems. An effective sysadmin understands the fundamentals first.

Bootstrapping has always been somewhat mysterious, but it was simpler in the days when manufacturers controlled every aspect of the system's hardware and software. Now that we have Linux and Solaris running on PC hardware, the boot procedure has to play by PC rules and deal with many potential configurations. Although we discuss the boot procedure for all our example systems in this chapter, you'll see that we have quite a bit more to say about the PC-based versions of UNIX than about the "captive" systems.

This chapter appears early in the book, but it refers to material that is not discussed in detail until many hundreds of pages later. In particular, familiarity with the material in Chapter 6, *The Filesystem*, and Chapter 13, *Drivers and the Kernel*, will prove helpful.

3.1 Bootstrapping

Bootstrapping is the standard term for "starting up a computer." The operating system's normal facilities are not available during the startup process, so the computer must "pull itself up by its own bootstraps." During bootstrapping, the kernel is loaded into memory and begins to execute. A variety of initialization tasks are performed, and the system is then made available to users.

Boot time is a period of special vulnerability. Errors in configuration, missing or unreliable equipment, and damaged filesystems can all prevent a computer from coming up. Boot configuration is often one of the first tasks an administrator must perform on a new system, especially when adding new hardware. Unfortunately, it is also one of the touchiest, and it requires some familiarity with many other aspects of the system.

When a computer is turned on, it first executes boot code that is stored in ROM. That code in turn attempts to figure out how to load and start the kernel. The kernel probes the system's hardware and then spawns the system's **init** process, which is always process number 1.

Before the system is fully booted, filesystems must be checked and mounted, and system daemons started. These procedures are managed by a series of shell scripts (sometimes called "init scripts") that are run in sequence by **init**. The exact layout of the startup scripts and the manner in which they are executed vary among systems. We cover the details later in this chapter.

Recovery boot to a shell

In normal operation, systems boot themselves independently and are then accessed remotely by administrators and users. However, administrators need a recovery tool they can use if a disk crashes or a configuration problem prevents the system from completing the normal boot process. Instead of shooting for full system operation, UNIX systems can boot just enough to run a shell on the system console. This option is traditionally known as booting to single-user mode, recovery mode, or maintenance mode, all terms that we use interchangeably in this chapter. As its name implies, single-user mode does not allow network operation; you need physical access to the system console to use it.

On most systems, you request a boot to single-user mode by passing an argument to the kernel at boot time. If the system is already up and running, you can bring it down to single-user mode with the **shutdown** or **telinit** command.

Steps in the boot process

A typical bootstrapping process consists of six distinct phases:

- Reading of the boot loader from the master boot record
- Loading and initialization of the kernel
- Device detection and configuration

- Creation of kernel processes
- Administrator intervention (single-user mode only)
- Execution of system startup scripts

Administrators have little interactive control over most of these steps. Instead, admins change most bootstrap configurations by editing config files for the system startup scripts or by changing the arguments the boot loader passes to the kernel.

Kernel initialization

See Chapter 13 for more information about the kernel.

The kernel is itself a program, and the first bootstrapping task is to get this program into memory so that it can be executed. The pathname of the kernel is vendor dependent, but it has traditionally been something like **/unix** or **/vmunix**. On Linux systems, the kernel is usually some variation of **/boot/vmlinuz**.

Most systems implement a two-stage loading process. During the first stage, the system ROM loads a small boot program into memory from disk. This program, called the boot loader, then arranges for the kernel to be loaded. This procedure occurs outside the domain of UNIX and so is not standardized among systems.

The kernel probes the system to learn how much RAM is available. Some of the kernel's internal data structures are statically sized, so the kernel sets aside some memory for itself when it starts. This memory is reserved for the kernel and cannot be used by user-level processes. The kernel prints a message on the console that reports the total amount of physical memory and the amount available to user processes.

Hardware configuration

One of the kernel's first chores is to scrutinize the machine's environment to see what hardware is present. As it probes the various system buses and inventories the hardware, the kernel prints out a line of cryptic information about each device it finds. In many cases, the kernel loads device drivers as independent kernel modules. For PC-based operating systems, vendors include kernels that work on most machine configurations and require minimal (if any) customization.

Hardware configuration should be a relatively transparent process for administrators, especially under Linux. Kernels distributed by vendors are extremely modular and will automatically detect most hardware. Nonetheless, you may encounter unrecognized hardware at some point. See Chapter 13, *Drivers and the Kernel*, for help with manual driver configuration.

Creation of kernel processes

Once basic initialization is complete, the kernel creates several "spontaneous" processes in user space. They're called spontaneous processes because they are not created through the normal system **fork** mechanism; see page 123 for details.

The exact number of spontaneous processes varies, although **init** is always PID 1. Most UNIX systems have **sched** as process 0.

Under Linux, there is no visible PID 0. **init** is accompanied by several memory and kernel handler processes, including those shown in Table 3.1. These processes all have low-numbered PIDs and can be identified by the brackets around their names in **ps** listings (e.g., [kacpid]). Sometimes the process names have a slash and a digit at the end, such as [kblockd/0]. The number indicates the processor on which the thread is running, which may be of interest on a multiprocessor system.

Table 3.1 Some common kernel processes on Linux systems

Thread	What it does
kjournald	Commits filesystem journal updates to disk[a]
kswapd	Swaps processes when physical memory is low
ksoftirqd	Handles soft interrupts if they can't be dealt with at context switch time
khubd	Configures USB devices

a. There is one **kjournald** for each mounted ext3 or ext4 filesystem.

Among these processes, only **init** is really a full-fledged user process. The others are actually portions of the kernel that have been dressed up to look like processes for scheduling or architectural reasons.

UNIX systems create similar kernel processes, but since these processes represent aspects of the kernel implementation, none of the names or functions are necessarily common among systems. Fortunately, administrators never need to interact with these processes directly.

Once these processes have been created, the kernel's role in bootstrapping is complete. However, none of the processes that handle basic operations (such as accepting logins) have been created, nor have most system daemons been started. All of these tasks are taken care of (indirectly, in some cases) by **init**.

Operator intervention (recovery mode only)

See Chapter 4 for more information about the root account.

If the system is to be brought up in recovery mode, a command-line flag passed in by the kernel notifies **init** of this fact as it starts up. During a single-user boot on sane systems, you are prompted to enter the root password. If you enter the right password, the system spawns a root shell. You can type <Control-D> instead of a password to bypass single-user mode and continue with a normal boot. See page 86 for more details.

See Chapter 6 for more information about filesystems and mounting.

From the single-user shell, you can execute commands in much the same way as when logged in on a fully booted system. However, sometimes only the root partition is mounted; you must mount other filesystems by hand to use programs that don't live in **/bin**, **/sbin**, or **/etc**.

In many single-user environments, the filesystem root directory starts off being mounted read-only. If **/etc** is part of the root filesystem (the usual case), it will be impossible to edit many important configuration files.[1] To fix this problem, you'll have to begin your single-user session by remounting / in read/write mode. In Linux, the command

```
# mount -o rw,remount /
```

usually does the trick. On most other systems, you can run **mount** / to make **mount** consult the **fstab** or **vfstab** file and determine how the filesystem should be mounted.

Red Hat's single-user mode is a bit more aggressive than normal. By the time you reach the shell prompt, it has usually tried to mount all local filesystems. Although this is usually helpful, it can be problematic if you have a sick filesystem.

The **fsck** command is run during a normal boot to check and repair filesystems. When you bring the system up in single-user mode, you may need to run **fsck** by hand. See page 259 for more information about **fsck**.

Once the single-user shell exits, the system attempts to continue booting in the normal fashion.

Execution of startup scripts

By the time the system is ready to run its startup scripts, it is recognizably UNIX. Even though it doesn't quite look like a fully booted system yet, no more "magic" steps are left in the boot process. The startup scripts are just normal shell scripts, and they're selected and run by **init** according to an algorithm that, though sometimes tortuous, is relatively comprehensible.

The care, feeding, and taxonomy of startup scripts merits a major section of its own. It's taken up in more detail starting on page 97. For a quick course in shell scripting itself, see Chapter 2, *Scripting and the Shell.*

Boot process completion

See page 1171 for more information about the login process.

After the initialization scripts have run, the system is fully operational. System daemons, such as DNS and SMTP servers, are accepting and servicing connections. Keep in mind that **init** continues to perform an important role even after booting is complete.

init defines one single-user and several network-enabled "run levels" that determine which of the system's resources are enabled. Run levels are described later in this chapter, starting on page 88.

1. For example, one common use of single-user mode is to reset a lost root password. This operation requires modification of the **/etc/shadow** file.

3.2 Booting PCs

At this point we've seen the general outline of the boot process. We now revisit several of the more important (and complicated) steps and discuss the details relevant to Intel systems.

PC booting is a lengthy ordeal that requires quite a bit of background information to explain. When a machine boots, it begins by executing code stored in ROMs. The exact location and nature of this code varies, depending on the type of machine you have. On a machine designed explicitly for UNIX or another proprietary operating system, the code is typically firmware that knows how to use the devices connected to the machine, how to talk to the network on a basic level, and how to understand disk-based filesystems. Such intelligent firmware is convenient for system administrators. For example, you can just type in the filename of a new kernel, and the firmware will know how to locate and read that file.

On PCs, the initial boot code is generally called a BIOS (Basic Input/Output System), and it is extremely simplistic compared to the firmware of a proprietary workstation. Actually, a PC has several levels of BIOS: one for the machine itself, one for the video card, one for the SCSI card if the system has one, and sometimes components for other peripherals such as network cards.

The built-in BIOS knows about some of the devices that live on the motherboard, typically the IDE and SATA controllers (and disks), network interfaces, power and temperature meters, and system hardware. SCSI cards are usually only aware of the devices that are connected to them. Thankfully, the complex interactions needed to make these devices work together have been standardized in the past few years, and little manual intervention is required on current systems.

The BIOS normally lets you select which devices you want the system to try to boot from. You can usually specify an ordered list of preferences such as "Try to boot from a DVD, then a USB drive, then the hard disk." Network booting with PXE (see *Netbooting PCs* on page 363) is also a common option.

Once the BIOS has figured out what device to boot from, it tries to read the first block of the device. This 512-byte segment is known as the master boot record or MBR. The MBR contains a program that tells the computer from which partition to load a secondary boot program, the "boot loader." For more information on PC-style disk partitions and the MBR, refer to Chapter 8, *Storage*.

The default MBR contains a simple program that tells the computer to get its boot loader from the first partition on the disk. Some systems offer a more sophisticated MBR that knows how to deal with multiple operating systems and kernels. Once the MBR has chosen a partition to boot from, it tries to load the boot loader specific to that partition. This loader is then responsible for loading the kernel.

3.3 GRUB: The GRand Unified Boot loader

GRUB, developed by the GNU project, is the default boot loader for most UNIX and Linux systems with Intel processors. GRUB ships with most Linux distributions, and with x86-based Solaris systems since version 10. GRUB's job is to choose a kernel from a previously assembled list and to load that kernel with options specified by the administrator.

There are two branches of the GRUB lineage: the original GRUB, now called "GRUB Legacy," and the newer GRUB 2. The name GRUB 2 is a bit deceptive since GRUB 2 releases actually have version numbers between 1 and 2. All of our example systems currently use GRUB Legacy, and that's the version we describe in this book. GRUB 2 is similar in concept but varies in its config file syntax.

By default, GRUB reads its default boot configuration from **/boot/grub/menu.lst** or **/boot/grub/grub.conf**. GRUB reads the configuration file at startup time (which is a pretty impressive feat in itself), so it allows dynamic changes at each system boot. The **menu.lst** and **grub.conf** files are slightly different but have a similar syntax. Red Hat systems use **grub.conf**, and Solaris, SUSE, and Ubuntu still use **menu.lst**. Here's a sample **grub.conf** file:

```
default=0
timeout=10
splashimage=(hd0,0)/boot/grub/splash.xpm.gz
title Red Hat Enterprise Linux Server (2.6.18-92.1.10.el5)
    root (hd0,0)
    kernel /vmlinuz-2.6.18-92.1.10.el5 ro root=LABEL=/
```

This example configures only a single operating system, which GRUB boots automatically (default=0) if it doesn't receive any keyboard input within 10 seconds (timeout=10). The root filesystem for the "Red Hat Enterprise Linux Server" configuration is the GRUB device (hd0,0), which is GRUB-ese for the first partition on the system's first hard disk ("first" being defined by the BIOS).

GRUB loads the kernel from **/vmlinuz-2.6.18-92.1.10.el5** and displays a splash screen from the file **/boot/grub/splash.xpm.gz** when it is loaded. Kernel paths are relative to the boot partition, which is usually mounted in **/boot**.

GRUB supports a powerful command-line interface as well as facilities for editing configuration file entries on the fly. To enter command-line mode, type **c** from the GRUB boot screen. From the command line, you can boot operating systems that aren't in **grub.conf**, display system information, and perform rudimentary filesystem testing. You can also enjoy the command line's shell-like features, including command completion and cursor movement. Anything that can be done through the **grub.conf** file can be done through the GRUB command line as well.

Press the <Tab> key to obtain a quick list of possible commands. Table 3.2 lists some of the more useful ones.

Table 3.2 GRUB command-line options

Command	Meaning
reboot	Reboots the system
find	Finds files on all mountable partitions
root	Specifies the root device (a partition)
kernel	Loads a kernel from the root device
help	Gets interactive help for a command
boot	Boots the system from the specified kernel image

For detailed information about GRUB and its command line-options, refer to the official manual at gnu.org/software/grub/manual.

Kernel options

GRUB lets you pass command-line options to the kernel. These options typically modify the values of kernel parameters, instruct the kernel to probe for particular devices, specify the path to **init**, or designate a specific root device. Table 3.3 shows a few examples.

Table 3.3 Examples of kernel boot-time options

Option	Meaning
acpi=off	Disables Advanced Configuration and Power Interface components
init=/bin/bash	Starts only the **bash** shell; useful for emergency recovery
root=/dev/foo	Tells the kernel to use **/dev/foo** as the root device
single[a]	Boots to single-user mode

a. Linux only. Use **-s** on Solaris—this is a carry-over for administrators who are familiar with OpenBoot on other CPU architectures.

When edited at boot time, kernel options are not persistent. Edit the appropriate **kernel** line in **grub.conf** or **menu.lst** to make the change persist across reboots.

Security patches, bug fixes, and features are all regularly added to the Linux kernel. Unlike other software packages, however, new kernel releases typically do not replace old ones. Instead, the new kernels are installed side by side with the old versions so that you can return to an older kernel in the event of problems. This convention helps administrators back out of an upgrade if a kernel patch breaks their system. As time goes by, the GRUB boot menus fill up with all the different versions of the kernel. It's usually safe to use the default selection, but try choosing another kernel if your system doesn't boot after patching.

Multibooting

Since many operating systems run on PCs, it's fairly common practice to set up a machine to boot several different operating systems. To make this work, you need to configure a boot loader to recognize all the different operating systems on your disks. In the next few sections, we cover some common multiboot stumbling blocks and then review some example configurations.

Each disk partition can have its own second-stage boot loader. However, the boot disk has only one MBR. When setting up a multiboot configuration, you must decide which boot loader is going to be the "master." For better or worse, your choice will often be dictated by the vagaries of the operating systems involved. GRUB is really the only option for Intel-based UNIX and Linux systems. Always use GRUB over the Windows boot loader when dual booting a Windows system.

A multiboot GRUB system is much like its single-boot counterpart. Install all the desired operating systems before making changes to **grub.conf** or **menu.lst**.

A **grub.conf** configuration for booting Windows looks different from one for booting a UNIX or Linux system:

```
title Windows XP
    rootnoverify (hd0,0)
    chainloader +1
```

The chainloader option loads the boot loader from a the specified location (here, sector 1 on the first partition of the primary IDE drive). The rootnoverify option guarantees that GRUB will not try to mount the specified partition.

The **grub.conf** file below boots Windows XP from the first partition (the default), and Red Hat Enterprise Linux from the second:

```
default=0
timeout=5
splashimage=(hd0,2)/boot/grub/splash.xpm.gz
hiddenmenu
title Windows XP
    rootnoverify (hd0,0)
    chainloader +1
title Red Hat
    root (hd0,1)
    kernel /vmlinuz
```

The fact that GRUB solves many potential multibooting problems doesn't really alleviate our inherent skepticism of multiboot configurations. See page 1140 for some additional comments.

3.4 Booting to single-user mode

The beginnings of the boot process are system dependent. Systems with non-Intel processors have custom boot loader software, while PCs are mostly standardized thanks to GRUB.

Single-user mode with GRUB

You don't need to use the command line to boot single-user mode under GRUB. The GRUB authors realized that boot options should be easily modifiable and decided on the 'a' key as the appropriate tool. At the GRUB splash screen, highlight the desired kernel and press 'a' to append to the boot options. To boot into single-user mode, add the **single** (or **-s** on Solaris) flag to the end of the existing kernel options. An example for a typical configuration might be

```
grub append> ro root=LABEL=/ rhgb quiet single
```

Single-user mode on SPARC

To interrupt the boot procedure and enter the OpenBoot PROM on Sun hardware, press the L1 and 'a' keys simultaneously. L1 is sometimes labeled STOP on modern Sun keyboards. From the boot PROM, you can type **boot -s** to boot to single-user mode.

To boot an alternative kernel under Solaris, you usually have to type the full Solaris name of the device and the file. The Solaris device name is the long, bizarre string of characters you see when you do an **ls -l** on the **/dev** file:

```
% ls -l /dev/rdsk/c0t0d0s0
lrwxrwxrwx   1 root     root          55 Jan 15  1998 /dev/rdsk/c0t0d0s0 ->
      ../../devices/sbus@1f,0/SUNW,fas@e,8800000/sd@0,0:a,raw
```

To boot the kernel stored as **/kernel/backup** on this disk, you'd need to enter the following command at the boot PROM monitor:

```
boot /devices/sbus@1f,0/SUNW,fas@e,8800000/sd@0,0:a,raw/kernel/backup
```

Table 3.4 lists some of the more useful commands you can enter from Sun's boot PROM and a brief description of their functions.

Table 3.4 Boot PROM commands on Sun hardware

Command	Function
boot */path_to_kernel*	Boots an alternative kernel
boot -s	Boots into single-user mode
boot -r	Reconfigures the kernel and probes for new devices
boot -a /etc/system.bak	Makes kernel read **/etc/system.bak** instead of **/etc/system**
probe-scsi	Shows a list of all attached SCSI devices

HP-UX single-user mode

The procedure for booting single-user on an HP-UX machine seems to depend on the exact type of machine. The following example is from an HP 9000/735.

First, interrupt the boot process when prompted to do so. You'll receive a prompt. At that prompt, type **boot pri isl** to get to a smarter prompt that will let you boot single-user. This prompt should look something like this:

```
ISL> prompt:
```

The following command selects a kernel and boots the system into single-user mode:

```
ISL> prompt: hpux -iS /stand/vmunix
```

AIX single-user mode

AIX refers to single-user mode as "maintenance" mode. Select maintenance mode from the boot menu before the system starts, or use **telinit S** from the command line if the system has already been booted.

3.5 Working with startup scripts

After you exit from single-user mode (or, in the standard boot sequence, at the point at which the single-user shell would have run), **init** executes the system startup scripts. These scripts are really just garden-variety shell scripts that are interpreted by **sh** or **bash**. The exact location, content, and organization of the scripts vary enormously among vendors.

Most systems use an approach in which scripts are numbered and executed in order. Scripts are kept in **/etc/init.d**, and links to them are made in the directories **/etc/rc0.d**, **/etc/rc1.d**, and so on. This organization is clean, and because the scripts are executed in order, the system can accommodate dependencies among services. These "startup" scripts both start and stop services, so this architecture also allows the system to be shut down in an orderly manner.

Some tasks that are often performed in the startup scripts are

- Setting the name of the computer
- Setting the time zone
- Checking the disks with **fsck**
- Mounting the system's disks
- Removing old files from the **/tmp** directory
- Configuring network interfaces
- Starting up daemons and network services

Startup scripts are quite verbose and print a description of everything they are doing. These status messages can be a tremendous help if the system hangs midway through booting or if you are trying to locate an error in one of the scripts.

Administrators should not modify startup scripts. The ones that accept configuration information read it in the form of a separate and site-specific configuration file, usually itself a shell script. You can modify the accessory configuration script and have confidence that it won't be overwritten by updates.

init scripts are used to some degree by all six of our example operating systems. Solaris 10's startup process was rewritten from the ground up and is discussed starting on page 97. Ubuntu uses an **init** replacement known as Upstart, but we cover it in this section because of its similarities to the traditional **init**.

In the sections below, we first describe the general idea of the system, then cover each OS's individual quirks.

init and its run levels

init is the first process to run after the system boots, and in many ways it is the most important daemon. It always has a PID of 1 and is an ancestor of all user processes and all but a few system processes. **init** implementations vary slightly among systems.

init defines at least seven run levels, each of which represents a particular complement of services that the system should be running. The exact definition of each run level varies among systems, but the following points are all generally true:

- At level 0, the system is completely shut down.
- Levels 1 and S represent single-user mode.
- Levels 2 through 5 include support for networking.
- Level 6 is a "reboot" level.

Levels 0 and 6 are special in that the system can't actually remain in them; it shuts down or reboots as a side effect of entering them. On most systems, the general default run level is 2 or 3. Under Linux, run level 5 is often used for X Windows login processes. Run level 4 is rarely used.

Single-user mode was traditionally **init** level 1. It shut down all network and remote login processes and made sure the system was running a minimal complement of software. Since single-user mode permits root access to the system, however, administrators wanted the system to prompt for the root password whenever it was booted into single-user mode.

The S run level was created to address this need. It spawns a process that prompts for the root password. On Solaris and AIX, S is the "real" single-user run level, but on Linux, it serves only to prompt for the root password and is not a destination in itself.

There seem to be more run levels defined than are strictly necessary or useful. The traditional explanation for this is that a phone switch had 7 run levels, so it was thought that a UNIX system should have at least that many. Linux and AIX actually support up to 10 run levels, but most of these are undefined. On AIX, only run level 2 is meaningful in the default configuration. Levels 0 and 1 are reserved for the operating system, and levels 3–9 are open for use by admins.

The **/etc/inittab** file tells **init** what to do at each run level. Its format varies from system to system, but the basic idea is that **inittab** defines commands that are to be run (or kept running) when the system enters each level.

As the machine boots, **init** ratchets its way up from run level 0 to the default run level, which is also set in **/etc/inittab**. To accomplish the transition between each pair of adjacent run levels, **init** runs the actions spelled out for that transition in **/etc/inittab**. The same progression is made in reverse order when the machine is shut down.

The **telinit** command changes **init**'s run level once the system is up. For example, **telinit 3** forces **init** to go to run level 3. **telinit**'s most useful argument is **-q**, which causes **init** to reread the **/etc/inittab** file.

Unfortunately, the semantics of the **inittab** file are fairly crude, and they don't mesh well with the way that services are actually started and stopped on UNIX systems. To map the facilities of the **inittab** file into something a bit more usable, **init** implements another layer of abstraction. This layer usually takes the form of a "change run levels" command that's run out of **inittab**. This command in turn executes scripts from a run-level-dependent directory to bring the system to its new state.

This second layer is not well developed in AIX. Instead, AIX systems rely heavily on the **inittab** file itself to manage services. AIX's startup scripts are also slightly different from those of other systems.

These days, most Linux distributions boot to run level 5 by default, which may not be appropriate for systems that don't need to run a window server. The default run level is easy to change. This line from a SUSE machine's **inittab** defaults to run level 5:

```
id:5:initdefault:
```

System administrators usually don't have to deal directly with **/etc/inittab** because the script-based interface is adequate for most applications. In the following discussion, we mostly ignore the **inittab** file and the other glue that attaches **init** to the execution of startup scripts. Just keep in mind that when we say that **init** runs such-and-such a script, the connection may not be quite so direct.

Overview of startup scripts

The master copies of the startup scripts live in the **/etc/init.d** directory. Each script is responsible for one daemon or one particular aspect of the system. The scripts understand the arguments **start** and **stop** to mean that the service they deal with should be initialized or halted. Most also understand **restart**, which is typically the same as a **stop** followed by a **start**. As a system administrator, you can manually start and stop individual services by running their associated **init.d** scripts by hand.

For example, here's a simple startup script that can start, stop, or restart **sshd**:

```
#!/bin/sh
test -f /usr/bin/sshd || exit 0
case "$1" in
    start)
        echo -n "Starting sshd: sshd"
        /usr/sbin/sshd
        echo "."
        ;;
    stop)
        echo -n "Stopping sshd: sshd"
        kill `cat /var/run/sshd.pid`
        echo "."
        ;;
    restart)
        echo -n "Stopping sshd: sshd"
        kill `cat /var/run/sshd.pid`
        echo "."
        echo -n "Starting sshd: sshd"
        /usr/sbin/sshd
        echo "."
        ;;
    *)
        echo "Usage: /etc/init.d/sshd start|stop|restart"
        exit 1
        ;;
esac
```

Although the scripts in **/etc/init.d** can start and stop individual services, the master control script run by **init** needs additional information about which scripts to run (and with what arguments) to enter any given run level. Instead of looking directly at the **init.d** directory when it takes the system to a new run level, the master script looks at a directory called **rc*level*.d**, where *level* is the run level to be entered (e.g., **rc0.d**, **rc1.d**, …).

These **rc*level*.d** directories contain symbolic links that point back to the scripts in the **init.d** directory. The names of the links start with **S** or **K** followed by a sequence number and the name of the service the script controls (e.g., **S34named**).

When **init** transitions from a lower run level to a higher one, it runs all the scripts that start with **S** in ascending numerical order with the argument **start**. When **init** transitions from a higher run level to a lower one, it runs all the scripts that start with **K** (for "kill") in descending numerical order with the argument **stop**.

This scheme gives administrators fine-grained control of the order in which services are started. For example, it doesn't make sense to start **sshd** before the network interfaces are up. Although the network and **sshd** are both configured to start at run level 3 in Red Hat, the **network** script has sequence number 10 and the **sshd** script has sequence number 55, so **network** is certain to be run first. Be sure to consider this type of dependency when you add a new service.

To tell the system when to start a daemon, you must place symbolic links into the appropriate directory. For example, to start **cupsd** (the printing daemon) at run level 2 and to stop it nicely before shutting down, the following pair of links would suffice:

```
# ln -s /etc/init.d/cups /etc/rc2.d/S80cups
# ln -s /etc/init.d/cups /etc/rc0.d/K80cups
```

The first line tells the system to run the **/etc/init.d/cups** startup script as one of the last things to do when entering run level 2 and to run the script with the **start** argument. The second line tells the system to run **/etc/init.d/cups** relatively soon when shutting down the system and to run the script with the **stop** argument. Some systems treat shutdown and reboot differently, so we should really put a symbolic link in the **/etc/rc6.d** directory as well to make sure the daemon shuts down properly when the system is rebooted.

Red Hat startup scripts

Startup scripts are one of the areas in which Linux distributions are most distinguished from each other. Red Hat uses a primarily **init**-script-based approach, with a few twists thrown in just to make life difficult for everyone.

At each run level, **init** invokes the script **/etc/rc.d/rc** with the new run level as an argument. **/etc/rc.d/rc** usually runs in "normal" mode, in which it just runs control scripts, but it can also run in "confirmation" mode, where it prompts you for confirmation before running each individual startup script.

Startup scripts store lock files in the **/var/lock/subsys** directory. The presence of a lock file with the same name as a startup script indicates that that service should already be running. Startup scripts create lock files when given a **start** command and remove them when performing a **stop**.

Red Hat supplies a **chkconfig** command to help you manage services. This command adds or removes startup scripts from the system, manages the run levels at which they operate, and lists the run levels for which a script is currently configured. See the man page for usage information for this simple and handy tool.

Red Hat also has an **/etc/rc.d/rc.local** script (not directory) that runs at boot time. It's the last script run as part of the startup process and is a good place to add site-specific tweaks or post-boot tasks.

Once you see the "Welcome to Red Hat Enterprise Linux" message during the boot process, you can press the 'i' key to enter confirmation mode. Unfortunately, Red Hat gives you no confirmation that you have pressed the right key. It continues to mount local filesystems, activate swap partitions, load keymaps, and locate its kernel modules. Only after **init** switches to run level 3 does the system actually start to prompt you for confirmation.

Interactive startup and single-user mode both begin at the same spot in the boot process. When the startup process is so broken that you cannot reach this point safely, you can use a DVD or USB drive to boot.

You can also pass the argument **init=/bin/sh** to the kernel to trick it into running a single-user shell before **init** even starts.[2] If you take this tack, you will have to do all the normal startup housekeeping by hand, including manually **fsck**ing and mounting local filesystems.

Much configuration of Red Hat's boot process can be achieved through manipulation of the config files in the **/etc/sysconfig** directory. Table 3.5 summarizes the function of some important items in this directory.

Table 3.5 Files and subdirectories of Red Hat's /etc/sysconfig directory

File/Dir	Function or contents
clock	Specifies the type of clock that the system has (almost always UTC)[a]
console	Is a mysterious directory that is always empty
crond	Lists arguments to pass to the **cron** daemon
i18n	Contains the system's locale settings (date formats, languages, etc.)
init	Configures the way messages from startup scripts are displayed
keyboard	Sets keyboard type (use "us" for the standard 101-key U.S. keyboard)
mouse	Sets the mouse type; used by X and **gpm**
network	Sets global network options (hostname, gateway, forwarding, etc.)
network-scripts	Contains accessory scripts and network config files
sendmail	Sets options for **sendmail**

a. If you multiboot your PC, all bets are off as to how the clock's time zone should be set.

Several of the items in Table 3.5 merit additional comments:

- The **network** file contains the system's default gateway, hostname, and other important settings that apply to all network interfaces.
- The **network-scripts** directory contains additional material related to network configuration. The only things you might need to change are the files named **ifcfg**-*interface*. For example, **network-scripts/ifcfg-eth0** contains the configuration parameters for the interface eth0. It sets the interface's IP address and networking options. See page 478 for more information about configuring network interfaces.

2. We once had a corrupted keymap file, and since the keymap file is loaded even in single-user mode, single-user was useless. Setting **init=/bin/sh** was the only way to boot the system to a usable single-user state to fix the problem. This can also be a useful trick in other situations.

- The **sendmail** file contains two variables: DAEMON and QUEUE. If the DAEMON variable is set to yes, the system starts **sendmail** in daemon mode (**-bd**) when the system boots. QUEUE tells **sendmail** how long to wait between queue runs (**-q**); the default is one hour.

SUSE startup scripts

SUSE's startup system resembles that of Red Hat, at least in terms of its general organization. However, SUSE's scripts are well organized, robust, and well documented. The folks that maintain this part of the operating system get a gold star.

As in Red Hat, **init** invokes the script **/etc/init.d/rc** at each run level and provides the new run level as an argument. Package-specific scripts live in the **/etc/init.d** directory, and their configuration files live in **/etc/sysconfig**. An excellent introduction to the SUSE startup process can be found in **/etc/init.d/README**.

Although both SUSE and Red Hat concentrate their boot configuration files in **/etc/sysconfig**, the specific files within this directory are quite different. (For one thing, SUSE's files are generally well commented.) You invoke options by setting shell environment variables, and these variables are then referenced by the scripts within **/etc/init.d**. Some subsystems require more configuration than others, and those that need multiple configuration files have private subdirectories, such as the **sysconfig/network** directory.

The **windowmanager** file is a typical example from the **sysconfig** directory:

```
## Path:          Desktop/Window manager
## Type:          string(gnome,startkde,startkde3,startxfce4,twm)
## Default:       kde
## Config:        profiles,kde,susewm

# Here you can set the default window manager (kde, fvwm, ...)
# changes here require at least a re-login

DEFAULT_WM="gnome"

## Type:          yesno
## Default:       yes

# install the SuSE extension for new users
# (theme and additional functions)

INSTALL_DESKTOP_EXTENSIONS="yes"

## Path:          Desktop
## Description:   default mouse cursor theme
## Type:          string
## Default:

# Name of mouse cursor theme for X11. Possible themes can be found
# in /usr/share/icons/

X_MOUSE_CURSOR="DMZ"
KDE_USE_IPV6="yes"
```

Each variable is preceded by YaST-readable[3] configuration information and a verbose description of the variable's purpose. For example, in the **windowmanager** file, the variable DEFAULT_WM sets the desktop window manager used by X.

SUSE also includes a **chkconfig** command for managing startup scripts. It's entirely different from the version provided by Red Hat, but it's an effective tool nonetheless and should be used in favor of manual script management.

Ubuntu startup scripts and the Upstart daemon

Starting with Feisty Fawn in early 2007, Ubuntu replaced the traditional **init** with Upstart, an event-driven service management system that is also used by some other Linux distributions. Upstart handles transitions in system state—such as hardware changes—more elegantly than does **init**. It also significantly reduces boot times.

Upstart starts and stops services in response to system events such as the addition of a device or the disconnection of a network drive. For compatibility, it also emulates the traditional run levels of **init**. However, startup and shutdown scripts are processed in a manner that is somewhat different from that used by **init**.

Upstart uses job definition files in the **/etc/event.d** directory instead of an **inittab** file. A job is similar in concept to a startup script: it performs a series of commands and then returns control to Upstart. The collection of jobs on an Ubuntu system looks like this:

```
ubuntu$ ls /etc/event.d
control-alt-delete  last-good-boot  logd  rc0  rc1  rc2  rc3  rc4  rc5  rc6
    rc-default  rcS  rcS-sulogin  sulogin  tty1  tty2  tty3  tty4  tty5  tty6
```

Over time, more startup scripts will be converted into native Upstart jobs. For now, Upstart uses run-level emulation scripts to boot the system. For example, the **rc2** script executes **/etc/rc2.d/rc**, which runs all the startup scripts for run level 2.

Because of the need to maintain this compatibility, Ubuntu administrators should use Ubuntu's **update-rc.d** command to maintain links to startup scripts within the **rc** directories. The syntax is

update-rc.d *service* { **start** | **stop** } *sequence runlevels* **.**

update-rc.d accepts a sequence number (the order in which the startup script should be run) and the applicable run levels as arguments. Use a terminating dot to end parsing.

Services that start later in a run-level transition should stop sooner when the system exits that level. For example, if CUPS starts at a sequence value of 80 during boot, it should stop at a sequence value of around 20, early in the shutdown process. The **update-rc.d** command to add the appropriate links would be

3. YaST is a SUSE-specific graphical configuration utility that maintains many aspects of a SUSE system.

```
ubuntu$ sudo update-rc.d cups start 80 2 3 4 5 . stop 20 S 1 6 .
 Adding system startup for /etc/init.d/cups ...
   /etc/rc1.d/K20cups -> ../init.d/cups
   /etc/rc6.d/K20cups -> ../init.d/cups
   /etc/rcS.d/K20cups -> ../init.d/cups
   /etc/rc2.d/S80cups -> ../init.d/cups
   /etc/rc3.d/S80cups -> ../init.d/cups
   /etc/rc4.d/S80cups -> ../init.d/cups
   /etc/rc5.d/S80cups -> ../init.d/cups
```

This command adds "start" instances at sequence 80 in run levels 2, 3, 4, and 5, and "stop" instances at sequence 20 in run levels S, 1, and 6.

The default run level is controlled by two telinit 2 lines in **/etc/event.d/rc-default**. Change the run level by editing **rc-default** with a text editor.

Upstart also controls logins on terminals through the jobs named **tty***.

HP-UX startup scripts

Under HP-UX, the actual startup scripts are kept in **/sbin/init.d**. The run-level directories are also in **/sbin**. Config files related to startup scripts generally live in **/etc/rc.config.d**. Their names correspond to the names of the startup scripts in **/sbin/init.d**. For example, the script

```
/sbin/init.d/SnmpMaster
```

gets its configuration information from

```
/etc/rc.config.d/SnmpMaster
```

and is actually invoked from **init** by way of the links

```
/sbin/rc2.d/S560SnmpMaster
/sbin/rc1.d/K440SnmpMaster
```

HP-UX saves the output of startup scripts in **/etc/rc.log**. If one of your startup scripts fails, check **/etc/rc.log** to see if it contains any relevant error messages or hints as to the source of the problem. This saving of startup script output is a most useful and excellent feature, and it's simple to implement, too. It's surprising that other vendors haven't caught on to it.

The config files in **/etc/rc.config.d** can be rather confusing, although they are generally well commented. Table 3.6 on the next page gives a short explanation of some of the more commonly modified files.

The default values in these files are usually OK. The most common files you might need to touch are **netconf**, **netdaemons**, and perhaps **nddconf**.

AIX startup

AIX takes a cruder approach to the boot process than our other example systems. During startup, AIX runs the **/sbin/rc.boot** script, which is written in **ksh**.

Table 3.6 Commonly modified HP-UX config files in /etc/rc.config.d

File(s)	Purpose
SnmpMaster	A master switch that turns all SNMP support on or off
Snmp*	Hold other SNMP-related options
acct	Turns process accounting on or off; see **acct**(1M)
auditing	Configures system auditing; see **audsys** and **audevent**
cde	Holds CDE (Common Desktop Environment) settings
clean*	Control various boot-time cleanup operations
hpetherconf	Configures Ethernet interfaces; see **lanadmin**
lp	Turns the print spooler on or off
mailservs	Starts **sendmail** or specifies a mail server
nameservs	Configures/starts the name server daemon
nddconf	Sets tunable kernel parameters at startup time using **ndd**
netconf	Specifies network device configuration (IP address, etc.)
netdaemons	Tells which networking daemons to start
nettl	Configures network tracing and logging[a]
nfsconf	Sets NFS configuration options
sshd	Configures the SSH daemon
vt	Starts **vtdaemon**; depends on **ptydaemon**
xfs	Turns the X Windows font server on or off

a. See **nettl**(1M), **nettlconf**(1M), and **nettlgen.conf**(4) for more information.

rc.boot is a poorly commented script that executes in three phases:

- Initialization of system hardware
- Mounting of filesystems
- Starting **/etc/init**, which processes entries in the **/etc/inittab** file

AIX relies more heavily on **/etc/inittab** than do its UNIX relatives. **init** reads each line of the **inittab** file and executes the lines in order. In some cases, **inittab** starts a daemon directly. For example, the following line starts or restarts **cron** at run levels 2 through 9:

```
cron:23456789:respawn:/usr/sbin/cron
```

Other **inittab** entries run a series of commands. For example, **/etc/rc.tcpip** (a **bsh** script), starts network daemons:

```
rctcpip:23456789:wait:/etc/rc.tcpip > /dev/console 2>&1 # Start TCP/IP daemons
```

Here, output from the script is routed to the system console. **init** waits for the script to exit before processing the next line in the file.

AIX includes a series of four simple commands for managing the **inittab** file: **mkitab**, **chitab**, **lsitab**, and **rmitab**. Predictably, these commands add, change, list, and remove entries from the **inittab**. We don't see the point and prefer to edit the file directly with a text editor such as **vi**.

3.6 Booting Solaris

With the introduction of its Service Management Facility, Sun revamped the boot process for Solaris 10 and OpenSolaris. SMF is a comprehensive and conceptually unique approach to managing services under UNIX. It wraps a new layer of logic around services to handle dependencies and automatically manage configuration errors and software failures.

SMF changes the boot procedure quite a bit. The traditional tableau of **init** and its **rc** scripts is, in theory, gone. Sun claims that modern applications and their interdependencies have become too complex for the standard scheme. They're kind of right. On the other hand, the standard architecture is much simpler, and we facetiously wonder how Linux and other popular operating systems could possibly be managing to limp along under the old system.

Before discussing the boot process, we need to take a general look at SMF.

The Solaris Service Management Facility

Sun defines a service as "an entity that provides a list of capabilities to applications and other services, local and remote." For our purposes, a service is roughly equivalent to a daemon: a web server, the **syslogd** system logger, or even **init**. Multiple instances of the same SMF service can exist. For example, you might run several email servers with different configurations and IP addresses. A service can also be defined as a collection of other services. This feature lets SMF subsume the role of **init**'s traditional run levels.

Each instance of a service is uniquely identified by a "fault management resource identifier" or FMRI. For example, the following equivalent FMRIs refer to the SSH service:

```
svc:/network/ssh:default
network/ssh:default
```

The ssh service is in the network category, and this particular FMRI describes the default instance. SMF includes several categories, such as application, device, network, and system. A special category called milestone encapsulates the concept of run levels.

You examine the status of services with the **svcs** command. Use **svcs -a** to see all services that have been defined, or omit the **-a** flag to see only services that are currently running. **svcs** can also examine an individual service. For example, the following command reviews the status of the SSH service:

```
solaris$ svcs -l svc:/network/ssh:default
fmri            svc:/network/ssh:default
name            SSH server
enabled         true
state           online
next_state      none
state_time      Mon Jul 13 15:56:19 2009
```

```
logfile          /var/svc/log/network-ssh:default.log
restarter        svc:/system/svc/restarter:default
contract_id      65
dependency       require_all/none svc:/system/filesystem/local (online)
dependency       optional_all/none svc:/system/filesystem/autofs (online)
dependency       require_all/none svc:/network/loopback (online)
dependency       require_all/none svc:/network/physical (online)
dependency       require_all/none svc:/system/cryptosvc (online)
dependency       require_all/none svc:/system/utmp (online)
dependency       require_all/restart file://localhost/etc/ssh/sshd_config (online)
```

This command line uses the full FMRI, but since there is only one instance of the service, **svcs -l ssh** would suffice. The state can assume the following values:

- online – enabled and successfully started
- disabled – not enabled and not running
- degraded – enabled but running with limitations
- legacy_run – running; used by the few services that haven't yet been converted to SMF and that still use traditional **init.d** scripts
- uninitialized – starting up and reading configuration
- maintenance – reporting that an error requiring administrative attention has occurred
- offline – enabled but off-line because the service is waiting on an unsatisfied dependency or cannot start for some other reason

In addition to the current service status, **svcs -l** lists the service's log file location, dependencies, and other essentials.

Dependencies allow the specification of arbitrarily complex relationships among services. This facility essentially replaces the system of numbered startup scripts used by the traditional **init** system, where a script prefixed with **S20** runs before one prefixed with **S90**.

In the example above, SSH requires local filesystems, network interfaces, cryptography services, **utmp**, and the existence of the **sshd_config** file. The filesystem automounter is marked as an optional dependency; SSH will run if the automounter is intentionally off-line (as set by the administrator) or if it is on-line and running.

The **svcadm** command changes the status of a service. To disable the SSH server (don't try this remotely!), use

```
solaris$ sudo svcadm disable ssh
```

This example uses the short FMRI for SSH, since it's unambiguous. The disabling is a persistent change; use **svcsadm -t** to disable SSH temporarily.

Under the hood, SMF configures services through XML files called manifests and profiles. A manifest describes the properties of a service, such as its dependencies and the instructions for starting and stopping it. Manifest files are stored in the **/var/svc/manifest** directory. Each instance of a service has its own manifest file.

The exec_method lines in a manifest file usually point to scripts that start and stop services, much like the scripts used in the **init.d** system. For instance, the startup process for the SSH daemon is defined in **/var/svc/manifest/ssh.xml** as

```
<exec_method
    type='method'
    name='start'
    exec='/lib/svc/method/sshd start'
    timeout_seconds='60'/>
```

The **/lib/svc/method/sshd** script that's referred to is an **sh** script that starts the service. It looks suspiciously like a script that might formerly have lived in **/etc/rc.d**—the more things change, the more they stay the same.

The service's profile file determines whether the instance is enabled or disabled. Profiles are kept in **/var/svc/profile**.

The persistent configuration for services is actually stored as a SQLite database in **/etc/svc/repository.db**. Therefore, you shouldn't directly modify the contents of the XML files. Instead, you can manage the manifests and profiles with the **svccfg** command. Use **inetadm** for services controlled by the **inetd** daemon. See the man pages for **svccfg**, **inetadm**, and **svc.configd** for more information.

One of the most touted features of SMF is the concept of "restarters," part of Solaris's much-hyped "predictive self-healing" technology. By contemplating the carefully defined dependency system, SMF can supposedly determine the reason that a service died and restart it if appropriate. The cause of a service failure might be a software bug, a hardware problem, an issue with a dependency, or even administrator error. A designated SMF restarter process, closely tied to the kernel, automatically performs the appropriate recovery actions.

A brave new world: booting with SMF

The boot process on a Solaris 10 or later system is initially very similar to traditional bootstrapping. SPARC booting is slightly different from booting on Intel systems, but the general concept is that low-level firmware (PROM for SPARC, BIOS for Intel) reads in a boot record, which loads the appointed OS kernel.

The kernel scans **/etc/system** for loadable kernel modules, then spins up **init**, which immediately starts the **svc.startd** process. **svc.startd** is the master SMF restarter and is responsible for starting services in dependency order, as defined in the SMF configuration repository.

Unfortunately, the run-level system and the **init** scripts from previous versions of Solaris are not completely dead. Some services—the ones that show as legacy-run in **svcs -a** output—still rely on scripts in the **/etc/rc.d** directories. The collision between SMF milestones and traditional run levels has left behind something of a pile of wreckage.

Booting

To avoid cutting your fingers on the sharp edges, keep in mind a few key points:

- Services in the legacy_run state were started from an **rc** script.
- Solaris defines eight run levels. See the man page for **init** for details.
- To change run levels, use **init** *n*, where *n* is the new run level. Do not try to use SMF to change milestones, which, according to Sun, "can be confusing and can lead to unexpected behavior."
- The **init** daemon is controlled through **/etc/inittab**, much as in Linux.

3.7 Rebooting and Shutting Down

Traditional UNIX and Linux machines were very touchy about how they were shut down. Modern systems have become less sensitive, especially when a robust filesystem is used, but it's always a good idea to shut down the machine nicely when possible. Improper shutdown can result in anything from subtle, insidious problems to a major catastrophe. Databases that aren't halted nicely are notorious for corruption and integrity issues.[4]

On consumer-oriented operating systems, rebooting the operating system is an appropriate first course of treatment for many problems. UNIX problems tend to be subtler and more complex, so blindly rebooting is effective in a smaller percentage of cases.

Whenever you modify a startup script or make significant system changes, you should reboot just to make sure that the system comes up successfully. If you don't discover a problem until several weeks later, you're unlikely to remember the details of your most recent changes.

shutdown: the genteel way to halt the system

The **shutdown** command is the safest, most considerate, and most thorough way to initiate a halt or reboot or to return the system to single-user mode. It dates back to the days of time-sharing systems, so its approach sometimes seems a bit anachronistic on desktop machines.

Unfortunately, almost every vendor has decided to tamper with **shutdown**'s arguments. We discuss the command in general, then tabulate the syntax and arguments you need on each platform.

You can ask **shutdown** to wait awhile before shutting down the system. During the waiting period, **shutdown** sends messages to logged-in users at progressively shorter intervals, warning them of the impending downtime. By default, the warnings simply say that the system is being shut down and give the time remaining until the event; you can also supply a short message of your own. Your message should explain why the system is being shut down and should estimate how long it will be before users can log in again (e.g., "back at 11:00 a.m."). Users can

4. In theory, databases should be particularly resistant to this form of corruption, but our experience in practice doesn't necessarily support this theory.

not log in when a **shutdown** is imminent, but they will see your message if you specified one.

Most versions of **shutdown** let you specify whether the machine should halt, go to single-user mode, or reboot. Sometimes, you can also specify whether you want to **fsck** the disks after a reboot. On modern systems with large disks, a complete **fsck** can take a long time; you can generally skip the checks if you shut the system down cleanly. (Most systems automatically skip the **fsck** checks whenever the filesystems were properly unmounted.)

Table 3.7 outlines **shutdown**'s command-line arguments on our example systems.

Table 3.7 The many faces of shutdown

System	Pathname	Time	R[a]	H	S	F
Linux	**/sbin/shutdown**	*time*	**-r**	**-h**	–	**-f**[b]
Solaris	**/usr/sbin/shutdown**	**-g***secs*	**-i6**	**-i0**	**-iS**	–
HP-UX	**/etc/shutdown**	*secs*	**-r**	**-h**	–	–
AIX	**/sbin/shutdown**	+*time*	**-r**	**-h**	**-m**	–

a. R = Reboot, H = Halt, S = Enter single-user mode, F = Skip **fsck**
b. Red Hat and SUSE, but not Ubuntu

For example, a Linux **shutdown** command that reminds users of scheduled maintenance and halts the system at 9:30 a.m. would look something like this:

```
$ sudo shutdown -h 09:30 "Going down for scheduled maintenance.
    Expected downtime is 1 hour."
```

It's also possible to specify a relative shutdown time. For example, the following command shuts down the system 15 minutes from when it is run:

```
$ sudo shutdown -h +15 "Going down for emergency disk repair."
```

halt and reboot: simpler ways to shut down

The **halt** command performs the essential duties required to shut the system down. It is called by **shutdown -h** but can also be used by itself. **halt** logs the shutdown, kills nonessential processes, executes the **sync** system call (called by and equivalent to the **sync** command), waits for filesystem writes to complete, and then halts the kernel.

halt -n prevents the **sync** call. It's used by **fsck** after it repairs the root partition. If **fsck** did not use **-n**, the kernel might overwrite **fsck**'s repairs with old versions of the superblock that were cached in memory.

reboot is almost identical to **halt**, but it causes the machine to reboot instead of halting. **reboot** is called by **shutdown -r**.

3.8 Exercises

E3.1 Is it really that bad to turn off a UNIX or Linux system with the power button on the computer case? What about unplugging the computer from the wall? Explain your answer. See if you can determine the likelihood of a bad outcome by doing Internet research.

E3.2 Use the GRUB command line to boot a kernel that isn't in **grub.conf**.

★ E3.3 Explain the concept of run levels. List the run levels defined on one of your local systems, and briefly describe each. Why is Ubuntu's run-level concept different from that of other Linux distributions?

★ E3.4 Write a startup script to start the "foo" daemon (**/usr/local/sbin/foo**), a network service. Show how you would glue it into the system to start automatically at boot time.

★★ E3.5 If a system is at run level 3 and you run the command **telinit 1**, what steps will be taken by **init**? What will be the final result of the command?

★★ E3.6 Draw a dependency graph that shows which daemons must be started before other daemons on your system.

★★ E3.7 List the steps used to create a working multiboot system that runs both Linux and Windows. Use GRUB.

4 Access Control and Rootly Powers

Access control is an area of active research, and it has long been one of the major challenges of operating system design. Generically speaking, operating systems define accounts for individual users, and they offer those users a smorgasbord of possible operations: editing text files, logging into remote computers, setting the system's hostname, installing new software, and so on. The access control system is the black box that considers potential actions (user/operation pairs) and issues rulings as to whether each action is permissible.

In the case of UNIX and Linux, there isn't really a single black box that implements access control. In fact, it's more like a warehouse full of black boxes—and the warehouse is running out of storage space. In this chapter, we first go back to the dawn of UNIX to understand how the access control situation got to be the way it is. We then look at modern UNIX and Linux access control systems in theory and in practice, then review some tools that help make the administration of access control (and especially, the management of the all-powerful root account) relatively painless.

Chapter 22, *Security*, describes how to avoid unwanted and embarrassing superuser access by others. Chapter 32, *Management, Policy, and Politics* covers the relevant political and administrative aspects.

4.1 Traditional UNIX access control

Even in earliest and simplest versions of UNIX, there was never a single-point access control system. There were, however, some general rules that shaped the system's design:

- Objects (e.g., files and processes) have owners. Owners have broad (but not necessarily unrestricted) control over their objects.
- You own new objects that you create.
- The special user account called "root" can act as the owner of any object.
- Only root can perform certain sensitive administrative operations.

There's no single "black box" of access control because the code that makes access control decisions is scattered about the system. For example, certain system calls (e.g., **settimeofday**) are restricted to root; the system call implementation simply checks the identity of the current user and rejects the operation if the user is not root. Other system calls (e.g., **kill**) implement different calculations that involve both ownership matching and special provisions for root. Finally, the filesystem implements its own access control system, one that is more sophisticated than that found anywhere else in the kernel. Only the filesystem uses the concept of UNIX groups for access control, for example.

See page 150 for more information about device files.

Complicating the picture is the fact that the kernel and the filesystem are intertwined. For example, you control and communicate with most devices through files that represent them in **/dev**. Since these device files are filesystem objects, they are subject to filesystem access control semantics.

Filesystem access control

In the traditional model, every file has both an owner and a group, sometimes referred to as the "group owner." The owner can set the permissions of the file. In particular, the owner can set them so restrictively that no one else can access it.[1] We talk more about file permissions in Chapter 6, *The Filesystem* (see page 152).

See page 181 for more information about groups.

Although the owner of a file is always a single person, many people can be group owners of the file, as long as they are all part of a single group. Groups are traditionally defined in the **/etc/group** file, but these days group information is more commonly stored on an NIS or LDAP server on the network; see Chapter 19, *Sharing System Files*, for details.

The owner of a file gets to specify what the group owners can do with it. This scheme allows files to be shared among members of the same project. For example, we use a UNIX group to control access to the source files for the admin.com web site.

The ownerships of a file can be determined with **ls -l** *filename*.

1. In fact, the permissions can be set so restrictively that even the owner of a file cannot access it.

For example:

```
aix$ ls -l /home/garth/todo
-rw------- 1 garth staff 1258 Jun 4 18:15 /home/garth/todo
```

This file is owned by the user garth and the group staff. The letters and dashes in the first column symbolize the permissions on the file; see page 154 for details on how to read this information.

*See page 176 for more information about the **/etc/passwd** file and page 186 for details on **/etc/group**.*

Both the kernel and the filesystem track owners and groups as numbers rather than as text names. In the most basic case, user identification numbers (UIDs for short) are mapped to usernames in the **/etc/passwd** file, and group identification numbers (GIDs) are mapped to group names in **/etc/group**. The text names that correspond to UIDs and GIDs are defined only for the convenience of the system's human users. When commands such as **ls** want to display ownership information in a human-readable format, they must look up each name in the appropriate file or database.

Process ownership

The owner of a process can send the process signals (see page 124) and can also reduce (degrade) the process's scheduling priority. Processes actually have multiple identities associated with them: a real, effective, and saved UID; a real, effective, and saved GID; and under Linux, a "filesystem UID" that is used only to determine file access permissions. Broadly speaking, the real numbers are used for accounting and the effective numbers are used for the determination of access permissions. The real and effective numbers are normally the same.

See page 690 for more information about NFS.

Saved IDs have no direct effect. They allow programs to park an inactive ID for later use, facilitating the parsimonious use of enhanced privileges. The filesystem UID is generally explained as an implementation detail of NFS and is usually the same as the effective UID.

The root account

The root account is UNIX's omnipotent administrative user. It's also known as the superuser account, although the actual username is "root".

The defining characteristic of the root account is its UID of 0. Nothing prevents you from changing the username on this account or from creating additional accounts whose UIDs are 0; however, these are both bad ideas. Such changes have a tendency to create inadvertent breaches of system security. They also create confusion when other people have to deal with the strange way you've configured your system.

Traditional UNIX allows the superuser (that is, any process whose effective UID is 0) to perform any valid operation on any file or process.[2]

2. "Valid" is the operative word here. Certain operations (such as executing a file on which the execute permission bit is not set) are forbidden even to the superuser.

Examples of restricted operations are

- Changing the root directory of a process with **chroot**
- Creating device files
- Setting the system clock
- Raising resource usage limits and process priorities
- Setting the system's hostname
- Configuring network interfaces
- Opening privileged network ports (those numbered below 1,024)
- Shutting down the system

An example of superuser powers is the ability of a process owned by root to change its UID and GID. The **login** program and its window system equivalents are a case in point; the process that prompts you for your password when you log in to the system initially runs as root. If the password and username that you enter are legitimate, the login program changes its UID and GID to your UID and GID and starts up your user environment. Once a root process has changed its ownerships to become a normal user process, it can't recover its former privileged state.

Setuid and setgid execution

Traditional UNIX access control is complemented by an identity substitution system that's implemented by the kernel and the filesystem in collaboration. The system is described in more detail on page 153; the short version is that it allows specially prepared executable files to run with elevated permissions, usually those of root. This mechanism lets developers and administrators set up structured ways for unprivileged users to perform privileged operations.

When the kernel runs an executable file that has its "setuid" or "setgid" permission bits set, it changes the effective UID or GID of the resulting process to the UID or GID of the file containing the program image rather than the UID and GID of the user that ran the command. The user's privileges are thus promoted for the execution of that specific command only.

For example, users must be able to change their passwords. But since passwords are stored in the protected **/etc/shadow** file, users need a setuid **passwd** command to mediate their access. The **passwd** command checks to see who's running it and customizes its behavior accordingly: users can only change their own passwords, but root can change any password. (This, incidentally, is yet another example of UNIX's ad hoc access control—the rules are written into the code of the **passwd** command.)

4.2 Modern access control

The preceding discussion leaves out a few details, but no major concepts in the traditional UNIX model have been omitted. Even though the traditional access control system can be summarized in a couple of pages, it has stood the test of time because it's simple, predictable, and capable of handling the majority of access control requirements at the average site. All UNIX and Linux variants continue to support this model, and it remains the default approach and the one that's most widely used today. And except when we discuss some specific alternatives, we assume throughout this book that it's the approach you're using.

Nevertheless, it has some obvious shortcomings:

- From a security perspective, the root account represents a potential single point of failure. If it's compromised, the integrity of the whole system is violated. There is no limit to the damage an attacker can inflict.
- The only way to subdivide the special privileges of the root account is by writing setuid programs. Unfortunately, as the Internet's steady stream of security updates demonstrates, it's difficult to write truly secure software. Besides, you shouldn't have to write custom software to express something as basic as "I'd like these three people to be able to perform backups on the file server."
- The security model isn't strong enough for use on a network. No computer to which an unprivileged user has physical access can be trusted to accurately represent the ownerships of the processes it's running. Who's to say that someone hasn't reformatted the disk and installed their own hacked copy of Windows or Linux, with UIDs of their choosing?
- Many high-security environments enforce conventions that simply can't be implemented with traditional UNIX security. For example, United States government standards require computer systems to forbid privileged users (e.g., those with Top Secret security clearance) from republishing high-security documents at a lower security level. Traditional UNIX security depends on the good will and skill of individual users in this regard.
- Because many access-control-related rules are embedded in the code of individual commands and daemons, you cannot redefine the system's behavior without modifying the source code and recompiling. But that's not practical in the real world.
- There is minimal support for auditing. You can easily see which groups a user belongs to, but you can't necessarily determine what those group memberships permit a user to do.

Because of these shortcomings, UNIX and Linux systems have undergone a variety of interventions over the years to enhance various aspects of the access control system and to help make UNIX systems more acceptable to sites with high security requirements. Some of the adjustments, such as PAM (see page 109), now have nearly universal support. Others are relatively idiosyncratic. The following sections outline the most common extensions.

Role-based access control

Role-based access control, sometimes known as RBAC, is a theoretical model formalized in 1992 by David Ferraiolo and Rick Kuhn. The basic idea is to add a layer of indirection to access control calculations. Instead of permissions being assigned directly to users, they are assigned to intermediate constructs known as "roles," and roles in turn are assigned to users. To make an access control decision, the access control library enumerates the roles of the current user and checks to see if any of those roles have the appropriate permissions.

You might detect some similarity between roles and UNIX groups, and in fact there is debate about whether these constructs are fully distinguishable. In practice, roles are more useful than groups because the systems that implement them allow them to be used outside the context of the filesystem. Roles can also have a hierarchical relationship to one another, a fact that greatly simplifies administration. For example, you might define a "senior administrator" role that has all the permissions of an "administrator" plus the additional permissions X, Y, and Z.

The RBAC model makes it practical to manage large collections of possible permissions. Most of the effort goes into defining the role hierarchy, but that is a one-time project. Day-to-day administration of users is simple. Accordingly, systems that support RBAC normally take advantage of it to split the omnipotent powers of the root account into many different fragments that can be separately assigned.

Solaris uses groups (**/etc/group**), authorizations (**/etc/security/auth_attr**), profiles (**/etc/security/prof_attr**), and bindings among users, authorizations, and profiles (**/etc/user_attr**) to implement roles. Authorizations have names such as solaris.admin.diskmgr, solaris.admin.patchmgr, and solaris.admin.printer. Many authorizations have a specific .read or .write granularity, too. There are 158 of them defined in the **auth_attr** file. The Solaris commands to manipulate roles are **roleadd**, **rolemod**, and **roledel**.

Since build 99 of OpenSolaris in May 2008, Solaris's RBAC system has been robust enough to allow the system to operate without a root account.

HP-UX also uses authorizations to define fine-grained rootly privileges, which are then assigned to roles associated with individual users and groups. The authorizations have names like hpux.admin.process.kill, hpux.admin.network.config, and hpux.admin.device.install. There are 137 authorizations predefined in the file **/etc/rbac/auths**. You manage roles with the **roleadm**, **authadm**, **cmdprivadm**, **privrun**, and **privedit** commands.

In AIX, roles have names like DomainAdmin, BackupRestore, AccountAdmin, SysConfig, and SecPolicy. Authorizations are at a similar granularity to those in Solaris or HP-UX. Some examples of authorization names are aix.device, aix.proc, aix.fs.manage.export, and aix.system.config.cron. Roles are tied to screens in the AIX sysadmin tool SMIT. Users can assume up to eight roles at once. AIX's role-related commands are **mkrole**, **chrole**, **rmrole**, **rolelist**, and **swrole**.

SELinux: security-enhanced Linux

SELinux is an NSA project that has been freely available since late 2000. It has been integrated into the 2.6 series of the Linux kernel and so is available on most current distributions. Some distributions ship with it enabled (and often in a somewhat dysfunctional state).

The primary focus of SELinux is to enable "mandatory access control," aka MAC, an access control system in which all permissions are assigned by administrators. Under MAC, users cannot delegate their access or set access control parameters on the objects they own. As such, it's primarily of interest to sites with specialized requirements.[3]

SELinux can also be used to implement a form of role-based access control, although this was not a primary objective of the system.

See page 923 for additional details.

POSIX capabilities (Linux)

Linux systems—even those that do not make use of the SELinux extensions—are theoretically capable of subdividing the privileges of the root account according to the POSIX standard for "capabilities." Capability specifications can also be assigned to executable programs. The programs then acquire the specified capabilities when they are executed. It's essentially a lower-risk form of setuid execution.

For various reasons, including problems with the current implementation, the capabilities facility is not as helpful or as relevant to system administrators as it might initially appear. For more comments on capabilities, see the discussion on page 818.

PAM: Pluggable Authentication Modules

PAM is an authentication technology rather than an access control technology. That is, rather than addressing the question "Does user X have permission to perform operation Y?", it helps answer the precursor question "How do I know this is really user X?" PAM is an important component of the access control chain on most systems.

In the past, user passwords were checked against the **/etc/shadow** file (or network equivalent) at login time so that an appropriate UID could be set for the user's shell or window system. Programs run by the user had to take the UID on faith. In the modern world of networks, cryptography, and biometric identification devices, a more flexible and open system is required. Hence, PAM.

3. One of our technical reviewers commented, "That's certainly not the intent. In fact, it's the average sites running basic DNS/web/email service that do best with SELinux. If you're doing unusual stuff, you end up in policy hell and turn it off. SELinux has actually gotten a lot better in recent times. Of course, I still turn it off…"

PAM is a wrapper for a variety of method-specific authentication libraries. Administrators specify the authentication methods they want the system to use, along with the appropriate contexts for each one. Programs that want to authenticate a user simply call the PAM system rather than implementing their own forms of authentication. PAM in turn calls the specific authentication library specified by the system administrator.

More details on PAM can be found in the *Security* chapter starting on page 908.

Kerberos: third-party cryptographic authentication

Like PAM, Kerberos deals with authentication rather than access control per se. But whereas PAM is an authentication *framework*, Kerberos is a specific authentication *method*. They're generally used together, PAM being the wrapper and Kerberos the actual implementation.

Kerberos uses a trusted third party (a server) to perform authentication for an entire network. Rather than authenticating yourself to the machine you are using, you provide your credentials to the Kerberos service, and it issues you cryptographic credentials that you can present to other services as evidence of your identity. Read more about Kerberos starting on page 924.

Access control lists

Since filesystem access control is so central to UNIX and Linux, it was an early target for elaboration. The most common addition has been support for access control lists (ACLs), a generalization of the traditional user/group/other permission model that accommodates permissions for multiple users and groups at once.

ACLs are part of the filesystem implementation, so they have to be explicitly supported by whatever filesystem you are using. Fortunately, all major UNIX and Linux filesystems now support them in one form or another.

See Chapter 18 for more information about NFS.

ACL support generally comes in one of two forms: an early POSIX draft standard that never quite made its way to formal adoption but was widely implemented anyway, and the system standardized by NFSv4, which is based on Microsoft Windows' ACLs. Both ACL standards are described in more detail in the filesystem chapter, starting on page 159.

4.3 Real-world access control

In spite of all the glamorous possibilities outlined in the last few sections, most sites still use the traditional root account for system administration. Many of the grievances lodged against the traditional system have some validity, but there tend to be equally compelling problems with the alternatives. In addition, add-on tools such as **sudo** (described on page 113) go a long way toward bridging the gap between simplicity and security.

Often, you can use a light dusting of POSIX capabilities or role-based access control to handle special circumstances (e.g., a printer or daemon that needs to be resettable by everyone who works in a particular department) while your administrative team continues to rely on **sudo** and the root account for daily use. The heavy-duty, high-impact systems such as SELinux should be reserved for sites that are required to use them for regulatory or contractual reasons.

Since root access is the *sine qua non* of system administration and also the pivot point for system security, proper husbandry of the root account is a crucial skill.

Choosing a root password

If you use the procedures and tools described in this chapter, you'll have surprisingly little use for the actual root password. Most of your administrative team won't need to know it at all.

Nevertheless, root does need a password. It should be something that's secure but also memorable at the infrequent intervals when you might actually use it. You can use a password vault or escrow system to help you "remember" the password, too; see page 117.

See page 916 for more information about password cracking.

The most important characteristic of a good password is length. The root password should be at least eight characters long; seven-character passwords are substantially easier to crack. On systems that use DES passwords, it doesn't help to use a password longer than eight characters because only the first eight are significant. See the section *Encrypted password* starting on page 179 for information about how to enable MD5 or Blowfish encryption for passwords. These can be longer and are more secure.

In theory, the most secure type of password consists of a random sequence of letters, punctuation, and digits. But because this type of password is hard to remember and usually difficult to type, it may not be optimally secure if administrators write it down or type it slowly.

We like the "shocking nonsense" approach defined by Grady Ward in an earlier version of the PGP Passphrase FAQ:

> *"Shocking nonsense" means to make up a short phrase or sentence that is both nonsensical and shocking in the culture of the user. That is, it contains grossly obscene, racist, impossible or otherwise extreme juxtapositions of ideas. This technique is permissible because the passphrase, by its nature, is never revealed to anyone with sensibilities to offend.*[4]
>
> *Shocking nonsense is unlikely to be duplicated anywhere because it does not describe a matter of fact that could be accidentally rediscovered by someone else. The emotional evocation makes it difficult for the creator to*

4. This FAQ was written for individual users of PGP. In the context of system administration, you should certainly consider the potential for offense. How will your shocking nonsense sound to the jury that's adjudicating your sexual harassment case?

forget. A mild example of such shocking nonsense might be, "Mollusks peck my galloping genitals." The reader can undoubtedly make up many far more shocking or entertaining examples for him or herself.

On systems that support passwords of arbitrary length, you can use the entire phrase as the password (it then becomes a "passphrase"). Or, you can reduce the phrase to a shorter password by recording only the second letter of each word or by some similar transformation. Password security is increased enormously if you include numbers, punctuation marks, and capital letters, and some systems now require this.

If your site has hundreds of computers, should you have hundreds of root passwords? It depends on your environment and risk tolerance, but probably not. A good rule of thumb is that machines that are clones (e.g., desktop workstations) should have the same root password. Servers should have unique passwords. In particular, every major piece of network and routing infrastructure should be separately protected.

Make sure you have accurate records that tell you which machines are sharing a root password. It's also important that you have a structured way to change root passwords on the machines that share them. Left-behinds are a security risk and an administrative headache.

Change the root password

- At least every three months or so
- Every time someone who knows the password leaves your site
- Whenever you think security may have been compromised

It's often said that passwords "should never be written down," but it's perhaps more accurate to say that they should never be left accessible to the wrong people. Root passwords and other important passwords probably *should* be written down or stored in a cryptographic vault so that there's some way for administrators to get to them in the event of an emergency. See page 117.

Logging in to the root account

Since root is just another user, you can log in directly to the root account and work your will upon the system. However, this turns out to be a bad idea. To begin with, it leaves no record of what operations were performed as root. That's bad enough when you realize that you broke something last night at 3:00 a.m. and can't remember what you changed; it's even worse when an access was unauthorized and you are trying to figure out what an intruder has done to your system. Another disadvantage is that the log-in-as-root scenario leaves no record of who was really doing the work. If several people have access to the root account, you won't be able to tell who used it and when.

For these reasons, most systems allow root logins to be disabled on terminals, through window systems, and across the network—everywhere but on the system console.[5] We suggest that you use these features. See *PAM: cooking spray or authentication wonder?* on page 908 to see how to implement this policy on your particular system.

su: substitute user identity

A marginally better way to access the root account is to use the **su** command. If invoked without arguments, **su** prompts for the root password and then starts up a root shell. Root privileges remain in effect until you terminate the shell by typing <Control-D> or the **exit** command. **su** doesn't record the commands executed as root, but it does create a log entry that states who became root and when.

The **su** command can also substitute identities other than root. Sometimes, the only way to reproduce or debug a user's problem is to **su** to their account so that you reproduce the environment in which the problem occurs.

If you know someone's password, you can access that person's account directly by executing **su** - *username*. As with an **su** to root, you will be prompted for the password for *username*. The - (dash) option makes **su** spawn the shell in login mode. The exact implications of login mode vary by shell, but it normally changes the number or identity of the startup files that the shell reads. For example, **bash** reads ~/**.bash_profile** in login mode and ~/**.bashrc** in nonlogin mode. When diagnosing other users' problems, it helps to reproduce their login environments as closely as possible.

On some systems, the root password allows an **su** or **login** to any account. On others, you must first **su** explicitly to root before **su**ing to another account; root can **su** to any account without entering a password.

Get in the habit of typing the full pathname to the **su** command (e.g., **/bin/su** or **/usr/bin/su**) rather than relying on the shell to find the command for you. This precaution gives you some protection against arbitrary programs called **su** that may have been sneaked into your search path with the intention of harvesting passwords.[6]

On some systems, you must be a member of the group "wheel" in order to use **su**.

We consider **su** to have been largely superseded by **sudo**, described in the next section. **su** is best reserved for emergencies.

sudo: limited su

Without RBAC or a system such as SELinux, it's hard to give someone the ability to do one task (backups, for example) without giving that person free run of the

5. Ubuntu Linux goes even further. By default, the system has no valid root password and requires the use of **sudo**, detailed later in this section.

6. For the same reason, do not include "." (the current directory) in your shell's search path. Although convenient, this configuration makes it easy to inadvertently run "special" versions of system commands that a user or intruder has left lying around as a trap. Naturally, this advice goes double for root.

system. And if the root account is used by several administrators, you really have only a vague idea of who's using it or what they've done.

The most widely used solution to these problems is a program called **sudo** that is currently maintained by Todd Miller. It runs on all of our example systems and is also available in source code form from sudo.ws.

solaris

Solaris's **pfexec** command implements a facility similar to **sudo** that is based on Solaris's own RBAC system.

sudo takes as its argument a command line to be executed as root (or as another restricted user). **sudo** consults the file **/etc/sudoers**, which lists the people who are authorized to use **sudo** and the commands they are allowed to run on each host. If the proposed command is permitted, **sudo** prompts for the *user's own* password and executes the command.

Additional **sudo** commands can be executed without the "sudoer" having to type a password until a five-minute period (configurable) has elapsed with no further **sudo** activity. This timeout serves as a modest protection against users with **sudo** privileges who leave terminals unattended.

See Chapter 11 for more information about syslog.

sudo keeps a log of the command lines that were executed, the hosts on which they were run, the people who requested them, the directory from which they were run, and the times at which they were invoked. This information can be logged by syslog or placed in the file of your choice. We recommend using syslog to forward the log entries to a secure central host.

A log entry for randy's executing **sudo /bin/cat /etc/sudoers** might look like this:

```
Dec 7 10:57:19 tigger sudo: randy: TTY=ttyp0 ; PWD=/tigger/users/randy;
    USER=root ; COMMAND=/bin/cat /etc/sudoers
```

The **sudoers** file is designed so that a single version can be used on many different hosts at once. Here's a typical example:

```
# Define aliases for machines in CS & Physics departments
Host_Alias   CS = tigger, anchor, piper, moet, sigi
Host_Alias   PHYSICS = eprince, pprince, icarus

# Define collections of commands
Cmnd_Alias  DUMP = /sbin/dump, /sbin/restore
Cmnd_Alias  PRINTING = /usr/sbin/lpc, /usr/bin/lprm
Cmnd_Alias  SHELLS = /bin/sh, /bin/tcsh, /bin/bash, /bin/ksh, /bin/bsh

# Permissions
mark, ed     PHYSICS = ALL
herb         CS = /usr/sbin/tcpdump : PHYSICS = (operator) DUMP
lynda        ALL = (ALL) ALL, !SHELLS
%wheel       ALL, !PHYSICS = NOPASSWD: PRINTING
```

The first five noncomment lines define groups of hosts and commands that are referred to in the permission specifications later in the file. The lists could be included literally in the specs, but the use of aliases makes the **sudoers** file easier to read and understand; it also makes the file easier to update in the future. It's also possible to define aliases for sets of users and for sets of users as whom commands may be run.

Each permission specification line includes information about

- The users to whom the line applies
- The hosts on which the line should be heeded
- The commands that the specified users can run
- The users as whom the commands can be executed

The first permission line applies to the users mark and ed on the machines in the PHYSICS group (eprince, pprince, and icarus). The built-in command alias ALL allows them to run any command. Since no list of users is specified in parentheses, **sudo** will only run commands as root.

The second permission line allows herb to run **tcpdump** on CS machines and dump-related commands on PHYSICS machines. However, the dump commands can only be run as operator, not as root. The actual command line that herb would type would be something like

```
ubuntu$ sudo -u operator /usr/sbin/dump 0u /dev/sda1
```

The user lynda can run commands as any user on any machine, except that she can't run several common shells. Does this mean that lynda really can't get a root shell? Of course not:

```
aix$ cp -p /bin/sh /tmp/sh
aix$ sudo /tmp/sh
```

Generally speaking, any attempt to allow "all commands except…" is doomed to failure, at least in a technical sense. However, it may still be worthwhile to set up the **sudoers** file this way as a reminder that root shells are frowned upon.

The final line allows users in group wheel to run **lpc** and **lprm** as root on all machines except eprince, pprince, and icarus. Furthermore, no password is required to run the commands.

Note that commands in **/etc/sudoers** are specified with full pathnames to prevent people from executing their own programs and scripts as root. Though no examples are shown above, it is possible to specify the arguments that are permissible for each command as well. In fact, this simple configuration only scratches the surface of the configuration options available in the **sudoers** file.

On AIX systems, you may find it helpful to include the following line in the defaults section of the **sudoers** file. It prevents **sudo** from removing the ODMDIR environment variable, which many administrative commands rely on to point them to the Object Data Manager configuration database.

```
Defaults env_keep = "ODMDIR"
```

To modify **/etc/sudoers**, you use the **visudo** command, which checks to be sure no one else is editing the file, invokes an editor on it, and then verifies the syntax of the edited file before installing it. This last step is particularly important because an invalid **sudoers** file might prevent you from **sudo**ing again to fix it.

The use of **sudo** has the following advantages:

- Accountability is much improved because of command logging.
- Operators can do chores without unlimited root privileges.
- The real root password can be known to only one or two people.[7]
- It's faster to use **sudo** than to use **su** or to log in as root.
- Privileges can be revoked without the need to change the root password.
- A canonical list of all users with root privileges is maintained.
- There is less chance of a root shell being left unattended.
- A single file can be used to control access for an entire network.

See page 916 for more information about password cracking.

There are a couple of disadvantages as well. The worst of these is that any breach in the security of a sudoer's personal account can be equivalent to breaching the root account itself. There is not much you can do to counter this threat other than caution your sudoers to protect their own accounts as they would the root account. You can also run a password cracker regularly on sudoers' passwords to ensure that they are making good password selections.

sudo's command logging can be subverted by tricks such as shell escapes from within an allowed program or by **sudo sh** and **sudo su** if you allow them.

If you think of **sudo** as a way of subdividing the privileges of the root account, it is superior in some ways to the built-in role-based access control systems offered by many versions of UNIX:

- You decide exactly how privileges will be subdivided. Your division may be coarser or finer than the off-the-shelf privileges defined for you by an RBAC system.
- Simple configurations—by far, the most common—are simple to set up, maintain, and understand.
- **sudo**'s aliases for groups of hosts, users, and commands are functionally similar to the roles in an RBAC system.
- **sudo** runs on all UNIX and Linux systems. You do not need to worry about using different RBAC systems on different platforms.
- You can share a single configuration file throughout your site.
- You get consistent, high-quality logging for free.

The major drawback of **sudo**-based access control is that the system remains vulnerable to catastrophic compromise if the root account is penetrated.

7. Or even zero people, if you have the right kind of password vault system in place.

Password vaults and password escrow

Five hundred miles north of the Norwegian mainland, on the island of Spitzbergen, a huge vault has been tunneled into the mountainside as a place for the world's countries to store seed samples against the possibility of future catastrophe. System administrators don't need a vault that large or that cold for passwords, but they do need a vault.

A password vault is a piece of software (or a combination of software and hardware) that stores passwords for your organization in a more secure fashion than "Would you like Windows to remember this password for you?" Several developments have made a password vault almost a necessity:

- The proliferation of passwords needed not just to log in to computers, but also to access web pages, configure routers and firewalls, and administer remote services
- The increasing need for strong (read "not very memorable") passwords as computers get so fast that weak passwords are easily broken
- Regulations that require access to certain data to be traceable to a single person—no shared logins such as root

Password management systems are emerging in the wake of legislation in the United States that attempts to impose accountability and security on various business sectors. In some cases, this legislation requires two-factor authentication; for example, a password or passphrase plus a challenge/response exchange. Password vaults are also a great boon for sysadmin support companies who must securely and traceably manage passwords not only for their own machines but also for their customers' machines.

Several password vault implementations are available. Free ones for individuals (e.g., KeePass) store passwords locally, give all-or-nothing access to the password database, and do no logging. Appliances suitable for huge enterprises (e.g., CyberArk) can cost tens of thousands of dollars. Many of the commercial offerings charge either by the user or by the number of passwords they remember.

We use a home-grown web-based system that has several nice features. One of our favorites features is the "break the glass" option, named for the hotel fire alarm stations that tell you to break the glass and pull the big red lever in the event of an emergency.

In this case, "breaking the glass" means obtaining a password that you wouldn't normally have access to. In the event of an emergency, you can go ahead and retrieve the password anyway. The system then notifies a list of other sysadmins and logs what you do with the password. When you have finished dealing with the emergency, you change the password and put the new password back in the vault.

A low-tech way to implement password escrow is to store passwords in tamper-evident, serial-numbered baggies of the type used by police to hold crime scene evidence. These bags are readily available on the Internet. As long as a baggie is present and unopened, you know that no one has accessed the password inside.

4.4 PSEUDO-USERS OTHER THAN ROOT

Root is generally the only user that has special status in the eyes of the kernel, but several other pseudo-users are defined by the system. You can identify these sham accounts by their low UIDs, usually less than 100. Most often, UIDs under 10 are system accounts, and UIDs between 10 and 100 are pseudo-users associated with specific pieces of software.

It's customary to replace the encrypted password field of these special users in **/etc/shadow** with a star so that their accounts cannot be logged in to. Set their shells to **/bin/false** or **/bin/nologin** as well, to protect against remote login exploits that use password alternatives such as SSH key files.

Files and processes that are part of the operating system but that need not be owned by root are sometimes given to the users bin or daemon. The theory was that this convention would help avoid the security hazards associated with ownership by root. It's not a very compelling argument, however, and current systems often just use the root account for this purpose.

On some systems, the user sys owns a number of special files such as the kernel's memory image in **/dev**. Few programs access these files, but those that do can run setuid to sys rather than root if this ownership convention is in use. On some systems, a group called kmem or sys is used instead of a sys user account.

See page 697 for more information about the nobody account.

The Network File System (NFS) uses the nobody account to represent root on other systems. For remote roots to be stripped of their rootly powers, the remote UID 0 has to be mapped to something other than the local UID 0. The nobody account acts as a generic alter ego for these remote roots. In NFSv4, it can be applied to remote users with no valid local account as well.

Since the nobody account is supposed to represent a generic and relatively powerless user, it shouldn't own any files. If nobody does own files, remote roots will be able to take control of them. Nobody shouldn't own no files!

A UID of -1 or -2 is traditional for nobody. The Linux kernel defaults to using UID 65,534, the 16-bit twos-complement version of -2. But really, the number is arbitrary: Red Hat uses 99, which makes more sense than 65,534 now that we have 32-bit UIDs. Solaris uses 60,001, which doesn't, but at least it's easy to remember as the 16-bit twos-complement version of -2, truncated—not rounded—to one significant digit, plus one.

The only snag with redefining nobody's UID is that **exportfs** does not seem to pay attention to the **passwd** file. You must explicitly tell it with the **anonuid** option to use a different UID for nobody.

4.5 Exercises

E4.1 Use the **find** command with the **-perm** option to locate five setuid files on your system. For each file, explain why the setuid mechanism is necessary for the command to function properly.

E4.2 Create two entries for the **sudoers** configuration file:

a) One entry that allows users matt and lisa to service the printer, unjam it, and restart printer daemons on the machine printserver

b) One entry that allows drew, smithgr, and jimlane to kill jobs and reboot the machines in a student lab

E4.3 Create three "shocking nonsense" passphrases but keep them to yourself. Run your three passphrases through **md5sum** and report these results. Based on the current state of cryptographic technology, is it safe to share the MD5 results? Why or why not?

☆ E4.4 Enumerate a sequence of commands that modify someone's password entry, and show how you could cover your tracks. Assume you had only **sudo** power (all commands allowed, but no shells or **su**).

☆ E4.5 Install **sudo** configured to send its mail tattling about misuse to you. Use it to test the **sudo** entries of the previous question with local usernames and machine names; verify that **sudo** is logging to syslog properly. Look at the syslog entries produced by your testing. (Requires root access; you'll most likely have to tweak **/etc/syslog.conf**, too.)

☆ E4.6 On a Solaris, HP-UX, or AIX system, set up an RBAC role that allows members to mount and unmount filesystems. Assign this role to two users. (Root access required.)

a) What steps are required? Can you limit the permitted operations to certain filesystems or types of filesystems?

b) Reimplement your solution as a **sudo** configuration. Is it more or less complicated to set up than the RBAC solution? Can you limit the permitted operations to certain filesystems or types of filesystems?

5 Controlling Processes

A process is the abstraction used by UNIX and Linux to represent a running program. It's the object through which a program's use of memory, processor time, and I/O resources can be managed and monitored.

It is part of the UNIX philosophy that as much work as possible be done within the context of processes, rather than handled specially by the kernel. System and user processes all follow the same rules, so you can use a single set of tools to control them both.

5.1 Components of a process

A process consists of an address space and a set of data structures within the kernel. The address space is a set of memory pages[1] that the kernel has marked for the process's use. It contains the code and libraries that the process is executing, the process's variables, its stacks, and various extra information needed by the kernel while the process is running. Because UNIX and Linux are virtual memory systems, there is no correlation between a page's location within a process's address space and its location inside the machine's physical memory or swap space.

1. Pages are the units in which memory is managed, usually between 1KiB and 8KiB in size.

The kernel's internal data structures record various pieces of information about each process. Here are some of the more important of these:

- The process's address space map
- The current status of the process (sleeping, stopped, runnable, etc.)
- The execution priority of the process
- Information about the resources the process has used
- Information about the files and network ports the process has opened
- The process's signal mask (a record of which signals are blocked)
- The owner of the process

An execution thread, usually known simply as a thread, is the result of a fork in execution within a process. A thread inherits many of the attributes of the process that contains it (such as the process's address space), and multiple threads can execute concurrently within a single process under a model called multithreading.

Concurrent execution is simulated by the kernel on old-style uniprocessor systems, but on multicore and multi-CPU architectures the threads can run simultaneously on different cores. Multithreaded applications such as BIND and Apache benefit the most from multicore systems since the applications can work on more than one request simultaneously. All our example operating systems support multithreading.

Many of the parameters associated with a process directly affect its execution: the amount of processor time it gets, the files it can access, and so on. In the following sections, we discuss the meaning and significance of the parameters that are most interesting from a system administrator's point of view. These attributes are common to all versions of UNIX and Linux.

PID: process ID number

The kernel assigns a unique ID number to every process.[2] Most commands and system calls that manipulate processes require you to specify a PID to identify the target of the operation. PIDs are assigned in order as processes are created.

PPID: parent PID

Neither UNIX nor Linux has a system call that initiates a new process running a particular program. Instead, an existing process must clone itself to create a new process. The clone can then exchange the program it's running for a different one.

When a process is cloned, the original process is referred to as the parent, and the copy is called the child. The PPID attribute of a process is the PID of the parent from which it was cloned.[3]

2. As pointed out by our reviewer Jon Corbet, Linux kernel 2.6.24 introduced process ID namespaces, which allow multiple processes with the same PID to exist concurrently. This feature was implemented to support container-based virtualization.

3. At least initially. If the original parent dies, **init** (process 1) becomes the new parent. See page 124.

The parent PID is a useful piece of information when you're confronted with an unrecognized (and possibly misbehaving) process. Tracing the process back to its origin (whether a shell or another program) may give you a better idea of its purpose and significance.

UID and EUID: real and effective user ID

See page 180 for more information about UIDs.

A process's UID is the user identification number of the person who created it, or more accurately, it is a copy of the UID value of the parent process. Usually, only the creator (aka the "owner") and the superuser can manipulate a process.

The EUID is the "effective" user ID, an extra UID used to determine what resources and files a process has permission to access at any given moment. For most processes, the UID and EUID are the same, the usual exception being programs that are setuid.

Why have both a UID and an EUID? Simply because it's useful to maintain a distinction between identity and permission, and because a setuid program may not wish to operate with expanded permissions all the time. On most systems, the effective UID can be set and reset to enable or restrict the additional permissions it grants.

Most systems also keep track of a "saved UID," which is a copy of the process's EUID at the point at which the process first begins to execute. Unless the process takes steps to obliterate this saved UID, it remains available for use as the real or effective UID. A conservatively written setuid program can therefore renounce its special privileges for the majority of its execution, accessing them only at the specific points at which extra privileges are needed.

Linux also defines a nonstandard FSUID process parameter that controls the determination of filesystem permissions. It is infrequently used outside the kernel and is not portable to other UNIX systems.

GID and EGID: real and effective group ID

See page 181 for more information about groups.

The GID is the group identification number of a process. The EGID is related to the GID in the same way that the EUID is related to the UID in that it can be "upgraded" by the execution of a setgid program. A saved GID is maintained. It is similar in intent to the saved UID.

The GID attribute of a process is largely vestigial. For purposes of access determination, a process can be a member of many groups at once. The complete group list is stored separately from the distinguished GID and EGID. Determinations of access permissions normally take into account the EGID and the supplemental group list, but not the GID.

The only time at which the GID really gets to come out and play is when a process creates new files. Depending on how the filesystem permissions have been set, new files may adopt the GID of the creating process. See page 154 for details.

Niceness

A process's scheduling priority determines how much CPU time it receives. The kernel uses a dynamic algorithm to compute priorities, allowing for the amount of CPU time that a process has recently consumed and the length of time it has been waiting to run. The kernel also pays attention to an administratively set value that's usually called the "nice value" or "niceness," so called because it tells how nice you are planning to be to other users of the system. We discuss niceness in detail on page 129.

In an effort to provide better support for low-latency applications, Linux has added "scheduling classes" to the traditional UNIX scheduling model. There are currently three classes, and each process is assigned to one class. Unfortunately, the real-time classes are neither widely used nor well supported from the command line. System processes use the traditional (niceness) scheduler, which is the only one we discuss in this book. See realtimelinuxfoundation.org for more discussion of issues related to real-time scheduling.

Control terminal

Most nondaemon processes have an associated control terminal. The control terminal determines default linkages for the standard input, standard output, and standard error channels. When you start a command from the shell, your terminal window normally becomes the process's control terminal. The concept of a control terminal also affects the distribution of signals, which are discussed starting on page 124.

5.2 The life cycle of a process

To create a new process, a process copies itself with the **fork** system call. **fork** creates a copy of the original process; that copy is largely identical to the parent. The new process has a distinct PID and has its own accounting information.

fork has the unique property of returning two different values. From the child's point of view, it returns zero. The parent receives the PID of the newly created child. Since the two processes are otherwise identical, they must both examine the return value to figure out which role they are supposed to play.

After a **fork**, the child process will often use one of the **exec** family of system calls to begin the execution of a new program.[4] These calls change the program that the process is executing and reset the memory segments to a predefined initial state. The various forms of **exec** differ only in the ways in which they specify the command-line arguments and environment to be given to the new program.

When the system boots, the kernel autonomously creates and installs several processes. The most notable of these is **init**, which is always process number 1. **init** is responsible for executing the system's startup scripts, although the exact manner

4. Actually, all but one are library routines rather than system calls.

in which this is done differs slightly between UNIX and Linux. All processes other than the ones the kernel creates are descendants of **init**. See Chapter 3 for more information about booting and the **init** daemon.

init also plays another important role in process management. When a process completes, it calls a routine named **_exit** to notify the kernel that it is ready to die. It supplies an exit code (an integer) that tells why it's exiting. By convention, 0 is used to indicate a normal or "successful" termination.

Before a process can be allowed to disappear completely, the kernel requires that its death be acknowledged by the process's parent, which the parent does with a call to **wait**. The parent receives a copy of the child's exit code (or an indication of why the child was killed if the child did not exit voluntarily) and can also obtain a summary of the child's use of resources if it wishes.

This scheme works fine if parents outlive their children and are conscientious about calling **wait** so that dead processes can be disposed of. If the parent dies first, however, the kernel recognizes that no **wait** will be forthcoming and adjusts the process to make the orphan a child of **init**. **init** politely accepts these orphaned processes and performs the **wait** needed to get rid of them when they die.

5.3 Signals

Signals are process-level interrupt requests. About thirty different kinds are defined, and they're used in a variety of ways:

- They can be sent among processes as a means of communication.
- They can be sent by the terminal driver to kill, interrupt, or suspend processes when keys such as <Control-C> and <Control-Z> are typed.[5]
- They can be sent by an administrator (with **kill**) to achieve various ends.
- They can be sent by the kernel when a process commits an infraction such as division by zero.
- They can be sent by the kernel to notify a process of an "interesting" condition such as the death of a child process or the availability of data on an I/O channel.

A core dump is a process's memory image. It can be used for debugging.

When a signal is received, one of two things can happen. If the receiving process has designated a handler routine for that particular signal, the handler is called with information about the context in which the signal was delivered. Otherwise, the kernel takes some default action on behalf of the process. The default action varies from signal to signal. Many signals terminate the process; some also generate a core dump.

5. The functions of <Control-Z> and <Control-C> can be reassigned to other keys with the **stty** command, but this is rare in practice. In this chapter we refer to them by their conventional bindings.

Specifying a handler routine for a signal within a program is referred to as catching the signal. When the handler completes, execution restarts from the point at which the signal was received.

To prevent signals from arriving, programs can request that they be either ignored or blocked. A signal that is ignored is simply discarded and has no effect on the process. A blocked signal is queued for delivery, but the kernel doesn't require the process to act on it until the signal has been explicitly unblocked. The handler for a newly unblocked signal is called only once, even if the signal was received several times while reception was blocked.

Table 5.1 lists some signals with which all administrators should be familiar. The uppercase convention for the names derives from C language tradition. You might also see signal names written with a SIG prefix (e.g., SIGHUP) for similar reasons.

Table 5.1 Signals every administrator should know[a]

#	Name	Description	Default	Can catch?	Can block?	Dump core?
1	HUP	Hangup	Terminate	Yes	Yes	No
2	INT	Interrupt	Terminate	Yes	Yes	No
3	QUIT	Quit	Terminate	Yes	Yes	Yes
9	KILL	Kill	Terminate	No	No	No
–[b]	BUS	Bus error	Terminate	Yes	Yes	Yes
11	SEGV	Segmentation fault	Terminate	Yes	Yes	Yes
15	TERM	Software termination	Terminate	Yes	Yes	No
–[b]	STOP	Stop	Stop	No	No	No
–[b]	TSTP	Keyboard stop	Stop	Yes	Yes	No
–[b]	CONT	Continue after stop	Ignore	Yes	No	No
–[b]	WINCH	Window changed	Ignore	Yes	Yes	No
–[b]	USR1	User-defined #1	Terminate	Yes	Yes	No
–[b]	USR2	User-defined #2	Terminate	Yes	Yes	No

a. A list of signal names and numbers is also available from the **bash** built-in command **kill -l**.
b. Varies among systems. See **/usr/include/signal.h** or **man signal** for more specific information.

Other signals, not shown in Table 5.1, mostly report obscure errors such as "illegal instruction." The default handling for signals like that is to terminate with a core dump. Catching and blocking are generally allowed because some programs may be smart enough to try to clean up whatever problem caused the error before continuing.

The BUS and SEGV signals are also error signals. We've included them in the table because they're so common: when a program crashes, it's usually one of these two signals that finally brings it down. By themselves, the signals are of no specific diagnostic value. Both of them indicate an attempt to use or access memory improperly.[6]

The signals named KILL and STOP cannot be caught, blocked, or ignored. The KILL signal destroys the receiving process, and STOP suspends its execution until a CONT signal is received. CONT may be caught or ignored, but not blocked.

TSTP is a "soft" version of STOP that might be best described as a request to stop. It's the signal generated by the terminal driver when <Control-Z> is typed on the keyboard. Programs that catch this signal usually clean up their state, then send themselves a STOP signal to complete the stop operation. Alternatively, programs can ignore TSTP to prevent themselves from being stopped from the keyboard.

Terminal emulators send a WINCH signal when their configuration parameters (such as the number of lines in the virtual terminal) change. This convention allows emulator-savvy programs such as text editors to reconfigure themselves automatically in response to changes. If you can't get windows to resize properly, make sure that WINCH is being generated and propagated correctly.[7]

The signals KILL, INT, TERM, HUP, and QUIT all sound as if they mean approximately the same thing, but their uses are actually quite different. It's unfortunate that such vague terminology was selected for them. Here's a decoding guide:

- KILL is unblockable and terminates a process at the kernel level. A process can never actually receive this signal.
- INT is sent by the terminal driver when you type <Control-C>. It's a request to terminate the current operation. Simple programs should quit (if they catch the signal) or simply allow themselves to be killed, which is the default if the signal is not caught. Programs that have an interactive command line (such as a shell) should stop what they're doing, clean up, and wait for user input again.
- TERM is a request to terminate execution completely. It's expected that the receiving process will clean up its state and exit.
- HUP has two common interpretations. First, it's understood as a reset request by many daemons. If a daemon is capable of rereading its configuration file and adjusting to changes without restarting, a HUP can generally be used to trigger this behavior.

6. More specifically, bus errors result from violations of alignment requirements or the use of nonsensical addresses. Segmentation violations represent protection violations such as attempts to write to read-only portions of the address space.

7. Which may be easier said than done. The terminal emulator (e.g., **xterm**), terminal driver, and user-level commands may all have a role in propagating SIGWINCH. Common problems include sending the signal to a terminal's foreground process only (rather than to all processes associated with the terminal) and failing to propagate notification of a size change across the network to a remote computer. Protocols such as Telnet and SSH explicitly recognize local terminal size changes and communicate this information to the remote host. Simpler protocols (e.g., direct serial lines) cannot do this.

Second, HUP signals are sometimes generated by the terminal driver in an attempt to "clean up" (i.e., kill) the processes attached to a particular terminal. This behavior is largely a holdover from the days of wired terminals and modem connections, hence the name "hangup."

Shells in the C shell family (**tcsh** et al.) usually make background processes immune to HUP signals so that they can continue to run after the user logs out. Users of Bourne-ish shells (**ksh**, **bash**, etc.) can emulate this behavior with the **nohup** command.

- QUIT is similar to TERM, except that it defaults to producing a core dump if not caught. A few programs cannibalize this signal and interpret it to mean something else.

The signals USR1 and USR2 have no set meaning. They're available for programs to use in whatever way they'd like. For example, the Apache web server interprets the USR1 signal as a request to gracefully restart.

5.4 KILL: SEND SIGNALS

As its name implies, the **kill** command is most often used to terminate a process. **kill** can send any signal, but by default it sends a TERM. **kill** can be used by normal users on their own processes or by root on any process. The syntax is

kill [-*signal*] *pid*

where *signal* is the number or symbolic name of the signal to be sent (as shown in Table 5.1) and *pid* is the process identification number of the target process.

A **kill** without a signal number does not guarantee that the process will die, because the TERM signal can be caught, blocked, or ignored. The command

kill -9 *pid*

"guarantees" that the process will die because signal 9, KILL, cannot be caught. Use **kill -9** only if a polite request fails. We put quotes around "guarantees" because processes can occasionally become so wedged that even KILL does not affect them (usually because of some degenerate I/O vapor lock such as waiting for a disk that has stopped spinning). Rebooting is usually the only way to get rid of these processes.

The **killall** command performs wildly different functions on UNIX and Linux. Under Linux, **killall** kills processes by name. For example, the following command kills all Apache web server processes:

ubuntu$ **sudo killall httpd**

The standard UNIX **killall** command that ships with Solaris, HP-UX, and AIX takes no arguments and simply kills all the current user's processes. Running it as root kills **init** and shuts down the machine. Oops.

The **pgrep** and **pkill** commands for Solaris, HP-UX, and Linux (but not AIX) search for processes by name (or other attributes, such as EUID) and display or signal them, respectively. For example, the following command sends a TERM signal to all processes running as the user ben:

```
$ sudo pkill -u ben
```

5.5 PROCESS STATES

A process is not automatically eligible to receive CPU time just because it exists. You need to be aware of the four execution states listed in Table 5.2.

Table 5.2 Process states

State	Meaning
Runnable	The process can be executed.
Sleeping	The process is waiting for some resource.
Zombie	The process is trying to die.
Stopped	The process is suspended (not allowed to execute).

A runnable process is ready to execute whenever CPU time is available. It has acquired all the resources it needs and is just waiting for CPU time to process its data. As soon as the process makes a system call that cannot be immediately completed (such as a request to read part of a file), the kernel puts it to sleep.

Sleeping processes are waiting for a specific event to occur. Interactive shells and system daemons spend most of their time sleeping, waiting for terminal input or network connections. Since a sleeping process is effectively blocked until its request has been satisfied, it will get no CPU time unless it receives a signal or a response to one of its I/O requests.

Some operations cause processes to enter an uninterruptible sleep state. This state is usually transient and not observed in **ps** output (indicated by a D in the STAT column; see Table 5.4 on page 132). However, a few degenerate situations can cause it to persist. The most common cause involves server problems on an NFS filesystem mounted with the "hard" option. Since processes in the uninterruptible sleep state cannot be roused even to service a signal, they cannot be killed. To get rid of them, you must fix the underlying problem or reboot.

Zombies are processes that have finished execution but have not yet had their status collected. If you see zombies hanging around, check their PPIDs with **ps** to find out where they're coming from.

Stopped processes are administratively forbidden to run. Processes are stopped on receipt of a STOP or TSTP signal and are restarted with CONT. Being stopped is similar to sleeping, but there's no way for a process to get out of the stopped state other than having some other process wake it up (or kill it).

5.6 NICE AND RENICE: INFLUENCE SCHEDULING PRIORITY

The "niceness" of a process is a numeric hint to the kernel about how the process should be treated in relation to other processes contending for the CPU. The strange name is derived from the fact that it determines how nice you are going to be to other users of the system. A high nice value means a low priority for your process: you are going to be nice. A low or negative value means high priority: you are not very nice.

The range of allowable niceness values varies among systems. The most common range is -20 to +19. Some systems use a range of a similar size beginning at 0 instead of a negative number (typically 0 to 39). The ranges used on our example systems are shown in Table 5.3 on the next page.

Despite their numeric differences, all systems handle nice values in much the same way. Unless the user takes special action, a newly created process inherits the nice value of its parent process. The owner of the process can increase its nice value but cannot lower it, even to return the process to the default niceness. This restriction prevents processes with low priority from bearing high-priority children. The superuser may set nice values arbitrarily.

It's rare to have occasion to set priorities by hand these days. On the puny systems of the 1970s and 80s, performance was significantly affected by which process was on the CPU. Today, with more than adequate CPU power on every desktop, the scheduler does a good job of servicing all processes. The addition of scheduling classes gives developers additional control when fast response is essential.

I/O performance has not kept up with increasingly fast CPUs, and the major bottleneck on most systems has become the disk drives. Unfortunately, a process's nice value has no effect on the kernel's management of its memory or I/O; high-nice processes can still monopolize a disproportionate share of these resources.

A process's nice value can be set at the time of creation with the **nice** command and adjusted later with the **renice** command. **nice** takes a command line as an argument, and **renice** takes a PID or (sometimes) a username.

Some examples:

```
$ nice -n 5 ~/bin/longtask        // Lowers priority (raise nice) by 5
$ sudo renice -5 8829             // Sets nice value to -5
$ sudo renice 5 -u boggs          // Sets nice value of boggs's procs to 5
```

Unfortunately, there is little agreement among systems about how the desired priorities should be specified; in fact, even **nice** and **renice** from the same system usually don't agree. Some commands want a nice value increment, whereas others want an absolute nice value. Some want their nice values preceded by a dash. Others want a flag (**-n**), and some just want a value.

To complicate things, a version of **nice** is built into the C shell and some other common shells (but not **bash**). If you don't type the full path to **nice**, you'll get the shell's version rather than the operating system's. This duplication can be confusing because shell-**nice** and command-**nice** use different syntax: the shell wants its priority increment expressed as *+incr* or *-incr*, but the stand-alone command wants an **-n** flag followed by the priority increment.[8]

Table 5.3 summarizes all these variations. A *prio* is an absolute nice value, while an *incr* is relative to the niceness of the shell from which **nice** or **renice** is run. Wherever an *-incr* or a *-prio* is called for, you can use a double dash to enter negative values (e.g., --**10**). Only the shell **nice** understands plus signs (in fact, it requires them); leave them out in all other circumstances.

Table 5.3 How to express priorities for various versions of nice and renice

System	Range	OS nice	csh nice	renice
Linux	-20 to 19	*-incr* or **-n** *incr*	*+incr* or *-incr*	*prio*
Solaris	0 to 39	*-incr* or **-n** *incr*	*+incr* or *-incr*	*incr* or **-n** *incr*
HP-UX	0 to 39	*-prio* or **-n** *prio*	*+incr* or *-incr*	**-n** *prio*[a]
AIX	-20 to 19	*-incr* or **-n** *incr*	*+incr* or *-incr*	**-n** *incr*

a. Uses absolute priority, but adds 20 to the value you specify.

The most commonly **nice**d process in the modern world is **ntpd**, the clock synchronization daemon. Since promptness is critical to its mission, it usually runs at a nice value about 12 below the default (that is, at a higher priority than normal).

If a problem drives the system's load average to 65, you may need to use **nice** to start a high-priority shell before you can run commands to investigate the problem. Otherwise, you may have difficulty running even simple commands.

5.7 PS: MONITOR PROCESSES

ps is the system administrator's main tool for monitoring processes. While versions of **ps** differ in their arguments and display, they all deliver essentially the same information. Part of the enormous variation among versions of **ps** can be traced back to differences in the development history of UNIX. However, **ps** is also a command that vendors tend to customize for other reasons. It's closely tied to the kernel's handling of processes, so it tends to reflect all of a vendors' underlying kernel changes.

ps can show the PID, UID, priority, and control terminal of processes. It also gives information about how much memory a process is using, how much CPU time it has consumed, and its current status (running, stopped, sleeping, etc.). Zombies show up in a **ps** listing as <exiting> or <defunct>.

8. Actually, it's worse than this: the stand-alone **nice** interprets **nice -5** to mean a *positive* increment of 5, whereas the shell built-in **nice** interprets this same form to mean a *negative* increment of 5.

Implementations of **ps** have become hopelessly complex over the last decade. Several vendors have abandoned the attempt to define meaningful displays and made their **ps**es completely configurable. With a little customization work, almost any desired output can be produced. As a case in point, the **ps** used by Linux is a trisexual and hermaphroditic version that understands multiple option sets and uses an environment variable to tell it what universe it's living in.

Do not be alarmed by all this complexity: it's there mainly for developers, not for system administrators. Although you will use **ps** frequently, you only need to know a few specific incantations.

On Linux and AIX, you can obtain a useful overview of all the processes running on the system with **ps aux**. The **a** option means to show all processes, **x** means to show even processes that don't have a control terminal, and **u** selects the "user oriented" output format. Here's an example of **ps aux** output on a machine running Red Hat (AIX output for the same command differs slightly):

```
redhat$ ps aux
  USER     PID %CPU%MEM  VSZ   RSS   TTY  STAT  TIME COMMAND
  root       1   0.1  0.2 3356  560   ?    S     0:00 init [5]
  root       2   0    0      0  0     ?    SN    0:00 [ksoftirqd/0]
  root       3   0    0      0  0     ?    S<    0:00 [events/0]
  root       4   0    0      0  0     ?    S<    0:00 [khelper]
  root       5   0    0      0  0     ?    S<    0:00 [kacpid]
  root      18   0    0      0  0     ?    S<    0:00 [kblockd/0]
  root      28   0    0      0  0     ?    S     0:00 [pdflush]
...
  root     196   0    0      0  0     ?    S     0:00 [kjournald]
  root    1050   0    0.1 2652  448   ?    S<s   0:00 udevd
  root    1472   0    0.3 3048  1008  ?    S<s   0:00 /sbin/dhclient -1
  root    1646   0    0.3 3012  1012  ?    S<s   0:00 /sbin/dhclient -1
  root    1733   0    0      0  0     ?    S     0:00 [kjournald]
  root    2124   0    0.3 3004  1008  ?    Ss    0:00 /sbin/dhclient -1
  root    2182   0    0.2 2264  596   ?    Ss    0:00 syslogd -m 0
  root    2186   0    0.1 2952  484   ?    Ss    0:00 klogd -x
   rpc    2207   0    0.2 2824  580   ?    Ss    0:00 portmap
rpcuser   2227   0    0.2 2100  760   ?    Ss    0:00 rpc.statd
  root    2260   0    0.4 5668  1084  ?    Ss    0:00 rpc.idmapd
  root    2336   0    0.2 3268  556   ?    Ss    0:00 /usr/sbin/acpid
  root    2348   0    0.8 9100  2108  ?    Ss    0:00 cupsd
  root    2384   0    0.6 4080  1660  ?    Ss    0:00 /usr/sbin/sshd
  root    2399   0    0.3 2780  828   ?    Ss    0:00 xinetd -stayalive
  root    2419   0    1.1 7776  3004  ?    Ss    0:00 sendmail: accept
...
```

Command names in brackets are not really commands at all but rather kernel threads scheduled as processes. The meaning of each field is shown in Table 5.4 on the next page.

Another useful set of arguments for Linux and AIX is **lax**, which provides more technical information. The **a** and **x** options are as above (show every process), and

Table 5.4 Explanation of ps aux output

Field	Contents
USER	Username of the process's owner
PID	Process ID
%CPU	Percentage of the CPU this process is using
%MEM	Percentage of real memory this process is using
VSZ	Virtual size of the process
RSS	Resident set size (number of pages in memory)
TTY	Control terminal ID
STAT	Current process status: R = Runnable D = In uninterruptible sleep S = Sleeping (< 20 sec) T = Traced or stopped Z = Zombie Additional flags: W= Process is swapped out < = Process has higher than normal priority N= Process has lower than normal priority L = Some pages are locked in core s = Process is a session leader
TIME	CPU time the process has consumed
COMMAND	Command name and arguments[a]

a. Programs can modify this info, so it's not necessarily an accurate representation of the actual command line.

l selects the "long" output format. **ps lax** is also slightly faster to run than **ps aux** because it doesn't have to translate every UID to a username—efficiency can be important if the system is already bogged down.

Shown here in an abbreviated example, **ps lax** includes fields such as the parent process ID (PPID), nice value (NI), and the type of resource on which the process is waiting (WCHAN).

```
redhat$ ps lax
  F  UID   PID   PPID PRI NI  VSZ   RSS  WCHAN  STAT TIME  COMMAND
  4    0     1      0  16  0 3356   560  select  S    0:00  init [5]
  1    0     2      1  34 19    0     0  ksofti  SN   0:00  [ksoftirqd/0
  1    0     3      1   5-10    0     0  worker  S<   0:00  [events/0]
  1    0     4      3   5-10    0     0  worker  S<   0:00  [khelper]
  5    0  2186      1  16  0 2952   484  syslog  Ss   0:00  klogd -x
  5   32  2207      1  15  0 2824   580  -       Ss   0:00  portmap
  5   29  2227      1  18  0 2100   760  select  Ss   0:00  rpc.statd
  1    0  2260      1  16  0 5668  1084  -       Ss   0:00  rpc.idmapd
  1    0  2336      1  21  0 3268   556  select  Ss   0:00  acpid
  5    0  2384      1  17  0 4080  1660  select  Ss   0:00  sshd
  1    0  2399      1  15  0 2780   828  select  Ss   0:00  xinetd -sta
  5    0  2419      1  16  0 7776  3004  select  Ss   0:00  sendmail: a
...
```

Under Solaris and HP-UX, **ps -ef** is a good place to start. The **e** option selects all processes, and the **f** option sets the output format. (**ps -ef** also works on AIX and Linux systems; note the dash.)

```
solaris$ ps -ef
 UID     PID   PPID   C    STIME    TTY    TIME   COMD
 root      0      0  80   Dec 21    ?      0:02   sched
 root      1      0   2   Dec 21    ?      4:32   /etc/init-
 root      2      0   8   Dec 21    ?      0:00   pageout
 root    171      1  80   Dec 21    ?      0:02   /usr/lib/sendmail-bd
trent   8482   8444  35 14:34:10  pts/7   0:00   ps-ef
trent   8444   8442 203 14:32:50  pts/7   0:01   -csh
...
```

The columns in the **ps -ef** output are explained in Table 5.5.

Table 5.5 Explanation of ps -ef output

Field	Content	Field	Content
UID	Username of the owner	STIME	Time the process was started
PID	Process ID	TTY	Control terminal
PPID	PID of the parent process	TIME	CPU time consumed
C	CPU use/scheduling info	COMD	Command and arguments

Like **ps lax** in the Linux and AIX worlds, **ps -elf** shows additional gory details on Solaris and HP-UX systems:

```
% ps -elf
 F S  UID   PID PPID   C  P  NI  ADDR      SZ   WCHAN    TIME   COMD
19 T  root    0    0  80  0  SY  f00c2fd8  0             0:02   sched
 8 S  root    1    0  65  1  20  ff26a800  88   ff2632c8 4:32   init-
 8 S  root  142    1  41  1  20  ff2e8000  176  f00cb69  0:00   syslogd
...
```

The STIME and TTY columns have been omitted to fit this page; they are identical to those produced with **ps -ef**. Nonobvious fields are described in Table 5.6 on the next page.

5.8 Dynamic monitoring with top, prstat, and topas

Since commands like **ps** offer only a one-time snapshot of your system, it is often difficult to grasp the big picture of what's really happening. **top** is a free utility that runs on many systems and provides a regularly updated summary of active processes and their use of resources. On AIX, an equivalent utility is **topas**, and on Solaris the analogous tool is **prstat**.

Table 5.6 Explanation of ps -elf output

Field	Contents
F	Process flags; possible values vary by system (rarely useful for sysadmins)
S	Process status: O = Currently running S = Sleeping (waiting for event) R = Eligible to run T = Stopped or being traced Z = Zombie D = Uninterruptible sleep (disk, usually)
C	Process CPU utilization/scheduling info
P	Scheduling priority (internal to the kernel, different from nice value)
NI	Nice value or SY for system processes
ADDR	Memory address of the process
SZ	Size (in pages) of the process in main memory
WCHAN	Address of the object the process is waiting for

For example:

```
ubuntu$ top
top - 16:37:08 up  1:42,  2 users,  load average: 0.01, 0.02, 0.06
Tasks:  76 total,   1 running,  74 sleeping,   1 stopped,   0 zombie
Cpu(s):  1.1% us,  6.3% sy,  0.6% ni, 88.6% id,  2.1% wa,  0.1% hi,  1.3% si
Mem:   256044k total,  254980k used,     1064k  free,   15944k  buffers
Swap:  524280k total,        0k  used,  524280k  free,  153192k  cached

  PID USER  PR   NI   VIRT   RES   SHR  S %CPU %MEM TIME+   COMMAND
 3175 root  15    0  35436  12m   4896  S  4.0   5.2 01:41.9 X
 3421 root  25   10  29916  15m   9808  S  2.0   6.2 01:10.5 rhn-applet-gui
    1 root  16    0   3356   560   480  S  0.0   0.2 00:00.9 init
    2 root  34   19      0     0  0     S  0.0   0   00:00.0 ksoftirqd/0
    3 root   5  -10      0     0  0     S  0.0   0   00:00.7 events/0
    4 root   5  -10      0     0  0     S  0.0   0   00:00.0 khelper
    5 root  15  -10      0     0  0     S  0.0   0   00:00.0 kacpid
   18 root   5  -10      0     0  0     S  0.0   0   00:00.0 kblockd/0
   28 root  15    0      0     0  0     S  0.0   0   00:00.0 pdflush
   29 root  15    0      0     0  0     S  0.0   0   00:00.3 pdflush
   31 root  13  -10      0     0  0     S  0.0   0   00:00.0 aio/0
   19 root  15    0      0     0  0     S  0.0   0   00:00.0 khubd
   30 root  15    0      0     0  0     S  0.0   0   00:00.2 kswapd0
  187 root   6  -10      0     0  0     S  0     0   00:00.0 kmirrord/0
  196 root  15    0      0     0  0     S  0     0   00:01.3 kjournald
...
```

By default, the display updates every 10 seconds. The most CPU-consumptive processes appear at the top. **top** also accepts input from the keyboard and allows you to send signals and to **renice** processes, so you can observe how your actions affect the overall condition of the machine.

Root can run **top** with the **-q** option to goose it up to the highest possible priority. This option can be very useful when you are trying to track down a process that has already brought the system to its knees.

5.9 THE /PROC FILESYSTEM

The Linux versions of **ps** and **top** read their process status information from the **/proc** directory, a pseudo-filesystem in which the kernel exposes a variety of interesting information about the system's state. Despite the name **/proc** (and the name of the underlying filesystem type, "proc"), the information is not limited to process information—a variety of status information and statistics generated by the kernel are represented here. You can even modify some parameters by writing to the appropriate **/proc** file. See page 421 for some examples.

Although some of the information is easier to access through front-end commands such as **vmstat** and **ps**, some of the less popular information must be read directly from **/proc**. It's worth poking around in this directory to familiarize yourself with everything that's there. **man proc** also lists some useful tips and tricks.

Because the kernel creates the contents of **/proc** files on the fly (as they are read), most appear to be empty when listed with **ls -l**. You'll have to **cat** or **more** the contents to see what they actually contain. But be cautious—a few files contain or link to binary data that can confuse your terminal emulator if viewed directly.

Process-specific information is divided into subdirectories named by PID. For example, **/proc/1** is always the directory that contains information about **init**. Table 5.7 lists the most useful per-process files.

Table 5.7 Process information files in Linux /proc (numbered subdirectories)

File	Contents
cmd	Command or program the process is executing
cmdline[a]	Complete command line of the process (null-separated)
cwd	Symbolic link to the process's current directory
environ	The process's environment variables (null-separated)
exe	Symbolic link to the file being executed
fd	Subdirectory containing links for each open file descriptor
maps	Memory mapping information (shared segments, libraries, etc.)
root	Symbolic link to the process's root directory (set with **chroot**)
stat	General process status information (best decoded with **ps**)
statm	Memory usage information

a. May be unavailable if the process is swapped out of memory.

Processes

The individual components contained within the **cmdline** and **environ** files are separated by null characters rather than newlines. You can filter their contents through **tr "\000" "\n"** to make them more readable.

The **fd** subdirectory represents open files in the form of symbolic links. File descriptors that are connected to pipes or network sockets don't have an associated filename. The kernel supplies a generic description as the link target instead.

The **maps** file can be useful for determining what libraries a program is linked to or depends on.

Solaris and AIX also have a **/proc** filesystem, but it does not include the extra status and statistical information found on Linux. A group of tools known collectively as the proc utilities display some useful information about running processes. For instance, the **procsig** command in AIX and its Solaris equivalent **psig** print the signal actions and handlers for a given process. Table 5.8 shows the most useful proc utilities and their functions.

Table 5.8 Commands for reading /proc information in AIX and Solaris

Solaris[a]	AIX	Description
pcred [*pid* | *core*]	**proccred** [*pid*]	Prints/sets real, effective, and saved UID/GID
pldd [-F] [*pid* | *core*]	**procldd** [*pid*]	Shows library dependencies (like **ldd**)
psig [*pid*]	**procsig** [*pid*]	Lists signal actions and handlers
pfiles [*pid*]	**procfiles** [*pid*]	Prints open files
pwdx [*pid*]	**procwdx** [*pid*]	Prints the current working directory
pwait [*pid*]	**procwait** [*pid*]	Waits for a process to exit

a. Some of the Solaris proc tools accept a core file as input. This is primarily a debugging tool.

HP-UX does not have a **/proc** filesystem or equivalent.

5.10 STRACE, TRUSS, AND TUSC: TRACE SIGNALS AND SYSTEM CALLS

It can sometimes be hard to figure out what a process is actually doing. You may have to make educated guesses based on indirect data from the filesystem and from tools such as **ps**.

Linux lets you directly observe a process with the **strace** command, which shows every system call the process makes and every signal it receives. A similar command for Solaris and AIX is **truss**. The HP-UX equivalent is **tusc**; however, **tusc** must be separately installed.

You can even attach **strace** or **truss** to a running process, snoop for a while, and then detach from the process without disturbing it.[9]

9. Well, usually. **strace** can interrupt system calls. The monitored process must then be prepared to restart them. This is a standard rule of UNIX software hygiene, but it's not always observed.

Although system calls occur at a relatively low level of abstraction, you can usually tell quite a bit about a process's activity from the output. For example, the following log was produced by **strace** run against an active copy of **top**:

```
redhat$ sudo strace -p 5810
gettimeofday({1116193814, 213881}, {300, 0})           = 0
open("/proc", O_RDONLY|O_NONBLOCK|O_LARGEFILE|O_DIRECTORY) = 7
fstat64(7, {st_mode=S_IFDIR|0555, st_size=0, ...})     = 0
fcntl64(7, F_SETFD, FD_CLOEXEC)                        = 0
getdents64(7, /* 36 entries */, 1024)                  = 1016
getdents64(7, /* 39 entries */, 1024)                  = 1016
stat64("/proc/1", {st_mode=S_IFDIR|0555, st_size=0, ...}) = 0
open("/proc/1/stat", O_RDONLY)                         = 8
read(8, "1 (init) S 0 0 0 0 -1 4194560 73"..., 1023)   = 191
close(8)                                               = 0
...
```

Not only does **strace** show you the name of every system call made by the process, but it also decodes the arguments and shows the result code the kernel returns.

strace is packed with goodies, most of which are documented in the man page. For example, the **-f** flag follows forked processes, which is useful for tracing daemons such as **httpd** that spawn many children. The **-e file** option displays only file operations, a feature that's especially handy for discovering the location of evasive configuration files.

In this example, **top** starts by checking the current time. It then opens and stats the **/proc** directory and reads the directory's contents, thereby obtaining a list of running processes. **top** goes on to stat the directory representing the **init** process and then opens **/proc/1/stat** to read the **init**'s status information.

Here's an even simpler example (the **date** command) using **truss** on Solaris:

```
solaris$ truss date
...
time()                                      = 1242507670
brk(0x00024D30)                             = 0
brk(0x00026D30)                             = 0
open("/usr/share/lib/zoneinfo/US/Mountain", O_RDONLY) = 3
fstat64(3, 0xFFBFFAF0)                      = 0
read(3, " T Z i f\0\0\0\0\0\0\0\0".., 877)  = 877
close(3)                                    = 0
ioctl(1, TCGETA, 0xFFBFFA94)                = 0
fstat64(1, 0xFFBFF9B0)                      = 0
write(1, " S a t   M a y   1 6   1".., 29)  = 29
Sat May 16 14:56:46 MDT 2009
_exit(0)
```

Here, after allocating memory and opening library dependencies (not shown), **date** uses the **time** system call to read the system time, opens the appropriate time zone file to determine the appropriate offset, and prints the date and time stamp by calling the **write** system call.

5.11 Runaway processes

See page 1131 for more information about runaway processes.

Runaway processes come in two flavors: user processes that consume excessive amounts of a system resource, such as CPU time or disk space, and system processes that suddenly go berserk and exhibit wild behavior. The first type of runaway is not necessarily malfunctioning; it might simply be a resource hog. System processes are always supposed to behave reasonably.

You can identify processes that use excessive CPU time by looking at the output of **ps** or **top**. If it's obvious that a user process is consuming more CPU than is reasonable, investigate the process. It can also be useful to look at the number of processes waiting to run. Use the **uptime** command to show the load averages (average numbers of runnable processes) over 1, 5, and 15-minute intervals.

There are two reasons to find out what a process is trying to do before tampering with it. First, the process may be both legitimate and important. It's unreasonable to kill processes at random just because they happen to use a lot of CPU. Second, the process may be malicious or destructive. In this case, you've got to know what the process was doing (e.g., cracking passwords) so that you can fix the damage.

Processes that make excessive use of memory relative to the system's physical RAM can cause serious performance problems. You can check the memory size of processes by using **top**. The VIRT column shows the total amount of virtual memory allocated by each process, and the RES column shows the portion of that memory that is currently mapped to specific memory pages (the "resident set"). On Linux systems, applications that use the video card (such as the X server) get a bad rap because video memory is included in the memory usage computations.

Both of these numbers can include shared resources such as libraries, and that makes them potentially misleading. A more direct measure of process-specific memory consumption is found in the DATA column, which is not shown by default. To add this column to **top**'s display, type the **f** key once **top** is running and select DATA from the list. The DATA value indicates the amount of memory in each process's data and stack segments, so it's relatively specific to individual processes (modulo shared memory segments). Look for growth over time as well as absolute size.

Runaway processes that produce output can fill up an entire filesystem, causing numerous problems. When a filesystem fills up, lots of messages will be logged to the console and attempts to write to the filesystem will produce error messages.

The first thing to do in this situation is to determine which filesystem is full and which file is filling it up. The **df -k** command shows filesystem use. Look for a filesystem that's 100% or more full.[10] Use the **du** command on the identified filesystem to find which directory is using the most space. Rinse and repeat with **du**

10. Most filesystem implementations reserve a portion (about 5%) of the storage space for "breathing room," but processes running as root can encroach on this space, resulting in a reported usage that is greater than 100%.

until the large files are discovered. If you can't determine which process is using the file, try using the **fuser** and **lsof** commands (covered in detail on page 144) for more information.

You may want to suspend all suspicious-looking processes until you find the one that's causing the problem, but remember to restart the innocents when you are done. When you find the offending process, remove the files it was creating. Sometimes it's smart to compress the file with **gzip** and rename it in case it contains useful or important data.

5.12 Recommended Reading

BOVET, DANIEL P., AND MARCO CESATI. *Understanding the Linux Kernel (3rd Edition).* Sebastopol, CA: O'Reilly Media, 2006.

MCKUSICK, MARSHALL KIRK, AND GEORGE V. NEVILLE-NEIL. *The Design and Implementation of the FreeBSD Operating System.* Reading, MA: Addison-Wesley Professional, 2004.

5.13 Exercises

E5.1 Explain the relationship between a file's UID and a running process's real UID and effective UID. Besides file access control, what is the purpose of a process's effective UID?

E5.2 Suppose that a user at your site has started a long-running process that is consuming a significant fraction of a machine's resources.

a) How would you recognize a process that is hogging resources?

b) Assume that the misbehaving process might be legitimate and doesn't deserve to die. Show the commands you would use to suspend the process temporarily while you investigate.

c) Later, you discover that the process belongs to your boss and must continue running. Show the commands you'd use to resume the task.

d) Alternatively, assume that the process needs to be killed. What signal would you send, and why? What if you needed to guarantee that the process died?

E5.3 Find a process with a memory leak (write your own program if you don't have one handy). Use **ps** or **top** to monitor the program's memory use as it runs.

★ E5.4 Write a simple Perl script that processes the output of **ps** to determine the total VSZ and RSS of the processes running on the system. How do these numbers relate to the system's actual amount of physical memory and swap space?

6 The Filesystem

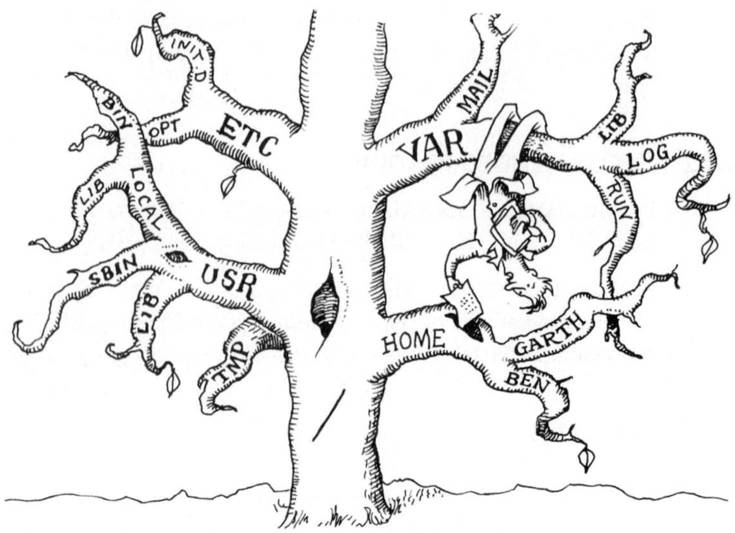

Quick: which of the following would you expect to find in a "filesystem"?

- Processes
- Audio devices
- Kernel data structures and tuning parameters
- Interprocess communication channels

If the system is UNIX or Linux, the answer is "all of the above, and more!" And yes, you might find some files in there, too.[1]

The basic purpose of a filesystem is to represent and organize the system's storage resources, but programmers have been eager to avoid reinventing the wheel when it comes to managing other types of objects. It has often proved convenient to map these objects into the filesystem namespace. This unification has some advantages (consistent programming interface, easy access from the shell) and some disadvantages (filesystem implementations akin to Frankenstein's monster), but like it or not, this is the UNIX (and hence, the Linux) way.

1. It's perhaps more accurate to say that these entities are *represented* within the filesystem. In most cases, the filesystem is used as a rendezvous point to connect clients with the drivers they are seeking.

The filesystem can be thought of as comprising four main components:

- A namespace – a way to name things and organize them in a hierarchy
- An API[2] – a set of system calls for navigating and manipulating objects
- A security model – a scheme for protecting, hiding, and sharing things
- An implementation – software to tie the logical model to the hardware

NFS, the Network File System, is described in Chapter 18.

Modern kernels define an abstract interface that accommodates many different back-end filesystems. Some portions of the file tree are handled by traditional disk-based implementations. Others are fielded by separate drivers within the kernel. For example, NFS and CIFS filesystems are handled by a driver that forwards the requested operations to a server on another computer.

Unfortunately, the architectural boundaries are not clearly drawn, and quite a few special cases exist. For example, device files furnish a way for programs to communicate with drivers inside the kernel. They are not really data files, but they're handled through the filesystem and their characteristics are stored on disk.

Another complicating factor is that the kernel supports more than one type of disk-based filesystem. In the modern best-of-breed category are the ext3 and ext4 filesystems that serve as many Linux distributions' default, along with Sun's ZFS, Veritas's VxFS, ReiserFS, JFS from IBM, and the still-in-development Btrfs.

There are also many implementations of foreign filesystems, such as the FAT and NTFS filesystems used by Microsoft Windows and the ISO 9660 filesystem used on older CD-ROMs. (Linux supports more filesystem types than any other variant of UNIX. Its extensive menu of choices gives you lots of flexibility and makes it easy to share files with other systems.)

The filesystem is a rich topic that we approach from several different angles. This chapter tells where to find things on your system and describes the characteristics of files, the meanings of permission bits, and the use of some basic commands that view and set attributes. Chapter 8, *Storage*, is where you'll find the more technical filesystem topics such as disk partitioning. Chapter 18, *The Network File System*, describes the file-sharing systems that are commonly used with Linux. You may also want to refer to Chapter 30, *Cooperating with Windows*, which discusses software you can use to share filesystems with computers running Windows.

With so many different filesystem implementations available, it may seem strange that this chapter reads as if there were only a single filesystem. We can be vague about the implementations because most modern filesystems either try to provide the traditional filesystem functionality in a faster and more reliable manner or they add extra features as a layer on top of the standard filesystem semantics. Some filesystems do both. For better or worse, too much existing software depends on the model described in this chapter for that model to be discarded.

2. Application Programming Interface, a generic term for the set of routines that a library, operating system, or software package provides for programmers to call.

6.1 Pathnames

The filesystem is presented as a single unified hierarchy that starts at the directory / and continues downward through an arbitrary number of subdirectories. / is also called the root directory. This single-hierarchy system differs from the one used by Windows, which retains the concept of partition-specific namespaces.

Absolute and relative paths

The list of directories that must be traversed to locate a particular file plus that file's filename form a pathname. Pathnames can be either absolute (**/tmp/foo**) or relative (**book4/filesystem**). Relative pathnames are interpreted starting at the current directory. You might be accustomed to thinking of the current directory as a feature of the shell, but every process has one. (Most processes never change their working directory, so they simply inherit the current directory of the process that started them.)

The terms *filename*, *pathname*, and *path* are more or less interchangeable—or at least, we use them interchangeably in this book. *Filename* and *path* can be used for both absolute and relative paths; *pathname* usually suggests an absolute path.

The filesystem can be arbitrarily deep. However, each component of a pathname (that is, each directory) must have a name no more than 255 characters long. There's also a limit on the path length you can pass into the kernel as a system call argument (4,095 bytes on Linux, 1,023 bytes on some older systems). To access a file with a pathname longer than this, you must **cd** to an intermediate directory and use a relative pathname.

Spaces in filenames

The naming of files and directories is essentially unrestricted, except that names are limited in length and must not contain slash characters or nulls. In particular, spaces are permitted. Unfortunately, UNIX has a long tradition of separating command-line arguments at whitespace, so legacy software tends to break when spaces appear within filenames.

Spaces in filenames were once found primarily on filesystems shared with Macs and PCs, but they have now metastasized into UNIX culture and are found in some standard software packages as well. There are no two ways about it: administrative scripts *must* be prepared to deal with spaces in filenames (not to mention apostrophes, asterisks, and various other menacing punctuation marks).

In the shell and in scripts, spaceful filenames can be quoted to keep their pieces together. For example, the command

```
$ less "My excellent file.txt"
```

preserves **My excellent file.txt** as a single argument to **less**. You can also escape individual spaces with a backslash. The filename completion feature of the common shells (usually bound to the <Tab> key) does this for you.

When you are writing scripts, a useful weapon to know about is **find**'s **-print0** option. In combination with **xargs -0**, this option makes the **find/xargs** combination work correctly regardless of the whitespace contained within filenames. For example, the command

```
$ find /home -type f -size +1M -print0 | xargs -0 ls -l
```

prints a long **ls** listing of every file in **/home** over one megabyte in size.

Unfortunately, HP-UX supports **find -print0** but not **xargs -0**, and AIX has neither option. However, you can install the GNU **findutils** package on either system to obtain current versions of both **find** and **xargs**. (Alternatively, you can use the **-exec** option to **find** instead of **xargs**, though it's fussier and less efficient.)

6.2 FILESYSTEM MOUNTING AND UNMOUNTING

The filesystem is composed of smaller chunks—also called filesystems—each of which consists of one directory and its subdirectories and files. It's normally apparent from context which type of "filesystem" is being discussed, but for clarity in the following discussion, we use the term "file tree" to refer to the overall layout and reserve the word "filesystem" for the chunks attached to the tree.

Most filesystems are disk partitions or disk-based logical volumes, but as we mentioned earlier, they can be anything that obeys the proper API: network file servers, kernel components, memory-based disk emulators, etc. Linux and Solaris even have a nifty "loopback" filesystem that lets you mount individual files as if they were distinct devices. It's great for developing filesystem images without having to worry about repartitioning your disks.

In most situations, filesystems are attached to the tree with the **mount** command.[3] **mount** maps a directory within the existing file tree, called the mount point, to the root of the newly attached filesystem. The previous contents of the mount point become inaccessible as long as another filesystem is mounted there. Mount points are usually empty directories, however.

For example,

```
$ sudo mount /dev/sda4 /users
```

installs the filesystem stored on the disk partition represented by **/dev/sda4** under the path **/users**. You could then use **ls /users** to see that filesystem's contents.

A list of the filesystems that are customarily mounted on a particular system is kept in the **/etc/fstab**, **/etc/vfstab** (Solaris), or **/etc/filesystems** (AIX) file. The

3. We say "in most situations" because Solaris's ZFS filesystem has adopted a rather different approach to mounting and unmounting, not to mention many other aspects of filesystem administration. Longtime readers may be expecting a snippy comment about gratuitous incompatibility at this point, but the ZFS scheme is a clear improvement and we look forward to the day that it's adopted by other systems. In the meantime, we must of necessity keep our ZFS coverage somewhat ghettoized. See page 264 for more details.

information contained in this file allows filesystems to be checked (with **fsck**) and mounted (with **mount**) automatically at boot time. It also serves as documentation for the layout of the filesystems on disk and enables short commands such as **mount /usr**. See page 260 for a discussion of the **fstab** file and its brethren.

You detach filesystems with the **umount** command. **umount** complains if you try to unmount a filesystem that is in use; the filesystem to be detached must not have open files or processes whose current directories are located there, and if the filesystem contains executable programs, they cannot be running.

Linux has a "lazy" unmount option (**umount -l**) that removes a filesystem from the naming hierarchy but does not truly unmount it until all existing file references have been closed. It's debatable whether this is a useful option. To begin with, there's no guarantee that existing references will ever close on their own. In addition, the "semi-unmounted" state can present inconsistent filesystem semantics to the programs that are using it; they can read and write through existing file handles but cannot open new files or perform other filesystem operations.

umount -f force-unmounts a busy filesystem and is supported on all our example systems. However, it's almost always a bad idea to use it on non-NFS mounts, and it may not work on certain types of filesystems (e.g., those that keep journals, such as ext3 or ext4).

Instead of reaching for **umount -f** when a filesystem you're trying to unmount turns out to be busy, run the **fuser** command to find out which processes hold references to that filesystem. **fuser -c** *mountpoint* prints the PID of every process that's using a file or directory on that filesystem, plus a series of letter codes that show the nature of the activity. For example,

```
$ fuser -c /usr
/usr:   157tm   315ctom   474tom   5049tom   84tm   496ctom   490tm
     16938c   16902ctm   358ctom   484tm
```

The exact letter codes vary from system to system. Table 6.1 summarizes the meanings of the codes, but the details are usually unimportant; the PIDs are what you want.

Table 6.1 Activity codes shown by fuser -c

Codes	Meaning
f,o	The process has a file open for reading or writing.
c	The process's current directory is on the filesystem.
e,t	The process is currently executing a file.
r	The process's root directory (set with **chroot**) is on the filesystem.
m,s	The process has mapped a file or shared library.

To investigate the offending processes, just run **ps** with the list of PIDs returned by **fuser**. For example,

```
$ ps -fp "157 315 5049"
     UID  PID  PPID C  STIME  TTY  TIME      CMD
    root  5049 490  0  Oct 14 ?    0:00      /usr/bin/X11/xdm
    root  157  1    0  Jun 27 ?    5:26      /usr/sbin/named
      lp  315  1    0  Jun 27 ?    0:00      /usr/lib/lpsched
     ...
```

Here, the quotation marks force the shell to pass the list of PIDs to **ps** as a single argument.

On Linux systems, you can avoid the need to launder PIDs through **ps** by running **fuser** with the **-v** flag. This option produces a more readable display that includes the command name.

```
$ fuser -cv /usr
            USER  PID   ACCESS COMMAND
/usr        root  444   ....m     atd
            root  499   ....m     sshd
            root  520   ....m     lpd
            ...
```

The letter codes in the ACCESS column are the same ones used in **fuser**'s nonverbose output.

A more elaborate alternative to **fuser** is the **lsof** utility by Vic Abell. **lsof** is a more complex and sophisticated program than **fuser**, and its output is correspondingly verbose. **lsof** is available from people.freebsd.org/~abe and works on all of our example systems.

Under Linux, scripts in search of specific information about processes' use of filesystems can read the files in **/proc** directly. However, **lsof -F**, which formats **lsof**'s output for easy parsing, is an easier and more portable solution. Use additional command-line flags to request just the information you need.

6.3 The organization of the file tree

Filesystems in the UNIX family have never been very well organized. Various incompatible naming conventions are used simultaneously, and different types of files are scattered randomly around the namespace. In many cases, files are divided by function and not by how likely they are to change, making it difficult to upgrade the operating system. The **/etc** directory, for example, contains some files that are never customized and some that are entirely local. How do you know which files to preserve during the upgrade? Well, you just have to know...

Despite several incremental improvements over the years (such as the designation of **/var** as a place to store system-specific data), UNIX and Linux systems are still pretty much a disorganized mess. Nevertheless, there's a culturally correct place for everything. Most software can be installed with little reconfiguration if your system is set up in a standard way. If you try to improve upon the default structure, you are asking for trouble.

See Chapter 13 for more information about configuring the kernel.

The root filesystem includes the root directory and a minimal set of files and subdirectories. The file that contains the OS kernel usually lives somewhere within the root filesystem, but it has no standard name or location; under Solaris, it is not really even a single file so much as a set of components.

Also part of the root filesystem are **/etc** for critical system and configuration files, **/sbin** and **/bin** for important utilities, and sometimes **/tmp** for temporary files. **/dev** is usually a real directory that's included in the root filesystem, but some or all of it may be overlaid with other filesystems if your system has virtualized its device support. (See page 419 for more information about this topic.)

Some systems keep shared library files and a few other odd things such as the C preprocessor in the **/lib** directory. Others have moved these items into **/usr/lib**, sometimes leaving **/lib** as a symbolic link.

See page 231 for some reasons why partitioning might be desirable and some rules of thumb to guide it.

The directories **/usr** and **/var** are also of great importance. **/usr** is where most standard programs are kept, along with various other booty such as on-line manuals and most libraries. It is not strictly necessary that **/usr** be a separate filesystem, but for convenience in administration it often is. Both **/usr** and **/var** must be available to enable the system to come up all the way to multiuser mode.

/var houses spool directories, log files, accounting information, and various other items that grow or change rapidly and that vary on each host. Since **/var** contains log files, which are apt to grow in times of trouble, it's a good idea to put **/var** on its own filesystem if that is practical.

Home directories of users are often kept on a separate filesystem, usually one that's mounted in the root directory. Dedicated filesystems can also be used to store bulky items such as source code libraries and databases.

Some of the more important standard directories are listed in Table 6.2. (Alternate rows have been shaded to improve readability.)

On many systems, a **hier** man page (**filesystem** man page on Solaris) outlines some general guidelines for the layout of the filesystem. Don't expect the actual system to conform to the master plan in every respect, however. The Wikipedia page for "UNIX directory structure" is a good general reference as well.

For Linux systems, the Filesystem Hierarchy Standard (pathname.com/fhs) attempts to codify, rationalize, and explain the standard directories. It's an excellent resource to consult when you're trying to figure out where to put something.

We discuss some additional rules and suggestions for the design of local hierarchies on page 407.

Table 6.2 Standard directories and their contents

Pathname	OS[a]	Contents
/bin	All	Core operating system commands[b]
/boot	LS	Kernel and files needed to load the kernel
/dev	All	Device entries for disks, printers, pseudo-terminals, etc.
/etc	All	Critical startup and configuration files
/home	All	Default home directories for users
/kernel	S	Kernel components
/lib	All	Libraries, shared libraries, and parts of the C compiler
/media	LS	Mount points for filesystems on removable media
/mnt	LSA	Temporary mount points, mounts for removable media
/opt	All	Optional software packages (not consistently used)
/proc	LSA	Information about all running processes
/root	LS	Home directory of the superuser (often just /)
/sbin	All	Commands needed for minimal system operability[c]
/stand	H	Stand-alone utilities, disk formatters, diagnostics, etc.
/tmp	All	Temporary files that may disappear between reboots
/usr	All	Hierarchy of secondary files and commands
/usr/bin	All	Most commands and executable files
/usr/include	All	Header files for compiling C programs
/usr/lib	All	Libraries; also, support files for standard programs
/usr/lib64	L	64-bit libraries on 64-bit Linux distributions
/usr/local	All	Software you write or install; mirrors structure of **/usr**
/usr/sbin	All	Less essential commands for administration and repair
/usr/share	All	Items that might be common to multiple systems
/usr/share/man	All	On-line manual pages
/usr/src	LSA	Source code for nonlocal software (not widely used)
/usr/tmp	All	More temporary space (preserved between reboots)
/var	All	System-specific data and configuration files
/var/adm	All	Varies: logs, setup records, strange administrative bits
/var/log	LSA	Various system log files
/var/spool	All	Spooling directories for printers, mail, etc.
/var/tmp	All	More temporary space (preserved between reboots)

a. L = Linux, S = Solaris, H = HP-UX, A = AIX.

b. On HP-UX and AIX, **/bin** is a symbolic link to **/usr/bin**.

c. The distinguishing characteristic of commands in **/sbin** is usually that they're linked with "static" versions of the system libraries and therefore don't have many dependencies on other parts of the system.

6.4 File types

Most filesystem implementations define seven types of files. Even when developers add something new and wonderful to the file tree (such as the process information under **/proc**), it must still be made to look like one of these seven types.

- Regular files
- Directories
- Character device files
- Block device files
- Local domain sockets
- Named pipes (FIFOs)
- Symbolic links

You can determine the type of an existing file with **ls -ld**. The first character of the **ls** output encodes the type. For example, the following command demonstrates that **/usr/include** is a directory:

```
$ ls -ld /usr/include
drwxr-xr-x   27 root    root        4096  Jul 15 20:57  /usr/include
```

ls uses the codes shown in Table 6.3 to represent the various types of files.

Table 6.3 File-type encoding used by ls

File type	Symbol	Created by	Removed by
Regular file	-	editors, **cp**, etc.	**rm**
Directory	d	**mkdir**	**rmdir**, **rm -r**
Character device file	c	**mknod**	**rm**
Block device file	b	**mknod**	**rm**
Local domain socket	s	**socket**(2)	**rm**
Named pipe	p	**mknod**	**rm**
Symbolic link	l	**ln -s**	**rm**

As Table 6.3 shows, **rm** is the universal tool for deleting files. But how would you delete a file named, say, **-f**? It's a legitimate filename under most filesystems, but **rm -f** doesn't work because **rm** interprets the **-f** as a flag. The answer is either to refer to the file by a longer pathname (such as **./-f**) or to use **rm**'s -- argument to tell it that everything that follows is a filename and not an option (i.e., **rm -- -f**).

Filenames that contain control characters present a similar problem since reproducing these names from the keyboard can be difficult or impossible. In this situation, you can use shell globbing (pattern matching) to identify the files to delete. When you use pattern matching, it's a good idea to get in the habit of using the **-i** option to **rm** to make **rm** confirm the deletion of each file. This feature protects you against deleting any "good" files that your pattern inadvertently matches. For example, to delete a file named **foo**<Control-D>**bar**, you could use

```
$ ls
foo?bar       foose       kde-root

$ rm -i foo*
rm: remove 'foo\004bar'? y
rm: remove 'foose'? n
```

Note that **ls** shows the control character as a question mark, which can be a bit deceptive.[4] If you don't remember that **?** is a shell pattern-matching character and try to **rm foo?bar**, you might potentially remove more than one file (although not in this example). **-i** is your friend!

To delete the most horribly named files, you may need to resort to **rm -i** *.

Another option for removing files with squirrely names is to use an alternative interface to the filesystem such as **emacs**'s dired mode or a visual tool such as Nautilus.

Regular files

Regular files consist of a series of bytes; filesystems impose no structure on their contents. Text files, data files, executable programs, and shared libraries are all stored as regular files. Both sequential access and random access are allowed.

Directories

A directory contains named references to other files. You can create directories with **mkdir** and delete them with **rmdir** if they are empty. You can delete non-empty directories with **rm -r**.

The special entries "." and ".." refer to the directory itself and to its parent directory; they may not be removed. Since the root directory has no parent directory, the path "/.." is equivalent to the path "/." (and both are equivalent to /).

A file's name is stored within its parent directory, not with the file itself. In fact, more than one directory (or more than one entry in a single directory) can refer to a file at one time, and the references can have different names. Such an arrangement creates the illusion that a file exists in more than one place at the same time.

These additional references ("links," or "hard links" to distinguish them from symbolic links, discussed below) are synonymous with the original file; as far as the filesystem is concerned, all links to the file are equivalent. The filesystem maintains a count of the number of links that point to each file and does not release the file's data blocks until its last link has been deleted. Hard links cannot cross filesystem boundaries.

You create hard links with **ln** and remove them with **rm**. It's easy to remember the syntax of **ln** if you keep in mind that it mirrors the syntax of **cp**. The command **cp oldfile newfile** creates a copy of **oldfile** called **newfile**, and **ln oldfile newfile** makes the name **newfile** an additional reference to **oldfile**. You can make hard links to directories as well as to flat files, but that's less commonly done.

You can use **ls -l** to see how many links to a given file exist. See the **ls** example output on page 154 for some additional detail.

4. **ls -b** shows the special characters as octal numbers, which can be helpful if you need to identify them specifically. <Control-A> is 1 (\001 in octal), <Control-B> is 2, and so on.

Hard links *are not* a distinct type of file. Instead of defining a separate "thing" called a hard link, the filesystem simply allows more than one directory entry to point to the same file. In addition to the file's contents, the underlying attributes of the file (such as ownerships and permissions) are also shared.

Character and block device files

See Chapter 13 for more information about devices and drivers.

Device files let programs communicate with the system's hardware and peripherals. The kernel includes (or loads) driver software for each of the system's devices. This software takes care of the messy details of managing each device so that the kernel proper can remain relatively abstract and hardware independent.

Device drivers present a standard communication interface that looks like a regular file. When the filesystem is given a request that refers to a character or block device file, it simply passes the request to the appropriate device driver. It's important to distinguish device *files* from device *drivers*, however. The files are just rendezvous points that communicate with drivers. They are not drivers themselves.

Character device files allow their associated drivers to do their own input and output buffering. Block device files are used by drivers that handle I/O in large chunks and want the kernel to perform buffering for them. In the past, a few types of hardware were represented by both block and character device files, but that configuration is unusual today.

Device files are characterized by two numbers, called the major and minor device numbers. The major device number tells the kernel which driver the file refers to, and the minor device number typically tells the driver which physical unit to address. For example, major device number 4 on a Linux system indicates the serial driver. The first serial port (**/dev/tty0**) would have major device number 4 and minor device number 0.

Drivers can interpret the minor device numbers that are passed to them in whatever way they please. For example, tape drivers use the minor device number to determine whether the tape should be rewound when the device file is closed.

In the distant past, **/dev** was a generic directory and the device files within it were created with **mknod** and removed with **rm**. A script called **MAKEDEV** helped standardize the work of creating device files for common pieces of equipment.

Unfortunately, this crude system was ill-equipped to deal with the endless sea of drivers and device types that have appeared over the last few decades. It also facilitated all sorts of potential configuration mismatches: device files that referred to no actual device, devices inaccessible because they had no device files, and so on.

These days, most systems implement some form of automatic device file management that lets the system take a more active role in the configuration of its own device files. In Solaris, for example, the **/dev** and **/devices** directories are fully virtualized. On Linux distributions, **/dev** is a standard directory, but the **udevd** daemon manages the files within it. (**udevd** creates and deletes device files in response to hardware changes reported by the kernel.) See Chapter 13, *Drivers and the Kernel*, for more information about each system's approach to this task.

Local domain sockets

Sockets are connections between processes that allow processes to communicate hygienically. UNIX defines several kinds of sockets, most of which involve the use of a network. Local domain sockets are accessible only from the local host and are referred to through a filesystem object rather than a network port. They are sometimes known as "UNIX domain sockets."

See Chapter 11 for more information about syslog.

Although socket files are visible to other processes as directory entries, they cannot be read from or written to by processes not involved in the connection. Syslog and the X Window System are examples of standard facilities that use local domain sockets.

Local domain sockets are created with the **socket** system call and removed with the **rm** command or the **unlink** system call once they have no more users.

Named pipes

Like local domain sockets, named pipes allow communication between two processes running on the same host. They're also known as "FIFO files" (FIFO is short for the phrase "first in, first out"). You can create named pipes with **mknod** and remove them with **rm**.

As with local domain sockets, real-world instances of named pipes are few and far between. They rarely require administrative intervention.[5]

Named pipes and local domain sockets serve similar purposes, and the fact that both exist is essentially a historical artifact. Neither of them would exist if UNIX and Linux were designed today; network sockets would stand in for both.

Symbolic links

A symbolic or "soft" link points to a file by name. When the kernel comes upon a symbolic link in the course of looking up a pathname, it redirects its attention to the pathname stored as the contents of the link. The difference between hard links and symbolic links is that a hard link is a direct reference, whereas a symbolic link is a reference by name. Symbolic links are distinct from the files they point to.

You create symbolic links with **ln -s** and remove them with **rm**. Since symbolic links can contain arbitrary paths, they can refer to files on other filesystems or to nonexistent files. Multiple symbolic links can also form a loop.

A symbolic link can contain either an absolute or a relative path. For example,

```
$ sudo ln -s archived/secure /var/log/secure
```

5. One reviewer commented, "Nagios (see page 887) uses them, and it sometimes needs help."

links **/var/log/secure** to **/var/log/archived/secure** with a relative path. It creates the symbolic link **/var/log/secure** with a target of "**archived/secure**", as demonstrated by this output from **ls**:

```
$ ls -l /var/log/secure
lrwxrwxrwx 1 root root 18 2009-07-05 12:54 /var/log/secure -> archived/secure[6]
```

The entire **/var/log** directory could then be moved elsewhere without causing the symbolic link to stop working (not that moving this directory is advisable).

It is a common mistake to think that the first argument to **ln -s** is interpreted relative to your current working directory. However, it is *not* resolved as a filename by **ln**; it's simply a literal string that becomes the target of the symbolic link.

6.5 File Attributes

Under the traditional UNIX and Linux filesystem model, every file has a set of nine permission bits that control who can read, write, and execute the contents of the file. Together with three other bits that primarily affect the operation of executable programs, these bits constitute the file's "mode."

The twelve mode bits are stored together with four bits of file-type information. The four file-type bits are set when the file is first created and cannot be changed, but the file's owner and the superuser can modify the twelve mode bits with the **chmod** (change mode) command. Use **ls -l** (or **ls -ld** for a directory) to inspect the values of these bits. An example is given on page 154.

The permission bits

Nine permission bits determine what operations may be performed on a file and by whom. Traditional UNIX does not allow permissions to be set per-user (although all systems now support access control lists of one sort or another; see page 159). Instead, three sets of permissions define access for the owner of the file, the group owners of the file, and everyone else (in that order).[7] Each set has three bits: a read bit, a write bit, and an execute bit (also in that order).

It's convenient to discuss file permissions in terms of octal (base 8) numbers because each digit of an octal number represents three bits and each group of permission bits consists of three bits. The topmost three bits (with octal values of 400, 200, and 100) control access for the owner. The second three (40, 20, and 10) control access for the group. The last three (4, 2, and 1) control access for everyone else ("the world"). In each triplet, the high bit is the read bit, the middle bit is the write bit, and the low bit is the execute bit.

6. The file permissions that **ls** shows for a symbolic link, lrwxrwxrwx, are dummy values. Permission to create, remove, or follow the link is controlled by the containing directory, whereas read, write, and execute permission on the link target are granted by the target's own permissions. Therefore, symbolic links do not need (and do not have) any permission information of their own.

7. If you think of the owner as "the user," you can easily remember the order of the permission sets with the word **Yugo** (like the car). This is also the letter coding used by the mnemonic version of **chmod**.

Each user fits into only one of the three permission sets. The permissions used are those that are most specific. For example, the owner of a file always has access determined by the owner permission bits and never the group permission bits. It is possible for the "other" and "group" categories to have more access than the owner, although this configuration would be highly unusual.

On a regular file, the read bit allows the file to be opened and read. The write bit allows the contents of the file to be modified or truncated; however, the ability to delete or rename (or delete and then recreate!) the file is controlled by the permissions on its parent directory because that is where the name-to-dataspace mapping is actually stored.

The execute bit allows the file to be executed. Two types of executable files exist: binaries, which the CPU runs directly, and scripts, which must be interpreted by a shell or some other program. By convention, scripts begin with a line similar to

```
#!/usr/bin/perl
```

that specifies an appropriate interpreter. Nonbinary executable files that do not specify an interpreter are assumed to be **bash** or **sh** scripts.[8]

For a directory, the execute bit (often called the "search" or "scan" bit in this context) allows the directory to be entered or passed through while a pathname is evaluated, but not to have its contents listed. The combination of read and execute bits allows the contents of the directory to be listed. The combination of write and execute bits allows files to be created, deleted, and renamed within the directory.

A variety of extensions such as access control lists (see page 159), SELinux (see page 923), and "bonus" permission bits defined by individual filesystems (see page 158) complicate or override the traditional nine-bit permission model. If you're having trouble explaining the system's observed behavior, check to see whether one of these factors might be interfering.

The setuid and setgid bits

The bits with octal values 4000 and 2000 are the setuid and setgid bits. When set on executable files, these bits allow programs to access files and processes that would otherwise be off-limits to the user that runs them. The setuid/setgid mechanism for executables is described on page 106.

When set on a directory, the setgid bit causes newly created files within the directory to take on the group ownership of the directory rather than the default group of the user that created the file. This convention makes it easier to share a directory of files among several users, as long as they belong to a common group. This interpretation of the setgid bit is unrelated to its meaning when set on an executable file, but no ambiguity can exist as to which meaning is appropriate.

8. The kernel understands the #! ("shebang") syntax and acts on it directly. However, if the interpreter is not specified completely and correctly, the kernel will refuse to execute the file. The shell then makes a second attempt to execute the script by calling **sh**.

On some systems, you can also set the setgid bit on nonexecutable plain files to request special locking behavior when the file is opened. However, we are not aware of any common cases in which this feature is used.

The sticky bit

The bit with octal value 1000 is called the sticky bit. It was of historical importance as a modifier for executable files on early UNIX systems. However, that meaning of the sticky bit is now obsolete and modern systems silently ignore it.

If the sticky bit is set on a directory, the filesystem won't allow you to delete or rename a file unless you are the owner of the directory, the owner of the file, or the superuser. Having write permission on the directory is not enough. This convention helps make directories like **/tmp** a little more private and secure.

Solaris and HP-UX are slightly less stringent in their handling of sticky directories: you can delete a file in a sticky directory if you have write permission on it, even if you aren't the owner. This actually makes a lot of sense, though it makes little practical difference.

ls: list and inspect files

The filesystem maintains about forty separate pieces of information for each file, but most of them are useful only to the filesystem itself. As a system administrator, you will be concerned mostly with the link count, owner, group, mode, size, last access time, last modification time, and type. You can inspect all of these with **ls -l** (or **ls -ld** for a directory; without the **-d** flag, **ls** lists the directory's contents).

An attribute change time is also maintained for each file. The conventional name for this time (the "ctime," short for "change time") leads some people to believe that it is the file's creation time. Unfortunately, it is not; it just records the time that the attributes of the file (owner, mode, etc.) were last changed (as opposed to the time at which the file's contents were modified).

Consider the following example:

```
$ ls -l /bin/gzip
-rwxr-xr-x  3  root  root  62100  May 28   2010  /bin/gzip
```

The first field specifies the file's type and mode. The first character is a dash, so the file is a regular file. (See Table 6.3 on page 148 for other codes.)

The next nine characters in this field are the three sets of permission bits. The order is owner-group-other, and the order of bits within each set is read-write-execute. Although these bits have only binary values, **ls** shows them symbolically with the letters r, w, and x for read, write, and execute. In this case, the owner has all permissions on the file and everyone else has read and execute permission.

If the setuid bit had been set, the x representing the owner's execute permission would have been replaced with an s, and if the setgid bit had been set, the x for the group would also have been replaced with an s. The last character of the permissions (execute permission for "other") is shown as t if the sticky bit of the file is turned on. If either the setuid/setgid bit or the sticky bit is set but the corresponding execute bit is not, these bits appear as S or T.

The next field in the listing is the file's link count. In this case it is 3, indicating that **/bin/gzip** is just one of three names for this file (the others are **/bin/gunzip** and **/bin/zcat**). Each time a hard link is made to a file, the file's link count is incremented by 1. Symbolic links do not affect the link count.

All directories have at least two hard links: the link from the parent directory and the link from the special file "." inside the directory itself.

The next two fields in the **ls** output are the owner and group owner of the file. In this example, the file's owner is root, and the file also belongs to the group named root. The filesystem actually stores these as the user and group ID numbers rather than as names. If the text versions (names) can't be determined, **ls** shows the fields as numbers. This might happen if the user or group that owns the file has been deleted from the **/etc/passwd** or **/etc/group** file. It could also indicate a problem with your NIS or LDAP database (if you use one); see Chapter 19.

The next field is the size of the file in bytes. This file is 62,100 bytes long. Next comes the date of last modification: May 28, 2010. The last field in the listing is the name of the file, **/bin/gzip**.

ls output is slightly different for a device file. For example:

```
$ ls -l /dev/tty0
crw-rw---- 1 root root 4, 0   Jun 11 20:41 /dev/tty0
```

Most fields are the same, but instead of a size in bytes, **ls** shows the major and minor device numbers. **/dev/tty0** is the first virtual console on this (Red Hat) system and is controlled by device driver 4 (the terminal driver).

One **ls** option that's useful for scoping out hard links is **-i**, which makes **ls** show each file's "inode number." Without going into too much detail about filesystem implementations, we'll just say that the inode number is an index into a table that enumerates all the files in the filesystem. Inodes are the "things" that are pointed to by directory entries; entries that are hard links to the same file have the same inode number. To figure out a complex web of links, you need both **ls -li** to show link counts and inode numbers and **find** to search for matches.[9]

Some other **ls** options that are important to know are **-a** to show all entries in a directory (even files whose names start with a dot), **-t** to sort files by modification time (or **-tr** to sort in reverse chronological order), **-F** to show the names of files in a way that distinguishes directories and executable files, **-R** to list recursively, and **-h** to show file sizes in human-readable form (e.g., 8K or 53M).

9. Try **find** *mountpoint* **-xdev -inum** *inode* **-print**.

chmod: change permissions

The **chmod** command changes the permissions on a file. Only the owner of the file and the superuser can change its permissions. To use the command on early UNIX systems, you had to learn a bit of octal notation, but current versions accept both octal notation and a mnemonic syntax. The octal syntax is generally more convenient for administrators, but it can only be used to specify an absolute value for the permission bits. The mnemonic syntax can modify some bits while leaving others alone.

The first argument to **chmod** is a specification of the permissions to be assigned, and the second and subsequent arguments are names of files on which permissions should be changed. In the octal case, the first octal digit of the specification is for the owner, the second is for the group, and the third is for everyone else. If you want to turn on the setuid, setgid, or sticky bits, you use four octal digits rather than three, with the three special bits forming the first digit.

Table 6.4 illustrates the eight possible combinations for each set of three bits, where r, w, and x stand for read, write, and execute.

Table 6.4 Permission encoding for chmod

Octal	Binary	Perms	Octal	Binary	Perms
0	000	---	4	100	r--
1	001	--x	5	101	r-x
2	010	-w-	6	110	rw-
3	011	-wx	7	111	rwx

For example, **chmod 711 myprog** gives all permissions to the owner and execute-only permission to everyone else.[10]

For the mnemonic syntax, you combine a set of targets (**u**, **g**, or **o** for user, group, other) with an operator (+, -, = to add, remove, or set) and a set of permissions. The **chmod** man page gives the details, but the syntax is probably best learned by example. Table 6.5 exemplifies some mnemonic operations.

The hard part about using the mnemonic syntax is remembering whether **o** stands for "owner" or "other"; "other" is correct. Just remember **u** and **g** by analogy to UID and GID; only one possibility is left.

On Linux and OpenSolaris systems, you can also specify the modes to be assigned by copying them from an existing file. For example, **chmod --reference=filea fileb** makes **fileb**'s mode the same as **filea**'s.

10. If **myprog** were a shell script, it would need both read and execute permission turned on. For the script to be run by an interpreter, it must be opened and read like a text file. Binary files are executed directly by the kernel and therefore do not need read permission turned on.

Table 6.5 Examples of chmod's mnemonic syntax

Spec	Meaning
u+w	Adds write permission for the owner of the file
ug=rw,o=r	Gives r/w permission to owner and group, and read permission to others
a-x	Removes execute permission for all categories (owner/group/other)
ug=srx,o=	Makes setuid/setgid and gives r/x permission to owner and group only
g=u	Makes the group permissions be the same as the owner permissions

With the **-R** option, **chmod** recursively updates the file permissions within a directory. However, this feat is trickier than it looks because the enclosed files and directories may not share the same attributes; for example, some might be executable files while others are text files. Mnemonic syntax is particularly useful with **-R** because it preserves bits whose values you don't set explicitly. For example,

```
$ chmod -R g+w mydir
```

adds group write permission to **mydir** and all its contents without messing up the execute bits of directories and programs.

If you *want* to adjust execute bits, be wary of **chmod -R**. It's blind to the fact that the execute bit has a different interpretation on a directory than it does on a flat file. Therefore, **chmod -R a-x** probably won't do what you intend.

chown and chgrp: change ownership and group

The **chown** command changes a file's ownership, and the **chgrp** command changes its group ownership. The syntax of **chown** and **chgrp** mirrors that of **chmod**, except that the first argument is the new owner or group, respectively.

To change a file's group, you must either be the owner of the file and belong to the group you're changing to or be the superuser. The rules for changing ownership are more complex and vary among systems. Most systems define some sort of process-specific capability that fine-tunes the behavior of **chown**.

Like **chmod**, **chown** and **chgrp** offer the recursive **-R** flag to change the settings of a directory and all the files underneath it. For example, the sequence

```
$ sudo chown -R matt ~matt/restore
$ sudo chgrp -R staff ~matt/restore
```

could be used to reset the owner and group of files restored from a backup for the user matt. If you're setting up a user's home directory, don't try to **chown** dot files with a command such as

```
$ sudo chown -R matt ~matt/.*
```

since the pattern will match **~matt/..** and will therefore end up changing the ownerships of the parent directory and probably the home directories of other users.

chown can change both the owner and group of a file at once with the syntax

chown *user:group file ...*

For example,

```
$ sudo chown -R matt:staff ~matt/restore
```

Linux and Solaris take this syntax to its logical end and let you omit either *user* or *group*, thus making the **chgrp** command superfluous. If you include the colon but no *group*, **chown** uses the user's default group.

umask: assign default permissions

You can use the built-in shell command **umask** to influence the default permissions given to the files you create. Every process has its own **umask** attribute; the shell's built-in **umask** command sets the shell's own **umask**, which is then inherited by commands that you run.

The **umask** is specified as a three-digit octal value that represents the permissions to *take away*. When a file is created, its permissions are set to whatever the creating program requests minus whatever the **umask** forbids. Thus, the individual digits of the **umask** allow the permissions shown in Table 6.6.

Table 6.6 Permission encoding for umask

Octal	Binary	Perms	Octal	Binary	Perms
0	000	rwx	4	100	–wx
1	001	rw–	5	101	–w–
2	010	r–x	6	110	––x
3	011	r––	7	111	–––

For example, **umask 027** allows all permissions for the owner but forbids write permission to the group and allows no permissions for anyone else. The default **umask** value is often 022, which denies write permission to the group and world but allows read permission.

See Chapter 7 for more information about startup files.

You cannot force users to have a particular **umask** value because they can always reset it to whatever they want. However, you can put a suitable default in the sample **.profile** file that you give to new users.

Linux bonus flags

Linux's ext2, ext3, and ext4 filesystems define some supplemental attributes you can turn on to request special semantics—"request" being the operative word, since many of the flags haven't actually been implemented. For example, one flag makes a file append-only and another makes it immutable and undeletable.

Since these flags don't apply to filesystems other than the ext* series, Linux uses special commands, **lsattr** and **chattr**, to view and change them. Table 6.7 lists the flags that currently work (about 50% of those mentioned in the man page).

Table 6.7 Ext2 and ext3 bonus flags

Flag	Meaning
A	Never update access time (`st_atime`; for performance)
a	Allow writing only in append mode (only root can set)
D	Force directory updates to be written synchronously
d	No backup—make **dump** ignore this file
i	Make file immutable and undeletable (only root can set)
j	Keep a journal for data changes as well as metadata
S	Force changes to be written synchronously (no buffering)

With the possible exception of the "no backup" flag, it's not clear that any of these features offer much day-to-day value. The immutable and append-only flags were largely conceived as ways to make the system more resistant to tampering by hackers or hostile code. Unfortunately, they can confuse software and protect only against hackers that don't know enough to use **chattr -ia**. Real-world experience has shown that these flags are more often used *by* hackers than *against* them.

The **S** and **D** options for synchronous writes also merit a special caution. Since they force all filesystem pages associated with a file or directory to be written out immediately on changes, they might seem to offer additional protection against data loss in the event of a crash. However, the order of operations for synchronous updates is unusual and has been known to confuse **fsck**; recovery of a damaged filesystem might therefore be made more difficult rather than more reliable. Filesystem journaling, as supported by ext3 and ext4, is usually a better option. The **j** option can force data journaling for specific files, albeit at some performance cost.

6.6 Access control lists

The traditional 9-bit owner/group/other access control system is powerful enough to accommodate most administrative needs. Although the system has clear limitations, it's very much in keeping with the UNIX traditions (some might say, "former traditions") of simplicity and predictability.

Virtually all non-UNIX operating systems use a more complicated way of regulating access to files: access control lists, aka ACLs. Each file or directory can have an associated ACL that lists the permission rules to be applied to it. Each of the rules within an ACL is called an access control entry, or ACE.

In general, an access control entry identifies the user or group to which it applies and specifies a set of permissions to be applied to those users. ACLs have no set length and can include permission specifications for multiple users or groups. Most OSes limit the length of an individual ACL, but the limit is high enough (usually at least 32 entries) that it rarely comes into play.

The more sophisticated ACL systems let administrators specify partial sets of permissions or negative permissions; some also have inheritance features that allow access specifications to propagate to newly created filesystem entities.

ACL systems are more powerful than the traditional UNIX model, but they are also an order of magnitude more complex, both for administrators and for software developers. Use them only with a degree of trepidation. Not only are ACLs complicated and tiresome to use, but they can also cause problematic interactions with ACL-unaware backup systems, network file service peers, and even simple programs such as text editors.

ACLs are entropy magnets. Over time, they tend to become increasingly complex and unmaintainable.

A short and brutal history of UNIX ACLs

The next few sections describe the various ACL systems supported by UNIX and Linux and the multiple sets of commands that manipulate them. Before we dive into those details, however, we should answer the underlying question those details are sure to provoke: "How did this ACL stuff get to be such a train wreck?"

As usual, the culprit is a tortured history of politics, money, and code forks. In this case, a basic understanding of the history helps impose some structure on the current reality.

A POSIX subcommittee first started work on an ACL facility for UNIX in the mid-1990s. To a first approximation, the POSIX ACL model simply extended the traditional UNIX `rwx` permission system to accommodate permissions for multiple groups and users.

Unfortunately, the POSIX draft never became a formal standard, and the working group was defunded in 1998. Several vendors implemented POSIX ACLs anyway. Other vendors created their own ACL systems. Since there was no clear leader, every implementation looked different.

Meanwhile, it became increasingly common for UNIX and Linux systems to share filesystems with Windows, which has its own ACL conventions. Here the plot thickens, because Windows makes a variety of distinctions that are not found in either the traditional UNIX model or its POSIX ACL equivalent. Windows ACLs are semantically more complex, too; for example, they allow negative permissions ("deny" entries) and have a complicated inheritance scheme.

See Chapter 18 for more information about NFS.

The architects of version 4 of the NFS protocol—the standard file-sharing protocol used by UNIX—wanted to incorporate ACLs as a first-class entity. Because of the UNIX/Windows split and the inconsistencies among UNIX ACL implementations, it was clear that the systems on the ends of an NFSv4 connection might often be of different types. Each system might understand NFSv4 ACLs, POSIX ACLs, Windows ACLs, or no ACLs at all. The NFSv4 standard would have to be interoperable with these various worlds without causing too many surprises or security problems.

Given this constraint, it's perhaps not surprising that NFSv4 ACLs are essentially a union of all preexisting systems. They are a strict superset of POSIX ACLs, so any POSIX ACL can be represented as an NFSv4 ACL without loss of information. At the same time, NFSv4 ACLs accommodate all the permission bits found on Windows systems, and they have most of Windows' semantic features as well.

ACL implementation

In theory, responsibility for maintaining and enforcing ACLs could be turned over to several different components of the operating system. ACLs could be implemented by the kernel on behalf of all the system's filesystems, by individual filesystems, or perhaps by higher-level software such as NFS and CIFS servers.

In practice, only filesystems can implement ACLs cleanly, reliably, and with acceptable performance. Hence, ACL support is both OS dependent and filesystem dependent. A filesystem that supports ACLs on one system may not support them on another, or it may feature a somewhat different implementation managed by different commands.

The standard UNIX system calls that manipulate files (**open**, **read**, **unlink**, and so on) make no provision for ACLs. However, they continue to work just fine on systems that have ACLs because the underlying filesystems do their own permission checking. Operations that are not allowed by the relevant ACL simply fail and return a generic "permission denied" error code.

ACL-aware programs use a separate system call or library routine to read or set files' ACLs. When an operating system first adds support for ACLs, it usually upgrades common utilities such as **ls** and **cp** to be at least minimally ACL-aware (for example, by making **cp -p** preserve ACLs if they are present). In addition, the system must add new commands or command extensions to let users read and set ACLs from the command line. Unfortunately, these commands are not standardized among operating systems, either.

Because ACL implementations are filesystem specific and because systems support multiple filesystem implementations, many systems end up supporting multiple types of ACLs. Even a given filesystem may offer several ACL options, as in IBM's JFS2. If multiple ACL systems are available, the commands to manipulate them might be the same or different; it depends on the system.

ACL support by system

In general, ACL support under UNIX and Linux is currently something of an ad hoc mess. Here are some particulars:

- As of this writing (2010), POSIX-based ACL systems have the lead in implementation and deployment, but NFSv4 ACLs are rapidly gaining ground and will likely become the de facto standard. Currently, only Sun's ZFS and IBM's JFS2 have native support for NFS4v4 ACLs.

- Under Linux, POSIX-style ACLs are supported by ReiserFS, XFS, JFS, Btrfs, and the ext* family of filesystems. They are usually disabled by default; use the **-o acl** option to **mount** to turn them on. The **getfacl** and **setfacl** commands read and manipulate POSIX ACL entries.

- Solaris supports POSIX ACLs on the older UFS filesystem and NFSv4 ACLs on ZFS. The Solaris versions of **ls** and **chmod** have been modified to display and edit both types of ACLs.[11] Solaris has **setfacl** and **getfacl** commands that are vaguely similar to those found on Linux distributions, but they're really just there for compatibility and work only for POSIX ACLs.

- HP-UX designed its own ACL system for its High-performance File System (HFS). When HP adopted Veritas's VxFS as its primary filesystem, it also incorporated support for POSIX-style ACLs.[12] Unfortunately, the two ACL systems are controlled by different sets of commands. HFS is now deprecated, but the HFS ACL commands remain behind for compatibility. We do not discuss the HFS ACLs in this book.

- AIX's JFS2 filesystem supports a proprietary ACL system known as AIXC. As of AIX 5.3.0, JFS2 also supports NFSv4-style ACLs. AIX uses the same commands (**aclget**, **aclput**, and **acledit**) to manipulate both types of ACLs, and it provides an **aclconvert** utility to facilitate migration from one format to another. We do not discuss AIXC in this book.

POSIX ACLs

POSIX ACLs are supported on many Linux filesystems and on HP-UX's VxFS filesystem port (known as JFS). They are also available under Solaris for the deprecated UFS filesystem only.

11. Make sure that your PATH environment variable puts **/bin** before **/usr/gnu/bin** so that you get the Solaris-specific versions of **ls** and **chown** instead of the GNU versions.
12. In an effort to keep customers disoriented and docile, HP has adopted a strategy of abducting the names of existing filesystems and applying them to proprietary products. For example, HP's HFS was so called to facilitate confusion with Apple's Hierarchical File System, also known as HFS. HP calls its VxFS port "JFS" to forestall the possibility that users might distinguish it from IBM's own unrelated JFS filesystem.

POSIX ACLs are a mostly straightforward extension of the standard 9-bit UNIX permission model. Read, write, and execute permission are the only capabilities that the ACL system deals with. Embellishments such as the setuid and sticky bits are handled exclusively through the traditional mode bits.

ACLs allow the rwx bits to be set independently for any combination of users and groups. Table 6.8 shows what the individual entries in an ACL can look like.

Table 6.8 Entries that can appear in an access control list

Format	Example	Sets permissions for
user::*perms*	user::rw-	The file's owner
user:*username*:*perms*	user:trent:rw-	A specific user
group::*perms*	group::r-x	The group that owns the file
group:*groupname*:*perms*	group:staff:rw-	A specific group
other::*perms*	other::---	All others
mask::*perms*	mask::rwx	All but owner and other[a]

a. Masks are somewhat tricky and are explained later in this section.

Users and groups can be identified by name or by UID/GID. The exact number of entries that an ACL can contain varies with the filesystem implementation and ranges from a low of 25 with XFS to a virtually unlimited number with ReiserFS and JFS. The ext* filesystems allow 32 entries, which is probably a reasonable limit for manageability in any case.

Interaction between traditional modes and ACLs

Files with ACLs retain their original mode bits, but consistency is automatically enforced and the two sets of permissions can never conflict. The following example (which uses the Linux command syntax) demonstrates that the ACL entries update automatically in response to changes made with old-style **chmod**:

```
$ touch /tmp/example
$ ls -l /tmp/example
-rw-rw-r-- 1 garth garth    0 Jun 14 15:57 /tmp/example
$ getfacl /tmp/example
getfacl: Removing leading '/' from absolute path names
# file: tmp/example
# owner: garth
# group: garth
user::rw-
group::rw-
other::r--
$ chmod 640 /tmp/example
$ getfacl --omit-header /tmp/example
user::rw-
group::r--
other::---
```

This enforced consistency allows older software with no awareness of ACLs to play reasonably well in the ACL world. However, there's a twist. Even though the group:: ACL entry in the example above appears to be tracking the middle set of traditional mode bits, that will not always be the case.

To understand why, suppose that a legacy program clears the write bits within all three permission sets of the traditional mode (e.g., **chmod ugo-w** *file*). The intention is clearly to make the file unwritable by anyone. But what if the resulting ACL were to look like this?

```
user::r--
group::r--
group:staff:rw-
other::r--
```

From the perspective of legacy programs, the file appears to be unmodifiable, yet it is actually writable by anyone in group staff. Not good. To reduce the chance of ambiguity and misunderstandings, the following rules are enforced:

- The user:: and other:: ACL entries are by definition identical to the "owner" and "other" permission bits from the traditional mode. Changing the mode changes the corresponding ACL entries, and vice versa.
- In all cases, the effective access permission afforded to the file's owner and to users not mentioned in another way are those specified in the user:: and other:: ACL entries, respectively.
- If a file has no explicitly defined ACL or has an ACL that consists only of one user::, one group::, and one other:: entry, these ACL entries are identical to the three sets of traditional permission bits. This is the case illustrated in the **getfacl** example above. (Such an ACL is termed "minimal" and need not actually be implemented as a logically separate ACL.)
- In more complex ACLs, the traditional group permission bits correspond to a special ACL entry called mask rather than the group:: ACL entry. The mask limits the access that the ACL can confer upon *all* named users, *all* named groups, *and* the default group.

In other words, the mask specifies an upper bound on the access that the ACL can assign to individual groups and users. It is conceptually similar to the **umask**, except that the ACL mask is always in effect and specifies the allowed permissions rather than the permissions to be denied. ACL entries for named users, named groups, and the default group can include permission bits that are not present in the mask, but the kernel simply ignores them.

As a result, the traditional mode bits can never understate the access allowed by the ACL as a whole. Furthermore, clearing a bit from the group portion of the traditional mode clears the corresponding bit in the ACL mask and thereby forbids this permission to everyone but the file's owner and those who fall in the category of "other."

When the ACL shown in the previous example is expanded to include entries for a specific user and group, **setfacl** automatically supplies an appropriate mask:

```
$ ls -l /tmp/example
-rw-r-----   1 garth  garth      0 Jun 14 15:57 /tmp/example
$ setfacl -m user::r,user:trent:rw,group:admin:rw /tmp/example
$ ls -l /tmp/example
-r--rw----+  1 garth  garth      0 Jun 14 15:57 /tmp/example
$ getfacl --omit-header /tmp/example
user::r--
user:trent:rw-
group::r--
group:admin:rw-
mask::rw-
other::---
```

As seen here, the Linux version of **setfacl** generates a mask that allows all the permissions granted in the ACL to take effect. If you want to set the mask by hand, include it in the ACL entry list given to **setfacl** or use the **-n** option to prevent **setfacl** from regenerating it. (The Solaris **setfacl** defaults to not recalculating the mask entry; use the **-r** flag to regenerate it.)

Note that after the **setfacl** command, **ls -l** shows a + sign at the end of the file's mode to indicate that it now has a real ACL associated with it. The first **ls -l** shows no + because at that point the ACL is "minimal." That is, it is entirely described by the 9-bit mode and so does not need to be stored separately.

If you use the traditional **chmod** command to manipulate the group permissions on an ACL-bearing file, be aware that your changes affect only the mask. To continue the previous example:

```
$ chmod 770 /tmp/example
$ ls -l /tmp/example
-rwxrwx---+ 1 garth  staff    0 Jun 14 15:57 /tmp/example
$ getfacl --omit-header /tmp/example
user::rwx
user:trent:rw-
group::r--
group:admin:rw-
mask::rwx
other::---
```

The **ls** output in this case is misleading. Despite the apparently generous group permissions, no one actually has permission to execute the file by reason of group membership. To grant such permission, you must edit the ACL itself.

Access determination

When a process attempts to access a file, its effective UID is compared to the UID that owns the file. If they are the same, access is determined by the ACL's user::

The Filesystem

permissions. Otherwise, if a matching user-specific ACL entry exists, permissions are determined by that entry in combination with the ACL mask.

If no user-specific entry is available, the filesystem tries to locate a valid group-related entry that provides the requested access; these entries are processed in conjunction with the ACL mask. If no matching entry can be found, the other:: entry prevails.

ACL inheritance

In addition to the ACL entry types listed in Table 6.8, the ACLs for directories can include default entries that are propagated to the ACLs of newly created files and subdirectories created within them. Subdirectories receive these entries both in the form of active ACL entries and in the form of copies of the default entries. Therefore, the original default entries may eventually propagate down through several layers of the directory hierarchy.

The connection between the parent and child ACLs does not continue once the default entries have been copied. If the parent's default entries change, the changes are not reflected in the ACLs of existing subdirectories.

NFSv4 ACLs

In this section, we discuss the characteristics of NFSv4 ACLs and briefly review the Solaris command syntax used to set and inspect them. AIX also supports NFSv4 ACLs, but it uses different commands (**aclget**, **aclput**, **acledit**, et al.) for this purpose. Rather than belaboring the details of any particular command set, we concentrate here on the theory behind the system. Once you understand basic principles, the system-specific commands are easy to pick up.

From a structural perspective, NFSv4 ACLs are similar to Windows ACLs. The main difference between them lies in the specification of the entity to which an access control entry refers.

In both systems, the ACL stores this entity as a string. For Windows ACLs, the string typically contains a Windows security identifier (SID), whereas for NFSv4, the string is typically of the form user:*username* or group:*groupname*. It can also be one of the special tokens owner@, group@, or everyone@. In fact, these latter entries are the most common because they correspond to the mode bits found on every file.

Systems such as Samba that share files between UNIX and Windows systems must provide some way of mapping between Windows and NFSv4 principals.

The Windows and NFSv4 permission model is more granular than the traditional UNIX read-write-execute model. The main refinements are as follows:

- NFSv4 distinguishes permission to create files within a directory from permission to create subdirectories.
- NFSv4 has a separate "append" permission bit.

- NFSv4 has separate read and write permissions for data, file attributes, extended attributes, and ACLs.
- NFSv4 controls a user's ability to change the ownership of a file through the standard ACL system. In traditional UNIX, the ability to change the ownership of files is usually reserved for root.

Table 6.9 shows the various permissions that can be assigned in the NFSv4 system. It also shows the one-letter codes used to represent them and the more verbose names displayed and accepted by Solaris's **ls** and **chmod** commands.

Table 6.9 NFSv4 file permissions

Code	Verbose name	Permission
r	read_data list_directory	Read data (file) or list directory contents (directory)
w	write_data add_file	Write data (file) or create file (directory)
p	append_data add_subdirectory	Append data (file) or create subdirectory (directory)
R	read_xattr	Read named ("extended") attributes
W	write_xattr	Write named ("extended") attributes
x	execute	Execute as a program
D	delete_child	Delete child within a directory
a	read_attributes	Read nonextended attributes
A	write_attributes	Write nonextended attributes
d	delete	Delete
c	read_acl	Read access control list
C	write_acl	Write access control list
o	write_owner	Change ownership
s	synchronize	Force writes to complete synchronously

Some permissions have multiple names because they are represented by the same flag value but are interpreted differently for files and directories. This kind of overloading should be familiar from the traditional UNIX permission system. (For example, an x in the traditional system indicates execute permission on a plain file and "traverse" permission on a directory.)

Although the NFSv4 permission model is fairly detailed, the individual permissions should mostly be self-explanatory. The "synchronize" permission allows a client to specify that its modifications to a file should be synchronous—that is, calls to **write** should not return until the data has actually been saved on disk.

An extended attribute is a named chunk of data that is stored along with a file; most modern filesystems support such attributes, although they are not yet widely used in the real world. At this point, the predominant use of extended attributes is to store ACLs themselves. However, the NFSv4 permission model treats ACLs separately from other extended attributes.

NFSv4 entities for which permissions can be specified

In addition to the garden-variety user:*username* and group:*groupname* specifiers, NFSv4 defines several special entities that may be assigned permissions in an ACL. Most important among these are owner@, group@, and everyone@, which correspond to the traditional categories in the 9-bit permission model.

The NFSv4 specification (RFC3530) defines a few more special entities such as dialup@ and batch@. From a UNIX perspective, they're all a bit peculiar. We are not aware of any actual real-world application for these entities; most likely, they exist to facilitate compatibility with Windows.

NFSv4 has several differences from POSIX. For one thing, it has no default entity, used in POSIX to control ACL inheritance. Instead, any individual access control entry (ACE) can be flagged as inheritable (see *ACL inheritance*, below). NFSv4 also does not use a mask to reconcile the permissions specified in a file's mode with its ACL. The mode is required to be consistent with the settings specified for owner@, group@, and everyone@, and filesystems that implement NFSv4 ACLs must preserve this consistency when either the mode or the ACL is updated.

Access determination

In the POSIX ACL system, the filesystem attempts to match the user's identity to the single most appropriate access control entry. That ACE then provides a complete set of controlling permissions for the file.

The NFSv4 system differs in that an ACE may specify only a partial set of permissions. Each NFSv4 ACE is either an "allow" ACE or a "deny" ACE; it acts more like a mask than an authoritative specification of all possible permissions.[13] Multiple ACEs can apply to any given situation.

When deciding whether to allow a particular operation, the filesystem reads the ACL in order, processing ACEs until either all requested permissions have been allowed or some requested permission has been denied. Only ACEs whose entity strings are compatible with the current user's identity are considered.

It's possible for the filesystem to reach the end of an NFSv4 ACL without having obtained a definitive answer to a permission query. The NFSv4 standard considers the result to be undefined, but most real-world implementations will choose to deny access, both because this is the convention used by Windows and because it's the only option that makes sense.

13. In addition to "allow" and "deny", the NFSv4 specification also allows "audit" and "alarm" entries that do not affect permission calculations but are potentially useful for logging and security control. The exact meaning of these entries is implementation dependent.

ACL inheritance

Like POSIX ACLs, NFSv4 ACLs allow newly created objects to inherit access control entries from their enclosing directory. However, the NFSv4 system is a bit more powerful and a lot more confusing. Here are the important points:

- Any ACE can be flagged as inheritable. Inheritance for newly created subdirectories (dir_inherit or d) and newly created files (file_inherit or f) are flagged separately.
- You can apply different access control entries to new files and new directories by creating separate access control entries on the parent directory and flagging them appropriately. You can also apply a single ACE to all new child entities (of whatever type) by turning on both the d and f flags.
- From the perspective of access determination, access control entries have the same effect on the parent (source) directory whether or not they are inheritable. If you want an entry to apply to children but not to the parent directory itself, turn on the ACE's inherit_only (i) flag.
- New subdirectories normally inherit two copies of each ACE: one with the inheritance flags turned off, which applies to the subdirectory itself; and one with the inherit_only flag turned on, which sets up the new subdirectory to propagate its inherited ACEs. You can suppress the creation of this second ACE by turning on the no_propagate (n) flag on the parent directory's copy of the ACE. The end result is that the ACE propagates only to immediate children of the original directory.
- Don't confuse the propagation of access control entries with true inheritance. Your setting an inheritance-related flag on an ACE simply means that the ACE will be copied to new entities. It does not create any ongoing relationship between the parent and its children. If you later change the ACE entries on the parent directory, the children are not updated.

Table 6.10 summarizes these various inheritance flags.

Table 6.10 NFSv4 ACE inheritance flags

Code	Verbose name	Meaning
f	file_inherit	Propagate this ACE to newly created files
d	dir_inherit	Propagate this ACE to newly created subdirectories
i	inherit_only	Propagate, but don't apply to the current directory
n	no_propagate	Propagate to new subdirectories, but not their children

NFSv4 ACL viewing in Solaris

Solaris has integrated its ACL support into **ls** and **chmod**, which is a nice approach and a straightforward extension of the commands' usual functions. Both

POSIX and NFSv4 ACLs are supported in this manner, although here we show only NFSv4 examples. The specific flavor of ACLs that you see or set depends on the underlying filesystem.

ls -v shows ACL information for filesystem objects. As with **-l**, you must include the **-d** option if you want to see the ACL for a directory; otherwise **ls -v** shows the ACL of every child of the directory. Here's a simple (!) example:

```
solaris$ mkdir /var/tmp/example
solaris$ ls -dv /var/tmp/example
drwxr-xr-x   2  garth  staff    2 Jan 11 07:19   /var/tmp/example
     0:owner@::deny
     1:owner@:list_directory/read_data/add_file/write_data/add_subdirectory
          /append_data/write_xattr/execute/write_attributes/write_acl
          /write_owner:allow
     2:group@:add_file/write_data/add_subdirectory/append_data:deny
     3:group@:list_directory/read_data/execute:allow
     4:everyone@:add_file/write_data/add_subdirectory/append_data/write_xattr
          /write_attributes/write_acl/write_owner:deny
     5:everyone@:list_directory/read_data/read_xattr/execute/read_attributes
          /read_acl/synchronize:allow
```

This newly created directory seems to have a complex ACL, but in fact it's a fake—this ACL is just the nine-bit mode shown on the first line of output translated into ACLese. It is not necessary for the filesystem to store an actual ACL because the ACL and the mode are equivalent. (Such ACLs are termed "trivial.") If the directory had an actual ACL, **ls** would show the mode bits with a + on the end (i.e., drwxr-xr-x+) to indicate the presence of the ACL.

Each numbered clause represents one access control entry. The format is

index:*entity*:*permissions*:*inheritance_flags*:*type*

The *index* numbers are added by **ls** for clarity and are not part of the actual ACL. They can be used in later **chmod** commands to identify a specific ACE to be replaced or deleted.

The *entity* can be the keywords owner@, group@, or everyone@, or a form such as user:*username* or group:*groupname*.

The *type* of an ACE is either allow or deny. Theoretically, alarm and audit are allowed as well, but ZFS doesn't implement these features.

Both the *permissions* and the *inheritance_flags* are slash-separated lists of options. Strangely, **ls** omits the *inheritance_flags* field (and one of the colon delimiters) if the flags are all turned off, but it does not do the same with the *permissions*.

For added confusion, **ls** displays multiple names for the r (read data/list directory), w (write data/add file), and p (append data/add subdirectory) permission bits, as if they were separate permissions. In fact, they are file- and directory-specific interpretations of the same bits and will always be present or absent together.

These quirks, together with the use of a colon as a subdivider within the *entity* field, make it tricky for scripts to parse **ls -v** output. If you need to process ACLs programmatically, look first for an existing library (such as the Solaris::ACL Perl module from the Comprehensive Perl Archive Network (CPAN) that facilitates the process. As a last resort, you can use the output of **ls -V** (described next), since this format is more amenable to parsing.

You can obtain a tabular display of ACL entries with **ls -V**. In this mode, permissions are represented by their one-letter codes as shown in Table 6.9 on page 167. All possible bits are displayed for each access control entry; those that are turned off are represented by dashes (just as **ls** displays a file's traditional mode).

```
solaris$ ls -dV /var/tmp/example
drwxr-xr-x   2  garth   staff    2 Jan 11 07:19   /var/tmp/example
          owner@:   --------------:-------:deny
          owner@:   rwxp---A-W-Co-:-------:allow
          group@:   -w-p----------:-------:deny
          group@:   r-x-----------:-------:allow
       everyone@:   -w-p---A-W-Co-:-------:deny
       everyone@:   r-x---a-R-c--s:-------:allow
```


Interactions between ACLs and modes

Several aspects of the translation of modes to ACLs merit further discussion. First, note that the group@ and everyone@ ACEs in the example above differ despite the fact that the corresponding clusters in the mode are both r-x. That's not because the translation rules are different for the group@ and everyone@ categories; rather, it's because certain permissions can't really be extrapolated from the traditional mode.

These "unspecified" permission bits receive default values through additions to the everyone@ ACEs only. The write_xattr, write_attributes, write_acl, and write_owner permissions are always denied, and the read_xattr, read_attributes, read_acl, and synchronize permissions are always allowed. If you factor out these permissions from the everyone@ set, you can see that the remaining ACEs for everyone@ are in fact the same as those for group@.

Of course, these "constant" permissions apply only to trivial ACLs. By editing the ACL directly, you can set the bits in any combination.

The mode and the ACL must remain consistent, so whenever you adjust one of these entities, the other updates automatically to conform to it. ZFS does a good job of determining the appropriate mode for a given ACL, but its algorithm for generating and updating ACLs in response to mode changes is rudimentary. The results aren't functionally incorrect, but they are often verbose, unreadable, and unmaintainable. In particular, the system may generate multiple and seemingly inconsistent sets of entries for owner@, group@, and everyone@ that depend on evaluation order for their aggregate effect.

As a general rule, never touch a file or directory's mode once you've applied an ACL. If worse comes to worst, remove the ACL with **chmod A-** *file* and start over.

Modifying NFSv4 ACLs in Solaris

Because ZFS enforces consistency between a file's mode and its ACL, all files have at least a trivial ACL (virtual or not). Ergo, ACL changes are always updates. You make ACL changes with **chmod**. The basic syntax is the same as always:

```
chmod [-R] acl_operation file ...
```

Table 6.11 shows the various types of ACL operations understood by **chmod**. Unfortunately, there is no ACL analog of **chmod**'s incremental, symbolic syntax for manipulating traditional modes. You cannot add or remove individual permissions from an ACE; you must replace the entire entry.

Table 6.11 ACL operations understood by Solaris's chmod

Operation	Function
A-	Replaces the entire ACL with its trivial version from the mode
A*index***-**	Deletes a single access control entry by position
A-*ace*	Deletes a given access control entry wherever it appears
A*index***=***ace*[,*ace*...]	Replaces one or more entire access control entries
A+*ace*	Adds an access control entry to the top of the ACL
A*index***+***ace*[,*ace*...]	Adds access control entries in front of *index*

The *index* numbers referred to in Table 6.11 are those shown by **ls -v**; they are the ordinals of the access control entries, starting at zero. You can encode the *ace* fields with either the verbose or one-letter permission names. For example, the command

```
solaris$ chmod A+user:ben:C:allow /var/tmp/example
```

gives the user ben permission to edit the ACL on the **/var/tmp/example** directory. Remember that access determination is an iterative process that works its way down the ACL, so ben retains any rights he had under the previous version of the ACL. The new access control entry goes at the start of the ACL (at index zero), so the command

```
solaris$ chmod A0- /var/tmp/example
```

removes the ACE that was just added and reverts the ACL to its original state.

6.7 Exercises

E6.1 What is a **umask**? Create a **umask** that would give no permissions to the group or the world.

E6.2 What is the difference between hard links and symbolic (soft) links? When is it appropriate to use one or the other?

☆ E6.3 What steps would be needed on your system for a Windows NTFS partition to be automatically mounted from a local hard disk? What's the most appropriate mount point for such a partition according to your system's conventions and the conventions in use at your site?

☆ E6.4 When installing a new system, it's important to set up the system volumes such that each filesystem (**/var**, **/usr**, etc.) has adequate space for both current and future needs. The Foobar Linux distribution uses the following defaults:

/	2GB
/var	100MB
/boot	100MB
<swap>	2GB
/usr	remaining space

What are some potential problems with this arrangement on a busy server box?

☆ E6.5 Why is it a good idea to put some partitions (such as **/var**, **/home**, and swap) on a separate drive from other data files and programs? What about **/tmp**? Give specific reasons for each of the filesystems listed.

☆ E6.6 Write a script that finds all the hard links on a filesystem.

☆ E6.7 Give commands to accomplish the following tasks.

a) Set the permissions on the file **README** to read/write for the owner and read for everyone else.

b) Turn on a file's setuid bit without changing (or knowing) the current permissions.

c) List the contents of the current directory, sorting by modification time and listing the most recently modified file last.

d) Change the group of a file called **shared** from "user" to "friends".

☆ E6.8 By convention, the **/tmp** directory is available to all users who care to create files there. What prevents one user from reading or deleting another's temporary files? What's to prevent a disgruntled user from filling up **/tmp** with junk files? What would be the consequences of such an attack?

7 Adding New Users

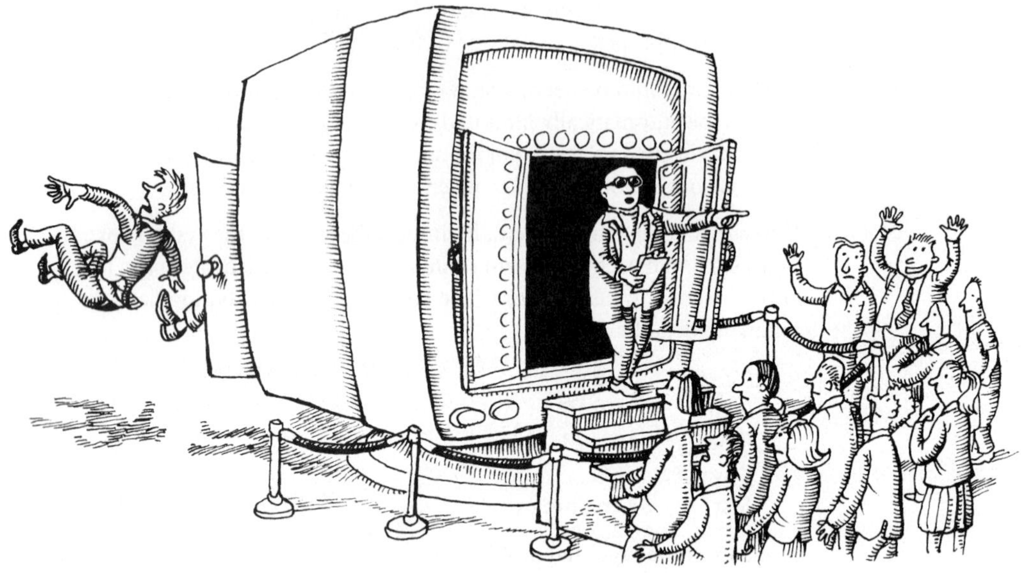

Adding and removing users is a routine chore on most systems. These tasks are simple, but they are also boring; most administrators tweak the tools provided with the operating system to automate the process and then delegate the actual work to an assistant or operator.

These days we are seeing a resurgence of centralized servers with login accounts for hundreds of people in addition to the distributed server with as few as two users. Administrators need a thorough understanding of the user account system in order to manage network services and to configure accounts appropriately for the local computing environment. Often, account management on servers is just one piece of the account-provisioning puzzle for an entire enterprise.

Today's enterprise environments need not just a tool for adding users to specific machines, but also a tool for managing users and their myriad accounts and passwords across the entire computing environment—an identity management system. Directory services such as Microsoft's Active Directory, OpenLDAP, and Fedora Directory Server are in widespread use, so we'll detail how these systems affect account management tasks. (As usual, myopic Microsoft does not play well with others unless you let Active Directory be in charge. Sigh.)

Some sites' needs may exceed the capabilities of even these systems. We do not cover the commercial identity management systems but will point you to a few candidates. They are probably the right solution for a very large site, especially where compliance with regulatory regimes such as HIPAA or Sarbanes-Oxley (in the United States) is required. See page 203.

Account hygiene is a key determinant of system security. Infrequently used accounts are prime targets for attackers, as are accounts with easily guessed passwords. Even if you use your system's automated tools to add and remove users, it's important to understand the changes the tools are making. For this reason, we start our discussion of account management with the flat files you must modify to add users to a single machine.

We then examine the automated tools distributed with each of our example operating systems and the configuration files that control their behavior. Surprisingly (or perhaps, confusingly), the user management tools are called **useradd**, **userdel**, and **usermod** on each of our example systems, even though the programs are not necessarily the same. (In addition, AIX achieves this naming conformity by wrapping its native **mkuser**, **rmuser**, and **chuser** tools with driver scripts.)

The default **useradd** tool is actually quite good and should be sufficient for most sites' needs. Unfortunately, **userdel** is not always as thorough as we would like.

Most systems also have simple GUI tools for adding and removing users, although these tools usually don't implement a batch mode or advanced localization. They are straightforward enough that we don't think it's helpful to review their operation in detail, but we'll point you to the vendors' documentation for each tool.

In this chapter, we focus specifically on adding and removing users. Many topics associated with user management actually live in other chapters and are only referenced here. For example,

- Pluggable authentication modules (PAM) for password encryption and the enforcement of strong passwords are covered in Chapter 22, *Security*. See the material on page 908.
- Password vaults for managing passwords are described in Chapter 4, *Access Control and Rootly Powers* (see page 117).
- Directory services such as NIS and OpenLDAP are outlined in Chapter 19, *Sharing System Files*, starting on page 728. Some comments on Active Directory can also be found in Chapter 30, *Cooperating with Windows*, on page 1154.
- Finally, policy and regulatory issues are major topics of Chapter 32, *Management, Policy, and Politics*.

That said, the next three sections present an overview of the primary files involved in user management.

7.1 THE /ETC/PASSWD FILE

The **/etc/passwd** file is a list of users recognized by the system. It can be extended or replaced by a directory service, so it's complete and authoritative only on standalone systems.

The system consults **/etc/passwd** at login time to determine a user's UID and home directory, among other things. Each line in the file represents one user and contains seven fields separated by colons:

- Login name
- Encrypted password placeholder (see page 179)
- UID (user ID) number
- Default GID (group ID) number
- "GECOS" information: full name, office, extension, home phone
- Home directory
- Login shell

For example, the following lines are all valid **/etc/passwd** entries:

```
root:x:0:0:The System,,x6096,:/:/bin/sh
jl:!:100:0:Jim Lane,ECOT8-3,,:/staff/jl:/bin/sh
dotty:x:101:20::/home/dotty:/bin/tcsh
```

Encrypted passwords used to live in the second field, but that is no longer safe; with fast hardware, they can be cracked (decrypted) in minutes. All versions of UNIX and Linux now hide the encrypted passwords by placing them in a separate file that is not world-readable. The **passwd** file contains an x in the encrypted password field on Linux, Solaris, and HP-UX and an ! or a * on AIX. (On AIX systems, * as a placeholder disables the account.)

The actual encrypted passwords are stored in **/etc/shadow** on Linux, Solaris, and HP-UX and in **/etc/security/passwd** on AIX. The formats vary.

See page 739 for more information about the ***nsswitch.conf*** *file.*

If user accounts are shared through a directory service such as NIS or LDAP, you might see special entries in the **passwd** file that begin with + or -. These entries tell the system how to integrate the directory service's data with the contents of **/etc/passwd**. This integration can also be set up in the **/etc/nsswitch.conf** file (**/etc/nscontrol.conf** on AIX).

The following sections discuss the **/etc/passwd** fields in more detail.

Login name

See page 728 for more information about NIS.

Login names (also known as usernames) must be unique and, depending on the operating system, may have length and character set restrictions. Table 7.1 shows the rules for our example systems. Login names can never contain colons or newlines because these characters are used as field separators and entry separators, respectively. If you use NIS or NIS+, login names are limited to eight characters, regardless of the operating system.

Table 7.1 Rules for forming login names

System	Len	Character set	First	Special rules
Linux	32[a]	a-z0-9_-	a-z	Some distros are more generous
Solaris	8[b]	A-Za-z0-9+.-_	A-Za-z	At least one lowercase letter
HP-UX	8	A-Za-z0-9_	A-Za-z	
AIX	8[c]	POSIX; no spaces, quotes, or #,=/?\	not -@~	Not all uppercase letters Not "default" or "ALL"

a. Although Linux allows 32 characters, legacy software (e.g., **top** and **rsh**) expects 8 or fewer.
b. Is being increased.
c. Can be changed in AIX 5.3 and later, see opposite page.

Originally, UNIX systems limited the permissible characters to alphanumerics and imposed an eight-character length limit. Since the rules for each system tend to be different, you should heed the most restrictive limits among your systems to avert potential conflicts. Such conservatism will guarantee that users can have the same login name on every machine. A combination of eight or fewer lowercase letters, numbers, and underscores is universally acceptable.

Login names are case sensitive; however, RFC822 calls for case to be ignored in email addresses. We are not aware of any problems caused by mixed-case login names, but lowercase names are traditional and also easier to type. Mail problems would likely ensue if the login names john and John were different people.

Login names should be easy to remember, so random sequences of letters do not make good login names. Avoid nicknames, even if your organization is informal. Names like DarkLord and QTPie belong in front of @hotmail.com. Even if your users have no self-respect, at least consider your site's overall credibility.

Since login names are often used as email addresses, it's useful to establish a standard way of forming them. It should be possible for users to make educated guesses about each other's login names. First names, last names, initials, or some combination of these all make reasonable naming schemes.

Any fixed scheme for choosing login names eventually results in duplicate names or names that are too long, so you will sometimes have to make exceptions. Choose a standard way of dealing with conflicts, such as adding a number to the end. In the case of a long name, you can use your mail system's aliasing features to equate two versions of the name, at least as far as mail is concerned.

It's common for large sites to implement a full-name email addressing scheme (e.g., John.Q.Public@mysite.com) that hides login names from the outside world. This is a good idea, but it doesn't obviate any of the naming advice given above. If for no other reason than the sanity of administrators, it's best if login names have a clear and predictable correspondence to users' actual names.

Login names should be unique in two senses. First, a user should have the same login name on every machine. This rule is mostly for convenience, both yours and the user's.

Second, a particular login name should always refer to the same person. Commands such as **ssh** can be set up to validate remote users according to their login names. If scott@boulder.colorado.edu and scott@refuge.colorado.edu are two different people, one Scott might be able to log in to the other's account without providing a password if the accounts are set up with relaxed security.

Experience also shows that duplicate names lead to email confusion. The mail system might be perfectly clear about which scott is which, but users will often send mail to the wrong address.

See page 756 for more information about mail aliases.

If your site has a global mail alias file, each new login name must be distinct from any alias in this file. If it is not, mail will be delivered to the alias rather than the new user.

AIX lets you change the maximum login name length with the **chdev** command. The relevant device is called sys0. You can run **lsattr -D -l sys0** to list the device's default attributes. Among them is the attribute max_logname, which controls the maximum length of login names. The following command shows you only that particular attribute:

```
aix$ lsattr -El sys0 -a max_logname
max_logname 9 Maximum login name length at boot time True
```

To adjust the limit, use the following commands. The change takes effect after the next reboot.[1]

```
aix$ sudo su -
aix# chdev -l sys0 -a max_logname=16
```

The default length is advertised as nine characters, but AIX's length specification is the size of the buffer and so must accommodate a null character to terminate the string. Hence, the actual default limit is eight characters, and our **chdev** command sets the limit to 15 characters.

AIX supports multibyte characters (for Asian languages, for example) but recommends against their use. The POSIX portable filename character set is the suggested alternative.

1. At first we could not make this work because we were using **sudo** (see page 113), and the environment variables set up by **sudo** *command* are usually different from those resulting from **sudo su** - and then running the command in a separate step. The **chdev** command cares. New versions (1.70 or later) of **sudo** have the **-i** flag to address this situation.

Encrypted password

Modern systems put a placeholder for the encrypted password in the **/etc/passwd** file and then prompt the user for a real password on first login. They also support several encryption schemes in addition to the standard UNIX **crypt** algorithm. The encrypted password is tagged to identify the form of encryption used to generate it. Our example systems support a variety of encryption algorithms: traditional **crypt** (based on DES), MD5, Blowfish, and an iterative version of MD5 inherited from the Apache web server project.

Password length is another important issue and is often determined by the algorithm used for encryption. Table 7.2 shows the default maximum and minimum password lengths and the encryption systems available on our example systems. Some systems let you type in arbitrarily long passwords but silently truncate them to the limit shown in the table.

Table 7.2 Password encryption algorithms and length limits

System	Min	Max	Algorithms	Where set
Linux	5	8	**crypt**, MD5, Blowfish[a]	**/etc/login.defs**
Solaris	6	8[b]	**crypt**, MD5, Blowfish, SHA256	**/etc/security/policy.conf** **/etc/security/crypt.conf**
HP-UX	6[c]	8	**crypt**	**/usr/include/limits.h**[d]
AIX	0	8	**crypt**, MD5 (BSD), Apache	Argument to **passwd** command

a. Blowfish is the default on SUSE and openSUSE systems; most others use MD5.
b. Maximum length depends on the algorithm chosen.
c. Root can set a user's password to any length.
d. This file contains many, many `#ifdef` constructs and so is not easy to read and understand.

If you choose to bypass your system's tools for adding users and edit **/etc/passwd** by hand (with **vipw**, of course—see page 188) to create a new account, put a star or an x in the encrypted password field. This measure prevents unauthorized use of the account until you or the user has set a real password. *Never, ever leave this field empty.* That introduces a jumbo-sized security hole because no password is required to access the account.

MD5 is slightly cryptographically better than the former DES standard used by **crypt**, and the MD5 scheme allows passwords of arbitrary length. Longer passwords are more secure—if you actually use them. Some cryptographic weaknesses have been demonstrated in MD5, but successful brute-force attacks have been mounted against DES. SHA256 and Blowfish are the current cryptographic strongmen in this arena. See page 906 for some hints on choosing passwords.

Encrypted passwords are of constant length (34 characters for MD5, 13 for DES) regardless of the length of the unencrypted password. Passwords are encrypted in combination with a random "salt" so that a given password can correspond to many different encrypted forms. If two users happen to select the same password, this fact usually cannot be discovered by inspection of the encrypted passwords. MD5 passwords are easy to spot because they always start with `$1$` or `$md5$`.[2] Blowfish passwords start with `$2a$` and SHA256 passwords with `$5$`.

SUSE defaults to Blowfish encryption for new passwords, which is a very reasonable default. Look for the `$2a$` prefix.

OpenSolaris now defaults to SHA256 (prefix `$5$`), although previous versions used MD5 by default.

UID (user ID) number

The UID identifies the user to the system. Login names are provided for the convenience of users, but software and the filesystem use UIDs internally. UIDs are usually unsigned 32-bit integers.

See page 105 for a description of the root account.

By definition, root has UID 0. Most systems also define pseudo-users such as bin and daemon to be the owners of commands or configuration files. It's customary to put such fake logins at the beginning of the **/etc/passwd** file and to give them low UIDs and a fake shell (e.g., **/bin/false**) to prevent anyone from logging in as those users. To allow plenty of room for nonhuman users you might want to add in the future, we recommend that you assign UIDs to real users starting at 500 or higher. (The desired range for new UIDs can be specified in the configuration files for **useradd**.)

See page 697 for more information about the nobody account.

Another special UID is that of the pseudo-user "nobody"; it is usually assigned a high value such as -1 or -2, which as unsigned integers in the UID field are the highest and next-highest possible UIDs. The "nobody" login is used when the root user on one machine tries to access files that are NFS-mounted from another machine that doesn't trust the first machine.

It's not a good idea to have multiple accounts with UID 0. While it might seem convenient to have multiple root logins with different shells or passwords, this setup just creates more potential security holes and gives you multiple logins to secure. If people need to have alternate ways to log in as root, you are better off if they use a program such as **sudo**.

Do not recycle UIDs, even when users leave your organization and you delete their accounts. This precaution prevents confusion if files are later restored from backups, where users may be identified by UID rather than by login name.

UIDs should be kept unique across your entire organization. That is, a particular UID should refer to the same login name and the same person on every machine that person is authorized to use. Failure to maintain distinct UIDs can result in security problems with systems such as NFS and can also result in confusion when a user moves from one workgroup to another.

2. `$1$` is the tag for the BSD MD5 algorithm; Sun uses its own MD5 implementation and tags it `$md5$`.

It can be hard to maintain unique UIDs when groups of machines are administered by different people or organizations. The problems are both technical and political. The best solution is to have a central database or directory server that contains a record for each user and enforces uniqueness. A simpler scheme is to assign each group within an organization a range of UIDs and let each group manage its own set. This solution keeps the UID spaces separate but does not address the parallel issue of unique login names.

LDAP is becoming a popular management tool for UIDs and user account information. It is briefly outlined in this chapter starting on page 202 and is covered more thoroughly in Chapter 19, *Sharing System Files*, starting on page 728.

Default GID number

Like a UID, a group ID number is a 32-bit integer. GID 0 is reserved for the group called root or system. As with UIDs, the system uses several predefined groups for its own housekeeping. Alas, there is no consistency among vendors. For example, the group bin has GID 1 on Red Hat and SUSE and GID 2 on Ubuntu, Solaris, HP-UX, and AIX.

In ancient times, when computing power was expensive, groups were used for accounting purposes so that the right department could be charged for your seconds of CPU time, minutes of login time, and kilobytes of disk used. Today, groups are used primarily to share access to files.

See page 153 for more information about setgid directories.

The **/etc/group** file defines the groups, with the GID field in **/etc/passwd** providing a default (or "effective") GID at login time. The default GID is not treated specially when access is determined; it is relevant only to the creation of new files and directories. New files are normally owned by your effective group, but if you want to share files with others in a project group, you must then remember to manually change the files' group owner.

To facilitate collaboration, you can set the setgid bit (02000) on a directory or mount filesystems with the **grpid** option. Both of these measures make newly created files default to the group of their parent directory.

GECOS field

The GECOS field is sometimes used to record personal information about each user. It has no well-defined syntax. Although you can use any formatting conventions you like, the **finger** command interprets comma-separated GECOS entries in the following order:

- Full name (often the only field used)
- Office number and building
- Office telephone extension
- Home phone number

See page 728 for more information about LDAP.

The **chfn** command lets users change their own GECOS information.[3] **chfn** is useful for keeping things like phone numbers up to date, but it can be misused. For example, a user can change the information to be either obscene or incorrect. Some systems can be configured to restrict which fields **chfn** can modify; most college campuses disable it entirely. On most systems **chfn** understands only the **/etc/passwd** file, so if you use LDAP or some other directory service for login information, **chfn** may not work at all.

On AIX, **chfn** accepts a **-R** *module* flag which loads the specified *module* to perform the actual update. The available modules are in **/usr/lib/security** and include one that deals with LDAP.

Home directory

A user's home directory is his or her default directory at login time. Be aware that if home directories are mounted over a network filesystem, they may be unavailable in the event of server or network problems. If the home directory is missing at login time, the system prints a message such as "no home directory"[4] and puts the user in /. On Linux, if **/etc/login.defs** sets DEFAULT_HOME to no, the login is not allowed to continue.

Login shell

The login shell is normally a command interpreter such as the Bourne shell or the C shell (**/bin/sh** or **/bin/csh**), but it can be any program. **sh** is the traditional default for UNIX, and **bash** (the GNU "Bourne again" shell) is the default for Linux and Solaris. AIX defaults to **ksh**, the Korn shell. **tcsh** is an enhanced C shell with command editing. On Linux systems, **sh** and **csh** are really just links to **bash** and **tcsh**, respectively.

Some systems permit users to change their shell with the **chsh** command, but as with **chfn**, this command may not work if you are using LDAP or some other directory service to manage login information. If you use the **/etc/passwd** file, a sysadmin can always change a user's shell by editing the **passwd** file with **vipw**.

Linux supports the **chsh** command and limits changes to shells listed in the file **/etc/shells**. SUSE enforces the **/etc/shells** list, but Red Hat just warns you if the selected shell is not on the list. If you add entries to the **shells** file, be sure to use absolute paths since **chsh** and other programs expect them.

On AIX systems, users can change their shells with **chsh** and are given a long list of shells to choose from.[5] The file **/etc/security/login.cfg** is the authoritative list

3. Except on Solaris, where **chfn** does not exist. The superuser can change a user's finger information with **passwd -g**.
4. This message appears when you log in on the console or on a terminal, but not when you log in through a display manager such as **xdm**, **gdm**, or **kdm**. Not only will you not see the message, but you will generally be logged out immediately because of the display manager's inability to write to the proper directory (e.g., **~/.gnome**).
5. Use the **chsec** command to change files in **/etc/security** rather than editing them directly.

of vetted shells. **/etc/shells** contains just a subset of these and is used only by the FTP daemon, **in.ftpd**. Many of the shells in the long list are just hard links to a single binary. For example **sh**, **ksh**, **rksh**, **psh**, and **tsh** (both in **/bin** and **/usr/bin**) are all the same program—it changes its behavior depending on the name it was called with. As with **chfn**, **chsh** takes an **-R** *module* flag to accommodate LDAP and other directory service systems.

solaris On Solaris, only the superuser can change a user's shell (using **passwd -e**). The file **/etc/shells** (which doesn't exist by default, although its man page does) contains a list of permitted shells.

7.2 THE /ETC/SHADOW AND /ETC/SECURITY/PASSWD FILES

A shadow password file is readable only by the superuser and serves to keep encrypted passwords safe from prying eyes and password cracking programs. It also includes some additional account information that wasn't provided for in the original **/etc/passwd** format. These days, shadow passwords are the default on nearly all systems.

IBM calls the file that stores the encrypted passwords **/etc/security/passwd**, while the rest of the world calls it **/etc/shadow**. The formats and contents are, of course, different. We'll look at **/etc/shadow** first.

The **shadow** file is not a superset of the **passwd** file, and the **passwd** file is not generated from it. You must maintain both files or use tools such as **useradd** that maintain both files on your behalf. Like **/etc/passwd**, **/etc/shadow** contains one line for each user. Each line contains nine fields, separated by colons:

- Login name
- Encrypted password
- Date of last password change
- Minimum number of days between password changes
- Maximum number of days between password changes
- Number of days in advance to warn users about password expiration
- **Linux**: Days after password expiration that account is disabled
  Solaris/HP-UX: Days before account automatically expires
- Account expiration date
- A reserved field that is currently always empty, except on Solaris

Only the values for the username and password are required. Absolute date fields in **/etc/shadow** are specified in terms of days (*not* seconds) since Jan 1, 1970, which is not a standard way of reckoning time on UNIX or Linux systems. However, you can convert from seconds to days since the UNIX epoch with

```
solaris$ expr 'date +%s' / 86400
```
[6]

6. There are 86,400 seconds in a day: 60 * 60 * 24.

Adding Users

A typical **shadow** entry looks like this:

```
millert:$md5$em5J8hL$a$iQ3pXe0sakdRaRFyy7Ppj.:14469:0:180:14:::
```

Here is a more complete description of each field:

- The login name is the same as in **/etc/passwd**. This field connects a user's **passwd** and **shadow** entries.
- The encrypted password is identical in concept and execution to the one previously stored in **/etc/passwd**; a fake Solaris MD5 password is shown.
- The last change field records the time at which the user's password was last changed. This field is filled in by the **passwd** command.
- The fourth field sets the number of days that must elapse between password changes. The idea is to force authentic changes by preventing users from immediately reverting to a familiar password after a required change. However, we think this feature could be somewhat dangerous when a security intrusion has occurred. We suggest setting this field to 0.
- The fifth field sets the maximum number of days allowed between password changes. This feature allows the administrator to enforce password aging; see page 906 for more information. Under Linux, the actual enforced maximum number of days is the sum of this field and the seventh (grace period) field.
- The sixth field sets the number of days before password expiration that **login** should begin to warn the user of the impending expiration.
- Solaris and HP-UX differ from Linux in their interpretation of the seventh field. Under Linux, the seventh field specifies how many days after the maximum password age has been reached to wait before treating the login as expired.

  The Solaris/HP-UX behavior is as follows: If a user has not logged in within the number of days specified in the seventh field, the account is disabled. Disused accounts are a favorite target of hackers, and this feature attempts to give you a way to take such accounts "off the market." However, it only works if the user can be found in the **/var/adm/lastlog** file; users that have never logged in will not be automatically disabled. Ergo, this feature does not really work in a networked environment because each host has its own **lastlog** file.
- The eighth field specifies the day (in days since Jan 1, 1970) on which the user's account will expire. The user may not log in after this date until the field has been reset by an administrator. If the field is left blank, the account will never expire.

  On Linux you can use **usermod** to set the expiration field; it takes dates in the format yyyy-mm-dd. Solaris's **usermod** also computes days since the epoch. It accepts dates in about 30 formats specified in **/etc/datemsk**, but alas, not in the yyyy-mm-dd format used by Linux.

- The ninth field is reserved for future use. Linux and HP-UX honor this use, but Solaris uses the last 4 bits to count failed login attempts.

Let's look again at our example **shadow** line:

```
millert:$md5$em5J8hL$a$iQ3pXe0sakdRaRFyy7Ppj.:14469:0:180:14:::
```

In this example, the user millert last changed his password on August 13, 2009. The password must be changed again within 180 days, and millert will receive warnings that the password needs to be changed for the last two weeks of this period. The account does not have an expiration date.

On Solaris, HP-UX, and Linux you can use the **pwconv** utility to reconcile the contents of the **shadow** file to those of the **passwd** file, picking up any new additions and deleting users that are no longer listed in **passwd**. On Linux, **pwconv** fills in most of the shadow parameters from defaults specified in **/etc/login.defs**.

Root on Solaris can use the command **passwd -f** *username* to force a user to change his or her password at the time of next login. This feature is useful if you regularly run **crack** to discover poorly-chosen (insecure) passwords. (Under Linux, that same **-f** flag lets users change their finger information.)

AIX does not use the term shadow passwords, but it does use the same concept. AIX's encrypted passwords are stored in the **/etc/security/passwd** file in a totally different format from that of the **/etc/passwd** file. Here's an example from a virgin AIX install, where the password algorithm defaults to **crypt**:[7]

```
trent:
    password = u10.OaYxRx4qI
    lastupdate = 1224876639
    flags = ADMCHG

evi:
    password = PiIr2qOPabZ.Q
    lastupdate = 1235785246
    flags =
```

The format should be self-explanatory. One or more blank lines separates entries. This same format is used for most AIX configuration files in **/etc/security**, with the username generalized to whatever object is being controlled or logged.

AIX provides a zillion knobs to control all aspects of logins and passwords. Some options are user oriented and some are port oriented (to control the TTY ports on which a given user can log in). See the comments in **/etc/security/login.cfg** and **/etc/security/user** for details. One handy command is **pwdadm**, which lets you force a user to change his or her password at next login.

7. Changing to a stronger encryption algorithm should be high on your to-do list for new AIX boxes.

7.3 THE /ETC/GROUP FILE

The **/etc/group** file contains the names of UNIX groups and a list of each group's members. Here's a portion of the **group** file from an AIX system:

```
system:!:0:root,pconsole,esaadmin
staff:!:1:ipsec,esaadmin,trent,ben,garth,evi
bin:!:2:root,bin
sys:!:3:root,bin,sys
adm:!:4:bin,adm
nobody:!:4294967294:nobody,lpd
```

Each line represents one group and contains four fields:

- Group name
- Encrypted password or a placeholder
- GID number
- List of members, separated by commas (be careful not to add spaces)

As in **/etc/passwd**, fields are separated by colons. Group names should be limited to eight characters for compatibility, although many systems do not actually require this. It is possible to enter a group password to allow users not belonging to a group to enter it with the **newgrp** command, but this is rarely done. Only Linux has real support for group passwords.[8] A password can be set with the **gpasswd** command; the encrypted form is stored in the **/etc/gshadow** file. Group passwords are rarely, if ever, used.

As with usernames and UIDs, group names and GIDs should be kept consistent among machines that share files through a network filesystem. Consistency can be hard to maintain in a heterogeneous environment since different operating systems use different GIDs for the same group names.

We've found that the best way to deal with this issue is to avoid using a system group as the default login group for a user. Some systems use group ownership together with the permission bits to control the execution of commands. GID inconsistencies among systems play havoc with site-wide systems for updating and installing software.

If a user defaults to a particular group in **/etc/passwd** but does not appear to be in that group according to **/etc/group**, **/etc/passwd** wins the argument. The group memberships granted at login time are really the union of those found in the **passwd** and **group** files.

Some systems limit the number of groups a user can belong to. Eight groups used to be a common limit, but it is now 16 on Solaris, 20 on HP-UX, and seemingly unlimited on AIX and Linux.

8. To set a group password under Solaris, you have to use **passwd** and cut and paste into **/etc/group**. There is no **/etc/gshadow** or equivalent file.

To minimize the potential for collisions with vendor-supplied GIDs, we suggest starting local groups at GID 500 or higher.

The UNIX tradition was originally to add new users to a group that represents their general category such as "students" or "finance." However, this convention increases the likelihood that users will be able to read one another's files because of slipshod permission setting, even if that is not really the intention of the files' owner. To avoid this problem, we prefer to create a unique group for each user. You can use the same name for both the user and the group. You can also make the GID the same as the UID.

The **useradd** utilities on all of our Linux distributions except SUSE default to placing users in their own personal groups. The UNIX systems default to putting all new users in the same group, but their **useradd**s can be configured to support personal groups, too.

A user's personal group should contain only that user. If you want to let users share files by way of the group mechanism, create separate groups for that purpose. The idea behind personal groups is not to discourage the use of groups per se—it's simply to establish a more restrictive *default* group for each user so that files are not shared inadvertently. You can also approach this goal through the shell's **umask** command (see page 158).

Linux, Solaris, and HP-UX all supply commands that create, modify, and delete groups: **groupadd**, **groupmod**, **groupdel**. AIX instead expects you to modify the **/etc/group** file with a text editor. However, it does provide the **grpck** command to check the file's syntax.

7.4 Adding users: the basic steps

Before you create an account for a new user at a corporate, government, or educational site, it's important that the user sign and date a copy of your local user agreement and policy statement. (What?! You don't have a user agreement and policy statement? See page 1215 for more information about why you need one and what to put in it.)

Users have no particular reason to want to sign a policy agreement, so it's to your advantage to secure their signatures while you still have some leverage. We find that it takes more effort to secure a signed agreement after an account has been released. If your process allows for it, have the paperwork precede the creation of the account.

Mechanically, the process of adding a new user consists of several steps required by the system, two steps that establish a useful environment for the new user, and several extra steps for your own convenience as an administrator.

Required:

- Have the new user sign your policy agreement.
- Edit the **passwd** and **shadow** files to define the user's account.
- Add the user to the **/etc/group** file (not really necessary, but nice).
- Set an initial password.
- Create, **chown**, and **chmod** the user's home directory.
- Configure roles and permissions (if you use RBAC; see page 190).

For the user:

- Copy default startup files to the user's home directory.
- Set the user's mail home and establish mail aliases.

For you:

- Verify that the account is set up correctly.
- Add the user's contact information and account status to your database.

This list cries out for a script or tool, and fortunately each of our example systems provides one in the form of a **useradd** command.

You must be root to add a user, or on AIX, you must have UserAdmin privileges. This is a perfect place to use **sudo**; see page 113.

Editing the passwd and group files

If you have to add a user by hand, use **vipw** to edit the **passwd** and **shadow** files. Although it sounds **vi**-centric, it actually uses your favorite editor as defined in the EDITOR environment variable. More importantly, it locks the file so that your editing and a user's password change operations do not collide.

On Solaris, and Red Hat systems, **vipw** automatically asks if you would like to edit the **shadow** file after you have edited the **passwd** file. SUSE and Ubuntu systems use **vipw -s** for this function.

Both HP-UX and AIX recommend that you not edit the password file by hand, with or without **vipw** (it is not even installed on AIX), but rather use **useradd** or their do-it-all sysadmin tools **smh** and SMIT, respectively. Our detailed coverage of **useradd** starts on page 191.

If the new user should be a member of more groups than just the default group specified in the **passwd** file, you must edit the **/etc/group** file and add the user's login name to each of the additional groups.

Setting a password

Rules for selecting good passwords are given on page 111.

Never leave a new account—or any account that has access to a shell—without a password. Password complexity can be enforced with configuration files; see the vendor-specific sections toward the end of this chapter to see which files and variables apply to your operating systems. Set a password for the new user with

```
$ sudo passwd newusername
```

You'll be prompted for the actual password. Some automated systems for adding new users do not require you to provide an initial password. Instead, they force the user to set a password on first login. Although this feature is convenient, it's a giant security hole: anyone who can guess new login names (or look them up in **/etc/passwd**) can swoop down and hijack the accounts before the intended users have had a chance to log in.

Creating the home directory and installing startup files

You can create the new user's home directory with a simple **mkdir**. You'll need to set ownerships and permissions on the new directory as well, but this is best done after you've installed any local startup files.

Startup files traditionally begin with a dot and end with the letters **rc**, short for "run command," a relic of the CTSS operating system. The initial dot causes **ls** to hide these "uninteresting" files from directory listings unless the **-a** option is used.

We recommend that you provide default startup files for each shell that is popular on your systems so that users continue to have a reasonable default environment if they change shells. Table 7.3 lists some common startup files.

Table 7.3 Common startup files and their uses

Command	Filename	Typical uses
sh	**.profile**	Sets search path, terminal type and environment
bash[a]	**.bashrc**	Sets the terminal type (if needed) Sets **biff** and **mesg** switches
	.bash_profile	Sets up environment variables Sets command aliases Sets the search path Sets the **umask** value to control permissions Sets CDPATH for filename searches Sets the PS1 (prompt) and HISTCONTROL variables
csh/tcsh	**.login**	Similar to **.bashrc** for **csh**
	.cshrc	Similar to **.login** for **csh**
vi/vim	**.exrc/.vimrc**	Sets **vi/vim** editor options
emacs	**.emacs**	Sets **emacs** editor options and key bindings
mail/mailx	**.mailrc**	Defines personal mail aliases Sets mail reader options (original UNIX mail client)
GNOME	**.gconf**	GNOME environment: user configuration via **gconf**
	.gconfpath	Path for additional user configuration via **gconf**
KDE	**.kde/**	KDE environment: directory of configuration files

a. **bash** also reads **.profile** or **/etc/profile** in emulation of **sh**.

Sample startup files are traditionally kept in **/etc/skel** (Linux, Solaris, HP-UX) or **/etc** (all systems). AIX, always a bit different, stashes them in **/etc/security**. If you customize your vendor's startup file examples, **/usr/local/etc/skel** is a reasonable place to put the modified copies. Linux also keeps tidbits of startup files in the **/etc/profile.d** directory, where shells look for pointers on coloring the output of **ls** to make it unreadable on a dark background, or the path to Kerberos binaries.

Depending on the user's shell, **/etc** may contain system-wide startup files that are processed before the user's own startup files. For example, **bash** and **sh** read **/etc/profile** before processing **~/.profile** and **~/.bash_profile**. These files are a good place in which to put site-wide defaults, but bear in mind that users can override your settings in their own startup files. For details on other shells, see the man page for the shell in question.

Be sure to set a reasonable default value for **umask**; we suggest 077, 027, or 022, depending on the friendliness and size of your site. If you do not use individual groups, we recommend umask 077 because it gives the owner full access but the group and the rest of the world no access. See page 158 for details on **umask**.

The startup files and directories listed for the GNOME and KDE desktop environments are just the tip of the iceberg. **gconf** is a tool that stores application preferences for programs run under GNOME, much like the Windows registry.

Setting permissions and ownerships

Now that the home directory is set up, turn it over to the user and make sure that the permissions on it are appropriate. The command

```
$ sudo chown -R newuser:newgroup ~newuser
```

should set ownerships properly. Note that you cannot use

```
$ sudo chown newuser:newgroup ~newuser/.*
```

to **chown** the dot files because *newuser* would then own not only his own files but also the parent directory ".." (e.g., **/home**) as well. This is a common and dangerous mistake.

Setting a mail home

It is convenient for each user to receive email on only one machine. This scheme is often implemented with an entry in the global aliases file **/etc/mail/aliases** or the **sendmail** userDB on the central mail server. See Chapter 20 for general information about email.

Configuring roles and administrative privileges

Role-based access control (RBAC) allows system privileges to be tailored for individual users and is available on many of our example systems. RBAC is not a traditional part of the UNIX or Linux access control model, but if your site uses it, role configuration must be a part of the process of adding users. RBAC is covered in detail starting on page 108 in the *Access Control and Rootly Powers* chapter.

See Chapter 32 for more information about SOX and GLBA

Legislation such as the Sarbanes-Oxley Act and the Gramm-Leach-Bliley Act in the United States has complicated many aspects of system administration in the corporate arena, including user management. Roles may be your only viable option for fulfilling some of the SOX/GLBA requirements.

Final steps

To verify that a new account has been properly configured, first log out, then log in as the new user and execute the following commands:

```
$ pwd        /* To verify the home directory */
$ ls -la     /* To check owner/group of startup files */
```

You will need to notify new users of their login names and initial passwords. Many sites send this information by email, but for security reasons that's usually not a good idea. Do it in person or over the phone, unless you are adding 500 new freshmen to the campus's CS-1 machines. Then, punt the problem to the instructor! This is also a good time to point users toward additional documentation on local customs if you have any.

See page 1227 for more information about written user contracts.

If your site requires users to sign a written policy agreement or appropriate use policy, be sure this step has been completed before releasing the account. This check will prevent oversights and strengthen the legal basis of any sanctions you might later need to impose.

Remind new users to change their passwords immediately. If you wish, you can enforce this by setting the password to expire within a short time. Another option is to have a script check up on new users and be sure their encrypted passwords in the **shadow** file have changed.[9]

In an environment in which you know the users personally, it's relatively easy to keep track of who's using a system and why. If you manage a large and dynamic user base, however, you'll need a more formal way to keep track of accounts. Maintaining a database of contact information and account statuses will help you figure out who someone is and why they have an account once the act of creating the account has faded from memory.

7.5 Adding users with useradd

Each system's **useradd** implements the same basic procedure outlined above. However, it is configurable, and you will probably want to customize it to fit your environment. Since each system has its own idea of what you should customize, where you should implement the customizations, and what the default behavior should be, we cover these details in vendor-specific sections.

9. Because the same password can have many encrypted representations, this method verifies only that the user has reset the password, not that it has actually been changed to a *different* password.

Table 7.4 is a handy summary of commands and configuration files related to managing users. Each of our example systems has a suite of commands for manipulating users, usually at least **useradd**, **usermod**, and **userdel**. Since the commands are all configured similarly, we show **useradd** as representative of all three and supplement its entry with other system-specific commands.

Please note that although each vendor has named its tools **useradd**, etc., the tools themselves are different from system to system.

Table 7.4 Commands and configuration files for user management

System	Cmds	Configuration files	Comments
Ubuntu	**useradd**	**/etc/login.defs** **/etc/default/useradd**	
	adduser	**/etc/adduser.conf**	Friendlier Perl version
SUSE	**useradd**	**/etc/login.defs** **/etc/default/useradd** **/etc/default/passwd**	
		/usr/sbin/useradd.local	For local customizations
		/usr/sbin/userdel.local	For local customizations
		/usr/sbin/userdel-pre.local	For local customizations
		/usr/sbin/userdel-post.local	For local customizations
Red Hat	**useradd**	**/etc/login.defs** **/etc/default/useradd**	
Solaris	**useradd**	**/etc/default/{login,passwd}** **/etc/security/policy.conf**	
HP-UX	**useradd**	**/etc/default/useradd** **/etc/default/security**	
	smh		GUI tool, also called **sam**
AIX	**useradd**	**/etc/security/user** **/etc/security/login.cfg** **/etc/security/mkuser.default**[a]	
	mkuser		Called by **useradd**
	chuser		Called by **usermod**
	rmuser		Called by **userdel**
	SMIT		GUI tool

a. This file is in **/usr/lib/security** on older AIX systems.

useradd on Ubuntu

Ubuntu provides two ways to add users: **adduser** and **useradd**. **adduser** is a Perl wrapper for **useradd** that is a bit more helpful (makes home directories, copies in startup files, etc.).

adduser is configured in **/etc/adduser.conf**, which includes options such as these:

- Rules for locating home directories: by group, by username, etc.
- Permission settings for new home directories
- UID and GID ranges for system users and general users
- An option to create individual groups for each user
- Disk quotas (Boolean only, unfortunately)
- Regex-based matching of usernames and group names

Other typical **useradd** parameters, such as rules for passwords, are set as parameters to the PAM module that does regular password authentication. (See page 908 for a discussion of PAM, aka Pluggable Authentication Modules.) **adduser** has a twin **addgroup** and cousins **deluser** and **delgroup**.

useradd on SUSE

SUSE's **useradd** does not create a new user's home directory or copy in startup files by default. You must request these niceties with the **-m** flag. (The startup files come from **/etc/skel**.) Nor does **useradd** create a mail spool file for new users.

SUSE's **useradd** also does not create user-specific groups; the default GID in the **passwd** file is set by the variable GROUP in **/etc/default/useradd**. New users are also added to the groups specified by the GROUPS variable. By default, these are the groups video and dialout, which allow access to the system's frame buffer and the dialup IP software **pppd**.

To make up for these deficiencies, SUSE's **useradd** calls **/usr/sbin/useradd.local**, a **bash** script to which you can add whatever customizations you wish.

The **/etc/login.defs** file on SUSE controls the following types of issues:

- Whether to allow logins if a user's home directory does not exist
- Degree of tolerance (delay and lockout) for failed login attempts
- Location of the "message of the day" and **ttytype** (terminal type) files
- Restrictions on the use of **chsh** and **chfn**
- Password aging
- Ranges of system and user UIDs and GIDs
- Rules for forming valid user and group names
- Users' **umask**s (the default is 022)
- Local scripts that piggyback on the **useradd** and **userdel** commands

Both the man page for **login.defs** and the comments in the file itself do a good job of describing the various parameters and their meanings.

useradd on Red Hat

The **useradd** program on Red Hat Enterprise Linux takes its configuration parameters from **/etc/login.defs**, where issues such as password aging controls, encryption algorithms, mail spool files, and UID/GID ranges are addressed. The comments in the file do a good job of explaining the various parameters.

useradd -D displays the defaults that **useradd** will use for new logins. Those defaults are set in the file **/etc/default/useradd**. On Red Hat, new users are placed in their own individual groups. The **passwd** file entry uses "x" as a password placeholder, and the shadow file uses "!!", a code that disables the login and requires a sysadmin to set a password for the new user. MD5 encryption is the default. A new user's home directory is populated with startup files from **/etc/skel**.

useradd on Solaris

On Solaris, some of the default parameters related to logins and passwords are stored in **/etc/default/login** and **/etc/default/passwd**; others are built into the **useradd** command itself. **useradd -D** shows the default values for several parameters. With additional flags, it can be used to reset some of those defaults.

The format of the **default/login** and **default/passwd** files is similar to that of Linux's **login.defs** file in that blank lines and lines beginning with # are ignored, and each noncomment line assigns a value to a variable. However, the syntax is

```
NAME=value
```

rather than

```
NAME <white-space> value
```

The **/etc/default/passwd** file controls the following:

- Minimum password length
- Password aging
- Required password complexity
- Checking for crackable passwords

/etc/default/login controls issues such as these:

- The time zone
- Limits on the size of files a user can create
- Whether root can log in only on the console
- Whether a password is required for each user
- Handling of failed login attempts
- Users' initial search path
- Users' default **umask** (defaults to 022)
- Whether to log root and failed logins through syslog

The files **/etc/security/policy.conf** and **/etc/security/crypt.conf** determine the encryption algorithms that can be used for passwords.

useradd on HP-UX

By default, HP-UX's **useradd** command does not create home directories or put the user in an individual group. However, with the **-m** option, **useradd** does create home directories and populate them with startup files from **/etc/skel**.

Configuration parameters for **useradd** are set in the files **/etc/default/useradd** and **/etc/default/security**, with the **useradd** file adopting the Linux-style format of NAME <white-space> value and the **security** using the Solaris NAME=value style. Geez, HP, make up your mind! The syntax should be clear from other entries in each file, but if you use the wrong form, the variable you tried to set will be silently ignored. No syntax error message is generated.

The **/etc/default/useradd** file controls options such as:

- Default group and shell
- Root of the home directory tree
- Account expiration
- Whether to create home directories
- Whether to allow duplicate UIDs

The file **/etc/default/security** contains additional configuration parameters, some of which relate to user management:

- Whether to allow logins with a missing home directory
- Whether to allow null passwords
- Minimum password length
- Handling of failed login attempts
- Handling of inactive accounts
- Default **umask** for new users (default 027)

The variable names in this file are long and well-chosen to explain exactly what each variable controls.

Adding Users

useradd on AIX

AIX's **useradd** is really just a **ksh** wrapper for its native AIX equivalent, **mkuser**. Likewise, **usermod** invokes **chuser**, and **userdel** calls **rmuser**. Man pages exist for these commands under both their original names and their rest-of-the-world-compliant names.

Configuration files control numerous aspects of logins and passwords and are kept in the **/etc/security** directory. There are three relevant files: **login.cfg**, **user**, and **mkuser.default**. The first two use the * as a comment character; the third has no comments. These files are organized in stanzas of the following form:

```
label:
    attribute = value
    next-attribute = value

next-label:
    attribute = value
```

For example, in the **/etc/security/user** file, the labels are usernames (or the word default); the possible attributes are shown in Table 7.5 on the next page.

Table 7.5 User account options in /etc/security/user (AIX)

Option	Type	Meaning
account_locked	Boolean	Prevents login if true
admin	Boolean	Gives admin privileges if true
auth1	Method list	Primary authentication method
auth2	Method list	Secondary authentication method
dictionlist	Filenames	Dictionaries that must exclude passwords
expires	Date	Expiration date of the user account
histexpire	Weeks	Period when a user cannot reuse a pwd
histsize	Number	# of previous pwds that can't be reused
login	Boolean	Can log in? Good for logins like bin
loginretries	Number	# of login tries before account is locked
logintimes	Time range	Limits when the user can log in
maxexpired	Weeks	Grace period for expired pwds
maxrepeats	Number	# of times a character can appear in pwd
minage, maxage	Weeks	Minimum and maximum age of a pwd
minalpha	Number	Minimum # of alpha characters in pwd
mindiff	Chars	# of old pwd chars allowed in new pwd
minlen	Number	Minimum length of pwd (don't set to 0)
minother	Number	Minimum # of nonalpha character in pwd
pwdchecks	Filenames	Functions to call to check for safe pwds
pwdwarntime	Days	Grace period warning user to change pwd
rlogin	Boolean	Can user **rlogin** or **telnet** to this account?
su	Boolean	Can other users **su** to this account?
ttys	Device list	Terminals on which this user can log in
umask	Octal	Default permissions for user-created files

Whew, what a list! Comments in the file often give the default values, which are fairly reasonable for a low-security installation. We recommend changing a few:

- Change umask from 022 to 077.
- Change loginretries from 0 (unlimited) to a small integer, say 5.
- Change minlen from 0 (no password OK) to at least 6 or 7.
- Change expires from 0 (never) to a year (only if you have a tool to refresh the expiration dates on valid users periodically).

See page 908 for more information about PAM.

Unfortunately, that's just one of the configuration files that controls a new user's login. The file **/etc/security/login.cfg** contains parameters to control bad logins (the delay inserted between prompts for the login and password, the number of bad logins allowed before disabling the account, how long to disable the account, when to reinstate it, etc.), the times at which logins are allowed, the prompt to print when requesting the user's password, a list of valid shells, the maximum permissible number of simultaneous logins, the length of time to wait for a user password, the type of login authorization to use (here is where you would specify

PAM[10] if you were to use it), and the password encryption algorithm (the default is **crypt**). Infinitely, perhaps pathologically, configurable. And to confuse you further, some parameters appear in both files, sometimes with the same name (e.g., logintimes) and sometimes with different names (loginretries vs. logindisable). Yikes! Clutter and complexity galore.

useradd on AIX does not provide a **-D** option to show the default values for new users. It puts new users in a single group and does not create their home directories unless invoked with the **-m** flag (in which case it also copies in a **.profile** file from the **/etc/security** directory).

useradd example

To create a new user "hilbert" using the system defaults on a Linux system, you could simply run

```
$ sudo useradd hilbert
```

This command would create the following entry in **/etc/passwd**:

```
hilbert:x:1005:20::/home/hilbert:/bin/sh
```

useradd disables the account by putting an x in the password field. You must assign a real password to make the account usable.

A more realistic example is shown below. We specify that hilbert's primary group should be "faculty" and that he should also be added to the "famous" group. We override the default home directory location and shell, and ask **useradd** to create the home directory if it does not already exist:

```
$ sudo useradd -c "David Hilbert" -d /home/math/hilbert -g faculty -G
    famous -m -s /bin/tcsh hilbert
```

This command creates the following **passwd** entry:

```
hilbert:x:1005:30:David Hilbert:/home/math/hilbert:/bin/tcsh
```

The assigned UID is one higher than the highest UID on the system, and the corresponding **shadow** entry is

```
hilbert:!:14322:0:99999:7:0::
```

The password placeholder character(s) in the **passwd** and **shadow** file vary depending on the operating system. **useradd** also adds hilbert to the appropriate groups in **/etc/group**, creates the directory **/home/math/hilbert**, and populates it from the **/etc/skel** directory.

7.6 Adding users in bulk with newusers (Linux)

Linux's **newusers** creates multiple accounts at one time from the contents of a text file. It's pretty gimpy, but it can be handy when you need to add a lot of users at

10. PAM is a relatively recent addition to AIX; it should be fully functional in versions 5.3 and later.

once, such as when creating class-specific accounts. **newusers** expects an input file of lines just like the **/etc/passwd** file, except that the password field contains the initial password in clear text. Oops… better protect that file.

newusers honors the password aging parameters set in the **/etc/login.defs** file, but it does not copy in the default startup files as **useradd** does. The only startup file it provides is **.xauth**.

At a university, what's really needed is a batch **adduser** script that can use a list of students from enrollment or registration data to generate the input for **newusers**, with usernames formed according to local rules and guaranteed to be locally unique, with strong passwords randomly generated, and with UIDs and GIDs increasing for each user. You're probably better off writing your own wrapper for **useradd** in Perl or Python than in trying to get **newusers** to do what you need.

7.7 Removing users

When a user leaves your organization, that user's login account and files should be removed from the system. This procedure involves the removal of all references to the login name that were added by you or your **useradd** program. If you remove a user by hand, you may want to use the following checklist:

- Remove the user from any local user databases or phone lists.
- Remove the user from the **aliases** file or add a forwarding address.
- Remove the user's crontab file and any pending **at** jobs or print jobs.
- Kill any of the user's processes that are still running.
- Remove the user from the **passwd**, **shadow**,[11] **group**, and **gshadow** files.
- Remove the user's home directory.
- Remove the user's mail spool.
- Clean up entries on shared calendars, room reservation systems, etc.
- Delete or transfer ownership of any mailing lists run by the deleted user.

Before you remove someone's home directory, be sure to relocate any files that are needed by other users. You usually can't be sure which files those might be, so it's always a good idea to make an extra backup of the user's home directory and mail spool before deleting them.

Once you have removed a user, you may want to verify that the user's old UID no longer owns files on the system. To find the paths of orphaned files, you can use the **find** command with the **-nouser** argument. Because **find** has a way of "escaping" onto network servers if you're not careful, it's usually best to check filesystems individually with **-xdev**:

```
$ sudo find filesystem -xdev -nouser
```

Killing the deleted user's running processes can be tricky in a distributed environment. Shared calendars and room reservation systems may have ongoing items

11. **/etc/security/**{**passwd,group**} on AIX

scheduled by the now-defunct user that are suddenly orphaned and need to be cleaned up. There are probably several more places in your environment where the user needs to be removed—make your own list, perhaps in the form of a cleanup script.

If your organization assigns individual workstations to users, it's generally simplest and most efficient to reimage the entire system from a master template before turning the system over to a new user. Before you do the reinstallation, however, it's a good idea to back up any local files on the system's hard disk in case they are needed in the future.

Each of our example systems has a **userdel** command that automates the process of removing a user. It will probably not do quite as thorough a job as you might like, unless you have religiously added functionality to it as you expanded the number of places where user-related information is stored.

Ubuntu's **deluser** is a Perl script that calls the usual **userdel**; it undoes all the things **adduser** does. It calls **deluser.local**, if it exists, to provide for easy localization. The configuration file **/etc/deluser.conf** lets you set options such as these:

- Whether to remove the user's home directory and mail spool
- Whether to back up the user's files, and where to put the backup
- Whether to remove all files owned by the user
- Whether to delete a group if it now has no members

SUSE supports a set of pre- and postexecution scripts as well as a **userdel.local** script that assists **userdel** and helps you make the default tools aware of your local customs. Configure it in **/etc/login.defs**.

Red Hat has the **userdel.local** script but no pre- and postexecution scripts to automate things like backing up the about-to-be-removed user's files.

Solaris and AIX have some extra crevices in which they stash user info, primarily in the files that control roles and authorization classes. Therefore, these systems' **userdel** commands have a bit more work to do to remove all references to a deleted user.

For example, in addition to the **/etc/passwd** and **/etc/group** file, Solaris' **userdel** updates **/etc/shadow**, **/etc/project**, and **/etc/user_attr**. AIX's **userdel** touches the following files in the **/etc/security** directory: **user**, **user.roles**, **lastlog**, **environ**, **audit/config**, **limits**, **passwd**, and **group**. Solaris is not as thorough as one might like: its **userdel** left a test login with a profile configured in **user_attr** that should have been cleaned up.

HP-UX's **userdel** is a ho-hum, run-of-the-mill-type guy who removes the changes made by **useradd**. It touches only the **passwd**, **shadow**, and **group** files.

Adding Users

7.8 Disabling logins

On occasion, a user's login must be temporarily disabled. A straightforward way to do this is to put a star or some other character in front of the user's encrypted password in the **/etc/security/passwd** (AIX) or **/etc/shadow** file. This measure prevents most types of password-regulated access because the password no longer decrypts to anything sensible. Commands such as **ssh** that do not necessarily check the system password may continue to function, however.

On all our Linux distributions, the **usermod -L** *user* and **usermod -U** *user* commands provide an easy way to lock and unlock passwords. They are just shortcuts for the password twiddling described above: the **-L** puts an ! in front of the encrypted password in the **/etc/shadow** file, and the **-U** removes it.

Root on Solaris can lock an account with **passwd -l** *loginname,* force a user to change his or her password with the **-f** flag, or unlock the account with **-u**. Locking an account adds `*LK*` to the password field of **/etc/shadow**. This is also the value set by **useradd** for new users.

HP-UX supports only **crypt**-encoded passwords. The * character can never belong to a **crypt**-generated password field, so adding a * to the encrypted password prevents the user from logging in.

On AIX, if the password placeholder field of **/etc/passwd** contains a * instead of an !, the account is locked. AIX's **pwdadm** command can force a user to change his or her password, or it can lock the account so that only an administrator can change the password.

Unfortunately, modifying a user's password simply makes logins fail. It does not notify the user of the account suspension or explain why the account no longer works. An alternative way to disable logins is to replace the user's shell with a program that prints an explanatory message and supplies instructions for rectifying the situation. The program then exits, terminating the login session.

This approach has both advantages and disadvantages. Any forms of access that check the password but do not pay attention to the shell will not be disabled. To facilitate the "disabled shell" trick, many daemons that provide nonlogin access to the system (e.g., **ftpd**) check to see if a user's login shell is listed in **/etc/shells** and deny access if it is not. This is the behavior you want. Unfortunately, it's not universal, so you may have to do some fairly comprehensive testing if you decide to use shell modification as a way of disabling accounts.

Another issue is that your carefully written explanation of the suspended account might never be seen if the user tries to log in through a window system or through a terminal emulator that does not leave output visible after a logout.

By default, **sendmail** will not deliver mail to a user whose shell does not appear in **/etc/shells**. It's a bad idea to interfere with the flow of mail, even if the recipient is not able to read it immediately. You can defeat **sendmail**'s default behavior by adding a fake shell named **/SENDMAIL/ANY/SHELL/** to the **/etc/shells** file.

7.9 Managing users with system-specific tools

HP-UX and AIX provide a comprehensive system administration tool that knows how to manage users, at least in a rudimentary fashion. In AIX it's SMIT, the System Management Interface Tool, and in HP-UX it's now called **smh**, the System Management Homepage. (It was called **sam**, the System Administration Manager, in earlier HP-UX releases.) Each of these tools has screens for adding and managing users, either with a windows-based GUI or with a terminal interface based on the **curses** library. If you are a brand new sysadmin or an old hand on a new and different operating system, these tools are a reasonable place to start for many of the common sysadmin tasks.

AIX's **smitty** has a handy feature: if you hit F6, it shows you the command and arguments that it is planning to execute. It also logs all interactions and keeps a script file of the commands it executed on your behalf. This can be a good learning tool as you become familiar with AIX's quirks. HP-UX's **smh** has nice single-character shortcuts for its **curses** interface. They are shown on each menu page so you can quickly get to the command you need.

7.10 Reducing risk with PAM

Pluggable Authentication Modules (PAM), are covered in the *Security* chapter starting on page 908. They centralize the management of the system's authentication facilities through standard library routines so that programs like **login**, **sudo**, **passwd**, and **su** do not have to supply their own tricky authentication code. PAM reduces the risk inherent in writing secured software, allows administrators to set site-wide security policies, and defines an easy way to add new authentication methods to the system.

Adding and removing users doesn't involve twiddling the PAM configuration, but the tools involved operate under PAM's rules and constraints. In addition, many of the PAM configuration parameters are similar to those used by **useradd** or **usermod**. If you change a parameter as described in this chapter and **useradd** doesn't seem to be paying attention to it, check to see if the system's PAM configuration is overriding your new value.

7.11 Centralizing account management

Some form of centralized account management is essential for medium-to-large enterprises of all types, be they corporate, academic, or governmental. Users need the convenience and security of a single login name, UID, and password across the site. Administrators need a centralized system that allows changes (such as account revocations) to be instantly propagated everywhere.

Such centralization can be achieved in a variety of ways, most of which (including Microsoft's Active Directory system) involve LDAP, the Lightweight Directory Access Protocol, in some capacity. Options range from bare-bones LDAP installations based on open source software to elaborate commercial identity management systems that come with a hefty price tag.

LDAP and Active Directory

See the section starting on page 728 for more information about LDAP and LDAP implementations.

LDAP is a generalized, database-like repository that can store user management data as well as other types of data. It uses a hierarchical client/server model that supports multiple servers as well as multiple simultaneous clients. One of LDAP's big advantages as a site-wide repository for login data is that it can enforce unique UIDs and GIDs across systems. It also plays well with Windows, although the reverse is only marginally true.

Microsoft's Active Directory uses LDAP and Kerberos and can manage lots of kinds of data including user information. It's a bit egotistical and wants to be the boss if it is interacting with UNIX or Linux LDAP repositories. If you need a single authentication system for a site that includes Windows desktops as well as UNIX and Linux systems, it is probably easiest to let Active Directory be in control and to use your UNIX LDAP databases as secondary servers.

To implement this configuration, you will need Active Directory and Microsoft's Services for UNIX, or a commercial Active Directory integration platform such as Quest Authentication Services (formerly Vintela Authorization Services). Sun's Virtual Directory can help to glue together several different authorization/authentication systems.

Each of our example systems has LDAP support built in, although sometimes just the client side (HP-UX, for example). LDAP is often coupled with PAM for performing authentication.

LDAP is a database, so the information stored there must fit a well-defined schema. Schemas are expressed as XML files, with the field names coming from the relevant RFCs, primarily RFC2307 for user management data. See Chapter 19, *Sharing System Files*, for the nitty-gritty details.

Single sign-on systems

Single sign-on (SSO) systems balance user convenience with security issues. The idea is that a user can sign on once (to a login prompt, web page, or Windows box) and be authenticated at that time. The user then obtains authentication credentials (usually implicitly, so that no active management is required), which can then be used to access other machines and applications. The user only has to remember one login and password sequence instead of many.

This scheme allows credentials to be more complex (since the user does not need to remember or even deal with them), which theoretically increases security. However, the impact of a compromised account is greater because one login gives an attacker access to multiple machines and applications. SSO systems make walking away from a desktop machine while you are still logged in a significant vulnerability. In addition, the authentication server becomes a critical bottleneck. If it's down, all useful work grinds to a halt across the enterprise.

Although SSO is a simple idea, it implies a lot of back-end complexity because the various applications and machines that a user might want to access must understand the authentication process and SSO credentials. Kerberos manages users' credentials in some SSO systems; it is covered in more detail in the *Security* chapter, starting on page 924.

Several open source SSO systems exist:

- JOSSO, an open source SSO server written in Java
- CAS, the Central Authentication Service, from Yale (also Java)
- Likewise Open, an integration tool that makes Microsoft Active Directory play nice with Linux and UNIX systems

A host of commercial systems are also available, most of them integrated with identity management suites, which are covered in the next section.

Identity management systems

"Identity management" is the latest buzzword in user management. In plain language, it means identifying the users of your systems, authenticating their identities, and granting privileges based on those authenticated identities. The standardization efforts in this realm are led by the World Wide Web Consortium and by The Open Group.

Commercial identity management systems combine several key UNIX concepts into a warm and fuzzy GUI replete with marketing jargon. Fundamental to all such systems is a database of user authentication and authorization data, often stored in LDAP format. Control is achieved with concepts such as UNIX groups, and limited administrative privileges are enforced through tools such as **sudo**. Most such systems have been designed with an eye toward regulatory requirements of accountability, tracking, and audit trails.

There are many commercial systems in this space: Oracle's Identity Management, Sun Identity Management Suite,[12] Courion, Avatier Identity Management Suite (AIMS), and BMC Identity Management Suite, to name a few. In evaluating identity management systems, look for the following features:

- Generation of globally unique user IDs
- The ability to create, change, and delete user accounts across the enterprise, on all types of hardware and operating systems

12. Now that Oracle has purchased Sun, it's unclear if this system will survive as a product after the merger is complete.

- A secure web interface for management that's accessible both inside and outside the enterprise
- The ability to easily display all users who have a certain set of privileges
- An easy way to see all the privileges granted to a particular user
- The ability to let users change (and reset) their own passwords, with enforcement of rules for picking strong passwords
- The ability for users to change their passwords globally in one operation
- A workflow engine; for example, tiered approvals before a user is given certain privileges
- The ability to coordinate with a personnel database to automatically delete access for employees who are terminated or laid off
- Configurable logging of all changes and administrative actions
- Configurable reports based on logging data (by user, by day, etc.)
- Role-based access control, including user account provisioning by role
- An interface through which hiring managers can request that accounts be provisioned according to role
- Exceptions to role-based provisioning, including a workflow for the approval of exceptions

Consider also how the system is implemented at the point at which authorizations and authentications actually take place. Does the system require a custom agent to be installed everywhere, or does it conform itself to the underlying systems?

7.12 Recommended Reading

"The Complete Buyer's Guide for Identity Management." Sun Microsystems white paper. 2008. sun.systemnews.com/articles/129/4/sec/20930.

7.13 Exercises

E7.1 How is a user's default group determined? How would you change it?

E7.2 Explain the differences among the following umask values: 077, 027, 022, and 755. How would you set one of these values as a site-wide default for new users? Can you impose a umask standard on your users?

E7.3 What is the purpose of the shadow password file?

☆ E7.4 Determine what authentication system the **login** program on your system uses. If it uses PAM, determine what other programs on the system also use PAM.

☆ E7.5 List the steps needed to add a user to a system without using **useradd**. What extra steps are needed for your local environment?

☆ E7.6 Determine the naming convention for new users at your site. What are the rules? How is uniqueness preserved? Can you think of any drawbacks? How are users removed?

☆☆ E7.7 Find a list of names (from a local on-line telephone directory, perhaps) and use it as the input to a script that forms login names according to the naming convention at your site. How many users can you accommodate before you have a collision? How many collisions are there overall? Use the data to evaluate your site's naming convention, and suggest improvements.

☆☆ E7.8 Write a script to help monitor the health of your **/etc/passwd** file. (Parts b and e require root access unless you're clever.)

a) Find any entries that have UID 0.
b) Find any entries that have no password (needs **/etc/shadow**).
c) Find any sets of entries that have duplicate UIDs.
d) Find any entries that have duplicate login names.
e) Find any entries that have no expiration date (needs **/etc/shadow**).

☆☆☆☆☆ E7.9 Write a PAM module to perform authentication by randomly generating a PIN code, sending it to the user's cell phone as an SMS message, and prompting the user to enter the PIN code for verification. Install your module and configure it into the PAM login stack to achieve two-factor authentication.

8 Storage

UNIX storage is looking more and more like a giant set of Lego blocks that you can put together in an infinite variety of configurations. What will you build? A fighter jet? A dump truck? An advanced technology helicopter with air bags and a night-vision camera?

Traditional hard disks remain the dominant medium for on-line storage, but they're increasingly being joined by solid state drives (SSDs) for performance-sensitive applications. Running on top of this hardware are a variety of software components that mediate between the raw storage devices and the filesystem hierarchy seen by users. These components include device drivers, partitioning conventions, RAID implementations, logical volume managers, systems for virtualizing disks over a network, and the filesystem implementations themselves.

In this chapter, we discuss the administrative tasks and decisions that occur at each of these layers. We begin with "fast path" instructions for adding a basic disk to each of our example systems. We then review storage-related hardware technologies and look at the general architecture of storage software. We then work our way up the storage stack from low-level formatting up to the filesystem level. Along the way, we cover disk partitioning, RAID systems, logical volume managers, and systems for implementing storage area networks (SANs).

Although vendors all use standardized disk hardware, there's a lot of variation among systems in the software domain. Accordingly, you'll see a lot of vendor-specific details in this chapter. We try to cover each system in enough detail that you can at least identify the commands and systems that are used and can locate the necessary documentation.

8.1 I JUST WANT TO ADD A DISK!

Before we launch into many pages of storage architecture and theory, let's first address the most common scenario: you want to install a hard disk and make it accessible through the filesystem. Nothing fancy: no RAID, all the drive's space in a single logical volume, and the default filesystem type.

Step one is to attach the drive and reboot. Some systems allow hot-addition of disk drives, but we don't address that case here. Beyond that, the recipes differ slightly among systems.

Regardless of your OS, it's critically important to *identify and format the right disk drive*. A newly added drive is not necessarily represented by the highest-numbered device file, and on some systems, the addition of a new drive can change the device names of existing drives. Double-check the identity of the new drive by reviewing its manufacturer, size, and model number before you do anything that's potentially destructive.

Linux recipe

Run **sudo fdisk -l** to list the system's disks and identify the new drive. Then run any convenient partitioning utility to create a partition table for the drive. For drives 2TB and below, install a Windows MBR partition table. **cfdisk** is the easiest utility for this, but you can also use **fdisk**, **sfdisk**, **parted**, or **gparted**. Larger disks require a GPT partition table, so you must partition with **parted** or its GNOME GUI, **gparted**. **gparted** is a lot easier to use but isn't usually installed by default.

Put all the drive's space into one partition of unspecified or "unformatted" type. Do not install a filesystem. Note the device name of the new partition before you leave the partitioning utility; let's say it's **/dev/sdc1**.

Next, run the following command sequence, selecting appropriate names for the volume group (*vgname*), logical volume (*volname*), and mount point. (Examples of reasonable choices: homevg, home, and **/home**.)

```
$ sudo pvcreate /dev/sdc1                           # Prepare for use w/LVM
$ sudo vgcreate vgname /dev/sdc1                    # Create volume group
$ sudo lvcreate -l 100%FREE -n volname vgname       # Create logical volume
$ sudo mkfs -t ext4 /dev/vgname/volname             # Create filesystem
$ sudo mkdir mountpoint                             # Create mount point
$ sudo vi /etc/fstab                                # Set mount opts, mntpoint
```

In the **/etc/fstab** file, copy the line for an existing filesystem and adjust it. The device to be mounted is **/dev/***vgname***/***volname*. If your existing **fstab** file identifies volumes by UUID, replace the UUID=*xxx* clause with the device file; UUID identification is not necessary for LVM volumes.

Finally, run **sudo mount** *mountpoint* to mount the filesystem.

See page 224 for more details on Linux device files for disks. See page 236 for partitioning information and page 251 for logical volume management. The ext4 filesystem family is discussed starting on page 255.

Solaris recipe

Run **sudo format** and inspect the menu of known disks to identify the name of the new device. Let's say it's **c9t0d0**. Type <Control-C> to abort.

Run **zpool create** *poolname* **c9t0d0**. Choose a simple *poolname* such as "home" or "extra." ZFS creates a filesystem and mounts it under /*poolname*.

See page 225 for more details on disk devices in Solaris. See page 264 for a general overview of ZFS.

HP-UX recipe

Run **sudo ioscan -fNn -C disk** to identify the device files for the new disk; let's say they are **/dev/disk/disk4** and **/dev/rdisk/disk4**.

Next, run the following command sequence, selecting appropriate names for the volume group (*vgname*), logical volume (*volname*), and mount point. (An example of reasonable choices: homevg, home, and **/home**.)

```
$ sudo pvcreate /dev/rdisk/disk4                # Prepare for use w/LVM
$ sudo vgcreate vgname /dev/disk/disk4          # Create volume group
$ vgdisplay vgname                              # View VG stats
...
Free PE          freespace                      # Note this value
...
$ sudo lvcreate -l freespace -n volname vgname  # Create logical volume
$ sudo mkfs /dev/vgname/volname                 # Create filesystem
$ sudo mkdir mountpoint                         # Create mount point dir
$ sudo vi /etc/fstab                            # Set mounting options
```

In the **/etc/fstab** file, copy the line for an existing filesystem and adjust it. The device to be mounted is **/dev/***vgname***/***volname*.

Finally, run **sudo mount** *mountpoint* to mount the filesystem.

See page 225 for more details on HP-UX disk device files. See page 251 for logical volume management information. The VxFS filesystem is discussed starting on page 256.

AIX recipe

Run **lsdev -C -c disk** to see a list of the disks the system is aware of, then run **lspv** to see which disks are already set up for volume management. The device that appears in the first list but not the second is your new disk. Let's say it's **hdisk1**.

Next, run the following command sequence, selecting appropriate names for the volume group (*vgname*), logical volume (*volname*), and mount point. (Examples of reasonable choices: homevg, home, and **/home**.)

```
$ sudo mkvg -y vgname hdisk1            # Create volume group
$ lsvg vgname                           # Note freespace value
...
MAX LVs:  256     FREE PPs:  325 (freespace megabytes)
...
$ sudo crfs -v jfs2 -g vgname -m mountpoint -a size=freespaceM
$ sudo mkdir mountpoint
$ sudo mount mountpoint
```

See page 226 for more details on AIX disk device files, and see page 253 for AIX logical volume management information. The JFS2 filesystem is discussed starting on page 257.

8.2 Storage hardware

See page 301 for a summary of current tape technologies.

Even in today's post-Internet world, there are only a few basic ways to store computer data: hard disks, flash memory, magnetic tapes, and optical media. The last two technologies have significant limitations that disqualify them from use as a system's primary filesystem. However, they're still commonly used for backups and for "near-line" storage—cases in which instant access and rewritability are not of primary concern.

After 40 years of hard disk technology, system builders are finally getting a practical alternative in the form of solid state disks (SSDs). These flash-memory-based devices offer a different set of tradeoffs from a standard disk, and they're sure to exert a strong influence over the architectures of databases, filesystems, and operating systems in the years to come.

At the same time, traditional hard disks are continuing their exponential increases in capacity. Twenty years ago, a 60MB hard disk cost $1,000. Today, a garden-variety 1TB drive runs $80 or so. That's 200,000 times more storage for the money, or double the MB/$ every 1.15 years—nearly twice the rate predicted by Moore's Law. During that same period, the sequential throughput of mass-market drives has increased from 500 kB/s to 100 MB/s, a comparatively paltry factor of 200. And random-access seek times have hardly budged. The more things change, the more they stay the same.

A third—hybrid—category, hard disks with large flash-memory buffers, was widely touted a few years ago but never actually materialized in the marketplace. It's not clear to us whether the drives were delayed by technical, manufacturing, or marketing concerns. They may yet appear on the scene, but the implications for system administrators remain unclear.

See page 14 for more information on IEC units (gibibytes, etc.).

Disk sizes are specified in gigabytes that are billions of bytes, as opposed to memory, which is specified in gigabytes (gibibytes, really) of 2^{30} (1,073,741,824) bytes. The difference is about 7%. Be sure to check your units when estimating and comparing capacities.

Hard disks and SSDs are enough alike that they can act as drop-in replacements for each other, at least at the hardware level. They use the same hardware interfaces and interface protocols. And yet they have different strengths, as summarized in Table 8.1. Performance and cost values are as of mid-2010.

Table 8.1 Comparison of hard disk and SSD technology

Characteristic	HD	SSD
Size	Terabytes	Gigabytes
Random access time	8ms	0.25ms
Sequential read	100 MB/s	250 MB/s
Random read	2 MB/s	250 MB/s
Cost	$0.10/GB	$3/GB
Reliability	Moderate	Unknown
Limited writes	No	Yes

In the next sections, we take a closer look at each of these technologies.

Hard disks

A typical hard drive contains several rotating platters coated with magnetic film. They are read and written by tiny skating heads that are mounted on a metal arm that swings back and forth to position them. The heads float close to the surface of the platters but do not actually touch.

Reading from a platter is quick; it's the mechanical maneuvering needed to address a particular sector that drives down random-access throughput. There are two main sources of delay.

First, the head armature must swing into position over the appropriate track. This part is called seek delay. Then, the system must wait for the right sector to pass underneath the head as the platter rotates. That part is rotational latency. Disks can stream data at tens of MB/s if reads are optimally sequenced, but random reads are fortunate to achieve more than a few MB/s.

A set of tracks on different platters that are all the same distance from the spindle is called a cylinder. The cylinder's data can be read without any additional movement of the arm. Although heads move amazingly fast, they still move much slower than the disks spin around. Therefore, any disk access that does not require the heads to seek to a new position will be faster.

Rotational speeds have increased over time. Currently, 7,200 RPM is the mass-market standard for performance-oriented drives, and 10,000 RPM and 15,000 RPM drives are popular at the high end. Higher rotational speeds decrease latency and increase the bandwidth of data transfers, but the drives tend to run hot.

Hard disks fail frequently. A 2007 Google Labs study of 100,000 drives surprised the tech world with the news that hard disks more than two years old had an average annual failure rate (AFR) of more than 6%, much higher than the failure rates manufacturers predicted based on their extrapolation of short-term testing. The overall pattern was a few months of infant mortality, a two-year honeymoon of annual failure rates of a few percent, and then a jump up to the 6%–8% AFR range. Overall, hard disks in the Google study had less than a 75% chance of surviving a five-year tour of duty.

Interestingly, Google found no correlation between failure rate and two environmental factors that were formerly thought to be important: operating temperature and drive activity. The complete paper can be found at tinyurl.com/fail-pdf.

Disk failures tend to involve either platter surfaces (bad blocks) or the mechanical components. The firmware and hardware interface usually remain operable after a failure, so you can query the disk for details (see page 230).

Drive reliability is often quoted by manufacturers in terms of mean time between failures (MTBF), denominated in hours. A typical value for an enterprise drive is around 1.2 million hours. However, MTBF is a statistical measure and should not be read to imply that an individual drive will run for 140 years before failing.

MTBF is the inverse of AFR in the drive's steady-state period—that is, after break-in but before wear-out. A manufacturer's MTBF of 1.2 million hours corresponds to an AFR of 0.7% per year. This value is almost, but not quite, concordant with the AFR range observed by Google (1%–2%) during the first two years of their sample drives' lives.

Manufacturers' MTBF values are probably accurate, but they are cherry-picked from the most reliable phase of each drive's life. MTBF values should therefore be regarded as an upper bound on reliability; they do not predict your actual expected failure rate over the long term. Based on the limited data quoted above, you might consider dividing manufacturers' MTBFs by a factor of 7.5 or so to arrive at a more realistic estimate of five-year failure rates.

Hard disks are commodity products, and one manufacturer's model is much like another's, given similar specifications for spindle speed, hardware interface, and reliability. These days, you need a dedicated qualification laboratory to make fine distinctions among competing drives.

Solid state disks

SSDs spread reads and writes across banks of flash memory cells, which are individually rather slow in comparison to modern hard disks. But because of parallelism, the SSD as a whole meets or exceeds the bandwidth of a traditional disk. The great strength of SSDs is that they continue to perform well when data is read or written at random, an access pattern that's predominant in real-world use.

Storage device manufacturers like to quote sequential transfer rates for their products because the numbers are impressively high. But for traditional hard disks, these sequential numbers have almost no relationship to the throughput observed with random reads and writes. For example, Western Digital's high-performance Velociraptor drives can achieve nearly 120 MB/s in sequential transfers, but their random read results are more on the order of 2 MB/s. By contrast, Intel's current-generation SSDs stay above 30 MB/s for all access patterns.

This performance comes at a cost, however. Not only are SSDs more expensive per gigabyte of storage than are hard disks, but they also introduce several new wrinkles and uncertainties into the storage equation.

Each page of flash memory in an SSD (typically 4KiB on current products) can be rewritten only a limited number of times (usually about 100,000, depending on the underlying technology). To limit the wear on any given page, the SSD firmware maintains a mapping table and distributes writes across all the drive's pages. This remapping is invisible to the operating system, which sees the drive as a linear series of blocks. Think of it as virtual memory for storage.

A further complication is that flash memory pages must be erased before they can be rewritten. Erasing is a separate operation that is slower than writing. It's also impossible to erase individual pages—clusters of adjacent pages (typically 128 pages or 512KiB) must be erased together. The write performance of an SSD can drop substantially when the pool of pre-erased pages is exhausted and the drive must recover pages on the fly to service ongoing writes.

Rebuilding a buffer of erased pages is harder than it might seem because filesystems typically do not mark or erase data blocks they are no longer using. A storage device doesn't know that the filesystem now considers a given block to be free; it only knows that long ago someone gave it data to store there. In order for an SSD to maintain its cache of pre-erased pages (and thus, its write performance), the filesystem has to be capable of informing the SSD that certain pages are no longer needed. As of this writing, ext4 and Windows 7's NTFS are the only common filesystems that offers this feature. But given the enormous interest in SSDs, other filesystems are sure to become more SSD-aware in the near future.

Another touchy subject is alignment. The standard size for a disk block is 512 bytes, but that size is too small for filesystems to deal with efficiently.[1] Filesystems

1. The 512-byte standard for hard disks may not hold out much longer; see lwn.net/Articles/377895.

manage the disk in terms of clusters of 1KiB to 8KiB in size, and a translation layer maps filesystem clusters into ranges of disk blocks for reads and writes.

On a hard disk, it makes no difference where a cluster begins or ends. But because SSDs can only read or write data in 4KiB pages (despite their emulation of a hard disk's traditional 512-byte blocks), filesystem cluster boundaries and SSD page boundaries should coincide. You wouldn't want a 4KiB logical cluster to correspond to half of one 4KiB SSD cluster and half of another—with that layout, the SSD might have to read or write twice as many physical pages as it should to service a given number of logical clusters.

Since filesystems usually count off their clusters starting at the beginning of whatever storage is allocated to them, the alignment issue can be finessed by aligning disk partitions to a power-of-2 boundary that is large in comparison with the likely size of SSD and filesystem pages (e.g., 64KiB). Unfortunately, the Windows MBR partitioning scheme that Linux has inherited does not make such alignment automatic. Check the block ranges that your partitioning tool assigns to make sure they are aligned, keeping in mind that the MBR itself consumes a block. (Windows 7 aligns partitions suitably for SSDs by default.)

The theoretical limits on the rewritability of flash memory are probably less of an issue than they might initially seem. Just as a matter of arithmetic, you would have to stream 100 MB/s of data to a 150GB SSD for more than four continuous years to start running up against the rewrite limit. The more general question of long-term SSD reliability is as yet unanswered, however. SSDs are an immature product category, and early adopters should expect quirks.

The controllers used inside SSDs are rapidly evolving, and there are currently marked differences in performance among manufacturers. The market should eventually converge to a standard architecture for these devices, but that day is still a year or two off. In the short term, careful shopping is essential.

Anand Shimpi's March 2009 article on SSD technology is a superb introduction to the promise and perils of the SSD. It can be found at tinyurl.com/dexnbt.

8.3 Storage hardware interfaces

These days, only a few interface standards are in common use. If a system supports several different interfaces, use the one that best meets your requirements for speed, redundancy, mobility, and price.

- ATA (Advanced Technology Attachment), known in earlier revisions as IDE, was developed as a simple, low-cost interface for PCs. It was originally called Integrated Drive Electronics because it put the hardware controller in the same box as the disk platters and used a relatively high-level protocol for communication between the computer and the disks. This is now the way that all hard disks work, but at the time it was something of an innovation.

The traditional parallel ATA interface (PATA) connected disks to the motherboard with a 40- or 80-conductor ribbon cable. This style of disk is nearly obsolete, but the installed base is enormous. PATA disks are often labeled as "IDE" to distinguish them from SATA drives (below), but they are true ATA drives. PATA disks are medium to fast in speed, generous in capacity, and unbelievably cheap.

- Serial ATA, SATA, is the successor to PATA. In addition to supporting much higher transfer rates (currently 3 Gb/s, with 6 Gb/s soon to arrive), SATA simplifies connectivity with tidier cabling and a longer maximum cable length. SATA has native support for hot-swapping and (optional) command queueing, two features that finally make ATA a viable alternative to SCSI in server environments.
- Though not as common as it once was, SCSI is one of the most widely supported disk interfaces. It comes in several flavors, all of which support multiple disks on a bus and various speeds and communication styles. SCSI is described in more detail on page 216.

  Hard drive manufacturers typically reserve SCSI interfaces for their highest-performing and most rugged drives. You'll pay more for these drives, but mostly because of the drive features rather than the interface.
- Fibre Channel is a serial interface that is popular in the enterprise environment thanks to its high bandwidth and to the large number of storage devices that can be attached to it at once. Fibre Channel devices connect with a fiber optic or twinaxial copper cable. Speeds range from roughly 1–40 Gb/s depending on the protocol revision.

  Common topologies include loops, called Fibre Channel Arbitrated Loops (FC-AL), and fabrics, which are constructed with Fibre Channel switches. Fibre Channel can speak several different protocols, including SCSI and even IP. Devices are identified by a hardwired, 8-byte ID number (a "World Wide Name") that's similar to an Ethernet MAC address.
- The Universal Serial Bus (USB) and FireWire (IEEE1394) serial communication systems have become popular for connecting external hard disks. Current speeds are 480 Mb/s for USB and 800 Mb/s for FireWire; both systems are too slow to accommodate a fast disk streaming data at full speed. Upcoming revisions of both standards will offer more competitive speeds (up to 5 Gb/s with USB 3.0).

  Hard disks never provide native USB or FireWire interfaces—SATA converters are built into the disk enclosures that feature these ports.

ATA and SCSI are by far the dominant players in the disk drive arena. They are the only interfaces we discuss in detail.

The PATA interface

PATA (Parallel Advanced Technology Attachment), also called IDE, was designed to be simple and inexpensive. It is most often found on PCs or low-cost workstations. The original IDE became popular in the late 1980s. A succession of protocol revisions culminating in the current ATA-7 (also known as Ultra ATA/133) added direct memory access (DMA) modes, plug and play features, logical block addressing (LBA), power management, self-monitoring capabilities, and bus speeds up to 133 MB/s. Around the time of ATA-4, the ATA standard also merged with the ATA Packet Interface (ATAPI) protocol, which allows CD-ROM and tape drives to work on an IDE bus.

The PATA connector is a 40-pin header that connects the drive to the interface card with a clumsy ribbon cable. ATA standards beyond Ultra DMA/66 use an 80-conductor cable with more ground pins and therefore less electrical noise. Some nicer cables that are available bundle up the ribbon into a thick cable sleeve, tidying up the chassis and improving air flow. Power cabling for PATA uses a chunky 4-conductor Molex plug.

If a cable or drive is not keyed, be sure that pin 1 on the drive goes to pin 1 on the interface jack. Pin 1 is usually marked with a small "1" on one side of the connector. If it is not marked, a rule of thumb is that pin 1 is usually the one closest to the power connector. Pin 1 on a ribbon cable is usually marked in red. If there is no red stripe on one edge of your cable, just make sure you have the cable oriented so that pin 1 is connected to pin 1 and mark the cable with a red sharpie.

Most PCs have two PATA buses, each of which can host two devices. If you have more than one device on a PATA bus, you must designate one as the master and the other as the slave. A "cable select" jumper setting on modern drives (which is usually the default) lets the devices work out master vs. slave on their own. Occasionally, it does not work correctly and you must explicitly assign the master and slave roles.

No performance advantage accrues from being the master. Some older PATA drives do not like to be slaves, so if you are having trouble getting one configuration to work, try reversing the disks' roles. If things are still not working out, try making each device the master of its own PATA bus.

Arbitration between master and slave devices on a PATA bus can be relatively slow. If possible, put each PATA drive on its own bus.

The SATA interface

As data transfer rates for PATA drives increased, the standard's disadvantages started to become obvious. Electromagnetic interference and other electrical issues caused reliability concerns at high speeds. Serial ATA, SATA, was invented to address these problems. It is now the predominant hardware interface for storage.

SATA smooths many of PATA's sharp edges. It improves transfer rates (potentially to 750 MB/s with the upcoming 6 Gb/s SATA) and includes superior error checking. The standard supports hot-swapping, native command queuing, and sundry performance enhancements. SATA eliminates the need for master and slave designations because only a single device can be connected to each channel.

SATA overcomes the 18-inch cable limitation of PATA and introduces new data and power cable standards of 7 and 15 conductors, respectively.[2] These cables are infinitely more flexible and easier to work with than their ribbon cable predecessors—no more curving and twisting to fit drives on the same cable. They do seem to be a bit more quality-sensitive than the old PATA ribbon cables, however. We have seen several of the cheap pack-in SATA cables that come with motherboards fail in actual use.[3]

SATA cables slide easily onto their mating connectors, but they can just as easily slide off. Cables with locking catches are available, but they're a mixed blessing. On motherboards with six or eight SATA connectors packed together, it can be hard to disengage the locking connectors without a pair of needle-nosed pliers.

SATA also introduces an external cabling standard called eSATA. The cables are electrically identical to standard SATA, but the connectors are slightly different. You can add an eSATA port to a system that has only internal SATA connectors by installing an inexpensive converter bracket.

Be leery of external multidrive enclosures that have only a single eSATA port—some of these are smart (RAID) enclosures that require a proprietary driver. (The drivers rarely support UNIX or Linux.) Others are dumb enclosures that have a SATA port multiplier built in. These are potentially usable on UNIX systems, but since not all SATA host adapters support port expanders, pay close attention to the compatibility information. Enclosures with multiple eSATA ports—one per drive bay—are always safe.

Parallel SCSI

SCSI, the Small Computer System Interface, defines a generic data pipe that can be used by all kinds of peripherals. In the past it was used for disks, tape drives, scanners, and printers, but these days most peripherals have abandoned SCSI in favor of USB.

Many flavors of SCSI interface have been defined since 1986, when SCSI-1 was first adopted as an ANSI standard. Traditional SCSI uses parallel cabling with 8 or 16 conductors.

Unfortunately, there has been no real rhyme or reason to the naming conventions for parallel SCSI. The terms "fast," "wide," and "ultra" were introduced at various times to mark significant developments, but as those features became standard, the descriptors vanished from the names. The nimble-sounding Ultra SCSI is in

2. That's right: for some reason, the power cable is more complicated than the data cable.
3. In the United States, an excellent source for good quality but cheap SATA cables is monoprice.com.

fact a 20 MB/s standard that no one would dream of using today, so it has had to give way to Ultra2, Ultra3, Ultra-320, and Ultra-640 SCSI. For the curious, the following regular expression matches all the various flavors of parallel SCSI:

(Fast(-Wide)?|Ultra((Wide)?|2 (Wide)?|3|-320|-640)?) SCSI|SCSI-[1-3]

Many different connectors have been used as well. They vary depending on the version of SCSI, the type of connection (internal or external), and the number of data bits sent at once. Exhibit A shows pictures of some common ones. Each connector is shown from the front, as if you were about to plug it into your forehead.

Exhibit A Parallel SCSI connectors (front view, male except where noted)

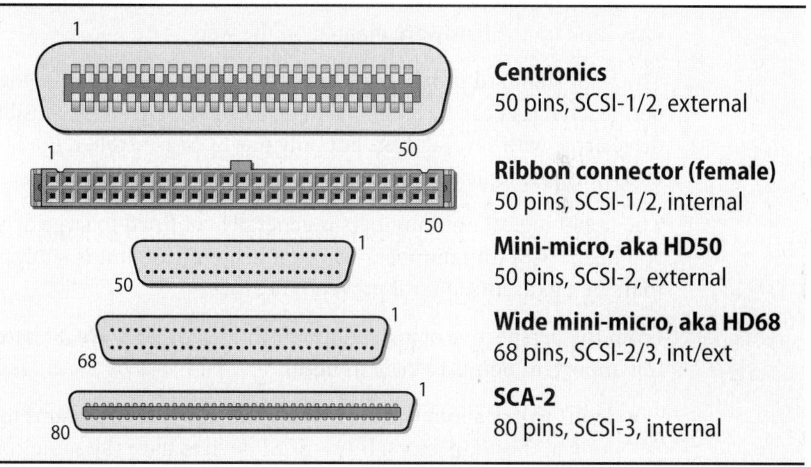

The only one of these connectors still being manufactured today is the SCA-2, which is an 80-pin connector that includes both power and bus connections.

Each end of a parallel SCSI bus must have a terminating resistor ("terminator"). These resistors absorb signals as they reach the end of the bus and prevent noise from reflecting back onto the bus. Terminators take several forms, from small external plugs that you snap onto a regular port to sets of tiny resistor packs that install onto a device's circuit boards. Most modern devices are autoterminating.

If you experience seemingly random hardware problems on your SCSI bus, first check that both ends of the bus are properly terminated. Improper termination is one of the most common SCSI configuration mistakes on old SCSI systems, and the errors it produces can be obscure and intermittent.

Parallel SCSI buses use a daisy chain configuration, so most external devices have two SCSI ports.[4] The ports are identical and interchangeable—either one can be

4. "Daisy chaining" is the common description, but it's perhaps a bit misleading. Parallel SCSI is physically wired as a chain, but it is electrically a single bus.

the input. Internal SCSI devices (including those with SCA-2 connectors) are attached to a ribbon cable, so only one port is needed on the device.

Each device has a SCSI address or "target number" that distinguishes it from the other devices on the bus. Target numbers start at 0 and go up to 7 or 15, depending on whether the bus is narrow or wide. The SCSI controller itself counts as a device and is usually target 7. All other devices must have their target numbers set to unique values. It is a common error to forget that the SCSI controller has a target number and to set a device to the same target number as the controller.

If you're lucky, a device will have an external thumbwheel with which the target number can be set. Other common ways of setting the target number are DIP switches and jumpers. If it is not obvious how to set the target number on a device, look up the hardware manual on the web.

The SCSI standard supports a form of subaddressing called a "logical unit number." Each target can have several logical units inside it. A plausible example is a drive array with several disks but only one SCSI controller. If a SCSI device contains only one logical unit, the LUN usually defaults to 0.

The use of logical unit numbers is generally confined to large drive arrays. When you hear "SCSI unit number," you should assume that it is really a target number that's being discussed until proven otherwise.

From the perspective of a sysadmin dealing with legacy SCSI hardware, here are the important points to keep in mind:

- Don't worry about the exact SCSI versions a device claims to support; look at the connectors. If two SCSI devices have the same connectors, they are compatible. That doesn't necessarily mean that they can achieve the same speeds, however. Communication will occur at the speed of the slower device.
- Even if the connectors are different, the devices can still be made compatible with an adapter if both connectors have the same number of pins.
- Many older workstations have internal SCSI devices such as tape and floppy drives. Check the listing of current devices before you reboot to add a new device.
- After you have added a new SCSI device, check the listing of devices discovered by the kernel when it reboots to make sure that everything you expect is there. Most SCSI drivers do not detect multiple devices that have the same SCSI address (an illegal configuration). SCSI address conflicts lead to strange behavior.
- If you see flaky behavior, check for a target number conflict or a problem with bus termination.
- Remember that your SCSI controller uses one of the SCSI addresses.

Serial SCSI

As in the PATA world, parallel SCSI is giving way to Serial Attached SCSI (SAS), the SCSI analog of SATA. From the hardware perspective, SAS improves just about every aspect of traditional parallel SCSI.

- Chained buses are passé. Like SATA, SAS is a point-to-point system. SAS allows the use of "expanders" to connect multiple devices to a single host port. They're analogous to SATA port multipliers, but whereas support for port multipliers is hit or miss, expanders are always supported.
- SAS does not use terminators.
- SCSI target IDs are no longer used. Instead, each SAS device has a Fibre-Channel-style 64-bit World Wide Name (WWN) assigned by the manufacturer. It's analogous to an Ethernet MAC address.
- The number of devices in a SCSI bus ("SAS domain," really) is no longer limited to 8 or 16. Up to 16,384 devices can be connected.

SAS currently operates at 3 Gb/s, but speeds are scheduled to increase to 6 Gb/s and then to 12 Gb/s by 2012.

Which is better, SCSI or SATA?

In past editions of this book, SCSI was the obvious interface choice for server applications. It offered the highest available bandwidth, out-of-order command execution (aka tagged command queueing), lower CPU utilization, easier handling of large numbers of storage devices, and access to the market's most advanced hard drives.

The advent of SATA has removed or minimized most of these advantages, so SCSI simply does not deliver the bang for the buck that it used to. SATA drives compete with (and in some cases, outperform) equivalent SCSI disks in nearly every category. At the same time, both SATA devices and the interfaces and cabling used to connect them are cheaper and far more widely available.

SCSI still holds a few trump cards:

- Manufacturers continue to use the SATA/SCSI divide to stratify the storage market. To help justify premium pricing, the fastest and most reliable drives are still available with only SCSI interfaces.
- SATA is limited to a queue depth of 32 pending operations. SCSI can handle thousands.
- SAS can handle many storage devices (hundreds or thousands) on a single host interface. But keep in mind that all those devices share a single pipe to the host; you are still limited to 3 Gb/s of aggregate bandwidth.

The SAS vs. SATA debate may ultimately be moot because the SAS standard includes support for SATA drives. SAS and SATA connectors are similar enough that a single SAS backplane can accommodate drives of either type. At the logical layer, SATA commands are simply tunneled over the SAS bus.

This convergence is an amazing technical feat, but the economic argument for it is less clear. The expense of a SAS installation is mostly in the host adapter, backplane, and infrastructure; the SAS drives themselves aren't outrageously priced. Once you've invested in a SAS setup, you might as well stick with SAS from end to end. (On the other hand, perhaps the modest price premiums for SAS drives are a *result* of the fact that SATA drives can easily be substituted for them.)

8.4 Peeling the onion: the software side of storage

If you're used to plugging in a disk and having your Windows system ask if you want to format it, you may be a bit taken aback by the apparent complexity of storage management on UNIX and Linux systems. Why is it all so complicated?

To begin with, much of the complexity is optional. On some systems, you can log in to your system's desktop, connect that same USB drive, and have much the same experience as on Windows. You'll get a simple setup for personal data storage. If that's all you need, you're good to go.

As usual in this book, we're primarily interested in enterprise-class storage systems: filesystems that are accessed by many users (both local and remote) and that are reliable, high-performance, easy to back up, and easy to adapt to future needs. These systems require a bit more thought, and UNIX and Linux give you plenty to think about.

Exhibit B shows a typical set of software components that can mediate between a raw storage device and its end users. The specific architecture shown in Exhibit B is for Linux, but our other example systems include similar features, although not necessarily in the same packages.

The arrows in Exhibit B mean "can be built on." For example, a Linux filesystem can be built on top of a partition, a RAID array, or a logical volume. It's up to the administrator to construct a stack of modules that connect each storage device to its final application.

Sharp-eyed readers will note that the graph has a cycle, but real-world configurations do not loop. Linux allows RAID and logical volumes to be stacked in either order, but neither component should be used more than once (though it is technically possible to do this).

Here's what the pieces in Exhibit B represent:

- A **storage device** is anything that looks like a disk. It can be a hard disk, a flash drive, an SSD, an external RAID array implemented in hardware, or even a network service that provides block-level access to a remote device. The exact hardware doesn't matter, as long as the device allows random access, handles block I/O, and is represented by a device file.

Exhibit B Storage management layers

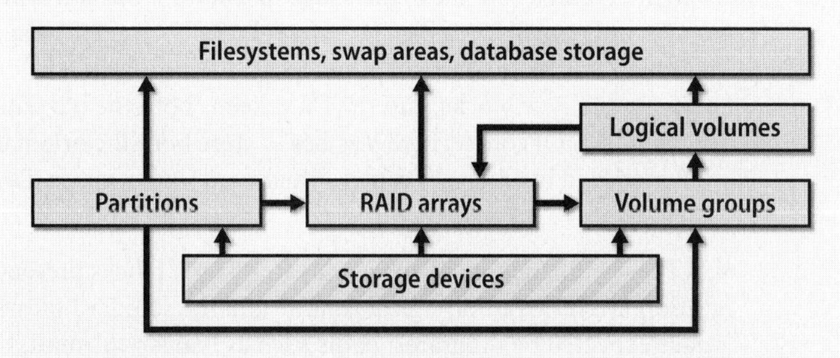

- A **partition** is a fixed-size subsection of a storage device. Each partition has its own device file and acts much like an independent storage device. For efficiency, the same driver that handles the underlying device usually implements partitioning. Most partitioning schemes consume a few blocks at the start of the device to record the ranges of blocks that make up each partition.

  Partitioning is becoming something of a vestigial feature. Linux and Solaris drag it along primarily for compatibility with Windows-partitioned disks. HP-UX and AIX have largely done away with it in favor of logical volume management, though it's still needed on Itanium-based HP-UX systems.

- A **RAID array** (a redundant array of inexpensive/independent disks) combines multiple storage devices into one virtualized device. Depending on how you set up the array, this configuration can increase performance (by reading or writing disks in parallel), increase reliability (by duplicating or parity-checking data across multiple disks), or both. RAID can be implemented by the operating system or by various types of hardware.

  As the name suggests, RAID is typically conceived of as an aggregation of bare drives, but modern implementations let you use as a component of a RAID array anything that acts like a disk.

- **Volume groups** and **logical volumes** are associated with logical volume managers (LVMs). These systems aggregate physical devices to form pools of storage called volume groups. The administrator can then subdivide this pool into logical volumes in much the same way that disks of yore were divided into partitions. For example, a 750GB disk and a 250GB disk could be aggregated into a 1TB volume group and then split into two 500GB logical volumes. At least one volume would include data blocks from both hard disks.

Since the LVM adds a layer of indirection between logical and physical blocks, it can freeze the logical state of a volume simply by making a copy of the mapping table. Therefore, logical volume managers often provide some kind of a "snapshot" feature. Writes to the volume are then directed to new blocks, and the LVM keeps both the old and new mapping tables. Of course, the LVM has to store both the original image and all modified blocks, so it can eventually run out of space if a snapshot is never deleted.

- A **filesystem** mediates between the raw bag of blocks presented by a partition, RAID array, or logical volume and the standard filesystem interface expected by programs: paths such as **/var/spool/mail**, UNIX file types, UNIX permissions, etc. The filesystem determines where and how the contents of files are stored, how the filesystem namespace is represented and searched on disk, and how the system is made resistant to (or recoverable from) corruption.

  Most storage space ends up as part of a filesystem, but swap space and database storage can potentially be slightly more efficient without "help" from a filesystem. The kernel or database imposes its own structure on the storage, rendering the filesystem unnecessary.

If it seems to you that this system has a few too many little components that simply implement one block storage device in terms of another, you're in good company. The trend over the last few years has been toward consolidating these components to increase efficiency and remove duplication. Although logical volume managers did not originally function as RAID controllers, most have absorbed some RAID-like features (notably, striping and mirroring). As administrators get comfortable with logical volume management, partitions are disappearing, too.

On the cutting edge today are systems that combine a filesystem, a RAID controller, and an LVM system all in one tightly integrated package. Sun's ZFS filesystem is the leading example, but the Btrfs filesystem in development for Linux has similar design goals. We have more to say about ZFS on page 264.

Most setups are relatively simple. Exhibit C illustrates a traditional partitions-and-filesystems schema as it might be found on a couple of data disks on a Linux system. (The boot disk is not shown.) Substitute logical volumes for partitions and the setup is similar on other systems.

In the next sections, we look in more detail at the steps involved in various phases of storage configuration: device wrangling, partitioning, RAID, logical volume management, and the installation of a filesystem. Finally, we double back to cover ZFS and storage area networking.

Exhibit C Traditional data disk partitioning scheme (Linux device names)

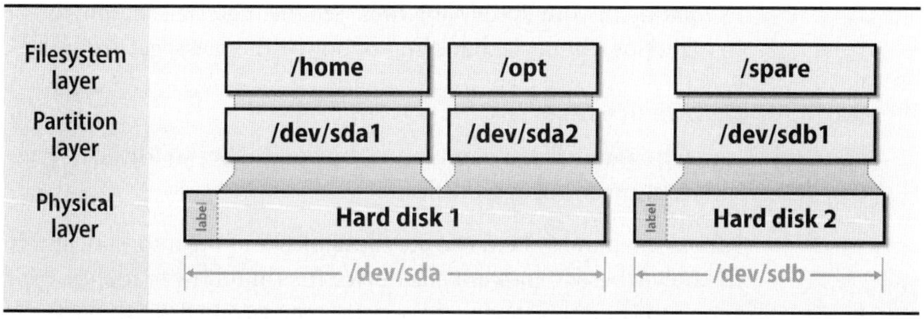

8.5 Attachment and low-level management of drives

The way a disk is attached to the system depends on the interface that is used. The rest is all mounting brackets and cabling. Fortunately, SAS and SATA connections are virtually idiot-proof.

For parallel SCSI, double-check that you have terminated both ends of the SCSI bus, that the cable length is less than the maximum appropriate for the SCSI variant you are using, and that the new SCSI target number does not conflict with the controller or another device on the bus.

Even on hot-pluggable interfaces, it's conservative to shut the system down before making hardware changes. Some older systems such as AIX default to doing device configuration only at boot time, so the fact that the hardware is hot-pluggable may not translate into immediate visibility at the OS level. In the case of SATA interfaces, hot-pluggability is an implementation option. Some host adapters don't support it.

Installation verification at the hardware level

After you install a new disk, check to make sure that the system acknowledges its existence at the lowest possible level. On a PC this is easy: the BIOS shows you IDE and SATA disks, and most SCSI cards have their own setup screen that you can invoke before the system boots.

On other types of hardware, you may have to let the system boot and check the diagnostic output from the kernel as it probes for devices. For example, one of our test systems showed the following messages for an older SCSI disk attached to a BusLogic SCSI host adapter.

```
scsi0 : BusLogic BT-948
scsi : 1 host.
  Vendor: SEAGATE   Model: ST446452W        Rev: 0001
  Type:   Direct-Access                     ANSI SCSI revision: 02
Detected scsi disk sda at scsi0, channel 0, id 3, lun 0
scsi0: Target 3: Queue Depth 28, Asynchronous
SCSI device sda: hdwr sector=512 bytes. Sectors=91923356 [44884 MB] [44.9 GB]
```

You may be able to review this information after the system has finished booting by looking in your system log files. See the material starting on page 352 for more information about the handling of boot-time messages from the kernel.

Disk device files

A newly added disk is represented by device files in **/dev**. See page 150 for general information about device files.

All our example systems create these files for you automatically, but you still need to know where to look for the device files and how to identify the ones that correspond to your new device. Formatting the wrong disk device file is a rapid route to disaster. Table 8.2 summarizes the device naming conventions for disks on our example systems. Instead of showing the abstract pattern according to which devices are named, Table 8.2 simply shows a typical example for the name of the system's first disk.

Table 8.2 Device naming standards for disks

System	Block device	Raw device	Partition
Linux	**/dev/sda**	*not used*	**/dev/sda1**
Solaris	**/dev/dsk/c0t0d0s2**	**/dev/rdsk/c0t0d0s2**	**/dev/dsk/c0t0d0s0**
HP-UX[a]	**/dev/disk/disk0**	**/dev/rdisk/disk0**	**/dev/disk/disk0_p1**[b]
AIX	**/dev/hdisk0**	**/dev/rhdisk0**	*not used*

a. HP-UX also uses Solaris-style device names for legacy compatibility.
b. Itanium-based systems only; non-Itanium systems do not have partitions.

The block and raw device columns show the path for the disk as a whole, and the partition column shows the path for an example partition.

Disk devices for Linux

Linux disk names are assigned in sequence as the kernel enumerates the various interfaces and devices on the system. Adding a disk can cause existing disks to change their names. In fact, even rebooting the system can cause name changes.[5] *Never* make changes without verifying the identity of the disk you're working on, even on a stable system.

Linux provides a couple of ways around the "dancing names" issue. Subdirectories under **/dev/disk** list disks by various stable characteristics such as their manufacturer ID or connection information. These device names (which are really just links back to **/dev/sd***) are stable, but they're long and awkward.

At the level of filesystems and disk arrays, Linux uses unique ID strings to persistently identify objects. In many cases, the existence of these long IDs is cleverly concealed so that you don't have to deal with them directly.

5. To deal with this issue, Linux uses UUIDs in the **/etc/fstab** file instead of device names; see page 262.

Linux doesn't have raw device files for disks or disk partitions, so just use the block device wherever you might be accustomed to specifying a raw device.

parted -l lists the sizes, partition tables, model numbers, and manufacturers of every disk on the system.

Disk devices for Solaris

Solaris disk device names are of the form **/dev/**[**r**]**dsk/c**W**t**X**d**Y**s**Z, where W is the controller number, X is the SCSI target number, Y is the SCSI logical unit number (or LUN, almost always 0), and Z is the partition (slice) number. There are a couple of subtleties: ATA drives show up as **c**W**d**Y**s**Z (with no **t** clause), and disks can have a series of DOS-style partitions, signified by **p**Z, as well as the Solaris-style slices denoted by **s**Z.

These device files are actually just symbolic links into the **/devices** tree, where the real device files live. More generally, Solaris makes an effort to give continuity to device names, even in the face of hardware changes. Once a disk has shown up under a given name, it can generally be found at that name in the future unless you switch controllers or SCSI target IDs.

By convention, slice 2 represents the complete, unpartitioned disk. Unlike Linux, Solaris gives you device files for every possible slice and partition, whether or not those slices and partitions actually exist. Solaris also supports overlapping partitions, but that's just crazy talk. Oracle may as well ship every Solaris system with a loaded gun.

Hot-plugging should work fine on Solaris. When you add a new disk, **devfsadmd** should detect it and create the appropriate device files for you. If need be, you can run **devfsadm** by hand.

Disk devices for HP-UX

HP-UX has traditionally used disk device names patterned after those of Solaris, which record a lot of hardware-specific information in the device path. As of HP-UX 11i v3, however, those pathnames have been deprecated in favor of "agile addresses" of the form **/dev/disk/disk1**. The latter paths are stable and do not change with the details of the system's hardware configuration.

Before you boot UNIX, you can obtain a listing of the system's SCSI devices from the PROM monitor. Unfortunately, the exact way in which this is done varies among machines. After you boot, you can list disks by running **ioscan**.

```
$ sudo ioscan -fNn -C disk
Class  I  H/W Path          Driver  S/W State H/W  TypeDescription
=====================================================================
disk   3  64000/0xfa00/0x0  esdisk  CLAIMED  DEVICE  TEACDV-28E-B
                 /dev/disk/disk3        /dev/rdisk/disk3
disk   4  64000/0xfa00/0x1  esdisk  CLAIMED  DEVICE  HP 73.4GMAS3735NC
                 /dev/disk/disk4        /dev/rdisk/disk4
                 /dev/disk/disk4_p1     /dev/rdisk/disk4_p1
```

Storage

```
                /dev/disk/disk4_p2   /dev/rdisk/disk4_p2
                /dev/disk/disk4_p3   /dev/rdisk/disk4_p3
disk   5 64000/0xfa00/0x2  esdisk  CLAIMED DEVICE  HP 73.4GMAS3735NC
                /dev/disk/disk5      /dev/rdisk/disk5
                /dev/disk/disk5_p1   /dev/rdisk/disk5_p1
                /dev/disk/disk5_p2   /dev/rdisk/disk5_p2
                /dev/disk/disk5_p3   /dev/rdisk/disk5_p3
```

The old-style device names are still around in the **/dsk** and **/rdsk** directories, and you can continue to use them if you wish—at least for now. Run **ioscan -m dsf** to see the current mapping between old- and new-style device names.

```
hp-ux$ ioscan -m dsf
Persistent DSF6          Legacy DSF(s)
========================================
/dev/rdisk/disk3         /dev/rdsk/c0t0d0
/dev/rdisk/disk4         /dev/rdsk/c2t1d0
/dev/rdisk/disk4_p1      /dev/rdsk/c2t1d0s1
/dev/rdisk/disk4_p2      /dev/rdsk/c2t1d0s2
/dev/rdisk/disk4_p3      /dev/rdsk/c2t1d0s3
/dev/rdisk/disk5         /dev/rdsk/c2t0d0
/dev/rdisk/disk5_p1      /dev/rdsk/c2t0d0s1
/dev/rdisk/disk5_p2      /dev/rdsk/c2t0d0s2
/dev/rdisk/disk5_p3      /dev/rdsk/c2t0d0s3
```

Note that partitions are now abbreviated **p** instead of **s** in the Solaris manner (for "slice"). Unlike Solaris, HP-UX uses names such as **disk3** with no partition suffix to represent the entire disk. On Solaris systems, partition 2 represents the whole disk; on HP-UX, it's just another partition.

The system from which this example comes is Itanium-based and so has disk partitions. Other HP systems use logical volume management instead of partitioning.

Disk devices for AIX

AIX's **/dev/hdisk***X* and **/dev/rhdisk***X* paths are refreshingly simple. Disk names are unfortunately subject to change when the hardware configuration changes. However, most AIX disks will be under logical volume management, so the hardware device names are not that important. The logical volume manager writes a unique ID to each disk as part of the process of inducting it into a volume group. This labeling allows the system to sort out the disks automatically, so changes in device names are less troublesome than they might be on other systems.

You can run **lsdev -C -c disk** to see a list of the disks the system is aware of.

Formatting and bad block management

All hard disks come preformatted, and the factory formatting is at least as good as any formatting you can do in the field. It is best to avoid doing a low-level format if it's not required. Don't reformat new drives as a matter of course.

6. DSF = device special file

If you encounter read or write errors on a disk, first check for cabling, termination, and address problems, all of which can cause symptoms similar to those of a bad block. If after this procedure you are still convinced that the disk has defects, you might be better off replacing it with a new one rather than waiting long hours for a format to complete and hoping the problem doesn't come back.

The formatting process writes address information and timing marks on the platters to delineate each sector. It also identifies bad blocks, imperfections in the media that result in areas that cannot be reliably read or written. All modern disks have bad block management built in, so neither you nor the driver need to worry about managing defects. The drive firmware substitutes known-good blocks from an area of backup storage on the disk that is reserved for this purpose.

Bad blocks that manifest themselves after a disk has been formatted may or may not be handled automatically. If the drive believes that the affected data can be reliably reconstructed, the newly discovered defect may be mapped out on the fly and the data rewritten to a new location. For more serious or less clearly recoverable errors, the drive aborts the read or write operation and reports the error back to the host operating system.

ATA disks are usually not designed to be formatted outside the factory. However, you may be able to obtain formatting software from the manufacturer, usually for Windows. Make sure the software matches the drive you plan to format and follow the manufacturer's directions carefully.[7]

SCSI disks format themselves in response to a standard command that you send from the host computer. The procedure for sending this command varies from system to system. On PCs, you can often send the command from the SCSI controller's BIOS. To issue the SCSI format command from within the operating system, use the **sg_format** command on Linux, the **format** command on Solaris, and the **mediainit** command on HP-UX.

Various utilities let you verify the integrity of a disk by writing random patterns to it and then reading them back. Thorough tests take a long time (hours) and unfortunately seem to be of little prognostic value. Unless you suspect that a disk is bad and are unable to simply replace it (or you bill by the hour), you should skip these tests. Barring that, let the tests run overnight. Don't be concerned about "wearing out" a disk with overuse or aggressive testing. Enterprise-class disks are designed for constant activity.

ATA secure erase

Since 2000, PATA and SATA disks have implemented a "secure erase" command that overwrites the data on the disk by using a method the manufacturer has determined to be secure against recovery efforts. Secure erase is NIST-certified for

7. On the other hand, at $80 for a 1TB drive, why bother?

most needs. Under the U.S. Department of Defense categorization, it's approved for use at security levels less than "secret."

Why is this feature even needed? First, filesystems generally do no erasing of their own, so an **rm -rf** * of a disk's data leaves everything intact and recoverable with software tools. It's critically important to remember this fact when disposing of disks, whether their destination is eBay or the trash.

Second, even a manual rewrite of every sector on a disk may leave magnetic traces that are recoverable by a determined attacker with access to a laboratory. Secure erase performs as many overwrites as are needed to eliminate these shadow signals. Magnetic remnants won't be a serious concern for most sites, but it's always nice to know that you're not exporting your organization's confidential data to the world at large.

Finally, secure erase has the effect of resetting SSDs to their fully erased state. This reset may improve performance in cases in which the ATA TRIM command (the command to erase a block) cannot be issued, either because the filesystem used on the SSD does not know to issue it or because the SSD is connected through a host adapter or RAID interface that does not propagate TRIM.

Unfortunately, UNIX support for sending the secure erase command remains elusive. At this point, your best bet is to reconnect drives to a Windows or Linux system for erasure. DOS software for secure erasing can be found at the Center of Magnetic Recording Research at tinyurl.com/2xoqqw. The MHDD utility also supports secure erase through its **fasterase** command—see tinyurl.com/2g6r98.

Under Linux, you can use the **hdparm** command:

```
$ sudo hdparm --user-master u --security-set-pass password /dev/sda[8]
$ sudo hdparm --user-master u --security-erase password /dev/sda
```

There is no analog in the SCSI world to ATA's secure erase command, but the SCSI "format unit" command described under *Formatting and bad block management* on page 226 is a reasonable alternative. Another option is to zero-out a drive's sectors with **dd if=/dev/zero of=***diskdevice* **bs=8k**.

Many systems have a **shred** utility that attempts to securely erase the contents of individual files. Unfortunately, it relies on the assumption that a file's blocks can be overwritten in place. This assumption is invalid in so many circumstances (any filesystem on any SSD, any logical volume that has snapshots, perhaps generally on ZFS) that **shred**'s general utility is questionable.

For sanitizing an entire PC system at once, another option is Darik's Boot and Nuke (dban.org). This tool runs from its own boot disk, so it's not a tool you'll use every day. It is quite handy for decommissioning old hardware, however.

8. The ATA secure erase command is password-protected to make it more difficult to access. Therefore, you must set the drive password before invoking the command. Don't bother to record the password, however; you can reset it at will. There is no danger of locking the drive.

hdparm: set disk and interface parameters (Linux)

Linux's **hdparm** command can do more than just send secure erase commands. It's a general way to interact with the firmware of SATA, IDE, and SAS hard disks. Among other things, **hdparm** can set drive power options, enable or disable noise reduction options, set the read-only flag, and print detailed drive information. A few of the options work on SCSI drives, too (under current Linux kernels).

The syntax is

> **hdparm** [*options*] *device*

Scores of options are available, but most are of interest only to driver and kernel developers. Table 8.3 shows a few that are relevant to administrators.

Table 8.3 Useful hdparm options for system administrators

Option	Function
-I[a]	Dumps lots of identifying and status information
-M *value*	Sets acoustic management options
-S *value*	Sets time delay for automatic standby (spin-down) mode
-y	Puts drive into standby mode immediately
-C	Queries the drive's current power management state
-T	Quick-tests interface bandwidth (no actual disk reads)
-t	Quick-tests overall platter-to-host sequential reads

a. This is an uppercase letter "eye" as in India.

Use **hdparm -I** to verify that each drive is using the fastest possible DMA transfer mode. **hdparm** lists all the disk's supported modes and marks the currently active mode with a star, as shown in the example below.

```
linux$ sudo hdparm -I /dev/sdf

/dev/sdf:

ATA device, with non-removable media
     Model Number:       WDC WD1001FALS-00J7B0
     Serial Number:      WD-WMATV0998277
     Firmware Revision:  05.00K05
     Transport:          Serial, SATA 1.0a, SATA II Extensions, SATA Rev 2.5
...
Capabilities:
     LBA, IORDY(can be disabled)
     Queue depth: 32
     Standby timer values: spec'd by Standard, with device specific minimum
     R/W multiple sector transfer: Max = 16  Current = 16
     Recommended acoustic management value: 128, current value: 254
     DMA: mdma0 mdma1 mdma2 udma0 udma1 udma2 udma3 udma4
          udma5 *udma6
```

```
        Cycle time: min=120ns recommended=120ns
   PIO: pio0 pio1 pio2 pio3 pio4
        Cycle time: no flow control=120ns  IORDY flow control=120ns
...
```

On any modern system, the optimal DMA mode should be selected by default; if this is not the case, check the BIOS and kernel logs for relevant information to determine why not.

Many drives offer acoustic management, which slows down the motion of the read/write head to attenuate the ticking or pinging sounds it makes. Drives that support acoustic management usually come with the feature turned on, but that's probably not what you want for production drives that live in a server room. Disable this feature with **hdparm -M 254**.

Most power consumed by hard disks goes to keep the platters spinning. If you have disks that see only occasional use and you can afford to delay access by 20 seconds or so as the motors are restarted, run **hdparm -S** to turn on the disks' internal power management feature. The argument to **-S** sets the idle time after which the drive enters standby mode and turns off the motor. It's a one-byte value, so the encoding is somewhat nonlinear. For example, values between 1 and 240 are in multiples of 5 seconds, and values from 241 to 251 are in units of 30 minutes. **hdparm** shows you its interpretation of the value when you run it; it's faster to guess, adjust, and repeat than to look up the detailed coding rules.

hdparm includes a simple drive performance test to help evaluate the impact of configuration changes. The **-T** option reads from the drive's cache and indicates the speed of data transfer on the bus, independent of throughput from the physical disk media. The **-t** option reads from the physical platters. As you might expect, physical reads are a lot slower.

```
$ sudo /sbin/hdparm -Tt /dev/hdb

/dev/sdf:
    Timing cached reads:   2092 MB in  2.00 seconds = 1046.41 MB/sec
    Timing buffered disk reads:  304 MB in  3.00 seconds = 101.30 MB/sec
```

100 MB/s or so is about the limit of today's mass-market 1TB drives, so these results (and the information shown by **hdparm -I** above) confirm that the drive is correctly configured.

Hard disk monitoring with SMART

Hard disks are fault-tolerant systems that use error-correction coding and intelligent firmware to hide their imperfections from the host operating system. In some cases, an uncorrectable error that the drive is forced to report to the OS is merely the latest event in a long crescendo of correctable but inauspicious problems. It would be nice to know about those omens before the crisis occurs.

ATA devices, including SATA drives, implement a detailed form of status reporting that is sometimes predictive of drive failures. This standard, called SMART for "self-monitoring, analysis, and reporting technology," exposes more than 50 operational parameters for investigation by the host computer.

The Google disk drive study mentioned on page 211 has been widely summarized in media reports as concluding that SMART data is not predictive of drive failure. That summary is not accurate. In fact, Google found that four SMART parameters were highly predictive of failure but that failure was not consistently preceded by changes in SMART values. Of failed drives in the study, 56% showed no change in the four most predictive parameters. On the other hand, predicting nearly half of failures sounds pretty good to us!

Those four sensitive SMART parameters are scan error count, reallocation count, off-line reallocation count, and number of sectors "on probation." Those values should all be zero. A nonzero value in these fields raises the likelihood of failure within 60 days by a factor of 39, 14, 21, or 16, respectively.

To take advantage of SMART data, you need software that queries your drives to obtain it and then judges whether the current readings are sufficiently ominous to warrant administrator notification. Unfortunately, reporting standards vary by drive manufacturer, so decoding isn't necessarily straightforward. Most SMART monitors collect baseline data and then look for sudden changes in the "bad" direction rather than interpreting absolute values. (According to the Google study, taking account of these "soft" SMART indicators in addition to the Big Four predicts 64% of all failures.)

The standard software for SMART wrangling on UNIX and Linux systems is the smartmontools package from smartmontools.sourceforge.net. It's installed by default on SUSE and Red Hat systems; on Ubuntu, you'll have to run **apt-get install smartmontools**. The package does run on Solaris systems if you build it from the source code.

The smartmontools package consists of a **smartd** daemon that monitors drives continuously and a **smartctl** command you can use for interactive queries or for scripting. The daemon has a single configuration file, normally **/etc/smartd.conf**, which is extensively commented and includes plenty of examples.

SCSI has its own system for out-of-band status reporting, but unfortunately the standard is much less granular in this respect than is SMART. The smartmontools attempt to include SCSI devices in their schema, but the predictive value of the SCSI data is less clear.

8.6 Disk partitioning

Partitioning and logical volume management are both ways of dividing up a disk (or pool of disks, in the case of LVM) into separate chunks of known size. All our example systems support logical volume management, but only Linux, Solaris, and sometimes HP-UX allow traditional partitioning.

You can put individual partitions under the control of a logical volume manager, but you can't partition a logical volume. Partitioning is the lowest possible level of disk management.

On Solaris, partitioning is required but essentially vestigial; ZFS hides it well enough that you may not even be aware that it's occurring. This section contains some general background information that may be useful to Solaris administrators, but from a procedural standpoint, the Solaris path diverges rather sharply from that of Linux, HP-UX, and AIX. Skip ahead to *ZFS: all your storage problems solved* on page 264 for details. (Or don't: **zpool create** *newpool newdevice* pretty much covers basic configuration.)

Both partitions and logical volumes make backups easier, prevent users from poaching each other's disk space, and confine potential damage from runaway programs. All systems have a root "partition" that includes / and most of the local host's configuration data. In theory, everything needed to bring the system up to single-user mode is part of the root partition. Various subdirectories (most commonly **/var**, **/usr**, **/tmp**, **/share**, and **/home**) may be broken out into their own partitions or volumes. Most systems also have at least one swap area.

Opinions differ on the best way to divide up disks, as do the defaults used by various systems. Here are some general points to guide you:

- It's a good idea to have a backup root device that you can boot to if something goes wrong with the normal root partition. Ideally, the backup root lives on a different disk from the normal root so that it can protect against both hardware problems and corruption. However, even a backup root on the same disk has some value.[9]
- Verify that you can boot from your backup root. The procedure is often nontrivial. You may need special boot-time arguments to the kernel and minor configuration tweaks within the alternate root itself to get everything working smoothly.
- Since the root partition is often duplicated, it should also be small so that having two copies doesn't consume an unreasonable amount of disk space. This is the major reason that **/usr** is often a separate volume; it holds the bulk of the system's libraries and data.
- Putting **/tmp** on a separate filesystem limits temporary files to a finite size and saves you from having to back them up. Some systems use a memory-based filesystem to hold **/tmp** for performance reasons. The memory-based filesystems are still backed by swap space, so they work well in a broad range of situations.

9. Solaris and HP-UX even have "dynamic root disk" systems to facilitate the maintenance and use of multiple roots. See the man pages for **beadm** or **lucreate** for Solaris and **drd** for HP-UX.

- Since log files are kept in **/var**, it's a good idea for **/var** to be a separate disk partition. Leaving **/var** as part of a small root partition makes it easy to fill the root and bring the machine to a halt.
- It's useful to put users' home directories on a separate partition or volume. Even if the root partition is corrupted or destroyed, user data has a good chance of remaining intact. Conversely, the system can continue to operate even after a user's misguided shell script fills up **/home**.
- Splitting swap space among several physical disks increases performance. This technique works for filesystems, too; put the busy ones on different disks. See page 1129 for notes on this subject.
- As you add memory to your machine, you should also add swap space. See page 1124 for more information about virtual memory.
- Backups of a partition may be simplified if the entire partition can fit on one piece of media. See page 294.
- Try to cluster quickly-changing information on a few partitions that are backed up frequently.

Traditional partitioning

Systems that allow partitions implement them by writing a "label" at the beginning of the disk to define the range of blocks included in each partition. The exact details vary; the label must often coexist with other startup information (such as a boot block), and it often contains extra information such as a name or unique ID that identifies the disk as a whole. Under Windows, the label is known as the MBR, or master boot record.

The device driver responsible for representing the disk reads the label and uses the partition table to calculate the physical location of each partition. Typically, one or two device files represent each partition (one block device and one character device; Linux has only block devices). Also, a separate set of device files represents the disk as a whole.

Solaris calls partitions "slices," or more accurately, it calls them slices when they are implemented with a Solaris-style label and partitions when they are implemented with a Windows-style MBR. Slice 2 includes the entire expanse of the disk, illustrating the rather frightening truth that more than one slice can claim a given disk block. Perhaps the word "slices" was selected because "partition" suggests a simple division, whereas slices can overlap. The terms are otherwise interchangeable.

Despite the universal availability of logical volume managers, some situations still require or benefit from traditional partitioning.

- On PC hardware, the boot disk must have a partition table. Most systems require MBR partitioning (see *Windows-style partitioning*, next), but

Itanium systems require GPT partitions (page 235). Data disks may remain unpartitioned.

See page 85 for more information about dual booting with Windows.

- Installing a Windows-style MBR makes the disk comprehensible to Windows, even if the contents of the individual partitions are not. If you want to interoperate with Windows (say, by dual booting), you'll need to install a Windows MBR. But even if you have no particular ambitions along those lines, it may be helpful to consider the ubiquity of Windows and the likelihood that your disk will one day come in contact with it.

  Current versions of Windows are well behaved and would never *dream* of writing randomly to a disk they can't decipher. However, they will certainly suggest this course of action to any administrator who logs in. The dialog box even sports a helpful "OK, mess up this disk!" button.[10] Nothing bad will happen unless someone makes a mistake, but safety is a structural and organizational process.

- Partitions have a defined location on the disk, and they guarantee locality of reference. Logical volumes do not (at least, not by default). In most cases, this fact isn't terribly important. However, short seeks are faster than long seeks, and the throughput of a disk's outer cylinders (those containing the lowest-numbered blocks) can exceed the throughput of its inner cylinders by 30% or more.[11] For situations in which every ounce of performance counts, you can use partitioning to gain an extra edge. (You can always use logical volume management *inside* partitions to regain some of the lost flexibility.)

- RAID systems (see page 237) use disks or partitions of matched size. A given RAID implementation may accept entities of different sizes, but it will probably only use the block ranges that all devices have in common. Rather than letting extra space go to waste, you can isolate it in a separate partition. If you do this, however, you should use the spare partition for data that is infrequently accessed; otherwise, use of the partition will degrade the performance of the RAID array.

Windows-style partitioning

The Windows MBR occupies a single 512-byte disk block, most of which is consumed by boot code. Only enough space remains to define four partitions. These are termed "primary" partitions because they are defined directly in the MBR.

You can define one of the primary partitions to be an "extended" partition, which means that it contains its own subsidiary partition table. The extended partition is a true partition, and it occupies a defined physical extent on the disk. The subsidiary partition table is stored at the beginning of that partition's data.

10. OK, OK, it probably just says "Format" or "OK," but this is what it *should* say.
11. Using only the outer cylinders of a disk to improve performance is known as "short stroking," the stroke in question being the travel of the head armature.

Partitions that you create within the extended partition are called secondary partitions. They are proper subsets of the extended partition.

Keep the following rules of thumb in mind when setting up Windows-partitioned disks. The first is an actual rule. The others exist only because certain BIOSes, boot blocks, or operating systems may require them.

- There can be only one extended partition on a disk.
- The extended partition should be the last of the partitions defined in the MBR; no primary partitions should come after it.
- Some older operating systems don't like to be installed in secondary partitions. To avoid trouble, stick to primary partitions for OS installations.

The Windows partitioning system lets one partition be marked "active." Boot loaders look for the active partition and try to load the operating system from it.

Each partition also has a one-byte type attribute that is supposed to indicate the partition's contents. Generally, the codes represent either filesystem types or operating systems. These codes are not centrally assigned, but over time some common conventions have evolved. They are summarized by Andries E. Brouwer at tinyurl.com/part-types.

The MS-DOS command that partitioned hard disks was called **fdisk**. Most operating systems that support Windows-style partitions have adopted this name for their own partitioning commands, but there are many variations among **fdisk**s. Windows itself has moved on: the command-line tool in recent versions is called **diskpart**. Windows also has a partitioning GUI that's available through the Disk Management plug-in of **mmc**.

It does not matter whether you partition a disk with Windows or some other operating system. The end result is the same.

GPT: GUID partition tables

Intel's extensible firmware interface (EFI) project aims to replace the rickety conventions of PC BIOSes with a more modern and functional architecture.[12] Although systems that use full EFI firmware are still uncommon, EFI's partitioning scheme has gained widespread support among operating systems. The main reason for this success is that MBR does not support disks larger than 2TB in size. Since 2TB disks are already widely available, this problem has become a matter of some urgency.

The EFI partitioning scheme, known as a "GUID partition table" or GPT, removes the obvious weaknesses of MBR. It defines only one type of partition, and you can create arbitrarily many of them. Each partition has a type specified by a 16-byte ID code (the globally unique ID, or GUID) that requires no central arbitration.

12. EFI has more recently become UEFI, a "unified" EFI effort supported by multiple vendors. However, EFI remains the more common term in general use. UEFI and EFI are essentially interchangeable.

Significantly, GPT retains primitive compatibility with MBR-based systems by dragging along an MBR as the first block of the partition table. This “fakie” MBR makes the disk look like it’s occupied by one large MBR partition (at least, up to the 2TB limit of MBR). It isn’t useful per se, but the hope is that the decoy MBR may at least prevent naïve systems from attempting to reformat the disk.

Versions of Windows from the Vista era forward support GPT disks for data, but only systems with EFI firmware can boot from them. Linux and its GRUB boot loader have fared better: GPT disks are supported by the OS and bootable on any system. Intel-based Mac OS systems use both EFI and GPT partitioning. Solaris understands GPT partitioning, and ZFS uses it by default. However, Solaris boot disks cannot use GPT partitioning.

Although GPT has already been well accepted by operating system kernels, its support among disk management utilities is still spotty. GPT remains a “bleeding edge” format. There is no compelling reason to use it on disks that don’t require it (that is, disks 2TB in size or smaller).

Linux partitioning

Linux systems give you several options for partitioning. **fdisk** is a basic command-line partitioning tool. GNU’s **parted** is a fancier command-line tool that understands several label formats (including Solaris’s native one) and can move and resize partitions in addition to simply creating and deleting them. A GUI version, **gparted**, runs under GNOME. Another possibility is **cfdisk**, which is a nice, terminal-based alternative to **fdisk**.

parted and **gparted** can theoretically resize several types of filesystems along with the partitions that contain them, but the project home page describes this feature as “buggy and unreliable.” Filesystem-specific utilities are likely to do a better job of adjusting filesystems, but unfortunately, **parted** does not have a “resize the partition but not the filesystem” command. Go back to **fdisk** if this is what you need.

In general, we recommend **gparted** over **parted**. Both are simple, but **gparted** lets you specify the size of the partitions you want instead of specifying the starting and ending block ranges. For partitioning the boot disk, most distributions’ graphical installers are the best option since they typically suggest a partitioning plan that works well with that particular distribution’s layout.

Solaris partitioning

ZFS automatically labels disks for you, applying a GPT partition table. However, you can also partition disks manually with the **format** command. On x86 systems, an **fdisk** command is also available. Both interfaces are menu driven and relatively straightforward.

format gives you a nice list of disks to choose from, while **fdisk** requires you to specify the disk on the command line. Fortunately, **format** has an **fdisk** command that runs **fdisk** as a subprocess, so you can use **format** as a kind of wrapper to help you pick the right disk.

Solaris understands three partitioning schemes: Windows MBR, GPT, and old-style Solaris partition tables, known as SMI. You must use MBR or SMI for the boot disk, depending on the hardware and whether you are running Solaris or OpenSolaris. For now, it's probably best to stick to these options for all manually partitioned disks under 2TB.

HP-UX partitioning

HP uses disk partitioning only on Itanium (Integrity) boot disks, on which a GPT partition table and an EFI boot partition are required. The **idisk** command prints and creates partition tables. Rather than being an interactive partitioning utility, it reads a partitioning plan from a file or from standard input and uses that to construct the partition table.

An **idisk** partitioning specification is mercifully straightforward. The first line contains only a number that specifies the number of partitions to create. Each following line contains a partition type (EFI, HPUX, HPDUMP, or HPSP for swap), a space character, and a size specification such as 128MB or 100%. If a percentage is used, it is interpreted relative to the space remaining on the drive after the preceding partitions have been allocated.

Storage

8.7 RAID: REDUNDANT ARRAYS OF INEXPENSIVE DISKS

Even with backups, the consequences of a disk failure on a server can be disastrous. RAID, "redundant arrays of inexpensive disks," is a system that distributes or replicates data across multiple disks.[13] RAID not only helps avoid data loss but also minimizes the downtime associated with hardware failures (often to zero) and potentially increases performance.

RAID can be implemented by dedicated hardware that presents a group of hard disks to the operating system as a single composite drive. It can also be implemented simply by the operating system's reading or writing multiple disks according to the rules of RAID.

Software vs. hardware RAID

Because the disks themselves are always the most significant bottleneck in a RAID implementation, there is no reason to assume that a hardware-based implementation of RAID will necessarily be faster than a software- or OS-based implementation. Hardware RAID has been predominant in the past for two main reasons: lack of software alternatives (no direct OS support for RAID) and hardware's ability to buffer writes in some form of nonvolatile memory.

13. RAID is sometimes glossed as "redundant arrays of independent disks," too. Both versions are historically accurate.

The latter feature does improve performance because it makes writes appear to complete instantaneously. It also protects against a potential corruption issue called the "RAID 5 write hole," which we describe in more detail starting on page 241. But beware: many of the common "RAID cards" sold for PCs have no non-volatile memory at all; they are really just glorified SATA interfaces with some RAID software onboard. RAID implementations on PC motherboards fall into this category as well. You're really much better off using the RAID features in Linux or OpenSolaris on these systems.

We recently experienced a disk controller failure on an important production server. Although the data was replicated across several physical drives, a faulty hardware RAID controller destroyed the data on all disks. A lengthy and ugly tape restore process ensued, and it was more than two months before the server had completely recovered. The rebuilt server now relies on the kernel's software to manage its RAID environment, removing the possibility of another RAID controller failure.

RAID levels

RAID can do two basic things. First, it can improve performance by "striping" data across multiple drives, thus allowing several drives to work simultaneously to supply or absorb a single data stream. Second, it can replicate data across multiple drives, decreasing the risk associated with a single failed disk.

Replication assumes two basic forms: mirroring, in which data blocks are reproduced bit-for-bit on several different drives, and parity schemes, in which one or more drives contain an error-correcting checksum of the blocks on the remaining data drives. Mirroring is faster but consumes more disk space. Parity schemes are more disk-space-efficient but have lower performance.

RAID is traditionally described in terms of "levels" that specify the exact details of the parallelism and redundancy implemented by an array. The term is perhaps misleading because "higher" levels are not necessarily "better." The levels are simply different configurations; use whichever versions suit your needs.

In the following illustrations, numbers identify stripes and the letters a, b, and c identify data blocks within a stripe. Blocks marked p and q are parity blocks.

- "Linear mode," also known as JBOD (for "just a bunch of disks") is not even a real RAID level. And yet, every RAID controller seems to implement it. JBOD concatenates the block addresses of multiple drives to create a single, larger virtual drive. It provides no data redundancy or performance benefit. These days, JBOD functionality is best achieved through a logical volume manager rather than a RAID controller.

- RAID level 0 is used strictly to increase performance. It combines two or more drives of equal size, but instead of stacking them end-to-end, it stripes data alternately among the disks in the pool. Sequential reads and writes are therefore spread among several disks, decreasing write and access times.

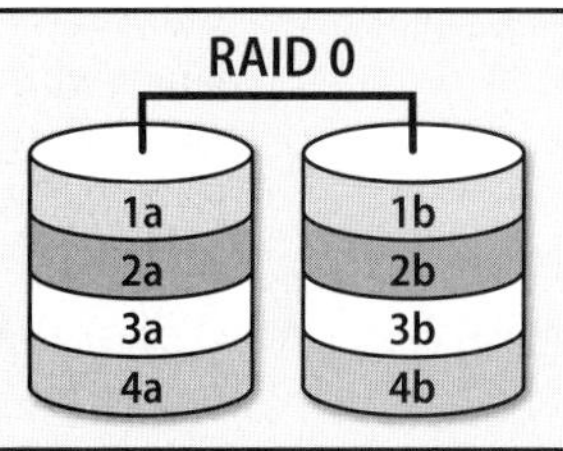

  Note that RAID 0 has reliability characteristics that are significantly *inferior* to separate disks. A two-drive array has roughly double the annual failure rate of a single drive, and so on.

- RAID level 1 is colloquially known as mirroring. Writes are duplicated to two or more drives simultaneously. This arrangement makes writes slightly slower than they would be on a single drive. However, it offers read speeds comparable to RAID 0 because reads can be farmed out among the several duplicate disk drives.

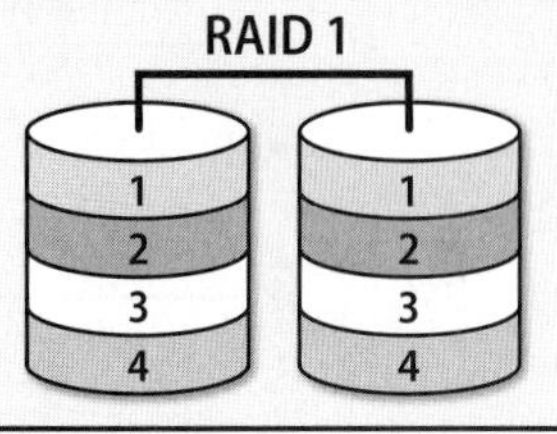

- RAID levels 1+0 and 0+1 are stripes of mirror sets or mirrors of stripe sets. Logically, they are concatenations of RAID 0 and RAID 1, but many controllers and software implementations provide direct support for them. The goal of both modes is to simultaneously obtain the performance of RAID 0 and the redundancy of RAID 1.

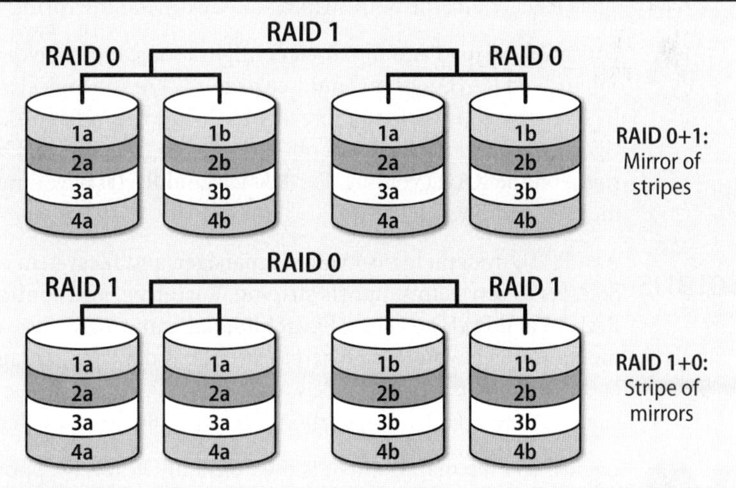

- RAID level 5 stripes both data and parity information, adding redundancy while simultaneously improving read performance. In addition, RAID 5 is more efficient in its use of disk space than is RAID 1. If there are N drives in an array (at least three are required), N–1 of them can store data. The space-efficiency of RAID 5 is therefore at least 67%, whereas that of mirroring cannot be higher than 50%.

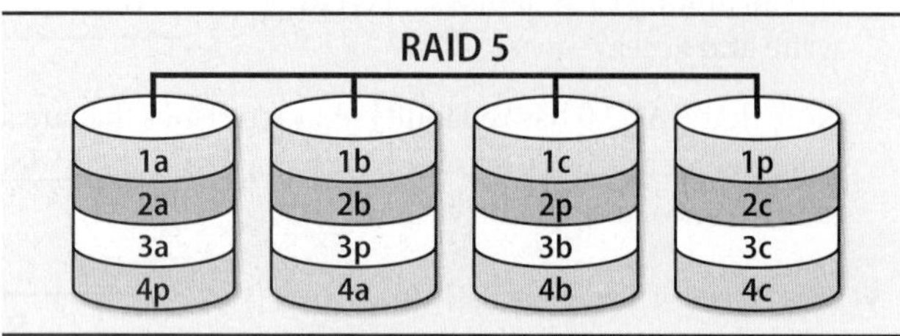

- RAID level 6 is similar to RAID 5 with two parity disks. A RAID 6 array can withstand the complete failure of two drives without losing data.

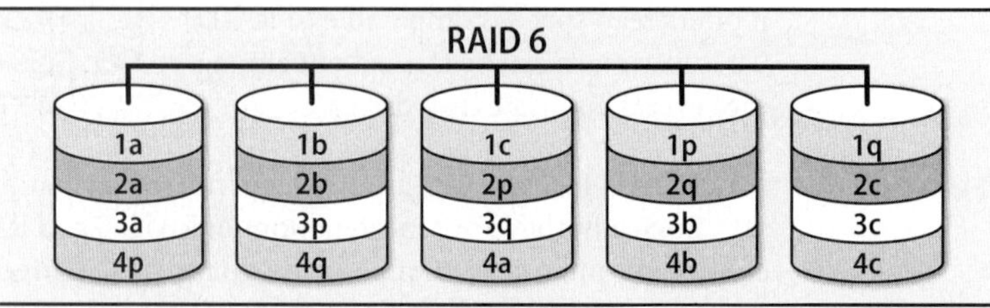

RAID levels 2, 3, and 4 are defined but are rarely deployed. Logical volume managers usually include both striping (RAID 0) and mirroring (RAID 1) features.

For simple striped and mirrored configurations, Linux gives you a choice of using a dedicated RAID system (**md**; see page 242) or the logical volume manager. The LVM approach is perhaps more flexible, while the **md** approach may be a bit more rigorously predictable. If you opt for **md**, you can still use LVM to manage the space on the RAID volume. For RAID 5 and RAID 6, you must use **md** to implement software RAID.

As a RAID system, logical volume manager, and filesystem all rolled into one, Solaris's ZFS system supports striping, mirroring, and configurations similar to RAID 5 and RAID 6. The ZFS architecture puts mirroring and parity arrangements on the lowest level, whereas striping is done per storage pool (one level up) and is automatic. This is a nice way to arrange the features because it preserves the clarity of the RAID configuration. See page 264 for more details on ZFS.

Logical volume management is the extent of OS-level support for RAID on HP-UX and AIX. (HP even makes you purchase the mirroring feature separately, although it is bundled in certain enterprise configurations.) If you want a parity-based system, you'll need some additional hardware. AIX does come with tools for administering RAID hardware already integrated, however: see Disk Array under Devices in SMIT.

Disk failure recovery

The Google disk failure study cited on page 211 should be pretty convincing evidence of the need for some form of storage redundancy in most production environments. At an 8% annual failure rate, your organization needs only 150 hard disks in service to expect an average of one failure per month.

JBOD and RAID 0 modes are of no help when hardware problems occur; you must recover your data manually from backups. Other forms of RAID enter a degraded mode in which the offending devices are marked as faulty. The RAID arrays continue to function normally from the perspective of storage clients, although perhaps at reduced performance.

Bad disks must be swapped out for new ones as soon as possible to restore redundancy to the array. A RAID 5 array or two-disk RAID 1 array can only tolerate the failure of a single device. Once that failure has occurred, the array is vulnerable to a second failure.

The specifics of the process are usually pretty simple. You replace the failed disk with another of similar or greater size, then tell the RAID implementation to replace the old disk with the new one. What follows is an extended period during which the parity or mirror information is rewritten to the new, blank disk. Often, this is an overnight operation. The array remains available to clients during this phase, but performance is likely to be very poor.

To limit downtime and the vulnerability of the array to a second failure, most RAID implementations let you designate one or more disks as "hot" spares. When a failure occurs, the faulted disk is automatically swapped for a spare, and the process of resynchronizing the array begins immediately. Where supported, hot spares should be used as a matter of course.

Drawbacks of RAID 5

RAID 5 is a popular configuration, but it has some weaknesses, too. The following issues apply to RAID 6 also, but for simplicity we frame the discussion in terms of RAID 5.

See Chapter 10, Backups, for general advice about backing up the system.

First, it's critically important to note that RAID 5 does not replace regular off-line backups. It protects the system against the failure of one disk—that's it. It does not protect against the accidental deletion of files. It does not protect against controller failures, fires, hackers, or any number of other hazards.

Second, RAID 5 isn't known for its great write performance. RAID 5 writes data blocks to N–1 disks and parity blocks to the Nth disk.[14] Whenever a random block

14. Parity data is distributed among all the drives in the array; each stripe has its parity stored on a different drive. Since there's no dedicated parity disk, it's unlikely that any single disk will act as a bottleneck.

is written, at least one data block and the parity block for that stripe must be updated. Furthermore, the RAID system doesn't know what the new parity block should contain until it has read the old parity block and the old data. Each random write therefore expands into four operations: two reads and two writes. (Sequential writes may fare better if the implementation is smart.)

Finally, RAID 5 is vulnerable to corruption in certain circumstances. Its incremental updating of parity data is more efficient than reading the entire stripe and recalculating the stripe's parity based on the original data. On the other hand, it means that at no point is parity data ever validated or recalculated. If any block in a stripe should fall out of sync with the parity block, that fact will never become evident in normal use; reads of the data blocks will still return the correct data.

Only when a disk fails does the problem become apparent. The parity block will likely have been rewritten many times since the occurrence of the original desynchronization. Therefore, the reconstructed data block on the replacement disk will consist of essentially random data.

This kind of desynchronization between data and parity blocks isn't all that unlikely, either. Disk drives are not transactional devices. Without an additional layer of safeguards, there is no simple way to guarantee that either two blocks or zero blocks on two different disks will be properly updated. It's quite possible for a crash, power failure, or communication problem at the wrong moment to create data/parity skew.

This problem is known as the RAID 5 "write hole," and it has received increasing attention over the last five years or so. One helpful resource is the web site of the Battle Against Any Raid Five,[15] baarf.org, which points to a variety of editorials on the subject. You'll have to decide for yourself whether the problem is significant or overblown. (We lean more toward "significant.")

The implementors of Solaris's ZFS filesystem claim that because ZFS uses variable-width stripes, it is immune to the RAID 5 write hole. That's also why ZFS calls its RAID implementation RAID-Z instead of RAID 5, though in practice the concept is similar.

Another potential solution is "scrubbing," validating parity blocks one by one while the array is relatively idle. Many RAID implementations include some form of scrubbing function.

mdadm: Linux software RAID

The standard software RAID implementation for Linux is called **md**, the "multiple disks" driver. It's front-ended by the **mdadm** command. **md** supports all the RAID configurations listed above as well as RAID 4. An earlier system known as **raidtools** is no longer used.

15. Slogan: "Enough is enough. You can either join BAARF. Or not."

The following example scenario configures a RAID 5 array composed of three identical 500GB hard disks. Although **md** can use raw disks as components, we prefer to give each disk a partition table for consistency, so we start by running **gparted**, creating an MBR partition table on each disk (**gparted** refers to this as the "msdos" style of partition table), and assigning all the disk's space to a single partition of type "unformatted" (which is unfortunately about as close as you can get to the actual use). It's not strictly necessary to set the partition type, but it's a useful reminder to anyone who might inspect the table later. There is also a "raid" flag bit you can set on a partition, although **gparted** doesn't make this easy: you must create the partition, execute the pending operations, and then go back to the new partition and edit its flags.

The following command builds a RAID 5 array from our three SCSI partitions:

```
linux$ sudo mdadm --create /dev/md0 --level=5 --raid-devices=3 /dev/sdb1
    /dev/sdc1 /dev/sdd1
mdadm: array /dev/md0 started.
```

The virtual file **/proc/mdstat** always contains a summary of **md**'s status and the status of all the system's RAID arrays. It is especially useful to keep an eye on the **/proc/mdstat** file after adding a new disk or replacing a faulty drive. (**watch cat /proc/mdstat** is a handy idiom.)

```
linux$ cat /proc/mdstat
Personalities : [linear] [multipath] [raid0] [raid1] [raid6] [raid5] [raid4] [raid10]
md0 : active raid5 sdd1[3] sdc1[1] sdb1[0]
      1023404544 blocks level 5, 64k chunk, algorithm 2 [3/2] [UU_]
      [>....................]  recovery =  0.1% (672640/511702272) finish=75.9min
    speed=112106K/sec

unused devices: <none>
```

The **md** system does not keep track of which blocks in an array have been used, so it must manually synchronize all the parity blocks with their corresponding data blocks. **md** calls the operation a "recovery" since it's essentially the same procedure used when you swap out a bad hard disk. It can take hours on a large array.

Some helpful notifications appear in the **/var/log/messages** file, too.

```
md0:RAID5 conf printout:
--- rd:3 wd:2
disk 0, o:1, dev:sdb1
disk 1, o:1, dev:sdc1
disk 2, o:1, dev:sdd1
md: recovery of RAID array md0
md: minimum _guaranteed_ speed: 1000 KB/sec/disk.
md: using max available idle IO bandwidth (but not more than 200000 KB/sec)
for recovery.
md: using 128k window, over a total of 511702272 blocks.
```

The initial creation command also serves to "activate" the array (make it available for use), but on subsequent reboots it may be necessary to activate the array as a separate step, usually out of a startup script. Red Hat and SUSE include sample startup scripts for RAID, and Ubuntu starts arrays by default.

mdadm does not technically require a configuration file, although it will use a configuration file if one is supplied (typically, **/etc/mdadm.conf**). We strongly recommend the use of a configuration file. It documents the RAID configuration in a standard way, thus giving administrators an obvious place to look for information when problems occur. The alternative to the use of a configuration file is to specify the configuration on the command line each time the array is activated.

mdadm --detail --scan dumps the current RAID setup into a configuration file. Unfortunately, the configuration it prints is not quite complete. The following commands build a complete configuration file for our example setup:

```
linux$ sudo sh -c 'echo DEVICE /dev/sdb1 /dev/sdc1 /dev/sdd1 >
    /etc/mdadm.conf'
linux$ sudo sh -c 'mdadm --detail --scan >> /etc/mdadm.conf'
linux$ cat /etc/mdadm.conf
DEVICE /dev/sdb1 /dev/sdc1 /dev/sdd1
ARRAY /dev/md0 level=raid5 num-devices=3 metadata=00.90 spares=1
    UUID=f18070c5:e2b6aa18:e368bf24:bd0fce41
```

mdadm can now read this file at startup or shutdown to easily manage the array. To enable the array at startup by using the freshly created **/etc/mdadm.conf**, we would execute

```
$ sudo mdadm -As /dev/md0
```

To stop the array manually, we would use the command

```
$ sudo mdadm -S /dev/md0
```

Once you've set up the **mdadm.conf** file, print it out and tape it to the side of the server. It's not always trivial to reconstruct the components of a RAID setup when something goes wrong.

mdadm has a **--monitor** mode in which it runs continuously as a daemon process and notifies you by email when problems are detected on a RAID array. Use this feature! To set it up, add a MAILADDR line to your **mdadm.conf** file to specify the recipient to whom warnings should be sent, and arrange for the monitor daemon to run at boot time. All our example distributions have an **init** script that does this for you, but the names and procedures for enabling are slightly different.

```
ubuntu$ sudo update-rc.d mdadm enable
suse$ sudo chkconfig -s mdadmd on
redhat$ sudo chkconfig mdmonitor on
```

What happens when a disk actually fails? Let's find out! **mdadm** offers a handy option that simulates a failed disk.

```
$ sudo mdadm /dev/md0 -f /dev/sdc1
mdadm: set /dev/sdc1 faulty in /dev/md0

$ sudo tail /var/log/messages
May 30 16:14:55 harp kernel: raid5: Disk failure on sdc, disabling device.
     Operation continuing on 2 devices
kernel: RAID5 conf printout:
kernel:  --- rd:3 wd:2 fd:1
kernel:  disk 0, o:1, dev:sdb1
kernel:  disk 1, o:0, dev:sdc1
kernel:  disk 2, o:1, dev:sdd1
kernel: RAID5 conf printout:
kernel:  --- rd:3 wd:2 fd:1
kernel:  disk 0, o:1, dev:sdb1
kernel:  disk 2, o:1, dev:sdd1

$ cat /proc/mdstat
Personalities : [raid6] [raid5] [raid4] [linear] [multipath] [raid0] [raid1] [raid10]
md0 : active raid5 sdb1[0] sdd1[2] sdc1[3](F)
        1023404544 blocks level 5, 64k chunk, algorithm 2 [3/2] [U_U]

unused devices: <none>
```

Because RAID 5 is a redundant configuration, the array continues to function in degraded mode, so users will not necessarily be aware of the problem.

To remove the drive from the RAID configuration, use **mdadm -r**:

```
$ sudo mdadm /dev/md0 -r /dev/sdc1
mdadm: hot removed /dev/sdc1
```

Once the disk has been logically removed, you can shut down the system and replace the drive. Hot-swappable drive hardware lets you make the change without turning off the system or rebooting.

If your RAID components are raw disks, you should replace them with an identical drive only. Partition-based components can be replaced with any partition of similar size, although for bandwidth matching it's best if the drive hardware is similar. (If your RAID configuration is built on top of partitions, you must run a partitioning utility to define the partitions appropriately before adding the replacement disk to the array.)

In our example, the failure is just simulated, so we can add the drive back to the array without replacing any hardware:

```
$ sudo mdadm /dev/md0 -a /dev/sdc1
mdadm: hot added /dev/sdc1
```

md will immediately start to rebuild the array. As always, you can see its progress in **/proc/mdstat**. A rebuild may take hours, so consider this fact in your disaster recovery plans.

8.8 Logical volume management

Imagine a world in which you don't know exactly how large a partition needs to be. Six months after creating the partition, you discover that it is much too large, but that a neighboring partition doesn't have enough space… Sound familiar? A logical volume manager lets you reallocate space dynamically from the greedy partition to the needy partition.

Logical volume management is essentially a supercharged and abstracted version of disk partitioning. It groups individual storage devices into "volume groups." The blocks in a volume group can then be allocated to "logical volumes," which are represented by block device files and act like disk partitions.

However, logical volumes are more flexible and powerful than disk partitions. Here are some of the magical operations a volume manager lets you carry out:

- Move logical volumes among different physical devices
- Grow and shrink logical volumes on the fly
- Take copy-on-write "snapshots" of logical volumes
- Replace on-line drives without interrupting service
- Incorporate mirroring or striping in your logical volumes

The components of a logical volume can be put together in various ways. Concatenation keeps each device's physical blocks together and lines the devices up one after another. Striping interleaves the components so that adjacent virtual blocks are actually spread over multiple physical disks. By reducing single-disk bottlenecks, striping can often provide higher bandwidth and lower latency.

LVM implementations

All our example systems support logical volume management, and with the exception of Solaris's ZFS, the systems are all quite similar.

In addition to ZFS, Solaris supports a previous generation of LVM called the Solaris Volume Manager, formerly Solstice DiskSuite. This volume manager is still supported, but new deployments should use ZFS.

Linux's volume manager, called LVM2, is essentially a clone of HP-UX's volume manager, which is itself based on software by Veritas. The commands for the two systems are essentially identical, but we show examples for both systems because their ancillary commands are somewhat different. AIX's system has similar abstractions but different command syntax. Table 8.4 illustrates the parallels among these three systems.

In addition to commands that deal with volume groups and logical volumes, Table 8.4 also shows a couple of commands that relate to "physical volumes." A physical volume is a storage device that has had an LVM label applied; applying such a label is the first step to using the device through the LVM. Linux and HP-UX use **pvcreate** to apply a label, but AIX's **mkvg** does it automatically. In addition to bookkeeping information, the label includes a unique ID to identify the device.

Table 8.4 Comparison of LVM commands

	Operation	Linux	HP-UX	AIX
Physical vol	Create	**pvcreate**	**pvcreate**	–
	Inspect	**pvdisplay**	**pvdisplay**	**lspv**
	Modify	**pvchange**	**pvchange**	**chpv**
	Check	**pvck**	**pvck**	–
Volume group	Create	**vgcreate**	**vgcreate**	**mkvg**
	Modify	**vgchange**	**vgchange**	**chvg**
	Extend	**vgextend**	**vgextend**	**extendvg**
	Inspect	**vgdisplay**	**vgdisplay**	**lsvg**
	Check	**vgck**	–	–
	Enable	**vgscan**	**vgscan**	**varyonvg**
Logical vol	Create	**lvcreate**	**lvcreate**	**mklv**
	Modify	**lvchange**	**lvchange**	**chlv**
	Resize	**lvresize**	**lvextend, lvreduce**	**extendlv**
	Inspect	**lvdisplay**	**lvdisplay**	**lslv**

"Physical volume" is a somewhat misleading term because physical volumes need not have a direct correspondence to physical devices. They *can* be disks, but they can also be disk partitions or RAID arrays. The LVM doesn't care.

Linux logical volume management

You can control Linux's LVM implementation (LVM2) with either a large group of simple commands (the ones illustrated in Table 8.4) or with the single **lvm** command and its various subcommands. These options are for all intents and purposes identical; in fact, the individual commands are really just links to **lvm**, which looks to see how it's been called to know how to behave. **man lvm** is a good introduction to the system and its tools.

A Linux LVM configuration proceeds in a few distinct phases:

- Creating (defining, really) and initializing physical volumes
- Adding the physical volumes to a volume group
- Creating logical volumes on the volume group

LVM commands start with letters that make it clear at which level of abstraction they operate: **pv** commands manipulate physical volumes, **vg** commands manipulate volume groups, and **lv** commands manipulate logical volumes. A few commands with the prefix **lvm** (e.g., **lvmchange**) operate on the system as a whole.

In the following example, we set up the **/dev/md0** RAID 5 device we created on page 243 for use with LVM and create a logical volume. Since striping and redundancy have already been addressed by the underlying RAID configuration, we won't make use of the corresponding LVM2 features, although they exist.

```
$ sudo pvcreate /dev/md0
Physical volume "/dev/md0" successfully created
```

Our physical device is now ready to be added to a volume group:

```
$ sudo vgcreate DEMO /dev/md0
Volume group "DEMO" successfully created
```

Although we're using only a single physical device in this example, we could of course add additional devices. In this case, it would be strange to add anything but another RAID 5 array since there is no benefit to partial redundancy. DEMO is an arbitrary name that we've selected.

To step back and examine our handiwork, we use the **vgdisplay** command:

```
$ sudo vgdisplay DEMO
--- Volume group ---
VG Name                 DEMO
System ID
Format                  lvm2
Metadata Areas          1
Metadata Sequence No    1
VG Access               read/write
VG Status               resizable
MAX LV                  0
Cur LV                  0
Open LV                 0
Max PV                  0
Cur PV                  1
Act PV                  1
VG Size                 975.99 GB
PE Size                 4.00 MB
Total PE                249854
Alloc PE / Size         0 / 0
Free                    PE / Size249854 / 975.99 GB
VG UUID                 NtbRLu-RqiQ-3Urt-iQZn-vEvJ-u0Th-FVYKWF
```

A "PE" is a physical extent, the allocation unit according to which the volume group is subdivided.

The final steps are to create the logical volume within DEMO and then to create a filesystem within that volume. We make the logical volume 100GB in size:

```
$ sudo lvcreate -L 100G -n web1 DEMO
Logical volume "web1" created
```

Most of LVM2's interesting options live at the logical volume level. That's where striping, mirroring, and contiguous allocation would be requested if we were using those features.

We can now access the volume through the device **/dev/DEMO/web1**. We discuss filesystems in general starting on page 254, but here is a quick overview of creating a standard filesystem so that we can demonstrate a few additional LVM tricks.

```
$ sudo mkfs /dev/DEMO/web1
...
$ sudo mkdir /mnt/web1
$ sudo mount /dev/DEMO/web1 /mnt/web1
```

Volume snapshots

You can create copy-on-write duplicates of any LVM2 logical volume, whether or not it contains a filesystem. This feature is handy for creating a quiescent image of a filesystem to be backed up on tape, but unlike ZFS snapshots, LVM2 snapshots are unfortunately not very useful as a general method of version control.

The problem is that logical volumes are of fixed size. When you create one, storage space is allocated for it up front from the volume group. A copy-on-write duplicate initially consumes no space, but as blocks are modified, the volume manager must find space in which to store both the old and new versions. This space for modified blocks must be set aside when you create the snapshot, and like any LVM volume, the allocated storage is of fixed size.

Note that it does not matter whether you modify the original volume or the snapshot (which by default is writable). Either way, the cost of duplicating the blocks is charged to the snapshot. Snapshots' allocations can be pared away by activity on the source volume even when the snapshots themselves are idle.

If you do not allocate as much space for a snapshot as is consumed by the volume of which it is an image, you can potentially run out of space in the snapshot. That's more catastrophic than it sounds because the volume manager then has no way to maintain a coherent image of the snapshot; additional storage space is required *just to keep the snapshot the same.* The result of running out of space is that LVM stops maintaining the snapshot, and the snapshot becomes irrevocably corrupt.

So, as a matter of practice, LVM snapshots should be either short-lived or as large as their source volumes. So much for "lots of cheap virtual copies."

To create **/dev/DEMO/web1-snap** as a snapshot of **/dev/DEMO/web1**, we would use the following command:

```
$ sudo lvcreate -L 100G -s -n web1-snap DEMO/web1
```

Note that the snapshot has its own name and that the source of the snapshot must be specified as *volume_group/volume.*

In theory, **/mnt/web1** should really be unmounted first to ensure the consistency of the filesystem. In practice, ext4 will protect us against filesystem corruption, although we may lose a few of the most recent data block updates. This is a perfectly reasonable compromise for a snapshot used as a backup source.

To check on the status of your snapshots, run **lvdisplay**. If **lvdisplay** tells you that a snapshot is "inactive," that means it has run out of space and should be deleted. There's very little you can do with a snapshot once it reaches this point.

Resizing filesystems

Filesystem overflows are more common than disk crashes, and one advantage of logical volumes is that they're much easier to juggle and resize than are hard partitions. We have experienced everything from servers used for personal MP3 storage to a department full of email pack rats.

The logical volume manager doesn't know anything about the contents of its volumes, so you must do your resizing at both the volume and filesystem levels. The order depends on the specific operation. Reductions must be filesystem-first, and enlargements must be volume-first. Don't memorize these rules: just think about what's actually happening and use common sense.

Suppose that in our example, **/mnt/web1** has grown more than we predicted and needs another 10GB of space. We first check the volume group to be sure additional space is available.

```
$ sudo vgdisplay DEMO
--- Volume group ---
VG Name                 DEMO
System ID
Format                  lvm2
Metadata Areas          1
Metadata Sequence No    18
VG Access               read/write
VG Status               resizable
MAX LV                  0
Cur LV                  2
Open LV                 1
Max PV                  0
Cur PV                  1
Act PV                  1
VG Size                 975.99 GB
PE Size                 4.00 MB
Total PE                249854
Alloc PE / Size         51200 / 200.00 GB
Free                    PE / Size198654 / 775.99 GB
VG UUID                 NtbRLu-RqiQ-3Urt-iQZn-vEvJ-u0Th-FVYKWF
```

Plenty of space is available, so we unmount the filesystem and use **lvresize** to add space to the logical volume.

```
$ sudo umount /mnt/web1
$ sudo lvchange -an DEMO/web1
$ sudo lvresize -L +10G DEMO/web1
$ sudo lvchange -ay DEMO/web1
Extending logical volume web1 to 110.00 GB
Logical volume web1 successfully resized
```

The **lvchange** commands are needed to deactivate the volume for resizing and to reactivate it afterwards. This part is only needed because there is an existing snapshot of web1 from our previous example. After the resize operation, the snapshot will “see” the additional 10GB of allocated space, but since the filesystem it contains is only 100GB in size, the snapshot will still be usable.

We can now resize the filesytem with **resize2fs**. (The **2** comes from the original ext2 filesystem, but the command supports all versions of ext.) Since **resize2fs** can determine the size of the new filesystem from the volume, we don’t need to specify the new size explicitly. We would have to do so when shrinking the filesystem.

```
$ sudo resize2fs /dev/DEMO/web1
resize2fs 1.41.9 (22-Aug-2009)
Please run 'e2fsck -f /dev/DEMO/web1' first.
```

Oops! **resize2fs** forces you to double-check the consistency of the filesystem before resizing.

```
$ sudo e2fsck -f /dev/DEMO/web1
e2fsck 1.41.9 (22-Aug-2009)
Pass 1: Checking inodes, blocks, and sizes
...
/dev/DEMO/web1: 6432/6553600 files (0.1% non-contiguous), 473045/26214400
    blocks
$ sudo resize2fs /dev/DEMO/web1
resize2fs 1.41.9 (22-Aug-2009)
Resizing the filesystem on /dev/DEMO/web1 to 28835840 (4k) blocks.
The filesystem on /dev/DEMO/web1 is now 28835840 blocks long.
```

That’s it! Examining the output of **df** again shows the changes:

```
$ sudo mount /dev/DEMO/web1 /mnt/web1
$ df -h /mnt/web1
Filesystem              Size   Used   Avail   Use%   Mounted on
/dev/mapper/DEMO-web   1109G   188M    103G     1%    /mnt/web1
```

HP-UX logical volume management

As of HP-UX 10.20, HP provides a full logical volume manager. It’s a nice addition, especially when you consider that HP-UX formerly did not even support the notion of disk partitions. The volume manager is called LVM, just as on Linux, although the HP-UX version is in fact the original. (Really, it’s Veritas software…)

As a simple example of LVM wrangling, here’s how you would configure a 75GB hard disk for use with the logical volume manager. If you have read through the Linux example above, the following procedure will seem eerily familiar. There are a few minor differences, but the overall process is essentially the same.

The **pvcreate** command identifies physical volumes.

```
$ sudo pvcreate /dev/rdisk/disk4
Creating "/etc/lvmtab_p".
Physical volume "/dev/rdisk/disk4" has been successfully created.
```

If you will be using the disk as a boot disk, add the **-B** option to **pvcreate** to reserve space for a boot block, then run **mkboot** to install it.

Storage

After defining the disk as a physical volume, you add it to a new volume group with the **vgcreate** command. Two metadata formats exist for volume groups, versions 1.0 and 2.0. You specify which version you want with the **-V** option when creating a volume group; version 1.0 remains the default. Version 2.0 has higher size limits, but it's not usable for boot devices or swap volumes. Even version 1.0 metadata has quite generous limits, so it should be fine for most uses. You can see the exact limits with **lvmadm**. For reference, here are the limits for 1.0:

```
$ sudo lvmadm -t -V 1.0
--- LVM Limits ---
VG Version                 1.0
Max VG Size (Tbytes)       510
Max LV Size (Tbytes)       16
Max PV Size (Tbytes)       2
Max VGs                    256
Max LVs                    255
Max PVs                    255
Max Mirrors                2
Max Stripes                255
Max Stripe Size (Kbytes)   32768
Max LXs per LV             65535
Max PXs per PV             65535
Max Extent Size (Mbytes)   256
```

You can add extra disks to a volume group with **vgextend**, but this example volume group contains only a single disk.

```
$ sudo vgcreate vg01 /dev/disk/disk4
Increased the number of physical extents per physical volume to 17501.
Volume group "/dev/vg01" has been successfully created.
Volume Group configuration for /dev/vg01 has been saved in
    /etc/lvmconf/vg01.con
```

Once your disks have been added to a convenient volume group, you can split the volume group's pool of disk space back into logical volumes. The **lvcreate** command creates a new logical volume. Specify the size of the volume in megabytes with the **-L** flag or in logical extents (typically 4MiB) with the **-l** flag. Sizes specified in MiB are rounded up to the nearest multiple of the logical extent size.

To assess the amount of free space remaining in a volume group, run **vgdisplay** *vgname* as root. The output includes the extent size and the number of unallocated extents.

```
$ sudo lvcreate -L 25000 -n web1 vg01
Logical volume "/dev/vg01/web1" has been successfully created with character
    device "/dev/vg01/rweb1".
Logical volume "/dev/vg01/web1" has been successfully extended.
Volume Group configuration for /dev/vg01 has been saved in
    /etc/lvmconf/vg01.conf
```

The command above creates a 25GB logical volume named web1. Once you've created your logical volumes, you can verify them by running **vgdisplay -v /dev/***vgname* to double-check their sizes and make sure they were set up correctly.

In most scenarios, you would then go on to create a filesystem on **/dev/vg01/web1** and arrange for it to be mounted at boot time. See page 258 for details.

Another common way to create a logical volume is to use **lvcreate** to create a zero-length volume and then use **lvextend** to add storage to it. That way, you can specify exactly which physical volumes in the volume group should compose the logical volume. If you allocate space with **lvcreate** (as we did above), it simply uses free extents from any available physical volumes in the volume group—good enough for most situations.

As in Linux, striping (which HP-UX's LVM refers to as "distributed allocation") and mirroring are features at the logical volume level. You can request them at the time the logical volume is created with **lvcreate**, or later with **lvchange**. In contrast to Linux, the logical volume manager does not allow snapshots. However, temporary snapshots are available as a feature of HP's VxFS filesystem.

If you plan to use a logical volume as a boot or swap device or to store system core dumps, you must specify contiguous allocation and turn off bad block remapping with the **-C** and **-r** flags to **lvcreate**, as shown below.[16]

```
# lvcreate -C y -r n -L 1500 -n root vg01
Logical volume "/dev/vg01/root" has been successfully created with character
    device "/dev/vg01/rroot".
Logical volume "/dev/vg01/root" has been successfully extended.
Volume Group configuration for /dev/vg01 has been saved in
    /etc/lvmconf/vg01.conf
# lvcreate -C y -r n -L 500 -n swap vg01
Logical volume "/dev/vg01/swap" has been successfully created with character
    device "/dev/vg01/rswap".
...
```

You must then run the **lvlnboot** command to notify the system of the new root and swap volumes. See the man page for **lvlnboot** for more information about the special procedures for creating boot, swap, and dump volumes.

AIX logical volume management

AIX's logical volume manager uses a different command set from the volume managers of Linux and HP-UX, but its underlying architecture and approach are similar. One potentially confusing point is that AIX calls the objects more commonly known as extents (that is, the units of space allocation within a volume group) "partitions." Because the entities normally referred to as partitions do not

16. HP-UX limitations require swap space to reside in the first 2GiB of the physical disk and the boot volume to be the first logical volume. The 1.5GB root and 500MB swap shown here were chosen to work around these constraints. You can have a root partition that is larger than these values, but you must then have separate boot and root volumes. See the man page for **lvlnboot** for more details.

Storage

exist in AIX, there is no ambiguity within the AIX sphere itself. However, tourists visiting from other systems may wish to bring along an AIX phrase book.

In other respects—physical volume, volume group, logical volume—AIX terminology is standard. The SMIT interface for logical volume management is pretty complete, but you can also use the commands listed in Table 8.4.

The following four commands create a volume group called webvg, a logical volume called web1 within it, and a JFS2 filesystem inside web1. The filesystem is then mounted in **/mnt/web1**.

```
$ sudo mkvg -y webvg hdisk1
webvg
$ sudo crfs -v jfs2 -g webvg -m /mnt/web1 -a size=25G
File system created successfully.
26213396 kilobytes total disk space.
New File System size is 52428800
$ sudo mkdir /mnt/web1
$ sudo mount /mnt/web1
```

AIX does not require you to label disks to turn them into physical volumes. **mkvg** and **extendvg** automatically label disks as part of the induction process. Note that **mkvg** takes a device name and not the path to a disk device.

You can create the logical volume and the filesystem inside it in separate steps (with **mklv** and **mkfs**, respectively), but **crfs** performs both tasks for you and updates **/etc/filesystems** as well. The exact name of the logical volume device that holds the filesystem is made up for you in the **crfs** scenario, but you can determine it by inspecting **/etc/filesystems** or running **mount**. (On the other hand, it can be hard to unscramble filesystems in the event of problems if the volumes all have generic names.)

If you run **mklv** directly, you can specify not only a device name of your choosing but also various options to the volume manager such as striping and mirroring configurations. Snapshots are implemented through the JFS2 filesystem and not through the volume manager.

8.9 Filesystems

Even after a hard disk has been conceptually divided into partitions or logical volumes, it is still not ready to hold files. All the abstractions and goodies described in Chapter 6, *The Filesystem*, must be implemented in terms of raw disk blocks. The filesystem is the code that implements these, and it needs to add a bit of its own overhead and data.

The Berkeley Fast File System implemented by McKusick et al. in the 1980s was an early standard that spread to many UNIX systems. With some small adjustments, it eventually became known as the UNIX File System (UFS) and formed the basis of several other filesystem implementations, including Linux's ext series, Solaris's UFS, and IBM's JFS.

Early systems bundled the filesystem implementation into the kernel, but it soon became apparent that support for multiple filesystem types was an important design goal. UNIX systems developed a well-defined kernel interface that allowed multiple types of filesystems to be active at once. The filesystem interface also abstracted the underlying hardware, so filesystems see approximately the same interface to storage devices as do other UNIX programs that access the disks through device files in **/dev**.

Support for multiple filesystem types was initially motivated by the need to support NFS and filesystems for removable media. But once the floodgates were opened, the "what if" era began; many different groups started to work on improved filesystems. Some were system specific, and others (such as ReiserFS) were not tied to any particular OS.

Given that you may have a choice of filesystems, should you investigate the various alternatives and choose the "best" one? Unless you're setting up a data disk for a very specific application, no. In nearly all situations, it's better to stick with the system's defaults. That's what the system's documentation and administrative tools probably assume.

Only a few features are truly non-negotiable:

- Good performance
- Tolerance for crashes and power outages without filesystem corruption
- The ability to handle disks and filesystems large enough for your needs

Fortunately, modern systems' default filesystems already cover these bases. Any improvement you might see from changing filesystems will be marginal and context dependent at best.

The next sections discuss the default filesystems on Linux, HP-UX, and AIX. The ZFS filesystem used by Solaris is administered differently and merits an entire section of its own; that section starts on page 264.

Linux filesystems: the ext family

The "second extended filesystem," ext2, was for a long time the mainstream Linux standard. It was designed and implemented primarily by Rémy Card, Theodore Ts'o, and Stephen Tweedie. Although the code for ext2 was written specifically for Linux, it is functionally similar to the Berkeley Fast File System.

Ext3 adds journaling capability to the existing ext2 code, a conceptually simple modification that increases reliability enormously. Even more interestingly, the ext3 extensions were implemented without changing the fundamental structure of ext2. In fact, you can still mount an ext3 filesystem as an ext2 filesystem—it just won't have journaling enabled.

Ext3 sets aside an area of the disk for the journal. The journal is allocated as if it were a regular file in the root of the filesystem, so it is not really a distinct structural component.

When a filesystem operation occurs, the required modifications are first written to the journal. When the journal update is complete, a "commit record" is written to mark the end of the entry. Only then is the normal filesystem modified. If a crash occurs during the update, the filesystem uses the journal log to reconstruct a perfectly consistent filesystem.[17]

Journaling reduces the time needed to perform filesystem consistency checks (see the **fsck** section on page 259) to approximately one second per filesystem. Barring some type of hardware failure, the state of an ext3 filesystem can almost instantly be assessed and restored.

Ext4 is a comparatively incremental update that raises a few size limits, increases the performance of certain operations, and allows the use of "extents" (disk block ranges) for storage allocation rather than just individual disk blocks. The on-disk format is compatible enough that ext2 and ext3 filesystems can be mounted as ext4 filesystems. Furthermore, ext4 filesystems can be mounted as if they were ext3 filesystems provided that the extent system has not been used.

Use of ext4 over the previous versions is recommended as of Linux kernel 2.6.28.[18] It is the default on Ubuntu and SUSE; Red Hat remains on ext3.

It's easy to add a journal to an existing ext2 filesystem, thereby promoting it to ext3 or ext4 (the distinction is vague because of backward compatibility). Just run **tune2fs** with the **-j** option. For example:

```
# tune2fs -j /dev/hda4
```

You would then need to modify the corresponding entry in **/etc/fstab** to read ext4 rather than ext2 (see page 260 for more information on the **fstab** file).

HP-UX filesystems: VxFS and HFS

VxFS is the mainstream HP-UX filesystem. It's based on a filesystem originally developed by Veritas Software, now part of Symantec. Since it includes a journal, HP sometimes refers to it as JFS, the Journaled File System. Don't confuse this JFS with AIX's JFS2, though; they are different filesystems.

VxFS is nearly unique among mainstream filesystems in that it supports clustering; that is, simultaneous modification by multiple, independent computers. This mode of operation involves some performance costs because the filesystem must

17. In most cases, only metadata changes are journaled. The actual data to be stored is written directly to the filesystem. However, you can change this behavior with the **data** mount option. See the **mount** man page for specifics.

18. Some say that the recommendation for ext4 in kernel 2.6.28 was, in retrospect, premature. Current versions are solid, however.

take extra steps to ensure cache coherency among computers. By default, clustering features are turned off; use the **-o cluster** option to **mount** to turn them on.

HFS is HP's previous mainstream filesystem. It's based on the UNIX File System and is now deprecated, though still supported.

AIX's JFS2

JFS2 is yet another filesystem that traces its roots back to the Berkeley Fast File System. The J stands for "journaled," but JFS2 has some other tricks up its sleeve, including extents, dynamic allocation of inodes, and the use of a B+ tree structure to store directory entries.

JFS2 is also interesting in that it's available under the GNU General Public License. It runs on Linux, too.

Filesystem terminology

Largely because of their common history with UFS, many filesystems share some descriptive terminology. The implementations of the underlying objects have often changed, but the terms are still widely used by administrators as labels for fundamental concepts.

"Inodes" are fixed-length table entries that each hold information about one file. They were originally preallocated at the time a filesystem was created, but some filesystems now create them dynamically as they are needed. Either way, an inode usually has an identifying number that you can see with **ls -i**.

Inodes are the "things" pointed to by directory entries. When you create a hard link to an existing file, you create a new directory entry, but you do not create a new inode.

On systems that preallocate inodes, you must decide in advance how many to create. It's impossible to predict exactly how many will someday be needed, so filesystem-building commands use an empirical formula, based on the size of the volume and an average file size, to guesstimate an appropriate number. If you anticipate storing zillions of small files, you may need to increase this number.

A superblock is a record that describes the characteristics of the filesystem. It contains information about the length of a disk block, the size and location of the inode tables, the disk block map and usage information, the size of the block groups, and a few other important parameters of the filesystem. Because damage to the superblock could erase some extremely crucial information, several copies of it are maintained in scattered locations.

Filesystems cache disk blocks to increase efficiency. All types of blocks can be cached, including superblocks, inode blocks, and directory information. Caches are normally not "write-through," so there may be some delay between the point at which an application thinks it has written a block and the point at which the block is actually saved to disk. Applications can request more predictable behavior for a file, but this option lowers throughput.

The **sync** system call flushes modified blocks to their permanent homes on disk, possibly making the on-disk filesystem fully consistent for a split second. This periodic save minimizes the amount of data loss that might occur if the machine were to crash with many unsaved blocks. Filesystems can do syncs on their own schedule or leave this up to the OS. Modern filesystems have journaling mechanisms that minimize or eliminate the possibility of structural corruption in the event of a crash, so sync frequency now mostly has to do with how many data blocks might be lost in a crash.

A filesystem's disk block map is a table of the free blocks it contains. When new files are written, this map is examined to devise an efficient layout scheme. The block usage summary records basic information about the blocks that are already in use. On filesystems that support extents, the information may be significantly more complex than the simple bitmap used by older filesystems.

Filesystem polymorphism

Filesystems are software packages with multiple components. One part lives in the kernel (or even potentially in user space under Linux; google for FUSE) and implements the nuts and bolts of translating the standard filesystem API into reads and writes of disk blocks. Other parts are user-level commands that initialize new volumes to the standard format, check filesystems for corruption, and perform other format-specific tasks.

Long ago, the standard user-level commands knew about "the filesystem" that the system used, and they simply implemented the appropriate functionality. **mkfs** created new filesystems, **fsck** fixed problems, and **mount** mostly just invoked the appropriate underlying system calls. These days filesystems are more modular, so these commands call filesystem-specific implementations of each utility.

The exact implementation varies. For example, the Linux wrappers look for discrete commands named **mkfs.***fsname*, **fsck.***fsname*, and so on in the normal directories for system commands. (You can run these commands directly, but it's rarely necessary.) AIX has a central **/etc/vfs** switch that records metainformation for filesystems (not to be confused with Solaris's **/etc/vfstab**, which is equivalent to the **fstab** or **filesystems** file on other systems; it's not needed for ZFS, though).

mkfs: format filesystems

The general recipe for creating a new filesystem is

```
mkfs [-T fstype] [-o options] rawdevice
```

The default *fstype* may be hard-coded into the wrapper, or it might be specified in **/etc/default/fs**. The available *options* are filesystem specific, but it's rare that you'll need to use them. Linux uses **-t** instead of **-T**, omits the **-o** designator, and does not have raw disk device files. AIX uses **-V** instead of **-T**.

AIX's **crfs** can allocate a new logical volume, create a filesystem on it, and update the **/etc/filesystems** file all in one step.

Two options you may consider tweaking are those that enable snapshots for filesystems that support them (JFS2 and VxFS) and locating the filesystem journal on a separate disk. The latter option can give quite a performance boost in the right circumstances.

fsck: check and repair filesystems

Because of block buffering and the fact that disk drives are not really transactional devices, filesystem data structures can potentially become self-inconsistent. If these problems are not corrected quickly, they propagate and snowball.

The original fix for corruption was a command called **fsck** ("filesystem consistency check," spelled aloud or pronounced "FS check" or "fisk") that carefully inspected all data structures and walked the allocation tree for every file. It relied on a set of heuristic rules about what the filesystem state might look like after failures at various points during an update.

The original **fsck** scheme worked surprisingly well, but because it involved reading all a disk's data, it could take hours on a large drive. An early optimization was a "filesystem clean" bit that could be set in the superblock when the filesystem was properly unmounted. When the system restarted, it would see the clean bit and know to skip the **fsck** check.

Now, filesystem journals let **fsck** pinpoint the activity that was occurring at the time of a failure. **fsck** can simply rewind the filesystem to the last known consistent state.

Disks are normally **fsck**ed automatically at boot time if they are listed in the system's **/etc/fstab**, **/etc/vfstab**, or **/etc/filesystems** file. The **fstab** and **vfstab** files have legacy "**fsck** sequence" fields that were normally used to order and parallelize filesystem checks. But now that **fsck**s are fast, the only thing that really matters is that the root filesystem be checked first.

You can run **fsck** by hand to perform an in-depth examination more akin to the original **fsck** procedure, but be aware of the time required.

Linux ext-family filesystems can be set to force a recheck after they have been remounted a certain number of times or after a certain period of time, even if all the unmounts were "clean." This precaution is good hygiene, and in most cases the default value (usually around 20 mounts) is acceptable. However, on systems that mount filesystems frequently, such as desktop workstations, even that frequency of **fsck**s can become tiresome. To increase the interval to 50 mounts, use the **tune2fs** command:

```
$ sudo /sbin/tune2fs -c 50 /dev/sda3
tune2fs 1.41.9 (22-Aug-2009)
Setting maximal mount count to 50
```

If a filesystem appears damaged and **fsck** cannot repair it automatically, *do not* experiment with it before making an ironclad backup. The best insurance policy is to **dd** the entire disk to a backup file or backup disk.

Most filesystems create a **lost+found** directory at the root of each filesystem in which **fsck** can deposit files whose parent directory cannot be determined. The **lost+found** directory has some extra space preallocated so that **fsck** can store orphaned files there without having to allocate additional directory entries on an unstable filesystem. Don't delete this directory.[19]

Since the name given to a file is recorded only in the file's parent directory, names for orphan files are not available and the files placed in **lost+found** are named with their inode numbers. The inode table does record the UID of the file's owner, however, so getting a file back to its original owner is relatively easy.

Filesystem mounting

A filesystem must be mounted before it becomes visible to processes. The mount point for a filesystem can be any directory, but the files and subdirectories beneath it are not accessible while a filesystem is mounted there. See *Filesystem mounting and unmounting* on page 143 for more information.

After installing a new disk, you should mount new filesystems by hand to be sure that everything is working correctly. For example, the command

```
$ sudo mount /dev/sda1 /mnt/temp
```

mounts the filesystem in the partition represented by the device file **/dev/sd1a** (device names will vary among systems) on a subdirectory of **/mnt**, which is a traditional path used for temporary mounts.

You can verify the size of a filesystem with the **df** command. The example below uses the Linux **-h** flag to request "human readable" output. Unfortunately, most systems' **df** defaults to an unhelpful unit such as "disk blocks," but there is usually a flag to make **df** report something specific such as kibibytes or gibibytes.

```
$ df -h /mnt/web1
Filesystem               Size  Used  Available  Use%   Mounted on
/dev/mapper-DEMO-web1    109G  188M       103G    1%   /mnt/web1
```

Setup for automatic mounting

You will generally want to configure the system to mount local filesystems at boot time. A configuration file in **/etc** lists the device names and mount points of all the system's disks (among other things). On most systems this file is called **/etc/fstab** (for "filesystem table"), but under both Solaris and AIX it has been restructured and renamed: **/etc/vfstab** on Solaris and **/etc/filesystems** on AIX. Here, we use the generic term "filesystem catalog" to refer to all three files.

19. Some systems have a **mklost+found** command you can use to recreate this directory if it is deleted.

By default, ZFS filesystems mount themselves automatically and do not require **vfstab** entries. However, you can change this behavior by setting ZFS filesystem properties. Swap areas and nonfilesystem mounts should still appear in **vfstab**.

mount, **umount**, **swapon**, and **fsck** all read the filesystem catalog, so it is helpful if the data presented there is correct and complete. **mount** and **umount** use the catalog to figure out what you want done if you specify only a partition name or mount point on the command line. For example, with the Linux **fstab** configuration shown on page 262, the command

```
$ sudo mount /media/cdrom0
```

would have the same effect as typing

```
$ sudo mount -t udf -o user,noauto,exec,utf8 /dev/scd0 /media/cdrom0
```

The command **mount -a** mounts all regular filesystems listed in the filesystem catalog; it is usually executed from the startup scripts at boot time.[20] The **-t**, **-F**, or **-v** flag (**-t** for Linux, **-F** for Solaris and HP-UX, **-v** for AIX) with an *fstype* argument constrains the operation to filesystems of a certain type. For example,

```
$ sudo mount -at ext4
```

mounts all local ext4 filesystems. The **mount** command reads **fstab** sequentially. Therefore, filesystems that are mounted beneath other filesystems must follow their parent partitions in the **fstab** file. For example, the line for **/var/log** must follow the line for **/var** if **/var** is a separate filesystem.

The **umount** command for unmounting filesystems accepts a similar syntax. You cannot unmount a filesystem that a process is using as its current directory or on which files are open. There are commands to identify the processes that are interfering with your **umount** attempt; see page 144.

The HP-UX **fstab** file is the most traditional of our example systems. Here are entries for a system that has only a single volume group:

```
# Device          Mount point  Type   Options     Seq

/dev/vg00/lvol3   /            vxfs   delaylog    0  1
/dev/vg00/lvol1   /stand       vxfs   tranflush   0  1
/dev/vg00/lvol4   /tmp         vxfs   delaylog    0  2
/dev/vg00/lvol5   /home        vxfs   delaylog    0  2
/dev/vg00/lvol6   /opt         vxfs   delaylog    0  2
/dev/vg00/lvol7   /usr         vxfs   delaylog    0  2
/dev/vg00/lvol8   /var         vxfs   delaylog    0  2
```

There are six fields per line, separated by whitespace. Each line describes a single filesystem. The fields are traditionally aligned for readability, but alignment is not required.

20. The noauto mount option excludes a given filesystem from automatic mounting by **mount -a**.

Storage

See Chapter 18 for more information about NFS.

The first field gives the device name. The **fstab** file can include mounts from remote systems, in which case the first field contains an NFS path. The notation *server:/export* indicates the */export* directory on the machine named *server*.

The second field specifies the mount point, and the third field names the type of filesystem. The exact type name used to identify local filesystems varies among machines.

The fourth field specifies **mount** options to be applied by default. There are many possibilities; see the man page for **mount** for the ones that are common to all filesystem types. Individual filesystems usually introduce options of their own. All the options shown above are specific to VxFS. For example, the delaylog option sacrifices some reliability for speed. See the **mount_vxfs** man page for more information about this and other VxFS mount options.

The fifth and sixth fields are vestigial. They are supposedly a "dump frequency" column and a column used to control **fsck** parallelism. Neither is important on contemporary systems.

Below are some additional examples culled from an Ubuntu system's **fstab**. The general format is the same, but Linux systems often include some additional flourishes.

```
proc            /proc            proc           defaults                    0  0
UUID=a8e3...8f8a  /              ext4           errors=remount-ro           0  1
UUID=13e9...b8d2  none           swap           sw                          0  0
/dev/scd0       /media/cdrom0    udf,iso9660    user,noauto,exec,utf8       0  0
/dev/scd1       /media/cdrom1    udf,iso9660    user,noauto,exec,utf8       0  0
/dev/fd0        /media/floppy0   auto           rw,user,noauto,exec,utf8    0  0
```

The first line addresses the **/proc** filesystem, which is in fact presented by a kernel driver and has no actual backing store. The proc device listed in the first column is just a placeholder.

The second and third lines use partition IDs (UUIDs, which we've truncated to make the excerpt more readable) instead of device names to identify volumes. This alternative is useful on Linux systems because the device names of disk partitions are unstable; adding or removing a disk can cause all the other disks to change names (e.g., from **/dev/sdb1** to **/dev/sdc1**). The UUID is linked only to the content of the partition, so it allows the partition to be tracked down wherever it might be hiding. Note that this convention works for the swap partition as well as the root.

The last three lines configure support for CD-ROM and floppy disk devices. The noauto option prevents the system from trying to mount these devices at boot time. (If no media were inserted, the mount attempt would fail and prolong the boot process.) The user option makes all the files on these removable drives appear to be owned by the user who mounts them.

On Solaris systems, the **/etc/vfstab** file has a slightly reorganized format with the order of some fields being swapped relative to the Linux and HP-UX scheme. However, the data is still tabular and is easily readable without much decoding effort. The distinguishing features of the **vfstab** format are that it has a separate "device to **fsck**" column and a separate "mount at boot" column.

AIX's **/etc/filesystems** file is organized as a series of property lists somewhat reminiscent of YAML or JSON, although the format is a bit different. Here's an example configuration for one filesystem:

```
/opt:
        dev       = /dev/hd10opt
        vfs       = jfs2
        log       = /dev/hd8
        mount     = true
        check     = true
        vol       = /opt
        free      = false
```

This format is nice in that it allows arbitrary properties to be associated with each filesystem, so filesystem-type-specific parameters can easily be recorded in the **filesystems** catalog. AIX automatically maintains this file when you perform disk wrangling operations through SMIT, but it's fine to edit the file directly, too.

USB drive mounting

Floppy disks have finally gone the way of the dodo, and good riddance. In their place are friendly, fast, and fun USB drives. These devices come in many flavors: personal "thumb" drives, digital cameras, iPods, and large external disks, to name a few. Most of these are supported by UNIX systems as data storage devices.

In the past, special tricks were necessary to manage USB devices. But now that operating systems have embraced dynamic device management as a fundamental requirement, USB drives are just one more type of device that shows up or disappears without warning.

From the perspective of storage management, the issues are

- Getting the kernel to recognize a device and to assign a device file to it
- Finding out what assignment has been made

The first step usually happens automatically, but systems have commands (such as AIX's **cfgmgr**) that you can use to goose the system if need be. Once a device file has been assigned, you can use the normal procedures described in *Disk device files* on page 224 to find out what it is.

For additional information about dynamic device management, see Chapter 13, *Drivers and the Kernel*.

Enabling swapping

Raw partitions or logical volumes, rather than structured filesystems, are normally used for swap space. Instead of using a filesystem to keep track of the swap area's contents, the kernel maintains its own simplified mapping from memory blocks to swap space blocks.

On some systems, it's also possible to swap to a file in a filesystem partition. With older kernels this configuration can be slower than using a dedicated partition, but it's still very handy in a pinch. In any event, logical volume managers eliminate most of the reasons you might want to use a swap file rather than a swap volume.

See page 1129 for more information about splitting swap areas.

The more swap space you have, the more virtual memory your processes can allocate. The best virtual memory performance is achieved when the swap area is split among several drives. Of course, the best option of all is to not swap; consider adding RAM if you find yourself needing to optimize swap performance.

On Linux systems, swap areas must be initialized with **mkswap**, which takes the device name of the swap volume as an argument.

You can manually enable swapping to a particular device with **swapon** *device* on most systems or **swap -a** *device* on Solaris. However, you will generally want to have this function performed automatically at boot time. Except on AIX, you can list swap areas in the regular filesystem catalog (**fstab** or **vfstab**) by giving them a filesystem type of swap. AIX has a separate file that lists the system's swap areas, **/etc/swapspaces**.

To review the system's current swapping configuration, run **swapon -s** on Linux systems, **swap -s** on Solaris and AIX, or **swapinfo** on HP-UX.

On AIX systems, you can use the **mkps** command to create a logical volume for swapping, add it to the **/etc/swapspaces** file, and start using it. This is the command called by the SMIT interface.

8.10 ZFS: ALL YOUR STORAGE PROBLEMS SOLVED

ZFS was introduced in 2005 as a component of OpenSolaris, and it quickly made its way to Solaris 10 and to various BSD-based distributions. In 2008, it became usable as a root filesystem, and it has been the front-line filesystem of choice for Solaris ever since.

Although ZFS is usually referred to as a filesystem, it is in fact a comprehensive approach to storage management that includes the functions of a logical volume manager and a RAID controller. It also redefines many common aspects of storage administration to make them simpler, easier, and more consistent. Although the current version of ZFS has a few limitations, most fall into the "not yet implemented" category rather than the "can't do for architectural reasons" category.

The advantages of ZFS's integrated approach are clear. If you're not already familiar with ZFS, we predict that you'll enjoy working with it. There is little doubt that the system will be widely emulated over the next decade. The open question is how long we'll have to wait to get ZFS-style features on other systems. Although ZFS is open source software, the terms of its current license unfortunately prevent inclusion in the Linux kernel.

Oracle's Btrfs filesystem project ("B-tree file system," officially pronounced "butter FS," though it's hard not to think "butter face") aims to repeat many of ZFS's advances on the Linux platform. It is already included in current Linux kernels as a technology preview. Ubuntu and SUSE users can experiment with it by installing the **btrfs-tools** or **btrfsprogs** packages, respectively. However, Btrfs is not production-ready, and now that Oracle has acquired Sun, the exact futures of both Btrfs and ZFS are uncertain.

ZFS architecture

Exhibit D shows a schematic of the major objects in the ZFS system and their relationship to each other.

Exhibit D ZFS architecture

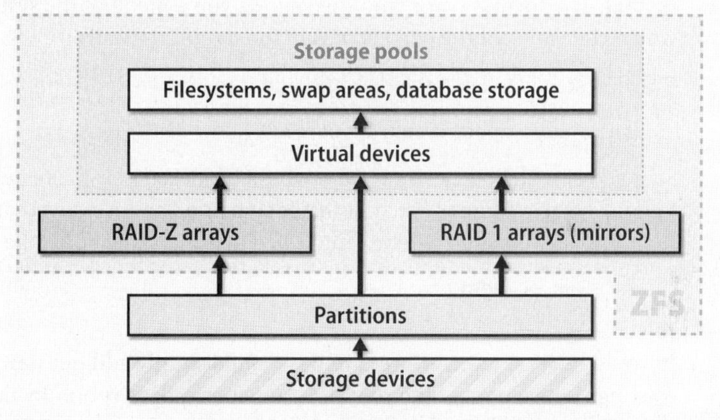

A ZFS "pool" is analogous to a "volume group" in other logical volume management systems. Each pool is composed of "virtual devices," which can be raw storage devices (disks, partitions, SAN devices, etc.), mirror groups, or RAID arrays. ZFS RAID is similar in spirit to RAID 5 in that it uses one or more parity devices to provide redundancy for the array. However, ZFS calls the scheme RAID-Z and uses variable-sized stripes to eliminate the RAID 5 write hole. All writes to the storage pool are striped across the pool's virtual devices, so a pool that contains only individual storage devices is effectively an implementation of RAID 0, although the devices in this configuration are not required to be of the same size.

Unfortunately, the current ZFS RAID is a bit brittle in that you cannot add new devices to an array once it has been defined; nor can you permanently remove a device. As in most RAID implementations, devices in a RAID set must be the same size; you can force ZFS to accept mixed sizes, but the size of the smallest volume then dictates the overall size of the array. To use disks of different sizes efficiently in combination with ZFS RAID, you must partition the disks ahead of time and define the leftover regions as separate devices.

Although you can turn over raw, unpartitioned disks to ZFS's care, ZFS secretly writes a GPT-style partition table onto them and allocates all of each disk's space to its first partition.

Most configuration and management of ZFS is done through two commands: **zpool** and **zfs**. Use **zpool** to build and manage storage pools. Use **zfs** to create and manage the entities created from pools, chiefly filesystems and raw volumes used as swap space and database storage.

Example: Solaris disk addition

Before we descend into the details of ZFS, let's start with a high-level example. Suppose you've added a new disk to your Solaris system and the disk has shown up as **/dev/dsk/c8d1**. (An easy way to determine the correct device is to run **sudo format**. The **format** command then shows you a menu of the system's disks from which you can spot the correct disk before typing <Control-C>.)

The first step is to label the disk and add it to a new storage pool:

```
solaris$ sudo zpool create demo c8d1
```

Step two is… well, there is no step two. ZFS labels the disk, creates the pool "demo," creates a filesystem root inside that pool, and mounts that filesystem as **/demo**. The filesystem will be remounted automatically when the system boots.

```
solaris$ ls -a /demo
.    ..
```

It would be even more impressive if we could simply add our new disk to the existing storage pool of the root disk, which is called "rpool" by default. (The command would be **sudo zpool add rpool c8d1**.) Unfortunately, the root pool can only contain a single virtual device. Other pools can be painlessly extended in this manner, however.

Filesystems and properties

It's fine for ZFS to automatically create a filesystem on a new storage pool because by default, ZFS filesystems consume no particular amount of space. All filesystems that live in a pool can draw from the pool's available space.

Unlike traditional filesystems, which are independent of one another, ZFS filesystems are hierarchical and interact with their parent and child filesystems in several ways. You create new filesystems with **zfs create**.

```
solaris$ sudo zfs create demo/new_fs
solaris$ zfs list -r demo
NAME          USED   AVAIL  REFER   MOUNTPOINT
demo          100K   488G     21K   /demo
demo/new_fs    19K   488G     19K   /demo/new_fs
```

The **-r** flag to **zfs list** makes it recurse through child filesystems. Most other **zfs** subcommands understand **-r**, too. Ever helpful, ZFS automounts the new filesystem as soon as we create it.

To simulate traditional filesystems of fixed size, you can adjust the filesystem's properties to add a "reservation" (an amount of space reserved in the storage pool for the filesystem's use) and a quota. This adjustment of filesystem properties is one of the keys to ZFS management, and it's something of a paradigm shift for administrators who are used to other systems. Here, we set both values to 1GB:

```
solaris$ sudo zfs set reservation=1g demo/new_fs
solaris$ sudo zfs set quota=1g demo/new_fs
solaris$ zfs list -r demo
NAME          USED   AVAIL  REFER   MOUNTPOINT
demo          1.00G   487G    21K   /demo
demo/new_fs    19K  1024M     19K   /demo/new_fs
```

The new quota is reflected in the AVAIL column for **/demo/new_fs**. Similarly, the reservation shows up immediately in the USED column for **/demo**. That's because the reservations of **/demo**'s descendant filesystems are included in its size tally.[21]

Both property changes are purely bookkeeping entries. The only change to the actual storage pool is the update of a block or two to record the new settings. No process goes out to format the 1GB of space reserved for **/demo/new_fs**. Most ZFS operations, including the creation of new storage pools and new filesystems, are similarly lightweight.

Using this hierarchical system of space management, you can easily group several filesystems to guarantee that their collective size will not exceed a certain threshold; you do not need to specify limits on individual filesystems.

You must set both the **quota** and **reservation** properties to properly emulate a traditional fixed-size filesystem.[22] The reservation alone simply ensures that the filesystem will have enough room available to grow *at least* that large. The quota limits the filesystem's maximum size *without* guaranteeing that space will be available for this growth; another object could snatch up all the pool's free space, leaving no room for **/demo/new_fs** to expand.

21. The REFER column shows the amount of data referenced by the active copy of each filesystem. **/demo** and **/demo/new_fs** have similar REFER values because they're both empty filesystems, not because there's any inherent relationship between the numbers.

22. The **reservation** and **quota** properties take into account all storage costs of the filesystem, including the space consumed for snapshots. If you want to limit only the size of the active copy of the filesystem, use the **refreservation** and **refquota** properties instead. The **ref** prefix indicates "amount of data referred to" by the active filesystem, the same total shown in the REFER column in **zfs list** output.

On the other hand, there are few reasons to set up a filesystem this way in real life. We show the use of these properties simply to demonstrate ZFS's space accounting system and to emphasize that ZFS is compatible with the traditional model, should you wish to enforce it.

Property inheritance

Many properties are naturally inherited by child filesystems. For example, if we wanted to mount the root of the demo pool in **/opt/demo** instead of **/demo**, we could simply set the root's **mountpoint** parameter:

```
solaris$ sudo zfs set mountpoint=/opt/demo demo
solaris$ zfs list -r demo
NAME          USED   AVAIL  REFER   MOUNTPOINT
demo          1.00G   487G    21K   /opt/demo
demo/new_fs    19K  1024M    19K   /opt/demo/new_fs
solaris$ ls /opt/demo
new_fs
```

Setting the **mountpoint** parameter automatically remounts the filesystems, and the mount point change affects child filesystems in a predictable and straightforward way. The usual rules regarding filesystem activity still apply, however; see page 143.

Use **zfs get** to see the effective value of a particular property; **zfs get all** dumps them all. The SOURCE column tells you why each property has its particular value: local means that the property was set explicitly, and a dash means that the property is read-only. If the property value is inherited from an ancestor filesystem, SOURCE shows the details of that inheritance as well.

```
solaris$ zfs get all demo/new_fs
solaris$ zfs get all demo/new_fs
NAME         PROPERTY       VALUE                   SOURCE
demo/new_fs  type           filesystem              -
demo/new_fs  creation       Wed Mar 17 17:57 2010   -
demo/new_fs  used           19K                     -
demo/new_fs  available      1024M                   -
demo/new_fs  referenced     19K                     -
demo/new_fs  compressratio  1.00x                   -
demo/new_fs  mounted        yes                     -
demo/new_fs  quota          1G                      local
demo/new_fs  reservation    1G                      local
demo/new_fs  mountpoint     /opt/demo/new_fs        inherited from demo
... <many more, about 40 in all>
```

Vigilant readers may notice that the available and referenced properties look suspiciously similar to the AVAIL and REFER columns shown by **zfs list**. In fact, **zfs list** is just a different way of displaying filesystem properties. If we had included the full output of our **zfs get** command above, there would be a used property in there, too. You can specify the properties you want **zfs list** to show with the **-o** option.

It wouldn't make sense to assign values to used and to the other size properties, so these properties are read-only. If the specific rules for calculating used don't meet your needs, other properties such as usedbychildren and usedbysnapshots may give you better insight into how your disk space is being consumed. See the ZFS admin guide for a complete list.

You can set additional, nonstandard properties on filesystems for your own use and for the use of your local scripts. The process is the same as for standard properties. The names of custom properties must include a colon to distinguish them from standard properties.

One filesystem per user

Since filesystems consume no space and take no time to create, the optimal number of them is closer to "a lot" than "a few." If you keep users' home directories on a ZFS storage pool, it's recommended that you make each home directory a separate filesystem. There are several reasons for this convention.

- If you need to set disk usage quotas, home directories are a natural granularity at which to do this. You can set quotas on both individual users' filesystems and on the filesystem that contains all users.
- Snapshots are per filesystem. If each user's home directory is a separate filesystem, the user can access old snapshots through **~/.zfs**.[23] This alone is a huge time saver for administrators because it means that users can service most of their own file restore needs.
- ZFS lets you delegate permission to perform various operations such as taking snapshots and rolling back the filesystem to an earlier state. If you wish, you can give users control over these operations for their own home directories. We do not describe the details of ZFS permission management in this book; see the *ZFS Administration Guide.*

Snapshots and clones

ZFS is organized around the principle of copy-on-write. Instead of overwriting disk blocks in place, ZFS allocates new blocks and updates pointers. This approach makes ZFS resistant to corruption because operations can never end up half-completed in the event of a power failure or crash. Either the root block is updated or it's not; the filesystem is consistent either way (though a few recent changes may be "undone").

Just as in a logical volume manager, ZFS brings copy-on-write to the user level by allowing you to create instantaneous snapshots. However, there's an important difference: ZFS snapshots are implemented per-filesystem rather than per-volume, so they have arbitrary granularity. Solaris uses this feature to great effect in the Time Slider widget for the GNOME desktop. Much like Mac OS's Time

23. This directory is hidden by default; it does not appear in **ls -a** output. You can make it visible with **zfs set snapdir=visible** *filesystem*.

Storage

Machine, the Time Slider is a combination of scheduled tasks that create and manage snapshots at regular intervals and a UI that makes it easy for you to reach older versions of your files.

On the command line, you create snapshots with **zfs snapshot**. For example, the following command sequence illustrates creation of a snapshot, use of the snapshot through the filesystem's **.zfs/snapshot** directory, and reversion of the filesystem to its previous state.

```
solaris$ sudo touch /opt/demo/new_fs/now_you_see_me
solaris$ ls /opt/demo/new_fs
now_you_see_me
solaris$ sudo zfs snapshot demo/new_fs@snap1
solaris$ sudo rm /opt/demo/new_fs/now_you_see_me
solaris$ ls /opt/demo/new_fs
solaris$ ls /opt/demo/new_fs/.zfs/snapshot/snap1
now_you_see_me
solaris$ sudo zfs rollback demo/new_fs@snap1
solaris$ ls /opt/demo/new_fs
now_you_see_me
```

You assign a name to each snapshot at the time it's created. The complete specifier for a snapshot is usually written in the form *filesystem@snapshot*.

Use **zfs snapshot -r** to create snapshots recursively. The effect is the same as executing **zfs snapshot** on each contained object individually: each subcomponent receives its own snapshot. All the snapshots have the same name, but they're logically distinct.

ZFS snapshots are read-only, and although they can bear properties, they are not true filesystems. However, you can instantiate a snapshot as a full-fledged, writable filesystem by "cloning" it.

```
solaris$ sudo zfs clone demo/new_fs@snap1 demo/subclone
solaris$ ls /opt/demo/subclone
now_you_see_me
solaris$ sudo touch /opt/demo/subclone/and_me_too
solaris$ ls /opt/demo/subclone
and_me_too      now_you_see_me
```

The snapshot that is the basis of the clone remains undisturbed and read-only. However, the new filesystem (**demo/subclone** in this example) retains a link to both the snapshot and the filesystem on which it's based, and neither of those entities can be deleted as long as the clone exists.

Cloning isn't a common operation, but it's the only way to create a branch in a filesystem's evolution. The **zfs rollback** operation demonstrated above can only revert a filesystem to its most recent snapshot, so to use it you must permanently delete (**zfs destroy**) any snapshots made since the snapshot that is your reversion target. Cloning lets you go back in time without losing access to recent changes.

For example, suppose that you've discovered a security breach that occurred some time within the last week. For safety, you want to revert a filesystem to its state of a week ago to be sure it contains no hacker-installed back doors. At the same time, you don't want to lose recent work or the data for forensic analysis. The solution is to clone the week-ago snapshot to a new filesystem, **zfs rename** the old filesystem, and then **zfs rename** the clone in place of the original filesystem.

For good measure, you should also **zfs promote** the clone; this operation inverts the relationship between the clone and the filesystem of origin. After promotion, the main-line filesystem has access to all the old filesystem's snapshots, and the old, moved-aside filesystem becomes the "cloned" branch.

Raw volumes

You create swap areas and raw storage areas with **zfs create**, just as you create filesystems. The **-V** *size* argument makes **zfs** treat the new object as a raw volume instead of a filesystem. The *size* can use any common unit, for example, **128m**.

Since the volume does not contain a filesystem, it is not mounted; instead, it shows up in the **/dev/zvol/dsk** and **/dev/zvol/rdsk** directories and can be referenced as if it were a hard disk or partition. ZFS mirrors the hierarchical structure of the storage pool in these directories, so **sudo zfc create -V 128m demo/swap** creates a 128MB swap volume located at **/dev/zvol/dsk/demo/swap**.

You can create snapshots of raw volumes just as you can with filesystems, but because there's no filesystem hierarchy in which to put a **.zfs/snapshot** directory, the snapshots show up in the same directory as their source volumes. Clones work too, just as you'd expect.

By default, raw volumes receive a space reservation equal to their specified size. You're free to reduce the reservation or do away with it entirely, but note that this can make writes to the volume return an "out of space" error. Clients of raw volumes may not be designed to deal with such an error.

Filesystem sharing filesystem through NFS, CIFS, and iSCSI

Just as ZFS redefines many aspects of traditional filesystem management, it also changes the way that filesystems are shared over a network. In particular, you can set the **sharenfs** or **sharesmb** property of a filesystem to **on** to make it available through NFS or Solaris's built-in CIFS server. See Chapter 18, *The Network File System*, for more information about NFS, and see the section *Sharing files with Samba and CIFS* on page 1142 for more information about CIFS.

If you leave these properties set to **off**, that does not mean the filesystems are unsharable; it just means that you must do your own export management with tools such as **sharemgr**, **share**, and **unshare** instead of having ZFS take care of this for you. The **sharenfs** and **sharesmb** properties can also take on values other than **on** and **off**. If you set a more detailed value, it's assumed that you want sharing turned on, and the value is passed through **zfs share** and on to **share** in the form of command-line arguments.

In a similar vein, **shareiscsi=on** on a raw volume makes that volume available as an iSCSI target. See page 274 for more information about iSCSI.

By default, all the **share*** properties are inheritable. If you share **/home** over NFS, for example, you automatically share the individual home directories beneath it, even if they are defined as separate filesystems. Of course, you can override this behavior by setting an explicit **sharenfs=no** value on each sub-filesystem.

ZFS uses the NFSv4 standard for access control lists. The nuances of that standard are discussed in more detail in Chapter 6, *The Filesystem*, starting on page 166. The executive summary is that ZFS provides excellent ACL support for both Windows and NFS clients.

Storage pool management

Now that we've peeked at some of the features that ZFS offers at the filesystem and block-client level, let's take a longer swim in ZFS's storage pools.

Up to this point, we've used a pool called "demo" that we created from a single disk back on page 266. Here it is in the output of **zpool list**:

```
solaris$ zpool list
NAME   SIZE    USED   AVAIL   CAP   HEALTH    ALTROOT
demo   496G    240K    496G    0%   ONLINE    -
rpool  748G  23.78G    724G    3%   ONLINE    -
```

The pool named rpool contains the bootable root filesystem. Bootable pools are currently restricted in several ways: they can only contain a single virtual device, and that device must be either a mirror array or a single disk drive; it cannot be a RAID array. If it is a disk, it cannot have a GPT partition table.

zpool status adds more detail about the virtual devices that make up a storage pool and reports their current status.

```
solaris$ zpool status demo
  pool: demo
 state: ONLINE
 scrub: none requested
config:

        NAME      STATE     READ  WRITE  CKSUM
        demo      ONLINE       0      0      0
          c8d1    ONLINE       0      0      0
```

Let's get rid of this demo pool and set up something a bit more sophisticated. We've attached five 500GB SCSI drives to our example system. We first create a pool called "monster" that includes three of those drives in a RAID-Z single-parity configuration.

```
solaris$ sudo zpool destroy demo
solaris$ sudo zpool create monster raidz1 c9t0d0 c9t1d0 c9t2d0
solaris$ zfs list monster
NAME          USED    AVAIL   REFER    MOUNTPOINT
monster       91.2K    981G   25.3K    /monster
```

ZFS also understands **raidz2** and **raidz3** for double and triple parity configurations. The minimum number of disks is always one more than the number of parity devices. Here, one drive out of three is used for parity, so roughly 1TB is available for use by filesystems.

For illustration, we then add the remaining two drives configured as a mirror.

```
solaris$ sudo zpool add monster mirror c9t3d0 c9t4d0
invalid vdev specification
use '-f' to override the following errors:
mismatched replication level: pool uses raidz and new vdev is mirror
solaris$ sudo zpool add -f monster mirror c9t3d0 c9t4d0
```

zpool initially balks at this configuration because the two virtual devices have different redundancy schemes. This particular configuration is OK since both vdevs have some redundancy. In actual use, you should not mix redundant and nonredundant vdevs since there's no way to predict which blocks might be stored on which devices; partial redundancy is useless.

```
solaris$ zpool status monster
   pool: monster
  state: ONLINE
  scrub: none requested
 config:

        NAME          STATE     READ  WRITE  CKSUM
        monster       ONLINE       0      0      0
          raidz1      ONLINE       0      0      0
            c9t0d0    ONLINE       0      0      0
            c9t1d0    ONLINE       0      0      0
            c9t2d0    ONLINE       0      0      0
          mirror      ONLINE       0      0      0
            c9t3d0    ONLINE       0      0      0
            c9t4d0    ONLINE       0      0      0
```

ZFS distributes writes among all a pool's virtual devices. As demonstrated in this example, it is not necessary for all virtual devices to be the same size.[24] However, the components within a redundancy group should be of similar size. If they are not, only the smallest size is used on each component. If you use multiple simple disks together in a storage pool, that is essentially a RAID 0 configuration.

You can add additional vdevs to a pool at any time. However, existing data will not be redistributed to take advantage of parallelism. Unfortunately, you cannot currently add additional devices to an existing RAID array or mirror.

24. In this example the *disks* are all the same size, but the virtual devices are not (1TB vs. 500GB).

ZFS has an especially nice implementation of read caching that makes good use of SSDs. To set up this configuration, just add the SSDs to the storage pool as vdevs of type **cache**. The caching system uses an adaptive replacement algorithm developed at IBM that is smarter than a normal LRU (least recently used) cache. It knows about the frequency at which blocks are referenced as well as their recency of use, so reads of large files are not supposed to wipe out the cache.

Hot spares are handled as vdevs of type **spare**. You can add the same disk to multiple storage pools; whichever pool experiences a disk failure first gets to claim the spare disk.

8.11 Storage area networking

There are several ways to attach storage resources to a network. Chapter 18, *The Network File System*, describes NFS, the traditional UNIX protocol used for file sharing. Windows systems use the protocol known variously as CIFS or SMB for similar purposes. The predominant implementation of CIFS for UNIX and Linux is Samba; see *Sharing files with Samba and CIFS* on page 1142 for more details.

NFS and CIFS are examples of "network-attached storage" (NAS) systems. They are high-level protocols, and their basic operations are along the lines of "open file X and send me the first 4KiB of data" or "adjust the ACL on file Y as described in this request." These systems are good at arbitrating access to filesystems that many clients want to read or write at once.

A storage area network (SAN) is a lower-level system for abstracting storage, one that makes network storage look like a local hard disk. SAN operations consist primarily of instructions to read or write particular "disk" blocks (though, of course, the block addressing is virtualized by the server in some way). If a client wants to use SAN storage to hold a filesystem, it must provide its own filesystem implementation. On the other hand, SAN volumes can also be used to store swap areas or other data that doesn't need the structure or overhead of a filesystem.

With the exception of HP's VxFS, mainstream filesystems are not designed to be updated by multiple clients that are unaware of each other's existence (at least, not at the level of raw disk blocks).[25] Therefore, SAN storage is not typically used as a way of sharing files. Instead, it's a way to replace local hard disks with centralized storage resources.

Why would you want to do this? Several reasons:

- Every client gets to share the benefits of a sophisticated storage facility that's optimized for performance, fault tolerance, and disaster recovery.

25. Just to be clear, many such filesystems exist. They are known generically as cluster (or clustered) filesystems. Special locking and synchronization algorithms must be used to implement clustering, so clustered filesystems are typically slower than standard filesystems on local disks. VxFS can operate in clustered or nonclustered mode, so it's a serviceable option for either situation.

- Utilization efficiency is increased because every client can have exactly as much storage as it needs. Although space allocations for virtual disks are fixed, they are not limited to the standard sizes of physical hard disks. In addition, virtual disk blocks that the client never writes need never actually be stored on the server.
- At the same time, a SAN makes storage infinitely more flexible and trivial to reconfigure. A "hard disk upgrade" can now be performed in a command or two from an administrator's terminal window.
- Duplicate block detection techniques can reduce the cost of storing files that are the same on many machines.
- Backup strategy for the enterprise can be unified through the use of shadow copies of block stores on the SAN server. In some cases, every client gets access to advanced snapshot facilities such as those found on logical volume managers, regardless of its operating system or the filesystem it's using.

Performance is always of interest to system administrators, but it's hard to make general statements about the effect of a SAN on a server's I/O performance without knowing more about the specific implementation. Networks impose latency costs and bandwidth restrictions that local disks do not. Even with advanced switching hardware, networks are semi-shared resources that can be subject to bandwidth contention among clients. On the positive side, large SAN servers come packed to the gills with memory and SSD caches. They use premium components and spread their physical I/O across many disks. In general, a properly implemented SAN is significantly faster than local storage.

That kind of setup isn't cheap, however. This is a domain of specialized, enterprise-class hardware, so get that $80 hard disk from Fry's out of your mind right from the start. Some major players in the SAN space are EMC, NetApp, HP, IBM, and perhaps surprisingly, Dell.

SAN networks

Because network concerns are a major determinant of SAN performance, serious installations have traditionally relied on Fibre Channel networks for their infrastructure. Mainstream Fibre Channel speeds are typically 4 or 8 Gb/s, as opposed to the 1 Gb/s speed of a typical Ethernet.

Ethernet is rapidly gaining ground, however. There are several reasons for this, the two most important being the growing availability of inexpensive 10 Gb/s Ethernets and the increasing prevalence of virtualized servers; virtualization systems generally have better support for Ethernet than for Fibre Channel. Of course, it's also helpful that Ethernet-based systems don't require the installation of an expensive secondary physical network infrastructure.

Several communication protocols can implement SAN functionality over Ethernet. The common theme among these protocols is that they each emulate a particular hardware interface that many systems already understand.

The predominant protocol is iSCSI, which presents the virtual storage device to the system as if it lived on a local SCSI bus. Other options are ATA-over-Ethernet (AoE) and Fibre-Channel-over-Ethernet (FCoE). These last options are Ethernet-specific (and therefore limited in their geographical extent), whereas iSCSI runs on top of IP. At present, iSCSI has about 20% of the SAN market, true Fibre Channel has about 60%, and other solutions account for the remaining 20%.

The details of implementing a Fibre Channel deployment are beyond the scope of this book, so here we review only iSCSI in detail. From the host operating system's perspective, Fibre Channel SAN drives typically look like a pile of SCSI disks, and they can be managed as such.

iSCSI: SCSI over IP

iSCSI lets you implement a SAN with your existing, cheap network hardware rather than a dedicated Fibre Channel network and expensive Fibre Channel host bus adapters. Your SAN servers will still likely be task-specific systems, but they too can take advantage of commodity hardware.

Borrowing a bit of terminology from traditional SCSI, iSCSI refers to a server that makes virtual disks available over the network as an iSCSI "target." A client that mounts these disks is called an "initiator," which makes sense if you keep in mind that the client originates SCSI commands and the server responds to them.

The software components that implement the target and initiator sides of an iSCSI relationship are separate. All modern operating systems include an initiator, although it's often an optional component. Most systems also have a standard target implementation.

iSCSI is formally specified in RFC3720. Unlike most RFCs, the specification is several hundred pages long, mostly because of the complexity of the underlying SCSI protocol. For the most part, iSCSI administration is simple unless you use the optional Internet Storage Name Service (iSNS) for structured management and discovery of storage resources. iSNS, defined in RFC4171, is an adaptation of Fibre Channel's management and discovery protocols to IP, so it's primarily of interest to sites that want to use both Fibre Channel and iSCSI.

Without iSNS, you simply point your initiator at the appropriate server, specify the name of the iSCSI device you want to access, and specify a username and password with which to authenticate. By default, iSCSI authentication uses the Challenge Handshake Authentication Protocol (CHAP) originally defined for the Point-to-Point Protocol (PPP) (see RFC1994), so passwords are not sent in plaintext over the network. Optionally, the initiator can authenticate the target through the use of a second shared secret.

iSCSI can run over IPsec, although that is not required. If you don't use an IPsec tunnel, data blocks themselves are not encrypted. According to RFC3720, connections that don't use IPsec must use CHAP secrets at least 12 characters long.

Targets and initiators both have iSCSI names, and several naming schemes are defined. The names in common use are iSCSI Qualified Names (IQNs), which have the following bizarre format:

iqn.*yyyy-mm.reversed_DNS_domain*:*arbitrary_name*

In most cases, everything up to the colon is a fixed (i.e., essentially irrelevant) prefix that's characteristic of your site. You implement your own naming scheme in the *arbitrary_name* portion of the IQN. The month and year (*mm* and *yyyy*) qualify the DNS domain to guard against the possibility of a domain changing hands. Use the original DNS registration date. An actual name looks something like this:

```
iqn.1995-08.com.example:disk54.db.engr
```

Despite the specificity of the IQN name format, it is not important that the prefix reflect your actual DNS domain or inception date. Most iSCSI implementations default to using the vendor's domain as an IQN, and this works fine. It is not even necessary that the IQNs involved in a service relationship have matching prefixes.

Storage

Booting from an iSCSI volume

If you're going to put your important data on a SAN, wouldn't it be nice to eliminate local hard disks entirely? Not only could you eliminate many of the special procedures needed to manage local disks, but you could also allow administrators to "swap" boot drives with a simple reboot, bringing instant upgrades and multiple boot configurations within reach even of Windows systems.

Unfortunately, the use of an iSCSI volume as a boot device is not widely supported. At least, not straightforwardly and not as a mainstream feature. Various Linux projects have made a go of it, but the implementations are necessarily tied to specific hardware and to specific iSCSI initiator software, and no current iSCSI boot project cooperates with the now-predominant initiator software, Open-iSCSI. Similarly, iSCSI boot support for Solaris and OpenSolaris is being worked on, but there's no production-ready solution yet.

The lone exception among our example systems is AIX, which has a long history of good support for iSCSI. AIX versions 5.3 and later running on POWER hardware have full support for iSCSI booting over IPv4.

Vendor specifics for iSCSI initiators

There have been at least four different iSCSI initiator implementations for Linux. Several have died off and others have merged. The sole survivor at this point seems to be Open-iSCSI, which is the standard initiator packaged with all our example Linux distributions. To get it up and running, install the **open-scsi** package on Ubuntu and SUSE and the **iscsi-initiator-utils** package on Red Hat.

The project's home page is open-iscsi.org, but don't go there looking for documentation. None seems to exist other than the man pages for **iscsid** and **iscsiadm**, which represent the implementation and the administrative interface for the system, respectively. Unfortunately, the administrative model for Open-iSCSI is best described as "creative."

In Open-iSCSI's world, a "node" is an iSCSI target, the thing that's named with an IQN. Open-iSCSI maintains a database of the nodes it knows about in a hierarchy underneath the directory **/etc/iscsi/nodes**. Configuration parameters for individual nodes are stored in this tree. Defaults are set in **/etc/iscsi/iscsid.conf**, but they are sometimes copied to newly defined nodes, so their function is not entirely predictable. The process of setting per-target parameters is painful; **iscsiadm** tortures you by making you change one parameter at a time and by making you list the IQN and server on each command line.

The saving grace of the system is that **iscsid.conf** and all the database files are just editable text files. Therefore, the sane approach is to use **iscsiadm** for the few things it does well and to circumvent it for the others.

To set up the system for simple, static operation with a single username and password for all iSCSI targets, first edit the **iscsid.conf** file and make sure the following lines are configured as shown:

```
node.startup = automatic
node.session.auth.authmethod = CHAP
node.session.auth.username = chap_name
node.session.auth.password = chap_password
```

We show these lines together, but they'll be separated in the actual file. The file is actually quite nicely commented and contains a variety of commented-out configuration options. Make sure you don't introduce duplicates.

Next, point **iscsiadm** at your target server and let it create node entries for each of the targets it discovers by reading that server's directory. Here, we'll configure the target called test from the server named iserver.

```
ubuntu$ sudo iscsiadm -m discovery -t st -p iserver
192.168.0.75:3260,1 iqn.1994-11.com.admin:test
```

iscsiadm creates a subdirectory in **/etc/iscsi/nodes** for each target. If there are targets you don't want to deal with, it's fine to just **rm -rf** their configuration directories. If the server offers many targets and you'd rather just specify the details of the one you want, you can do that, too:

```
ubuntu$ sudo iscsiadm -m node -o new -p iserver
    -T iqn.1994-11.com.admin:test
New iSCSI node [tcp:[hw=default,ip=,net_if=default,iscsi_if=default]
    iserver,3260,-1 iqn.1994-11.com.admin:test] added
```

Strangely, these two methods achieve similar results but create different hierarchies under **/etc/iscsi/nodes**. Whichever version you use, check the text files that are the leaves of the hierarchy to be sure the configuration parameters are set appropriately. If you entered the target manually, you may need to set the property node.startup to automatic by hand.

You can then connect to the remote targets with **iscsiadm -m node -l**:

```
ubuntu$ sudo iscsiadm -m node -l
Logging in to [iface: default, target: iqn.1994-11.com.admin:test, portal:
    192.168.0.75,3260]
Login to [iface: default, target: iqn.1994-11.com.admin:test, portal:
    192.168.0.75,3260]: successful
```

You can verify that the system now sees the additional disk by running **fdisk -l**. (The device files for iSCSI disks are named like those for any other SCSI disk.) If you have set up the configuration files as described above, the connections should be restored automatically at boot time.

For iSCSI target service on Linux systems, the preferred implementation is the iSCSI Enterprise Target package hosted at iscsitarget.sourceforge.net. It's usually available as a package called **iscsitarget**.

Solaris includes target and initiator packages; both are optional. All packages related to iSCSI have "iscsi" in their names. For the initiator side, install the package SUNWiscsi; you'll have to reboot afterward.

There is no configuration file; all configuration is performed with the **iscsiadm** command, which has a rather strange syntax. Four top-level verbs (**add**, **modify**, **list**, and **remove**) can be applied to a variety of different aspects of the initiator configuration. The following steps perform basic configuration of the initiator as a whole and connect to a target on the server iserver.

```
solaris$ sudo iscsiadm modify initiator-node -a CHAP -H testclient
solaris$ sudo iscsiadm modify initiator-node -C
Enter secret: <password for testclient>
Re-enter secret: <password for testclient>
solaris$ sudo iscsiadm modify discovery -s enable
solaris$ sudo iscsiadm add static-config iqn.1994-11.com.admin:test,iserver
solaris$ sudo iscsiadm list target -S
Target: iqn.1994-11.com.admin:test
    Alias: -
    TPGT: 1
    ISID: 4000002a0000
    Connections: 1
    LUN: 0
        Vendor:  IET
        Product:  VIRTUAL-DISK
        OS Device Name: /dev/rdsk/c10t3d0s2
```

At this point you can simply configure the disk normally (for example, by running **zpool create iscsi c10t3d0**).

The first command sets the initiator's authentication mode to CHAP and sets the CHAP username to testclient. The **-C** option sets the password; you cannot combine this option with any others. It's also possible to set the name and password individually for each target if you prefer.

The **modify discovery** command enables the use of statically configured targets, and the **add** command designates the server and IQN of a specific target. All this configuration is persistent across reboots.

To serve iSCSI targets to other systems, you'll need to install the SUNWiscsitgt package. Administration is structured similarly to the initiator side, but the command is **iscsitadm** instead of **iscsiadm**.

To use iSCSI on HP-UX systems, download the iSCSI initiator software from software.hp.com and install it with HP-UX's Software Distributor tool. A kernel rebuild and reboot are required. Fortunately, the system is well documented in a stand-alone manual, the *HP-UX iSCSI Software Initiator Support Guide*, available from docs.hp.com.

Most initiator configuration is performed with the **iscsiutil** command, installed in **/opt/iscsi/bin**. Use **iscsiutil -l** *iqn* to set the initiator's IQN, **iscsiutil -u -N** *user* to set the global CHAP username (it can also be set per-server or per-target), and **iscsiutil -u -W** *password* to set the global CHAP password.

You can then add targets from a particular server with **iscsiutil -a -I** *server*. Run **ioscan -NH 64000** to activate the server connections and to create virtual disk devices. You can check the status of the system with **iscsiutil -p -o**.

AIX's iSCSI initiator comes installed and ready to go. In typical AIX style, most configuration is done through the system's ODM database. The iscsi0 device represents the configuration of the initiator as a whole, and individual target devices can be defined as ODM entries or in text configuration files in **/etc/iscsi**. The text configuration files seem to work somewhat more reliably.

AIX does not distinguish between the initiator's IQN and its CHAP username. The IQN is set on the iscsi0 device; therefore, you should plan on using the same CHAP username on every server. The first step on the fast configuration path is to set that IQN to an appropriate value.

```
aix$ sudo chdev -l iscsi0 -a initiator_name='iqn.1994-11.com.admin:client'
```

We used a different CHAP username for this example than for other systems since "testclient" isn't technically a valid IQN for the initiator (although in fact it works fine as well).

In the **/etc/iscsi/targets** file, we add the following entry:

```
iserver 3260 iqn.1994-11.com.admin:test "chap_password"
```

The 3260 is the standard server port for iSCSI; we include it here only because the port is required by the file format. To activate the new iSCSI disk, we need only run **cfgmgr -l iscsi0**. The **cfgmgr** command prints no confirmation messages, but we can see that the new device has appeared by looking in the **/dev** directory (on our example system, the new disk is **/dev/hdisk2**) or by running **smitty devices**, navigating to the Fixed Disk category, and listing the entries. The latter option is perhaps safer since **smitty** explicitly shows that **hdisk2** is an iSCSI volume.

To disconnect an iSCSI device, you must not only edit the configuration file and reload the configuration with **cfgmgr** but you must also delete the disk from **smitty**'s Fixed Disk list.

8.12 Exercises

E8.1 Describe any special considerations that an administrator should take into account when designing a storage architecture for each of the following applications.

a) A server that will host the home directories of about 200 users
b) A swap area for a site's primary DNS server
c) Storage for the mail queue at a large spam house
d) A large InnoDB (MySQL) database

E8.2 Logical volume managers are powerful but can be confusing if not well understood. Practice adding, removing, and resizing disks in a volume group. Show how you would remove a device from one volume group and add it to another. What would you do if you wanted to move a logical volume from one volume group to another?

★ E8.3 Using printed or Internet resources, identify the best-performing SCSI and SATA drives. Do the benchmarks used to evaluate these drives reflect the way that a busy server would use its boot disk? What cost premium would you pay for SCSI, and how much performance improvement (if any) would you get for the money?

★ E8.4 Add a disk to your system and set up a partition or logical volume on the new disk as a backup root partition. Make sure you can boot from the backup root and that the system runs normally when so booted. Keep a journal of all the steps required to complete this task. You may find the **script** command helpful. (Requires root access.)

★ E8.5 What is a superblock and what is it used for? Look up the definition of the ext4 superblock structure in the kernel header files and discuss what each of the fields in the structure represents.

★ E8.6 Use **mdadm** and its **-f** option to simulate a failed disk in a Linux RAID array. Remove the disk from the array and add it back. How does **/proc/mdstat** look at each step?

Storage

★★ E8.7 What fields are stored in an inode on an ext4 filesystem? List the contents of the inode that represents the **/etc/motd** file. Where is this file's filename stored? (Tools such as **hexdump** and **ls -i** might help.)

★★ E8.8 Examine the contents of a directory file with a program such as **od** or **hexdump**. Each variable-length record represents a file in that directory. Look up the on-disk structure of a directory and explain each field, using an example from a real directory file. Next, look at the **lost+found** directory on a filesystem that uses them. Why are there so many names there when the **lost+found** directory is empty?

★★★★★ E8.9 Write a program that traverses the filesystem and prints the contents of the **/etc/motd** and **/etc/magic** files. But don't open the files directly; open the raw device file for the root partition and use the **seek** and **read** system calls to decode the filesystem and find the appropriate data blocks. **/etc/motd** is usually short and will probably contain only direct blocks. **/etc/magic** should require you to decode indirect blocks. (If it doesn't, pick a larger text file.)

Hint: when reading the system header files, be sure you have found the filesystem's on-disk inode structure, not the in-core inode structure. (Requires root access.)

9 Periodic Processes

Scripting and automation are the keys to consistency and reliability. For example, an **adduser** program can add new users faster than you can, with a smaller chance of making mistakes. Almost any task can be encoded in a Perl or Python script.

It's often useful to have a script or command executed without any human intervention. For example, you might want to have a script verify (say, every half-hour) that your network routers and switches are working correctly, and have the script send you email when problems are discovered.[1]

9.1 CRON: SCHEDULE COMMANDS

The **cron** daemon is the standard tool for running commands on a predetermined schedule. It starts when the system boots and runs as long as the system is up.

cron reads configuration files that contain lists of command lines and the times at which they are to be invoked. The command lines are executed by **sh**, so almost anything you can do by hand from the shell can also be done with **cron**.[2]

1. Many sites go further than this and send a text message to an administrator's phone as soon as a problem is detected. See Chapter 21, *Network Management and Debugging*, for more details.
2. You can configure **cron** to use other shells as well.

A **cron** configuration file is called a "crontab," short for "cron table." Crontabs for individual users are stored under **/var/spool/cron**. There is (at most) one crontab file per user: one for root, one for jsmith, and so on. Crontab files are named with the login names of the users to whom they belong, and **cron** uses these filenames to figure out which UID to use when running the commands contained in each file. The **crontab** command transfers crontab files to and from this directory.

Although the exact implementations vary, all versions of **cron** try to minimize the time they spend reparsing configuration files and making time calculations. The **crontab** command helps maintain **cron**'s efficiency by notifying **cron** when the crontabs change. Ergo, you shouldn't edit crontab files directly, since this may result in **cron** not noticing your changes. If you do get into a situation where **cron** doesn't seem to acknowledge a modified crontab, a HUP signal will force it to reload on most systems.

See Chapter 11 for more information about syslog.

cron normally does its work silently, but most versions can keep a log file (usually **/var/cron/log** or **/var/adm/cron/log**) that lists the commands that were executed and the times at which they ran. See Table 9.2 on page 287 for logging defaults.

On some systems, creating the log file enables logging, and removing the log file turns logging off. On other systems, the log is turned on or off in a configuration file. Yet another variation is for **cron** to use syslog. The log file grows quickly and is rarely useful; leave logging turned off unless you're debugging a specific problem or have specific auditing requirements.

9.2 THE FORMAT OF CRONTAB FILES

All the crontab files on a system share a similar format. Comments are introduced with a pound sign (#) in the first column of a line. Each noncomment line contains six fields and represents one command:

```
minute hour dom month weekday command
```

The first five fields tell **cron** when to run the *command*. They're separated by whitespace, but within the *command* field, whitespace is passed along to the shell. The fields in the time specification are interpreted as shown in Table 9.1.

Table 9.1 Crontab time specifications

Field	Description	Range
minute	Minute of the hour	0 to 59
hour	Hour of the day	0 to 23
dom	Day of the month	1 to 31
month	Month of the year	1 to 12
weekday	Day of the week	0 to 6 (0 = Sunday)

Each of the time-related fields may contain

- A star, which matches everything
- A single integer, which matches exactly
- Two integers separated by a dash, matching a range of values
- A range followed by a slash and a step value, e.g., 1-10/2 (Linux only)
- A comma-separated list of integers or ranges, matching any value

For example, the time specification

```
45 10 * * 1-5
```

means "10:45 a.m., Monday through Friday." A hint: never put a star in the first field unless you want the command to be run every minute.

There is a potential ambiguity to watch out for with the *weekday* and *dom* fields. Every day is both a day of the week and a day of the month. If both *weekday* and *dom* are specified, a day need satisfy only one of the two conditions in order to be selected. For example,

```
0,30 * 13 * 5
```

means "every half-hour on Friday, and every half-hour on the 13th of the month," not "every half-hour on Friday the 13th."

The *command* is the **sh** command line to be executed. It can be any valid shell command and should not be quoted. The *command* is considered to continue to the end of the line and may contain blanks or tabs.

Although **sh** is involved in executing the *command*, the shell does not act as a login shell and does not read the contents of **~/.profile** or **~/.bash_profile**. As a result, the command's environment variables may be set up somewhat differently from what you expect. If a command seems to work fine when executed from the shell but fails when introduced into a crontab file, the environment is the likely culprit. If need be, you can always wrap your command into a script that sets up the appropriate environment variables.

Percent signs (%) indicate newlines within the *command* field. Only the text up to the first percent sign is included in the actual command. The remaining lines are given to the command as standard input.

Here are some examples of legal crontab commands:

```
echo The time is now `date` > /dev/console
mail -s Reminder evi@anchor % Don't forget to write your chapters.
cd /etc; /bin/mail -s "Password file" evi < passwd
```

And below are some additional examples of complete crontab entries:

```
30 2 * * 1      (cd /home/joe/project; make)
```

Cron

This entry runs **make** in the directory **/home/joe/project** every Monday morning at 2:30 a.m. An entry like this might be used to start a long compilation at a time when other users would not be using the system. Usually, any output produced by a **cron** command is mailed to the owner of the crontab.[3]

```
20 1 * * *        find /tmp -atime +3 -type f -exec rm -f {} ';'
```

This command runs at 1:20 each morning. It removes all files in the **/tmp** directory that have not been accessed in 3 days.

```
55 23 * * 0-3,6  /staff/trent/bin/checkservers
```

This line runs **checkservers** at 11:55 p.m. every day except Thursdays and Fridays.

cron does not try to compensate for commands that are missed while the system is down. However, the Linux and HP-UX **cron**s are smart about small time adjustments such as shifts into and out of daylight saving time. Other versions of **cron** may skip commands or run them twice if they are scheduled during the transition period (usually between 1:00 and 3:00 a.m. in the United States, for example).[4]

9.3 Crontab management

crontab *filename* installs *filename* as your crontab, replacing any previous version. **crontab -e** checks out a copy of your crontab, invokes your editor on it (as specified by the EDITOR environment variable), and then resubmits it to the crontab directory. **crontab -l** lists the contents of your crontab to standard output, and **crontab -r** removes it, leaving you with no crontab file at all.

Root can supply a *username* argument to edit or view other users' crontabs. For example, **crontab -r jsmith** erases the crontab belonging to the user jsmith, and **crontab -e jsmith** edits it. Linux allows both a *username* and a *filename* argument in the same command, so the username must be prefixed with **-u** to disambiguate (e.g., **crontab -u jsmith crontab.new**).

Without command-line arguments, most versions of **crontab** will try to read a crontab from standard input. If you enter this mode by accident, don't try to exit with <Control-D>; doing so will erase your entire crontab. Use <Control-C> instead. Linux requires you to supply a dash as the *filename* argument if you want to make **crontab** pay attention to its standard input. Smart.

Two config files, **cron.deny** and **cron.allow**, specify which users may submit crontab files. They're located in a different directory on every system; see Table 9.2 for a summary.

3. That is, the user after whom the crontab file is named. On most (but not all) systems, the actual owner of crontab files is root.

4. One of our contributors reports having seen a case in which **cron** consumed 100% of the CPU because the system date had been set to the UNIX epoch. The local time zone was a negative offset from GMT, so with the offset taken into account, the local time appeared to be a negative number, and **cron** was confused. Most systems power their on-board clocks with a battery, so clock resets are not as unusual as you might think. Time instability is a common symptom of a dead or dying battery.

Table 9.2 Locations of cron permission and log files

System	Allow/deny	Default	Default log
Linux	**/etc**	All users	via syslog
Solaris	**/etc/cron.d**	All users	**/var/cron/log**
HP-UX	**/usr/lib/cron**	Only root	**/var/adm/cron/log**
AIX	**/var/adm/cron**	All users	**/var/adm/cron/log**

If the allow file exists, then it contains a list of all users that may submit crontabs, one per line. No unlisted person can invoke the **crontab** command. If the allow file doesn't exist, then the deny file is checked. It, too, is just a list of users, but the meaning is reversed: everyone except the listed users is allowed access.

If neither the allow file nor the deny file exists, systems default (apparently at random, there being no dominant convention) to allowing all users to submit crontabs or to limiting crontab access to root. In practice, a starter **cron.allow** or **cron.deny** file is often included in the default OS installation, so the question of how **crontab** behaves without configuration files is moot. Among our example systems, only HP-UX defaults to blocking **crontab** access for unprivileged users.

It's important to note that on most systems, access control is implemented by **crontab**, not by **cron**. If a user is able to sneak a crontab file into the appropriate directory by other means, **cron** will blindly execute the commands it contains.

Solaris is a bit different in this regard. Its **cron** daemon checks to be sure that the user's account hasn't been locked with an *LK* in **/etc/shadow**. If it has, **cron** won't run the user's jobs. The rationale is to prevent disabled users from running jobs, whether inadvertently or maliciously. If you want a user to have a valid account from **cron**'s perspective but not a valid password, run **passwd -N** *user*.

9.4 Linux and Vixie-cron extensions

The version of **cron** included on Linux distributions (including our three examples) is usually the one known as ISC **cron** or "Vixie-**cron**," named after its author, Paul Vixie. It's a modern rewrite that provides a bit of added functionality with less mess.

A primary difference is that in addition to looking for user-specific crontabs, Vixie-**cron** also obeys system crontab entries found in **/etc/crontab** and in the **/etc/cron.d** directory. These files have a slightly different format from the per-user crontab files in that they allow commands to be run as an arbitrary user. An extra *username* field comes before the command name. The *username* field is not present in garden-variety crontab files because the crontab's filename provides this same information (even on Linux systems).

cron treats the **/etc/crontab** and **/etc/cron.d** entries in exactly the same way. In general, **/etc/crontab** is intended as a file for system administrators to maintain by hand, whereas **/etc/cron.d** is provided as a depot into which software packages can install any crontab entries they might need. Files in **/etc/cron.d** are by convention named after the packages that install them, but **cron** doesn't care about or enforce this convention.

Time ranges in Vixie-**cron** crontabs can include a step value. For example, the series 0,3,6,9,12,15,18 can be written more concisely as 0-18/3. You can also use three-letter text mnemonics for the names of months and days, but not in combination with ranges. As far as we know, this feature works only with English names.

You can specify environment variables and their values in a Vixie-**cron** crontab file. See the **crontab**(5) man page for more details.

Vixie-**cron** logs its activities through syslog using the facility "cron," with most messages submitted at level "info." Default syslog configurations generally send **cron** log data to its own file.

For reasons that are unclear, **cron** has been renamed **crond** on Red Hat. But it is still the same Vixie-**cron** we all know and love.

9.5 Some common uses for cron

A number of standard tasks are especially suited for invocation by **cron**, and these usually make up the bulk of the material in root's crontab. In this section we look at a few common chores and the crontab lines used to implement them.

Systems often come with crontab entries preinstalled. If you want to deactivate the standard entries, comment them out by inserting a pound sign (#) at the beginning of each line. Don't delete them; you might want to refer to them later.

In addition to the **/etc/cron.d** mechanism, Linux distributions also preinstall crontab entries that run the scripts in a set of well-known directories, thereby providing another way for software packages to install periodic jobs without any editing of a crontab file. For example, scripts in **/etc/cron.daily** are run once a day, and scripts in **/etc/cron.weekly** are run once a week. You can put files in these directories by hand as well.

Many sites have experienced subtle but recurrent network glitches that occur because administrators have configured **cron** to run the same command on hundreds of machines at exactly the same time. Clock synchronization with NTP exacerbates the problem. The problem is easy to fix with a random delay script or config file adjustment, but it can be tricky to diagnose because the symptoms resolve so quickly and completely.

Simple reminders

It's not going to put Google Calendar out of business, but **cron** can be quite useful in its own geeky way for simple reminders: birthdays, due dates, recurrent tasks, etc. That's especially true when the reminder process has to integrate with other home-grown software such as a trouble ticket manager.

The following crontab entry implements a simple email reminder. (Lines have been folded to fit the page. In reality, this is one long line.)

```
30  4  25  *  *      /usr/bin/mail -s "Time to do the TPS reports"
    owen@atrust.com%TPS reports are due at the end of the month! Get
    busy!%%Sincerely,%cron
```

Note the use of the % character both to separate the command from the input text and to mark line endings within the input. This entry sends email once on the 25th day of each month.

Filesystem cleanup

Some of the files on any system are worthless junk (no, not the system files). For example, when a program crashes, the kernel may write out a file (usually named **core**, **core.***pid*, or *program***.core**) that contains an image of the program's address space. Core files are useful for developers, but for administrators they are usually a waste of space. Users often don't know about core files, so they tend not to delete them on their own.[5]

NFS, the Network File System, is described in Chapter 18.

NFSv3 is another source of extra files. Because NFSv3 servers are stateless, they have to use a special convention to preserve files that have been deleted locally but are still in use by a remote machine. Most implementations rename such files to **.nfs***xxx*, where *xxx* is a number. Various situations can result in these files being forgotten and left around after they are supposed to have been deleted.

Many programs create temporary files in **/tmp** or **/var/tmp** that aren't erased for one reason or another. Some programs, especially editors, like to make a backup copy of each file they work with.

A partial solution to the junk file problem is to institute some sort of nightly disk space reclamation out of **cron**. Modern systems usually come with something of this sort set up for you, but it's a good idea to review your system's default behavior to make sure it's appropriate for your situation.

Below are several common idioms implemented with the **find** command.

```
find / -xdev -type f '(' -name core -o name 'core.[0-9]*' -o name '*.core' ')'
    -atime +7 -exec rm -f {} ';'
```

This command removes core images that have not been accessed in a week. The **-xdev** argument makes sure that **find** won't cross over to filesystems other than the root; this restraint is important on networks where many filesystems may be cross-mounted.[6] If you want to clean up more than one filesystem, use a separate command for each. (Note that **/var** is typically a separate filesystem.)

5. Many systems' kernels can be configured to put core dumps in a particular directory, or optionally, not generate them at all. For example, see **man core** on Linux or **man coreadm** on Solaris.

6. Not all versions of **find** support the **-xdev** argument. On some systems, it's called **-x**.

Cron

The **-type f** argument is important because the Linux kernel source contains a directory called **core**. You wouldn't want to be deleting that, would you?[7]

```
find / -xdev -atime +3 '(' -name '#*' -o -name '.#*' -o -name '*.CKP' -o
    -name '*~' -o -name '.nfs*' ')' -exec rm -f {} ';'
```

This command deletes files that have not been accessed in three days and that begin with # or **.#** or **.nfs** or end with ~ or **.CKP**. These patterns are typical of various sorts of temporary and editor backup files.

See page 143 for more information about mount options.

For performance reasons, some administrators use the noatime mount option to prevent the filesystem from maintaining access time stamps. That configuration will confuse both of the **find** commands shown above because the files will appear to have been unreferenced even if they were recently active. Unfortunately, the failure mode is to delete the files; be sure you are maintaining access times before using these commands as shown.

```
cd /tmp; find . ! -name . ! -name lost+found -type d -mtime +3
    -exec /bin/rm -rf {} ';'
```

This command recursively removes all subdirectories of **/tmp** not modified in 72 hours. On most systems, plain files in **/tmp** are removed at boot time by the system startup scripts. However, some systems do not remove directories. If a directory named **lost+found** exists, it is treated specially and is not removed. This is important if **/tmp** is a separate filesystem. See page 260 for more information about **lost+found**.

If you use any of these commands, make sure that users are aware of your cleanup policies before disaster strikes!

Network distribution of configuration files

See Chapter 19 for more information about sharing configuration files.

If you are running a network of machines, it's often convenient to maintain a single, network-wide version of configuration files such as the mail aliases database. Usually, the underlying sharing mechanism is some form of polling or periodic distribution, so this is an ideal task for **cron**. Master versions of system files can be distributed every night with **rsync** or **rdist**.

Sometimes, postprocessing is required. For example, you might need to run the **newaliases** command to convert a file of mail aliases to the hashed format used by **sendmail** because the AutoRebuildAliases option isn't set in your **sendmail.cf** file. You might also need to load files into an administrative database such as NIS.

Log file rotation

Systems vary in the quality of their default log file management, and you will probably need to adjust the defaults to conform to your local policies. To "rotate"

7. Bryan Helvey, one of our technical reviewers, has worked in the oil industry and notes that **core** in that context is as likely to refer to a core sample as to a core dump. More generally, we acknowledge that it's inherently dangerous to delete files base on their names alone.

a log file means to divide it into segments by size or by date, keeping several older versions of the log available at all times. Since log rotation is a recurrent and regularly scheduled event, it's an ideal task for **cron**. See Chapter 11, *Syslog and Log Files* for more details.

9.6 EXERCISES

E9.1 A local user has been abusing his crontab privileges by running expensive tasks at frequent intervals. After asking him to stop several times, you are forced to revoke his privileges. List the steps needed to delete his current crontab and make sure he can't add a new one.

E9.2 Think of three tasks (other than those mentioned in this chapter) that might need to be run periodically. Write crontab entries for each task and specify where they should go on your system.

E9.3 Choose three entries from your system's crontab files. Decode each one and describe when it runs, what it does, and why you think the entry is needed. (Requires root access.)

☆ E9.4 Write a script that keeps your startup files (~/.**[a-z]***) synchronized among all the machines on which you have an account. Schedule this script to run regularly from **cron**. (Is it safe to blindly copy every file whose name starts with a dot? How will you handle directories? Should files being replaced on the destination machines be backed up before they are overwritten?)

10 Backups

At most sites, the information stored on computers is worth far more than the computers themselves. It is also much harder to replace. Protecting this information is one of the system administrator's most important (and, unfortunately, most tedious) tasks.

There are hundreds of creative and not-so-creative ways to lose data. Software bugs routinely corrupt documents. Users accidentally delete data files. Hackers and disgruntled employees erase disks. Hardware problems and natural disasters take out entire machine rooms.

If executed correctly, backups allow an administrator to restore a filesystem (or any portion of a filesystem) to the condition it was in at the time of the last backup. Backups must be done carefully and on a strict schedule. The backup system and backup media must also be tested regularly to verify that they are working correctly.

The integrity of your backup procedures directly affects your company's bottom line. Senior management needs to understand what the backups are actually capable of doing, as opposed to what they *want* the backups to do. It may be OK to lose a day's work at a university computer science department, but it probably isn't OK at a commodity trading firm.

We begin this chapter with some general backup philosophy, followed by a discussion of the most commonly used backup devices and media (their strengths, weaknesses, and costs). Next, we talk about how to design a backup scheme and review the mechanics of the popular **dump** and **restore** utilities.

We then discuss some additional backup and archiving commands and suggest which commands are best for which situations. Finally, we take a look at Bacula, a free network backup package, and offer some comments about other open source and commercial alternatives.

10.1 MOTHERHOOD AND APPLE PIE

Before we get into the meat and potatoes of backups, we want to pass on some general hints that we have learned over time (usually, the hard way). None of these suggestions is an absolute rule, but you will find that the more of them you follow, the smoother your backups and restores will go.

Perform all backups from a central location

Many backup utilities allow you to perform dumps over the network. Although there is some performance penalty for doing dumps that way, the increase in ease of administration makes it worthwhile. If you manage only a handful of servers, it's probably easiest to run a script from a central location that executes **dump** (by way of **ssh**) on each machine that needs to be dumped. If you have more than a few servers, you should use a software package (commercial or free) to automate this process.

Even if your backups are too large to be funneled through a single server, you should still try to keep your backup system as centralized as possible. Centralization facilitates administration and lets you restore data to alternate servers. Depending on the media you are using, you can often put more than one media device on a server without affecting performance.

Dumps created with **dump** can only be restored on machines that have the same byte order as the dump host (and in most cases, only on machines running the same OS). You can sometimes use **dd** to take care of byte swapping problems, but this simple fix won't resolve differences among incompatible versions of **dump.**

If you are backing up so much data across a network that the network's bandwidth becomes an issue, consider creating a LAN dedicated to backup traffic. Many organizations find this approach effective for alleviating network bottlenecks.

Label your media

Label each piece of backup media clearly and completely—an unlabeled tape is a scratch tape. Directly label each piece of media to uniquely identify its contents. On the cases for the media, write detailed information such as lists of filesystems, backup dates, the format of the backups, the exact syntax of the commands used to create them, and any other information you would need to restore the system without referring to on-line documentation.

Free and commercial labeling programs abound. Save yourself a major headache and invest in one. Vendors of laser printer labels can usually provide templates for each of their labels. Better yet, buy a dedicated label printer. They are inexpensive and work well.

Your automated dump system should record the name of each filesystem it has dumped. Good record keeping allows you to quickly skip forward to the correct filesystem when you want to restore a file. It's also a good idea to record the order of the filesystems on the tape or case.

If you can afford it, buy an autochanger or tape drive that reads bar codes. This feature ensures that your electronic tape labels always match the physical ones.

Pick a reasonable backup interval

The more often backups are done, the less data is lost in a crash. However, backups use system resources and an operator's time. You must provide adequate data integrity at a reasonable cost of time and materials. In general, costs increase as you move toward more granular restoration capabilities.

On busy systems, it is generally appropriate to back up home directories every workday. On systems that are used less heavily or on which the data is less volatile, you might decide that performing backups several times a week is sufficient. On a small system with only one user, performing backups once a week is probably adequate. How much data are your users willing to lose?

Choose filesystems carefully

Filesystems that are rarely modified do not need to be backed up as frequently as users' home directories. If only a few files change on an otherwise static filesystem (such as **/etc/passwd** in the root filesystem), you can copy these files every day to another partition that is backed up regularly.

If **/tmp** is a separate filesystem, it should not be backed up. The **/tmp** directory should not contain anything essential, so there is no reason to preserve it. If this seems obvious, you are in better shape than many sites we've visited.

Make daily dumps fit on one piece of media

*See Chapter 9 for more information about **cron**.*

In a perfect world, you could do daily dumps of all your important filesystems onto a single tape. High-density media such as DLT, AIT, and LTO make this goal practical for some sites. However, as our work habits change and telecommuting becomes more popular, the range of "good" times to do backups is shrinking. More and more network services must be available around the clock, and large backups take time.

Another major problem is the rapid expansion of disk space that has resulted from the ever-lower price of hard disks. You can no longer purchase a stock desktop machine with less than 250GB of disk space. Why clean up your disks and enforce quotas when you can just throw a little money at the problem and add more disk space? Unfortunately, it's all too easy for the amount of on-line storage to outstrip your ability to back it up.

Backup utilities are perfectly capable of dumping filesystems to multiple pieces of media. However, if a dump spans multiple tapes, an operator or tape library robot must be present to change the media, and the media must be carefully labeled to allow restores to be performed easily. Unless you have a good reason to create a really large filesystem, don't do it.

If you can't fit your daily backups on one tape, you have several options:

- Buy a higher-capacity backup device.
- Buy a stacker or library and feed multiple pieces of media to one device.
- Change your dump sequence.
- Use multiple backup devices.

Keep media off-site

First, baby steps: you should always have an off-*line* copy of your data.That is, a protected copy that is not stored on a hard disk on the machine of origin. Snapshots and RAID arrays are not substitutes for real backups!

Most organizations also keep backups off-*site* so that a disaster such as a fire cannot destroy both the original data and the backups. "Off-site" can be anything from a safe deposit box at a bank to the President's or CEO's home. Companies that specialize in the secure storage of backup media guarantee a secure and climate-controlled environment for your archives. Always make sure your off-site storage provider is reputable, bonded, and insured. There are on-line (but off-site) businesses today that specialize in safeguarding your data.

The speed with which backup media are moved off-site should depend on how often you need to restore files and on how much latency you can accept. Some sites avoid making this decision by performing two dumps to different backup devices, one that stays on-site and one that is moved immediately.[1]

Protect your backups

Dan Geer, a security consultant, said, "What does a backup do? It reliably violates file permissions at a distance." Hmmm.

Encryption of backup media is usually a no-brainer and is required by security standards such as the Payment Card Industry Data Security Standard (PCI DSS).

1. A large financial institution located in the World Trade Center kept its "off-site" backups one or two floors below their offices. When the building was bombed (the first time), the backup tapes (as well as the computers) were destroyed. Make sure "off-site" really is.

Many backup utilities make encryption relatively painless. However, you must be sure that the encryption keys cannot be lost or destroyed and that they are available for use in an emergency.

Physically secure your backup media as well. Not only should you keep your media off-site, but you should also keep them under lock and key. If you use a commercial storage facility for this purpose, the company you deal with should guarantee the confidentiality of the tapes in their care.

Some companies feel so strongly about the importance of backups that they make duplicates, which is really not a bad idea at all.

Limit activity during backups

Filesystem activity should be limited during backups because changes can cause your backup utility to make mistakes. One way to limit activity is to do dumps when few active users are around (in the middle of night or on weekends). To automate the process, mount your backup media every day before leaving work and let **cron** execute the backup for you. That way, dumps occur at a time when files are less likely to be changing, and the dumps have minimal impact on users.

In practice, it is next to impossible to find a disk that doesn't always have at least a little activity. Users want 24/7 access to data, services run around the clock, and databases require special backup procedures. Most databases must be temporarily stopped or put in a special degraded mode so that backups can accurately capture data at a single point in time. Sites with a lot of data may not be able to tolerate the downtime necessary to perform a traditional backup of their database. These days the only way to do a backup with no disk activity is to first create a snapshot.

See page 274 for more information about SANs.

Most SAN controllers, and all our example operating systems, provide some way to create a snapshot of a filesystem. This feature lets you make relatively safe backups of an active filesystem, even one on which files are currently open. On Linux, snapshots are implemented through the logical volume manager (see page 249), and on our other example systems they are created through the filesystem.

Snapshots can be created almost instantaneously thanks to a clever copy-on-write scheme. No data is actually copied or moved at the time the snapshot is created. Once the snapshot exists, changes to the filesystem are written to new locations on disk. In this way, two (or more) images can be maintained with minimal use of additional storage. Snapshots are similar in concept to incremental backups, except that they operate at the block level rather than the filesystem level.

In this context, snapshots are primarily a tool for creating "real" backups of a filesystem. They are never a replacement for off-line backups. Snapshots also help facilitate database backups, since the database only needs to be paused for a second while the snapshot completes. Later, the relatively slow tape backup can be performed against the snapshot as the live database goes happily on its way serving up queries.

Verify your media

We've heard many horror stories about system administrators who did not discover problems with their dump regime until after a serious system failure. It is essential that you continually monitor your backup procedure and verify that it is functioning correctly. Operator error ruins more dumps than any other problem.

The first check is to have your backup software attempt to reread tapes immediately after it has finished dumping.[2] Scanning a tape to verify that it contains the expected number of files is a good check. It's best if every tape is scanned, but this no longer seems practical for a large organization that uses many tapes every day. A random sample would be most prudent in this environment.

*See page 310 for more information about **restore**.*

It is often useful to generate a table of contents for each filesystem (**dump** users can use **restore -t**) and to store the resulting catalogs on disk. These catalogs should be named in a way that relates them to the appropriate tape; for example, **okra:usr.Jan.13**. A database of these records makes it easy to discover what piece of media a lost file is on. Just **grep** for the filename and pick the newest instance.

In addition to providing a catalog of tapes, successfully reading the table of contents from the tape is a good indication that the dump is OK and that you will probably be able to read the media when you need to. A quick attempt to restore a random file gives you even more confidence in your ability to restore from that piece of media.[3]

You should periodically attempt to restore from random media to make sure that restoration is still possible. Every so often, try to restore from an old (months or years) piece of dump media.[4] Tape drives have been known to wander out of alignment over time and become unable to read their old tapes. The media can be recovered by a company that specializes in this service, but it is expensive.

A related check is to verify that you can read the media on hardware other than your own. If your machine room burns, it does not do much good to know that the backup could have been read on a tape drive that has now been destroyed. DAT tapes have been particularly susceptible to this problem in the past, but more recent versions of the technology have improved.

Develop a media life cycle

All media have a finite life. It's great to recycle your media, but be sure to abide by the manufacturer's recommendations regarding the life of the media. Most tape manufacturers quantify this life in terms of the number of passes that a tape can stand: a backup, a restore, and an **mt fsf** (file skip forward) each represent one

2. GNU versions of **restore** include the **-C** option to verify a dump tape against a directory tree.
3. For example, **restore -t** reads only the table of contents for the dump, which is stored at the beginning of the tape. When you actually restore a file, you are testing a more extensive region of the medium.
4. It's helpful to treat users who request the restoration of accidentally deleted files as colleagues who are spot-checking your backup system rather than as incompetent, file-deleting annoyances. A positive attitude makes the experience more pleasant for both of you and increases the number of spot-checks.

pass. Nontape technologies have a much longer life that is sometimes expressed as a mean time to failure (MTTF), but all hardware and media have a finite lifetime. Think of media life in dog-years rather than real years.

Before you toss old tapes in the trash, remember to erase or render them unreadable. A bulk tape eraser (a large electromagnet) can help with this, but be sure to keep it far, far away from computers and active media. Cutting or pulling out part of a backup tape does not really do much to protect your data, because tape is easy to splice or respool. Document-destruction companies shred tapes for a fee.

In the case of hard disks used as backup media, remember that drive recovery services cost less than a thousand dollars and are just as available to bad guys as they are to you. Consider performing a secure erase (page 227) or SCSI format operation before a drive leaves your site.

Design your data for backups

With disks so cheap and new storage architectures so reliable, it's tempting to throw your hands and not back up all your data. Don't give up! A sensible storage architecture—designed rather than grown willy-nilly as disk needs increase—can make backups much more tractable.

Start by taking an inventory of your storage needs:

- The various kinds of data your site deals with
- The expected volatility of each type of data
- The backup frequency needed for comfort with potential losses
- The network and political boundaries over which the data is spread

Use this information to design your site's storage architecture, keeping backups and potential growth in mind. For example, putting project directories and users' home directories on a dedicated file server can make it easier to manage your data and ensure its safety.

With the advent of powerful system-imaging and disk-building solutions, it is often easier to re-image a broken system than to troubleshoot and restore corrupt or missing files. Many administrators configure their users' workstations to store all data on a centralized server. Others manage farms of servers that have near-identical configurations and data (such as the content for a busy web site). In such an environment, it's reasonable not to back up vast arrays of duplicated systems. On the other hand, security mavens encourage generous backups so that data is available for forensic analysis in the event of an incident.

Prepare for the worst

After you have established a backup procedure, explore the worst case scenario: your site is completely destroyed. Determine how much data would be lost and how long it would take to get your system back to life. (Include in your calculations the time it would take to acquire new hardware.) Then determine whether you can live with your answers.

More formal organizations often designate a Recovery Time Objective (RTO) and a Recovery Point Objective (RPO) for information on specific servers or filesystems. When these numbers are available, they provide valuable guidance.

An RTO represents the maximum amount of time that the business can tolerate waiting for a recovery to complete. Typical RTOs for user data range from hours to days. For production servers, RTOs can range from hours to seconds.

An RPO indicates how recent a backup is required for the restore and influences the granularity at which backups must be retained. Depending on how frequently the dataset changes and how important it is, an RPO might range from weeks to hours to seconds. Tape backups clearly can't satisfy near-real-time RPOs, so such requirements usually imply large investments and specialized storage devices located in multiple data centers.

Although the process of defining these metrics may seem somewhat arbitrary, it is a useful way to get the "owners" of the data on the same page as the technical folks. The process requires balancing cost and effort against the business's need for recoverability. It's a difficult but important venture.

10.2 Backup devices and media

Many failures can damage several pieces of hardware at once, so backups should be written to some sort of removable media. A good rule of thumb is to create offline backups that no single disgruntled system administrator could destroy.

Backing up one hard disk to another on the same machine or in the same data center provides little protection against a server failure, although it is certainly better than no backup at all. Companies that back up your data over the Internet are becoming more popular, but most backups are still created locally.

The following sections describe some of the media that can be used for backups. The media are presented in rough order of increasing capacity.

Manufacturers like to specify their hardware capacities in terms of compressed data; they often optimistically assume a compression ratio of 2:1 or more. In the sections below, we ignore compression in favor of the actual number of bytes that can physically be stored on each piece of media.

The compression ratio also affects a drive's throughput rating. If a drive can physically write 1 MB/s to tape but the manufacturer assumes 2:1 compression, the throughput magically rises to 2 MB/s. As with capacity figures, we have ignored throughput inflation below.

Optical media: CD-R/RW, DVD±R/RW, DVD-RAM, and Blu-ray

At a cost of about $0.30 each, CDs and DVDs are an attractive option for backups of small, isolated systems. CDs hold about 700MB and DVDs hold 4.7GB. Dual-layer DVDs clock in at about 8.5GB.

Drives that write these media are available for every common bus (SCSI, IDE, USB, SATA, etc.) and are in many cases are so inexpensive as to be essentially free. Now that CD and DVD prices have equilibrated, there's no reason to use CDs rather than DVDs. However, we still see quite a few CDs used in the real world for reasons that are not entirely clear.

Optical media are written through a photochemical process that involves the use of a laser. Although hard data on longevity has been elusive, it is widely believed that optical media have a substantially longer shelf life than magnetic media. However, the write-once versions (CD-R, DVD-R, and DVD+R) are not as durable as manufactured (stamped) CDs and DVDs.

Today's fast DVD writers offer speeds as fast as—if not faster than—tape drives. The write-once versions are DVD-R and DVD+R. DVD-RW, DVD+RW, and DVD-RAM are rewritable. The DVD-RAM system has built-in defect management and is therefore more reliable than other optical media. On the other hand, it is much more expensive.

Manufacturers estimate a potential life span of hundreds of years for these media if they are properly stored. Their recommendations for proper storage include individual cases, storage at a constant temperature in the range 41°F–68°F with relative humidity of 30%–50%, no exposure to direct sunlight, and marking only with water-soluble markers. Under average conditions, a reliable shelf life of 1–5 years is probably more realistic.

As borne out by numerous third-party evaluations, the reliability of optical media has proved to be exceptionally manufacturer dependent. This is one case in which it pays to spend money on premium quality media. Unfortunately, quality varies from product to product even within a manufacturer's line, so there is no safe-bet manufacturer.

A recent entry to the optical data storage market is the Blu-ray disc, whose various flavors store from 25–100 GB of data. This high capacity is a result of the short wavelength (405nm) of the laser used to read and write the disks (hence the "blue" in Blu-ray). As the cost of media drops, this technology promises to become a good solution for backups.

Portable and removable hard disks

External storage devices that connect through a USB 2.0 or eSATA port are common. The underlying storage technology is usually some form of hard disk, but flash memory devices are common at the low end (the ubiquitous "jump drives"). Capacities for conventional hard drives range from less than 250GB to over 2TB. Solid state drives (SSDs) are based on flash memory and are currently available in sizes up to 160GB. The limit on USB flash memory devices is about 64GB, but it is growing fast.

The lifetime of flash memory devices is mostly a function of the number of write cycles. Midrange drives usually last at least 100,000 cycles.

The main limitation of such drives as backup media is that they are normally on-line and so are vulnerable to power surges, heating overload, and tampering by malicious users. For hard drives to be effective as backup media, they must be manually unmounted or disconnected from the server. Removable drives make this task easier. Specialized "tapeless backup" systems that use disks to emulate the off-line nature of tapes are also available.

Magnetic tapes in general

Many kinds of media store data by adjusting the orientation of magnetic particles. These media are subject to damage by electrical and magnetic fields. You should beware of the following sources of magnetic fields: audio speakers, transformers and power supplies, unshielded electric motors, disk fans, CRT monitors, and even prolonged exposure to the Earth's background radiation.

All magnetic tapes eventually become unreadable over a period of years. Most tape media will keep for at least three years, but if you plan to store data longer than that, you should either use media that are certified for a longer retention period or rerecord the data periodically.

Small tape drives: 8mm and DDS/DAT

Various flavors of 8mm and Digital Data Storage/Digital Audio Tape drives compose the low end of the tape storage market. Exabyte 8mm tape drives were early favorites, but the drives tended to become misaligned every 6–12 months, requiring a trip to the repair depot. It was not uncommon for tapes to be stretched in the transport mechanism and become unreliable. The 2–7 GB capacity of these tapes makes them inefficient for backing up today's desktop systems, let alone servers.

DDS/DAT drives are helical scan devices that use 4mm cartridges. Although these drives are usually referred to as DAT drives, they are really DDS drives; the exact distinction is unimportant. The original format held about 2GB, but successive generations have significantly improved DDS capacity. The current generation (DAT 160) holds up to 80GB of data at a transfer rate of 6.9 MB/s. The tapes should last for 100 backups and are reported to have a shelf life of 10 years.

DLT/S-DLT

Digital Linear Tape/Super Digital Linear Tape is a mainstream backup medium. These drives are reliable, affordable, and capacious. They evolved from DEC's TK-50 and TK-70 cartridge tape drives. DEC sold the technology to Quantum, which popularized the drives by increasing their speed and capacity and by dropping their price. In 2002, Quantum acquired Super DLT, a technology by Benchmark Storage Innovations that tilts the recording head back and forth to reduce crosstalk between adjacent tracks.

Quantum now offers two hardware lines: a performance line and a value line. You get what you pay for. The tape capacities vary from DLT-4 at 800GB to DLT-4 in the value line at 160GB, with transfer rates of 60 MB/s and 10 MB/s, respectively.

Manufacturers boast that the tapes will last 20 to 30 years—that is, if the hardware to read them still exists. How many 9-track tape drives are still functioning and on-line these days?

The downside of S-DLT is the price of media, which runs $90–100 per 800GB tape. A bit pricey for a university; perhaps not for a Wall Street investment firm.

AIT and SAIT

Advanced Intelligent Tape is Sony's own 8mm product on steroids. In 1996, Sony dissolved its relationship with Exabyte and introduced the AIT-1, an 8mm helical scan device with twice the capacity of 8mm drives from Exabyte. Today, Sony offers AIT-4, with a capacity of 200GB and a 24 MB/s maximum transfer rate, and AIT-5, which doubles the capacity while keeping the same transfer speed.

SAIT is Sony's half-height offering, which uses larger media and has greater capacity than AIT. SAIT tapes holds up to 500GB of data and sport a transfer rate of 30 MB/s. This product is most common in the form of tape library offerings—Sony's are especially popular.

The Advanced Metal Evaporated (AME) tapes used in AIT and SAIT drives have a long life cycle. They also contain a built-in EEPROM that gives the media itself some smarts. Software support is needed to make any actual use of the EEPROM, however. Drive and tape prices are both roughly on par with DLT.

VXA/VXA-X

The VXA and VXA-X technologies were originally developed by Exabyte and were acquired by Tandberg Data in 2006. The VXA drives use what Exabyte describes as a packet technology for data transfer. The VXA-X products still rely on Sony for the AME media; the V series is upgradable as larger-capacity media become available. The VXA and X series claim capacities in the range of 33–160 GB, with a transfer rate of 24 MB/s.

LTO

Linear Tape-Open was developed by IBM, HP, and Quantum as an alternative to the proprietary format of DLT. LTO-4, the latest version, has an 800GB capacity at a speed of 120 MB/s. LTO media has an estimated storage life of 30 years but is susceptible to magnetic exposure. As with most technology, the previous generation LTO-3 drives are much less expensive and are still adequate for use in many environments. The cost of media is about $40 for LTO-4 tapes and $25 for the 400GB LTO-3 tapes.

Jukeboxes, stackers, and tape libraries

With the low cost of disks these days, most sites have so much disk space that a full backup requires many tapes, even at 800GB per tape. One possible solution for these sites is a stacker, jukebox, or tape library.

A stacker is a simple tape changer that is used with a standard tape drive. It has a hopper that you load with tapes. The stacker unloads full tapes as they are ejected from the drive and replaces them with blank tapes from the hopper. Most stackers hold about ten tapes.

A jukebox is a hardware device that can automatically change removable media in a limited number of drives, much like an old-style music jukebox that changed records on a single turntable. Jukeboxes are available for all the media discussed here. They are often bundled with special backup software that understands how to manipulate the changer. Storage Technology (now part of Oracle) and Sony are two large manufacturers of these products.

Tape libraries, also known as autochangers, are a hardware backup solution for large data sets—terabytes, usually. They are large-closet-sized mechanisms with multiple tape drives (or optical drives) and a robotic arm that retrieves and files media on the library's many shelves. As you can imagine, they are quite expensive to purchase and maintain, and they have special power, space, and air conditioning requirements.

Most purchasers of tape libraries also purchase an operations contract from the manufacturer to optimize and run the device. The libraries have a software component, of course, which is what really runs the device. Storage Technology (Oracle), Spectra Logic, and HP are leading manufacturers of tape libraries.

Hard disks

The decreasing cost of hard drives makes disk-to-disk backups an attractive option to consider. Although we suggest that you not duplicate one disk to another within the same physical machine, hard disks can be a good, low-cost solution for backups over a network and can dramatically decrease the time required to restore large datasets.

One obvious problem is that hard disk storage space is finite and must eventually be reused. However, disk-to-disk backups are an excellent way to protect against the accidental deletion of files. If you maintain a day-old disk image in a well-known place that's shared over NFS or CIFS, users can recover from their own mistakes without involving an administrator.

Remember that on-line storage is usually not sufficient protection against malicious attackers or data center equipment failures. If you are not able to actually store your backups off-line, at least shoot for geographic diversity when storing them on-line.

Internet and cloud backup services

Service providers have recently begun to offer Internet-hosted storage solutions. Rather than provisioning storage in your own data center, you lease storage from a cloud provider. Not only does this approach provide on-demand access to almost limitless storage, but it also gives you an easy way to store data in multiple geographic locations.

Internet storage services start at 10¢/GB/month and get more expensive as you add features. For example, some providers let you choose how many redundant copies of your data will be stored. This pay-per-use pricing allows you to pick the reliability that is appropriate for your data and budget.

Internet backups only work if your Internet connection is fast enough to transmit copies of your changes every night without bogging down "real" traffic. If your organization handles large amounts of data, it is unlikely that you can back it up across the Internet. But for smaller organizations, cloud backups can be an ideal solution since there is no up-front cost and no hardware to buy. Remember, any sensitive data that transits the Internet or is stored in the cloud must be encrypted.

Summary of media types

Whew! That's a lot of possibilities. Table 10.1 summarizes the characteristics of the media discussed in the previous sections.

Table 10.1 Backup media compared

Medium	Capacity[a]	Speed[a]	Drive	Media	Cost/GB[a]	Reuse?	Random?[b]
CD-R	700MB	7MB/s	$15	15¢	21¢	No	Yes
CD-RW	700MB	4MB/s	$20	30¢	42¢	Yes	Yes
DVD±R	4.7GB	30MB/s	$30	30¢	6¢	No	Yes
DVD+R DL[c]	8.5GB	30MB/s	$30	$1	12¢	No	Yes
DVD±RW	4.7GB	10MB/s	$30	40¢	9¢	Yes	Yes
Blu-ray	25GB	30MB/s	$100	$3	12¢	No	Yes
DDS-4 (4mm)	20GB	30MB/s	$100	$5	25¢	Yes	No
DLT/S-DLT	160GB	16MB/s	$500	$10	6¢	Yes	No
DLT-S4	800GB	60MB/s	$2,500	$100	13¢	Yes	No
AIT-4 (8mm)	200GB	24MB/s	$1,200	$40	20¢	Yes	No
AIT-5	400GB	24MB/s	$2,500	$50	13¢	Yes	No
VXA-320	160GB	12MB/s	$800	$60	38¢	Yes	No
LTO-3	400GB	80MB/s	$200	$25	6¢	Yes	No
LTO-4	800GB	120MB/s	$1,600	$40	5¢	Yes	No

a. Uncompressed capacity and speed
b. Allows random access to any part of the media
c. Dual-layer

What to buy

When you buy a backup system, you pretty much get what you see in Table 10.1. All the media work reasonably well, and among the technologies that are close in price, there generally isn't a compelling reason to prefer one over another. Buy a system that meets your specifications and your budget. If you are deploying new hardware, make sure it is supported by your OS and backup software.

Although cost and media capacity are both important considerations, it's important to consider throughput as well. Fast media are more pleasant to deal with, but be careful not to purchase a tape drive that overpowers the server it is attached to. If the server can't shovel data to the drive at an acceptable pace, the drive will be forced to stop writing while it waits on the server. You sure don't want a tape drive that is too slow, but you also don't want one that is too fast.

Similarly, choose backup media that is appropriately sized for your data. It doesn't make any sense to splurge on DLT-S4 tapes if you have only a few hundred GB of data to protect. You will just end up taking half-full tapes off-site.

Optical media, DDS, and LTO drives are excellent solutions for small workgroups and for individual machines with a lot of storage. The startup costs are relatively modest, the media are widely available, and several manufacturers are using each standard. All of these systems are fast enough to back up beaucoup data in a finite amount of time.

DLT, AIT, and LTO are all roughly comparable for larger environments. There isn't a clear winner among the three, and even if there were, the situation would no doubt change within a few months as new versions of the formats were deployed. All of these formats are well established and would be easy to integrate into your environment, be it a university or corporation.

In the remainder of this chapter, we use the generic term "tape" to refer to the media chosen for backups. Examples of backup commands are phrased in terms of tape devices.

10.3 Saving space and time with incremental backups

Almost all backup tools support at least two different kinds of backups: full backups and incremental backups. A full backup includes all of a filesystem's contents. An incremental backup includes only files that have changed since the previous backup. Incremental backups are useful for minimizing the amount of network bandwidth and tape storage consumed by each day's backups. Because most files never change, even the simplest incremental schedule eliminates many files from the daily dumps.

Many backup tools support additional kinds of dumps beyond the basic full and incremental procedures. In general, these are all more-sophisticated varieties of incremental dump. The only way to back up less data is to take advantage of data that's already been stored on a backup tape somewhere.

Some backup software identifies identical copies of data even if they are found in different files on different machines. The software then ensures that only one copy is written to tape. This feature is usually known as deduplication, and it can be very helpful for limiting the size of backups.

The schedule that is right for you depends on

- The activity of your filesystems
- The capacity of your dump device
- The amount of redundancy you want
- The number of tapes you want to buy

When you do a backup with **dump**, you assign it a backup level, which is an integer. A level N dump backs up all files that have changed since the last dump of level less than N. A level 0 backup places the entire filesystem on the tape. With an incremental backup system, you may have to restore files from several sets of backup tapes to reset a filesystem to the state it was in during the last backup.[5]

Historically, **dump**, supported levels 0 through 9, but newer versions support thousands of dump levels. As you add additional levels to your dump schedule, you divide the relatively few active files into smaller and smaller segments. A complex dump schedule confers the following benefits:

- You can back up data more often, limiting your potential losses.
- You can use fewer daily tapes (or fit everything on one tape).
- You can keep multiple copies of each file to protect against media errors.
- You can reduce the network bandwidth and time needed for backups.

These benefits must be weighed against the added complexity of maintaining the system and of restoring files. Given these constraints, you can design a schedule at the appropriate level of sophistication. Below, we describe a couple of possible sequences and the motivation behind them. One of them might be right for your site—or, your needs might dictate a completely different schedule.

A simple schedule

If your total amount of disk space is smaller than the capacity of your tape device, you can use a trivial dump schedule. Do level 0 dumps of every filesystem each day. Reuse a group of tapes, but every N days (where N is determined by your site's needs), keep the tape forever. This scheme costs you

(365/N) * (price of tape)

per year. Don't reuse the exact same tape for every night's dump. It's better to rotate among a set of tapes so that even if one night's dump is blown, you can still fall back to the previous night.

This schedule guarantees massive redundancy and makes data recovery easy. It's a good solution for a site with lots of money but limited operator time (or skill).

5. Actually, most versions of **dump** do not keep track of files that have been deleted. If you restore from incremental backups, deleted files are recreated.

From a safety and convenience perspective, this schedule is the ideal. Don't stray from it without a specific reason (e.g., to conserve tapes or labor).

A moderate schedule

A more reasonable schedule for most sites is to assign a tape to each day of the week, each week of the month (you'll need 5), and each month of the year. Every day, do a level 9 dump to the daily tape. Every week, do a level 5 dump to the weekly tape. And every month, do a level 3 dump to the monthly tape. Do a level 0 dump whenever the incrementals get too big to fit on one tape, which is most likely to happen on a monthly tape. Do a level 0 dump at least once a year.

The choice of levels 3, 5, and 9 is arbitrary. You could use levels 1, 2, and 3 with the same effect. However, the gaps between dump levels give you some breathing room if you later decide you want to add another level of dumps. Other backup software uses the terms full, differential, and incremental rather than numeric dump levels.

This schedule requires 24 tapes plus however many tapes are needed for the level 0 dumps. Although it does not require too many tapes, it also does not afford much redundancy.

10.4 Setting up a backup regime with dump

The **dump** and **restore** commands are the most common way to create and restore from backups. These programs have been around for a very long time, and their behavior is well known. At most sites, **dump** and **restore** are the underlying commands used by automated backup software.

You may have to explicitly install **dump** and **restore** on your Linux systems, depending on the options you selected during the original installation. A package is available for easy installation on all our example distributions. The current Red Hat release offers a system administration package at installation time that includes **dump**.

On Solaris systems, **dump** and **restore** are called **ufsdump** and **ufsrestore**. A **dump** command exists, but it's not backup-related. As the names suggest, the **ufs*** commands work only with the older UFS filesystem; they do not work on ZFS filesystems. See page 316 for a discussion of ZFS backup options.

ufsdump accepts the same flags and arguments as other systems' traditional **dump**, but it parses arguments differently. **ufsdump** expects all the flags to be contained in the first argument and the flags' arguments to follow in order. For example, where most commands would want **-a 5 -b -c 10**, on Solaris **ufsdump** would want **abc 5 10**.

ufsdump is only supposed to be used on unmounted filesystems. If you need to back up a live filesystem, be sure to run Solaris's **fssnap** command and then run **ufsdump** against the snapshot.

On AIX, the **dump** command is called **backup**, although **restore** is still called **restore**. A **dump** command exists, but it's not backup-related.

For simplicity, we refer to the backup commands as **dump** and **restore** and show their traditional command-line flags. Even on systems that call the commands something else, they function similarly. Given the importance of reliable dumps, however, you *must* check these flags against the man pages on the machine you are dumping; most vendors have tampered with the meaning of at least one flag.

Dumping filesystems

dump builds a list of files that have been modified since a previous dump, then packs those files into a single large file to archive to an external device. **dump** has several advantages over most of the other utilities described in this chapter.

- Backups can span multiple tapes.
- Files of any type (even devices) can be backed up and restored.
- Permissions, ownerships, and modification times are preserved.
- Files with holes are handled correctly.[6]
- Backups can be performed incrementally (with only recently modified files being written out to tape).

The GNU version of **tar** used on Linux provides all these features as well. However, **dump**'s handling of incremental backups is a bit more sophisticated than **tar**'s. You may find the extra horsepower useful if your needs are complex.

Unfortunately, the version of **tar** shipped with most major UNIX distributions lacks many of GNU **tar**'s features. If you must support backups for both Linux and UNIX variants, **dump** is your best choice. It is the only command that handles these issues (fairly) consistently across platforms, so you can be an expert in one command rather than being familiar with two. If you are lucky enough to be in a completely homogeneous Linux environment, pick your favorite. **dump** is less filling, but **tar** tastes great!

On Linux systems, **dump** natively supports filesystems in the ext family. You may have to download and install other versions of **dump** to support other filesystems.

The **dump** command understands the layout of raw filesystems, and it reads a filesystem's inode table directly to decide which files must be backed up. This knowledge of the filesystem makes **dump** very efficient, but it also imposes a couple of limitations.[7]

See Chapter 18 for more information about NFS.

The first limitation is that every filesystem must be dumped individually. The other limitation is that only filesystems on the local machine can be dumped; you

6. Holes are blocks that have never contained data. If you open a file, write one byte, seek 1MB into the file, then write another byte, the resulting "sparse" file takes up only two disk blocks even though its logical size is much bigger. Files created by Berkeley DB or **ndbm** contain many holes.
7. **dump** requires access to raw disk partitions. Anyone allowed to do dumps can read all the files on the system with a little work.

cannot dump an NFS filesystem you have mounted from a remote machine. However, you can dump a local filesystem to a remote tape drive.[8]

dump does not care about the length of filenames. Hierarchies can be arbitrarily deep, and long names are handled correctly.

The first argument to **dump** is the incremental dump level. **dump** uses the **/etc/dumpdates** file to determine how far back an incremental dump must go.

The **-u** flag causes **dump** to automatically update **/etc/dumpdates** when the dump completes. The date, dump level, and filesystem name are recorded. If you never use the **-u** flag, all dumps become level 0s because no record of your having previously dumped the filesystem is ever created. If you change a filesystem's name, you can edit the **/etc/dumpdates** file by hand.

See page 418 for information about device numbers.

dump sends its output to some default device, usually the primary tape drive. To specify a different device, use the **-f** flag. If you are placing multiple dumps on a single tape, make sure you specify a non-rewinding tape device (a device file that does not cause the tape to be rewound when it is closed—most tape drives have both a standard and a non-rewinding device entry).[9] Read the man page for the tape device to determine the exact name of the appropriate device file. Table 10.2 gives some hints for our four example systems.

Table 10.2 Device files for the default SCSI tape drive

System	Rewinding	Non-rewinding
Linux	**/dev/st0**	**/dev/nst0**
Solaris	**/dev/rmt/0**	**/dev/rmt/0n**
HP-UX	**/dev/rmt/0m**	**/dev/rmt/0mn**
AIX	**/dev/rmt0**	**/dev/rmt0.1**

If you choose the rewinding device by accident, you end up saving only the last filesystem dumped. Since **dump** does not have any idea where the tape is positioned, this mistake does not cause errors. The situation only becomes apparent when you try to restore files.

To dump to a remote system, you specify the identity of the remote tape drive as *hostname:device*; for example,

```
$ sudo dump -0u -f anchor:/dev/nst0 /spare
```

Permission to access remote tape drives should be controlled through an SSH tunnel. See page 926 for more information.

8. Legacy systems may use a separate **rdump** command to perform dumps to a remote tape drive. Modern **dumps** accept a **-f** *hostname:tapedevice* argument.

9. All the entries for a tape unit use the same major device number. The minor device number tells the tape device driver about special behaviors (rewinding, byte swapping, etc.).

Backups

In the past, you had to tell **dump** exactly how long your tapes were so that it could stop writing before it ran off the end of a tape. Modern tape drives can tell when they have reached the end of a tape and report that fact back to **dump**, which then rewinds and ejects the current tape and requests a new one. Since the variability of hardware compression makes the "virtual length" of each tape somewhat indeterminate, it's always best to rely on the end-of-tape (EOT) indication.

All versions of **dump** understand the **-d** and **-s** options, which specify the tape density in bytes per inch and the tape length in feet, respectively. A few more-sensible versions let you specify sizes in kilobytes with the **-B** option. For versions that don't, you must do a little bit of arithmetic to express the size you want.

For example, let's suppose we want to do a level 5 dump of **/work** to a DDS-4 (DAT) drive whose native capacity is 20GB (with a typical compressed capacity of about 40GB). DAT drives can report EOT, so we need to lie to **dump** and set the tape size to a value that's much bigger than 40GB, say, 50GB. That works out to about 60,000 feet at 6,250 bpi:

```
# dump -5u -s 60000 -d 6250 -f /dev/nst0 /work
DUMP: Date of this level 5 dump: Wed Nov 18 14:28:05 2009
DUMP: Date of last level 0 dump: Sun Nov 15 21:11:05 2009
DUMP: Dumping /dev/hda2 (/work) to /dev/nst0
DUMP: mapping (Pass I) [regular files]
DUMP: mapping (Pass II) [directories]
DUMP: estimated 18750003 tape blocks on .23 tape(s)
....
```

The flags **-5u** are followed by the parameters **-s** (size: 60,000 feet), **-d** (density: 6,250 bpi), and **-f** (tape device: **/dev/nst0**). Finally, the filesystem name (**/work**) is given; this argument is required. Most versions of **dump** allow you to specify the filesystem by its mount point, as in the example above. Some require you to specify the raw device file.

The last line of output shown above verifies that **dump** will not attempt to switch tapes on its own initiative, since it believes that only about a quarter of a tape is needed for this dump. It is fine if the number of estimated tapes is more than 1, as long as the specified tape size is larger than the actual tape size. **dump** will reach the actual EOT before it reaches its own computed limit.

Restoring from dumps with restore

The program that extracts data from tapes written with **dump** is called **restore**. We first discuss restoring individual files (or a small set of files), then explain how to restore entire filesystems.

Normally, the **restore** command is dynamically linked, so you need the system's shared libraries available to do anything useful. Building a statically linked version of **restore** takes some extra effort but makes it easier to recover from a disaster because **restore** is then completely self-contained.

When you are notified of a lost file, first determine which tapes contain versions of the file. Users often want the most recent version, but that is not always the case. For example, a user who loses a file by inadvertently copying another file on top of it would want the version that existed before the incident occurred. It's helpful if you can browbeat users into telling you not only what files are missing but also when they were lost and when they were last modified. We find it helpful to structure users' responses with a request form.

If you do not keep on-line catalogs, you must mount tapes and repeatedly attempt to restore the missing files until you find the correct tape. If the user remembers when the files were last changed, you may be able to make an educated guess about which tapes the files might be on.

After determining which tapes you want to extract from, create and **cd** to a temporary directory such as **/var/restore** where a large directory hierarchy can be created; most versions of **restore** must create all the directories leading to a particular file before that file can be restored. Do not use **/tmp**—your work could be wiped out if the machine crashes and reboots before the restored data has been moved to its original location.

The **restore** command has many options. Most useful are **-i** for interactive restores of individual files and directories and **-r** for a complete restore of an entire filesystem. You might also need **-x**, which requests a noninteractive restore of specified files—be careful not to overwrite existing files.

restore -i reads the table of contents from the tape and then lets you navigate through it as you would a normal directory tree, using commands called **ls**, **cd**, and **pwd**. You mark the files that you want to restore with the **add** command. When you finish selecting, type **extract** to pull the files off the tape.

*See page 317 for a description of **mt**.*

If you placed multiple dumps on a single tape, you must use the **mt** command to position the tape at the correct dump file before running **restore**. Remember to use the non-rewinding device!

For example, to restore the file **/users/janet/iamlost** from a remote tape drive, you might issue the following commands. Let's assume that you have found the right tape, mounted it on **tapehost:/dev/nst0**, and determined that the filesystem containing janet's home directory is the fourth one on the tape.

```
$ sudo mkdir /var/restore
$ cd /var/restore
$ sudo ssh tapehost mt -f /dev/nst0 fsf 3
$ sudo restore -i -f tapehost:/dev/nst0
restore> ls
.:
janet/  garth/  lost+found/ lynda/
restore> cd janet
restore> ls
afile bfile cfile iamlost
```

```
restore> add iamlost
restore> ls[10]
afile bfile cfile iamlost*
restore> extract
You have not read any volumes yet.
Unless you know which volume your files are on you should
start with the last volume and work towards the first.
Specify next volume #: 1
set owner/mode for '.'? [yn] n
```

Volumes (tapes) are enumerated starting at 1, not 0, so for a dump that fits on a single tape, you specify 1. When **restore** asks if you want to set the owner and mode, it's asking whether it should set the current directory to match the root of the tape. Unless you are restoring an entire filesystem, you probably do not want to do this.

Once the **restore** has completed, give the file to janet:

```
$ cd /var/restore
$ ls janet
iamlost
$ ls ~janet
afile bfile cfile
$ sudo cp -p janet/iamlost ~janet/iamlost.restored
$ sudo chown janet ~janet/iamlost.restored
$ sudo chgrp staff ~janet/iamlost.restored
$ cd /; sudo rm -rf /var/restore
$ mail janet
Your file iamlost has been restored as requested and has
been placed in /users/janet/iamlost.restored.

Your name, Humble System Administrator
```

Some administrators prefer to restore files into a special directory and allow users to copy their files out by hand. In that scheme, the administrator must protect the privacy of the restored files by verifying their ownership and permissions. If you choose to use such a system, remember to clean out the directory every so often.

If you originally wrote a backup to a remote tape drive and are unable to restore files from it locally, try hosting the tape on the same remote host that was used for the original backup.

restore -i is usually the easiest way to restore a few files or directories from a dump. However, it does not work if the tape device cannot be moved backwards a record at a time (a problem with some 8mm drives). If **restore -i** fails, try **restore -x** before jumping out the window. **restore -x** requires you to specify the complete path of the file you want to restore (relative to the root of the dump) on the command line. The following sequence of commands repeats the previous example, but with **-x**.

10. The star next to **iamlost** indicates that it has been marked for extraction.

```
$ sudo mkdir /var/restore
$ cd /var/restore
$ sudo ssh tapehost mt -f /dev/nst0 fsf 3
$ sudo restore -x -f tapehost:/dev/nst0 ./janet/iamlost
```

Restoring entire filesystems

With luck, you will never have to restore an entire filesystem after a system failure. However, the situation does occasionally arise. Before attempting to restore the filesystem, be absolutely sure that whatever problem caused the filesystem to be destroyed in the first place has been taken care of. It's pointless to spend hours spinning tapes only to lose the filesystem once again.

Before you begin a full restore, create and mount the target filesystem. See Chapter 8, *Storage*, for more information about how to prepare the filesystem. To start the restore, **cd** to the mount point of the new filesystem, put the first tape of the most recent level 0 dump in the tape drive, and type **restore -r**.

restore prompts for each tape in the dump. After the level 0 dump has been restored, mount and restore the incremental dumps. Restore incremental dumps in the order in which they were created. Because of redundancy among dumps, it may not be necessary to restore every incremental. Here's the algorithm for determining which dumps to restore:

Step 1: Restore the most recent level 0 dump.

Step 2: Restore the lowest-level dump made after the dump you just restored. If multiple dumps were made at that level, restore the most recent one.

Step 3: If that was the last dump that was ever made, you are done.

Step 4: Otherwise, go back to step 2.

Here are some examples of dump sequences. You would need to restore only the levels shown in boldface.

0 0 0 0 0 **0**
0 5 5 5 **5**
0 3 **2** 5 **4** **5**
0 9 9 5 9 9 **3** 9 9 **5** 9 **9**
0 3 5 9 **3** **5** **9**

Let's take a look at a complete command sequence. If the most recent dump was the first monthly after the annual level 0 in the "moderate" schedule on page 307, the commands to restore **/home**, residing on the logical volume **/dev/vg01/lvol5**, would look like this:

```
$ sudo mkfs /dev/vg01/lvol5
$ sudo mount /dev/vg01/lvol5 /home
$ cd /home
```

```
/* Mount first tape of level 0 dump of /home. */
$ sudo restore -r
/* Mount the tapes requested by restore. */
/* Mount first tape of level 3 monthly dump. */
$ sudo restore -r
```

If you had multiple filesystems on one dump tape, you'd use the **mt** command to skip forward to the correct filesystem before running each **restore**. See page 317 for a description of **mt**.

This sequence would restore the filesystem to the state it was in when the level 3 dump was done, except that all deleted files would be resurrected. This problem can be especially nasty when you are restoring an active filesystem or are restoring to a disk that is nearly full. It is possible for a **restore** to fail because the filesystem has been filled up with ghost files.[11]

Restoring to new hardware

When an entire system has failed, you must perform what is known as "bare metal recovery." Before you can follow the filesystem restoration steps above, you will at least need to

- Provision replacement hardware
- Install a fresh copy of the operating system
- Install backup software (such as **dump** and **restore**)
- Configure the local tape drive or configure access to a tape server

After these steps, you can follow the restoration process described above.

10.5 Dumping and restoring for upgrades

We recommend that when you perform a major OS upgrade, you back up all filesystems with a level 0 dump and, possibly, restore them. The restore is needed only if the new OS uses a different filesystem format or if you restructure your disks. However, you *must* do backups as insurance against any problems that might occur during the upgrade. A complete set of backups also gives you the option to reinstall the old OS if the new version does not prove satisfactory. Fortunately, with the progressive upgrade systems used by most distributions these days, you are unlikely to need these tapes.

Be sure to back up all system and user partitions. Depending on your upgrade path, you may choose to restore only user data and system-specific files that are in the root filesystem or in **/usr**, such as **/etc/passwd**, **/etc/shadow**, or **/usr/local**. UNIX's directory organization mixes local files with vendor-distributed files, making it quite difficult to pick out your local customizations.

11. Some versions of **dump** and **restore** are rumored to keep track of deletions. We believe Solaris and Linux to be among these.

You should do a complete set of level 0 **dumps** immediately after an upgrade, too. Most vendors' upgrade procedures set the modification dates of system files to the time when they were mastered rather than to the current time. Ergo, incremental dumps made relative to the pre-upgrade level 0 are not sufficient to restore your system to its post-upgrade state in the event of a crash.

10.6 Using other archiving programs

dump is not the only program you can use to archive files to tapes; however, it is usually the most efficient way to back up an entire system. **tar** and **dd** can also move files from one medium to another.

tar: package files

tar reads multiple files or directories and packages them into one file, often a tape device. **tar** is a useful way to back up any files whose near-term recovery you anticipate. For instance, if you have a bunch of old data files and the system is short of disk space, you can use **tar** to put the files on a tape and then remove them from the disk.

tar is also useful for moving directory trees from place to place, especially if you are copying files as root. **tar** preserves ownership and time information, but only if you ask it to. For example,

```
sudo tar -cf - fromdir | ( cd todir ; sudo tar -xpf - )
```

creates a copy of the directory tree *fromdir* in *todir*. Avoid using **..** in the *todir* argument since symbolic links and automounters can make it mean something different from what you expect. We've been bitten several times.

Most versions of **tar** do not follow symbolic links by default, but they can be told to do so. Consult your **tar** manual for the correct flag; it varies from system to system. The biggest drawback of **tar** is that non-GNU versions do not allow multiple tape volumes. If the data you want to archive will not fit on one tape, you may need to upgrade your version of **tar**.

Another problem with some non-GNU versions of **tar** is that pathnames are limited by default to 100 characters. This restriction prevents **tar** from archiving deep hierarchies. If you're creating **tar** archives on your Linux systems and exchanging them with others, remember that people with the standard **tar** may not be able to read the tapes or files you create.[12]

tar's **-b** option lets you specify a "blocking factor" to use when writing a tape. The blocking factor is specified in 512-byte blocks; it determines how much data **tar** buffers internally before performing a write operation. Some DAT devices do not

12. The GNU implementation includes a filename mapping table as one of the files in the archive. Users of the standard **tar** can extract the contents of the archive and fix it up by hand, but the process is tedious.

work correctly unless the blocking factor is set to a special value, but other drives do not require this setting.

On some systems, certain blocking factors may yield better performance than others. The optimal blocking factor varies widely, depending on the computer and tape drive hardware. In many cases, you will not notice any difference in speed. When in doubt, try a blocking factor of 20.

tar expands holes in files and is intolerant of tape errors.[13]

dd: twiddle bits

dd is a file copying and conversion program. Unless you tell it to do some sort of conversion, **dd** just copies from its input file to its output file. If a user brings you a tape that was written on a non-UNIX system, **dd** may be the only way to read it.

One historical use for **dd** was to create a copy of an entire filesystem. However, a better option these days is to **mkfs** the destination filesystem and then run **dump** piped to **restore**. **dd** can sometimes clobber partitioning information if used incorrectly. It can only copy filesystems between partitions of exactly the same size.

You can also use **dd** to make a copy of a magnetic tape. With two tape drives, say, **/dev/st0** and **/dev/st1**, you'd use the command

```
$ dd if=/dev/st0 of=/dev/st1 cbs=16b
```

With one drive (**/dev/st0**), you'd use the following sequence:

```
$ dd if=/dev/st0 of=tfile cbs=16b
/* Change tapes. */
$ dd if=tfile of=/dev/st0 cbs=16b
$ rm tfile
```

Of course, if you have only one tape drive, you must have enough disk space to store an image of the entire tape.

dd is also a popular tool among forensic specialists. Because it creates a bit-for-bit, unadulterated copy of a volume, **dd** can be used to duplicate electronic evidence for use in court.

ZFS backups

See page 264 for a more general introduction to ZFS.

Solaris's ZFS incorporates the features of a logical volume manager and RAID controller as well as a filesystem. It is in many ways a system administrator's dream, but backup is something of a mixed bag.

ZFS makes it easy and efficient to create filesystem snapshots. Past versions of a filesystem are available through the **.zfs** directory in the filesystem's root, so users can easily restore their own files from past snapshots without administrator intervention. From the perspective of on-line version control, ZFS gets a gold star.

13. GNU's **tar** handles holes intelligently if you invoke the **-S** option when creating an archive.

However, snapshots stored on the same media as the active filesystem shouldn't be your only backup strategy. ZFS knows this, too: it has a very nice **zfs send** facility that summarizes a filesystem snapshot to a linear stream. You can save the stream to a file or pipe it to a remote system. You can write the stream to a tape. You can even send the stream to a remote **zfs receive** process to replicate the filesystem elsewhere (optionally, with all its history and snapshots). If you like, **zfs send** can serialize only the incremental changes between two snapshots. Two gold stars: one for the feature, and one for the fact that the full documentation is just a page or two (see the man page for **zfs**).

The fly in the ointment is that **zfs receive** deals only with complete filesystems. To restore a few files from a set of serialized **zfs send** images, you must restore the entire filesystem and then pick out the files you want. Let's hope you've got plenty of time and free disk space and that the tape drive isn't needed for other backups.

In fairness, several arguments help excuse this state of affairs. ZFS filesystems are lightweight, so you're encouraged to create many of them. Restoring all of **/home** might be traumatic, but restoring all of **/home/ned** is likely to be trivial.[14] More importantly, ZFS's on-line snapshot system eliminates 95% of the cases in which you would normally need to refer to a backup tape.

On-line snapshots don't replace backup tapes or reduce the frequency with which those tapes must be written. However, snapshots do reduce the frequency at which tapes must be read.

10.7 Using multiple files on a single tape

A magnetic tape contains one long string of data. However, it's often useful to store more than one "thing" on a tape, so tape drives and their drivers conspire to afford a bit more structure. When **dump** or some other command writes a stream of bytes out to a tape device and then closes the device file, the driver writes an end-of-file marker on the tape. This marker separates the stream from other streams that are written subsequently. When the stream is read back in, reading stops automatically at the EOF.

You can use the **mt** command to position a tape at a particular stream or "fileset," as **mt** calls them. **mt** is especially useful if you put multiple files (for example, multiple dumps) on a single tape. It also has some of the most interesting error messages of any UNIX utility. The basic format of the command is

mt [**-f** *tapename*] *command* [*count*]

There are numerous choices for *command*. They vary from platform to platform, so we discuss only the ones that are essential for doing backups and restores.

14. On the other hand, if you **zfs send -R** the **/home** filesystem and its descendants, there's currently no way to restore only **/home/ned**; you must restore **/home**. As an administrator, you probably don't want to have to schedule every home directory for independent backups.

rew rewinds the tape to the beginning.

offl puts the tape off-line. On most tape drives, this command causes the tape to rewind and pop out of the drive. Most scripts use this command to eject the tape when they are done, clearly indicating that everything finished correctly.

status prints information about the current state of the tape drive (whether a tape is loaded, etc.).

fsf [*count*] fast-forwards the tape. If no *count* is specified, **fsf** skips forward one file. With a numeric argument, it skips the specified number of files. Use this command to skip forward to the correct filesystem on a tape with multiple dumps.

bsf [*count*] should backspace *count* files. The exact behavior of this directive depends on the tape drive hardware and its associated driver. In some situations, the current file is counted. In others, it is not. On some equipment, **bsf** does nothing, silently. If you go too far forward on a tape, your best bet is to run **mt rew** on it and start again from the beginning.

Consult the **mt** man page for a list of all the supported commands.

If you're fortunate enough to have a robotic tape library, you may be able to control its tape changer by installing the **mtx** package, an enhanced version of **mt**. For example, we use it for unattended tape swapping with our groovy Dell PowerVault LTO-3 tape cartridge system. Tape changers with barcode readers will even display the scanned tape labels through the **mtx** interface. Look ma, no hands!

10.8 Bacula

Bacula is an enterprise-level client/server backup solution that manages backup, recovery, and verification of files over a network. The Bacula server components run on Linux, Solaris, and FreeBSD. The Bacula client backs up data from many platforms, including all our example operating systems and Microsoft Windows.

In previous editions of this book, Amanda was our favorite noncommercial backup tool. If you need Amanda information, see a previous edition of this book or amanda.org.

The feature list below explains why Bacula is our new favorite.

- It has a modular design.
- It backs up UNIX, Linux, Windows, and Mac OS systems.
- It supports MySQL, PostgreSQL, or SQLite for its back-end database.
- It supports an easy-to-use, menu-driven command-line console.
- It's available under an open source license.
- Its backups can span multiple tape volumes.
- Its servers can run on multiple platforms.

- It creates SHA1 or MD5 signature files for each backed-up file.
- It allows encryption of both network traffic and data stored on tape.
- It can back up files larger than 2GiB.
- It supports tape libraries and autochangers.
- It can execute scripts or commands before and after backup jobs.
- It centralizes backup management for an entire network.

The Bacula model

To deploy Bacula, you should understand its major components. Exhibit A illustrates Bacula's general architecture.

Exhibit A Bacula components and their relationships

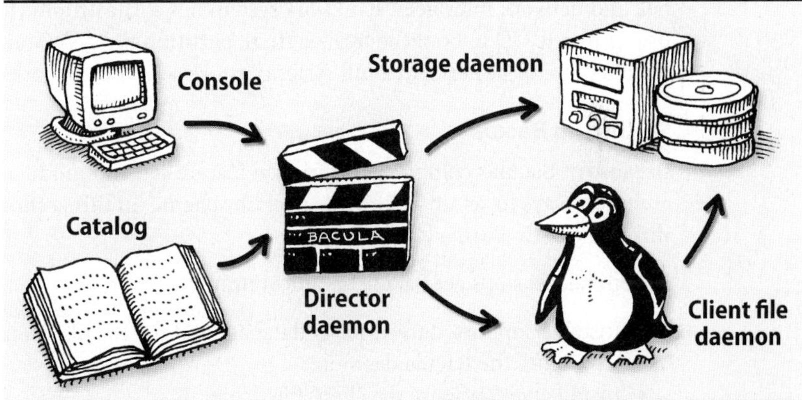

The Bacula director is the daemon that coordinates backup, restore, and verification operations. You can submit backup or restore jobs to the director daemon by using the Bacula console. You can also ask the director daemon to query the Bacula storage daemon or the file daemons located on client computers.

You communicate with the director daemon through the Bacula console, which can be run as a GNOME or MS Windows GUI or as a command-line tool. The console can run anywhere; it doesn't have to be located on the same computer as the director daemon.

A storage daemon is the Bacula component that reads and writes tapes or other backup media. This service must run on the machine that is connected to the tape drive or storage device used for backups, but it does not have to be installed on the same server as the director (although it can be).

A Bacula file daemon runs on each system that is to be backed up. File daemon implementations for each supported operating system send the appropriate file data and attributes to the storage daemon as backup jobs are executed.

The final Bacula component is the catalog, a relational database in which Bacula stores information about every file and volume that is backed up. The catalog makes Bacula fast and efficient during a restore because the entire backup history is available on-line; Bacula knows what storage volumes are needed to restore a particular fileset before it reads a single tape. Bacula currently supports three different databases: MySQL, PostgreSQL, and SQLite. The catalog database need not reside on the same server as the director.

An additional, optional component is the Bacula Rescue CD-ROM. This component is a separately downloadable package that creates individualized, bootable rescue CDs for Linux systems to use for "bare metal" recovery. The CDs contain a statically linked copy of the system's file daemon as well as customized shell scripts that incorporate configuration information about the system's disks, kernel, and network interfaces. If a Linux system has a catastrophic failure, you can use its rescue CD to boot the fresh system, partition the disk, and connect to the Bacula director to perform a full system restore over the network.

Setting up Bacula

Because of Bacula's complexity, advanced feature set, and modular design, there are many ways to set up a site-wide backup scheme. In this section we walk through a basic Bacula configuration.

In general, six steps get Bacula up and running:

- Install a supported third-party database and the Bacula daemons.
- Configure the Bacula daemons.
- Install and configure the client file daemons.
- Start the Bacula daemons.
- Add media to media pools with the Bacula console.
- Perform a test backup and restore.

A minimal setup consists of a single backup server machine and one or more clients. The clients run only a file daemon. The remaining four Bacula components (director daemon, storage daemon, catalog, and console) all run on the server. In larger environments it's advisable to distribute the server-side Bacula components among several machines, but the minimal setup works great for backing up at least a few dozen systems.

Installing the database and Bacula daemons

It's important to run the same (major) version of Bacula on every system. In the past, some major releases have been incompatible with one another.

Before you can install Bacula, you must first install the back-end database for its catalog. For sites backing up just a few systems, SQLite provides the easiest installation. If you are backing up more systems, it's advisable to use a more scalable database. Our experience with MySQL in this role has been positive, and we assume MySQL in the following examples.

Stability and reliability are a must when you are dealing with a backup platform, so once you have installed the database, we recommend that you download and install the latest stable source code from the Bacula web site. Step-by-step installation documentation is included with the source code in the **docs** directory. The documentation is also on-line at bacula.org, where it is available in both HTML and PDF format. Helpful tutorials and developer guides can also be found there.

After unpacking the source code, run **./configure --with-mysql** followed by **make** to compile the binaries, and, finally, run **make install** to complete the installation.

Once Bacula has been installed, the next step is to create the actual MySQL database and the data tables inside it. Bacula includes three shell scripts that prepare MySQL to store the catalog. The **grant_mysql_privileges** script sets up the appropriate MySQL permissions for the Bacula user. The **create_mysql_database** script creates the Bacula database, and, finally, the **make_mysql_tables** script populates the database with the required tables. Analogous scripts are included for PostgreSQL and SQLite. Bacula's prebuilt database creation scripts can be found in the **src/cats** directory of the Bacula source code distribution.

Bacula saves a table entry for every file backed up from every client, so your database server should have plenty of memory and disk space. Database tables for a medium-sized network can easily grow to millions of entries. For MySQL, you should probably dedicate at least the resources defined in the **my-large.cnf** file included in the distribution. If you eventually find that your catalog database has grown to become unmanageable, you can always set up a second instance of MySQL and use separate catalogs for different groups of clients.

Backups

Configuring the Bacula daemons

After setting up the database that will store the catalog, you must configure the other four Bacula components. By default, all configuration files are located in the **/etc/bacula** directory. Bacula has a separate configuration file for each component. Table 10.3 lists the filenames and the machines on which each configuration file is needed.

Table 10.3 Bacula configuration filenames (in /etc/bacula)

Component	File	Which machines
Director daemon	**bacula-dir.conf**	The server that runs the director daemon
Storage daemon	**bacula-sd.conf**	Every server that has a storage device
File daemon	**bacula-fd.conf**	Every client that is to be backed up
Management console	**bconsole.conf**	Every machine used as a control console

It might seem silly that you have to configure each Bacula component independently when you have a single server, but this modular design allows Bacula to scale incredibly well. Tape backup server at capacity? Add a second server with its own storage daemon. Want to back up to an off-site location? Install a storage daemon on a server there. Need to back up new clients? Install and configure the clients' file daemons. New backup administrator? Install the management console on his or her workstation.

The configuration files are human-readable text files. The sample configuration files included in the Bacula distribution are well documented and are a great starting place for a typical configuration.

Before we begin a more detailed discussion of our example setup, let's first define some key Bacula terms.

- "Jobs" are the fundamental unit of Bacula activity. They come in two flavors: backup and restore. A job comprises a client, a fileset, a storage pool, and a schedule.
- "Pools" are groups of physical media that store jobs. For example, you might use two pools, one for full backups and another for incrementals.
- "Filesets" are lists of filesystems and individual files. Filesets can be explicitly included in or excluded from backup or restore jobs.
- "Messages" are inter-daemon communiqués (log entries, really) regarding the status of daemons and jobs. Messages can also be sent by email and written to log files.

We do not cover all the possible configuration parameters in this chapter. Instead, we begin each section with a general overview and then point out some parameters that we think are either particularly useful or hard to grasp.

Common configuration sections

The Bacula configuration files are composed of sections known generically as "resources." Each resource section is enclosed in curly braces. Some resources appear in multiple configuration files. Comments are introduced with a # sign in all Bacula configuration files.

All four configuration files contain a Director resource:

```
# Sample Bacula director configuration file, /etc/bacula-dir.conf

Director {
    Name = bull-dir # a canonical name for our Bacula director
    DIRport = 9101
    Query File = "/etc/bacula/query.sql"
    Working Directory = "/var/Bacula/working"
    Pid Directory = "/var/run"
    Maximum Concurrent Jobs = 1
    Password = "zHpScUnHN9"
    Messages = Standard
}
```

The Director resource is more or less the mother ship of the Bacula sea. Its parameters define the name and basic behavior of the director. Options set the communication port through which the other daemons communicate with the director, the location in which the director stores its temporary files, and the number of concurrent jobs that the director can handle.

Passwords are strewn throughout the Bacula configuration files, and they serve a variety of purposes. Exhibit B shows how the passwords on different machines and in different configuration files should correspond.

Exhibit B Passwords in the Bacula configuration files

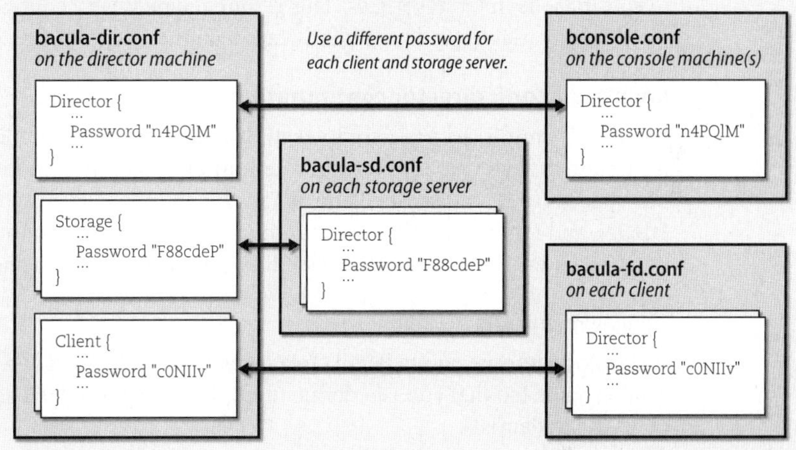

Although passwords appear as plaintext in the configuration files, they are never transmitted over the network in this form.

In our example configuration, the director and console are hosted on the same machine. However, a password is still required in both configuration files.

The director, storage, and file daemons all have a Messages resource that tells Bacula how to handle specific message types generated by each Bacula daemon. In a typical configuration, the storage and file daemons forward their messages back to the director:

```
Messages {
    Name = Standard
    director = bull-dir = all
}
```

In the director's configuration file, the Messages resource is more complex. The example on the next page tells Bacula to save messages to a log file and to forward them by email.

```
Messages {
    Name = Standard
    mailcommand = "/sbin/bsmtp -h localhost -f \"\(Bacula\)
        bacula@admin.com\" -s \"Bacula: %t %e of %c %l\" %r"
    operatorcommand = "/sbin/bsmtp -h localhost -f \"\(Bacula\)
        bacula@admin.com\" -s \"Bacula: Intervention needed for %j\" %r"
    mail = backups-admins@admin.com = all, !skipped
    operator = backups-tapeadmins@admin.com = mount
    console = all, !skipped, !saved
    append = "/var/log/bacula.log" = all, !skipped
}
```

You can define multiple Messages resources for the director and then assign them to specific jobs in Job resources. This resource type is very configurable; a complete list of variables and commands can be found in the on-line documentation.

bacula-dir.conf: director configuration

bacula-dir.conf is the most complex of Bacula's configuration files. It requires a minimum of seven types of resource definitions in addition to the Director and Messages resources described above: Catalog, Storage, Pool, Schedule, Client, FileSet, and Job. We highlight each resource definition here with a brief example, but start your own configuration by editing the sample files included with Bacula.

Catalog resources

A Catalog resource points Bacula to a particular catalog database. It includes a catalog name (so that you can define multiple catalogs), a database name, and database credentials.

```
Catalog {
    Name = MYSQL
    dbname = "bacula"; dbuser = "bacula"; dbpassword = "9p6NLm6CnQ"
}
```

Storage resources

A Storage resource describes how to communicate with a particular storage daemon, which in turn is responsible for interfacing with its local backup devices. Storage resources are hardware-independent; the storage daemon has its own configuration file that describes the storage hardware in detail.

```
Storage {
    Name = TL4000
    Address = bull
    SDPort = 9103
    Password = "jiKkrZuE00"
    Device = TL4000
    Autochanger = yes
    Maximum Concurrent Jobs = 2
    Media Type = LTO-3
}
```

Pool resources

A Pool resource groups backup media, typically tapes, into sets that are used by specific backup jobs. It may be useful to separate tapes that you use for off-site archival storage from those that you use for nightly incrementals. Each piece of media is assigned to a single Pool, so it's easy to automatically recycle some tapes and archive others.

```
Pool {
    Name = Full_Pool
    Pool Type = Backup
    Recycle = yes
    AutoPrune = yes
    Storage = TL4000
    Volume Retention = 365 days
}
```

Schedule resources

Schedule resources define the timetables for backup jobs. The name, date, and time specification are the only required parameters, but as you can see from the example below, you can sneak in additional parameter values. These values then override the default parameters set in a Job specification.

Below, full backups run on the first Tuesday of each month at 8:10 p.m. The incremental backups use a different tape pool and run every week from Wednesday through Monday at 8:10 p.m.

```
Schedule {
    Name = "Nightly"
    Run = Level=Full Pool=FullPool 1st tue at 20:10
    Run = Level=Incremental Pool=IncrementalPool wed-mon at 20:10
}
```

Client resources

Client resources identify the computers to be backed up. Each resource has a unique name, IP address, and password; one is required for each client. The catalog for storing backup metadata is also specified.The parameters File Retention and Job Retention specify how long file and job records for this client should be kept in the catalog. If the AutoPrune parameter is set, expired data is deleted from the catalog. Pruning affects only the catalog records and not the actual files stored on backup tapes; recycling of tapes is configured in the Pool resource.

```
Client {
    Name = harp
    Address = 192.168.1.28
    FDPort = 9102
    Catalog = MYSQL
    Password = "TbEpJqrcqy"
}
```

FileSet resources

A FileSet resource defines the files and directories to be included in or excluded from a backup job. Unless you have systems with identical partitioning schemes, you'll probably need a different fileset for each client. FileSet resources can define multiple Include and Exclude parameters, along with individual Options such as regular expressions. By default, Bacula recursively backs up directories but does not span partitions, so take care to list in separate File parameters all the partitions you want to back up.

In the example below, we enable software compression as well as the signature option, which computes a hash value for each file backed up. These options increase the CPU overhead for backups but can save tape capacity or help identify files that have been modified during a suspected security incident.

```
FileSet {
    Name = "harp"
    Include {
        Options {
            signature=SHA1
            compression=GZIP
        }
        File = "/"
        File = "/boot"
        File = "/var"
    }
    Exclude = { /proc /tmp /.journal /.fsck }
}
```

Job resources

A Job resource defines the overall characteristics of a particular backup job by tying together Client, FileSet, Storage, Pool, and Schedule resources. In general, there is one Job definition per client, although you can easily set up multiple jobs if you want to back up different FileSets at different frequencies.

You can supply an (optional) JobDefs resource to set the defaults for all backup jobs. Use of this resource can simplify the per-job configuration data.

```
Job {
    Name = "Harp"
    JobDefs = DefaultJob
    Level = Full
    Write Bootstrap = "/bacula/bootstraps/harp.bsr"
    Client = harp
    FileSet = harp
    Pool = Full_Pool
    Incremental Backup Pool = Incremental_Pool
    Schedule = "Nightly"
    Prefer Mounted Volumes = no
    Max Run Time = 36000
}
```

A "bootstrap" file is a special text file, created by Bacula, that contains information about files to restore. Bootstrap files list the files and volumes needed for a restore job and are incredibly helpful for bare-metal restores. They are not mandatory but are highly recommended.

Bootstrap files are created during restores, or during backups if you have defined the Write Bootstrap parameter for the job. Write Bootstrap tells Bacula where to save the bootstrap information. Bootstrap files are overwritten during full backups and appended to during incremental backups.

bacula-sd.conf: storage daemon configuration

Storage daemons accept data from file daemons and transfer it to the actual storage media (or vice versa, in the case of a restore). The resources Storage, Device, and Autochanger are defined within the **bacula-sd.conf** file, along with the common Messages and Director resources.

The Director resource

The Director resource controls which directors are permitted to contact the storage daemon. The password in the Storage resource of **bacula-dir.conf** must match the password in the Director resource of **bacula-sd.conf**.

```
Director {
    Name = bull-dir
    Password = "jiKkrZuE00"
}
```

The Storage resource

The Storage resource is relatively straightforward. It defines some basic working parameters such as the daemon's network port and working directory.

```
Storage {
    Name = bull-sd
    SDPort = 9103
    WorkingDirectory = "/var/bacula/working"
    Pid Directory = "/var/run"
    Maximum Concurrent Jobs = 2
}
```

Device resources

Each storage device gets its own Device resource definition. This resource specifies details about the physical backup hardware, be it tape, optical media, or online storage. The details include media type, capabilities, and autochanger information for devices that are managed by a tape changer or media robot.

The example below defines an LTO-3 drive with an automatic tape changer. Note that **/dev/nst0** is a non-rewinding device, which is almost invariably what you want. The Name parameter defines a symbolic name that's used to associate the

Backups

drive with its corresponding Autochanger resource. The Name also helps you remember which piece of equipment the resource describes.

The AlwaysOpen parameter tells Bacula to keep the device open unless an administrator explicitly requests an unmount. This option saves time and tape stress because it avoids rewinding and positioning operations between jobs.

```
Device {
    Name = TL4000-Drive0
    Media Type = LTO-3
    Archive Device = /dev/nst0
    AutomaticMount = yes
    AlwaysOpen = yes
    RemovableMedia = yes
    RandomAccess = no
    Autochanger = yes
}
```

Autochanger resources

The optional Autochanger resource definition is only required if you are lucky enough to have a tape changer. It associates the storage devices to the autochanger and specifies the command that makes the changer swap tapes.

```
Autochanger {
    Name = TL4000
    Device = TL4000-Drive0,TL4000-Drive1
    Changer Command = "/etc/bacula/mtx-changer %c %o %S %a %d"
    Changer Device = /dev/changer
}
```

bconsole.conf: console configuration

The console program communicates with the director to schedule jobs, check the status of jobs, or restore data. **bconsole.conf** tells the console how to communicate with the director. The parameters in this file must correspond to those given in the Director resource in the director's configuration file (**bacula-dir.conf**), with the exception of the Address parameter.

```
# Console configuration file, bconsole.conf

Director {
    Name = bull-dir
    DIRport = 9101
    Address = bull
    Password = "zHpScUnHN9"
}
```

Installing and configuring the client file daemon

The file daemon installed on backup clients communicates with the Bacula storage daemon as backups and restores are executed. A file daemon must be installed and configured on every computer that is to be backed up with Bacula.

Bacula is available in binary form for many platforms, including Windows and various Linux distributions. On UNIX systems, you can install the file daemon from the original source tree by running **./configure --enable-client-only** followed by **make** and **make install**. You can hard-code defaults for many file daemon options at configuration time, but maintenance is easier if you just list them in your **bacula-fd.conf** file. By default, binaries are installed in **/sbin** and configuration files in **/etc/bacula**.

After installing the file daemon, configure it by editing **bacula-fd.conf**, which is broken into three parts. The first part consists of the `Director` resource, which tells the file daemon which director is allowed to schedule backups for this client. The `Director` resource also includes a `Password` parameter, which must be identical to the password listed in the `Client` resource in the director's own configuration file.

The second part of the **bacula-fd.conf** file is the `FileDaemon` resource, which names the client and specifies the port on which the file daemon listens for commands from the director daemon.

The final component is the `Messages` resource (refer back to page 323), which defines how local messages are to be handled.

Starting the Bacula daemons

With the server daemons installed and a test client configured, the next step is to fire up the daemons by running the startup script in the server's installation directory (**./bacula start**). This same command is also used on each client to start the client's file daemon.

The **bacula** startup script should be configured to run at boot time. Depending on your system and installation method, this may or may not be done for you. See Chapter 3, *Booting and Shutting Down*, for some additional details on how to start services at boot time on our example systems.

Once the daemons are running, you can use the console program (**bconsole** in the installation directory) to check their status, add media to pools, and execute backup and restore jobs. You can run **bconsole** from any computer as long as it has been properly installed and configured.

```
$ sudo ./bconsole
Connecting to Director bull:9101
1000 OK: bull-dir Version: 2.4.4 (23 December 2009)
Enter a period to cancel a command.
*
```

Use the console's **help** command to see a list of the commands it supports.

Adding media to pools

Before you can run a backup job, you need to label a tape and assign it to one of the media pools defined in the director's configuration file. Use the console's **label** command to write a software "label" to a blank tape and assign it to a Bacula pool.

Backups

Always match your Bacula label to the physical label on your tape. If you have an autochanger that supports bar codes, you can use the **label barcode** command to automatically label any blank tapes with the human-readable values from their bar-coded labels.

Use the **list media** command to verify that the tape has been added to the correct pool and marked as appendable.

Running a manual backup

Use the console's **run** command to perform a manual backup. No arguments are needed; the console displays all the backup jobs defined in the director's configuration file. You can modify any option within the **run** command by following the console's menu-driven prompts.

The following example shows a manual full backup of the server harp, using the defaults specified in our configuration files.

```
* run harp
Run Backup job
JobName:  harp
Level:    Full
Client:   harp
FileSet:  harp
Pool:     FullPool
Storage:  SureStore
When:     2009-10-08 10:56:41
Priority: 10
OK to run? (yes/mod/no): yes
Run command submitted.
```

After the backup job has been successfully submitted to the director, you can track its status with the console's **status** command. You can also use the **messages** command to obtain blow-by-blow updates as they arrive. Depending on how you have set up the system's Message resources, a detailed summary report may also be emailed to the Bacula administrator.

Running a restore job

To restore files, start up the console and run the **restore** command. Like the **run** command, **restore** is menu driven. It starts by helping you identify which jobs need to be read to restore the target files. **restore** presents you with several methods of specifying the relevant job IDs. Once you have selected a set of jobs, you can then select the files from those jobs to restore.

```
* restore
To select the JobIds, you have the following choices:
    1: List last 20 Jobs run
    2: List Jobs where a given File is saved
    3: Enter list of comma separated JobIds to select
    4: Enter SQL list command
```

```
    5: Select the most recent backup for a client
    6: Select backup for a client before a specified time
    7: Enter a list of files to restore
    8: Enter a list of files to restore before a specified time
    9: Find the JobIds of the most recent backup for a client
    10: Find the JobIds for a backup for a client before a specified time
    11: Enter a list of directories to restore for found JobIds
    12: Cancel
Select item:  (1-12):
```

The three most useful options are probably "Select the most recent backup for a client" (#5), "Select backup for a client before a specified time" (#6), and "List Jobs where a given File is saved" (#2). The first two of these options provide a shell-like environment for selecting files, similar to that of **restore -i**. The third option comes in handy for those pesky users that can never seem to remember exactly where the file they removed really lives. Another powerful way to find job IDs is option #4, "Enter SQL list command," which lets you enter any properly formatted SQL query. (Of course, you must be familiar with the database schema.)

Suppose that a user needs a recent copy of his **pw_expire.pl** script restored. However, he's not sure in which directory he kept the file. In addition, he would like the files restored to the **/tmp** directory of the original machine. A request like this would set many a system administrator to grumbling around the water cooler, but for the Bacula administrator it's a snap. (Unfortunately, Bacula's format for search results is so wide that we had to truncate it below.)

```
* restore
...
To select the JobIds, you have the following choices:
    1: List last 20 Jobs run
    2: List Jobs where a given File is saved
    ...
Select item:  (1-12): 2
Defined Clients:
    1: bull
    2: harp
    ...
Select the Client (1-12): 2
Enter Filename (no path): pw_expire.pl
+-------+---------------------------------------------+-----------------------+----------
| JobId | Name                                        | StartTime             | JobType...
+-------+---------------------------------------------+-----------------------+----------
| 4484 | /home/jim/development/pw_expire.pl | 2009-11-03 20:11:35 | B...
| 4251 | /home/jim/development/pw_expire.pl | 2009-10-21 18:03:01 | B...
| 4006 | /home/jim/development/pw_expire.pl | 2009-10-06 20:10:02 | B...
+-------+---------------------------------------------+-----------------------+----------
```

Bacula's list of **pw_expire.pl** instances reveals several recent backups and their associated job IDs. Bacula then returns us to the **restore** menu, where we can use option #3 (enter job IDs) to focus on a specific job.

Backups

```
Select item: (1-12): 3
Enter JobId(s), comma separated, to restore: 4484
You have selected the following JobId: 4484
Building directory tree for JobId 4484 ... 1 Job, 779,470 files
You are now entering file selection mode where you add (mark) and
remove (unmark) files to be restored. No files are initially added, unless
you used the "all" keyword on the command line.
Enter "done" to leave this mode.
cwd is: /
$ cd /home/jim/development
cwd is: /home/jim/development
$ dir
...
-rwxr-xr-x 1 jim atrust   923  2009-10-25 12:05:43 /home/jim/development/pw_exp...
$ mark pw_expire.pl
1 files marked.
$ done
```

It's not shown in this example, but Bacula sometimes displays job IDs with a comma (e.g., 4,484). You must omit the comma any time you enter an ID back into Bacula; otherwise, Bacula interprets your entry as a comma-separated list.

```
Bootstrap records written to /var/bacula/working/restore.bsr
The restore job will require the following Volumes:

    000879L3

1 file selected to be restored.

Defined Clients:
    1: bull
    2: harp
    ...
Select the Client (1-2): 2
```

Bacula now writes the bootstrap file that it will use to perform the restore, displays the names of the tape volumes it requires, and prompts you to select a client to which it should restore the files. For this example, we restored the file back to the original host harp.

```
Run Restore Job
JobName:        RestoreFiles
Bootstrap:      /bacula/bacula/working/jf-dir.restore.4.bsr
Where:          /var/restore
Replace:        always
FileSet:        Full Set
Backup Client:  harp
Restore Client: harp
Storage:        LTO3-TL4000
When:           2009-11-23 15:13:05
Catalog:        MYSQL
Priority:       10
OK to run? (yes/mod/no):
```

Before we run this particular job, we want to modify the default settings. Specifically, we need to change the destination of this restore to **/tmp** to accommodate the user's request.

```
OK to run? (yes/mod/no): mod
Parameters to modify:
     1: Level
     2: Storage
     3: Job
     4: FileSet
     5: Restore Client
     6: When
     7: Priority
     8: Bootstrap
     9: Where
     10: File Relocation
     11: Replace
     12: JobId
Select parameter to modify (1-12): 9
Please enter path prefix for restore (/ for none): /tmp
Run Restore job
JobName:          RestoreFiles
Bootstrap:        /var/Bacula/working/restore.bsr
Where:            /tmp
...
OK to run? (yes/mod/no): yes
Run command submitted.
Restore command done.
```

After making the changes, we submit the job to the director, which executes it. We could then use the **messages** command to view the job's logging output.

Backing up Windows clients

You can download prebuilt binaries for Windows clients from bacula.org.

Bacula is great for backing up Windows data files, but it takes an extra step to create a bomb-proof level 0 backup of a Windows system. Unfortunately, Bacula has no understanding of the Windows registry or system state, and it does not understand Windows' locking of open files. At a minimum, you should configure a pre-execution script that triggers Windows' built-in System Restore feature. System Restore will make a local backup of the system state, and your Bacula backup will then receive the current state in its archived form. To capture locked files correctly, you may also need to make use of the Windows Volume Shadow Copy Service (VSS).

Check the **examples** directory in the Bacula source tree for other Windows-related goodies, including a clever script that "pushes" Windows file daemon updates to clients through Bacula's built-in restore system. The Windows client in the latest version of Bacula supports Windows 7 clients and 64-bit clients. It even has experimental support for Microsoft Exchange backups.

Monitoring Bacula configurations

System administration requires vigilance, and backups are the last place to be making an exception. Backups will fail, and if not fixed quickly, critical data will surely be lost.

Bacula jobs produce a job report that is routed according to the job's Message resource in the director daemon's configuration file. The report includes basic information about the volumes used, the number and size of files backed up, and any errors that may have occurred. The report usually gives you enough information to troubleshoot any minor problems. We recommend that you configure important messages to go to your email inbox, or perhaps even to your pager.

You can use the console's **status** command to query the various Bacula daemons for information. The output includes information about upcoming jobs, currently running jobs, and jobs that were terminated. The **messages** command is an easy way to review recent log entries.

Bacula includes a contributed Nagios plug-in, which makes it easy to integrate backups into your existing monitoring infrastructure. See page 887 for general information about Nagios.

Bacula tips and tricks

Two issues that come up frequently are client file daemons that aren't running and storage daemons that cannot find any appendable tape volumes. In the example below, the director daemon reports that a backup job terminated with a fatal error because it could not communicate with the file daemon on host harp. This error can be seen repeatedly at the end of the summary report.

```
...
SD termination status:  Waiting on FD
Termination:            *** Backup Error ***

11-Nov 21:06 bull-dir JobId 259: Warning: bsock.c:123 Could not connect to
    Client: harp on 192.168.1.3:9102. ERR=Connection refused Retrying ...
11-Nov 21:31 bull-dir JobId 259: Warning: bsock.c:123 Could not connect to
    Client: harp on 192.168.1.3:9102. ERR=Connection refused
```

The example below shows the storage daemon reporting that no tape volumes from the appropriate pool are available to perform a requested backup. You can fix the problem either by adding a new volume to the pool or by purging and recycling an existing volume. There's no need to restart the job; Bacula should continue to execute it unless you cancel it explicitly.

```
06-May 23:01 bull-sd JobId 1545: Job Southernfur.2009-05-06_19.03.00.07
    waiting. Cannot find any appendable volumes.
Please use the "label"  command to create a new Volume for:
    Storage:     "TL4000-Drive0" (/dev/nst0)
    Pool:        Full_Pool
    Media type:  LTO-3
```

If you ever need to see more detailed information about what the daemons are doing, you can have them send a slew of debugging information to the console by appending the option **-d***nnn* to the startup command. For example,

```
$ sudo ./bacula start -d100
```

The *nnn* represents the debug level. Typical values range between 50 and 200. The higher the number, the more information displayed. You can also enable debugging from within the console with the **setdebug** command.

Alternatives to Bacula

Several other free or shareware backup tools are available for download. The following packages are particularly noteworthy; all are still actively developed.

- Amanda: a very popular and proven system that backs up UNIX and Linux systems to a single tape drive. See amanda.org.
- **rsync**: a free tool that runs on all of our example platforms and is included by default on many Linux distributions. It can synchronize files from one computer to another and can run in conjunction with SSH to transfer data securely over the Internet. **rsync** is smart about only transferring differences in files, so it uses network bandwidth efficiently. See page 725 for additional discussion of **rsync**. Note that **rsync** alone usually isn't sufficient for backups since it does not save multiple copies. Nor does it create off-line backups.
- **star**: a faster implementation of **tar**. **star** is included with Linux and is available for all types of UNIX.
- Mondo Rescue: a utility that backs up Linux systems to CD-R, DVD-R, tape, or hard disk. This tool is particularly useful for bare-metal recovery. Read more at mondorescue.org.

10.9 COMMERCIAL BACKUP PRODUCTS

We would all like to think that UNIX is the only OS in the world, but unfortunately, that is not the case. When looking at commercial backup solutions, you should consider whether they can handle any other operating systems that you are responsible for backing up. Most contemporary products address cross-platform issues and let you include UNIX, Windows, and Mac OS workstations in your backup scheme. You must also consider non-UNIX storage arrays and file servers.

Users' laptops and other machines that are not consistently connected to your network should also be protected from failure. When looking at commercial products, you may want to ask if each product is smart enough not to back up identical files from every laptop. How many copies of **command.com** do you really need?

Since we find that Bacula works well for us, we don't have much experience with commercial products. We asked some of our big-bucks buddies at commercial sites for quick impressions of the systems they use. Their comments are reproduced here.

ADSM/TSM

The ADSM product was developed by IBM and later purchased by Tivoli. It is marketed today as the Tivoli Storage Manager (TSM), although the product is once again owned by IBM. TSM is a data management tool that also handles backups. More information can be found at ibm.com/tivoli.

Pros:

- Owned by IBM; it's here to stay
- Attractive pricing and leasing options
- Very low failure rate
- Uses disk cache; useful for backing up slow clients
- Deals with Windows clients
- Excellent documentation (priced separately)

Cons:

- Poorly designed GUI interface
- Every 2 files =1kB in the database
- The design is incremental forever

Veritas NetBackup

Veritas merged with Symantec in 2005. They sell backup solutions for a variety of systems. When you visit their web site (symantec.com), make sure you select the product that's appropriate for you. NetBackup is the most enterprise-ish product, but smaller shops can probably get away with BackupExec.

Pros:

- Decent GUI interface
- Connects to storage area networks and NetApp filers
- Push install for UNIX and Windows
- Can write tapes in GNU **tar** format
- Centralized database, but can support a distributed backup system

Cons:

- Some bugs
- Pricing is confusing and annoying
- Client notorious for security vulnerabilities

EMC NetWorker

Storage behemoth EMC acquired Legato NetWorker back in 2003. At the time, Veritas and Legato were the two market leaders for enterprise backup.

Pros:

- Competitively priced
- Server software can run on each of our example platforms
- Supports diverse client platforms
- Slick, integrated bare-metal restorations

Cons:

- Significant overlap among EMC products

Other alternatives

W. Curtis Preston, author of the O'Reilly book *Backup & Recovery*, maintains a web page about backup-related topics (disk mirroring products, advanced filesystem products, remote system backup products, off-site data-vaulting products, etc.) at backupcentral.com.

10.10 Recommended Reading

PRESTON, W. CURTIS. *Backup & Recovery: Inexpensive Backup Solutions for Open Systems*. Sebastopol, CA: O'Reilly Media, 2007.

10.11 Exercises

E10.1 Investigate the backup procedure used at your site. Which machines perform the backups? What type of storage devices are used? Where are tapes stored? Suggest improvements to the current system.

E10.2 What steps are needed to restore files on a system that uses Bacula? How do you find the right tape?

Exercises continue on the next page.

★ E10.3 Given the following output from **df** and **/etc/dumpdates**, identify the steps needed to perform the three restores requested. Enumerate your assumptions. Assume that the date of the restore request is January 18.

df output from the machine khaya.cs.colorado.edu:

```
/dev/hda8      256194    81103   161863   33%  /
/dev/hda1       21929     4918    15879   24%  /boot
/dev/hda6     3571696    24336  3365924    1%  /local
/dev/hda10     131734     5797   119135    5%  /tmp
/dev/hda5     1815580  1113348   610004   65%  /usr
/dev/hda7      256194    17013   225953    7%  /var
```

/etc/dumpdates from khaya.cs.colorado.edu:

```
/dev/hda8          2 Sun Jan  17  22:59:23 2010
/dev/hda6          3 Sun Jan  17  22:51:51 2010
/dev/hda7          3 Sun Jan  17  22:50:24 2010
/dev/hda5          9 Sun Jan  17  22:46:25 2010
/dev/hda5          1 Tue Jan  12  22:45:42 2010
/dev/hda7          0 Tue Jan  12  23:14:47 2010
/dev/hda6          1 Tue Jan  12  23:14:32 2010
/dev/hda8          1 Tue Jan  12  23:14:17 2010
/dev/hda6          0 Sun Jan  10  22:47:31 2010
/dev/hda1          1 Fri Jan   8  22:16:05 2010
/dev/hda7          1 Thu Jan   7  22:08:09 2010
/dev/hda1          4 Sun Jan   3  22:51:53 2010
/dev/hda7          2 Thu Dec  24  22:53:52 2009
/dev/hda5          0 Tue Nov   3  22:46:21 2009
/dev/hda1          0 Mon Sep  21  22:46:29 2009
/dev/hda8          0 Mon Aug  24  23:01:24 2009
/dev/hda1          3 Wed Jul  29  22:52:20 2009
/dev/hda6          2 Wed Jul  29  23:01:32 2009
```

a) "Please restore my entire home directory (**/usr/home/clements**) from some time in the last few days. I seem to have lost the entire code base for my senior project."

b) "Umm, I accidentally did a **sudo rm -rf /*** on my machine khaya. Could you restore all the filesystems from the latest backups?"

c) "All my MP3 files that I have been collecting from BitTorrent over the last month are gone. They were stored in **/tmp/mp3/**. Could you please restore them for me?"

☆ E10.4 Design a backup plan for the following scenarios. Assume that each computer has a 400GB disk and that users' home directories are stored locally. Choose a backup device that balances cost vs. support needs and explain your reasoning. List any assumptions you make.

a) A research facility has 50 machines. Each machine holds a lot of important data that changes often.

b) A small software company has 10 machines. Source code is stored on a central server that has 4TB of disk space. The source code changes throughout the day. Individual users' home directories do not change very often. Cost is of little concern and security is of utmost importance.

c) A home network has two machines. Cost is the most important consideration, and the users are not system administrators.

☆ E10.5 Design a restore strategy for each of the three situations described in Exercise 10.4.

☆ E10.6 Write Bacula configuration statements that implement the backup plans you came up with for Exercise 10.4.

☆ E10.7 Outline the steps you would take to perform a **dump** to a remote tape drive through a secure SSH tunnel.

11 Syslog and Log Files

System daemons, the kernel, and various utilities and services all emit data that is logged and eventually ends up on your finite-sized disks. Most of that data has a limited useful life and needs to be summarized, compressed, archived, and eventually thrown away. Access and audit data may need to be managed closely according to regulatory retention rules or site security policies.

Experienced administrators review logs sooner rather than later. Log files often contain important hints that point toward the resolution of vexing configuration problems. When a daemon refuses to start or a chronic error continues to plague a booting system, check the logs first.

UNIX has historically tried to use an integrated system known as syslog for one-stop log shopping, but this effort has met with mixed success at best. Although the **syslogd** daemon still reigns as the designated king of logging, plenty of applications, network daemons, startup scripts, and other vigilantes still write to their own ad hoc log files. This lawlessness has resulted in a complement of logs that varies significantly among flavors of UNIX and even among Linux distributions.

In most cases, a log event is captured as a single line of text that includes the time and date, the type and severity of the event, and any other relevant details. The various components of the message may be separated by spaces, tabs, or punctuation, depending on the specific file.

Since most logs are text files, they can be viewed or parsed with standard tools such as **cat**, **grep**, **tail**, and Perl. Most modern systems also include log management tools that rotate, compress, and monitor log files on a daily or weekly basis.

Log files managed by syslog usually contain events from multiple sources. For example, complaints from the kernel and from a network daemon may appear adjacent to each other. At sites that have set up a centralized logging server, events from multiple hosts may be aggregated and processed together.

The snippet below shows typical events from a centralized syslog server:

```
Dec 18 15:12:42 av18.cs.colorado.edu sbatchd[495]: sbatchd/main: ls_info()
    failed: LIM is down; try later; trying ...
Dec 18 15:14:28 proxy-1.cs.colorado.edu pop-proxy[27283]: Connection from
    128.138.198.84
Dec 18 15:14:30 mroe.cs.colorado.edu pingem[271]: maltese-
    office.cs.colorado.edu has not answered 42 times
Dec 18 15:15:05 schwarz.cs.colorado.edu vmunix: Multiple softerrors: Seen 100
    Corrected Softerrors from SIMM J0201
Dec 18 15:15:16 coyote.cs.colorado.edu PAM_unix[17405]: (sshd) session closed
    for user trent
Dec 18 15:15:48 proxy-1.cs.colorado.edu pop-proxy[27285]: Connection from
    12.2.209.183
Dec 18 15:15:50 av18.cs.colorado.edu last message repeated 100 times
```

See page 908 for more information on PAM.

This example contains entries from several different hosts (av18, proxy-1, mroe, schwarz, and coyote) and from several programs: **sbatchd**, **pop-proxy**, **pingem**, and the Pluggable Authentication Modules library.

The importance of having a well-defined, site-wide logging strategy has grown along with the adoption of formal IT standards such as COBIT and ISO 27002 as well as the maturing of industry regulations. Today, these external standards may require you to maintain a centralized, hardened, enterprise-wide repository for log activity, with time stamps provided through NTP and a strict retention schedule. We discuss some specific strategies later in this chapter.

11.1 Finding log files

UNIX is often criticized for being inconsistent, and indeed it is. Just take a look at a directory of log files and you're sure to find some with names like **maillog**, some like **ftp.log**, and maybe even some like **lpNet**, **lpd-errs**, or **console_log**. In addition to having random names, log files are often scattered across directories and filesystems. By default, most of these files are found in **/var/adm** or **/var/log**.

Linux systems are generally a bit more sane, although each distribution has its own way of naming and dividing up the log files. For the most part, Linux packages send their logging information to files in the **/var/log** directory.

Table 11.1 compiles information about some of the more common log files on our example systems. Specifically, it lists the following:

- The log files to archive, summarize, or truncate
- The program that creates each
- An indication of how each filename is specified
- The frequency of cleanup that we consider reasonable
- The systems (among our examples) that use the log file
- A description of the file's contents

Filenames in Table 11.1 are relative to **/var/adm**, **/var/log**, or **/var/log/syslog** unless otherwise noted.

Log files are generally owned by root, although conventions for the ownership and mode of log files vary. In some cases, a less privileged daemon such as **httpd** or **mysqld** may require write access and set the ownership and mode appropriately. You may need to use **sudo** to view sensitive log files that have tight permissions. Alternatively, for log files that don't contain sensitive system details, it's usually safe to change the permissions to be world-readable. We usually recommend the latter method for log files that you need to view regularly, such as Apache's logs in **/var/log/httpd**.

Syslog maintains many of the log files in Table 11.1, but its default configuration varies widely among systems. With a consistent **/etc/syslog.conf** file, the log files would have more in common among operating systems.

Log files can grow large very quickly, especially the logs for busy services such as email, web, and DNS servers. An out-of-control log file can fill up the disk and bring the system to its knees. For this reason, we like to keep a separate partition for the noisiest and busiest log files. On Linux systems, **/var** or **/var/log** is a good choice. Other systems' conventions vary, but plan ahead when building a new box.

Files *not* to manage

Most logs are text files to which lines are written as interesting events occur. But a few of the logs listed in Table 11.1 have a rather different context.

wtmp (sometimes **wtmpx**) contains a record of users' logins and logouts as well as entries that record when the system was rebooted or shut down. It's a fairly generic log file in that new entries are simply added to the end of the file. However, the **wtmp** file is maintained in a binary format. Use the **last** command to decode the information.

See the footnote on page 308 for more info about sparse files.

lastlog contains similar information to that in **wtmp**, but it records only the time of last login for each user. It is a sparse, binary file that's indexed by UID. It will stay smaller if your UIDs are assigned in some kind of numeric sequence, although this is certainly nothing to lose sleep over in the real world. **lastlog** doesn't need to be rotated because its size stays constant unless new users log in.

Table 11.1 Log files on parade

File	Program	Where[a]	Freq[a]	Systems[a]	Contents
acpid	**acpid**	F	64k	RZ	Power-related events
auth.log	**sudo**, etc.[b]	S	M	U	Authorizations
apache2/*	**httpd** (v2)	F	D	ZU	Apache HTTP server logs (v2)
apt*	APT	F	M	U	Aptitude package installations
boot.log	**rc** scripts	F[c]	M	R	Output from system startup scripts
boot.msg	kernel	H	–	Z	Dump of kernel message buffer
cron, cron/log	**cron**	S	W	RAH	**cron** executions and errors
cups/*	CUPS	F	W	ZRU	Printing-related messages (CUPS)
daemon.log	various	S	W	U	All daemon facility messages
debug	various	S	D	U	Debugging output
dmesg	kernel	H	–	RU	Dump of kernel message buffer
dpkg.log	**dpkg**	F	M	U	Package management log
faillog[d]	**login**	H	W	RZU	Unsuccessful login attempts
httpd/*	**httpd**	F	D	R	Apache HTTP server logs (in **/etc**)
kern.log	kernel	S	W	U	All kern facility messages
lastlog	**login**	H	–	RZ	Last login time per user (binary)
mail*	mail-related	S	W	all	All mail facility messages
messages	various	S	W	RZUS	The main system log file
rpmpkgs	**cron.daily**	H	D	R	List of installed RPM packages
samba/*	**smbd**, etc.	F	W	–	Samba (Windows/CIFS file-sharing)
secure	**sshd**, etc.	S	M	R	Private authorization messages
sulog	**su**	F	–	SAH	**su** successes and failures
syslog*	various	S	W	SUH	The main system log file
warn	various	S	W	Z	All warning/error-level messages
wpars/*	**wpar**	F	–	A	Workload partition events
wtmp	**login**	H	M	all	Login records (binary)
xen/*	Xen	F	1m	RZU	Xen virtual machine information
Xorg.*n*.log	**Xorg**	F	W	RS	X Windows server errors
yum.log	**yum**	F	M	R	Package management log

a. Where: S = Syslog, H = Hardwired, F = Configuration file
Freq: D = Daily, W = Weekly, M = Monthly, NN[km] = Size-based, in kB or MB
Systems: U = Ubuntu, Z = SUSE, R = Red Hat and CentOS, S = Solaris, H = HP-UX, A = AIX

b. **passwd**, **login**, and **shutdown** also write to the authorization log. It's in **/var/adm**.

c. Actually logs through syslog, but the facility and level are configured in **/etc/initlog.conf**.

d. Binary file that must be read with the **faillog** utility.

utmp attempts to keep a record of each user that is currently logged in. It is sometimes wrong, usually because a shell was killed with an inappropriate signal and the parent of the shell did not clean up properly. **utmp** is often world-writable.

Vendor specifics

Vendors seem to have hidden log files all over the disk. Careful detective work with your daemons' config files and your syslog configuration file will find many of them. This section details some of the more obscure nooks and crannies in which log files have been hidden.

Linux distributions win the grand prize for simplified log management. Logs are clearly named and consistently stored in **/var/log**. All our example distributions also include a superior tool, **logrotate**, for rotating, truncating, and managing them. New software packages can drop a config file into the **/etc/logrotate.d** directory to set up a management strategy for their logs. (**logrotate** is covered in detail later in this chapter; see page 356.)

By contrast, Solaris has the most disorganized collection of log files ever. With a directory called **/var/log** it shouldn't be so hard. A few pointers:

- **/var/log/***
- **/var/cron/log**
- **/var/lp/logs/***
- **/var/saf/_log**
- **/var/saf/zsmon/log**
- **/var/svc/log**
- **/var/adm/***

You can run the vendor-supplied **/usr/lib/newsyslog** script out of **cron** to rotate the main log files, **/var/adm/messages** and **/var/log/syslog**.

HP-UX log files are in **/var/adm**. A lot of odd little mystery files live in this directory, many of which are not logs, so be careful what you touch. **nettl.LOG000** is a network control and statistics file; see man **nettl** for details. By default, log entries submitted through syslog go into the **/var/adm/syslog** directory.

11.2 Syslog: the system event logger

Syslog, originally written by Eric Allman, is a comprehensive logging system. It has two important functions: to liberate programmers from the tedious mechanics of writing log files, and to put administrators in control of logging. Before syslog, every program was free to make up its own logging policy. System administrators had no control over what information was kept or where it was stored.

Syslog is flexible. It lets you sort messages by their source and importance ("severity level") and route them to a variety of destinations: log files, users' terminals, or even other machines. Syslog's ability to centralize the logging for a network is one of its most valuable features.

Syslog was long ago adopted by every major variant of UNIX and Linux with the exception of AIX. Even AIX includes the syslog daemon and library routines, but it supplies no default syslog configuration and uses its own proprietary daemon for error reporting. See page 353 later in this chapter for details. Since syslog is so commonly used by add-on software, we believe that a thorough understanding of syslog is important even for AIX administrators.

Syslog architecture

Syslog consists of three parts:

- **syslogd**, the logging daemon (and its config file, **/etc/syslog.conf**)
- **openlog** et al., library routines that submit messages to **syslogd**
- **logger**, a user-level command that submits log entries from the shell

syslogd is started at boot time and runs continuously; it cannot be managed with **inetd**. Programs that are syslog-aware write log entries (by calling the **syslog** library routine) to the special file **/dev/log**, a UNIX domain socket. **syslogd** reads messages from this file, consults its configuration file, and dispatches each message to the appropriate destination.

Signals are described on page 124.

A hangup signal (HUP, signal 1) causes **syslogd** to close its log files, reread its configuration file, and start logging again. If you modify **/etc/syslog.conf**, you must send a hangup signal to **syslogd** to make your changes take effect. A TERM signal makes **syslogd** exit.

syslogd writes its process ID to a file in **/var/run** (**/etc** on AIX). This convention makes it easy to send signals to **syslogd** from a script. For example, the following command sends a hangup signal:

```
solaris$ sudo kill -HUP `/bin/cat /var/run/syslogd.pid`
```

Trying to compress or rotate a log file that **syslogd** has open for writing is not healthy and has unpredictable results. Refer to page 356 for information on sane log rotation with the **logrotate** utility.

The preferred method of restarting **syslogd** on AIX is to use **refresh**:

```
aix$ sudo refresh -s syslogd
```

refresh contacts the System Resource Controller, which manages subsystems such as logging. See the **refresh** man page for more information.

Syslog

Configuring syslogd

The **/etc/syslog.conf** file controls **syslogd**'s behavior. It is a text file with a relatively simple format. Blank lines and lines with a pound sign (#) in column one are ignored. The basic format is

```
selector <Tab> action
```

For example, the line

```
mail.info       /var/log/maillog
```

causes messages from the email system to be saved in **/var/log/maillog**. The *selector* and *action* fields must be separated by one or more tabs; spaces don't work (in most versions) and become invisible errors that are very hard to track down. Cutting and pasting with your mouse is one way to introduce such errors.

Selectors identify the program ("facility") that is sending a log message and the message's severity level with the syntax

```
facility.level
```

Both facility names and severity levels must be chosen from a short list of defined values; programs can't make up their own. Facilities are defined for the kernel, for common groups of utilities, and for locally written programs. Everything else is classified under the generic facility "user."

Selectors can contain the special keywords * and none, meaning all or nothing, respectively. A selector can include multiple facilities separated by commas. Multiple selectors can be combined with semicolons.

In general, selectors are ORed together: a message matching any selector will be subject to the line's *action*. However, a selector with a level of none excludes the listed facilities regardless of what other selectors on the same line may say.

Here are some examples of ways to format and combine selectors:

```
facility.level                      action
facility1,facility2.level           action
facility1.level1;facility2.level2   action
*.level                             action
*.level;badfacility.none            action
```

Table 11.2 lists the valid facility names. There are currently 21 facilities.

Table 11.2 Syslog facility names

Facility	Programs that use it
*	All facilities except "mark"
auth	Security and authorization-related commands
authpriv	Sensitive/private authorization messages
cron	The **cron** daemon
daemon	System daemons
ftp	The FTP daemon, **ftpd**
kern	The kernel
local0-7	Eight flavors of local message
lpr	The line printer spooling system
mail	**sendmail** and other mail-related software
mark	Time stamps generated at regular intervals
news	The Usenet news system (obsolete)
syslog	**syslogd** internal messages
user	User processes (the default if not specified)
uucp	Obsolete, ignore

Don't take syslog's distinction between auth and authpriv too seriously. *All* authorization-related messages are sensitive, and none should be world-readable.

syslogd itself produces time stamp messages, which are logged if the "mark" facility appears in **syslog.conf** to specify a destination for them. Time stamps can help you figure out that your machine crashed between 3:00 and 3:20 a.m., not just "sometime last night." This information can be a big help when you are debugging problems that seem to occur regularly.

Table 11.3 lists syslog's severity levels in order of descending importance.

Table 11.3 Syslog severity levels (descending severity)

Level	Approximate meaning
emerg	Panic situations
alert	Urgent situations
crit	Critical conditions
err	Other error conditions
warning	Warning messages
notice	Things that might merit investigation
info	Informational messages
debug	For debugging only

The severity level of a message specifies its importance. The distinctions between the various levels are sometimes fuzzy. There's a clear difference between notice and warning and between warning and err, but the exact shade of meaning expressed by alert as opposed to crit is a matter of conjecture.

In the **syslog.conf** file, levels indicate the *minimum* importance that a message must have in order to be logged. For example, a message from the mail system at level warning would match the selector mail.warning as well as the selectors mail.info, mail.notice, mail.debug, *.warning, *.notice, *.info, and *.debug. If **syslog.conf** specifies that mail.info messages be logged to a file, mail.warning messages will go there also.

As a refinement of the basic syntax, the Linux version of syslog also allows the characters = and ! to be prefixed to priority levels to indicate "this priority only" and "except this priority and higher," respectively. Table 11.4 shows examples.

Table 11.4 Examples of Linux priority level qualifiers in syslog.conf

Selector	Meaning
mail.info	Mail-related messages of info priority and higher
mail.=info	Only messages at info priority
mail.info;mail.!err	Only priorities info, notice, and warning
mail.debug;mail.!=warning	All priorities except warning

The *action* field tells syslog what to do with each message. The options are listed in Table 11.5.

Table 11.5 Syslog actions

Action	Meaning
filename	Appends the message to a file on the local machine
@hostname	Forwards the message to the **syslogd** on *hostname*
@ipaddress	Forwards the message to the **syslogd** on host *ipaddress*
|*fifoname*	Writes the message to the named pipe *fifoname* [a]
user1,user2,...	Writes the message to the screens of *users* if they are logged in
*	Writes the message to all users who are currently logged in

a. See **info mkfifo** for more information (Linux versions of **syslogd** only).

If a *filename* (or *fifoname*) action is used, the name should be an absolute path. If you specify a nonexistent filename on a Linux system, **syslogd** will create the file when a message is first directed to it. On other systems, the file must already exist; **syslogd** will not create it.

On Linux distributions, you can preface a *filename* action with a dash to indicate that the filesystem should not be **sync**ed after each log entry is written. **sync**ing helps preserve as much logging information as possible in the event of a crash, but for busy log files it can be devastating in terms of system performance. We recommend including the dashes (and thereby inhibiting **sync**ing) as a matter of course. Remove the dashes only temporarily when investigating a problem that is causing kernel panics.

If you specify a *hostname* in lieu of an IP address, it must of course be resolvable through a translation mechanism such as DNS or NIS.

Solaris's syslog implementation runs the **syslog.conf** file through the **m4** macro preprocessor. Check your manual pages and use quotes liberally so that your configuration means what you intend. For example, you must quote anything that is an **m4** keyword or contains a comma. Here is a typical **m4**-style entry:

```
auth.notice                    ifdef(`LOGHOST', `/var/log/authlog', `@loghost')
```

Note that the quotes used are the back-tick and the single apostrophe. This line directs messages to the file **/var/log/authlog** if LOGHOST is not defined. Otherwise, messages are forwarded to the machine loghost. **m4**'s ifdef statements are very powerful; they allow sysadmins to create a single **syslog.conf** that can be used on all machines.

Although multiple facilities and levels are allowed in a selector, there is no provision for multiple actions. To send a message to two places (such as to a local file and to a central logging host), you simply include two lines in the configuration file that have the same selectors.

Because syslog messages can be used to mount a form of denial of service attack, the **syslogd** daemon on most Linux distributions does not accept log messages from other machines unless it is started with the **-r** flag. And by default, **syslogd** also refuses to act as a third-party message forwarder; messages that arrive from one network host cannot be sent on to another. Use the **-h** flag to override this behavior. Edit the syslog startup scripts to make the change permanent. On RHEL, syslog configuration should be edited in **/etc/sysconfig/syslog**.

Config file examples

Since it's relatively easy to read a **syslog.conf** file, we do not review our example systems' config files in detail; they're all pretty straightforward. Instead, we look at some common ways that you might want to set up logging if you choose to depart from or expand on your system's default.

Below are three sample **syslog.conf** files that correspond to a stand-alone machine on a small network, a client machine on a larger network, and the central logging host on that same large network. The central host is called netloghost.[1]

Stand-alone machine

A basic configuration for a stand-alone machine is shown below:

```
# syslog.conf file for small network or stand-alone machines

# emergencies: tell everyone who is logged on
*.emerg[2]                                        *
#  important messages
*.warning;daemon,auth.info;user.none  /var/log/messages
#  printer errors
lpr.debug                                         /var/log/lpd-errs
```

The first noncomment line writes emergency messages to the screens of all current users. An example of emergency messages are those generated by **shutdown** when the system is about to be turned off.

The second line writes important messages to **/var/log/messages**. The info level is below warning, so the daemon,auth.info clause includes additional logging from **passwd**, **su**, and daemon programs. The third line writes printer error messages to **/var/log/lpd-errs**.

Network logging client

A network client forwards serious messages to a central logging machine, as shown in the example on the next page.

1. More accurately, it uses "netloghost" as one of its hostname aliases. This setup allows the identity of the log host to be modified with little reconfiguration. An alias can be added in **/etc/hosts** or set up with a CNAME record in DNS. See page 585 for more information about DNS CNAME records.

2. Unless users running X have the **xconsole** program running, they won't get these messages.

```
# syslog.conf file for nonmaster machines

# Emergencies: tell everyone who is logged on
*.emerg;user.none                          *

# Forward important messages to the central logger
*.warning;lpr,local1.none                  @netloghost
daemon,auth.info                           @netloghost

# Send some local stuff to the central logger too
local2.info;local7.debug                   @netloghost

# Keep printer errors local
lpr.debug                                  /var/log/lpd-errs

# sudo logs to local2 - keep a copy here too
local2.info                                /var/log/sudo.log

# Keep kernel messages local
kern.info                                  /var/log/kern.log
```

This configuration does not keep much log information locally. It's worth mentioning that if netloghost is down or unreachable, log messages will be irretrievably lost. You may want to keep local duplicates of important messages to guard against this possibility.

At a site with local software installed, lots of messages can be logged inappropriately to facility user, level emerg. In this example, user/emerg has been specifically excluded with the user.none clause in the first noncomment line.

*See page 113 for more information about **sudo**.*

The second and third lines forward all important messages to the central logging host; messages from the printing system and the campus-wide card access system (local1) are explicitly excluded. The fourth line forwards a subset of local logging information to netloghost as well. The last three entries keep local copies of printer errors, **sudo** messages, and kernel messages.

Central logging host

This example is for netloghost, the central, secure logging host for a moderate-sized network of about 7,000 hosts.

```
# syslog.conf file for master logging host

# Emergencies to the console and log file, with timing marks
*.emerg                                 /dev/console
*.err;kern,mark.debug;auth.notice       /dev/console
*.err;kern,mark.debug;user.none         /var/log/console.log
auth.notice                             /var/log/console.log

# Send non-emergency messages to the usual log files
*.err;user.none;kern.debug              /var/log/messages
daemon,auth.notice;mail.crit            /var/log/messages
lpr.debug                               /var/log/lpd-errs
mail.debug                              /var/log/mail.log
```

```
# Local authorization messages, e.g., sudo and npasswd
local2.debug                    /var/log/sudo.log
local2.alert                    /var/log/sudo-errs.log
auth.info                       /var/log/auth.log

# Other local stuff
local0.info                     /var/adm/nbl.log
local4.notice                   /var/admlog/da.log
local6.debug                    /var/adm/annex-isn.log
local7.debug                    /var/admlog/tcp.log

# Local messages (the default if no facility is specified)
user.info                       /var/admlog/user.log
```

Messages arriving from local programs and **syslogd**s on the network are written to log files. In some cases, the output from each facility is put into its own file.

The central logging host generates the time stamp for each message as it writes the message out. The time stamps do not reflect the time on the originating host. If you have machines in several time zones or your system clocks are not synchronized, the time stamps can be somewhat misleading.

Syslog debugging

The **logger** command is useful for submitting log entries from shell scripts. You can also use it to test changes in **syslogd**'s configuration file. For example, if you have just added the line

```
local5.warning          /tmp/evi.log
```

and want to verify that it is working, run

```
hp-ux$ logger -p local5.warning "test message"
```

A line containing "test message" should be written to **/tmp/evi.log**. If this doesn't happen, perhaps you forgot to create the **evi.log** file, to give the file appropriate permissions, or to send **syslogd** a hangup signal. Or perhaps you've used spaces instead of tabs?

Alternatives to syslog

Although syslog has long been the reigning logging system for UNIX and Linux, several alternatives have been developed in an attempt to address some of syslog's shortcomings. One of these, syslog-ng (syslog, next generation), is now used on SUSE systems by default. From a configuration standpoint it is quite different from the standard syslog, and we do not describe it in detail in this book. It's available from balabit.com if you would like to try it on a non-SUSE system.

Syslog-ng adds additional configuration facilities, filtering based on message content, message integrity, and better support for firewall restrictions when messages are forwarded over the network.

SDSC Secure Syslog (from the San Diego Supercomputing Center) is also known as high-performance syslog. It provides a forensically sound auditing system by implementing the specifications of RFC3195 (*Reliable Delivery for syslog*). It was designed with high-traffic sites in mind and contains a number of performance optimizations. You can download the source code from SourceForge:

sourceforge.net/projects/sdscsyslog

Rsyslog, another powerful, next-generation alternative, is the default shipped with several popular Linux distributions, including Fedora. Rsyslog is multithreaded and aims for high reliability and robust security. It supports logging over TCP (as opposed to UDP, used by the original syslog) and can use SSL, which may be required at some sites for regulatory reasons. Rsyslog can even log to databases. Learn more at rsyslog.com.

Linux kernel and boot-time logging

The kernel and the system startup scripts present some special challenges in the domain of logging. In the case of the kernel, the problem is to create a permanent record of the boot process and the operation of the kernel without building in dependencies on any particular filesystem or filesystem organization. In the case of the startup scripts, the challenge is to capture a coherent narrative of the startup procedure without permanently tying any of the system daemons to a startup log file, interfering with any program's own logging, or gooping up the startup scripts with double entries or output redirections.

Kernel logging is dealt with by having the kernel store its log entries in an internal buffer of limited size. The buffer is large enough to accommodate messages about all the kernel's boot-time activities. Once the system has come all the way up, a user process accesses the kernel's log buffer and makes a final disposition of its contents. The **dmesg** command is the best way to view the kernel buffer; the output even contains messages that were generated before **init** started.

The kernel's ongoing logging is handled by a daemon called **klogd**. The functions of **klogd** are actually a superset of those of **dmesg**; in addition to dumping the kernel log and exiting, it can also read messages out of the kernel buffer as they are generated and pass them along to a file or to syslog. In normal operation, **klogd** runs in this latter mode. Syslog processes the messages according to the instructions for the "kern" facility. They are typically sent to **/var/log/messages** or **/var/log/syslog**.

Our example distributions' startup scripts do not use **dmesg**'s **-c** flag when they make their initial dump of log messages, so the kernel's message buffer is read but not reset. When **klogd** starts up, it finds the same set of messages seen by **dmesg** in the buffer and submits them to syslog. For this reason, some entries appear in both the **dmesg** or **boot.msg** file and in the system's primary syslog file.

Another issue in kernel logging is the appropriate management of the system console. As the system is booting, it's important for all the output to come to the console. However, once the system is up and running, console messages may be more an annoyance than a help, particularly if the console is used for logins.

Both **dmesg** and **klogd** let you set the kernel's console logging level with a command-line flag. For example:

```
ubuntu$ sudo dmesg -n 2
```

Level 7 is the most verbose and includes debugging information. Level 1 includes only panic messages (the lower-numbered levels are the most severe). All kernel messages continue to go to the central buffer (and to syslog) regardless of whether they are forwarded to the console.

The kernel provides some control files underneath the **/proc/sys** directory to allow floods of repeated log messages to be choked off at the source. See the section *Tuning Linux kernel parameters* starting on page 421 for more information about the general mechanism through which kernel parameters are set. The specific control files are **/proc/sys/kernel/printk_ratelimit**, which specifies the minimum number of seconds that must elapse between kernel messages once the choke has been activated (default 5), and **/proc/sys/kernel/printk_ratelimit_burst**, which specifies how many grouped messages to let through before activating the choke (default 10). These parameters are advisory, so they do not absolutely guarantee that a heavy flow of messages will be stanched. They also apply only to messages created in the kernel with the **printk_ratelimit()** function.

Logging for the system startup scripts is unfortunately not as well managed as kernel logging.

Red Hat Enterprise Linux uses an **initlog** command to capture the output of startup commands and submit it to syslog. Unfortunately, **initlog** must be mentioned explicitly whenever a command is run, so the information comes at the cost of some complexity. Messages eventually make their way to **/var/log/boot.log**.

Our other example systems make no coherent effort to capture a history of the startup scripts' output. Some information is logged by individual commands and daemons, but much goes unrecorded.

11.3 AIX LOGGING AND ERROR HANDLING

AIX manages its logs differently from other UNIX systems. Although syslog is present in the default installation, it is not configured. Instead, AIX relies on a proprietary daemon called **errdemon** for system error reporting. **errdemon** is intended to handle system diagnostic messages (such as notifications of hardware failures or full filesystems) but not to handle logging for individual daemons. Thus, the prudent system administrator will rely on the wisdom of **errdemon** for

AIX-specific diagnostics and on a custom-configured syslog for centralized application logs.

errdemon starts at system boot in **/etc/rc.bootc** and reads error events from the special file **/dev/error**. Both the kernel and some AIX userland applications write errors to this file according to predefined templates in **/dev/adm/ras/errtmplt**. **errdemon** compares new entries to the templates and writes the output in a binary format to the file **/var/adm/ras/errlog**. AIX loves binary formats!

errlog is a circular file, so it overwrites the first event with the most recent when the file reaches its maximum size, 1MB by default. **errdemon** also buffers events that haven't yet been written to the log. The settings can be viewed or adjusted by running **/usr/lib/errdemon** directly. See the man page for invocation details.

Because **errlog** is not a text file, you use another proprietary tool called **errpt** to read its contents. Without any arguments, **errpt** prints a list of all events in the log in a short form. Add the **-a** argument for detailed output. A sample entry from our AIX systems looks like this:

```
aix$ errpt -a
---------------------------------------------------------------------------
LABEL:              DMPCHK_NOSPACE
IDENTIFIER:         F89FB899

Date/Time:          Sat Mar 21 15:00:01 MST 2009
Sequence Number:    224
Machine Id:         0001A4C4D700
Node Id:            ibm
Class:              O
Type:               PEND
WPAR:               Global
Resource Name:      dumpcheck

Description
The copy directory is too small.

Probable Causes
There is not enough free space in the file system containing the copy
directory to accommodate the dump.

          Recommended Actions
          Increase the size of that file system.

Detail Data
File system name
/var/adm/ras

Current free space in kb
          108476
Current estimated dump size in kb
          197836
---------------------------------------------------------------------------
...
```

This particular event indicates that the system dump will not fit in the specified destination filesystem. Most of the section labels are self-explanatory, but see **man errpt** for further details.

Although **errdemon** is a useful source of log data on a stand-alone AIX system, its use can interfere with a more broadly defined enterprise logging strategy. You may have to do some scripting to capture **errdemon** events in syslog format or to forward them for central archiving. IBM's extensive on-line documentation also shows how to send error reports to syslog through the Object Data Manager.

You may need to delete entries from the error logs, and IBM provides the **errclear** command for this purpose. **errclear** deletes all messages older than the number of days specified as an argument. For example, **errclear 7** deletes error messages older than one week.

Run **errclear 0** to clear all error messages or **errclear -j** *identifier* **0** to clear a specific message.

Syslog configuration under AIX

By default, AIX's **syslog.conf** file consists of a long list of comments and no parsable configuration data. It's up to the system administrator to configure syslog in a manner consistent with settings on other systems.

Always the renegade, AIX provides a native log rotation facility within **syslogd**. Logs can be rotated at regular intervals or rotated when they reach a given size. They can optionally be compressed and archived to a new location. Although we appreciate the convenience of these features, they cannot manage files that are outside syslog's control, such as logs that are generated by non-syslog-aware applications. To implement comprehensive log management, you'll probably need a combination of the native **syslogd** rotation features and one of the tools covered later in this chapter.

Syslog

To replicate a Linux-style syslog configuration, append the following lines to **/etc/syslog.conf** and run **refresh -s syslogd**. Don't forget to use tabs in place of spaces and to create each file in advance.

```
mail.debug      /var/log/mail
user.debug      /var/log/user
kern.debug      /var/log/kern
syslog.debug    /var/log/messages
daemon.debug    /var/log/daemon
auth.debug      /var/log/secure
local2.debug    /var/log/sudo
```

You specify log rotation in **syslog.conf** by appending the term `rotate` to the end of a configuration line. Logs can be rotated when they reach a given file size or after a given time increment. If you set up both size and time constraints, **syslogd** rotates the file as soon as either criterion is met. Furthermore, files can be compressed or archived to a new location. Table 11.6 summarizes these options.

Table 11.6 AIX log rotation options in syslog.conf

Option	Meaning
rotate	Indicates that the specified file should be rotated
size *N*[km][a]	Rotates when the file reaches the specified size[b]
files N	Keeps the specified number of versions in the rotation
time N[hdwmy][c]	Rotates after the specified time interval has elapsed[b]
compress	Compresses the rotated file with **compress**
archive *location*	Moves the rotated file to *location*

a. k = kilobytes, m = megabytes
b. There must be no space between *N* and the unit. For example, 3m is correct, but 3 m is not.
c. h = hours, d = days, w = weeks, m = months, y = years

For example, here are some **syslog.conf** configuration lines from the previous example that have been expanded to include rotation options:

```
# Rotate at 500MB, keep 4 files
mail.debug    /var/log/mail          rotate size 500m files 4

# Rotate after 1 week, keep 10 files, compress the file
user.debug    /var/log/user         rotate files 10 time 1w compress

# Rotate after 100KB or 2 months, whichever occurs first, keeping 4 files
kern.debug    /var/log/kern         rotate size 100k files 4 time 2m

# Keep 1 year of weekly logs, compress the file, move the file to /logs
syslog.debug /var/log/messages  rotate files 52 time 1w compress archive /logs
```

11.4 LOGROTATE: MANAGE LOG FILES

Erik Troan's excellent **logrotate** utility implements a variety of log management policies and is standard on all our example Linux distributions. It also runs on Solaris, HP-UX, and AIX, but you'll have to install it. We prefer **logrotate** to the inferior **logadm** package that's provided with Solaris.

A **logrotate** configuration file consists of a series of specifications for groups of log files to be managed. Options that appear outside the context of a log file specification (such as errors, rotate, and weekly in the following example) apply to all following specifications. They can be overridden within the specification for a particular file and can also be respecified later in the file to modify the defaults.

Here's a somewhat contrived example that handles several different log files:

```
# Global options
errors errors@book.admin.com
rotate 5
weekly
```

```
# Logfile rotation definitions and options
/var/log/messages {
      postrotate
            /bin/kill -HUP `cat /var/run/syslogd.pid`
      endscript
}
/var/log/samba/*.log {
      notifempty
      copytruncate
      sharedscripts
      postrotate
            /bin/kill -HUP `cat /var/lock/samba/*.pid`
      endscript
}
```

This configuration rotates **/var/log/messages** every week. It keeps five versions of the file and notifies **syslogd** each time the file is reset. Samba log files (of which there may be several) are also rotated weekly, but instead of being moved aside and restarted, they are copied and then truncated. The Samba daemons are sent HUP signals only after all log files have been rotated.

Table 11.7 lists the most useful **logrotate.conf** options.

Table 11.7 logrotate options

Option	Meaning
compress	Compresses all noncurrent versions of the log file
daily, weekly, monthly	Rotates log files on the specified schedule
delaycompress	Compresses all versions but current and next-most-recent
endscript	Marks the end of a prerotate or postrotate script
errors *emailaddr*	Emails error notifications to the specified *emailaddr*
missingok	Doesn't complain if the log file does not exist
notifempty	Doesn't rotate the log file if it is empty
olddir *dir*	Specifies that older versions of the log file be placed in *dir*
postrotate	Introduces a script to run after the log has been rotated
prerotate	Introduces a script to run before any changes are made
rotate *n*	Includes *n* versions of the log in the rotation scheme
sharedscripts	Runs scripts only once for the entire log group
size *logsize*	Rotates if log file size > *logsize* (e.g., 100K, 4M)

logrotate is normally run out of **cron** once a day. Its standard configuration file is **/etc/logrotate.conf**, but multiple configuration files (or directories containing configuration files) can appear on **logrotate**'s command line. This feature is used to great effect by Linux distributions, which define the **/etc/logrotate.d** directory as a standard place for **logrotate** config files. **logrotate**-aware software packages (of which there are many) can drop in log management instructions as part of their installation procedure, greatly simplifying administration.

In addition to **logrotate**, Ubuntu provides a simpler program called **savelog** that manages rotation for individual files. It's more straightforward than **logrotate** and doesn't use (or need) a config file. Some packages prefer to use their own **savelog** configurations rather than **logrotate**.

11.5 Condensing log files to useful information

Syslog is great for sorting and routing log messages, but when all is said and done, its end product is still a bunch of log files. While they may contain all kinds of useful information, those files aren't going to come and find you when something goes wrong. Another layer of software is needed to analyze the logs and make sure that important messages don't get lost amid the chatter.

A variety of free tools are available to fill this niche, and most of them are remarkably similar: they scan recent log entries, match them against a database of regular expressions, and process the important messages in some attention-getting way. Tools differ primarily in their degree of flexibility and in the size of their off-the-shelf database of patterns.

Two of the more commonly used log postprocessors are Todd Atkins' **swatch** and Craig Rowland's **logcheck**. Both are available from sourceforge.net (**logcheck** comes with the sentrytools package: sourceforge.net/projects/sentrytools).

swatch is a Perl script that gets its marching orders from a configuration file. The configuration syntax is fairly flexible, and it provides access to the full pattern-matching mojo of Perl. While **swatch** can process an entire file in a single bound, it's primarily intended to be left running so that it can review new messages as they arrive, a la **tail -f**. A disadvantage of **swatch** is that you must build your own configuration essentially from scratch; it doesn't know about specific systems and the actual log messages they might generate.

logcheck is a more basic script written in **sh**. The distribution also includes a C program that **logcheck** uses to help it record its place within a log file. **logcheck** knows how far it has read in a log file, so there is perhaps less chance of a message slipping by at startup or shutdown time. In addition, **logcheck** can run at intervals from **cron** rather than running continuously.

logcheck comes with sample databases for several different versions of UNIX and Linux. Even if you don't want to use the actual script, it's worth looking over the patterns to see if there are any you might want to steal for your own use.

These tools have the disadvantage of working on only a single log file at a time. If your syslog configuration sorts messages into many different files, you might want to duplicate some of the messages into a central file that is frequently truncated or rotated, then use that summary file to feed a postprocessing script. That's easier than setting up a complicated network of scripts to handle multiple files.

Splunk (splunk.com) unites log and status messages from many different sources into a single, searchable message database. A basic version is free.

SEC, the Simple Event Correlator, is a different type of log management tool. It's a Perl script that reads lines from files, named pipes, or standard input and converts them into various classes of "input events" by matching them to regular expressions. Configuration rules then specify how input events should be transmogrified into output events such as the execution of a particular script or the emission of a message to a specified pipe or file.

The SEC distribution is available from kodu.neti.ee/~risto/sec and contains an extensive man page with examples. Additional examples are available at the web site. SEC isn't as "off the shelf" as the other tools listed above, but it's a good base on which to build a custom log analysis tool.

No matter what system you use to scan log files, there are a couple of things you should be sure to check for:

- Most security-related messages should receive a prompt review. It's often helpful to monitor failed login, **su**, and **sudo** attempts in order to catch potential break-ins before they happen. If someone has just forgotten his password (as is usually the case), a proactive offer of help will make a good impression and cement your reputation for clairvoyance.
- Messages about disks that have filled up should be flagged and acted on immediately. Full disks often bring useful work to a standstill.
- Events that are repeated many times deserve attention, if only in the name of hygiene.

11.6 Logging policies

Over the years, log events have emigrated from the realm of system administration minutia and become a formidable enterprise event management challenge. Security incident handling, IT standards, and legislative edicts may all require a holistic and systematic approach to the management of log data.

The log data from a single system has a relatively inconsequential effect on storage, but a centralized register of events from hundreds of servers and dozens of applications is a different story entirely. Thanks in large part to the mission-critical nature of web services, application and daemon logs have become as important as those generated by the operating system.

Keep these questions in mind when designing your logging strategy:

- How many systems and applications will be included?
- What type of storage infrastructure is available?
- How long must logs be retained?
- What types of events are important?

The answers to these questions depend on business requirements and on any applicable standards or regulations. For example, one standard from the Payment Card Industry Security Standards Council requires that logs be retained on an easy-access medium (e.g., a locally mounted hard disk) for three months and archived to long-term storage for at least one year. The same standard also includes specific requirements about the types of data that must be included.

However you answer the questions above, be sure to gather input from your information security and compliance departments if your organization has them.

UNIX systems and applications have highly configurable log and audit settings. Depending on the usage volume, it may be necessary to tone down the verbosity of logs. Conversely, a sensitive or important application may require additional event-related data. For most applications, consider capturing at least the following information:

- Username or user ID
- Event success or failure
- Source address for network events
- Date and time (from an authoritative source, such as NTP)
- Sensitive data added, altered, or removed
- Event details

Most sites today are trending towards a centralized approach to log collection and analysis. Such centralization has multiple benefits: simplified storage requirements, simpler automated analysis and alerting, and improved security. Copying events to a central system also improves the integrity of the logs, since it is much harder for an attacker to cover his tracks.

See page 237 for more information about RAID.

A log server should have a carefully considered storage strategy. For example, logs may reside on a local RAID array for 30 days, a locally mounted SAN for an additional year, and finally be archived to tape for inclusion in the enterprise backup rotation for another three years. Storage requirements may evolve over time, and a successful implementation will adapt easily to these changing conditions.

Access to centralized log servers should be limited to high-level system administrators and to software and personnel involved with addressing compliance and security issues. These systems have no real role in the organization's daily business beyond satisfying auditability requirements, so application administrators, end users, and the help desk have no business accessing them. Access to log files on the central servers should itself be logged.

Centralization takes work, and at smaller sites it may not represent a net benefit. We suggest twenty servers as a reasonable threshold for considering centralization. Below that size, just ensure that logs are rotated properly and are archived frequently enough to avoid filling up a disk. Include log files in a monitoring solution that will alert you if a log file stops growing.

11.7 Exercises

E11.1 What are the main reasons for keeping old log files?

E11.2 What is the difference between **lastlog** and **wtmp**? What is a reasonable rotation policy for each?

E11.3 Dissect and understand the following **syslog.conf** line:

```
*.notice;kern.debug;lpr.info;mail.crit;news.err /var/log/messages
```

Does it seem sensible?

E11.4 Look through your log files for entries from the SSH service. What events are logged when a login attempt is successful? What if a login attempt fails? What steps would you take to increase the logging verbosity of the SSH daemon?

E11.5 Many IT industry standards and regulations impose logging or auditing requirements. Choose one of these standards and discuss how you might tune a syslog configuration to achieve compliance.

☆ E11.6 Where would you find the boot log for your Linux machine? What issues affect logging at boot time? How does **klogd** solve these issues?

☆ E11.7 Investigate the logging policy in use at your site, including the log file rotation policy. How much disk space is dedicated to logging? How long are log files kept? Can you foresee circumstances in which your site's policy would not be adequate? What solution would you recommend? (Requires root access.)

☆ E11.8 Some log messages are extremely important and should be reviewed by an administrator immediately. What system could you set up to make sure that this happens as quickly as possible?

12 Software Installation and Management

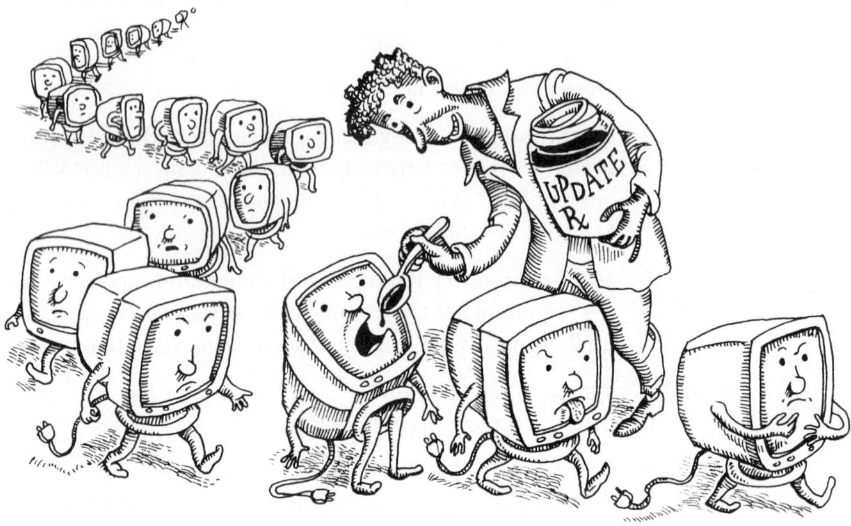

The installation, configuration, and management of software is a large part of most sysadmins' jobs. Administrators respond to installation and configuration requests from users, apply updates to fix security problems, and supervise transitions to new software releases that may offer both new features and incompatibilities. Generally speaking, administrators perform all of the following tasks:

- Automating mass installations of operating systems
- Maintaining custom OS configurations for the local environment
- Keeping systems and applications patched and up to date
- Managing add-on software packages

The process of configuring an off-the-shelf distribution or software package to conform to your needs (and to your local conventions for security, file placement, and network topology) is often referred to as "localization." This chapter explores some techniques and applications that help reduce the pain of software installation and make these tasks scale more gracefully. We also discuss the installation procedure for each of our example operating systems, including some options for automated deployment that use common (platform-specific) tools.

12.1 INSTALLING LINUX AND OPENSOLARIS

Current Linux distributions all have straightforward procedures for basic installation. OpenSolaris has adopted many of the same conventions, so its installation process is similar, especially on PC hardware.

Installation typically involves booting from a DVD, answering a few basic questions, optionally configuring disk partitions, and then telling the installer which software packages to install. Some systems, such as Ubuntu and OpenSolaris, include a "live" option on the installation media that lets you run the operating system without actually installing it on a local disk. This used to be a big deal, but these days it's becoming a standard feature of most distributions.

Installing the base operating system from local media is fairly trivial thanks to the GUI applications that shepherd you through the process. Table 12.1 lists pointers to detailed installation instructions for each of our example distributions.

Table 12.1 Installation documentation for Linux and OpenSolaris

Distribution	Documentation source
Red Hat Enterprise Linux	redhat.com/docs/manuals/enterprise
SUSE	en.opensuse.org/Installation
Ubuntu	help.ubuntu.com/community/Installation
OpenSolaris	dlc.sun.com/osol/docs/content/dev/getstart

Netbooting PCs

If you have to install the operating system on more than one computer, you will quickly reach the limits of interactive installation. It's time consuming, error prone, and boring to repeat the standard installation process on hundreds of systems. You can minimize human errors by using a localization checklist, but even this measure does not remove all potential sources of variation.

To alleviate some of these problems, most systems include network installation options that simplify large-scale deployments. The most common methods use DHCP and TFTP to boot the system sans physical media, then retrieve the installation files from a network server through HTTP, NFS, or FTP. Network installations are appropriate for sites with more than ten or so systems.

The Preboot eXecution Environment, also known as PXE, is a standard from Intel that allows systems to boot from a network interface. PXE acts like a miniature OS sitting in a ROM on your network card. It exposes its network capabilities through a standardized API for the system BIOS to use. This cooperation makes it possible for a single boot loader to netboot any PXE-enabled PC without the need to supply special drivers for each network card.

See page 469 for more information about DHCP.

The external (network) portion of the PXE protocol is straightforward and is similar to the netboot procedures used on other architectures. A host broadcasts a DHCP "discover" request with the PXE flag turned on, and a DHCP server or proxy responds with a DHCP packet that includes PXE options (the name of a boot server and boot file). The client downloads its boot file by using TFTP (or, optionally, multicast TFTP) and then executes it.

Setting up PXE for Linux

Several PXE-based netboot systems exist, but the one that works best at this time is H. Peter Anvin's PXELINUX, which is part of his SYSLINUX suite of boot loaders for every occasion. Check it out at syslinux.zytor.com.

PXELINUX provides a boot file that you install in your server's **tftpboot** directory and that is downloaded to the booting PC when PXE goes into action. The PC then executes the boot file and downloads its configuration from the server; the configuration specifies which kernel to use. This chain of events can occur without intervention, or you can choose to create a custom boot menu.

PXELINUX uses the PXE API for its downloads and is therefore hardware independent all the way through the boot process. Despite the name, PXELINUX is not limited to booting Linux. It can boot other OSes and can even boot older image types (such as those made from floppy disks) if you use the MEMDISK kernel, which is also part of the SYSLINUX package.

On the server side, ISC's (the Internet Systems Consortium's) DHCP server is your best bet for providing PXE information. See also the material at netboot.me and boot.kernel.org.

Netbooting non-PCs

PXE is an Intel product and is limited to IA-32 and IA-64 hardware. Other architectures have their own methods of booting over the net, and these are almost always more elegant than PXE. An interesting twist to the netboot story is that now that Linux has spread beyond the Intel architecture, many of these "dedicated" UNIX systems now have the option of netbooting Linux instead of their native operating systems.

SPARC machines and most PowerPC boxes use Open Firmware, which is easy to netboot (type **boot net**).

IBM and HP systems also have netbooting capabilities, but the procedures are heavily dependent on the Network Installation Manager and Ignite-UX software packages, respectively. We cover these tools below, but only in the context of mass system installations. Refer to the documentation from IBM and HP for netboot specifics.

Using Kickstart: the automated installer for Red Hat Enterprise Linux

Kickstart is Red Hat's tool for performing automated installations. It is really just a scripting interface to the standard Red Hat installer, Anaconda, and it is dependent on both the base distribution and RPM packages. Kickstart is flexible and quite smart about autodetecting the system's hardware.

Setting up a Kickstart configuration file

Kickstart's behavior is controlled by a single configuration file, generally called **ks.cfg**. The format of this file is straightforward. If you're visually inclined, Red Hat provides a handy GUI tool called **system-config-kickstart** that lets you point and click your way to **ks.cfg** nirvana.

The **ks.cfg** file is also quite easy to generate programmatically. For example, suppose that you wanted to install a different set of packages on servers and clients and that you also have two offices that require slightly different customizations. You could write a small Perl script that used a master set of parameters to generate a config file for the servers and clients in each office. Changing the complement of packages would become just a matter of changing this one Perl script rather than changing every config file. There may even be some cases in which you need to generate an individualized config file for each host. In this situation, you would certainly want the files to be automatically generated.

A Kickstart config file consists of three ordered parts. The first part is the command section, which specifies options such as the language, keyboard, and time zone. This section also specifies the source of the distribution with the url option (in the following example, it's a host called installserver).

Here's an example of a complete command section:

```
text
lang en_US                     # lang is used during the installation...
langsupport en_US              # ...and langsupport at run time.
keyboard us                    # Use an American keyboard.
timezone --utc America/EST     # --utc means hardware clock is on UTC (GMT)
mouse
rootpw --iscrypted $1$NaCl$X5jRlREy9DqNTCXjHp075/
reboot                         # Reboot after installation. Always a good idea.
bootloader --location=mbr      # Install default boot loader in the MBR.
install                        # Install a new system instead of upgrading.
url --url http://installserver/redhat
clearpart --all --initlabel    # Clear all existing partitions.
part / --fstype ext3 --size 4096
part swap --size 1024
part /var --fstype ext3 -size 1 --grow
network --bootproto dhcp
auth --useshadow --enablemd5
firewall --disabled
xconfig --defaultdesktop=GNOME --startxonboot --resolution 1280x1024
    --depth 24
```

Kickstart uses graphical mode by default, which defeats the goal of unattended installation. The text keyword at the top of the example fixes this.

The rootpw option sets the new machine's root password. The default is to specify the password in cleartext, which presents a serious security problem. You should always use the --iscrypted flag to specify a pre-encrypted password. Password entries from an **/etc/shadow** file work fine for the encrypted password, or you can try the **/sbin/grub-md5-crypt** tool on an already built system.

The clearpart and part directives specify a list of disk partitions with sizes. You can use the --grow option to ask one of the partitions to expand to fill any remaining space on the disk. This feature makes it easy to accommodate systems that have different sizes of hard disk. Advanced partitioning options, such as the use of LVM, are supported by Kickstart but not by the **system-config-kickstart** tool. Refer to Red Hat's on-line documentation for full disk layout options.

The second section is a list of packages to install, beginning with a %packages directive. The list can contain individual packages, collections such as @ GNOME, or the notation @ Everything to include the whole shebang. When selecting individual packages, specify only the package name, not the version or the **.rpm** extension. Here's an example:

```
%packages
@ Networked Workstation
@ X Window System
@ GNOME
mylocalpackage
```

In the third section of the Kickstart configuration file, you can specify arbitrary shell commands for Kickstart to execute. There are two possible sets of commands: one introduced with %pre that runs before installation, and one introduced with %post that runs afterward. Both sections have some restrictions on the ability of the system to resolve hostnames, so it's safest to use IP addresses if you want to access the network. In addition, the postinstall commands are run in a **chroot**ed environment, so they cannot access the installation media.

Building a Kickstart server

Kickstart expects its installation files to be laid out as they are on the distribution CD, with packages stored in a directory called **RedHat/RPMS** on the server. You can easily add your own packages to this directory. There are, however, a couple of issues to be aware of.

First, if you tell Kickstart to install all packages (with an @ Everything in the packages section of your **ks.cfg**), it installs the add-on packages in alphabetical order after the base packages have been laid down. If your package depends on other packages that are not in the base set, you may want to call your package something like **zzmypackage.rpm** to make sure that it gets installed last.

If you don't want to install all packages, either list your supplemental packages individually in the %packages section of the **ks.cfg** file or add your packages to one or more of the collection lists. Collection lists are specified by entries such as @ GNOME and stand for a predefined set of packages whose members are enumerated in the file **RedHat/base/comps** on the server. Unfortunately, the **comps** file format is not well documented. The collections are the lines that begin with 0 or 1; the number specifies whether the collection is selected by default. In general, it's not a good idea to tamper with the standard collections. We suggest that you leave them as Red Hat defined them and explicitly name all your supplemental packages in the **ks.cfg** file.

Pointing Kickstart at your config file

Once you've created a config file, you have a couple of ways to get Kickstart to use it. The officially sanctioned method is to boot with a DVD and ask for a Kickstart installation by specifying **linux ks** at the initial boot: prompt. If you don't specify additional arguments, the system determines its network address by using DHCP. It then obtains the DHCP boot server and boot file options, attempts to mount the boot server with NFS, and uses the value of the boot file option as its Kickstart configuration file. If no boot file has been specified, the system looks for a file called **/kickstart/***host_ip_address***-kickstart**.

Alternatively, you can tell Kickstart to get its configuration file in some other way by providing a path as an argument to the **ks** option. There are several possibilities. The instruction

```
boot: linux ks=http:server:/path
```

tells Kickstart to use HTTP to download the file instead of NFS. Using **ks=floppy** tells Kickstart to look for **ks.cfg** on a local floppy drive.

To eliminate the use of boot media entirely, you'll need to graduate to PXE. See page 363 for more information about that.

Using AutoYaST: SUSE's automated installation tool

YaST2 is SUSE's all-in-one installation and configuration tool. It comes with a nice GUI and is fun to use when installing a single system. AutoYaST, its automated equivalent, is the most powerful automated installation software of all the distributions described in this book. You can download detailed documentation from suse.com/~ug/autoyast_doc.

SUSE splits the autoinstallation process into three phases: preparation, installation, and configuration. Initial preparation is performed with the YaST2 AutoYaST module:

```
suse$ /sbin/yast2 autoyast
```

This module helps you define the details of your desired setup. The result of running it is an XML control file that tells the installer how to configure a SUSE system. The structure of the file is described in the on-line documentation mentioned above.

A couple of shortcuts can speed the configuration process. The AutoYaST module can read Kickstart configuration files to help you upgrade from "legacy" systems. If you want to duplicate the configuration of the machine you are currently working on, an option automates this as well.

To perform an actual installation, you need three network services:

- A DHCP server on the same subnet as the machine you want to set up
- A SUSE installation server or package repository
- A server that provides the configuration information for the installation

The last of these servers can supply the configuration files through your choice of HTTP, NFS, or TFTP.

In the most basic setup, you produce a control file for each machine you want to install. AutoYaST uses the IP address of the client to determine which control file to use. This approach is not especially efficient if you have to install a series of slightly different machines.

You can create more complex setups by using a rules system. Different control files are matched to the target system based on system properties such as disk size, host ID, or PCMCIA availability. The contents of all selected control files are merged, with the last control file overriding earlier ones in the case of conflicts. (A control file does not have to specify all aspects of a system's configuration, so this merging does make sense.)

Control files can also define "classes" of machines based on hostnames or IP address ranges, and each class may have yet another subsidiary control file associated with it. Machines can belong to zero, one, or multiple classes, and their configurations will incorporate the contents of all the appropriate class control files.

Thanks to its ability to integrate the contents of multiple control files, the AutoYaST structure allows complex setups to be defined with minimal redundancy. The XML control files are somewhat cumbersome for humans to read, but the files are simple to process and edit with any of the commonly available XML processing tools.

Automating installation with the Ubuntu installer

Ubuntu relies on the underlying Debian installer (named, appropriately enough, **debian-installer**) for "preseeding," the recommended method for automated installation. As in Kickstart, a preconfiguration file answers questions asked by the installer. Preseeded installations cannot use existing partitions; they must either use existing free space or repartition the entire disk.

All the interactive parts of the Debian installer use the **debconf** utility to decide which questions to ask and what default answers to use. By providing **debconf** with a database of preformulated answers, you fully automate the installer. You can either generate the database by hand (it's a text file), or you can perform an interactive installation on an example system and then dump out your **debconf** answers with the following commands:

```
ubuntu$ sudo debconf-get-selections --installer > preseed.cfg
ubuntu$ sudo debconf-get-selections >> preseed.cfg
```

Make the config file available on the net and then pass it to the kernel at installation time with the following kernel argument:

```
preseed/url=http://host/path/to/preseed
```

The syntax of the preseed file, usually called **preseed.cfg**, is simple and reminiscent of Red Hat's **ks.cfg**. The sample below has been shortened for simplicity.

```
d-i debian-installer/locale string en_US
d-i console-setup/ask_detect boolean false
d-i console-setup/layoutcode string us
d-i netcfg/choose_interface select auto
d-i netcfg/get_hostname string unassigned-hostname
d-i netcfg/get_domain string unassigned-domain
d-i netcfg/wireless_wep string
...
d-i partman-auto/disk string /dev/sda
d-i partman-auto/method string lvm
d-i partman-auto/choose_recipe select atomic
...
d-i passwd/user-fullname string Daffy Duck
d-i passwd/username string dduck
d-i passwd/user-password-crypted password $1$/mkq9/$G//i6tN.x6670.95lVSM/
d-i user-setup/encrypt-home boolean false
tasksel tasksel/first multiselect ubuntu-desktop
d-i grub-installer/only_debian boolean true
d-i grub-installer/with_other_os boolean true
d-i finish-install/reboot_in_progress note
xserver-xorg xserver-xorg/autodetect_monitor boolean true
...
```

Several options in this list simply disable dialogs that would normally require user interaction. For example, the ask_detect disables keymap selection. Similarly, the wireless_wep option forestalls a question about WEP keys.

This configuration tries to identify a network interface that's actually connected to a network (choose_interface select auto) and obtains network information through DHCP. The system hostname and domain values are presumed to be provided by DHCP and are not overridden.

The partman* lines are evidence that the partman-auto package is being used for disk partitioning. You must specify a disk to install to unless the system has only one. In this case, **/dev/sda** is used.

Several partitioning "recipes" are provided:

- atomic puts all the system's files in one partition.
- home creates a separate partition for **/home**.
- multi creates separate partitions for **/home**, **/usr**, **/var**, and **/tmp**.

You can create users through the passwd series of directives. As with Kickstart configuration, we strongly recommend providing MD5 hashed password values. Preseed files are often stored on HTTP servers and are apt to be discovered by curious users. (Of course, an MD5 password is still subject to brute force attack.)

The task selection (tasksel) option chooses the type of Ubuntu system to install. Available values include standard, ubuntu-desktop, dns-server, lamp-server, kubuntu-desktop, edubuntu-desktop, and xubuntu-desktop.

The sample preseed file shown above comes from the Ubuntu installation documentation found at help.ubuntu.com. The guide contains full documentation for the syntax and usage of the preseed file.

Although Ubuntu does not descend from the Red Hat lineage, it has grafted compatibility with Kickstart control files onto its own underlying installer. Ubuntu also includes the **system-config-kickstart** tool for creating these files. The Kickstart functionality in Ubuntu's installer is missing a number of important features that are supported by Red Hat's Anaconda, such as LVM and firewall configuration. We recommend sticking with the Debian installer unless you have a good reason to choose Kickstart.

12.2 Installing Solaris

Like most hardware vendors, Sun ships new servers with Solaris preinstalled. Administrators need only answer a few quick questions and reboot the server before the operating system is ready for localization. We've appreciated this preinstallation feature over the years because the Solaris installer was abysmal. The OpenSolaris team has seen the light, however, and the new installer (originally code named "Caiman") is the bee's knees.

The Solaris media is now a live CD that provides a "try before you buy" experience, similar to Ubuntu. The installation process is extremely straightforward and asks only a few questions before installing to the local drive.

As in the Linux world, Solaris administrators need a way to implement mass deployments over the network. Solaris systems running Intel processors can use PXE servers for network boot assistance, like their Linux-wielding siblings. Systems with SPARC processors use the OpenBoot PROM, aka OBP. The OBP is usually accessed with the STOP+A key combination on Sun keyboards. It identifies and tests hardware, detects error conditions, and hands over the boot process to a more sophisticated boot loader, much like the BIOS on Intel systems. OBP has more features than most PC BIOSes, however, including built-in support for booting over a network.

The network boot feature obtains an IP address through DHCP or RARP, then downloads a kernel via TFTP. When booted for automated installation, the kernel connects to an HTTP server or mounts an NFS share to download an appropriate system image and start the installation.

Solaris offers two automatic network installation methods:

- JumpStart, the traditional installer service developed by Sun
- Automated Installer, a replacement service used by OpenSolaris

JumpStart is a veteran installation tool that first appeared in Solaris 2.6 and can be used in all releases through Solaris 10. Like most automatic installation methods, JumpStart uses a predefined answers file and rule-based client selection to make installation choices automatically.

The biggest drawback to JumpStart is its poor scalability. Each client must be manually added to the install server by MAC address. Configuration files specify installation types, configuration values, and other parameters on a per-client basis. This gives the administrator power and flexibility, but it becomes cumbersome when you have hundreds or thousands of systems.

The Automated Installer (sometimes referred to as AI) is the new kid on the block. Its primary development goals were improved scalability and reduced configuration. AI has its roots in JumpStart but distances itself in part through the use of new terminology. At the time of this writing, AI remains a work in progress, but it's more or less ready for production use. Notably, AI is limited to recent releases of OpenSolaris and currently does not work at all with traditional Solaris.

Network installations with JumpStart

JumpStart's original purpose was just to allow Solaris to be installed over a network, but it does have some facilities for automatic installation as well. Over the years, Sun realized that more granular control was needed over the automated installations, so they added the advanced features that are now dubbed Custom JumpStart. An automated Custom JumpStart network installation involves several components:

- An install server that hosts the installation media. A single install server can host media for more than one installation type; for example, different versions of Solaris or support for multiple platforms.
- A boot server that helps clients boot and points them toward the install servers. A boot server is only needed when the client system and the install server are on different subnets.
- A series of files that identify clients, answer configuration questions, and select packages.
- An NFS or HTTP server that shares packages, installation files, and configuration information.

Server-side components can all be located on the same machine. The servers are release- and platform independent. For example, a SPARC-based Solaris 9 boot and install server can offer installation services for x86 Solaris 10 clients.

Since netboot parameters can be included in DHCP responses, you can use a DHCP server as an alternative to a dedicated JumpStart boot server. DHCP is probably the better option for x86 systems that use PXE booting and for client systems on a different subnet from the install server. We discuss only the same-subnet case here; refer to docs.sun.com/doc/817-5504 for more details.

Setting up an install server is straightforward. The setup tools are on the Solaris CD or DVD media. Insert the Solaris medium into the drive on the install server and run commands such as the following to configure a simple install server:

```
solaris$ sudo mkdir -p /jumpstart/s10sparc
solaris$ cd /cdrom/cdrom0/s0/Solaris_10/Tools
solaris$ sudo ./setup_install_server /jumpstart/s10sparc
```

Here, we transfer the SPARC installation files to the **/jumpstart/s10sparc** directory on the install server. The **setup_install_server** script copies the files and adds the appropriate hooks for network-based installations. If only CD media are available, use the **add_to_install_server** command to replicate the contents of multiple CDs to the server.

Several files configure the automated installation tasks:

- A **rules** file identifies clients and assigns installation profiles.
- Individual profile files specify disk partition layout, packages to install, and other system details.
- A **sysidcfg** file provides preconfigured answers to installation questions.
- Optionally, shell scripts can run before and after the installation process.

When a client requests a network installation, JumpStart uses the **rules** file to identify it according to attributes such as the client's hostname, subnet, or model. If the attributes match, JumpStart reads installation details from the appropriate profile, answers installation questions with **sysidcfg**, and executes any custom scripts before and after installation.

The first step in creating a JumpStart configuration is to create a directory to hold all the various configuration files:

```
solaris$ sudo mkdir -m 755 /jumpstart/config
```

This directory must be shared through NFS or HTTP so that clients can access it. For example, to share by NFS, add the line

```
share -F nfs /jumpstart
```

to **/etc/dfs/dfstab** and run **shareall** to initiate NFS service.

The syntax of the **rules** file is simple but powerful. Systems can be identified by network, hostname, model, domain name, or by many other attributes.[1] The following **rules** file specifies one profile for systems on the 192.168.10.0 network and another profile for SPARC systems that have 2–4 GiB of memory:

```
network 192.168.10.0 - profile_a -
arch sparc && memsize 2048-4096 begin profile_b end
```

In the network example, there are no custom scripts, and the installation profile called **profile_a** is used. The other example uses scripts called **begin** and **end** and a profile file named **profile_b**.

Profile files are also simple. Keywords (of which there are many) specify filesystems and installation types. A sample profile might look something like this:

```
install_type initial_install
system_type standalone
partitioning default
filesys any 512 swap        # Specify size of /swap
cluster SUNWCpall
```

An initial_install starts with a clean slate, as opposed to performing an upgrade. This profile uses a default disk partitioning scheme. The cluster SUNWCpall line identifies an "installation group" of packages to install—in this case, all available Solaris packages.

The **sysidcfg** file, which preconfigures other aspects of the installation, consists of lines of the form

keyword=value

Keywords are case insensitive and, except for the network_interface keyword, can only be used once. If a keyword appears more than once, only the first instance takes effect.

Some keywords depend on others and are enclosed in curly braces. These dependent keywords cannot be used unless the corresponding parent (independent) keyword has also been specified. Table 12.2 on the next page lists the independent keywords. See the man page for **sysidcfg** for information about dependent keywords.

Software

As an alternative to **sysidcfg**, a limited set of preconfiguration options can also be specified through DHCP or a network service such as DNS. However, we recommend the use of **sysidcfg** because of the limited number of options available through the alternative pathways.

The following **sysidcfg** example configures a system called sake that has one network interface.

1. Google "Custom JumpStart and Advanced Installations" to access Sun's guide, which contains full details on the rules and profiles files.

Table 12.2 Independent keywords for the JumpStart sysidcfg file

Keyword	What it specifies
keyboard	Keyboard layout and language
name_service	Name service configuration for NIS, DNS, or LDAP
network_interface	Net connection details: hostname, IP address, etc.
nfs4_domain	Domain to use for NFS version 4
root_password	Encrypted root password
security_policy	Kerberos network authentication
service_profile	Available network services
system_locale	System language
terminal	Terminal type
timeserver	Network date and time server
timezone	System time zone

```
keyboard=US-English
system_locale=en_US
timezone=US/Mountain
terminal=sun-cmd
timeserver=time.nist.gov
name_service=DNS {domain_name=solaris.booklab.atrust.com
    name_server=192.168.2.10
    search=atrust.com,booklab.atrust.com}
nfs4_domain=dynamic
root_password=m4QPOWNY
network_interface=e1000g0 {hostname=sake
    default_route=192.168.10.254
    ip_address=192.168.10.15
    netmask=255.255.255.0}
```

If you're distributing the same **sysidcfg** file to many clients, the IP address will of course need to differ between systems. You can leave out the network interface details to force them to be configured the first time the system boots. Or, to obtain a network address from DHCP rather than assigning it statically, use the line

```
network_interface=e1000g0 {dhcp}
```

After you've set up the **rules** file, the **sysidcfg** file, and your profiles, copy them all to the **/jumpstart/config** directory and run Sun's **check** tool, which validates the configuration. The **check** script should be run from the **config** directory, and its use is mandatory; it creates a **rules.ok** file that certifies to JumpStart that the files are syntactically acceptable. *Do not skip this step or JumpStart will not work.*

```
solaris$ sudo cp /jumpstart/s10sparc/Solaris_10/Misc/jumpstart_sample/check
    /jumpstart/config
solaris $ sudo ./check
Validating rules...
Validating profile profile_A...
The custom JumpStart configuration is ok.
```

At the end of the configuration process, your **/jumpstart/config** directory should look something like this:

```
solaris$ ls -l
-rwxr-xr-x   1 root   root  52152   Aug 23 19:42 check
-rw-r--r--   1 root   root    413   Aug 23 19:29 profile_a
-rw-r--r--   1 root   root     48   Aug 23 19:13 rules
-rw-r--r--   1 root   root     62   Aug 23 19:43 rules.ok
-rw-r--r--   1 root   root    314   Aug 23 17:35 sysidcfg
```

You must add each client to be set up through JumpStart to the install server; this is a two-step process. First, add the MAC address of the client to the server's **/etc/ethers** file. Second, run the **add_install_client** tool to add the client to the configuration database, as shown here:

```
solaris$ cd /jumpstart/s10sparc/Solaris_10/Tools
solaris$ sudo ./add_install_client -c server:/jumpstart sake sun4v
```

In this case, the client called sake will use the JumpStart NFS share on the host server for installation. You start the actual network installation on the client from the OBP prompt:

```
ok boot net - install
```

This complicated process allows for highly customized and flexible installations at the expense of a few brain cells.

Network installations with the Automated Installer

The OpenSolaris developers assessed the complexity of JumpStart and decided to create a new deployment tool for OpenSolaris. This tool, the Automated Installer, mirrors the style of JumpStart in several ways but abstracts away some of the complexity through a convenient tool called **installadm**. In its simplest form, server installation can now be achieved with a single command. All the files you need to get started with AI are contained in the SUNWinstalladm-tools package.

An AI server offers one or more "installation services," each of which represents an OS installation option and is discovered by clients at boot time through multicast DNS. Different services might serve different installation needs; for example, one service for site-specific web servers and another for database servers.

Once a client locates an installer, it searches for a configuration, or manifest, that matches its system description. The client performs an installation with data from the manifest files. No client configuration is required, although custom client installations are available if you need them.

An AI server installation bundles all the necessary parts together in a convenient package, including DHCP and TFTP services. Be sure to check with your network administrator before adding these to the network.

Behind the scenes, AI creates three XML-formatted manifest files.

- The AI manifest file contains disk partitioning and packaging details, roughly equivalent to a JumpStart profile file.
- The SC manifest file contains system configuration details, such as time zone and account information, much like JumpStart's **sysidcfg** file.
- The criteria manifest file matches the other two manifest files to client devices, just like the **rules** file in JumpStart.

If you find XML intellectually stimulating, you can edit the manifests by hand to create custom configurations. Normally, you just run **installadm** to add, remove, enable, disable, and list new installation services and to create custom client configurations.

For example, the following **installadm** command creates a new installation service that you can use to install a client. In this example, the OpenSolaris 0906 release ISO image is used as an installation source. The **-c 10** option makes the DHCP server offer up to 10 dynamic addresses starting at 192.168.1.200. The installation image is copied to **/export/install**.

```
solaris$ sudo installadm create-service -s ~/osol-0906-x86.iso
    -i 192.168.1.200 -c 10 /export/install
Setting up the target image at /export/install ...
Warning: Using default manifest </usr/share/auto_install/default.xml>
Registering the service _install_service_46501._OSInstall._tcp.local
Creating DHCP Server
Created DHCP configuration file.
Created dhcptab.
Added "Locale" macro to dhcptab.
Added server macro to dhcptab - opensolaris.
DHCP server started.
dhtadm: Unable to signal the daemon to reload the dhcptab
Added network macro to dhcptab - 192.168.1.0.
Created network table.
adding tftp to /etc/inetd.conf
Converting /etc/inetd.conf
copying boot file to /tftpboot/pxegrub.I86PC.OpenSolaris-1
Service discovery fallback mechanism set up
```

To install the client, perform a network boot as usual. The server uses the predefined rules to pick an installation image, download it to the client, and start the installation.

Automated Installer is changing rapidly. After installing the package, refer to **/usr/share/doc/auto_install/index.html** for current details.

12.3 Installing HP-UX

As a server-oriented operating system aimed almost exclusively at large applications that require a lot of heavy lifting, HP-UX does not attempt to provide a flashy, next-generation installation process. Its text-based installation software is utilitarian and guides you through the basic configuration options: disk partitioning, network settings, software to install, etc.

For sites that need network-based and automated installations, HP's Ignite-UX option is available. Ignite-UX can install multiple HP-UX systems simultaneously over the network. PA-RISC clients boot by using BOOTP, and Itanium systems use DHCP. You can configure multiple software repositories. For example, installation packages might be provided from one location, patches from another, and application packages from a third. As an added bonus, Ignite-UX also includes a recovery service that restores a machine's configuration from a recent image.

The following steps are needed to set up Ignite-UX:

- Install the Ignite-UX software and HP-UX packages on the server.
- Configure Ignite-UX to offer the appropriate installation options.
- Enable Ignite-UX service dependencies, such as NFS and BOOTP.
- Add client MAC and IP addresses to the server.

After you've configured the server, you can add a boot option on the client systems (through HP's EFI Boot Manager) to make them install HP-UX from an Ignite-UX server. Alternatively, for systems already running HP-UX, you can use the **bootsys** command to push the installation from the server to the client.

On our example system, Ignite-UX came preinstalled, but if your system doesn't have it, try the command **swinstall -s /dvdrom Ignite-UX**. Here, **/dvdrom** is the mount point for a DVD that contains the operating system media, or "operating environment" in HP's terminology. The installation results in a number of installed packages, some of which are listed below.

```
hp-ux$ sudo swlist Ignite-UX
...
# Ignite-UX                     C.7.5.142   HP-UX System Installation Services
Ignite-UX.BOOT-COMMON-IA        C.7.5.142   Boot Components for IPF clients
Ignite-UX.BOOT-COMMON-PA        C.7.5.142   Boot Components for PA-RISC clients
Ignite-UX.BOOT-KRN-11-11        C.7.5.142   Boot Kernel for B.11.11 clients
Ignite-UX.BOOT-KRN-11-23        C.7.5.142   Boot Kernel for B.11.23 clients
Ignite-UX.BOOT-KRN-11-31        C.7.5.142   Boot Kernel for B.11.31 clients
Ignite-UX.BOOT-SERVICES         C.7.5.142   Boot Services for Installations
...
```

Ignite-UX scatters its configuration files and binaries haphazardly across the filesystem. Table 12.3 on the next page lists the most important components.

Table 12.3 Important binaries, directories, and configuration files used by Ignite-UX

Filename	Purpose
/etc/bootptab	Acts as a plain-text "database" for **bootpd**
/etc/opt/ignite/instl_boottab	Records IP addresses for booting PA-RISC clients
/opt/ignite/bin/bootsys	Updates clients that are already running HP-UX
/opt/ignite/bin/make_config	Creates config info file using an installation depot
/opt/ignite/bin/make_depots	Creates install depots from some source media
/opt/ignite/bin/manage_index	Adds a depot to the Ignite-UX index
/opt/ignite/lbin/setup_server	Shares **/var/opt/ignite/clients** over NFS
/var/opt/ignite/clients	Stores client configuration files (dir)
/var/opt/ignite/data	Traditionally used for installation depots (dir)
/var/opt/ignite/INDEX	Indexes all installation depots known to Ignite-UX

The **make_depots** command extracts installation packages and sets them up as an operating environment depot for installation to clients. After you create a depot, run **make_config** to read the depot's contents and create a configuration file that describes them. The configuration becomes known to Ignite-UX by way of the **manage_index** command, which adds configurations to an **INDEX** file. A sample series of commands for version 11i v3 is shown below.

```
hp-ux$ cd /opt/ignite/bin
hp-ux$ sudo ./make_depots -s /dev/dsk/c2t2d0
    -d /var/opt/ignite/depots/Rel_B.11.31/oe_media
hp-ux$ sudo ./make_config -s /var/opt/ignite/depots/Rel_B.11.31/core_media
  -c /var/opt/ignite/data/Rel_B.11.31/oe_media_cfg
hp-ux$ sudo ./manage_index -n "HP-UX B.11.31 Default" -c "11i v3"
hp-ux$ sudo ./manage_index -a
    -f /var/opt/ignite/data/Rel_B.11.31/oe_media_cfg -c "11i v3"
```

Before the server can be used by clients, you must enable BOOTP and share the **clients** directory. Individual clients must also be added to the **instl_boottab** or **bootptab** file, depending upon whether they are PA-RISC or Itanium machines.

To share the config directory via NFS, just run **/opt/ignite/lbin/setup_server**. Behind the scenes, this command just creates an NFS share in **/etc/dfs/sharetab**.

You can turn on BOOTP by uncommenting the bootps line in **/etc/inetd.conf**. Then ask **inetd** to reread its configuration by running **/usr/sbin/inetd -c**.

Before Ignite-UX will offer installation services to a client, it must normally recognize the client by MAC address. However, to lighten your administrative burden, we recommend that you use HP's concept of "anonymous clients," which are not associated with particular MAC addresses.

PA-RISC and Itanium systems rely on different boot mechanisms, and the two services are configured slightly differently. To configure Ignite-UX boot services for PA-RISC systems, edit the file **/etc/opt/ignite/instl_boottab**. Lines in this file are of the form:

```
IP_address:MAC_address:datetime_last_used [ :reserve ]
```

The *IP_address* field assigns an IP address for the new client to use while accessing installation services. The optional *MAC_address* field identifies a specific client machine; if you leave it out, any client can use this IP address (but note the interaction with the reserve keyword). The third field is used and maintained by Ignite-UX; leave it blank when adding new entries.

If the keyword reserve is present in the last column, the IP address is reserved for the use of the client whose MAC address appears in field two. If reserve is not specified, field two simply shows the last MAC address that used that IP address.

The **/etc/bootptab** and **/etc/dhcptab** files, used to boot Itanium systems, have a very different format. The files are well commented and littered liberally with examples, which we won't repeat here. (Note that a single daemon, **bootpd**, serves both BOOTP and DHCP requests on HP-UX systems.) DHCP is the preferred boot method for Itanium systems since it can provide anonymous client services. See the comments in **/etc/bootptab** and **/etc/dhcpv6tab** for full details.

Once you've configured an Ignite-UX server as discussed above, clients can boot from it over the network. On the client side, interrupt the normal boot process, enter the EFI Boot Manager, and add a network device. The client will request an IP address, and the Ignite-UX server will respond and begin the installation.

This method works best for systems that share a subnet with the Ignite-UX server. For configurations in which the client is not on the server's subnet, HP lists a number of options in the *Ignite-UX Administration Guide.*

Automating Ignite-UX installations

Ignite-UX network boot configuration is a prerequisite for automated installation, but configuring Ignite-UX without specifying automatic boot details results in an interactive installation. Ignite-UX can also

- Use the saved configuration from a previous installation to automate future installations.
- Rely on configuration files that can be set up per client, per release, or at the whim of the administrator.
- Specify default values for some configuration options, such as DNS servers, and leave others to be selected during interactive installation.

The automated installation files are located in **/opt/ignite/data**, and several examples and sample configurations are included in the Ignite-UX installation package. The **release** and **example** subdirectories are a good place to get started.

12.4 Installing AIX with the Network Installation Manager

Network Installation Manager, or NIM, is AIX's answer to Kickstart, JumpStart, and Ignite-UX. Versions of NIM since AIX 5.3 can also install Linux systems. A NIM "master" server installs clients from one or more installation images, where a client can be a stand-alone machine, a diskless or dataless workstation, or a workload partition.[2] Installations rely on TFTP, NFS, and DHCP or BOOTP, much as on other systems.[3] NIM is included on the standard AIX installation media.

All NIM environments have at least one "resource server" that offers some set of software to be used by clients. The resource server may or may not be the same system as the master. Environments that have complex network topologies or geographically separated locations should use localized resource servers to improve installation performance.

There are three ways to configure NIM:

- By using the web-based system manager
- By using the **smit nim** or **smit eznim** fast paths
- From the command line with the **nim** tool

We find SMIT to be the fastest and most convenient interface for configuring a NIM environment. The "EZ" version covers most of the common NIM tasks such as quick setup of a master server, updating, backing up, or reinstalling existing clients, and configuring new clients. The full-featured **smit nim** version adds some complexity over EZ NIM but adds more configuration options, such as the ability to include custom software packages and more granular control over the installed clients.

If you insist on command-line operation, the **nim_master_setup** tool is the best place to get started. (SMIT's EZ-NIM options for configuring a master server really just call **nim_master_setup** with the specified options.) This tool initializes filesystems for the NIM software resources, creates the necessary configuration files, and copies in a sample client configuration file that you can edit for your local clients.

The most basic usage is **nim_master_setup -a device=/dev/cd0**, where **/dev/cd0** is the drive that contains the installation media for the target AIX release. Unlike most of the other installation systems described in this chapter, a NIM master server can install releases of AIX only at the same revision level or earlier; an AIX 5.2 server cannot install AIX 6.1 releases.

Table 12.4 lists some of the most useful NIM-related command-line tools.

2. A diskless client has no hard disk for local filesystems and relies on network services for storage. A dataless client has only has local swap space and perhaps **/tmp** and **/home** filesystems.

3. Since vendors all use approximately the same protocols and architectures, aren't you glad that they cooperated and settled on a standard installation system? :-)

Table 12.4 NIM command-line tools

Tool	What it does
nim_master_setup	Installs and configures a NIM master server
nim_update_all	Updates installation resources and clients
nim_clients_setup	Defines new clients and initiates OS installation
nim_master_recover	Restores the master NIM database to a new server
nim	Multiple: configures resources, defines clients, etc.
nimclient	Pulls resources (e.g., updates) from a server (run on clients)

12.5 Managing packages

UNIX and Linux variants all use some form of packaging system to facilitate the job of software management. Packages have traditionally been used to distribute software, but they can be used to wrap configuration files and administrative data as well. They have several advantages over the traditional unstructured **.tar.gz** archives. Perhaps most importantly, they try to make the installation process as atomic as possible. If an error occurs, the package can be backed out or reapplied.

Package installers are typically aware of configuration files and will not normally overwrite local customizations performed by a system administrator. They will either back up the existing config files that they change or provide example config files under a different name (e.g., **pkg.conf.rpmnew**). If you find that a newly installed package breaks something on your system, you can, at least in theory, back it out to restore your system to its original state. Of course, theory != practice, so don't try this out on a production system without testing it first.

Packaging systems define a dependency model that allows package maintainers to ensure that the libraries and support infrastructure on which their applications depend are properly installed. Some packaging systems do a more complete job of dependency management than others.

Packages can also run scripts at various points during the installation, so they can do much more than just disgorge new files.

Packages are also a nice way to distribute your own localizations. You can create a package that, when installed, reads localization information about a machine (or gets it from central database) and uses that information to set up local configuration files. You can also bundle up your local applications as packages, complete with dependencies, or make packages for third-party applications that aren't normally distributed in package format. You can versionize your packages and use the dependency mechanism to upgrade machines automatically when a new version of your localization package is installed.

You can also use the dependency mechanism to create groups of packages. For example, it's possible to create a package that installs nothing of its own but depends on many other patches. Installing the package with dependencies turned on results in all the patches being installed in a single step.

12.6 Managing Linux packages

Two package formats are in common use on Linux systems. Red Hat, SUSE, and several other distributions use RPM, the Red Hat Package Manager. Ubuntu uses the separate but equally popular **.deb** format (named after the Debian distribution on which Ubuntu was originally based). The two formats are functionally similar.

It's easy to convert between the two package formats with a tool such as **alien** from kitenet.net/programs/alien. **alien** knows nothing about the software inside a package, so if the contents are not already compatible with your distribution, **alien** will not help. In general, it's best to stick with the native package mechanism used by your distribution.

Both the RPM and **.deb** packaging systems now function as dual-layer soup-to-nuts configuration management tools. At the lowest level are the tools that install, uninstall, and query packages: **rpm** for RPM and **dpkg** for **.deb**.

On top of these commands are systems that know how to find packages on the Internet, analyze interpackage dependencies, and upgrade all the packages on a system. **yum**, the Yellowdog Updater, Modified, works with the RPM system. The Red Hat Network is specific to Red Hat Enterprise Linux and uses RPM. The Advanced Package Tool (APT) originated in the **.deb** universe but works well with both **.deb** and RPM packages.

On the next couple of pages, we review the low-level commands **rpm** and **dpkg**. In the section *Using high-level Linux package management systems* starting on page 384, we discuss the comprehensive update systems (e.g., APT and **yum**) that build on these low-level facilities.

rpm: manage RPM packages

The **rpm** command installs, verifies, and queries the status of packages. It formerly built them as well, but this function has now been broken out into a separate command called **rpmbuild**. **rpm** options have complex interactions and can be used together only in certain combinations. It's most useful to think of **rpm** as if it were several different commands that happen to share the same name.

The mode you tell **rpm** to enter (such as **-i** or **-q**) specifies which of **rpm**'s multiple personalities you are hoping to access. **rpm --help** lists all the options broken down by mode, but it's worth your time to read the man page in some detail if you will frequently be dealing with RPM packages.

The bread-and-butter options are **-i** (install), **-U** (upgrade), **-e** (erase), and **-q** (query). The **-q** option is a bit tricky in that it serves only to enable other options; you must supply an additional command-line flag to pose a specific question. For example, the command **rpm -qa** lists all the packages installed on the system.

Let's look at an example. Suppose you need to install a new version of OpenSSH because of a recent security fix. Once you've downloaded the package, you could run **rpm -U** to replace the older version with the newer.

```
redhat$ sudo rpm -U openssh-2.9p2-12.i386.rpm
error: failed dependencies:
openssh = 2.9p2-7 is needed by openssh-askpass-2.9p2-7
openssh = 2.9p2-7 is needed by openssh-askpass-gnome-2.9p2-7
openssh = 2.9p2-7 is needed by openssh-clients-2.9p2-7
openssh = 2.9p2-7 is needed by openssh-server-2.9p2-7
```

D'oh! Perhaps it's not so simple after all. Here we see that the currently installed version of OpenSSH, 2.9p2-7, is required by a number of other packages. **rpm** won't let us upgrade OpenSSH because the change might affect the operation of these other packages. This type of conflict happens all the time, and it's a major motivation for the development of systems like APT and **yum**. In real life we wouldn't attempt to untangle the dependencies by hand, but let's continue with **rpm** alone for the purpose of this example.

We could force the upgrade with the **--force** option, but that's usually a bad idea. The dependency information is there to save you time and trouble, not just to get in your way. There's nothing like a broken SSH on a remote system to ruin a sysadmin's morning.

Instead, we'll grab updated versions of the dependent packages as well. If we were smart, we could have determined that other packages depended on OpenSSH before we even attempted the upgrade:

```
redhat$ rpm -q --whatrequires openssh
openssh-askpass-2.9p2-7
openssh-askpass-gnome-2.9p2-7
openssh-clients-2.9p2-7
openssh-server-2.9p2-7
```

Suppose that we've obtained updated copies of all the packages. We could install them one at a time, but **rpm** is smart enough to handle them all at once. If you list multiple RPMs on the command line, **rpm** sorts them by dependency before installation.

```
redhat$ sudo rpm -U openssh-*
```

Cool! Looks like it succeeded, and sure enough:

```
redhat$ rpm -q openssh
openssh-2.9p2-12
```

Note that **rpm** understands which package we are talking about even though we didn't specify the package's full name or version.

Software

dpkg: manage .deb packages in Ubuntu

Just as RPM packages have the all-in-one **rpm** command, Debian packages have the **dpkg** command. Useful options include **--install**, **--remove**, and **-l** to list the packages that have been installed on the system. A **dpkg --install** of a package that's already on the system removes the previous version before installing.

Running **dpkg -l | grep** *package* is a convenient way to determine if a particular package is installed. For example, to search for an HTTP server, try:

```
ubuntu$ dpkg -l | grep -i http
ii  lighttpd 1.4.13-9ubuntu4 A fast webserver with minimal memory footpri
```

This search found the **lighttpd** software, an excellent open source, lightweight web server. The leading ii indicates that the software is installed.

Suppose that the Ubuntu security team recently released a fix to **nvi** to patch a potential security problem. After grabbing the patch, we run **dpkg** to install it. As you can see, it's much chattier than **rpm** and tells us exactly what it's doing:

```
ubuntu$ sudo dpkg --install ./nvi_1.79-16a.1_i386.deb
(Reading database ... 24368 files and directories currently installed.)
Preparing to replace nvi 1.79-14 (using ./nvi_1.79-16a.1_i386.deb) ...
Unpacking replacement nvi ...
Setting up nvi (1.79-16a.1) ...
Checking available versions of ex, updating links in /etc/alternatives ...
(You may modify the symlinks there yourself if desired - see 'man ln'.)
Leaving ex (/usr/bin/ex) pointing to /usr/bin/nex.
Leaving ex.1.gz (/usr/share/man/man1/ex.1.gz) pointing to
    /usr/share/man/man1/nex.1.gz.
...
```

We can now use **dpkg -l** to verify that the installation worked. The **-l** flag accepts an optional prefix pattern to match, so we can just search for **nvi**:

```
ubuntu$ dpkg -l nvi
Desired=Unknown/Install/Remove/Purge
| Status=Not/Installed/Config-files/Unpacked/Failed-config/Half-installed
|/ Err?=(none)/Hold/Reinst-required/X=both-problems (Status,Err: uppercase=bad)
||/ Name          Version          Description
+++-===========-==============-==================================
ii  nvi           1.79-16a.1       4.4BSD re-implementation of vi.
```

Our installation seems to have gone smoothly.

12.7 Using high-level Linux package management systems

Metapackage management systems such as APT, **yum**, and the Red Hat Network share several goals:

- To simplify the task of locating and downloading packages
- To automate the process of updating or upgrading systems
- To facilitate the management of interpackage dependencies

Clearly, there is more to these systems than just client-side commands. They all require that distribution maintainers organize their offerings in an agreed-upon way so that the software can be accessed and reasoned about by clients.

Since no single supplier can encompass the entire "world of Linux software," the systems all allow for the existence of multiple software repositories. Repositories can be local to your network, so these systems make a dandy foundation for creating your own internal distribution system.

The Red Hat Network is closely tied to Red Hat Enterprise Linux. It's a commercial service that costs money and offers more in terms of attractive GUIs and automation ability than do APT and **yum**. The Red Hat Network is a shiny, public version of Red Hat's expensive and proprietary Satellite Server. The client side can reference **yum** and APT repositories, and this ability has allowed distributions such as CentOS to adapt the client GUI for nonproprietary use.

APT is better documented than the Red Hat Network, is significantly more portable, and is free. It's also more flexible in terms of what you can do with it. APT originated in the world of Debian and **dpkg**, but it has been extended to encompass RPMs, and versions that work with all of our example distributions are available. It's the closest thing we have at this point to a universal standard for software distribution.

yum is an RPM-specific analog of APT. It's the default package manager for Red Hat Enterprise Linux version 5, although it runs on any RPM-based system, provided that you can point it toward appropriately formatted repositories.

We like APT and consider it a solid choice if you want to set up your own automated package distribution network. See the section *APT: the Advanced Package Tool* on page 387 for more information. However, in most cases it's safest to stick with the package management tool that ships with your distribution of choice.

SUSE implements its own RPM-based package management tool known as ZYpp, with a command-line interface called Zypper. In addition to the usual features such as repository configuration, package installation, and status queries, Zypper shines in its implementation of dependency resolution. Zypper 1.0 was released with openSUSE 11.1. We discuss Zypper beginning on page 392.

Package repositories

Linux distributors maintain software repositories that work hand-in-hand with their chosen package management systems. The default configuration for the package management system usually points to one or more well-known web or FTP servers that are under the distributor's control.

However, it isn't immediately obvious what such repositories should contain. Should they include only the sets of packages blessed as formal, major releases? Formal releases plus current security updates? Up-to-date versions of all the packages that existed in the formal releases? Useful third-party software not officially supported by the distributor? Source code? Binaries for multiple hardware architectures? When you run **apt-get upgrade**, **yum upgrade,** or **zypper dup** to bring the system up to date, what exactly should that mean?

In general, package management systems must answer all these questions and must make it easy for sites to select the cross-sections they want to include in their software "world." The following concepts help structure this process.

- A "release" is a self-consistent snapshot of the package universe. Before the Internet era, named OS releases were more or less immutable and were associated with one specific point in time; security patches were made available separately. These days, a release is a more nebulous concept. Releases evolve over time as packages are updated. Some releases, such as Red Hat Enterprise Linux, are specifically designed to evolve slowly; by default, only security updates are incorporated. Other releases, such as beta versions, change frequently and dramatically. But in all cases, the release is the baseline, the target, the "thing I want to update my system to look like."
- A "component" is a subset of the software within a release. Distributions partition themselves differently, but one common distinction is that between core software blessed by the distributor and extra software made available by the broader community. Another distinction that's common in the Linux world is the one between the free, open source portions of a release and the parts that are tainted by some kind of restrictive licensing agreement.

  Of particular note from an administrative standpoint are minimally active components that include only security fixes. Some releases allow you to combine a security component with an immutable baseline component to create a relatively stable version of the distribution, even though the mainline distribution may evolve much faster.
- An "architecture" represents a specific class of hardware. The expectation is that machines within an architecture class will be similar enough that they can all run the same binaries. Architectures are specific instances of releases, for example, "Ubuntu Karmic Koala for x86_64." Since components are subdivisions of releases, there's a corresponding architecture-specific instance for each of them as well.
- Individual packages are the elements that make up components, and therefore, indirectly, releases. Packages are usually architecture specific and are versioned independently of the main release and of other packages. The correspondence between packages and releases is implicit in the way the network repository is set up.

The existence of components that aren't maintained by the distributor (e.g., Ubuntu's "universe" and "multiverse") raises the question of how these components relate to the core OS release. Can they really be said to be "a component" of the specific release, or are they some other kind of animal entirely? From a package management perspective, the answer is clear: extras are a true component. They are associated with a specific release, and they evolve in tandem with it. The separation of control is interesting from an administrative standpoint, but it doesn't affect the package distribution systems, except that they may need to be manually added by the administrator.

RHN: the Red Hat Network

With Red Hat having gracefully departed from the consumer Linux business, the Red Hat Network has become the system management platform for Red Hat Enterprise Linux. You purchase the right to access the Red Hat Network by subscribing. At its simplest, you can use the Red Hat Network as a glorified web portal and mailing list. Used in this way, the Red Hat Network is not much different from the patch notification mailing lists that have been run by various UNIX vendors for years. But more features are available if you're willing to pay for them. For current pricing and features, see rhn.redhat.com.

The Red Hat Network provides a web-based interface for downloading new packages as well as a command-line alternative. Starting with Red Hat Enterprise 5, the CLI tool is **yum**; before that it was the unwieldy, dependency-headache-inducing tool called **up2date**. **yum** even lets you download and install new packages without human intervention. Once you register, your machines get all the patches and bug fixes that they need without you ever having to intervene.

The downside of automatic registration is that Red Hat decides what updates you need. You might consider how much you really trust Red Hat (and the software maintainers whose products they package) not to screw things up. Given some of the interesting choices Red Hat has made in the past when it comes to little things like which compiler to ship, some folks might remain skeptical.

A reasonable compromise might be to sign up one machine in your organization for automatic updates. You can take snapshots from that machine at periodic intervals to test as possible candidates for internal releases.

APT: the Advanced Package Tool

APT is one of the most mature package management systems. It's possible to upgrade an entire system full of software with a single **apt-get** command or even (as with the Red Hat Network) to have your boxes continuously keep themselves up to date without human intervention.

The first rule of using **apt-get** on Ubuntu systems (and indeed all management of Debian packages) is to ignore the existence of **dselect**, which acts as a front end for the Debian package system. It's not a bad idea, but the user interface is poor and can be intimidating to the novice user. Some documentation will try to steer you toward **dselect**, but stay strong and stick with APT.

If you are using **apt-get** to manage a stock Ubuntu installation from a standard mirror, the easiest way to see the available packages is to visit the master list at packages.ubuntu.com. The web site includes a nice search interface. If you set up your own **apt-get** server (see page 390), then of course you will know what packages you have made available and you can list them in whatever way you want.

Distributions commonly include dummy packages that exist only to claim other packages as prerequisites. **apt-get** downloads and upgrades prerequisite packages as needed, so the dummy packages make it easy to install or upgrade several packages as a block. For example, installing the **gnome-desktop-environment** package obtains and installs all the packages necessary to run the GNOME UI.

Once you have set up your **/etc/apt/sources.list** file (described in detail below) and know the name of a package that you want, the only remaining task is to run **apt-get update** to refresh **apt-get**'s cache of package information. After that, just run **apt-get install** *package-name* as a privileged user to install the package. The same command updates a package that has already been installed.

Suppose we want to install a new version of the **sudo** package that fixes a security bug. First, it's always wise to do an **apt-get update**:

```
ubuntu$ sudo apt-get update
Get:1 http://http.us.debian.org stable/main Packages [824kB]
Get:2 http://non-us.debian.org stable/non-US/main Release [102B]
...
```

Now we can actually fetch the package. Note that we are using **sudo** as we fetch the new **sudo** package—**apt-get** can even upgrade packages that are in use!

```
ubuntu$ sudo apt-get install sudo
Reading Package Lists... Done
Building Dependency Tree... Done
1 packages upgraded, 0 newly installed, 0 to remove and 191 not upgraded.
Need to get 0B/122kB of archives. After unpacking 131kB will be used.
(Reading database ... 24359 files and directories currently installed.)
Preparing to replace sudo 1.6.1-1 (using .../sudo_1.6.9p10-1ubuntu3.4_i386.deb)
   ...
Unpacking replacement sudo ...
Setting up sudo (1.6.2p2-2) ...
Installing new version of config file /etc/pam.d/sudo ...
```

apt-get configuration

Configuring **apt-get** is straightforward; pretty much everything you need to know can be found in Ubuntu's community documentation on package management:

help.ubuntu.com/community/AptGet/Howto

The most important **apt-get** configuration file is **/etc/apt/sources.list**, which tells **apt-get** where to get its packages. Each line specifies the following:

- A type of package, currently deb or deb-src for Debian-style packages or rpm or rpm-src for RPMs
- A URL that points to a file, CD-ROM, HTTP server, or FTP server from which to fetch packages

- A "distribution" (really, a release name) that lets you deliver multiple versions of packages. Distributors use this for major releases, but you can use it however you want for internal distribution systems.
- A potential list of components (categories of packages within a release)

Unless you want to set up your own APT repository or cache, the default configuration generally works fine. Source packages are downloaded from the entries beginning with deb-src.

On Ubuntu systems, you'll almost certainly want to include the "universe" component, which gives access to the larger world of Linux open source software. The "multiverse" packages include non-open-source content, such as some VMware tools and components.

As long as you're editing the **sources.list file**, you should retarget the individual entries to point to your closest mirror. A full list of Ubuntu mirrors can be found at launchpad.net/ubuntu/+archivemirrors. This is a dynamic (and long) list of mirrors that changes regularly, so be sure to keep an eye on it between releases.

Make sure that security.ubuntu.com is listed as a source so that you have access to the latest security patches.

An example /etc/apt/sources.list file

The following example uses us.archive.ubuntu.com as a package source for the "main" components of Ubuntu (those that are fully supported by the Ubuntu team). In addition, this **sources.list** includes unsupported but open source "universe" packages, and non-free, unsupported packages in the "multiverse" component. There is also a repository for updates, or bug-fixed packages, in each component. Finally, the last six lines are for security updates.

```
# General format: type uri distribution [components]
deb http://us.archive.ubuntu.com/ubuntu/ karmic main restricted
deb-src http://us.archive.ubuntu.com/ubuntu/ karmic main restricted
deb http://us.archive.ubuntu.com/ubuntu/ karmic-updates main restricted
deb-src http://us.archive.ubuntu.com/ubuntu/ karmic-updates main restricted
deb http://us.archive.ubuntu.com/ubuntu/ karmic universe
deb-src http://us.archive.ubuntu.com/ubuntu/ karmic universe
deb http://us.archive.ubuntu.com/ubuntu/ karmic-updates universe
deb-src http://us.archive.ubuntu.com/ubuntu/ karmic-updates universe
deb http://us.archive.ubuntu.com/ubuntu/ karmic multiverse
deb-src http://us.archive.ubuntu.com/ubuntu/ karmic multiverse
deb http://us.archive.ubuntu.com/ubuntu/ karmic-updates multiverse
deb-src http://us.archive.ubuntu.com/ubuntu/ karmic-updates multiverse
deb http://security.ubuntu.com/ubuntu karmic-security main restricted
deb-src http://security.ubuntu.com/ubuntu karmic-security main restricted
deb http://security.ubuntu.com/ubuntu karmic-security universe
deb-src http://security.ubuntu.com/ubuntu karmic-security universe
deb http://security.ubuntu.com/ubuntu karmic-security multiverse
deb-src http://security.ubuntu.com/ubuntu karmic-security multiverse
```

The *distribution* and *components* fields help **apt-get** navigate the fileystem hierarchy of the Ubuntu repository, which has a standardized layout. The root distribution is the working title given to each release, such as intrepid, jaunty, or karmic. The available components are typically called main, universe, multiverse, and restricted. Only add the universe and multiverse repositories if you are comfortable having unsupported (and license restricted, in the case of multiverse) software in your environment.

Creation of a local repository mirror

If you plan to use **apt-get** on a large number of machines, you will probably want to cache packages locally—downloading a copy of each package for every machine is not a sensible use of external bandwidth. A mirror of the repository is easy to configure and convenient for local administration. Just make sure to keep it updated with the latest security patches.

The best tool for the job is the handy **apt-mirror** package, which is available from apt-mirror.sourceforge.net. You can also install the package from the universe component with **sudo apt-get install apt-mirror**.

Once installed, **apt-mirror** drops a file called **mirror.list** in **/etc/apt**. It's a shadow version of **sources.list**, but it's used only as a source for mirroring operations. By default, **mirror.list** conveniently contains all the repositories for the running version of Ubuntu.

To actually mirror the repositories in **mirror.list**, just run **apt-mirror** as root:

```
ubuntu$ sudo apt-mirror
Downloading 57 index files using 20 threads...
Begin time: Sat Aug 29 18:53:44 2009
[20]... [19]... [18]... [17]... [16]... [15]... [14]...
```

By default, **apt-mirror** puts its repository copies in **/var/spool/apt-mirror**. Feel free to change this by uncommenting the set base_path directive in **mirror.list**, but be aware that you must then create **mirror**, **skel**, and **var** subdirectories under the new mirror root.

apt-mirror takes a long time to run on its first pass because it is mirroring many gigabytes of data (currently ~40 GB per Ubuntu release). Subsequent executions are faster and should be run automatically out of **cron**. You can run the **clean.sh** script from the **var** subdirectory of your mirror to clean out obsolete files.

To start using your mirror, share the base directory via HTTP using a web server of your choice. We like to use symbolic links to the web root. For instance:

```
ln -s /var/spool/apt-mirror/us.archive.ubuntu.com/ubuntu /var/www/ubuntu
```

To make clients use your local mirror, edit their **sources.list** files just as if you were selecting a nonlocal mirror.

apt-get automation

You can run **apt-get** on a regular schedule from **cron**. Even if you don't install packages automatically, you may want to run **apt-get update** regularly to keep your package summaries up to date.

apt-get dist-upgrade downloads and installs new versions of any packages that are currently installed on the local machine. **dist-upgrade** is similar to **upgrade** but has slightly more intelligent dependency handling. **dist-upgrade** may want to delete some packages that it views as irreconcilably incompatible with the upgraded system, so be prepared for potential surprises.

If you really want to play with fire, have machines perform the upgrade in an unattended fashion by using the **-yes** option. It answers any confirmation questions that **apt-get** might ask with an enthusiastic "Yes!" Be aware that some updates, such as kernel packages, may not take effect until after a system reboot.

It's probably not a good idea to perform automated upgrades directly from a distribution's mirror. However, in concert with your own APT servers, packages, and release control system, this is a perfect way to keep clients in sync. A quickie shell script like the following keeps a box up to date with its APT server:

```
#!/bin/sh
apt-get update
apt-get -yes dist-upgrade
```

Call this script from a **cron** job if you want to run it nightly. You can also refer to it from a system startup script to make the machine update at boot time. See Chapter 9, *Periodic Processes*, for more information about **cron**; see Chapter 3, *Booting and Shutting Down*, for more information about startup scripts.

If you run updates out of **cron** on many machines, it's a good idea to use time randomization to make sure that everyone doesn't try to update at once. The short Perl script on page 727 can help with this task.

If you don't quite trust your source of packages, consider automatically downloading all changed packages without installing them. Use **apt-get**'s **--download-only** option to request this behavior, then review the packages by hand and install the ones you want to update. Downloaded packages are put in **/var/cache/apt**, and over time this directory can grow to be quite large. Clean out the unused files from this directory with **apt-get autoclean**.

yum: release management for RPM

yum, the Yellowdog Updater, Modified, is a metapackage manager based on RPM.[4] It may be a bit unfair to call **yum** an **apt-get** clone, but it's thematically and implementationally similar, although cleaner and slower in practice. **yum** is the official package management system for Red Hat Enterprise Linux and comes

4. Not to be confused with Yum Fish Bait with Live Prey Technology (LPT), yum3x.com.

preinstalled on many other distributions. If necessary, you can obtain the latest version from the distribution's repository of packages.

As with **apt-get**, a server-side command (**yum-arch**) compiles a database of header information from a large set of packages (often an entire release). The header database is then shared along with the packages through HTTP or FTP. Clients use the **yum** command to fetch and install packages; **yum** figures out dependency constraints and does whatever additional work is needed to complete the installation of the requested packages. If a requested package depends on other packages, **yum** downloads and installs those packages as well.

The similarities between **apt-get** and **yum** extend to the command-line options they understand. For example, **yum install foo** downloads and installs the most recent version of the foo package (and its dependencies, if necessary). There is at least one treacherous difference, though: **apt-get update** refreshes **apt-get**'s package information cache, but **yum update** updates every package on the system (it's analogous to **apt-get upgrade**). To add to the confusion, **yum upgrade** is the same as **yum update** but with obsolescence processing enabled.

yum does not match on partial package names unless you include shell globbing characters (such as * and ?) to explicitly request this behavior. For example, **yum update 'perl*'** refreshes all packages whose name starts with "perl". Remember to quote the globbing characters so the shell doesn't interfere with them.

Unlike **apt-get**, **yum** defaults to validating its package information cache against the contents of the network repository every time you run it. Use the **-C** option to prevent the validation and **yum makecache** to update the local cache (it takes a while to run). Unfortunately, the **-C** option doesn't do much to improve **yum**'s sluggish performance.

yum's configuration file is **/etc/yum.conf**. It includes general options and pointers to package repositories. Multiple repositories can be active at once, and each repository can be associated with multiple URLs.

Zypper package management for SUSE: now with more ZYpp!

After years of fairly lax package management, SUSE systems now offer a best-of-breed option in the form of Zypper, a full-featured, next-generation package manager based on RPM. Of all the tools covered here, Zypper offers the most flexible and powerful options for installing, removing, and querying packages. It is also the only tool that includes repository management from the command line.

Getting to know the tool is easy for anyone that understands **apt-get** or **yum**. Table 12.5 shows the basic **zypper** commands, which should be eerily familiar.

In the example below, we've used **zypper sh** to open a Zypper shell where commands can be typed directly.

Table 12.5 Zypper commands

Command	What it does
zypper addrepo *uri*	Adds a repository to the working set
zypper dist-upgrade	Updates to the current distribution release
zypper info *packages*	Displays information about *packages*
zypper install *packages*	Downloads and installs *packages*
zypper list-updates	Lists all updated packages in the repository
zypper modifyrepo *uri*	Modifies the properties of a repository
zypper refresh	Updates the local cache's repository metadata
zypper remove *packages*	Uninstalls *packages*
zypper repos	Lists repositories in the current working set
zypper search *string*	Searches for packages with matching names
zypper shell (or **sh**)	Starts an interactive **zypper** session
zypper update	Installs updated versions of all current packages

```
suse$ zypper sh
zypper> repos
# | Alias            | Name                     | Enabled  | Refresh
--+------------------+--------------------------+----------+----------
1 | openSUSE 11.1-0  | openSUSE 11.1-0          | Yes      | No
2 | repo-debug       | openSUSE-11.1-Debug      | No       | Yes
3 | repo-non-oss     | openSUSE-11.1-Non-Oss    | Yes      | Yes
4 | repo-oss         | openSUSE-11.1-Oss        | Yes      | Yes
5 | repo-source      | openSUSE-11.1-Source     | No       | Yes
6 | repo-update      | openSUSE-11.1-Update     | Yes      | Yes
```

Rather than having to run **zypper refresh** by hand to ensure that package data is up to date, you can enable automatic refreshing with **zypper -f**.

Zypper configuration files, including software repository configuration, are found in **/etc/zypp**. Most administrators won't need to touch these files, but they're verbosely commented if the need arises.

12.8 Managing packages for UNIX

Software installation and packaging is one area in which Linux has a clear advantage over traditional UNIX operating systems. Installing, upgrading, and searching for software on a Linux system is an almost trivial task for the end user or administrator. The search features are powerful, the user communities are large, and the active developers number in the thousands.

By contrast, UNIX systems leave administrators with far fewer packages to choose from and looser control over those that do exist. In this section, we examine the packaging software that's prevalent on each of our example UNIX systems.

Solaris packaging

Since SunOS 2.0, Solaris packaging was traditionally managed by SVR4 with some incremental improvements that kept the system hobbling along for twenty years or so. Unfortunately, SVR4 is deficient in many areas, including dependency management, usability, support for new technologies such as ZFS, and support for network repositories. For OpenSolaris, the developers decided to scrap the old system and start fresh.

OpenSolaris now uses the Image Packaging System (IPS), which is a great leap forward over SVR4. It incorporates network repositories as a key architectural theme. In addition to standard package management functionality, the system offers tools for package developers that simplify the creation and centralization of packages. IPS also offers backward compatibility with legacy SVR4 packages.

At the moment, IPS packages are markedly dissimilar to those in formats such as **.deb** or RPM. An IPS package is not a single file that you can easily copy among systems. Rather, a package is a collection of files, dependencies, and other data that must be served from a repository by IPS's **pkg.depotd** daemon. IPS remains under development, and a more palatable format is promised someday.

You use the **pkg** command for most IPS operations—installation, removal, searching, status queries, etc. **pkg** also manages repositories, though they're referred to as "publishers" in the **pkg** documentation and command syntax.[5] **pkg install**, **pkg uninstall**, **pkg search**, and **pkg info** all perform the expected functions. The **pkg image-update** command is similar to APT's **dist-upgrade**; it updates all installed packages to the latest available versions.

By default, the OpenSolaris release repository is the default publisher. It currently hosts around 1,700 packages.[6]

```
solaris$ pkg publisher
PUBLISHER                  TYPE    STATUS  URI
opensolaris.org (preferred) origin  online  http://pkg.opensolaris.org/rele...
```

See **man -s5 pkg** for further details on IPS, or **man pkg** for information on the **pkg** command.

HP-UX packaging

HP's packaging system, formally known as Software Distributor or SD, has offered HP-UX users robust package management since version 10. It's a no-nonsense tool with a bundle of features that's sure to make any system administrator giddy with excitement:

- Most tools offer graphical, **curses**-based, and command-line operating modes, depending on how they are invoked.

5. The development team distinguishes between the terms "repository" and "publisher," but we'll treat them as equivalent here.
6. Contrast with more than 30,000 in Ubuntu Karmic Koala.

- Software can be managed on remote systems by way of **swagentd**, a daemon that starts at boot time and speaks over either UDP and TCP.[7]
- Software depots can be located on local media or in network directories.
- A job browser lets administrators monitor remote systems' installation status in real time.

A series of executables whose names begin with **sw** (well, mostly) make up the SD toolkit. Table 12.6 lists the individual tools and their functions.

Table 12.6 Software Distributor command list

Command	GUI?	What it does
install-sd	–	Reinstalls the Software Distributor system
sd	Y[a]	Manages remote jobs: creation, scheduling, monitoring
swacl	–	Configures SD security options
swask	–	Runs interactive installation scripts
swconfig	–	Configures (or reconfigures) installed software
swcopy	Y	Copies packages to a repository for future installation
swinstall	Y	Installs software packages from a repository
swjob	–	Command-line alternative to the **sd** command
swlist	Y	Lists installed software or software located in a depot
swmodify	–	Modifies the catalog of software installed on the system[b]
swpackage	–	Creates new software packages
swreg	–	Registers a software depot
swremove	Y	Removes packages from the system or from a depot
swverify	–	Confirms the integrity of installed software
swagentd	–	Acts as the SD command agent (starts at boot time)

a. This tool is GUI-only; it has no command line. **swjob** is the command-line equivalent.
b. Also known as the installed products database or IPD

Software

Most of the SD commands support a peculiar **-x** flag that modifies default options specific to that tool. For example, among the options for the **swinstall** command are **allow_incompatible**, which permits installation of a package meant for a different architecture, and **autoreboot**, which reboots the system after installation if necessary. The full list of options for each tool is given in its man page or in the file **/usr/lib/sw/sys.defaults**. Even more strangely, per-user defaults can be configured in a **~/.swdefaults** file.

The **swinstall** command is most often used by administrators, especially those that diligently install security patches as they are released. **swinstall -i** forces an interactive installation. The GUI starts if X is running; otherwise, you get the text interface.

7. Actually, **swagentd** invokes **swagent**, but this process is transparent to the user.

Sadly, HP-UX does not have a convenient on-line software repository from which you can easily install patches. The closest thing to it is the HP-UX Software Assistant tool, which analyzes the system with reference to an HP-provided catalog of patches, downloads the appropriate patch bundles, and builds a software depot from which you can use **swinstall** to patch the system.

Let's look at a few examples. To install security patch PHKL_40197 from an NFS-based software depot on the host hpux.booklab, we'd run the command

```
hp-ux$ sudo swinstall -s hpux.booklab:/hpux/patches PHKL_40197
```

swinstall runs configuration scripts automatically during installation. If you later need to reconfigure a package, use the **swconfig** command. **swconfig** customizes a software package for the local system (e.g., by making modifications to a file in **/etc** or changing the permissions on a directory). To reconfigure the **sudo** package, we'd run the following command:

```
hp-ux$ sudo swconfig -x reconfigure=true sudo
```

To remove this package, we'd run **swremove sudo**. **swverify** examines a package and performs an integrity check on its essential components. Use **swverify** to fix problems such as broken defaults files or missing directories.

swlist shows you the software installed on the system or available in a depot. The interactive interface is generally handier for searching, but here's a simple command line that lists the Java-related packages on our example HP-UX system:

```
hp-ux$ sudo swlist 'Java*'
# Initializing...
# Contacting target "hpux11"...

# Target:  hpux11:/

# Java15JDK          1.5.0.11.00   Java 1.5 JDK for HP-UX
  Java15JDK.Jdk15    1.5.0.11.00   Java 1.5 JDK
  Java15JDK.Jre15    1.5.0.11.00   Java 1.5 JRE
# Java15JRE          1.5.0.11.00   Java 1.5 JRE for HP-UX
  Java15JRE.Jre15    1.5.0.11.00   Java 1.5 JRE
```

Remote operation is a powerful feature of Software Distributor. The remote features allows sysadmins to push software to remote systems (optionally, on a predefined schedule). Most commands support remote operations, and some, such as **swinstall**, also support them in their GUIs. Remote operations are performed with remote procedure calls (RPC), and security is controlled with access control lists. See **man 5 sd** to configure remote operations.

Software management in AIX

Most UNIX vendors have at least attempted to keep up with Linux in the software management space, but IBM has opted for something of a Stone Age approach in AIX. The SMIT **install_software** fastpath is recommended in most cases; behind the curtains, it invokes the **installp** command. The SMIT **easy_install** fastpath is another option that requires fewer keystrokes than **install_software**.

installp processes an IBM-proprietary package format called Backup File Format, or **.bff**, as well as an older version of the RPM format used by many Linux systems. Unfortunately, **installp** is missing many features that spoiled administrators have come to take for granted, such as package installation from a network depot and even effective package querying. We always use **smit install_software** or **smit easy_install** when we add packages to our AIX systems.

AIX's **lslpp** command lists the installed software packages, which IBM refers to as "filesets." **lslpp -L all** lists all software products on the system—you can also use the **smit list_installed_sw** fastpath to similar effect. Installed software has state and type codes that indicate the condition and origin of each package. The state can be one of applied, broken, committed, locked, obsolete, or inconsistent. The type is an **installp** fileset, product, component, feature, RPM, or fix.

12.9 Revision control

Mistakes are a fact of life. Therefore, it's important to keep track of the configuration changes you make so that when these changes cause problems, you can easily revert to a known-good configuration. In this section we discuss some common ways of managing changes at the level of individual files. Choose the tools that match your needs and the complexity of your site.

Backup file creation

This command probably looks familiar:

```
$ cp bigfile.conf bigfile.bak
```

It probably seems a bit shameful, as well—surely, real system administrators do something more sophisticated?

In fact, there's much to be said in favor of this kind of impromptu backup. Backup files are simple to create, easy to **diff**, and they create an audit trail, at least to the extent that backup files can be ordered by modification time. They require no additional software, and there's no possibility that someone will leave the backup system in an ambiguous state.

We suggest a couple of tweaks, however. It's best to create backup files by moving the original file aside to its new name with **mv** and then copying it back to its original name. Use **cp -p** to preserve the file's attribute settings. This procedure preserves the original file's modification time and handles cases in which a process has an open reference to the original file.

Better yet, add a short scriptlet like the one below to your ~/**.bash_profile** or ~/**.profile** file. It defines a **backup** "command" (a **bash** function, really) that picks a backup filename and does the switcheroo for you.

```
function backup () {
    newname=$1.`date +%Y%m%d.%H%M.bak`;
    mv $1 $newname;
    echo "Backed up $1 to $newname.";
    cp -p $newname $1;
}
```

For example:

```
$ backup hello.py
Backed up hello.py to hello.py.20091030.1612.bak.
```

The filename encodes the date and time at which the backup occurred, and the file's modification time records the time at which the contents were last changed prior to your new (still-to-be-made) updates. Both pieces of information are potentially useful. This script encodes the time in such a way that an alpha sort of the filenames also sorts the backup files correctly by date.

Systems that are regularly backed up to tape can still benefit from the use of manually created backup files. Recovery from a backup file is faster and easier than recovery from a tape, and manual backups preserve an additional layer of history.

Formal revision control systems

At the next level of complexity and robustness are formal revision control systems, which are software packages that track, archive, and provide access to multiple revisions of files. These packages originated in the world of software development, but they are quite useful for system administrators, too.

Revision control systems address several problems. First, they provide an organized way to trace the history of modifications to a file so that changes can be understood in context and so that earlier versions can be recovered. Second, they extend the concept of versioning beyond the level of individual files. Related groups of files can be versioned together in a manner that takes account of their interdependencies. Finally, revision control systems coordinate the activities of multiple editors so that race conditions cannot cause anyone's changes to be permanently lost[8] and so that incompatible changes from multiple editors do not become active simultaneously.

The last few years have witnessed a boom in open source version control systems, and the available choices have expanded by almost an order of magnitude. Major contenders among the newer systems include Arch, Mercurial, and Bazaar-NG. Git, originally developed by Linux creator Linus Torvalds, has gained quick traction in the open source community and is now used for management of the Linux kernel source code. A time-tested system called Subversion from the previous generation remains in wide use and offers an outstanding Windows GUI.

8. For example, suppose that sysadmins Alice and Bob both edit the same file and that each makes some changes. Alice saves first. When Bob saves his copy of the file, it overwrites Alice's version. If Alice has quit from the editor, her changes are completely gone and unrecoverable.

Several commercial revision control systems are also available. You may already have access to one of them if you work in a development shop, and you might be tempted to use it for administrative data. Tread carefully, though; our experience has been that these commercial systems are usually overkill for sysadmin use.

The most popular systems today are Subversion and Git. Either system works well for system administration, but Git has an edge in that it makes setting up new repositories a fast and simple operation. For other advantages of Git, see Scott Chacon's whygitisbetterthanx.com web site.

Subversion

In the Subversion model, a central server or directory acts as a project's authoritative repository. By default, the Subversion server is a module in the Apache web server, which is convenient for distributed software development but maybe not so good for administrative uses. Fortunately, the Subversion folks provide an alternative type of server in the form of a daemon called **svnserve**. You can run **svnserve** from your home directory while experimenting with Subversion, but in production use it should have its own user account and be run from **inetd**.

Setting up a repository is easy. For example, the following steps create a new Subversion repository called **admin**:

```
# cd /home/svn
# mkdir repositories
# cd repositories
# svnadmin create admin
# chmod 700 admin
```

If you peek inside the **admin** directory, you will find a well-organized repository structure, including a **README** file. The configuration file **svnserve.conf** can be found in the **conf** subdirectory. This file tells the server daemon how to provide access to the new repository. Here's an example configuration appropriate for administrative files:

```
[general]
anon-access = none
auth-access = write
password-db = passwd
realm = The Sysadmin Repository
```

Because one of Subversion's design goals was to facilitate collaboration among people at different sites, it has an access control model that is separate from that of the operating system. The file **passwd** (in the same directory) contains a list of users and their plaintext (!) passwords. The plaintext bit is not nice, but the saving grace is that the passwords are never transmitted over the network. They are also never typed from memory by users, so you may as well assign passwords that are long enough and random enough to be secure.

For example:

```
[users]
tobi = lkadslfkjasdljkhe8938uhau7623rhkdfndf
evi = 09uqalkhlkasdgfprghkjhsdfjj83yyouhfuhe
fritz = kd939hjahkjaj3hkuyasdfaadfk3ijdkjhf
```

Naturally, permissions on the **passwd** file should be set restrictively.

All that remains is to start the server on the new repository:

```
# svnserve --daemon --root /home/svn/repositories
```

As an unprivileged user, you can now check out the **admin** archive from anywhere on the network.

```
$ svn checkout --username tobi svn://server.atrust.com/admin checkout
Authentication realm: <svn://server.atrust.com:3690> The Sysadmin Repository
Password for 'tobi': <password>
```

When you enter the password for the first time, Subversion squirrels away a copy in a **.subversion** directory that it creates in your home. To add or move files within your local copy of the project, use the **svn** command:

```
$ cd checkout
$ vi foo.c
$ svn add foo.c
```

Once you are done, commit your changes to the repository:

```
$ svn commit -m "Initial checkin; added foo.c"
```

It is not necessary to list the changed files you want to commit, although you can do so if you wish; **svn** will figure it out on its own. If you omit the **-m** option, **svn** starts an editor for you so that you can edit the commit message.

To get the latest updates from the repository, run **svn update** within the project. Subversion performs a merge operation on any files that have been modified in both your local copy of the project and the master repository. Files with unresolvable conflicts are marked as "conflicted," and Subversion does not allow you to check them in until you have fixed the problems and told Subversion that the conflicts have been resolved:

```
$ svn resolved foo.c
```

If you want to know who has changed which lines in a file, you can ask Subversion to dish out the blame:

```
$ svn blame bar.c
```

This command prints an annotated version of the file that shows when and by whom each line was last modified. (Those of a more forgiving or optimistic nature can use the synonym **svn praise**.) It's also easy to get diffs relative to a particular date or version. For example, if you want to know what has changed in **foo.c** since July 4, 2010, the following command will tell you:

```
$ svn diff -r "{2010-07-04}" foo.c
```

You can download the latest version of Subversion from subversion.tigris.org. The standard documentation is the book *Version Control with Subversion*, published by O'Reilly. The full text is available on-line at svnbook.red-bean.com.

Subversion's exceptionally good Windows GUI is called TortoiseSVN; we used it to manage the source files for this book. See tortoisesvn.tigris.org for details.

Git

Git's shtick is that it has no central repository. Instead of checking out a particular version of a project's files, you simply copy the repository (including its entire history) and carry it around with you like a hermit crab lugging its shell. Your commits to the repository are local operations, so they're fast and you don't have to worry about communicating with a central server.

Git uses an intelligent compression system to reduce the cost of storing the entire history, and in most cases this system is quite effective. In many cases, working requirements for storage space are even lower than with Subversion.

Git is great for developers because they can pile their source code onto a laptop and work without being connected to a network while still making use of all the benefits of revision control. When the time comes to integrate multiple developers' work, their changes can be integrated from one copy of the repository to another in any fashion that suits the organization's workflow. It's always possible to unwind two copies of a repository back to their common ancestor state, no matter how many changes and iterations have occurred after the split.

Git's promiscuous copying-and-branching strategy isn't terribly relevant to the context of system administration, but its use of a local repository is a big leap forward for system administrators—or perhaps more accurately, it's a big leap backward, but in a good way. Early revision control systems (e.g., RCS and CVS) used local repositories but were unable to handle collaboration, change merging, and independent development. Now we've come full circle to a point where putting files under revision control is once again a fast, simple, local operation. At the same time, all of Git's advanced collaboration features are available for use in situations that require them.

Software

Before you start using Git, set your name and email address:

```
$ git config --global user.name "John Q. Ulsah"
$ git config --global user.email "ulsah@book.admin.com"
```

To track garden-variety changes to configuration files, you'll generally want to use in-situ repositories that are never duplicated and therefore never need to be reconciled or integrated. This convention makes the Git wrangling pretty simple, but since commits will be done as root, it's important to make sure that all potential committers set their names and email addresses as shown above. (Git uses your personal information for log entries even when you're running it through **sudo**.)

To create a repository that covers the **/etc** directory, you'd run these commands:

```
$ cd /etc
$ sudo git init
Initialized empty Git repository in /etc/.git/
$ sudo git add .
$ sudo git commit -m "Initial commit"
Created initial commit ed25c29: Initial commit
2538 files changed, 259122 insertions(+), 0 deletions(-)
  create mode 100644 .java/.systemPrefs/.system.lock
  create mode 100644 .java/.systemPrefs/.systemRootModFile
...
```

In the sequence above, **git init** creates the repository's infrastructure in the **/etc/.git** directory. **git add .** puts **/etc** and everything beneath it on Git's "staging" list, which is the list of files to be committed by the next **git commit** operation. The **-m** flag to **git commit** includes the log message on the command line. If you leave it out, **git** starts up an editor with which you can compose the log message.

Let's now make a change and check it into the repository.

```
$ sudo vi mdadm/mdadm.conf
$ sudo git commit mdadm/mdadm.conf -m "Added spare to svr4west array"
Created commit 901bd39: Added spare to svr4west array
  1 files changed, 1 insertions(+), 0 deletions(-)
```

Naming modified files on the **git commit** command line bypasses Git's normal use of the staging area and creates a revision that includes only changes to the named files. The existing staging area remains unchanged, and Git ignores any other files that may have been modified.

If a change involves multiple files, you have a couple of options. If you know exactly which files were changed, you can always list them all on the command line as shown above. If you're lazy, you can run **git commit -a** to make Git add all modified files to the staging area before doing the commit. This last option has a couple of pitfalls, however.

First, there may be modified files that have nothing to do with your changes. For example, the **/etc/mtab** file on Linux systems is maintained by the system, so it can change even in the absence of configuration changes. Allowing this file to participate in the commit sets you up for problems in the future because it's not really part of your current changes. If you later have to revert your changes, it would be a mistake to revert the **mtab** file as well.

The second pitfall is that **git commit -a** only checks for changes to files that are currently under revision control. It does not pick up new files.

To avoid these stumbling blocks, run **git status** and assess the situation manually. This command informs you of new files, modified files, and staged files all at once. For example, suppose that we edited **/etc/mdadm/mdadm.conf** as in the previous example and also installed a new system daemon, **foobard**, whose configuration file is **/etc/foobard/foobard.conf**. Git might show the following:[9]

```
$ sudo git status
# On branch master
# Changed but not updated:
#    (use "git add <file>..." to update what will be committed)
#
#         modified:     mdadm/mdadm.conf
#         modified:     mtab
#         modified:     passwd
# Untracked files:
#    (use "git add <file>..." to include in what will be committed)
#
#         foobard/
no changes added to commit (use "git add" and/or "git commit -a")
```

The **foobard.conf** file is not listed by name because Git doesn't yet see beneath the **foobard** directory that contains it. We can see that both **mtab** and **passwd** have unexpected changes. The **mtab** changes are certainly spurious, but the **passwd** changes might or might not be. Perhaps the installation script for **foobard** created a dedicated system account for it, or perhaps someone else edited the **passwd** file and forgot to commit their changes to the repository.

To resolve the question, you can run **git diff passwd** to see the actual changes in the **passwd** file. Let's assume that in this case the **passwd** changes are unrelated to our recent activities. Therefore, we'll probably want to check in these changes separately from the ones we just made:

```
$ sudo git commit passwd -m "Checking in existing passwd changes"
Created commit 6f7853c: Checking in existing passwd changes
  1 files changed, 1 insertions(+), 0 deletions(-)
```

We can make Git ignore the **mtab** file, now and forever; however, two steps are required. First, we'll "delete" **mtab** from the current repository image:

```
$ sudo git rm --cached mtab
rm 'mtab'
```

The **--cached** option prevents Git from actually deleting the **mtab** file, so don't leave it out! In essence, we're stuffing a virtual file deletion operation into Git's staging area. Git will behave as if we had deleted the file with **rm**.

The second step to eradicating **mtab** from Git's universe is to add it to Git's list of files to ignore in the future. That's done by creating or editing a **.gitignore** file.

9. Even though this command makes no changes, it must still be run as root because it creates lock files in the **.git** directory.

```
$ sudo sh -c "echo mtab >> .gitignore"
```
[10]

Finally, we'll commit all the remaining changes:

```
$ sudo git add .
$ sudo git commit -m "Installed foobard; added RAID spare"
Created commit 32978e6: Installed foobard; added RAID spare
  4 files changed, 3 insertions(+), 1 deletion(-)
  create mode 100644 .gitignore
  create mode 100644 foobard/foobard.conf
  delete mode 100644 mtab
```

Note that the **.gitignore** file itself becomes part of the managed set of files. It's fine to re-add files that are already under management, so **git add .** is an easy way to say "I want to make the new repository image look like the current directory." You couldn't just do a **git commit -a** in this situation because that would pick up neither **foobard.conf** nor **.gitignore**; these files are new to management by Git and must be explicitly added.

In an effort to fool you into thinking that it manages files' permissions as well as their contents, Git shows you file modes when adding new files to the repository. It's lying; Git does not track modes, owners, or modification times. If you use Git to revert changes to system files, double-check that their attributes remain OK. A corollary is that you can't count on using Git to recover complex file hierarchies from scratch in situations where the ownerships and permissions are important.

Using Git for basic revision control isn't significantly more painful than making manual backup copies. The hard part is getting your entire administrative team up to speed with the system and making sure that it's used consistently.

12.10 Software localization and configuration

Adapting computers to your local environment is one of the prime battlegrounds of system administration: tell the system about all the printers available on the network, start the special licensing daemon, add the **cron** job that cleans the **/scratch** directory once a week, integrate support for that special scanner they use over in the graphics department, and on and on. Taking care of these issues in a structured and reproducible way is a central goal of architectural thinking.

Keep the following points in mind:

- Users do not have root privileges. Any need for root privileges in the course of normal operations is suspicious and probably indicates that something is fishy with your local configuration.
- Users do not wreck the system intentionally. Design internal security so that it guards against unintentional errors and the widespread dissemination of administrative privileges.

10. The explicit call to **sh** forces the redirection operator to be evaluated in the context of a root shell. If we simply typed **echo mtab >> .gitignore**, the shell would try to open **.gitignore** before running **sudo**.

- Users that misbehave in minor ways should be interviewed before being chastised. Users frequently respond to inefficient administrative procedures by attempting to subvert them, so consider the possibility that noncompliance is an indication of architectural problems.
- Be customer-centered. Talk to users and ask them which tasks they find difficult. Find ways to make these tasks simpler.
- Your personal preferences are yours. Let your users have their own. Offer choices wherever possible.
- When administrative decisions affect users' experience of the system, be aware of the reasons for your decisions. Let your reasons be known.
- Keep your local documentation up to date and easily accessible. See page 1200 for more information on this topic.

Organizing your localization

If your site has a thousand computers and each computer has its own configuration, you will spend a major portion of your working time figuring out why one box has a particular problem and another doesn't. Clearly, the solution is to make every computer the same—right? But real-world constraints and the varying needs of your users typically make this impossible.

There's a big difference in administrability between *multiple* configurations and *countless* configurations. The trick is to split your setup into manageable bits. You will find that some parts of the localization apply to all managed hosts, others apply to only a few, and still others are specific to individual boxes.

In addition to performing installations from scratch, you will also need to continually roll out updates. Keep in mind that individual hosts have different needs for currency, stability, and uptime.

A prudent system administrator should not roll out new software releases en masse. Instead, rollouts should be staged according to a gradual plan that accommodates other groups' needs and allows time for problems to be discovered while their potential to cause damage is still limited. Never update critical servers until you have some confidence in the changes you are contemplating, and avoid Fridays unless you're prepared for a long weekend in front of the terminal.[11]

However you design your localization system, make sure that all original data is kept in a revision control system. This precaution lets you keep track of which changes have been thoroughly tested and are ready for deployment. In addition, it lets you identify the originator of any problematic changes. The more people involved in the process, the more important this last consideration becomes.

11. Security patches are a possible exception to this rule. Plug security holes as soon as they are found. On the other hand, security patches do sometimes introduce bugs.

It is advantageous to separate the base OS release from the localization release. Depending on the stability needs of your environment, you may use minor local releases only for bug fixing. However, we have found that adding new features in small doses yields a smoother operation than queuing up changes into "horse pill" releases that risk a major disruption of service.

It's often a good idea to specify a maximum number of "releases" you are willing to have in play at any given time. Some administrators believe that there is no reason to fix software that isn't broken. They point out that gratuitously upgrading systems costs time and money and that "cutting edge" all too often means "bleeding edge." Those who put these principles into practice must be willing to collect an extensive catalog of active releases.

By contrast, the "lean and mean" crowd point to the inherent complexity of releases and the difficulty of comprehending (let alone managing) a random collection of releases dating years into the past. Their trump cards are security patches, which must typically be applied universally and on a tight schedule. Patching outdated versions of the operating system is often infeasible, so administrators are faced with the choice of skipping updates on some computers or crash-upgrading these machines to a newer internal release. Not good.

Neither of these perspectives is provably correct, but we tend to side with those who favor a limited number of releases. Better to perform your upgrades on your own schedule rather than one dictated by an external emergency.

Testing

It's important to test changes before unleashing them on the world. At a minimum, this means that you need to test your own local configuration changes. However, you should really test the software that your vendor releases as well. A major UNIX vendor once released a patch that, when applied a certain way, performed an **rm -rf** /. Imagine installing this patch throughout your organization without testing it first.

Testing is an especially pertinent issue if you use a service that offers an automatic patching capability, such as most of the packaging systems discussed in this chapter. Mission-critical systems should never be directly connected to a vendor-sponsored update service. Identify a sacrificial machine to be connected to the service, and roll out the changes from this box to other machines at your site only after appropriate testing. Disable updates during your testing phase; otherwise, upstream changes can sneak their way prematurely onto your production systems in the middle of the testing process.

See page 1191 for more information about trouble tracking.

If you foresee that an update may cause user-visible problems or changes, notify users well in advance and give them a chance to communicate with you if they have concerns regarding your intended changes or timing. Make sure that users have an easy way to report bugs.

If your organization is geographically distributed, make sure that other offices help with testing. International participation is particularly valuable in multilingual environments. If no one in the U.S. office speaks Japanese, for example, you had better get the Tokyo office to test anything that might affect kanji support. A surprising number of system parameters vary with location. Does the U.S. office test changes to the printing infrastructure with A4 paper, or will the non-U.S. offices be in for a surprise?

Compiling locally

In the old days of UNIX, when there were many different architectures, programs were generally distributed in the form of source archives, usually **.tar.gz** files that you would uncompress and then compile. Once the program was built, you would then install the software in a location such as **/usr/local**. Today, the use of package management systems means that fewer programs need to be installed this way. It also means that administrators make fewer decisions since packages specify where their contents are installed.

Even with easy package management, some people still prefer to compile their own software.[12] Running your own build gives you more control over the software's compiled-in options. It also lets you be more paranoid because you can inspect the source code you are compiling. Some people seem to think that this once-over is important, but unless you've got the time and skill to inspect every line of a 20,000-line software package, the added security value is minimal.

Since not every piece of software in the world has been packaged for every Linux distribution and UNIX flavor, it's likely that you will run across at least a few programs that you need to compile and install yourself, especially if your computers are not 32-bit Intel systems. What's more, if yours is a development site, you will have to consider where to put your site's own locally developed software.

Historically, the most common location for local software has been **/usr/local**, and this convention is still widely followed today. The UNIX/Linux Filesystem Hierarchy Standard (FHS) specifies that **/usr/local** be present and empty after the initial OS installation, and many packages expect to install themselves there.

Although **/usr/local** is traditional, many sites find it to be an unmanageable dumping ground. The traditional way it's laid out (basically the same as **/usr**, with binaries in **/usr/local/bin**, man pages in **/usr/local/man**, and so on) creates a raft of problems in some environments: it's hard to have multiple versions of the same software installed, the directories can be large, it's a pain to manage multiple architectures, etc.

12. Hard-core compile-it-yourselfers should check out the Gentoo Linux distribution, which is designed to be recompiled from scratch on the destination system.

Distributing localizations

A localization system must handle both initial installation and incremental updates. The updates can be especially tricky. Efficiency is a major concern since you probably do not want to repeat the entire localization dance to update the permissions of a single file. Even though the process is automated, the rebuild-from-scratch model makes updates an expensive and time-consuming process.

A simple and scalable way to organize localizations is to maintain files in a tree structure that mimics the (skeletonized) filesystem of a production machine. A dedicated installation script can copy the tree to the destination machine and perform any additional editing that is required.

This type of setup has several advantages. You can maintain as many localization trees as are necessary to implement your local administrative scheme. Some of the trees will be alternatives, with each machine getting only one of the available choices. Other trees will be overlays that can be copied on top of the trees that came before them. Localization trees can overwrite files if necessary, or they can be completely disjoint. Each tree that is potentially installed independently should be represented by a separate revision control project.

The overlay-tree approach allows flexibility in implementation. If you use a packaging system to distribute your local customizations, the overlays can simply be rolled up into independent packages. The appropriate customization scripts can be included in the package and set to run as part of the installation process.

Another good implementation idea is to use **rsync** to bring destination machines into compliance with their overlay trees. **rsync** copies only files that are out of date, so it can be very efficient for distributing incremental changes. This behavior is hard to simulate with a packaging system alone. Refer to page 725 for more information about **rsync**.

12.11 Using configuration management tools

Localization systems tend to be home-grown. Part of the reason for this is that all sites are different and each has its own bizarre quirks. However, the "not invented here" syndrome is also a significant contributor. Perhaps the lack of a dominant open source tool for performing configuration management has conditioned us to think of this problem as lying outside the domain of standardized tools.

Nevertheless, the tools exist and are worth your review, if only to give yourself some clarity about why you choose not to make use of them. The following sections outline a few common systems in rough order of popularity and similarity.

cfengine: computer immune system

One of the best-known localization tools is Mark Burgess' **cfengine**. It was envisioned as a sort of "computer immune system" that bases its operation on a model of how the system should be configured. When it detects a discrepancy between the model and the reality, **cfengine** takes the appropriate steps to bring the system into compliance. Because of this underlying model, **cfengine** is useful for ongoing configuration maintenance.

cfengine can make backup copies of the files it modifies and can keep a detailed log of its changes. It can also be run in a no-action mode in which it describes the changes it would make without actually implementing them.

You use **cfengine**'s own special language to describe how you want your computers to be configured. You can specify rules such as, "The file **xyz** must exist in **/etc**, have permissions 644, and belong to root." You can also write rules regarding the content of individual files. For example, you can specify that **/etc/hosts** must contain the line "router 192.168.0.1". **cfengine** then adds this line if it is missing.

cfengine's configuration language lets you turn on individual rules depending on factors such as the hostname, the OS, or the subnet. This feature makes it easy to write a single configuration file that covers the needs of all the machines in your administrative domain.

The following is a simple example from the UNIX world. It makes sure that **/bin** is a symlink to **/usr/bin** on Suns, does some additional link checking on legacy OSF boxes, and removes everything from **/var/scratch** that is older than seven days:

```
control:
actionsequence = ( links tidy )
links:
    sun4::
        /bin -> /usr/bin
        # other links
    osf::
        # some osf specific links
tidy:
    /var/scratch pattern=* age=7 recurse=inf
```

See the **cfengine** home page at cfengine.org for more information.

LCFG: a large-scale configuration system

LCFG was originally developed by Paul Anderson at Edinburgh University in 1993. In its latest incarnation it is known as LCFG(ng) and has gained a number of users outside the university. LCFG is primarily geared toward managing large Solaris or Linux installations. The LCFG web site is lcfg.org.

Like **cfengine**, LCFG defines a specialized configuration language. The configurations of all managed machines are stored on a central server in a set of master configuration files. From these, LCFG generates customized XML files that describe the configuration of each managed host. A daemon on the central server monitors the master configuration files for changes and regenerates the XML files as required.

The XML files are published on an internal web server from which clients can then pull their own configurations. The clients use a variety of component scripts to configure themselves according to the XML blueprints.

Template Tree 2: cfengine helper

Template Tree 2 was created at the Swiss Federal Institute of Technology (ETH) by Tobias Oetiker. It is a component-based system driven by a central configuration. It reduces complexity by taking a two-level approach to defining a site's configuration and can deal with the relocated root directories of diskless machines.

On the lower level, the system consists of a number of "feature packs." A feature pack is a collection of files accompanied by a **META** file that describes how these files must be installed on the target system. A feature can be anything from a network configuration to the latest version of OpenSSH. Features can expose configurable parameters that can be set in the master configuration file.

The upper level of configuration is a master site configuration file in which you pull the features together and associate them to machines or groups of machines. At this level, you must specify values for the unbound configuration parameters exposed by each feature. For example, one of the parameters for a mail server feature might be the name of the mail domain.

Template Tree 2 combines the information from the master configuration file and the individual features' **META** files to generate a **cfengine** configuration file for the whole site. Because each feature must contain documentation about its purpose and usage, Template Tree 2 can also generate composite documentation.

DMTF/CIM: the Common Information Model

The Distributed Management Task Force (DMTF), a coalition of "more than 3,000 active participants," has been working since 1992 to develop its Common Information Model (CIM) in an attempt to create standards for an object-oriented, cross-platform management system.

In DMTF's own words, CIM is "a management schema...provided to establish a common conceptual framework at the level of a fundamental topology both with respect to classification and association, and with respect to the basic set of classes intended to establish a common framework for a description of the managed environment." Or whatever.

All major vendors from Microsoft to Sun are members of the DMTF. Unfortunately, the standards they have produced demonstrate an impressive mastery of the arts of obfuscation and buzzword husbandry. The companies involved seem eager to demonstrate their willingness to standardize no matter what. The standards center on XML and object orientation. However, we have yet to see a sensible product built on top of them.

If there is an upside to this quagmire, it is that the DMTF efforts at least require vendors to provide programmatically accessible configuration interfaces to their systems based on an open standard. For UNIX and Linux environments this is nothing new, but the DMTF is not a UNIX creature. It includes Cisco, Microsoft, Symantec, and many other companies with little history of providing sensible ways of scripting their systems. Giving these products a configuration API is a good thing, even if the implementations are still lacking.

12.12 Sharing software over NFS

Where should extra software actually be installed: on individual clients or on a central file server from which it can be shared over NFS? The standard answer is "on the clients," but the NFS solution makes updates quicker (it's faster and more reliable to update ten NFS servers than 1,000 clients) and saves disk space on clients (not that this matters much in the world of 1TB disks).

The question really boils down to manageability versus reliability. Network filesystem-based access is centralized and easier to manage from day to day, and it makes bug fixes and new packages instantaneously available on all clients. However, running over the network may be a bit slower than accessing a local disk. In addition, the network server model adds dependencies on the network and the file server, not only because it adds potential points of failure but also because it requires that clients and servers agree on such things as the shared libraries that will be available and the version of those libraries that will be installed. The bottom line is that NFS software libraries are an advanced administrative technique and should only be attempted in environments that allow for a high degree of central coordination.

In general, networks of heterogeneous systems derive the most benefit from shared software repositories. If your site has standardized on one operating system and that operating system provides reasonable package management facilities, you're likely to be better off sticking with the native system.

Package namespaces

Traditional UNIX sprays the contents of new packages across multiple directories. Libraries go to **/usr/lib**, binaries to **/usr/bin**, documentation to **/usr/share/docs**, and so on. Linux inherits more or less the same system, although the Filesystem Hierarchy Standard helps make the locations somewhat more predictable. (See pathname.com/fhs for more information about the FHS.)

The advantage of this convention is that files show up in well-known places. As long your PATH environment variable points to **/usr/bin** and the other standard binary directories, for example, newly installed programs will be readily available.

The downsides are that the origins of files must be explicitly tracked (by means of package management systems) and that the scattered files are difficult to share on a network. Fortunately, sysadmins willing to put in some extra work have a reasonable way out of this dilemma: package namespaces.

The gist of the scheme is to install every package into its own separate root directory. For example, you might install **gimp** into **/tools/graphics/gimp**, with the binary being located at **/tools/graphics/gimp/bin/gimp**. You can then recreate an aggregate binary directory for your collection of tools by placing symbolic links into a directory such as **/tools/bin**:

```
/tools/bin/gimp -> /tools/graphics/gimp/bin/gimp
```

Users can then add the directory **/tools/bin** to their PATH variables to be assured of picking up all the shared tools.

There are various options for structuring the **/tools** directory. A hierarchical approach (e.g., **/tools/graphics**, **/tools/editors**, etc.) facilitates browsing and speeds performance. You may want to include the software version, hardware architecture, operating system, or responsible person's initials in your naming conventions to allow the same collection of tools to be served to many types of clients. For example, Solaris users might include **/tools/sun4/bin** in their PATHs, and Ubuntu users include **/tools/ubuntu/bin**.

When you install a new version of a major tool, it's a good idea to keep older versions around indefinitely, particularly when users may have significant time and effort invested in projects that use the tool. Ideally, new versions of tools would be backward compatible with old data files and software, but in practice, disasters are common. It's fine to require users to go through some configuration trouble to access an older version of a package; it's not fine to just break their existing work and make them deal with the consequences.

Dependency management

Some packages depend on libraries or on other software packages. When you install software locally through a package-management system, you get lots of help with resolving these issues. However, when you build your own site-wide network software repository, you must address these issues explicitly.

If you manage libraries in the same way you manage applications, you can compile your tools to use libraries from within the shared **/tools** directory. This convention lets you keep multiple versions of a library active simultaneously. Because dependent applications are linked against specific versions of the library, the setup remains stable even when new versions of the library are released. The downside is that this type of setup can be quite complicated to use and maintain over time.

Resist the temptation to link against a global **/tools/lib** directory that contains generically named links to common libraries. If you change the links, you may run into unexpected and difficult-to-diagnose problems. Shared library systems are designed to address some of the potential headbutts, but it makes sense to play it safe in a complicated setup.

The exact steps needed to make the linker use a specific version of a shared library vary from system to system. Under Linux, you can set the LD_LIBRARY_PATH environment variable or use the linker's -**R** option.

Wrapper scripts

Unfortunately, library-level compatibility is only half the story. The fact that tools invoke one another directly raises another opportunity for conflict. For example, suppose the utility named **foo** makes frequent use of the utility named **bar**. If you update the default version of **bar**, you may find that **foo** suddenly stops working. In this case, you can conclude that **foo** depended on some behavior of **bar** that is no longer supported (or at least is no longer the default).

If your software repository supports multiple versions (e.g., **/tools/util/bar-1.0** and **/tools/util/bar-2.0**), you can fix this problem by moving the original version of **foo** to **foo.real** and replacing it with a little wrapper script:

```
#!/bin/sh
# make sure the program finds any files co-packaged with it
# first even if it does not use an explicit path.
PATH=/tools/util/bar-1.0/bin:$PATH
export PATH
exec /tools/util/foo-1.0/bin/foo.real "$@"
```

Now **foo** will be launched with a customized PATH environment variable, and it will call the old version of **bar** in preference to the new one.

Wrappers are a powerful tool that can address not only package dependencies but also issues such as security, architecture- or OS-dependence, and usage tracking. Some sites wrap all shared binaries.

12.13 Recommended reading

Intel Corporation and SystemSoft. *Preboot Execution Environment (PXE) Specification, v2.1.* 1999. pix.net/software/pxeboot/archive/pxespec.pdf

PXELinux Questions. syslinux.zytor.com/wiki/index.php/PXELINUX

Rodin, Josip. *Debian New Maintainers' Guide.* debian.org/doc/maint-guide This document contains good information about **.deb** packages.

Silva, Gustavo Noronha. *APT HOWTO.* debian.org/doc/manuals/apt-howto

Hohndel, Dirk, and Fabian Herschel. *Automated Installation of Linux Systems Using YaST.* usenix.org/events/lisa99/full_papers/hohndel/hohndel_html

Stückelberg, Marc Vuilleumier, and David Clerc. *Linux Remote-Boot mini-HOWTO: Configuring Remote-Boot Workstations with Linux, DOS, Windows 95/98 and Windows NT.* 1999. tldp.org/HOWTO/Remote-Boot.html

The Red Hat Enterprise Linux System Administration Guide. redhat.com/docs

WACHSMANN, ALF. *How to Install Red Hat Linux via PXE and Kickstart.* stanford.edu/~alfw/PXE-Kickstart/PXE-Kickstart.html

BURGESS, MARK. *Cfengine: A Site Configuration Engine.* USENIX Computing Systems, Vol 8, No 3. 1995. cfengine.org

HP Ignite-UX Administration Guide. docs.hp.com/en/5992-5309/5992-5309.pdf

NIM from A to Z. www.redbooks.ibm.com/redbooks/pdfs/sg247296.pdf. This is a thorough Network Installation Manager guide.

Solaris Advanced Installation Guide. docs.sun.com/app/docs/doc/802-5740

12.14 EXERCISES

E12.1 Outline the differences between Kickstart, JumpStart, and Ignite-UX. What are some of the advantages and disadvantages of each?

E12.2 Install Subversion from subversion.tigris.org. Set up **svnserve** and create a repository. How can you make the repository usable from anywhere on the local network but still maintain reasonable security?

E12.3 Review the way that local software is organized at your site. Will the system scale? Is it easy to use? Discuss.

E12.4 What are some of the most important features of a configuration management system? What are the security implications of distributing configuration files over the network?

★★ E12.5 Set up the network installer of your choice and install a new machine by using your server. Outline all the steps needed to perform this task. What were some of the stumbling blocks? What are some of the scalability issues you discovered with the installer you chose?

13 Drivers and the Kernel

The kernel hides the system's hardware underneath an abstract, high-level programming interface. It furnishes many of the facilities that users and user-level programs take for granted. For example, the kernel creates all the following concepts from lower-level hardware features:

- Processes (time-sharing, protected address spaces)
- Signals and semaphores
- Virtual memory (swapping, paging, mapping)
- The filesystem (files, directories, namespace)
- General input/output (specialty hardware, keyboard, mouse, USB)
- Interprocess communication (pipes and network connections)

The kernel incorporates device drivers that manage its interaction with specific pieces of hardware; the rest of the kernel is, to a large degree, device independent. The relationship between the kernel and its device drivers is similar to the relationship between user-level processes and the kernel. When a process asks the kernel to "Read the first 64 bytes of **/etc/passwd**," the kernel (or more accurately, a filesystem driver) might translate this request into a device driver instruction such as "Fetch block 3,348 from device 3." The disk driver would further break up this command into bit patterns to be presented to the device's control registers.

The kernel is written mostly in C, with a sprinkling of assembly language to help it interface with hardware- or chip-specific functions that are not accessible through normal compiler directives.

One of the advantages of Linux and other open source environments is that the availability of source code makes it relatively easy to roll your own device drivers and kernel modules. In the early days of Linux, having skills in this area was a necessity because it was difficult to administer Linux systems without being able to mold the system to a specific environment. Development for other flavors of UNIX is more difficult without specialized knowledge. (Kudos to IBM for having excellent driver development documentation, as they do in many other areas.)

Fortunately, sysadmins can be perfectly effective without ever soiling their hands with kernel code. In fact, such activities are better left to kernel and driver developers. Administrators should focus more on the overall needs of the user community. Sysadmins can tune the kernel or add preexisting modules as described in this chapter, but they don't need to take a crash course in C or assembly language programming to survive. (This was not always true!)

13.1 Kernel adaptation

All the UNIX platforms covered in this book run monolithic kernels, in which the entire operating system runs in kernel space, a section of memory reserved for privileged operating system functions. In a monolithic kernel, services such as device drivers, interprocess communication, virtual memory, and scheduling run in the same address space. This approach contrasts with a "microkernel" architecture, in which many of these services run in user mode (i.e., as regular processes). The pros and cons of the two architectures have been hotly debated for years, but most kernel developers agree that both approaches have merit.

Linux is also a monolithic kernel at heart, but it allows user-space drivers for many devices. The Gelato, UIO, FUSE, and FUSD projects each provide interfaces to devices in user space. Nevertheless, most drivers are still implemented in kernel mode, generally for performance reasons.

Modern monolithic kernels support on-demand loading of modules, so you can incorporate device drivers and other kernel functions as needed without rebuilding the kernel and rebooting. Drivers, filesystems, and new system calls are all commonly implemented as modules. The memory used by a module is allocated and freed as the code is loaded or removed. This feature is particularly useful for embedded systems with limited memory since developers can tune the kernel to eliminate unneeded devices.

A kernel can learn about the system's hardware in several ways. The most basic way is that you explicitly inform the kernel about the hardware it should expect to find (or pretend not to find, as the case may be). In addition, the kernel prospects for many devices on its own, either at boot time or dynamically (once the system is running). The latter method is the most typical for USB devices: memory sticks, digital cameras, printers, and so on. Linux has reasonable support for a wide array of such devices. AIX and HP-UX have very limited support, and Solaris falls somewhere in between.

Table 13.1 shows the location of the kernel build directory and the standard name of the installed kernel on each of our example systems.

Table 13.1 Kernel build directory and location by system

System	Build directory	Kernel
Linux	**/usr/src/linux**	**/vmlinuz** or **/boot/vmlinuz**
Solaris	–[a]	**/platform/***hardware-class-name***/unix**
HP-UX	**/stand**	**/stand/vmunix**
AIX	–[b]	**/usr/lib/boot/unix**

a. Administrators rarely build Solaris kernels, and when they do, the administrator creates an arbitrary build directory.

b. The AIX kernel is never rebuilt, even when new modules and devices are added.

13.2 Drivers and device files

A device driver is a program that manages the system's interaction with a particular type of hardware. The driver translates between the hardware commands understood by the device and the stylized programming interface used by the kernel. The driver layer helps keep the kernel reasonably device independent.

In most cases, device drivers are part of the kernel; they are not user processes. However, a driver can be *accessed* both from within the kernel and from user space. User-level access to devices is usually through special device files that live in the **/dev** directory. The kernel maps operations on these files into calls to the code of the driver.

With the remarkable pace at which new hardware is developed, it is practically impossible to keep mainline OS distributions up to date with the latest hardware. Ergo, you will occasionally need to add a device driver to your system to support a new piece of hardware.

Device drivers are system specific, and they are often specific to a particular range of kernel revisions as well. Drivers for other operating systems (e.g., Windows) will not work, so keep this in mind when you purchase new hardware.[1] In addition, devices vary in their degree of compatibility and functionality when used with various Linux distributions, so it's wise to pay some attention to the results other sites have obtained with any hardware you are considering.

1. The NDISwrapper project enables Windows drivers for some networking devices to be used under Linux. See sourceforge.net/projects/ndiswrapper for full details.

Hardware vendors are becoming more aware of the UNIX and Linux markets, and they sometimes provide UNIX and Linux drivers for their products. In the optimal case, your vendor furnishes you with both drivers and installation instructions. Occasionally, you only find the driver you need on some sketchy-looking and uncommented web page. For either case, this section shows you what is really going on when you add a driver to your system.

Device files and device numbers

Most devices have a corresponding file in **/dev**; network devices are notable exceptions on modern operating systems. Complex servers may support hundreds of devices. Solaris handles this complexity quite nicely by using a separate subdirectory of **/dev** for each type of device: **disk**, **cdrom**, **terminal**, etc.

By virtue of being device files, the files in **/dev** each have a major and minor device number associated with them. The kernel uses these numbers to map device-file references to the corresponding driver.

The major device number identifies the driver with which the file is associated (in other words, the type of device). The minor device number usually identifies which particular instance of a given device type is to be addressed. The minor device number is sometimes called the unit number.

You can see the major and minor number of a device file with **ls -l**:

```
linux$ ls -l /dev/sda
brw-rw----  1 root disk 8, 0 Jul 13 01:38 /dev/sda
```

This example shows the first SCSI disk on a Linux system. It has a major number of 8 and a minor number of 0.

The minor device number is sometimes used by the driver to select or enable certain characteristics particular to that device. For example, a tape drive can have one file in **/dev** that rewinds the drive automatically when it is closed and another file that does not. The driver is free to interpret the minor device number in whatever way it wants. Look up the man page for the driver to determine what convention it's using.

There are actually two primary types of device files: block device files and character device files. A block device is read or written one block (a group of bytes, usually a multiple of 512) at a time; a character device can be read or written one byte at a time. Disks and tapes lead dual lives; terminals and printers do not.

Device drivers present a standard interface to the kernel. Each driver has routines for performing some or all of the following functions:

```
attach     close     dump      ioctl   open    probe
psize      read      receive   reset   select  stop
strategy   timeout   transmit  write
```

It is sometimes convenient to implement an abstraction as a device driver even when it controls no actual device. Such phantom devices are known as pseudo-devices. For example, a user who logs in over the network is assigned a PTY (pseudo-TTY) that looks, feels, and smells like a serial port from the perspective of high-level software. This trick allows programs written in the days when everyone used a terminal to continue to function in the world of windows and networks. **/dev/zero**, **/dev/null**, and **/dev/random** are some other examples of pseudo-devices.

When a program performs an operation on a device file, the kernel intercepts the reference, looks up the appropriate function name in a table, and transfers control to the appropriate part of the driver. To perform an unusual operation that doesn't have a direct analog in the filesystem model (for example, ejecting a floppy disk), a program can use the **ioctl** system call to pass a message directly from user space into the driver.

Device file creation

Device files can be created manually with the **mknod** command, with the syntax

mknod *filename type major minor*

where *filename* is the device file to be created, *type* is **c** for a character device or **b** for a block device, and *major* and *minor* are the major and minor device numbers. If you are manually creating a device file that refers to a driver that's already present in your kernel, check the documentation for the driver to find the appropriate major and minor device numbers.

Under Linux, the udev system dynamically manages the creation and removal of device files according to the actual presence (or absence) of devices. The **udevd** daemon listens for messages from the kernel regarding device status changes. Based on configuration information in **/etc/udev** and **/lib/udev**, **udevd** can take a variety of actions when a device is discovered or disconnected. By default, it just creates device files in **/dev**. Udev is covered in detail beginning on page 437.

On Solaris systems, **/dev** is actually composed of symbolic links to files in the **/devices** directory, which is a separate filesystem. The Device File System (devfs) manages the device files in **/devices**. These files are created automatically at boot time by **devfsadmd**, which continues to run after boot to handle update notifications from the kernel. Administrators can use **devfsadm** to tweak this process, but most administrators will not need to use it.

The HP-UX kernel creates devices files at boot time. If new devices are attached later, administrators must create the device files manually by running the **mksf**, **insf**, and **mknod** commands. The **smh** tool also incorporates a limited interface for viewing device information.

In AIX, the **cfgmgr** command runs at boot time to configure devices and to install drivers for devices that weren't formerly present. It prints warnings for any devices for which the software or drivers are not installed. Once a device is detected, AIX remembers it by placing an identifier in the Object Data Manager, which we discuss on page 432. **cfgmgr** creates files in **/dev** for devices that are successfully detected and initialized.

Given the existence of these various tools for automating the creation of device files, system administrators running current releases of UNIX and Linux should never need to manually manage device files with **mknod**.

Naming conventions for devices

Naming conventions for devices are somewhat random. They are often holdovers from the way things were done under UNIX on a DEC PDP-11, as archaic as that may sound in this day and age.

For devices that have both block and character identities, the character device name is usually prefaced with the letter **r** for "raw" (e.g., **/dev/da0** vs. **/dev/rda0**). An alternative convention is to store character device files in a subdirectory that has a name that starts with **r** (e.g., **/dev/dsk/dks0d3s0** vs. **/dev/rdsk/dks0d3s0**). However, an **r** does not always imply a raw device file.

See Chapter 31 for more information about serial ports.

Serial device files are usually named **tty** followed by a sequence of letters that identify the interface the port is attached to. TTYs are sometimes represented by more than one device file; the extra files usually afford access to alternative flow control methods or locking protocols.

The names of tape devices often include not only a reference to the drive itself but also an indication of whether the device rewinds after the tape device is closed. Each vendor has a different scheme.

The naming conventions for the files that represent hard disks and SSDs are rather complex on most systems. See *Disk device files* on page 224 for details.

Custom kernels versus loadable modules

When the system is installed, it comes with a generic kernel that's designed to run most applications on most hardware. The generic kernel includes many different device drivers and option packages. Some drivers may also be dynamically inserted into the running kernel. On Linux, the udev system can also manage real-time device changes, such as the insertion of a USB device.

There are various schools of thought on whether production servers should have custom-built kernels. Although there is some potential for performance gains, especially in embedded systems without much memory, the manageability tradeoff for patching and system upgrades is usually a deal breaker. Unless there's a legitimate need to wring every last ounce of performance out of the system, we recommend using the vendor's stock kernel.

When it comes to kernel device support, the wise administrator is usually also the laziest. Use the dynamic module approach whenever possible. Avoid building a custom kernel unless it is strictly necessary. On Linux systems, most USB devices can be attached with no administrator intervention.

13.3 LINUX KERNEL CONFIGURATION

You can use any one of four basic methods to configure a Linux kernel. Chances are you'll have the opportunity to try all of them eventually. The methods are

- Modifying tunable (dynamic) kernel configuration parameters
- Building a kernel from scratch (really, this means compiling it from the source code, possibly with modifications and additions)
- Loading new drivers and modules into an existing kernel on the fly
- Providing operational directives at boot time through the kernel loader, GRUB. See page 82 for more information.

These methods are each applicable in slightly different situations. Modifying tunable parameters is the easiest and most common, whereas building a kernel from source files is the hardest and least often required. Fortunately, all these approaches become second nature with a little practice.

Tuning Linux kernel parameters

Many modules and drivers in the kernel were designed with the knowledge that one size doesn't fit all. To increase flexibility, special hooks allow parameters such as an internal table's size or the kernel's behavior in a particular circumstance to be adjusted on the fly by the system administrator. These hooks are accessible through an extensive kernel-to-userland interface represented by files in the **/proc** filesystem (aka procfs). In some cases, a large user-level application (especially an "infrastructure" application such as a database) may require a sysadmin to adjust kernel parameters to accommodate its needs.

You can view and set kernel options at run time through special files in **/proc/sys**. These files mimic standard Linux files, but they are really back doors into the kernel. If a file in **/proc/sys** contains a value you want to change, you can try writing to it. Unfortunately, not all files are writable (regardless of their apparent permissions), and not much documentation is available. If you have the kernel source tree installed, you may be able to read about some of the values and their meanings in the subdirectory **Documentation/syscnt**.

For example, to change the maximum number of files the system can have open at once, try something like

```
linux$ cat /proc/sys/fs/file-max
34916
linux$ sudo sh -c "echo 32768 > /proc/sys/fs/file-max"
```

Once you get used to this unorthodox interface, you'll find it quite useful. A word of caution, however: changes are not remembered across reboots.

Table 13.2 lists some commonly tuned parameters. Default values vary widely among distributions.

Table 13.2 Files in /proc/sys for some tunable kernel parameters

Dir[a]	File	Function and commentary
C	**autoeject**	Autoejects CD-ROM on dismount
F	**file-max**	Sets the maximum number of open files; on a system that handles a large number of files, try increasing this to 16384
F	**inode-max**	Sets the maximum number of open inodes per process; useful to tinker with if an app opens tens of thousands of file handles
K	**ctrl-alt-del**	Reboots on Ctrl-Alt-Delete sequence; may be a matter of personal preference or may increase security on unsecured consoles
K	**printk_ratelimit**	Minimum seconds between kernel messages
K	**printk_ratelimit_burst**	Sets the number of messages in succession before the **printk** rate limit is actually enforced
K	**shmmax**	Sets the maximum amount of shared memory
N	**conf/default/rp_filter**	Enables IP source route verification; this anti-spoofing mechanism makes the kernel drop packets received from "impossible" paths
N	**icmp_echo_ignore_all**	Ignores ICMP pings when set to 1
N	**icmp_echo_ignore_broadcasts**	Ignores broadcast pings when set to 1; almost always a good idea to set this to 1
N	**ip_forward**	Allows IP forwarding when set to 1; only set to 1 if you're using your Linux box as a router
N	**ip_local_port_range**	Specifies local port range allocated during connection setup; for servers that initiate many outbound connections, enlarge this to 1024–65000 for improved performance
N	**tcp_fin_timeout**	Specifies seconds to wait for a final FIN packet; set to a lower value (~20) on high-traffic servers to increase peformance
N	**tcp_syncookies**	Protects against SYN flood attacks; turn on if you suspect denial of service (DOS) attacks

a. F = **/proc/sys/fs**, N = **/proc/sys/net/ipv4**, K = **/proc/sys/kernel**, C = **/proc/sys/dev/cdrom**

A more permanent way to modify these same parameters is to use the **sysctl** command. **sysctl** can set individual variables either from the command line or by reading a list of *variable=value* pairs from a file. By default, **/etc/sysctl.conf** is read at boot time and its contents are used to set initial (custom) parameter values.

For example, the command

```
linux$ sudo sysctl net.ipv4.ip_forward=0
```

turns off IP forwarding. (Alternatively, you can just edit **/etc/sysctl.conf** manually.) You form the variable names used by **sysctl** by replacing the slashes in the **/proc/sys** directory structure with dots.

Building a Linux kernel

Because Linux evolves rapidly, it is likely that you'll eventually be faced with the need to build a Linux kernel. Kernel patches, device drivers, and new functionality continually arrive on the scene. This is really something of a mixed blessing. On one hand, it's convenient to always support the "latest and greatest," but on the other hand, it can become quite time consuming to keep up with the constant flow of new material.

It's less likely that you'll need to build a kernel on your own if you're running a "stable" version. Originally, Linux adopted a versioning scheme in which the second part of the version number indicated whether the kernel was stable (even numbers) or in development (odd numbers). For example, kernel version 2.6.6 would be a "stable" kernel, whereas 2.7.4 would be a "development" kernel. Today, this scheme isn't religiously followed, so you'd best check the home page at kernel.org for the official word on this issue. The kernel.org site is also the best source for Linux kernel source code if you aren't relying on a particular distribution (or vendor) to provide you with a kernel.

If it ain't broke, don't fix it

A good system administrator carefully weighs needs and risks when planning kernel upgrades and patches. Sure, the new release may be the latest and greatest, but is it as stable as the current version? Could the upgrade or patch be delayed and installed with another group of patches at the end of the month? It's important to resist the temptation to let "keeping up with the Joneses" (in this case, the kernel hacking community) dominate the best interests of your user community.

A good rule of thumb is to upgrade or apply patches only when the productivity gains you expect to obtain (usually measured in terms of reliability and performance) will exceed the effort and lost time required to perform the installation. If you're having trouble quantifying the specific gain, that's a good sign that the patch can wait for another day. (Of course, security-related patches should be installed promptly.)

Configuring kernel options

In this chapter we use *path_to_kernel_src* as a placeholder for whichever directory you choose for kernel source code. Most distributions install kernel source files in **/usr/src**. In all cases, you need to install the kernel source package before you can build a kernel on your system; see page 380 for tips on package installation.

The kernel configuration process revolves around the **.config** file at the root of the kernel source directory. All the kernel configuration information is specified in this file, but its format is somewhat cryptic. Use the decoding guide in

path_to_kernel_src/**Documentation/Configure.help**

to find out what the various options mean.

To save folks from having to edit the **.config** file directly, Linux has several **make** targets that let you configure the kernel with different interfaces. If you are running KDE, the prettiest configuration interface is provided by **make xconfig**. Likewise, if you're running GNOME, **make gconfig** is probably the best option. These commands bring up a graphical configuration screen on which you can pick the devices to add to your kernel (or compile as loadable modules).

If you are not running KDE or GNOME, you can use a terminal-based alternative invoked with **make menuconfig**. Finally, the older-style **make config** prompts you to respond to every single configuration option available without letting you later go back if you change your mind. We recommend **make xconfig** or **make gconfig** if your environment supports them; otherwise, use **make menuconfig**. Avoid **make config**, the least flexible and most painful text-based **make** target.

If you're migrating an existing kernel configuration to a new kernel version (or tree), you can use the **make oldconfig** target to read in the previous config file and to ask only the questions that are new.

These tools are straightforward as far as the options you can turn on, but unfortunately they are painful to use if you want to maintain several versions of the kernel for multiple architectures or hardware configurations.

The various configuration interfaces described above all generate a **.config** file that looks something like this:

```
# Automatically generated make config: don't edit
# Code maturity level options

CONFIG_EXPERIMENTAL=y

# Processor type and features

# CONFIG_M386 is not set
# CONFIG_M486 is not set
# CONFIG_M586 is not set
# CONFIG_M586TSC is not set
CONFIG_M686=y
CONFIG_X86_WP_WORKS_OK=y
CONFIG_X86_INVLPG=y
CONFIG_X86_BSWAP=y
CONFIG_X86_POPAD_OK=y
CONFIG_X86_TSC=y
CONFIG_X86_GOOD_APIC=y
...
```

As you can see, the contents are cryptic and do not describe what the CONFIG tags mean. Each CONFIG line refers to a specific kernel configuration option. The value y compiles the option into the kernel; the value m enables the option as a loadable module.

Some things can be configured as modules and some can't. You just have to know which is which; it's not clear from the **.config** file. Nor are the CONFIG tags easily mapped to meaningful information.

Building the kernel binary

Setting up an appropriate **.config** file is the most important part of the Linux kernel configuration process, but you must jump through several more hoops to turn that file into a finished kernel.

Here's an outline of the entire process:

- Change directory (**cd**) to the top level of the kernel source directory.
- Run **make xconfig**, **make gconfig**, or **make menuconfig**.
- Run **make dep** (not required for kernels 2.6.x and later).
- Run **make clean**.
- Run **make**.
- Run **make modules_install**.
- Copy **arch/i386/boot/bzImage** to **/boot/vmlinuz**.
- Copy **arch/i386/boot/System.map** to **/boot/System.map**.
- Add a configuration line for the new kernel to **/boot/grub/grub.conf**.

The **make clean** step is not always strictly necessary, but it is generally a good idea to start with a clean build environment. In practice, many problems can be traced back to this step having been skipped.

Adding a Linux device driver

On Linux systems, device drivers are typically distributed in one of three forms:

- A patch against a specific kernel version
- A loadable module
- An installation script or package that installs the driver

The most common form is the installation script or package. If you're lucky enough to have one of these for your new device, you should be able to follow the standard procedure for installing new software.

In situations where you have a patch against a specific kernel version, you can in most cases install the patch with the following procedure:

```
linux# cd path_to_kernel_src ; patch -p1 < patch_file
```

If neither of these cases applies, you are likely in a situation in which you must manually integrate the new device driver into the kernel source tree. In the following pages, we demonstrate how to manually add a hypothetical network "snarf" driver to the kernel. Linux actually makes this a rather tedious process, especially when compared to some other versions of UNIX.

Within the **drivers** subdirectory of the kernel source tree, find the subdirectory that corresponds to the type of device you are dealing with. A directory listing of **drivers** looks like this:

```
linux$ ls -F path_to_kernel_src/drivers
acorn/      char/     i2c/        Makefile  net/      s390/    telephony/
acpi/       dio/      ide/        md/       nubus/    sbus/    usb/
atm/        fc4/      ieee1394/   media/    parport/  scsi/    video/
block/      gsc/      input/      message/  pci/      sgi/     zorro/
bluetooth/  hil/      isdn/       misc/     pcmcia/   sound/
cdrom/      hotplug/  macintosh/  mtd/      pnp/      tc/
```

The most common directories to which drivers are added are **block**, **char**, **net**, **scsi**, **sound**, and **usb**. These directories contain drivers for block devices (such as IDE disk drives), character devices (such as serial ports), network devices, SCSI cards, sound cards, and USB devices, respectively. Some of the other directories contain drivers for the buses themselves (e.g., **pci**, **nubus**, and **zorro**); it's unlikely that you will need to add drivers to these directories. Some directories contain platform-specific drivers, such as **macintosh**, **s390**, and **acorn**.

Since our example device is a network-related device, we add the driver to the directory **drivers/net**. We modify the following files:

- **drivers/net/Makefile** so that our driver will be compiled
- **drivers/net/Kconfig** so that our device will appear in the config options

After putting the **.c** and **.h** files for the driver in **drivers/net/snarf**, we add the driver to **drivers/net/Makefile**. The line we add (near the end of the file) is

```
obj-$(CONFIG_SNARF_DEV) += snarf/
```

This configuration adds the snarf driver (stored in the **snarf/** directory) to the build process.

After adding the device to the **Makefile**, we have to make sure we can configure the device when we configure the kernel. All network devices must be listed in the file **drivers/net/Kconfig**. To add the device so that it can be built either as a module or as part of the kernel (consistent with what we claimed in the **Makefile**), we add the following line:

```
config SNARF_DEV
tristate 'Snarf device support'
```

The first token after config is the configuration macro, which must match the token following CONFIG_ in the **Makefile**. The tristate keyword means that we can build the device as a module. If the device cannot be built as a module, we would use the keyword bool instead of tristate. The next token is the string to display on the configuration screen. It can be any arbitrary text, but it should identify the device that is being configured.

Having managed to link a new device driver into the kernel, how do you tell the kernel it needs to use the new driver? In kernel versions before 2.6, this was a tedious task that required programming knowledge. As part of the recent architectural changes made to the device driver model, there is now a standard way for drivers to associate themselves with the kernel.

It's beyond the scope of this chapter to explain how that happens in detail, but the result is that device drivers written for version 2.6 (and later) register themselves with the macro MODULE_DEVICE_TABLE. This macro makes the appropriate behind-the-scenes connections so that other utilities such as **modprobe** (discussed in the *Loadable kernel modules* section starting on page 434) can enable new devices in the kernel.

13.4 Solaris Kernel Configuration

At boot time, the Solaris kernel probes for devices and initializes a driver for each device it finds. It makes extensive use of loadable modules and loads code only for the devices that are actually present, unless forced to do otherwise.

Depending on your point of view, this automatic configuration makes configuring a custom kernel more or less of a necessity under Solaris than on other systems. In an ideal world, the kernel would correctly identify its hardware environment 100% of the time. Unfortunately, flaky, nonstandard, or just plain buggy hardware (or drivers) can occasionally turn this creature comfort into a torment.

That said, let's look at how to custom-configure a Solaris kernel, should you ever need to do so.

The Solaris kernel area

To make on-demand module loading work correctly, Solaris relies heavily on a particular directory organization. Solaris expects to find certain directories in certain places, and these directories must contain specific types of modules:

- **/kernel** – modules common to machines that share an instruction set
- **/platform/***platform-name***/kernel** – modules specific to one type of machine, such as a Sun Fire T200
- **/platform/***hardware-class-name***/kernel** – modules specific to one class of hardware; for example, all sun4u machines
- **/usr/kernel** – similar to **/kernel**

You can determine your *platform-name* and *hardware-class-name* with **uname -i** and **uname -m**, respectively.

Drivers/Kernel

Here's an example:

```
solaris$ uname -i
SUNW,Sun-Fire-T200
solaris$ uname -m
sun4v
```

When Solaris boots, it searches the path

/platform/*platform-name***/kernel:/kernel:/usr/kernel**

in an attempt to find a kernel. It first looks for files named **unix**, and then it looks for files named **genunix**. **genunix** is a generic kernel that represents the platform-independent portion of the base kernel.

Each of the directories listed above can contain several standard subdirectories, listed in Table 13.3. Since the subdirectories can exist within any of the kernel directories, we use the generic name **KERNEL** to symbolize any and all kernel directories.

Table 13.3 Subdirectories of Solaris kernel directories

Subdir	What it contains
drv	Loadable object files for device drivers Configuration files that list probe addresses for each device
misc	Loadable object files for miscellaneous kernel routines
cpu	CPU-specific module for UltraSPARC
strmod	STREAMS modules
sparcv9	The 64-bit kernel
fs	Filesystem-related kernel modules
exec	Modules for decoding executable file formats
sched	Operating system schedulers
sys	Loadable system calls
genunix	Generic platform-independent kernel
unix	The base platform-specific kernel

You should not normally have to change any files in these directories unless you install a new device driver. The one exception to this rule may be the **.conf** files in the **KERNEL/drv** directory, which specify device-specific configuration parameters. It's rarely necessary to change them, however, and you should really only do it if a device's manufacturer tells you to.

Configuring the kernel with /etc/system

Solaris's **/etc/system** file serves as the master configuration file for the kernel. Table 13.4 shows the directives and variables that can appear in this file. Directives are keywords in their own right; variables must be assigned a value with the `set` directive.

Table 13.4 Directives and variables used in /etc/system

Name	Type[a]	Meaning
rootfs	D	Specifies the filesystem type of the root partition
rootdev	D	Specifies the location of the root partition
forceload	D	Specifies drivers ("modules") that should be loaded
exclude	D	Specifies modules that should *not* be loaded
moddir	D	Specifies a new path to modules
set	D	Sets kernel tuning variables (such as maxusers)
maxusers	V	Controls table sizes and various other parameters
pt_cnt	V	Sets the number of available PTYs
max_nproc	V	Sets the maximum number of processes
maxuprc	V	Sets the maximum number of user processes

a. D = directive, V = variable

/etc/system is consulted at boot time and can be so badly mutilated that the system no longer boots. **boot -a** lets you specify a backup copy of **/etc/system** if you made one. (If you don't have a backup copy and your existing one doesn't work, you can use **/dev/null**.)

Let's look at a sample **/etc/system** file for a simple kernel.

```
rootfs:ufs
rootdev:/sbus@1,f8000000/esp@0,800000/sd@3,0:a
```

These lines specify that the root filesystem will be of type UFS (UNIX File System) and that it will reside on the sd3a disk partition. The syntax used to specify the root device is identical to that used by Sun's **openprom** monitor. It varies from platform to platform, so consult your hardware manual or follow the symlinks in **/dev** that map the weird names to sensible ones. An **ls -l** after the link has been followed will show the exact long name.

```
moddir: /platform/SUNW,Sun-Fire-T200/kernel:/platform/sun4v/kernel:/kernel:
    /usr/kernel
```

This line (which has been wrapped to fit the page) specifies the search path for loadable modules. This value is suggested by the **kernel** man page; however, it is not the default, so you must specify it explicitly.

```
exclude: lofs
forceload: drv/sd
```

The first line excludes the loopback filesystem from the kernel, and the second forces the generic SCSI driver (sd) to be loaded.

```
set maxusers=64
```

This line sizes the kernel's tables appropriately for 64 simultaneous logins.

Adding a Solaris device driver

Solaris drivers are usually distributed as packages. Use **pkgadd** to add the device driver to the system. When drivers are not distributed as a package or when package addition fails, it's trivial to add the drivers by hand because they are all implemented as loadable kernel modules.

Solaris drivers are almost always distributed as object files, not as source code as is common on Linux systems. In this example, we add the device "snarf" to Solaris. The snarf driver should come with at least two files, including **snarf.o** (the actual driver) and **snarf.conf** (a configuration file). Both files should go into the directory **/platform/'uname -m'/kernel/drv**.

Once the **.conf** file has been copied over, you can edit it to specify particular device parameters. You should not normally need to do this, but sometimes configuration options are available for fine-tuning the device for your application.

After the files have been copied into place, you need to load the module with the **add_drv** command. (More on loadable kernel modules later in this chapter.) In this case, we load snarf into the kernel by running the command **add_drv snarf**. That's it! This is definitely the least painful of our examples.

Debugging a Solaris configuration

Since Solaris makes up its view of the world on the fly, debugging a troubled machine can be frustrating. Fortunately, Solaris provides several tools that display the machine's current configuration.

The **prtconf** command prints the machine's general configuration, including its machine type, model number, amount of memory, and some information about the configured hardware devices. Lines that describe devices (drivers, really) are indented to show the dependencies among them. The handy **prtconf -D** option shows the name of the driver for each device.

In the following snippet of **prtconf** output, several lines state "driver not attached." This message can have multiple meanings: there is no driver for a device, the device is configured but not attached to the system, or the device is unused and no driver has been loaded.

```
solaris$ sudo prtconf
System Configuration:  Sun Microsystems  i86pc
Memory size: 580 Megabytes
System Peripherals (Software Nodes):

i86pc
    scsi_vhci, instance #0
    isa, instance #0
      i8042, instance #0
        keyboard, instance #0
        mouse, instance #0
      lp, instance #0 (driver not attached)
```

```
        asy, instance #0 (driver not attached)
        asy, instance #1 (driver not attached)
        fdc, instance #0
          fd, instance #0 (driver not attached)
        pit_beep, instance #0
```

The **prtconf -D** display shows which drivers to load in **/etc/system**.

```
solaris$ sudo prtconf -D
System Configuration: Sun Microsystems i86pc
Memory size: 580 Megabytes
System Peripherals (Software Nodes):

i86pc (driver name: rootnex)
    scsi_vhci, instance #0 (driver name: scsi_vhci)
    isa, instance #0 (driver name: isa)
      i8042, instance #0 (driver name: i8042)
        keyboard, instance #0 (driver name: kb8042)
        mouse, instance #0 (driver name: mouse8042)
      lp, instance #0 (driver name: ecpp)
      asy, instance #0 (driver name: asy)
      asy, instance #1 (driver name: asy)
      fdc, instance #0 (driver name: fdc)
        fd, instance #0 (driver name: fd)
      pit_beep, instance #0 (driver name: pit_beep)
```

sysdef is **prtconf** on steroids. In addition to the information given by **prtconf**, it also lists pseudo-device drivers, tunable kernel parameters, and the filenames of loaded modules. If you modify the default kernel for an important machine, consider including the output of **sysdef** in your documentation for the machine.

The **modinfo** command reports information about dynamically loaded modules. Solaris dynamically loads device drivers, STREAMS modules, and filesystem drivers, among other things. Don't be surprised if **modinfo**'s output contains more than 200 entries. See page 435 for more information about **modinfo**.

13.5 HP-UX KERNEL CONFIGURATION

HP-UX's kernel is the most monolithic among our example operating systems, and it prefers to load most modules statically. It also has a complex and confusing configuration file. Fortunately, HP provides a handy configuration tool known as **kcweb**, which runs as a GUI if X Windows and a browser are available, or on the command line otherwise. To force command-line operation, use **kcweb -t**.

HP-UX reads kernel configuration parameters (such as modules and tunable values) from the **/stand/system** file. This file is maintained by **kcweb** and other tools, and administrators should not modify it directly.

Modules and configuration options can be static or dynamic. A static value or module is one that requires a kernel rebuild and a reboot to change or install.

Dynamic modules are loaded and unloaded as they are used, without requiring a reboot. Likewise, dynamically tunable values take effect immediately.

Table 13.5 lists a few of the more useful tunable properties of the HP-UX kernel.

Table 13.5 HP-UX kernel tunable configuration values (useful ones)

Variable	Type	Default	Meaning
maxfiles_lim	Dynamic	4096	Hard limit on open files per process
maxfiles	Static	2048	Soft limit on open files per process
maxuprc	Dynamic	256	Maximum number of user processes
nproc	Dynamic	4200	Maximum number of processes
nflocks	Dynamic	4096	Maximum number of file locks
ninode	Static	8192	Maximum number of open inodes
npty	Static	60	Maximum number of PTYs
nstrtel	Static	60	Maximum number of **telnet** session devices
nkthread	Dynamic	8416	Maximum number of kernel threads

If you request changes to static modules or static tunable values, **kcweb** automatically runs the **mk_kernel** command to build a new kernel. The new kernel takes effect at the next system reboot.

13.6 Management of the AIX kernel

The AIX kernel never requires a rebuild. New devices are configured dynamically through IBM's mysterious black box known as the Object Data Manager (ODM).

It's an enigmatic setup. Many parameters that are commonly tunable on other kernels, such as shared memory settings, cannot be tuned at all on AIX. Instead, they are managed independently by the kernel. Other configurable options are managed through a series of six tuning commands.

The Object Data Manager

Rather than keeping device configuration information in text files or scripts, AIX squirrels it away in the Object Data Manager (ODM) attribute/value database. Another layer of glue associates these property lists with specific devices (driver instances, really) and binds the drivers to the configuration information.

AIX's intent is to support persistence for device configuration. Rather than having one way to configure devices on the fly (e.g., **ifconfig** or **ndd**) and a parallel system of configuration files and scripts that do configuration at boot time, AIX's scheme attempts to unify these functions so that most device changes are automatically sticky across reboots.

However, if you take the red pill and look at what's actually going on within the system, the underlying complexity can be daunting. The system has more entry points than traditional UNIX, and the interactions among the components aren't always obvious. Here's an outline of the various layers:

- The Object Data Manager is a configuration repository that's analogous to the registry in Microsoft Windows. It's actually a bit more sophisticated than the Windows registry in that it has the concept of object schemas and instances rather than just arbitrary property lists.
- Programs access ODM through library routines, but you can also work with the ODM database through the **odmadd**, **odmcreate**, **odmdrop**, **odmshow**, **odmget**, **odmchange**, and **odmdelete** commands.[2]
- The command family **chdev**, **lsdev**, **lsattr**, **mkdev**, **rmdev**, **lsconn**, and **lsparent** maps ODM configuration information to specific devices. AIX's **chdev** is actually quite similar to the Solaris and HP-UX **ndd** command (see page 498), but by default **chdev** writes your changes both to the active driver and to the ODM configuration database. Even common parameters such as the system hostname and the details of static routes are stored as device attributes (the device in this case being an instance of the "inet" driver).
- Several administration utilities provide front ends to the **chdev** family. For example, **mktcpip** is sort of like a persistent **ifconfig** that converts its arguments into a series of **chdev** calls on network interfaces, affecting both the active and saved configurations. (Would you guess that its syntax mirrors that of **ifconfig**? You guessed wrong.)
- ODM is a user-level facility, so drivers don't access it directly. Just as with traditional text-file configuration, some software must read the ODM configurations at boot time and poke the appropriate values into the running drivers.

Fortunately, most administrators need not touch the complexities of ODM thanks to SMIT and to higher-level tools such as **mktcpip**.

One indispensable utility for managing AIX devices is the **cfgmgr** command. Run it as root with no arguments after adding new hardware to the system; the new hardware will miraculously be recognized and become available for use. Well, usually. If the device drivers haven't already been loaded into the ODM database, **cfgmgr** will helpfully suggest a package for you to install from the AIX installation media. See the **cfgmgr** man page for further details.

2. Dan Foster, one of our technical reviewers, commented, "Direct manipulation of the ODM with the **odm*** tools is *not* recommended if you don't know exactly what you're doing. These commands do no error checking on the data you modify, whereas the normal **ch*/mk*/rm*** tools validate data prior to making changes. The **odm*** tools are like a loaded AK-47 with no safety mechanism: one quick touch, and you've discharged several rounds into an eviscerated target."

Kernel tuning

AIX has six categories of tunable values and supplies six corresponding commands for tweaking them. Most of the values relate to performance optimization. Table 13.6 captures each command and its purpose. Breaking from standard AIX convention, the commands share a common syntax. The parameters can also be managed through the SMIT interface with the incantation **smit tuning.** See the man page for each command for detailed information.

Table 13.6 Commands for setting tunable kernel parameters in AIX

Command	Domain	Examples of things you can configure
vmo	Virtual memory	Minimum number of free pages
ioo	Input/Output	Asynchronous I/O behavior JFS2 configuration
schedo	Process scheduling	Process time slices and priorities Virtual process management
no	Network	IP forwarding TCP and UDP socket buffer sizes Packet time-to-live values
nfso	NFS	UTF-8 support Delegation support Maximum number of NFS connections
raso	Reliability	Only a few tunables, none of which are particularly valuable to administrators

The commands are simple to use. To enable IP forwarding, for example, run

```
aix$ sudo no -o ipforwarding=1
```

To list all available tunables for the I/O subsystem, type

```
aix$ sudo ioo -a
```

You can add the **-r** flag to any of the commands to ensure that your changes persist after a reboot.

13.7 Loadable kernel modules

Loadable kernel modules (LKMs) are now common to nearly all flavors of UNIX. Each of our example systems implements some form of dynamic loading facility, although the exact implementations vary.

Loadable kernel module support allows a device driver—or any other kernel service—to be linked into and removed from the kernel while it is running. This facility makes the installation of drivers much easier since the kernel binary does not need to be changed. It also allows the kernel to be smaller because drivers are not loaded unless they are needed.

Although loadable drivers are convenient, they are not 100% safe. Any time you load or unload a module, you risk causing a kernel panic. So don't try out an untested module when you are not willing to crash the machine.

Like other aspects of device and driver management, the implementation of loadable modules is OS dependent. The sections below outline the commands and caveats appropriate for Solaris and Linux, which support more devices and allow more administrator configuration than do our other example systems.

Loadable kernel modules in Linux

Linux is both more and less sophisticated than Solaris in its handling of loadable kernel modules, at least from the system administrator's point of view. Under Linux, almost anything can be built as a loadable kernel module. The exceptions are the root filesystem type, the device on which the root filesystem resides, and the PS/2 mouse driver.

Loadable kernel modules are conventionally stored under **/lib/modules/***version*, where *version* is the version of your Linux kernel as returned by **uname -r**. You can inspect the currently loaded modules with the **lsmod** command:

```
redhat$ sudo /sbin/lsmod
Module                  Size  Used by
ipmi_devintf           13064  2
ipmi_si                36648  1
ipmi_msghandler        31848  2 ipmi_devintf,ipmi_si
iptable_filter          6721  0
ip_tables              21441  1 iptable_filter
...
```

Loaded on this machine are the Intelligent Platform Management Interface modules and the **iptables** firewall.

As an example of manually loading a kernel module, here's how we would insert the snarf module that we set up in the previous section:

```
redhat$ sudo insmod /path/to/snarf.ko
```

We can also pass parameters to loadable kernel modules; for example,

```
redhat$ sudo insmod /path/to/snarf.ko io=0xXXX irq=X
```

Once a loadable kernel module has been manually inserted into the kernel, it can only be removed if you explicitly request its removal or if the system is rebooted. We could use **rmmod snarf** to remove our snarf module.

You can use **rmmod** at any time, but it works only if the number of current references to the module (listed in the Used by column of **lsmod**'s output) is 0.

You can also load Linux LKMs semiautomatically with **modprobe**, a wrapper for **insmod** that understands dependencies, options, and installation and removal procedures. **modprobe** uses the **/etc/modprobe.conf** file to figure out how to handle each individual module.

You can dynamically generate an **/etc/modprobe.conf** file that corresponds to all your currently installed modules by running **modprobe -c**. This command generates a long file that looks like this:

```
#This file was generated by: modprobe -c
path[pcmcia]=/lib/modules/preferred
path[pcmcia]=/lib/modules/default
path[pcmcia]=/lib/modules/2.6.6
path[misc]=/lib/modules/2.6.6
...
# Aliases
alias block-major-1 rd
alias block-major-2 floppy
...
alias char-major-4 serial
alias char-major-5 serial
alias char-major-6 lp
...
alias dos msdos
alias plip0 plip
alias ppp0 ppp
options ne io=x0340 irq=9
```

The path statements tell where a particular module can be found. You can modify or add entries of this type if you want to keep your modules in a nonstandard location.

The alias statement maps between block major device numbers, character major device numbers, filesystems, network devices, and network protocols and their corresponding module names.

The options lines are not dynamically generated but rather must be manually added by an administrator. They specify options that should be passed to a module when it is loaded. For example, we could use the following line to tell the snarf module its proper I/O address and interrupt vector:[3]

```
options snarf io=0xXXX irq=X
```

modprobe also understands the statements install and remove. These statements allow commands to be executed when a specific module is inserted into or removed from the running kernel.

Loadable kernel modules in Solaris

In Solaris, virtually everything is a loadable module. The **modinfo** command lists the modules that are currently loaded.

3. If you're using really oddball PC hardware, it can be a challenge to create a configuration in which device interrupt request vectors (IRQs) and I/O ports do not overlap. You can view the current assignments on your system by examining the contents of **/proc/interrupts** and **/proc/ioports**, respectively. The overlap isn't typically an issue with current mainstream PC hardware.

The output looks like this:

```
solaris$ modinfo
Id  Loadaddr  Size   Info  Rev  ModuleName
 1  ff07e000  3ba0   1     1    specfs (filesystem for specfs)
 2  ff086000  1340   -     1    swapgeneric (root/swap config)
 3  ff082000  1a56   1     1    TS (time sharing sched class)
 4  ff084000  49c    -     1    TS_DPTBL (Timesharing dispatch)
 5  ff095000  15248  2     1    ufs (filesystem for ufs)
 6  ff0b8000  20e0   1     1    rootnex (sun4c root nexus)
 7  ff084a00  170    57    1    options (options driver)
 8  ff08dc00  2f4    62    1    dma (Direct Memory Access)
 9  ff08c000  968    59    1    sbus (SBus nexus driver)
...
```

On our Solaris system, the list continued for 80-odd lines. Many elements that are hardwired into the kernel on other versions of UNIX (such as UFS, the local filesystem) are loadable drivers in Solaris. This organization should make it much easier for third parties to write packages that integrate easily and seamlessly into the kernel, at least in theory.

As described in *Linux kernel configuration* earlier in this chapter, you can add a driver with the **add_drv** command. This command loads the driver into the kernel and makes the appropriate device links (all links are rebuilt each time the kernel boots). Once you **add_drv** a driver, it remains a part of the system until you actively remove it. You can unload drivers by hand with **rem_drv**.

Whenever you add a driver by running **add_drv**, it is a good idea to also run **drvconfig**. This command reconfigures the **/devices** directory and adds any files that are appropriate for the newly loaded driver.

Loadable modules that are not accessed through device files can be loaded and unloaded with **modload** and **modunload**.

13.8 Linux udev for fun and profit

Device files have been a tricky problem for many years. When systems supported only a few types of devices, manual maintenance of device files was manageable. As the number of available devices has grown, however, the **/dev** filesystem has become cluttered, often with files irrelevant to the current system. Red Hat Enterprise Linux version 3 included more than 18,000 device files, one for every possible device that could be attached to the system! The creation of static device files quickly became a crushing problem and an evolutionary dead end.

USB, FireWire, PCMCIA, and other device interfaces introduce additional wrinkles. For example, if a user connects two external hard drives, it would be convenient for the system to recognize and automount each drive with a persistent device name. Ideally, a drive that is initially recognized as **/dev/sda** would remain available as **/dev/sda** despite intermittent disconnections and regardless of the activity of other devices and buses. The presence of dynamic devices such as cameras, printers, scanners, and other types of removable media clouds the water and makes the persistent identity problem even worse.

Udev is an elegant solution to these issues. It is a device management system implemented in user space (rather than inside the kernel) that informs end-user applications about devices as they are attached and removed. Udev relies on sysfs, described below, to learn what's going on with the system's devices, and it uses a series of udev-specific rules to understand appropriate naming conventions. Udev maintains device files in **/dev** automatically and with minimal disruption. Only devices that are currently available to the system have files in **/dev**.

Linux administrators should understand how udev's rule system works and should know how to use the **udevadm** command. Before peering into those details, however, let's first review the underlying technology of sysfs.

Linux sysfs: a window into the souls of devices

Sysfs was added to the Linux kernel at version 2.6. It is a virtual, in-memory filesystem that provides detailed and well-organized information about the system's available devices, their configurations, and their state. Sysfs device information is accessible both from within the kernel and from user space.

You can explore the **/sys** directory, where sysfs is typically mounted, to find out everything from what IRQ a device is using to how many blocks have been queued for writing on a disk controller. One of the guiding principles of sysfs is that each file in **/sys** should represent only one attribute of the underlying device. This convention imposes a certain amount of structure on an otherwise chaotic data set.

Table 13.7 shows the directories in the **/sys** root directory, each of which is a subsystem that is registered with sysfs. These directories vary slightly by distribution.

Table 13.7 Subdirectories of /sys

Directory	Description
block	Information about block devices such as hard disks
bus	Buses known to the kernel: PCI-E, SCSI, USB, and others
class	A tree organized by functional types of devices, e.g., sound and graphic cards, input devices, and network interfaces
dev	Device information split between character and block devices
devices	An ancestrally correct representation of all discovered devices
firmware	Interfaces to platform-specific subsystems such as ACPI
fs	A directory for some, but not all, filesystems known to the kernel
kernel	Kernel internals such as cache and virtual memory status
module	Dynamic modules loaded by the kernel
power	A few details about the system's power state; mostly unused

Originally, if information about device configuration was available at all, it was found in the **/proc** filesystem. Although **/proc** continues to hold run-time information about processes and the kernel, we anticipate that all device-specific information will move to **/sys** over time.

Exploring devices with udevadm

The **udevadm** command queries device information, triggers events, controls the **udevd** daemon, and monitors udev and kernel events. Its primary use for administrators is to build and test rules, which are covered in the next section.

udevadm expects one of six commands as its first argument: **info**, **trigger**, **settle**, **control**, **monitor**, or **test**. Of particular interest to system administrators are **info**, which prints device-specific information, and **control**, which starts and stops udev or forces it to reload its rules files. The **monitor** command displays events as they occur.

The following command shows all udev attributes for the device sdb. The output is truncated here, but in reality it goes on to list all parent devices—such as the USB bus—that are ancestors of sdb in the device tree.

```
linux$ udevadm info -a -n sdb
...
looking at device '/devices/pci0000:00/0000:00:11.0/0000:02:03.0/usb1/1-1/1-1:
    1.0/host6/target6:0:0/6:0:0:0/block/sdb':
  KERNEL=="sdb"
  SUBSYSTEM=="block"
  DRIVER==""
  ATTR{range}=="16"
  ATTR{ext_range}=="256"
  ATTR{removable}=="1"
  ATTR{ro}=="0"
  ATTR{size}=="1974271"
  ATTR{capability}=="53"
  ATTR{stat}=="      71      986     1561      860        1        0        1
    12        0      592      872"
...
```

All paths in **udevadm** output, such as **/devices/pci0000:00/...**, are relative to **/sys**.

The output is formatted so that you can feed it back to udev when constructing rules. For example, if the ATTR{size}=="1974271" clause were unique to this device, you could copy that snippet into a rule as the identifying criteria.

Refer to the man page on **udevadm** for additional options and syntax.

Constructing rules and persistent names

Udev relies on a set of rules to guide its management and naming of devices. The default rules reside in the **/lib/udev/rules.d** directory, but local rules belong in **/etc/udev/rules.d**. There is no need to edit or delete the default rules—you can ignore or override a file of default rules by creating a new file with the same name in the custom rules directory.

The master configuration file for udev is **/etc/udev/udev.conf**; however, the default behaviors are reasonable. The **udev.conf** files on our example distributions contain only comments, with the exception of one line that enables error logging.

Sadly, because of political bickering among distributors and developers, there is little rule synergy among distributions. Many of the filenames in the default rules directory are the same from distribution to distribution, but the contents of the files differ significantly.

Rule files are named according to the pattern *nn-description*.**rules**, where *nn* is usually a two-digit number. Files are processed in lexical order, so lower numbers are processed first. Files from the two rules directories are combined before the udev daemon, **udevd**, parses them. The **.rules** suffix is mandatory; files without it are ignored.

Rules are of the form

```
match_clause, [match_clause, ...] assignment_clause [,assignment_clause ...]
```

The *match_clauses* define the situations in which the rule is to be applied. Each match clause consists of a key, an operator, and a value. For example, the clause ATTR{size}=="1974271" was referred to above as a potential component of a rule; it selects all devices whose size attribute is exactly 1,974,271.

Most match keys refer to device properties (which **udevd** obtains from the **/sys** filesystem), but some refer to other context-dependent attributes, such as the operation being handled (e.g., device addition or removal). All match clauses must match in order for a rule to be activated.

Table 13.8 shows the match keys understood by udev.

Table 13.8 Udev match keys

Match key	Function
ACTION	Matches the event type, e.g., add or remove
DEVPATH	Matches a specific device path
KERNEL[a]	Matches the kernel's name for the device
SUBSYSTEM[a]	Matches a specific subsystem
DRIVER[a]	Matches the driver used by a device
ATTR{*filename*}[a]	Matches a device's sysfs values; the *filename* is a leaf in the sysfs tree that corresponds to a specific attribute
ENV{*key*}	Matches the value of an environment variable
TEST{*omask*}	Tests whether a file exists; the *omask* is optional
PROGRAM	Runs an external command; matches if the return code is 0
RESULT	Matches the output of the last call through PROGRAM

a. A plural version is also available. It searches up the device path to match the value.

For matching rules, the *assignment_clauses* specify the actions **udevd** should take to handle the event. Their format is similar to that for match clauses.

The most important assignment key is NAME, which indicates what udev should name the device. The optional SYMLINK assignment key creates a symbolic link to the device through its desired path in **/dev**.

Let's put these components together with an example: a USB flash drive. Suppose that we want to make the drive's device name persist across insertions and that we want the drive to be mounted and unmounted automatically.

To start with, we insert the flash drive and check to see how the kernel identifies it. There are a couple of ways to do this. By running the **lsusb** command, we can inspect the USB bus directly:

```
ubuntu$ lsusb
Bus 001 Device 007: ID 1307:0163 Transcend, Inc. USB Flash Drive
Bus 001 Device 001: ID 1d6b:0002 Linux Foundation 2.0 root hub
Bus 002 Device 001: ID 1d6b:0001 Linux Foundation 1.1 root hub
```

Alternatively, we can check for log entries submitted to **/var/log/messages**. In our case, the attachment leaves an extensive audit trail:

```
Aug  9 19:50:03 ubuntu kernel: [42689.253554] scsi 8:0:0:0: Direct-Access
     Ut163    USB2FlashStorage 0.00 PQ: 0 ANSI: 2
Aug  9 19:50:03 ubuntu kernel: [42689.292226] sd 8:0:0:0: [sdb] 1974271 512-
     byte hardware sectors: (1.01 GB/963 MiB)
...
Aug  9 19:50:03 ubuntu kernel: [42689.304749] sd 8:0:0:0: [sdb] 1974271 512-
     byte hardware sectors: (1.01 GB/963 MiB)
Aug  9 19:50:03 ubuntu kernel: [42689.307182]  sdb: sdb1
Aug  9 19:50:03 ubuntu kernel: [42689.427785] sd 8:0:0:0: [sdb] Attached SCSI
     removable disk
Aug  9 19:50:03 ubuntu kernel: [42689.428405] sd 8:0:0:0: Attached scsi generic
     sg3 type 0
```

The log messages above indicate that the drive was recognized as sdb, which gives us an easy way to identify the device in **/sys**. We can now examine the **/sys** filesystem with **udevadm** in search of some rule snippets that are characteristic of the device and might be usable in udev rules.

```
ubuntu$ udevadm info -a -p /block/sdb/sdb1
looking at device '/devices/pci0000:00/0000:00:11.0/0000:02:03.0/usb1/1-1/1-1:
     1.0/host30/target30:0:0/30:0:0:0/block/sdb/sdb1':
       KERNEL=="sdb1"
       SUBSYSTEM=="block"
       DRIVER==""
       ATTR{partition}=="1"
       ATTR{start}=="63"
       ATTR{size}=="1974208"
       ATTR{stat}=="      71      792      1857      808       0       0       0
     0        0     512       808"
```

```
looking at parent device '/devices/pci0000:00/0000:00:11.0/0000:02:03.0/usb1/1-
   1/1-1:1.0/host30/target30:0:0/30:0:0:0/block/sdb':
      KERNELS=="sdb"
      SUBSYSTEMS=="block"
      DRIVERS==""
...
      ATTRS{scsi_level}=="3"
      ATTRS{vendor}=="Ut163    "
      ATTRS{model}=="USB2FlashStorage"
...
```

The output from **udevadm** show several opportunities for matching. One possibility is the size field, which is likely to be unique to this device. However, if the size of the partition were to change, the device would not be recognized. Instead, we can use a combination of two values: the kernel's naming convention of sd plus an additional letter, and the contents of the model attribute, USB2FlashStorage. For creating rules specific to this particular flash drive, another good choice would be the device's serial number (not displayed here).

We'll put our rules for this device in the file **/etc/udev/rules.d/10-local.rules**. Because we have multiple objectives in mind, we need a series of rules.

First, we take care of creating device symlinks in **/dev**. The following rule uses our knowledge of the ATTRS and KERNEL match keys, gleaned from **udevadm**, to identify the device:

```
ATTRS{model}=="USB2FlashStorage", KERNEL=="sd[a-z]1", SYMLINK+="ate-
    flash%n"
```

When the rule triggers, **udevd** sets up **/dev/ate-flash***N* as a symlink to the device. We don't really expect more than one of these devices to appear on the system. If more copies do appear, they receive unique names in **/dev**, but the exact names depend on the insertion order of the devices.

Next, we use the ACTION key to run some commands whenever the device appears on the USB bus. The RUN assignment key lets us create an appropriate mount point directory and mount the device there.

```
ACTION=="add", ATTRS{model}=="USB2FlashStorage", KERNEL=="sd[a-z]1",
    RUN+="/bin/mkdir -p /mnt/ate-flash%n"
ACTION=="add", ATTRS{model}=="USB2FlashStorage", KERNEL=="sd[a-z]1",
    PROGRAM=="/lib/udev/vol_id -t %N", RESULT=="vfat", RUN+="/bin/mount
    -t vfat /dev/%k /mnt/ate-flash%n"
```

The PROGRAM and RUN keys look similar, but PROGRAM is a match key that's active during the rule selection phase, whereas RUN is an assignment key that's part of the rule's actions once triggered. The second rule above verifies that the flash drive contains a Windows filesystem before mounting it with the **-t vfat** option to the **mount** command.

Similar rules clean up when the device is removed:

```
ACTION=="remove", ATTRS{model}=="USB2FlashStorage", KERNEL=="sd[a-z]1",
    RUN+="/bin/umount -l /mnt/ate-flash%n"
ACTION=="remove", ATTRS{model}=="USB2FlashStorage", KERNEL=="sd[a-z]1",
    RUN+="/bin/rmdir /mnt/ate-flash%n"
```

Now that our rules are in place, we must notify **udevd** of our changes. **udevadm**'s **control** command is one of the few that require root privileges.

```
ubuntu$ sudo udevadm control --reload-rules
```

Typos are silently ignored after a reload, even with the **--debug** flag, so be sure to double-check the rules' syntax.

That's it! Now when the flash drive is plugged into a USB port, **udevd** creates a symbolic link called **/dev/ate-flash1** and mounts the drive as **/mnt/ate-flash1**.

```
ubuntu$ ls -l /dev/ate*
lrwxrwxrwx 1 root root 4 2009-08-09 21:22 /dev/ate-flash1 -> sdb1

ubuntu$ mount | grep ate
/dev/sdb1 on /mnt/ate-flash1 type vfat (rw)
```

13.9 Recommended reading

Bovet, Daniel P., and Marco Cesati. *Understanding the Linux Kernel (3rd Edition)*. Sebastopol, CA: O'Reilly Media, 2006.

Corbet, Jonathan, et al. *Linux Device Drivers (3rd Edition)*. Sebastopol, CA: O'Reilly Media, 2005. This book is also available on-line at lwn.net/Kernel/LDD3.

Love, Robert. *Linux Kernel Development (2nd Edition)*. Indianapolis, IN: Novell Press, 2005.

McDougall, Richard, and Jim Mauro. *Solaris Internals: Solaris 10 and Open-Solaris Kernel Architecture (2nd Edition)*. Upper Saddle River, NJ: Prentice Hall PTR, 2006.

13.10 EXERCISES

E13.1 Describe what the kernel does. Explain the difference between loading a driver as a module and linking it statically into the kernel.

E13.2 A process on an HP-UX system crashed and reported a cryptic error: "Too many open files: file permissions deny server access." What might be the cause of this error? What change needs to occur to fix the underlying issue?

★ E13.3 Do AIX systems offer loadable kernel modules? How would a developer add support for a new filesystem or for new system calls to an AIX kernel? When might this functionality be needed?

★ E13.4 At a local flea market, you get a great deal on a laptop card that gives you Ethernet connectivity through a parallel port. What steps would you need to perform to make Linux recognize this new card? Should you compile support directly into the kernel or add it as a module? Why? (Bonus question: if your hourly consulting fee is $80, estimate the value of the labor needed to get this cheapie Ethernet interface working.)

★★ E13.5 In the lab, configure a Linux kernel with **xconfig** or **menuconfig** and build a kernel binary. Install and run the new system. Turn in **dmesg** output from the old and new kernels and highlight the differences. (Requires root access.)

SECTION TWO

NETWORKING

14 TCP/IP Networking

It would be hard to overstate the importance of networks to modern computing, although that doesn't seem to stop people from trying. At many sites—perhaps even the majority—web and email access are the primary uses of computers. As of 2010, internetworldstats.com estimates the Internet to have nearly 1.5 billion users, or more than 21% of the world's population. In North America, Internet penetration approaches 75%.

TCP/IP is the networking system that underlies the Internet. TCP/IP does not depend on any particular hardware or operating system, so devices that speak TCP/IP can all exchange data ("interoperate") despite their many differences.

TCP/IP works on networks of any size or topology, whether or not they are connected to the outside world. This chapter introduces the TCP/IP protocols in the political and technical context of the Internet, but stand-alone networks are quite similar at the TCP/IP level.

14.1 TCP/IP and its relationship to the Internet

TCP/IP and the Internet share a history that goes back several decades. The technical success of the Internet is due largely to the elegant and flexible design of

TCP/IP and to the fact that TCP/IP is an open and nonproprietary protocol suite. In turn, the leverage provided by the Internet has helped TCP/IP prevail over several competing protocol suites that were favored at one time or another for political or commercial reasons.

The progenitor of the modern Internet was a research network called ARPANET established in 1969 by the U.S. Department of Defense. By the end of the 1980s the network was no longer a research project and we transitioned to the commercial Internet. Today's Internet is a collection of private networks owned by Internet service providers (ISPs) that interconnect at many so-called peering points.

Who runs the Internet?

Oversight of the Internet and the Internet protocols has long been a cooperative and open effort, but its exact structure has changed as the Internet has evolved into a public utility and a driving force in the world economy. Current Internet governance is split roughly into administrative, technical, and political wings, but the boundaries between these functions are often vague. The major players are listed below:

- ICANN, the Internet Corporation for Assigned Names and Numbers: if any one group can be said to be in charge of the Internet, this is probably it. It's the only group with any sort of actual enforcement capability. ICANN controls the allocation of Internet addresses and domain names, along with various other snippets such as protocol port numbers. It is organized as a nonprofit corporation headquartered in California and operates under a memorandum of understanding with the U.S. Department of Commerce. (icann.org)
- ISOC, the Internet Society: ISOC is an open-membership organization that represents Internet users. Although it has educational and policy functions, it's best known as the umbrella organization for the technical development of the Internet. In particular, it is the parent organization of the Internet Engineering Task Force (ietf.org), which oversees most technical work. ISOC is an international nonprofit organization with offices in Washington, D.C. and Geneva. (isoc.org)
- IGF, the Internet Governance Forum: a relative newcomer, the IGF was created by the United Nations in 2005 to establish a home for international and policy-oriented discussions related to the Internet. It's currently structured as a yearly conference series, but its importance is likely to grow over time as governments attempt to exert more control over the operation of the Internet. (intgovforum.org)

Of these groups, ICANN has the toughest job: establishing itself as the authority in charge of the Internet, undoing the mistakes of the past, and foreseeing the future, all while keeping users, governments, and business interests happy.

Network standards and documentation

If your eyes haven't glazed over just from reading the title of this section, you've probably already had several cups of coffee. Nonetheless, accessing the Internet's authoritative technical documentation is a crucial skill for system administrators, and it's more entertaining than it sounds.

The technical activities of the Internet community are summarized in documents known as Requests for Comments or RFCs. Protocol standards, proposed changes, and informational bulletins all usually end up as RFCs. RFCs start their lives as Internet Drafts, and after lots of email wrangling and IETF meetings they either die or are promoted to the RFC series. Anyone who has comments on a draft or proposed RFC is encouraged to reply. In addition to standardizing the Internet protocols, the RFC mechanism sometimes just documents or explains aspects of existing practice.

RFCs are numbered sequentially; currently, there are about 5,600. RFCs also have descriptive titles (e.g., *Algorithms for Synchronizing Network Clocks*), but to forestall ambiguity they are usually cited by number. Once distributed, the contents of an RFC are never changed. Updates are distributed as new RFCs with their own reference numbers. Updates may either extend and clarify existing RFCs or supersede them entirely.

RFCs are available from numerous sources, but rfc-editor.org is dispatch central and will always have the most up-to-date information. Look up the status of an RFC at rfc-editor.org before investing the time to read it; it may no longer be the most current document on that subject.

The Internet standards process itself is detailed in RFC2026. Another useful meta-RFC is RFC5540, *40 Years of RFCs*, which describes some of the cultural and technical context of the RFC system.

Don't be scared away by the wealth of technical detail found in RFCs. Most contain introductions, summaries, and rationales that are useful for system administrators even when the technical details are not. Some RFCs are specifically written as overviews or general introductions. RFCs may not be the gentlest way to learn about a topic, but they are authoritative, concise, and free.

Not all RFCs are full of boring technical details. Here are some of our favorites on the lighter side (usually written on April 1st):

- RFC1149 – *Standard for Transmission of IP Datagrams on Avian Carriers*[1]
- RFC1925 – *The Twelve Networking Truths*
- RFC3251 – *Electricity over IP*
- RFC3514 – *The Security Flag in the IPv4 Header*
- RFC4041 – *Requirements for Morality Sections in Routing Area Drafts*

1. A group of Linux enthusiasts from BLUG, the Bergen (Norway) Linux User Group, actually implemented the Carrier Pigeon Internet Protocol (CPIP) as specified in RFC1149. For details, see the web site blug.linux.no/rfc1149.

In addition to being assigned its own serial number, an RFC can also be assigned an FYI (For Your Information) number, a BCP (Best Current Practice) number, or a STD (Standard) number. FYIs, STDs, and BCPs are subseries of the RFCs that include documents of special interest or importance.

FYIs are introductory or informational documents intended for a broad audience. They can be a good place to start research on an unfamiliar topic if you can find one that's relevant. Unfortunately, this series has languished recently and not many of the FYIs are up to date.

BCPs document recommended procedures for Internet sites; they consist of administrative suggestions and for system administrators are often the most valuable of the RFC subseries.

STDs document Internet protocols that have completed the IETF's review and testing process and have been formally adopted as standards.

RFCs, FYIs, BCPs, and STDs are numbered sequentially within their own series, so a document can bear several different identifying numbers. For example, RFC1713, *Tools for DNS Debugging*, is also known as FYI27.

14.2 Networking road map

Now that we've provided a bit of context, let's look at the TCP/IP protocols themselves. TCP/IP is a protocol "suite," a set of network protocols designed to work smoothly together. It includes several components, each defined by a standards-track RFC or series of RFCs:

- IP, the Internet Protocol, which routes data packets from one machine to another (RFC791)
- ICMP, the Internet Control Message Protocol, which provides several kinds of low-level support for IP, including error messages, routing assistance, and debugging help (RFC792)
- ARP, the Address Resolution Protocol, which translates IP addresses to hardware addresses (RFC826)[2]
- UDP, the User Datagram Protocol, which provides unverified, one-way data delivery (RFC768)
- TCP, the Transmission Control Protocol, which implements reliable, full duplex, flow-controlled, error-corrected conversations (RFC793)

These protocols are arranged in a hierarchy or "stack", with the higher-level protocols making use of the protocols beneath them. TCP/IP is conventionally described as a five-layer system (as shown in Exhibit A), but the actual TCP/IP protocols inhabit only three of these layers.

2. This is actually a little white lie. ARP is not really part of TCP/IP and can be used with other protocol suites. However, it's an integral part of the way TCP/IP works on most LAN media.

Exhibit A TCP/IP layering model

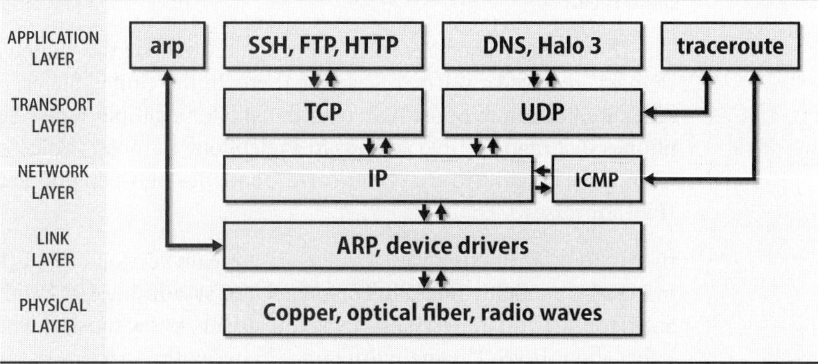

IPv4 and IPv6

The version of TCP/IP that has been in widespread use for three decades is protocol revision 4, aka IPv4. It uses four-byte IP addresses. A modernized version, IPv6, expands the IP address space to 16 bytes and incorporates several other lessons learned from the use of IPv4. It removes several features of IP that experience has shown to be of little value, making the protocol potentially faster and easier to implement. IPv6 also integrates security and authentication into the basic protocol.

All modern operating systems and many network devices already support IPv6. However, active use of IPv6 remains essentially zero in the real world.[3] Experience suggests that it's probably best for administrators to defer production use of IPv6 to the extent that this is possible. Everyone will eventually be forced to switch to IPv6, but as of 2010 that day is still years away. At the same time, the transition is not so far in the future that you can ignore it when purchasing new network devices. Insist on IPv6 compatibility for new acquisitions.

The development of IPv6 was to a large extent motivated by the concern that we are running out of 4-byte IPv4 address space. And indeed we are: projections indicate that the current IPv4 allocation system will collapse some time around 2011. (See ipv4.potaroo.net for a daily update.) Even so, mainstream adoption of IPv6 throughout the Internet is probably still not in the cards anytime soon.

More likely, another round of stopgap measures on the part of ISPs and ICANN (or more specifically, its subsidiary IANA, the Internet Assigned Numbers Authority) will extend the dominance of IPv4 for another few years. We expect to see wider use of IPv6 on the Internet backbone, but outside of large ISPs, academic sites involved in Internet research, and universal providers such as Google, our

3. A Google study presented at RIPE 57 in October 2008 indicated that overall IPv6 penetration (actual use, not capability) was 0.24%. No country had IPv6 penetration greater than 0.76%.

guess is that IPv6 will not be directly affecting most sysadmins' work in the immediate future.

The IPv4 address shortage is felt more acutely outside the United States, and so IPv6 has received a warmer welcome there. In the United States, it may take a killer application to boost IPv6 over the hill: for example, a new generation of cell phones that map an IPv6 address to a telephone number. (Voice-over-IP systems would also benefit from a closer correspondence between phone numbers and IPv6 addresses.)

In this book, we focus on IPv4 as the mainstream version of TCP/IP. IPv6-specific material is explicitly marked. Fortunately for sysadmins, IPv4 and IPv6 are highly analogous. If you understand IPv4, you already know most of what you need to know about IPv6. The main difference between the versions lies in their addressing schemes. In addition to longer addresses, IPv6 introduces a few additional addressing concepts and some new notation. But that's about it.

Packets and encapsulation

TCP/IP supports a variety of physical networks and transport systems, including Ethernet, token ring, MPLS (Multiprotocol Label Switching), wireless Ethernet, and serial-line-based systems. Hardware is managed within the link layer of the TCP/IP architecture, and higher-level protocols do not know or care about the specific hardware being used.

Data travels on a network in the form of *packets*, bursts of data with a maximum length imposed by the link layer. Each packet consists of a header and a payload. The header tells where the packet came from and where it's going. It can also include checksums, protocol-specific information, or other handling instructions. The payload is the data to be transferred.

The name of the primitive data unit depends on the layer of the protocol. At the link layer it is called a *frame*, at the IP layer a *packet*, and at the TCP layer a *segment*. In this book, we use "packet" as a generic term that encompasses these various cases.

As a packet travels down the protocol stack (from TCP or UDP transport to IP to Ethernet to the physical wire) in preparation for being sent, each protocol adds its own header information. Each protocol's finished packet becomes the payload part of the packet generated by the next protocol. This nesting is known as encapsulation. On the receiving machine, the encapsulation is reversed as the packet travels back up the protocol stack.

For example, a UDP packet being transmitted over Ethernet contains three different wrappers or envelopes. On the Ethernet wire, it is framed with a simple header that lists the source and next-hop destination hardware addresses, the length of the frame, and the frame's checksum (CRC). The Ethernet frame's payload is an IP packet, the IP packet's payload is a UDP packet, and the UDP packet's payload is the data being transmitted. Exhibit B shows the components of such a frame.

Exhibit B A typical network packet[4]

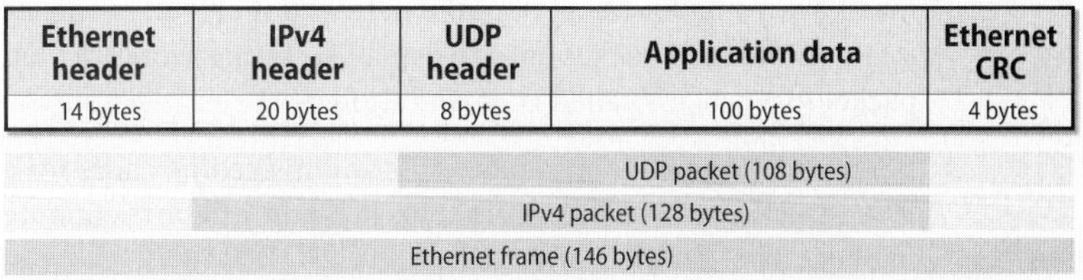

Ethernet header	IPv4 header	UDP header	Application data	Ethernet CRC
14 bytes	20 bytes	8 bytes	100 bytes	4 bytes

UDP packet (108 bytes)
IPv4 packet (128 bytes)
Ethernet frame (146 bytes)

Ethernet framing

One of the main chores of the link layer is to add headers to packets and to put separators between them. The headers contain each packet's link-layer addressing information and checksums, and the separators ensure that receivers can tell where one packet stops and the next one begins. The process of adding these extra bits is known generically as framing.

The link layer is actually divided into two parts: MAC, the Media Access Control sublayer, and LLC, the Link Layer Control sublayer. The MAC layer deals with the media and transmits packets onto the wire. The LLC layer handles the framing.

Today, a single standard for Ethernet framing is in common use: DIX Ethernet II. Historically, several slightly different standards based on IEEE 802.2 were also used, especially on Novell networks.

Maximum transfer unit

The size of packets on a network may be limited both by hardware specifications and by protocol conventions. For example, the payload of a standard Ethernet frame is traditionally 1,500 bytes. The size limit is associated with the link-layer protocol and is called the maximum transfer unit or MTU. Table 14.1 shows some typical values for the MTU.

Table 14.1 MTUs for various types of network

Network type	Maximum transfer unit
Ethernet	1,500 bytes (1,492 with 802.2 framing)[a]
FDDI	4,470 bytes (4,352 for IP/FDDI)
Token ring	Configurable[b]
PPP modem link	Configurable, often 512 or 576 bytes
Point-to-point WAN links (T1, T3)	Configurable, often 1,500 or 4,500 bytes

a. See page 541 for some comments on "jumbo" Ethernet packets.
b. Common values are 552; 1,064; 2,088; 4,508; and 8,232. Sometimes 1,500 to match Ethernet.

4. For specificity, RFCs that describe protocols often use the term "octet" instead of "byte."

The IP layer splits packets to conform to the MTU of a particular network link. If a packet is routed through several networks, one of the intermediate networks may have a smaller MTU than the network of origin. In this case, an IPv4 router that forwards the packet onto the small-MTU network further subdivides the packet in a process called fragmentation.

Fragmentation of in-flight packets is an unwelcome chore for a busy router, so IPv6 largely removes this feature. Packets can still be fragmented, but the originating host must do the work itself.

Senders can discover the lowest-MTU link through which a packet must pass by setting the packet's "do not fragment" flag. If the packet reaches an intermediate router that cannot forward the packet without fragmenting it, the router returns an ICMP error message to the sender. The ICMP packet includes the MTU of the network that's demanding smaller packets, and this MTU then becomes the governing packet size for communication with that destination.

The TCP protocol does path MTU discovery automatically, even in IPv4. UDP is not so nice and is happy to shunt extra work to the IP layer.

Fragmentation problems can be insidious. Although path MTU discovery should automatically resolve MTU conflicts, an administrator must occasionally intervene. If you are using a tunneled architecture for a virtual private network, for example, you should look at the size of the packets that are traversing the tunnel. They are often 1,500 bytes to start with, but once the tunneling header is added, they become 1,540 bytes or so and must be fragmented. Setting the MTU of the link to a smaller value averts fragmentation and increases the overall performance of the tunneled network. Consult the **ifconfig** man page to see how to set an interface's MTU.

14.3 Packet addressing

Like letters or email messages, network packets must be properly addressed in order to reach their destinations. Several addressing schemes are used in combination:

- MAC (media access control) addresses for use by hardware
- IPv4 and IPv6 network addresses for use by software
- Hostnames for use by people

Hardware (MAC) addressing

Each of a host's network interfaces usually has one link-layer MAC address that distinguishes it from other machines on the physical network, plus one or more IP addresses that identify the interface on the global Internet. This last part bears repeating: IP addresses identify *network interfaces, not machines*. (To users the distinction is irrelevant, but administrators must know the truth.)

The lowest level of addressing is dictated by network hardware. For example, Ethernet devices are assigned a unique 6-byte hardware address at the time of manufacture. These addresses are traditionally written as a series of 2-digit hex bytes separated by colons; for example, 00:50:8D:9A:3B:DF.

Token ring interfaces have a similar address that is also six bytes long. Some point-to-point networks (such as PPP) need no hardware addresses at all; the identity of the destination is specified as the link is established.

A 6-byte Ethernet address is divided into two parts. The first three bytes identify the manufacturer of the hardware, and the last three bytes are a unique serial number that the manufacturer assigns. Sysadmins can sometimes identify the brand of machine that is trashing a network by looking up the 3-byte identifier in a table of vendor IDs. A current vendor table is available from

iana.org/assignments/ethernet-numbers

The 3-byte codes are actually IEEE Organizationally Unique Identifiers (OUIs), so you can also look up them up directly in the IEEE's database at

standards.ieee.org/regauth/oui

Of course, the relationships among the manufacturers of chipsets, components, and systems are complex, so the vendor ID embedded in a MAC address can be misleading, too.

In theory, Ethernet hardware addresses are permanently assigned and immutable. However, many network interfaces now let you override the hardware address and set one of your own choosing. This feature can be handy if you have to replace a broken machine or network card and for some reason must use the old MAC address (e.g., all your switches filter it, or your DHCP server hands out addresses based on MAC addresses, or your MAC address is also a software license key). Spoofable MAC addresses are also helpful if you need to infiltrate a wireless network that uses MAC-based access control. But for simplicity, it's generally advisable to preserve the uniqueness of MAC addresses.

IP addressing

At the next level up from the hardware, Internet addressing (more commonly known as IP addressing) is used. IP addresses are globally unique[5] and hardware independent.

See page 468 for more information about ARP.

The mapping from IP addresses to hardware addresses is implemented at the link layer of the TCP/IP model. On networks such as Ethernet that support broadcasting (that is, networks that allow packets to be addressed to "all hosts on this

5. In general, an IP address identifies a specific and unique destination. However, several special cases muddy the water. NAT (page 462) uses one interface's IP address to handle traffic for multiple machines. IP private address spaces (page 462) are addresses that multiple sites can use at once, as long as the addresses are not visible to the Internet. Anycast addressing shares one IP address among several machines.

physical network"), senders use the ARP protocol to discover mappings without assistance from a system administrator. In IPv6, an interface's MAC address can be used as part of the IP address, making the translation between IP and hardware addressing virtually automatic.

Hostname "addressing"

See Chapter 17 for more information about DNS.

IP addresses are sequences of numbers, so they are hard for people to remember. Operating systems allow one or more hostnames to be associated with an IP address so that users can type rfc-editor.org instead of 128.9.160.27. Under UNIX and Linux, this mapping can be set up in several ways, ranging from a static file (**/etc/hosts**) to the LDAP database system to DNS, the world-wide Domain Name System. Keep in mind that hostnames are really just a convenient shorthand for IP addresses, and as such, they refer to network interfaces rather than computers.

Ports

IP addresses identify a machine's network interfaces, but they are not specific enough to address individual processes or services, many of which may be actively using the network at once. TCP and UDP extend IP addresses with a concept known as a port, a 16-bit number that supplements an IP address to specify a particular communication channel. Standard services such as email, FTP, and HTTP associate themselves with "well known" ports defined in **/etc/services**.[6] To help prevent impersonation of these services, UNIX systems restrict server programs from binding to port numbers under 1,024 unless they are run as root. (Anyone can communicate with a server running on a low port number; the restriction applies only to the program listening on the port.)

Address types

The IP layer defines several broad types of address, some of which have direct counterparts at the link layer:

- Unicast – addresses that refer to a single network interface
- Multicast – addresses that simultaneously target a group of hosts
- Broadcast – addresses that include all hosts on the local subnet
- Anycast – addresses that resolve to any one of a group of hosts

Multicast addressing facilitates applications such as video conferencing in which the same set of packets must be sent to all participants. The Internet Group Management Protocol (IGMP) constructs and manages sets of hosts that are treated as one multicast destination.

Multicast is largely unused on today's Internet, but it's slightly more mainstream in IPv6. IPv6 broadcast addresses are really just specialized forms of multicast addressing.

6. You can find a full list of assigned ports at iana.org/assignments/port-numbers.

Anycast addresses bring load balancing to the network layer by allowing packets to be delivered to whichever of several destinations is closest in terms of network routing. You might expect that they'd be implemented similarly to multicast addresses, but in fact they are more like unicast addresses.

Most of the implementation details for anycast support are handled at the level of routing rather than IP. The novelty of anycast addressing is really just the relaxation of the traditional requirement that IP addresses identify unique destinations. Anycast addressing is formally described for IPv6, but the same tricks can be applied to IPv4, too—for example, as is done for root DNS name servers.

14.4 IP ADDRESSES: THE GORY DETAILS

With the exception of multicast addresses, Internet addresses consist of a network portion and a host portion. The network portion identifies a logical network to which the address refers, and the host portion identifies a node on that network. In IPv4, addresses are four bytes long and the boundary between network and host portions is set administratively. In IPv6, addresses are 16 bytes long and the network portion and host portion are always eight bytes each.

IPv4 addresses are written as decimal numbers, one for each byte, separated by periods; for example, 209.85.171.147. The leftmost byte is the most significant and is always part of the network portion.

When 127 is the first byte of an address, it denotes the "loopback network," a fictitious network that has no real hardware interface and only one host. The loopback address 127.0.0.1 always refers to the current host. Its symbolic name is "localhost". (This is another small violation of IP address uniqueness since every host thinks 127.0.0.1 is a different computer: itself.)

IPv6 addresses and their text-formatted equivalents are a bit more complicated. They're discussed in the section *IPv6 addressing* starting on page 464.

An interface's IP address and other parameters are set with the **ifconfig** command. Jump ahead to page 478 for a detailed description of **ifconfig**.

IPv4 address classes

Historically, IP addresses had an inherent "class" that depended on the first bits of the leftmost byte. The class determined which bytes of the address were in the network portion and which were in the host portion. Today, an explicit mask identifies the network portion, and the boundary can fall between two adjacent bits, not just between bytes. However, the traditional classes are still used as defaults when no explicit division is specified.

Classes A, B, and C denote regular IP addresses. Classes D and E are used for multicasting and research addresses. Table 14.2 on the next page describes the characteristics of each class. The network portion of an address is denoted by N, and the host portion by H.

Table 14.2 Historical Internet address classes

Class	1st byte[a]	Format	Comments
A	1-127	N.H.H.H	Very early networks, or reserved for DoD
B	128-191	N.N.H.H	Large sites, usually subnetted, were hard to get
C	192-223	N.N.N.H	Easy to get, often obtained in sets
D	224-239	–	Multicast addresses, not permanently assigned
E	240-255	–	Experimental addresses

a. The value 0 is special and is not used as the first byte of regular IP addresses. 127 is reserved for the loopback address.

It's rare for a single physical network to have more than 100 computers attached to it, so class A and class B addresses (which allow for 16,777,214 hosts and 65,534 hosts per network, respectively) are really quite silly and wasteful. For example, the 127 class A networks use up half the available address space. Who knew that IPv4 address space would become so precious!

Subnetting

To make better use of these addresses, you can now reassign part of the host portion to the network portion by specifying an explicit 4-byte "subnet mask" or "netmask" in which the 1s correspond to the desired network portion and the 0s correspond to the host portion. The 1s must be leftmost and contiguous. At least eight bits must be allocated to the network part and at least two bits to the host part. Ergo, there are really only 22 possible values for an IPv4 netmask.

For example, the four bytes of a class B address would normally be interpreted as N.N.H.H. The implicit netmask for class B is therefore 255.255.0.0 in decimal notation. With a netmask of 255.255.255.0, however, the address would be interpreted as N.N.N.H. Use of the mask turns a single class B network address into 256 distinct class-C-like networks, each of which can support 254 hosts.

*See page 478 for more information about **ifconfig**.*

Netmasks are assigned with the **ifconfig** command as each network interface is set up. By default, **ifconfig** uses the inherent class of an address to figure out which bits are in the network part. When you set an explicit mask, you simply override this behavior.

Netmasks that do not end at a byte boundary can be annoying to decode and are often written as /XX, where XX is the number of bits in the network portion of the address. This is sometimes called CIDR (Classless Inter-Domain Routing; see page 460) notation. For example, the network address 128.138.243.0/26 refers to the first of four networks whose first bytes are 128.138.243. The other three networks have 64, 128, and 192 as their fourth bytes. The netmask associated with these networks is 255.255.255.192 or 0xFFFFFFC0; in binary, it's 26 ones followed by 6 zeros. Exhibit C breaks out these numbers in a bit more detail.

Exhibit C Netmask base conversion

IP address	128	.	138	.	243	.	0
Decimal netmask	255	.	255	.	255	.	192
Hex netmask	f f	.	f f	.	f f	.	c 0
Binary netmask	1111 1111	.	1111 1111	.	1111 1111	.	1100 0000

A /26 network has 6 bits left (32 – 26 = 6) to number hosts. 2^6 is 64, so the network has 64 potential host addresses. However, it can only accommodate 62 actual hosts because the all-0 and all-1 host addresses are reserved (they are the network and broadcast addresses, respectively).

In our 128.138.243.0/26 example, the extra two bits of network address obtained by subnetting can take on the values 00, 01, 10, and 11. The 128.138.243.0/24 network has thus been divided into four /26 networks:

- 128.138.243.0/26 (0 in decimal is **00**000000 in binary)
- 128.138.243.64/26 (64 in decimal is **01**000000 in binary)
- 128.138.243.128/26 (128 in decimal is **10**000000 in binary)
- 128.138.243.192/26 (192 in decimal is **11**000000 in binary)

The boldfaced bits of the last byte of each address are the bits that belong to the network portion of that byte.

Tricks and tools for subnet arithmetic

It's confusing to do all this bit twiddling in your head, but some tricks can make it simpler. The number of hosts per network and the value of the last byte in the netmask always add up to 256:

last netmask byte = 256 – net size

For example, 256 – 64 = 192, which is the final byte of the netmask in the preceding example. Another arithmetic fact is that the last byte of an actual network address (as opposed to a netmask) must be evenly divisible by the number of hosts per network. We see this fact in action in the 128.138.243.0/26 example, where the last bytes of the networks are 0, 64, 128, and 192—all divisible by 64.[7]

Given an IP address (say, 128.138.243.100), we cannot tell without the associated netmask what the network address and broadcast address will be. Table 14.3 on the next page shows the possibilities for /16 (the default for a class B address), /24 (a plausible value), and /26 (a reasonable value for a small network).

The network address and broadcast address steal two hosts from each network, so it would seem that the smallest meaningful network would have four possible

7. Of course, 0 counts as being divisible by any number…

Table 14.3 Example IPv4 address decodings

IP address	Netmask	Network	Broadcast
128.138.243.100/16	255.255.0.0	128.138.0.0	128.138.255.255
128.138.243.100/24	255.255.255.0	128.138.243.0	128.138.243.255
128.138.243.100/26	255.255.255.192	128.138.243.64	128.138.243.127

hosts: two real hosts—usually at either end of a point-to-point link—and the network and broadcast addresses. To have four values for hosts requires two bits in the host portion, so such a network would be a /30 network with netmask 255.255.255.252 or 0xFFFFFFFC. However, a /31 network is in fact treated as a special case (see RFC3021) and has no network or broadcast address; both of its two addresses are used for hosts, and its netmask is 255.255.255.254.

A handy web site called the IP Calculator by Krischan Jodies (it's available at jodies.de/ipcalc) helps with binary/hex/mask arithmetic. IP Calculator displays everything you might need to know about a network address and its netmask, broadcast address, hosts, etc. A tarball for a command-line version of the tool, **ipcalc**, is also available.

On Ubuntu you can install **ipcalc** through **apt-get**.

Here's some sample IP Calculator output, munged a bit to help with formatting:

```
Address:   24.8.175.69             00011000.00001000.10101111 .01000101
Netmask:   255.255.255.0 = 24  11111111.11111111.11111111 .00000000
Wildcard:  0.0.0.255               00000000.00000000.00000000 .11111111
=>
Network:   24.8.175.0/24           00011000.00001000.10101111 .00000000  (Class A)
Broadcast: 24.8.175.255            00011000.00001000.10101111 .11111111
HostMin:   24.8.175.1              00011000.00001000.10101111 .00000001
HostMax:   24.8.175.254            00011000.00001000.10101111 .11111110
```

The output provides both easy-to-understand versions of the addresses and "cut and paste" versions. Very useful.

Red Hat includes a similar but unrelated program that's also called **ipcalc**. However, it's relatively useless because it only understands default IP address classes.

If a dedicated IP calculator isn't available, the standard utility **bc** makes a good backup utility since it can do arithmetic in any base. Set the input and output bases with the **ibase** and **obase** directives. Set the **obase** first; otherwise, it's interpreted relative to the new **ibase**.

CIDR: Classless Inter-Domain Routing

CIDR is defined in RFC1519.

Like subnetting, of which it is a direct extension, CIDR relies on an explicit netmask to define the boundary between the network and host parts of an address. But unlike subnetting, CIDR allows the network portion to be made *smaller* than would be implied by an address's implicit class. A short CIDR mask may have the effect of aggregating several networks for purposes of routing. Hence, CIDR is sometimes referred to as supernetting.

CIDR simplifies routing information and imposes hierarchy on the routing process. Although CIDR was only intended as an interim solution along the road to IPv6, it has proved to be sufficiently powerful to handle the Internet's growth problems for the better part of a decade.

For example, suppose that a site has been given a block of eight class C addresses numbered 192.144.0.0 through 192.144.7.0 (in CIDR notation, 192.144.0.0/21). Internally, the site could use them as

- 1 network of length /21 with 2,046 hosts, netmask 255.255.248.0
- 8 networks of length /24 with 254 hosts each, netmask 255.255.255.0
- 16 networks of length /25 with 126 hosts each, netmask 255.255.255.128
- 32 networks of length /26 with 62 hosts each, netmask 255.255.255.192

and so on. But from the perspective of the Internet, it's not necessary to have 32, 16, or even 8 routing table entries for these addresses. They all refer to the same organization, and all the packets go to the same ISP. A single routing entry for 192.144.0.0/21 suffices. CIDR makes it easy to allocate portions of class A and B addresses and thus increases the number of available addresses manyfold.

Inside your network, you can mix and match regions of different subnet lengths as long as all the pieces fit together without overlaps. This is called variable length subnetting. For example, an ISP with the 192.144.0.0/21 allocation could define some /30 networks for point-to-point customers, some /24s for large customers, and some /27s for smaller folks.

All the hosts on a network must be configured with the same netmask. You can't tell one host that it is a /24 and another host on the same network that it is a /25.

Address allocation

Only network numbers are formally assigned; sites must define their own host numbers to form complete IP addresses. You can subdivide the address space that has been assigned to you into subnets in whatever manner you like.

Administratively, ICANN (the Internet Corporation for Assigned Names and Numbers) has delegated blocks of addresses to five regional Internet registries, and these regional authorities are responsible for doling out subblocks to ISPs within their regions (see Table 14.4 on the next page). These ISPs in turn divide up their blocks and hand out pieces to individual clients. Only large ISPs should ever have to deal directly with one of the ICANN-sponsored address registries.

The delegation from ICANN to regional registries and then to national or regional ISPs has allowed for further aggregation in the backbone routing tables. ISP customers who have been allocated address space within the ISP's block do not need individual routing entries on the backbone. A single entry for the aggregated block that points to the ISP suffices.

Table 14.4 Regional Internet registries

Name	Site	Region covered
ARIN	arin.net	North America, part of the Caribbean
APNIC	apnic.net	Asia/Pacific region, including Australia and New Zealand
AfriNIC	afrinic.net	Africa
LACNIC	lacnic.net	Central and South America, part of the Caribbean
RIPE NCC	ripe.net	Europe and surrounding areas

Private addresses and network address translation (NAT)

Another factor that has helped decelerate the rate at which IPv4 addresses are consumed is the use of private IP address spaces, described in RFC1918. These addresses are used by your site internally but are never shown to the Internet (or at least, not intentionally). A border router translates between your private address space and the address space assigned by your ISP.

RFC1918 sets aside 1 class A network, 16 class B networks, and 256 class C networks that will never be globally allocated and can be used internally by any site. Table 14.5 shows the options. (The "CIDR range" column shows each range in the more compact CIDR notation; it does not add additional information.)

Table 14.5 IP addresses reserved for private use

IP class	From	To	CIDR range
Class A	10.0.0.0	10.255.255.255	10.0.0.0/8
Class B	172.16.0.0	172.31.255.255	172.16.0.0/12
Class C	192.168.0.0	192.168.255.255	192.168.0.0/16

The original idea was that sites would choose an address class from among these options to fit the size of their organizations. But now that CIDR and subnetting are universal, it probably makes the most sense to use the class A address (subnetted, of course) for all new private networks.

To allow hosts that use these private addresses to talk to the Internet, the site's border router runs a system called NAT (Network Address Translation). NAT intercepts packets addressed with these internal addresses and rewrites their source addresses, using a real external IP address and perhaps a different source port number. It also maintains a table of the mappings it has made between internal and external address/port pairs so that the translation can be performed in reverse when answering packets arrive from the Internet.

NAT's use of port number mapping multiplexes several conversations onto the same IP address so that a single external address can be shared by many internal hosts. In some cases, a site can get by with only one "real" IP address. For example, this is the default configuration for most mass-market routers used with cable and DSL modems.

A site that uses NAT must still request a small section of address space from its ISP, but most of the addresses thus obtained are used for NAT mappings and are not assigned to individual hosts. If the site later wants to choose another ISP, only the border router and its NAT configuration need be updated, not the configurations of the individual hosts.

Large organizations that use NAT and RFC1918 addresses must institute some form of central coordination so that all hosts, independently of their department or administrative group, have unique IP addresses. The situation can become complicated when one company that uses RFC1918 address space acquires or merges with another company that's doing the same thing. Parts of the combined organization must often renumber.

It is possible to have a UNIX or Linux box perform the NAT function, but most sites prefer to delegate this task to their routers or network connection devices.[8] See the vendor-specific sections later in this chapter for details.

An incorrect NAT configuration can let private-address-space packets escape onto the Internet. The packets may get to their destinations, but answering packets won't be able to get back. CAIDA,[9] an organization that collects operational data from the Internet backbone, finds that 0.1% to 0.2% of the packets on the backbone have either private addresses or bad checksums. This sounds like a tiny percentage, but it represents thousands of packets every minute on a busy circuit. See caida.org for other interesting statistics and network measurement tools.

One issue raised by NAT is that an arbitrary host on the Internet cannot initiate connections to your site's internal machines. To get around this limitation, NAT implementations let you preconfigure externally visible "tunnels" that connect to specific internal hosts and ports.[10]

Another issue is that some applications embed IP addresses in the data portion of packets; these applications are foiled or confused by NAT. Examples include some media streaming systems, routing protocols, and FTP commands. NAT sometimes breaks VPNs (virtual private networks), too.

NAT hides interior structure. This secrecy feels like a security win, but the security folks say NAT doesn't really help for security and does not replace the need for a firewall. Unfortunately, NAT also foils attempts to measure the size and

8. Of course, many routers now run embedded Linux kernels. Even so, these dedicated systems are still generally more proficient and more secure than general-purpose computers that also forward packets.
9. CAIDA, pronounced "kay duh," is the Cooperative Association for Internet Data Analysis at the San Diego Supercomputer Center on the UCSD campus (caida.org).
10. Many routers also support the Universal Plug and Play (UPnP) standards promoted by Microsoft, one feature of which allows interior hosts to set up their own dynamic NAT tunnels. This can be either a godsend or a security risk, depending on your perspective. The feature is easily disabled at the router if you wish to do so.

topology of the Internet. See RFC4864, *Local Network Protection for IPv6*, for a good discussion of both the real and illusory benefits of NAT in IPv4.

IPv6 addressing

IPv6 addresses are 128 bits long. These long addresses were originally intended to solve the problem of IP address exhaustion. But now that they're here, they are being exploited to help with issues of routing, mobility, and locality of reference.

IPv4 addresses were not designed to be geographically clustered in the manner of phone numbers or zip codes, but clustering was added after the fact in the form of the CIDR conventions. (Of course, the relevant "geography" is really routing space rather than physical location.) CIDR was so technically successful that hierarchical subassignment of network addresses is now assumed throughout IPv6. Your IPv6 ISP assigns you an address prefix that you simply prepend to the local parts of your addresses, usually at your border router.

The boundary between the network portion and the host portion of an IPv6 address is fixed at /64, so there can be no disagreement or confusion about how long an address's network portion "really" is. Stated another way, true subnetting no longer exists in the IPv6 world, although the term "subnet" lives on as a synonym for "local network." Even though network numbers are always 64 bits long, routers needn't pay attention to all 64 bits when making routing decisions. They can route packets based on prefixes, just as they do under CIDR.

An early scheme outlined in RFC2374 called for four standardized subdivision levels within the network portion of an IPv6 address. But in light of the positive experience with letting ISPs manage their own IPv4 address subdivisions, that plan was withdrawn in RFC3587. ISPs are now free to set delegation boundaries wherever they wish.

The 64-bit host ID can potentially be derived from the hardware interface's 48-bit MAC address.[11] This scheme allows for automatic host numbering, which is a nice feature for sysadmins since only the subnet needs to be managed.

The fact that the MAC address can be seen at the IP layer has both good and bad implications. The good part is that host number configuration can be completely automatic. The bad part is that the brand and model of interface card are encoded in the first half of the MAC address, so prying eyes and hackers with code for a particular architecture will be helped along. The IPv6 standards point out that sites are not *required* to use MAC addresses to derive host IDs; they can use whatever numbering system they want.

11. More specifically, it is the MAC address with the two bytes 0xFFFE inserted in the middle and one bit (bit 6 of the first byte, numbering bits from the left, starting at 0) complemented; see RFC4291. The standard for converting 48-bit MAC addresses into 64-bit IP host numbers is known as EUI-64.

Here are some useful sources of additional IPv6 information:

- ipv6tf.org – An IPv6 information portal
- ipv6.org – FAQs and technical information
- ipv6forum.com – Marketing folks and IPv6 propaganda

- RFC3587 – *IPv6 Global Unicast Address Format*
- RFC4291 – *IP Version 6 Addressing Architecture*

Various schemes have been proposed to ease the transition from IPv4 to IPv6, mostly focusing on ways to tunnel IPv6 traffic through the IPv4 network to compensate for gaps in IPv6 support. The two tunneling systems in common use are called 6to4 and Teredo; the latter, named after a family of wood-boring shipworms, can be used on systems behind a NAT device.

14.5 Routing

Routing is the process of directing a packet through the maze of networks that stand between its source and its destination. In the TCP/IP system, it is similar to asking for directions in an unfamiliar country. The first person you talk to might point you toward the right city. Once you were a bit closer to your destination, the next person might be able to tell you how to get to the right street. Eventually, you get close enough that someone can identify the building you're looking for.

Routing information takes the form of rules ("routes"), such as "To reach network A, send packets through machine C." There can also be a default route that tells what to do with packets bound for a network to which there is no explicit route.

Routing information is stored in a table in the kernel. Each table entry has several parameters, including a mask for each listed network. To route a packet to a particular address, the kernel picks the most specific of the matching routes—that is, the one with the longest mask. If the kernel finds no relevant route and no default route, then it returns a "network unreachable" ICMP error to the sender.

The word "routing" is commonly used to mean two distinct things:

- Looking up a network address in the routing table to forward a packet toward its destination

- Building the routing table in the first place

In this section we examine the forwarding function and look at how routes can be manually added to or deleted from the routing table. We defer the more complicated topic of routing protocols that build and maintain the routing table until Chapter 15.

Routing tables

You can examine a machine's routing table with **netstat -r**. Use **netstat -rn** to avoid DNS lookups and present all the information numerically, which is generally more useful. We discuss **netstat** in more detail starting on page 868, but here is a short example to give you a better idea of what routes look like:

```
redhat$ netstat -rn
Kernel IP routing table
Destination     Genmask          Gateway          Fl  MSS   Iface
132.236.227.0   255.255.255.0    132.236.227.93   U   1500  eth0
default         0.0.0.0          132.236.227.1    UG  1500  eth0
132.236.212.0   255.255.255.192  132.236.212.1    U   1500  eth1
132.236.220.64  255.255.255.192  132.236.212.6    UG  1500  eth1
127.0.0.1       255.255.255.255  127.0.0.1        U   3584  lo
```

This host has two network interfaces: 132.236.227.93 (eth0) on the network 132.236.227.0/24 and 132.236.212.1 (eth1) on the network 132.236.212.0/26.

The destination field is usually a network address, although you can also add host-specific routes (their genmask is 255.255.255.255 since all bits are consulted). An entry's gateway field must contain the full IP address of a local network interface or adjacent host; on Linux kernels it can be 0.0.0.0 to invoke the default gateway.

For example, the fourth route in the table above says that to reach the network 132.236.220.64/26, packets must be sent to the gateway 132.236.212.6 through interface eth1. The second entry is a default route; packets not explicitly addressed to any of the three networks listed (or to the machine itself) are sent to the default gateway host, 132.236.227.1.

A host can only route packets to gateway machines that are reachable through a directly connected network. The local host's job is limited to moving packets one hop closer to their destinations, so it is pointless to include information about nonadjacent gateways in the local routing table. Each gateway that a packet visits makes a fresh next-hop routing decision based on its own local routing database.[12]

*See page 481 for more information about the **route** command.*

Routing tables can be configured statically, dynamically, or with a combination of the two approaches. A static route is one that you enter explicitly with the **route** command. Static routes remain in the routing table as long as the system is up; they are often set up at boot time from one of the system startup scripts. For example, the Linux commands

```
route add -net 132.236.220.64 netmask 255.255.255.192
    gw 132.236.212.6 eth1
route add default gw 132.236.227.1 eth0
```

12. The IP source routing feature is an exception to this rule; see page 473.

add the fourth and second routes displayed by **netstat -rn** above. (The first and third routes in that display were added by **ifconfig** when the eth0 and eth1 interfaces were configured.)

The final route is also added at boot time. It configures the loopback interface, which prevents packets sent from the host to itself from going out on the network. Instead, they are transferred directly from the network output queue to the network input queue inside the kernel.

In a stable local network, static routing is an efficient solution. It is easy to manage and reliable. However, it requires that the system administrator know the topology of the network accurately at boot time and that the topology not change often.

Most machines on a local area network have only one way to get out to the rest of the network, so the routing problem is easy. A default route added at boot time suffices to point toward the way out. Hosts that use DHCP (see page 469) to get their IP addresses can also obtain a default route with DHCP.

For more complicated network topologies, dynamic routing is required. Dynamic routing is implemented by a daemon process that maintains and modifies the routing table. Routing daemons on different hosts communicate to discover the topology of the network and to figure out how to reach distant destinations. Several routing daemons are available. See Chapter 15, *Routing*, for details.

ICMP redirects

Although IP generally does not concern itself with the management of routing information, it does define a naive damage control feature called an ICMP redirect. When a router forwards a packet to a machine on the same network from which the packet was originally received, something is clearly wrong. Since the sender, the router, and the next-hop router are all on the same network, the packet could have been forwarded in one hop rather than two. The router can conclude that the sender's routing tables are inaccurate or incomplete.

In this situation, the router can notify the sender of its problem by sending an ICMP redirect packet. In effect, a redirect says, "You should not be sending packets for host *xxx* to me; you should send them to host *yyy* instead."

In theory, the recipient of a redirect can adjust its routing table to fix the problem. In practice, redirects contain no authentication information and are therefore untrustworthy. Dedicated routers usually ignore redirects, but most UNIX and Linux systems accept them and act on them by default. You'll need to consider the possible sources of redirects in your network and disable their acceptance if they could pose a problem.

Under Linux, the variable **accept_redirects** in the **/proc** hierarchy controls the acceptance of ICMP redirects. See page 504 for instructions on examining and resetting this variable.

On Solaris, use **ndd -set /dev/ip ip_ignore_redirect 1** to disregard ICMP redirects. See page 498 for more details.

Although HP-UX also uses the **ndd** command to control its IP protocol stack, the underlying IP implementation lacks the ability to ignore ICMP redirects. However, you can arrange to have the routes that result from these redirects deleted from the routing table a second later with

```
ndd -set /dev/ip ip_ire_redirect_interval 1000
```

Some versions of HP-UX have enforced minima of 5 or 60 seconds on this parameter (which is expressed in milliseconds), but HP-UX 11 appears to accept smaller values without complaint.

On AIX, the command to ignore ICMP redirects is **no -p -o ipignoreredirects=1**. The **-p** option makes it a permanent change; omit this to test the change temporarily. See page 507 for more details.

14.6 ARP: The Address Resolution Protocol

ARP is defined in RFC826.

Although IP addresses are hardware-independent, hardware addresses must still be used to actually transport data across a network's link layer.[13] ARP, the Address Resolution Protocol, discovers the hardware address associated with a particular IP address. It can be used on any kind of network that supports broadcasting but is most commonly described in terms of Ethernet.

If host A wants to send a packet to host B on the same Ethernet, it uses ARP to discover B's hardware address. If B is not on the same network as A, host A uses the routing system to determine the next-hop router along the route to B and then uses ARP to find that router's hardware address. Since ARP uses broadcast packets, which cannot cross networks,[14] it can only be used to find the hardware addresses of machines directly connected to the sending host's local network.

Every machine maintains a table in memory called the ARP cache, which contains the results of recent ARP queries. Under normal circumstances, many of the addresses a host needs are discovered soon after booting, so ARP does not account for a lot of network traffic.

ARP works by broadcasting a packet of the form "Does anyone know the hardware address for 128.138.116.4?" The machine being searched for recognizes its own IP address and replies, "Yes, that's the IP address assigned to one of my network interfaces, and the corresponding Ethernet address is 8:0:20:0:fb:6a."

The original query includes the IP and Ethernet addresses of the requestor so that the machine being sought can reply without issuing an ARP query of its own.

13. Except on point-to-point links, on which the identity of the destination is sometimes implicit.
14. Routers can in fact be configured to flood broadcast packets to other networks, but this is generally a bad idea. If you find yourself wanting to forward broadcasts, there is most likely something amiss with your network or server architecture.

Thus, the two machines learn each other's ARP mappings with only one exchange of packets. Other machines that overhear the requestor's initial broadcast can record its address mapping, too.

The **arp** command examines and manipulates the kernel's ARP cache, adds or deletes entries, and flushes or shows the table. **arp -a** displays the contents of the ARP cache; output formats vary.

The **arp** command is generally useful only for debugging and for situations that involve special hardware. For example, if two hosts on a network are using the same IP address, one has the right ARP table entry and one is wrong. You can use the **arp** command to track down the offending machine.

14.7 DHCP: THE DYNAMIC HOST CONFIGURATION PROTOCOL

DHCP is defined in RFCs 2131 and 2132.

When you plug a device or computer into a network, it usually obtains an IP address for itself on the local network, sets up an appropriate default route, and connects itself to a local DNS server. The Dynamic Host Configuration Protocol (DHCP) is the hidden Svengali that makes this magic happen.

The protocol lets a DHCP client "lease" a variety of network and administrative parameters from a central server that is authorized to distribute them. The leasing paradigm is particularly convenient for PCs that are turned off when not in use and for networks that must support transient guests such as laptops.

Leasable parameters include

- IP addresses and netmasks
- Gateways (default routes)
- DNS name servers
- Syslog hosts
- WINS servers, X font servers, proxy servers, NTP servers
- TFTP servers (for loading a boot image)

There are dozens more—see RFC2132. Real-world use of the more exotic parameters is rare, however.

Clients must report back to the DHCP server periodically to renew their leases. If a lease is not renewed, it eventually expires. The DHCP server is then free to assign the address (or whatever was being leased) to a different client. The lease period is configurable, but it's usually quite long (hours or days).

Even if you want each host to have its own permanent IP address, DHCP can save you time and suffering. Once the server is up and running, clients can use it to obtain their network configuration at boot time. No fuss, no mess, and most importantly, a minimum of local configuration on the client machines.

DHCP software

ISC, the Internet Systems Consortium, maintains a very nice open source reference implementation of DHCP. Major versions 2, 3, and 4 of ISC's software are all in common use, and all of these versions work fine for basic service. Version 3 supports backup DHCP servers, and version 4 supports IPv6. Server, client, and relay agents are all available from isc.org.

Major Linux distributions all use some version of the ISC software, although you may have to install the server portion explicitly. The server package is called **dhcp** on Red Hat, **dhcp3-server** on Ubuntu, and **dhcp-server** on SUSE.

Non-Linux systems often have their own home-grown DCHP implementations, and unfortunately all our example UNIX systems fall into this category.

It's best not to tamper with the client side of DHCP, since that part of the code is relatively simple and comes preconfigured and ready to use. Changing the client side of DHCP is not trivial.

However, if you need to run a DHCP *server*, we recommend the ISC package over vendor-specific implementations. In a typical heterogeneous network environment, administration is greatly simplified by standardizing on a single implementation. The ISC software provides a reliable, open source solution that builds without incident on most versions of UNIX.

In the next few sections, we briefly discuss the DHCP protocol, explain how to set up the ISC server that implements it, and review some client configuration issues.

How DHCP works

DHCP is a backward-compatible extension of BOOTP, a protocol originally devised to help diskless UNIX workstations boot. DHCP generalizes the parameters that can be supplied and adds the concept of a lease period for assigned values.

A DHCP client begins its interaction with a DHCP server by broadcasting a "Help! Who am I?" message.[15] If a DHCP server is present on the local network, it negotiates with the client to provide an IP address and other networking parameters. If there is no DHCP server on the local net, servers on different subnets can receive the initial broadcast message through a separate piece of DHCP software that acts as a relay agent.

When the client's lease time is half over, it attempts to renew its lease. The server is obliged to keep track of the addresses it has handed out, and this information must persist across reboots. Clients are supposed to keep their lease state across reboots too, although many do not. The goal is to maximize stability in network configuration. In theory, all software should be prepared for network configurations to change at a moment's notice, but a lot of software still makes unwarranted assumptions about the continuity of the network.

15. Clients initiate conversations with the DHCP server by using the generic all-ones broadcast address. The clients don't yet know their subnet masks and therefore can't use the subnet broadcast address.

ISC's DHCP software

ISC's server daemon is called **dhcpd**, and its configuration file is **dhcpd.conf**, usually found in **/etc** or **/etc/dhcp3**. The format of the config file is a bit fragile; leave out a semicolon and you may receive a cryptic, unhelpful error message.

When setting up a new DHCP server, you must also make sure that an empty lease database file has been created. Check the summary at the end of the man page for **dhcpd** to find the correct location for the lease file on your system. It's usually somewhere underneath **/var**.

To set up the **dhcpd.conf** file, you need the following information:

- The subnets for which **dhcpd** should manage IP addresses, and the ranges of addresses to dole out
- A list of static IP address assignments you want to make (if any), along with the MAC (hardware) addresses of the recipients
- The initial and maximum lease durations, in seconds
- Any other options the server should pass to DHCP clients: netmask, default route, DNS domain, name servers, etc.

The **dhcpd** man page outlines the configuration process, and the **dhcpd.conf** man page covers the exact syntax of the config file. In addition to setting up your configuration, make sure **dhcpd** is started automatically at boot time. (See Chapter 3, *Booting and Shutting Down*, for instructions.) It's helpful to make startup of the daemon conditional on the existence of the **dhcpd.conf** file if your system doesn't do this for you automatically.

Below is a sample **dhcpd.conf** file from a Linux box with two interfaces, one internal and one that connects to the Internet. This machine performs NAT translation for the internal network (see page 462) and leases out a range of 10 IP addresses on this network as well.

Every subnet must be declared, even if no DHCP service is provided on it, so this **dhcpd.conf** file contains a dummy entry for the external interface. It also includes a host entry for one particular machine that needs a fixed address.

```
# global options

option domain-name "synack.net";
option domain-name-servers gw.synack.net;
option subnet-mask 255.255.255.0;
default-lease-time 600;
max-lease-time 7200;

subnet 192.168.1.0 netmask 255.255.255.0 {
    range 192.168.1.51 192.168.1.60;
    option broadcast-address 192.168.1.255;
    option routers gw.synack.net;
}
```

```
subnet 209.180.251.0 netmask 255.255.255.0 {
}

host gandalf {
    hardware ethernet 08:00:07:12:34:56;
    fixed-address gandalf.synack.net;
}
```

See Chapter 17 for more information about DNS.

Unless you make static IP address assignments such as the one for gandalf above, you'll need to consider how your DHCP configuration will interact with DNS. The easy option is to assign a generic name to each dynamically leased address (e.g., dhcp1.synack.net) and allow the names of individual machines to float along with their IP addresses. Alternatively, you can configure **dhcpd** to update the DNS database as it hands out addresses. The dynamic update solution is more complicated, but it has the advantage of preserving each machine's hostname.

ISC's DHCP relay agent is a separate daemon called **dhcrelay**. It's a simple program with no configuration file of its own, although Linux distributions often add a startup harness that feeds it the appropriate command-line arguments for your site. **dhcrelay** listens for DHCP requests on local networks and forwards them to a set of remote DHCP servers that you specify. It's handy both for centralizing the management of DHCP service and for provisioning backup DHCP servers.

ISC's DHCP client is similarly configuration free. It stores status files for each connection in the directory **/var/lib/dhcp** or **/var/lib/dhclient**. The files are named after the interfaces they describe. For example, **dhclient-eth0.leases** would contain all the networking parameters that **dhclient** had set up on behalf of the eth0 interface.

14.8 Security issues

We address the topic of security in a chapter of its own (Chapter 22), but several security issues relevant to IP networking merit discussion here. In this section, we briefly look at a few networking features that have acquired a reputation for causing security problems and recommend ways to minimize their impact. The details of our example systems' default behavior on these issues (and the appropriate methods for changing them) vary considerably and are discussed in the system-specific material starting on page 484.

IP forwarding

A UNIX or Linux system that has IP forwarding enabled can act as a router. That is, it can accept third-party packets on one network interface, match them to a gateway or destination host on another interface, and retransmit the packets.

Unless your system has multiple network interfaces and is actually supposed to function as a router, it's advisable to turn this feature off. Hosts that forward packets can sometimes be coerced into compromising security by making external packets appear to have come from inside your network. This subterfuge can help an intruder's packets evade network scanners and packet filters.

It is perfectly acceptable for a host to use multiple network interfaces for its own traffic without forwarding third-party traffic.

ICMP redirects

ICMP redirects (see page 467) can maliciously reroute traffic and tamper with your routing tables. Most operating systems listen to ICMP redirects and follow their instructions by default. It would be bad if all your traffic were rerouted to a competitor's network for a few hours, especially while backups were running! We recommend that you configure your routers (and hosts acting as routers) to ignore and perhaps log ICMP redirect attempts.

Source routing

IP's source routing mechanism lets you specify an explicit series of gateways for a packet to transit on the way to its destination. Source routing bypasses the next-hop routing algorithm that's normally run at each gateway to determine how a packet should be forwarded.

Source routing was part of the original IP specification; it was intended primarily to facilitate testing. It can create security problems because packets are often filtered according to their origin. If someone can cleverly route a packet to make it appear to have originated within your network instead of the Internet, it might slip through your firewall. We recommend that you neither accept nor forward source-routed packets.

Broadcast pings and other directed broadcasts

Ping packets addressed to a network's broadcast address (instead of to a particular host address) are typically delivered to every host on the network. Such packets have been used in denial of service attacks; for example, the so-called Smurf attacks. (The "Smurf attacks" Wikipedia article has details.)

Broadcast pings are a form of "directed broadcast" in that they are packets sent to the broadcast address of a distant network. The default handling of such packets has been gradually changing. For example, versions of Cisco's IOS up through 11.x forwarded directed broadcast packets by default, but IOS releases since 12.0 do not. It is usually possible to convince your TCP/IP stack to ignore broadcast packets that come from afar, but since this behavior must be set on each interface, the task can be nontrivial at a large site.

IP spoofing

The source address on an IP packet is normally filled in by the kernel's TCP/IP implementation and is the IP address of the host from which the packet was sent. However, if the software creating the packet uses a raw socket, it can fill in any source address it likes. This is called IP spoofing and is usually associated with some kind of malicious network behavior. The machine identified by the spoofed source IP address (if it is a real address at all) is often the victim in the scheme. Error and return packets can disrupt or flood the victim's network connections.

You should deny IP spoofing at your border router by blocking outgoing packets whose source address is not within your address space. This precaution is especially important if your site is a university where students like to experiment and may be tempted to carry out digital vendettas.

If you are using private address space internally, you can filter at the same time to catch any internal addresses escaping to the Internet. Such packets can never be answered (because they lack a backbone route) and always indicate that your site has an internal configuration error.

In addition to detecting outbound packets with bogus source addresses, you must also protect against a attacker's forging the source address on external packets to fool your firewall into thinking that they originated on your internal network. A heuristic known as "unicast reverse path forwarding" (uRPF) helps with this. It makes IP gateways discard packets that arrive on an interface that is different from the one on which they would be transmitted if the source address were the destination. It's a quick sanity check that uses the normal IP routing table as a way to validate the origin of network packets. Dedicated routers implement uRPF, but so does the Linux kernel. On Linux, it's enabled by default.

If your site has multiple connections to the Internet, it may be perfectly reasonable for inbound and outbound routes to be different. In this situation, you'll have to turn off uRPF to make your routing work properly. If your site has only one way out to the Internet, then turning on uRPF is usually safe and appropriate.

Host-based firewalls

Traditionally, a network packet filter or firewall connects your local network to the outside world and controls traffic according to a site-wide policy. Unfortunately, Microsoft has warped everyone's perception of how a firewall should work with its notoriously insecure Windows systems. The last few Windows releases all come with their own personal firewalls, and they complain bitterly if you try to turn the firewall off.

Our example systems all include packet filtering software, but you should not infer from this that every UNIX or Linux machine needs its own firewall. It does not. The packet filtering features are there to allow these machines to serve as network gateways.

However, we don't recommend using a workstation as a firewall. Even with meticulous hardening, full-fledged operating systems are too complex to be fully trustworthy. Dedicated network equipment is more predictable and more reliable—even if it secretly runs Linux.

Even sophisticated software solutions like those offered by Check Point (whose products run on UNIX, Linux, and Windows hosts) are not as secure as a dedicated device such as Cisco's Adaptive Security Appliance series. The software-only solutions are nearly the same price, to boot.

A more thorough discussion of firewall-related issues begins on page 932.

Virtual private networks

Many organizations that have offices in several locations would like to have all those locations connected to one big private network. Such organizations can use the Internet as if it were a private network by establishing a series of secure, encrypted "tunnels" among their various locations. A network that includes such tunnels is known as a virtual private network or VPN.

VPN facilities are also needed when employees must connect to your private network from their homes or from the field. A VPN system doesn't eliminate every possible security issue relating to such ad hoc connections, but it's secure enough for many purposes.

See page 943 for more information about IPsec.

Some VPN systems use the IPsec protocol, which was standardized by the IETF in 1998 as a relatively low-level adjunct to IP. Others, such as OpenVPN, implement VPN security on top of TCP using Transport Layer Security (TLS), formerly known as the Secure Sockets Layer (SSL). TLS is also on the IETF's standards track, although it hasn't yet been fully adopted.

A variety of proprietary VPN implementations are also available. These systems generally don't interoperate with each other or with the standards-based VPN systems, but that's not necessarily a major drawback if all the endpoints are under your control.

The TLS-based VPN solutions seem to be the marketplace winners at this point. They are just as secure as IPsec and considerably less complicated. Having a free implementation in the form of OpenVPN doesn't hurt either. (Unfortunately, it doesn't run on HP-UX or AIX yet.)

To support home and portable users, a common paradigm is for users to download a small Java or ActiveX component through their web browser. This component then provides VPN connectivity back to the enterprise network. The mechanism is convenient for users, but be aware that the browser-based systems differ widely in their implementations: some provide VPN service through a pseudo-network-interface, while others forward only specific ports. Still others are little more than glorified web proxies.

Be sure you understand the underlying technology of the solutions you're considering, and don't expect the impossible. True VPN service (that is, full IP-layer connectivity through a network interface) requires administrative privileges and software installation on the client, whether that client is Windows or a UNIX laptop. Check browser compatibility too, since the voodoo involved in implementing browser-based VPN solutions often doesn't translate among browsers.

14.9 PPP: THE POINT-TO-POINT PROTOCOL

PPP is defined in RFC1331.

PPP represents an underlying communication channel as a virtual network interface. However, since the underlying channel need not have any of the features of an actual network, communication is restricted to the two hosts at the ends of the link—a virtual network of two. PPP has the distinction of being used on both the slowest and the fastest IP links, but for different reasons.

In its asynchronous form, PPP is best known as the protocol used to provide dial-up Internet service over phone lines and serial links. These channels are not inherently packet oriented, so the PPP device driver encodes network packets into a unified data stream and adds link-level headers and markers to separate packets.

In its synchronous form, PPP is the encapsulation protocol used on high-speed circuits that have routers at either end. It's also commonly used as part of the implementation of DSL and cable modems for broadband service. In these latter situations, PPP not only converts the underlying network system (often ATM in the case of DSL) to an IP-friendly form, but it also provides authentication and access control for the link itself. In a surreal, down-the-rabbit-hole twist, PPP can implement Ethernet-like semantics on top of an actual Ethernet, a configuration known as "PPP over Ethernet" or PPPoE.

Designed by committee, PPP is the "everything *and* the kitchen sink" encapsulation protocol. In addition to specifying how the link is established, maintained, and torn down, PPP implements error checking, authentication, encryption, and compression. These features make it adaptable to a variety of situations.

PPP as a dial-up technology was once an important topic for UNIX and Linux system administrators, but the widespread availability of broadband has made dial-up configuration largely irrelevant. At the same time, the high-end applications of PPP have mostly retreated into various pieces of dedicated network hardware. These days, the primary use of PPP is to connect through cellular modems.

14.10 BASIC NETWORK CONFIGURATION

Only a few steps are involved in adding a new machine to an existing local area network, but every system does it slightly differently. Systems typically provide a control panel GUI for basic network configuration, but more elaborate (or automated) setups may require you to edit the configuration files directly.

Before bringing up a new machine on a network that is connected to the Internet, secure it (Chapter 22, *Security*) so that you are not inadvertently inviting attackers onto your local network.

The basic steps to add a new machine to a local network are as follows:

- Assign a unique IP address and hostname.
- Make sure network interfaces are properly configured at boot time.
- Set up a default route and perhaps fancier routing.
- Point to a DNS name server to allow access to the rest of the Internet.

If you rely on DHCP for basic provisioning, most of the configuration chores for a new machine are performed on the DHCP server rather than on the new machine itself. New OS installations typically default to getting their configuration through DHCP, so new machines may require no network configuration at all. Refer to the DHCP section starting on page 469 for general information.

After any change that might affect booting, you should always reboot to verify that the machine comes up correctly. Six months later when the power has failed and the machine refuses to boot, it's hard to remember what change you made that might have caused the problem. (Refer also to Chapter 21, *Network Management and Debugging*.)

The process of designing and installing a physical network is touched on in Chapter 16, *Network Hardware*. If you are dealing with an existing network and have a general idea of how it is set up, it may not be necessary for you to read too much more about the physical aspects of networking unless you plan to extend the existing network.

In this section, we review the various commands and issues involved in manual network configuration. This material is general enough to apply to any UNIX or Linux system. In the vendor-specific sections starting on page 484, we address the unique twists that distinguish UNIX from Linux and separate the various vendors' systems.

As you work through basic network configuration on any machine, you'll find it helpful to test your connectivity with basic tools such as **ping** and **traceroute**. Those tools are actually described in the *Network Management and Debugging* chapter; see the sections starting on page 861 for more details.

Hostname and IP address assignment

See Chapter 17 for more information about DNS.

Administrators have various heartfelt theories about how the mapping from hostnames to IP addresses is best maintained: through the **hosts** file, LDAP, the DNS system, or perhaps some combination of those options. The conflicting goals are scalability, consistency, and maintainability versus a system that is flexible enough to allow machines to boot and function when not all services are available. *Prioritizing sources of administrative information* starting on page 739 describes how the various options can be combined.

Another consideration you might take into account when designing your addressing system is the possible need to renumber your hosts in the future. Unless you are using RFC1918 private addresses (see page 462), your site's IP addresses may change when you switch ISPs. Such a transition becomes daunting if you must visit each host on the network to reconfigure its address. To expedite renumbering, you can use hostnames in configuration files and confine address mappings to a few centralized locations such as the DNS database and your DHCP configuration files.

The **/etc/hosts** file is the oldest and simplest way to map names to IP addresses. Each line starts with an IP address and continues with the various symbolic names by which that address is known.

Here is a typical **/etc/hosts** file for the host lollipop:

```
127.0.0.1        localhost
192.108.21.48    lollipop.atrust.com lollipop loghost
192.108.21.254   chimchim-gw.atrust.com chimchim-gw
192.108.21.1     ns.atrust.com ns
192.225.33.5     licenses.atrust.com license-server
```

A minimalist version would contain only the first two lines. localhost is commonly the first entry in the **/etc/hosts** file; this entry is unnecessary on many systems, but it doesn't hurt to include it. IPv6 addresses can go in this file as well.

Because **/etc/hosts** contains only local mappings and must be maintained on each client system, it's best reserved for mappings that are needed at boot time (e.g., the host itself, the default gateway, and name servers). Use DNS or LDAP to find mappings for the rest of the local network and the rest of the world. You can also use **/etc/hosts** to specify mappings that you do not want the rest of the world to know about and therefore do not publish in DNS.[16]

The **hostname** command assigns a hostname to a machine. **hostname** is typically run at boot time from one of the startup scripts, which obtains the name to be assigned from a configuration file. (Of course, each system does this slightly differently. See the system-specific sections beginning on page 484 for details.) The hostname should be fully qualified: that is, it should include both the hostname and the DNS domain name, such as anchor.cs.colorado.edu.

See page 728 for more information about LDAP.

At a small site, you can easily dole out hostnames and IP addresses by hand. But when many networks and many different administrative groups are involved, it helps to have some central coordination to ensure uniqueness. For dynamically assigned networking parameters, DHCP takes care of the uniqueness issues. Some sites now use LDAP databases to manage their hostnames and IP addresses assignments.

ifconfig: configure network interfaces

ifconfig enables or disables a network interface, sets its IP address and subnet mask, and sets various other options and parameters. It is usually run at boot time with command-line parameters taken from config files, but you can also run it by

16. You can also use a split DNS configuration to achieve this goal; see page 617.

hand to make changes on the fly. Be careful if you are making **ifconfig** changes and are logged in remotely—many a sysadmin has been locked out this way and had to drive in to fix things.

An **ifconfig** command most commonly has the form

ifconfig *interface [family] address options...*

For example, the command

```
ifconfig eth0 192.168.1.13 netmask 255.255.255.0 up
```

sets the IPv4 address and netmask associated with the interface eth0 and readies the interface for use.

interface identifies the hardware interface to which the command applies. It is usually a two- or three-character name followed by a number, but Solaris interface names can be longer. Some common names are ie0, le0, le1, ln0, en0, we0, qe0, hme0, eth0, and lan0. The loopback interface is lo on Linux and lo0 on Solaris, HP-UX, and AIX. On most systems, **ifconfig -a** lists the system's network interfaces and summarizes their current settings. Use **netstat -i** for this on HP-UX.

Under Solaris, network interfaces must be "attached" with **ifconfig** *interface* **plumb** before they become configurable and visible to **ifconfig -a**. You can use the **dladm** command to list interfaces regardless of whether they have been plumbed.

The *family* parameter tells **ifconfig** which network protocol ("address family") you want to configure. You can set up multiple protocols on an interface and use them all simultaneously, but they must be configured separately. The main options here are **inet** for IPv4 and **inet6** for IPv6; **inet** is assumed if you leave the parameter out. Linux systems support a handful of other legacy protocols such as AppleTalk and Novell IPX.

The *address* parameter specifies the interface's IP address. A hostname is also acceptable here, but the hostname must be resolvable to an IP address at boot time. For a machine's primary interface, this means that the hostname must appear in the local **hosts** file, since other name resolution methods depend on the network having been initialized.

The keyword **up** turns the interface on; **down** turns it off. When an **ifconfig** command assigns an IP address to an interface, as in the example above, the **up** parameter is implicit and does not need to be mentioned by name.

ifconfig understands lots of other options. The most common ones are mentioned below, but as always, consult your man pages for the final word on your particular system. **ifconfig** options all have symbolic names. Some options require an argument, which should be placed immediately after the option name and separated from the option name by a space.

The **netmask** option sets the subnet mask for the interface and is required if the network is not subnetted according to its address class (A, B, or C). The mask can be specified in dotted decimal notation or as a 4-byte hexadecimal number beginning with **0x**. As usual, bits set to 1 are part of the network number, and bits set to 0 are part of the host number.

The **broadcast** option specifies the IP broadcast address for the interface, expressed in either hex or dotted quad notation. The default broadcast address is one in which the host part is set to all 1s. In the **ifconfig** example above, the autoconfigured broadcast address is 192.168.1.255.

You can set the broadcast address to any IP address that's valid for the network to which the host is attached. Some sites have chosen weird values for the broadcast address in the hope of avoiding certain types of denial of service attacks that are based on broadcast pings, but this is risky and probably overkill. Failure to properly configure every machine's broadcast address can lead to broadcast storms, in which packets travel from machine to machine until their TTLs expire.[17]

A better way to avoid problems with broadcast pings is to prevent your border routers from forwarding them and to tell individual hosts not to respond to them. See Chapter 22, *Security*, for instructions on how to implement these constraints.

solaris

Solaris integrates the **ifconfig** command with its DHCP client daemon. **ifconfig** *interface* **dhcp** configures the named interface with parameters leased from a local DHCP server, then starts **dhcpagent** to manage the leases over the long term. Other systems keep **ifconfig** ignorant of DHCP, with the DHCP software operating as a separate layer.

You can also get the configuration for a single interface with **ifconfig** *interface*:

```
solaris$ ifconfig e1000g0

e1000g0: flags=1000843<UP,BROADCAST,RUNNING,MULTICAST,IPv4> mtu 1500
     index 2 inet 192.168.10.10 netmask ffffff00 broadcast 192.168.10.255

redhat$ ifconfig eth0
eth0  Link encap:Ethernet  HWaddr 00:02:B3:19:C8:86
        inet addr:192.168.1.13  Bcast:192.168.1.255  Mask:255.255.255.0
        UP BROADCAST RUNNING MULTICAST  MTU:1500  Metric:1
        RX packets:206983 errors:0 dropped:0 overruns:0 frame:0
        TX packets:218292 errors:0 dropped:0 overruns:0 carrier:0
        collisions:0 txqueuelen:100
        Interrupt:7 Base address:0xef00
```

The lack of collisions on the Ethernet interface in the second example may indicate a very lightly loaded network or, more likely, a switched network. On a shared

17. Broadcast storms occur because the same link-layer broadcast address must be used to transport packets no matter what the IP broadcast address has been set to. For example, suppose that machine X thinks the broadcast address is A1 and machine Y thinks it is A2. If X sends a packet to address A1, Y will receive the packet (because the link-layer destination address is the broadcast address), will see that the packet is not for itself and also not for the broadcast address (because Y thinks the broadcast address is A2), and may then forward the packet back to the net. If two machines are in Y's state, the packet circulates until its TTL expires. Broadcast storms can erode your bandwidth, especially on a large switched net.

network (one built with hubs instead of switches, or one that uses old-style coaxial Ethernet), check this number to ensure that it is below about 5% of the output packets. Lots of collisions indicate a loaded network that needs to be watched and possibly split into multiple subnets or migrated to a switched infrastructure.

Now that you know how to configure a network interface by hand, you need to figure out how the parameters to **ifconfig** are set when the machine boots, and you need to make sure that the new values are entered correctly. You normally do this by editing one or more configuration files; see the vendor-specific sections starting on page 484 for more information.

One additional comment regarding **ifconfig**: you can assign more than one IP address to an interface by making use of the concept of "virtual network interfaces" or "IP aliases." Administrators can do this to allow one machine to host several web sites. See page 967 for more information.

Network hardware options

Network hardware often has configurable options that are specific to its media type and have little to do with TCP/IP per se. One common example of this is modern-day Ethernet, wherein an interface card may support 10, 100, 1000, or even 10000 Mb/s in either half-duplex or full-duplex mode. Most equipment defaults to autonegotiation mode, in which both the card and its upstream connection (usually a switch port) try to guess what the other wants to use.

Historically, autonegotiation has worked about as well as a blindfolded cowpoke trying to rope a calf. Modern network devices play better together, but autonegotiation is still a common source of failure. High packet loss rates (especially for large packets) are a common artifact of failed autonegotiation.

If you're having problems with mysterious packet loss, turn off autonegotiation everywhere as your first course of action. Lock the interface speed and duplex on both servers and the switch ports to which they are connected. Autonegotiation is useful for ports in public areas where roving laptops may stop for a visit, but it serves no useful purpose for statically attached hosts other than avoiding a small amount of administration.

The exact method by which hardware options like autonegotiation are set varies widely, so we defer discussion of those details to the system-specific sections starting on page 484.

route: configure static routes

The **route** command defines static routes, explicit routing table entries that never change, even if you run a routing daemon. When you add a new machine to a local area network, you usually need to specify only a default route.

This book's discussion of routing is split between this section and Chapter 15, *Routing*. Although most of the basic information about routing and the **route** command is found in this section, you might find it helpful to read the first few sections of Chapter 15 if you need more information.

Routing is performed at the IP layer. When a packet bound for some other host arrives, the packet's destination IP address is compared with the routes in the kernel's routing table. If the address matches a route in the table, the packet is forwarded to the next-hop gateway IP address associated with that route.

There are two special cases. First, a packet may be destined for some host on a directly connected network. In this case, the "next-hop gateway" address in the routing table is one of the local host's own interfaces, and the packet is sent directly to its destination. This type of route is added to the routing table for you by the **ifconfig** command when you configure an interface.

Second, it may be that no route matches the destination address. In this case, the default route is invoked if one exists. Otherwise, an ICMP "network unreachable" or "host unreachable" message is returned to the sender.

Many local area networks have only one way out, so all they need is a single default route that points to the exit. On the Internet backbone, the routers do not have default routes. If there is no routing entry for a destination, that destination cannot be reached.

Each **route** command adds or removes one route. Unfortunately, **route** is one of a handful of UNIX commands that function identically across systems and yet have somewhat different syntax everywhere. Here's a prototypical **route** command that works almost everywhere:

```
# route add -net 192.168.45.128/25 zulu-gw.atrust.net
```

This command adds a route to the 192.168.45.128/25 network through the gateway router zulu-gw.atrust.net, which must be either an adjacent host or one of the local host's own interfaces. (Linux requires the option name **gw** in front of the gateway address.) Naturally, **route** must be able to resolve zulu-gw.atrust.net into an IP address. Use a numeric IP address if your DNS server is on the other side of the gateway!

Linux also accepts an interface name (e.g., eth0) as the destination for a route. It has the same effect as specifying the interface's primary IP address as the gateway address. That is, the IP stack attempts direct delivery on that interface rather than forwarding to a separate gateway. Routing entries that were set up this way show their gateway addresses as 0.0.0.0 in **netstat -r** output. You can tell where the route really goes by looking in the Iface column for the interface name.

Destination networks were traditionally specified with separate IP addresses and netmasks, but all versions of **route** except that of HP-UX now understand CIDR notation (e.g., 128.138.176.0/20). CIDR notation is clearer and relieves you of the need to fuss over some of the system-specific syntax issues. Even Linux accepts CIDR notation, although the Linux man page for **route** doesn't admit this.

Solaris has a nifty **-p** option to **route** that makes your changes persistent across reboots. In addition to being entered in the kernel's routing table, the changes are recorded in **/etc/inet/static_routes** and restored at boot time.

Some other tricks:

- To inspect existing routes, use the command **netstat -nr**, or **netstat -r** if you want to see names instead of numbers. Numbers are often better if you are debugging, since the name lookup may be the thing that is broken. An example of **netstat** output is shown on page 466.
- Use the keyword **default** instead of an address or network name to set the system's default route.
- Use **route delete** or **route del** to remove entries from the routing table.
- UNIX systems use **route -f** or **route flush** to initialize the routing table and start over. Linux does not support this option.
- IPv6 routes are set up similarly to IPv4 routes. You'll need to tell **route** that you're working in IPv6 space with the **-inet6** or **-A inet6** option.
- **/etc/networks** maps names to network numbers, much like the **hosts** file maps hostnames to IP addresses. Commands such as **route** that expect a network number can accept a name if it is listed in the **networks** file. Network names can also be listed in an NIS database or in DNS; see RFC1101.
- You can use **route add -host** to set up a route that's specific to a single IP address. It's essentially the same as a route with a netmask of 255.255.255.255, but it's flagged separately in the routing table.

DNS configuration

To configure a machine as a DNS client, you need only set up the **/etc/resolv.conf** file. DNS service is not, strictly speaking, required (see page 739), but it's hard to imagine a situation in which you'd want to eliminate it completely.

The **resolv.conf** file lists the DNS domains that should be searched to resolve names that are incomplete (that is, not fully qualified, such as anchor instead of anchor.cs.colorado.edu) and the IP addresses of the name servers to contact for name lookups. A sample is shown here; for more details, see page 561.

```
search cs.colorado.edu colorado.edu
nameserver 128.138.242.1
nameserver 128.138.243.151
nameserver 192.108.21.1
```

/etc/resolv.conf should list the "closest" stable name server first. Servers are contacted in order, and the timeout after which the next server in line is tried can be quite long. You can have up to three nameserver entries. If possible, you should always have more than one.

If the local host obtains the addresses of its DNS servers through DHCP, the DHCP client software stuffs these addresses into the **resolv.conf** file for you when it obtains the leases. Since DHCP configuration is the default for most systems, you generally do not need to configure the **resolv.conf** file manually if your DHCP server has been set up correctly.

Many sites use Microsoft's Active Directory DNS server implementation. That works fine with the standard UNIX and Linux **resolv.conf**; there's no need to do anything differently.

14.11 System-specific network configuration

On early UNIX systems, you configured the network by editing the system startup scripts and directly changing the commands they contained. Modern systems have read-only scripts; they cover a variety of configuration scenarios and choose among them by reusing information from other system files or consulting configuration files of their own.

Although this separation of configuration and implementation is a good idea, every system does it a little bit differently. The format and use of the **/etc/hosts** and **/etc/resolv.conf** files are relatively consistent among UNIX and Linux systems, but that's about all you can count on for sure.

Most systems provide some sort of GUI interface for basic configuration tasks, but the mapping between the visual interface and the configuration files behind the scenes is often unclear. In addition, the GUIs tend to ignore advanced configurations, and they are relatively inconvenient for remote and automated administration. In the next sections, we pick apart some of the variations among our example systems, describe what's going on under the hood, and cover the details of network configuration for each of our supported operating systems. In particular, we cover

- Basic configuration
- DHCP client configuration
- Dynamic reconfiguration and tuning
- Security, firewalls, filtering, and NAT configuration
- Quirks

However, not all of our operating systems need discussion for each topic.

Keep in mind that most network configuration happens at boot time, so there's some overlap between the information here and the information presented in Chapter 3, *Booting and Shutting Down*.

14.12 Linux networking

Linux is always one of the first networking stacks to include new features. The Linux folks are sometimes so quick that the rest of the networking infrastructure cannot interoperate. For example, the Linux implementation of explicit congestion notification (ECN), specified in RFC2481, collided with incorrect default settings on an older Cisco firewall product, causing all packets with the ECN bit set to be dropped. Oops.

Linux developers love to tinker, and they often implement features and algorithms that aren't yet accepted standards. One example is the Linux kernel's addition of pluggable congestion control algorithms in release 2.6.13. The several options include variations for lossy networks, high-speed WANs with lots of packet loss, satellite links, and more. The standard TCP "reno" mechanism (slow start, congestion avoidance, fast retransmit, and fast recovery) is still used by default, but a variant may be more appropriate for your environment.

After any change to a file that controls network configuration at boot time, you may need to either reboot or bring the network interface down and then up again for your change to take effect. You can use **ifdown** *interface* and **ifup** *interface* for this purpose on most Linux systems, although the implementations are not identical. (Under SUSE, **ifup** and **ifdown** only work when networking is not under the control of NetworkManager.)

NetworkManager

Linux support for mobile networking was relatively scattershot until the advent of NetworkManager in 2004. It consists of a service that's designed to be run continuously, along with a system tray app for configuring individual network interfaces. In addition to various kinds of wired network, NetworkManager also handles transient wireless networks, wireless broadband, and VPNs. It continually assesses the available networks and shifts service to "preferred" networks as they become available. Wired networks are most preferred, followed by familiar wireless networks.

This system represents quite a change for Linux network configuration. In addition to being more fluid than the traditional static configuration, it's also designed to be run and managed by users rather than system administrators. NetworkManager has been widely adopted by Linux distributions, including all of our examples, but in an effort to avoid breaking existing scripts and setups, it's usually made available as a sort of "parallel universe" of network configuration in addition to whatever traditional network configuration was used in the past.

SUSE makes you choose whether you want to live in the NetworkManager world or use the legacy configuration system, which is managed through YaST. Ubuntu runs NetworkManager by default, but keeps the statically configured network interfaces out of the NetworkManager domain. Red Hat Enterprise Linux doesn't run NetworkManager by default at all.

NetworkManager is primarily of use on laptops, since their network environment may change frequently. For servers and desktop systems, NetworkManager isn't necessary and may in fact complicate administration. In these environments, it should be ignored or configured out.

Ubuntu network configuration

As shown in Table 14.6, Ubuntu configures the network in **/etc/hostname** and **/etc/network/interfaces**, with a bit of help from the file **/etc/network/options**.

Table 14.6 Ubuntu network configuration files in /etc

File	What's set there
hostname	Hostname
network/interfaces	IP address, netmask, default route

The hostname is set in **/etc/hostname**. The name in this file should be fully qualified; its value is used in a variety of contexts, some of which require qualification.

The IP address, netmask, and default gateway are set in **/etc/network/interfaces**. A line starting with the iface keyword introduces each interface. The iface line can be followed by indented lines that specify additional parameters. For example:

```
auto lo eth0
iface lo inet loopback
iface eth0 inet static
    address 192.168.1.102
    netmask 255.255.255.0
    gateway 192.168.1.254
```

The **ifup** and **ifdown** commands read this file and bring the interfaces up or down by calling lower-level commands (such as **ifconfig**) with the appropriate parameters. The auto clause specifies the interfaces to be brought up at boot time or whenever **ifup -a** is run.

The inet keyword in the iface line is the address family a la **ifconfig**. The keyword static is called a "method" and specifies that the IP address and netmask for eth0 are directly assigned. The address and netmask lines are required for static configurations; earlier versions of the Linux kernel also required the network address to be specified, but now the kernel is smarter and can figure out the network address from the IP address and netmask. The gateway line specifies the address of the default network gateway and is used to install a default route.

SUSE network configuration

SUSE makes you choose between NetworkManager and the traditional configuration system. You make the choice inside of YaST; you can also use the YaST GUI to configure the traditional system. Here, we assume the traditional system. In addition to configuring network interfaces, YaST provides straightforward UIs for the **/etc/hosts** file, static routes, and DNS configuration. Table 14.7 shows the underlying configuration files.

Table 14.7 SUSE network configuration files in /etc/sysconfig/network

File	What's set there
ifcfg-*interface*	Hostname, IP address, netmask, and more
ifroute-*interface*	Interface-specific route definitions
routes	Default route and static routes for all interfaces
config	Lots of less commonly used network variables

With the exceptions of DNS parameters and the system hostname, SUSE sets most networking options in **ifcfg-***interface* files in the **/etc/sysconfig/network** directory. One file should be present for each interface on the system.

In addition to specifying the IP address, gateway, and broadcast information for an interface, the **ifcfg-*** files can tune many other network dials. Take a look at the **ifcfg.template** file for a well-commented rundown of the possible parameters. Here's a simple example with our comments:

```
BOOTPROTO='static'       # Static is implied but it doesn't hurt to be verbose.
IPADDR='192.168.1.4/24'  # The /24 defines the NETWORK and NETMASK vars
NAME='AMD PCnet - Fast 79C971' # Used to start and stop the interface.
STARTMODE='auto'         # Start automatically at boot
USERCONTROL='no'         # Disable control through kinternet/cinternet GUI
```

Global static routing information for a SUSE system (including the default route) is stored in the **routes** file. Each line in this file is like a **route** command with the option names omitted and includes destination, gateway, netmask, interface, and optional extra parameters to be stored in the routing table for use by routing daemons. For the host configured above, which has only a default route, the **routes** file contains the line

```
default 192.168.1.254 - -
```

Routes unique to specific interfaces are kept in **ifroute-***interface* files, where the nomenclature of the *interface* component is the same as for the **ifcfg-*** files. The contents have the same format as the **routes** file.

Red Hat network configuration

Red Hat's network configuration GUI is called **system-config-network**; it's also accessible from the System->Administration menu under the name Network. This tool provides a simple UI for configuring individual network interfaces and static routes. It also has panels for setting up IPsec tunnels, configuring DNS, and adding **/etc/hosts** entries.

Table 14.8 shows the underlying configuration files that this GUI edits.

You set the machine's hostname in **/etc/sysconfig/network**, which also contains lines that specify the machine's DNS domain and default gateway.

Table 14.8 Red Hat network configuration files in /etc/sysconfig

File	What's set there
network	Hostname, default route
static-routes	Static routes
network-scripts/ifcfg-*ifname*	Per-interface parameters: IP address, netmask, etc.

For example, here is a **network** file for a host with a single Ethernet interface:

```
NETWORKING=yes
NETWORKING_IPV6=no
HOSTNAME=redhat.toadranch.com
DOMAINNAME=toadranch.com       ### optional
GATEWAY=192.168.1.254
```

Interface-specific data is stored in **/etc/sysconfig/network-scripts/ifcfg-***ifname*, where *ifname* is the name of the network interface. These configuration files set the IP address, netmask, network, and broadcast address for each interface. They also include a line that specifies whether the interface should be configured "up" at boot time.

A generic machine will have files for an Ethernet interface (eth0) and for the loopback interface (lo). For example,

```
DEVICE=eth0
IPADDR=192.168.1.13
NETMASK=255.255.255.0
NETWORK=192.168.1.0
BROADCAST=192.168.1.255
ONBOOT=yes
```

and

```
DEVICE=lo
IPADDR=127.0.0.1
NETMASK=255.0.0.0
NETWORK=127.0.0.0
BROADCAST=127.255.255.255
ONBOOT=yes
NAME=loopback
```

are the **ifcfg-eth0** and **ifcfg-lo** files for the machine redhat.toadranch.com described in the **network** file above. A DHCP-based setup for eth0 is even simpler:

```
DEVICE=eth0
BOOTPROTO=dhcp
ONBOOT=yes
```

After changing configuration information in /**etc/sysconfig**, run **ifdown** *ifname* followed by **ifup** *ifname* for the appropriate interface. If you reconfigure multiple interfaces at once, you can use the command **service network restart** to reset all

networking. (This is really just a shorthand way to run **/etc/rc.d/init.d/network**, which is invoked at boot time with the **start** argument.)

The startup scripts can also configure static routes. Any routes added to the file **/etc/sysconfig/static-routes** are entered into the routing table at boot time. The entries specify arguments to **route add**, although in a different order:

```
eth0 net 130.225.204.48 netmask 255.255.255.248 gw 130.225.204.49
eth1 net 192.38.8.0 netmask 255.255.255.224 gw 192.38.8.129
```

The interface is specified first, but it is actually shuffled to the end of the **route** command line, where it forces the route to be associated with the given interface. (You'll see this architecture in the GUI as well, where the routes are configured as part of the setup for each interface.) The rest of the line consists of **route** arguments. The **static-routes** example above would produce the following commands:

```
route add -net 130.225.204.48 netmask 255.255.255.248 gw 130.225.204.49 eth0
route add -net 192.38.8.0 netmask 255.255.255.224 gw 192.38.8.129 eth1
```

Current Linux kernels do not use the metric parameter to **route**, but they allow it to be entered into the routing table for use by routing daemons.

Linux network hardware options

The **ethtool** command queries and sets a network interface's media-specific parameters such as link speed and duplex. It replaces the old **mii-tool** command, but some systems still include both.

You can query the status of an interface just by naming it. For example, this eth0 interface (a generic NIC on a PC motherboard) has autonegotiation enabled and is currently running at full speed:

```
ubuntu# ethtool eth0
Settings for eth0:
        Supported ports: [ TP MII ]
        Supported link modes:   10baseT/Half     10baseT/Full
                                100baseT/Half    100baseT/Full
                                1000baseT/Half   1000baseT/Full
        Supports auto-negotiation: Yes
        Advertised link modes:  10baseT/Half     10baseT/Full
                                100baseT/Half    100baseT/Full
                                1000baseT/Half   1000baseT/Full
        Advertised auto-negotiation: Yes
        Speed: 1000Mb/s
        Duplex: Full
        Port: MII
        PHYAD: 0
        Transceiver: internal
        Auto-negotiation: on
        Supports Wake-on: pumbg
        Wake-on: g
        Current message level: 0x00000033 (51)
        Link detected: yes
```

To lock this interface to 100 Mb/s full duplex, use the command

```
ubuntu# ethtool -s eth0 speed 100 duplex full
```

If you are trying to determine whether autonegotiation is reliable in your environment, you may also find **ethtool -r** helpful. It forces the parameters of the link to be renegotiated immediately.

Another useful option is **-k**, which shows what protocol-related tasks have been assigned to the network interface rather than being performed by the kernel. Most interfaces can calculate checksums, and some can assist with segmentation as well. Unless you have reason to think that a network interface is not doing these tasks reliably, it's always better to offload them. You can use **ethtool -K** in combination with various suboptions to force or disable specific types of offloading. (The **-k** option shows current values and the **-K** option sets them.)

Any changes you make with **ethtool** are transient. If you want them to be enforced consistently, you'll have to make sure that **ethtool** gets run as part of the system's network configuration. It's best to do this as part of the per-interface configuration; if you just arrange to have some **ethtool** commands run at boot time, your configuration will not properly cover cases in which the interfaces are restarted without a reboot of the system.

On Red Hat systems, you can include an ETHTOOL_OPTS= line in the configuration file for the interface underneath **/etc/sysconfig/network-scripts**. **ifup** passes the entire line as arguments to **ethtool**.

SUSE's provision for running **ethtool** is similar to Red Hat's, but the option is called ETHTOOL_OPTIONS and the per-interface configuration files are kept in **/etc/sysconfig/network**.

In Ubuntu, you can run the **ethtool** commands from a post-up script specified in the interface's configuration in **/etc/network/interfaces**.

Linux TCP/IP options

Linux puts a representation of each tunable kernel variable into the **/proc** virtual filesystem. The networking variables are in **/proc/sys/net/ipv4**. Here's a trimmed list of some of the most interesting ones for illustration:

```
ubuntu$ cd /proc/sys/net/ipv4; ls -F
...                              ...                      tcp_no_metrics_save
conf/                            tcp_congestion_control   tcp_orphan_retries
icmp_echo_ignore_all             tcp_dma_copybreak        tcp_reordering
icmp_echo_ignore_broadcasts      tcp_dsack                tcp_retrans_collapse
...                              tcp_ecn                  tcp_retries1
icmp_ratelimit                   tcp_fack                 tcp_retries2
icmp_ratemask                    tcp_fin_timeout          tcp_rfc1337
igmp_max_memberships             tcp_frto                 tcp_rmem
igmp_max_msf                     tcp_frto_response        tcp_sack
inet_peer_gc_maxtime             tcp_keepalive_intvl      ,,,
inet_peer_gc_mintime             tcp_keepalive_probes     tcp_stdurg
```

```
inet_peer_maxttl          tcp_keepalive_time       tcp_synack_retries
inet_peer_minttl          tcp_low_latency          tcp_syncookies
inet_peer_threshold       tcp_max_orphans          tcp_syn_retries
ip_default_ttl            tcp_max_ssthresh         tcp_timestamps
ip_dynaddr                tcp_max_syn_backlog      ...
ip_forward                tcp_max_tw_buckets       udp_mem
...                       tcp_mem                  udp_rmem_min
neigh/                    tcp_moderate_rcvbuf      udp_wmem_min
route/                    tcp_mtu_probing
```

Many of the variables with rate and max in their names are used to thwart denial of service attacks. The **conf** subdirectory contains variables that are set per interface. It contains subdirectories **all** and **default** and a subdirectory for each interface (including the loopback). Each subdirectory contains the same set of files.

```
ubuntu$ cd conf/default; ls -F
accept_redirects       disable_policy        promote_secondaries
accept_source_route    disable_xfrm          proxy_arp
arp_accept             force_igmp_version    rp_filter
arp_announce           forwarding            secure_redirects
arp_filter             log_martians          send_redirects
arp_ignore             mc_forwarding         shared_media
bootp_relay            medium_id             tag
```

If you change a variable in the **conf/eth0** subdirectory, for example, your change applies to that interface only. If you change the value in the **conf/all** directory, you might expect it to set the corresponding value for all existing interfaces, but this is not in fact what happens. Each variable has its own rules for accepting changes via **all**. Some values are ORed with the current values, some are ANDed, and still others are MAXed or MINed. As far as we are aware, there is no documentation for this process outside of the kernel source code, so the whole debacle is probably best avoided. Just confine your modifications to individual interfaces.

If you change a variable in the **conf/default** directory, the new value propagates to any interfaces that are later configured. On the other hand, it's nice to keep the defaults unmolested as reference information; they make a nice sanity check if you want to undo other changes.

The **/proc/sys/net/ipv4/neigh** directory also contains a subdirectory for each interface. The files in each subdirectory control ARP table management and IPv6 neighbor discovery for that interface. Here is the list of variables; the ones starting with gc (for garbage collection) determine how ARP table entries are timed out and discarded.

```
ubuntu$ cd neigh/default; ls -F
anycast_delay              gc_stale_time     proxy_delay
app_solicit                gc_thresh1        proxy_qlen
base_reachable_time        gc_thresh2        retrans_time
base_reachable_time_ms     gc_thresh3        retrans_time_ms
delay_first_probe_time     locktime          ucast_solicit
gc_interval                mcast_solicit     unres_qlen
```

To see the value of a variable, use **cat**; to set it, use **echo** redirected to the proper filename. For example, the command

```
ubuntu$ cat icmp_echo_ignore_broadcasts
0
```

shows that this variable's value is 0, meaning that broadcast pings are not ignored. To set it to 1 (and avoid falling prey to Smurf-type denial of service attacks), run

```
ubuntu$ sudo sh -c "echo 1 > icmp_echo_ignore_broadcasts"
```
[18]

from the **/proc/sys/net** directory.

You are typically logged in over the same network you are tweaking as you adjust these variables, so be careful! You can mess things up badly enough to require a reboot from the console to recover, which might be inconvenient if the system happens to be in Point Barrow, Alaska, and it's January. Test-tune these variables on your desktop system before you even think of tweaking a production machine.

To change any of these parameters permanently (or more accurately, to reset them every time the system boots), add the appropriate variables to **/etc/sysctl.conf**, which is read by the **sysctl** command at boot time. The format of the **sysctl.conf** file is *variable=value* rather than **echo value > variable** as you would run from the shell to change the variable by hand. Variable names are pathnames relative to **/proc/sys**; you can also use dots instead of slashes if you prefer. For example, either of the lines

```
net.ipv4.ip_forward=0
net/ipv4/ip_forward=0
```

in the **/etc/sysctl.conf** file would turn off IP forwarding on this host.

Some of the options under **/proc** are better documented than others. Your best bet is to look at the man page for the protocol in question in section 7 of the manuals. For example, **man 7 icmp** documents four of the six available options. (You must have man pages for the Linux kernel installed to see man pages about protocols.)

You can also take a look at the **ip-sysctl.txt** file in the kernel source distribution for some good comments. If you don't have kernel source installed, just google for ip-sysctl-txt to reach the same document.

Security-related kernel variables

Table 14.9 shows Linux's default behavior with regard to various touchy network issues. For a brief description of the implications of these behaviors, see page 472. We recommend that you verify the values of these variables so that you do not answer broadcast pings, do not listen to routing redirects, and do not accept

18. If you try this command in the form **sudo echo 1 > icmp_echo_ignore_broadcasts**, you just generate a "permission denied" message—your shell attempts to open the output file before it runs **sudo**. You want the **sudo** to apply to both the **echo** command and the redirection. Ergo, you must create a root subshell in which to execute the entire command.

source-routed packets. These should be the defaults on current distributions except for **accept_redirects** and sometimes **accept_source_route**.

Table 14.9 Default security-related network behaviors in Linux

Feature	Host	Gateway	Control file (in /proc/sys/net/ipv4)
IP forwarding	off	on	**ip_forward** for the whole system **conf/***interface***/forwarding** per interface[a]
ICMP redirects	obeys	ignores	**conf/***interface***/accept_redirects**
Source routing	*varies*	*varies*	**conf/***interface***/accept_source_route**
Broadcast ping	ignores	ignores	**icmp_echo_ignore_broadcasts**

a. The *interface* can be either a specific interface name or **all**.

Linux NAT and packet filtering

Linux traditionally implements only a limited form of Network Address Translation (NAT) that is more properly called Port Address Translation, or PAT. Instead of using a range of IP addresses as a true NAT implementation would, PAT multiplexes all connections onto a single address. The details and differences aren't of much practical importance, though.

iptables implements not only NAT but also packet filtering. In earlier versions of Linux this functionality was a bit of a mess, but **iptables** makes a much cleaner separation between the NAT and filtering features.

Packet filtering features are covered in more detail in the *Security* chapter starting on page 932. If you use NAT to let local hosts access the Internet, you *must* use a full complement of firewall filters when running NAT. The fact that NAT "isn't really IP routing" doesn't make a Linux NAT gateway any more secure than a Linux router. For brevity, we describe only the actual NAT configuration here; however, this is but a small part of a full configuration.

To make NAT work, you must enable IP forwarding in the kernel by setting the **/proc/sys/net/ipv4/ip_forward** kernel variable to 1. Additionally, you must insert the appropriate kernel modules:

```
ubuntu$ sudo /sbin/modprobe iptable_nat
ubuntu$ sudo /sbin/modprobe ip_conntrack
ubuntu$ sudo /sbin/modprobe ip_conntrack_ftp
```

Many other connection-tracking modules exist; see the **net/netfilter** subdirectory underneath **/lib/modules** for a more complete list and enable the ones you need.

The **iptables** command to route packets using NAT is of the form

```
sudo iptables -t nat -A POSTROUTING -o eth1 -j SNAT --to 63.173.189.1
```

In this example, eth0 is the interface connected to the Internet. The eth0 interface does not appear directly in the command line above, but its IP address is the one that appears as the argument to **--to**. The eth1 interface is the one connected to the internal network.

To Internet hosts, it appears that all packets from hosts on the internal network have eth0's IP address. The host performing NAT receives incoming packets, looks up their true destinations, rewrites them with the appropriate internal network IP address, and sends them on their merry way.

14.13 Solaris networking

Solaris comes with a bounteous supply of startup scripts. At a trade show, we once scored a tear-off calendar with sysadmin trivia questions on each day's page. The question for January 1 was to name all the files you had to touch to change the hostname and IP address on a machine running Solaris. A quick peek at the answers showed six files. This is modularization taken to bizarre extremes. That said, let's look at Solaris network configuration.

Solaris basic network configuration

Solaris stashes some network configuration files in **/etc** and some in **/etc/inet**. Many are duplicated through the magic of symbolic links, with the actual files living in **/etc/inet** and the links in **/etc**.

To set the hostname, enter it into the file **/etc/nodename**. The change will take effect when the machine is rebooted. Some sites use just the short hostname; others use the fully qualified domain name.

See page 739 for more information about the name service switch.

The **/etc/defaultdomain** file's name suggests that it might be used to specify the DNS domain, but it actually specifies the NIS or NIS+ domain name. The DNS domain is specified in **/etc/resolv.conf** as usual.

Solaris uses **/etc/nsswitch.conf** to set the order in which **/etc/hosts**, NIS, NIS+, and DNS are consulted for hostname resolution. We recommend looking at the **hosts** file, then DNS for easy booting. The line from **nsswitch.conf** would be

```
hosts:   files  dns
```

This is the default configuration if the host receives the addresses of its DNS servers through DHCP.

Solaris networking can run in traditional mode or in "Network Auto-Magic" (NWAM) mode, where networking is managed autonomously by the **nwamd** daemon. NWAM mode is fine for workstations, but it has limited configurability and allows only one network interface to be active at a time. The discussion below assumes traditional mode.

To see which networking mode is active, run **svcs svc:/network/physical**. There should be two configuration lines, one for NWAM and one for the traditional mode ("default"). Run **svcadm** to switch the configuration. For example, the following exchange shows the system being taken from NWAM to traditional mode.

```
solaris$ svcs svc:/network/physical
STATE       STIME     FMRI
disabled    Mar_31    svc:/network/physical:default
online      Mar_31    svc:/network/physical:nwam
solaris$ sudo svcadm disable svc:/network/physical:nwam
solaris$ sudo svcadm enable svc:/network/physical:default
```

Solaris configures the IP address of each network interface through a file called **/etc/hostname.***interface*, where *interface* is the usual name of the interface. These files can contain either a hostname that appears in the **hosts** file or an IP address. The value in a **hostname.***interface* file is used as the *address* parameter to **ifconfig**, so it's safest to use an address, even though the configuration filename implies that a hostname is expected.

Any special **ifconfig** options can also be put in the **hostname.***interface* file on the same line as the hostname or IP address; it is all one big **ifconfig** command line. The startup scripts try to discover the IP addresses of any interfaces without corresponding **hostname** files by using DHCP.[19]

As shipped, the Solaris startup files rely on using the **ifconfig** options **netmask +** and **broadcast +**. The pluses mean to look in **/etc/netmasks** for the netmask value and to figure out the broadcast address value from it. The **/etc/netmasks** file lists network numbers and their corresponding netmask values. Any network that is subnetted differently from its inherent network class (A, B, or C) must be represented in the file. Here is an example of a **netmasks** file:

```
# CS Department network masks database
# Network         netmask
# =======         =======
#
128.138.0.0       255.255.255.192    # default for dept.
#
128.138.192.64    255.255.255.192    # drag
128.138.192.192   255.255.255.192    # csops
128.138.193.0     255.255.255.224    # bcrg
128.138.193.32    255.255.255.224    # database
128.138.198.0     255.255.255.0      # slip
...
```

The first line sets a default of /26 for the class B address 128.138.0.0, which is then overridden with specific masks that vary from the default. All networks are listed, even though many use the default value and could in fact be left out. On the systems from which this example is taken, the **netmasks** file is centrally maintained and distributed to all hosts. No single host has interfaces on all these networks.

19. Solaris network interfaces must be scoped out with **ifconfig plumb** to make them accessible. You might have to run this command by hand when performing manual configuration.

In older versions of Solaris, the network startup scripts were files in **/etc/init.d** (chiefly **rootusr**, **inetinit**, **sysid.net**, and **inetsvc**). Solaris 10 radically restructured the way that startup files and system services are managed. The scripts have been refactored and now live in **/lib/svc/method**. See page 97 for an overview of Solaris's Service Management Facility.

If **/etc/defaultrouter** exists, it is assumed to contain the identity (which again can be either a hostname or a numeric address) of the default gateway, and no further routing configuration is performed. As usual, a numeric address is preferable; using a name requires an **/etc/hosts** entry or a DNS server on the local network.

Solaris used to run **routed** (which it actually called **in.routed**) whenever no default gateway was specified, but in Solaris 10 and later you must enable **routed** explicitly with **svcadm enable routing/route**. Use the command **svcs route** to determine the service's current state.

Beware: **routed** will go into server (talkative) mode automatically if the machine has more than one network interface or the file **/etc/gateways** exists. This is generally not what you want. You can prevent routed from squawking by turning on the "quiet mode" flag:

```
solaris# svccfg -s routing/route:default setprop routing/quiet_mode = true
```

Solaris configuration examples

Here are some examples of the commands needed to bring up a Solaris interface and add a route to a default gateway:

```
solaris$ sudo ifconfig e1000g0 plumb
solaris$ sudo ifconfig e1000g0 192.108.21.48 netmask 255.255.255.0 up
solaris$ sudo route add default 192.108.21.254
```

The following examples show how to see the status of network interfaces and routing tables. Commands prefaced with **sudo** must be run as root. The final example shows a feature of the Solaris **route** command that is not present on our other architectures: the **get** argument shows the next hop to a particular destination. We have taken some liberties to make the examples fit on the page.

```
solaris$ ifconfig -a
lo0: flags=2001000849<UP,LOOPBACK,RUNNING,MULTICAST,IPv4,VIRTUAL>
     mtu 8232 index 1 inet 127.0.0.1 netmask ff000000
e1000g0: flags=1000843<UP,BROADCAST,RUNNING,MULTICAST,IPv4> mtu 1500
     index 2 inet 192.108.21.48 netmask ffffff00 broadcast 192.108.21.255

solaris$ sudo ifconfig e1000g0
e1000g0: flags=1000843<UP,BROADCAST,RUNNING,MULTICAST,IPv4> mtu 1500
     index 2 inet 192.108.21.48 netmask ffffff00 broadcast 192.108.21.255
     ether 0:14:4f:e:e6:1c
```

Notice that when run as root, **ifconfig** shows the hardware address, but when run as a user, it does not.

```
solaris$ netstat -nr
Routing Table: IPv4
Destination     Gateway             Flags  Ref   Use   Interface
--------------- -------------------- ------- ----- ------ ---------
default         192.108.21.254      UG      1    9959
192.108.21.0    192.108.21.48       U       1    4985   e1000g0
127.0.0.1       127.0.0.1           UH      1     107   lo0

solaris$ sudo route get google.com
      route to: gw-in-f100.google.com
   destination: default
          mask: default
       gateway: 192.108.21.254
     interface: e1000g0
         flags: <UP,GATEWAY,DONE,STATIC>
recvpipe  sendpipe  ssthresh  rtt,ms  rttvar,ms  hopcount  mtu   expire
    0         0         0        0        0          0     1500     0
```

Solaris DHCP configuration

Solaris includes a DHCP client and wins the prize for the easiest and most sensible DHCP client configuration:

```
solaris$ sudo ifconfig interface dhcp
```

It just works! **ifconfig** calls the **dhcpagent** program to get the parameters for the interface from DHCP and to configure the interface with them. You can include several options on the **ifconfig** command line to specify the interface as the primary one, set timeouts, increase lease times, or display the status of the interface. To manually unconfigure DHCP, just run

```
solaris$ sudo ifconfig interface drop
```

This is all very nice, but you probably want DHCP to be automatically consulted at boot time. You can set this up either by providing no configuration files for an interface at all (thus relying on autoconfiguration, similar to Linux's Network-Manager) or by creating an **/etc/dhcp.***interface* file to go with the corresponding **/etc/hostname.***interface* file. If you like, the **dhcp.***interface* file can contain additional command-line parameters to be passed to the **ifconfig** command.

The **hostname.***interface* file must still exist to get the interface to be plumbed; however, it can be left empty. If the **hostname.***interface* file is not empty, the startup scripts will first statically configure the interface by using its contents and then later reconfigure the interface by using DHCP.

dhcpagent manages the interface from DHCP's point of view. Among other tasks, it negotiates extensions to leases and cancels leases when they are no longer needed. If an interface that has been configured with DHCP is later reconfigured by hand, **dhcpagent** will discontinue management of that interface.

dhcpagent collects the leased values from the DHCP server (default route, domain, name servers, etc.), but it does not act on most of them directly. Instead, it makes the parameters available through the **dhcpinfo** command. The service management scripts consult **dhcpinfo** for various pieces of information, which are then used as arguments to **route**, put into the **resolv.conf** file, etc.

dhcpagent transmits errors to syslog with facility daemon and priorities info through critical. Debug-level syslog output is available with the **-d** flag.

You can check the files in **/etc/dhcp** to view the configuration of a particular interface. However, the existence of an *interface*.**dhc** file for an interface does not necessarily mean that **dhcpagent** is currently controlling the interface—the lease may have expired.

ndd: TCP/IP and interface tuning for Solaris

Solaris's **ndd** command reconfigures the TCP/IP protocol stack on a running system. Perhaps "reconfigure" is too strong a word; each module exposes parameters that can be examined and in some cases adjusted on the fly.

The basic syntax is

```
ndd [-set] device ? | variable [value]
```

If you give the argument **?** (which must be protected from the shell as **\?**), **ndd** returns a list of variables understood by the driver for the specified device. If you supply the name of a *variable*, **ndd** returns the value of that variable. If you use the **-set** flag and supply a *value*, the specified *variable* is set to the value you specify.

Unfortunately, the **ndd** man page doesn't tell you the possible names of devices, and it doesn't tell you that you must be root to run **ndd** on some devices (**ip** and **hme**, for example) and not on others (**tcp** and **udp**). Table 14.10 slips you a quick cheat sheet.

Table 14.10 Devices you can probe with Solaris's ndd command

Device	Description	Variable names
/dev/tcp	TCP protocol variables	tcp_*
/dev/udp	UDP protocol variables	udp_*
/dev/ip	IP protocol variables	ip_* and ip6_*
/dev/icmp	ICMP protocol variables	icmp_*
/dev/rawip	Identical to **/dev/icmp**	icmp_*
/dev/arp	ARP protocol variables	arp_*

Interface-specific variable names in the **/dev/ip** category control IP forwarding on specific network interfaces. For example, e1000g0:ip_forwarding controls IP forwarding on **/dev/e1000g0**. There's a global ip_forwarding variable, too.

If you have access to an HP-UX machine, run **ndd** there with the **-h** flag (for help) and it will give you device names, variable names, and the meaning of each of the variables. Many variable names are the same, so you can partially work around Sun's minimal **ndd** man page.

Interface-specific options such as link speed, autonegotiation, and jumbo packet support are also set with **ndd**; run **ndd** directly on the device file for the interface (e.g., **/dev/e1000g0**). Unfortunately, the way Sun has set up this convention makes the names of the configuration parameters dependent on the specific driver, so there isn't a universal recipe for, say, locking a network interface to 100 Mb/s.

To change speeds, you'll need to identify the writable "capability" variables for each speed (usually named *_cap) and turn off (set to zero) all the ones you want to disallow. Turn off the *_autoneg_cap variable, too, to disable autonegotiation. For example, the following script sets **/dev/e1000g0** to 100 Mb/s full duplex on one of our lab machines:

```
#!/bin/sh
ndd -set /dev/e1000g0 adv_autoneg_cap 0
ndd -set /dev/e1000g0 adv_1000fdx_cap 0
ndd -set /dev/e1000g0 adv_100fdx_cap 1
ndd -set /dev/e1000g0 adv_100hdx_cap 0
ndd -set /dev/e1000g0 adv_10fdx_cap 0
ndd -set /dev/e1000g0 adv_10hdx_cap 0
```

Solaris security

Table 14.11 shows Solaris's default behavior with regard to various touchy network issues. For a brief description of the implications of these behaviors, see *Security issues* starting on page 472. You can adjust most of these settings with **ndd**.

Table 14.11 Security-related network behaviors in Solaris

Feature	Default	ndd variable
IP forwarding	off	ip_forwarding
ICMP redirects	obeys	Can't be changed[a]
Source routing	ignores	ip_forward_src_routed
Broadcast ping (respond)	on	ip_respond_to_echo_broadcast
Broadcast ping (forward)	off	ip_forward_directed_broadcasts

a. You can only modify the entries' time-to-live.

Solaris firewalls and filtering

As mentioned in the *Security issues* section, you generally shouldn't use a UNIX, Linux, or Windows box as a firewall or NAT gateway. Use a dedicated piece of network hardware instead. Solaris used to make it easy to follow this rule by not including any filtering software, but Darren Reed's free IPFilter software has now been bundled into the basic distribution. If you must use a UNIX-based filter, this is a good choice—it was always our favorite of the add-on filters for Solaris.

The IPFilter suite implements IP filtering, NAT, and transparent port forwarding. It is free, open source, and works on either SPARC or Intel hardware. The IPFilter package includes **ipf** for configuring a firewall, **ipfstat** for printing out the filtering rules that have been installed, and **ipnat** for implementing NAT.

See Chapter 22, *Security*, for details on packet filtering with IPFilter. The section about this topic starts on page 939. Here, we discuss only IPFilter's NAT features.

Solaris NAT

To make NAT work, you must tell the kernel what addresses to map from, what addresses to map to, and what port range to use to extend the address space. See page 462 for a general discussion of NAT and the mechanisms it uses to bridge from private to public address space.

To configure NAT, you supply rules to the **ipnat** command. The rules are similar to those used with **ipf** to implement packet filtering. But beware: like **ipf** rules, **ipnat** rules are ordered. However, they have opposite precedence. Just to keep you on your toes, the *first* matching rule is selected, not the last.

Below are some examples of **ipnat** rules. To be activated at boot time, these would go in the **/etc/ipf/ipnat.conf** file:

```
map eth1 192.168.1.0/24 -> 128.138.198.0/26 portmap tcp/udp 20000:65000
map eth1 192.168.1.0/24 -> 128.138.198.0/26
```

We have assumed that eth1 is our interface to the Internet and that our internal network is numbered with the class C private address space range. These rules map addresses from a /24 network into addresses from a /26 network. Since a /26 network can accommodate only one-quarter of the hosts that a /24 network can, it's potentially possible to run out of target addresses in this configuration. But the portmap clause extends the address range by allowing each address to be used with 45,000 different source ports.

The first rule above covers all TCP and UDP traffic but does not affect ICMP; ICMP does not use the concept of a port. The second rule catches ICMP messages and tries to get them routed back to the right host. If the kernel can't unambiguously determine who should receive a particular ICMP message, it sends the packet out as a broadcast; machines that receive it out of context can just ignore it.

On a home machine, you might be assigned just a single real IP address by your ISP or your ISP's DHCP server. If you're given a static address assignment, just give the target network in the map line a /32 designation and a large enough port range to accommodate the needs of all your local hosts. If you get a different dynamic address each time you connect, use the notation 0/32 in the map line; it will make **ipnat** read the address directly from the network interface. For example, here is a line you might use for a single, dynamically assigned address:

```
map eth1 192.168.1.0/24 -> 0/32 portmap tcp/udp 20000:65000
```

To test out the configuration, run

```
solaris$ sudo ipnat -CF -f /etc/ipf/ipnat.conf
```

These options first delete all existing rules and then load the complete set of rules from the **/etc/ipf/ipnat.conf** file.

Solaris networking quirks

The output of **ifconfig -a** is different when it is run as root than when it is run as a regular user. When run as root, it shows the link-level Ethernet addresses in addition to the IP addresses and parameters.

Solaris lets you change the link-level (MAC) address of a network interface with the **ifconfig** command and the address family **ether**. This feature can be useful if you need to worm your way onto a MAC-restricted wireless network.

14.14 HP-UX NETWORKING

HP-UX network configuration is easy: all configuration parameters are set in the file **/etc/rc.config.d/netconf**. The values in this file (and all the other files in the **rc.config.d** directory) are read into the environment at boot time and used by the **/sbin/rc** script as the machine boots. **netconf** is liberally scattered with comments that tell you just which variables must be set and what they mean.

Basic network configuration for HP-UX

To assign a hostname to a machine and configure its first network interface, edit the **netconf** file and assign a value to the following variables:

```
HOSTNAME
INTERFACE_NAME[0]
IP_ADDRESS[0]
SUBNET_MASK[0]
```

For example:

```
HOSTNAME=disaster
INTERFACE_NAME[0]=lan0
IP_ADDRESS[0]=192.108.21.99
SUBNET_MASK[0]=255.255.255.0
```

A second network interface would have subscript 1, and its existence would be indicated by the variable NET_CARDS being set to 2.

The **netconf** file also contains variables to configure static routes and start a routing daemon. To establish a default route, set the following variables:

```
ROUTE_DESTINATION[0]=default
ROUTE_MASK[0]=""
ROUTE_GATEWAY[0]=192.108.21.254
ROUTE_COUNT[0]=1
```

The ROUTE_MASK variable is needed for a network in which the netmask differed from the default for the class of addresses used. The ROUTE_COUNT variable should be 0 if the gateway is the local machine and 1 if it is remote. To add more static routes, just enter their parameters to a set of ROUTE_* variables with indexes [1], [2], etc. These arguments are passed directly to the **route** command. For example, the destination parameter can be the word **default** as above or **net** *netaddr* or **host** *hostaddr*.

HP-UX supplies **gated** but not **routed**; to use **gated**, set the variable GATED to 1 and GATED_ARGS to the arguments you want **gated** started with. See Chapter 15, *Routing*, for a bit more information about **gated**. The HP-UX man page on routing (**man routing**) contains a lot of good background information.

Many fields in the **netconf** file can contain either a hostname or an IP address. If a hostname is used, it *must* be defined in **/etc/hosts**. At boot time, HP-UX looks only at **/etc/hosts** and does not use any other name lookup mechanism. The machines in **/etc/hosts** should have their fully qualified domain names listed first, followed by their short names and any aliases.

HP uses the **lanscan** command to show information about the network interfaces on a machine. **ifconfig -a** does not work, but **ifconfig** *interface* does. Network interface names begin with either "lan" or "snap": lan for Ethernet link-layer encapsulation and snap for IEEE 802.3 encapsulation. The first interface is lan0, the second is lan1, and so on.

HP-UX has the same sort of "plumbing" concept that Solaris does, but interfaces are automatically plumbed when they are assigned an IP address by **ifconfig**.

SMH is HP's system administration tool, which is alleged to make UNIX system administration a breeze. It is a menu-based system and can be used to configure network interfaces, as well as to perform many other sysadmin chores.

HP-UX configuration examples

To bring up an HP-UX network interface and add a default route by hand, you'd use commands such as the following:

```
hp-ux$ sudo ifconfig lan0 192.108.21.99 netmask 0xffffff00
hp-ux$ sudo route add default 192.108.21.254 1[20]
```

HP's **lanscan** command lists the network interfaces in the system and the characteristics of the device driver that controls them. **lanscan -v** shows slightly more information. The examples below were munged to fit the page. The MAC entry with value ETHER implies that the network device name should be lan0, not snap0; **ifconfig** shows this to be true.

20. On HP-UX 11, the hop count field is not required; it defaults to 0 if not explicitly specified. Earlier versions required the count field to be present.

```
$ lanscan
Hardware  Station   Crd  Hdw   Net-Int      NM  MAC    HP-DLPI  DLPI
Path      Address   In#  State NamePPA      ID  Type   Support  Mjr#
8/0/20/0  0x001...  0    UP    lan0 snap0   1   ETHER  Yes      130

$ ifconfig lan0
lan0: flags=843<UP,BROADCAST,RUNNING,MULTICAST> inet 192.108.21.99
    netmask ffffff00 broadcast 192.108.21.255

$ ifconfig snap0
ifconfig: no such interface
```

netstat -i shows network interface names, and **netstat -nr** displays routing tables:

```
$ netstat -i
Name    Mtu   Network        Address                Ipkts  Opkts
lan0    1500  192.108.21.0   disaster.atrust.com     6047   3648
lo0     4136  127.0.0.0      localhost.atrust.com     231    231

$ netstat -nr
Routing tables
Dest/Netmask      Gateway           Flags  Refs   Use   Int    Pmtu
127.0.0.1         127.0.0.1         UH        0   231   lo0    4136
192.108.21.99     192.108.21.99     UH        8         lan0   4136
192.108.21.0      192.108.21.99     U         2     0   lan0   1500
127.0.0.0         127.0.0.1         U         0     0   lo0    4136
default           192.108.21.254    UG        0     0   lan0   1500
```

The **lanadmin** command displays a summary of the network traffic that each interface has seen. It can also manipulate and monitor interfaces. It's a menu-based program with useful help lists to lead you to the information you want. Here is an example that displays the statistics for the lan0 interface:

```
% lanadmin
   LOCAL AREA NETWORK ONLINE ADMINISTRATION, Version 1.0
            Copyright 1994 Hewlett Packard Company.
                    All rights are reserved.
Test Selection mode.

    lan     = LAN Interface Administration
    menu    = Display this menu
    quit    = Terminate the Administration
    terse   = Do not display command menu
    verbose = Display command menu

Enter command: lan

LAN Interface test mode. LAN Interface PPA Number = 0
    clear   = Clear statistics registers
    display = Display LAN Interface status/statistics
    end     = End LAN Interface Admin., go up 1 level
    menu    = Display this menu
    ppa     = PPA Number of the LAN Interface
```

```
    quit     = Terminate the Admin, return to shell
    reset    = Reset LAN Interface, execute selftest
    specific = Go to Driver specific menu

Enter command: display

                    LAN INTERFACE STATUS DISPLAY
                      Tue , Jun 2,2009 00:41:24
PPA Number                     = 0
Description                    = lan0 Intel PCI Pro 10/100Tx Server Adapter
Type (value)                   = ethernet-csmacd(6)
MTU Size                       = 1500
Speed                          = 100000000
Station Address                = 0x00306eea9237
Administration Status (value)  = up(1)
Operation Status (value)       = up(1)
...
Inbound Unicast Packets        = 45691
Inbound Non-Unicast Packets    = 2630
...
Deferred Transmissions         = 0
Late Collisions                = 0
Excessive Collisions           = 0
...
```

HP-UX DHCP configuration

As with other network configuration parameters, you turn on the use of DHCP at boot time by setting variables in the **/etc/rc.config.d/netconf** file. In this case, the variable names start with DHCP_ENABLE. The index [0] refers to the first interface, [1] to the second interface, and so on. For example,

```
DHCP_ENABLE[0]=1
```

sets the first network interface to DHCP mode. It will get its IP address, netmask, and other networking parameters from the DHCP server on the local network. Setting the variable equal to 0 would disable DHCP; you'd have to assign a static address in the **netconf** file. If no DHCP_ENABLE clause is present, the variable defaults to 1.

The **/sbin/auto_parms** script does the real legwork of contacting the DHCP server. The program **dhcpdb2conf** enters the DHCP parameters secured by **auto_parms** into the **netconf** file, from which boot-time configuration information is taken.

HP-UX dynamic reconfiguration and tuning

*See page 498 for more details about **ndd**.*

As in Solaris, you can use **ndd** to tune many different networking parameters. When used interactively, **ndd** tunes values on the fly. To change values permanently, enter them in **/etc/rc.config.d/nddconf**, which is read at boot time.

On an HP-UX system, **ndd**'s **-h** (help) option is quite useful. With no arguments, it lists all the parameters you can tune. If you also specify a variable name, **ndd -h** describes what the variable does and shows its minimum, maximum, and default values. For example:

```
$ ndd -h | grep source
ip_forward_src_routed -  Controls forwarding of source routed packets

$ ndd -h ip_forward_src_routed
ip_forward_src_routed:
  Set to 1 to forward source-routed packets; set to 0 to
  disable forwarding. If disabled, an ICMP Destination
  Unreachable message is sent to the sender of source-
  routed packets needing to be forwarded. [0,1] Default: 1
```

ndd's output claims that this version of HP-UX allows forwarding of source-routed packets by default. That may be the kernel's preference, but in fact the default **/etc/rc.config.d/nddconf** file on our lab system disables this behavior:

```
TRANSPORT_NAME[2]=ip
NDD_NAME[2]=ip_forward_src_routed
NDD_VALUE[2]=0
```

The 2s here indicate the third of ten possible variables to be set in **nddconf**. For the next variable that you wanted to change, you would add another copy of the same three lines with appropriate values and with subscript 3 instead of 2. Unfortunately, only 10 parameters can be set through **nddconf**.

To view and change the value of the ip_forward_src_routed variable by hand, use **ndd -get** and **ndd -set** (the syntax is slightly different from that on Solaris systems):

```
$ ndd -get /dev/ip ip_forward_src_routed
0
$ sudo ndd -set /dev/ip ip_forward_src_routed 1
$ ndd -get /dev/ip ip_forward_src_routed
1
```

HP-UX security, firewalls, filtering, and NAT

Table 14.12 shows HP-UX's default behavior with regard to various touchy network issues. For a brief description of the implications of these behaviors, see *Security issues* on page 472. You can modify most of them with **ndd**.

Table 14.12 Security-related network behaviors in HP-UX

Feature	Default	Control through ndd
IP forwarding	dynamic[a]	Set ip_forwarding: 0 = off, 1 = on, 2 = dynamic
ICMP redirects	obeys[b]	Set ip_ire_redirect_interval to 0 to disable
Source routing	ignores	Set ip_forward_src_routed to 1 to enable
Broadcast ping (forward)	blocked	Set ip_forward_directed_broadcasts
Broadcast ping (respond)	ignores	Set ip_respond_to_echo_broadcast

a. On with >1 network interface; off otherwise.
b. The redirect entries are by default preserved for five minutes.

Like Solaris, HP-UX includes Darren Reed's IPFilter package for packet filtering and NAT translation. See *IPFilter for UNIX systems* on page 939 and *Solaris NAT* on page 500 for some additional detail. The IPFilter part is all the same, although HP-UX configures the package differently at startup. Instead of using **svcadm** to enable IPFilter, edit **/etc/rc.config.d/ipfconf** and turn on the options you want. Configuration files for **ipf** and **ipnat** should go in **/etc/opt/ipf** instead of **/etc/ipf**.

HP-UX's version of **inetd** has built-in TCP wrapper functionality that you configure in the file **/var/adm/inetd.sec**.

If you wonder in exactly what ways HP has shipped you an insecure system, take a look at Kevin Steves' article about the steps needed to turn an HP-UX 11 system into a bastion host on an unprotected network: tinyurl.com/5sffy2. This document is a bit old (2002), but it's an excellent description of all the creature comforts in HP-UX that must be turned off if the machine is to be secure on the open Internet. We wish we knew of a document like this for our other example systems.

14.15 AIX NETWORKING

Rather than keeping network configuration information in text files or scripts, AIX squirrels it away in the Object Data Manager (ODM) attribute/value database. Another layer of glue associates these property lists with specific devices (driver instances, really) and binds the drivers to the configuration information.

The Object Data Manager on page 432 describes the ODM system in general. The overall scheme is rather complex, and it allows access to the network configuration at multiple layers. Table 14.13 shows a variety of AIX commands for setting an interface's network address. They vary chiefly in whether they affect the running configuration, the boot-time configuration, or both.

Table 14.13 Eight ways to set an interface's IP address in AIX

Command	Affects Current?	Affects Boot?
smitty mktcpip *(and fill out the form)*	Yes	Yes
mktcpip -i en3 -a 192.168.0.1	Yes	Yes
chdev -l en3 -a netaddr=192.168.0.1	Yes	Yes
chdev -l en3 -a netaddr=192.168.0.1 -P	No	Yes
chdev -l en3 -a netaddr=192.168.0.1 -T	Yes	No
ifconfig en3 inet 192.168.0.1	Yes	No
odmchange -o CuAt -q'name=en3 AND attribute=netaddr' < config[a]	No	Yes
echo 'Hey! I set the network address!'	No	No

a. **odmchange** requires an attribute/value list as input. You cannot specify attribute values on the command line.

To be fair, **mktcpip** does more than just set device configuration parameters—it also runs the **rc.tcpip** script to start relevant network daemons.

SMIT's network configuration facilities are relatively complete, so you can, and should, rely on SMIT for most basic configuration. Look under the "Communications Applications and Services" topic for TCP/IP configuration options.

Most sysadmins will never need to operate below the level of **chdev/lsattr** et al. However, this layer can be useful for seeing the authoritative list of configuration options for a device. For example, the following query shows the configurable parameters for the network interface en3:

```
aix$ lsattr -H -E -l en3
attribute      value           description                          settable
alias4                         IPv4 Alias including Subnet Mask     True
alias6                         IPv6 Alias including Prefix Length   True
arp            on              Address Resolution Protocol (ARP)    True
authority                      Authorized Users                     True
broadcast      192.168.10.255  Broadcast Address                    True
mtu            1500            Maximum IP Packet Size               True
netaddr        192.168.10.11   Internet Address                     True
netaddr6                       IPv6 Internet Address                True
netmask        255.255.255.0   Subnet Mask                          True
prefixlen                      Prefix Length for IPv6 Address       True
remmtu         576             Max. Packet Size for REMOTE Nets     True
security       none            Security Level                       True
state          up              Current Interface Status             True
tcp_mssdflt                    Set TCP Maximum Segment Size         True
tcp_nodelay                    Enable/Disable TCP_NODELAY Option    True
tcp_recvspace                  Set Socket Buffer Space for Receiving True
tcp_sendspace                  Set Socket Buffer Space for Sending  True
```

The **-H** option asks for the output columns to be labeled, the **-E** option requests current ("effective," as opposed to default) values, and the **-l** option identifies the device to probe. Many of the devices that **chdev** et al. can operate on have no entries in **/dev**. You can run **lsdev -C** to see a complete list of the available devices.

To set a value, use **chdev**. For example, to set the MTU for en3 above to 1450, you could use the command

```
aix$ sudo chdev -l en3 -a mtu=1450
```

no: manage AIX network tuning parameters

AIX breaks out its system-wide TCP/IP options into a separate, parallel world of persistent attribute/value pairs that are accessed through the **no** command rather than through **chdev**. (The difference is that **no** is for system-wide configuration, whereas **chdev** configures instances of specific drivers or devices.)

You can run **no -a** to see a list of all the available variables—there are currently more than 125. Table 14.14 lists some of the ones with security implications.

Table 14.14 Security-related TCP/IP tuning variables for AIX

Variable	Meaning	Default
bcastping	Respond to broadcast pings	0
directed_broadcast	Allow forwarding of broadcast packets	0
ipforwarding	Allow IP forwarding	0
ipignoreredirects	Ignore ICMP redirects	0[a]
ipsrcrouteforward	Forward source-routed IP packets	1[a]
ipsrcrouterecv	Accept source-routed IP packets	0
ipsrcroutesend	Block sending of source-routed packets	1

a. Probably advisable to change

To set a variable, use

```
no -p -o variable=value
```

For example, to prevent the TCP/IP stack from forwarding source-routed packets, you would use the command

```
aix$ sudo no -p -o ipsrcrouteforward=0
```

The **-p** option makes the change effective both immediately and after a reboot.

14.16 Recommended Reading

STEVENS, W. RICHARD. *TCP/IP Illustrated, Volume One: The Protocols.* Reading, MA: Addison-Wesley, 1994.

WRIGHT, GARY R., AND W. RICHARD STEVENS. *TCP/IP Illustrated, Volume Two: The Implementation.* Reading, MA: Addison-Wesley, 1995.

These two books are an excellent and thorough guide to the TCP/IP protocol stack. A bit dated, but still solid.

STEVENS, W. RICHARD. *UNIX Network Programming.* Upper Saddle River, NJ: Prentice Hall, 1990.

STEVENS, W. RICHARD, BILL FENNER, AND ANDREW M. RUDOFF. *UNIX Network Programming, Volume 1, The Sockets Networking API (3rd Edition).* Upper Saddle River, NJ: Addison-Wesley, 2003.

STEVENS, W. RICHARD. *UNIX Network Programming, Volume 2: Interprocess Communications (2nd Edition).* Upper Saddle River, NJ: Addison-Wesley, 1999.

These books are the student's bibles in networking classes that involve programming. If you need only the Berkeley sockets interface, the original edition is still a fine reference. If you need the STREAMS interface too, then the third edition, which includes IPv6, is a good bet. All three are clearly written in typical Rich Stevens style.

TANENBAUM, ANDREW. *Computer Networks (4th Edition).* Upper Saddle River, NJ: Prentice Hall PTR, 2003.

This was the first networking text, and it is still a classic. It contains a thorough description of all the nitty-gritty details going on at the physical and link layers of the protocol stack. The latest edition includes coverage on wireless networks, gigabit Ethernet, peer-to-peer networks, voice over IP, and more.

SALUS, PETER H. *Casting the Net, From ARPANET to INTERNET and Beyond.* Reading, MA: Addison-Wesley Professional, 1995.

This is a lovely history of the ARPANET as it grew into the Internet, written by a historian who has been hanging out with UNIX people long enough to sound like one of them!

COMER, DOUGLAS. *Internetworking with TCP/IP Volume 1: Principles, Protocols, and Architectures (5th Edition).* Upper Saddle River, NJ: Prentice Hall, 2006.

Doug Comer's *Internetworking with TCP/IP* series was for a long time the standard reference for the TCP/IP protocols. The books are designed as undergraduate textbooks and are a good introductory source of background material.

HUNT, CRAIG. *TCP/IP Network Administration (3rd Edition).* Sebastopol, CA: O'Reilly Media, 2002.

Like other books in the nutshell series, this book is directed at administrators of UNIX systems. Half the book is about TCP/IP, and the rest deals with higher-level UNIX facilities such as email and remote login.

FARREL, ADRIAN. *The Internet and Its Protocols: A Comparative Approach.* San Francisco, CA: Morgan Kaufmann Publishers, 2004.

KOZIERAK, CHARLES M. *The TCP/IP Guide: A Comprehensive, Illustrated Internet Protocols Reference.* San Francisco, CA: No Starch Press, 2005.

An excellent collection of documents about the history of the Internet and its various technologies can be found at isoc.org/internet/history.

14.17 EXERCISES

E14.1 How could listening to (i.e., obeying) ICMP redirects allow an unauthorized user to compromise the network?

E14.2 What is the MTU of a network link? What happens if the MTU for a given link is set too high? Too low?

★ E14.3 The network 134.122.0.0/16 has been subdivided into /19 networks.

a) How many networks are there? List them. What is their netmask?
b) How many hosts could there be on each network?
c) Determine which network the address 134.122.67.124 belongs to.
d) What is the broadcast address for each network?

★ E14.4 Host 128.138.2.4 on network 128.138.2.0/24 wants to send a packet to host 128.138.129.12 on network 128.138.129.0/24. Assume that

- Host 128.138.2.4 has a default route through 128.138.2.1.
- Host 128.138.2.4 just booted and has not sent or received any packets.
- All other machines on the network have been running for a long time.
- Router 128.138.2.1 has a direct link to 128.138.129.1, the gateway for the 128.138.129.0/24 subnet.

a) List all the steps that are needed to send the packet. Show the source and destination Ethernet and IP addresses of all packets transmitted.

b) If the network were 128.138.0.0/16, would your answer change? How or why not?

c) If the 128.138.2.0 network were a /26 network instead of a /24, would your answer change? How or why not?

★ E14.5 DHCP lease times are configurable on the server. If there many more assignable IP addresses than potential clients, should you make the lease time as long as possible (say, weeks)? Why or why not? What about other DHCP parameters?

★★ E14.6 After installing a new Linux system, how would you address the security issues mentioned in this chapter? Check to see if any of the security problems have been dealt with on the Linux systems in your lab. (May require root access.)

★★ E14.7 What steps are needed to add a new machine to the network in your lab environment? In answering, use parameters appropriate for your network and local situation. Assume that the operating system has already been installed on the new machine.

★★ E14.8 Create a configuration file for ISC's DHCP server that assigns addresses in the range 128.138.192.[1-55]. Use a lease time of two hours and make sure that the host with Ethernet address 00:10:5A:C7:4B:89 always receives IP address 128.138.192.55.

15 Routing

Keeping track of where network traffic should flow next is no easy task. Chapter 14 briefly introduced IP packet forwarding. In this chapter, we examine the forwarding process in more detail and investigate several network protocols that allow routers to automatically discover efficient routes. Routing protocols not only lessen the day-to-day administrative burden of maintaining routing information, but they also allow network traffic to be redirected quickly if a router, link, or network should fail.

It's important to distinguish between the process of actually forwarding IP packets and the management of the routing table that drives this process, both of which are commonly called "routing." Packet forwarding is simple, whereas route computation is tricky; consequently, the second meaning is used more often in practice. This chapter describes only unicast routing; multicast routing (sending packets to groups of subscribers) involves an array of very different problems and is beyond the scope of this book.

For most cases, the information covered in Chapter 14, *TCP/IP Networking*, is all you need to know about routing. If the appropriate network infrastructure is already in place, you can set up a single static route (as described in the *Routing* section starting on page 465) and voilà, you have enough information to reach just about anywhere on the Internet. If you must survive within a complex network topology or if you are using UNIX or Linux systems as part of your network infrastructure, then this chapter's information about dynamic routing protocols and tools can come in handy.

IP routing is "next hop" routing. At any given point, the system handling a packet only needs to determine the *next* host or router in the packet's journey to its final destination. This is a different approach from that of many legacy protocols, which determine the exact path a packet will travel before it leaves its originating host, a scheme known as source routing.[1]

15.1 Packet Forwarding: A Closer Look

Before we jump into the management of routing tables, let's take a more detailed look at how the tables are used. Consider the network shown in Exhibit A.

Exhibit A Example network

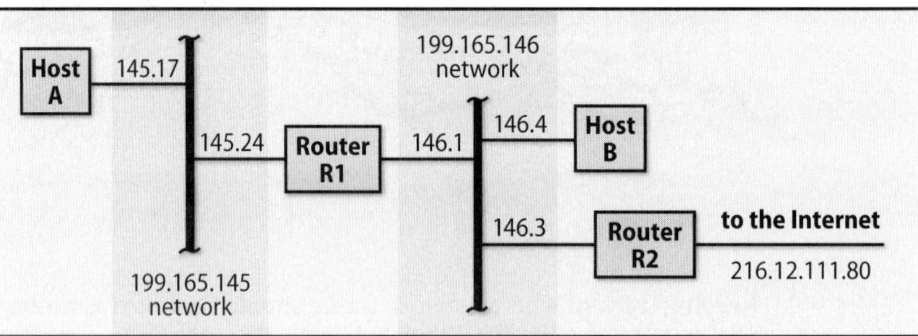

Router R1 connects two networks, and router R2 connects one of the nets to the outside world. For now, we assume that R1 and R2 are general-purpose computers rather than dedicated routers. (We assume Linux and IPv4 for all systems involved in this example, but the commands and principles are similar under IPv6 and on UNIX systems.) Let's look at some routing tables and some specific packet forwarding scenarios. First, host A's routing table:

```
A$ netstat -rn
Kernel IP routing table
Destination    Gateway         Genmask         Flags MSS  Window  irtt  Iface
199.165.145.0  0.0.0.0         255.255.255.0   U       0  0          0  eth0
127.0.0.0      0.0.0.0         255.0.0.0       U       0  0          0  lo
0.0.0.0        199.165.145.24  0.0.0.0         UG      0  0          0  eth0
```

*See page 478 for more information about **ifconfig**.*

Host A has the simplest routing configuration of the four machines. The first two routes describe the machine's own network interfaces in standard routing terms. These entries exist so that forwarding to directly connected networks need not be

1. IP packets can also be source-routed—at least in theory—but this is almost never done. The feature is not widely supported because of security considerations.

handled as a special case. eth0 is host A's Ethernet interface, and lo is the loopback interface, a virtual interface emulated in software. Entries such as these are normally added automatically by **ifconfig** when a network interface is configured.

Some systems treat the loopback route as a "host route" to one particular IP address rather than an entire network. Since 127.0.0.1 is the only IP address that will ever exist on the loopback network, it doesn't really matter how it's defined. The only changes you'd see in the routing table would be 127.0.0.1 in the destination column instead of 127.0.0.0 and an H in the Flags column.

See the discussion of netmasks starting on page 458.

There is no substantive difference between a host route and a network route. They are treated exactly the same when the kernel goes to look up addresses in the routing table; only the length of the implicit mask is different.

The default route on host A forwards all packets not addressed to the loopback address or to the 199.165.145 network to the router R1, whose address on this network is 199.165.145.24. The G flag indicates that this route goes to a gateway, not to one of A's local interfaces. Gateways must be only one hop away.

See page 454 for more information about addressing.

Suppose a process on A sends a packet to B, whose address is 199.165.146.4. The IP implementation looks for a route to the target network, 199.165.146, but none of the routes match. The default route is invoked and the packet is forwarded to R1. Exhibit B shows the packet that actually goes out on the Ethernet (the addresses in the Ethernet header are the MAC addresses of A's and R1's interfaces on the 145 net).

Exhibit B Ethernet packet

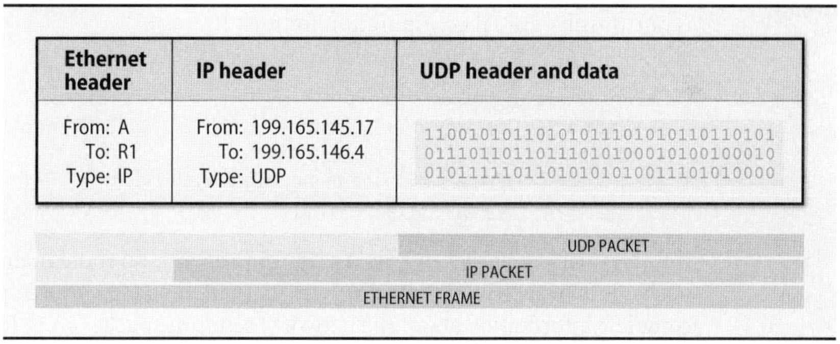

Ethernet header	IP header	UDP header and data
From: A To: R1 Type: IP	From: 199.165.145.17 To: 199.165.146.4 Type: UDP	11001010110101011101010110110101 01110110110111010100010100100010 01011111011010101010011101010000

UDP PACKET
IP PACKET
ETHERNET FRAME

The Ethernet destination hardware address is that of router R1, but the IP packet hidden within the Ethernet frame does not mention R1 at all. When R1 inspects the packet it has received, it sees from the IP destination address that it is not the ultimate destination of the packet. It then uses its own routing table to forward the packet to host B without rewriting the IP header; the header still shows the packet coming from A.

Here's the routing table for host R1:

```
R1$ netstat -rn
Kernel IP routing table
Destination     Gateway         Genmask         Flags MSS  Window  irtt  Iface
127.0.0.0       0.0.0.0         255.0.0.0       U       0  0          0  lo
199.165.145.0   0.0.0.0         255.255.255.0   U       0  0          0  eth0
199.165.146.0   0.0.0.0         255.255.255.0   U       0  0          0  eth1
0.0.0.0         199.165.146.3   0.0.0.0         UG      0  0          0  eth1
```

This table is similar to that of host A, except that it shows two physical network interfaces. The default route in this case points to R2, since that's the gateway through which the Internet can be reached. Packets bound for either of the 199.165 networks can be delivered directly.

Like host A, host B has only one real network interface. However, B needs an additional route to function correctly because it has direct connections to two different routers. Traffic for the 199.165.145 net must travel through R1, while other traffic should go out to the Internet through R2.

```
B$ netstat -rn
Kernel IP routing table
Destination     Gateway         Genmask         Flags MSS  Window  irtt  Iface
127.0.0.0       0.0.0.0         255.0.0.0       U       0  0          0  lo
199.165.145.0   199.165.146.1   255.255.255.0   U       0  0          0  eth0
199.165.146.0   0.0.0.0         255.255.255.0   U       0  0          0  eth0
0.0.0.0         199.165.146.3   0.0.0.0         UG      0  0          0  eth0
```

See page 467 for an explanation of ICMP redirects.

In theory, you can configure host B with initial knowledge of only one gateway and rely on help from ICMP redirects to eliminate extra hops. For example, here is one possible initial configuration for host B:

```
B$ netstat -rn
Kernel IP routing table
Destination     Gateway         Genmask         Flags MSS  Window  irtt  Iface
127.0.0.0       0.0.0.0         255.0.0.0       U       0  0          0  lo
199.165.146.0   0.0.0.0         255.255.255.0   U       0  0          0  eth0
0.0.0.0         199.165.146.3   0.0.0.0         UG      0  0          0  eth0
```

If B then sends a packet to host A (199.165.145.17), no route matches and the packet is forwarded to R2 for delivery. R2 (which, being a router, presumably has complete information about the network) sends the packet on to R1. Since R1 and B are on the same network, R2 also sends an ICMP redirect notice to B, and B enters a host route for A into its routing table:

```
199.165.145.17 199.165.146.1  255.255.255.255 UGHD 0  0          0  eth0
```

This route sends all future traffic for A directly through R1. However, it does not affect routing for other hosts on A's network, all of which have to be routed by separate redirects from R2.

Some sites use ICMP redirects this way as a sort of low-rent routing "protocol," thinking that this approach is dynamic. Unfortunately, systems and routers all handle redirects differently. Some hold on to them indefinitely. Others remove them from the routing table after a relatively short period (5–15 minutes). Still others ignore them entirely, which is probably the correct approach from a security perspective.

Redirects have several other potential disadvantages: increased network load, increased load on R2, routing table clutter, and dependence on extra servers, to name a few. Therefore, we don't recommend their use. In a properly configured network, redirects should never appear in the routing table.

15.2 ROUTING DAEMONS AND ROUTING PROTOCOLS

In simple networks such as the one shown in Exhibit A, it is perfectly reasonable to configure routing by hand. At some point, however, networks become too complicated to be managed this way. Instead of having to explicitly tell every computer on every network how to reach every other computer and network, it would be nice if the computers could just cooperate and figure it all out. This is the job of routing protocols and the daemons that implement them.

Routing protocols have a major advantage over static routing systems in that they can react and adapt to changing network conditions. If a link goes down, then the routing daemons can discover and propagate alternative routes to the networks served by that link, if any such routes exist.

Routing daemons collect information from three sources: configuration files, the existing routing tables, and routing daemons on other systems. This information is merged to compute an optimal set of routes, and the new routes are then fed back into the system routing table (and possibly fed to other systems through a routing protocol). Because network conditions change over time, routing daemons must periodically check in with one another for reassurance that their routing information is still current.

The exact manner in which routes are computed depends on the routing protocol. Two general types of protocols are in common use: distance-vector protocols and link-state protocols.

Distance-vector protocols

Distance-vector (aka "gossipy") protocols are based on the general idea, "If router X is five hops away from network Y, and I'm adjacent to router X, then I must be six hops away from network Y." You announce how far you think you are from the networks you know about. If your neighbors don't know of a better way to get to each network, they mark you as being the best gateway. If they already know a shorter route, they ignore your advertisement. Over time, everyone's routing tables are supposed to converge to a steady state.

This is really a very elegant idea. If it worked as advertised, routing would be relatively simple. Unfortunately, the basic algorithm does not deal well with changes in topology.[2] In some cases, infinite loops (e.g., router X receives information from router Y and sends it on to router Z, which sends it back to router Y) can prevent routes from converging at all. Real-world distance-vector protocols must avoid such problems by introducing complex heuristics or by enforcing arbitrary restrictions such as the RIP (Routing Information Protocol) notion that any network more than 15 hops away is unreachable.

Even in nonpathological cases, it can take many update cycles for all routers to reach a steady state. Therefore, to guarantee that routing will not jam for an extended period, the cycle time must be made short, and for this reason distance-vector protocols as a class tend to be talkative. For example, RIP requires that routers broadcast all their routing information every 30 seconds. EIGRP sends updates every 90 seconds.

On the other hand, BGP, the Border Gateway Protocol, transmits the entire table once and then transmits changes as they occur. This optimization substantially reduces the potential for "chatty" (and mostly unnecessary) traffic.

Table 15.1 lists the distance-vector protocols in common use today.

Table 15.1 Common distance-vector routing protocols

Proto	Long name	Application
RIP	Routing Information Protocol	Internal LANs (if that)
RIPng	Routing Information Protocol, next generation	IPv6 LANs
EIGRP[a]	Enhanced Interior Gateway Routing Protocol	WANs, corporate LANs
BGP	Border Gateway Protocol	Internet backbone routing

a. This protocol (EIGRP) is proprietary to Cisco.

Link-state protocols

Link-state protocols distribute information in a relatively unprocessed form. The records traded among routers are of the form "Router X is adjacent to router Y, and the link is up." A complete set of such records forms a connectivity map of the network from which each router can compute its own routing table. The primary advantage that link-state protocols offer over distance-vector protocols is the ability to quickly converge on an operational routing solution after a catastrophe occurs. The tradeoff is that maintaining a complete map of the network at each node requires memory and CPU power that would not be needed by a distance-vector routing system.

2. The problem is that changes in topology can lengthen the optimal routes. Some DV protocols such as EIGRP maintain information about multiple possible routes so that they always have a fallback plan. The exact details are not important.

Because the communications among routers in a link-state protocol are not part of the actual route-computation algorithm, they can be implemented in such a way that transmission loops do not occur. Updates to the topology database propagate across the network efficiently, at a lower cost in network bandwidth and CPU time.

Link-state protocols tend to be more complicated than distance-vector protocols, but this complexity can be explained in part by the fact that link-state protocols make it easier to implement advanced features such as type-of-service routing and multiple routes to the same destination.

Only two link-state protocols are in general use: OSPF and IS-IS. Although IS-IS has been widely implemented, it is not widely used and we do not recommended it for new deployments. See page 520 for some additional comments on IS-IS.

Cost metrics

For a routing protocol to determine which path to a network is shortest, it has to define what is meant by "shortest." Is it the path involving the fewest number of hops? The path with the lowest latency? The largest minimal intermediate bandwidth? The lowest financial cost?

For routing, the quality of a link is represented by a number called the cost metric. A path cost is the sum of the costs of each link in the path. In the simplest systems, every link has a cost of 1, leading to hop counts as a path metric. But any of the considerations mentioned above can be converted to a numeric cost metric.

Routing protocol designers have labored long and hard to make the definition of cost metrics flexible, and some protocols even allow different metrics to be used for different kinds of network traffic. Nevertheless, in 99% of cases, all this hard work can be safely ignored. The default metrics for most systems work just fine.

You may encounter situations in which the actual shortest path to a destination may not be a good default route for political reasons. To handle these cases, you can artificially boost the cost of the critical links to make them seem less appealing. Leave the rest of the routing configuration alone.

Interior and exterior protocols

An "autonomous system" (AS) is a group of networks under the administrative control of a single entity. The definition is vague; real-world autonomous systems can be as large as a world-wide corporate network or as small as a building or a single academic department. It all depends on how you want to manage routing. The general tendency is to make autonomous systems as large as possible. This convention simplifies administration and makes routing as efficient as possible.

Routing within an autonomous system is somewhat different from routing between autonomous systems. Protocols for routing among ASes ("exterior" protocols) must often handle routes for many networks (e.g., the entire Internet), and they must deal gracefully with the fact that neighboring routers are under other people's control. Exterior protocols do not reveal the topology inside an autonomous system, so in a sense they can be thought of as a second level of routing hierarchy that deals with collections of nets rather than individual hosts or cables.

In practice, small- and medium-sized sites rarely need to run an exterior protocol unless they are connected to more than one ISP. With multiple ISPs, the easy division of networks into local and Internet domains collapses, and routers must decide which route to the Internet is best for any particular address. (However, that is not to say that *every* router must know this information. Most hosts can stay stupid and route their default packets through an internal gateway that is better informed.)

While exterior protocols are not so different from their interior counterparts, this chapter concentrates on the interior protocols and the daemons that support them. If your site must use an external protocol as well, see the recommended reading list on page 528 for some suggested references.

15.3 Protocols on parade

Several routing protocols are in common use. In this section, we introduce the major players and summarize their main advantages and weaknesses.

RIP and RIPng: Routing Information Protocol

RIP is an old Xerox protocol that was adapted for IP networks. The IP version was originally specified in RFC1058, circa 1988. The protocol has existed in three versions: RIP, RIPv2, and the IPv6-only RIPng ("next generation").

All versions of RIP are simple distance-vector protocols that use hop counts as a cost metric. Because RIP was designed in an era when computers were expensive and networks small, RIPv1 considers any host fifteen or more hops away to be unreachable. Later versions of RIP have maintained the hop-count limit, mostly to encourage the administrators of complex sites to migrate to more sophisticated routing protocols.

See page 460 for information about classless addressing, aka CIDR.

RIPv2 is a minor revision of RIP that distributes netmasks along with next-hop addresses, so its support for subnetted networks and CIDR is better than RIPv1's. A vague gesture toward increasing the security of RIP was also included.

RIPv2 can be run in a compatibility mode that preserves most of its new features without entirely abandoning vanilla RIP receivers. In most respects, RIPv2 is identical to the original protocol and should be used in preference to it.

See page 451 for details on IPv6.

RIPng is a restatement of RIP in terms of IPv6. It is an IPv6-only protocol, and RIP remains IPv4-only. If you want to route both IPv4 and IPv6 with RIP, you'll need to run RIP and RIPng as separate protocols.

Although RIP is known for its profligate use of broadcasting, it does a good job when a network is changing often or when the topology of remote networks is not known. However, it can be slow to stabilize after a link goes down.

It was originally thought that the advent of more sophisticated routing protocols such as OSPF would make RIP obsolete. However, RIP continues to fill a need for a simple, easy-to-implement protocol that doesn't require much configuration, and it works well on low-complexity networks. The reports of RIP's death are greatly exaggerated.

RIP is widely implemented on non-UNIX platforms. A variety of common devices, from printers to SNMP-manageable network components, can listen to RIP advertisements to learn about network gateways. In addition, some form of RIP client is available for all versions of UNIX and Linux, so RIP is a de facto lowest-common-denominator routing protocol. Often, RIP is used for LAN routing, and a more featureful protocol is used for wide-area connectivity.

Some sites run passive RIP daemons (usually **routed** or Quagga's **ripd**) that listen for routing updates on the network but do not broadcast any information of their own. The actual route computations are performed with a more efficient protocol such as OSPF (see the next section). RIP is used only as a distribution mechanism.

OSPF: Open Shortest Path First

OSPF is the most popular link-state protocol. "Shortest path first" refers to the mathematical algorithm used to calculate routes; "open" is used in the sense of "nonproprietary." RFC2328 defines the basic protocol (OSPF version 2), and RFC5340 extends it to include support for IPv6 (OSPF version 3). OSPF version 1 is obsolete and is not used.

OSPF is an industrial-strength protocol that works well for large, complicated topologies. It offers several advantages over RIP, including the ability to manage several paths to a single destination and the ability to partition the network into sections ("areas") that share only high-level routing information. The protocol itself is complex and hence only worthwhile at sites of significant size, where routing protocol behavior really makes a difference. To use OSPF effectively, your site's IP addressing scheme should be reasonably hierarchical.

The OSPF protocol specification does not mandate any particular cost metric. Cisco's implementation uses a bandwidth-related value by default.

EIGRP: Enhanced Interior Gateway Routing Protocol

EIGRP is a proprietary routing protocol that runs only on Cisco routers. Its predecessor IGRP was created to address some of the shortcomings of RIP before robust standards like OSPF existed. IGRP has now been deprecated in favor of EIGRP, which accommodates CIDR masks. IGRP and EIGRP are configured similarly despite being quite different in their underlying protocol design.

EIGRP supports IPv6, but as with other routing protocols, the IPv6 world and IPv4 world are configured separately and act as separate, though parallel, routing domains.

EIGRP is a distance-vector protocol, but it's designed to avoid the looping and convergence problems found in other DV systems. It's widely regarded as the most evolved distance-vector protocol. For most purposes, EIGRP and OSPF are equally functional.

IS-IS: the ISO "standard"

IS-IS, the Intra-domain Intermediate System to Intermediate System Routeing Protocol, is the International Organization for Standardization's answer to OSPF. It was originally designed to manage "routeing" for the OSI network protocols and was later extended to handle IP routing.

Both IS-IS and OSPF were developed in the early 90s when ISO protocols were politically in vogue. Early attention from the IETF helped lend IS-IS a veneer of legitimacy, but it seems to be falling farther and farther behind OSPF in popularity. Today, the use of IS-IS is extremely rare outside of vendor certification test environments. The protocol itself is mired with lots of ISO baggage and generally should be avoided.

Router Discovery Protocol and Neighbor Discovery Protocol

IPv4's Router Discovery Protocol uses ICMP messages sent to the IP multicast address 224.0.0.1 to announce and learn about other routers on a network. Unfortunately, not all routers currently make these announcements, and not all hosts listen to them. The hope was that someday the use of RDP would become more widespread, but chicken-and-egg issues have largely prevented other protocols from relying on it.

See page 468 for more information about ARP.

IPv6's Neighbor Discovery Protocol subsumes the functions of both RDP and ARP, the Address Resolution Protocol used to map IPv4 addresses to hardware addresses on local networks. Because it's a core component of IPv6, NDP is available wherever IPv6 is found and IPv6 routing protocols typically build on it.

BGP: the Border Gateway Protocol

BGP is an exterior routing protocol; that is, a protocol that manages traffic among autonomous systems rather than among individual networks. There were once several exterior routing protocols in common use, but BGP has outlasted them all.

BGP is now the standard protocol used for Internet backbone routing. As of mid-2010, the Internet routing table contains about 320,000 prefixes. It should be clear from this number that backbone routing has very different scaling requirements from local routing.

15.4 Routing strategy selection criteria

Routing for a network can be managed at essentially four levels of complexity:

- No routing
- Static routes only
- Mostly static routes, but clients listen for RIP updates
- Dynamic routing everywhere

The topology of the overall network has a dramatic effect on each individual segment's routing requirements. Different nets may need very different levels of routing support. The following rules of thumb can help you choose a strategy:

- A stand-alone network requires no routing.
- If a network has only one way out, clients (nongateway machines) on that network should have a static default route to the lone gateway. No other configuration is necessary, except perhaps on the gateway itself.
- A gateway with a small number of networks on one side and a gateway to "the world" on the other side can have explicit static routes pointing to the former and a default route to the latter. However, dynamic routing is advisable if both sides have more than one routing choice.
- Use dynamic routing at points where networks cross political or administrative boundaries, even if the complexity of the networks involved would not otherwise suggest the use of a routing protocol.
- RIP works OK and is widely supported. Don't reject it out of hand just because it's an older protocol with a reputation for chattiness.

  The problem with RIP is that it doesn't scale indefinitely; an expanding network will eventually outgrow it. That fact makes RIP something of a transitional protocol with a narrow zone of applicability. That zone is bounded on one side by networks too simple to require any routing protocol and on the other side by networks too complicated for RIP. If your network plans include continued growth, it's probably reasonable to skip over the "RIP zone" entirely.
- Even when RIP isn't a good choice for your global routing strategy, it's still a good way to distribute routes to leaf nodes. But don't use it where it's not needed: systems on a network that has only one gateway never need dynamic updates.
- EIGRP and OSPF are about equally functional, but EIGRP is proprietary to Cisco. Cisco makes excellent and cost-competitive routers; nevertheless, standardizing on EIGRP limits your choices for future expansion.
- Routers connected to the Internet through multiple upstream providers must use BGP. However, most routers have only one upstream path and can therefore use a simple static default route.

A good default strategy for a medium-sized site with a relatively stable local structure and a connection to someone else's net is to use a combination of static and dynamic routing. Routers within the local structure that do not lead to external networks can use static routing, forwarding all unknown packets to a default machine that understands the outside world and does dynamic routing.

A network that is too complicated to be managed with this scheme should rely on dynamic routing. Default static routes can still be used on leaf nets, but machines on networks with more than one router should run **routed** or some other RIP receiver in passive mode.

15.5 Routing daemons

We don't recommend the use of UNIX and Linux systems as routers for production networks. Dedicated routers are simpler, more reliable, more secure, and faster (even if they are secretly running a Linux kernel). That said, it's nice to have the option to set up a new subnet using only a $15 network card and a $40 switch. That's a reasonable approach for lightly populated test and auxiliary networks.

Systems that act as gateways to such subnets don't need any help managing their own routing tables. Static routes are perfectly adequate, both for the gateway machine and for the machines on the subnet itself. However, if you want the subnet to be reachable by other systems at your site, you need to advertise the subnet's existence and to identify the router to which packets bound for that subnet should be sent. The usual way to do this is to run a routing daemon on the gateway.

UNIX and Linux systems can participate in most routing protocols through the use of various routing daemons. The notable exception is EIGRP, which as far as we are aware has no widely available UNIX or Linux implementation.

Because the use of routing daemons is uncommon on production systems, we don't describe their use and configuration in detail. However, the following sections outline the common software options and point to detailed configuration information.

routed: obsolete RIP implementation

routed was for a long time the only standard routing daemon, and it's still included on a few systems. **routed** speaks only RIP, and poorly at that: even support for RIPv2 is scattershot. **routed** does not speak RIPng, implementation of that protocol being confined to modern daemons such as Quagga or HP-UX's **ramd**.

Where available, **routed** is useful chiefly for its "quiet" mode (**-q**), in which it listens for routing updates but does not broadcast any information of its own. Aside from the command-line flag, **routed** normally does not require configuration. It's an easy and cheap way to get routing updates without having to deal with much configuration hassle.

See page 481 for more about ***route****.*

routed adds its discovered routes to the kernel's routing table. Routes must be reheard at least every four minutes or they will be removed. However, **routed** knows which routes it has added and does not remove static routes that were installed with the **route** command.

gated: first-generation multiprotocol routing daemon

gated is an elegantly designed and once-freely-available routing framework that allows the simultaneous use of multiple routing protocols. It gives administrators precise control over advertised routes, broadcast addresses, trust policies, and metrics. **gated** shares routes among several protocols, allowing routing gateways to be constructed between areas that have standardized on different routing systems. It also has one of the nicest administrative interfaces and configuration file designs of any administrative software.

Alas, **gated** is dead (or at least, dead-ish), though its memory lives on in slow-to-change releases such as HP-UX and AIX, which bundle versions 3.5.9 and 6.0, respectively.

gated is an object lesson in the perils of attempting to compete with open source software. It started out as freely distributable software, but in 1992 it was privatized and turned over to a development consortium; updates then became available only to members of the consortium. The consortium was eventually disbanded, and the rights to the commercial version of **gated** changed hands several times. Meanwhile, the open source Zebra and Quagga projects rose to take over **gated**'s role as the mainstream open source routing package. These days, **gated** is extinct both as a commercial product and as an open source project, a sad end to a useful and well-designed package.

Quagga: mainstream routing daemon

Quagga (quagga.net) is a development fork of Zebra, a GNU project started by Kunihiro Ishiguro and Yoshinari Yoshikawa to implement multiprotocol routing with a collection of independent daemons instead of a single monolithic application. In real life, the quagga—a subspecies of zebra last photographed in 1870—is extinct, but in the digital realm it is Quagga that survives and Zebra that is no longer under active development.

Quagga currently implements RIP (all versions), OSPF (versions 2 and 3), BGP, and IS-IS. It runs on Linux, Solaris, and various flavors of BSD. On Solaris and our example Linux systems, Quagga is either installed by default or is available as an optional package through the system's standard software repository.

In the Quagga system, the **zebra** daemon acts as a central clearing-house for routing information. It manages the interaction between the kernel's routing table and the daemons for individual routing protocols (**ripd**, **ripngd**, **ospfd**, **ospf6d**, **bgpd**, and **isisd**). It also controls the flow of routing information among protocols. Each daemon has its own configuration file in the **/etc/quagga** directory.

You can connect to any of the Quagga daemons through a command-line interface (**vtysh** on Linux, **quaggaadm** on Solaris) to query and modify its configuration. The command language itself is designed to be familiar to users of Cisco's IOS operating system; see the section on Cisco routers starting on page 525 for some additional details. As in IOS, you use **enable** to enter "superuser" mode, **config term** to enter configuration commands, and **write** to save your configuration changes back to the daemon's configuration file.

The official documentation at quagga.net is available in HTML or PDF form. Although complete, it's for the most part a workmanlike catalog of options and does not provide much of an overview of the system. The real documentation action is on the wiki, wiki.quagga.net. Look there for well-commented example configurations, FAQs, and tips.

Although the configuration files have a simple format and are not complex, you'll need to understand the protocols you're configuring and have some idea of which options you want to enable or configure. See the recommended reading list on page 528 for some good books on routing protocols.

Solaris and Red Hat include a selection of helpful configuration file examples for the various Quagga daemons in the **/etc/quagga** directory. Solaris includes a nice **README.Solaris** file as well. However, you're still best off referring to the wiki.

ramd: multiprotocol routing system for HP-UX

HP-UX includes a suite of routing daemons that are eerily similar in their general architecture to Zebra and Quagga. We are not sure whether the similarity is attributable to emulation, convergent evolution, or perhaps to an early fork from the Zebra code base.

In any event, the similarity is only superficial. Some notable points of divergence are that HP's system supports only IPv6 and external routing protocols (RIPng, BGP, and IS-IS) and that it does not support OSPF at all. The configuration language is different, and the control utility (**rdc**, as opposed to Quagga's **vtysh** or **quaggaadm**) accepts only command-line arguments; it does not function as an independent shell environment.

HP calls its system the Route Administration Manager Daemon, and the suite's **ramd** daemon plays the same role as **zebra** in the Quagga universe. As in Quagga, the protocol-specific daemons are called **ripngd**, **isisd**, and **bgpd**.

XORP: router in a box

XORP, the eXtensible Open Router Platform project, was started at around the same time as Zebra, but its ambitions are more general. Instead of focusing on routing, XORP aims to emulate all the functions of a dedicated router, including packet filtering and traffic management. Check it out at xorp.org.

One interesting aspect of XORP is that in addition to running under several operating systems (Linux, various BSD derivatives, Mac OS X, and Windows Server

2003), it's also available as a live CD that runs directly on PC hardware. The live CD is secretly based on Linux, but it does go a long way toward turning a generic PC into a dedicated routing appliance.

Vendor specifics

Quagga is the go-to routing software for Linux. All of our example distributions either install it by default or make it readily available from the distributor's repository. Quagga has become so entrenched that most distributions no longer include **routed**. Even where they do, it's a vestigial version without RIPv2 support.

Solaris includes a functional **routed** (actually called **in.routed**) that understands RIPv2. It also includes Quagga; you can take your pick. For any sort of IPv6 routing, you'll need to use Quagga.

in.routed is the default routing solution, and it's started automatically at boot time if you haven't specified a default network gateway in the **/etc/defaultrouter** file. Solaris continues to supply the **in.rdisc** router discovery daemon, which is curious since its functionality is now included in **in.routed**.

HP-UX's primary routing system, **ramd**, is discussed above (see page 524). HP also provides a copy of **gated** 3.5.9, which is quite old and has no support for IPv6. If you want to manage both IPv4 and IPv6 routing under HP-UX, you'll have to use **gated** for the former and **ramd** for the latter. Unfortunately, Quagga does not currently run on HP-UX.

AIX provides three routing daemons: **gated** v6.0, a **routed** that speaks only RIPv1, and **ndpd-router**, an implementation of RIPng and NDP. AIX's **gated** speaks RIPng, too; however, if you want to use **gated** for IPv6 routing, you may need to run both **gated** and **ndpd-router**. See the documentation for details.

15.6 Cisco routers

Routers made by Cisco Systems, Inc., are the de facto standard for Internet routing today. Having captured over 60% of the router market, Cisco's products are well known, and staff that know how to operate them are relatively easy to find. Before Cisco, UNIX boxes with multiple network interfaces were often used as routers. Today, dedicated routers are the favored gear to put in datacom closets and above ceiling tiles where network cables come together.

Most of Cisco's router products run an operating system called Cisco IOS, which is proprietary and unrelated to UNIX. Its command set is rather large; the full documentation set fills up about 4.5 feet of shelf space. We could never fully cover Cisco IOS here, but knowing a few basics can get you a long way.

By default, IOS defines two levels of access (user and privileged), both of which are password protected. By default, you can simply **telnet** to a Cisco router to enter user mode.

You are prompted for the user-level access password:

```
$ telnet acme-gw.acme.com[3]
Connected to acme-gw.acme.com.
Escape character is '^]'.

User Access Verification
Password:
```

Upon entering the correct password, you receive a prompt from Cisco's EXEC command interpreter.

```
acme-gw.acme.com>
```

At this prompt, you can enter commands such as **show interfaces** to see the router's network interfaces or **show ?** to list the other things you can see.

To enter privileged mode, type **enable** and when asked, type the privileged password . Once you have reached the privileged level, your prompt ends in a #:

```
acme-gw.acme.com#
```

BE CAREFUL—you can do anything from this prompt, including erasing the router's configuration information and its operating system. When in doubt, consult Cisco's manuals or one of the comprehensive books published by Cisco Press.

You can type **show running** to see the current running configuration of the router and **show config** to see the current nonvolatile configuration. Most of the time, these are the same.

Here's a typical configuration:

```
acme-gw.acme.com# show running
Current configuration:
version 12.1
hostname acme-gw
enable secret xxxxxxxx
ip subnet-zero

interface Ethernet0
  description Acme internal network
    ip address 192.108.21.254 255.255.255.0
    no ip directed-broadcast
interface Ethernet1
  description Acme backbone network
    ip address 192.225.33.254 255.255.255.0
    no ip directed-broadcast

ip classless
line con 0
transport input none
```

3. Modern versions of IOS support a variety of access methods, including SSH. **telnet**, of course, is entirely insecure. If your site already uses Cisco routers, contact your network administrator to find out which methods have been enabled.

```
line aux 0
  transport input telnet
line vty 0 4
  password xxxxxxxx
  login

end
```

The router configuration can be modified in a variety of ways. Cisco offers graphical tools that run under some versions of UNIX/Linux and Windows. Real network administrators never use these; the command prompt is always the "sure bet." It is also possible to **scp** a config file to or from a router so that you can edit it with your favorite editor.

To modify the configuration from the command prompt, type **config term**:

```
acme-gw.acme.com# config term
Enter configuration commands, one per line.  End with CNTL/Z.
acme-gw(config)#
```

You can then type new configuration commands exactly as you want them to appear in the **show running** output. For example, if we wanted to change the IP address of the Ethernet0 interface in the example above, we could enter

```
interface Ethernet0
ip address 192.225.40.253 255.255.255.0
```

When you've finished entering configuration commands, press <Control-Z> to return to the regular command prompt. If you're happy with the new configuration, enter **write mem** to save the configuration to nonvolatile memory.

Here are some tips for a successful Cisco router experience:

- Name the router with the **hostname** command. This precaution helps prevent accidents caused by configuration changes to the wrong router. The hostname always appears in the command prompt.
- Always keep a backup router configuration on hand. You can **scp** or **tftp** the running configuration to another system each night for safekeeping.
- It's often possible to store a copy of the configuration in NVRAM or on a removable jump drive. Do so!
- Once you have configured the router for SSH access, turn off the Telnet protocol entirely.
- Control access to the router command line by putting access lists on the router's VTYs (VTYs are like PTYs on a UNIX system). This precaution prevents unwanted parties from trying to break into your router.

- Control the traffic flowing through your networks (and possibly to the outside world) by setting up access lists on each interface. See *Packet-filtering firewalls* on page 932 for more information about how to set up access lists.
- Keep routers physically secure. It's easy to reset the privileged password if you have physical access to a Cisco box.

If you have multiple routers and multiple router wranglers, check out the free tool RANCID from shrubbery.net. With a name like RANCID it practically markets itself, but here's the elevator pitch: RANCID logs into your routers every night to retrieve their configuration files. It diffs the configurations and lets you know about anything that's changed. It also keeps the configuration files under revision control (see page 397) automatically.

15.7 Recommended reading

PERLMAN, RADIA. *Interconnections: Bridges, Routers, Switches, and Internetworking Protocols (2nd Edition)*. Reading, MA: Addison-Wesley, 2000.

This is the definitive work in this topic area. If you buy just one book about networking fundamentals, this should be it. Also, don't ever pass up a chance to hang out with Radia—she's a lot of fun and holds a shocking amount of knowledge in her brain.

DOOLEY, KEVIN AND IAN J. BROWN. *Cisco IOS Cookbook (2nd Edition)*. Sebastopol, CA: O'Reilly Media, 2007.

DOYLE, JEFF, AND JENNIFER CARROLL. *Routing TCP/IP, Volume I (2nd Edition)*. Indianapolis, IN: Cisco Press, 2005.

DOYLE, JEFF, AND JENNIFER DEHAVEN CARROLL. *Routing TCP/IP, Volume II*. Indianapolis, IN: Cisco Press, 2001.

This pair of volumes is an in-depth introduction to routing protocols and is independent of any particular implementation. *Volume I* covers interior protocols, and *Volume II* covers exterior protocols, NAT, and multicast routing.

HALABI, SAM. *Internet Routing Architectures (2nd Edition)*. Indianapolis, IN: Cisco Press, 2000.

This well-regarded book concentrates on BGP.

HUITEMA, CHRISTIAN. *Routing in the Internet (2nd Edition)*. Upper Saddle River, NJ: Prentice Hall PTR, 2000.

This book is a clear and well-written introduction to routing from the ground up. It covers most of the protocols in common use and also some advanced topics such as multicasting.

There are many routing-related RFCs. The main ones are shown in Table 15.2.

Table 15.2 Routing-related RFCs

RFC	Title	Authors
1075	Distance Vector Multicast Routing Protocol	Waitzman et al.
1256	ICMP Router Discovery Messages	Deering
1724	RIP Version 2 MIB Extension	Malkin, Baker
2080	RIPng for IPv6	Malkin, Minnear
2328	OSPF Version 2	Moy
2453	Routing Information Protocol Version 2	Malkin
4271	A Border Gateway Protocol 4 (BGP-4)	Rekhter, Li, et al.
4552	Authentication/Confidentiality for OSPFv3	Gupta, Melam
4822	RIPv2 Cryptographic Authentication	Atkinson, Fanto
4861	Neighbor Discovery for IPv6	Narten et al.
5175	IPv6 Router Advertisement Flags Option	Haberman, Hinden
5308	Routing IPv6 with IS-IS	Hopps
5340	OSPF for IPv6	Coltun et al.
5643	Management Information Base for OSPFv3	Joyal, Manral, et al.

Exercises begin on the next page.

15.8 Exercises

E15.1 Investigate the Linux **route** command and write a short description of what it does. Using **route**, how would you

a) Add a default route to 128.138.129.1 using interface eth1?

b) Delete a route to 128.138.129.1?

c) Determine whether a route was added by a program such as **routed** or an ICMP redirect?

E15.2 Compare static and dynamic routing, listing several advantages and disadvantages of each. Describe situations in which each would be appropriate and explain why.

★ E15.3 Consider the following **netstat -rn** output from a Linux system. Describe the routes and figure out the network setup. Which network, 10.0.0.0 or 10.1.1.0, is closer to the Internet? Which process added each route?

```
Destination    Gateway       Genmask         Flags MSS  Window  irtt  Iface
10.0.0.0       0.0.0.0       255.255.255.0   U      40  0          0  eth1
10.1.1.0       0.0.0.0       255.255.255.0   U      40  0          0  eth0
0.0.0.0        10.0.0.1      0.0.0.0         UG     40  0          0  eth1
```

★★ E15.4 Figure out the routing scheme that is used at your site. What protocols are in use? Which machines directly connect to the Internet? You can use **tcpdump** to look for routing update packets on the local network and **traceroute** to explore beyond the local net. (Requires root access.)

★★ E15.5 If you were a medium-sized ISP that provided dial-in accounts and virtual hosting, what sort of routing setup up would you use? Make sure that you consider not only the gateway router(s) between the Internet backbone and your own network but also any interior routers that may be in use. Draw a network diagram that outlines your routing architecture.

16 Network Hardware

Whether you're using Google on your cell phone,[1] banking on-line, or receiving Skype video calls from your cousins in Belgium, just about everything in the world these days is handled in digital form. Moving data from one place to another is on everyone's mind. Behind all this craziness is fancy network hardware and—you guessed it—a whole bunch of stuff that originated in the deep, dark caves of UNIX. If there's one area in which UNIX technology has touched human lives, it's in the practical realization of large-scale packetized data transport.

Many network-layer technologies have been promoted over the years, but one has emerged as a clear winner: Ethernet. Now that Ethernet is found on everything from game consoles to refrigerators, a thorough understanding of this system is critical to success as a system administrator.

It goes without saying that the speed and reliability of your network have a direct effect on your organization's productivity. But today, networking is so pervasive that the state of the network can affect our ability to perform basic human interactions, such as placing a telephone call. A poorly designed network is a personal and professional embarrassment that can have catastrophic social effects. It can also be very expensive to fix.

1. Did you know that iPhones run a form of embedded UNIX?

At least four major factors contribute to success:

- Development of a reasonable network design
- Selection of high-quality hardware
- Proper installation and documentation
- Competent ongoing operations and maintenance

This chapter focuses on understanding, installing, and operating Ethernet networks. We also touch briefly on "last mile" network technologies such as DSL (Digital Subscriber Line), which are normally presented to the end customer in the form of—surprise!—Ethernet.

16.1 Ethernet: the Swiss Army knife of networking

Having captured over 95% of the world-wide Local Area Network (LAN) market, Ethernet can be found just about everywhere in its many forms. It started as Bob Metcalfe's Ph.D. thesis at MIT but is now described in a variety of IEEE standards.

Ethernet was originally specified at 3 Mb/s (mega*bits* per second), but it moved to 10 Mb/s almost immediately. Once a 100 Mb/s standard was finalized in 1994, it became clear that Ethernet would evolve rather than be replaced. This touched off a race to build increasingly faster version of Ethernet, and that race goes on today. Table 16.1 highlights the evolution of the various Ethernet standards.[2]

How Ethernet works

The underlying model used by Ethernet can be described as a polite dinner party at which guests (computers) don't interrupt each other but rather wait for a lull in the conversation (no traffic on the network cable) before speaking. If two guests start to talk at once (a collision) they both stop, excuse themselves, wait a bit, and then one of them starts talking again.

The technical term for this scheme is CSMA/CD:

- Carrier Sense: you can tell whether anyone is talking.
- Multiple Access: everyone can talk.
- Collision Detection: you know when you interrupt someone else.

The actual delay on collision detection is somewhat random. This convention avoids the scenario in which two hosts simultaneously transmit to the network, detect the collision, wait the same amount of time, and then start transmitting again, thus flooding the network with collisions. This was not always true!

Today, the importance of the CSMA/CD conventions has been lessened by the advent of switches, which typically limit the number of hosts in a given collision domain to two. (To continue the "dinner party" analogy, you might think of this

2. We have omitted a few goofy Ethernet standards that have withered on the vine, such as 100BaseT4 and 100BaseVG-AnyLAN.

Table 16.1 The evolution of Ethernet

Year	Speed	Common name	IEEE#	Dist	Media[a]
1973	3 Mb/s	Xerox Ethernet	–	?	Coax
1976	10 Mb/s	Ethernet 1	–	500m	RG-11 coax
1982	10 Mb/s	DIX Ethernet (Ethernet II)	–	500m	RG-11 coax
1985	10 Mb/s	10Base5 ("Thicknet")	802.3	500m	RG-11 coax
1985	10 Mb/s	10Base2 ("Thinnet")	802.3	180m	RG-58 coax
1989	10 Mb/s	10BaseT	802.3	100m	Cat 3 UTP copper
1993	10 Mb/s	10BaseF	802.3	2km 25km	MM fiber SM fiber
1994	100 Mb/s	100BaseTX ("100 meg")	802.3u	100m	Cat 5 UTP copper
1994	100 Mb/s	100BaseFX	802.3u	2km 20km	MM fiber SM fiber
1998	1 Gb/s	1000BaseSX	802.3z	260m 550m	62.5-μm MM fiber 50-μm MM fiber
1998	1 Gb/s	1000BaseLX	802.3z	440m 550m 3km	62.5-μm MM fiber 50-μm MM fiber SM fiber
1998	1 Gb/s	1000BaseCX	802.3z	25m	Twinax
1999	1 Gb/s	1000BaseT ("Gigabit")	802.3ab	100m	Cat 5e, 6 UTP copper
2002	10 Gb/s	10GBase-SR 10GBase-LR 10GBase-ER 10GBase-ZR	802.3ae 802.3aq 	300m 10km 40km 80km	MM fiber SM fiber SM fiber SM fiber
2006	10 Gb/s	10GBase-T ("10 Gig")	802.3an	100m	Cat 6a, 7, 7a UTP
2009	40 Gb/s	40GBase-CR4 40GBase-SR4	P802.3ba	10m 100m	UTP Copper MM fiber
2009	100 Gb/s	100GBase-CR10 100Gbase-SR10	P802.3ba	10m 100m	UTP Copper MM fiber
2012[b]	1 Tb/s	TBD	TBD	TBD	CWDM fiber
2015[b]	10 Tb/s	TBD	TBD	TBD	DWDM fiber

a. MM = Multimode, SM = Single-mode, UTP = Unshielded twisted pair, CWDM = Coarse wavelength division multiplexing, DWDM = Dense wavelength division multiplexing.
b. Industry projection

variant as being akin to the scene sometimes found in old movies where two people sit at opposite ends of a long, formal dining table.)

Ethernet topology

The Ethernet topology is a branching bus with no loops; a packet can travel between two hosts on the same network in only one way. Three types of packets can be exchanged on a segment: unicast, multicast, and broadcast. Unicast packets are addressed to only one host. Multicast packets are addressed to a group of hosts. Broadcast packets are delivered to all hosts on a segment.

A "broadcast domain" is the set of hosts that receive packets destined for the hardware broadcast address. Exactly one broadcast domain is defined for each logical Ethernet segment. Under the early Ethernet standards and media (e.g., 10Base5), physical segments and logical segments were exactly the same because all the packets traveled on one big cable with host interfaces strapped onto the side of it.[3]

With the advent of switches, today's logical segments usually consist of many (possibly dozens or hundreds) physical segments (or, in some cases, wireless segments) to which only two devices are connected: the switch port and the host. The switches are responsible for escorting multicast and unicast packets to the physical (or wireless) segments on which the intended recipients reside. Broadcast traffic is forwarded to all ports in a logical segment.

A single logical segment can consist of physical (or wireless) segments operating at different speeds (10 Mb/s, 100 Mb/s, 1 Gb/s, or 10 Gb/s). Hence, switches must have buffering and timing capabilities that let them smooth over any potential timing conflicts.

Unshielded twisted pair cabling

Unshielded twisted pair (UTP) is the preferred cable medium for Ethernet. It is based on a star topology and has several advantages over other media:

- It uses inexpensive, readily available copper wire. (Sometimes, existing building wiring can be used.)
- UTP wire is much easier to install and debug than is coax or fiber. Custom lengths are easy to make.
- UTP uses RJ-45 connectors, which are cheap, reliable, and easy to install.
- The link to each machine is independent (and private!), so a cabling problem on one link is unlikely to affect other hosts on the network.

The general "shape" of a UTP network is illustrated in Exhibit A.

UTP wire suitable for use in modern LANs is commonly broken down into eight classifications. The performance rating system was first introduced by Anixter, a large cable supplier. These standards were formalized by the Telecommunications Industry Association (TIA) and are known today as Category 1 through Category 7, with a few special variants such as Category 5e and Category 6a thrown in for good measure.

The International Organization for Standardization (ISO) has also jumped into the exciting and highly profitable world of cable classification. They promote standards that are exactly or approximately equivalent to the higher-numbered

3. No kidding! Attaching a new computer involved boring a hole into the outer sheath of the cable with a special drill to reach the center conductor. A "vampire tap" that bit into the outer conductor was then clamped on with screws.

Exhibit A A UTP installation

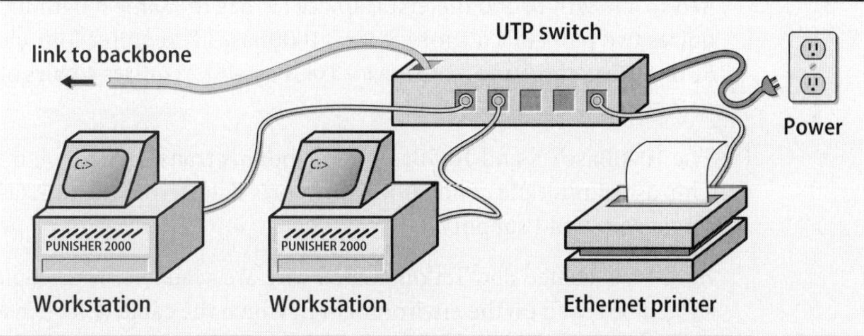

TIA categories. For example, TIA Category 5 cable is equivalent to ISO Class D cable. For the geeks in the audience, Table 16.2 illustrates the major differences among the various modern-day classifications. This is good information to memorize so you can impress your friends at parties.

Table 16.2 UTP cable characteristics

Parameter[a]	Units	Cat 5 Class D[b]	Cat 5e	Cat 6 Class E	Cat 6a Class EA	Cat 7 Class F	Cat 7a Class FA
Frequency range	MHz	100	100	250	500	600	1000
Attenuation	dB	24	24	21.7	18.4	20.8	60
NEXT	dB	27.1	30.1	39.9	59	62.1	60.4
ELFEXT	dB	17	17.4	23.2	43.1	46.0	35.1
Return loss	dB	8	10	12	32	14.1	61.93
Propagation delay	ns	548	548	548	548	504	534

a. NEXT = Near-end crosstalk, ELFEXT = Equal level far-end crosstalk
b. Includes additional TIA and ISO requirements TSB95 and FDAM 2, respectively

In practice, Category 1 and Category 2 cables are suitable only for voice applications (if that). Category 3 cable is as low as you can go for a LAN; it is the standard for 10 Mb/s 10BaseT but should only be used today as a last resort. Category 4 is something of an orphan and is not ideally suited for any particular application.

Category 5 cable can support 100 Mb/s. Category 5e, Category 6, and Category 6a cabling support 1 Gb/s and are the most common standard currently in use for data cabling. Category 6a is the cable of choice for new installations because it is particularly resistant to interference from older Ethernet signaling standards (e.g., 10BaseT), a problem that has plagued some Category 5/5e installations. Category 7 and Category 7a cable are intended for 10 Gb/s use.

See page 545 for more information about wiring.

10BaseT connections require two pairs of Category 3 wire, and each link is limited to a length of 100 meters; 100BaseTX has the same length limitation but requires two pairs of Category 5 wire. 1000BaseTX requires four pairs of Category 5e or Category 6/6a wire. Likewise 10GBase-TX requires 4 pairs of Category 6a, 7, or 7a wire.

The 1000BaseTX and 10GBase-TX standards transmit data on multiple pairs. This use of multiple conductors transports data across the link faster than any single pair could support.

Both PVC-coated and Teflon-coated wire are available. Your choice of jacketing should be based on the environment in which the cable will be installed. Enclosed areas that feed into the building's ventilation system ("return air plenums") typically require Teflon.[4] PVC is less expensive and easier to work with but produces toxic fumes if it catches fire (hence the need to keep it out of air plenums).

See page 1163 for more information about the RS-232 standard.

For terminating the four-pair UTP cable at patch panels and RJ-45 wall jacks, we suggest that you use the TIA/EIA-568A RJ-45 wiring standard. This standard, which is compatible with other uses of RJ-45 (e.g., RS-232), is a convenient way to keep the wiring at both ends of the connection consistent, regardless of whether you can easily access the cable pairs themselves. Table 16.3 shows the pinouts.

Table 16.3 TIA/EIA-568A standard for wiring four-pair UTP to an RJ-45 jack

Pair	Colors	Wired to	Pair	Colors	Wired to
1	White/Blue	Pins 5/4	3	White/Green	Pins 1/2
2	White/Orange	Pins 3/6	4	White/Brown	Pins 7/8

Existing building wiring may or may not be suitable for network use, depending on how and when it was installed. Many old buildings were retrofitted with new cable in the 1980s. Unfortunately, this cable usually won't support anything beyond 100 Mb/s.

Optical fiber

Optical fiber is used to transmit data in cases where copper cable isn't adequate, for one reason or another. Fiber carries signals farther than copper. Fiber is also more resistant to electrical interference, which is an attractive feature for some applications. Where fiber isn't absolutely necessary, copper is normally preferred because it's less expensive and easier to work with.

"Multimode" and "single mode" fiber are the two common types. Multimode fiber is typically used for applications within a building or campus. It's thicker than single-mode fiber and can carry multiple rays of light; this feature permits the use of less expensive electronics (e.g., LEDs as a light source).

4. Check with your fire marshall or local fire department to determine the requirements in your area.

Single-mode fiber is most often found in long-haul applications, such as intercity or interstate connections. It can carry only a single ray of light and requires expensive precision electronics on the endpoints.

TIA-598C recommends color-coding the common types of fiber as shown in Table 16.4. The key rule to remember is that everything must match. The fiber that connects the endpoints, the fiber cross-connect cables, and the endpoint electronics must all be of the same type and size. Note that although both OM1 and OM2 are colored orange, they are not interchangeable—check the size imprint on the cables to make sure they match. You will experience no end of difficult-to-isolate problems if you don't follow this rule.

Table 16.4 Attributes of standard optical fibers

Mode	ISO name[a]	Core diameter	Cladding diameter	Color
Multi	OM1	62.5 µm	125 µm	Orange
Multi	OM2	50 µm	125 µm	Orange
Multi	OM3	50 µm[b]	125 µm	Aqua
Single	OS1	8–10 µm	125 µm	Yellow

a. According to ISO 11801.
b. OM3 is optimized for carrying laser light.

More than 30 types of connectors are used on the ends of optical fibers, and there is no real rhyme or reason as to which connectors are used where. The connectors you need to use in a particular case will most often be dictated by the equipment vendors or by your existing building fiber plant. The good news is that conversion jumpers are fairly easy to obtain.

Connecting and expanding Ethernets

Ethernets can be connected through several types of devices. The options below are ranked by approximate cost, with the cheapest options first. The more logic that a device uses to move bits from one network to another, the more hardware and embedded software the device needs to have and the more expensive it is likely to be.

Hubs

See page 451 for more on network layers.

Hubs are also referred to as concentrators or repeaters. They are active devices that connect Ethernet segments at the physical layer. They require external power.

Acting as a repeater, a hub retimes and reconstitutes Ethernet frames but does not interpret them; it has no idea where packets are going or what protocol they are using. With the exception of extremely special cases, *hubs should no longer be used in enterprise networks*, and we discourage their use in residential (consumer) networks as well. (Why? Because switches make significantly more efficient use of network bandwidth and are just as cheap these days.)

Switches

Switches connect Ethernets at the link layer. Their purpose is to join two physical networks in a way that makes them seem like one big physical network. Switches are the industry standard for connecting Ethernet devices today.

Switches receive, regenerate, and retransmit packets in hardware. Switches use a dynamic learning algorithm. They notice which source addresses come from one port and which from another. They forward packets between ports only when necessary. At first all packets are forwarded, but in a few seconds the switch has learned the locations of most hosts and can be more selective.

Since not all packets are forwarded among networks, each segment of cable that connects to a switch is less saturated with traffic than it would be if all machines were on the same cable. Given that most communication tends to be localized, the increase in apparent bandwidth can be dramatic. And since the logical model of the network is not affected by the presence of a switch, few administrative consequences result from installing one.

Switches can sometimes become confused if your network contains loops. The confusion arises because packets from a single host appear to be on two (or more) ports of the switch. A single Ethernet cannot have loops, but as you connect several Ethernets with routers and switches, the topology can include multiple paths to a host. Some switches can handle this situation by holding alternative routes in reserve in case the primary route goes down. They perform a pruning operation on the network they see until the remaining sections present only one path to each node on the network. Some switches can also handle duplicate links between the same two networks and route traffic in a round robin fashion.

Switches must scan every packet to determine if it should be forwarded. Their performance is usually measured by both the packet scanning rate and the packet forwarding rate. Many vendors do not mention packet sizes in the performance figures they quote; therefore, actual performance may be less than advertised.

Although Ethernet switching hardware is getting faster all the time, it is still not a reasonable technology for connecting more than a hundred hosts in a single logical segment. Problems such as "broadcast storms" often plague large switched networks since broadcast traffic must be forwarded to all ports in a switched segment. To solve this problem, use a router to isolate broadcast traffic between switched segments, thereby creating more than one logical Ethernet.

Choosing a switch can be difficult. The switch market is a highly competitive segment of the computer industry, and it's plagued with marketing claims that aren't even partially true. When selecting a switch vendor, you should rely on independent evaluations ("bakeoffs" such as those that appear in magazine comparisons) rather than any data supplied by vendors themselves. In recent years, it has been common for one vendor to have the "best" product for a few months but then completely destroy its performance or reliability when trying to make improvements, thus elevating another manufacturer to the top of the heap.

In all cases, make sure that the backplane speed of the switch is adequate—that's the number that really counts at the end of a long day. A well-designed switch should have a backplane speed that exceeds the sum of the speeds of all its ports.

VLAN-capable switches

Large sites can benefit from switches that partition their ports (through software configuration) into subgroups called Virtual Local Area Networks or VLANs. A VLAN is a group of ports that belong to the same logical segment, as if the ports were connected to their own dedicated switch. Such partitioning increases the ability of the switch to isolate traffic, and that capability has beneficial effects on both security and performance.

Traffic between VLANs is handled by a router, or in some cases, by a routing module or routing software layer within the switch. An extension of this system known as "VLAN trunking" (such as is specified by the IEEE 802.1Q protocol) allows physically separate switches to service ports on the same logical VLAN.

Routers

Routers (aka "layer 3 switches") direct traffic at the network layer, layer 3 of the OSI network model. They shuttle packets to their final destinations in accordance with the information in the TCP/IP protocol headers. In addition to simply moving the packets from one place to another, routers can also perform other functions such as packet filtering (for security), prioritization (for quality of service), and big-picture network topology discovery. See all the gory details of how routing really works in Chapter 15.

Routers take one of two forms: fixed configuration and modular. Fixed configuration routers have specific network interfaces permanently installed at the factory. They are usually suitable for small, specialized applications. For example, a router with a T1 interface and an Ethernet interface might be a good choice to connect a small company to the Internet.

Modular routers have a slot or bus architecture to which interfaces can be added by the end user. Although this approach is usually more expensive, it ensures greater flexibility down the road.

Depending on your reliability needs and expected traffic load, a dedicated router may or may not be cheaper than a UNIX or Linux system configured to act as a router. However, the dedicated router usually results in superior performance and reliability. This is one area of network design in which it's usually advisable to spend the extra money up front to avoid headaches later.

Autonegotiation

With the introduction of a variety of Ethernet standards came the need for devices to identify how their neighbors were configured and to adjust their settings accordingly. For example, the network won't work if one side of a link thinks the network is running at 1 Gb/s and the other side of the link thinks it's running at 10 Mb/s. The Ethernet autonegotiation feature of the IEEE standards is designed to detect and solve this problem. And in some cases, it does. In other cases, it is easily misapplied and simply compounds the problem.

The two golden rules of autonegotiation are these:

- You *must* use autonegotiation on all interfaces capable of 1 Gb/s or above. It's required by the standard.
- On interfaces limited to 100 Mb/s or below, you must either configure *both* ends of a link in autonegotiation mode, or you must *manually* configure the speed and duplex (half vs. full) on *both* sides. If you configure only one side in autonegotiation mode, it will not (in most cases) "learn" how the other side has been configured. The result will be a configuration mismatch and poor performance.

To see how to set a network interface's autonegotiation policy, see the system-specific sections in the *TCP/IP Networking* chapter; they start on page 484.

Power over Ethernet

Power over Ethernet (PoE) is an extension of UTP Ethernet (standardized as IEEE 802.3af) that transmits power to devices over the same UTP cable that carries the Ethernet signal. It's especially handy for Voice over IP (VoIP) telephones or wireless access points (to name just two examples) that need a relatively small amount of power and a network connection wherever they live.

The power supply capacity of PoE systems has been stratified into four classes that range from 3.84 to 12.95 watts. Never satisfied, the industry is currently working on a higher power standard (802.3at) that may provide more than 60 watts. Won't it be convenient to operate an Easy-Bake oven off the network port in the conference room?[5]

PoE has two ramifications that are significant for sysadmins:

- You need to be aware of PoE devices in your infrastructure so that you can plan the availability of PoE-capable switch ports accordingly. They are more expensive than non-PoE ports.
- The power budget for data closets that house PoE switches must include the wattage of the PoE devices. Note that you don't have to budget the same amount of extra cooling for the closet because most of the heat generated by the consumption of PoE power will be dissipated outside the closet (usually, in an office).

5. Sadly, we discovered during technical review that Easy-Bake ovens require a 100 watt light bulb (if they use a bulb at all; some now have heating elements), thus dashing the industry's hopes for IEEE 802.3at compatibility. And for those of you that are wondering: yes, it is possible to boot a small Linux system off a PoE port. Specific hardware is left as an exercise for the reader.

Jumbo frames

Ethernet is standardized for a typical packet size of 1,500 bytes (1,518 with framing), a value chosen long ago when networks were slow and memory for buffers was scarce. Today, these 1,500-byte packets look pretty shrimpy in the context of a gigabit Ethernet. Because every packet consumes overhead and introduces latency, network throughput can be higher if larger packet sizes are allowed.

Unfortunately, the IEEE standards for the various types of Ethernet forbid large packets because of interoperability concerns. But just as highway traffic often mysteriously flows faster than the stated speed limit, illicit king-size Ethernet packets are a common sight on today's networks. Egged on by impatient customers, manufacturers of network equipment have quietly flouted the IEEE and built support for large frames into their gigabit products.

To use these so-called jumbo frames, all you need do is bump up your network interfaces' MTUs. Throughput gains vary with traffic patterns, but large transfers over TCP (e.g., NFSv4 or CIFS file service) benefit the most. Expect a modest but measurable improvement on the order of 10%.

Be aware of these points, though:

- All network equipment on a subnet must support and use jumbo frames, including switches and routers. You cannot mix and match.
- Because jumbo frames are nonstandard, you usually have to enable them explicitly. Devices may accept jumbo frames by default, but they probably will not generate them.
- Since jumbo frames are a form of outlawry, there's no universal consensus on exactly how large a jumbo frame can or should be. The most common value is 9,000 bytes, or 9,018 bytes with framing. You'll have to investigate your devices to determine the largest packet size they have in common. Frames larger than 9K or so are sometimes called "super jumbo frames," but don't be scared off by the extreme-sounding name. Larger is generally better, at least up to 64K or so.
- Jumbo frames are only viable for internal use. The Internet does not transport jumbo frames.

We endorse the use of jumbo frames on gigabit Ethernets, but only where it's easy and safe (i.e., probably not in complex enterprise environments). Be prepared to do some extra debugging if things go wrong. It's perfectly reasonable to deploy new networks with the default MTU and to convert to jumbo frames later once the reliability of the underlying network has been confirmed.

16.2 Wireless: Ethernet for Nomads

A wireless network consists of Wireless Access Points (WAPs, or simply APs) and wireless clients. WAPs can be connected to traditional wired networks (the typical configuration) or wirelessly connected to other access points, a configuration known as a "wireless mesh."

WAPs are usually dedicated appliances that consist of one or more radios and some form of embedded network operating system, often a stripped-down version of Linux. A single WAP can provide a connection point for multiple clients, but not for an unlimited number of clients. A good rule of thumb is to serve no more than eight simultaneous clients from a single enterprise-grade WAP. Any device that communicates through a wireless standard supported by your WAPs can act as a client.

The common wireless standards today are IEEE 802.11g and 802.11n. 802.11g operates in the 2.4 GHz frequency band and provides LAN-like access at up to 54 Mb/s. Operating range varies from 100 meters to 40 kilometers, depending on equipment and terrain.

802.11n delivers up to 600 Mb/s[6] of bandwidth and can use both the 5 GHz frequency band and the 2.4 GHz band (though 5 GHz is recommended for deployment). Typical operating range is approximately double that of 802.11g.

Today, 802.11g (and its grandfather, 802.11b) are commonplace. The transceivers are inexpensive and are built into most laptops. Add-in cards are widely and cheaply available for desktop PCs, too.

You can configure a Linux box to act as an 802.11a/b/g access point if you have the right hardware and driver. Since most PC-based wireless cards are still designed for Microsoft Windows, they may not come from the factory with Linux drivers.

An excellent stand-alone 802.11b/g wireless base station for the home or small office is Apple's AirPort Express, a wall-wart-like product that is inexpensive (around $99) and highly functional.[7] Another option is to consider running a stripped down version of Linux (such as OpenWRT) on a commercial WAP. See openwrt.org for more information and a list of compatible hardware.

Literally dozens of vendors are hawking wireless access points. You can buy them at Home Depot and even at the grocery store. Predictably, the adage that "you get what you pay for" applies. El cheapo access points (those in the $50 range) are likely to perform poorly when handling large file transfers or more than one active client.

Debugging a wireless network is something of a black art. You must consider a range of variables when dealing with problems. If you are deploying a wireless network at an enterprise scale, you'll probably need to invest in a wireless network analyzer. We highly recommend the analysis products made by AirMagnet.

6. The 600 Mb/s bandwidth of 802.11n is largely theoretical. In practice, bandwidth in the neighborhood of 400 Mb/s is a more realistic expectation for an optimized configuration. The environment and the capabilities and hardware of the client devices explain most of the difference between theoretical and real-life throughput. When it comes to wireless, your mileage may vary!

7. In fact, it will also connect to your stereo to play music wirelessly from your PC or laptop.

Wireless security

The security of wireless networks has traditionally been very poor. Wired Equivalent Privacy (WEP) is a protocol used in conjunction with 802.11b networks to encrypt packets traveling over the airwaves. Unfortunately, this standard contains a fatal design flaw that renders it little more than a speed bump for snoopers. Someone sitting outside your building or house can access your network directly and undetectably, usually in under a minute.

More recently, the Wi-Fi Protected Access (WPA) security standards have engendered new confidence in wireless security. Today, WPA (specifically, WPA2) should be used instead of WEP in all new installations.Without WPA2, wireless networks should be considered completely insecure and should never be found inside an enterprise firewall. Don't even use WEP at home!

To remember that it's WEP that's insecure and WPA that's secure, just remember that WEP stands for Wired Equivalent Privacy. The name is accurate; WEP gives you as much protection as letting someone connect directly to your wired network. (That is, no protection at all—at least at the IP level.)

Wireless switches and lightweight access points

In much the same way that Ethernet hubs grew up to become Ethernet switches, wireless products are undergoing a gradual makeover for use in large enterprises. A number of vendors (such as Cisco) now make "wireless switches" that work in conjunction with a fleet of access points that you deploy throughout a campus. The theory is that you can deploy hordes of inexpensive access points and then manage them centrally through an "intelligent" switch. The switch maintains the WAPs' configuration information and smoothly supports authentication and roaming. LWAPP (Lightweight Wireless Access Point Protocol) is one standard protocol that provides this functionality.

If you need ubiquitous wireless service throughout a medium-to-large organization, it's definitely worth your time to evaluate this category of products. Not only do these products decrease management time, but most also include a means to monitor and manage the quality of the wireless service delivered to users.

One particularly neat trick is to deploy an 802.11g/n network throughout your facility and use it to support hand-held VoIP phones for your staff. It's like a cellular network for free!

16.3 DSL AND CABLE MODEMS: THE LAST MILE

It's easy to move large amounts of data among businesses and other large data facilities. Carrier-provided technologies such as T1, T3, SONET, MPLS, and frame relay provide relatively simple conduits for moving bits from place to place. However, these technologies are not realistic options for connecting individual houses and home offices. They cost too much, and the infrastructure they require is not universally available.

Digital Subscriber Line (DSL) uses ordinary copper telephone wire to transmit data at speeds of up to 24 Mb/s (although typical DSL connections yield between 256 kb/s and 5 Mb/s). Since most homes and businesses already have existing telephone wiring, DSL is a viable way to complete the "last mile" of connectivity from the telephone company to the building. DSL connections are usually terminated in a box that acts as a TCP/IP router and connects to other devices within the building over an Ethernet.

Unlike regular POTS (Plain Old Telephone Service) and ISDN connections, which require you to "dial up" an endpoint, most DSL implementations supply a dedicated service that is always connected. This feature makes DSL even more attractive because there is no setup or connection delay when a user wants to transfer data.

DSL comes in several forms, and as a result it's often referred to as xDSL, with the x representing a specific subtechnology such as A for asymmetric, S for symmetric, H for high speed, RA for rate-adaptive, and I for DSL-over-ISDN (useful for locations too far from the central office to support faster forms of DSL). The exact technology variants and data transfer speeds available in your area depend on the central office equipment that your telephone company or carrier has deployed.

The race for "last mile" connectivity to hundreds of millions of homes is a hot one. It's also highly politicized, well capitalized, and overpublicized. The DSL approach leverages the copper infrastructure that is common among the Incumbent Local Exchange Carriers (ILECs), who often favored higher profit margins over infrastructure investments as the networking revolution of the 1980s and 90s passed them by.

Cable television companies, which already have fiber infrastructure in most neighborhoods, are promoting their own "last mile" solutions. Compared to DSL, cable modems typically yield higher (though asymmetric) bandwidth. The cable modem industry has become enlightened about data standards and is currently converging on the Data Over Cable Service Interface Specification (DOCSIS) standard. This standard defines the technical specs for both cable modems and the equipment used at the cable company, and it allows various brands of equipment to interoperate.

All in all, the fight between cable modem and DSL technologies largely boils down to who can deliver the highest bandwidth to a particular user's home at the lowest cost. The good news for us is that as Big Cable and Big Telecom compete for customers, they are forced to invest in infrastructure to serve residential neighborhoods.

16.4 Network testing and debugging

One major advantage of the large-scale migration to Ethernet (and other UTP-based technologies) is the ease of network debugging. Since these networks can be analyzed link by link, hardware problems can often be isolated in seconds rather than days.

The key to debugging a network is to break it down into its component parts and to test each piece until you've isolated the offending device or cable. The "idiot lights" on switches and hubs (such as "link status" and "packet traffic") often hold immediate clues to the source of the problem. Top-notch documentation of your wiring scheme is essential for making these indicator lights work in your favor.

As with most tasks, having the right tools for the job is a big part of being able to get the job done right and without delay. The market offers two major types of network debugging tools (although they are quickly growing together).

The first is the hand-held cable analyzer. This device can measure the electrical characteristics of a given cable, including its length (with a groovy technology called "time domain reflectrometry"). Usually, these analyzers can also point out simple faults such as a broken or miswired cable. Our favorite product for LAN cable analysis is the Fluke LanMeter. It's an all-in-one analyzer that can even perform IP pings across the network. High-end versions have their own web server that can show you historical statistics. For WAN (telco) circuits, the T-BERD line analyzer is the cat's meow. It's made by JDSU (jdsu.com).

The second type of debugging tool is the network sniffer. A sniffer captures the bytes that travel across the wire and disassembles network packets to look for protocol errors, misconfigurations, and general snafus. Sniffers operate at the link layer of the network rather than the electrical layer, so they can't diagnose cabling problems or electrical issues that may be affecting network interfaces.

Commercial sniffers are available, but we find that the freely available program Wireshark (wireshark.org) running on a fat laptop is usually the best option.[8] See the *Packet sniffers* section starting on page 874 of Chapter 21, *Network Management and Debugging*, for more details.

16.5 BUILDING WIRING

If you're embarking on a building wiring project, the most important advice we can give you is to "do it right the first time." This is not an area in which to skimp or cut corners. Buying quality materials, selecting a competent wiring contractor, and installing extra connections (drops) will save you years of frustration and heartburn down the road.

UTP cabling options

Category 6a wire typically offers the best price vs. performance tradeoff in today's market. Its normal format is four pairs per sheath, which is just right for a variety of data connections from RS-232 to gigabit Ethernet.

8. Like so many popular programs, Wireshark is often the target of attacks by hackers. Make sure you stay up to date with the current version.

Category 6a specifications require that the twist be maintained to the point of contact. Special training and termination equipment are necessary to satisfy this requirement. You must use Category 6a jacks and patch panels. We've had the best luck with parts manufactured by Siemon (siemon.com).

Connections to offices

One connection per office is clearly not enough. But should you use two or four? We recommend four, for several reasons:

- They can be used with voice telephones.
- They can be used to accommodate visitors or demo machines.
- The cost of the materials is typically only 5%–10% of the total cost.
- Your best guess doubled is often a good estimate.
- It's much cheaper to do it once rather than adding wires later.
- When ports run low, people add 4- or 8-port switches purchased from the nearest office supply store, then complain to the help desk about connection speed.

If you're in the process of wiring your entire building, you might consider installing a few outlets in the hallways, conference rooms, lunch rooms, bathrooms, and of course, ceilings (for wireless access points). Don't forget to keep security in mind, however, and put publicly accessible ports on a "guest" VLAN that doesn't have access to your internal network resources.

Wiring standards

Modern buildings often require a large and complex wiring infrastructure to support all the various activities that take place inside. Walking into the average telecommunications closet can be a shocking experience for the weak of stomach, as identically colored, unlabeled wires often cover the walls.

In an effort to increase traceability and standardize building wiring, the Telecommunications Industry Association in February 1993 released the TIA/EIA-606 Administration Standard for the telecommunication infrastructure of commercial buildings. EIA-606 specifies requirements and guidelines for the identification and documentation of telecommunications infrastructure.

Items covered by EIA-606 include

- Termination hardware
- Cables
- Cable pathways
- Equipment spaces
- Infrastructure color coding
- Symbols for standard components

In particular, the standard specifies colors to be used for wiring. Table 16.5 shows the details.

Table 16.5 EIA-606 color chart

Termination type	Color	Code[a]	Comments
Demarcation point	Orange	150C	Central office terminations
Network connections	Green	353C	Also used for aux circuit terminations
Common equipment[b]	Purple	264C	Major switching/data eqpt. terminations
First-level backbone	White	–	Cable terminations
Second-level backbone	Gray	422C	Cable terminations
Station	Blue	291C	Horizontal cable terminations
Interbuilding backbone	Brown	465C	Campus cable terminations
Miscellaneous	Yellow	101C	Maintenance, alarms, etc.
Key telephone systems	Red	184C	–

a. According to the Pantone Matching System®
b. PBXes, hosts, LANs, muxes, etc.

Pantone sells software to map between the Pantone systems for ink-on-paper, textile dyes, and colored plastic. Hey, you could color-coordinate the wiring, the uniforms of the installers, and the wiring documentation! On second thought…

16.6 Network design issues

This section addresses the logical and physical design of the network. It's targeted at medium-sized installations. The ideas presented here will scale up to a few hundred hosts but are overkill for three machines and inadequate for thousands. We also assume that you have an adequate budget and are starting from scratch, which is probably only partially true.

Most of network design consists of the specification of

- The types of media that will be used
- The topology and routing of cables
- The use of switches and routers

Another key issue in network design is congestion control. For example, file-sharing protocols such as NFS and CIFS tax the network quite heavily, and so file serving on a backbone cable is undesirable.

The issues presented in the following sections are typical of those that must be considered in any network design.

Network architecture vs. building architecture

The network architecture is usually more flexible than the building architecture, but the two must coexist. If you are lucky enough to be able to specify the network before the building is constructed, be lavish. For most of us, both the building and a facilities management department already exist and are somewhat rigid.

In existing buildings, the network must use the building architecture, not fight it. Modern buildings often contain utility raceways for data and telephone cables in addition to high-voltage electrical wiring and water or gas pipes. They often use drop ceilings, a boon to network installers. Many campuses and organizations have underground utility tunnels that facilitate network installation.

The integrity of fire walls[9] must be maintained; if you route a cable through a fire wall, the hole must be snug and filled in with a noncombustible substance. Respect return air plenums in your choice of cable. If you are caught violating fire codes, you may be fined and will be required to fix the problems you have created, even if that means tearing down the entire network and rebuilding it correctly.

Your network's logical design must fit into the physical constraints of the buildings it serves. As you specify the network, keep in mind that it is easy to draw a logically good solution and then find that it is physically difficult or impossible to implement.

Expansion

It is very difficult to predict needs ten years into the future, especially in the computer and networking fields. Therefore, design the network with expansion and increased bandwidth in mind. As cable is installed, especially in out-of-the-way, hard-to-reach places, pull three to four times the number of pairs you actually need. Remember: the majority of installation cost is labor, not materials.

Even if you have no plans to use fiber, it's wise to install some when wiring your building, especially in situations where it will be hard to install cable later. Run both multimode and single-mode fiber. The kind you need in the future is always the kind you didn't install.

Congestion

A network is like a chain: it is only as good as its weakest or slowest link. The performance of Ethernet, like that of many other network architectures, degrades nonlinearly as the network gets loaded.

Overtaxed switches, mismatched interfaces, and low-speed links can all lead to congestion. It is helpful to isolate local traffic by creating subnets and by using interconnection devices such as routers. Subnets can also be used to cordon off machines that are used for experimentation. It's difficult to run an experiment that involves several machines if you cannot isolate those machines both physically and logically from the rest of the network.

9. This type of fire wall is a concrete, brick, or flame-retardant wall that prevents flames from spreading and burning down a building. While much different from a network security firewall, it's probably just as important.

Maintenance and documentation

We have found that the maintainability of a network correlates highly with the quality of its documentation. Accurate, complete, up-to-date documentation is absolutely indispensable.

Cables should be labeled at all termination points. It's a good idea to post copies of local cable maps inside communications closets so that the maps can be updated on the spot when changes are made. Once every few weeks, have someone copy down the changes for entry into a wiring database.

Joints between major population centers in the form of switches or routers can facilitate debugging by allowing parts of the network to be isolated and debugged separately. It's also helpful to put joints between political and administrative domains, for similar reasons.

16.7 Management issues

If the network is to work correctly, some things need to be centralized, some distributed, and some local. Reasonable ground rules and "good citizen" guidelines need to be formulated and agreed on.

A typical environment includes

- A backbone network among buildings
- Departmental subnets connected to the backbone
- Group subnets within a department
- Connections to the outside world (e.g., Internet or field offices)

Several facets of network design and implementation must have site-wide control, responsibility, maintenance, and financing. Networks with charge-back algorithms for each connection grow in bizarre but predictable ways as departments try to minimize their own local costs. Prime targets for central control are

- The network design, including the use of subnets, routers, switches, etc.
- The backbone network itself, including the connections to it
- Host IP addresses, hostnames, and subdomain names
- Protocols, mostly to ensure that they interoperate
- Routing policy to the Internet

Domain names, IP addresses, and network names are in some sense already controlled centrally by authorities such as ARIN (American Registry for Internet Numbers) and ICANN. However, your site's use of these items must be coordinated locally as well.

A central authority has an overall view of the network: its design, capacity, and expected growth. It can afford to own monitoring equipment (and the staff to run it) and to keep the backbone network healthy. It can insist on correct network design, even when that means telling a department to buy a router and build a subnet to connect to the campus backbone. Such a decision might be necessary to ensure that a new connection does not adversely impact the existing network.

If a network serves many types of machines, operating systems, and protocols, it is almost essential to have a smart router (e.g., Cisco) as a gateway between nets.

16.8 Recommended vendors

In the past 20+ years of installing networks around the world, we've gotten burned more than a few times by products that didn't quite meet specs or were misrepresented, overpriced, or otherwise failed to meet expectations. Below is a list of vendors in the United States that we still trust, recommend, and use ourselves today.

Cables and connectors

AMP (part of Tyco) (800) 522-6752 amp.com	Anixter (800) 264-9837 anixter.com	Black Box Corporation (724) 746-5500 blackbox.com
Belden Cable (800) 235-3361 (765) 983-5200 belden.com	Newark Electronics (800) 463-9275 newark.com	Siemon (860) 945-4395 siemon.com

Test equipment

Fluke (800) 443-5853 fluke.com	JDSU (866) 228-3762 jdsu.com	Siemon (860) 945-4395 siemon.com

Routers/switches

Cisco Systems (415) 326-1941 cisco.com	Juniper Networks (408) 745-2000 juniper.net

16.9 Recommended reading

Barnett, David, David Groth, and Jim McBee. *Cabling: The Complete Guide to Network Wiring (3rd Edition)*. San Francisco: Sybex, 2004.

Seifert, Rich. *Gigabit Ethernet: Technology and Applications for High Speed LANs*. Reading, MA: Addison-Wesley, 1998.

ANSI/TIA/EIA-568-A, *Commercial Building Telecommunications Cabling Standard*, and ANSI/TIA/EIA-606, *Administration Standard for the Telecommunications Infrastructure of Commercial Buildings*, are the telecommunication industry's standards for building wiring. Unfortunately, they are not free. See tiaonline.org.

Spurgeon, Charles. "Guide to Ethernet." ethermanage.com/ethernet

16.10 Exercises

E16.1 Today, most office buildings house computer networks and are wired with UTP Ethernet. Some combination of routers and switches is needed to support these networks. List the advantages and disadvantages of each.

☆ E16.2 Draw a simple, imaginary network diagram that connects a machine in your computer lab to Amazon.com. Include LAN, MAN, and WAN components. Show what technology is used for each component. Show some switches and routers.

☆ E16.3 Research WPA2's Temporal Key Integrity Protocol. Detail what advantages this has over WEP, and what types of attacks it prevents.

☆☆ E16.4 TTCP is a tool that measures TCP and UDP performance. Install TTCP on two networked machines and measure the performance of the link between them. What happens to the bandwidth if you adjust buffer sizes up or down? How do your observed numbers compare with the theoretical capacity of the physical medium?

17 DNS: The Domain Name System

Zillions of hosts are connected to the Internet. How do we keep track of them all when they belong to so many different countries, networks, and administrative groups? Two key pieces of infrastructure hold everything together: the Domain Name System (DNS), which keeps track of who the hosts are, and the Internet routing system, which keeps track of how they are connected.

Although DNS has come to serve several different purposes, its primary job is to map between hostnames and IP addresses. Users and user-level programs like to refer to machines by name, but low-level network software understands only IP addresses (that is, numbers). DNS provides the glue that keeps everyone happy. It has also come to play an essential role in the routing of email, web server access, and many other services.

DNS is a distributed database. "Distributed" means that my site stores the data about my computers, your site stores the data about your computers, and our sites cooperate and share data when one site needs to look up the other's data. From an administrative point of view, your DNS servers answer queries from the outside world about names in your domain, and they query other domains' servers on behalf of your users.

See page 449 for more information about the RFC system.

The DNS system is defined by a series of RFCs, 108 of them at last count. Several implementations exist, varying in functionality, focus, and adherence to the RFCs. Table 17.1 shows the major players. The market shares shown in Table 17.1 were measured with respect to Internet-facing name servers, not internal name servers.

Table 17.1 Some popular implementations of DNS

Name	Author	Source	Share[a]	Comments
BIND	ISC	isc.org	80.3%	Auth or caching
Microsoft DNS	Microsoft	microsoft.com	15.4%	Myriad sins
djbdns[b]	Dan Bernstein	tinydns.org	2.6%	Violates some RFCs
PowerDNS	PowerDNS BV	powerdns.com	0.7%	Auth only
NSD[c]	NLnet Labs	nlnetlabs.nl	< 0.1%	Auth only, very fast
Unbound	NLnet Labs	unbound.net	–	Caching only, fast

a. Market share from isc.org's July 2009 Internet Domain Survey
b. Also known as tinydns, which is the server component of the djbdns package
c. Originally designed for root and top-level domain servers; now in general use

This chapter includes general information about DNS and the sysadmin chores associated with the BIND, NSD, and Unbound name server implementations. Examples are drawn from BIND 9.7, NSD 3.2.4, and Unbound 1.4.1.

You might ask why we waste space on NSD and Unbound when their market share is so small, especially in a chapter that is already so long. Three reasons:

- First, to deploy a truly robust DNS environment, you should not have all servers running the same software. A successful attack on your site's DNS service essentially takes your site off the Internet. Diversity of software, hardware, and network connectivity are the keys to surviving the Darwinian pressure of the Internet. Add geographical location and sysadmin skills to your diversity pile and you will be in fine shape.
- The second reason is performance: NSD and Unbound are significantly faster than BIND.
- Finally, of all the name server implementations, only BIND and NSD/Unbound implement DNSSEC, the cryptographic security extensions to DNS. DNSSEC is better tested and more robust in the NSD/Unbound implementations than in BIND.

Today, many sites (most?) use neither BIND nor NSD/Unbound internally, but rather Microsoft's Active Directory instead. We cover Active Directory briefly in Chapter 30, *Cooperating with Windows*, beginning on page 1154.

17.1 Who needs DNS?

DNS defines

- A hierarchical namespace for hosts and IP addresses
- A distributed database of hostname and address information
- A "resolver" to query this database
- Improved routing and sender authentication for email
- A mechanism for finding services on a network
- A protocol used by name servers to exchange information

DNS is a client/server system. Servers ("name servers") load the data from your DNS files into memory and use it to answer queries both from internal clients and from clients and other servers out on the Internet. All of your hosts should be DNS clients, but relatively few need to be DNS servers.

Managing your DNS

If your organization is small (a few hosts on a single network), you can run servers on your own hosts or ask your ISP to supply DNS service on your behalf. A medium-sized site with several subnets should run multiple DNS servers to reduce query latency and improve reliability. A very large site can divide its DNS domain into subdomains and run several servers for each subdomain.

DNS forward mappings associate a hostname with an IP address. Reverse mappings go from the IP address to the hostname. A domain's forward and reverse mappings should be managed in the same place whenever possible. Some ISPs are happy to let you manage the forward files but are reluctant to relinquish control of the reverse mappings. Such split management can lead to synchronization problems. See page 585 for an elegant hack that makes delegation work even for tiny pieces of address space.

DNS domains must be served by at least two servers, though we recommend at least three, geographically dispersed. Typically, one of the servers is designated as a master server (also called a primary server) that owns the reference copy of the domain's data. The other servers are called slave servers or secondary servers; they copy their data from the master server.

Some sites operate their own master server and let their ISP's servers act as slaves. Once the system has been configured, the ISP's servers automatically download host data from the master server. Changes to the DNS configuration are propagated to the slaves through a mechanism known as a zone transfer.

Another common arrangement is to outsource all DNS service and to rely on the outsourcing firm's diversity, robustness, and geographic distribution.

If you run local servers, don't put all of them on the same network. When DNS stops working, the network effectively stops for your users. Spread your DNS servers around so that you don't end up with a fragile system and a single point of failure. DNS is quite robust if designed well and configured carefully.

17.2 How DNS works

Each host that uses DNS is either a client of the system or simultaneously a client and a server. If you do not plan to run any DNS servers, it's not essential that you read the next few sections. Just skip ahead to page 561 for details on configuring a machine to be a client of DNS.

Resource records

Each site maintains one or more pieces of the distributed database that makes up the world-wide DNS system. Your piece of the database consists of text files that contain records for each of your hosts; these are known as "resource records." Each record is a single line consisting of a name (usually a hostname), a record type, and some data values. The name field can be omitted if its value is the same as that of the previous line.

For example, the lines

```
nubark      IN  A     63.173.189.1
            IN  MX    10 mailserver.atrust.com.
```

in the "forward" file (called **atrust.com**), and the line

```
1           IN  PTR   nubark.atrust.com.
```

in the "reverse" file (called **63.173.189.rev**) associate nubark.atrust.com with the IP address 63.173.189.1. The MX record reroutes email addressed to this machine to the host mailserver.atrust.com.

Resource records are the lingua franca of DNS and are independent of the configuration files that control the operation of any given DNS server implementation. They are also the pieces of data that flow around the DNS system and become cached at various locations.

Delegation

All name servers read the identities of the root servers from a local config file or have them built into the code. The root servers know the name servers for com, net, edu, fi, de, and other top-level domains. Farther down the chain, edu knows about colorado.edu, berkeley.edu, and so on. Each domain can delegate authority for its subdomains to other servers.

Let's inspect a real example. Suppose we want to look up the address for the machine vangogh.cs.berkeley.edu from the machine lair.cs.colorado.edu. The host lair asks its local name server, ns.cs.colorado.edu, to figure out the answer. The following illustration (Exhibit A) shows the subsequent events.

Exhibit A DNS query process for vangogh.cs.berkeley.edu

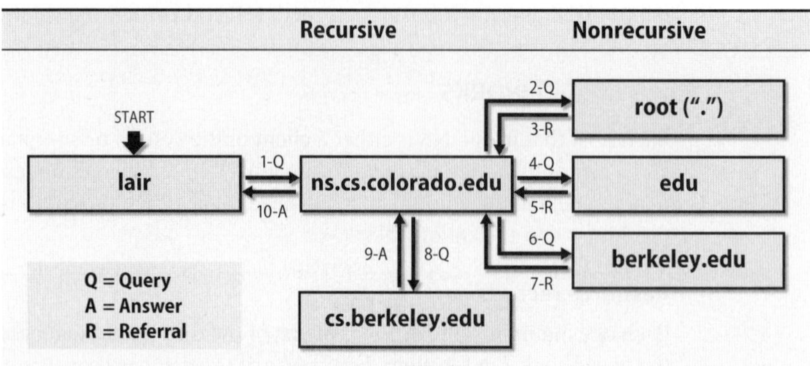

The numbers on the arrows between servers show the order of events, and a letter indicates the type of transaction (query, referral, or answer). We assume that none of the required information was cached before the query, except for the names and IP addresses of the servers of the root domain.

The local server doesn't know vangogh's address. In fact, it doesn't know anything about cs.berkeley.edu or berkeley.edu or even edu. It does know servers for the root domain, however, so it queries a root server about vangogh.cs.berkeley.edu and receives a referral to the servers for edu.

The local name server is a recursive server. When the answer to a query consists of a referral to another server, the local server resubmits the query to the new server. It continues to follow referrals until it finds a server that has the data it's looking for.

In this case, the local name server sends its query to a server of the edu domain (asking, as always, about vangogh.cs.berkeley.edu) and gets back a referral to the servers for berkeley.edu. The local name server then repeats the query in the berkeley.edu domain. If the Berkeley server doesn't have the answer cached, it returns a referral to the servers for cs.berkeley.edu. The cs.berkeley.edu server is authoritative for the requested information, looks the answer up in its zone files, and returns vangogh's address.

When the dust settles, ns.cs.colorado.edu has cached vangogh's address. It has also cached data on the servers for edu, berkeley.edu, and cs.berkeley.edu.

You can view the query process in detail with **dig +trace** or **drill -T**.[1]

Caching and efficiency

Caching increases the efficiency of lookups: a cached answer is almost free and is usually correct because hostname-to-address mappings change infrequently. An

1. **dig** and **drill** are DNS query tools: **dig** from the BIND distribution and **drill** from NLnet Labs.

answer is saved for a period of time called the "time to live" (TTL), which is specified by the owner of the data record in question. Most queries are for local hosts and can be resolved quickly. Users also inadvertently help with efficiency because they repeat many queries; after the first instance of a query, the rest are more or less free.

Under normal conditions, your site's resource records should use a TTL that is somewhere between 1 hour and 1 day. The longer the TTL, the less network traffic will be consumed by Internet clients obtaining fresh copies of the record.

If you have a specific service that is load balanced across logical subnets (often called "global server load balancing"), you may be required by your load balancing vendor to choose a shorter TTL, such as 10 seconds or 1 minute. (The short TTL lets the load balancer react quickly to inoperative servers and denial of service attacks.) The system still works correctly with short TTLs, but your name servers have to work hard. In the vangogh example above, the TTLs were 42 days for the roots, 2 days for edu, 2 days for berkeley.edu, and 1 day for vangogh.cs.berkeley.edu. These are reasonable values. If you are planning a massive renumbering, you can change the TTLs to a shorter value well before you start.

DNS servers also implement negative caching. That is, they remember when a query fails and do not repeat that query until the negative caching TTL value has expired. Negative caching saves answers of the following types:

- No host or domain matches the name queried.
- The type of data requested does not exist for this host.
- The server to ask is not responding.
- The server is unreachable because of network problems.

BIND caches the first two types of negative data; Unbound caches all four. Each implementation allows the negative cache times to be configured.

Multiple answers

A name server often receives multiple records in response to a query. For example, the response to a query for the name servers of the root domain would list all 13 servers. Most name servers return the answers in random order as a primitive form of load balancing.

You can take advantage of this balancing effect for your own servers by assigning a single hostname to several different IP addresses (which in reality are different machines):

```
www          IN  A    192.168.0.1
             IN  A    192.168.0.2
             IN  A    192.168.0.3
```

Busy web servers such as Yahoo! or Google are not really a single machine; they're just a single name in the DNS.

17.3 DNS FOR THE IMPATIENT

Before we start with the details of DNS, let's first take a brief detour to address everyone's most frequently asked questions:

- How do I add a new machine to a network that's using a name server?
- How do I configure that new machine as a client of DNS?

What follows is a cookbook-style recipe that does not define or explain any terminology and that probably does not fit exactly with your local sysadmin policies and procedures. Use it with caution and refer to RFC1912, *Common DNS Operational and Configuration Errors.*

Adding a new machine to DNS

If your network is set up to use the Dynamic Host Configuration Protocol (DHCP) you may not need to perform any manual configuration for DNS. When a new computer is connected, the DHCP server informs it of the DNS servers it should use for queries. Hostname-to-IP-address mappings for use by the outside world were most likely set up when the DHCP server was configured and are automatically entered through DNS's dynamic update facility.

For networks that do not use DHCP, the following recipe shows how to update the DNS configuration by copying and modifying the records for a similar computer.

Step 1: Choose an unused hostname and IP address for the new machine in conjunction with local sysadmins or your upstream ISP.

Step 2: Identify a similar machine on the same subnet. You'll use that machine's records as a model for the new ones. In this example, we use a machine called template.example.com on the subnet 208.77.188.0/24 as the model.

Step 3: Log in to the master name server machine. If you don't know which machine is the master server, you probably shouldn't be messing with it, but you can use the **dig** command (**dig SOA** *domainname*) to identify it. (You can also use **drill** if **dig** is not installed.)

Step 4a, for sites running BIND servers:

- Find the name server configuration file, usually **/etc/named.conf**.
- Within the options statement in **named.conf**, find the directory line that tells where zone data files are kept at your site (see page 603). The zone files contain the actual host and IP address data.
- From the zone statements, find the filenames for the forward zone file and reverse zone file appropriate for your new IP address (page 612).
- Verify from the zone statements that this server is in fact the master server (type master, not slave or some other value) for the domain. If it's not, you're on the wrong system! The forward zone statement in **/etc/named.conf** should look something like this:

```
zone "example.com" {
   type master;
   file "filename";
...
```

The reverse zone statement should look like this:

```
zone "188.77.208.in-addr.arpa" {
   type master;
   file "filename";
...
```

- Make a note of the filenames listed as arguments to file in the forward and reverse zone definitions.

Step 4b, for sites running NSD:

- Open the NSD configuration file, **/etc/nsd/nsd.conf**.
- Find the zone statement for your domain in **nsd.conf** (the name keyword identifies each zone).
- Verify that you are in fact on the master server. You can tell because the zone section for your domain will include a provide-xfr clause. If it contains a request-xfr clause, it's a slave server for that zone and you're on the wrong machine. The zone statement for the forward zone should look like:

```
zone:
   name: example.com
   zonefile: /var/nsd/primary/example.com
   provide-xfr: ip-addr tsig.key.name
   notify: ip-addr NOKEY
```

The reverse zone statement looks like:

```
zone:
   name: 188.77.208.in-addr.arpa
   zonefile: /var/nsd/primary/188.77.208.in-addr.arpa
   provide-xfr: ip-addr tsig.key.name
   notify: ip-addr NOKEY
```

- Make a note of the filenames listed as arguments to the zonefile keywords in the forward and reverse zone definitions.

Step 5: Go to the zone file directory and edit the forward zone file. Find the records for the template host you identified earlier. They'll look something like this:

```
template     IN   A     208.77.188.100
             IN   MX    10 mail-hub
             IN   MX    20 template
```

Your version might not include the MX lines, which are used for mail routing. Your zone files also might not include the IN specifier (it's the default) or use capital letters.

Step 6: Duplicate those records and change them appropriately for your new host. The zone file might be sorted by hostname; follow the existing convention.

Step 7: Change the serial number in the SOA record at the beginning of the file—it's the first of the five numbers in the SOA record. The serial number should only increase. Add 1 if your site uses an arbitrary serial number, or set the field to the current date if your site uses that convention.[2]

Step 8: Edit the reverse zone file and look for a record like this:

```
100             IN   PTR   template.example.com.
```

Duplicate this record with the appropriate changes. Note that there is a trailing dot after the hostname; don't omit it. If your reverse zone file shows more than just the last byte of each host's IP address, you must enter the bytes in reverse order. For example, the record

```
100.188         IN   PTR   template.example.com.
```

corresponds to the IP address 208.77.188.100 (here, the reverse zone is relative to 77.208.in-addr.arpa rather than 188.77.208.in-addr.arpa).

Step 9: Update the serial number in the SOA record of the reverse zone file, as described in step 7.

Step 10a: If you are using BIND and are lazy, run **rndc reload**. If the server is a busy one, you can reload only the domains (or views) that you changed:

```
$ sudo rndc reload forward-zone-name
$ sudo rndc reload reverse-zone-name
```

Step10b: If you are using NSD, run **nsdc rebuild** followed by **nsdc restart**.

Step 11: Check the configuration with **dig** or **drill**; see page 677. You can also try to **ping** or **traceroute** to your new host's name, even if the new host has not yet been set up. A "host unknown" message means you goofed; "host not responding" means that everything is probably OK.

The most common errors are

- Forgetting to update the zone serial numbers (steps 7 and 9)
- Forgetting to reload the name server (step 10)
- Forgetting to add a dot at the end of the hostname in the PTR resource record in the reverse zone (step 8)

2. The date convention also includes a two-digit change number, so you can have 99 changes per day.

Configuring a DNS client

Each host on the network must be a name server client. You configure the client side of DNS in the file **/etc/resolv.conf**, which lists the DNS servers the host can query when a user attempts to resolve a hostname (i.e., requests a web page, sends an email message, or uses the Internet).[3]

If your host gets its IP address and network parameters from a DHCP server, the **/etc/resolv.conf** file should be set up for you automatically. Otherwise, you must edit the file by hand. The format is

```
search domainname ...
option optionname ...
nameserver ipaddr
```

Up to three name servers can be listed. Here's a complete example:

```
search atrust.com booklab.atrust.com
nameserver 63.173.189.1       ; ns1
nameserver 174.129.219.225   ; ns2
```

Comments were never defined for the **resolv.conf** file. They are somewhat supported in that anything that is not recognized is ignored. It's safe to put comments at the end of nameserver lines because the parser just looks for an IP address and ignores the rest of the line. But because the search line can contain multiple arguments, comments there could cause problems.

The search line lists the domains to query if a hostname is not fully qualified. If a user issues the command **ssh coraline**, for example, the resolver completes the name with the first domain in the search list (in the example above, atrust.com) and looks for coraline.atrust.com. If no such name exists, the resolver also tries coraline.booklab.atrust.com. The number of domains that can be specified in a search directive is resolver specific; most allow between six and eight, with a limit of 256 characters.

The name servers listed in **resolv.conf** must be configured to allow your host to submit queries and must answer them completely (be recursive), not refer you to other name servers. They are contacted in order. As long as the first one continues to answer queries, the others are ignored. If a problem occurs, the query times out and the next name server is tried. Each server is tried in turn, up to four times. The timeout interval increases with every failure. The default timeout interval is 5 seconds, which seems like forever to impatient users.

The options clause can change the timeout interval, the number of retries, and the default behavior for choosing among the listed name servers. The options available are determined by the resolver library implementation. ISC's **libbind** behavior is described below and is accurate for all our example systems except HP-UX.

3. In Windows, the client-side DNS information can be configured through the TCP/IP configuration panel for each network adapter. The exact procedure varies with the version of Windows.

It's common to put the best and closest name server first in the nameserver lines, but if you want to load balance between equally competent name servers, you should use the rotate option. For example:

```
options rotate timeout:2 attempts:2
```

rotates between the listed name servers, times out in 2 seconds, and queries each server at most twice.

HP-UX does not fully support the options clause illustrated above; the timeout and number of retries variables are set directly in **resolv.conf** as follows:

```
retrans timeout-value-in-milliseconds
retry #-of-attempts
```

Most resolvers allow you to list a maximum of three name servers. If you list more, they are silently ignored. Table 17.2 summarizes the defaults.

Table 17.2 /etc/resolv.conf defaults

OS	Max NS	Max search length	Timeout	Retries
Linux	3	6 domains, 256 chars	5 sec	2
Solaris	3	6 domains, 256 chars	5 sec	2
HP-UX	3	6 domains, 256 chars	5 sec	4
AIX	3	6 domains, 1024 chars	5 sec	2

If a host is itself a name server, it should be listed first in its own **resolv.conf** file. If no name servers are listed, localhost is assumed.

The **resolv.conf** file also understands the domain directive as an alternative to search; it specifies a single domain to add to names that are not fully qualified. It's an older form; we recommend replacing domain directives with search directives when you encounter them. The directives are mutually exclusive, so only one should be present. If you inadvertently include both directives, only the last one listed takes effect.

If there is no **/etc/resolv.conf** file, AIX uses **/etc/netsvc.conf** to decide how to perform name resolution and extracts the default domain name from the hostname, which must be fully qualified. AIX provides a sample **resolv.conf** file in **/usr/lpp/tcpip/samples/resolv.conf** that you can copy. Just in case adding a couple of lines to a text file is too hard for you, AIX provides the **namerslv** command as an interface for adding, deleting, and changing name servers in **resolv.conf**. But wait! You also get the **mknamsv**, **rmnamsv**, **chnamsv**, and **lsnamsv** commands as high-level interfaces to **namerslv**. (Of course, a sysadmin can't be expected to master a sophisticated set of tools like this overnight, so you'll probably need a GUI to start out with; try **smitty resolv.conf**.)

Once **/etc/resolv.conf** has been configured, the system will start using DNS for name service as long as DNS hasn't been disabled in the file that prioritizes sources of administrative data (**/etc/nsswitch.conf**, or **/etc/netsvc.conf** on AIX; see page 739).

After configuring **/etc/resolv.conf**, you should be able to refer to other machines by name rather than by IP address. Try **ping** *hostname*. If you try to reach another local machine and the command just hangs, try referring to the machine by its IP address. If that works, then your DNS configuration is the problem. Verify that the name server IP addresses in **/etc/resolv.conf** are correct and that the servers you point to allow queries from your network (see page 606). **dig** from a working machine can answer these questions.

17.4 Name servers

A name server performs several chores:

- It answers queries about your site's hostnames and IP addresses.
- It asks about both local and remote hosts on behalf of your users.
- It caches the answers to queries so that it can answer faster next time.
- It transfers data between your name servers to keep them synchronized.

Name servers deal with zones, where a "zone" is essentially a domain minus its subdomains. You will often see the term "domain" used where "zone" is what's really meant, even in this book.

The NSD/Unbound suite separates the function of answering queries about your hosts (the NSD part) from the function of issuing queries about other domains on behalf of your users (the Unbound part). This separation is healthy.

Name servers can operate in several different modes. The distinctions among them fall along several axes, so the final categorization is often not very tidy. To make things even more confusing, a single server can play different roles with respect to different zones. Table 17.3 on the next page lists some of the adjectives used to describe name servers.

These categorizations are based on the name server's source of data (authoritative, caching, master, slave), on the type of data saved (stub), on the query path (forwarder), on the completeness of answers handed out (recursive, nonrecursive), and finally, on the visibility of the server (distribution). The next few sections provide some additional details on the most important of these distinctions; the others are described elsewhere in this chapter.

Authoritative and caching-only servers

Master, slave, and caching-only servers are distinguished by two characteristics: where the data comes from and whether the server is authoritative for the domain. BIND can be all three types, NSD can be a master or slave, and Unbound is caching-only.

Table 17.3 A name server taxonomy

Type of server	Description
authoritative	An official representative of a zone
master	The master server for a zone; gets its data from a disk file
primary	Another name for the master server
slave	Copies its data from the master
secondary	Another name for a slave server
stub	Like a slave, but copies only name server data (not host data)
distribution	A server advertised only within a domain (aka "stealth server")
nonauthoritative[a]	Answers a query from cache; doesn't know if the data is still valid
caching	Caches data from previous queries; usually has no local zones
forwarder	Performs queries on behalf of many clients; builds a large cache
recursive	Queries on your behalf until it returns either an answer or an error
nonrecursive	Refers you to another server if it can't answer a query

a. Strictly speaking, "nonauthoritative" is an attribute of a DNS query response, not a server.

Each zone typically has one master name server.[4] The master server keeps the official copy of the zone's data on disk. The system administrator changes the zone's data by editing the master server's data files.

See page 639 for more information about zone transfers.

A slave server gets its data from the master server through a "zone transfer" operation. A zone can have several slave name servers and *must* have at least one. A stub server is a special kind of slave that loads only the NS (name server) records from the master. See page 614 for an explanation of why you might want this behavior. It's fine for the same machine to be both a master server for some zones and a slave server for other zones.

A caching-only name server loads the addresses of the servers for the root domain from a startup file and accumulates the rest of its data by caching answers to the queries it resolves. A caching-only name server has no data of its own and is not authoritative for any zone (except perhaps the localhost zone).

An authoritative answer from a name server is "guaranteed"[5] to be accurate; a nonauthoritative answer might be out of date. However, a very high percentage of nonauthoritative answers are perfectly correct. Master and slave servers are authoritative for their own zones, but not for information they may have cached about other domains. Truth be told, even authoritative answers can be inaccurate if a sysadmin changes the master server's data but forgets to propagate the changes (e.g., doesn't change the zone's serial number).

Name servers should be located on machines that are stable, do not have many users, are secure, and are on an uninterruptible power supply. One slave is

4. Some sites use multiple masters or even no masters; we describe the single-master case.

5. Guaranteed here just means that the answer came from an authoritative server's in-memory database and not from the cache of a random nonauthoritative server.

required. Ideally, there should be at least two slaves, one of which is off-site. On-site slaves should live on different networks and different power circuits. When name service stops, all normal network access stops, too.

Although they are not authoritative, caching-only servers can reduce the latency seen by your users and the amount of DNS traffic on your internal networks. At most sites, desktop machines send their queries about machines on the Internet through a caching server. Larger sites should have several caching servers.

Security and general DNS hygiene argue for separating the functions of serving your authoritative data to the world from serving the world's data to your users. In an implementation like NSD/Unbound, this separation is enforced architecturally. But even with BIND, which uses a single name server binary (**named**), you can run separate copies of the server for each purpose: one as an authoritative server and one as a caching, recursive server.

Recursive and nonrecursive servers

Name servers are either recursive or nonrecursive. If a nonrecursive server has the answer to a query cached from a previous transaction or is authoritative for the domain to which the query pertains, it provides an appropriate response. Otherwise, instead of returning a real answer, it returns a referral to the authoritative servers of another domain that are more likely to know the answer. A client of a nonrecursive server must be prepared to accept and act on referrals.

Although nonrecursive servers may seem lazy, they usually have good reason not to take on extra work. Authoritative-only servers (e.g., root servers and top-level domain servers) are all nonrecursive, but since they may process tens of thousands of queries per second we can excuse them for cutting corners.

A recursive server returns only real answers and error messages. It follows referrals itself, relieving clients of this responsibility. In other respects, the basic procedure for resolving a query is essentially the same.

For security reasons, an organization's externally accessible name servers should always be nonrecursive. Recursive name servers that are visible to the world may be vulnerable to cache poisoning attacks.

Resolver libraries *do not* understand referrals; any local name server listed in a client's **resolv.conf** file must be recursive.

One side effect of having a name server follow referrals is that its cache acquires information about intermediate domains. On a local network, this caching is often the behavior you want since it allows subsequent lookups from any host on the network to benefit from the name server's previous work. On the other hand, the server for a top-level domain such as com or edu should not save up information requested by a host several domains below it.

Name servers generate referrals hierarchically. For example, if a server can't supply an address for lair.cs.colorado.edu, it refers to the servers for cs.colorado.edu, colorado.edu, edu, or the root domain. A referral must include addresses for the servers of the referred-to domain, so the choice is not arbitrary; the server must refer to a domain for which it already knows the servers.

The longest answer (the one with the most components) is returned. If the address of lair was not known but the name servers for cs.colorado.edu were known, then those servers' addresses would be returned. If cs.colorado.edu was unknown but colorado.edu was known, then the addresses of name servers for colorado.edu would be returned, and so on.

Name servers preload their caches from a "hints" file that lists the servers for the root domain. Some referral can always be made, even if it's just "Ask a root server."

17.5 The DNS namespace

The DNS namespace is organized into a tree with two top-level branches: forward mappings and reverse mappings. Forward mappings map hostnames to IP addresses, and reverse mappings map IP addresses to hostnames. Every fully qualified hostname (e.g., nubark.atrust.com) is a node in the forward branch of the tree, and every IP address is a node in the reverse branch. Periods separate levels of the tree; the root of the tree (the top) is ".", aka "dot".

Fully qualified hostnames can be viewed as a notation in which the "most significant part" is on the right. For example, in the name nubark.atrust.com, nubark is in atrust and atrust is in com. IP addresses, on the other hand, have the "most significant part" on the left. In the address 128.138.243.100, for example, host 100 is on subnet 243, which is part of network 128.138.

To allow the same DNS system to service both kinds of data, the IP branch of the namespace is inverted by listing the octets of the IP address backwards. For example, if host nubark.atrust.com has IP address 63.173.189.1, the corresponding node of the forward branch of the naming tree is "nubark.atrust.com." and the node of the reverse branch is "1.189.173.63.in-addr.arpa.".[6] Both of these names end with a dot, just as the full pathnames of files always start with a slash.

A "fully qualified domain name" is the full path to a DNS object, including a final dot. For example, a host named nubark in the atrust.com domain has the FQDN "nubark.atrust.com.".

A "domain" is a subtree of the DNS naming tree. For example, the atrust.com *domain* contains atrust.com and all of atrust.com's subdomains and hosts. By contrast, a "zone" is a domain minus any subdomains that have been delegated to other name servers.

If the atrust.com domain were further subdivided into the subdomains engineering, marketing, and booklab, then the domain atrust.com would contain four zones: the original atrust.com plus engineering.atrust.com, marketing.atrust.com,

6. The in-addr.arpa portion of the name is a fixed suffix.

and booklab.atrust.com. The atrust.com zone contains all the hosts in atrust.com except those in engineering, marketing, and booklab.

Name servers are associated with zones, not domains. You can determine whether a given name (such as booklab.atrust.com) identifies a subdomain rather than a host by checking DNS. Subdomains have name server (NS) records associated with them.

Domain names originally had to be made up of letters, numbers, and dashes, with each component (label) being at most 63 characters long and an entire FQDN being less than 256 characters. FQDNs are not case sensitive, but they are usually written in lowercase letters. Domain names were liberalized by RFC2181.

The ongoing internationalization of domain names is forcing changes to these rules to allow longer FQDNs. Characters in nonroman alphabets are represented through an encoding called Punycode, similar in spirit to Unicode but with different implementation details.

There are two types of top-level domains: country code domains (ccTLDs) and generic top level domains (gTLDs). ICANN, the Internet Corporation for Assigned Names and Numbers, accredits various agencies to be part of its shared registry project for registering names in the gTLDs such as com, net, and org. As of this writing, you have something like 1,000 choices for a registrar and 21 gTLDs in which to register. Check icann.org for the definitive list. ICANN is in the process of creating many more gTLDs.

To register for a ccTLD name, check the IANA (Internet Assigned Numbers Authority) web page iana.org/cctld to find the registry in charge of a particular country's registration.

Registering a second-level domain name

To obtain a second-level domain name, you must apply to a registrar for the appropriate top-level domain. To complete the domain registration forms, you must choose a name that is not already taken and identify a technical contact person, an administrative contact person, and at least two hosts that will be name servers for your domain. Fees vary among registrars, but these days they are all generally quite inexpensive.

Creating your own subdomains

The procedure for creating a subdomain is similar to that for creating a second-level domain, except that the central authority is now local (or more accurately, within your own organization). Specifically, the steps are as follows.

- Choose a name that is unique in the local context.
- Identify two or more hosts to be servers for your new domain.[7]
- Coordinate with the administrator of the parent domain.

7. Technically, since you make the rules for your subdomain, one or more will do.

Parent domains should check to be sure that a child domain's name servers are up and running before performing the delegation. If the servers are not working, a "lame delegation" results, and you might receive nasty email asking you to clean up your DNS act. Page 678 covers lame delegations in more detail.

17.6 DESIGNING YOUR DNS ENVIRONMENT

Many factors affect the design of a robust and efficient DNS system for your environment: the size of your organization, whether you use RFC1918 private IP addresses on your local network, whether you use DHCP, whether you use Microsoft's Active Directory, whether your internal network is routed or switched, and where your firewall is in relation to your DNS servers, to name a few. You may find it helpful to split the problem into three parts:

- Managing the namespace hierarchy: subdomains, multiple levels, etc.
- Serving the authoritative data about your site to the outside world
- Providing name lookups for your users

Namespace management

If your site is small and independent, the use of subdomains is neither necessary nor desirable unless your management requires them for some nontechnical reason. On the other hand, in a medium-sized organization with several independent sysadmin groups, subdomains can reduce the need for site-wide coordination. (Subdomains divided along geographic or departmental lines are most common.) A large organization has little hope of enforcing unique names throughout its site and therefore needs subdomains, perhaps at multiple levels.

Recent additions to DNS have defined zone-level records (SPF and DKIM/ADSP) that help to prevent other sites from forging mail that appears to originate from your domain. Optimal use of these features may require you to define subdomains based on the sensitivity of the information your organization sends by email. See page 591 for more details.

The creation of subdomains requires communication and cooperation between the sysadmins responsible for the parent domain and those responsible for the subdomain. At the time the subdomain is delegated and set up, be sure to make a note of whom to contact if you want to add, change, or delete servers. Make sure your firewall does not block access to the subdomain's servers if you want the subdomain to be accessible from outside your organization.

If you use subdomains to manage your namespace, run the **doc** (domain obscenity control) tool from **cron** once a week to be sure that your delegations stay synchronized and that you don't inadvertently create lame delegations. The DNS tools section (see page 667) describes **doc** and several other tools that help keep DNS healthy.

Authoritative servers

The DNS specifications require at least two authoritative servers for each domain. Master and slave servers are authoritative; caching and stub servers are not. Ideally, a site has multiple authoritative servers, each on a separate network and power circuit. Many sites maintain an authoritative server off-site, often hosted by their ISP. If your ISP does not offer this service, you can purchase it from a DNS service provider or trade with a local firm (ideally, not a competitor) or university.

A few years ago, Microsoft got caught violating the rule of separate networks. They had all three of their authoritative servers on the same subnet, and when the router that connected that subnet to the Internet failed, the servers became unreachable. Two hours later, as cached records expired, microsoft.com and all their other domains dropped off the Internet. The number of queries for Microsoft-related names at the root servers increased to 25% of the total load (10,000 queries/second), up from its typical value of 0.000001%. Problems persisted for a couple of days. When the dust settled, Microsoft had fixed the router and outsourced their DNS service.

Authoritative servers keep their data synchronized by using zone transfers. Use TSIG (transaction signature) keys to authenticate and control the zone transfers from your master server to your slave servers. See page 645 for TSIG configuration information.

You may want the query responses provided by your authoritative servers to depend to some extent on who is asking. A query from outside your network might receive one answer, while the same query originating inside your organization would receive a different (or more complete) answer. This configuration is called "split DNS" and is implemented at the zone level, not the name server level.

Each version of the zone is called a "view," after the view statement with which it is configured in the BIND configuration file. External folks see one view of the data, and internal folks see another. This feature is commonly used to conceal the existence of internal machines from prying eyes and to ensure that machines using RFC1918 private IP addresses do not leak them onto the Internet. Views are tricky to debug, but BIND's extensive logging capabilities, together with clever use of the **dig** command, can help; see page 667 for some hints.

NSD does not support views and split DNS. However, you can simulate this feature by running two instances of NSD with different configurations. (Of course, you can do that with BIND, too.)

Caching servers

Recursive caching servers answer local users' queries about sites on the Internet. Each computer at your site should have ready access to a local caching server.

Some organizations use a hierarchy in which one or more machines are designated as "forwarders" through which the local subnets' caching servers pass their queries. The forwarders thereby develop a rich cache that is available to the entire site. Depending on the size of your site, forwarders can be independent or arranged in a hierarchy. The configuration of forwarders is covered on page 606 for BIND and on page 638 for Unbound.

If a caching server dies, the network essentially stops working for all the users that were primary clients of that server.[8] (And your phone starts ringing.) Start your caching name servers with a script that restarts them after a few seconds if they die. Here is an example of a nanny script from a machine that runs **named** for several TLDs:

```
#!/bin/sh

PATH=/usr/local/sbin:/usr/sbin:/sbin:$PATH
export PATH

trap "" 1
while :; do
    named -f -c /var/named/named.conf >> /var/log/named 2>&1
        < /dev/null
    logger "named restart"
    sleep 15
done
exit
```

When **named** crashes, the script submits a syslog entry with the **logger** command, then waits 15 seconds (an arbitrary value) before restarting **named**. BIND ships with a nanny script in the **contrib** directory, although it's not as necessary as it once was.

On Solaris, you can have SMF do your nannying for you; see page 97.

Hardware requirements

Name servers need to be well provisioned in three dimensions: CPU, memory, and network bandwidth. Of these, CPU is probably the least critical for now, but it will become more of an issue as DNSSEC is fully deployed and zone signing and signature validation are required. If possible, use dedicated machines for your busy name servers and separate authoritative servers from recursive ones.

Busy name servers get thousands of queries per second and therefore need multiple network interfaces and high bandwidth connections. The traffic usually consists of zillions of small UDP packets.

Recursive servers need enough memory to cache all the answers your users demand. The best way to determine if a name server machine has enough memory is to run it for a while and watch the size of the name server process. It takes a week or two to converge on a stable size at which old cache records are expiring at

8. If a client's **/etc/resolv.conf** file lists multiple name servers, the resolver should fail over to one of the backup servers. But all too often, only a single name server is configured.

about the same rate that new ones are being inserted. Once stable, the system should not be swapping, and its paging rates should be reasonable.

If your name server runs on a dedicated machine, a good rule of thumb is for the machine to have double the amount of memory consumed by the name server daemon after it has been running for a week. The **top** and **vmstat** commands show memory usage; see *Analyzing memory usage* on page 1125 for more details.

Authoritative servers need enough memory to store all the data for which they are authoritative. Most sites can manage this, but servers for top-level domains and DNS hosting sites may need either huge memories or special software that facilitates storing part of the data on disk.

You can control the amount of resources that a name server uses through configuration options. See the list of tuning options for BIND on page 608 and for NSD on page 630.

Security

DNS security is covered in a whole section of its own, starting on page 642. We won't duplicate that discussion here except to remind you that if you use a firewall, be sure that your DNS system does not emit queries to which your firewall blocks the answers. Make sure that your DNS administrators have ongoing communication with your security and network administrators.

By default, DNS uses UDP with random unprivileged source ports (>1023) for queries; the answers are UDP packets addressed to those same ports. With DNSSEC and internationalized domain names, DNS responses may be larger than the path MTU and therefore arrive fragmented. Ergo, your firewall should not block fragmented UDP packets. If a UDP query fails due to fragmentation, often it is reissued as a TCP query, so your firewall should be kind to TCP DNS replies, too.

Summing up

Exhibit B illustrates the design recommended in the previous paragraphs.

Exhibit B DNS server architecture

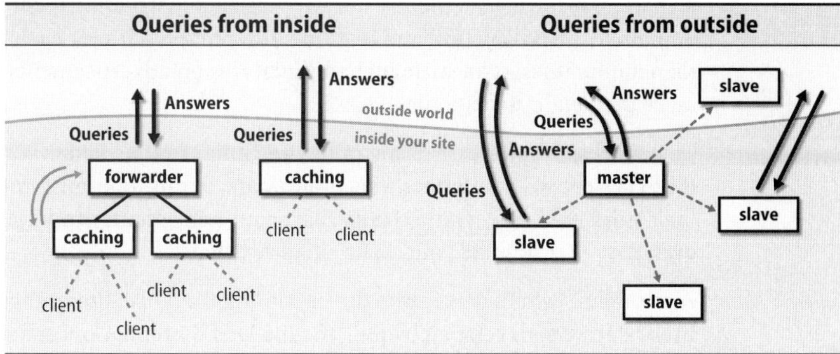

Exhibit B shows clear separation of caching servers (on the left) for your users and authoritative servers (on the right) for your data. Also note the use of the off-site slave server, which is highly recommended.

See page 457 for more information about anycast addressing.

The University of California at Berkeley (berkeley.edu) uses anycast IP addresses to replicate their caching servers. Clients all appear to contact the same set of servers, but the routing system (OSPF in this case) routes them to whichever caching server is nearest. This configuration results in easy and consistent client configuration and a robust DNS environment for users.

17.7 What's new in DNS

One of the neatest new developments in the DNS world is the use of DNS records to authenticate and verify the integrity of email messages. This system, called DomainKeys Identified Mail (DKIM), helps expose phishing (e.g., mail that appears to come from your bank and asks you to "verify" your account information). DKIM also helps detect spammers who forge the sender's address.

In the DKIM system, originating email servers sign outbound messages with a cryptographic private key. The corresponding public key is published as a DNS TXT record. Email receivers can verify the integrity and origin of a message by looking up the DKIM (public) key of the message's ostensible origin and checking it against the message's signatures.

The DKIM system does not require a change to your DNS software, but it does require the cooperation of your outgoing email server (to sign messages) and incoming email server or mail reader (to verify the signatures). From DNS's point of view, only the configuration and data files need to change to support a new subdomain called _domainkey.

Even better, a construct called the Author Domain Signing Practice (ADSP) declaration allows a site to say whether it signs all, part, or none of its outgoing email for each DNS zone. Receiving sites can use this policy statement to decide how to treat unsigned messages and messages whose signatures cannot be verified.

For example, a bank that generates several categories of email (e.g., marketing messages, account statements, and wire transfer instructions) could create a subdomain for each function and institute different policies for each. Receivers can then ignore missing or mismatched signatures on advertisements but reject messages that ought to be secure.

This mechanism for expressing policy is similar to the Sender Policy Framework (SPF) system, which defines a way for organizations to publish the identities of their valid mail servers in DNS so that spammers who try to forge the From address can be recognized and their email rejected.

Also on our "what's new" list is the upcoming BIND 10, the next generation of the BIND software developed by ISC, the Internet Systems Consortium, which has maintained BIND since version 4. The BIND 10 effort has been funded by sponsoring organizations around the world, mostly domain registrars.

BIND 10 will continue to be an open source reference implementation of DNS. It will be partially built on BIND 9 and will focus on improving modularity, customizability, clusterization, integration, resilience, and run-time control.

BIND 9 and earlier versions stored the DNS database in memory; BIND 10 will support multiple data storage systems. Another planned feature is a nice user interface API so folks can build GUI interfaces to populate zones and control the software. See isc.org/bind10 for details.

Several of our older "what's new" issues from previous editions are still in the proposed-standard-but-not-yet-widely-adopted pile. Some examples are DNSSEC-bis (security), IDN (internationalized domain names), and IPv6. These initiatives are progressing, but slowly. We include them at the end of Table 17.4, which lists new topics, relevant RFCs, and references to the pages in this book where the details are covered.

Table 17.4 Recent developments in DNS and BIND

Page	RFCs	Description
603	5001	NSID, name server identification for anycast servers
591	5518, 5016, 4871, 4686	DKIM requirements, signatures, third-party signing, ADSP sender signing practice
590	4470	SPF mail server identification
594	4255	SSHFP, SSH host key fingerprint
574	5198, 4952, 4690, 4290, 4185, 3492	Internationalized domain names (via Punycode, in top-level domains, exchange format)
482	4472, 4339, 4159, 3901	IPv6, operational issues, host configuration, ip6.arpa not ip6.int for reverse mappings, current best practices
648	5155, 5011, 4641, 4509, 4470, 4033–5	DNSSEC, authentication, delegation signer (DS) resource records, operational practices, trust anchors, denial of existence (NXDOMAIN)

Some of these new features are enormous projects that the IETF has not yet finished standardizing. The working groups that are writing the standards have good writers but lack vigilant code warriors, leading to the occasional specification that is difficult or even impossible to implement. The current releases of BIND, NSD, and Unbound include most of the new features.

IPv6 is described in more detail in Chapter 14.

Two massive new features, IPv6 support and DNSSEC, warrant a bit of commentary. IPv6 increases the length of IP addresses from 32 bits to 128 bits. If ever fully implemented, it will have an enormous impact on the Internet. BIND, NSD, and Unbound support the pieces of IPv6 that have been standardized so far, but it appears unlikely that IPv6 will be widely deployed during the lifetime of this book. Therefore, our coverage of IPv6 support is brief. There's enough in this chapter to give you the general flavor, but not enough to enable you to migrate your site to IPv6 and configure DNS for it.

The DNSSEC standard adds authentication data to the DNS database and its servers. It uses public key cryptography to verify the source and integrity of DNS data and uses DNS to distribute keys as well as host data.

Sites that want to deploy DNSSEC-signed zones will run up against a bootstrapping problem until the root and top-level domains are signed, because the DNSSEC trust model requires signatures to be chained from the root down. However, a new stopgap scheme called DLV, domain lookaside validation, is poised to step in and glue islands of trust together until the root and gTLDs are fully onboard with DNSSEC. See page 661 for details.

The introduction of internationalized domain names, which allow the use of non-English characters, is proceeding by way of a hack that maps Unicode characters back to ASCII. A system called Punycode performs the mapping uniquely and reversibly by using an algorithm known as Bootstring; see RFC3492 for details. Internationalized domain names effectively reduce the maximum length (both per-component and total) allowed for DNS names. The Punycode representation of a name begins with the string xn--, so if you see strange queries that start with those four characters, you'll know what they represent.

Each of these major issues (IPv6, DNSSEC, and internationalization) significantly increases the size of DNS data records, thereby making it more likely that DNS will bump into limits on UDP packet sizes and require the EDNS0 (Extended DNS, version 0) protocol to increase its packet size from 512 bytes (the default) to a larger value, say 4,096 bytes. As of 2009, statistics collected at the K root name server show that approximately 35% of queries are not using EDNS0 and so would receive truncated or fragmented DNS answers from sites that use larger packets.[9]

17.8 The DNS database

A zone's DNS database is a set of text files maintained by the system administrator on the zone's master name server. These text files are often called zone files. They contain two types of entries: parser commands (things like $ORIGIN and $TTL) and resource records. Only the resource records are really part of the database; the parser commands just provide some shorthand ways to enter records.

Commands in zone files

Zone file commands are standardized in RFCs 1035 and 2308.

Commands can be embedded in a zone files to make them more readable and easier to maintain. The commands either influence the way that the parser interprets subsequent records or they expand into multiple DNS records themselves.

9. See k.root-servers.org/statistics/GLOBAL/monthly for current data.

Once a zone file has been read and interpreted, none of these commands remain a part of the zone's data (at least, not in their original forms).

Three commands are standard in DNS, and a fourth, $GENERATE, is found only in BIND. See page 587 for an example of $GENERATE in action. The standard directives are

```
$ORIGIN domain-name
$INCLUDE filename [origin]
$TTL default-ttl
```

Commands must start in the first column and occur on a line by themselves.

Zone files are read and parsed from top to bottom in a single pass. As the name server reads a zone file, it adds the default domain (or "origin") to any names that are not already fully qualified. The origin defaults to the domain name specified in the name server's configuration file. However, you can set the origin or change it within a zone file by using the $ORIGIN directive.

The use of relative names where fully qualified names are expected saves lots of typing and makes zone files much easier to read.

Many sites use the $INCLUDE directive in their zone database files to separate overhead records from data records, to separate logical pieces of a zone file, or to keep cryptographic keys in a file with restricted permissions. The syntax of the $INCLUDE directive is

```
$INCLUDE filename [origin]
```

The specified file is read into the database at the point of the $INCLUDE directive. If *filename* is not an absolute path, it is interpreted relative to the home directory of the running name server.

If you supply an *origin* value, the parser acts as if an $ORIGIN directive precedes the contents of the file being read. Watch out: the origin does not revert to its previous value after the $INCLUDE has been executed. You'll probably want to reset the origin, either at the end of the included file or on the line following the $INCLUDE statement.

The $TTL directive sets a default value for the time-to-live field of the records that follow it. It must be the first line of the zone file. The default units for the $TTL value are seconds, but you can also qualify numbers with h for hours, m for minutes, d for days, or w for weeks. For example, the lines

```
$TTL 86400
$TTL 24h
$TTL 1d
```

all set the $TTL to one day.

Resource records

Each zone of the DNS hierarchy has a set of resource records associated with it. The basic format of a resource record is

```
[name] [ttl] [class] type data
```

Fields are separated by whitespace (tabs or spaces) and can contain the special characters shown in Table 17.5.

Table 17.5 Special characters used in resource records

Character	Meaning
;	Introduces a comment
@	The current zone name
( )	Allows data to span lines
*	Wild card[a] (*name* field only)

a. See page 584 for some cautionary statements.

The *name* field identifies the entity (usually a host or domain) that the record describes. If several consecutive records refer to the same entity, the name can be omitted after the first record as long as the subsequent records begin with whitespace. If it is present, the *name* field must begin in column one.

A name can be either relative or absolute. Absolute names end with a dot and are complete. Internally, the software deals only with absolute names; it appends the current domain and a dot to any name that does not already end in a dot. This feature allows names to be shorter, but it also invites mistakes.

For example, if cs.colorado.edu was the current domain, the name "anchor" would be interpreted as "anchor.cs.colorado.edu.". If by mistake you entered the name as "anchor.cs.colorado.edu", the lack of a final dot would still imply a relative name, resulting in the name "anchor.cs.colorado.edu.cs.colorado.edu."—this kind of mistake is common.

The *ttl* (time to live) field specifies the length of time, in seconds, that the data item can be cached and still be considered valid. It is often omitted, except in the root server hints file. It defaults to the value set by the $TTL directive (see page 596 for format details), which must be the first line of the zone data file.

See Chapter 19 for more information about NIS.

Increasing the value of the *ttl* parameter to about a week substantially reduces network traffic and DNS load. However, once records have been cached outside your local network, you cannot force them to be discarded. If you plan a massive renumbering and your old *ttl* was a week, lower the $TTL value (e.g., to one hour) at least a week before your intended renumbering. This preparatory step makes sure that records with week-long *ttl*s are expired and replaced with records that have one-hour *ttls*. You can then be certain that all your updates will propagate together within an hour. Set the *ttls* back to their original value after you've completed your update campaign.

Some sites set the TTL on the records for Internet-facing servers to a low value so that if a server experiences problems (network failure, hardware failure, denial of service attack, etc.), the administrators can respond by changing the server's name-to-IP-address mapping. Because the original TTLs were low, the new values will propagate quickly. For example, the name google.com has a five-minute TTL, but Google's name servers have a TTL of four days (345,600 seconds):

```
google.com.          300  IN  A   209.85.171.100
google.com.       345600  IN  NS  ns1.google.com.
ns1.google.com.   345600  IN  A   216.239.32.10
```

We used the **dig** command to recover this data; the output is truncated here.

The *class* specifies the network type. Three values are recognized:

- IN for the Internet, which is the default
- HS for Hesiod, a directory service used locally by some sites
- CH, used internally by name servers to identify themselves

The default value for the class is IN. It is often specified explicitly in zone data files even though as the default, it can be omitted. Hesiod, developed at MIT, is a database service built on top of BIND.

CH originally stood for ChaosNet, a now-obsolete network protocol formerly used by Symbolics Lisp machines. Today, only two pieces of identification data are normally tucked away in the CH class: the version number of the name server software and the name of the host on which the server is running. These data nuggets can be extracted with **dig** or **drill** as shown on page 598.

Administrators and hackers use the name server version number to identify servers in need of upgrades, and admins use the host identification to debug name servers that are replicated through the use of anycast routing. Making this information available through the CH class was originally a feature of BIND, but the convention has now been adopted by other DNS implementations as well.

Many different types of DNS records are defined, but fewer than 10 are in common use; IPv6 adds a few more. We divide the resource records into four groups:

- Zone infrastructure records identify domains and their name servers.
- Basic records map between names and addresses and route mail.[10]
- Security records add authentication and signatures to zone files.
- Optional records provide extra information about hosts or domains.

10. MX mail routing records fit in both the zone infrastructure pile and the basic records pile because they can refer to entire zones as well as individual hosts.

The contents of the *data* field depend on the record type. A DNS query for a particular domain and record type returns all matching resource records from the zone file. Table 17.6 lists the common record types.

Table 17.6 DNS record types

	Type	Name	Function
Zone	SOA	Start Of Authority	Defines a DNS zone
	NS	Name Server	Identifies servers, delegates subdomains
Basic	A	IPv4 Address	Name-to-address translation
	AAAA	IPv6 Address	Name-to-IPv6-address translation
	PTR	Pointer	Address-to-name translation
	MX	Mail Exchanger	Controls email routing
Security and DNSSEC	DS	Delegation Signer	Hash of signed child zone's key-signing key
	DNSKEY	Public Key	Public key for a DNS name
	NSEC	Next Secure	Used with DNSSEC for negative answers
	NSEC3[a]	Next Secure v3	Used with DNSSEC for negative answers
	RRSIG	Signature	Signed, authenticated resource record set
	DLV	Lookaside	Nonroot trust anchor for DNSSEC
	SSHFP	SSH Fingerprint	SSH host key, allows verification via DNS
	SPF	Sender Policy	Identifies mail servers, inhibits forging
	DKIM	Domain Keys	Verify email sender and message integrity
Optional	CNAME	Canonical Name	Nicknames or aliases for a host
	SRV	Services	Gives locations of well-known services
	TXT	Text	Comments or untyped information[b]

a. The original NSEC system allows hackers handy with the **dig** command to easily list all of a zone's records. NSEC3 has fixed this weakness but is more expensive to compute; both are currently in use.

b. TXT records are increasingly being used to try out new ideas without having to get full IETF blessing for new record types. For example, SPF and DKIM records were first implemented as TXT records.

Some record types are obsolete, experimental, or not widely used. See your name server's implementation documentation for a complete list. Most records are maintained by hand (by editing text files), but the security resource records require cryptographic processing and so must be managed with software tools. These records are described in the DNSSEC section beginning on page 648.

The order of resource records in the zone file is arbitrary, but traditionally the SOA record is first, followed by the NS records. The records for each host are usually kept together. It's common practice to sort by the *name* field, although some sites sort by IP address so that it's easier to identify unused addresses. The zone files on slave servers are not managed by humans, but rather are written by the name server software; the record order is scrambled.

As we describe each type of resource record in detail in the next sections, we inspect some sample records from the atrust.com domain's data files. The default domain in this context is "atrust.com.", so a host specified as "bark" really means "bark.atrust.com.".

See page 449 for more information about RFCs.

The format and interpretation of each type of resource record is specified by the IETF in the RFC series. In the upcoming sections, we list the specific RFCs relevant to each record (along with their years of origin) in a margin note.

The SOA record

SOA records are specified in RFC1035 (1987).

An SOA (Start of Authority) record marks the beginning of a zone, a group of resource records located at the same place within the DNS namespace. The data for a DNS domain usually includes at least two zones: one for translating hostnames to IP addresses, called the forward zone, and others that map IP addresses back to hostnames, called reverse zones.

Each zone has exactly one SOA record. The SOA record includes the name of the zone, the primary name server for the zone, a technical contact, and various timeout values. Comments are introduced by a semicolon. Here's an example:

```
; Start of authority record for atrust.com
atrust.com.     IN   SOA   ns1.atrust.com. hostmaster.atrust.com. (
                           2009070200   ; Serial number
                           10800        ; Refresh      (3 hours)
                           1200         ; Retry        (20 minutes)
                           3600000      ; Expire       (40+ days)
                           3600 )       ; Minimum      (1 hour)
```

*For configuration details see page 597 for **named.conf** and page 625 for **nsd.conf**.*

The *name* field of the SOA record (atrust.com. in this example) often contains the symbol @, which is shorthand for the name of the current zone. The value of @ is the domain name specified in the zone statement of **named.conf** or in the zone's name entry in the **nsd.conf** file. This value can be changed from within the zone file with the $ORIGIN parser directive (see page 596).

This example has no *ttl* field. The class is IN for Internet, the type is SOA, and the remaining items form the *data* field. The numerical parameters in parentheses are timeout values and are often written on one line without comments.

"ns1.atrust.com." is the zone's master name server.[11]

"hostmaster.atrust.com." is the email address of the technical contact in the format "*user.host.*" rather than the standard *user@host*. Just replace that first dot with an @ and remove the final dot if you need to send mail to a domain's administrator. Sites often use an alias such as admin or hostmaster in place of an actual login name. The sysadmin responsible for hostmaster duties may change, and it's easier to change one entry in the **aliases** file (see page 756) than to change all your zone files when you need to update the contact person.

11. Actually, any name server for the zone can be listed in the SOA record unless you are using dynamic DNS. In that case, the SOA record must name the master server.

The parentheses continue the SOA record over several lines.

The first numeric parameter is the serial number of the zone's configuration data. The serial number is used by slave servers to determine when to get fresh data. It can be any 32-bit integer and should be incremented every time the data file for the zone is changed. Many sites encode the file's modification date in the serial number. For example, 2009070200 is the first change to the zone on July 2, 2009.

Serial numbers need not be continuous, but they must increase monotonically. If by accident you set a really large value on the master server and that value is transferred to the slaves, then correcting the serial number on the master will not work. The slaves request new data only if the master's serial number is larger than theirs.

There are two ways to fix this problem.

- One fix is to exploit the properties of the sequence space in which the serial numbers live. This procedure involves adding a large value (2^{31}) to the bloated serial number, letting all the slave servers transfer the data, and then setting the serial number to just what you want. This weird arithmetic, with explicit examples, is covered in detail in the O'Reilly DNS book; RFC1982 describes the sequence space.
- A sneaky but more tedious way to fix the problem is to change the serial number on the master, kill the slave servers, remove the slaves' backup data files so they are forced to reload from the master, and restart the slaves. It does not work to just remove the files and reload; you must kill and restart the slave servers. This method gets hard if you follow best-practices advice and have your slave servers geographically distributed, especially if you are not the sysadmin for those slave servers.

It is a common mistake to change the data files but forget to update the serial number. Your name server will punish you by failing to propagate your changes to the slave servers.

The next four entries in the SOA record are timeout values, in seconds, that control how long data can be cached at various points throughout the world-wide DNS database. Times can also be expressed in units of minutes, hours, days, or weeks by addition of a suffix of `m`, `h`, `d`, or `w`, respectively. For example, `1h30m` means 1 hour and 30 minutes. Timeout values represent a tradeoff between efficiency (it's cheaper to use an old value than to fetch a new one) and accuracy (new values should be more accurate). The four timeout fields are called *refresh*, *update*, *expire*, and *minimum*.

The *refresh* timeout specifies how often slave servers should check with the master to see if the serial number of the zone's configuration has changed. Whenever the zone changes, slaves must update their copy of the zone's data. The slave compares the serial numbers; if the master's serial number is larger, the slave requests a zone transfer to update the data. Common values for the *refresh* timeout range from one to six hours (3,600 to 21,600 seconds).

Instead of just waiting passively for slave servers to time out, master servers for BIND (always) and NSD (if so configured) notify their slaves every time a zone changes. It's possible for an update notification to be lost because of network congestion, so the refresh timeout should still be set to a reasonable value.

If a slave server tries to check the master's serial number but the master does not respond, the slave tries again after the *retry* timeout period has elapsed. Our experience suggests that 20–60 minutes (1,200–3,600 seconds) is a good value.

If a master server is down for a long time, slaves will try to refresh their data many times but always fail. Each slave should eventually decide that the master is never coming back and that its data is surely out of date. The *expire* parameter determines how long the slaves will continue to serve the domain's data authoritatively in the absence of a master. The system should be able to survive if the master server is down for a few days, so this parameter should have a longish value. We recommend a week to a month or two.

The *minimum* parameter in the SOA record sets the time to live for negative answers that are cached. The default for positive answers (i.e., actual records) is specified at the top of the zone file with the $TTL directive. Experience suggests values of several hours to a few days for $TTL and an hour to a few hours for the *minimum*. BIND silently discards any *minimum* values greater than 3 hours.

The $TTL, *expire*, and *minimum* parameters eventually force everyone that uses DNS to discard old data values. The initial design of DNS relied on the fact that host data was relatively stable and did not change often. However, DHCP, mobile hosts, and the Internet explosion have changed the rules. Name servers are desperately trying to cope with the dynamic update and incremental zone transfer mechanisms described later. For more information about TTLs, see page 576.

NS records

NS records are specified in RFC1035 (1987).

NS (name server) records identify the servers that are authoritative for a zone (that is, all the master and slave servers) and delegate subdomains to other organizations. NS records are usually placed directly after the zone's SOA record.

The format is

```
zone [ttl] [IN] NS hostname
```

For example:

```
            NS  ns1.atrust.com.
            NS  ns2.atrust.com.
booklab     NS  ubuntu.booklab.atrust.com.
            NS  ns1.atrust.com.
```

The first two lines define name servers for the atrust.com domain. No *name* is listed because it is the same as the *name* field of the SOA record that precedes the records; the *name* can therefore be left blank. The *class* is also not listed because IN is the default and does not need to be stated explicitly.

The third and fourth lines delegate a subdomain called booklab.atrust.com to the name servers ubuntu.booklab and ns1. These records are really part of the booklab subdomain, but they must also appear in the parent zone, atrust.com, in order for the delegation to work. In a similar fashion, NS records for atrust.com are stored in the .com zone file to define the atrust.com subdomain and identify its servers. The .com servers refer queries about hosts in atrust.com to the servers listed in NS records for atrust.com within the .com domain.

See page 596 for more information about delegation.

The list of name servers in the parent zone should be kept up to date with those in the zone itself, if possible. Nonexistent servers listed in the parent zone can delay name service, although clients will eventually stumble onto one of the functioning name servers. If none of the name servers listed in the parent exist in the child, a so-called lame delegation results; see page 678.

Extra servers in the child are OK as long as at least one of the child's servers still has an NS record in the parent. Check your delegations with **dig** or **drill** occasionally to be sure they specify an appropriate set of servers; see page 677.

A records

A records are specified in RFC1035 (1987).

A (address) records are the heart of the DNS database. They provide the mapping from hostnames to IP addresses that was formerly specified in the **/etc/hosts** file. A host usually has one A record for each of its network interfaces. The format is

```
hostname [ttl] [IN] A ipaddr
```

For example:

```
ns1            IN  A      63.173.189.1
```

In this example, the *name* field is not dot-terminated, so the name server adds the default domain to it to form the fully qualified name "ns1.atrust.com.". The record associates that name with the IP address 63.173.189.1.

PTR records

PTR records are specified in RFC1035 (1987).

PTR (pointer) records map from IP addresses back to hostnames. As described on page 566, reverse mapping records live under the in-addr.arpa domain and are named with the bytes of the IP address in reverse order. For example, the zone for the 189 subnet in this example is 189.173.63.in-addr.arpa.

The general format of a PTR record is

```
addr [ttl] [IN] PTR hostname
```

For example, the PTR record in the 189.173.63.in-addr.arpa zone that corresponds to ns1's A record above is

```
1              IN  PTR   ns1.atrust.com.
```

The name 1 does not end in a dot and therefore is relative. But relative to what? Not atrust.com—for this sample record to be accurate, the default zone has to be "189.173.63.in-addr.arpa.".

You can set the zone by putting the PTR records for each subnet in their own file. The default domain associated with the file is set in the name server configuration file. Another way to do reverse mappings is to include records such as

```
1.189          IN   PTR   ns1.atrust.com.
```

with a default domain of 173.63.in-addr.arpa. Some sites put all reverse records in the same file and use $ORIGIN directives (see page 596) to specify the subnet. Note that the hostname ns1.atrust.com ends with a dot to prevent the default domain, 173.63.in-addr.arpa, from being appended to its name.

Since atrust.com and 189.173.63.in-addr.arpa are different regions of the DNS namespace, they constitute two separate zones. Each zone must have its own SOA record and resource records. In addition to defining an in-addr.arpa zone for each real network, you should also define one that takes care of the loopback network (127.0.0.0), at least if you run BIND. See page page 619 for an example.

This all works fine if subnets are defined on byte boundaries. But how do you handle the reverse mappings for a subnet such as 63.173.189.0/26, where that last byte can be in any of four subnets: 0-63, 64-127, 128-191, or 192-255? An elegant hack defined in RFC2317 exploits CNAME resource records to accomplish this feat; see page 585.

The reverse mappings provided by PTR records are used by any program that authenticates inbound network traffic. For example, **sshd** may allow[12] remote logins without a password if the machine of origin is listed, by name, in a user's **~/.shosts** file. When the destination host receives a connection request, it knows the source machine only by IP address. It uses DNS to convert the IP address to a hostname, which is then compared to the appropriate file. **netstat**, **sendmail**, **tcpd**, **sshd**, X Windows, and **ftpd** all do reverse mappings to get hostnames from IP addresses.

It's important that A records match their corresponding PTR records. Mismatched and missing PTR records cause authentication failures that can slow your system to a crawl. This problem is annoying in itself; it can also facilitate denial of service attacks against any application that requires the reverse mapping to match the A record.

MX records

MX records are specified in RFC1035 (1987).

The mail system uses mail exchanger (MX) records to route mail more efficiently. An MX record preempts the destination specified by the sender of a message, in most cases directing the message to a hub at the recipient's site. This feature puts the flow of mail into a site under the control of local sysadmins instead of senders.

The format of an MX record is

name [*ttl*] [IN] MX *preference host* …

12. But really shouldn't, for security reasons.

The records below route mail addressed to user@somehost.atrust.com to the machine mailserver.atrust.com if it is up and accepting email. If mailserver is not available, mail goes to mail-relay3.atrust.com. If neither machine named in the MX records is accepting mail, the fallback behavior is to deliver the mail as originally addressed.

```
somehost        IN  MX  10 mailserver.atrust.com.
                IN  MX  20 mail-relay3.atrust.com.
```

Hosts with low preference values are tried first: 0 is the most desirable, and 65,535 is as bad as it gets. (It might seem that this example configuration is not very robust because both mail servers are at atrust.com. However, the two servers are in fact on different networks and are not co-located.)

MX records are useful in many situations:

- When you have a central mail hub for incoming mail
- When you want to filter mail for spam or viruses before delivering it
- When the destination host is down
- When the destination host isn't directly reachable from the Internet
- When the local sysadmin knows where mail should be sent better than your correspondents do (i.e., always)

Every host that the outside world knows about should have MX records. Other entities in DNS need them, too. For example, hosts that can never or should never receive email (e.g., network printers) should have MX records. The domain itself should have an MX record that points to a mail hub machine so that mail to user@domain will work as senders expect. (But note that this configuration does require that usernames be unique across all machines in the domain.)

A machine that accepts email on behalf of another host may need to configure its mail transport program to enable this function. See pages 784 and 835 for a discussion of how to set up this configuration on **sendmail** and Postfix email servers, respectively.

Wild card MX records are also sometimes seen in the DNS database:

```
*               IN  MX  10 mailserver.atrust.com.
```

At first glance, this record seems like it would save lots of typing and add a default MX record for all hosts. But wild card records don't quite work as you might expect. They match anything in the *name* field of a resource record that is *not* already listed as an explicit name in another resource record.

Thus, you *cannot* use a star to set a default value for all your hosts. But perversely, you can use it to set a default value for names that are not your hosts. This setup causes lots of mail to be sent to your hub only to be rejected because the hostname matching the star really does not belong to your domain. Ergo, avoid wild card MX records.

CNAME records

CNAME records are specified in RFC1035 (1987).

CNAME records assign additional names to a host. These nicknames are commonly used either to associate a function with a host or to shorten a long hostname. The real name is sometimes called the canonical name (hence, "CNAME"). Some examples:

```
ftp        IN  CNAME  anchor
kb         IN  CNAME  kibblesnbits
```

The format of a CNAME record is

nickname [*ttl*] [IN] CNAME *hostname*

When DNS software encounters a CNAME record, it stops its query for the nickname and requeries for the real name. If a host has a CNAME record, other records (A, MX, NS, etc.) for that host must refer to its real name, not its nickname.[13]

CNAME records can nest eight deep. That is, a CNAME record can point to another CNAME, and that CNAME can point to a third CNAME, and so on, up to seven times; the eighth target must be the real hostname. If you use CNAMEs, the PTR record should point to the real name, not a nickname.

You can avoid CNAMEs altogether by publishing A records for both a host's real name and its nicknames. This configuration makes lookups slightly faster because the extra layer of indirection is not needed.

The CNAME hack

See page 460 for more information about CIDR.

CNAMEs are also used to torture the existing semantics of DNS into supporting reverse zones for networks that are not subnetted on a byte boundary. Before CIDR addressing was commonplace, most subnet assignments were on byte boundaries or within the same organization, and the reverse delegations were easy to manage. For example, if the class B network 128.138 was subnetted into a set of class C-like networks, each subnet would make a tidy package for the in-addr.arpa domain. The reverse zone for the 243 subnet would be 243.138.128.in-addr.arpa.

But what happens if the 243 subnet is further divided into, say, four pieces as a /26 network? If all four pieces are assigned to the same organization, there is actually no problem. The four subnets can still share a single file that contains all of their PTR records. However, if the 243 subnet is assigned to an ISP that wants to delegate each /26 network to a different customer, a more complicated solution is necessary. The ISP must either maintain the reverse records on behalf of each client, or it must find a way to take the third octet of the IP address (243 in this case) and divide it into four different pieces that can be delegated independently.

13. This rule for CNAMEs was explicitly relaxed for DNSSEC, which adds digital signatures to each DNS resource record set. The RRSIG record for the CNAME refers to the nickname.

When an administrative boundary falls in the middle of a byte, you have to be sneaky. You must also work closely with the domain above or below you. The trick is this: for each possible host address in the natural in-addr.arpa zone, add a CNAME that deflects the lookup to a zone controlled by the owner of the appropriate subnet. This scheme makes for messy zone files on the parent, but it does let you delegate authority to the actual users of each subnet.

Here is the scheme in gory detail. The parent organization (in our case, the ISP) creates CNAME records for each possible IP address with an extra fake component (dot-separated chunk) that represents the subnet. For example, in the /26 scenario just described, the first quarter of the addresses would have a "0-63" component, the second quarter would have a "64-127" component, and so on. Here's what it looks like:

```
$ORIGIN 243.138.128.in-addr.arpa.
1               IN   CNAME  1.0-63
2               IN   CNAME  2.0-63
...
63              IN   CNAME  63.0-63
64              IN   CNAME  64.64-127
65              IN   CNAME  65.64-127
...
```

To delegate the 0-63 piece of the reverse zone to the customer that has been assigned that subnet, we'd add the following NS records:

```
0-63            IN   NS       ns1.customer1.com.
0-63            IN   NS       ns2.customer1.com.
...
```

customer1.com's site would have a zone file that contained the reverse mappings for the 0-63.243.138.128.in-addr.arpa zone.

For example,

```
1               IN   PTR      host1.customer1.com.
2               IN   PTR      host2.customer1.com.
...
```

By adding this extra component, we create a new "cut" at which to perform delegation. When someone looks up the reverse mapping for 128.138.243.1, for example, the CNAME record at 1.243.138.128.in-addr.arpa refocuses the search to the name 1.0-63.243.138.128.in-addr.arpa, which is controlled by the customer.

The customer's files are clean; it's only the ISP that must deal with an inelegant configuration mess. But things can get even more complicated. Customer1 could itself be an ISP that wants to further subdivide its addresses. But that's OK: chains of CNAMEs can be up to eight links long, and since a byte has only eight bits, we can never run out. CNAME chains are discouraged but not forbidden in the RFCs; they do slow down name resolution since each link in a CNAME chain causes the link to be followed and a new query for the target to be initiated.

Early in the life of the CNAME hack, the $GENERATE command was added to BIND's repertoire to facilitate the creation of resource records in the parent zone. For example, the following lines produce the records for the first subnet:

```
$ORIGIN 243.138.128.in-addr.arpa.
$GENERATE 0-63 $ CNAME $.0-63
0-63            NS  ns1.customer1.com.
0-63            NS  ns2.customer1.com.
```

The $ in the $GENERATE command (itself a BIND extension) iterates from 0 to 63 and creates 64 different CNAME records. The other three /26 networks would be handled similarly.

SRV records

SRV records are specified in RFC2782 (2000).

An SRV record specifies the location of services within a domain. For example, the SRV record lets you query a remote domain for the name of its FTP server. Before SRV, you had to hope the remote sysadmins had followed the prevailing custom and added a CNAME for "ftp" to their server's DNS records.

SRV records make more sense than CNAMEs for this application and are certainly a better way for sysadmins to move services around and control their use. However, SRV records must be explicitly sought and parsed by clients, so it will be a while before their effects are really felt. They are used extensively by Windows.

SRV records resemble generalized MX records with fields that let the local DNS administrator steer and load-balance connections from the outside world. The format is

```
service.proto.name [ttl] [IN] SRV pri wt port target
```

where *service* is a service defined in the IANA assigned numbers database (see iana.org/numbers.htm), *proto* is either tcp or udp, *name* is the domain to which the SRV record refers, *pri* is an MX-style priority, *wt* is a weight used for load balancing among several servers, *port* is the port on which the service runs, and *target* is the hostname of the server that provides the service. To avoid a second round trip, DNS servers usually return the A record of the target with the answer to a SRV query.

A value of 0 for the *wt* parameter means that no special load balancing should be done. A value of "." for the target means that the service is not run at this site.

Here is an example snitched from the RFC2782 and adapted for atrust.com:

```
_ftp._tcp           SRV    0  0  21    ftp-server.atrust.com.

; 1/4 of the connections to old box, 3/4 to the new one
_ssh._tcp           SRV    0  1  22    old-slow-box.atrust.com.
                    SRV    0  3  22    new-fast-box.atrust.com.

; main server on port 80, backup on new box, port 8000
_http._tcp          SRV    0  0  80    www-server.atrust.com.
                    SRV   10  0  8000  new-fast-box.atrust.com.
```

```
; so both http://www.atrust.com and http://atrust.com work
_http._tcp.www      SRV    0  0  80    www-server.atrust.com.
                    SRV   10  0  8000  new-fast-box.atrust.com.

; block all other services (target = .)
*._tcp              SRV    0  0  0     .
*._udp              SRV    0  0  0     .
```

This example illustrates the use of both the weight parameter (for SSH) and the priority parameter (HTTP). Both SSH servers are used, with the work being split between them. The backup HTTP server is only used when the principal server is unavailable. All other services are blocked, both for TCP and UDP. However, the fact that other services do not appear in DNS does not mean that they are not actually running, just that you can't locate them through DNS.

MS Exchange servers use SRV records to help Outlook clients find them and to provide automatic configuration for Outlook Anywhere. The SRV records are the fourth thing tried, after Active Directory and some predefined auto-discovery URLs. Windows uses a GUI tool called DNS Manager to set up SRV records.

TXT records

TXT *records are specified in RFC1035 (1987).*

A TXT record adds arbitrary text to a host's DNS records. For example, some sites have a TXT record that identifies them:

```
                IN   TXT    "Applied Trust Engineering, Boulder, CO, USA"
```

This record directly follows the SOA and NS records for the atrust.com zone and so inherits the *name* field from them.

The format of a TXT record is

```
name [ttl] [IN] TXT info ...
```

All *info* items must be quoted. You can use a single quoted string or multiple strings that are individually quoted. Be sure the quotes are balanced—missing quotes wreak havoc with your DNS data because all the records between the missing quote and the next occurrence of a quote mysteriously disappear.

As with other resource records, servers return TXT records in random order. To encode long items such as addresses, use long text lines rather than a collection of several TXT records.

Because TXT records have no particular format, they are sometimes used to test prospective new types of DNS records without requiring changes to the DNS system itself. For example, SPF records (see page 590) were originally implemented as TXT records. Now that a dedicated record type has been created, use of the TXT version is no longer recommended, but many sites still do it.

IPv6 resource records

The IPv6 records are specified in RFC1886 (1995).

See Chapter 14 for a more detailed discussion of IPv6.

IPv6 is a new version of the IP protocol. It has spent over 15 years in the specification process and has spawned about 250 RFCs, yet it still isn't really done.[14] IPv6 was originally motivated by a perceived need for more IP network addresses. However, the stopgap solutions to this problem (CIDR, private addresses, NAT, and stricter control of addresses) have been so successful that a mass migration to IPv6 has turned out not to be as essential as originally envisioned—at least, not quite yet. The adoption of IPv6 is now being driven by Asia, where IPv4 addresses are spread more thinly.

IPv6 DNS records are totally separate from the transport protocol used to deliver them. Publishing IPv6 records in your DNS zones does not mean that you must answer queries for them with IPv6. About half the query load on the K root name server (k.root-servers.net) consists of queries for IPv4 A records, and one quarter consists of queries for IPv6 AAAA records. However, 99% of all the actual queries use IPv4 transport.

IPv6 forward records – AAAA

The format of an AAAA record is

```
hostname [ttl] [IN] AAAA ipaddr
```

For example:

```
f.root-servers.net.    IN    AAAA    2001:500:2f::f
```

Each colon-separated chunk of the address represents four hex digits, with leading zeros usually omitted. Two adjacent colons stand for "enough zeros to fill out the 128 bits of a complete IPv6 address." An address can contain at most one such double colon.

IPv6 reverse records – PTR

See page 582 for a discussion of the IPv4 version of PTR records.

In IPv6, the reverse mapping information corresponding to an AAAA address record is a PTR record in the ip6.arpa top-level domain.

The "nibble" format reverses an AAAA address record by expanding each colon-separated address chunk to the full 4 hex digits and then reversing the order of those digits and tacking on ip6.arpa at the end. For example, the PTR record that corresponds to our sample AAAA record above would be

```
f.0.0.0.0.0.0.0.0.0.0.0.0.0.0.0.0.0.0.0.f.2.0.0.0.0.5.0.1.0.0.2.ip6.arpa.
    PTR f.root-servers.net.
```

(This line has been folded to fit the page.) It's unfortunately not very friendly for a sysadmin to have to type or debug or even read. Of course, in your actual DNS zone files, the $ORIGIN statement could hide some of the complexity.

14. Tony Li, an active member of the IETF community, once described IPv6 as "too little, too soon."

SPF records

SPF records are specified in RFCs 4406 and 4408 (2006).

SPF (Sender Policy Framework) records are an attempt to identify email messages with forged From headers, which are often spam or phishing. If the site receiving a message determines that the headers are forged, it can drop the mail, filter it, or tag it before delivering it to the recipient. This functionality was first implemented with TXT records, but we now have a dedicated SPF record type that uses the same syntax as the TXT version. Sites can have SPF records, TXT records in SPF format, both, or neither.

Unfortunately, there are two competing ways of using SPF records: Microsoft's Sender ID system and the rest of the world's system. The IETF's working groups could not reach consensus on the best option, so both approaches were published as experimental RFCs. The main difference is whether the tests are done on the envelope sender's address or the header sender's address.

Both the SPF and Sender ID specifications have a serious flaw: email that is forwarded fails the SPF check because the receiver compares the sender's SPF record with the forwarder's IP address. Therefore, sites need to be careful with the disposition of mail that fails the SPF check.

Here, we describe a subset of the syntax and semantics of the RFC4408 version of SPF records. The complete specification is infinitely flexible, with macros, redirects, includes, and such yielding a dozen ways to achieve a given policy. We concentrate on a simple, efficient subset of that dozen.

An SPF record lists the IP addresses of servers that originate the zone's legitimate email. For example, **dig gmail.com spf**[15] returns the following record:

```
gmail.com.          300 IN  SPF   "v=spf1 redirect=_spf.google.com"
```

This SPF record redirects clients to the _spf subdomain at google.com. A followup query, **dig _spf.google.com spf**, yields

```
_spf.google.com.   300 IN  SPF   "v=spf1 ip4:216.239.32.0/19 ip4:64.233.160.0/19
        ip4:66.249.80.0/20 ip4:72.14.192.0/18 ip4:209.85.128.0/17 ip4:66.102.0.0/20
        ip4:74.125.0.0/16 ip4:64.18.0.0/20 ip4:207.126.144.0/20 ?all"
```

Rather than listing specific hosts, this SPF record enumerates the IP networks of Google's mail servers. This is all one long SPF record, but we have inserted line breaks to make it fit on the page.

Quoted strings are limited to 255 bytes, so if you need more than 255 characters for your entry, you must use multiple quoted strings. Multiple strings are concatenated with no extra white space. Try to keep the total length below about 450 bytes, though, so that query responses can still fit in a single 512-byte UDP packet. SPF strings are case insensitive.

15. This is a little white lie; Google and many other sites implement their SPF records with TXT records because the SPF resource record type is new and is only recently supported by popular name server software. But in looking to the future, we have taken editorial license and shown SPF records instead of TXT records. The **dig**s were also for TXT records, not SPFs.

Let's dissect that record in a bit more detail:

- v=spf1 indicates that the record conforms to version 1 of the SPF protocol, described in RFC4408. v=spf2.0 would indicate Microsoft's Sender ID system, described in RFC4406.
- The ip4 tags indicate that the following data value is a normal IP network or host address. Multiple clauses can be included, as is done here.
- ?all indicates "done" to the checking function that interprets the record.

The complexity of the full SPF language is disheartening. Other tags are available to list hostnames, MX records, PTR records, IPv6 addresses, and so on. Some of these forms require a second DNS lookup, so although they may add convenience or flexibility, they are less efficient than the ip4 tag. The examples at the end of RFC4408 are a good reference if you want to get fancy with your SPF records.

Here is another example, obtained with **dig sendmail.com txt**:

```
sendmail.com.           IN  TXT  "v=spf1 ip4:209.246.26.40 ip4:209.246.26.41 ip4:
    63.211.143.38 ip4:209.246.26.36 ip4:209.246.26.39 ip4:209.246.26.24 ip4:
    209.246.26.25 ip4:209.246.26.10 ip4:209.246.26.53 ip4:72.32.154.224/27
    ptr:constantcontact.com ~all"
```

This record specifies complete server IP addresses rather than entire networks. At the tail end of the IP address list is a ptr: clause that permits constantcontact.com to send mail purporting to be from sendmail.com. This clause should only take effect if constantcontact.com has a matching PTR record, which isn't currently the case—as of this writing, the PTR maps back to www.constantcontact.com, not constantcontact.com. Either email receivers are not checking the PTR record rigorously or the SPF record has a small bug.

Surveys (sendmail.org/dkim/survey) of about 1,000 U.S. banks and Fortune 1,000 companies showed that SPF was supported by more than 90% of the sites, with the Sender ID format being used by only 1%–2%. Some email readers (e.g., Gmail) print a bright red warning banner across a message that has failed an SPF check and might be phishing.

sendmail, Postfix, and **exim** support SPF processing; Microsoft Exchange supports Sender ID. See page 768 for more SPF information.

DKIM and ADSP records

DKIM records are specified in RFCs 4871 (2007) and 5617 (2009).

DKIM stands for DomainKeys Identified Mail and is a merge and enhancement of two systems: DomainKeys from Yahoo! and Identified Internet Mail from Cisco. It's a signature system for email. The receiver of a message can authenticate the sender (no forgeries) and guarantee the message's integrity (no meddling).

A lot of work has gone into the DKIM specifications so that edge cases like mailing lists and outsourced email solutions will work correctly. Another focus of the DKIM design is to make implementation easy; it requires no per-user or per-host changes. Here, we cover only the DNS aspects of DKIM. The email implications are described in Chapter 20, *Electronic Mail*, starting on page 845.

DKIM resource records have not yet been standardized as a DNS record type; TXT records in a special format are used instead. They use a DNS record name formed from a "selector" concatenated with the string _domainkey. The record's data is the site's DKIM public key. Multiple selectors may exist so that keys can be easily rolled over and revoked.

A site using DKIM signatures computes a signature over specified header fields and the body of the message with its DKIM private key. It puts the signature into the outbound message in the form of a header field called DKIM-Signature.

The corresponding public key is available through the sending site's DNS zone as a TXT record associated with the name *selector*._domainkey.*domain*. The receiving site does a DNS lookup for this key and uses it to validate the message signature. Successful signature verification authenticates the message as having come from the purported sending domain and verifies that the message has not been modified in transit.

Here is an example of a DKIM-Signature header line from a signed message:

```
DKIM-Signature: v=1; a=rsa-sha256; c=relaxed/relaxed; d=gmail.com; s=gamma;
    h=domainkey-signature:mime-version:received:reply-to:date:message-id:
    subject:from:to:content-type;
    bh=24HfUvt1AO4JxRNBmg94pN6ZJUPdqSbkOd4Zppou4sI=;
    b=UtYWupx/Udqi7Sd1n0h5zIDKq7R/Gg+HwYBxM0LcshlwhqrHhyHy1ea3So8
    EnMXJEYI3jyzj3VNGemOAOSUqHlMmdlSLdP7AvxptY0VfLgYGM9ID4uw
    B0l4a7ZJuoiVHJmsEA/ExK48rvq10ZJY+AgRdDpbx6/56phSfVJt+a+A=
```

The various tags in the signature are explained in Table 17.7.

Table 17.7 Tags in the DKIM-Signature email header

Tag	Example value	What it is
v	1	Version number; must be 1
a	rsa-sha256	Encryption algorithm: rsa-sha1 or rsa-sha256
c	relaxed/relaxed	Canonicalization algorithm:[a] simple or relaxed
d	gmail.com	Domain of the sender
s	gamma	Selector or key name
h	domain...	Header fields to include in the header signature
bh	24HfUvt1...	Cryptographic hash of the body of the message
b	UtYWupx...	Cryptographic signature of the whole message

a. The algorithm specifies how the header and body are munged before encryption.

The selector tag, s=gamma, tells us the name of the public key, and the d= tag gives the parent domain. To get our hands on the public key, we **dig** for the TXT record for the pseudo-host gamma._domainkey.gmail.com.

```
gamma._domainkey.gmail.com. 300 IN TXT "k=rsa\; t=y\;
    p=MIGfMA0GCSqGSIb3DQEBAQUAA4GNADCBiQKBgQDIhyR3oItOy22ZOaBrI
    Ve9m/iME3RqOJeasANSpg2YTHTYV+Xtp4xwf5gTjCmHQEMOs0qYu0FYiNQP
    QogJ2t0Mfx9zNu06rfRBDjiIU9tpx2T+NGlWZ8qhbiLo5By8apJavLyqTLavyPSrv
    sx0B3YzC63T4Age2CDqZYA+OwSMWQIDAQAB"
```

This is a pretty messy record to have to type into your zone files—thank goodness for cut and paste. The k= tag identifies the type of key; the only value defined to date is rsa. The t=y flag means that you are just testing DKIM and so receiving sites should be lenient if your signatures don't verify. The p= clause is the public key itself. Semicolons must be escaped with backslashes because they are comment symbols in DNS data files.

The DKIM TXT record often contains a version tag, v=DKIM1. As in all TXT records, everything must be in double quotes.

To generate an RSA key pair in the appropriate format for your zone files, use the following **openssl** commands to generate a private key and extract the corresponding public key from it:

```
$ openssl genrsa -out rsa.private 1024
$ openssl rsa -in rsa.private -out rsa.public -pubout -outform PEM
```

Then cut and paste the public key from **rsa.public** into the p= clause of your text record. It cannot contain any spaces or newlines, so be careful that the cut and paste does not introduce any additional characters.

You can choose any name as your selector.

In the Gmail example above, the _domainkey.gmail.com segment of the name gamma._domainkey.gmail.com is not a true subzone of gmail.com from the DNS perspective. You can verify this observation by searching for the zone's name servers (**dig _domainkey.gmail.com ns**), which would have to exist if it was a proper delegated subzone. The example below from yahoo.com implements _domainkey as a proper subdomain.

RFC5617 defines a TXT record you can stash in a special subdomain to express your overall policy with respect to signing messages. This record was just recently standardized (2009) and is called an ADSP (Author Domain Signing Policy) text record. The subdomain is _adsp._domainkey.*domain*.

Inside the TXT record, you include a dkim= clause to declare your site's signing policy. The possible values are

- all, for domains that sign all outgoing email messages
- unknown, for domains that might sign some email messages
- discardable, for domains that sign all email and recommend that recipients discard messages whose signature cannot be verified

As an example, the discardable tag might be used by a bank that sends sensitive customer account information from a subdomain created for this purpose. A user's acting on instructions from forged email that appears to emanate from this domain could have disastrous consequences, so it's best if such email can be refused or discarded without reaching the addressee.

The ADSP TXT record can also include a t=y clause if you are just testing out DKIM and don't want recipients to take your signatures too seriously.

During the development of the ADSP system, prior to RFC5617, a domain's ADSP TXT record was kept in a different subdomain (_domainkey.*domain*, with no _adsp prefix) and had a slightly different syntax. o=~ meant that the domain signed some of its email, and o=- meant that it signed all email.

Since the two conventions use different subdomains, they can coexist. As of this writing, the original form remains predominant. If you are serious about getting recipients to scrutinize your signatures, it's probably best to use both conventions for the next few years until everyone has become RFC5617-compliant.

Let's look at an example. Gmail does not have an ADSP record, but Yahoo! does:

```
_domainkey.yahoo.com.    7200  IN  TXT   "t=y\; o=~\;
    n=http://antispam.yahoo.com/domainkeys"
```

The n= clause is a comment that points a human user to more information about Yahoo!'s use of DKIM records.[16] Some sites include an email address (without any @s, to avoid spam) instead. Here is yahoo.com's DKIM TXT record for the key (selector) s1024:

```
s1024._domainkey.yahoo.com.   86400   IN   TXT   "k=rsa\; t=y\;
    p=MIGfMA0GCSqGSIb3DQEBAQUAA4GNADCBiQKBgQDrEee0Ri4Juz+QfiWYui
    /E9UGSXau/2P8LjnTD8V4Unn+2FAZVGE3kL23bzeoULYv4PeleB3gfm"
    "JiDJOKU3Ns5L4KJAUUHjFwDebt0NP+sBK0VKeTATL2Yr/S3bT/xhy+1xtj4Rkd
    V7fVxTn56Lb4udUnwuxK4V5b5PdOKj/+XcwIDAQAB\; n=A 1024 bit key\;"
```

Here again, the n= clause is a comment, this time about the key itself.

The DKIM records shown in this section are all TXT records, but they will eventually migrate to the DKIM record type, which has the same format. In the interim, sites can use both record types to be sure there are no transition issues.

Chapter 20 covers the steps needed to implement DKIM within your mail system.

SSHFP resource records

SSHFP records are specified in RFC4255 (2006).

SSH, the secure shell, allows secure remote logins over an insecure network. It uses two authentication schemes, one for the host itself and one for the user attempting to log in. Unfortunately, users typically accept whatever host key **ssh** presents to them without verifying it. DNS's SSHFP record type lets **ssh** verify the host key automatically, ensuring that the user has reached the intended machine and not an impostor.

16. However, the given URL currently redirects to sourceforge.net's page about DomainKeys, the old standard that has been mostly abandoned.

To keep packet sizes down, SSHFP records do not store a complete copy of a host's public keys. Instead, they store digests (i.e., cryptographic hashes) of those keys. Here's the syntax:

```
name [ttl] [IN] SSHFP algorithm# fingerprint_algorithm# fingerprint
```

The *algorithm#* identifies the public key cryptosystem used to generate the host's key. This algorithm is not actually used in the verification process; it is just compared with the key presented by the remote host to be sure that both parties are talking about the same kind of key. RSA is algorithm 1 and DSA is algorithm 2.

The *fingerprint* is the hash to be matched, and the *fingerprint_algorithm#* tells how to process the public key presented by the remote host to produce a hash for comparison. Only one hashing algorithm (SHA-1) is currently defined, so the contents of this field are currently always 1.

Here's an example from RFC4255:

```
host.example.      SSHFP  2  1  123456789abcdef67890123456789abcdef67890
```

SSH typically creates both RSA and DSS host key pairs; they're usually stored in **/etc/ssh** with names like **ssh_host_rsa_key.pub** and **ssh_host_dsa_key.pub**. On the user's end, SSH stores accepted host public keys in the **.ssh/known_hosts** file in the user's home directory.

You can grab the host keys from that directory to build your SSHFP resource records. Recent versions of **ssh-keygen** can generate the SSHFP DNS records with the **-r** and **-g** flags. There is also an **sshfp** command on Linux and available for UNIX (freshports.org/dns/sshfp) that converts the keys to fingerprints and produces the necessary DNS records.

See page 928 for more information about SSHFP records.

You can ask OpenSSH to use SSHFP records by setting the VerifyHostKeyDNS option to yes. SSH supports multiple authentication and verification methods, and since SSHFP records are not yet widely used, you shouldn't make them the only possible option. Try SSHFP first, and if that fails, fall back to prompting the user to confirm the host key manually as was done before we had SSHFP. See page 926 in Chapter 22, *Security*, for more information about configuring SSH.

Like SPF and DKIM records, the SSHFP system more or less assumes that you are using DNSSEC and that DNS records are therefore trustworthy. That probably isn't true right now, but DNSSEC is gaining traction and will eventually see the light of day. See page 648 for our DNSSEC coverage.

DNSSEC resource records

Six resource record types are currently associated with DNSSEC. DS, DLV, and DNSKEY are for storing various types of keys or fingerprints. RRSIGs contain the signatures of other records in the zone (record sets, really). Finally, NSEC and NSEC3 give DNS servers a way to sign nonexistent records, providing cryptographic security for negative answers to queries. These six records are different from most in that they are generated with software tools rather than being typed in by hand.

DNSSEC is a big topic in its own right, so we discuss these records and their use in the DNSSEC section that begins on page 648.

Glue records: links between zones

Each zone stands alone with its own set of data files, name servers, and clients. But zones need to be connected to form a coherent hierarchy: booklab.atrust.com is a part of atrust.com, and we need some kind of DNS linkage between them.

Since DNS referrals occur only from parent domains to child domains, it is not necessary for a name server to know anything about the domains (or more accurately, zones) above it in the DNS hierarchy. However, the servers of a parent domain must know the IP addresses of the name servers for all of its subdomains. In fact, *only* the name servers known to the parent zone can be returned as referrals in response to external queries.

In DNS terms, the parent zone needs to contain the NS records for each delegated zone. Since NS records are written in terms of hostnames rather than IP addresses, the parent server must also have a way to resolve the hostnames, either by making a normal DNS query (if this does not create a dependency loop) or by having copies of the appropriate A records.

There are two ways in which you can meet this requirement: by including the necessary records directly, or by using stub zones.

With the first method, you simply include the necessary NS and A records in the parent zone. For example, the atrust.com zone file could contain these records:

```
; subdomain information

booklab          IN  NS  ns1.atrust.com.
                 IN  NS  ubuntu.booklab.atrust.com.
                 IN  NS  ns.cs.colorado.edu.
testlab          IN  NS  ns1.atrust.com.
                 IN  NS  ns.testlab.atrust.com.

; glue records

ubuntu.booklab   IN  A   63.173.189.194
ns.testlab       IN  A   63.173.189.17
```

The "foreign" A records are called glue records because they don't really belong in this zone. They're only reproduced here to connect the new domain to the naming tree. Missing or incorrect glue records leave part of your namespace inaccessible, and users trying to reach it get "host unknown" errors.

It is a common error to include glue records for hostnames that don't need them. For example, ns1.atrust.com in the example above is part of the atrust.com zone, and its A record is stored elsewhere in the file. The address of ns.cs.colorado.edu is also not needed in the glue section since it can be determined with a normal DNS query. An A record in this zone would initially just be unnecessary, but it could later become out of date and wrong if ns.cs.colorado.edu's address were to change. The rule of thumb is to include A records only for hosts that are within the current domain or any of its subdomains. BIND and NSD ignore unnecessary glue records, and BIND logs their presence as an error.

The scheme just described is the standard way of connecting zones, but it requires the child to keep in touch with the parent and tell the parent about any changes or additions to its name server fleet. Since parent and child zones are often run by different sites, updates can be a tedious manual task that requires coordination across administrative boundaries. A corollary is that in the real world, this type of configuration is often out of date.

The second way to maintain links is to use stub zones. A stub zone is essentially the same thing as a slave zone, but it includes only the zone's NS records and the corresponding A records of those name servers. Like a slave, a stub zone is automatically updated and so eliminates the need for communication between the administrators of the parent and child zones.

An important caveat is that stub zones must be configured identically on both the master and slave servers *of the parent zone*. It might just be easiest to keep in touch manually with your parent domain and to verify its configuration a couple of times a year (especially if it is local).

You can use the **dig** command to see which of your servers your parent domain is currently advertising. First run

```
$ dig parent-domain ns
```

to determine the name servers for your parent domain. Pick one and then run

```
$ dig @name-server.parent-domain child-domain ns
```

to see your list of public name servers. One situation in which stub zones are very useful is when your internal network uses RFC1918 private IP address space and you need to keep the RFC1918 delegations in sync.

We have now covered most of the background information that applies to the Domain Name System generally and to its database. In the next section, we cover configuration details specific to the BIND implementation. The NSD/Unbound implementation is covered beginning on page 625.

17.9 The BIND software

BIND, the Berkeley Internet Name Domain system, is an open source software package from ISC that implements the DNS protocol for Linux, UNIX, Mac OS, and Windows systems. There have been three main flavors of BIND: BIND 4, BIND 8, and BIND 9, with BIND 10 currently under development by ISC. We cover only BIND 9 in this book.

Version determination

It often doesn't seem to occur to vendors to document which version of an external software package they have included with their systems, so you might have to do some sleuthing to find out exactly what software you are dealing with. You can sometimes determine the version number with a sneaky query with **dig**, a command that comes with BIND. The command

```
$ dig @server version.bind txt chaos
```

returns the version number unless someone has decided to withhold that information by changing it in BIND's configuration file. First, determine the name of the name server for the domain in question with

```
$ dig domain ns
```

and then do the version.bind query. For example, the command works at isc.org:

```
$ dig @ns-ext.isc.org version.bind txt chaos
version.bind.          0  CH  TXT  "9.5.1"
```

But it doesn't work at cs.colorado.edu:

```
$ dig @mroe.cs.colorado.edu version.bind txt chaos
version.bind.          0  CH  TXT  "wouldn't you like to know..."[17]
```

Some sites configure BIND to conceal its version number on the theory that this provides some degree of "security through obscurity." We don't really endorse this practice, but it might help fend off some of the script kiddies. See page 603 for a more detailed discussion of this topic.

This same query works for some other DNS software; for example,

```
$ dig @k.root-servers.net version.bind txt chaos
version.bind.          0  CH  TXT  "NSD 2.3.7"
```

shows that the K root name server is running NSD.

Another piece of data in the CHAOS class identifies the name of the server queried. But wait—if you just queried the server, you must know its name, right? Actually some of the busiest servers (e.g., the root name servers) are really multiple machines scattered around the globe that all have the same server name and IP address. This replication scheme is called "anycast routing." The routing system takes you to the "closest" instance. If you are the sysadmin trying to debug a problem, however, it may be important to distinguish which of the replicated servers you have reached. For example,

```
$ dig @k.root-servers.net hostname.bind txt chaos
hostname.bind.         0  CH  TXT  "k2.nap.k.ripe.net"
```

17. The 0 in the answer is the TTL for the data value. One of our reviewers reported once seeing the answer to this query come up as "Name is Bind, James Bind!"

or

```
$ dig @k.root-servers.net id.server txt chaos
id.server.              0  CH  TXT  "k2.nap.k.ripe.net"
```

The IETF tried to standardize these odd CHAOS-class names into implementation-independent forms, version.server and id.server, but only id.server made it through the entire process; version.server ended up in an IETF draft that never became an RFC. NSD uses all four forms, BIND only the three approved forms.

See Chapter 11 for more information about syslog.

As an administrator, you can start the name server (**named** or **nsd**) with the **-v** flag to make it print its version to standard output and exit. On Linux, you can ask your package manager which version is installed. You can also usually tell what BIND version you have by inspecting the log files in **/var/log** or its equivalent on your system. The BIND name server logs its version number to syslog (facility "daemon") as it starts up. **grep** for BIND to get lines like this:

```
Jul 13 07:19:55 nubark named[757]: starting BIND 9.5.0-P2 -u named
```

If all else fails, **dig**'s version number usually parallels **named**'s, and **dig** is often installed even when **named** is not. **dig**'s first line of output includes the version number as a comment.

Table 17.8 shows the versions of BIND that are included with our example systems. It's always safest to use the current release.

Table 17.8 Versions of BIND shipped with our example systems

System	OS vers	BIND vers	BIND release date
ISC	–	9.6.1-P3	January, 2010
Ubuntu	9.04	9.5.1-P2	March, 2009
SUSE	10.2	9.4.2	November, 2007
RHEL	5.3	9.3.4-P1	July, 2007
Solaris	5.10	9.3.4-P1	July, 2007
OpenSolaris	2009.06	9.6.1-P1	July, 2009
HP-UX	11	9.3.2	December, 2005
AIX	6.1	8.3.3+ or 9.2.1	January, 2004

AIX ships both BIND 8 and BIND 9 binaries, called **named8** and **named9**, respectively. As shipped, the generic form **named** is linked to **named8**. The + in the version number is short for "+Fix_for_CERT_till_07_15_04"; not exactly current.

Most vendors back-port security fixes to their installed version of an older release rather than upgrade to the latest release from ISC, so version numbers can be deceiving. As you can see, many of our vendors are not very current, so your first DNS sysadmin chore might be to upgrade the software.

Components of BIND

The BIND distribution has four major components:

- A name server daemon called **named** that answers queries
- A resolver library that queries DNS servers on behalf of users
- Command-line interfaces to DNS: **nslookup**, **dig**, and **host**
- A program to remotely control **named** called **rndc**

The hardest BIND-related sysadmin chore is probably sorting through all the myriad options and features that BIND supports and determining which ones make sense for your situation.

Configuration files

The complete configuration for **named** consists of the config file, the zone data files that contain address mappings for each host, and the root name server hints file. Authoritative servers need a config file and zone data files for each zone for which they are the master server; caching servers need the config file and the root hints file. **named**'s config file has its own format; all the other files are collections of individual DNS data records whose formats were discussed in the *The DNS database* section beginning on page 574.

named's configuration file, **named.conf**, specifies the roles (master, slave, stub, or caching-only) of this host and the manner in which it should obtain its copy of the data for each zone it serves. It's also the place where options are specified—both global options related to the overall operation of **named** and server- or zone-specific options that apply to only a portion of the DNS traffic.

The config file consists of a series of statements whose syntax we describe as they are introduced in subsequent sections. The format is unfortunately quite fragile—a missing semicolon or unbalanced quotes can wreak havoc.

Fortunately, BIND includes a couple of handy tools to check the syntax of the config file (**named-checkconf**) and the zone data files (**named-checkzone**). They look for both errors and omissions. For example, **named-checkzone** tells you if you've forgotten to include a $TTL directive. Unfortunately, it doesn't catch everything. For example, missing glue records (see page 596) are not reported and cause heavy loads on the root and gTLD servers.

Comments can appear anywhere that whitespace is appropriate. C, C++, and shell-style comments are all understood:

```
/* This is a comment and can span lines. */
// Everything to the end of the line is a comment.
# Everything to the end of the line is a comment.
```

Each statement begins with a keyword that identifies the type of statement. There can be more than one instance of each type of statement, except for `options` and `logging`. Statements and parts of statements can also be left out, invoking default behavior for the missing items. Table 17.9 lists the available statements; the Page column points to our discussion of each statement in the upcoming sections.

Table 17.9 Statements used in named.conf

Statement	Page	Function
include	602	Interpolates a file
options	602	Sets global configuration options/defaults
acl	609	Defines access control lists
key	609	Defines authentication information
trusted-keys	610	Uses preconfigured cryptographic keys
server	610	Specifies per-server options
masters	611	Defines a list of masters for stub and slave zones
logging	612	Specifies logging categories and their destinations
statistics-channels	612	Outputs real-time statistics in XML
zone	612	Defines a zone of resource records
controls	615	Defines channels used to control **named** with **rndc**
view	617	Defines a view of the zone data
lwres	–	Specifies that **named** should be a resolver, too

Before describing these statements and the way they are used to configure **named**, we need to describe a data structure that is used in many of the statements, the address match list. An address match list is a generalization of an IP address that can include the following items:

- An IP address, either v4 or v6 (e.g., 199.165.145.4)
- An IP network specified with a CIDR[18] netmask (e.g., 199.165/16)
- The name of a previously defined access control list (see page 609)
- The name of a cryptographic authentication key
- The ! character to negate things

Address match lists are used as parameters to many statements and options. Some examples:

```
{ ! 1.2.3.13; 1.2.3/24; };
{ 128.138/16; 198.11.16/24; 204.228.69/24; 127.0.0.1; };
```

The first of these lists excludes the host 1.2.3.13 but includes the rest of the 1.2.3.0/24 network; the second defines the networks assigned to the University of Colorado. The braces and final semicolon are not really part of the address match lists but are included for illustration; they would be part of the enclosing statements of which the address match lists are a part.

When an IP address or network is compared to a match list, the list is searched in order until a match is found. This "first match" algorithm makes the ordering of

18. CIDR netmasks are described starting on page 460.

entries important. For example, the first address match list above would not have the desired effect if the two entries were reversed, because 1.2.3.13 would succeed in matching 1.2.3.0/24 and the negated entry would never be encountered.

Now, on to the statements! Some are short and sweet; others almost warrant a chapter unto themselves.

The include statement

To break up or better organize a large configuration, you can put different portions of the configuration in separate files. Subsidiary files are brought into **named.conf** with an include statement:

```
include "path";
```

If the *path* is relative, it is interpreted relative to the directory specified in the directory option. A common use of the include statement is to bring in cryptographic keys that should not be world-readable. Rather than closing read access to the whole **named.conf** file, some sites keep keys in files with restricted permissions that only **named** can read. Those files are then included into **named.conf**.

Many sites put zone statements in a separate file and use the include statement to pull them in. This configuration helps separate the parts of the configuration that are relatively static from those that are likely to change frequently.

The options statement

The options statement specifies global options, some of which may later be overridden for particular zones or servers. The general format is

```
options {
    option;
    option;
    ...
};
```

If no options statement is present in **named.conf**, default values are used.

BIND has a lot of options—too many, in fact. The 9.7 release has more than 150, which is a lot for sysadmins to wrap their heads around. Unfortunately, as soon as the BIND folks think about removing some of the options that were a bad idea or that are no longer necessary, they get pushback from sites who use and need those obscure options. We do not cover the whole gamut of BIND options here; we have biased our coverage and discuss only the ones whose use we recommend. (We also asked the BIND developers for their suggestions on which options to cover, and followed their advice.)

For more complete coverage of the options, see one of the books on DNS and BIND listed at the end of this chapter. You can also refer to the documentation shipped with BIND. The **ARM** document in the **doc** directory of the distribution describes each option and shows both syntax and default values. The file **doc/misc/options** also contains a complete list of options.

As we wind our way through about a quarter of the possible options, we have added a margin note as a mini index entry. The default values are listed in square brackets beside each option. For most sites, the default values are just fine. Options are listed in no particular order.

File locations

```
directory "path";          [directory where the server was started]
key-directory "path";      [same as directory entry]
```

The directory statement causes **named** to **cd** to the specified directory. Wherever relative pathnames appear in **named**'s configuration files, they are interpreted relative to this directory. The *path* should be an absolute path. Any output files (debugging, statistics, etc.) are also written in this directory. The key-directory is where cryptographic keys are stored; it should not be world-readable.

We like to put all the BIND-related configuration files (other than **named.conf** and **resolv.conf**) in a subdirectory beneath **/var** (or wherever you keep your configuration files for other programs). We use **/var/named** or **/var/domain**.

Name server identity

```
version "string";          [real version number of the server]
hostname "string";         [real hostname of the server]
server-id "string";        [none]
```

The version string identifies the version of the name server software running on the server. The hostname string identifies the server itself, as does the server-id string. These options let you lie about the true values. Each of them puts data into CHAOS-class TXT records where curious onlookers can search for them with the **dig** command.

We discourage tampering with these values. It is very handy to be able to query your name servers and find out what version they are running, for example, if you want to know whether your vendor is shipping a current release, or if you need to verify that you have upgraded all of your servers to the latest revision. If you must hide the version number, at least enter a string that communicates version information to your sysadmins but isn't obviously doing so. (The new NSID resource record does exactly this. The data portion of this TXT-ish record is a string value that your sysadmins set to have meaning to them but not the rest of the world.)

The hostname and server-id parameters are recent additions motivated by the use of anycast routing to duplicate instances of the root and gTLD servers.

Zone synchronization

```
notify yes | master-only | explicit | no;     [yes]
also-notify servers_ipaddrs;                  [empty]
allow-notify address-match-list;              [empty]
```

The notify and also_notify clauses apply only to master servers, and allow-notify applies only to slave servers.

Early versions of BIND synchronized zone files between master and slave servers only when the refresh timeout in the zone's SOA record had expired. These days the master **named** automatically notifies its peers whenever the corresponding zone database has been reloaded, as long as notify is set to yes. The slave servers can then rendezvous with the master to see if the file has changed, and if so, to update their copies of the zone data.

You can use notify both as a global option and as a zone-specific option. It makes the zone files converge much more quickly after you make changes. By default, every authoritative server sends updates to every other authoritative server (a system termed "splattercast" by Paul Vixie). If notify is set to master-only, this talkativeness is curbed and notifications are sent only to slave servers of zones for which this server is the master. If the notify option is set to explicit, then **named** only notifies the servers listed in the also-notify clause.

See page 614 for more information about stub zones.

named normally figures out which machines are slave servers of a zone by looking at the zone's NS records. If also-notify is specified, a set of additional servers that are not advertised with NS records can also be notified. This tweak is sometimes necessary when your site has internal servers. Don't also-notify stub servers; they are only interested in the zone's NS records and can wait for the regular update cycle.

The target of an also-notify is a list of IP addresses and, optionally, ports. For servers with multiple network interfaces, additional options specify the IP address and port to use for outgoing notifications. Localhost zones are a good place to turn off notification, since they never change. You must use the allow-notify clause if you want a name server other than the master to notify secondaries.

Query recursion

```
recursion yes | no;                               [yes]
allow-recursion { address_match_list };           [all hosts]
```

The recursion option specifies whether **named** should process queries recursively on behalf of your users. You can enable this option on an authoritative server of your zones' data, but that's frowned upon. The best-practice recommendation is to keep authoritative servers and caching servers separate.

If this name server should be recursive for your clients, set recursion to yes and include an allow-recursion clause so that **named** can distinguish queries that originate at your site from remote queries. **named** will act recursively for the former and nonrecursively for the latter. If your name server answers recursive queries for everyone, it is called an open resolver and can become a reflector for certain kinds of attacks; see RFC5358.

Cache memory use

```
recursive-clients number;                         [1000]
max-cache-size number;                            [unlimited]
```

If your server has limited memory, you may need to tweak the recursive-clients and max-cache-size options. recursive-clients controls the number of recursive lookups the server will process simultaneously; each requires about 20KiB of memory. max-cache-size limits the amount of memory the server will use for caching answers to queries. If the cache grows too large, **named** deletes records before their TTLs expire, to keep memory use under the limit.

IP port utilization

```
use-v4-udp-ports { range beg end; };     [range 1024 65535]
use-v6-udp-ports { range beg end; };     [range 1024 65535]

avoid-v4-udp-ports { port_list };        [empty]
avoid-v6-udp-ports { port_list };        [empty]

query-source v4-address [ port ]         [any]      # CAUTION, don't use port
query-source-v6 v6-address [ port ]      [any]      # CAUTION, don't use port
```

Source ports have become important in the DNS world because of a weakness in the DNS protocol discovered by Dan Kaminsky that allows DNS cache poisoning when name servers use predictable source ports and query IDs. The use- and avoid- options for UDP ports together with changes to the **named** software have mitigated this attack. Do not use the query-source address options to specify a fixed outgoing port for DNS queries or you will undo the Kaminsky protection that a large range of random ports provides.

The defaults for the use-v*-udp-ports are fine and you shouldn't need to change them. If your firewall blocks certain ports in this range (for example, port 2049 for SunRPC) then you have a small problem. When your name server sends a query and uses one of the blocked ports as its source, the firewall blocks the answer, and the name server eventually stops waiting and sends out the query again. Not fatal, but annoying to the user caught in the crossfire.

To avoid this problem, use the avoid-v*-udp-ports options to make BIND stay away from the blocked ports. Any high-numbered UDP ports blocked by your firewall should be included in the list.[19] If you update your firewall in response to some threatened attack, be sure to update the port list here, too.

The query-source options let you specify the IP address to be used on outgoing queries. For example, you might need to use a specific IP address to get through your firewall or to distinguish between internal and external views.

Queries go out from random high-numbered ports, and the answers come back to those same ports. Ergo, your firewall must be prepared to accept UDP packets on random high-numbered ports. Some sysadmins used to set a specific outgoing port number so that they can configure the firewall to recognize it and accept UDP packets only for that port. However, this configuration is no longer safe in the post-Kaminsky era.

If you use the query-source option, specify only the IP address from which you want queries to be sent; do not specify a port number.

19. Some firewalls are stateful and may be smart enough to recognize the DNS answer as being paired with the corresponding query of a second ago. Such firewalls don't need help from this option.

Use of forwarding

```
forwarders { in_addr; in_addr; ... };    [empty list]
forward only | first;                     [first]
```

Instead of having every name server perform its own external queries, you can designate one or more servers as forwarders. A run-of-the-mill server can look in its cache and in the records for which it is authoritative. If it doesn't find the answer it's looking for, it can then send the query on to a forwarder host. That way, the forwarders build up caches that benefit the entire site. The designation is implicit—nothing in the configuration file of the forwarder explicitly says "Hey, you're a forwarder."

The forwarders option lists the IP addresses of the servers you want to use as forwarders. They are queried in turn. The use of a forwarder circumvents the normal DNS procedure of starting at a root server and following the chain of referrals. Be careful not to create forwarding loops.

A forward-only server caches answers and queries forwarders, but it never queries anyone else. If the forwarders do not respond, queries fail. A forward-first server prefers to deal with forwarders, but if they do not respond, the forward-first server will complete queries itself.

Since the forwarders option has no default value, forwarding does not occur unless it has been specifically configured. You can turn on forwarding either globally or within individual zone statements.

Permissions

```
allow-query { address_match_list };          [all hosts]
allow-query-cache { address_match_list };    [all hosts]
allow-transfer { address_match_list };       [all hosts]
allow-update { address_match_list };         [none]
blackhole { address_match_list };            [empty]
```

These options specify which hosts (or networks) can query your name server or its cache, request block transfers of your zone data, or dynamically update your zones. These match lists are a low-rent form of security and are susceptible to IP address spoofing, so there's some risk in relying on them. It's probably not a big deal if someone tricks your server into answering a DNS query, but avoid the allow_update and allow_transfer clauses; use cryptographic keys instead.

The blackhole address list identifies servers that you never want to talk to; **named** does not accept queries from these servers and will never ask them for answers.

Packet sizes

```
edns-udp-size number;     [4096]
max-udp-size number;      [4096]
```

All machines on the Internet must be capable of reassembling a fragmented UDP packet of 512 bytes or fewer. Although this conservative requirement made sense in the 1980s, it is laughably small by modern standards. Modern routers and firewalls can handle much larger packets, but it only takes one bad link in the IP chain to spoil the whole path.

Since DNS uses UDP for queries and since DNS responses are often larger than 512 bytes, DNS administrators have to worry about large UDP packets being dropped. If a large reply gets fragmented and your firewall only lets the first fragment through, the receiver gets a truncated answer and retries the query with TCP. TCP is much more expensive, and busy servers at the root or TLDs don't need increased TCP traffic because of everybody's broken firewalls.

The edns-udp-size option sets the reassembly buffer size that the name server advertises through EDNS0, the extended DNS protocol. The max-udp-size option sets the maximum packet size that the server will actually send. Both sizes are in bytes. Reasonable values are in the 512–4,096 byte range.

Both values default to 4,096 bytes to help accommodate new features such as DNSSEC, IPv6, and internationalized domain names. However, some (broken) firewalls do not allow UDP packets larger than 512 bytes, and others are configured to block all but the first packet of a fragmented UDP response. The only real solution is to fix the firewalls.

To get an idea of what packet size is OK for your site, try running the command **dig rs.dns-oarc.net txt** and see what comes back; see page 652 for more details about the DNS-OARC reply-size server. If this tool shows a small size, the problem is probably at your perimeter and you will need to fix your firewalls.

As an interim solution, try setting the max-udp-size parameter to the value shown by the reply-size server. This setting makes **named** squeeze its answers into packets that might get through unfragmented. Set edns-udp-size to the same value so that you can get packets flowing in both directions. Don't forget to set the values back to 4,096 after you fix your firewalls!

Avoid these options unless you are sure you have a packet size problem, since they also limit the size of packets along paths that can handle a full 4,096 bytes.

DNSSEC control

```
dnssec-enable yes | no;                              [yes]
dnssec-validation yes | no;                          [yes]
dnssec-lookaside domain trust-anchor domain;         [".", "dlv.isc.org"]
dnssec-must-be-secure domain yes | no;               [none]
```

These options configure support for DNSSEC. See the sections starting on page 648 for a general discussion of DNSSEC and a detailed description of how to set up DNSSEC at your site.

An authoritative server needs the dnssec-enable option turned on. A recursive server needs the dnssec-enable and dnssec-validation options turned on and a trust anchor specified with a trusted-keys statement.

If there is no trust anchor for the domain in question, the software tries to find one by using the dnssec-lookaside option, which skirts the issue of the parent domains not using DNSSEC.

dnssec-enable and dnssec-validation are turned on by default, which has various implications:

- An authoritative server of a signed zone answering a query with the DNSSEC-aware bit turned on answers with the requested resource records and their signatures.
- An authoritative server of a signed zone answering a query with the DNSSEC-aware bit *not* set answers with just the requested resource records, as in the pre-DNSSEC era.
- An authoritative server of an unsigned zone answers queries with just the requested resource records; there are no signatures to include.
- A recursive server sends queries on behalf of users with the DNSSEC-aware bit set.
- A recursive server validates the signatures included with signed replies before returning data to the user.

The dnssec-lookaside option takes two domains as parameters. For example, the defaults are equivalent to the following configuration line:

```
dnssec-lookaside "." trust-anchor "dlv.isc.org";
```

This configuration tells name servers trying to establish a chain of trust to look to dlv.isc.org if they cannot get secure delegation information from the root of the DNS naming tree. Once the root and top-level domains have been signed and are served with DNSSEC, lookaside validation will not be necessary. See page 661 for a discussion of the pros and cons of DLV and its privacy implications.

The dnssec-must-be-secure option allows you to specify that you will only accept secure answers from particular domains, or, alternatively, that you don't care and that insecure answers are OK. For example, you might say yes to the domain important-stuff.mybank.com and no to the domain marketing.mybank.com. The domains in question must be covered by your trusted-keys clause or registered with the DLV server.

Statistics

```
zone-statistics yes | no             [no]
```

This option makes **named** maintain per-zone statistics as well as global statistics. See page 676 for more information about the statistics **named** compiles and how to display them.

Performance tuning

```
clients-per-query int;      [10]        # Clients waiting on the same query
max-clients-per-query int;  [100]       # Max clients before server drops 'em
datasize int;               [unlimited] # Max memory server may use
files int;                  [unlimited] # Max no. of concurrent open files
lame-ttl int;               [10min]     # Seconds to cache lame server data
max-acache-size int;        [ ]         # Cache size for additional data
max-cache-size int;         [ ]         # Max memory for cached answers
```

```
max-cache-ttl int;          [1week]    # Max TTL for caching positive data
max-journal-size int;       [ ]        # Max size of transaction journal file
max-ncache-ttl int;         [3hrs]     # Max TTL for caching negative data
tcp-clients int;            [100]      # Max simultaneous TCP clients
```

This long list of options can be used to tune **named** to run well on your hardware. We don't describe them in detail, but if you are having performance problems, these may suggest a starting point for your tuning efforts.

Whew, we are finally done with the options. Let's get on to the rest of the configuration language!

The acl statement

An access control list is just an address match list with a name:

```
acl acl_name {
    address_match_list
};
```

You can use an *acl_name* anywhere an address match list is called for.

An acl must be a top-level statement in **named.conf**, so don't try sneaking it in amid your other option declarations. **named.conf** is read in a single pass, so access control lists must be defined before they are used. Four lists are predefined:

- any – all hosts
- localnets – all hosts on the local network(s)
- localhost – the machine itself
- none – nothing

The localnets list includes all of the networks to which the host is directly attached. In other words, it's a list of the machine's network addresses modulo their netmasks.

The (TSIG) key statement

The key statement defines a "shared secret" (that is, a password) that authenticates communication between two servers; for example, between the master server and a slave for a zone transfer, or between a server and the **rndc** process that controls it. Background information about BIND's support for cryptographic authentication is given in the *Security issues* section starting on page 642. Here, we touch briefly on the mechanics of the process.

To build a key record, you specify both the cryptographic algorithm that you want to use and the shared secret, represented as a base-64-encoded string (see page 645 for details):

```
key key-id {
    algorithm string;
    secret string;
};
```

As with access control lists, the *key-id* must be defined with a key statement before it is used. To associate the key with a particular server, just include *key-id* in the keys clause of that server's server statement. The key is used both to verify requests from that server and to sign the responses to those requests.

The shared secret is sensitive information and should not be kept in a world-readable file. Use an include statement to bring it into the **named.conf** file.

The trusted-keys statement

In theory, DNSSEC parent zones authenticate their child zones' public keys, allowing signatures to be chain-authenticated all the way back to the DNS root. In practice, the root and top-level domains do not yet support DNSSEC, so some other method of validating a zone's public keys is needed.

The trusted-keys statement is a brute-force way of telling **named**, "The proper public key for zone XXX.com is YYY," thus bypassing the usual DNSSEC mechanisms for obtaining and verifying zone keys. Such a declaration is sometimes known as a "trust anchor." It's intended for use when a zone is signed but its parent zone is not.

Of course, XXX.com must be important enough to your site to merit this special treatment, and you must have some secure, out-of-band way to determine the proper value of the key. There's no magic way to get the correct key; the foreign zone's administrator has to read it to you over the telephone or send it to you in some other way that can be authenticated. An HTTPS secure web page is often used for this purpose. You must go through the whole process again whenever the key changes.

The format of the trusted-keys statement is

```
trusted-keys {
    domain flags protocol algorithm key;
    domain flags protocol algorithm key;
    ...
}
```

Each line represents the trust anchor for a particular domain. The *flags*, *protocol*, and *algorithm* are nonnegative integers. The *key* is a base-64-encoded string matching the DNSKEY resource record used to sign the zone.

DNSSEC is covered in more detail starting on page 648.

The server statement

named can potentially talk to many servers, not all of which are running current software and not all of which are even nominally sane. The server statement tells **named** about the characteristics of its remote peers. The server statement can override defaults for a particular server; it's not required unless you want to configure keys for zone transfers.

```
server ip_addr {
    bogus yes | no;                              [no]
    provide-ixfr yes | no;                       [yes]
    request-ixfr yes | no;                       [yes]
    keys { key-id; key-id; ... };                [none]
    transfer-source ip-address [port];           [closest interface]
    transfer-source-v6 ipv6-address [port];      [closest interface]
};
```

You can use a server statement to override the values of global configuration options for individual servers. Just list the options for which you want nondefault behavior. We have not shown all the server-specific options, just the ones we think you might need. See the BIND documentation for a complete list.

If you mark a server as being bogus, **named** won't send any queries its way. This directive should be reserved for servers that really are bogus. bogus differs from the global option blackhole in that it suppresses only outbound queries. By contrast, the blackhole option completely eliminates all forms of communication with the listed servers.

A BIND name server acting as master for a dynamically updated zone performs incremental zone transfers if provide-ixfr is set to yes. Likewise, a server acting as a slave requests incremental zone transfers from the master if request-ixfr is set to yes. Dynamic DNS is discussed in detail on page 640.

The keys clause identifies a key ID that has been previously defined in a key statement for use with TSIG transaction signatures (see page 645). Any requests sent to the remote server are signed with this key. Requests originating at the remote server are not required to be signed, but if they are, the signature will be verified.

The transfer-source clauses give the IPv4 or IPv6 address of the interface (and optionally, the port) that should be used as a source address (port) for zone transfer requests. This clause is only needed when the system has multiple interfaces and the remote server has specified a specific IP address in its allow-transfer clause; the addresses must match.

The masters statement

How can there be more than one master? See page 614.

The masters statement lets you name a set of one or more master servers by specifying their IP addresses and cryptographic keys. You can then use this defined name in the masters clause of zone statements instead of repeating the IP addresses and keys.

The masters facility is helpful when multiple slave or stub zones get their data from the same remote servers. If the addresses or cryptographic keys of the remote servers change, you can update the masters statement that introduces them rather than changing many different zone statements.

The syntax is

```
masters name { ip_addr [port ip_port] [key key] ; ... } ;
```

The logging statement

named is the current holder of the "most configurable logging system on Earth" award. Syslog put the prioritization of log messages into the programmer's hands and the disposition of those messages into the sysadmin's hands. But for a given priority, the sysadmin had no way to say, "I care about this message but not about that message." BIND added categories that classify log messages by type, and channels that broaden the choices for the disposition of messages. Categories are determined by the programmer, and channels by the sysadmin.

Since logging requires quite a bit of explanation and is somewhat tangential, we discuss it in the debugging section beginning on page 667.

The statistics-channels statement

The statistics-channels statement lets you connect to a running **named** with a browser to view statistics as they are accumulated. Since the stats of your name server might be sensitive, you should restrict access to this data to trusted hosts at your own site. The syntax is

```
statistics-channels {
    inet (ip-addr | *) port port# allow { address_match_list } ;
    ...
}
```

You can include multiple inet-port-allow sequences. The defaults are open, so be careful! The IP address defaults to any, the port defaults to port 80 (normal HTTP), and the allow clause defaults to letting anyone connect. To use statistics channels, you must compile **named** with **libxml2**.

The zone statement

zone statements are the heart of the **named.conf** file. They tell **named** about the zones for which it is authoritative and set the options that are appropriate for managing each zone. A zone statement is also used by a caching server to preload the root server hints —the names and addresses of the root servers, which bootstrap the DNS lookup process.

The exact format of a zone statement varies, depending on the role that **named** is to play with respect to that zone. The possible zone types are master, slave, hint, forward, stub, and delegation-only. We do not describe the stub-type zones (used by BIND only) or the delegation-only type (used to stop the use of wild card records in top-level zones to advertise a registrar's services). The following brief sections describe the other zone types.

Many of the global options covered earlier can become part of a zone statement and override the previously defined values. We have not repeated those options here, except to mention certain ones that are frequently used.

Configuring the master server for a zone

Here's the format you need for a zone of which this **named** is the master server:

```
zone "domain_name" {
    type master;
    file "path";
};
```

The *domain_name* in a zone specification must always appear in double quotes.

The zone's data is kept on disk in a human-readable (and human-editable) file. Since there is no default for the filename, you must provide a file statement when declaring a master zone. A zone file is just a collection of DNS resource records in the formats described starting on page 574.

Other server-specific attributes are also frequently specified within the zone statement. For example:

```
allow-query { address_match_list };       [any]
allow-transfer { address_match_list };    [any]
allow-update { address_match_list };      [none]
zone-statistics yes | no                  [no]
```

The access control options are not required, but it's a good idea to use them. They each take either an IP address or a TSIG encryption key. As usual, the encryption key is safer. If dynamic updates are used for this zone, the allow-update clause must be present with an address match list that limits the hosts from which updates can occur. Dynamic updates apply only to master zones; the allow-update clause cannot be used for a slave zone. Be sure that this clause includes just your own machines (e.g., DHCP servers) and not the whole Internet.[20]

The zone-statistics option makes **named** keep track of query/response statistics such as the number and percentage of responses that were referrals, that resulted in errors, or that demanded recursion. See the examples on page 676.

With all these zone-specific options (and about 40 more we have not covered), the configuration is starting to sound complicated. However, a master zone declaration consisting of nothing but a pathname to the zone file is perfectly reasonable. Here is an example, slightly modified, from the BIND documentation:

```
zone "example.com" {
    type master;
    file "forward/example.com";
    allow-query { any; };
    allow-transfer { my-slaves; };
}
```

Here, my-slaves would be an access control list you had previously defined.

20. You also need ingress filtering at your firewall; see page 932. Better yet, use TSIG for authentication.

Configuring a slave server for a zone

The zone statement for a slave is similar to that of a master:

```
zone "domain_name" {
     type slave;
     file "path";
     masters { ip_addr [port ip_port] [key keyname]; ... };   [no default]
     allow-query { address_match_list };                      [any]
};
```

Slave servers normally maintain a complete copy of their zone's database. The file statement specifies a local file in which the replicated database can be stored. Each time the server fetches a new copy of the zone, it saves the data in this file. If the server crashes and reboots, the file can then be reloaded from the local disk without being transferred across the network.

You shouldn't edit this cache file, since it's maintained by **named**. However, it can be interesting to look at if you suspect you have made an error in the master server's data file. The slave's disk file shows you how **named** has interpreted the original zone data—relative names and origin directives have all been expanded. If you see a name in the data file that looks like one of these

128.138.243.151.cs.colorado.edu.
anchor.cs.colorado.edu.cs.colorado.edu.

you can be pretty sure that you forgot a trailing dot somewhere.

The masters clause lists the IP addresses of one or more machines from which the zone database can be obtained. It can also contain the name of a masters list defined with a previous masters statement.

We have said that only one machine can be the master for a zone, so why is it possible to list more than one address? Two reasons. First, the master machine might have more than one network interface and therefore more than one IP address. It's possible for one interface to become unreachable (because of network or routing problems) while others are still accessible. Therefore, it's a good practice to list all of the master server's topologically distinct addresses.

Second, **named** really doesn't care where the zone data comes from. It can pull the database just as easily from a slave server as from the master. You could use this feature to allow a well-connected slave server to serve as a sort of backup master, since the IP addresses are tried in order until a working server is found. In theory, you can also set up a hierarchy of servers, with one master serving several second-level servers, which in turn serve many third-level servers.

Setting up the root server hints

Another form of zone statement points **named** toward a file from which it can preload its cache with the names and addresses of the root name servers.

```
zone "." {
    type hint;
    file "path";
};
```

The "hints" are a set of DNS records that list servers for the root domain. They're needed to give a recursive, caching instance of **named** a place to start searching for information about other sites' domains. Without them, **named** would only know about the domains it serves and their subdomains.

When **named** starts, it reloads the hints from one of the root servers. Ergo, you'll be fine as long as your hints file contains at least one valid, reachable root server. As a fallback, the root server hints are also compiled into **named**.

The hints file is often called **root.cache**. It contains the response you would get if you queried any root server for the name server records in the root domain. In fact, you can generate the hints file this way by running **dig**. For example:

```
$ dig @f.root-servers.net . ns > root.cache
```

Mind the dot. If f.root-servers.net is not responding, you can run the query without specifying a particular server:

```
$ dig . ns > root.cache
```

The output will be similar; however, you will be obtaining the list of root servers from the cache of a local name server, not from an authoritative source. That should be just fine—even if you have not rebooted or restarted your name server for a year or two, it has been refreshing its root server records periodically as their TTLs expire.

Setting up a forwarding zone

A zone of type forward overrides **named**'s default query path (ask the root first, then follow referrals as described on page 606) for a particular domain:

```
zone "domain_name" {
    type forward;
    forward only | first;
    forwarders { ip_addr; ip_addr; ... };
};
```

You might use a forward zone if your organization had a strategic working relationship with some other group or company and you wanted to funnel traffic directly to that company's name servers, bypassing the standard query path.

The controls statement for rndc

The controls statement limits the interaction between the running **named** process and **rndc**, the program a sysadmin can use to signal and control it. **rndc** can start and stop **named**, dump its state, put it in debug mode, etc. **rndc** is a network program, and with improper configuration it might let anyone on the Internet mess with your name server. The syntax is

```
controls {
    inet ip_addr port ip-port allow { address_match_list } keys { key_list };
}
```

The port that **rndc** uses to talk to **named** defaults to port 953 if it is not specified with the port clause.

Allowing your name server to be controlled remotely is both handy and dangerous. Strong authentication through a key entry in the allow clause is required; keys in the address match list are ignored and must be explicitly stated in the keys clause of the controls statement.

You can use the **rndc-confgen** command to generate an authentication key for use between **rndc** and **named**. There are essentially two ways to set this up: you can have both **named** and **rndc** consult the same configuration file to learn the key (**/etc/rndc.key**), or you can include the key in both the **rndc** and **named** configuration files (**/etc/rndc.conf** for **rndc** and **/etc/named.conf** for **named**). The latter option is more complicated, but it's necessary when **named** and **rndc** will be running on different computers. **rndc-confgen -a** sets up keys for localhost access.

When no controls statement is present, BIND defaults to the loopback address for the address match list and looks for the key in **/etc/rndc.key**. Because strong authentication is mandatory, the **rndc** command cannot control **named** if there is no key. This precaution may seem draconian, but consider: even if **rndc** worked only from 127.0.0.1 and this address was blocked from the outside world at your firewall, you would still be trusting all local users to not tamper with your name server. Any user could **telnet** to the control port and type "stop"—quite an effective denial of service attack.

Here is an example of the output (to standard out) from **rndc-confgen** when a 256-bit key is requested. We chose 256 bits because it fits on the page. You would normally choose a longer key and redirect the output to **/etc/rndc.conf**. The comments at the bottom of the output show the lines you need to add to **named.conf** to make **named** and **rndc** play together.

```
$ ./rndc-confgen -b 256
# Start of rndc.conf
key "rndc-key" {
    algorithm hmac-md5;
    secret "orZuz5amkUnEp52zlHxD6cd5hACldOGsG/elP/dv2IY=";
};

options {
    default-key "rndc-key";
    default-server 127.0.0.1;
    default-port 953;
};
# End of rndc.conf
```

```
# Use with the following in named.conf, adjusting the allow list as needed:
# key "rndc-key" {
#       algorithm hmac-md5;
#       secret "orZuz5amkUnEp52zlHxD6cd5hACldOGsG/elP/dv2IY=";
# };
#
# controls {
#       inet 127.0.0.1 port 953
#     allow { 127.0.0.1; } keys { "rndc-key"; };
# };
# End of named.conf
```

Split DNS and the view statement

Many sites want the internal view of their network to be different from the view seen from the Internet. For example, you might reveal all of a zone's hosts to internal users but restrict the external view to a few well-known servers. Or, you might expose the same set of hosts in both views but supply additional (or different) records to internal users. For example, the MX records for mail routing might point to a single mail hub machine from outside the domain but point to individual workstations from the perspective of internal users.

See page 462 for more information about private address spaces.

A split DNS configuration is especially useful for sites that use RFC1918 private IP addresses on their internal networks. For example, a query for the hostname associated with IP address 10.0.0.1 can never be answered by the global DNS system, but it is meaningful within the context of the local network. Of the queries arriving at the root name servers, 4%–5% are either *from* an IP address in one of the private address ranges or *about* one of these addresses. Neither can be answered; both are the result of misconfiguration, either of BIND's split DNS or Microsoft's "domains."

The view statement packages up a couple of access lists that control which clients see which view, some options that apply to all the zones in the view, and finally, the zones themselves. The syntax is

```
view view-name {
     match-clients { address_match_list } ;        [any]
     match-destinations { address_match_list } ;  [any]
     match-recursive-only yes | no;                [no]
     view_option; ...
     zone_statement; ...
} ;
```

Views have always had a match-clients clause that filters on the source IP address in the query packet and is typically used to serve internal and external views of a site's DNS data. For finer control, you can now also filter on the query destination address and can require recursive queries. The match-destinations clause looks at the destination address in the query packet and is useful on multihomed machines when you want to serve different DNS data depending on the interface on which the query arrived. The match-recursive-only clause requires queries to be recursive as well as to originate at a permitted client. Iterative queries let you see what is in a site's cache; this option prevents it.

Views are processed in order, so put the most restrictive views first. Zones in different views can have the same names but take their data from different files. Views are an all-or-nothing proposition; if you use them, all zone statements in your **named.conf** file must appear in the context of a view.

Here is an example from the BIND 9 documentation. The two views define the same zone, but with different data.

```
view "internal" {
    match-clients { our_nets; };          // Only internal networks
    recursion yes;                        // Internal clients only
    zone "example.com" {                  // Complete view of zone
        type master;
        file "example-internal.db";
    };
};

view "external" {
    match-clients { any; };               // Allow all queries
    recursion no;                         // But no recursion
    zone "example.com" {                  // Only "public" hosts
        type master;
        file "example-external.db";
    }
};
```

If the order of the views were reversed, no one would ever see the internal view. Internal hosts would match the any value in the match-clients clause of the external view before they reached the internal view.

Our second DNS configuration example starting on page 620 provides an additional example of views.

17.10 BIND CONFIGURATION EXAMPLES

Now that we have explored the wonders of **named.conf**, let's look at some complete configuration examples. In the following sections, we discuss samples from several contexts:

- The localhost zone
- A small security company that uses split DNS
- The experts: isc.org, the Internet Systems Consortium

The localhost zone

The address 127.0.0.1 refers to a host itself and should be mapped to the name "localhost.".[21] Some sites map the address to "localhost.*localdomain*." and some do both. The corresponding IPv6 address is ::1.

If you forget to configure the localhost zone, your site may end up querying the root servers for localhost information. The root servers receive so many of these queries that the operators are considering adding a generic mapping between localhost and 127.0.0.1 at the root level. In measurements at the K root server in Europe in January 2010 (k.root-servers.org/statistics), "local" was the fourth most popular domain queried, just behind com, arpa, and net. That's a lot of useless queries (1,500/second) for a busy name server. Other unusual names in the popular "bogus TLD" category are lan, home, localdomain, and domain.

The forward mapping for the name localhost can be defined in the forward zone file for the domain (with an appropriate $ORIGIN statement) or in its own file. Each server, even a caching server, is usually the master for its own reverse localhost domain.

Here are the lines in **named.conf** that configure localhost:

```
zone "localhost" {                  // localhost forward zone
    type master;
    file "localhost";
    allow-update { none; };
};

zone "0.0.127.in-addr.arpa" {       // localhost reverse zone
    type master;
    file "127.0.0";
    allow-update { none; };
};
```

The corresponding forward zone file, **localhost**, contains

```
$TTL 30d
; localhost.
@            IN   SOA   localhost. postmaster.localhost. (
                          1998050801    ;serial
                          3600          ;refresh
                          1800          ;retry
                          604800        ;expiration
                          3600 )        ;minimum

                  NS    localhost.
                  A     127.0.0.1
```

21. Actually, the whole class A network 127/8 refers to localhost, but most folks just use 127.0.0.1.

and the reverse file, **127.0.0**:

```
$TTL 30d
; 0.0.127.in-addr.arpa
@            IN   SOA   localhost. postmaster.localhost. (
                          1998050801   ;serial
                          3600         ;refresh
                          1800         ;retry
                          604800       ;expiration
                          3600 )       ;minimum

                  NS    localhost.
1                 PTR   localhost.
```

The mapping for the localhost address (127.0.0.1) never changes, so the timeouts can be large. Note the serial number, which encodes the date; the file was last changed in 1998. Also note that only the master name server is listed for the localhost domain. The meaning of @ here is "0.0.127.in-addr.arpa.".

A small security company

Our first real example is for a small company that specializes in security consulting. They run BIND 9 on a recent version of Red Hat Enterprise Linux and use views to implement a split DNS system in which internal and external users see different host data. They also use private address space internally; queries about those addresses should never escape to the Internet to clutter up the global DNS system. Here is their **named.conf** file, reformatted and commented a bit:

```
options {
    directory "/var/domain";
    version "root@atrust.com";
    allow-transfer {82.165.230.84; 71.33.249.193; 127.0.0.1; };
    listen-on { 192.168.2.10; 192.168.2.1; 127.0.0.1; 192.168.2.12; };
};

include "atrust.key";                     // Defn of atkey in mode 600 file

controls {
    inet 127.0.0.1 allow { 127.0.0.1; } keys { atkey; };
};

view "internal" {

    match-clients { 192.168.0.0/16; 206.168.198.192/28; 172.29.0.0/24; };
    recursion yes;

    include "infrastructure.zones";      // Root hints, localhost forw + rev

    zone "atrust.com" {                  // Internal forward zone
        type master;
        file "internal/atrust.com";
    };
```

```
    zone "1.168.192.in-addr.arpa" {        // Internal reverse zone
        type master;
        file "internal/192.168.1.rev";
        allow-update { none; };
    };
    ...                                    // Lots of zones omitted
    include "internal/trademark.zones"; // atrust.net, atrust.org, etc. slaves

}; // End of internal view

view "world" {                             // External view

    match-clients { any; };
    recursion no;

    zone "atrust.com" {                    // External forward zone
        type master;
        file "world/atrust.com";
        allow-update { none; };
    };
    zone "189.173.63.in-addr.arpa" {       // External reverse zone
        type master;
        file "world/63.173.189.rev";
        allow-update { none; };
    };
    include "world/trademark.zones";       // atrust.net, atrust.org, etc. masters
    zone "admin.com" {                     // Master zones only in world view
        type master;
        file "world/admin.com";
        allow-update { none; };
    };
    ...                                    // Lots of master+slave zones omitted

}; // End of external view
```

The file **atrust.key** defines the key named atkey:

```
key "atkey" {
    algorithm hmac-md5;
    secret "shared secret key goes here";
};
```

The file **infrastructure.zones** contains the root hints and localhost files, and **trademark.zones** includes variations on the name atrust.com, both in different top-level domains (net, org, us, info, etc.) and with different spellings (applied-trust.com, etc.).

Zones are organized by view (internal or world) and type (master or slave), and the naming convention for zone data files reflects this scheme. This server is recursive for the internal view, which includes all local hosts, including many that use private addressing. The server is not recursive for the external view, which contains only selected hosts at atrust.com and the external zones for which they provide either master or slave DNS service.

Snippets of the files **internal/atrust.com** and **world/atrust.com** are shown below. First, the **internal** file:

```
; atrust.com - internal file

$TTL 86400
$ORIGIN atrust.com.
@               3600  SOA   ns1.atrust.com. trent.atrust.com. (
                              2010032900 10800 1200 3600000 3600 )
                3600  NS    NS1.atrust.com.
                3600  NS    NS2.atrust.com.
                3600  MX    10 mailserver.atrust.com.
                3600  A     66.77.122.161

ns1                   A     192.168.2.11
ns2                   A     66.77.122.161
www                   A     66.77.122.161
mailserver            A     192.168.2.11
exchange              A     192.168.2.100
secure                A     66.77.122.161
...
```

RFC1918 private addresses are used. Also, note that rather than use CNAMEs to assign nicknames to a host, this site uses multiple A records. This scheme is faster because encountering a CNAME results in an additional query. PTR records should point to only one of the multiple names that are mapped to the same IP address. This site also delegates subdomains for their DHCP networks, our book writing lab, and their Microsoft infrastructure (not shown).

Here is the external view of that same domain from the file **world/atrust.com**:

```
; atrust.com - external file

$TTL 57600
$ORIGIN atrust.com.
@                     SOA   ns1.atrust.com. trent.atrust.com. (
                              2010030400 10800 1200 3600000 3600 )
                      NS    NS1.atrust.com.
                      NS    NS2.atrust.com.
                      MX    10 mailserver.atrust.com.
                      A     66.77.122.161
ns1.atrust.com.       A     206.168.198.209
ns2.atrust.com.       A     66.77.122.161
www                   A     66.77.122.161
mailserver            A     206.168.198.209
secure                A     66.77.122.161

; reverse maps
exterior1             A     206.168.198.209
209.198.168.206       PTR   exterior1.atrust.com.
exterior2             A     206.168.198.213
213.198.168.206       PTR   exterior2.atrust.com.
...
```

As in the internal view, nicknames are implemented with A records. Very few hosts are actually visible in the external world view, although that's not immediately apparent from these truncated excerpts. Note that machines that appear in both views (for example, ns1.atrust.com) have RFC1918 private addresses internally but real addresses externally.

The TTL in these zone files is set to 16 hours (57,600 seconds). For internal zones, the TTL is one day (86,400 seconds). Most individual records in zone files are not assigned an explicit TTL value.

The bizarre PTR records at the end of the external file allow atrust.com's ISP to delegate the reverse mapping of a very small piece of address space. CNAME records at the ISP's site enable this variation of the CNAME hack to work; see page 585 for more information.

The Internet Systems Consortium, isc.org

ISC is the author and maintainer of BIND as well as the operator of the F root name server. ISC also runs a TLD server that serves many top-level domains. That's why we call them the experts!

Below are snippets from their configuration files. Notice that they are using both IPv4 and IPv6. They also use TSIG encryption to authenticate between master and slave servers for zone transfers. The transfer-source options ensure that the source IP addresses for outgoing zone transfer requests conform to the specifications in the allow-transfers statements on the master servers.

The **named.conf** file:

```
// isc.org TLD name server

options {
    directory "/var/named";
    datasize 1000M;
    listen-on { 204.152.184.64; };
    listen-on-v6 { 2001:4f8:0:2::13; };
    recursion no;
    transfer-source 204.152.184.64;
    transfer-source-v6 2001:4f8:0:2::13;
};

// rndc key
key rndc_key {
    algorithm hmac-md5;
    secret "<secret>";
};

// TSIG key for name server ns-ext
key ns-ext {
    algorithm hmac-md5;
    secret "<secret>";
};
```

```
server 204.152.188.234 { keys { ns-ext; }; };

controls {
    inet 204.152.184.64 allow { any; } keys { rndc_key; };
};

include "inf/named.zones";          // Root, localhost, 127.0.0.1, ::1
include "master.zones";             // Zones we master
include "slave.zones";              // Lots of slaves
```

These include statements keep the **named.conf** file short and tidy. If you serve lots of zones, consider breaking up your configuration into bite-sized pieces like this. More importantly, set up your filesystem hierarchy so that you don't have a directory with a thousand zone files in it. Modern filesystems handle large directories efficiently, but they can be a management hassle.

Here's more from the file **master.zones**:

```
zone "isc.org" {
    type master;
    file "master/isc.org";
    allow-update { none; };
    allow-transfer { none; };
};

zone "sfo2.isc.org" {
    type master;
    file "master/sfo2.isc.org";
    allow-update { none; };
    allow-transfer { none; };
};

// Lots of zones truncated
```

And from **slaves.zones**:

```
zone "vix.com" {
    type slave;
    file "secondary/vix.com";
    masters { 204.152.188.234; };
};

zone "cix.net" {
    type slave;
    file "secondary/cix.net";
    masters { 204.152.188.234; };
};
```

The allow-transfer clause set to none in the **master.zones** file implies that ISC is using multiple master servers—someone has to implement zone transfers to the slave servers.

17.11 THE NSD/UNBOUND SOFTWARE

With BIND configuration out of the way, we now introduce an alternative DNS server implementation that offers some nice features along with speedy performance. NSD, the Name Server Daemon, was developed by NLnet Labs in 2003. The original intention of the project was to develop an authoritative server implementation independent of BIND that could be used on root servers, thus making the root zone more robust through software diversity. Three root servers and several top-level domains now use NSD, but you don't have to be a root server or TLD to benefit from NSD's robustness, speed, and simplicity.

Two programs form the core of the NSD software suite: **zonec**, a zone file precompiler that converts text-format DNS zone files into databases; and **nsd**, the name server daemon itself. NSD precomputes and indexes all possible answers to the valid queries it might receive, so unlike BIND, which creates its answers on the fly, NSD has the answers in an outgoing packet in a single memory copy, making it blindingly fast.

Unbound is a recursive DNS server that is complementary to NSD. It was developed in C by NLnet Labs from a Java implementation by VeriSign, Nominet, Kirei, and EP.NET. Together, NSD and Unbound provide flexible, fast, secure DNS service appropriate for most sites. The NLnet Labs components are not as mature as BIND and do not have as many bells and whistles, but they are fine solutions for most sites.

ldns, a library of routines that make it easier to write DNS software tools, is also available for use with the NSD and Unbound distributions. It includes a directory of examples: several tools aimed primarily at DNSSEC, a DNSSEC signer tool, and **drill**, a debugging tool similar to BIND's **dig**. You can download them all from nlnetlabs.nl. NLnet Labs has also built a tool called Autotrust that does RFC5011 key rollover and key management. It is being integrated into Unbound; however, we do not cover it here.

The DNSSEC code in NSD/Unbound is more robust and better tested than that in BIND. It's also faster. For example, Unbound is about five times faster than BIND at verifying DNSSEC signatures. BIND still has an edge in some areas, though, notably in documentation and in extra features. For a really robust DNS regime, run both!

Installing and configuring NSD

First, create a user called nsd on the system where the **nsd** name server will run. Then log in as nsd, download the NSD/Unbound packages (currently, three of them: NSD, Unbound, and the separate **ldns**), and unpack. To install **nsd**, follow the directions in the **doc/README** file in the distribution, basically:

```
$ ./configure
$ make
$ sudo make install
```

Table 17.10 shows where NSD installs or expects things to be by default.

Table 17.10 NSD installation directories

Item	Directory
Binaries	**/usr/local/sbin**
Sample config file	**/etc/nsd**
Man pages	**/usr/local/share**
Text zone files	**/etc/nsd**
Compiled zone files	**/var/db/nsd**
PID file	**/var/run**

It seems a bit rude for NSD to put the zone files beneath **/etc**, especially if your zones are large. Consider moving the files to somewhere in **/usr/local** or **/var**. You can use **configure** to change things if you don't like NSD's choices; the makefile is quite readable. The output of **configure** goes to the file **config.log** in the install directory, so you can sort through it if there is a problem.

The NSD suite installs seven programs:

- **nsd** – the name server daemon
- **nsdc** – a script that controls **nsd** by sending it signals
- **zonec** – converts text zone files to database files
- **nsd-notify** – sends notification messages (deprecated)
- **nsd-xfer** – receives zone transfers (deprecated)
- **nsd-checkconf** – checks the syntax of **nsd.conf**
- **nsd-patch** – reflects incremental database updates back to zone files

Fundamental differences from BIND

If you are used to BIND, a few things in NSD will seem strange at first. For example, there is no root hints file and no need to include localhost zones. NSD also has no support for views, so if your site publishes different versions of the DNS data inside and outside your organization, you will have to stick with BIND or use multiple instances of **nsd**. Dynamic updates are also unsupported. Since **nsd** is an authoritative-only server, many of BIND's bells and whistles do not apply.

BIND reads zone files and keeps them in memory; NSD precompiles zone files into a database format and uses both memory and disk for the database.

nsd's configuration language is simpler than BIND's. There are no semicolons to forget, no braces to group things, and only three top-level statements: server, zone, and key. Comments are introduced with the # sign. Options under each of the three statements have the form

```
attribute: value
```

There can be only one server statement. It specifies global options. zone statements list zone-specific options, and key statements define cryptographic keys, which are required for communication between master and slave servers and for controlling **nsd**. Whitespace separates attributes from values. Values can be quoted, but they don't have to be.

Like BIND, **nsd** generalizes IP addresses, but in a slightly different manner than BIND's address match list construct. It is called an *ip-spec* and can be

- A plain IP address (IPv4 or IPv6)
- A subnet in CIDR notation, e.g., 1.2.3.0/24
- A subnet with an explicit mask, e.g., 1.2.3.4&255.255.255.0
- A range of IP addresses such as 1.2.3.4-1.2.3.25

Spaces are not allowed in any of these forms.

Another fundamental difference is the use of key values for authentication of zone transfers and notification messages. In BIND, a key is associated with an IP address, and communication to and from that address is signed and validated with that key. In NSD, the key is finer grained, so **nsd** could have one key for notifications, a different key for sending a zone transfer, and yet a third key for receiving that transfer. Useful? Well…

The semantics of notify in **nsd** are analogous to BIND's notify explicit clause: only servers explicitly listed are notified. (By default, BIND notifies all name servers listed in the zone file for the domain in question.)

The NSD documentation refers to master and slave zones, whereas the BIND documentation uses those adjectives to refer to servers. These are basically the same thing. An "instance" of a name server is the master server or slave server for a specific zone.

nsd favors sensible default behavior over configurability. For example, DNSSEC is turned on by default for signed zones and off for unsigned zones. By default, **nsd** listens on both IPv4 and IPv6 sockets. Logging is either on or off rather than having the infinite shades and gradations of the BIND paradigm. **nsd** uses TSIG for communication among servers (zone transfers, notifications, etc.).

The file **doc/NSD-FOR-BIND-USERS** gives a quick description of the differences between BIND and NSD and includes a sample config file. The man page for the configuration file, **nsd.conf**, and the **doc/README** file also have examples, but sadly there is no consistency between them.[22]

NSD configuration example

We have taken some editorial license and merged the three samples from the distribution and added our own editorial commentary to give you a feel for NSD configuration before covering the various options in more detail. Here we have

22. To display the man pages without installing them, do: **groff -man -T ascii** *man-page-filename* **| less**.

configured **nsd** to be the master server for the domain atrust.com and a slave server for the domain admin.com.

```
server:
    username: nsd                       # User nsd should run as after chroot
    database: /var/db/nsd/nsd.db        # Precompiled zone database file
    logfile: /var/log/nsd.log           # Log file, default is to stderr + syslog
    pidfile: /var/run/nsd.pid           # nsd process id
key:
    name: tsig.atrust.com.              # Key for atrust..com zone transfers
    algorithm: hmac-md5
    secret: "base64 secret goes here"
zone:
    name: atrust.com                          # Name of the zone
    zonefile: /var/nsd/primary/atrust.com
    provide-xfr: 1.2.3.4 tsig.atrust.com.     # Address of atrust.com slave
    notify: 1.2.3.4 tsig.atrust.com           # And key for notify or xfrs.
    provide-xfr: 1.2.30.40 tsig.atrust.com.   # Address of another slave
    notify: 1.2.30.40 tsig.atrust.com         # And key for notify or xfrs.
key:
    name: tsig.admin.com.                     # Key to get admin.com slave data
    algorithm: hmac-md5
    secret: "base64 secret goes here"
zone:
    name: admin.com                           # Zone we are a slave for
    zonefile: "/var/nsd/secondary/admin.com.signed"
    allow-notify: 5.6.7.8 NOKEY               # Its master server
    request-xfr: 5.6.7.8 tsig.admin.com.      # And key for xfrs
```

This sample **nsd.conf** file configures the server to be the master for atrust.com and to notify and provide zone transfers to two slave servers, one at IP address 1.2.3.4 and the other at IP address 1.2.30.40. The server will use the TSIG key called tsig.atrust.com to authenticate both slave servers for transfers and notifications. (You could, and probably should, use a separate key for each slave server.)

This server is also a slave server for the signed zone admin.com, whose master server is at IP address 5.6.7.8. We can receive notifications of zone data changes without a key, but must use the tsig.admin.com key to receive zone transfers. Master zones have provide-xfr clauses and slave zones have a request-xfr clause.

After you've installed **nsd** and set up your configuration file, use **nsd-checkconf** to check the config file's syntax. Its error reports are a bit terse; for example, "error: syntax error" and a line number. After fixing **nsd-checkconf**'s gripes, run it again and repeat the process until **nsd-checkconf** reports no more errors.

NSD key definitions

A key clause defines a named key to be used in subsequent access control options. Each key has three attributes: a name, an algorithm, and a shared secret (aka password). Consider putting key definitions, or at least their secret portions, into files that have restricted permissions. You can use the include statement to import them into **nsd.conf**—just put include: *filename* wherever you want the text from *filename* to be inserted.

Here is the syntax of the key statement:

Key definitions

```
name: key-name
algorithm: alg
secret: password-base-64
```

There can be multiple key statements.

The name field identifies the key. Choose names that reflect the zone and the servers involved in the secure communication. The algorithm can be hmac-md5, hmac-sha1, or hmac-sha256. You can use the **ldns-keygen** command to generate TSIG keys, even though it is really designed for generating DNSSEC private/public key pairs. You can run **ldns-keygen -a list** to get a list of algorithms.

Here's an example using hmac-sha1:

```
$ ldns-keygen -a hmac-sha1 example.com
```

This command produces a file called **Kexample.com.+158+*12345*.key** that contains the TSIG key. Just cut and paste the secret part into your key specification. The **158** in the filename stands for the hmac-sha1 algorithm. hmac-md5 is **157**, and hmac-sha256 is **159**. The number *12345* is just a placeholder for a random 5-digit key tag. If you have multiple keys, this tag helps you keep them straight.

NSD global configuration options

We divide NSD's options into two groups: global options for the server, and zone-specific options that can be applied to any zones served by a given instance of **nsd**. Some options can be overridden by command-line flags as **nsd** is started.

Server options generally have sensible defaults and require attention only if your directory structure is nonstandard or you want to do something fancy. Below, we show default values in square brackets. As with the BIND options, we have added margin notes describing each group of options to make navigation easier.

Include a file

```
include: filename
```

The include: directive can appear anywhere in the configuration file. The specified *filename* is read into the config file, and its contents replace the directive.

IP addresses and port

```
ip-address: ip_addresses          [all IP addresses]
ip4-only: yes | no                [no]
ip6-only: yes | no                [no]
port: portnum                     [53]
```

By default, NSD binds to port 53 on all network interfaces, both IPv4 and IPv6. If you list the addresses with an ip-address: clause, **nsd** bypasses the kernel's routing tables and ensures that a query to one IP address does not receive its answer from a different IP address; many resolvers require this. If your machine has only one network interface, this option is not useful. The ip4-only and ip6-only options limit **nsd** to a particular protocol, and port sets the network port on which to listen for incoming queries.

You should not normally need any of these options, as the defaults are fine.

ID variables

```
identity: string                [hostname]
hide-version: yes | no          [no]
```

This pair of options controls whether **nsd** tells the truth about its version and hostname when queried for the CHAOS class names id.server and version.server. As explained on page 598, we recommend not tampering with these values.

Logging, statistics

```
logfile: filename               [stderr and syslog]
verbosity: level                [0]
debug-mode: yes | no            [no]
statistics: #secs               [0] # no statistics
```

Logging is, by default, to standard error and to syslog (facility daemon), with the amount of logging determined by the verbosity option. The range of possible values is 0–5; higher numbers mean that more data should be logged. The logfile parameter diverts log messages to a file instead sending them to syslog.

If you specify debug-mode, **nsd** does not fork extra copies of itself and stays attached to your terminal so that you can see messages sent to standard error.

If you want to keep statistics, set *#secs* to the number of seconds between dumps. Statistics are like other log messages, so they go to the log file or to syslog if no log file has been specified. It's best to watch the stats output for a bit to make sure you have chosen a sensible dump interval and are not filling your disks with information that no one will ever look at.

Filenames

```
database: filename     [/var/db/nsd/nsd.db]
difffile: filename     [/var/db/nsd/ixfr.db]
xfrdfile: filename     [/var/db/nsd/xfrd.state]
pid-file: filename     [OS-specific, usually /var/run/nsd.pid]
zonesdir: directory    [/etc/nsd]
```

Compiled zone files and zone transfer info default to living in **/var/db/nsd**; it's unlikely that you will need to change this. The PID file should go where your operating system puts other PID files, usually in **/var/run**. By default, human-editable zone files go in **/etc/nsd**, which feels like a bad choice. Consider moving them beneath **/var**, perhaps to **/var/nsd/zones**.

Tuning

```
tcp-count: int              [10]
server-count: int           [1]
xfrd-reload-timeout: #sec   [10]
```

tcp-count limits the number of concurrent TCP connections the server can use for zone transfers. You'll know you've exceeded the limit when you see "xfrd: max number of TCP connections (10) reached" in the log. If that happens frequently, you should increase this limit.

The server-count option specifies the number of instances of **nsd** to start. For multi-CPU machines, you may want to increase this value. xfrd-reload-timeout throttles reloads after zone transfers by waiting at least the specified number of seconds since the last reload before reloading again.

Security

```
username: login          [nsd]
chroot: directory        [none]
```

nsd must start running as root in order to open a privileged socket (port 53), but it can then drop back to the privileges of a normal user as long as all the files it needs are owned by that user. Hence, the dedicated nsd account.

For added security, you can also run **nsd** in a **chroot**ed jail as long as the zone files, database file, **xfrdfile**, **difffile**, PID file, and syslog socket (or log file) are accessible through the jail directory.

NSD zone-specific configuration options

Unlike global options, zone-specific options do generally require some configuration, especially the access control lists.

Zone definitions

```
name: zonename
zonefile: filename
```

A zone is defined by a zone name and a file of resource records.

Master ACLs

```
notify: ip-address ( key-name | NOKEY )23
provide-xfr: ip-spec ( key-name | NOKEY | BLOCKED )23
```

The master server for a zone notifies its slaves of updates to the zone. Then, when requested by the slaves, it initiates zone transfers to transmit the modified data. Therefore, a zone for which this server is the master must have the notify and provide-xfr access lists specified. The values of these options will normally be the same. Notification messages are signed with the listed *key-name* unless you specify the NOKEY option.

Keep in mind that unlike **named**, **nsd** does not automatically notify the slave servers of a zone; you must list them explicitly in the notify and provide-xfr clauses. There may be multiple instances of these statements.

Slave ACLs

```
allow-notify: ip-spec ( key-name | NOKEY | BLOCKED )23
request-xfr: [ AXFR | UDP ] ip-address ( key-name | NOKEY )23
```

A slave server for a zone must explicitly allow the master to send notification messages. Any messages received from servers that are not listed in the allow-notify list (or that are tagged as BLOCKED) are ignored.

The request-xfr clause makes the slave server request a zone transfer from the master server at the listed *ip-address* using the specified *key-name*. If you include the AXFR argument, only AXFR transfers (that is, transfers of the entire zone, as

23. The parentheses are here to show grouping; do not include them in an actual value.

opposed to incremental updates) will be requested. The UDP argument specifies that the request for a zone transfer be sent with UDP transport rather than the default TCP. It's best just to use TCP.

Source IP address

```
outgoing-interface: ip-spec
```

This list controls the IP address used by a slave server to request a zone transfer or by a master to send notifications. The addresses must match; that is, the access control clause in the master's zone configuration must use the same address as the corresponding clause in the slave's zone configuration.

Running nsd

Once you have configured **nsd**, run the **nsd-checkconf** program to be sure there are no syntax errors in your **nsd.conf** file. Then put your zone files in the right directory (the one specified in **nsd.conf**) and use **nsdc**, the NSD control script, to compile them into database files. Finally start the name server with **nsdc**.

```
$ sudo nsdc rebuild
$ sudo nsdc start
```

Test the name server with **dig** or **drill**, and if you're happy with the results, add **nsdc start** to your operating system's startup sequence and **nsdc stop** to its shutdown sequence. You can also set up a crontab job to run **nscd patch** once a day to update the text zone files from the database files.

Installing and configuring Unbound

Unbound is a recursive, caching, validating DNS name server from the same folks (NLnet Labs) that produce NSD. It was originally developed for UNIX and Linux, but it's now is available for Windows, too.

To install, create a new user called "unbound", log in as this user, and download the distribution from unbound.net. Unbound requires the **ldns** and OpenSSL libraries and can use the **libevent** libraries (monkey.org/~provos/libevent) as well if they are available. Like NSD, Unbound initially runs as root, but then falls back to running under its dedicated user account.

To build:

```
$ ./configure
$ make
$ sudo make install
```

Unbound also comes with an extensive test suite that you can run with **make test**. The distribution installs the following binaries:

- **unbound** – the recursive name server
- **unbound-checkconf** – syntax checker of the **unbound.conf** file
- **unbound-control**, **unbound-control-setup** – secure remote control
- **unbound-host** – simple query tool

unbound-host is not as verbose as **dig** or **drill**, but it's handy for command-line validation when DNSSEC is tested.

Table 17.11 shows the locations of Unbound components.

Table 17.11 Unbound installation directories

Item	Directory
Binaries	**/usr/local/sbin**
Libraries	**/usr/local/lib**
Configuration file	**/usr/local/etc/unbound/unbound.conf**
Man pages	**/usr/local/share**
Secure jail	**/usr/local/etc/unbound**
PID file	**/usr/local/etc/unbound**

unbound's configuration file, **unbound.conf**, is similar to that of **nsd**. The basic syntax is

```
attribute: value
```

with comments initiated by # and lasting until the end of the line. You can run **unbound-checkconf** to check the validity of your config file.

Here is a small example of an **unbound.conf** file, adapted from the man page with saner paths and some additional comments:

```
server:
    directory: "/var/unbound/etc"
    username: unbound
    chroot: "/var/unbound"
    pidfile: "/var/run/unbound.pid"

root-hints: "root.cache"
    interface: 0.0.0.0                  # Listen on all IPv4 interfaces
    interface: ::0                      # And on all IPv6 interfaces
    access-control: 10.0.0.0/8 allow    # Local private networks
    access-control: 2001:DB8::/64 allow # Local IPv6 networks
```

This example listens on all interfaces and allows queries from the local IPv6 networks and from the unrouted private net 10. It logs to syslog with facility daemon (the default) and runs in a **chroot**ed jail as user unbound.

With recursion come lots of options; the **unbound** option list approaches half the size (70+) of BIND's (150+). Our coverage is selective. See the man page and the how-to documents at unbound.net for the full story.

unbound's config language has four top-level clauses: server, remote-control, stub-zone, and forward-zone.[24] Global options appear beneath the server clause. Here are a few of the more important ones.

24. It also has hooks for the Python scripting language.

Locations

```
directory: directory            [/usr/local/etc/unbound]
pidfile: filename               [/usr/local/etc/unbound/unbound.pid]
root-hints: filename            [none]
```

The directory option sets the server's working directory. **unbound** defaults to a directory under **/usr/local/etc**, but many sites prefer **/var**. The location of the PID file defaults to **unbound**'s working directory, but it also works fine in more traditional places such as **/var/run**.

Root hints are built into **unbound**'s code, so the hints file is not required. However, you can provide one if you like since the addresses in the code may eventually become out of date. Use **dig . ns** to obtain a fresh copy occasionally, or if you are really paranoid, try **dig @a.root-servers.net . ns** for an authoritative copy.

Logging

```
use-syslog: yes | no            [yes]
logfile: filename               [none]
log-time-ascii: yes | no        [no]
verbosity: level                [1]
```

Logging information can go either to syslog or to a file. Choose between them with the use-syslog and logfile options. If you want normal time instead of UNIX time (seconds since 1/1/1970) in log messages, turn on the log-time-ascii option. The verbosity determines the amount of logging; see page 673 for details.

Statistics

```
statistics-interval: seconds      [0, i.e., disabled]
statistics-cumulative: yes | no   [no]
extended-statistics: yes | no     [no]
```

Statistics are turned off by default because they slow down the name server. If you turn them on by setting the statistics-interval option to a nonzero number of seconds, statistics will be written to the log file (or to syslog) at the specified interval. By default, the statistics counters are reset to 0 each time they are written out; use the statistics-cumulative option to make them accumulate over time.

Setting extended-statistics to yes generates more data that you can dump using **unbound-control**.

See page 886 for more information about Cacti and RRDtool.

The distribution's **contrib** directory contains plug-ins that connect Cacti or Munin to the running name server and that graph real-time statistics with RRDtool. See the statistics how-to at unbound.net for details.

Query access

```
access-control: netblock action         [allow only localhost]
```

The access-control option is the key to configuring **unbound** to be a recursive name server for your own users and not for the rest of the world. Use multiple access-control lines to allow multiple networks. The *action* parameter can take on four values:

- deny – blocks all queries from the specified network or host
- refuse – blocks queries and sends a REFUSED message back
- allow – answers queries from clients requesting recursion
- allow-snoop – answers queries from recursive and iterative clients

The refuse action is more conformant to the DNS specification than deny because clients assume that unanswered queries were lost on the network rather than having been administratively dropped for policy reasons. The allow action is the one to use for normal DNS clients.

allow-snoop answers iterative queries as well as recursive queries. You can use it to investigate the contents of the server's cache, since an iterative query succeeds only if the answer is already in-cache. allow snoop can also be exploited for unwholesome purposes, so limit this action to your sysadmins' hosts.

Security

```
chroot: directory                [/usr/local/etc/unbound]
username: name                   [unbound]
```

The username option specifies the unprivileged user as whom **unbound** should run once it has completed its startup housekeeping.

The chroot directive tells **unbound** to run in a **chroot**ed jail. You will have to jump through some hoops to make sure that everything **unbound** needs is available from the jail directory, but recent versions of the code make this pretty easy.

The code is smart about mapping global pathnames into the **chroot**ed world. Most paths can be specified as absolute global paths, as absolute paths within the jail directory, or as paths relative to the working directory. **unbound** performs the appropriate mapping when necessary.

A couple of fine points about running **unbound** in jail: Reading the config file of course predates the **chroot**, so the config file specified on **unbound**'s command line should be a global path. The PID file, the unbound-control key files, and the syslog socket can all remain outside the jail directory because they are opened before **unbound** performs its **chroot**.

unbound reads **/dev/random** before **chroot**ing, but it's still a good idea to make **/dev/random** available after the **chroot**; **unbound** may need to return to it later to obtain more random data. If **unbound** cannot reach **/dev/random**, it uses a default source of randomness and logs a warning message.

Under Linux, you can make **/dev/random** available in the jail with the following incantation (which assumes that **/var/unbound** is your jail directory):

```
linux$ sudo mount --bind -n /dev/random /var/unbound/dev/random
```

ID variables

The following options control whether **unbound** tells the truth about its version and hostname when queried for the CHAOS names id.server and version.server:

```
hide-identity: yes | no          [no]
identity: string                 [hostname]
hide-version: yes | no           [no]
version: string                  [name server version]
```

As explained on page 598, we recommend not tampering with these values.

IP addresses

```
interface: ip-address                    [localhost]
outgoing-port-avoid: number-or-range     [none]
```

unbound has several options that control the interfaces on which it listens for queries and the port numbers used for receiving and sending queries. The defaults are fine for most sites and are not vulnerable to Kaminsky-type cache poisoning attacks. However, the interface and outgoing-port-avoid options should be configured explicitly.

The interface option specifies the interfaces on which **unbound** listens for queries. It needs to be set explicitly because the default is localhost—fine if every machine runs **unbound**, but not so fine if you run one name server per subnet or per site. Add an interface statement for each interface on which clients might try to submit queries.

You should also configure outgoing-port-avoid to exclude any ports that are blocked by your firewall and any ports used by another program. **unbound** already excludes ports below 1,024 and IANA-assigned ports.

DNSSEC

```
module-config: module-names          [none]
trust-anchor-file: filename          [none]
trust-anchor: resource-record        [none]
trusted-keys-file: filename          [none]
dlv-anchor-file: filename            [none]
dlv-anchor: resource-record          [none]
```

These options all deal with DNSSEC deployment; they allow you to express trust anchors by listing the files in which they live or by stuffing the resource record directly into the option's value. There can be at most one DLV anchor.

Setting module-config to validator iterator turns on DNSSEC validation and must be accompanied by trust anchors, either explicitly configured or via DLV. See *DNSSEC* on page 648 for more info.

Signatures

```
val-*: <various>                     [signature options, defaults are ok]
```

The val-* series of options deal with the validation process for signatures of signed zones. They tweak various parameters (such as maximum permissible clock skew) that can affect validation. The default values are fine unless you are debugging your DNSSEC deployment. Setting val-log-level to 1 logs validation failures, which is also helpful for debugging.

Tuning

unbound supports several performance-tuning options. An important one is num-threads, which should be set to the number of cores available on the server (i.e., the number of cores per processor times the number of processors).

The tuning defaults are fine for most sites, so rather than list them all here, we refer you to the man page for **unbound.conf** and the how-tos at unbound.net. Toward the end of the man page is a helpful example that tunes performance on a small-memory machine.

Private addresses

```
private-address: ip-address-or-subnet     [none]
private-domain: domain-name               [none]
```

The private-address statement blocks the listed IP addresses from being returned in query results. It's normally used in conjunction with RFC1918 private IP address spaces (see page 462) to keep these shameful addresses from escaping onto the Internet. This behavior is generally what you want for external sites, but if you are actually using RFC1918 addresses internally, you probably don't want to be blacklisting your own internal addresses. The private-domain statement resolves this conflict by allowing the specified domain and all its subdomains to contain private addresses.

The next set of configuration options pertains to the remote-control statement, which controls communication between **unbound** and the **unbound-control** program. That communication is controlled by self-signed SSL/TLS certificates in X.509 format that are set up by the **unbound-control-setup** program. There are only a few options, so we list them all:

*Controlling **unbound***

```
control-enable: yes | no                      [no]
control-interface: ip-address                 [localhost (127.0.0.1 and ::1)]
control-port: port                            [953]
server-key-file: private-key-file             [unbound_server.key]
server-cert-file: certificate-file-pem        [unbound_server.pem]
control-key-file: private-key-file            [unbound_control.key]
control-cert-file: certificate-file-pem       [unbound_control.pem]
```

You can control **unbound** from anywhere on the Internet. To set up authentication, run **unbound-control-setup** to create the necessary certificate files, set the control-enable option to yes, and set the control-interface to the network interface on which the server should listen for control commands. You can use 0.0.0.0 (and ::0) to enable all interfaces. The default is to require the controller to be logged in to the same machine as **unbound**, which is probably safest.

Stub zones

```
stub-zone:
    name: domain-name                [none]
    stub-host: hostname              [none]
    stub-addr: ip-address[@port]     [none]
```

A stub-zone clause lets you tunnel queries for a particular domain to an authoritative server that you designate rather than resolving them in the usual hierarchical fashion from the root. For example, you might want your users to see a private view of your local network that includes more hosts than are seen by DNS queriers on the outside. The name "stub zone" is unfortunate and has no connection to the stub zones used in the BIND world.

To implement this configuration, you'd run an authoritative server on a different host (or on the same host at a different port) to serve your local version of the zone. You'd then point **unbound** to that server by using the stub-zone options. You can specify either the *hostname* of the server (stub-host) or its IP address (stub-addr). You can also specify the *port*, which defaults to 53. The address form protects against chicken-and-egg problems if **unbound** cannot look up the name without access to the destination zone.

You can have as many stub zones as you want.

Forwarding

```
forward-zone:
    name: domain-name                          [none]
    forward-host: server-name                  [none]
    forward-addr: ip-address[@port]            [none]
```

The forward-zone option lets **unbound** act as a forwarder, forwarding all queries (or just some, depending on the value of the name parameter) to another server to help that server build up a bigger cache. Forwarding occurs only if **unbound** cannot answer a query from its own cache. See page 569 for general information about forwarders and reasons why you might want to use them.

There may be multiple forward-zone statements. If you specify the name as . (a single period), all queries are forwarded.

17.12 Updating zone files

To change a domain's data (e.g., to add or delete a host), you update the zone data files on the master server. You must also increment the serial number in the zone's SOA record. Finally, you must get your name server software to pick up and distribute your changes. This final step varies depending on your software:

- BIND: Run **rndc reload** to signal **named** to pick up the changes. You can also kill and restart **named**, but if your server is both authoritative for your zone and recursive for your users, this operation discards cached data from other domains.
- NSD: Run **nsdc rebuild**, followed by **nsdc reload**. **nsd** does no caching, so it is not adversely affected by being restarted.

Updated zone data is propagated to slave servers of BIND masters right away because the notify option is on by default. In NSD, you must configure the notify ACL to get this (desirable) effect. If notifications are not turned on, your slave servers will not pick up the changes until after *refresh* seconds, as set in the zone's SOA record (typically an hour later).

If you have the notify option turned off, you can force BIND slaves to update themselves by running **rndc reload** on each slave. This command makes the slave check with the master, see that the data has changed, and request a zone transfer. The corresponding NSD command is **nsdc reload**.

Don't forget to modify both the forward and reverse zones when you change a hostname or IP address. Forgetting the reverse files leaves sneaky errors: some commands work and some won't.

Changing the data files but forgetting to change the serial number makes the changes take effect on the master server (after a reload) but not on the slaves.

Do not edit data files on slave servers. These files are maintained by the name server and sysadmins should not meddle with them. It's fine to look at the BIND data files as long as you don't make changes. The NSD files are databases and so cannot be directly inspected. However, changes are by default written back to the text zone files by **nsd-patch**.

BIND allows zone changes to be made through a programmatic API, as specified in RFC2136. This feature, called dynamic updates, is necessary to support autoconfiguration protocols like DHCP. The dynamic update mechanism is described on page 640.

Zone transfers

DNS servers are synchronized through a mechanism called a zone transfer. A zone transfer can include the entire zone (called AXFR) or just the recent changes (called IXFR). By default, zone transfers use the TCP protocol on port 53. BIND logs transfer-related information with category "xfer-in" or "xfer-out"; NSD includes it in the regular logging stream.

A slave that wants to refresh its data requests a zone transfer from the master server and makes a backup copy of the zone data on disk. If the data on the master has not changed, as determined by a comparison of the serial numbers (not the actual data), no update occurs and the backup files are just touched. (That is, their modification times are set to the current time.)

Both the sending and receiving servers remain available to answer queries during a zone transfer. Only after the transfer is complete does the slave begin to use the new data.

When zones are huge (like com) or dynamically updated (see the next section), changes are typically small relative to the size of the entire zone. With IXFR, only the changes are sent (unless they are larger than the complete zone, in which case a regular AXFR transfer is done). The IXFR mechanism is analogous to the **patch** program in that it makes changes to an old database to bring it into conformity with a new database.

In BIND, IXFR is the default for any zones configured for dynamic update, and **named** maintains a transaction log called *zonename*.**jnl**. You can set the options provide-ixfr and request-ixfr in the server statements for individual peers. The provide-ixfr option enables or disables IXFR service for zones for which this server is the master. The request-ixfr option requests IXFRs for zones for which this server is a slave.

```
provide-ixfr yes ;          # In BIND server statement
request-ixfr yes ;          # In BIND server statement
```

IXFRs work for zones that are edited by hand, too. Use the BIND zone option called ixfr-from-differences to enable this behavior. IXFR requires the zone file to be sorted in a canonical order. **named** takes care of this chore for you, but it costs the server some memory and CPU. IXFRs trade these costs in exchange for reduced network traffic.

When requesting a zone transfer, NSD slaves ask for an IXFR but fall back to AXFR if that is all the master server supports. Because NSD's data lives in a compiled database format, sorting is not required for IXFRs. NSD stores the transfer daemon's state in the file specified by the xfrdfile attribute in case the transfer is interrupted.

Reloads after IXFRs can be throttled by the xfrd-reload-timeout attribute. It defaults to 10 seconds, so IXFR changes are batched to some degree.

In BIND, an IXFR request to a server that does not support it automatically falls back to the standard AXFR zone transfer. You can prohibit AXFR fallback in NSD by setting allow-axfr-fallback to no.

In both systems, much effort has been expended to ensure that a server crash during an IXFR does not leave zones with trashed data.

BIND dynamic updates

The DNS system is built on the premise that name-to-address mappings are relatively stable and do not change frequently. However, a site that uses DHCP to dynamically assign IP addresses as machines boot and join the network breaks this rule constantly. There are two classical solutions: add generic entries to the DNS database, or continually edit the DNS files. For many sites, neither solution is satisfactory.

The first solution should be familiar to anyone who has looked up the PTR record for the IP address assigned to them by a mass-market (home) ISP. The DNS configuration usually looks something like this:

```
dhcp-host1.domain.        IN  A  192.168.0.1
dhcp-host2.domain.        IN  A  192.168.0.2
...
```

Although this is a simple solution, it means that hostnames are permanently associated with particular IP addresses and that computers therefore change hostnames whenever they receive a new IP address. Hostname-based logging and security measures become very difficult in this environment.

BIND's dynamic update feature offers an alternative solution. It allows the DHCP daemon to notify BIND of the address assignments it makes, thus updating the contents of the DNS database on the fly. Dynamic updates can add, delete, or modify resource records. When dynamic updates are enabled, **named** maintains a journal of dynamic changes (*zonename*.**jnl**) that it can consult in the event of a server crash. **named** recovers the in-memory state of the zone by reading the original zone files and then replaying the changes from the journal.

You cannot hand-edit a dynamically updated zone without first stopping the dynamic update stream. **rndc freeze** *zone* or **rndc freeze** *zone class view* will do the trick. These commands sync the journal file to the master zone file on disk and then delete the journal. You can then edit the zone file by hand. Unfortunately, the original formatting of the zone file will have been destroyed by **named**'s monkeying—the file will look like those maintained by **named** for slave servers.

Dynamic update attempts are refused while the zone is frozen. Use **rndc thaw** with the same arguments you froze with to reload the zone file from disk and reenable dynamic updates.

The **nsupdate** program supplied with BIND 9 comes with a command-line interface for making dynamic updates. It runs in batch mode, taking commands from the keyboard or a file. A blank line or the **send** command signals the end of an update and sends the changes to the server. Two blank lines signify the end of input. The command language includes a primitive if statement to express constructs such as "if this hostname does not exist in DNS, add it." As predicates for an **nsupdate** action, you can require a name to exist or not exist, or require a resource record set to exist or not exist.

For example, here is a simple **nsupdate** script that adds a new host and also adds a nickname for an existing host if the nickname is not already in use. The angle bracket prompt is produced by **nsupdate** and is not part of the command script.

```
$ nsupdate
> update add newhost.cs.colorado.edu 86400 A 128.138.243.16
>
> prereq nxdomain gypsy.cs.colorado.edu
> update add gypsy.cs.colorado.edu CNAME evi-laptop.cs.colorado.edu
```

Dynamic updates to DNS are scary. They can potentially provide uncontrolled write access to your important system data. Don't try to use IP addresses for access control—they are too easily forged. TSIG authentication with a shared-secret key is better; it's available and is easy to configure. BIND 9 supports both:

```
$ nsupdate -k keydir:keyfile
```

or

```
$ nsupdate -y keyname:secretkey
```

Since the password goes on the command line in the **-y** form, anyone running **w** or **ps** at the right moment can see it. For this reason, the **-k** form is preferred. For more details on TSIG, see the section starting on page 645.

Dynamic updates to a zone are enabled in **named.conf** with an allow-update or update-policy clause. allow-update grants permission to update any records in accordance with IP- or key-based authentication. update-policy is a BIND 9 extension that allows fine-grained control for updates according to the hostname or record type. It requires key-based authentication. Both are zone options.

Use update-policy to allow clients to update their A or PTR records but not to change the SOA record, NS records, or KEY records. You can also use update-policy to allow a host to update only its own records. The parameters let you express names explicitly, as a subdomain, as a wild card, or as the keyword self, which sets a general policy for machines' access to their own records. Resource records are identified by class and type. The syntax of an update-policy rule is

```
update-policy ( grant | deny ) identity nametype name [types] ;
```

The *identity* is the name of the cryptographic key needed to authorize the update. The *nametype* has one of four values: name, subdomain, wildcard, or self. The *name* is the zone to be updated, and the *types* are the resource record types that can be updated. If no types are specified, all types except SOA, NS, RRSIG, and NSEC or NSEC3 can be updated. Here's an example:

```
update-policy { grant dhcp-key subdomain dhcp.cs.colorado.edu A } ;
```

This configuration allows anyone who knows the key dhcp-key to update address records in the dhcp.cs.colorado.edu subdomain. This statement would appear in the master server's **named.conf** file within the zone statement for the domain dhcp.cs.colorado.edu. There would be a key statement to define dhcp-key as well.

The snippet below from the **named.conf** file at the Computer Science Department at the University of Colorado uses the update-policy statement to allow students in a system administration class to update their own subdomains but not to mess with the rest of the DNS environment.

```
// saclass.net
zone "saclass.net" {
    type master;
    file "saclass/saclass.net";
    update-policy {
        grant feanor_mroe. subdomain saclass.net.;
        grant mojo_mroe. subdomain saclass.net.;
        grant dawdle_mroe. subdomain saclass.net.;
        grant pirate_mroe. subdomain saclass.net.;
        ...
    };
...
```

17.13 Security issues

DNS started out as an inherently open system, but it has steadily grown more and more secure—or at least, securable. By default, anyone on the Internet can investigate your domain with individual queries from tools such as **dig**, **host**, **nslookup**, and **drill**. In some cases, they can dump your entire DNS database.

To address such vulnerabilities, name servers support various types of access control based on host and network addresses or on cryptographic authentication. Table 17.12 summarizes the security features that can be configured in **named.conf**, **nsd.conf**, or **unbound.conf**. The Page column shows where in this book to look for more information.

Table 17.12 Security features in BIND, NSD, and Unbound

	Feature	Context	Page	What it specifies
BIND	acl	Various	609	Access control lists
	allow-query	options, zone	606	Who can query a zone or server
	allow-recursion	options	604	Who can make recursive queries
	allow-transfer	options, zone	606	Who can request zone transfers
	allow-update	zone	613	Who can make dynamic updates
	blackhole	options	606	Servers to completely ignore
	bogus	server	611	Servers never to query
	update-policy	zone	641	Use of dynamic updates
NSD/Unbound	access-control	server	634	Permitted queriers (Unbound)
	allow-notify	Slave zone	631	Permitted notifiers (NSD)
	chroot	server	631/635	Directory to **chroot** to
	notify	Master zone	631	Slave servers to notify (NSD)
	provide-xfr	Master zone	631	Zone transfer receivers (NSD)
	request-xfr	Slave zone	631	Zone transfer providers (NSD)
	username	server	631/635	User to run as from **chroot** jail

All three name servers can run in a **chroot**ed environment under an unprivileged UID to minimize security risks; **unbound** does so by default. They can all use transaction signatures to control communication between master and slave servers (BIND and NSD) and between the name servers and their control programs (BIND and Unbound). Each also supports the whole DNSSEC hairball. These topics are taken up in the next few sections.

Access control lists in BIND, revisited

ACLs are named address match lists that can appear as arguments to statements such as allow-query, allow-transfer, and blackhole. Their basic syntax was described on page 609. ACLs can help beef up DNS security in a variety of ways.

Every site should at least have one ACL for bogus addresses and one ACL for local addresses. For example:

```
acl bogusnets {                // ACL for bogus networks
    0.0.0.0/8 ;                // Default, wild card addresses
    1.0.0.0/8 ;                // Reserved addresses
    2.0.0.0/8 ;                // Reserved addresses
    169.254.0.0/16 ;           // Link-local delegated addresses
```

```
        192.0.2.0/24 ;          // Sample addresses, like example.com
        224.0.0.0/3 ;           // Multicast address space
        10.0.0.0/8 ;            // Private address space (RFC1918)25
        172.16.0.0/12 ;         // Private address space (RFC1918)
        192.168.0.0/16 ;        // Private address space (RFC1918)
    } ;

    acl cunets {                // ACL for University of Colorado networks
        128.138.0.0/16 ;        // Main campus network
        198.11.16/24 ;
        204.228.69/24 ;
    };
```

In the global options section of your config file, you could then include

```
allow-recursion { cunets; } ;
blackhole { bogusnets; } ;
```

It's also a good idea to restrict zone transfers to legitimate slave servers. An ACL makes things nice and tidy.

```
acl ourslaves {
    128.138.242.1 ;         // anchor
    ...
} ;
acl measurements {
    198.32.4.0/24 ;         // Bill manning's measurements, v4 address
    2001:478:6:0::/48 ;     // Bill manning's measurements, v6 address
} ;
```

The actual restriction is implemented with a line such as

```
allow-transfer { ourslaves; measurements; } ;
```

Here, transfers are limited to our own slave servers and to the machines of an Internet measurement project that walks the reverse DNS tree to determine the size of the Internet and the percentage of misconfigured servers. Limiting transfers in this way makes it impossible for other sites to dump your entire database with a tool such as **dig** (see page 677).

Of course, you should still protect your network at a lower level through router access control lists and standard security hygiene on each host. If those measures are not possible, you can refuse DNS packets except to a gateway machine that you monitor closely.

Open resolvers

An open resolver is a recursive, caching name server that accepts and answers queries from anyone on the Internet. Open resolvers are bad. Outsiders can consume your resources without your permission or knowledge, and if they are bad guys, they may be able to poison your resolver's cache.

25. Don't make private addresses bogus if you use them and are configuring your internal DNS servers!

Worse, open resolvers are sometimes used by bad guys to amplify distributed denial of service attacks. The attacker sends queries to your resolver with a faked source address that points back to the victim of the attack. Your resolver dutifully answers the queries and sends some nice fat packets to the victim. The victim didn't initiate the queries, but it still has to route and process the network traffic. Multiply by a bunch of open resolvers and it's real trouble for the victim.

Statistics show that between 75% and 80% of caching name servers are currently open resolvers—yikes! The site dns.measurement-factory.com/tools can help you test your site. Go there, select the "open resolver test," and type in the IP addresses of your name servers. You can also test all the name servers on your network or all the servers at your site by using your whois identifier.

Use access control lists in **named.conf** or **unbound.conf** to limit your caching name servers to answering queries from your own users.

Running in a chrooted jail

If hackers compromise your name server, they can potentially gain access to the system under the guise of the user as whom it runs. To limit the damage that someone could do in this situation, you can run the server in a **chroot**ed environment, run it as an unprivileged user, or both.

For **named**, the command-line flag **-t** specifies the directory to **chroot** to, and the **-u** flag specifies the UID under which **named** should run. For example,

```
$ sudo named -u 53
```

initially starts **named** as root, but after **named** completes its rootly chores, it relinquishes its root privileges and runs as UID 53.

For **nsd** and **unbound**, the config file server options username and chroot do the same job. These options can also be specified on the **nsd** command line with the same flags as BIND: **-u** and **-t**, respectively.

Many sites don't bother to use the **-u** and **-t** flags, but when a new vulnerability is announced, they must be faster to upgrade than the hackers are to attack.

The **chroot** jail cannot be an empty directory since it must contain all the files the name server normally needs in order to run: **/dev/null**, **/dev/random**, the zone files, configuration files, keys, syslog target files and the syslog UNIX-domain socket, **/var**, etc. It takes a bit of work to set this all up. The **chroot** system call is performed after libraries have been loaded, so it is not necessary to copy shared libraries into the jail.

Secure server-to-server communication with TSIG and TKEY

While DNSSEC (covered in the next section) was being developed, the IETF developed a simpler mechanism, called TSIG (RFC2845), to allow secure communication among servers through the use of "transaction signatures." Access control based on transaction signatures is more secure than access control based on IP source addresses alone. TSIG can secure zone transfers between a master server and its slaves, and in BIND can secure dynamic updates.

The TSIG signature on a message authenticates the peer and verifies that the data has not been tampered with. Signatures are checked at the time a packet is received and are then discarded; they are not cached and do not become part of the DNS data.

TSIG uses symmetric encryption. That is, the encryption key is the same as the decryption key. This single key is called the "shared secret." The TSIG specification allows multiple encryption methods. BIND implements MD5, SHA-1, SHA-224, and SHA-256. NSD implements the same set but without SHA-224. Use a different key for each pair of servers that want to communicate securely.

TSIG is much less expensive computationally than public key cryptography, but because it requires manual configuration, it is only appropriate for a local network on which the number of pairs of communicating servers is small. It does not scale to the global Internet.

Setting up TSIG for BIND

First, use BIND's **dnssec-keygen** utility to generate a shared-secret host key for the two servers, say, master and slave1:

```
$ dnssec-keygen -a HMAC-MD5 -b 128 -n HOST master-slave1
```

The **-b 128** flag tells **dnssec-keygen** to create a 128-bit key. We use 128 bits here just to keep the keys short enough to fit on our printed pages. In real life, you might want to use a longer key; 512 bits is the maximum allowed.

This command produces two files: **Kmaster-slave1.+157+09068.private** and **Kmaster-slave1.+157+09068.key**. The **157** stands for the HMAC-MD5 algorithm, and the **09068** is a number used as a key identifier in case you have multiple keys for the same pair of servers.[26]

Both files include the same key, just in different formats. The **.private** file looks like this:

```
Private-key-format: v1.2
Algorithm: 157 (HMAC_MD5)
Key: jxopbeb+aPc71Mm2vc9R9g==
```

and the **.key** file like this:

```
master-slave1. IN KEY 512 3 157 jxopbeb+aPc71Mm2vc9R9g==
```

Note that **dnssec-keygen** has added a dot to the end of the key names in both the filenames and the contents of the **.key** file. The motivation for this convention is that when **dnssec-keygen** is used for DNSSEC keys that are added to zone files, the key names must be fully qualified domain names and must therefore end in a

26. The number looks random, but it is really just a hash of the TSIG key.

dot. There should probably be two tools, one for shared-secret keys and one for public-key key pairs.

You don't actually need the **.key** file—it's another artifact of **dnssec-keygen** being used for two different jobs. Just delete it. The 512 in the KEY record is not the key length but rather a flag bit that identifies the record as a DNS host key.

After all this complication, you may be disappointed to learn that the generated key is really just a long random number. You could generate the key manually by writing down an ASCII string of the right length (divisible by 4) and pretending that it's a base-64 encoding of something, or you could use **mmencode** to encode a random string. The way you create the key is not important; it just has to exist on both machines.

***scp** is part of the OpenSSH suite. See page 926 for details.*

Copy the key from the **.private** file to both master and slave1 with **scp**, or cut and paste it. *Do not* use **telnet** or **ftp** to copy the key; even internal networks may not be secure.

The key must be included in both machines' **named.conf** files. Since **named.conf** is usually world-readable and keys should not be, put the key in a separate file that is included in **named.conf**. The key file should have mode 600 and should be owned by the **named** user.

For example, you could put the snippet

```
key master-slave1. {
    algorithm hmac-md5 ;
    secret "shared-key-you-generated" ;
} ;
```

in the file **master-slave1.tsig**. In the **named.conf** file, add the line

```
include "master-slave1.tsig" ;
```

near the top.

This part of the configuration simply defines the keys. For them to actually be used to sign and verify updates, the master needs to require the key for transfers and the slave needs to identify the master with a server statement and keys clause. For example, you might add the line

```
allow-transfer { key master-slave1. ;} ;
```

to the zone statement on the master server, and the line

```
server master's-IP-address { keys { master-slave1. ; } ; } ;
```

to the slave's **named.conf** file. If the master server allows dynamic updates, it can also use the key in its allow-update clause in the zone statement.

Our example key name is pretty generic. If you use TSIG keys for many zones, you may want to include the name of the zone in the key name to help you keep everything straight.

To test your TSIG configuration, run **named-checkconf** to verify that you have the syntax right. Then use **dig** to attempt a zone transfer (**dig** @*master* **axfr**) from both slave1 and from some other machine. The first should succeed and the second should fail with the diagnostic "Transfer failed." To be absolutely sure everything is right, remove the allow-transfer clause and try the **dig** commands again. This time, both should succeed. (Don't forget to put the allow-transfer back in!) As a final test, increase the serial number for the zone on the master server, run **rndc reload**, and watch the log file on the slave to see if it picks up the change and transfers the zone.

When you first start using transaction signatures, run **named** at debug level 1 (see page 667 for information about debug mode) for a while to see any error messages that are generated. Ancient versions of BIND do not understand signed messages and complain about them, sometimes to the point of refusing to load the zone.

See page 1195 for more information about NTP.

When using TSIG keys and transaction signatures between master and slave servers, you should keep the clocks of the servers synchronized with NTP. If the clocks are too far apart (more than about 5 minutes), signature verification will not work. This problem can be very hard to identify.

TKEY is a BIND mechanism that lets two hosts generate a shared-secret key automatically, without phone calls or secure copies to distribute the key. It uses an algorithm called the Diffie-Hellman key exchange in which each side makes up a random number, does some math on it, and sends the result to the other side. Each side then mathematically combines its own number with the transmission it received to arrive at the same key. An eavesdropper might overhear the transmission but will be unable to reverse the math.[27]

Microsoft servers use TSIG in a nonstandard way called GSS-TSIG that exchanges the shared secret through TKEY. If you need a Microsoft server to communicate with BIND, use the tkey-domain and tkey-gssapi-credential options.

SIG(0) is another mechanism for signing transactions between servers or between dynamic updaters and the master server. It uses public key cryptography; see RFCs 2535 and 2931 for details.

TSIG in NSD

You can use the **ldns-keygen** command in the **examples** directory of the **ldns** distribution to generate TSIG keys for NSD's access control lists. For details, see page 655. NSD does not support SIG(0) keys or the TKEY Diffie-Hellman key exchange system.

DNSSEC

DNSSEC is a set of DNS extensions that authenticate the origin of zone data and verify its integrity by using public key cryptography. That is, the extensions allow

27. The math involved is called the discrete log problem and relies on the fact that for modular arithmetic, taking powers is easy but taking logs to undo the powers is close to impossible.

DNS clients to ask the questions "Did this DNS data really come from the zone's owner?" and "Is this really the data sent by that owner?"

DNSSEC relies on a cascading chain of trust. The root servers provide validation information for the top-level domains, the top-level domains provide validation information for the second-level domains, and so on. Or at least, that's the original design of the system. As of early 2010, the root and most top-level domains remain unsigned.

ICANN and the U.S. Department of Commerce are dragging their feet on signing the root, although this change has been promised for a while. It might happen in mid-2010. VeriSign appears to be in no rush to sign the .com and .net zones. The zones are already huge, and the signed versions will be even larger, requiring servers to be reprovisioned. Furthermore, VeriSign's X.509 certificate service represents a significant portion of its revenue, and DNSSEC may replace these certificates for certain applications. Nevertheless, VeriSign has promised to sign the .com zone by 2011, just in time for the scheduled renegotiation of its contract with ICANN in 2012.

Fortunately, the concept of trust anchors lets us bootstrap the DNSSEC validation process and secure portions of the DNS tree in advance of the availability of signed root and top-level domains.

Public key cryptosystems use two keys: one to encrypt (sign) and a different one to decrypt (verify). Publishers sign their data with the secret "private" key. Anyone can verify the validity of a signature with the matching "public" key, which is widely distributed. If a public key correctly decrypts a zone file, then the zone must have been encrypted with the corresponding private key. The trick is to make sure that the public keys you use for verification are authentic. Public key systems allow one entity to sign the public key of another, thereby vouching for the legitimacy of the key; hence the term "chain of trust."

The data in a DNS zone is too voluminous to be encrypted with public key cryptography—the encryption would be too slow. Instead, since the data is not secret, a secure hash (e.g., an MD5 checksum) is run on the data and the results of the hash are signed (encrypted) by the zone's private key. The results of the hash are like a fingerprint of the data and are called a digital signature. The signatures are appended to the data they authenticate as RRSIG records in the signed zone file.

To verify the signature, you decrypt it with the public key of the signer, run the data through the same secure hash algorithm, and compare the computed hash value with the decrypted hash value. If they match, you have authenticated the signer and verified the integrity of the data.

In the DNSSEC system, each zone has its own public and private keys. In fact, it has two sets of keys: a zone-signing key pair and a key-signing key pair. The private zone-signing key signs each RRset (that is, each set of records of the same type for the same host). The public zone-signing key verifies the signatures and is included in the zone's data in the form of a DNSKEY resource record.

Parent zones contain DS records that are a hash of the child's self-signed key-signing key DNSKEY records. A name server verifies the authenticity of a child zone's DNSKEY record by checking it against the parent zone's signature. To verify the authenticity of the parent zone's key, the name server can check the parent's parent, and so on back to the root. The public key for the root zone would be widely published and included in the root hints file.

The DNSSEC specifications require that if a zone has multiple keys, each is tried until the data is validated. This behavior is required so that keys can be rolled over (changed) without interruptions in DNS service. If a DNSSEC-aware recursive name server queries an unsigned zone, the unsigned answer that comes back is accepted as valid. But problems occur when signatures expire or when parent and child zones do not agree on the child's current DNSKEY record.

Before we jump into the mechanics of generating keys and signing zones, we need to outline the real-world status of DNSSEC and its impact on sysadmins. It is ready to deploy, but a couple of problems remain. On the plus side:

- Current versions of the DNS software (both **named** and **nsd/unbound**) are ready. Tools exist to sign zones and verify signatures.
- Momentum toward signed zones is building. As of early 2010, .gov, .org, and several ccTLDs (mostly in Europe) are now signed. (Sweden was the first signed TLD.) The root will be signed in 2010, and the other gTLDs will follow a year or two later. The U.S. government has required all sites within .gov to be signed as well.
- The IETF standards seem to be functional and deployable.

However, two thorny problems remain: key distribution and packet size.

With the root and TLDs not signed, the chain of trust is currently broken. Sites that want to sign their zones have to find other ways to publish their keys. A lookaside validation scheme (RFCs 4431 and 5074) designed by Sam Weiler of Sparta allows a convenient workaround for this problem by enabling third-party organizations such as ISC to validate sites' keys. This is a good interim solution, but also a single point of failure. ISC is used to running critical servers (they run the F root server), but accidents do happen. There are also potential privacy issues with a third party having knowledge of all the sites your users visited. (Of course, these same privacy concerns apply to all root server operators.) Another interim solution is the use of so-called ITARs (itar.iana.org); see page 661.

Strong keys are long, and some sites like to distribute several of them. This means bigger packets. DNSSEC requires EDNS0, the extended DNS protocol, which supports UDP packets larger than 512 bytes. However, not all implementations support it; those folks may not be able to use DNSSEC.

Even for EDNS0-aware servers, the MTU over the path between two servers may be smaller than a big fat signed packet stuffed with keys. If the packet is too large, it should in theory be fragmented at the IP layer, but problems remain. Some implementations of TCP/IP fragment TCP packets but not UDP packets. Some firewall devices do not have enough saved state to properly reassemble fragmented UDP packets. And finally, some firewalls drop UDP packets to port 53 that are larger than 512 bytes. Oops. When a UDP response is mutilated or fails to get through, the client then switches to TCP, which causes performance problems of its own.

A few other issues:

- Russia refuses to use the RSA algorithm, and RSA is currently the only algorithm that DNSSEC-aware name servers are required to implement. Russia has standardized on an algorithm called GOST, a symmetric cipher, that is similar in design to DES.[28]
- China (among other countries) has its own root, .com, and .net servers, thus fracturing the DNS naming tree. How will DNSSEC work with a fractured root?
- RFC5011, a proposed standard for automated updates of DNSSEC trust anchors, inflates the key handling overhead by adding keys to your DNSKEY resource record sets. This extension would exacerbate the MTU problem mentioned above and seems to be a bad idea. There are also situations in which use of the RFC5011 scheme would leave a site's keys in a revoked state even though cached data might still require those keys for verification.
- Linux distributions ship with a list of keys to get you started. This seems like a bad idea since the keys will inevitably become out of date and wrong. Your DNS will slowly degrade without you really knowing why. (Key lists themselves are not necessarily a bad idea. For example, you can use lists from the RIPE and IANA web sites to cross-check keys you obtain through DNS until the root and TLDs are signed.)
- Maybe we need a well-known hostname (analogous to www for web servers) that sites can use to publish their public keys while we wait for the top of the DNS tree to be signed—key.*domain-name*, or something like that.

Sysadmins need to start thinking about signing their domains and setting up a shiny new server or two. We do recommend that you deploy DNSSEC at this point, but stage it carefully on a test network well before you plan to deploy it on production networks.

28. GOST is secure (as far as we know) and has a much shorter key length than other algorithms. Since it is a symmetric cipher and not a public key system, it can replace TSIG but cannot be used for DNSSEC. Proposals to allow GOST are winding their way through the IETF standardization process.

DNSSEC deployment can be done in two independent steps:

- Sign your zones and serve signed data to DNSSEC-aware clients.
- Validate the answers to your users' queries.

Check out UCLA's handy SecSpider tool at secspider.cs.ucla.edu. It probes your DNSSEC setup from several locations around the globe to verify that your keys are available and that large packets containing them can reach those locations. (It was in fact SecSpider that first discovered the path MTU issue with DNSSEC.) SecSpider also identifies DNSSEC misconfigurations, and using it may help out a grad student trying to gather enough data to write his thesis. You can also obtain copies of the public keys for other signed zones from the SecSpider web site (secspider.cs.ucla.edu/trust-anchors.conf).

The DNS-OARC (DNS Operations, Analysis, and Research Center) has implemented a reply-size test server that you can query with **dig** to find out how large a DNS UDP reply packet can transit between that server and your site:

```
$ dig +short rs.dns-oarc.net txt
rst.x1014.rs.dns-oarc.net.
rst.x1202.x1014.rs.dns-oarc.net.
rst.x1382.x1202.x1014.rs.dns-oarc.net.
"63.231.83.113 DNS reply size limit is at least 1382 bytes"
"63.231.83.113 sent EDNS buffer size 4096"
```

This example tells you that DNS replies of size 1,382 can get through, but not much larger, even though you are advertising a buffer size of 4,096. In this case, the problem is likely that the firewall is not admitting UDP fragments.

Other common sizes are 486, indicating a server that does not support EDNS0 and limits UDP packets to 512 bytes, and 4,023, which indicates that the full 4,096-byte buffer size can be used. If you use the *@server* argument to **dig**, you will see the packet size limitations from the DNS-OARC machine to that server. For more information, see dns-oarc.net/oarc/services/replysizetest.

If you are about to implement DNSSEC and either SecSpider or DNS-OARC indicates a problem with packet sizes, it might be time to talk to your firewall folks and try to get things fixed before you deploy.

DNSSEC policy

Before you begin deployment of DNSSEC, there are a few policies and procedures that you should nail down or at least think about. For example:

- What size keys will you use? Longer keys are more secure, but they make for larger packets.
- How often will you change keys in the absence of a security incident?
- How will you distribute your public keys? How will sites that need your keys verify that they are authentic?

We suggest that you keep a key log that records the date you generated each key, the hardware and operating system used, the key tag assigned, the version of the key generator software, the algorithm used, the key length, and the signature validity period. If a cryptographic algorithm is later compromised, you can check your log to see if you are vulnerable.

DNSSEC resource records

DNSSEC uses six resource record types that were referenced in the DNS database section back on page 590 but were not described in detail: DS, DLV, DNSKEY, RRSIG, NSEC, and NSEC3. We describe them here in general and then outline the steps involved in signing a zone. Each of these records is created by DNSSEC tools rather than by being typed into a zone file with a text editor.

The DS (Designated Signer) record appears only in the parent zone and indicates that a subzone is secure (signed). It also identifies the key used by the child to self-sign its own KEY resource record set. The DS record includes a key identifier (a five-digit number), a cryptographic algorithm, a digest type, and a digest of the public key record allowed (or used) to sign the child's key resource record.

If your parent zone is not signed, you can establish a trust anchor at ISC by using a DLV (domain lookaside validation) record with the same format. Here are examples of each:[29]

```
example.com.              IN DS   682 5 1 12898DCF9F7AD20DBCE159E7...
example.com.dlv.isc.org.  IN DLV  682 5 1 12898DCF9F7AD20DBCE159E7...
```

The question of how to change existing keys in the parent and child zones has been a thorny one that seemed destined to require cooperation and communication between parent and child. The creation of the DS record, the use of separate key-signing and zone-signing keys, and the use of multiple key pairs have helped address this problem.

Keys included in a DNSKEY resource record can be either key-signing keys (KSKs) or zone-signing keys (ZSKs). A new flag, called SEP for "secure entry point," distinguishes between them. Bit 15 of the flags field is set to 1 for KSKs and to 0 for ZSKs. This convention makes the flags field of KSKs odd and of ZSKs even when they are treated as decimal numbers. The values are currently 257 and 256, respectively.

Multiple keys can be generated and signed so that a smooth transition from one key to the next is possible. The child may change its zone-signing keys without notifying the parent; it must only coordinate with the parent if it changes its key-signing key. As keys roll over, both the old key and the new key are valid for a certain interval. Once cached values on the Internet have expired, the old key can be retired.

29. In this section, base-64-encoded hashes and keys have all been truncated to save space and better illustrate the structure of the records.

An RRSIG record is the signature of a resource record set (that is, the set of all records of the same type and name within a zone). RRSIG records are generated by zone-signing software and added to the signed version of the zone file.

An RRSIG record contains a wealth of information:

- The type of record set being signed
- The signature algorithm used, encoded as a small integer
- The number of labels (dot-separated pieces) in the name field
- The TTL of the record set that was signed
- The time the signature expires (as *yyyymmddhhssss*)
- The time the record set was signed (also *yyyymmddhhssss*)
- A key identifier (a 5-digit number)
- The signer's name (domain name)
- And finally, the digital signature itself (base-64 encoded)

Here's an example:

```
RRSIG   NS 5 2 57600 20090919182841 (
          20090820182841 23301 example.com.
          pMKZ76waPVTbIguEQNUojNVlVewHau4p...== )
```

NSEC or NSEC3 records are also produced as a zone is signed. Rather than signing record sets, they certify the intervals *between* record set names and so allow for a signed answer of "no such domain" or "no such resource record set." For example, a server might respond to a query for A records named bork.atrust.com with an NSEC record that certifies the nonexistence of any A records between bark.atrust.com and borrelia.atrust.com.

Unfortunately, the inclusion of the endpoint names in NSEC records allows someone to walk through the zone and obtain all of its valid hostnames. NSEC3 fixes this feature by including hashes of the endpoint names rather than the endpoint names themselves, but it is more expensive to compute: more security, less performance. NSEC and NSEC3 are both in current use, and you can choose between them when you generate your keys and sign your zones.

Unless protecting against a zone walk is critically important for your site, we recommend that you use NSEC for now. Only recent versions of BIND (9.6 and later) and NSD (3.1 and later) understand NSEC3 records.

Turning on DNSSEC

Since NSD is an authoritative-only name server, it only needs to be concerned with serving signed data to DNSSEC-aware clients. There is no need to explicitly turn DNSSEC on. If a zone is signed, NSD uses DNSSEC.

BIND is a bit more complicated. Current BIND releases have removed OpenSSL from the distribution, so if you want to use DNSSEC, you will have to either obtain a preconfigured package that includes DNSSEC support or obtain the SSL libraries directly from openssl.org. If you take the latter route, you'll have to then recompile BIND with cryptographic support turned on (use the **--with-openssl** option to **./configure**). If you don't do this, **dnssec-keygen** will complain. However, it will still work for generating TSIG keys, since those don't require OpenSSL. BIND displays a lovely warning page if your version of OpenSSL is so old that it has known security vulnerabilities.

Two separate workflows are involved in using signed zones: one that creates keys and signs zones, and a second that serves the contents of those signed zones. These duties need not be implemented on the same machine. In fact, it is better to quarantine the private key and the CPU-intensive signing process on a machine that is not publicly accessible from the Internet. (Of course, the machine that serves the data must be visible to the Internet.)

The first step in setting up DNSSEC is to organize your zone files so that all the data files for a zone are in a single directory. The tools that manage DNSSEC zones expect this organization.

Next, enable DNSSEC on your servers with the **named.conf** options

```
options {
    dsnsec-enable yes;
}
```

for authoritative servers and

```
options {
    dsnsec-enable yes;
    dnssec-validation yes;
}
```

for recursive servers. The dnssec-enable option tells your authoritative servers to include DNSSEC record set signatures in their responses when answering queries from DNSSEC-aware name servers. The dnssec-validation option makes **named** verify the legitimacy of signatures it receives in responses from other servers.

Key pair generation

You must generate two key pairs for each zone you want to sign: a zone-signing (ZSK) pair and a key-signing (KSK) pair. Each pair consists of a public key and a private key. The KSK's private key signs the ZSK and creates a secure entry point for the zone. The ZSK's private key signs the zone's resource records. The public keys are then published to allow other sites to verify your signatures.

The BIND commands

```
$ dnssec-keygen -a RSASHA1 -b 1024 -n ZONE example.com
Kexample.com.+005+23301
$ dnssec-keygen -a RSASHA1 -b 2048 -n ZONE -f KSK example.com
Kexample.com.+005+00682
```

or the NSD commands

```
$ ldns-keygen -a RSASHA1 -b 1024 example.com
Kexample.com.+005+23301
$ ldns-keygen -a RSASHA1 -b 2048 -k example.com
Kexample.com.+005+00682
```

generate for example.com a 1,024-bit ZSK pair that uses the RSA and SHA-1 algorithms and a corresponding 2,048-bit KSK pair.[30] The outstanding issue of UDP packet size limits suggests that it's best to use short zone-signing keys, but to change them often. You can use longer key-signing keys to help recover some security. It takes awhile to generate the keys—a minute or two for short keys, and a half-hour or more for longer keys on a tired old laptop.

Both key generators print the base filename of the key they have generated to standard out. In this example, **example.com** is the name of the key, **005** is the identifier of the RSA/SHA-1 algorithm suite, and **23301** and **00682** are hashes called the key identifiers, key footprints, or key tags.[31] Each run of the BIND key generator creates two files (**.key** and **.private**), and the NSD key generator produces three files (**.key**, **.private**, and **.ds**):

```
Kexample.com.+005+23301.key          # Public zone-signing key
Kexample.com.+005+23301.private      # Private zone-signing key
Kexample.com.+005+23301.ds           # DS record for ZSK (NSD only)

Kexample.com.+005+00682.key          # Public key-signing key
Kexample.com.+005+00682.private      # Private key-signing key
Kexample.com.+005+00682.ds           # DS record for KSK (NSD only)
```

Several encryption algorithms are available, each with a range of possible key lengths. You can run **dnssec-keygen** with no arguments or **ldns-keygen -a list** to see the current list of supported algorithms. BIND and NSD can both use keys generated by other software.

Depending on the version of your software, some of the available algorithm names may have NSEC3 appended or prepended to them. If you want to use NSEC3 records instead of NSEC records for signed negative answers, you must generate NSEC3-compatible keys with one of the NSEC3-specific algorithms; see the man pages for **ldns-signzone** or **dnssec-keygen**.

The **.key** files each contain a single DNSKEY resource record for example.com. For example, here is the zone-signing public key, truncated to fit the page. You can tell it's a ZSK because the flags field is 256, rather than 257 for a KSK.

```
example.com.      IN DNSKEY 256 3 5 AwEAAex7tHe60w5va8sPpnRe4RX8MgI...
```

30. 2,048 bits is surely overkill; many sites use 1,500 or fewer.

31. To make it easier to compare the BIND and NSD processes, we finagled the key footprints to make the BIND and NSD sets match. In real life, every key would have a different footprint.

These public keys must be $INCLUDEd or inserted into the zone file, either at the end or right after the SOA record. To copy the keys into the zone file, you can append them with **cat**[32] or paste them in with a text editor.

The **.ds** files produced by NSD's key generator, **ldns-keygen**, contain DS records; the one that corresponds to the KSK would be stored in the parent zone if DNSSEC were fully deployed. The DS record can be generated from the KSK's DNSKEY resource record, and some signed zones require it instead of or in addition to the KSK's DNSKEY record. Here is what DS records look like:

```
example.com.    3600  IN  DS  23301 1 1 5bd844108f8d8fea341b3bc2f2135e...
example.com.    3600  IN  DS  00682 1 1 0dbf80886b7168633ff8273255de09...
```

Ideally, the private key portion of any key pair would be kept off-line, or at least on a machine that is not on the public Internet. This precaution is impossible for dynamically updated zones and impractical for zone-signing keys, but it is perfectly reasonable for key-signing keys, which are presumably quite long-lived. Consider a hidden master server that is not accessible from outside for the ZSKs. Print out the private KSK or write it to a USB memory stick and then lock it in a safe until you need it again.

While you're locking away your new private keys, it's also a good time to enter the new keys into your key log file. You don't need to include the keys themselves, just the IDs, algorithms, date, purpose, and so on.

The default signature validity periods are one month for RRSIG records (ZSK signatures of resource record sets) and three months for DNSKEY records (KSK signatures of ZSKs). Current best practice suggests ZSKs of length 1,024 that are used for three months to a year and KSKs of length 1,280 that are used for a year or two.[33] Since the recommended key retention periods are longer than the default signature validity periods, you must either specify a longer validity period when signing zones or periodically re-sign the zones, even if the key has not changed.

Zone signing

Now that you've got keys, you can sign your zones with the **dnssec-signzone** (BIND) or **ldns-signzone** (NSD) commands, which add RRSIG and NSEC or NSEC3 records for each resource record set. These commands read your original zone file and produce a separate, signed copy named *zonefile***.signed**.

The BIND syntax is

dnssec-signzone [**-o** *zonename*] [**-N increment**] [**-k** *KSKfile*] *zonefile* [*ZSKfile*]

where *zonename* defaults to *zonefile* and the key files default to the filenames produced by **dnssec-keygen** as outlined above.

32. Use a command like **cat Kexample.com.+*.key** >> **zonefile**. The >> appends to the **zonefile** rather than replacing it entirely, as > would. (Don't mess this one up!)

33. The web site keylength.com tabulates a variety of organizations' recommendations regarding the suggested lengths of cryptographic keys.

If you name your zone data files after the zones and maintain the names of the original key files, the command reduces to

```
dnssec-signzone [-N increment] zonefile
```

The **-N increment** flag automatically increments the serial number in the SOA record so that you can't forget. You can also specify the value **unixtime** to update the serial number to the current UNIX time (seconds since January 1, 1970) or the value **keep** to prevent **dnssec-signzone** from modifying the original serial number. The serial number is incremented in the signed zone file but not in the original zone file.

Here's a spelled-out example that uses the keys generated above:

```
$ sudo dnssec-signzone -o example.com -N increment
    -k Kexample.com+005+00682 example.com Kexample.com+005+23301
```

The signed file is sorted in alphabetical order and includes the DNSKEY records we added by hand and the RRSIG and NSEC records generated during signing. The zone's serial number has been incremented.

If you generated your keys with the NSEC3RSASHA1 algorithm, you would sign the zone as above but with the **-3** *salt* flag.

Some other useful options to **dnssec-signzone** are

- **-g** to generate DS record(s) to be included in the parent zone
- **-l** to generate DLV record(s) for use if the parent zone is not signed
- **-s** *start-time* to set the time that the signatures become valid
- **-e** *end-time* to set the time that the signatures expire
- **-t** to print statistics

The dates for signature validity can be expressed as absolute times in the format *yyyymmddhhmmss* or as a time relative to now in the format +*N*, where *N* is in seconds. The default signature validity period is from an hour in the past to 30 days in the future. Here is an example in which we specify that signatures should be valid until the end of the calendar year 2010:

```
$ dnssec-signzone -N increment -e 20101231235959 example.com
```

Under NSD, the syntax for signing a zone is

```
ldns-signzone [-o zonename] zonename key [key ...]
```

You can just list both keys and let **ldns-signzone** figure out which is the KSK and which is the ZSK. For example:

```
$ sudo ldns-signzone example.com Kexample.com.+005+00682
    Kexample.com.+005+23301
```

As with **dnssec-signzone**, you can use the **-e** *yyyymmdd* flag to set the expiration date for signatures. To generate NSEC3 records instead of NSEC records for signing gaps, use the flags **-n -s** *salt*.

Signed zone files are typically four to ten times larger than the original zone, and all your nice logical ordering is lost. A line such as

```
mail-relay                    A      63.173.189.2
```

becomes several lines:

```
mail-relay.example.com.    57600 A      63.173.189.2
                           57600 RRSIG  A 5 3 57600 20090722234636 (
                                  20090622234636 23301 example.com.
                                  Y7s9jDWYuuXvozeU7zGRdFCl+rzU8cLiwoev
                                  0I2TGfLlbhsRgJfkpEYFVRUB7kKVRNguEYwk
                                  d2RSkDJ9QzRQ+w== )
                   3600  NSEC   mail-relay2.example.com. A RRSIG NSEC
                   3600  RRSIG  NSEC 5 3 3600 20090722234636 (
                                  20090622234636 23301 example.com.
                                  42QrXP8vpoChsGPseProBMZ7twf7eS5WK+4O
                                  WNsN84hF0notymRxZRIZypqWzLIPBZAUJ77R
                                  HP0hLfBDoqmZYw== )
```

In practical terms, a signed zone file is no longer human-readable, and it cannot be edited by hand because of the RRSIG and NSEC or NSEC3 records. No user-serviceable parts inside!

With the exception of DNSKEY records, each resource record set (resource records of the same type for the same name) gets one signature from the ZSK. DNSKEY resource records are signed by both the ZSK and the KSK, so they have two RRSIGs. The base-64 representation of a signature ends in however many equal signs are needed to make the length a multiple of 4.

For clarity in subsequent examples, we assume that the zone file is named for the zone and that the zone files and the key files are in the same directory. In real life it's actually a good idea to specify the key files explicitly, especially when you are rolling over keys and need to be sure the command uses the right ones.

Once your zones are signed, all that remains is to point your name server at the signed versions of the zone files. If you're using BIND, look for the zone statement that corresponds to each zone in **named.conf** and change the file parameter from **example.com** to **example.com.signed**. For NSD, the corresponding configuration file is **nsd.conf** and you're looking for zonefile lines.

Finally, restart the name server daemon, telling it to reread its configuration file. For BIND, do **sudo rndc reconfig** followed by **sudo rndc flush**. For NSD, try **sudo nsdc rebuild** followed by **sudo nsdc restart**.

We are now serving a DNSSEC signed zone! To make changes, you can edit either the original unsigned zone or the signed zone and then re-sign the zone. Editing a signed zone is something of a logistical nightmare, but it is much quicker than re-signing the entire zone. Be sure to remove the RRSIG records that correspond to any records that you change. You probably want to make identical changes to the unsigned zone to avoid version skew.

If you pass a signed zone as the argument to **dnssec-signzone** or **ldns-signzone**, any unsigned records are signed and the signatures of any records that are close to expiring are renewed. "Close to expiring" is defined as being three-quarters of the way through the validity period. Re-signing typically results in changes, so make sure you increment the zone's serial number by hand or, with BIND, use the **-N increment** clause on the **dnssec-signzone** command line to automatically increment the zone's serial number.

That's all there is to the local part of DNSSEC configuration. What's left is the thorny problem of getting our island of secure DNS connected to other trusted, signed parts of the DNS hierarchy. We either need to get our DS records into the signed parent zone, or we need to use the domain lookaside validation workaround. The next sections cover these tasks.

The DNSSEC chain of trust

Continuing with our example DNSSEC setup, example.com is now signed and its name servers have DNSSEC enabled. This means that when querying they use EDNS0, the extended DNS protocol, and set the DNSSEC-aware option in the DNS header of the packet. When answering a query that arrives with that bit set, they include the signature data with their answer.

A client that receives signed answers can validate the response by checking the record's signatures with the appropriate public key. But it gets this key from the zone's own DNSKEY record, which is rather suspicious if you think about it. What's to stop an impostor from serving up both fake records and a fake public key that validates them?

There are several possible answers to this question. Your site must implement at least one of them; otherwise, all your DNSSEC work is for naught.

The canonical solution is that you give your parent zone a DS record to include in its zone file. By virtue of coming from the parent zone, the DS record is certified by the parent's private key. If the client trusts your parent zone, it should then trust that the parent zone's DS record accurately reflects your zone's public key.

The parent zone is in turn certified by its parent, and so on back to the root. When DNSSEC is fully deployed, the only key you will need to know a priori is the public key used to sign the root, which can be put in the root hints file that bootstraps the whole DNS process.

If you're lucky enough to have a signed parent, just give your parent's administrators a DS record and the key-signing DNSKEY used to sign it.[34] The **-g** flag to BIND's **dnssec-signzone** generates files called **dsset-domain** and **keyset-domain** that can be securely delivered to your parent to be added directly to the parent's zone file. Similarly, NSD's **ldns-keygen** produces the required DS record in the **.ds** file and the DNSKEY record in the **.key** file as the keys are generated. Note that

34. How can you tell if your parent is signed? Try **dig +dnssec** or **drill -D**.

you must publish your DNSKEY record in your own zone before your parent installs the corresponding DS record.

If your parent zone isn't signed, you must provide some other way for the outside world to verify that the public key published in your DNS is really yours. There are three different ways to do this:

- Use one or more of the trusted anchor repositories (TAR) to publish your public key; for example, the one from SecSpider. To use TAR keys on your own servers, get the key lists from SecSpider, from the ITAR run by the IANA (contains only TLDs), or from the RIPE-NCC TAR (contains only their own zones, mostly European TLDs and reverse zones). Put these in a `trusted-keys` clause in your name server config file.
- Use a domain lookaside validation server such as that provided by ISC, the Internet Systems Consortium. This service essentially makes isc.org your adoptive DNS parent. It's easy and free; see isc.org/ops/dlv. Other DLV servers exist, but you can use only one, and ISC's is well established and well run.
- Use Vantages (vantage-points.org), a daemon that partners with copies of itself that belong to friends you trust, thus forming a social network of daemons who can obtain keys independently from different sites on the Internet and compare their results to decide if the keys are authentic.

We describe the DLV solution in more detail in the next section. But keep in mind that all three of these options are interim solutions designed to help with incremental DNSSEC deployment. If your parent zone is already signed, don't even consider these options. Just give your parent the appropriate DS record.

DLV: domain lookaside validation

A DNSSEC-aware caching server that receives a signed query response first verifies that the record signatures match the domain's public key as specified by its DNSKEY record. The client then attempts to validate the key itself by looking in the parent zone for a DS record. If no DS record is available, the client looks for a DLV record in the original domain; that record redirects to dlv.isc.org or whichever DLV server is acting as the zone's foster parent. Once the client gets hold of the DLV record from dlv.isc.org, it can verify the chain of trust. Setting up DLV service for your zone is therefore a matter of generating the appropriate DLV records and putting them in the right places.

A DLV record is really just a DS record in disguise. The record type is different, but the body of the record is the same. The record's *name* field is also modified to place the record into the DLV provider's zone. For example, example.com might become example.com.dlv.isc.org.

In BIND, **dnssec-signzone -l** (lowercase letter L) generates the DLV record:

```
$ sudo dnssec-signzone -l dlv.isc.org example.com
```

This command re-signs the zone and writes a file called **dlvset-example.com.** containing a DLV record ready for the DLV provider's zone.

NSD/Unbound users must generate the DLV record themselves. Copy the **.ds** file created when you generated your KSK key and change the record type from DS to DLV. Then adjust the *name* field. For example, change

```
example.com.              3600  IN  DS   25069 1 1 0dbf80886b716863de09...
```

to

```
example.com.dlv.isc.org.  3600  IN  DLV  25069 1 1 0dbf80886b716863de09...
```

The changes are shown in bold.

Once you've collected the DLV record and the key files used to sign your zone, go to the dlv.isc.org web page and follow the directions to have isc.org be your DLV server. ISC makes you jump through some hoops to verify that you own your domain, are authorized to manage it, and have provided its public key securely. But the process is not difficult.

ISC will give you some new lines for your trusted-keys clause in **named.conf**:

```
trusted-keys {
    dlv.isc.com 257 3 5 "hex mumbo jumbo of the key goes here";
    dlv.isc.com 257 3 5 "hex mumbo jumbo of another key goes here";
    ...
}
```

BIND users must also add a line to the **named.conf** options section:

```
dnssec-lookaside "." trusted-anchor "dlv.isc.org" ;
```

For NSD, add the DLV record to the zone and re-sign the zone. To enable DLV validation in **unbound**, get dlv.isc.org's KSK DNSKEY record from the ISC web site or from SecSpider and verify its signature. (SecSpider verifies that keys are consistent as seen from multiple locations; see page 652.) Don't just **dig** for the key, as that's insecure until you have DNSSEC deployed. Put the key in a file in **unbound**'s working directory, say, **dlv.isc.org.key**, and add the line

```
dlv-anchor-file: "dlv.isc.org.key"
```

to your **unbound.conf** file in the server section.

DNSSEC key rollover

Key rollover has always been a thorny issue in DNSSEC. In fact, the original specifications were changed specifically to address the issue of the communication needed between parent and child zones whenever keys were created, changed, or deleted. The new specifications are called DNSSEC-bis.

ZSK rollover is relatively straightforward and does not involve your parent zone or any trust anchor issues. The only tricky part is the timing. Keys have an expiration time, so rollover must occur well before that. However, they also have a TTL, defined in the zone file. For the sake of illustration, let's assume that the TTL is one day and that keys don't expire for another week. The steps involved are then

- Generate a new ZSK.
- Include it in the zone file.
- Sign or re-sign the zone with the KSK and the *old* ZSK.
- Signal the name server to reload the zone; the new key is now there.
- Wait 24 hours (the TTL); now everyone has both the old and new keys.
- Sign the zone again with the KSK and the *new* ZSK.
- Signal the name server to reload the zone.
- Wait another 24 hours; now everyone has the new signed zone.
- Remove the old ZSK at your leisure, e.g., the next time the zone changes.

This scheme is called prepublishing. Needless to say, you must start the process at least two TTLs before the point at which you need to have everyone using the new key. The waiting periods guarantee that any site with cached values always has a cached key that corresponds to the cached data.

Another variable that affects this process is the time it takes for your slowest slave server to update its copy of your zone when notified by the master server. So don't wait until the last minute to start your rollover process or to re-sign zones whose signatures are expiring. Expired signatures do not validate, so sites that verify DNSSEC signatures will not be able to do DNS lookups for your domain.

The mechanism to roll over a KSK is called double signing and it's also pretty straightforward. However, you will need to communicate your new DS record to your parent or communicate a DLV record to your surrogate parent. Make sure you have positive acknowledgement from the parent or trust anchor repository before you switch to just the new key. Here are the steps:

- Create a new KSK.
- Include it in the zone file.
- Sign the zone with both old and new KSKs and the ZSK.
- Signal the name server to reload the zone.
- Wait 24 hours (the TTL); now everyone has the new key.
- Notify anyone with a trust anchor for you of the new KSK value.
- After confirmation, delete the old KSK record from the zone.
- Re-sign the zone with the new KSK and ZSK.

DNSSEC tools

Four tool sets for dealing with DNSSEC deployment and testing exist in addition to those that come with the BIND and NSD/Unbound distributions: **ldns**, Sparta, RIPE, and Vantages. At least two more sets are under development: OpenDNSSEC (opendnssec.org) and DNSSHIM. OpenDNSSEC hopes to manage all the mess and complexity that comes with DNSSEC automatically, which sounds wonderful. DNSSHIM is an authoritative DNS server implementation with automatic configuration of slaves and DNSSEC goo written in Java and Python.

***ldns** tools, nlnetlabs.nl/projects/ldns*

ldns, from the folks at NLnet Labs, is a library of routines for writing DNS tools and a set of example programs that use the library. We list the tools below along with a brief statement of what each one does. The tools are all in the **examples** directory except for **drill**, which has its own directory in the distribution. Man pages can be found with the commands. The top-level **README** file gives very brief installation instructions.

- **ldns-keygen** generates TSIG keys and DNSSEC key pairs.
- **ldns-signzone** signs a zone file with either NSEC or NSEC3.
- **ldns-verify-zone** makes sure RRSIG, NSEC, and NSEC3 records are OK.
- **ldns-key2ds** converts a DNSKEY record to a DS record.
- **ldns-rrsig** prints out human-readable expiration dates from RRSIGs.
- **ldns-nsec3-hash** prints the NSEC3 hash for a name.
- **ldns-revoke** sets the revoke flag on a DNSKEY key RR (RFC5011).
- **ldns-chaos** shows the name server ID info stored in the CHAOS class.
- **ldns-keyfetcher** fetches DNSSEC public keys for zones.
- **ldns-read-zone** reads a zone and prints it out in various formats.
- **ldns-update** sends a dynamic update packet.
- **ldns-walk** walks through a zone, using the DNSSEC NSEC records.
- **ldns-zsplit** splits a zone into chunks so it can be signed in parallel.
- **ldns-zcat** reassembles zone files split with **ldns-zsplit**.
- **ldns-compare-zones** shows the differences between two zone files.
- **ldns-notify** makes a zone's slave servers check for updates.
- **ldns-dpa** analyzes DNS packets in **tcpdump** trace files.

Many of these tools are very simple and do only one tiny DNS chore. They were written as examples of using the **ldns** library and demonstrate how simple the code becomes when the library does all the hard bits for you.

Sparta tools, dnssec-tools.org

The Sparta tool set builds on the BIND tools for DNSSEC and includes the following commands:

- **zonesigner** generates keys and signs zones.
- **donuts** analyzes zone files and finds errors and inconsistencies.
- **donutsd** runs **donuts** at intervals and warns of problems.
- **rollerd**, **rollctl**, and **rollinit** automate key rollovers using the prepublishing scheme for ZSKs and the double signature method for KSKs. See page 662 for the details of these schemes.
- **trustman** manages trust anchors and includes an implementation of RFC5011 key rollover.
- **dnspktflow** traces the flow of DNS packets during a query/response sequence captured by **tcpdump** and produces a cool diagram.
- **mapper** maps your zone files, showing secure and insecure portions.
- **validate** is a command-line signature validation tool.

The web site contains good documentation and tutorials for all of these tools. The source code is available for download and is covered by the BSD license.

Sparta maintains DNSSEC libraries written in Perl that are distributed through CPAN. It also distributes patches to several popular software packages (including Firefox, Thunderbird, Postfix, **sendmail**, **libSPF**, and OpenSSH) to make them more DNSSEC aware.

RIPE tools, ripe.net

RIPE's tools act as a front end to BIND's DNSSEC tools and focus on key management. They have friendlier messages as they run and package up the many arguments and commands into more intuitive forms.

Vantages tools, vantage-points.org

Vantages is a framework for distributed monitoring that is based at Colorado State University. Its current focus is on operational issues related to DNSSEC, and Vantages tools can be used to help maintain your DNSSEC deployment.

The project's chief product is **vantaged**, a daemon that gathers DNSKEY records and compares their values with those obtained by other **vantaged**s around the Internet. If lots of **vantaged**s get the same answer, the key is likely to be accurate and not spoofed; a spoofer would have to compromise all sites running the Vantage software to get this result. Vantages collects keys from DNS, HTTP, and HTTPS sources and classifies them into one of four states: confirmed, provisional, unknown, and conflict. It adds confirmed keys to your `trusted-keys` statement in **named.conf**.

Vantages has some additional tools as well:

- **d-sync** monitors the consistency of DS record keys between parent and child zones, which is especially useful during key rollovers.
- **dnsfunnel** determines the path MTU between you and any other site. It looks a bit like **traceroute**.
- **dnskey-grab** gets the DNSKEYs for a zone from its authoritative servers.

Debugging DNSSEC

DNSSEC has been designed to interoperate with both signed and unsigned zones, and with both DNSSEC-aware and DNSSEC-oblivious name servers. So incremental deployment is possible, and it usually just works. But not always.

DNSSEC is a distributed system with lots of moving parts. Authoritative servers, client resolvers, and the paths between them can all experience problems. A problem seen locally may originate far away, so tools like SecSpider and Vantages that monitor the distributed state of the system can be very helpful. Those tools, the utilities mentioned in the previous section, and your name server log files are your primary weapons on the debugging front.

Make sure that you route the DNSSEC logging category in **named.conf** to a file on the local machine. It's helpful to separate out the DNSSEC-related messages so that you don't route any other logging categories to this file. Here is an example logging specification for **named**:

```
channel dnssec-log {
    file "/var/log/named/dnssec.log" versions 4 size 10m ;
    print-time yes ;
    print-category yes ;
    print-severity yes;
    severity debug 3;
} ;
category dnssec { dnssec-log; } ;
```

In BIND you must set the debugging level to 3 or higher to see the validation steps taken by a recursive BIND server trying to validate a signature. This logging level produces about two pages of logging output per signature verified. If you are monitoring a busy server, log data from multiple queries will likely be interleaved. Sorting through the mess can be challenging and tedious.

For NSD and Unbound, set the verbosity level higher than the defaults (0 and 1, respectively) in their config files or, for Unbound, just adjust the verbosity on the fly with the **verbosity** *level* flag to **unbound-control**. Like BIND, Unbound must be at log level 3 to show the steps for signature validation.

Once things are working OK, set Unbound's val-log-level to 1 to print a one-line error message for each signature that fails to verify. This level of detail helps you keep track of sites that are giving you trouble. You can further explore the failures with either the signature chase option to **drill** or with **unbound-host -v -d** (or even **-dddd** to get lots of debugging info) on the problem name. You must pass both **drill** and **unbound-host** the relevant public keys.

drill has two particularly useful flags: **-T** to trace the chain of trust from the root to a specified host, and **-S** to chase the signatures from a specified host back to the root. Here's some mocked-up sample output from **drill -S** snitched from the *DNSSEC HOWTO* at NLnet Labs:

```
$ drill -S -k ksk.keyfile example.net SOA
DNSSEC Trust tree:
example.net. (SOA)
|---example.net. (DNSKEY keytag: 17000)
    |---example.net. (DNSKEY keytag: 49656)
    |---example.net. (DS keytag: 49656)
        |---net. (DNSKEY keytag: 62972)
            |---net. (DNSKEY keytag: 13467)
            |---net. (DS keytag: 13467)
                |---. (DNSKEY keytag: 63380)
                    |---. (DNSKEY keytag: 63276)   ;; Chase successful
```

If a validating name server cannot verify a signature, it returns a SERVFAIL indication. The underlying problem could be a configuration error by someone at one of the zones in the chain of trust, bogus data from an interloper, or a problem in the setup of the validating recursive server itself. Try **drill** to chase the signatures along the chain of trust and see where the problem is. If the signatures all verify, then try querying the troublesome site with **dig** and then with **dig +cd**. (The **cd** flag turns off validation.) Try this at each of the zones in the chain of trust to see if you can find the problem. You can work your way up or down the chain of trust. The likely result will be an expired trust anchor or expired signatures.

17.14 Microsoft and DNS

For years, ISC and BIND struggled to interoperate with Microsoft's DNS tools and Active Directory product. Microsoft was accused of being intentionally incompatible with the standards and of not documenting the protocol extensions they were using. However, it now appears that Microsoft was not really trying to be incompatible; they were just slightly incompetent and were working with buggy software (their ASN.1 encoder and parser) that tweaked the packets just enough so that BIND could not make sense of them. Now, all is well. The bugs have been fixed, and both BIND and Microsoft follow the IETF protocols and can interoperate. That's the good news.

The bad news is that Active Directory is tightly integrated with Kerberos and LDAP and follows its own twisty little passages (all alike!). Replacing any of the pieces—for example, the Kerberos key distribution center—with a comparable open source implementation is doomed to failure. BIND can do authentication with Active Directory by using GSS-TSIG, but authorization is still nearly impossible because AD stores everything in an LDAP database from hell.

See Chapter 30, *Cooperating with Windows*, for hints on peaceful coexistence with Active Directory. It starts on page 1135.

17.15 Testing and debugging

Both BIND and NSD/Unbound provide three basic debugging tools: logging, a control program, and a command-line query tool. BIND's fleet is the most mature, but since BIND is also the most complicated, things even out.

Logging in BIND

See Chapter 11 for more information about syslog.

named's logging facilities are flexible enough to make your hair stand on end. BIND originally just used syslog to report error messages and anomalies. Recent versions generalize the syslog concepts by adding another layer of indirection and support for logging directly to files. Before we dive in, let's take a look at the mini-glossary of BIND logging terms shown in Table 17.13 on the next page.

You configure BIND logging with a logging statement in **named.conf**. You first define channels, the possible destinations for messages. You then tell various categories of message to go to particular channels.

Table 17.13 A BIND logging lexicon

Term	What it means
channel	A place where messages can go: syslog, a file, or **/dev/null**[a]
category	A class of messages that **named** can generate; for example, messages about dynamic updates or messages about answering queries
module	The name of the source module that generates a message
facility	A syslog facility name. DNS does not have its own specific facility, but you have your pick of all the standard ones.
severity	The "badness" of an error message; what syslog refers to as a priority

a. **/dev/null** is a pseudo-device that throws away all input.

When a message is generated, it is assigned a category, a module, and a severity at its point of origin. It is then distributed to all the channels associated with its category and module. Each channel has a severity filter that tells what severity level a message must have in order to get through. Channels that lead to syslog are also filtered according to the rules in **/etc/syslog.conf**.

Here's the outline of a logging statement:

```
logging {
    channel_def;
    channel_def;
    ...
    category category_name {
        channel_name;
        channel_name;
        ...
    };
};
```

Channels

A *channel_def* looks slightly different depending on whether the channel is a file channel or a syslog channel. You must choose file or syslog for each channel; a channel can't be both at the same time.

```
channel channel_name {
    file path [versions numvers | unlimited] [size sizespec];
    syslog facility;
    severity severity;

    print-category yes | no;
    print-severity yes | no;
    print-time yes | no;
};
```

For a file channel, *numvers* tells how many backup versions of a file to keep, and *sizespec* specifies how large the file should be allowed to grow (examples: 2048,

100k, 20m, unlimited, default) before it is automatically rotated. If you name a file channel **mylog**, the rotated versions are **mylog.0**, **mylog.1**, and so on.

See page 346 for a list of syslog facility names.

In the syslog case, *facility* specifies what syslog facility name is used to log the message. It can be any standard facility. In practice, only daemon and local0 through local7 are reasonable choices.

The rest of the statements in a *channel_def* are optional. *severity* can have the values (in descending order) critical, error, warning, notice, info, or debug (with an optional numeric level, e.g., severity debug 3). The value dynamic is also recognized and matches the server's current debug level.

The various print options add or suppress message prefixes. Syslog prepends the time and reporting host to each message logged, but not the severity or the category. The source filename (module) that generated the message is also available as a print option. It makes sense to enable print-time only for file channels—syslog adds its own time stamps, so there's no need to duplicate them.

The four channels listed in Table 17.14 are predefined by default. These defaults should be fine for most installations.

Table 17.14 Predefined logging channels in BIND

Channel name	What it does
default_syslog	Sends to syslog, facility daemon, severity info
default_debug	Logs to the file **named.run**, severity set to dynamic
default_stderr	Sends to standard error of the **named** process, severity info
null	Discards all messages

Categories

Categories are determined by the programmer at the time the code is written. They organize log messages by topic or functionality instead of just by severity. Table 17.15 on the next page shows the current list of message categories.

Log Messages

The default logging configuration is:

```
logging {
    category default { default_syslog; default_debug; };
};
```

You should watch the log files when you make major changes to BIND and perhaps increase the logging level. Later, reconfigure to preserve only serious messages once you have verified that **named** is stable.

Query logging can be quite educational. You can verify that your allow clauses are working, see who is querying you, identify broken clients, etc. It's a good check to

Table 17.15 BIND logging categories

Category	What it includes
client	Client requests
config	Configuration file parsing and processing
database	Messages about database operations
default	Default for categories without specific logging options
delegation-only	Queries forced to NXDOMAIN by delegation-only zones
dispatch	Dispatching of incoming packets to server modules
dnssec	DNSSEC messages
edns-disabled	Info about broken servers
general	Catchall for unclassified messages
lame-servers	Servers that are supposed to be serving a zone, but aren't [a]
network	Network operations
notify	Messages about the "zone changed" notification protocol
queries	A short log message for every query the server receives (!)
resolver	DNS resolution, e.g., recursive lookups for clients
security	Approved/unapproved requests
unmatched	Queries **named** cannot classify (bad class, no view)
update	Messages about dynamic updates
update-security	Approval or denial of update requests
xfer-in	Zone transfers that the server is receiving
xfer-out	Zone transfers that the server is sending

a. Either the parent zone or the child zone could be at fault; impossible to tell without investigating.

perform after major reconfigurations, especially if you have a good sense of what your query load looked like before the changes.

To start query logging, just direct the queries category to a channel. Writing to syslog is less efficient than writing directly to a file, so use a file channel on a local disk when you are logging every query. Have lots of disk space and be ready to turn query logging off once you obtain enough data. (**rndc querylog** toggles query logging on and off dynamically.)

Views can be pesky to debug, but fortunately, the view that matched a particular query is logged along with the query.

Some common log messages are listed below:

- *Lame server resolving xxx.* If you get this message about one of your own zones, you have configured something incorrectly. The message is harmless if it's about some zone out on the Internet; it's someone else's problem. A good one to throw away by directing it to the null channel.
- *... query (cache) xxx denied.* This can be either misconfiguration of the remote site, abuse, or a case in which someone has delegated a zone to you, but you have not configured it.

- *Too many timeouts resolving xxx: disabling EDNS.* This message can result from a broken firewall not admitting UDP packets over 512 bytes long or not admitting fragments. It can also indicate problems at the specified host. Verify that the problem is not your firewall and consider redirecting these messages to the null channel.
- *Unexpected RCODE (SERVFAIL) resolving xxx.* This can be an attack or, more likely, a sign of something repeatedly querying a lame zone.
- *Bad referral.* This message indicates a miscommunication among a zone's name servers.
- *Not authoritative for.* A slave server is unable to get authoritative data for a zone. Perhaps it's pointing to the wrong master, or perhaps the master had trouble loading the zone in question.
- *Rejected zone.* **named** rejected a zone file because it contained errors.
- *No NS RRs found.* A zone file did not include NS records after the SOA record. It could be that the records are missing, or it could be that they don't start with a tab or other whitespace. In the latter case, the records are not attached to the zone of the SOA record and are therefore misinterpreted.
- *No default TTL set.* The preferred way to set the default TTL for resource records is with a $TTL directive at the top of the zone file. This error message indicates that the $TTL is missing; it is required in BIND 9.
- *No root name server for class.* Your server is having trouble finding the root name servers. Check your hints file and the server's Internet connectivity.
- *Address already in use.* The port on which **named** wants to run is already being used by another process, probably another copy of **named**. If you don't see another **named** around, it might have crashed and left an **rndc** control socket open that you'll have to track down and remove. A good way to fix the problem is to stop the **named** process with **rndc** and then restart **named**:

  ```
  $ sudo rndc stop
  $ sudo /usr/sbin/named ...
  ```

- *... updating zone xxx: update unsuccessful.* A dynamic update for a zone was attempted but refused, most likely because of the allow-update or update-policy clause in **named.conf** for this zone. This is a common error message and often is caused by misconfigured Windows boxes.

Sample BIND logging configuration

The following snippet from the ISC **named.conf** file for a busy TLD name server illustrates a comprehensive logging regimen.

```
logging {
    channel default_log { # Default channel, to a file
        file "log/named.log" versions 3 size 10m;
        print-time yes;
        print-category yes;
        print-severity  yes;
        severity info;
    };
    channel xfer-log { # Zone transfers channel, to a file
        file "log/xfer.log" versions 3 size 10m;
        print-category yes;
        print-severity yes;
        print-time yes;
        severity info;
    };

    channel dnssec-log { # DNSSEC channel, to a file
        file "log/dnssec.log" versions 3 size 1M;
        severity debug 1;
        print-severity yes;
        print-time yes;
    };
    category default { default_log; default_debug; };
    category dnssec { dnssec-log; };
    category xfer-in { xfer-log; };
    category xfer-out { xfer-log; };
    category notify { xfer-log; };
};
```

Debug levels in BIND

named debug levels are indicated by integers from 0 to 100. The higher the number, the more verbose the output. Level 0 turns debugging off. Levels 1 and 2 are fine for debugging your configuration and database. Levels beyond about 4 are appropriate for the maintainers of the code.

You invoke debugging on the **named** command line with the **-d** flag. For example,

```
$ sudo named -d2
```

would start **named** at debug level 2. By default, debugging information is written to the file **named.run** in the current working directory from which **named** is started. The **named.run** file grows very fast, so don't go out for a beer while debugging or you will have bigger problems when you return.

You can also turn on debugging while **named** is running with **rndc trace**, which increments the debug level by 1, or with **rndc trace** *level*, which sets the debug level to the value specified. **rndc notrace** turns debugging off completely. You can also enable debugging by defining a logging channel that includes a severity specification such as

```
severity debug 3;
```

which sends all debugging messages up to level 3 to that particular channel. Other lines in the channel definition specify the destination of those debugging messages. The higher the severity level, the more information is logged.

Watching the logs or the debugging output illustrates how often DNS is misconfigured in the real world. That pesky little dot at the end of names (or rather, the lack thereof) accounts for an alarming amount of DNS traffic. The dot is required at the end of each fully qualified domain name.

Logging in NSD/Unbound

Logging in NSD and Unbound is simple in comparison to BIND. According to NSD's **doc/README** file, "NSD doesn't do any logging." What that really means is that NSD does not do any DNS traffic logging or monitoring; however, it does log important software events to syslog.

By default, log messages go to standard error and to syslog with facility daemon. However, if the logfile attribute of the server statement in either **unbound.conf** or **nsd.conf** is set, then logging goes to the specified file.

The amount of data logged (aside from errors, which are always included) is controlled by a verbosity level that you set in the config files. In the case of **unbound**, you can also set the verbosity level as a command-line option. Verbosity varies from 0–5; the default levels are 0 for **nsd** and 1 for **unbound**.

It can be a bit hard to get a handle on what the various verbosity levels mean for **nsd**. They map to syslog roughly as follows:

- Level 3 – syslog severity "error"
- Level 4 – syslog severity "warning"
- Level 5 – syslog severity "notice"
- Level 6 – syslog severity "info"

The meanings of the levels for **unbound** are documented in the config file's man page as follows:

- Level 0 – no information logged, only errors
- Level 1 – operational information
- Level 2 – detailed operational information
- Level 3 – query-level information on a per-query basis
- Level 4 – algorithm-level information
- Level 5 – cache misses and client identification

You can invoke **nsd** with the **-d** flag to turn on debugging mode. In this mode, **nsd** stays in the foreground instead of forking and exiting. This behavior is equivalent to what you get if you set debug-mode: yes in the server clause of **nsd.conf**. If you recompile **nsd** with DEBUG defined to a particular level, even more debugging information becomes available, but it's mostly of value to developers.

unbound also has a **-d** flag to turn on debugging mode. You can boost the verbosity of the debugging information with the **-v** flag; for more, try **-v -v**. Debugging output is separate from the verbosity of logging information set in the config file. You can configure additional logging to help debug DNSSEC signature validation issues; see page 666.

Name server control programs

All three of our name servers come with a control program: **nsdc** controls **nsd**, **rndc** controls **named**, and **unbound-control** controls **unbound**. **nsdc** works on the local machine only, but **rndc** and **unbound-control** can work across the Internet if you set them up that way.

rndc uses a network socket to communicate with **named** and uses TSIG authentication for security. **unbound-control** uses SSL/TLS, and **nsdc** uses signals.

Using BIND's ***rndc***

Table 17.16 shows some of the options accepted by **rndc**. Typing **rndc** with no arguments gives a list of available commands and a short description of what they do. Earlier incantations of **rndc** used signals as **nsdc** does, but with over 25 commands, the BIND folks ran out of signals long ago. Commands that produce files put them in whatever directory is specified as **named**'s home in **named.conf**.

rndc reload makes **named** reread its configuration file and reload zone files. The **reload** *zone* command is handy when only one zone has changed and you don't want to reload all the zones, especially on a busy server. You can also specify a *class* and *view* to reload only the selected view of the zone's data.

Note that **rndc reload** is not sufficient to add a completely new zone; that requires **named** to read both the **named.conf** file and the new zone file. For new zones, use **rndc reconfig**, which rereads the config file and loads any new zones without disturbing existing zones.

rndc freeze *zone* stops dynamic updates and reconciles the journal of dynamic updates to the data files. After freezing the zone, you can edit the zone data by hand. As long as the zone is frozen, dynamic updates are refused. Once you've finished editing, use **rndc thaw** *zone* to start accepting dynamic updates again.

rndc dumpdb makes **named** dump its database to **named_dump.db**. The dump file is big and includes not only local data but also any cached data the name server has accumulated.

Your versions of **named** and **rndc** must match or you will get an error message about a protocol version mismatch. They're normally installed together on individual machines, but version skew can be an issue when you are trying to control a **named** on another computer.

Table 17.16 rndc commands[a]

Command	Function
dumpdb	Dumps the DNS database to **named_dump.db**
flush [*view*]	Flushes all caches or those for a specified *view*
flushname *name* [*view*]	Flushes the specified *name* from the server's cache
freeze *zone* [*class* [*view*]]	Suspends updates to a dynamic *zone*
thaw *zone* [*class* [*view*]]	Resumes updates to a dynamic *zone*
halt	Halts **named** without writing pending updates
querylog	Toggles tracing of incoming queries
notify *zone* [*class* [*view*]]	Resends notification messages for *zone*
notrace	Turns off debugging
reconfig	Reloads the config file and loads any new zones
recursing	Dumps queries currently recursing, **named.recursing**
refresh *zone* [*class* [*view*]]	Schedules maintenance for a *zone*
reload	Reloads **named.conf** and zone files
reload *zone* [*class* [*view*]]	Reloads only the specified *zone* or *view*
restart[b]	Restarts the server
retransfer *zone* [*class* [*view*]]	Recopies the data for *zone* from the master server
stats	Dumps statistics to **named.stats**
status	Displays the current status of the running **named**
stop	Saves pending updates and then stops **named**
trace	Increments the debug level by 1
trace *level*	Changes the debug level to the value *level*
validation *newstate*	Enables/disables DNSSEC validation on the fly

a. The *class* argument here is the same as for resource records, typically IN for Internet.
b. Not yet implemented in BIND 9 (9.7.0), but it has been promised forever—must be hard to do.

Using NSD's ***nsdc***

NSD's control program, **nsdc**, is a shell script that uses signals to control the behavior of **nsd** and **zonec**, its zone precompiler companion. Because **nsdc** must be run on the same machine as **nsd**, keys are not needed.

nsdc has a smaller repertoire of commands than **rndc**, as shown in Table 17.17 on the next page. When run, **nsdc** reads the **nsd.conf** configuration file and uses the **nsd-checkconf** utility to verify that there are no syntax errors.

Using ***unbound-control***

unbound-control talks to the **unbound** name server through TLS, the transport layer security protocol (formerly known as SSL), which uses a key and a certificate for each end. These keys are configured in the remote-control section of the config file **unbound.conf**. More than 20 commands can be given remotely to modify the server's behavior. Rather than list all possible commands, we refer you to the man page for **unbound-control**, where they are well documented.

Table 17.17 nsdc commands

Command	Function
start	Starts the **nsd** server
stop	Stops the **nsd** server (sends SIGTERM)
reload	Reloads the compiled zone database
rebuild	Rebuilds the zone database with **zonec**
restart	Restarts **nsd**; that is, stops it and then starts it
running	Checks whether **nsd** is running; no output means all's well
update	Tries to update all slave zones
notify	Sends notify messages to all slave servers
patch	Merges zone transfer changes (database) back to zone files (text)

Among the 20 are the usual start, stop, and reread types, but also several options that allow fine-grained control of the cache and the local data zones that have been configured. Options such as forwarding can be configured or modified on the fly. You can dump or reload the cache as well.

Name server statistics

Each of our name servers collects statistics with varying granularity and can dump them to a file on request. Several options are configurable: what data to collect, where to write it, how often to update it, and so on. BIND's new statistics channel is the most flexible mechanism. NSD's attitude is that it's a sleek, speedy name server and that if you want statistics, another program should gather them and let NSD get on with it primary job. **unbound** is somewhere in the middle.

BIND and **unbound** can both send their statistics to another program for presentation and graphing. BIND uses the new statistics-channels statement (page 612) and XML. **unbound** uses plug-ins in the **contrib** directory to connect to either Munin or Cacti (see page 886).

named maintains summary information that can be dumped to **named.stats** in **named**'s working directory on receipt of a nudge from **rndc**:

```
$ sudo rndc stats
```

Here's a small snippet of the output from a server in the vix.com domain. Lots has been left out; about 20 groups of data are shown, but we include only two:

```
+++ Statistics Dump +++ (1248150900)
++ Incoming Queries ++
2650862 A
9105 NS
404378 SOA
85744 PTR
246258 MX
3208092 TXT
...
```

```
++ Name Server Statistics ++
10028960 IPv4 requests received
388015 IPv6 requests received
5896039 requests with EDNS(0) received
92403 TCP requests received
4363730 queries resulted in successful answer
766435 queries resulted in nxrrset
599672 queries resulted in NXDOMAIN
...
```

The statistics show the success vs. failure of lookups and categorize the various kinds of errors. This server received 10 million queries, with the majority of the query types being AAAA (the IPv6 address type) and TXT (perhaps for SPF or DKIM records). The logs showed quite a bit of bogus activity on this server (e.g., unauthorized zone transfer requests). Perhaps the unusually high number of AAAA and TXT record queries is part of this activity—A records are typically the most queried-for.

If **named** has been compiled with the XML library, the statistics-channels statement in **named.conf** sets up a real-time statistics feed that you can monitor with a web browser.

Debugging with dig

Four command-line tools query the DNS database: **nslookup**, **dig**, **host**, and **drill**. The first three are distributed with BIND, and **drill** comes with Unbound/**ldns**. **nslookup** and **host** are simple and have pretty output, but you need **dig** or **drill** to get all the details. **drill** is better for following DNSSEC signature chains. The name **drill** is a pun on **dig** (the **d**omain **i**nformation **g**roper), implying you can get even more info from DNS with **drill** than you can with **dig**.

By default, **dig** and **drill** query the name servers configured in **/etc/resolv.conf**. The @*nameserver* argument makes either command query a specific name server. The ability to query a particular server lets you check to be sure that any changes you make to a zone have been propagated to secondary servers and to the outside world. This feature is especially useful if you use views (split DNS) and need to verify that you have configured them correctly.

If you specify a record type, **dig** and **drill** query for that type only. The pseudo-type **ANY** is a bit sneaky: instead of returning all data associated with a name, it returns all *cached* data associated with the name. So, to get all records, you might have to do **dig** *domain* **NS** followed by **dig @ns1.***domain domain* **ANY**. (Authoritative data counts as cached in this context.)

dig has about 50 options and **drill** about half that many. Either command accepts an **-h** flag to list the various options. (You'll probably want to pipe the output through **less**.) For both tools, **-x** reverses the bytes of an IP address and does a reverse query. The **+trace** flag to **dig** or **-T** to **drill** shows the iterative steps in the resolution process from the roots down.

We have omitted samples of **dig** and **drill** output, since we have used them throughout this chapter to illustrate various DNS issues.

dig and **drill** include the notation aa in the output flags if an answer is authoritative (i.e., it comes directly from a master or slave server of that zone). The code ad indicates that an answer is "authentic" in the DNSSEC sense. When testing a new configuration, be sure that you look up data for both local and remote hosts. If you can access a host by IP address but not by name, DNS is probably the culprit.

Lame delegations

When you apply for a domain name, you are asking for a part of the DNS naming tree to be delegated to your name servers and your DNS administrator. If you never use the domain or you change the name servers or their IP addresses without coordinating with your parent zone, a "lame delegation" results.

The effects of a lame delegation can be very bad. If one of your servers is lame, your DNS system is less efficient. If all the name servers for a domain are lame, no one can reach you. All queries start at the root unless answers are cached, so lame servers and software that doesn't do negative caching of SERVFAIL errors increase the load of everyone on the path from the root to the lame domain.

There are two ways to find lame delegations: by reviewing the log files and by using a tool called **doc**, short for "domain obscenity control." We look at some **doc** examples in the next section, but let's first review some log entries.

Many sites point the lame-servers logging channel to **/dev/null** and don't bother fretting about other people's lame delegations. That's fine as long as your own domain is squeaky clean and is not itself a source or victim of lame delegations. One lame server slows DNS down; if all servers are lame, your domain is essentially off the air.

Here is a logging example. We have truncated the output to tame **dig**'s verbosity; the **+short** flag to **dig** limits the output even more.

```
Jul 19 14:37:50 nubark named[757]: lame server resolving 'w3w3.com' (in
    'w3w3.com'?): 216.117.131.52#53
```

Digging for name servers for w3w3.com at one of the .com gTLD servers yields

```
$ dig @e.gtld-servers.net w3w3.com ns
;; ANSWER SECTION:
w3w3.com.       172800  IN  NS  ns0.nameservices.net.
w3w3.com.       172800  IN  NS  ns1.nameservices.net.
```

But if we now ask each of these servers in turn that same question, we get an answer from ns0 and no answer from ns1:

```
$ dig @ns0.nameservices.net w3w3.com ns
;; ANSWER SECTION:
w3w3.com.       14400   IN  NS  ns0.nameservices.net.
w3w3.com.       14400   IN  NS  ns1.nameservices.net.
```

```
$ dig @ns1.nameservices.net w3w3.com ns
;; QUESTION SECTION:
;w3w3.com.      IN      NS

;; AUTHORITY SECTION:
com.            92152   IN  NS  M.GTLD-SERVERS.NET.
com.            92152   IN  NS  I.GTLD-SERVERS.NET.
com.            92152   IN  NS  E.GTLD-SERVERS.NET.
```

The name server ns1.nameservices.net has been delegated responsibility for w3w3.com by the .com servers, but it does not accept that responsibility. It is misconfigured, resulting in a lame delegation. Clients trying to look up w3w3.com will get slow service. If w3w3.com is paying nameservices.net for DNS service, they deserve a refund!

Sometimes when you **dig** at an authoritative server in an attempt to find lameness, **dig** returns no information. Try the query again with the **+norecurse** flag so that you can see exactly what the server in question knows.

DNS sanity checking tools

Several tools check various aspects of your DNS environment. **named-checkconf** and **named-checkzone** are shipped with BIND 9; they check the basic syntax (not semantics) of the **named.conf** file and of your zone files. NSD and Unbound include similar tools called **nsd-checkconf** and **unbound-checkconf**.

The original DNS checking tool is **nslint**, written by Craig Leres when he was at Lawrence Berkeley Labs. **doc**, the **d**omain **o**bscenity **c**ontrol program, which checks delegations and finds inconsistencies and errors in your deployed DNS, is discussed in more detail below. The tool **lamers** (from the same web site as **doc**) rifles through log files and sends email to the DNS administrators of offending sites telling them that they have a lame delegation and describing how to fix the problem. **DDT** by Jorge Frazao and Artur Romao debugs cached data.

dnswalk traverses your delegation tree and identifies inconsistencies between parent and child or between forward and reverse records. It also finds missing dots, unnecessary glue records, etc. It is a general DNS hygiene nag. **dnswalk** needs to be able to do zone transfers in order to work its magic.

Several DNSSEC debugging and management tools are described on page 663.

doc is a C shell script. It's currently maintained by Brad Knowles, from whose web site it can be downloaded: shub-internet.org/brad/dns (note: "shub", not "shrub"). If you plan to put **doc** in your path or run it from **cron**, you must edit the script and set the `auxd` variable to point to the installation directory.

doc checks delegations by making repeated calls to **dig**. It reports on inconsistencies, errors, and other problems related to a particular domain name. Its screen output summarizes the issues that it finds. It also produces a verbose log file in the current directory with details.

doc uses the local name server to do its digging. If your domain uses BIND's view statement and includes RFC1918 private addresses in the internal view, running **doc** on the internal view confuses **doc** and makes it report spurious errors. If you use views, run **doc** from outside the domain so that it sees what external users see.

Here's what **doc** has to say about w3w3.com, the lame domain above:

```
$ doc w3w3.com
Doc-2.2.3: doc w3w3.com
Doc-2.2.3: Starting test of w3w3.com.   parent is com.
Doc-2.2.3: Test date - Tue Jul 21 21:15:11 MDT 2009
Summary:
    ERRORS found for w3w3.com. (count: 1)
    WARNINGS issued for w3w3.com. (count: 1)
Done testing w3w3.com.  Tue Jul 21 21:15:21 MDT 2009
```

doc puts the details of the testing and the errors found (together, over 600 lines) in its log file, in this case **log.w3w3.com.**:

```
ERROR: no SOA record for w3w3.com. from ns1.nameservices.net.
```

doc didn't label w3w3.com as a "lame delegation" per se, but that's the underlying problem it has identified. Following the NS records from the parent zone, it checked with ns1.nameservices.net to be sure it was acting as an authoritative name server for w3w3.com; it wasn't.

If you manage a domain that includes subdomains (or don't trust the managers of your parent domain), consider running **doc** from **cron** once a week to verify that all delegations relating to your domain are correct.

Performance issues

BIND 9's performance on multiprocessor architectures is not as speedy as its developers might have hoped, but several root servers use BIND 9 and happily handle tens of thousands of queries per second. The performance is probably more than adequate for most sites. But NSD's and Unbound's performance is even better, especially for DNSSEC signed zones.

We've said this multiple times already, but it bears repeating: set your TTLs to reasonable values—weeks or days, not minutes or seconds. The use of short TTLs punishes both you (because you must constantly re-serve the same records) and your web clients (because they must constantly fetch them). It also provides a potential attacker with a cache poisoning opportunity. Some name servers selectively ignore TTLs they don't like (values that seem unreasonably long or unreasonably short).

Paging degrades server performance nonlinearly, so don't be stingy with memory on hosts that run name servers. You'll need to wait about a week for the memory footprint to stabilize for recursive servers; see page 571.

To estimate the memory **nsd** would need to serve your authoritative data, fill in the web form at nlnetlabs.net/nsd/nsd-memsize.html. Neat!

Use forwarders. See page 606 for a discussion of forwarding.

The **init** scripts that start **named** on many systems provide extra entry points (e.g., **reload**) that are intended for use by system administrators. But it's easier and more cross-platform efficient to use **rndc** instead.

*See page 1188 for more information about **inetd**.*

Do not use **inetd** or **xinetd** to manage a name server; it restarts the server every time it's needed, dramatically slowing response times and preventing any useful cache from being developed.

17.16 Vendor specifics

This section describes the status of name service software on our various vendors' platforms. Everyone ships BIND, although you may have to specify that you want it installed when you install the operating system or install it as a package later.

Linux distributions are for the most part far more agile at upgrading to recent releases of BIND than their UNIX cohorts. Even so, name service is crucially important. You might want to make a policy of getting the latest source distribution and building it yourself rather than waiting for packages to become available.

Ubuntu and Red Hat have the entire NSD/Unbound suite available in the form of packages; SUSE has only Unbound in their official repositories. Currently, all of the packaged versions are a bit out of date, so as with BIND, you might want to just get the latest source code from nlnetlabs.nl and build it yourself.

In this section, we include pointers to the configuration files, the release of BIND on which each vendor's software is based, and information about how to integrate BIND with other sources of administrative data such as flat files or NIS. A more complete discussion of this last topic is presented in Chapter 19. In particular, refer to the material beginning on page 739.

See page 87 for more information about system startup scripts.

We also include pointers to the startup scripts that should execute at boot time to start the name server. If name service dies, so does your network, your email, your web site—everything. Some sites use a keep-running script such as the **nanny** script in the BIND distribution.

Specifics for Linux

BIND packages for Linux install a startup script for **named** that's run through **init**: **/etc/init.d/bind9** for Ubuntu and **/etc/init.d/named** for RHEL and SUSE.

Linux's **named** packages install things in all the usual places. Table 17.18 shows the details. Red Hat has some extras that interact with their Network Manager tool through a **-D** command-line flag to **named**. Details can be found in the **doc/README-DBUS** file in the Red Hat BIND package.

Table 17.18 BIND files in Linux

File	Directory	Description
resolv.conf	**/etc**	Resolver library configuration file
named, lwres	**/usr/sbin**	Name server daemon
lwresd	**/usr/sbin**	Lightweight resolver
named.conf	**/etc**	**named** config file (RHEL and SUSE)
	/etc/bind	**named** config file (Ubuntu)
named-checkconf	**/usr/sbin**	Checks the syntax of the config file
named-checkzone	**/usr/sbin**	Checks the syntax of zone files
namedGetForwarders	**/usr/sbin**	Red Hat only, for Network Manager tool
namedSetForwarders	**/usr/sbin**	Red Hat only, for Network Manager tool
nsswitch.conf	**/etc**	Service switch file

Linux uses a switch file, **/etc/nsswitch.conf,** to specify how hostname-to-IP address mappings should be performed and whether DNS should be tried first, last, or not at all. If no switch file is present, the default behavior is

```
hosts: dns [!UNAVAIL=return] files
```

The !UNAVAIL clause means that if DNS is available but a name is not found there, the lookup attempt should fail rather than continuing to the next entry (in this case, the **/etc/hosts** file). If no name server were running (as might be the case during the boot process), the lookup process *would* consult the **hosts** file.

Our example distributions all provide the following default **nsswitch.conf** entry:

```
hosts: files dns
```

There is really no "best" way to configure the lookups—it depends on how your site is managed. In general, we prefer to keep as much host information as possible in DNS rather than in NIS or flat files, but we also try to preserve the ability to fall back to the static **hosts** file during the boot process if necessary.

Ubuntu is the most up-to-date of our Linux distributions, with its distributed package being just a few months old. Programs and files have owner root and group owner "bind" with permissions set to allow access if **named** is invoked as user "bind" instead of root.

Some useful sample files are stashed in **/etc/bind**. Included are a **named.conf** file and zone files for root hints, localhost, the broadcast addresses, and private address space. The supplied **named.conf** includes the files **named.conf.options** and **named.conf.local**. It sets BIND's default directory to **/var/cache/bind**; as shipped, the directory exists but is empty.

The logic behind the configuration info being in **/etc** and the zone info in **/var** is that if you are a secondary server for other sites, you do not control the size of the zone files that **named** will write. To avoid potentially filling up the root partition, you will probably want to keep the files in **/var**. Zones for which you are the primary server can live with the config files (use absolute paths in the **named.conf** file), or they can live in **/var/cache/bind**, too.

The sample **named.conf** file does not need to be modified if you want to run a caching-only server. You must add any zones for which you are authoritative, preferably to the supplied **named.conf.local** file.

The sample files provided by Ubuntu make use of some new BIND features to help your servers be good DNS citizens on the network. For example, they configure .com and .net as delegation-only zones to keep your users' typos from generating advertising revenue for VeriSign through its Site Finder tool. If you don't use private address space (RFC1918) internally, then the empty RFC1918 zone files prevent those addresses from escaping the local network. Go, Ubuntu!

The directory **/usr/share/doc/bind9** contains several useful references. Check out the **README.Debian** file (even on Ubuntu) to understand the strategy for configuring BIND.

The SUSE installation says what it is doing and produces a reasonable, well-documented name server installation. By default, **named** runs in a **chroot**ed environment beneath **/var/lib/named** as user and group "named". The installer creates the **chroot** jail directory and populates it with all the files needed to run **named**, even niceties such as the UNIX-domain socket for **syslog**. Extra configuration files (not **named.conf**) and zone files live in **/etc/named.d** and are copied to the jail when **named** is started. If you do not want to run **named** in jail, modify the line that says

```
NAMED_RUN_CHROOTED="yes"
```

in **/etc/sysconfig/named**. That's all you have to change; the startup scripts in **/etc/init.d** refer to this information and are able to start **named** in either fashion.

SUSE provides a sample **/etc/named.conf** file with helpful comments that explain many of the options. SUSE's **/etc/named.conf** file is not world-readable as it usually is on other systems. The default file imports a file called **named.conf.include**, which then imports the **rndc-access.conf** file from **/etc/named.d**, both of which are readable to the world. It's not entirely clear what SUSE has in mind here concerning security. **rndc** is preconfigured to accept control commands from localhost only.

SUSE's **named.conf** file can be used as-is to run a caching-only server. If you want to serve your own zones, put the zone files in the **/etc/named.d** directory and list the zones' names in the **/etc/named.conf.include** file.

The ISC BIND documentation lives in **/usr/share/doc/packages/bind9**.

Installing RHEL's BIND package puts the binaries in **/usr/sbin**, puts the man pages in **/usr/share/man**, adds a user and group called "named", and creates directories for zone files. The "named" user has access to the data files through group permissions.

Unless you change this in **/etc/sysconfig/named**, the **named.conf** file goes in **/etc** (as Paul Vixie and God intended), and the zone files go in **/var/named**. No sample files are provided, but the **bindconf** package should have them.

Specifics for Solaris

Solaris 10 ships with BIND 9.3.4-P1, vintage late 2007; you should consider upgrading. OpenSolaris is more up to date with BIND 9.6.1-P1 (2009). Solaris has always called their network programs **in.*progname*** and **named** was no exception, so that you often couldn't find it for a bit if you forgot that it was called **in.named**, and not **named**. Happily, this is no longer true and Solaris has come around to calling the name server plain old **named**, though the **in.named** name persists as a link. Like Linux, Solaris uses a service order file called **/etc/nsswitch.conf** to specify how BIND, NIS, NIS+ (Solaris 10 only), and the **/etc/hosts** file interact. Modifying the `hosts` line in that file to

```
hosts:   files dns
```

causes name resolution to try **/etc/hosts** first and then try DNS. The short-circuit clause `NOTFOUND=return` can modify any entry. Putting crucial servers and routers in the **/etc/hosts** file eases the chicken-and-egg problems that sometimes occur at boot time before name service is available. Solaris's name service is started by the SMF service svc:/network/dns/server:default. SMF options specify the command-line arguments.

Table 17.19 summarizes the BIND filenames and locations for Solaris.

Table 17.19 BIND 9 files in Solaris

File	Directory	Description
resolv.conf	**/etc**	Resolver library configuration file
named	**/usr/sbin**	Name server daemon
named-checkconf	**/usr/sbin**	Checks configuration file syntax
named-checkzone	**/usr/sbin**	Checks zone file syntax
named.conf	**/etc**	Configuration file for name server
nsswitch.conf	**/etc**	Service switch file

Specifics for HP-UX

HP-UX includes BIND 9.3.2, vintage late 2005; better upgrade! HP-UX provides several sample **nsswitch.conf** files for various combinations of databases and services. One lists the HP defaults. Copy the one that seems right for your environment to **/etc/nsswitch.conf**.

HP recommends

```
hosts:        dns [NOTFOUND=return] nis [NOTFOUND=return] files
```

but we prefer

```
hosts:        files [NOTFOUND=continue] dns
```

to avoid problems with booting. It's important to be able to configure the network in the boot sequence without looking up names in NIS or DNS, inasmuch as those services cannot run until the network is up. HP-UX's startup script for name service is in **/etc/rc.config.d/namesvrs_dns**.

HP-UX supplies well-commented sample files for just about everything in the directory **/usr/newconfig**, but alas, nothing for name service. However, it does have a couple of ancient commands related to name service: **hosts_to_named**, which transforms a **hosts** file into a zone file, and **sig_named**, which sends signals to the running **named** process to control it. The **/etc/hosts** file these days just contains localhost and the host itself, so the conversion routine is useless. And since BIND 9, **rndc** must be used to control **named**, not signals.

Table 17.20 summarizes the filenames and locations for name service on HP-UX.

Table 17.20 BIND files in HP-UX

File	Directory	Description
resolv.conf	/etc	Resolver library configuration file
named	/usr/sbin	Name server daemon
lwresd	/usr/sbin	Lightweight resolver daemon
named-checkconf	/usr/sbin	Checks the config file syntax
named-checkzone	/usr/sbin	Checks zone file syntax
named.conf	/etc/namedb	Configuration file for name server
nsswitch.conf	/etc	Service switch file

Specifics for AIX

AIX ships with both BIND 8 and BIND 9, with binaries **named8** and **named9**, respectively. As shipped, **named** is a link to **named8,** which is no longer supported by ISC. They ship versions 8.3.3+ and 9.2.1, vintage January 2004. Sloth-like upgrade performance here! AIX does not include the **named-checkconf** and **named-checkzones** commands—perhaps they entered the BIND distribution after 2004. The startup scripts for name service under AIX are in **/etc/rc.tcpip**.

We were starting to think these tables of file locations were silly since operating systems have largely converged to standard locations as far as BIND is concerned, but AIX settles that dispute. Table 17.21 on the next page shows the AIX the filenames and locations.

Table 17.21 BIND files in AIX

File	Directory	Description
resolv.conf	**/etc**	Resolver library configuration file
named8	**/usr/sbin**	BIND 8 name server daemon
named9	**/usr/sbin**	BIND 9 name server daemon
named	**/usr/sbin**	Link to **named8** [default] or **named9**
named.conf	**/etc**	Configuration file for name server
netsvc.conf	**/etc**	Service switch file
irs.conf	**/etc**	Another service switch file
NSORDER	*environment*	Service switch environment variable

In typical AIX fashion, there are three mechanisms that embody the "service switch" concept whereby you specify the order in which directory services are consulted. The NSORDER environment variable overrides what is specified in **/etc/netsvc.conf**, and the contents there override what is in **/etc/irs.conf**.

Not only are there three places to worry about, but the syntax is slightly different in each one. For example, to select DNS lookups for hostnames in the **netsvc.conf** file, you would use the value `bind`, but to do the same thing in the **irs.conf** file, the value is `dns`. The syntax allows you to specify what to do if the preferred service does not find an answer, but of course it's different from the notation used in the **nsswitch.conf** files of other systems. See *Prioritizing sources of administrative information* on page 739 for the details on service switches.

17.17 Recommended reading

DNS and BIND are described by a variety of sources, including the documentation that comes with the distributions, chapters in several books on Internet topics, books in the O'Reilly Nutshell series, books from other publishers, and various on-line resources. NSD and Unbound are new enough that their external documentation is thinner, but we have found one book with coverage along with several web documents.

Mailing lists and newsgroups

The following mailing lists are associated with BIND:

- bind-announce – mail bind-announce-request@isc.org to join
- namedroppers – mail namedroppers-request@internic.net to join
- bind-users – mail bind-users-request@isc.org to join
- bind9-workers – mail bind9-workers-request@isc.org (code warriors)

Send bug reports to bind9-bugs@isc.org.

The mailing lists for NSD/Unbound are

- nsd-users – join from the nlnetlabs.nl/projects/nsd web page
- unbound-users – join from the unbound.net web page
- ldns-users – join from nlnetlabs.nl/projects/ldns web page
- drill – join from nlnetlabs.nl/projects/drill web page

And finally, a DNS mailing list where operational issues for extreme sites (registrars, root servers, TLD servers, etc.) are discussed:

- dns-operations – join at the lists.dns-oarc.net web site

Books and other documentation

THE NOMINUM AND ISC BIND DEVELOPMENT TEAMS. *BINDv9 Administrator Reference Manual.* Available in the BIND distribution (**doc/arm**) from isc.org. This document outlines the administration and management of BIND 9. It's also available as a printed booklet:

REED, JEREMY C., EDITOR. *BIND 9 DNS Administration Reference Book*. Redwood City, CA: Reed Media Services, 2007.

ALBITZ, PAUL, AND CRICKET LIU. *DNS and BIND (5th Edition).* Sebastopol, CA: O'Reilly Media, 2006.

This popular and well-respected book about BIND includes coverage of both BIND 8 and BIND 9. It is very complete—the virtual DNS bible.

LIU, CRICKET. *DNS & BIND Cookbook*. Sebastopol, CA: O'Reilly Media, 2002.

This baby version of the O'Reilly DNS book is task oriented and gives clear instructions and examples for various name server chores. This book is a bit dated, but it's still useful.

AITCHISON, RON. *Pro DNS and BIND.* Berkeley, CA: Apress, 2005.

This is a newcomer in the DNS arena and includes a very good section on DNSSEC with examples and deployment strategy. We found a few typos but fortunately the author maintains a web site of corrections while awaiting the publisher's next print run. The depth of material and organization make it a better choice than *DNS and BIND* for many purposes, but as a DNS administrator you had better own both!

MENS, JAN-PIET. *Alternative DNS Servers: Choice and Deployment, and Optional SQL/LDAP Back-Ends*. Cambridge, England: UIT Cambridge Ltd., 2009.

This book covers about 10 different name server implementations, including NSD/Unbound. It explores various back ends for storing zone data, has nice diagrams, and offers a wealth of information.

On-line resources

The DNS Resources Directory, dns.net/dnsrd, is a useful collection of resources and pointers to resources, maintained by András Salamon.

The web sites isc.org, dns-oarc.net, ripe.net, nlnetlabs.nl, and f.root-servers.org or k.root-servers.org contain a wealth of DNS information, research, measurement results, presentations, and other good stuff.

Google has indexed DNS resources at

directory.google.com/Top/Computers/Internet/Protocols/DNS

All the nitty-gritty details of the DNS protocol, resource records, and the like are summarized at iana.org/assignments/dns-parameters. This document contains a nice mapping from a DNS fact to the RFC that specifies it.

The *DNSSEC HOWTO*, a tutorial in disguise by Olaf Kolkman, is a 70-page document that covers the ins and outs of deploying and debugging DNSSEC. Get it at nlnetlabs.nl/dnssec_howto/dnssec_howto.pdf.

The RFCs

The RFCs that define the DNS system are available from rfc-editor.org. We used to list a page or so of the most important DNS-related RFCs, but there are now so many (more than 100, with another 50 Internet drafts) that you are better off searching rfc-editor.org to access the entire archive. Refer to the **doc/rfc** and **doc/draft** directories of the current BIND distribution to see the whole fleet.

The original, definitive standards for DNS, vintage 1987, are

- RFC1034 – *Domain Names: Concepts and Facilities*
- RFC1035 – *Domain Names: Implementation and Specification*

17.18 Exercises

E17.1 Explain the function of each of the following DNS records: SOA, PTR, A, MX, and CNAME.

E17.2 What are glue records and why are they needed? Use **dig** or **drill** to find the glue records that connect your local zone to its parent.

E17.3 What are the implications of negative caching? Why is it important?

E17.4 Create SPF records for your site to help control spam.

☆ E17.5 What steps are needed to set up a new second-level domain? Include both technical and procedural factors.

☆ E17.6 What is the difference between an authoritative and a nonauthoritative answer to a DNS query? How could you ensure that an answer was authoritative?

☆ E17.7 What machine is your local name server? What steps must it take to resolve the name www.admin.com, assuming that no information about this domain is cached anywhere in DNS?

☆ E17.8 Explain the significance for DNS of the 512-byte limit on UDP packets. What are the potential problems, and what are the workarounds that address them?

☆ E17.9 Explore the 512-bit Russian GOST or 256-bit NIST P-256 ECDSA algorithms and their impact on the 512-byte UDP packet limit. Do they help things fit? How big are the keys and the signatures?

☆ E17.10 Create SSHFP records for your site and upgrade your **ssh** to use them.

☆ E17.11 Use the ISC DNS-OARC reply size server from various locations at your site to determine if there are any local configuration policies or practices that would inhibit DNSSEC deployment. What sizes do you see? Do they vary with your location? How about from home? Gather the same data with SecSpider or **dnsfunnel**. Are the numbers consistent? If not, which tool gives more accurate information?

☆☆ E17.12 Use the DNSSEC tools or libraries to build a script that determines whether a secure site is in sync with its parent's DS record and whether its signatures have expired. Set it up to run daily from **cron**.

☆☆ E17.13 Create DKIM records for your domain and set up your mail servers and clients to use them.

☆☆ E17.14 Create a subdomain at your site. Add a real host with lots of names and addresses, then secure it with DNSSEC and connect it to the Internet's trust network by creating a DLV record at ISC. Turn on logging and watch the logs for a few days. Document your procedures and problems.

18 The Network File System

The Network File System protocol, commonly known as NFS, lets you share filesystems among computers. NFS is nearly transparent to users, and no information is lost when an NFS server crashes. Clients can simply wait until the server returns and then continue as if nothing had happened.

NFS was introduced by Sun Microsystems in 1984. It was originally implemented as a surrogate filesystem for diskless clients, but the protocol proved to be well designed and useful as a general file-sharing solution. All UNIX vendors and Linux distributions provide some version of NFS; many use code licensed from Sun. The NFS protocol is now an open standard documented in RFCs (see RFCs 1094, 1813, and 3530 in particular).

18.1 Introduction to Network File Services

Sharing files over a network seems like a simple task, but in fact it's a confoundingly complex problem with many edge cases and subtleties. As evidence of the complexities involved, numerous issues in the NFS protocol have revealed themselves only as bugs encountered in unusual situations over more than a quarter century of use. Today's administrators can be confident that the most common file-sharing protocols (NFS and CIFS) will not regularly corrupt data or otherwise induce the wrath of upset users, but it's taken a lot of work and experience to get to this point.

Issues of state

One of the design decisions made when designing a network filesystem is determining what part of the system will track the files that each client has open, information referred to generically as "state." A server that does not record the status of files and clients is said to be stateless; one that does is stateful. Both approaches have been used over the years, and both have benefits and drawbacks.

Stateful servers keep track of all open files across the network. This mode of operation introduces many layers of complexity (more than you might expect) and makes recovery in the event of a crash far more difficult. When the server returns from a hiatus, a negotiation between the client and server must occur to reconcile the last known state of the connection. Statefulness allows clients to maintain more control over files and facilitates the management of files that are opened in read/write mode.

On a stateless server, each request is independent of the requests that have preceded it. If either the server or the client crashes, nothing is lost in the process. Under this design, it is painless for servers to crash or reboot, since no context is maintained. However, it's impossible for the server to know which clients have opened files for writing, so the server cannot manage concurrency.

Performance concerns

Network filesystems should provide users with a seamless experience. Accessing a file over the network should be no different from accessing a file on a local filesystem. Unfortunately, wide area networks have high latencies, which cause operations to behave erratically, and low bandwidth, which results in slow performance for larger files. Most file service protocols, including NFS, incorporate techniques to minimize performance problems on both local and wide area networks.

Most protocols try to minimize the number of network requests. For example, read-ahead caching preloads portions of a file into a local memory buffer to avoid delay when a new section of the file is read. A little extra network bandwidth is consumed in an effort to avoid a full round trip exchange with the server. Similarly, some systems cache writes in memory and send their updates in batches, reducing the delay incurred when communicating write operations to the server. These types of batch operations are generically referred to as request coalescing.

Security

Any service that provides convenient access to files on a network has great potential to cause security problems. Local filesystems implement complex access control algorithms, safeguarding files with granular access permissions. On a network, the problems are multiplied since there may be race conditions and differences in configuration among machines as well as bugs in the file service software and unresolved issues in the file-sharing protocol.

The rise of directory services and centralized authentication has improved the security of network file systems. In essence, no client can be trusted to authenticate itself sanely, so a trusted, central system must verify identities and approve access to files. The complexities of these services have slowed their adoption, but most sites today implement some form of centralized access control.

18.2 THE NFS APPROACH

The newest version of the NFS protocol is designed for platform independence, good performance over wide area networks like the Internet, and strong security. Most implementations also include diagnostic utilities to debug configuration and performance problems. A portion of both the server-side and client-side software resides in the kernel. However, these parts of NFS need no configuration and are largely transparent from an administrator's point of view.

Protocol versions and history

The first public release of the NFS protocol was version 2 in 1989. Version 2 clients cannot assume that a write operation is complete until they receive an acknowledgment from the server. To avoid discrepancies in the event of a crash, version 2 servers must commit each modified block to disk before replying. This constraint introduces a significant delay in NFS writes since modified blocks would normally be written only to the in-memory buffer cache.

NFS version 3, which dates from the early 1990s, eliminates this bottleneck with a coherency scheme that permits asynchronous writes. It also updates several other aspects of the protocol that were found to have caused performance problems and improves the handling of large files. The net result is that NFS version 3 is quite a bit faster than version 2. All sites should be using version 3 or 4 at this point.

NFS version 4 is a major overhaul that includes many new fixes and features. Highlighted enhancements include

- Compatibility and cooperation with firewalls and NAT devices
- Integration of the lock and mount protocols into the core NFS protocol
- Stateful operation
- Strong, integrated security
- Support for replication and migration
- Support for both UNIX and Windows clients
- Access control lists (ACLs)
- Support for Unicode filenames
- Good performance even on low-bandwidth connections

Although V4 is a significant step forward in many ways, the protocol changes haven't much altered the process of configuring and administering NFS.

The various protocol versions are not compatible, but NFS servers (including those on all our example systems) typically implement all three of them. In practice, all NFS clients and servers can interoperate using some version of the protocol. Always use the V4 protocol if both sides support it.

Transport protocols

NFS version 2 originally used UDP because that was what performed best on the LANs and computers of the 1980s. Although NFS does its own packet sequence reassembly and error checking, UDP and NFS both lack the congestion control algorithms that are essential for good performance on a large IP network.

To remedy these potential problems, NFS migrated to a choice of UDP or TCP in version 3, and to TCP only in version 4.[1] The TCP option was first explored as a way to help NFS work through routers and over the Internet. Over time, most of the original reasons for preferring UDP over TCP have evaporated in the warm light of fast CPUs, cheap memory, and faster networks.

State

A client must explicitly mount an NFS filesystem before using it, just as a client must mount a filesystem stored on a local disk. However, NFS versions 2 and 3 are stateless, and the server does not keep track of which clients have mounted each filesystem. Instead, the server simply discloses a secret "cookie" at the conclusion of a successful mount negotiation. The cookie identifies the mounted directory to the NFS server and so provides a way for the client to access its contents. Cookies persist between reboots of the server, so a crash does not leave the client in an unrecoverable muddle. The client can simply wait until the server is available again and resubmit the request.

NFSv4, on the other hand, is a stateful protocol: both client and server maintain information about open files and locks. When the server fails, the client assists in the recovery process by sending the server its pre-crash state information. A returning server waits during a predefined grace period for former clients to report their state information before it permits new operations and locks. The cookie management of V2 and V3 no longer exists in NFSv4.

File system exports

NFS servers maintain a list of directories (called "exports" or "shares") that they make available to clients over the network. By definition, all servers export at least one directory. In V2 and V3, each export is treated as an independent entity. In V4, each server exports a single hierarchical pseudo-filesystem that incorporates all its exported directories. Essentially, the pseudo-filesystem is the server's own filesystem namespace skeletonized to remove anything that is not exported.

1. Technically, any transport protocol that implements congestion control can be used, but TCP is the only reasonable choice today.

For example, consider the following list of directories, with the directories to be exported in boldface.

/www/domain1
/www/domain2
/www/domain3
/var/logs/httpd
/var/spool

In NFS version 3, each exported directory must be separately configured. Client systems must execute three different mount requests to obtain access to all the server's exports.

In NFS version 4, however, the pseudo-filesystem bridges the disconnected portions of the directory structure to create a single view for NFS clients. Rather than requesting a separate mount for each of **/www/domain1**, **/www/domain2**, and **/var/logs/httpd**, the client can simply mount the server's pseudo-root directory and browse the hierarchy.

The directories that are not exported, **/www/domain3** and **/var/spool**, do not appear during browsing. In addition, individual files contained in /, **/var**, **/www**, and **/var/logs** are not visible to the client because the pseudo-filesystem portion of the hierarchy includes only directories. Thus, the client view of the NFSv4-exported file system is

```
/
  /www
    /www/domain1
    /www/domain2
  /var
    /var/logs
      /var/logs/httpd
```

The server specifies the root of the exported filesystems in a configuration file known as the **exports** file.

File locking

File locking (as implemented by the **flock**, **lockf**, or **fcntl** systems calls) has been a sore point on UNIX systems for a long time. On local filesystems, it has been known to work less than perfectly. In the context of NFS, the ground is shakier still. By design, early versions of NFS servers are stateless: they have no idea which machines are using any given file. However, state information is needed to implement locking. What to do?

The traditional answer was to implement file locking separately from NFS. In most systems, the two daemons **lockd** and **statd** try to make a go of it. Unfortunately, the task is difficult for a variety of subtle reasons, and NFS file locking has generally tended to be flaky.

NFSv4 has removed the need for **lockd** and **statd** by folding locking (and hence, statefulness and all that it implies) into the core protocol. This change introduces significant complexity but obviates many of the related problems of earlier NFS versions. Unfortunately, separate **lockd**s and **statd**s are still needed to support V2 and V3 clients if your site has them. Our example systems all ship with the earlier versions of NFS enabled, so the separate daemons still run by default.

Security concerns

In many ways, NFS V2 and V3 are poster children for everything that is or ever has been wrong with UNIX and Linux security. The protocol was originally designed with essentially no concern for security, and convenience has its price. NFSv4 has addressed the security concerns of earlier versions by mandating support for strong security services and establishing better user identification.

All versions of the NFS protocol are intended to be security-mechanism independent, and most servers support multiple "flavors" of authentication. A few of the common flavors include

- AUTH_NONE – no authentication
- AUTH_SYS – UNIX-style user and group access control
- RPCSEC_GSS – a powerful flavor that ensures integrity and privacy in addition to authentication

Traditionally, most sites have used AUTH_SYS authentication, which depends on UNIX user and group identifiers. In this scheme, the client simply sends the local UID and GID of the user requesting access to the server. The server compares the values to those from its own **/etc/passwd** file[2] and determines whether the user should have access. Thus, if users mary and bob share the same UID on two different clients, they will have access to each other's files. Furthermore, users that have root access on a system can **su** to whatever UID they wish; the server will then give them access to the corresponding user's files.

Enforcing **passwd** file consistency among systems is essential in environments that use AUTH_SYS. But even this is only a security fig leaf; any rogue host (or heaven forfend, Windows machine) can "authenticate" its users however it likes and therefore subvert NFS security.

See page 924 for more information about Kerberos.

To prevent such problems, most sites should use a more robust authentication mechanism such as Kerberos in combination with the NFS RPCSEC_GSS layer. This configuration requires both the client and server to participate in a Kerberos realm. The Kerberos realm authenticates clients centrally, avoiding the problems of self-identification described above. Kerberos can also provide strong encryption and guaranteed integrity for files transferred over the network. All protocol-conformant NFS version 4 systems must implement RPCSEC_GSS, but it's optional in version 3.

2. Or its network database equivalent, such as NIS or LDAP.

See page 702 for more information about the ***exports*** *file.*

Access to NFS volumes is granted by a file called **/etc/exports** that enumerates the hostnames (or IP addresses) of systems that should have access to the server's shared filesystems. Unfortunately, this too is a weak form of security because the server trusts the clients to tell it who they are. It's easy to make clients lie about their identities and IP addresses, so this mechanism cannot be fully trusted. Nevertheless, you should export filesystems only to clients that you trust, and you should always check that you have not accidentally exported filesystems to the whole world.

See page 932 for more information about firewalls.

NFS version 4 uses only TCP as a transport protocol and typically communicates over port 2049. Since V4 does not rely on any other ports, opening access through a firewall is as simple as opening TCP port 2049. As with all access list configurations, be sure to specify source and destination addresses in addition to the port. If your site doesn't need to provide NFS services to hosts on the Internet, block access through the firewall or use a local packet filter.

File service over wide area networks with NFSv2 and V3 is not recommended because of the long history of bugs in the RPC protocols and the lack of strong security mechanisms. Administrators of NFS version 3 servers should block access to TCP and UDP ports 2049 and also the **portmap** port, 111.

Identity mapping in version 4

As discussed in Chapter 7, UNIX operating systems identify users through a collection of UIDs and GIDs in the local **passwd** file or administrative database. NFS version 4, on the other hand, represents users and groups as string identifiers of the form *user@nfs-domain* and *group@nfs-domain*. Both NFS clients and servers run an identity mapping daemon that maps UNIX identifier values to strings.

When a version 4 client performs an operation that returns identities, such as a file listing with **ls -l** (the underlying operation is a series of **stat** calls), the server's identity mapping daemon uses its local **passwd** file to convert the UID and GID of each file object to a string such as ben@atrust.com. The client's identity mapper then reverses the process, converting ben@atrust.com into local UID and GID values, which may or may not be the same as the server's. If the string value does not match any local identity, the nobody user account is used.

At this point, the remote filesystem call (**stat**) has completed and returned UID and GID values to its caller (here, the **ls** command). But since **ls** was called with the **-l** option, it needs to display text names instead of numbers. So, **ls** in turn retranslates the IDs back to textual names using the **getpwuid** and **getgrgid** library routines. These routines once again consult the **passwd** file or its network database equivalent. What a long, strange trip it's been.

Confusingly, the identity mapper is only used when retrieving and setting file attributes, typically ownerships. *Identity mapping plays no role in authentication or access control,* all of which is handled in the traditional form by RPC. Ergo, consistent **passwd** files are still essential for users of AUTH_SYS "security."

An unfortunate side effect of this identity and authentication ambiguity arises on systems that do not have synchronized **passwd** files. The identity mapper may do a better job of mapping than the underlying NFS protocol, causing the apparent file permissions to conflict with the permissions the NFS server will actually enforce. Consider, for example, the following commands on an NFSv4 client:

```
[ben@nfs-client]$ id ben
uid=1000(ben) gid=1000(ben) groups=1000(ben)

[ben@nfs-client]$ id john
uid=1010(john) gid=1010(john) groups=1010(john)

[ben@nfs-client]$ ls -ld ben
drwxr-xr-x  2  john  root        4096  May 27 16:42  ben

[ben@nfs-client]$ touch ben/file
[ben@nfs-client]$ ls -l ben/file
-rw-rw-r--   1  john  nfsnobody  0      May 27 17:07  ben/file
```

First, ben is shown to have UID 1000 and john to have UID 1010. An NFS-exported home directory called **ben** appears to have permissions 755 and is owned by john. However, ben is able to create a file in the directory even though the **ls -l** output indicates that he lacks write permission.

On the server, john has UID 1000. Since john has UID 1010 on the client, the identity mapper performs UID conversion as described above, with the result that "john" appears to be the owner of the directory. However, the identity mapping daemon plays no role in access control. For the file creation operation, ben's UID of 1000 is sent directly to the server, where it is interpreted as john's UID.

How do you know which operations are identity mapped and which are not? It's simple: whenever a UID or GID appears *in the filesystem API* (as with **stat** or **chown**), it is mapped. Whenever the user's own UIDs or GIDs are used *implicitly* for access control, they are routed through the designated authentication system.

Unfortunately for administrators, identity mapping daemons are not standardized across systems, so their configuration processes may be different. The specifics for each of our example systems are covered starting on page 709.

Root access and the nobody account

Although users should generally be given identical privileges wherever they go, it's traditional to prevent root from running rampant on NFS-mounted filesystems. By default, the NFS server intercepts incoming requests made on behalf of UID 0 and changes them to look as if they came from some other user. This modification is called "squashing root." The root account is not entirely shut out, but it is limited to the abilities of a normal user.

A placeholder account named "nobody" is defined specifically to be the pseudo-user as whom a remote root masquerades on an NFS server. The traditional UID for nobody is 65,534 (the 16-bit twos-complement equivalent of UID -2).[3] You can change the default UID and GID mappings for root in the **exports** file. Some systems have an all_squash option to map all client UIDs to the same UID on the server. This configuration eliminates all distinctions among users and creates a sort of public-access filesystem. On Solaris and HP-UX, access is denied altogether if root is mapped to UID -1.

The intent behind these precautions is good, but their ultimate value is not as great as it might seem. Remember that root on an NFS client can **su** to whatever UID it wants, so user files are never really protected. The only real effect of root squashing is to prevent access to files that are owned by root and not readable or writable by the world.

Performance considerations in version 4

NFSv4 was designed to achieve good performance over wide area networks. Most WANs have higher latency and lower bandwidth than LANs. NFS takes aim at these problems with the following refinements:

- An RPC called COMPOUND clumps multiple file operations into one request, reducing the latency incurred from multiple network requests.
- A delegation mechanism allows client-side caching of files. Clients can maintain local control over files, including those open for writing.

These features are part of the core NFS protocol and do not require much attention from system administrators.

Disk quotas

Remote disk quota information can be accessed through an out-of-band server, **rquotad**. NFS servers enforce disk quotas if they are enabled on the underlying filesystem, but users cannot view their quota information unless **rquotad** is running on the remote server.

We consider disk quotas to be largely obsolete; however, some organizations still depend on them to keep users from hogging all available disk space. If you're supporting one of these organizations, you can consult the quota man pages. We don't discuss **rquotad** further.

18.3 Server-side NFS

An NFS server is said to "export" a directory when it makes the directory available for use by other machines. Solaris and HP-UX use the word "share" instead. For consistency, we use "export" throughout this chapter.

3. Although the Red Hat NFS server defaults to UID -2, the nobody account in the **passwd** file uses UID 99. You can leave things as they are, add a **passwd** entry for UID -2, or change anonuid and anongid to 99 if you wish.

In NFS version 3, the process used by clients to mount a filesystem (that is, to learn its secret cookie) is separate from the process used to access files. The operations use separate protocols, and the requests are served by different daemons: **mountd** for mount requests and **nfsd** for actual file service. On some systems, these daemons are called **rpc.nfsd** and **rpc.mountd** as a reminder that they rely on RPC as an underlying protocol (and hence require **portmap** to be running). In this chapter, we omit the **rpc** prefix for readability.

NFSv4 does not use **mountd** at all. However, unless your NFS clients are all at version 4, **mountd** should remain running.

On an NFS server, both **mountd** and **nfsd** should start when the system boots, and both should remain running as long as the system is up. The system startup scripts typically run the daemons automatically if you have any exports configured. The names of the NFS server startup scripts for each of our example platforms are shown in Table 18.1.

Table 18.1 NFS server startup scripts

System	Paths to startup scripts
Ubuntu	**/etc/init.d/nfs-kernel-server** **/etc/init.d/nfs-common**
SUSE	**/etc/init.d/nfsserver**[a]
Red Hat	**/etc/rc.d/init.d/nfs**
Solaris	**/etc/init.d/nfs.server**
HP-UX	**/sbin/init.d/nfs.server**
AIX	**/etc/rc.nfs**

a. **/etc/init.d/nfs** mounts NFS client filesystems.

NFS uses a single access control database that tells which filesystems should be exported and which clients may mount them. The operative copy of this database is usually kept in a file called **xtab** (**sharetab** on Solaris and HP-UX) and also in tables internal to the kernel. Since **xtab** and **sharetab** aren't meant to be human readable, you use a helper command—**exportfs** or **share**—to add and modify entries. To remove entries from the exports table, use **exportfs -u** or **unshare**.

Maintaining a binary file by hand is not much fun, so most systems assume that you would rather maintain a text file that enumerates the system's exported directories and their access settings. The system can then consult this text file at boot time to automatically construct the **xtab** or **sharetab** file.

On most systems, **/etc/exports** is the canonical, human-readable list of exported directories. Its contents are read by **exportfs -a**. Under Solaris and HP-UX, the canonical list is **/etc/dfs/dfstab**, which is really just a script containing a series of **share** commands. (The **shareall** command greps the NFS-related commands out of **dfstab** and runs them. Since NFS is the only native file-sharing system that obeys this convention, **shareall** is equivalent to **sh /etc/dfs/dfstab**.)

Table 18.2 summarizes the last few paragraphs. It tells you what file to edit when you want to export a new filesystem and what to do to make your changes take effect once you've finished editing that file.

Table 18.2 Where to set up exported directories

System	Exports info in	What to do after changing it
Linux	**/etc/exports**	Run **/usr/sbin/exportfs -a**
Solaris	**/etc/dfs/dfstab**	Run **shareall**
HP-UX	**/etc/dfs/dfstab**	Run **shareall**
AIX	**/etc/exports**	Run **/usr/sbin/exportfs -a**

NFS deals with the logical layer of the filesystem. Any directory can be exported; it doesn't have to be a mount point or the root of a physical filesystem. However, for security, NFS does pay attention to the boundaries between filesystems and does require each device to be exported separately. For example, on a machine that has set up **/users** as a separate partition, you could export the root directory without exporting **/users**.[4]

Clients are usually allowed to mount subdirectories of an exported directory if they wish, although the protocol does not require this feature. For example, if a server exports **/chimchim/users**, a client could mount only **/chimchim/users/joe** and ignore the rest of the **users** directory.

Most versions of UNIX don't let you export subdirectories of an exported directory with different options, but this practice is OK under Linux.

The share command and dfstab file (Solaris, HP-UX)

/etc/dfs/dfstab executes the **share** command once for each exported filesystem. For example, on a server that shares **/home** with hosts monk and leopard (with monk allowed root access) and that shares **/usr/share/man** with hosts ross and harp, the **/etc/dfs/dfstab** file would contain the following commands:

```
share -F nfs -o rw=monk.atrust.com:leopard.atrust.com,root=monk.atrust.com
     /home
share -F nfs -o rw=ross.atrust.com:harp.atrust.com /usr/share/man
```

After editing **/etc/dfs/dfstab**, remember to run **shareall** to make your changes take effect. Since **shareall** simply runs the commands in the **dfstab** file, it will not unshare filesystems that you remove. Use the command **unshare** */path/to/fs* to explicitly remove a share. Table 18.3 lists the most common options for **share**.

4. Of course, you should never export the root directory.

Table 18.3 Options for the share command (Solaris, HP-UX)

Option	Description
ro	Exports read-only to the entire world (not recommended)
ro=*list*	Exports read-only with access only by listed hosts
rw	Exports read-write to the entire world (not recommended)
rw=*list*	Exports read-write with access only by listed hosts
root=*list*	Lists hosts permitted to access this filesystem as root; otherwise, root access from a client is equivalent to access by "nobody" (usually UID -2)
anon=*uid*	Specifies the UID to which root is remapped; the default is "nobody"
nosub	Forbids clients to mount subdirectories of the exported directory
nosuid	Prevents setuid and setgid files from being created through NFS

Wherever a *list* is called for in a **share** option, it should consist of a colon-separated group of the items shown in Table 18.4, all of which are ways of specifying hosts or groups of hosts.

Table 18.4 Client specifications for the share command

Type	Syntax	Meaning
Hostname	*hostname*	Individual hosts (must be fully qualified)
Netgroup	*groupname*	NIS netgroups (not frequently used)
DNS domains	*.domain.com*	Any host within the domain
IP networks	*@netname*	Network names as defined in **/etc/networks**[a]

a. CIDR-style specifications are also accepted; for example, **@128.138.92.128/25**.

The note in Table 18.4 regarding hostnames bears repeating: individual hostnames *must* be fully qualified or they will be ignored.

You can put a dash in front of an item to explicitly disallow it. The list is examined from left to right during each lookup until a matching item is found, so negations should precede the more general items that they modify. For example, the line

```
share -F nfs -o rw=-@192.168.10.0/24:.booklab.atrust.com /users
```

exports **/users** read-write to all hosts in the booklab.atrust.com DNS domain except for hosts on the 192.168.10 network. In the command, the **-F** flag indicates that **share** should use the **nfs** filesystem type, as opposed to any of the others in **/etc/dfs/fstypes**.

It's possible to export a directory read-only to some clients and read-write to others. Just include both the **rw=** and **ro=** options.

The **share** man page documents a few basic NFS options. For a complete list, refer to the **share_nfs** man page.

The exportfs command and the exports file (Linux, AIX)

The **exports** file consists of a list of exported directories in the leftmost column followed by lists of associated options. For example, the AIX **exports** line

```
/home                -vers=4,sec=sys,access=harp.atrust.com
```

permits **/home** to be mounted by the machine harp.atrust.com using version 4 of the NFS protocol and UNIX authentication (sec=sys).

Filesystems that are listed in the **exports** file without a specific set of hosts are usually mountable by *all* machines. This is a sizable security hole.

The exact options and syntax used in the **exports** file vary somewhat among systems, though there is a certain thematic similarity. The following sections describe the general formats for Linux and AIX. As always, be sure to check the man page for your system.

Exports in AIX

AIX has the most "classic" **exports** format of our example systems. The permissible options are shown in Table 18.5.

Table 18.5 Common export options for AIX

Option	Description
access=*list*	Lists the hosts that can mount the filesystem.
ro	Exports read-only to everyone; no clients may write on the filesystem.
rw	Exports for reading and writing to everyone (the default).
rw=*list*	Exports read-mostly. The *list* enumerates the hosts allowed to mount for writing; all others must mount read-only.
root=*list*	Lists hosts that can access the filesystem as root. Without this option, root access from a client is equivalent to access by the user nobody.
vers=*n*	Exports the directory to clients using version *n*. Valid values are 2, 3, and 4. Specifying either 2 or 3 includes both 2 and 3.
sec=*flavor*	Specifies a list of security methods for the exported directory. Values include sys (UNIX authentication), dh (DES), krb5 (Kerberos authentication), krb5i (Kerberos authentication and integrity), krb5p (Kerberos authentication, integrity, and privacy), and none (anonymous access, not recommended).
anon=*n*	Specifies the UID to which remote roots are mapped. Defaults to -2 (nobody). Setting this value to -1 denies root access entirely.

In Table 18.5, a *list* consists of a colon-separated series of hostnames and netgroup names. The options in Table 18.5 are similar to those understood by the **share** command. However, there are some subtle differences. For example, the option

```
rw=leopard.atrust.com:ross.atrust.com
```

in **share** syntax means to export the directory read-write with access only by the listed hosts. Under AIX, this option allows the entire world to mount the directory read-only. Gotcha! Under AIX, you must use the access clause to restrict mounting to a specified list of clients:

```
rw,access=leopard.atrust.com:ross.atrust.com
```

Read-write exporting is the default, so the rw clause could actually be eliminated. It doesn't hurt to include it explicitly, however.

Each line in an AIX **exports** file should consist of a directory path, whitespace, and then a dash followed by a comma-separated list of options. For instance, the following example shares the **/home** directory to the host leopard.atrust.com with AUTH_SYS security and version 4 of the protocol:

```
/home -vers=4,sec=sys,rw,access=leopard.atrust.com
```

Remember to run **exportfs -a** after changing the **/etc/exports** file.

Exports in Linux

As in AIX, the Linux **/etc/exports** file enumerates the filesystems exported through NFS and the clients that may access each of them. Whitespace separates the filesystem from the list of clients, and each client is followed by a parenthesized list of comma-separated options. Lines can be continued with a backslash.

Here's what the format looks like:

```
/home              harp(rw,no_root_squash) monk(rw)
/usr/share/man     *.atrust.com(ro)
```

There is no way to list multiple client specifications for a single set of options, although some client specifications refer to multiple hosts. Table 18.6 lists the four types of specifications that can appear in the **exports** file.

Table 18.6 Client specifications in the Linux /etc/exports file

Type	Syntax	Meaning
Hostname	*hostname*	Individual hosts
Netgroup	*@groupname*	NIS netgroups (not frequently used)
Wild cards	* and ?	FQDNs[a] with wild cards; "*" will not match a dot
IP networks	*ipaddr/mask*	CIDR-style specifications (e.g., 128.138.92.128/25)

a. Fully qualified domain names

Table 18.7 on the next page shows the most commonly used export options understood by Linux.

Linux's NFS server has the unusual feature of allowing subdirectories of exported directories to be exported with different options. Use the noaccess option to unexport subdirectories that you would rather not share.

Table 18.7 Common export options in Linux

Option	Description
ro	Exports read-only
rw	Exports for reading and writing (the default)
rw=*list*	Exports read-mostly. The *list* enumerates the hosts allowed to mount for writing; all others must mount read-only.
root_squash	Maps ("squashes") UID 0 and GID 0 to the values specified by anonuid and anongid.[a] This is the default.
no_root_squash	Allows normal access by root. Dangerous.
all_squash	Maps all UIDs and GIDs to their anonymous versions. Useful for supporting PCs and untrusted single-user hosts.
anonuid=*xxx*	Specifies the UID to which remote roots should be squashed
anongid=*xxx*	Specifies the GID to which remote roots should be squashed
secure	Requires remote access to originate at a privileged port
insecure	Allows remote access from any port
noaccess	Blocks access to this dir and subdirs (used with nested exports)
wdelay	Delays writes in hopes of coalescing multiple updates
no_wdelay	Writes data to disk as soon as possible
async	Makes server reply to write requests before actual disk write
nohide	Reveals filesystems mounted within exported file trees
hide	Opposite of nohide
subtree_check	Verifies that each requested file is within an exported subtree
no_subtree_check	Verifies only that file requests refer to an exported filesystem
secure_locks	Requires authorization for all lock requests
insecure_locks	Specifies less stringent locking criteria (supports older clients)
sec=*flavor*	Specifies a list of security methods for the exported directory. Values include sys (UNIX authentication), dh (DES), krb5 (Kerberos authentication), krb5i (Kerberos authentication and integrity), krb5p (Kerberos authentication, integrity, and privacy), and none (anonymous access, not recommended).
fsid=*num*	Specifies the V4 pseudo-filesystem root (usually 0)

a. Unlike most operating systems, Linux allows UIDs other than root to be collapsed. Look up the all_squash option for more details.

For example, the configuration

```
/home         *.atrust.com(rw)
/home/ben     (noaccess)
```

allows hosts in the atrust.com domain to access all the contents of **/home** except for **/home/ben**. The absence of a client name on the second line means that the option applies to all hosts; it's perhaps somewhat more secure this way.

The subtree_check option (the default) verifies that every file accessed by a client lies within an exported subdirectory. If you turn off this option, only the fact that the file is within an exported filesystem is verified. Subtree checking can cause occasional problems when a requested file is renamed while the client has the file open. If you anticipate many such situations, consider setting no_subtree_check.

The secure_locks option requires authorization and authentication in order for files to be locked. Some NFS clients don't send credentials with lock requests and do not work with secure_locks. In this case, you would only be able to lock world-readable files. Replacing these clients with ones that support credentials correctly is the best solution. However, you can specify the insecure_locks option as a stopgap.

Linux's **mountd** can be run out of **inetd** rather than run continuously. This configuration allows supplemental access control to be performed by the TCP wrapper program, **tcpd**. See page 917 for more information.

nfsd: serve files

Once a client's mount request has been validated by **mountd**, the client can request various filesystem operations. These requests are handled on the server side by **nfsd**, the NFS operations daemon.[5] **nfsd** need not be run on an NFS client machine unless the client exports filesystems of its own.

nfsd takes a numeric argument that specifies how many server threads to fork. Selecting the appropriate number of **nfsd**s is important and is unfortunately something of a black art. If the number is too low or too high, NFS performance can suffer.

The optimal number of **nfsd** threads depends on the operating system and the hardware in use. If you notice that **ps** usually shows the **nfsd**s in state D (uninterruptible sleep) and that some idle CPU is available, consider increasing the number of threads. If you find the load average (as reported by **uptime**) rising as you add **nfsd**s, you've gone too far; back off a bit from that threshold. You should also run **nfsstat** regularly to check for performance problems that might be associated with the number of **nfsd** threads. See page 710 for more details on **nfsstat**.

On a loaded NFS version 2 or 3 server with a lot of UDP clients, UDP sockets can overflow if requests arrive while all **nfsd** threads are already in use. You can monitor the number of overflows with **netstat -s**. Add more **nfsd**s until UDP socket overflows drop to zero. Overflows indicate a severe undersupply of server daemons, so you should probably add a few more than this metric would indicate.

The number of **nfsd** threads is configured in a system-wide NFS configuration file. The location of the file and the available settings differ widely. Table 18.8 on the next page shows the settings for our example systems. After making any changes to the **nfsd** configuration file, be sure to restart the services using the scripts in Table 18.1.

5. In reality, **nfsd** simply makes a nonreturning system call to NFS server code embedded in the kernel.

Table 18.8 How to specify the number of nfsd daemons

System	Config file (in /etc)	Option to set	Default
Ubuntu	**default/nfs-kernel-server**	RPCNFSDCOUNT	8
SUSE	**sysconfig/nfs**	USE_KERNEL_NFSD_NUMBER	4
Red Hat	**sysconfig/nfs**	RPCNFSDCOUNT	8
Solaris	**default/nfs**	NFSD_SERVERS	16
HP-UX	**default/nfs**	NFSD_SERVERS	16
AIX	*Use SMIT or* ***chnfs*** *to change the number of* ***nfsd*** *daemons.*		

18.4 Client-side NFS

NFS filesystems are mounted in much the same way as local disk filesystems. The **mount** command understands the notation *hostname:directory* to mean the path *directory* on the host *hostname*. As with local filesystems, **mount** maps the remote *directory* on the remote *host* into a directory within the local file tree. After the mount completes, you access an NFS-mounted filesystem just like a local filesystem. The **mount** command and its associated NFS extensions represent the most significant concerns to the system administrator of an NFS client.

Before an NFS file system can be mounted, it must be properly exported (see *Server-side NFS* on page 698). To verify that a server has properly exported its filesystems from the client's perspective, use the client's **showmount** command:

```
$ showmount -e monk
Export list for monk:
/home/ben harp.atrust.com
```

This example reports that the directory **/home/ben** on the server monk has been exported to the client system harp.atrust.com. If an NFS mount is not working, first verify that the filesystems have been properly exported on the server with **exportfs**. (You might have just forgotten to run **exportfs -a** after updating the **exports** file.) Next, check the **showmount** output.

See page 917 for more information about ***hosts.**** *files and TCP wrappers.*

If the directory is properly exported on the server but **showmount** returns an error or an empty list, you might double-check that all the necessary processes are running on the server (**portmap**, **mountd**, **nfsd**, **statd**, and **lockd**), that the **hosts.allow** and **hosts.deny** files allow access to those daemons, and that you are on the right client system.

The path information displayed by **showmount**, such as **/home/ben** above, is only valid for NFS version 2 and 3 servers. NFS version 4 servers export a single unified pseudo-filesystem. The traditional NFS concept of separate mount points doesn't jive with version 4's model, so **showmount** isn't applicable.

Unfortunately, there is no good replacement for **showmount** in NFSv4. On the server, the command **exportfs -v** shows the existing exports, but of course this only works locally. If you don't have direct access to the server, mount the root of the server's pseudo-filesystem and traverse the directory structure manually, noting each mount point.

To actually mount the filesystem in versions 2 and 3, you would use a command such as

```
$ sudo mount -o rw,hard,intr,bg monk:/home/ben /nfs/ben
```

To accomplish the same using version 4 on a Linux system, type

```
$ sudo mount -t nfs4 -o rw,hard,intr,bg monk:/ /nfs/ben
```

In this case, the options after **-o** specify that the filesystem should be mounted read-write (**rw**), that operations should be interruptible (**intr**), and that retries should be done in the background (**bg**). Table 18.9 introduces the most common mount options.

Table 18.9 NFS mount flags and options

Flag	Description
rw	Mounts the filesystem read-write (must be exported that way)
ro	Mounts the filesystem read-only
bg	If the mount fails (server doesn't respond), keeps trying it in the background and continues with other mount requests
hard	If a server goes down, causes operations that try to access it to block until the server comes back up
soft	If a server goes down, causes operations that try to access it to fail and return an error, thereby avoiding processes "hanging" on inessential mounts
intr	Allows users to interrupt blocked operations (and return an error)
nointr	Does not allow user interrupts
retrans=*n*	Specifies the number of times to repeat a request before returning an error on a soft-mounted filesystem
timeo=*n*	Sets the timeout period (in 10ths of a second) for requests
rsize=*n*	Sets the read buffer size to *n* bytes
wsize=*n*	Sets the write buffer size to *n* bytes
sec=*flavor*	Specifies the security flavor
vers=*n*[a]	Sets the NFS protocol version
proto=*proto*	Selects a transport protocol; must be tcp for NFS version 4

a. Although the vers flag is listed in the **mount** man pages on Linux systems, using it results in an error. To request a version 4 mount, use **mount -t nfs4** instead.

Filesystems mounted hard (the default) cause processes to hang when their servers go down. This behavior is particularly bothersome when the processes in question are standard daemons, so we do not recommend serving critical system binaries over NFS. In general, the use of the soft and intr options reduces the number of NFS-related headaches. However, these options can have their own undesirable side effects, such as aborting a 20-hour simulation after it has run for 18 hours just because of a transient network glitch.[6] Automount solutions such as autofs, discussed later, also provide some remedies for mounting ailments.

The read and write buffer sizes apply to both UDP and TCP mounts, but the optimal values differ. Because you can trust TCP to transfer data efficiently, the values should be higher; 32KiB is a good value. For UDP, 8KiB is a good value when server and client are on the same network. The default is 1KiB, but even the man page recommends increasing it to 8KiB for better performance.

You can test an NFS mount with **df** just as you would test a local filesystem:

```
$ df /nfs/ben
Filesystem          1k-blocks     Used  Available  Use%  Mounted on
leopard:/home/ben   17212156   1694128  14643692    11%  /nfs/ben
```

umount works on NFS filesystems just like it does on local filesystems. If the NFS filesystem is in use when you try to unmount it, you will get an error such as

```
umount: /nfs/ben: device is busy
```

Use **lsof** to find processes with open files on the filesystem. Kill them, or in the case of shells, change directories. If all else fails or your server is down, try running **umount -f** to force the filesystem to be unmounted.

The footnote to Table 18.9 is worth repeating: the Linux **mount** command defaults to a filesystem type of **nfs** when it recognizes the *hostname:directory* syntax on the command line. The **nfs** type is only valid for protocol versions 2 and 3. Use **mount -t nfs4** *hostname:directory* when requesting a version 4 mount.

Mounting remote filesystems at boot time

See page 711 for more information about autofs.

You can use the **mount** command to establish temporary network mounts, but you should list mounts that are part of a system's permanent configuration in **/etc/fstab** (**/etc/vfstab** in Solaris) so that they are mounted automatically at boot time. Alternatively, mounts can be handled by an automatic mounting service such as autofs.

The following **fstab** entries mount the filesystems **/home** and **/usr/local** from the hosts monk and ross:

```
# filesystem     mountpoint   fstype  flags                          dump  fsck
monk:/home       /nfs/home    nfs     rw,bg,intr,hard,nodev,nosuid   0     0
ross:/usr/local  /usr/local   nfs4    ro,bg,intr,soft,nodev,nosuid   0     0
```

The Solaris **/etc/vfstab** file is slightly different in format, but options are listed similarly. The NFS options are largely the same as those on other systems.

6. Jeff Forys, one of our technical reviewers, remarked, "Most mounts should use hard, intr, and bg, because these options best preserve NFS's original design goals. soft is an abomination, an ugly Satanic hack! If the user wants to interrupt, cool. Otherwise, wait for the server and all will eventually be well again with no data lost."

Use SMIT to configure boot-time NFS mounts on AIX systems. Do not modify the **/etc/filesystems** file by hand since it can be overwritten during volume group imports or exports.

*See page 260 for more information about the **fstab** file.*

When you add entries to **fstab/vfstab**, be sure to create the appropriate mount point directories with **mkdir**. You can make your changes take effect immediately (without rebooting) by running **mount -a -F nfs** on Solaris or HP-UX; use **-t** instead of **-F** on Linux, and for version 4 use **mount -a -t nfs4**. On AIX, you can mount NFS filesystems with **mount -v nfs -a**.

The flags field of **/etc/fstab** specifies options for NFS mounts; these options are the same ones you would specify on the **mount** command line.

Restricting exports to privileged ports

NFS clients are free to use any TCP or UDP source port they like when connecting to an NFS server. However, some servers may insist that requests come from a privileged port (a port numbered lower than 1,024). Others allow this behavior to be set as an option. In the world of PCs and desktop Linux boxes, the use of privileged ports provides little actual security.

Most NFS clients adopt the traditional (and still recommended) approach of defaulting to a privileged port to avert the potential for conflict. Under Linux, you can accept mounts from unprivileged ports with the insecure export option.

18.5 Identity mapping for NFS version 4

Unlike earlier versions of NFS, which identify users with raw UID and GID values, version 4 uses strings of the form *user@nfs-domain* and *group@nfs-domain*. On both NFS servers and clients, an identity mapping daemon translates between the string identifiers and the local UNIX UID and GID values. Mapped values are used to translate file attribute information, but they are not used for access control, which is handled separately.

All systems participating in an NFSv4 network should have the same NFS domain. In most cases, it's reasonable to use your DNS domain as the NFS domain. For example, atrust.com is a straightforward choice of NFS domain for the server harp.atrust.com. Clients in subdomains (e.g., booklab.atrust.com) may or may not want to use the shorter site-wide name (e.g., atrust.com) to facilitate NFS communication.

Unfortunately for administrators, there is no standard implementation of NFSv4 UID mapping, so the details of administration differ slightly among systems. Table 18.10 on the next page names the mapping daemon on each of our example systems and notes the location of its configuration file.

Other than having their NFS domains set, identity mapping services require little assistance from administrators. The daemons are started at boot time from the same scripts that manage NFS. After making configuration changes, you'll need

Table 18.10 Identity mapping daemons and configurations

System	Daemon	Configuration
Linux	**/usr/sbin/rpc.idmapd**	**/etc/idmapd.conf**
Solaris	**/usr/lib/nfs/nfsmapid**	**/etc/default/nfs**[a]
HP-UX	**/usr/sbin/nfsmapid**	**/etc/default/nfs**[a]
AIX	**/usr/sbin/nfsrgyd**	**chnfsdom** *domain*

a. The domain is set in the NFSMAPID_DOMAIN parameter.

to restart the daemon. Options such as verbose logging and alternate management of the nobody account are usually available; see the man page for the specific daemon.

18.6 NFSSTAT: DUMP NFS STATISTICS

nfsstat displays various statistics maintained by the NFS system. **nfsstat -s** shows server-side statistics, and **nfsstat -c** shows information for client-side operations. By default, **nfsstat** shows statistics for all protocol versions. For example:

```
$ nfsstat -c

Client rpc:
calls    badcalls  retrans  badxid  timeout  wait  newcred  timers
64235    1595      0        3       1592     0     0        886

Client nfs:
calls    badcalls  nclget   nclsleep
62613    3         62643    0
null     getattr   setattr  readlink  lookup   root   read
0%       34%       0%       21%       30%      0%     2%
write    wrcache   create   remove    rename   link   symlink
3%       0%        0%       0%        0%       0%     0%
mkdir    readdir   rmdir    fsstat
0%       6%        0%       0%
```

This example is from a relatively healthy NFS client. If more than 3% of RPC calls time out, it's likely that there is a problem with your NFS server or network. You can usually discover the cause by checking the badxid field. If badxid is near 0 with timeouts greater than 3%, packets to and from the server are getting lost on the network. You may be able to solve this problem by lowering the rsize and wsize mount parameters (read and write block sizes).

If badxid is nearly as high as timeout, then the server is responding, but too slowly. Either replace the server or increase the timeo mount parameter.

Running **nfsstat** and **netstat** occasionally and becoming familiar with their output will help you discover NFS problems before your users do.

18.7 Dedicated NFS file servers

Fast, reliable file service is an essential element of a production computing environment. Although you can certainly roll your own file servers from workstations and off-the-shelf hard disks, doing so is often not the best-performing or easiest-to-administer solution (though it is usually the cheapest).

Dedicated NFS file servers have been around for many years. They offer a host of potential advantages over the homebrew approach:

- They are optimized for file service and typically provide the best possible NFS performance.
- As storage requirements grow, they can scale smoothly to support terabytes of storage and hundreds of users.
- They are more reliable than stand-alone boxes thanks to their simplified software, redundant hardware, and use of disk mirroring.
- They usually provide file service for both UNIX and Windows clients. Most even contain integrated web, FTP, and SFTP servers.
- They are often easier to administer than UNIX file servers.
- They often include backup and checkpoint facilities that are superior to those found on vanilla UNIX systems.

Some of our favorite dedicated NFS servers are made by Network Appliance, Inc. (netapp.com). Their products run the gamut from very small to very large, and their pricing is OK. EMC is another player in the high-end server market. They make good products, but be prepared for sticker shock and build up your tolerance for marketing buzzwords. LeftHand Networks, owned by HP, is another player that has gained traction in recent years with lower-cost, high-performing, entry-level storage products.

Storage area network (SAN) systems are another option for high-performance storage management over a network. They differ from dedicated file servers in that they have no understanding of filesystems; they simply serve disk blocks. A SAN is therefore unencumbered by the overhead of an operating system and affords fast read/write access, but it's unable to manage concurrent access by multiple clients without the help of a clustered filesystem. See page 274 for more information about SANs.

18.8 Automatic mounting

Mounting filesystems at boot time by listing them in **/etc/fstab** or **/etc/vfstab** can cause several kinds of administrative headaches on large networks.

First, maintaining the **fstab** file on hundreds of machines can be tedious, even with help from scripts and configuration management systems. Each host may have slightly different needs and so require individual attention.

Second, if filesystems are mounted from many different hosts, clients become dependent on many different servers. Chaos ensues when one of those servers crashes. Every command that accesses the mount points will hang.

Third, when an important server crashes, it may cripple users by making important filesystems like **/usr/share** unavailable. In this situation, it's best if a copy of the partition can be mounted temporarily from a backup server. However, NFS has no built-in provision for backup servers.

You can moderate all these problems by using an automount daemon to mount filesystems when they are referenced and to unmount them when they are no longer being used. An automounter limits the number of active mount points and is largely transparent to users. Most automounters also accept a list of "replicated" (identical) filesystems so that the network can continue to function when a primary server becomes unavailable.

To implement this behind-the-scenes mounting and unmounting, the automounter mounts a virtual filesystem driver on the directories you've designated as locations for automatic mounting to occur. In the past, the automounter did this by posing as an NFS server, but this scheme suffers from some significant limitations and is rarely found on contemporary systems. These days, a kernel-resident filesystem driver called autofs is used.

Instead of mirroring an actual filesystem, the automounter "makes up" a virtual filesystem hierarchy according to the specifications given in its configuration file. When a user references a directory within the automounter's virtual filesystem, the automounter intercepts the reference and mounts the actual filesystem the user is trying to reach. On systems that support autofs, the NFS filesystem is mounted beneath the autofs filesystem in normal UNIX fashion. Other systems may require mounting to occur in a separate directory that is then pointed to by symbolic links.

The idea of an automounter originally comes from Sun, now part of Oracle. Sun's implementation, **automount**, is shipped with most Sun-derived NFS clients. Linux distributions supply a version that functionally mimics that of Sun, though it is an independent implementation. Similarly, AIX provides its own independent **automount** daemon that IBM calls "an administration tool for AutoFS."

The various **automount** implementations understand three different kinds of configuration files (referred to as "maps"): direct maps, indirect maps, and master maps.[7] Direct and indirect maps provide information about the filesystems to be automounted. A master map lists the direct and indirect maps that **automount** should pay attention to. Only one master map can be active at once; the default master map is kept in **/etc/auto_master** (**/etc/auto.master** under Linux).

On most systems, **automount** is a stand-alone command that reads its configuration files, sets up any necessary autofs mounts, and exits. Actual references to

7. A direct map can also be managed as an NIS database or in an LDAP directory, but this is tricky.

automounted filesystems are handled (through autofs) by a separate daemon process, **automountd**. The daemon does its work silently and does not need additional configuration.

On Linux systems, the daemon is called **automount** and the setup function is performed by the **/etc/init.d/autofs** startup script. Linux details are given in the section *Specifics for Linux* on page 717. In the following discussion, we refer to the setup command as **automount** and the daemon as **automountd**.

If you change the master map or one of the direct maps that it references, you must rerun **automount** to pick up the changes. With the **-v** option, **automount** will show you the adjustments it's making to its configuration.

automount also accepts a **-t** argument that tells how long (in seconds) an automounted filesystem may remain unused before being unmounted. The default is usually 10 minutes. Since an NFS mount whose server has crashed can cause programs that touch it to hang, it's good hygiene to clean up automounts that are no longer in use; don't raise the timeout too much.[8]

Indirect maps

Indirect maps automount several filesystems underneath a common directory. However, the path of the directory is specified in the master file, not in the map itself. For example, an indirect map for filesystems mounted under **/chimchim** might look like this:

```
users    harp:/harp/users
devel    -soft harp:/harp/devel
info     -ro harp:/harp/info
```

The first column names the subdirectory in which each automount should be installed, and subsequent items list the mount options and the NFS path of the filesystem. This example (perhaps stored in **/etc/auto.harp**) tells **automount** that it can mount the directories **/harp/users**, **/harp/devel**, and **/harp/info** from the server harp, with **info** being mounted read-only and **devel** being mounted soft.

In this configuration the paths on chimchim and the local host are the same. However, this correspondence is not required.

Direct maps

Direct maps list filesystems that do not share a common prefix, such as **/usr/src** and **/cs/tools**. A direct map (e.g., **/etc/auto.direct**) that described both of these filesystems to **automount** might look something like this:

```
/usr/src     harp:/usr/src
/cs/tools    -ro monk:/cs/tools
```

8. The other side of this issue is the fact that it takes a certain amount of time to mount a filesystem. System response will be faster and smoother if filesystems aren't being continually remounted.

Because they do not share a common parent directory, these automounts must each be implemented with a separate autofs mount. This configuration requires more overhead, but it has the added advantage that the mount point and directory structure are always accessible to commands such as **ls**. Using **ls** on a directory full of indirect mounts can be confusing to users because **automount** doesn't show the subdirectories until their contents have been accessed (**ls** doesn't look inside the automounted directories, so it does not cause them to be mounted).

Master maps

A master map lists the direct and indirect maps that **automount** should pay attention to. For each indirect map, it also specifies the root directory used by the mounts defined in the map.

A master map that made use of the direct and indirect maps shown in the previous examples would look something like this:

```
# Directory   Map
/harp         /etc/auto.harp -proto=tcp
/-            /etc/auto.direct
```

The first column is a local directory name for an indirect map or the special token /- for a direct map. The second column identifies the file in which the map is stored. You can have several maps of each type. When you specify mount options at the end of a line, they set the defaults for all mounts within the map. Linux administrators should always specify the -fstype=nfs4 mount flag for NFS version 4 servers.

On most systems, the default options set on a master map entry do not blend with the options specified in the direct or indirect map to which it points. If a map entry has its own list of options, the defaults are ignored. Linux merges the two sets, however. If the same option is specified in both places, the map entry's value overrides the default.

The master map can usually be replaced or augmented by a version shared through NIS. See your documentation for details.

Executable maps

If a map file is executable, it's assumed to be a script or program that dynamically generates automounting information. Instead of reading the map as a text file, the automounter executes it with an argument (the "key") that indicates which subdirectory a user has attempted to access. The script is responsible for printing an appropriate map entry; if the specified key is not valid, the script can simply exit without printing anything.

This powerful feature makes up for many of the deficiencies in **automounter**'s rather strange configuration system. In effect, it allows you to easily define a sitewide automount configuration file in a format of your own choice. You can write a simple script to decode the global configuration on each machine. Some systems come with a handy **/etc/auto.net** executable map that takes a hostname as a key and mounts all exported file systems on that host.

Since automount scripts run dynamically as needed, it's unnecessary to distribute the master configuration file after every change or to convert it preemptively to the **automounter** format; in fact, the global configuration file can have a permanent home on an NFS server.

Automount visibility

When you list the contents of an automounted filesystem's parent directory, the directory appears empty no matter how many filesystems have been automounted there. You cannot browse the automounts in a GUI filesystem browser.

An example:

```
$ ls /portal
$ ls /portal/photos
art_class_2010    florissant_1003              rmnp03
blizzard2008      frozen_dead_guy_Oct2009      rmnp_030806
boston021130      greenville.021129            steamboat2006
```

The **photos** filesystem is alive and well and is automounted under **/portal**. It's accessible through its full pathname. However, a review of the **/portal** directory does not reveal its existence. If you had mounted this filesystem through the **fstab** file or a manual **mount** command, it would behave like any other directory and would be visible as a member of the parent directory.

One way around the browsing problem is to create a shadow directory that contains symbolic links to automount points. For example, if **/automounts/photos** is a link to **/portal/photos**, you can **ls** the contents of **/automounts** to discover that **photos** is an automounted directory. References to **/automounts/photos** are still routed through the automounter and work correctly.

Unfortunately, these symbolic links require maintenance and can go out of sync with the actual automounts unless they are periodically reconstructed by a script.

Replicated filesystems and automount

In some cases, a read-only filesystem such as **/usr/share** may be identical on several different servers. In this case, you can tell **automount** about several potential sources for the filesystem. It will choose a server based on its own idea of which servers are closest given network numbers, NFS protocol versions, and response times to an initial query.

Although **automount** itself does not see or care how the filesystems it mounts are used, replicated mounts should represent read-only filesystems such as **/usr/share** or **/usr/local/X11**. There's no way for **automount** to synchronize writes across a set of servers, so replicated read-write filesystems are of little practical use.

Under Solaris and HP-UX, **automount** can smoothly switch from one server of a replicated mount to another when problems occur. This feature is only supposed to work properly for read-only mounts, but rumor has it that read-write mounts are handled more reasonably than the documentation would suggest. References to files that have been opened for writing will still hang when **automount** changes servers, however, which is yet another reason why replicated read-write mounts may not be so useful.

Although **automount** can select among replicated servers according to its own criteria for efficiency and locality, you can also assign explicit priorities if you like. The priorities are small integers, with larger numbers indicating lower priority. The default priority is 0, most eligible.

An **auto.direct** file that defines **/usr/man** and **/cs/tools** as replicated filesystems might look like this:

```
/usr/man    -ro harp:/usr/share/man monk(1):/usr/man
/cs/tools   -ro leopard,monk:/cs/tools
```

Note that server names can be listed together if the source path on each is the same. The (1) after monk in the first line sets that server's priority with respect to **/usr/man**. The lack of a priority after harp indicates an implicit priority 0.

Automatic automounts (V3; all but Linux)

Instead of listing every possible mount in a direct or indirect map, you can tell **automount** a little about your filesystem naming conventions and let it figure things out for itself. The key piece of glue that makes this work is that the **mountd** running on a remote server can be queried to find out what filesystems the server exports. In NFS version 4, the export is always /, which eliminates the need for this automation.

There are several ways to configure "automatic automounts," the simplest of which is the -hosts mount type. If you list -hosts as a map name in your master map file, **automount** then maps remote hosts' exports into the specified automount directory:

```
/net     -hosts -nosuid,soft
```

For example, if harp exported **/usr/share/man**, that directory could then be reached through the automounter at the path **/net/harp/usr/share/man**.

The implementation of -hosts does not enumerate all possible hosts from which filesystems can be mounted; that would be impossible. Instead, it waits for individual subdirectory names to be referenced, then runs off and mounts the exported filesystems from the requested host.

A similar but finer-grained effect can be achieved with the * and & wild cards in an indirect map file. Also, a number of macros available for use in maps expand to the current hostname, architecture type, and so on. See the **automount**(1M) man page for details.

Specifics for Linux

The Linux implementation of **automount** has diverged a bit from that of Sun. The changes mostly have to do with the naming of commands and files.

First, **automount** is the daemon that actually mounts and unmounts remote file systems. It fills the same niche as the **automountd** daemon on other systems and generally does not need to be run by hand.

The default master map file is **/etc/auto.master**. Its format and the format of indirect maps are as described previously. The documentation can be hard to find, however. The master map format is described in **auto.master**(5) and the indirect map format in **autofs**(5); be careful, or you'll get **autofs**(8), which documents the syntax of the **autofs** command. (As one of the man pages says, "The documentation leaves a lot to be desired.") To cause changes to the master map to take effect, run **/etc/init.d/autofs reload**, which is equivalent to **automount** in Sun-land.

The Linux implementation does not support the Solaris-style `-hosts` clause for automatic automounts.

18.9 Recommended reading

Callaghan, Brent. *NFS Illustrated.* Reading, MA: Addison-Wesley, 1999.

Stern, Hal, Mike Eisler, and Ricardo Labiaga. *Managing NFS and NIS (2nd Edition).* Sebastopol, CA: O'Reilly Media, 2001.

Table 18.11 lists the various RFCs for the NFS protocol.

Table 18.11 NFS-related RFCs

RFC	Title	Author	Date
1094	Network File System Protocol Specification	Sun Microsystems	Mar 1989
1813	NFS Version 3 Protocol Specification	B. Callaghan et al.	Jun 1995
2623	NFS Version 2 and Version 3 Security Issues	M. Eisler	Jun 1999
2624	NFS Version 4 Design Considerations	S. Shepler	Jun 1999
3530	NFS Version 4 Protocol	S. Shepler et al.	April 2003

18.10 Exercises

☆ E18.1 Explore your local NFS setup. Is NFS used, or is a different solution in place? Is automounting used? What tradeoffs have been made?

☆ E18.2 In NFS versions 2 and 3, what is the relationship between **mountd**, **nfsd**, and **portmap**? What does the NFS dependency on **portmap** mean in terms of security?

☆☆ E18.3 What are some of the conceptual changes between NFS versions 3 and 4? How does the issue of stateful versus stateless change other attributes of the protocol?

☆☆ E18.4 Your employer needs you to export **/usr** and **/usr/local** through NFS. You have been given the following information and requests:

a) Because of office politics, you want only your department (local subnet 192.168.123.0/24) to be able to use these exported filesystems. What lines must be added to which files to implement this configuration? Pay attention to the proper export options.

b) List the steps needed to make **mountd** and **nfsd** recognize these new shared filesystems. How could you verify that the directories were being shared without mounting them?

c) Outline a strategy that would make all machines on your local subnet automatically mount the exported directories on the mount points **/mnt/usr** and **/mnt/usr/local**.

19 Sharing System Files

We're all familiar with the concept of sharing data among computers, whether that's accomplished through email attachments, transfer protocols such as HTTP and FTP, or file-sharing services like those provided by NFS and CIFS. These mechanisms are designed primarily as a way for users to share files and application data. However, UNIX and Linux systems can benefit from another type of sharing: the distribution of administrative configuration data. This kind of sharing centralizes administrative control and promotes consistency among systems.

User logins and passwords are a real-world example of the need for this kind of sharing. You rarely want to add a user to a single machine; in most cases, you want to define that user on an entire class or network of machines. In addition, most organizations are now faced with the need to support a mix of platforms—some UNIX, some Linux, and some Windows—and users are increasingly annoyed when they have to remember (and change) a different password on each platform. Fortunately, it's not that hard to synchronize configuration and user information across different systems.

Sharing system files isn't as easy as it sounds. Attempts to develop distributed administrative databases for large networks go back several decades and have produced a number of interesting systems. However, none of the systems in general use seem exactly right in their approach. Some are simple but not secure and not scalable. Others are functional but unwieldy. All the systems have limitations that can prevent you from setting up the network the way you want to, and none of them manage all the information you may want to share across your machines.

In this chapter we first discuss some basic techniques for keeping configuration files synchronized on a network. Next, we address the Lightweight Directory Access Protocol (LDAP), a more sophisticated, platform-independent database system that is becoming a de facto standard in both the UNIX and Windows worlds. Most sites today are migrating toward LDAP, in large part because of Microsoft's adoption of (most of) the LDAP standard in their Active Directory product and the desire to better integrate Linux and Windows environments. Finally, we cover NIS, a historically popular database system that lingers on in some environments but probably should not be deployed at new sites.

Note that sharing system files is different from system configuration and software deployment. These domains have different needs, and in practice, they are addressed by different solutions. See Chapter 12, *Software Installation and Management*, for details about what goes on behind that particular wall.

19.1 What to share

Of the many configuration files on a UNIX or Linux system, only a subset can be usefully shared among machines. In modern times, the most pressing need for sharing relates to the contents of the **passwd**, **hosts**, and **aliases** files; however, other configuration files can become shared entities as well. Table 19.1 shows some of the most commonly shared files.

Table 19.1 System files that are commonly shared

Filename	Function
/etc/passwd	User account information database
/etc/shadow[a]	Holds user account passwords
/etc/group	Defines UNIX groups
/etc/hosts	Maps between hostnames and IP addresses
/etc/mail/aliases	Holds electronic mail aliases
/etc/sudoers	Grants privileges for the **sudo** command
/etc/skel/*	Holds default configuration files for new home directories

a. Not necessarily sharable among all flavors of UNIX since the encryption can vary; see page 179.

Table 19.1 is far from being a comprehensive list; your exact configuration depends on how similar you want the machines at your site to be. For the most part, though, additional configuration files are associated with specific applications and are not supported by administrative directory systems such as LDAP; you must share the files by copying them.

See page 908 for more information about PAM.

Many of the files in Table 19.1 are intended to be accessed through routines in the standard C library. For example, the **/etc/passwd** file can be searched with the **getpwuid**, **getpwnam**, and **getpwent** routines. These routines take care of opening, reading, and parsing the **passwd** file so that user-level programs don't have to do it themselves. Modern systems can also use pluggable authentication modules (PAM), which define a standard programming interface for performing security-related lookups. PAM allows systems such as Kerberos and LDAP to be easily integrated into the system. The exact complement of data sources that are consulted is set by the system administrator; see *Prioritizing sources of administrative information* on page 739 for details.

19.2 Copying files around

Brute-force file copying is not an elegant solution, but it works on every kind of machine and is easy to set up and maintain. It's a reliable system because it minimizes the interdependencies among machines (although it may also make it easier for machines to fall out of sync). File copying also offers the most flexibility in terms of what can be distributed, and how. It is often used to keep applications and data files, as well as system files, up to date.

Quite a few configuration files are not supported by any of the common database services. **/etc/ntp.conf**, which determines how hosts keep their clocks synchronized, is an example. To keep such files in sync, you really have no choice but to use some sort of file-copying system.

The NFS option

Some sites distribute configuration files by publishing them on an NFS server. This is perhaps the simplest possible technique from an automation point of view—all you need on the client is **cp**, at least in theory.

See Chapter 18, for more information about NFS.

NFS used to have security issues that made this approach a bit risky, but in NFSv4, those concerns have largely been addressed. For extra security, you can use encryption to protect sensitive files from inspection by prying eyes.

See page 925 for more information about PGP.

Another step that increases security is to have the publisher sign configuration files with a public key cryptography package such as PGP. Clients can then verify that the files they are being offered through NFS are authentic and unmodified before installing them.

Many software packages let you specify a nonstandard location for configuration files. Therefore, it's theoretically possible to point these packages at configuration files that live on an NFS filesystem, thus making no local copies at all. However, we *strongly* advise against this configuration. It makes every system in the world dependent on one NFS server, and that server then has to actively serve all those clients. Worse yet, many packages don't expect remote systems to be locking their configuration files or creating temporary files in their configuration directories; the setup may not even work correctly. More accurately, it may work perfectly almost all of the time but fail mysteriously and sporadically, leaving no evidence of what went wrong. Welcome to hell.

Push systems vs. pull systems

Once you get away from the shared filesystem model, file-copying systems generally use either a "push" model or a "pull" model. With push, the master server periodically distributes the freshest files to each client, whether the client wants them or not. Files can be pushed explicitly whenever a change is made, or they can simply be distributed on a regular schedule (perhaps with some files being transferred more often than others).

The push model has the advantage of keeping the distribution system centralized on one machine. Files, lists of clients, update scripts, and timetables are stored in one place, making the scheme easy to control. One disadvantage is that each client must let the master modify its system files, thereby creating a security hazard.

In a pull system, each client is responsible for updating itself from the server. This is a less centralized way of distributing files, but it is also more adaptable and more secure. When data is shared across administrative boundaries, a pull system is especially attractive because the master and client machines need not be run by the same administrative group or political faction.

rdist: push files

The **rdist** command is the easiest way to distribute files from a central server. It has something of the flavor of **make**: you use a text editor to create a specification of the files to be distributed, and then you use **rdist** to bring reality into line with your specification. **rdist** copies files only when they are out of date, so you can write your specification as if all files were to be copied and let **rdist** optimize out unnecessary work.

rdist preserves the owner, group, mode, and modification time of files. When it updates an existing file, **rdist** first deletes the old version before installing the new. This feature makes **rdist** suitable for transferring executables that might be in use during the update.[1]

rdist historically ran on top of **rsh** and used **rsh**'s authentication system to gain access to remote systems. However, this system is not secure and is disabled by default on modern operating systems. Even though the **rdist** documentation continues to talk about **rsh**, do not be fooled into thinking that **rsh** security is a reasonable choice.

Current versions of **rdist** are better in that they allow any command that understands the same syntax to be substituted for **rsh**. In practice, the substitute is **ssh**, which uses cryptography to verify the identity of hosts and to prevent network eavesdroppers from obtaining copies of your data. The downside is that you must

1. Though the old version disappears from the filesystem namespace, it continues to exist until all references have been released. You must also be aware of this effect when managing log files.

run remote **ssh** servers in a mode that does not require a password (but authenticates the client with a cryptographic key pair). This is a less secure configuration than we would normally recommend, but it is still a huge improvement over **rsh**. See page 926 for more information about **sshd** and its authentication modes.

Now that we've belabored the perils of **rdist**, let's look at how it actually works. Like **make**, **rdist** looks for a control file (**Distfile** or **distfile**) in the current directory. **rdist -f** *distfile* explicitly specifies the control file's pathname. Within the control file, tabs, spaces, and newlines are used interchangeably as separators. Comments are introduced with a pound sign (#).

The meat of a **Distfile** consists of statements of the form

```
label: pathnames -> destinations commands
```

The *label* field associates a name with the statement. From the shell, you can run **rdist** *label* to distribute only the files described in a particular statement.

The *pathnames* and *destinations* are lists of files to be copied and hosts to copy them to, respectively. If a list contains more than one entry, the list must be surrounded with parentheses and the elements separated by whitespace. The *pathnames* can include shell-style globbing characters (e.g., **/usr/man/man[123]** or **/usr/lib/***). The notation *~user* is also acceptable, but it is evaluated separately on the source and destination machines.

By default, **rdist** copies the files and directories listed in *pathnames* to the equivalent paths on each destination machine. You can modify this behavior by supplying a sequence of commands and terminating each with a semicolon.

The following commands are understood:

```
install options [destdir];
notify namelist;
except pathlist;
except_pat patternlist;
special [pathlist] string;
cmdspecial [pathlist] string;
```

The install command sets options that affect the way **rdist** copies files. Options typically control the treatment of symbolic links, the correctness (vs. efficiency) of **rdist**'s difference-checking algorithm, and the way that deletions are handled. The options, which must be preceded by -o, consist of a comma-separated list of option names. For example, the line

```
install -oremove,follow;
```

makes **rdist** follow symbolic links (instead of just copying them as links) and removes existing files on the destination machine that have no counterpart on the source machine. See the **rdist** man page for a complete list of options. The defaults are almost always what you want.

The name "install" is somewhat misleading, since files are copied whether or not an install command is present. Options are specified as they would be on the **rdist** command line, but when included in the **Distfile**, they apply only to the set of files handled by that install command.

The optional *destdir* specifies an installation directory on the destination hosts. By default, **rdist** uses the original pathnames.

The notify command takes a list of email addresses as its argument. **rdist** sends mail to these addresses whenever a file is updated. Any addresses that do not contain an at sign (@) are suffixed with the name of the destination host. For example, **rdist** would expand "pete" to "pete@anchor" when reporting a list of files updated on host anchor.

See the section starting on page 48 for more information about regular expressions.

The except and except_pat commands remove pathnames from the list of files to be copied. Arguments to except are matched literally, and those of except_pat are interpreted as regular expressions. These exception commands are useful because **rdist**, like **make**, allows macros to be defined at the beginning of its control file. You might want to use a similar list of files for several statements, specifying only the additions and deletions for each host.

The special command executes a shell command (the *string* argument, in quotation marks) on each remote host. If a *pathlist* is present, **rdist** executes the command once after copying each of the specified files. Without a *pathlist*, **rdist** executes the command after every file. cmdspecial is similar, but it executes the shell command once after all copying is complete. (The contents of the *pathlist* are passed to the shell as an environment variable.)

Here's a simple example of a **Distfile**:

```
SYS_FILES  = (/etc/passwd /etc/group /etc/mail/aliases)
GET_ALL    = (chimchim lollipop barkadon)
GET_SOME = (whammo spiff)

all: ${SYS_FILES} -> ${GET_ALL}
    notify barb;
    special /etc/mail/aliases "/usr/bin/newaliases";

some: ${SYS_FILES} -> ${GET_SOME}
    except /etc/mail/aliases;
    notify eddie@spiff;
```

*See page 760 for more information about **newaliases**.*

This configuration replicates the three listed system files on chimchim, lollipop, and barkadon and sends mail to barb@*destination* describing any updates or errors that occur. After **/etc/mail/aliases** is copied, **rdist** runs **newaliases** on each destination. Only two files are copied to whammo and spiff. **newaliases** is not run, and a report is mailed to eddie@spiff.

To get **rdist** working among machines, you must also tell **sshd** on the recipient hosts to trust the host from which you are distributing files. To do this, you generate a plaintext key for the master host and store a copy of the public portion in the file ~**root/.ssh/authorized_keys** on each recipient. It's probably also wise to restrict what this key can do and where it can log in from. See the description of "method B" on page 926 for more information.

rsync: transfer files more securely

__rsync__ is available from rsync.samba.org.

rsync, written by Andrew Tridgell and Paul Mackerras, is similar in spirit to **rdist** but with a somewhat different focus. It does not use a file-copying control file in the manner of **rdist** (although the server side does have a configuration file). **rsync** is a bit like a souped-up version of **scp** that is scrupulous about preserving links, modification times, and permissions. It is more network efficient than **rdist** because it looks inside individual files and attempts to transmit only the differences between versions.

From our perspective, the main advantage of **rsync** is the fact that receiving machines can run the remote side as a server process out of **xinetd** or **inetd**. The server (actually just a different mode of **rsync**, which must be installed on both the master and the clients) is quite configurable: it can restrict remote access to a set of given directories and can require the master to prove its identity with a password. Since no **ssh** access is necessary, you can set up **rsync** to distribute system files without making too many security compromises. (However, if you prefer to use **ssh** instead of an **inetd**-based server process, **rsync** lets you do that too.) What's more, **rsync** can also run in pull mode (pulling files down from the **rsync** server rather than letting the server push files to the local system), which is even more secure (see the section on pulling files, page 727).

Unfortunately, **rsync** isn't nearly as flexible as **rdist**, and its configuration is less sophisticated than **rdist**'s **distfile**. You can't execute arbitrary commands on the clients, and you can't **rsync** to multiple hosts at once.

As an example, the command

```
# rsync -gopt --password-file=/etc/rsync.pwd /etc/passwd lollipop::sysfiles
```

transfers the **/etc/passwd** file to the machine lollipop. The **-gopt** options preserve the permissions, ownerships, and modification times of the file. The double colon in **lollipop::sysfiles** makes **rsync** contact the remote **rsync** directly on port 873 instead of using **ssh**. The password stored in **/etc/rsync.pwd** authenticates the connection.[2]

This example transfers only one file, but **rsync** is capable of handling multiple files at once. In addition, the **--include** and **--exclude** flags let you specify a list of regular expressions to match against filenames, so you can set up a sophisticated set

2. Although the password is encrypted for transmission across the network, the transferred files are not. If you use **ssh** as the transport (**rsync -gopt -e ssh /etc/passwd /etc/shadow lollipop:/etc** – note the single colon), the connection will be encrypted, but **sshd** will have to be configured not to require a password. Name your poison!

of transfer criteria. If the command line gets too unwieldy, you can read the patterns from separate files with the **--include-file** and **--exclude-file** options.

Linux **rsync** packages usually include a **xinetd** configuration for **rsync**. However, you must edit **/etc/xinetd.d/rsync** and change disable = yes to disable = no to actually enable the server.

As of this writing, **rsync** isn't shipped as part of the Solaris distribution. You can download the source code from rsync.samba.org and install it, or google for a premade Solaris binary. You may need to use **inetconv** to convert the daemon's startup method to be compatible with Solaris's new SMF framework.

HP-UX doesn't include **rsync** either, but you can get precompiled HP-UX binaries in **swinstall** depot form from

hpux.connect.org.uk/hppd/hpux/Networking/Admin/rsync-3.0.6

An AIX version of **rsync** is available from

ftp://ftp.software.ibm.com/aix/freeSoftware/aixtoolbox/RPMS/ppc/rsync

As of this writing, an RPM package for AIX 6.1 is still under development. In the interim, many people have reported success in using the AIX 5.3 RPM on their AIX 6.1 systems.

Once you have enabled **rsync**, you need to set up a couple of config files to tell the **rsync** server how to behave. The main file is **/etc/rsyncd.conf**, which contains both global configuration parameters and a set of "modules," each of which is a directory tree to export or import. A reasonable configuration for a module that you can push to (i.e., that will accept incoming file transfers initiated by the connecting client) looks something like this:

```
# sysfiles is just an arbitrary title for the particular module.
[sysfiles]
# This is the path you allow files to be pushed to. It could be just /.
path = /etc
# This is the file specifying the user/password pair to authenticate the module
secrets file = /etc/rsyncd.secrets
# Can be read only if you are pulling files
read only = false
# UID and GID under which the transfer will be done
uid = root
gid = root
# List of hosts that are allowed to connect
hosts allow = distribution_master_hostname
```

Many other options can be set, but the defaults are reasonable. This configuration limits operations to the **/etc** directory and allows access only by the listed host. From the user's or client's point of view, you can **rsync** files to the server with the destination *hostname*::**sysfiles**, which maps to the module above. If you want to set up **rsync** in pull mode (pulling files from a central **rsync** server), the lines above will still work, but you may want to tighten things up a bit; for example, by setting the transfer mode to read-only.

The last thing you need to do is set up an **rsyncd.secrets** file. It's generally kept in **/etc** (although you can put it elsewhere) and contains the passwords that clients use to authenticate themselves. For example:

```
root:password
```

As a general rule, **rsync** passwords should be different from system passwords. Because the passwords are shown in plaintext, **rsyncd.secrets** must be readable only by root.

Pulling files

You can implement a pulling system in several ways. The most straightforward way is to make the files available on a central FTP or web server[3] and to have the clients automatically download them as needed. In historical times, administrators would roll their own utilities to do this (often scripting **ftp** with a system such as **expect**), but standard utilities can now do it for you.

One such utility that ships with most systems is the popular **wget**. It's a straightforward little program that fetches the contents of a URL (either FTP or HTTP). For example, to FTP a file with **wget**, just run

```
wget ftp://user:password@hostname/path/to/file
```

The specified *file* is deposited in the current directory.

An alternative option for FTP is **ncftp**, which ships with many systems. It's really just an enhanced FTP client that allows for easy scripting.

You can also use **rsync** as described in the previous section. If you run an **rsync** server on your central distribution host, clients can simply **rsync** the files down. Using this method is perhaps slightly more complex than using FTP, but you then have access to all of **rsync**'s features.

Whatever system you use, be careful not to overload your data server. If a lot of machines on the network try to access the server simultaneously (e.g., if everyone runs an update out of **cron** at the same time), you can cause an inadvertent denial of service attack. Large sites should keep this problem in mind and allow for staggering or randomization. A simple way to do this is to wrap **cron** jobs in a Perl script such as this:

```
#!/usr/bin/perl
sleep rand() * 600; # sleep between 0 and 600 seconds (i.e., 10 minutes)
system(command_to_copy_files_down);
```

3. Keep in mind that both HTTP and FTP transport data in plaintext. You should consider HTTPS or SFTP, respectively, if the contents of the transferred files are sensitive.

19.3 LDAP: The Lightweight Directory Access Protocol

UNIX and Linux sites need a good way to distribute their administrative configuration data; however, the problem is really more general than that. What about nonadministrative data such as telephone and email directories? What about information that you want to share with the outside world? What everyone really needs is a generalized directory service.

A directory service is just a database, but one that makes a few assumptions. Any data set that has characteristics matching the assumptions is a candidate for inclusion in the directory. The basic assumptions are as follows:

- Data objects are relatively small.
- The database will be widely replicated and cached.
- The information is attribute based.
- Data are read often but written infrequently.
- Searching is a common operation.

The current IETF standards-track system designed to fill this role is the Lightweight Directory Access Protocol (LDAP). The LDAP specifications don't really speak to the database itself, just the way that it's accessed through a network. But because they specify how the data is schematized and how searches are performed, they imply a fairly specific data model as well.

LDAP was originally designed as a gateway protocol that would allow TCP/IP clients to talk to an older directory service called X.500, which is now obsolete. Over time, it became apparent both that X.500 was going to die out and that UNIX really needed a standard directory of some sort. These factors have led to LDAP being developed as a full-fledged directory system in its own right (and perhaps to its no longer being quite so deserving of the L).[4]

At this point, LDAP has become quite mainstream, spurred perhaps in part by Microsoft's adoption of LDAP as the basis for its Active Directory service. On the UNIX and Linux side, the OpenLDAP package (openldap.org) has become the standard implementation. The 389 Directory Server (formerly known as Fedora Directory Server and Netscape Directory Server) is also open source and can be found at port389.org. It runs on Linux, Solaris, and HP-UX.

The structure of LDAP data

LDAP data takes the form of property lists, which are known in LDAP world as "entries." Each entry consists of a set of named attributes (such as `description` or `uid`) along with those attributes' values. Windows users might recognize this structure as being similar to that of the Windows registry. As in the registry, an individual attribute can have several values.

4. Because of LDAP's tortured history, many sources tend to go into great detail about LDAP's X.500 and OSI connections. However, this history is not relevant to contemporary use of LDAP. Ignore it.

As an example, here's a typical (but simplified) **/etc/passwd** line expressed as an LDAP entry:

```
uid: ghopper
cn: Grace Hopper
userPassword: {crypt}$1$pZaGA2RL$MPDJoc0afuhHY6yk8HQFp0
loginShell: /bin/bash
uidNumber: 1202
gidNumber: 1202
homeDirectory: /home/ghopper
```


This notation is a simple example of LDIF, the LDAP Data Interchange Format, which is used by most LDAP-related tools and server implementations. The fact that LDAP data can be easily converted back and forth from plain text is part of the reason for its success.

Entries are organized into a hierarchy through the use of "distinguished names" (attribute name: dn) that form a sort of search path. For example, the dn for the user above might be

```
dn: uid=ghopper,ou=People,dc=navy,dc=mil
```

As in DNS, the "most significant bit" goes on the right. Here, the DNS name navy.mil has been used to structure the top levels of the LDAP hierarchy. It has been broken down into two domain components (dc's), "navy" and "mil," but this is only one of several common conventions.

Every entry has exactly one distinguished name. Therefore, the entry hierarchy looks like a simple branching tree with no loops. There are, however, provisions for symbolic links between entries and for referrals to other servers.

LDAP entries are typically schematized through the use of an objectClass attribute. Object classes specify the attributes that an entry can contain, some of which may be required for validity. The schema also assigns a data type to each attribute. Object classes nest and combine in the traditional object-oriented fashion. The top level of the object class tree is the class named top, which specifies merely that an entry must have an objectClass attribute.

Table 19.2 shows some common LDAP attributes whose meanings might not be immediately apparent.

Table 19.2 Some common attribute names found in LDAP hierarchies

Attribute	Stands for	What it is
o	Organization	Often identifies a site's top-level entry[a]
ou	Organizational unit	A logical subdivision, e.g., "marketing"
cn	Common name	The most natural name to represent the entry
dc	Domain component	Used at sites that model their hierarchy on DNS
objectClass	Object class	Schema to which this entry's attributes conform

a. Typically not used by sites that model their LDAP hierarchy on DNS

The point of LDAP

Until you've had some experience with it, LDAP can be a slippery concept to grab hold of. LDAP by itself doesn't solve any specific administrative problem. There's no "primary task" that LDAP is tailor-made to handle, and sites diverge widely in their reasons for deploying LDAP servers. So before we move on to the specifics of installing and configuring OpenLDAP, it's probably worth reviewing some reasons why you might want to investigate LDAP for use at your site.

Here are the big ones:

- LDAP can act as a central repository for information about your users, including everything from their phone numbers and home addresses to their login names and passwords.

*See page 774 for more information about using LDAP with **sendmail**.*

- In a similar vein, you can use LDAP to distribute configuration information for ancillary applications. Most mail systems—including **sendmail**, Exim, and Postfix—can draw a large part of their routing information from LDAP, and this is in fact one of LDAP's most popular applications. Tools as varied as the Apache web server and the autofs automounter can be configured to pay attention to LDAP, too. It's likely that LDAP support will become more and more common over time.
- LDAP makes it easy for applications (even those written by other teams and other departments) to authenticate users without having to worry about the exact details of account management.
- Changes to LDAP data take effect immediately and are instantly visible to all hosts and client applications.
- It's easy to access LDAP data through command-line tools such as **ldapsearch**. In addition, LDAP is well supported by common scripting languages such as Perl and Python (through the use of libraries). Ergo, LDAP is a terrific way to distribute configuration information for locally written scripts and administrative utilities.
- Excellent web-based tools are available for managing LDAP, some examples being phpLDAPadmin (phpldapadmin.sourceforge.net) and Directory Administrator (diradmin.open-it.org). These tools are so easy to use that you can just rip the box open and start playing without reading the manual.
- LDAP is well supported as a public directory service. Most major email clients support the use of LDAP to access user directories. Simple LDAP searches are also supported by many web browsers through the use of an LDAP URL type.
- Microsoft's Active Directory architecture is based on LDAP, and the current release of Windows Server includes extensions (originally called "Services for UNIX," then "Windows Security and Directory Services for

UNIX," and now "Windows Server 2008 UNIX Interoperability Components") that facilitate the mapping of UNIX users and groups. See Chapter 30, *Cooperating with Windows*, for more information about integrating your UNIX systems with Active Directory-based LDAP.

LDAP documentation and specifications

A good general introduction to LDAP is *LDAP for Rocket Scientists*, which covers LDAP architecture and protocol. Find it on-line at zytrax.com/books/ldap. Another good source of information is the LDAP-related RFCs, which are numerous and varied. As a group, they tend to convey an impression of great complexity, which is somewhat unrepresentative of average use. Table 19.3 list some of the high points.

Table 19.3 Important LDAP-related RFCs

RFC	Title
2307	An Approach for Using LDAP as a Network Information Service
2820	Access Control Requirements for LDAP
2849	LDAP Data Interchange Format (LDIF)—Technical Specification
3112	LDAP Authentication Password Schema
3672	Subentries in the Lightweight Directory Access Protocol (LDAP)
4511	LDAP: The Protocol
4512	LDAP: Directory Information Models
4513	LDAP: Authentication Methods and Security Mechanisms
4514	LDAP: String Representation of Distinguished Names
4515	LDAP: String Representation of Search Filters
4516	LDAP: Uniform Resource Locator
4517	LDAP: Syntaxes and Matching Rules
4519	LDAP: Schema for User Applications

OpenLDAP: the traditional open source LDAP server

OpenLDAP is an extension of work originally done at the University of Michigan; it now continues as an open source project. It's shipped with most Linux distributions, though it is not necessarily included in the default installation. You'll need to download and install the software to run it on Solaris, HP-UX, or AIX. The documentation is perhaps best described as "brisk."

In the OpenLDAP distribution, **slapd** is the standard LDAP server daemon. In an environment with multiple OpenLDAP servers, **slurpd** runs on the master server and handles replication by pushing changes out to slave servers. A selection of command-line tools enable the querying and modification of LDAP data.

Setup is straightforward. First, create an **/etc/openldap/slapd.conf** file by copying the sample installed with the OpenLDAP server.

These are the lines you need to pay attention to:

```
database bdb
suffix "dc=mydomain, dc=com"
rootdn "cn=admin, dc=mydomain, dc=com"
rootpw {crypt}abJnggxhB/yWI
directory /var/lib/ldap
```

The database format defaults to Berkeley DB, which is fine for data that will live within the OpenLDAP system. You can use a variety of other back ends, including ad hoc methods such as scripts that create the data on the fly.

suffix is your "LDAP basename." It's the root of your portion of the LDAP namespace, similar in concept to your DNS domain name. In fact, this example illustrates the use of a DNS domain name as an LDAP basename, which is a common practice.

rootdn is your administrator's name, and rootpw is the administrator's UNIX-format (DES) password. Note that the domain components leading up to the administrator's name must also be specified. You can either copy and paste the password from **/etc/shadow** (if you don't use MD5 passwords) or generate it with a simple Perl one-liner

```
perl -e "print crypt('password','salt');"
```

where *password* is the desired password and *salt* is an arbitrary two-character string. Because of the presence of this password, make sure that the permissions on your **slapd.conf** file are 600 and that the file is owned by root.

Edit **/etc/openldap/ldap.conf** to set the default server and basename for LDAP client requests. It's pretty straightforward—just set the argument of the host entry to your server and set the base to the same value as the suffix in **slapd.conf**. (Make sure both lines are uncommented.)

At this point, you should be able to start up **slapd** by simply running it with no arguments.

389 Directory Server: alternative open source LDAP server

Like OpenLDAP, the 389 Directory Server (port389.org) is an extension of the work done at the University of Michigan. However, it spent some years in the commercial world (at Netscape) before returning as an open source project.

There are many reasons to consider the 389 Directory Server as an alternative to OpenLDAP, but its superior documentation is one clear advantage. The 389 Directory Server comes with several professional-grade administration and use guides, including detailed installation and deployment instructions.

A few other key features of the 389 Directory Server are

- Multimaster replication for fault tolerance and high write performance
- Active Directory user and group synchronization

- A graphical console for all facets of user, group, and server management
- On-line, zero downtime, LDAP-based update of schema, configuration, management and in-tree Access Control Information (ACIs)

As of this writing, the 389 Directory Server appears to have a more active development community than OpenLDAP. We generally recommend it over OpenLDAP for new installations.

From an administrative standpoint, the structure and operation of the two open source servers are strikingly similar. This fact is perhaps not too surprising since both packages were built on the same original code base.

LDAP instead of /etc/passwd and /etc/group

Client-side LDAP support is relatively easy to add. Some systems install the necessary **nss_ldap** package by default, but if not, they usually provide the package as an option. This package includes a PAM module that lets you use LDAP with pluggable authentication modules in addition to the name service switch. (See Chapter 30, *Cooperating with Windows*, for more information about integrating UNIX and Linux systems with Active Directory-based LDAP.)

Client-side LDAP defaults for **nss_ldap** are set in **/etc/ldap.conf**, which shares its format with **/etc/openldap/ldap.conf** (described on page 732) but which includes additional options specific to the name service and PAM contexts. You must also edit the **/etc/nsswitch.conf** file on each client to add `ldap` as a source for each type of data you want to LDAPify. (The **nsswitch.conf** changes make the C library pass requests to the **libnss_ldap** library, which then uses the **/etc/ldap.conf** information to figure out how to perform the LDAP queries. See *Prioritizing sources of administrative information* on page 739 for details.)

RFC2307 defines the standard mapping from traditional UNIX data sets, such as the **passwd** and **group** files, into the LDAP namespace. It's a useful reference document for sysadmins using LDAP in a UNIX environment, at least in theory. In practice, the specifications are a lot easier for computers to read than for humans; you're better off looking at examples.

Padl Software offers a free set of Perl scripts that migrate existing flat files or NIS maps to LDAP. It's available from padl.com/OSS/MigrationTools.html, and the scripts are straightforward to run. They can be used as filters to generate LDIF, or they can be run against a live server to upload the data directly. For example, the **migrate_group** script converts this line from **/etc/group**

```
csstaff:x:2033:evi,matthew,trent
```

to the following LDIF:

```
dn: cn=csstaff,ou=Group,dc=domainname,dc=com
cn: csstaff
objectClass: posixGroup
objectClass: top
```

```
userPassword: {crypt}x
gidNumber: 2033
memberuid: evi
memberuid: matthew
memberuid: trent
```

(Note the object class and distinguished name specifications, which were omitted from the **passwd** example on page 729.)

Once a database has been imported, you can verify that the transfer worked correctly by running the **slapcat** utility, which displays the entire database.

LDAP querying

To administer LDAP, you need to be able to see and manipulate the contents of the database. The phpLDAPadmin tool mentioned earlier is one of the nicer free tools for this purpose because it gives you an intuitive point-and-click interface. If phpLDAPadmin isn't an option, **ldapsearch** (distributed with both OpenLDAP and 389 Directory Server) is an analogous command-line tool that produces output in LDIF format. **ldapsearch** is especially useful for calling from scripts and for debugging environments in which Active Directory is acting as the LDAP server.

The following example query uses **ldapsearch** to look up directory information for every user whose cn starts with "ned". (In this case, there's only one result.) The meanings of the various flags are discussed below.

```
$ ldapsearch -h atlantic.atrust.com -p 389
    -x -D "cn=trent,cn=users,dc=boulder,dc=atrust,dc=com" -W
    -b "CN=users,DC=boulder,DC=atrust,DC=com" "cn=ned*"
Enter LDAP Password: password
# LDAPv3
# base <CN=users,DC=boulder,DC=atrust,DC=com> with scope sub
# filter: cn=ned*
# requesting: ALL
#
# ned, Users, boulder.atrust.com
dn: CN=ned,CN=Users,DC=boulder,DC=atrust,DC=com
objectClass: top
objectClass: person
objectClass: organizationalPerson
objectClass: user
cn: ned
sn: McClain
telephoneNumber: 303 245 4505
givenName: Ned
distinguishedName: CN=ned,CN=Users,DC=boulder,DC=atrust,DC=com
displayName: Ned McClain
memberOf: CN=Users,CN=Builtin,DC=boulder,DC=atrust,DC=com
```

```
memberOf: CN=Enterprise Admins,CN=Users,DC=boulder,DC=atrust,DC=com
name: ned
sAMAccountName: ned
userPrincipalName: ned@boulder.atrust.com
lastLogonTimestamp: 129086952498943974
mail: ned@atrust.com
```

ldapsearch's **-h** and **-p** flags specify the host and port of the LDAP server you want to query, respectively.

You usually need to authenticate yourself to the LDAP server. In this case, the **-x** flag requests simple authentication (as opposed to SASL). The **-D** flag identifies the distinguished name of a user account that has the privileges needed to execute the query, and the **-W** flag makes **ldapsearch** prompt you for the corresponding password.

The **-b** flag tells **ldapsearch** where in the LDAP hierarchy to start the search. This parameter is known as the baseDN; hence the **b**. By default, **ldapsearch** returns all matching entries below the baseDN; you can tweak this behavior with the **-s** flag.

The last argument is a "filter," which is a description of what you're searching for. It doesn't require an option flag. This filter, **cn=ned***, returns all LDAP entries that have a common name that starts with "ned". The filter is quoted to protect the star from shell globbing.

If you want to extract all entries below a given baseDN, just use **objectClass=*** as the search filter—or leave the filter out, since this is the default.

Any arguments that follow the filter select specific attributes to return. For example, if you added **mail givenName** to the command line above, **ldapsearch** would return only those attributes of matching entries.

LDAP and security

Traditionally, LDAP was used more in the manner of a phone directory than anything else, and for that purpose, sending data without encrypting it was usually acceptable. As a result, the "standard" LDAP implementation grants unencrypted access through TCP port 389. However, we strongly advise against the use of unencrypted LDAP for the transmission of authentication information, even if passwords are individually hashed or encrypted.

As an alternative, LDAP-over-SSL (known as LDAPS, usually running on TCP port 686) is available in most situations (including the Microsoft world) on both the client and server. This access method is preferred because it protects the information contained in both the query and the response. Use LDAPS when possible.

A system as complex as LDAP inevitably has the potential to be misconfigured in a way that weakens security. Of course, it is likely to contain some plain, old-fashioned security holes, too. Caveat administrator.

19.4 NIS: THE NETWORK INFORMATION SERVICE

NIS, released by Sun in the 1980s, was the first "prime time" administrative database. It was originally called the Sun Yellow Pages, but eventually had to be renamed for legal reasons. NIS commands still begin with the letters **yp**, so it's hard to forget the original name. NIS was widely adopted among UNIX vendors and is supported by every Linux distribution.

These days, however, NIS is an old grey mare. NIS should not be used for new deployments. We say this primarily because of the inevitable need to integrate with Windows systems, but also because of NIS's various security and scalability shortcomings.

Nevertheless, we include some brief coverage of NIS in deference to the large number of legacy sites where it's still in use.

The NIS model

The unit of sharing in NIS is the record, not the file. A record usually corresponds to one line in a config file. A master server maintains the authoritative copies of system files, which are kept in their original locations and formats and are edited with a text editor just as before. A server process makes the contents of the files available over the network. A server and its clients constitute an NIS "domain."[5]

Data files are preprocessed into database files by a hashing library to improve the efficiency of lookups. After editing files on the master server, you use **make** to tell NIS to convert them to their hashed format.

Only one key can be associated with each entry, so a system file may have to be translated into several NIS "maps." For example, the **/etc/passwd** file is translated into two different maps called **passwd.byname** and **passwd.byuid**. One map is used to look up entries by username and the other to look up entries by UID. Either map can be used to enumerate the entries in the **passwd** file. However, because hashing libraries do not preserve the order of records, there is no way to reconstruct an exact duplicate of the original file.

NIS lets you replicate the network maps on a set of slave servers. Providing more than one server helps relieve the load on the master and helps keep clients working even when some servers become unavailable. Whenever a file is changed on the master server, the corresponding NIS map must be pushed out to the slaves so that all servers provide the same data. Clients do not distinguish between the master server and the slaves.

Understanding how NIS works

NIS's data files are stored in one directory, usually **/var/yp**. Hereafter, we refer to this as "the NIS directory." Each NIS map is stored in a hashed database format in

5. Do not confuse NIS domains with DNS domains. They are completely separate and have nothing to do with each other.

a subdirectory of the NIS directory named for the NIS domain. The exact name and number of the map files depends on the hashing library being used. There is one map (file) for each key by which a file can be searched. For example, in the domain cssuns, the DB files for the **/etc/passwd** maps might be

```
/var/yp/cssuns/passwd.byname
/var/yp/cssuns/passwd.byuid
```

The **makedbm** command generates NIS maps from flat files. However, you need not invoke this command directly; a **Makefile** in **/var/yp** generates all the common NIS maps. After you modify a system file, **cd** to **/var/yp** and run **make**. The **make** command checks the modification time of each file against the modification times of the maps derived from it and runs **makedbm** for each map that needs to be rebuilt.

On HP-UX systems, a command called **ypmake** is used instead of **make**.

The **ypxfr** command copies maps from the master server to the slave servers. **ypxfr** is a pull command; it must be run on each slave server to make that server import the map. Slaves usually execute **ypxfr** every so often just to verify that they have the most recent maps; you can use **cron** to control how often this is done.

The default implementation of map copying is somewhat inefficient. On most systems, a daemon called **ypxfrd** (or **rpc.ypxfrd)** can be run on the master server to speed responses to **ypxfr** requests. **ypxfrd** sidesteps the normal NIS protocol and simply hands out copies of the map files. Unfortunately, map files are stored with different database formats and byte ordering on different systems, so the use of **ypxfrd** introduces some potential incompatibilities.

yppush is a "push" command that's used on the master server. It actually does not transfer any data but rather instructs each slave to execute a **ypxfr**. The **yppush** command is used by the **Makefile** in the NIS directory to ensure that newly updated maps are propagated to slaves.

The special map called **ypservers** does not correspond to any flat file. This map contains a list of all the servers of the domain. It's automatically constructed when the domain is set up with **ypinit**. Its contents are examined when the master server needs to distribute maps to slaves.

After initial configuration, the only active components of the NIS system are the **ypserv** and **ypbind** daemons. **ypserv** runs only on servers (both master and slave); it accepts queries from clients and answers them by looking up information in the hashed map files.

ypbind runs on every machine in the NIS domain, including servers. The C library contacts the local **ypbind** daemon when it needs to answer an administrative query (provided that **/etc/nsswitch.conf** says to do so). **ypbind** locates a **ypserv** in the appropriate domain and returns its identity to the C library, which then contacts the server directly.

Latter-day versions of **ypbind** periodically check to be sure they are dealing with the most responsive server for an NIS domain. This is an improvement over the traditional implementation, which fixates on a particular server.

NIS includes a number of minor commands that examine maps, find out which version of a map each server is using, and control the binding between clients and servers. A complete list of NIS commands and daemons is given in Table 19.4.

Table 19.4 NIS commands and daemons

Program	Description
ypserv	Is the NIS server daemon, started at boot time
ypbind	Is the NIS client daemon, started at boot time
domainname	Sets the NIS domain for a machine (runs at boot time)
ypxfr	Downloads current version of a map from master server
ypxfrd	Serves requests from **ypxfr** (runs on master server)
yppush	Makes slave servers update their versions of a map
makedbm	Builds a hashed map from a flat file
ypmake[a]	Rebuilds hashed maps from flat files that have changed
ypinit	Configures a host as a master or slave server
ypset	Makes **ypbind** connect to a particular server[b]
ypwhich	Finds out which server the current host is using
yppoll	Finds out what version of a map a server is using
ypcat	Prints the values contained in an NIS map
ypmatch	Prints map entries for a specified key
yppasswd	Changes a password on the NIS master server
ypchfn	Changes GECOS information on the NIS master server
ypchsh	Changes a login shell on NIS master server
yppasswdd	Is the server for **yppasswd**, **ypchsh**, and **ypchfn**
ypupdated[a]	Is the server for updating NIS maps (managed by **inetd**)

a. Not used or supported on all systems
b. Must be specifically enabled with **ypbind -ypsetme** or **ypbind -ypset** (dangerous)

NIS security

NIS is not secure. Broadcast mode is particularly bad; any host on a network can claim to serve a particular domain and then feed bogus administrative data to NIS clients. On Linux systems, you can mitigate this particular problem by explicitly enumerating the permissible NIS servers for each client.

If you're at all concerned about the security in your environment, you shouldn't use NIS to serve the **passwd** or **shadow** files. Use alternative distributed authentication mechanisms, such as LDAP, for this purpose.

Many security vulnerabilities have been found in older versions of NIS. Make sure you're running the current version.

19.5 Prioritizing sources of administrative information

Administrative information can be distributed in several ways. Every system understands flat files and knows how to use DNS to look up hostnames and Internet addresses. Since a given piece of information could come from several potential sources, there's also a way for you to specify the sources that are to be checked and the order in which the checks are made.

The **/etc/nsswitch.conf** (**/etc/netsvc.conf** on AIX) config file allows an explicit search path to be specified for each type of configuration information. A typical **nsswitch.conf** file looks something like this:

```
passwd:  files ldap
hosts:   files dns
group:   files
...
```

Each line configures one type of information (usually, one flat-file equivalent). The common sources are nis, nisplus, files, dns, ldap, and compat; they refer to NIS, NIS+,[6] vanilla flat files (ignoring tokens such as "+"), DNS, LDAP, and NIS-ified flat files, respectively. DNS is a valid data source only for host and network information.

Sources are tried from left to right until one of them produces an answer for the query. In the example above, the **gethostbyname** routine would first check the **/etc/hosts** file, and if the host was not listed there, would then check DNS. Queries about UNIX groups, on the other hand, would check only the **/etc/group** file.

If necessary, you can define the "failure" of a source more specifically by putting bracketed expressions after it. For example, the line

```
hosts:  dns [NOTFOUND=return] files
```

causes DNS to be used exclusively if it is available; a negative response from the name server makes queries return immediately (with a failure code) without checking flat files. However, flat files are used if no name server is available. The various types of failures are shown in Table 19.5; each can be set to return or continue, signifying whether the query should be aborted or forwarded to the next source.

Table 19.5 Failure modes recognized in /etc/nsswitch.conf

Condition	Meaning
UNAVAIL	The source doesn't exist or is down.
NOTFOUND	The source exists, but couldn't answer the query.
TRYAGAIN	The source exists but is busy.
SUCCESS	The source was able to answer the query.

6. An ill-starred successor to the original NIS, now discontinued by Sun but still supported by some systems for historical reasons.

System Files

By default, most systems ship with **nsswitch.conf** files that are reasonable for a stand-alone machine. All entries go to the flat files, with the exception of host lookups, which first consult flat files and then DNS. A few systems default to `compat` mode for **passwd** and **group**, which is probably worth changing. If you really use NIS, just explicitly put it in the **nsswitch.conf** file.

nscd: cache the results of lookups

On some Linux distributions, another finger in the system file pie belongs to **nscd**, the somewhat misleadingly titled name service cache daemon.

nscd works in conjunction with the C library to cache the results of library calls such as **getpwent**. **nscd** is simply a wrapper for these library routines; it knows nothing about the actual data sources being consulted. **nscd** should in theory improve the performance of lookups, but any improvement is largely unnoticeable from the user's viewpoint.

See Chapter 17 for more information about DNS.

We say that "name service cache daemon" is misleading because the term "name service" usually refers to DNS, the distributed database system that maps between hostnames and Internet addresses. **nscd** does in fact cache the results of DNS lookups (because it wraps **gethostbyname**, etc.), but it also wraps the library routines that access information from the **passwd** and **group** files and their network database equivalents. (For security, lookups to **/etc/shadow** are not cached.)

In concept, **nscd** should have no effect on the operation of the system other than to speed up repeated lookups. In practice, it can cause unexpected behavior because it maintains its own copy of the lookup results. Lookups are stored in the cache for a fixed amount of time (set in **nscd**'s configuration file, **/etc/nscd.conf**), and there is always the possibility that recent changes will not be reflected in **nscd**'s cache until the previous data has timed out. **nscd** is smart enough to monitor local data sources (such as **/etc/passwd**) for changes, so local updates should propagate within 15 seconds. For remote entries, such as those retrieved through NIS, you may have to wait for the full timeout period before changes take effect.

Among our example distributions, only SUSE runs **nscd** by default. Red Hat installs **nscd** but does not start it at boot time by default; to enable the use of **nscd**, run **chkconfig nscd on**. Ubuntu is **nscd** compatible but does not include **nscd** in the default installation; run **apt-get install nscd** to download it.

nscd starts at boot time and runs continuously. The default **/etc/nscd.conf** specifies a timeout of 10 minutes for **passwd** data and an hour for **hosts** and **group**, with a 20-second negative timeout (the amount of time before an unsuccessful lookup is retried). In practice, these values rarely need changing. If a change you recently made doesn't seem to show up, **nscd** is probably the reason.

19.6 RECOMMENDED READING

CARTER, GERALD. *LDAP System Administration*. Sebastopol, CA: O'Reilly Media, 2003.

MALÈRE, LUIZ ERNESTO PINHEIRO. *LDAP Linux HOWTO*. tldp.org

VOGLMAIER, REINHARD. *The ABCs of LDAP: How to Install, Run, and Administer LDAP Services*. Boca Raton, FL: Auerbach Publications, 2004.

LDAP for Rocket Scientists. zytrax.com/books/ldap

19.7 EXERCISES

E19.1 Why is a "pull" method of updating a local machine's files more secure than a "push" method?

E19.2 Explain the following excerpt from an **rdist** distfile:

```
LINUX_PASSWD = ( redhatbox ubuntubox susebox )

passwd:
      ( /etc/passwd ) -> ( ${LINUX_PASSWD} )
      install /etc/passwd.rdist;
      cmdspecial /etc/passwd.rdist "/usr/local/sbin/mkpasswd";
```

★ E19.3 Explain the differences between **rdist** and **rsync**. In what situations would it be better to use one than the other?

★ E19.4 What method does your site use to share system files? What security issues are related to that method? Suggest an alternative way to share system files at your site, and detail the concerns that it addresses. What, if any, are the drawbacks?

★★★★★ E19.5 Design an LDAP schema that stores user information such as login, password, shell, authorized machines, etc. Build a tool that enters new users into the database interactively or from a file containing a list of users. Build a tool that generates the **passwd**, **group**, and **shadow** files from the LDAP database for the machines in your lab. Allow users to have different passwords on each machine if they want. (Not all users are necessarily authorized to use each computer.) Your **adduser** system should be able to print lists of existing user login names and to print login/password pairs for new users.

20 Electronic Mail

Social networks and SMS messages have started to push email into the "old technology" category as they reduce the world to relationships and microthoughts. Nevertheless, email remains the universal standard for on-line communication. Everyone from grandmas to the stodgiest of corporations now routinely uses email to communicate with family, co-workers, partners, customers, and even the government. It's a mad, mad, mad email-enabled world.[1]

Email is easy and just works; if you know someone's email address, you type a message addressed to them and press Send. Voilà! Seconds later, the message is delivered to their electronic mailbox, whether they're next door or halfway around the world. From the user's perspective, nothing could be easier.

The underlying infrastructure that makes electronic mail possible on such a large scale is complex. There are several software packages you can run on your system to transport and manage electronic mail (three of which are discussed later in this chapter), but they all require a certain degree of configuration and management. In addition, it's important that you understand the underlying concepts and

1. Even as Evi is sailing in the middle of the ocean, she is almost always in email contact through her HAM/SSB radio and a "speedy" packet radio connection that approaches 30 baud at good times.

protocols associated with email so that you don't spoil your users' illusion that cross-platform interorganizational email is a gift from the gods that magically works every time.

Understanding and administering your own email infrastructure isn't your only option. Many providers now offer "managed" email service, which hosts your email system on remote servers in exchange for a monthly or yearly fee (possibly per-user). Likewise, a number of "free" hosted services, such as Google's Gmail, Yahoo! Mail, and MSN Hotmail have become popular for individuals. If you're an individual looking for a personal email account or an account for a small business, these may be viable options for you. In addition to offering personal email accounts, Gmail has an interesting step-up feature that hosts email for an entire domain. See google.com/a for details or google for "hosted Gmail" to find several useful how-to guides that describe the setup process.

Hosted services relieve you of multiple burdens, including storage, server management, software updates, configuration, spam filtering, backups, and security vigilance, to name a few. In return for the "free" services, you'll probably see some advertising and may wonder about your privacy and exactly who is reading your mail. It seems like a good deal in many cases; if the hosted option works for you, you at least get the benefit of not needing to read the rest of this huge chapter.

However, hosted email isn't the solution for everyone. Businesses and other large organizations that depend on email service often cannot take the risk of hosting email off-site. Such organizations may have a variety of reasons to host their own email systems, including security, performance, and availability. This chapter is for those people.

The sheer bulk of this chapter—almost 120 pages—attests to the complexity of email systems (or perhaps just to the wordiness of the authors). Table 20.1 presents a mini-roadmap.

Table 20.1 Roadmap to the giant email chapter

20.1 Mail systems

In theory, a mail system consists of several distinct components:

- A "mail user agent" (MUA or UA) that lets users read and compose mail
- A "mail submission agent" (MSA) that accepts outgoing mail from an MUA, grooms it, and submits it to the transport system
- A "mail transport agent" (MTA) that routes messages among machines
- A "delivery agent" (DA) that places messages in a local message store[2]
- An optional "access agent" (AA) that connects the user agent to the message store (e.g., through the IMAP or POP protocol)

Attached to some of these agents are tools for recognizing spam, viruses, and (outbound) internal company secrets. Exhibit A illustrates how the various pieces fit together as a message winds its way from sender to receiver.

Exhibit A Mail system components

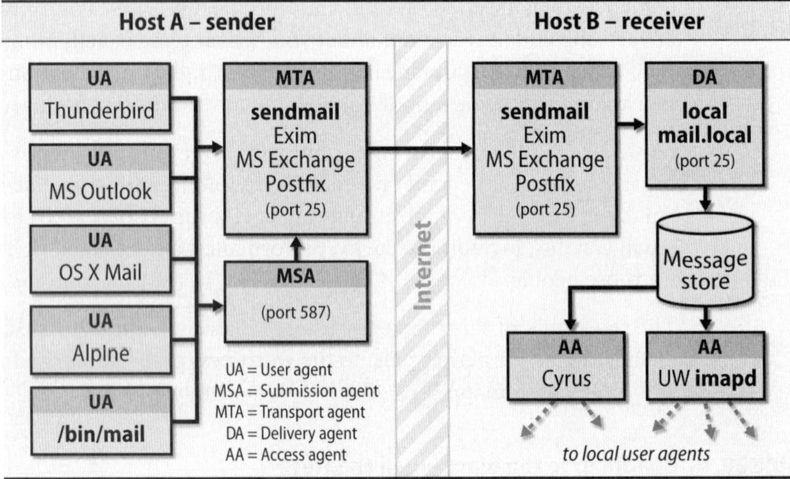

User agents

Email users employ a user agent (sometimes called an email client) to read and compose messages. Email messages originally consisted only of text, but a standard known as Multipurpose Internet Mail Extensions (MIME) is now used to encode text formats and attachments (including viruses) into email. It is supported by most user agents. Since MIME generally does not affect the addressing or transport of mail, we do not discuss it further.

/bin/mail was the original user agent, and it remains the "good ol' standby" for reading text email messages at a shell prompt. Since email on the Internet has

2. The receiving users' mailboxes or, sometimes, a database

moved beyond the text era, text-based user agents are no longer practical for most users. But we shouldn't throw **/bin/mail** away; it's still a handy interface for scripts and other programs. (One avid Linux user we know routes nightly emails from **cron** to calendaring software so that a glance at the calendar tells him the status of all his software builds. By default, **cron** uses **/bin/mail** to notify a user when it cannot run a scheduled job.)

One of the elegant features illustrated in Exhibit A is that a user agent doesn't necessarily need to be running on the same system—or even on the same platform—as the rest of your mail system. Users can reach their email from a Windows laptop or smartphone through access agent protocols like IMAP and POP.

Wikipedia's "comparison of e-mail clients" page contains a detailed listing of many, many email clients, the operating systems they run on, and the features they support. Popular clients include Thunderbird, Alpine, Zimbra, and of course, Microsoft Outlook. The "comparison of webmail providers" page has similar information for web-based services like Gmail, Hotmail, and Yahoo! Mail.

Submission agents

MSAs, a late addition to the email pantheon, were invented to offload some of the computational tasks of MTAs. MSAs make it easy for mail hub servers to distinguish incoming from outbound email (when making decisions about allowing relaying, for example) and give user agents a uniform and simple configuration for outbound mail.

The MSA is a sort of "receptionist" for new messages injected into the system by local user agents. An MSA sits between the user agent and the transport agent and takes over several functions that were formerly a part of the MTA's job. An MSA implements secure (encrypted and authenticated) communication with user agents and often does minor header rewriting and cleanup on incoming messages. In many cases, the MSA is really just the MTA listening on a different port with a different configuration applied.

MSAs speak the same mail transfer protocol used by MTAs, so they appear to be MTAs from the perspective of user agents. However, they typically listen for connections on port 587 rather than port 25, the MTA standard. For this scheme to work, user agents must connect on port 587 instead of port 25. If your user agents cannot be taught to use port 587, you can still run an MSA on port 25, but you must do so on a system other than the one that runs your MTA; only one process at a time can listen on a particular port.

An MSA can help with several spam-induced problems. Infected home PCs are being used to send large amounts of spam. As a result, many ISPs that offer home service either block outgoing connections to port 25 or require account verification as part of the SMTP conversation. A home PC could use the ISP's own mail server for outgoing mail, but some of the newer spam-fighting mechanisms such as SPF (page 767) and DKIM (page 845) require that mail that appears to be sent from an organization actually originate there.

If you use an MSA, be sure to configure your transport agent so that it doesn't duplicate any of the rewriting or header fix-up work done by the MSA. Duplicate processing won't affect the correctness of mail handling, but it does represent useless extra work.

Since your MSA uses your MTA to relay messages, the MSA and MTA must use SMTP-AUTH to authenticate each other. Otherwise, you will have a so-called open relay that spammers can exploit and that other sites will blacklist you for.

Transport agents

A transport agent must accept mail from a user agent or submission agent, understand the recipients' addresses, and somehow get the mail to the correct hosts for delivery. Transport agents speak the Simple Mail Transport Protocol (SMTP), which was originally defined in RFC821 but has now been superseded and extended by RFC5321. The extended version is called ESMTP.

An MTA's list of chores, as both a mail sender and receiver, includes

- Receiving email messages from remote mail servers
- Understanding the recipients' addresses
- Rewriting addresses to a form understood by the delivery agent
- Forwarding the message to the next responsible mail server or passing it to a local delivery agent to be saved to a user's mailbox

The bulk of the work involved in setting up a mail system relates to the configuration of the MTA. In this book, we cover three open source MTAs: **sendmail**, Exim, and Postfix.

Local delivery agents

A delivery agent, sometimes called a local delivery agent (LDA), accepts mail from a transport agent and delivers it to the appropriate recipients' mailboxes on the local machine. As originally specified, email can be delivered to a person, to a mailing list, to a file, or even to a program. However, the last two types of recipients can weaken the security and safety of your system.

MTAs usually include a built-in local delivery agent for easy deliveries. **procmail** (procmail.org) and Maildrop (courier-mta.org/maildrop) are LDAs that can filter or sort mail before delivering it. Some access agents (AAs) also have built-in LDAs that do both delivery and local housekeeping chores.

Message stores

The message store is the final resting place of an email message once it has completed its journey across the Internet and been delivered to recipients.

Mail has traditionally been stored in either **mbox** format or **Maildir** format. The former stores all mail in a single file, typically **/var/mail/***username*, with individual messages separated by a special From line. **Maildir** format stores each message in a separate file. A file for each message is more convenient but creates directories with many, many small files; some filesystems may not be amused.

These flat files are still common message stores, but ISPs with thousands or millions of email clients are looking to other technologies for their message stores, usually databases. Message stores are becoming more opaque.

Access agents

Two protocols are used to access message stores and download email messages to a local device (workstation, laptop, telephone, etc.): IMAP4 and POP. Earlier versions of these protocols had security issues. Be sure to use a version (IMAPS or POP3S) that incorporates SSL encryption and hence does not transmit passwords in cleartext over the Internet.

We like IMAP, the Internet Message Access Protocol, better than POP. It delivers your mail one message at a time rather than all at once, which is kinder to the network (especially on slow links) and better for someone who travels from location to location. IMAP is especially good at dealing with the giant attachments that some folks like to send: you can browse the headers of your messages and not download the attachments until you are ready to deal with them.

IMAP manages mail folders among multiple sites; for example, between your mail server and your PC. Mail that stays on the server can be part of the normal backup schedule. The Wikipedia page for IMAP contains lots of information and a list of available implementations.

POP, the Post Office Protocol, is similar to IMAP but assumes a model in which all email is downloaded from the server to the client. The mail can either be deleted from the server (in which case it might not be backed up) or saved on the server (in which case your mail spool file grows larger and larger). The "mailbox at a time" paradigm is hard on the network and less flexible for the user. It can be really slow if you are a pack rat and have a large mail spool file.

Some IMAP/POP server implementations are Courier, Cyrus IMAP, Dovecot, UW[3] **imapd**, and Zimbra. Dovecot and Zimbra[4] are our favorites. Nearly every email user agent supports both IMAP and POP.

So many pieces, so little time

With a mail system consisting of so many pieces (and we haven't even addressed spam and virus scanning!), the architecture of email probably sounds overly complex. But at smaller sites, the MTA can largely absorb the functions of the MSA and LDA, and that helps keep things simple. Larger sites may want to keep all the

3. University of Washington, Seattle, WA.
4. Zimbra is not just an access agent, but rather a complete industrial-strength mail system; see page 853.

pieces separated and run multiple instances of each piece to help spread load. The reality is that email handling systems can be as simple or as complicated as you want them to be. We cover design suggestions beginning on page 753.

20.2 THE ANATOMY OF A MAIL MESSAGE

A mail message has three distinct parts:

- The envelope
- The headers
- The body of the message

The envelope determines where the message will be delivered or, if the message can't be delivered, to whom it should be returned. The envelope is invisible to users and is not part of the message itself; it's used internally by the MTA.

The envelope addresses generally agree with the From and To lines of the header when the sender and recipient are individuals. The envelope and headers may not agree if the message was sent to a mailing list or was generated by a spammer who is trying to conceal his identity.

The headers are a collection of property/value pairs as specified in RFC5322. They record all kinds of information about the message, such as the date and time it was sent, the transport agents through which it passed on its journey, and who it is to and from. The headers are a bona fide part of the mail message, but user agents often hide the less interesting ones when displaying messages for the user.

The body of the message is the content to be sent. It usually consists of plain text, although that text often represents a mail-safe encoding of various types of binary content.

Reading mail headers

Dissecting mail headers and using them to locate problems within the mail system is an essential sysadmin skill. Many user agents hide the headers, but there is usually a way to see them, even if you have to use an editor on the message store. Below are most of the headers (with occasional truncations indicated by ...) from a typical nonspam message. We removed another half page of headers that Gmail uses as part of its spam filtering.

```
Delivered-To: sailingevi@gmail.com
Received: by 10.231.39.205 with SMTP id...; Fri, 16 Oct 2009 08:14:27 -700 (PDT)
Received: by 10.114.163.26 with SMTP id...; Fri, 16 Oct 2009 08:14:26 -700 (PDT)
Return-Path: <david@schweikert.ch>
Received: from mail-relay.atrust.com (mail-relay.atrust.com [63.173.189.2])
    by mx.google.com with ESMTP id 17si2166978pxi.34.2009.10.16.08.14.20;
    Fri, 16 Oct 2009 08:14:25 -0700 (PDT)
Received-SPF: fail (google.com: domain of david@schweikert.ch does not
    designate 63.173.189.2 as permitted sender) client-ip=63.173.189.2;
```

```
Authentication-Results: mx.google.com; spf=hardfail (google.com: domain of
     david@schweikert.ch does not designate 63.173.189.2 as permitted sender)
     smtp.mail=david@schweikert.ch
Received: from mail.schweikert.ch (nigel.schweikert.ch [88.198.52.145])
     by mail-relay.atrust.com (8.12.11/8.12.11) with ESMTP id n9GFEDKA029250
     for <evi@atrust.com>; Fri, 16 Oct 2009 09:14:14 -0600
Received: from localhost (localhost.localdomain [127.0.0.1])
     by mail.schweikert.ch (Postfix) with ESMTP id 3251112DA79;
     Fri, 16 Oct 2009 17:14:12 +0200 (CEST)
X-Virus-Scanned: Debian amavisd-new at mail.schweikert.ch
Received: from mail.schweikert.ch ([127.0.0.1])
     by localhost (mail.schweikert.ch [127.0.0.1]) (amavisd-new, port 10024)
     with ESMTP id dV8BpT7rhJKC; Fri, 16 Oct 2009 17:14:07 +0200 (CEST)
Received: by mail.schweikert.ch (Postfix, from userid 1000)
     id 2A15612DB89; Fri, 16 Oct 2009 17:14:07 +0200 (CEST)
Date: Fri, 16 Oct 2009 17:14:06 +0200
From: David Schweikert <david@schweikert.ch>
To: evi@atrust.com
Cc: Garth Snyder <garth@garthsnyder.com>
Subject: Email chapter comments
```

To read this beast, start reading the Received lines, but start from the bottom (sender side). This message went from David Schweikert's home machine in the schweikert.ch domain to his mail server (mail.schweikert.ch), where it was scanned for viruses. It was then forwarded to the recipient evi@atrust.com. However, the receiving host mail-relay.atrust.com sent it on to sailingevi@gmail.com, where it entered Evi's mailbox.

See page 767 for more information about SPF.

Midway through the headers, you see an SPF validation failure. This happened because Google checked the IP address of mail-relay.atrust.com and compared it to the SPF record at schweikert.ch; of course, it doesn't match. This is an inherent weakness of using SPF records to identify forgeries—they don't work for mail that has been relayed.

You can often see the MTAs that were used (Postfix at schweikert.ch, **sendmail** 8.12 at atrust.com), and in this case, you can also see that virus scanning was performed through **amavisd-new** on port 10,024 on a machine running Debian Linux. You can follow the progress of the message from the Central European Summer Time zone (CEST +0200), to Colorado (-0600), and on to the Gmail server (PDT -0700); the numbers are the differences between local time and UTC, Coordinated Universal Time. There is a lot of info stashed in the headers!

Here are the headers, again truncated, from a spam message:

```
Delivered-To: sailingevi@gmail.com
Received: by 10.231.39.205 with SMTP id...; Mon, 19 Oct 2009 08:59:32 -0700...
Received: by 10.231.5.143 with SMTP id...; Mon, 19 Oct 2009 08:59:31 -0700...
Return-Path: <smotheringl39@sherman.dp.ua>
Received: from mail-relay.atrust.com (mail-relay.atrust.com [63.173.189.2]) ...
```

```
Received-SPF: neutral (google.com: 63.173.189.2 is neither permitted nor denied
      by best guess record for domain of smotheringl39@sherman.dp.ua) client-
      ip=63.173.189.2;
Authentication-Results: mx.google.com; spf=neutral (google.com: 63.173.189.2 is
      neither permitted nor denied by best guess record for domain of
      smotheringl39@sherman.dp.ua) smtp.mail=smotheringl39@sherman.dp.ua
Received: from SpeedTouch.lan (187-10-167-249.dsl.telesp.net.br
      [187.10.167.249] (may be forged)) by mail-relay.atrust.com ...
Received: from 187.10.167.249 by relay2.trifle.net; Mon, 19 Oct 2009 13:59: ...
From: "alert@atrust.com" <alert@atrust.com>
To: <ned@atrust.com>
Subject: A new settings file for the ned@atrust.com mailbox
Date: Mon, 19 Oct 2009 13:59:12 -0300 ...
```

According to the From header, this message's sender is alert@atrust.com. But according to the Return-Path header, which contains a copy of the envelope sender, the originator was smotheringl39@sherman.dp.ua, an address in the Ukraine. The first MTA that handled the message is at IP address 187.10.167.249, which is in Brazil. Sneaky spammers...[5]

The SPF check at Google fails again, this time with a "neutral" result because the domain sherman.dp.ua does not have an SPF record with which to compare the IP address of mail-relay.atrust.com.

The recipient information is also at least partially untrue. The To header says the message is addressed to ned@atrust.com. However, the envelope recipient addresses must have included evi@atrust.com in order for the message to be forwarded to sailingevi@gmail.com for delivery.

20.3 THE SMTP PROTOCOL

The Simple Mail Transport Protocol (SMTP) and its extended version, ESMTP, have been standardized in the RFC series (RFC5321) and are used for most message hand-offs among the various pieces of the mail system:

- UA-to-MSA or -MTA as a message is injected into the mail system
- MSA-to-MTA as the message starts its delivery journey
- MTA- or MSA-to-antivirus or -antispam scanning programs
- MTA-to-MTA as a message is forwarded from one site to another
- MTA-to-DA as a message is delivered to the local message store

Because the format of messages and the transfer protocol are both standardized, my MTA and your MTA don't have to be the same or even know each other's identity; they just have to both speak SMTP or ESMTP. Your various mail servers can run different MTAs and interoperate just fine.

5. It's important to note that many of the lines in the header, including the Received lines, may have been forged. Use this data with extreme caution.

True to its name, SMTP is quite simple. An MTA connects to your mail server and says, in essence, "Here's a message; please deliver it to user@your.domain." Your MTA says "OK."

Requiring strict adherence to the SMTP protocol has become a technique for fighting spam and malware, so it's important for mail administrators to be somewhat familiar with the protocol. The language has only a few commands; Table 20.2 shows the most important ones.

Table 20.2 SMTP commands

Command	Function
HELO *hostname*	Identifies the connecting host if speaking SMTP
EHLO *hostname*	Identifies the connecting host if speaking ESMTP
MAIL FROM: *revpath*	Initiates a mail transaction (envelope sender)
RCPT TO: *fwdpath*[a]	Identifies envelope recipient(s)
VRFY *address*	Verifies that *address* is valid (deliverable)
EXPN *address*	Shows expansion of aliases and **.forward** mappings
DATA	Begins the message body[b]
QUIT	Ends the exchange and closes the connection
RSET	Resets the state of the connection
HELP	Prints a summary of SMTP commands

a. There can be multiple RCPT commands for a message.
b. You terminate the body by entering a dot on its own line.

You had me at EHLO

ESMTP speakers start conversations with EHLO instead of HELO. If the process at the other end understands and responds with an OK, then the participants negotiate supported extensions and agree on a lowest common denominator for the exchange. If the peer returns an error in response to the EHLO, then the ESMTP speaker falls back to SMTP. But today, almost everything uses ESMTP.

A typical SMTP conversation to deliver an email message goes as follows: HELO or EHLO, MAIL FROM:, RCPT TO:, DATA, and QUIT. The sender does most of the talking, with the recipient contributing error codes and acknowledgments.

SMTP and ESMTP are both text-based protocols, so you can use them directly when debugging the mail system. Just **telnet** to TCP port 25 or 587 and start entering SMTP commands. See the example on page 845 in the Postfix section.

SMTP error codes

Also specified in the RFCs that define SMTP are a set of temporary and permanent error codes. These were originally three-digit codes (e.g., 550), with each digit being interpreted separately. A first digit of 2 indicated success, a 4 signified a temporary error, and a 5 indicated a permanent error.

The three-digit error code system did not scale, so RFC3463 restructured it to create more flexibility. It defined an expanded error code format known as a delivery status notification or DSN. DSNs have the format X.X.X instead of the old XXX, and each of the individual Xs can be a multidigit number. The initial X must still be 2, 4, or 5. The second digit specifies a topic, and the third provides the details. The new system uses the second number to distinguish host errors from mailbox errors. We've listed a few of the DSN codes in Table 20.3. RFC3463's Appendix A shows them all.

Table 20.3 RFC3463 delivery status notifications

Temporary	Permanent	Meaning
4.2.1	5.2.1	Mailbox is disabled
4.2.2	5.2.2	Mailbox is full
4.2.3	5.2.3	Message is too long
4.4.1	5.4.1	No answer from host
4.4.4	5.4.4	Unable to route
4.5.3	5.5.3	Too many recipients
4.7.1	5.7.1	Delivery not authorized, message refused
4.7.*	5.7.*	Site policy violation

SMTP authentication

RFC4954 defines an extension to the original SMTP protocol that allows an SMTP client to identify and authenticate itself to a mail server. The server might then let the client relay mail through it. The protocol supports several different authentication mechanisms. The exchange is as follows:

- The client says EHLO, announcing that it speaks ESMTP.
- The server responds and advertises its authentication mechanisms.
- The client says AUTH and names a specific mechanism that it wants to use, optionally including its authentication data.
- The server accepts the data sent with AUTH or starts a challenge and response sequence with the client.
- The server either accepts or denies the authentication attempt.

To see what authentication mechanisms a server supports, you can **telnet** to port 25 and say EHLO. For example, here is a truncated conversation with the mail server mail-relay.atrust.com (the commands we typed are in bold):

```
solaris$ telnet mail-relay.atrust.com 25
Trying 192.168.2.10...
Connected to mail-relay.atrust.com.
Escape character is '^]'.
```

```
220 mail-relay.atrust.com ESMTP ATE Mail Service 24.1.2/24.1.2; Tue, 20 Oct
    2009 14:28:53 -0600
ehlo solaris.booklab.atrust.com
250-mail-relay.atrust.com Hello solaris.booklab.atrust.com, pleased to meet
    you
250-ENHANCEDSTATUSCODES
250-AUTH LOGIN PLAIN
...
250 HELP
quit
221 2.0.0 mail-relay.atrust.com closing connection
```

In this case, the mail server supports the LOGIN and PLAIN authentication mechanisms. **sendmail**, Exim, and Postfix all support SMTP authentication; details of configuration are covered on pages 801, 820, and 830, respectively.

20.4 Mail system design

The mail design we outline in this chapter is almost mandatory for keeping the administration of medium and large sites manageable and for protecting users from viruses and spam. However, it is also appropriate for small sites. The main concepts that lead to easy administration are

- Servers for incoming and outgoing mail; for really large sites, a hierarchy
- Filtering for spam and viruses before admitting messages to your site
- Filtering for spam, viruses, and data leaks before sending messages out
- For busy sites, a backup MTA for outgoing mail that fails on the first try
- Journaling and archiving ability for legal purposes (e.g., discovery)
- A mail home for each user at a physical site
- IMAP or POP to integrate PCs, Macs, cell phones, and remote clients

See page 583 for more information about MX records.

We discuss each of these key issues below and then give a few examples. Other subsystems must cooperate with the design of your mail system as well: DNS MX records must be set correctly, Internet firewalls must let mail in and out, the message store machine(s) must be identified, and so on.

Mail servers have at least five functions:

- To accept outgoing mail from MSAs or user agents
- To receive incoming mail from the outside world
- To filter mail for spam, viruses, and other malware
- To deliver mail to end-users' mailboxes
- To allow users to access their mailboxes with IMAP or POP

At a small site, the servers that implement these functions might all be the same machine wearing different hats. At larger sites, they should be separate machines. It is much easier to configure your network firewall rules if incoming mail arrives at only one machine and outgoing mail appears to originate from only one machine. The realities of today's unsecured Internet force content-scanning chores on mail servers as well.

Using mail servers

There are two basic types of mail server: Internet-facing servers, to handle incoming and outgoing mail; and internal servers, to interface with users. Here, we outline a mail system design that is secure, seems to scale well, and is relatively easy to manage. It centralizes the handling of both incoming and outgoing mail on servers dedicated to those purposes. Exhibit B illustrates one form of this system.

Exhibit B Mail system architecture

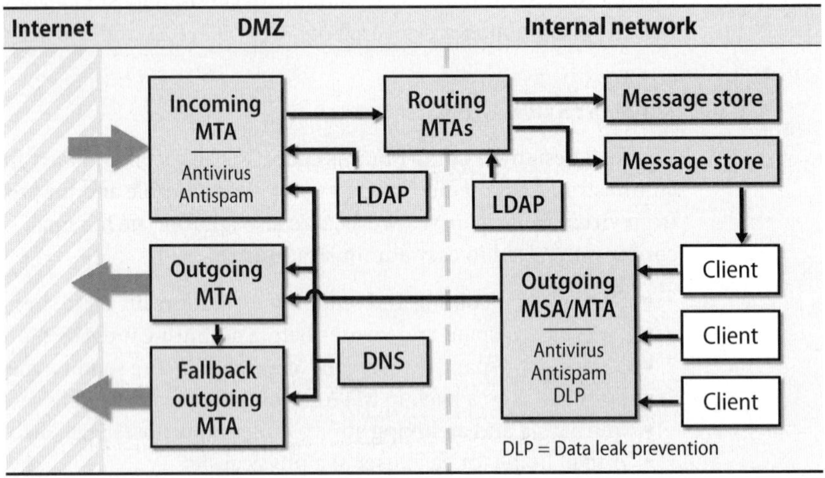

See page 932 for more information about firewalls.

The mail system depicted here shows two regions of your site: a DMZ (demilitarized zone) whose machines connect directly to the Internet, and an internal zone that is separated from the DMZ and the Internet by a firewall. In the DMZ are several servers:

- An MTA listening on port 25 and handing incoming mail to filters
- Virus and spam filters that reject or quarantine dangerous messages
- An LDAP (Lightweight Directory Access Protocol) database replica that contains mail routing information
- An outgoing MTA that tries to deliver mail submitted by the MSA
- A fallback MTA, for messages that fail on the first delivery attempt
- A caching DNS server: used by the outgoing MTA for MX lookups, and by the incoming MTA for blacklist lookups (senders' domains) and cryptographic lookups for signed messages

The server that accepts messages from the wild and woolly Internet is the most vulnerable one. It should be well secured, have few users, and have no extraneous processes or services running. Each message it handles should be checked to ensure that

- The sender's site is not on a blacklist.
- The sender's SPF record is OK.
- The local recipients are valid.
- If the message is signed, its DKIM signature can be verified.
- No malware is embedded in the message.
- The message is not spam.

All of this scanning can be done within the MTA or by a separate package such as **amavisd-new**. Spam and malware scanning are covered starting on page 761.

The server that handles outgoing mail must also be well maintained. If your site manages large mailing lists, a fallback MTA can improve overall performance by isolating problem recipients and handling them separately. We assume that the filtering and scanning of outbound mail happens at the MSA in the internal zone.

The servers in the internal zone are

- An internal routing MTA that routes accepted mail to message stores
- The original LDAP database, which includes mail routing information
- An outgoing MSA or MTA
- Filters for viruses, spam, and data leak prevention (DLP)

Outgoing mail should be scanned for viruses and spam to verify that local machines are not infected and to limit the spread of malware to other sites. If your site has concerns about the leakage of confidential or proprietary information (e.g., credit card or Social Security numbers), DLP filtering should be performed by the internal MSA before the message reaches the outgoing MTA in the more vulnerable DMZ.

Most current DLP filtering solutions seem to be embedded in commercial web/email products (e.g., ClearEmail, Cisco's IronPort, WebSense, Content Control, etc.) and include a large dose of marketing hype. Some have routines to recognize things like Social Security numbers and credit card numbers in addition to recognizing words or phrases that you configure. DLP scanning is in its infancy and has privacy ramifications. Make sure employee or use agreements mention that you intend to scan both incoming and outgoing email for spam, malware, and proprietary data.

At the end of the road are the users in the internal zone who access both the message stores (to read incoming mail) and the MSA (to send outgoing mail). These same users can be remote, in which case they should use SMTP-AUTH to authenticate themselves.

Both incoming and outgoing mail servers can be replicated if your mail load requires this. For example, multiple inbound mail servers can hide behind a load balancing box or can use DNS MX records to crudely balance load. Different client machines can route mail through different outbound servers.

In the opposite direction, sites with modest mail loads might carefully combine incoming and outgoing mail servers. Some types of processing, like BATV or Pen-pals backscatter, are easier to implement with a single server. BATV (bounce address tag validation) is a scheme for determining whether a bounce address is real or forged; it rejects email backscatter from bounces to forged sender addresses. Pen-pals (part of **amavisd-new**) is a scheme that lowers the spam score of a message if the sender is replying to email previously sent by one of your users.

See page 721 for a discussion of file distribution issues.

Most hosts at your site can use a minimal MSA/MTA configuration that forwards all outgoing mail to a smarter server for processing. They do not need to accept mail from the Internet and can all share the same configuration. You might want to distribute the configuration with a tool such as **rdist** or **rsync**.

Sites that use software such as Microsoft Exchange or Lotus Notes but are not comfortable directly exposing these applications to the Internet can use a design similar to the one outlined above in which Exchange assumes the routing role in the internal zone.

Whatever design you choose, make sure that your MTA configuration, your DNS MX records, and your firewall rules are all implementing the same policy with respect to mail.

20.5 Mail aliases

Aliases allow mail to be rerouted either by the system administrator or by individual users.[6] Aliases can define mailing lists, forward mail among machines, or allow users to be referred to by more than one name. Alias processing is recursive, so it's legal for an alias to point to other destinations that are themselves aliases.

Sysadmins often use role or functional aliases (e.g., printers@example.com) to route email about a particular issue to whatever person is currently handling that issue. Other examples might include an alias that receives the results of a nightly security scan or an alias for the postmaster in charge of email.

Mail systems typically support several aliasing mechanisms:

- Flat-file maps such as those generated from the **/etc/mail/aliases** file
- Various mail routing databases associated with a particular MTA
- LDAP databases
- Other sharing mechanisms such as NIS

See Chapter 19 for more information about LDAP.

Flat files such as the **/etc/mail/aliases** file (discussed later in this section) are by far the most straightforward and easiest way to set up aliases at small- to mid-sized sites. If you want to use the mail homes concept and you have a large,

6. Technically, aliases are configured only by sysadmins. A user's control of mail routing through the use of a **.forward** file is not really aliasing, but we have lumped them together here.

complex site, we recommend that you implement mail homes by storing aliases in an LDAP server.

Most user agents provide some sort of aliasing feature (usually called "my groups," "my mailing lists," or something like that). However, the user agent expands such aliases before the mail ever reaches the MSA or MTA. These aliases are internal to the user agent and don't require support from the rest of the mail system.

Another place where aliases can be defined is in a forwarding file in the home directory of each user (**~/.forward**). These aliases, which use a slightly nonstandard syntax, apply to all mail delivered to that particular user. They're often used to forward mail to a different account or to implement automatic "I'm on vacation" responses.

Transport agents look for aliases in the global **aliases** file (**/etc/mail/aliases** or **/etc/aliases**) and then in recipients' forwarding files. Aliasing is applied only to messages that the MTA considers to be local.

The format of an entry in the **aliases** file is

```
local-name: recipient1,recipient2,...
```

where *local-name* is the original address to be matched against incoming messages and the recipient list contains either recipient addresses or the names of other aliases. Indented lines are considered continuations of the preceding lines.

From mail's point of view, the **aliases** file supersedes **/etc/passwd**, so the entry

```
david: david@somewhere-else.edu
```

would prevent the local user david from ever receiving any mail. Therefore, administrators and **adduser** tools should check both the **passwd** file and the **aliases** file when selecting new usernames.

The **aliases** file should always contain an alias named "postmaster" that forwards mail to whoever maintains the mail system. Similarly, an alias for "abuse" is appropriate in case someone outside your organization needs to contact you regarding spam or suspicious network behavior that originates at your site. An alias for automatic messages from the MTA must also be present; it's usually called Mailer-Daemon and is often aliased to postmaster.

Sadly, there is so much abuse of the mail system these days that some sites configure these standard contact addresses to throw mail away instead of forwarding it to a human user. Entries such as

```
# Basic system aliases -- these MUST be present.
mailer-daemon:   postmaster
postmaster:      "/dev/null"
```

are common. We don't recommend this practice because humans having trouble reaching your site by email do write to the postmaster address.

A better paradigm might be

```
# Basic system aliases -- these MUST be present.
mailer-daemon:  "/dev/null"
postmaster:     root
```

You should redirect root's mail to your site's sysadmins or to someone who logs in every day. The bin, sys, daemon, nobody, and hostmaster accounts (and any other pseudo-user accounts you set up) should have similar aliases.

In addition to a list of users, aliases can refer to

- A file containing a list of addresses
- A file to which messages should be appended
- A command to which messages should be given as input

These last two targets should push your "What about security?" button because the sender of a message totally determines its content. Being able to append that content to a file or deliver it as input to a command sounds pretty scary. Many MTAs either do not allow these targets or severely limit the commands and file permissions that are acceptable.

Aliases can cause mail loops. MTAs try to detect loops that would cause mail to be forwarded back and forth forever and return the errant messages to the sender. To determine when mail is looping, an MTA can count the number of Received lines in a message's header and stop forwarding it when the count reaches a preset limit (usually 25). Each visit to a new machine is called a "hop" in email jargon; returning a message to the sender is known as "bouncing" it. So a more typically jargonized summary of loop handling would be, "Mail bounces after 25 hops."[7] Another way MTAs can detect mail loops is by adding a Delivered-To header for each host to which a message is forwarded. If an MTA finds itself wanting to send a message to a host that's already mentioned in a Delivered-To header, it knows the message has traveled in a loop.

Getting aliases from files

The :include: directive in the **aliases** file (or a user's **.forward** file) allows the list of targets for the alias to be taken from the specified file. It is a great way to let users manage their own local mailing lists. The included file can be owned by the user and changed without involving a system administrator. However, such an alias can also become a tasty and effective spam expander, so don't let email from outside your site be directed there. If users outside your site need to send mail to the alias, use mailing list software such as Mailman (covered on page 760) to help keep the system secure.

7. We have been inconsistent with terminology in this chapter, sometimes calling a returned message a "bounce" and sometimes calling it an "error." What we really mean is that a delivery status notification (DSN, a specially formatted email message) has been generated. Such a notification usually means that a message was undeliverable and is therefore being returned to the sender.

When setting up a list to use :include:, the sysadmin must enter the alias into the global **aliases** file, create the included file, and **chown** the included file to the user that is maintaining the mailing list. For example, the **aliases** file might contain

```
sa-book: :include:/usr/local/mail/ulsah.authors
```

The file **ulsah.authors** should be on a local filesystem and should be writable only by its owner. To be really complete, we should also include aliases for the mailing list's owner so that errors (bounces) are sent to the owner of the list and not to the sender of a message addressed to the list:

```
owner-sa-book: evi
```

See page 760 for more information about mailing lists and their interaction with the **aliases** file.

Mailing to files

If the target of an alias is an absolute pathname (double-quoted if it includes special characters), messages are appended to the specified file. The file must already exist. For example:

```
cron-status: /usr/local/admin/cron-status-messages
```

It's useful to be able to send mail to files, but this feature arouses the interest of the security police and is therefore restricted. This syntax is only valid in the **aliases** file and in a user's **.forward** file (or in a file that's interpolated into one of these files with the :include: directive). A filename is not understood as a normal address, so mail addressed to /etc/passwd@example.com would bounce.

If the destination file is referenced from the **aliases** file, it must be world-writable (not advisable), setuid but not executable, or owned by the MTA's default user. The identity of the default user is set in the MTA's configuration file.

If the file is referenced in a **.forward** file, it must be owned and writable by the original message recipient, who must be a valid user with an entry in the **passwd** file and a valid shell that's listed in **/etc/shells**. For files owned by root, use mode 4644 or 4600, setuid but not executable.

Mailing to programs

An alias can also route mail to the standard input of a program. This behavior is specified with a line such as

```
autoftp: "|/usr/local/bin/ftpserver"
```

It's even easier to create security holes with this feature than with mailing to a file, so once again it is only permitted in **aliases**, **.forward**, or :include: files, and often requires the use of a restricted shell.

Aliasing by example

Here are some typical aliases that a system administrator might use.

```
# General redirections for pseudo-accounts.
bin: root
daemon: root
adm: root
abuse: root
junk: "/dev/null"
root: ned

# Pager aliases
pigdog: :include:/usr/local/etc/pigdog
tier1coverage: :include:/usr/local/etc/tier1coverage
tier2coverage: :include:/usr/local/etc/tier2coverage

# Sysadmin conveniences
diary: "/usr/local/admin/diary"
info: "|/usr/local/bin/sendinfo"

# Class aliases that change every semester
sa-class: real-sa-class@nag.cs.colorado.edu
real-sa-class: :include:/usr/local/adm/sa-class.list
```

The sa-class alias has two levels so that the data file containing the list of students only needs to be maintained on a single machine, nag. The diary alias is a nice convenience and works well as a documentation extraction technique for squirrelly student sysadmins who bristle at documenting what they do. Sysadmins can easily memorialize important events in the life of the machine (OS upgrades, hardware changes, crashes, etc.) by sending mail to the diary file.

Building the hashed alias database

Since entries in the **aliases** file are in no particular order, it would be inefficient for the MTA to search this file directly. Instead, a hashed version is constructed with the Berkeley DB system. This hashing significantly speeds alias lookups, especially when the file gets big.

The file derived from **/etc/mail/aliases** is called **aliases.db**. Every time you change the **aliases** file, you must rebuild the hashed database with the **newaliases** command. Save the error output if you run **newaliases** automatically—you might have introduced formatting errors.

Using mailing lists and list wrangling software

A mailing list is a giant alias that sends a copy of each message posted to it to each person who has joined the list. Some mailing lists have thousands of recipients.

Mailing lists are usually specified in the **aliases** file but maintained in an external file. Some standard naming conventions are understood by MTAs and most mailing list software. Experienced users have come to rely on them as well. The most common are the "-request" suffix and the "owner-" prefix, which are used to reach the maintainers of the list. The conventions are illustrated by the following aliases:

```
mylist: :include:/etc/mail/include/mylist
owner-mylist: mylist-request
mylist-request: evi
owner-owner: postmaster
```


In this example, mylist is the name of the mailing list. The members are read from the file **/etc/mail/include/mylist**. Bounces generated by mailing to the list are sent to the list's owner, evi, as are requests to join the list. The indirection from owner-mylist to mylist-request to evi is useful because the owner's address (in this case, mylist-request) becomes the Return-Path address on each message sent to the list. The mylist-request alias is a bit more appropriate for this field than the address of the actual maintainer. Errors in messages to the owner-mylist alias (evi, really) would be sent to owner-owner.

If you use a site-wide aliases file, you need to add an extra level of indirection pointing mylist to myreallist@master so that the data file containing the list of members only needs to exist in one place.

Software packages for maintaining mailing lists

Two software packages, Mailman and Sympa, that automate the maintenance of mailing lists have clawed their way to "best of breed" status from a pack of about ten major contenders. These packages typically let users obtain information about the list and give users an easy way to subscribe and unsubscribe. They facilitate moderation of the list and filter it for spam and viruses. Each package is available in several (spoken, not programming) languages.

Both Mailman (gnu.org/software/mailman), written in Python, and Sympa (sympa.org), written in Perl, have web interfaces that let users subscribe and unsubscribe without involving the list manager.

20.6 Content scanning: spam and malware

This section covers the generic issues involved in fighting spam and viruses, including the use of an external antivirus tool, **amavis-new**. The details specific to a particular MTA are covered in each MTA's section.

Some issues to decide before you implement content scanning include

- Where to scan: in the DMZ or on the internal network?
- When to scan: at the initial connection or after a message is accepted?
- In what order to scan?
- What to do with the viruses and spam messages you identify?

Incoming mail is traditionally scanned at the incoming mail hub in the DMZ. Ideally, it should be scanned in-line so that bad messages can be refused while the original SMTP connection is still open. Outgoing email can be scanned for viruses and spam on an internal smart host through which all messages are routed.

We suggest the following order of operations for sanity-checking a message:

- Checking RFC compliance of the sender's SMTP implementation
- Verifying the existence of local recipients
- IP blacklisting; see page 766
- Reputation checking; see page 766
- DKIM and SPF verification; see page 767
- Antispam filtering; see pages 764 and 765
- Antivirus scanning; see pages 768 and 769

Many spam robots do not follow the SMTP protocol correctly; they typically start talking before the EHLO response. A slight delay by your server can often expose their "early talker" behavior. You can use this information either to reject the connection or to increase the spam score of the received messages.

Checking recipients to verify that they are valid local users is good unless your later checks might transform the recipients' addresses. Early checking minimizes the work your mail server has to do for mail that will eventually turn out to be undeliverable. It also eliminates a lot of "shotgun" spam. However, it does let the sender probe your user address space.

The order of the other checks is primarily driven by their cost. Check quick and easy things before more time-consuming things, so that, on average, bad messages are refused as soon possible.

Once you have identified a message as bad, what do you do with it? Refuse it, drop it, quarantine it, archive it? We recommend that you quarantine and archive while you are testing your setup. When you are satisfied that the system is doing what you want, refuse or drop all viruses and refuse or archive spam, according to your users' preferences. Delete archived spam that is more than a month old; meanwhile, users can move false positives from the spam box to their regular mailbox.

Spam

Spam is the jargon word for junk mail, also known as unsolicited commercial email or UCE. It has become a serious problem because although the response rate is low, the responses per dollar spent is high. (A list of 30 million email addresses costs about $40.) If it didn't work for the spammers, it wouldn't be such a problem. Surveys show that 95%–98% of all mail is spam. Refer to spamological sites such spamlinks.net for the latest numbers.

Our main recommendation regarding spam is that you use the preventive measures and publicly maintained blacklists that are available to you. A good one is zen.spamhaus.org. Another possibility is to redirect your incoming email to an outsourced spam fighting company such as Postini (now part of Google) or

Message Labs (now part of Symantec). However, this option may entail some compromises in performance, privacy, or reliability.

Advise your users to simply delete the spam they receive. Many spam messages contain instructions on how recipients can be removed from the mailing list. If you follow those instructions, the spammers may remove you from the current list, but they immediately add you to several other lists with the annotation "reaches a real human who reads the message." Your email address is then worth even more.

Folks that sell email addresses to spammers use a form of dictionary attack to harvest addresses. Starting with a list of common last names, the scanning software adds different first initials in hopes of hitting on a valid email address. To check the addresses, the software connects to the mail servers at, say, 50 large ISPs and does a VRFY, EXPN, or RCPT on each of zillions of addresses. MTAs can block the SMTP commands VRFY and EXPN, but not RCPT. Such actions hammer your mail server and interfere with it being able to accept and deliver real email promptly. To protect themselves from this sort of abuse, MTAs can rate-limit the number of RCPTs from a single source.

Forgeries

Forging email is trivial; many user agents let you fill in the sender's address with anything you want. MTAs can use SMTP authentication between local servers, but that doesn't scale to Internet sizes. Some MTAs add warning headers to outgoing local messages that they think might be forged.

Any user can be impersonated in mail messages. Be careful if email is your organization's authorization vehicle for things like door keys, access cards, and money. You should warn administrative users of this fact and suggest that if they see suspicious mail that appears to come from a person in authority, they should verify the validity of the message. Caution is doubly appropriate if the message asks that unreasonable privileges be given to an unusual person.

Message privacy

See page 925 for more information about PGP and GPG.

Message privacy essentially does not exist unless you use an external encryption package such as Pretty Good Privacy (PGP), its GNU-ified clone (GPG), or S/MIME. By default, all mail is sent unencrypted. End-to-end encryption requires support from mail user agents. Tell your users that they must do their own encryption if they want their mail to be private.

Both S/MIME and PGP are documented in the RFC series, with S/MIME being on the standards track. However, we prefer PGP and GPG; they're more widely available. PGP was designed by an excellent cryptographer, Phil Zimmermann, whom we trust.

These standards offer a basis for email confidentiality, authentication, message integrity assurance, and nonrepudiation of origin. However, traffic analysis is still possible since the headers and envelope are sent as plaintext.

Spam filtering

The spam problem has led to an arms race between the spam abatement folks and the spammers, with ever-more-sophisticated techniques being deployed on both sides. Some of the current control measures are

- Greylisting: temporary deferrals (a form of RFC compliance checking)
- SpamAssassin, a heuristic, pattern-matching spam recognition tool
- Blacklists: lists of known bad guys in the spam world, often DNS-based
- Whitelists: lists of known good guys, DNS-based, avoid false positives
- Mail filters ("milters") that scan both the headers and body of a message
- SPF and DKIM/ADSP records to identify senders' domains and policies
- **amavisd-new** and MailScanner: antivirus/antispam filtering systems

We cover each of these options in more detail later in this section.

When to filter

When to filter is a fundamental question, and one with no perfect answer. The main question is whether you filter "in line" during the SMTP transaction with the sender or after the mail has been accepted. There are advantages and disadvantages to both schemes. The advantages of in-line (pre-queue) filtering include the following:

- You can reject the mail and thus not take responsibility for delivery. (This may even be required for legal reasons in some countries!)

- The sender is notified reliably about why the mail couldn't be delivered. You don't need to trust the sender of the mail; you just state the reason for rejecting the message and let the originating server deal with informing the sender. Much cleaner and more reliable than accepting the mail and then bouncing it.

However, there are advantages to post-queue filtering, too:

- The performance of your Internet-facing mail server is not dragged down by extensive spam checking. This is especially valuable when bursts of mail arrive at the same time.

- Filtering after a message has been queued is simpler and more robust.

At first glance you might think post-queue filtering is best. It doesn't impact your mail server and is easier on your sysadmins. However, the bounce messages generated by post-queue filtering become their own type of spam when the sender's address is forged—as it usually is on spam.

This problem is called "backscatter spam," and a system called BATV (bounce address tag validation) has been devised to help with it. But problems remain. BATV can determine the validity of the bounce address (envelope address of the sender) if the original submitter of the message has signed the envelope address. BATV milters are available to help sites send only valid bounce messages.

A reasonable compromise might be to do basic virus and spam scanning in-line and then do additional scanning after messages have been queued.

Greylisting/DCC

Greylisting is a scheme in which you configure your mail server to defer all connections from new, unrecognized IP addresses for, say, 15 minutes to an hour. The server rejects the mail with a "try again later" message. Real MTAs sending real users' email will wait and then try again; spambots will move on down their lists and won't retry.

Greylisting has been implemented for a host of MTAs; see greylisting.org for current details. It is especially effective as part of a spam-fighting tool called DCC (the Distributed Checksum Clearinghouses; see rhyolite.com/dcc) that detects the "bulkiness" of a message by computing a fuzzy checksum and seeing how many other mail servers have seen that same checksum. It is not really a spam detector per se, but a bulk email detector. If you whitelist all the bulk email you expect to receive (such as mailing lists you belong to), then the remaining detections consist of unsolicited bulk email, which is pretty much the definition of spam.

DCC can do greylisting as well; it is used as a milter and can greylist or reject in-line during an SMTP session. Because DCC does not do pattern matching as SpamAssassin-type tools do, it is not fooled by spammers who add randomness to their messages in an attempt to foil the pattern matchers.

The effectiveness of greylisting has declined (from more than 97% effective to below 90%) as spambots have begun to take it seriously and spruced up their SMTP implementations. However, it is still effective when used in combination with blacklists because the automated blacklist maintainers often manage to get spamming sites onto the blacklist before the retry period has elapsed. Go Zen!

SpamAssassin

SpamAssassin (spamassassin.apache.org) is an open source Perl module written by Habeeb Dihu and maintained by Ian Justman. It does a pretty good job of identifying spam. It can be invoked through a milter and is used in lots of antispam products.

SpamAssassin uses a variety of ad hoc rules to identify spam. The rules used to be updated frequently, but they seem to be less actively maintained these days. SpamAssassin catches essentially all the real spam but has occasional false positives, especially if configured with the auto-Bayes option turned on. Be sure to scrutinize your haul of spam carefully as you are setting up SpamAssassin and tuning its parameters.

SpamAssassin uses a point system to score messages. If a message accumulates too many points (configurable on both a site-wide and per-user basis), SpamAssassin tags the message as spam. You can then refile suspicious messages in a spam folder, either by running a server-side filter such as Cyrus's **sieve** or by configuring your user agent. You can even teach SpamAssassin about good and bad messages ("ham" and "spam") by using its Bayesian filter feature.

Blacklists

See Chapter 17 for more information about DNS.

Several organizations (e.g., spamhaus.org) compile lists of spammers and publish them in the DNS. MTAs can be configured to check these blacklists (also known as Realtime Black Lists or RBLs) and reject mail that comes from listed sites.

There are also lists of open relays, that is, mail servers that are willing to forward a message from the Internet to a user outside their local site without authenticating the sending server. Spammers use open relays to obfuscate the origin of their messages and to foist the work of sending their huge volumes of email onto other sites.

Whitelists

Whitelists are DNS-based reputation lists that are essentially the opposite of the blacklists described above. They are used to reduce the number of false positives generated by spam filters. One whitelist, dnswl.org, rates domains as follows:

- High – never sends spam
- Medium – rarely sends spam, fixes spam problems when they occur
- Low – occasionally sends spam, slower to correct it
- None – legitimate mail server but might send spam

They recommend that you omit some of your usual mail scanning based on the rating in the whitelist:

- Skip both blacklisting and greylisting for every domain with a rating.
- Skip spam filtering for domains with ratings of high or medium.
- Never skip virus scanning.

The web site includes details for using the whitelist with each of the MTAs we describe in this book. Lookups are done through DNS, as with blacklists. For example, if you want to know the rating of IP address 1.2.3.4, you do a DNS query for the pseudo-host 4.3.2.1.list.dnswl.org. The return value is an IP address of the form 127.0.*x*.*y*, where *x* is a number that identifies the sending domain's general category of business (e.g., financial services or email marketing) and *y* is the site's whitelist rating from 0–3 (0 = none, 3 = high).

To speed up whitelist evaluations, you can download the data for the entire whitelist and **rsync** it daily to keep current; don't choose the even hour or half hour for your **cron** job.

You can check your own site's status at the dnswl.org web site. Here is typical output for a nonspammy site, caida.org:

```
IP range            192.172.226.32/32
Domain/Hostname     jungle.caida.org
Score               med

IP range            192.172.226.36/32
Domain/Hostname     fido.caida.org
Score               med

IP range            192.172.226.78/32
Domain/Hostname     rommie.caida.org
Score               med
```

The domain hotmail.com yielded about ten pages of entries, all with score "none."

Miltering: mail filtering

The developers of **sendmail** created an API that lets third-party programs filter the headers and content of mail messages as they are being processed by the MTA. These "milters" are used for spam fighting, virus detection, statistical analysis, encryption, and a host of other purposes. Milters are fully supported in both the **sendmail** and Postfix MTAs; Exim uses filters and ACLs instead. See milter.org for a catalog of available milters, complete with user ratings, license information, and statistics on downloads and updates.

MTAs invoke milters on incoming messages while they are still connected to the sending site. Milters can recognize the profile of a virus or spam message and report back to the MTA, discard the message, create log entries, or take whatever other action you feel is appropriate. Milters have access to both metadata and message content.

Miltering is potentially a powerful tool both for fighting spam and viruses and for violating users' privacy. A touchy situation evolves when managers want to know exactly what proprietary information is leaving the organization by email, while employees feel that their email should be private. Make sure employee agreements are explicit about any kind of scanning you intend to do.

SPF and Sender ID

The best way to fight spam is to stop it at its source. This sounds simple and easy, but in reality it's almost an impossible challenge. The structure of the Internet makes it difficult to track the real source of a message and to verify its authenticity. The community needs a sure-fire way to verify that the entity sending an email is really who or what it claims to be.

Many proposals have addressed this problem, but SPF and Sender ID have achieved the most traction. SPF, or Sender Policy Framework, has been described by the IETF in RFC4408. SPF defines a set of DNS records (see page 588) through which an organization can identify its official outbound mail servers. MTAs can then refuse email purporting to be from that organization's domain if the email does not originate from one of these official sources. Of course, the system only works well if the majority of organizations publish SPF records. Several milters available for download implement SPF-checking functionality.

Sender ID and SPF are virtually identical in form and function. However, key parts of Sender ID are patented by Microsoft, and hence it has been the subject of much controversy. As of this writing, Microsoft is still trying to strong-arm the industry into adopting its proprietary standards. The IETF chose not to choose and published RFC4406 on Sender ID and RFC4408 on SPF. Both are classified as experimental, so it's up to the marketplace to decide between them.

Messages that are relayed break SPF and Sender ID, which is a serious flaw in both systems. The receiver consults the SPF record for the original sender to discover its list of authorized servers. However, those addresses won't match any relay machines that were involved in transporting the message. Be careful what decisions you make based on SPF failures.

DomainKeys, DKIM, and ADSP

See Chapter 17 for more information about DKIM in DNS.

DKIM (DomainKeys Identified Mail) is a cryptographic signature system for email messages. It lets the receiver verify not only the sender's identity but also the fact that a message has not been tampered with in transit. The system uses DNS records to publish a domain's cryptographic keys and message-signing policy.

The original DomainKeys system is a precursor to DKIM that offers similar functionality and was championed by Yahoo!. It is still in use. DKIM and DomainKeys do not collide, and sites can verify signatures of both types. For signing new messages, it's best to use DKIM.

ADSP (Author Domain Signing Practice) DNS records let senders declare their signing policies for each subdomain. For example, a bank might state that it signs all mail from transactions.mybank.com. Anyone who receives unsigned mail (or mail on which the signature can't be verified) that claims to be from that domain should refuse or quarantine it. However, marketing.mybank.com might not sign its messages at all.

For a while, ADSP was called SSP (sender signing policy), so you might still see either type of DNS TXT record. DKIM is supported by all the MTAs described in this chapter, but real-world deployment has been slow. We are not sure why.

Even if you don't want to refuse messages based on DKIM or SPF verification failures, you can still use the information to increase the messages' spam score or to change your behavior to accord with the sender's reputation.

MTA-specific antispam features

Each MTA has configuration options that can help ameliorate spam problems. For example, some MTAs can determine that they are being asked to do a zillion

RCPTs and can introduce a delay of, say, 15 seconds between RCPTs for connections that are abusing them.

We cover spam-related configuration options with the rest of the details of MTA configuration. For **sendmail**, see page 789; for Exim, see page 818; and for Postfix, see page 840. DKIM and ADSP are discussed in more detail on page 845 of this chapter and in Chapter 17, beginning on page 590.

MailScanner

Julian Field's MailScanner (mailscanner.info) is an actively maintained, flexible, open source scanner for mail hubs; it recognizes spam, viruses, and phishing attempts. It's written in Perl and uses external antivirus (ClamAV and 25 other tools) and antispam (SpamAssassin) software. Its antiphishing component, called ScamNailer (scamnailer.info), is independent and does not depend on MailScanner. You can adjust MailScanner's configuration rulesets at the granularity of users, domains, or IP addresses.

MailScanner is not a milter, but rather a stand-alone program that operates on the MTA's mail queues. For example, you might configure the MTA in your DMZ to accept messages (after in-line checks with milters, blacklists, etc.) and put them in an inbound queue. You'd have MailScanner read messages from that queue, do its antispam, antivirus, and antiphishing magic, and transfer the messages that pass muster into a separate outbound queue. Another instance of the MTA could then process the outbound queue and deliver the messages.

One disadvantage of this system is that mail rejected by MailScanner creates bounce messages and can therefore contribute to backscatter spam.

Although MailScanner is free, commercial support is available. It also has an active user mailing list and a dedicated IRC channel that is monitored 24/7. It's well documented both on-line and in the book *MailScanner: A User Guide and Training Manual* by Julian Field. MailScanner's configuration file comes with so many comments that the configuration primitives almost get lost; once you're an expert, you might want to delete some of the boilerplate.

You can capture statistics from MailScanner through a web front-end called MailWatch. MRTG can graph the data, as illustrated in Exhibit C (next page). Note the huge spike that occurred on September 19th, probably an attack of some type.

amavisd-new

amavisd-new is an interface between MTAs and various virus and spam scanners such as ClamAV and SpamAssassin. It was originally based on AMaViS (A Mail Virus Scanner) but has little in common with the original these days. It's written in Perl and is developed by Mark Martinec; the web site is ijs.si/software/amavisd. We follow the maintainers' conventions in referring to the overall package as (boldfaced) **amavisd-new**; however, the daemon itself is called **amavisd**.

Exhibit C MRTG graph of mail traffic

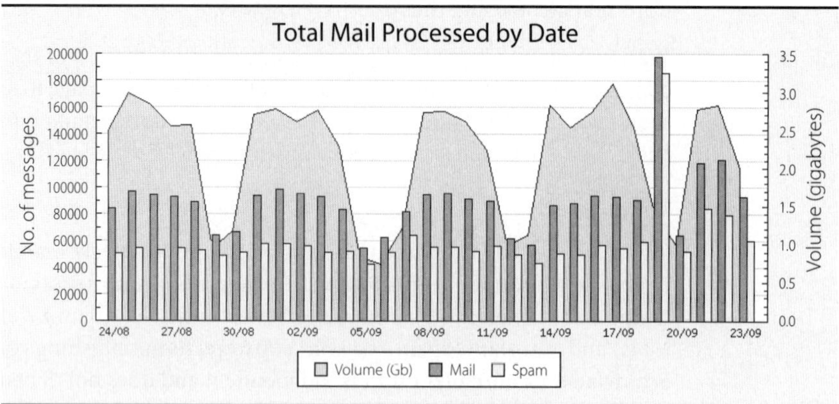

amavisd-new communicates with the MTA through a local domain or TCP socket. It can filter either in-line (when used as a milter, before the MTA has accepted a message) or after a message has been accepted but before it is delivered to the recipients.

Why use another piece of software when your MTA can do its own scanning with milters and the like? One answer is that it's convenient to keep the configuration of all your filters in one place. It's also likely to be easier to respond to a new attack or to include a new tool if all your filtering is coordinated through one interface. Another benefit is that the scanner can run on a separate machine and thereby distribute some of the load of accepting and processing messages on a busy server. A good compromise is to do easy, quick checks in your MTA and to hand the more expensive checks to a tool like **amavisd**.

amavisd can interface to many antispam and antivirus scanning packages. It is quite powerful but has a couple of disadvantages:

- The documentation is a bit scattered, and it's not clear what is current and what is old and no longer true.
- The configuration is complicated. There are lots of parameters and subtly different variants of those parameters.

How amavisd works

amavisd stands between the MTA that holds the message to be vetted and the software that will actually do the checking. **amavisd** listens for connections from the MTA on TCP port 10,024, speaks SMTP or LMTP to receive messages, and returns its answers to the MTA on port 10,025. It can also use a local domain socket if it is running on the same machine as the MTA.

If **amavisd** hands the scanned message and results back to the MTA from which the message was originally received, filtering can be done in-line and the message rejected during the MTA's initial SMTP session. If **amavisd** instead queues messages for an internal mail hub, the filtering is off-line and naughty messages can be dropped or bounced.

See Chapter 21 for more information about SNMP.

amavisd is meticulous about not losing mail, not letting messages slip by without being checked, honoring individual recipients' wishes, and following the standards laid out in the various email-related RFCs. Despite being written in Perl, **amavisd** has pretty good performance. It scans each message only once, no matter how many recipients are associated with it. Logging can be quite extensive, and tools in the distribution can monitor filtering through SNMP. **amavisd** does not need to run as root and has a good security history.

amavisd installation

Download the latest version of the software from ijs.si/software/amavisd or grab a Linux package and skip the steps detailed in the **INSTALL** file at the top of the distribution hierarchy. The project home page has pointers to precompiled packages. **amavisd** expects to run as user and group vscan or amavis, so it might be easiest to create that user and group and then log in as vscan to get the software and install it. After you have **amavisd** installed and working correctly, change the account's login shell to **/bin/false** or some other restricted shell.

The file **amavisd.conf-default** contains a list of every possible configuration parameter and its default value. **amavisd.conf-sample** is a more typical commented sample config file. Finally, **amavisd.conf** is a minimal starting place (but still over 750 lines long!) with some comments for variables that must be changed. The configuration language is Perl.

Basic amavisd configuration

Here is a basic **amavisd** configuration for a host called mail.example.com, where the MTA and **amavisd** are running on the same machine and using TCP and the SMTP protocol to communicate with each other.

```
use strict;

$myhostname = 'mail.example.com';
@local_domains_maps = (['.example.com']);
@mynetworks = qw(127.0.0.0/8 192.168.0.0/16);

$forward_method = 'smtp:[127.0.0.1]:10025';
$enable_db = 1;
$enable_global_cache = 1;
$max_servers = 5;
$DO_SYSLOG = 1;
$SYSLOG_LEVEL = "mail.info";
$bypass_decode_parts = 1;
```

```
$final_virus_destiny = D_REJECT;
$final_banned_destiny = D_REJECT;
$final_bad_header_destiny = D_PASS;
$log_recip_templ = undef;

@av_scanners = (
    ['ClamAV-clamd',
        \&ask_daemon, ["CONTSCAN {}\n", "/var/run/clamav/clamd"],
        qr/\bOK$/m, qr/\bFOUND$/m,
        qr/^.*?: (?!Infected Archive)(.*) FOUND$/m ],
);
1;
```

More than 40 antispam and antivirus programs are listed in the sample configuration's av_scanners array; this excerpt shows only ClamAV. The 1; at the end of the file is a Perlism that ensures that the file itself will evaluate to true in any Perl context that reads it.

amavisd-new tools

The **amavisd-new** distribution includes two handy tools: **amavisd-nanny** and **amavisd-agent**. The nanny monitors the health of **amavisd**, and the agent provides access to lots of SNMP-like counters and gauges in real time. Both require the Berkeley DB library.

amavisd-nanny shows the state of all **amavisd** processes, what messages they are working on, what they are doing, and how long they have been doing it. Running it with the **-h** flag shows a usage message and also a list of states that **amavisd** can be in. Most interesting are S for spam scanning, V for virus scanning, and a dot (period) for being idle. A state character is printed every second with a colon character every ten to make it easier to count. You should run the **amavisd-nanny** occasionally just to see how the system is doing. Here's an example:

```
$ sudo amavisd-nanny
process-id  task-id    elapsed in    elapsed-bar (dots indicate idle)
            or state   idle or busy
PID 01422:               0:09:51     .........:.........:.........:.....
PID 26784:  26784-18     0:00:01     ==
PID 01422:               0:09:53     .........:.........:.........:.....
PID 26784:               0:00:03     ...
```

amavisd-agent is an SNMP-like agent that collects statistics from all the running daemons and can show things like the number of messages processed, the time to process each, the percent that contain viruses, the most common viruses, etc. Here is a massively truncated example:

```
$ sudo amavisd-agent
entropy           STR ipwvEIo5VA
sysContact        STR
sysDescr          STR amavisd-new-2.6.1 (20080629)
sysLocation       STR
sysObjectID       OID 1.3.6.1.4.1.15312.2.1
```

```
sysServices         INT 64
sysUpTime           Timeticks 111090596 (12 days, 20:35:05.96)
...
ContentVirusMsgs              1274      3/h          0.5%    (InMsgs)...
InMsgs                        247458    515/h        100.0%  (InMsgs)...
InMsgsRecips                  297574    619/h        120.3%  (InMsgs)...
InMsgsSize                    28728MB   60MB/h       100.0%  (InMsgsSize)...
TimeElapsedTotal              62518s    0.253s/msg           (InMsgs)...
virus.byname.W32/MyDoom-N     9         0/h          15.5%   (ContentVirusM...
virus.byname.Troj/BredoZp-H   8         0/h          13.8%   (ContentVirusM...
```

The first numerical column is the absolute count of an item, followed by the calculated rate and a percentage value in relation to the baseline of which it's a subset, shown in parentheses.

In this case, the mail server processed 247,458 messages in 12 days with an average of 1.2 recipients per message (InMsgsRecips is 120.3% of InMsgs). The server detected 1,274 viruses, which represents about 0.5% of the total mail traffic. The scanners required 0.253 seconds on average to process a mail message. The two most frequent viruses were MyDoom-N and BredoZp-H.

Tests of your MTA's scanning effectiveness

When testing that your MTA is correctly identifying viruses and other malware, you need to use real, infected messages to verify that your countermeasures are actually identifying them and dealing with them appropriately. So don't do this in a production environment in case things get out of hand. Set up a secure, physically separate test lab that is not connected to your production network.

Antivirus researchers have compiled a small test file and given it to EICAR, the European Expert Group for IT-Security (eicar.org/anti_virus_test_file.htm) to distribute. It is not actually a virus, just a distinctive sequence of bytes that antivirus applications add to their databases as a virus (usually under a descriptive name such as EICAR-AV-Test). You can email, share, and reproduce the test file freely without worrying about starting a virus outbreak. EICAR provides several versions of the file so that you can test for the file in various wrappers such as ZIP.

GTUBE, the generic test for unsolicited bulk email, is a similar file for testing spam filters. It's available from spamassassin.apache.org/gtube.

If you are testing and debugging by speaking SMTP to your MTA, check out the SWAKS tool (SWiss Army Knife SMTP, jetmore.org/john/code/#swaks) by John Jetmore. It's written in Perl and lets you test SMTP conversations easily with command-line arguments. The man page or **swaks --help** gets you documentation. It requires the libraries **libnet-ssleay-perl** and **libnet-dns-perl** if you want to test SMTP authentication. It's not rocket science, but it's definitely faster than typing SMTP commands by hand.

20.7 EMAIL CONFIGURATION

The heart of an email system is its MTA, or mail transport agent. **sendmail** was the original UNIX MTA, written by Eric Allman while he was a graduate student at UC Berkeley many years ago. Since then, a host of other MTAs have been developed. Some of them are commercial products and some are open source implementations. In this chapter, we cover three open source mail transport agents: **sendmail**, Postfix by Wietse Venema of IBM Research, and Exim by Philip Hazel of the University of Cambridge.

After the top-level design of the mail system, configuration of the MTA is the next big sysadmin chore. Fortunately, the default or sample configurations that ship with MTAs are often very close to what the average site needs. You don't have to start from scratch when configuring your MTA.

SecuritySpace (securityspace.com) does a monthly survey to determine the market share of the various MTAs. In their December 2009 survey, 1.7 million out of 2 million MTAs responded, and 950,000 replied with a banner that identified the MTA software in use. Table 20.4 shows these results, as well as the SecuritySpace results for 2007 and some 2001 values from a different survey.

Table 20.4 Mail transport agent market share

MTA	Source	Market share 2009	2007	2001
Exim	exim.org	30%	20%	8%
Postfix	postfix.org	20%	15%	2%
MS Exchange	microsoft.com/exchange	20%	22%	4%
sendmail	sendmail.org	19%	29%	60%
All others	–	<3% each	<3% each	< 3% each

The trend is clearly away from **sendmail** and toward Exim and Postfix, with Microsoft gaining market share and then leveling off. Among our example operating systems, the UNIX variants all ship **sendmail**. Ubuntu is moving from Postfix to Exim, SUSE ships Postfix, and Red Hat includes all three but defaults to **sendmail**.

For each of our MTAs, we include details on the configuration necessary to accomplish many of the features of our suggested mail system design, including

- Configuration of simple clients
- Configuration of an Internet-facing mail server
- Control of both inbound and outbound mail routing
- Stamping of mail as coming from a central server or the domain itself
- Security
- Debugging

If you are implementing a mail system from scratch and have no site politics or biases to deal with, it may be hard to choose an MTA. **sendmail** and Exim are certainly the most complex and probably the most configurable and most powerful options. Postfix is simpler, faster, and was designed with security as a primary goal. If your site or your sysadmins have a history with a particular MTA, it's probably not worth switching unless you need functionality that's not available in your old MTA.

sendmail configuration is covered in the next section. Exim configuration begins on page 807, and Postfix configuration on page 828.

20.8 SENDMAIL

The **sendmail** distribution in source form is available from sendmail.org, but it's rarely necessary to build it from scratch these days. If you have to, refer to the top-level **INSTALL** file. If you need to tweak some of the build defaults, you can find **sendmail**'s assumptions in **devtools/OS/***your-OS-name,* and you can add features by editing **devtools/Site/site.config.m4**. **sendmail** uses the **m4** macro preprocessor not only during compilation but also for configuration. An **m4** configuration file is usually named *hostname***.mc** and is then translated from a slightly user-friendly syntax into a totally inscrutable low-level language in the file *hostname***.cf**, which is in turn installed as **/etc/mail/sendmail.cf**.

To see what version of **sendmail** is installed on your system and how it was compiled, try the following command:

```
linux$ /usr/sbin/sendmail -d0.1 -bt < /dev/null
Version 8.13.8
 Compiled with: DNSMAP HESIOD HES_GETMAILHOST LDAPMAP LOG
     MAP_REGEX MATCHGECOS MILTER MIME7TO8 MIME8TO7 NAMED_BIND
     NETINET NETINET6 NETUNIX NEWDB NIS PIPELINING SASLv2 SCANF
     SOCKETMAP STARTTLS TCPWRAPPERS USERDB USE_LDAP_INIT
============ SYSTEM IDENTITY (after readcf) ============
      (short domain name) $w = ross
  (canonical domain name) $j = ross.atrust.com
         (subdomain name) $m = atrust.com
              (node name) $k = ross.atrust.com
=========================================================
```

This command puts **sendmail** in address test mode (**-bt**) and debug mode (**-d0.1**) but gives it no addresses to test (**</dev/null**). A side effect is that **sendmail** tells us its version and the compiler flags it was built with. Once you know the version number, you can look at the sendmail.org web site to see if any known security vulnerabilities are associated with that release.

To find the **sendmail** files on your system, look at the beginning of the installed **/etc/mail/sendmail.cf** file. The comments there mention the directory in which the configuration was built. That directory should in turn lead you to the **.mc** file that is the original source of the configuration.

Most vendors that ship **sendmail** include not only the binary but also the **cf** directory from the distribution tree, which they hide somewhere among the operating system files. Table 20.5 will help you find it.

Table 20.5 sendmail configuration directory location

System	Directory
Ubuntu	**/usr/share/sendmail**
SUSE	**/usr/share/sendmail**
Red Hat	**/usr/share/sendmail-cf**
Solaris	**/etc/mail/cf**
HP-UX	**/usr/newconfig/etc/mail/cf**
AIX	**/usr/samples/tcpip/sendmail/cf**

The switch file

The service switch is covered in more detail in Chapter 19.

Most systems have a "service switch" configuration file, **/etc/nsswitch.conf**, that enumerates the methods that can satisfy various standard queries such as user and host lookups. If more than one resolution method is listed for a given type of query, the service switch file also determines the order in which the various methods are consulted.

The existence of the service switch is normally transparent to software. However, **sendmail** likes to exert fine-grained control over its lookups, so it currently ignores the system switch file and uses its own internal service configuration file (**/etc/mail/service.switch**) instead.

Two fields in the switch file impact the mail system: aliases and hosts. The possible values for the hosts service are dns, nis, nisplus, and files. For aliases, the possible values are files, nis, nisplus, and ldap. Support for the mechanisms you use (except files) must be compiled into **sendmail** before the service can be used.

Starting sendmail

sendmail should not be controlled by **inetd** or **xinetd**, so it must be explicitly started at boot time. See Chapter 3, *Booting and Shutting Down*, for startup details. The flags that **sendmail** is started with determine its behavior. You can run **sendmail** in several modes, selected with the **-b** flag. **-b** stands for "be" or "become" and is always used with another flag that determines the role **sendmail** will play. Table 20.6 lists the legal values and also includes the **-A** flag, which selects between MTA and MSA behavior.

If you are configuring a server that will accept incoming mail from the Internet, run **sendmail** in daemon mode (**-bd**). In this mode, **sendmail** listens on network port 25 and waits for work.[8] You will usually specify the **-q** flag, too—it sets the

8. The ports that **sendmail** listens on are determined by DAEMON_OPTIONS; port 25 is the default.

Table 20.6 Command-line flags for sendmail's major modes

Flag	Meaning
-Ac	Uses the **submit.cf** config file and acts as an MSA
-Am	Uses the **sendmail.cf** config file and acts as an MTA
-ba	Runs in ARPANET mode (expects CR/LF at the ends of lines)
-bd	Runs in daemon mode and listens for connections on port 25
-bD	Runs in daemon mode, but in the foreground rather than the background[a]
-bh	Views recent connection info (same as **hoststat**)
-bH	Purges disk copy of outdated connection info (same as **purgestat**)
-bi	Initializes hashed aliases (same as **newaliases**)
-bm	Runs as a mailer, delivers mail in the usual way (default)
-bp	Prints mail queue (same as **mailq**)
-bP	Prints the number of entries in queues via shared memory
-bs	Enters SMTP server mode (on standard input, not port 25)
-bt	Enters address test mode
-bv	Verifies mail addresses only; doesn't send mail

a. This mode is used for debugging so that you can see the error and debugging messages.

interval at which **sendmail** processes the mail queue. For example, **-q30m** runs the queue every thirty minutes, and **-q1h** runs it every hour.

sendmail normally tries to deliver a message immediately, saving it in the queue only momentarily to guarantee reliability. But if your host is too busy or the destination machine is unreachable, **sendmail** queues the message and tries to send it again later. **sendmail** uses persistent queue runners that are usually started at boot time. It does locking, so multiple, simultaneous queue runs are safe. The "queue groups" configuration feature helps with large mailing lists and queues. It is covered in more detail starting on page 802.

sendmail reads its configuration file, **sendmail.cf**, only when it starts up. Therefore, you must either kill and restart **sendmail** or send it a HUP signal when you change the config file. **sendmail** creates a **sendmail.pid** file that contains its process ID and the command that started it. You should start **sendmail** with an absolute path because it re-**exec**s itself on receipt of the HUP signal. The **sendmail.pid** file allows the process to be HUPed with the command

```
$ sudo kill -HUP `head -1 sendmail.pid`
```

The location of the PID file is OS-dependent. It's usually **/var/run/sendmail.pid** or **/etc/mail/sendmail.pid** but can be set in the config file with the confPID_FILE option:

```
define(confPID_FILE, `/var/run/sendmail.pid')
```

Mail queues

sendmail uses at least two queues: **/var/spool/mqueue** when acting as an MTA on port 25, and **/var/spool/clientmqueue** when acting as an MSA on port 587.[9] All messages make at least a brief stop in the queue before being sent on their way.

A queued message is saved in pieces in several different files. Each filename has a two-letter prefix that identifies the piece, followed by a random ID built from **sendmail**'s process ID. Table 20.7 shows the six possible pieces.

Table 20.7 Prefixes for files in the mail queue

Prefix	File contents
qf	The message header and control file
df	The body of the message
tf	A temporary version of the **qf** file while the **qf** file is being updated
Tf	Signifies that 32 or more failed locking attempts have occurred
Qf	Signifies that the message bounced and could not be returned
xf	Temporary transcript file of error messages from mailers

If subdirectories **qf**, **df**, or **xf** exist in a queue directory, then those pieces of the message are put in the proper subdirectory. The **qf** file contains not only the message header but also the envelope addresses, the date at which the message should be returned as undeliverable, the message's priority in the queue, and the reason the message is in the queue. Each line begins with a single-letter code that identifies the rest of the line.

Each message that is queued must have a **qf** and **df** file. All the other prefixes are used by **sendmail** during attempted delivery. When a machine crashes and reboots, the startup sequence for **sendmail** should delete the **tf**, **xf**, and **Tf** files from each queue. The sysadmin responsible for mail should check occasionally for **Qf** files in case local configuration is causing the bounces. An occasional glance at the queue directories lets you spot problems before they become disasters.

The mail queue opens up several opportunities for things to go wrong. For example, the filesystem can fill up (avoid putting **/var/spool/mqueue** and **/var/log** on the same partition), the queue can become clogged, or orphaned mail messages can get stuck in the queue. **sendmail** has configuration options to help with performance on very busy machines; we have collected these in the performance section starting on page 802.

20.9 SENDMAIL CONFIGURATION

sendmail's actions are controlled by a single configuration file, typically called **/etc/mail/sendmail.cf** for a **sendmail** running as an MTA or **/etc/mail/submit.cf**

9. **sendmail** can use multiple queues beneath **mqueue** to increase performance; see page 802.

for a **sendmail** acting as an MSA. The flags with which **sendmail** is started determine which config file it uses: **-bm**, **-bs**, and **-bt** use **submit.cf** if it exists, and all other modes use **sendmail.cf**. You can change these names with command-line flags or config file options, but it is best not to.

The raw config file format was designed to be easy to parse by machines, not humans. The **m4** source (**.mc**) file from which the **.cf** file is generated is an improvement, but its picky and rigid syntax isn't going to win any awards for user friendliness, either. Fortunately, many of the paradigms you might want to set up have already been hammered out by others with similar needs and are supplied in the distribution as prepackaged features.

sendmail configuration involves several steps:

- Deciding the role of the machine you are configuring: client, server, Internet-facing mail receiver, etc.
- Choosing the features needed to implement that role and building an **.mc** file for the configuration
- Compiling the **.mc** file with **m4** to produce a **.cf** config file

We cover the features commonly used for site-wide, Internet-facing servers and for little desktop clients. For more detailed coverage, we refer you to two key pieces of documentation on the care and feeding of **sendmail**: the O'Reilly book *sendmail* by Bryan Costales et al. and the file **cf/README** from the distribution.

The m4 preprocessor

m4, originally intended as a front end for programming languages, lets users write more readable (or perhaps more cryptic) programs. **m4** is powerful enough to be useful in many input transformation situations, and it works nicely for **sendmail** configuration files.

m4 macros have the form

```
name(arg1, arg2, ..., argn)
```

There cannot be any space between the name and the opening parenthesis. Left and right single quotes designate strings as arguments. **m4**'s quote conventions are weird, since the left and right quotes are different characters. Quotes nest, too.

m4 has some built-in macros, and users can also define their own. Table 20.8 on the next page lists the most common built-in macros that are used in **sendmail** configuration.

The sendmail configuration pieces

The **sendmail** distribution includes a **cf** subdirectory beneath which are all the pieces necessary for **m4** configuration. Table 20.5 on page 776 shows the location of the **cf** directory if you did not install the **sendmail** source but relied on your vendor. The **README** file there is **sendmail**'s configuration documentation. The

Table 20.8 m4 macros commonly used with sendmail

Macro	Function
define	Defines a macro named *arg1* with value *arg2*
undefine	Discards a previous definition of macro named *arg1*
include	Includes (interpolates) the file named *arg1*
dnl	Discards characters up to and including the next newline
divert	Manages output streams

subdirectories, listed in Table 20.9, contain examples and snippets you can include in your own configuration.

Table 20.9 sendmail configuration subdirectories

Directory	Contents
cf	Sample **.mc** (master configuration) files
domain	Sample **m4** files for various domains at Berkeley
feature	Fragments that implement various features
hack	Special features of dubious value or implementation
m4	The basic config file and other core files
ostype	OS-dependent file locations and quirks
mailer	**m4** files that describe common mailers (delivery agents)
sh	Shell scripts used by **m4**

The **cf/cf** directory contains examples of **.mc** files. In fact, it contains so many examples that yours may get lost in the clutter. We recommend that you keep your own **.mc** files separate from those in the distributed **cf** directory. Either create a new directory named for your site (**cf/***sitename*) or move the **cf** directory aside to **cf.examples** and create a new **cf** directory. If you do this, copy the **Makefile** and **Build** script over to your new directory so the instructions in the **README** file still work. Alternatively, you can copy all of your own configuration **.mc** files to a central location rather than leaving them inside the **sendmail** distribution. The **Build** script uses relative pathnames, so you'll have to modify it if you want to build a **.cf** file from an **.mc** file and are not in the **sendmail** distribution hierarchy.

The files in the **cf/ostype** directory configure **sendmail** for each specific operating system. Many are predefined, but if you have moved things around on your system, you might have to modify one or create a new one. Copy one that is close to reality for your system and give it a new name.

The **cf/feature** directory is where you will shop for all the configuration pieces you might need. There is a feature for just about anything that any site running **sendmail** has found useful.

The other directories beneath **cf** are pretty much boilerplate and do not need to be tweaked or even understood—just use them.

A configuration file built from a sample .mc file

Before we dive into the details of the various configuration macros, features, and options you might use in a **sendmail** configuration, let's put the cart before the horse and create a "no frills" configuration to illustrate the general process. Our example is for a leaf node, myhost.example.com; the master configuration file is called **myhost.mc**. Here's the complete **.mc** file:

```
divert(-1)
#### basic .mc file for example.com
divert(0)
VERSIONID(`$Id$')
OSTYPE(`linux')
MAILER(`local')
MAILER(`smtp')
```

Except for the diversions and comments, each line invokes a prepackaged macro. The first four lines are boilerplate; they insert comments in the compiled file to note the version of **sendmail**, the directory the configuration was built in, etc. The OSTYPE macro includes the **../ostype/linux.m4** file. The MAILER lines allow for local delivery (to users with accounts on myhost.example.com) and for delivery to Internet sites.

To build the real configuration file, just run the **Build** command you copied over to the new **cf** directory:

```
$ ./Build myhost.cf
```

Finally, install **myhost.cf** in the right spot—normally **/etc/mail/sendmail.cf**, but some vendors move it. Favorite vendor hiding places are **/etc** and **/usr/lib**.

At a larger site, you may want to create a separate **m4** file to hold site-wide defaults; put it in the **cf/domain** directory. Individual hosts can then include the contents of this file by using the DOMAIN macro. Not every host needs a separate config file, but each group of similar hosts (same architecture and same role: server, client, etc.) will probably need its own configuration.

The order of the macros in the **.mc** file is not arbitrary. It should be

```
VERSIONID
OSTYPE
DOMAIN
FEATURE
local macro definitions
MAILER
```

Even with **sendmail**'s easy **m4** configuration system, you still have to make several configuration decisions for your site. As you read about the features described below, think about how they might fit into your site's organization. A small site will probably have only a hub node and leaf nodes and thus will need only two versions of the config file. A larger site may need separate hubs for incoming and outgoing mail and, perhaps, a separate POP/IMAP server.

Whatever the complexity of your site and whatever face it shows to the outside world (exposed, behind a firewall, or on a virtual private network, for example), it's likely that the **cf** directory contains some appropriate ready-made configuration snippets just waiting to be customized and put to work.

20.10 SENDMAIL CONFIGURATION PRIMITIVES

sendmail configuration commands are case sensitive. By convention, the names of predefined macros are all caps (e.g., OSTYPE), **m4** commands are all lower case (e.g., define), and configurable option names usually start with lowercase conf and end with an all-caps variable name (e.g., confFALLBACK_MX). Macros usually refer to an **m4** file called **../***macroname***/***arg1***.m4**. For example, the reference OSTYPE(`linux') causes the file **../ostype/linux.m4** to be included.

Tables and databases

Before we dive into specific configuration primitives, we must first discuss tables (sometimes called maps or databases), which **sendmail** can use to do mail routing or address rewriting. Most are used in conjunction with the FEATURE macro.

A table is a cache (usually a text file) of routing, aliasing, policy, or other information that is converted to a database format with the **makemap** command and then used as an information source for one or more of **sendmail**'s various lookup operations. Although the data usually starts as a text file, data for **sendmail** tables can come from DNS, NIS, LDAP, or other sources. The use of a centralized IMAP server relieves **sendmail** of the chore of chasing down users and obsoletes some of its tables.

Two database libraries are supported: the **dbm/ndbm** library that is standard with most versions of UNIX and Linux, and Berkeley DB, which is a more extensible library that supports multiple storage schemes. We recommend BDB if your system has it or you can install it. It's faster than **dbm** and creates smaller files.

sendmail defines three database map types:

- dbm – uses an extensible hashing algorithm (**dbm/ndbm**)
- hash – uses a standard hashing scheme (DB)
- btree – uses a B-tree data structure (DB)

For most table applications in **sendmail**, the hash database type—the default—is the best. Use the **makemap** command to build the database file from a text file; you specify the database type and the output file base name. The text version of the database should appear on **makemap**'s standard input. For example:

```
$ sudo makemap hash /etc/mail/access < /etc/mail/access
```

At first glance this command looks like a mistake that would cause the input file to be overwritten by an empty output file. However, **makemap** tacks on an appropriate suffix, so the actual output file is **/etc/mail/access.db** and in fact there is no conflict. Each time the text file is changed, the database file must be rebuilt with **makemap** (but **sendmail** need not be HUPed).

Comments can appear in the text files from which maps are produced. They begin with # and continue until the end of the line.

In most circumstances, the longest possible match is used for database keys. As with any hashed data structure, the order of entries in the input text file is not significant. FEATUREs that expect a database file as a parameter default to hash as the database type and **/etc/mail/***tablename***.db** as the filename for the database.

Generic macros and features

Table 20.10 lists common configuration primitives, whether they are typically used (yes, no, maybe), and a brief description of what they do. More details and examples are given in the sections following the table.

Table 20.10 Sendmail generic configuration primitives

Primitive	Used?	Description
OSTYPE	Yes	Includes OS-specific paths and mailer flags
DOMAIN	No	Includes site-specific configuration details
MAILER	Yes	Enables mailers, typically smtp and local
FEATURE	Maybe	Enables a variety of **sendmail** features
use_cw_file	Yes (servers)	Lists hosts for which you accept mail
redirect	Maybe (servers)	Bounces mail nicely when users move
always_add_domain	Yes	Fully qualifies hostnames if UA didn't
access_db	Maybe (servers)	Sets database of hosts to relay mail for
virtusertable	Maybe (servers)	Turns on domain aliasing (virtual domains)
ldap_routing	Maybe (servers)	Routes incoming mail using LDAP
MASQUERADE_AS	Yes	Makes all mail seem to come from one place
EXPOSED_USER	Yes	Lists users who shouldn't be masqueraded
MAIL_HUB	Yes (servers)	Specifies mail server for incoming mail
SMART_HOST	Yes (clients)	Specifies mail server for outgoing mail

OSTYPE macro

An OSTYPE file packages a variety of vendor-specific information, such as the expected locations of mail-related files, paths to commands that **sendmail** needs, flags to mailer programs, etc. See **cf/README** for a list of all the variables that can be defined in an OSTYPE file.[10]

10. So where is the OSTYPE macro itself defined? In a file in the **cf/m4** directory, which is magically prepended to your config file when you run the **Build** script.

Each of our example systems except SUSE includes the appropriate OSTYPE file from the **sendmail** distribution. SUSE instead has its own **suse_linux.m4** file. That file is long (over 80 lines compared to 5 lines in the comparable **linux.m4** file) and contains numerous FEATUREs and other macros that are usually found in a site's master configuration file (the **.mc** file) and not in the OSTYPE file. This hides the real configuration from the sysadmin—a mixed blessing, perhaps, but not a practice we recommend.

DOMAIN macro

The DOMAIN directive lets you specify site-wide generic information in one place (**cf/domain/***filename***.m4**) and then include it in each host's config file with

```
DOMAIN(`filename')
```

MAILER macro

You must include a MAILER macro for every delivery agent you want to enable. You'll find a complete list of supported mailers in the directory **cf/mailers**, but typically you need only local, smtp, and maybe cyrus. MAILER lines are generally the last thing in the **.mc** file.

FEATURE macro

The FEATURE macro enables a whole host of common scenarios (56 at last count!) by including **m4** files from the **feature** directory. The syntax is

```
FEATURE(keyword, arg, arg, ...)
```

where *keyword* corresponds to a file *keyword***.m4** in the **cf/feature** directory and the *args* are passed to it. There can be at most nine arguments to a feature.

use_cw_file feature

The **sendmail** internal class w (hence the name **cw**) contains the names of all local hosts for which this host accepts and delivers mail. This feature specifies that mail be accepted for the hosts listed, one per line, in **/etc/mail/local-host-names**. The configuration line

```
FEATURE(`use_cw_file')
```

invokes the feature. A client machine does not really need this feature unless it has nicknames, but your incoming mail hub machine does. The **local-host-names** file should include any local hosts and virtual domains for which you accept email, including sites whose backup MX records point to you.

Without this feature, **sendmail** delivers mail locally only if it is addressed to the machine on which **sendmail** is running.

If you add a new host at your site, you must add it to the **local-host-names** file and send a HUP signal to **sendmail** to make your changes take effect. Unfortunately, **sendmail** reads this file only when it starts.

redirect feature

When people leave your organization, you usually either forward their mail or let mail to them bounce back to the sender with an error. The redirect feature provides support for a more elegant way of bouncing mail.

If Joe Smith has graduated from oldsite.edu (login smithj) to newsite.com (login joe), then enabling redirect with

```
FEATURE(`redirect')
```

and adding the line

```
smithj: joe@newsite.com.REDIRECT
```

to the **aliases** file at oldsite.edu causes mail to smithj to be returned to the sender with an error message suggesting that the sender try the address joe@newsite.com instead. The message itself is not automatically forwarded.

always_add_domain feature

The always_add_domain feature makes all email addresses fully qualified. It should always be used.

access_db feature

The access_db feature controls relaying and other policy issues. Typically, the raw data that drives this feature either comes from LDAP or is kept in a text file called **/etc/mail/access**. In the latter case, the text file must be converted to some kind of indexed format with the **makemap** command, as described on page 782. To use the flat file, use FEATURE(`access_db') in the configuration file; for the LDAP version, use FEATURE(`access_db', `LDAP').[11]

The key field in the access database is an IP network or a domain name with an optional tag such as Connect:, To:, or From:. The value field specifies what to do with the message.

The most common values are OK to accept the message, RELAY to allow it to be relayed, REJECT to reject it with a generic error indication, or ERROR:"*error code and message*" to reject it with a specific message. Other possible values allow for finer-grained control. Here is a snippet from a sample **/etc/mail/access** file:

```
localhost     RELAY
127.0.0.1     RELAY
192.168.1.1   RELAY
192.168.1.17  RELAY
66.77.123.1   OK
fax.com       OK
61            ERROR:"550 We don't accept mail from spammers"
67.106.63     ERROR:"550 We don't accept mail from spammers"
```

11. This form uses the default LDAP schema defined in the file **cf/sendmail.schema**; if you want a different schema file, use additional arguments in your FEATURE statement.

virtusertable feature

The virtusertable feature supports domain aliasing for incoming mail. This feature allows multiple virtual domains to be hosted on one machine and is used frequently at web hosting sites. The key field of the table contains either an email address (*user@host.domain*) or a domain specification (*@domain*). The value field is a local or external email address. If the key is a domain, the value can either pass the *user* field along as the variable %1 or route the mail to a different user. Here are some examples:

```
@appliedtrust.com        %1@atrust.com
unix@book.admin.com      sa-book-authors@atrust.com
linux@book.admin.com     sa-book-authors@atrust.com
webmaster@example.com    billy.q.zakowski@colorado.edu
info@testdomain.net      ausername@hotmail.com
```

All the host keys on the left side of the data mappings must be listed in the **cw** file, **/etc/mail/local-host-names**, or be included in the VIRTUSER_DOMAIN list. If they are not, **sendmail** will not know to accept the mail locally and will try to find the destination host on the Internet. But DNS MX records will point **sendmail** back to this same server and you will get a "local configuration error" message in the resulting bounce message. Unfortunately, **sendmail** cannot tell that the error message for this instance should really be "virtusertable key not in cw file."

ldap_routing feature

LDAP, the Lightweight Directory Access Protocol, can be a source of data for aliases or mail routing information as well general tabular data as described earlier. The **cf/README** file has a long section on LDAP with lots of examples.

To use LDAP in this way, you must have built **sendmail** to include LDAP support. In your **.mc** file, add the lines

```
define(`confLDAP_DEFAULT_SPEC', `-h server -b searchbase')
FEATURE(`ldap_routing')
LDAPROUTE_DOMAIN(`my_domain')
```

Those lines tell **sendmail** that you want to use an LDAP database to route incoming mail addressed to the specified domain. The LDAP_DEFAULT_SPEC option identifies the LDAP server and the LDAP basename for searches. LDAP uses port 389 unless you specify a different port by adding -p *ldap_port* to the define.

sendmail uses the values of two tags in the LDAP database:

- mailLocalAddress for the addressee on incoming mail
- mailRoutingAddress for the destination to which email should be sent

sendmail also supports the tag mailHost, which if present routes mail to the MX-designated mail handler for the specified host. The recipient address remains the value of the mailRoutingAddress tag.

LDAP database entries support a wild card entry, *@domain*, that reroutes mail addressed to anyone at the specified domain (as was done in the virtusertable).

By default, mail addressed to user@host1.mydomain would first trigger a lookup on user@host1.mydomain. If that failed, **sendmail** would try @host1.mydomain but not user@mydomain. Including the line

```
LDAPROUTE_EQUIVALENT(`host1.mydomain')
```

would also try the keys user@mydomain and @mydomain. This feature enables a single database to route mail at a complex site. You can also take the entries for the LDAPROUTE_EQUIVALENT clauses from a file, which makes the feature quite usable. The syntax for that form is

```
LDAPROUTE_EQUIVALENT_FILE(`filename')
```

Additional arguments to the ldap_routing feature let you specify more details about the LDAP schema and control the handling of addressee names that have a *+detail* part. As always, see the **cf/README** file for exact details.

Masquerading features

An email address is usually made up of a username, a host, and a domain, but many sites do not want the names of their hosts exposed on the Internet. The MASQUERADE_AS macro lets you specify a single identity for other machines to hide behind. All mail appears to emanate from the designated machine or domain. This is fine for regular users, but for debugging purposes, system users such as root should be excluded from the masquerade.

For example, the sequence

```
MASQUERADE_AS(`atrust.com')
EXPOSED_USER(`root')
EXPOSED_USER(`Mailer-Daemon')
```

would stamp mail as coming from user@atrust.com unless it was sent by root or the mail system; in these cases, the mail would carry the name of the originating host. MASQUERADE_AS is just the tip of a vast masquerading iceberg that extends downward through a dozen variations and exceptions. The allmasquerade and masquerade_envelope features (in combination with MASQUERADE_AS) hide just the right amount of local info. See the **cf/README** for details.

MAIL_HUB and SMART_HOST macros

Masquerading makes all mail appear to come from a single host or domain by rewriting the headers and, optionally, the envelope. But most sites will want all mail to *actually* come from (or go to) a single machine so that they can control the flow of viruses, spam, and company secrets. You can achieve this control with a combination of MX records in the DNS, the MAIL_HUB macro for incoming mail, and the SMART_HOST macro for outgoing mail.

See page 583 for more information about DNS MX records.

For example, in the architectural diagram on page 754, MX records would direct incoming email from the Internet to the MTA in the demilitarized zone. After verification that the received email was free of viruses and spam and was directed to valid local users, the mail could be relayed, with the following define, to the internal routing MTA for delivery:

```
define(`MAIL_HUB', `smtp:routingMTA.mydomain')
```

See the next section for more about nullclient.

Likewise, client machines would relay their mail to the SMART_HOST designated in the nullclient feature in their configuration. The SMART_HOST could then filter for viruses and spam so that mail from your site did not pollute the Internet.

The syntax of SMART_HOST parallels that of MAIL_HUB, and the default delivery agent is again relay. For example:

```
define(`SMART_HOST', `smtp:outgoingMTA.mydomain')
```

You can use the same machine as the server for both incoming and outgoing mail. Both the SMART_HOST and the MAIL_HUB must allow relaying, the first from clients inside your domain and the second from the MTA in the DMZ.

Client configuration

If your site follows the paradigms illustrated in the mail system design section (page 753), most of your machines will need to be configured as clients who just submit outgoing mail generated by users and don't receive mail at all. One of **sendmail**'s FEATUREs, nullclient, is just right for this situation. It creates a config file that forwards all mail to a central hub via SMTP. The entire config file, after the VERSIONID and OSTYPE lines, would be simply

```
FEATURE(`nocanonify')
FEATURE(`nullclient', `mailserver')
EXPOSED_USER(`root')
```

where *mailserver* is the name of your central hub. The nocanonify feature tells **sendmail** not to do DNS lookups or rewrite addresses with fully qualified domain names. All of that work will be done by the *mailserver* host. This feature is similar to SMART_HOST and assumes that the client will MASQUERADE_AS *mailserver.* The EXPOSED_USER clause exempts root from the masquerading and so facilitates debugging.

The *mailserver* machine must allow relaying from its null clients. That permission is granted in the access_db, described on page 785. The null client must have an associated MX record that points to *mailserver* and must also be included in the *mailserver*'s **cw** file (usually **/etc/mail/local-host-names**). These settings allow the *mailserver* to accept mail for the client.

sendmail should run as an MSA (without the -**bd** flag) if the user agents on the client machine can be taught to use port 587 for submitting mail. If not, you can run **sendmail** in daemon mode (-**bd**) but set the DAEMON_OPTIONS configuration option to listen for connections only on the loopback interface.

SUSE provides a sample **.mc** file for a null client in **/etc/mail/linux.nullclient.mc**. Fill in the name of your mail server, build the **sendmail.cf** file, and you're done.

Configuration options

You set config file options with **m4**'s define command. A complete list of options that are accessible as **m4** variables (along with their default values) is given in the **cf/README** file.

The defaults are OK for a typical site that is not too paranoid about security and not too concerned with performance. The defaults try to protect you from spam by turning off relaying, by requiring addresses to be fully qualified, and by requiring that senders' domains resolve to an IP address. If your mail hub machine is very busy and services a lot of mailing lists, you may need to tweak some of the performance values.

Table 20.11 on the next page lists some options that you might need to adjust (about 10% of over 175 configuration options). Their default values are shown in parentheses. To save space, the option names are shown without their conf prefix; for example, the FALLBACK_MX option is really named confFALLBACK_MX. We divided the table into subsections that identify the kind of issue the variable addresses: resource management, performance, security and spam abatement, and miscellaneous options. Some options fit in more than one category, but we listed them only once.

Spam-related features in sendmail

sendmail has a variety of features and configuration options that can help you control spam and viruses:

- Rules that control third-party (aka promiscuous, aka open) relaying; that is, the use of your mail server by one off-site user to send mail to another off-site user. Spammers often use relaying to mask the true source of their mail and thereby avoid detection by ISPs. Relaying also lets spammers use *your* cycles and save their own.
- The access database for filtering recipient addresses. This feature is rather like a firewall for email.
- Blacklists that catalog open relays and known spam-friendly sites that **sendmail** can check against.
- Throttles that can slow down mail acceptance when certain types of bad behavior are detected.
- Header checking and input mail filtering by means of a generic mail filtering interface called **libmilter**. It allows arbitrary scanning of message headers and content and lets you reject messages that match a particular profile. Milters are plentiful and very powerful; see milter.org.

Table 20.11 Basic sendmail configuration options

	Option name	Description (default value)
Resources	MAX_DAEMON_CHILDREN	Max number of child processes[a] (no limit)
	MAX_MESSAGE_SIZE	Max size in bytes of a single message (infinite)
	MIN_FREE_BLOCKS	Min filesystem space to accept mail (100)
	TO_*lots_of_stuff*	Timeouts for all kinds of things (various)
Performance	DELAY_LA	Load avg. to slow down deliveries (0 = no limit)
	FALLBACK_MX	See page 803 for description (no default)
	FAST_SPLIT	Suppresses MX lookups as recipients are sorted and split across queues (1 = true)
	HOST_STATUS_DIRECTORY	See page 803 for description (no default)
	MCI_CACHE_SIZE	# of open outgoing TCP connections cached (2)
	MCI_CACHE_TIMEOUT	Time to keep cached connections open (5m)
	MIN_QUEUE_AGE	Minimum time jobs must stay in queue; makes a busy machine handle the queue better (0)
	QUEUE_LA	Load average at which mail should be queued instead of delivered immediately (8 * #CPUs)
	REFUSE_LA	Load avg. at which to refuse mail (12 * #CPUs)
Security and spam	AUTH_MECHANISMS	SMTP auth mechanisms for Cyrus SASL[b]
	CONNECTION_RATE_THROTTLE	Slows DOS attacks by limiting the rate at which mail connections are accepted (no limit)
	DONT_BLAME_SENDMAIL	Overrides **sendmail**'s security and file checking; don't change casually! (safe)
	MAX_MIME_HEADER_LENGTH	Sets max size of MIME headers (no limit)[c]
	MAX_RCPTS_PER_MESSAGE	Slows spam delivery; defers extra recipients and sends a temporary error msg (infinite)
	PRIVACY_FLAGS	Limits info given out by SMTP (authwarnings)
Misc	DOUBLE_BOUNCE_ADDRESS	Catches a lot of spam; some sites use **/dev/null**, but that can hide serious problems (postmaster)
	LDAP_DEFAULT_SPEC	Map spec for LDAP database, including the host and port the server is running on (undefined)

a. More specifically, the maximum number of child processes that can run at once. When the limit is reached, **sendmail** refuses connections. This option can prevent (or create) denial of service attacks.

b. The default value is EXTERNAL GSSAPI KERBEROS_V4 DIGEST-MD5 CRAM-MD5; don't add PLAIN LOGIN, because the password is transmitted as cleartext. That may be OK internally, but not on the Internet unless the connection is also secured through the use of SSL.

c. This option can prevent user agent buffer overflows. "256/128" is a good value to use—it means 256 bytes per header and 128 bytes per parameter to that header.

Couple these with techniques like greylisting (page 764), content scanning with **amavisd-new** (page 769), and the new DNS records for email authentication (page 767), and you might stand a fighting chance against the spammers.

Relay control

sendmail accepts incoming mail, looks at the envelope addresses, decides where the mail should go, and then passes it along to an appropriate destination. That destination can be local or it can be another transport agent farther along in the delivery chain. When an incoming message has no local recipients, the transport agent that handles it is said to be acting as a relay.

Only hosts that are tagged with RELAY in the access database (see page 785) or that are listed in **/etc/mail/relay-domains** are allowed to submit mail for relaying. Some types of relaying are useful and legitimate. How can you tell which messages to relay and which to reject? Relaying is actually necessary in only three situations:

- When the transport agent acts as a gateway for hosts that are not reachable in any other way; for example, hosts that are not always turned on (laptops, Windows PCs) and virtual hosts. In this situation, all the recipients for which you want to relay lie within the same domain.
- When the transport agent is the outgoing mail server for other, not-so-smart hosts. In this case, all the senders' hostnames or IP addresses will be local (or at least enumerable).
- When you have agreed to be a backup MX destination for another site.

Any other situation that appears to require relaying is probably just an indication of bad design (with the possible exception of support for mobile users). You can obviate the first use of relaying (above) by designating a centralized server to receive mail, with POP or IMAP being used for client access. The second case should always be allowed, but only for your own hosts. You can check IP addresses or hostnames. In the third case, you can list the other site in your access database and allow relaying just for that site's IP address blocks.

Although **sendmail** comes with relaying turned off by default, several features have been added to turn relaying back on, either fully or in a limited and controlled way. These features are listed below for completeness, but our recommendation is that you be careful about opening things up too much. The access_db feature is the safest way to allow limited relaying.

- FEATURE(`relay_entire_domain') – allows relaying for just your domain
- RELAY_DOMAIN(`*domain, …*') – adds more domains to be relayed
- RELAY_DOMAIN_FILE(`*filename*') – same; takes domain list from a file
- FEATURE(`relay_hosts_only') – affects RELAY_DOMAIN, accessdb

You will need to make an exception if you use the SMART_HOST or MAIL_HUB designations to route mail through a particular mail server machine. That server will have to be set up to relay mail from local hosts. Configure it with

```
FEATURE(`relay_entire_domain')
```

If you consider turning on relaying in some form, consult the **sendmail** documentation in **cf/README** to be sure you don't inadvertently become a friend of spammers. When you are done, have one of the relay-checking sites verify that you did not inadvertently create an open relay—try spamhelp.org.

User or site blacklisting

If you have local users or hosts to which you want to block mail, use

```
FEATURE(`blacklist_recipients')
```

which supports the following types of entries in your access file:

```
To:nobody@                  ERROR:550 Mailbox disabled for this user
To:printer.mydomain         ERROR:550 This host does not accept mail
To:user@host.mydomain       ERROR:550 Mailbox disabled for this user
```

These lines block incoming mail to user nobody on any host, to host printer, and to a particular user's address on one machine. The use of the To: tag lets these users send messages, just not receive them; some printers have that capability.

To include a DNS-style blacklist for incoming email, use the dnsbl feature:

```
FEATURE(`dnsbl', `zen.spamhaus.org')
```

This feature makes **sendmail** reject mail from any site whose IP address is in any of the three blacklists of known spammers (SBL, XBL, and PBL) maintained at spamhaus.org. Other lists catalog sites that run open relays and known blocks of addresses that are likely to be a haven for spammers. These blacklists are distributed through a clever tweak of the DNS system; hence the name dnsbl. See page 766 for a more complete explanation of how the system works.

You can pass a third argument to the dnsbl feature to specify the error message you would like returned. If you omit this argument, **sendmail** returns a fixed error message from the DNS database that contains the records.

You can include the dnsbl feature several times to check different lists of abusers.

Throttles, rates, and connection limits

Table 20.12 lists several **sendmail** controls that can slow down mail processing when clients' behavior appears suspicious.

Table 20.12 sendmail's "slow down" configuration primitives

Primitive	Description
BAD_RCPT_THROTTLE	Slows down spammers collecting addresses
MAX_RCPTS_PER_MESSAGE	Defers delivery if a message has too many recipients
ratecontrol feature	Limits the rate of incoming connections
conncontrol feature	Limits the number of simultaneous connections
greet_pause feature	Delays HELO response, requires strict SMTP compliance

After the no-such-login count reaches the limit set in the BAD_RCPT_THROTTLE option, **sendmail** sleeps for one second after each rejected RCPT command, slowing a spammer's address harvesting to a crawl. To set that threshold to 3, use

```
define(`confBAD_RCPT_THROTTLE', `3')
```

Setting the MAX_RCPTS_PER_MESSAGE option causes the sender to queue extra recipients for later. This is a cheap form of greylisting for messages that have a suspiciously large number of recipients.

The ratecontrol and conncontrol features allow per-host or per-net limits on the rate at which incoming connections are accepted and the number of simultaneous connections, respectively. Both use the **/etc/mail/access** file to specify the limits and the domains to which that they should apply, the first with the tag ClientRate: in the key field and the second with tag ClientConn:. To enable rate controls, insert lines like these in your **.mc** file:[12]

```
FEATURE(`ratecontrol', `nodelay',`terminate')
FEATURE(`conncontrol', `nodelay',`terminate')
```

Then, add to your **/etc/mail/access** file the list of hosts or nets to be controlled and their restriction thresholds. For example, the lines

```
ClientRate:192.168.6.17    2
ClientRate:170.65.3.4      10
```

limit the hosts 192.168.6.17 and 170.65.3.4 to two new connections per minute and ten new connections per minute, respectively. The lines

```
ClientConn:192.168.2.8     2
ClientConn:175.14.4.1      7
ClientConn:                10
```

set limits of two simultaneous connections for 192.168.2.8, seven for 175.14.4.1, and ten simultaneous connections for all other hosts.

Another nifty feature is greet_pause. When a remote MTA connects to your **sendmail** server, the SMTP protocol mandates that it wait for your server's welcome greeting before speaking. However, it's common for spam mailers to blurt out an EHLO/HELO command immediately. This behavior is partially explainable as poor implementation of the SMTP protocol in spam-sending tools, but it may also be a feature that aims to save time on the spammer's behalf. Whatever the cause, this behavior is suspicious and is known as "slamming."

The greet_pause feature makes **sendmail** wait for a specified period of time at the beginning of the connection before greeting its newfound friend. If the remote MTA does not wait to be properly greeted and proceeds with an EHLO or HELO command during the planned awkward moment, **sendmail** logs an error and refuses subsequent commands from the remote MTA.

12. FEATURE(`access_db') must be there too.

You can enable greeting pauses with this entry in the **.mc** file:

```
FEATURE(`greet_pause', `700')
```

This line causes a 700 millisecond delay at the beginning of every new connection. You can set per-host or per-net delays with a GreetPause: prefix in the access database, but most sites use a blanket value for this feature.

Milter configuration in sendmail

Miltering in general is introduced on page 767; this section describes how to configure miltering in **sendmail**. The configuration directives INPUT_MAIL_FILTER and MAIL_FILTER control the miltering action. A slew of options give you fine-grained control over exactly when in the SMTP conversation each filter is applied (MILTER_MACROS_*). For example, the line

```
INPUT_MAIL_FILTER(`filtername', `S=mailer:/var/run/filtername.socket')
```

passes each incoming message to the **/etc/mail/filtername** program through the socket specified in the second argument. Below is a more realistic example that uses milters to connect to SpamAssassin through a local domain socket and to check DKIM signatures with the **dkim-filter** program through a TCP socket at port 8699.

```
dnl # Enable SpamAssassin
INPUT_MAIL_FILTER(`spamassassin',
`S=local:/var/run/spamass-milter.sock, F=, T=C:15m;S:4m;R:4m;E:10m')

dnl # Enable DomainKeys and DKIM
INPUT_MAIL_FILTER(`dkim-filter', `S=inet:8699@127.0.0.1, T=R:2m')

define(`confMILTER_MACROS_CONNECT', `j, {daemon_name}')
define(`confMILTER_MACROS_ENVFROM', `i, {auth_type}')
```

The last two statements set parameters passed to the milters when the session connection starts and after the MAIL FROM command, respectively.

For more information, see **libmilter/README** or the HTML documentation in the **libmilter/docs** directory of the **sendmail** distribution. The **README** file gives an overview and a simple example of a filter that logs messages to a file. The files in **docs** describe the library interface and tell how to use the various calls to build your own mail filtering programs. milter.org is a great reference.

amavisd and sendmail connection

amavisd is an external, industrial strength virus and spam scanner introduced on page 769. This section illustrates how to use it with **sendmail**.

The easiest way to connect **sendmail** and **amavisd** is to use two mail servers: one that receives mail from the Internet and passes it to **amavisd**; the other that runs in queue-only mode, receives scanned messages from **amavisd**, and transmits them on their way, either for local delivery or to the Internet. **amavisd** sits in the middle, acting as a MAIL_HUB for incoming mail and a SMART_HOST for outgoing mail.

Unfortunately, this scheme scans messages off-line, after **sendmail** has already accepted them for delivery. To use **amavisd** in-line, see the file **README.milter** in the **amavisd-new** documentation.

The key configuration lines on the Internet-facing server—the ones that pass all mail to the **amavisd** process listening on port 10,024—are

```
FEATURE(`stickyhost')
define(`MAIL_HUB', `esmtp:[127.0.0.1]')
define(`SMART_HOST', `esmtp:[127.0.0.1]')
define(`confDELIVERY_MODE', `q')
define(`ESMTP_MAILER_ARGS', `TCP $h 10024')
DAEMON_OPTIONS(`Name=receivingMTA')
```

This last line makes debugging the configuration much easier because you can then tell which process (the receiving **sendmail**, the transmitting **sendmail**, or **amavisd**) is logging what messages.

After scanning, **amavisd** passes messages to the queueing-only **sendmail** process listening on port 10,025 (not port 25 as usual), and from there, queue runners either complete local delivery or ship the messages out to the Internet.

On the transmitting server, setting

```
DAEMON_OPTIONS(`Addr=127.0.0.1, Port=10025, Name=transmittingMTA')
```

tells **sendmail** to listen on port 10,025 for messages returning from **amavisd**. It logs any info or error messages with the name transmittingMTA to distinguish it from the receivingMTA.

There are more settings you can tweak (for example, performance limits) to make sure the two instances of **sendmail** play well together. Some thought needs to go into deciding exactly what checks will be done, which process will do them, and in what order they will occur.

The file **README_FILES/README.sendmail-dual** in the **amavisd-new** distribution is a good reference.

20.11 Security and sendmail

With the explosive growth of the Internet, programs such as **sendmail** that accept arbitrary user-supplied input and deliver it to local users, files, or shells have frequently provided an avenue of attack for hackers. **sendmail**, along with DNS and even IP, is flirting with authentication and encryption as a built-in solution to some of these fundamental security issues.

sendmail supports both SMTP authentication and encryption with TLS, Transport Layer Security (formerly known as SSL, the Secure Socket Layer). TLS brought with it six new configuration options for certificate files and key files. New actions for access database matches can require that authentication must have succeeded.

In this section, we describe **sendmail**'s permissions model, ownerships, and privacy protection. We then briefly discuss TLS and SASL (the Simple Authentication and Security Layer) and their use with **sendmail**.

sendmail carefully inspects file permissions before it believes the contents of, say, a **.forward** or an **aliases** file. Although this tightening of security is generally welcome, it's sometimes necessary to relax the tough policies. To this end, **sendmail** introduced the DontBlameSendmail option, so named in hopes that the name will suggest to sysadmins that what they are doing is considered unsafe.

This option has many possible values—55 at last count. The default is safe, the strictest possible. For a complete list of values, see **doc/op/op.ps** in the **sendmail** distribution or the O'Reilly **sendmail** book. Or just leave the option set to safe.

Ownerships

Three user accounts are important in the **sendmail** universe: the DefaultUser, the RunAsUser, and the TrustedUser.

By default, all of **sendmail**'s mailers run as the DefaultUser unless the mailer's flags specify otherwise. If a user mailnull, sendmail, or daemon exists in the **/etc/passwd** file, DefaultUser will be that. Otherwise, it defaults to UID 1 and GID 1. We recommend the use of the mailnull account and a mailnull group. Add it to **/etc/passwd** with a star as the password, no valid shell, no home directory, and a default group of mailnull. You'll have to add the mailnull entry to the **group** file, too. The mailnull account should not own any files. If **sendmail** is not running as root, the mailers must be setuid.

If RunAsUser is set, **sendmail** ignores the value of DefaultUser and does everything as RunAsUser. If you are running **sendmail** setgid (to smmsp), then the submission **sendmail** just passes messages to the real **sendmail** through SMTP. The real **sendmail** does not have its setuid bit set, but it runs as root from the startup files.

The RunAsUser is the UID that **sendmail** runs under after opening its socket connection to port 25. Ports numbered less than 1,024 can be opened only by the superuser; therefore, **sendmail** must initially run as root. However, after performing this operation, **sendmail** can switch to a different UID. Such a switch reduces the risk of damage or access if **sendmail** is tricked into doing something bad. Don't use the RunAsUser feature on machines that support user accounts or other services; it is meant for use on firewalls or bastion hosts only.[13]

13. Bastion hosts are specially hardened hosts intended to withstand attack when placed in a DMZ or outside a firewall.

By default, **sendmail** does not switch identities and continues to run as root. If you change the RunAsUser to something other than root, you must change several other things as well. The RunAsUser must own the mail queue, be able to read all maps and include files, be able to run programs, etc. Expect to spend a few hours finding all the file and directory ownerships that must be changed.

sendmail's TrustedUser can own maps and alias files. The TrustedUser is allowed to start the daemon or rebuild the **aliases** file. This facility exists mostly to support GUI interfaces to **sendmail** that need to provide limited administrative control to certain users. If you set TrustedUser, be sure to guard the account that it points to because this account can easily be exploited to gain root access. The TrustedUser is different from the TRUSTED_USERS class, which determines who can rewrite the From line of messages.[14]

Permissions

File and directory permissions are important to **sendmail** security. Use the settings listed in Table 20.13 to be safe.

Table 20.13 Owner and permissions for sendmail-related directories

Path	Owner	Mode	What it contains
/var/spool/clientmqueue	smmsp:smmsp	770	Queue for initial submissions
/var/spool/mqueue	RunAsUser	700	Mail queue directory
/, /var, /var/spool	root	755	Path to **mqueue**
/etc/mail/*	TrustedUser	644	Maps, the config file, aliases
/etc/mail	TrustedUser	755	Parent directory for maps
/etc	root	755	Path to **mail** directory

sendmail refuses to read files that have lax permissions (for example, files that are group- or world-writable or that live in group- or world-writable directories). In particular, **sendmail** is *very* picky about the complete path to any alias file or forward file. This pickiness sometimes clashes with the way sites like to manage mailing list aliases. To see where you stand with respect to **sendmail**'s ideas about permissions, run **sendmail -v -bi**. The **-bi** flag initializes the alias database and warns you of inappropriate permissions.

Solaris has a handy program, **check-permissions**, that understands **sendmail**'s security standards and reports unsafe paths or files. It follows includes in aliases and **.forward** files. It can check either the invoking user or all users, depending on the command-line flags.

sendmail no longer reads **.forward** files that have link counts greater than 1 if the directory paths that lead to them have lax permissions. This rule bit Evi when one of her **.forward** files, which she usually hard-linked to either **.forward.to.boulder**

14. The TRUSTED_USERS feature is typically used to support mailing list software.

or **.forward.to.sandiego**, silently failed to forward her mail from a small site at which she did not receive much mail. It was months before she realized that "I never got your mail" was her own fault and not a valid excuse.

You can turn off many of the restrictive file access policies mentioned above with the DontBlameSendmail option. But don't do that.

Safer mail to files and programs

We recommend that you use **smrsh** instead of **/bin/sh** as your program mailer and that you use **mail.local** instead of **/bin/mail** as your local mailer. Both programs are included in the **sendmail** distribution. To incorporate them into your configuration, add the lines

```
FEATURE(`smrsh', `path-to-smrsh')
FEATURE(`local_lmtp', `path-to-mail.local')
```

to your **.mc** file. If you omit the explicit paths, the commands are assumed to live in **/usr/libexec**. You can use **sendmail**'s confEBINDIR option to change the default location of the binaries to whatever you want. Table 20.14 may help you find where our friendly vendors have stashed things.

Table 20.14 Location of sendmail's restricted delivery agents

OS	smrsh	mail.local	sm.bin
sendmail	**/usr/libexec**	**/usr/libexec**	**/usr/adm**
Ubuntu	**/usr/lib/sm.bin**	**/usr/lib/sm.bin**	**/usr/adm**
SUSE	**/usr/lib/sendmail.d/bin**	**/usr/lib/sendmail.d/bin**	–
Red Hat	**/usr/sbin**	–	**/etc/smrsh**
Solaris	**/usr/lib**	**/usr/lib**	**/var/adm**
HP-UX	**/usr/sbin**	–	**/usr/adm**[a]
AIX	**/usr/sbin**	–	**/usr/adm**[a]

a. This directory does not exist on either HP-UX or AIX as shipped, so you must create it.

smrsh is a restricted shell that executes only the programs contained in one directory (**/usr/adm/sm.bin** by default). **smrsh** ignores user-specified paths and tries to find any requested commands in its own known-safe directory. **smrsh** also blocks the use of certain shell metacharacters such as <, the input redirection symbol. Symbolic links are allowed in **sm.bin**, so you don't need to make duplicate copies of the programs you allow. The **vacation** program is a good candidate for **sm.bin**. Don't put **procmail** there; it's insecure.

Here are some example shell commands and their possible **smrsh** interpretations:

```
vacation eric                  # Executes /usr/adm/sm.bin/vacation eric
cat /etc/passwd                # Rejected, cat not in sm.bin
vacation eric < /etc/passwd    # Rejected, no < allowed
```

sendmail's SafeFileEnvironment option controls where files can be written when email is redirected to a file by **aliases** or a **.forward** file. It causes **sendmail** to execute a **chroot** system call, making the root of the filesystem no longer / but rather **/safe** or whatever path you specified in the SafeFileEnvironment option. An alias that directed mail to the **/etc/passwd** file, for example, would really be written to **/safe/etc/passwd**.

The SafeFileEnvironment option also protects device files, directories, and other special files by allowing writes only to regular files. Besides increasing security, this option ameliorates the effects of user mistakes. Some sites set the option to **/home** to allow access to home directories while keeping system files off-limits.

Mailers can also be run in a **chroot**ed directory.

Privacy options

sendmail also has privacy options that control

- What external folks can determine about your site through SMTP
- What you require of the host on the other end of an SMTP connection
- Whether your users can see or run the mail queue

Table 20.15 lists the possible values for the privacy options as of this writing; see the file **doc/op/op.ps** in the distribution for current information.

Table 20.15 Values of the PrivacyOption variable

Value	Meaning
public	Does no privacy/security checking
needmailhelo	Requires SMTP HELO (identifies remote host)
noexpn	Disallows the SMTP EXPN command
novrfy	Disallows the SMTP VRFY command
needexpnhelo	Does not expand addresses (EXPN) without a HELO
needvrfyhelo	Does not verify addresses (VRFY) without a HELO
noverb[a]	Disallows verbose mode for EXPN
restrictmailq	Allows only **mqueue** directory's group to see the queue
restrictqrun	Allows only **mqueue** directory's owner to run the queue
restrictexpand	Restricts info displayed by the **-bv** and **-v** flags[b]
noetrn[c]	Disallows asynchronous queue runs
authwarnings	Adds warning header if outgoing message seems forged
noreceipts	Turns off delivery status notification for success return receipts
nobodyreturn	Does not return message body in a DSN
goaway	Disables all SMTP status queries (EXPN, VRFY, etc.)

a. Verbose mode follows **.forward** files when an EXPN command is given and reports more information on the whereabouts of a user's mail. Use noverb or, better yet, noexpn, on any machine exposed to the outside world.

b. Unless executed by root or the TrustedUser.

c. ETRN is an ESMTP command intended for use by dial-up hosts. It requests that the queue be run just for messages to that host.

We recommend conservatism; in your **.mc** file, use

```
define(`confPRIVACY_OPTIONS', ``goaway, authwarnings, restrictmailq,
    restrictqrun'')
```

sendmail's default value for the privacy options is authwarnings; the line above would reset that value. Notice the double sets of quotes; some versions of **m4** require them to protect the commas in the list of privacy option values. Red Hat, Solaris, and AIX default to authwarnings; SUSE and Ubuntu to authwarnings, needmailhelo, novrfy, noexpn, and noverb; and HP-UX defaults to restrictqrun, goaway, and authwarnings, the most secure—go, HP!

Running a chrooted sendmail (for the truly paranoid)

If you are worried about the access that **sendmail** has to your filesystem, you can start it in a **chroot**ed jail. (See page 913 in Chapter 22, *Security*, for more information about **chroot**.) Create a minimal filesystem in your jail, including things like **/dev/null**, **/etc** essentials (**passwd**, **group**, **resolv.conf**, **sendmail.cf**, any map files, **mail/***), the shared libraries that **sendmail** needs, the **sendmail** binary, the mail queue directory, and any log files. You will probably have to fiddle with the list to get it just right. Use the **chroot** command to start a jailed **sendmail**. For example:

```
$ sudo chroot /jail /usr/sbin/sendmail -bd -q30m
```

Denial of service attacks

Denial of service attacks are difficult to prevent because there is no a priori way to determine that a message is an attack rather than a valid piece of email. Attackers can try various nasty things, including flooding the SMTP port with bogus connections, filling disk partitions with giant messages, clogging outgoing connections, and mail bombing. **sendmail** has some configuration parameters that can help slow down or limit the impact of a denial of service attack, but these parameters can also interfere with legitimate mail. Milters can help sysadmins thwart a prolonged denial of service attack.

The MaxDaemonChildren option limits the number of **sendmail** processes. It prevents the system from being overwhelmed with **sendmail** work, but it also allows an attacker to easily shut down SMTP service. The MaxMessageSize option can help prevent the mail queue directory from filling, but if you set it too low, legitimate mail will bounce. (You might mention your limit to users so that they aren't surprised when their mail bounces. We recommend a fairly high limit anyway, since some legitimate mail is huge.) The ConnectionRateThrottle option, which limits the number of permitted connections per second, can slow things down a bit. And finally, setting MaxRcptsPerMessage, which controls the maximum number of recipients allowed on a single message, might help.

sendmail has always been able to refuse connections (option REFUSE_LA) or queue email (QUEUE_LA) according to the system load average. A variation,

DELAY_LA, keeps the mail flowing, but at a reduced rate. See page 803 in the performance section for details.

In spite of all these protections for your mail system, someone mail bombing you will still interfere with legitimate mail. Mail bombing can be quite nasty.

SASL: the Simple Authentication and Security Layer

sendmail supports the SMTP authentication system defined in RFC4954. It's based on SASL, the Simple Authentication and Security Layer (RFCs 4422 and 4752). SASL is a shared-secret system that is typically host-to-host; you must make explicit arrangements for each pair of servers that are to mutually authenticate. It is usually used between user agents and MSAs or between MSAs and MTAs within a site.

SASL is a generic authentication mechanism that can be integrated into a variety of protocols. The SASL framework (it's a library) has two fundamental concepts: an authorization identifier (like a login name) and an authentication identifier (like a password). It can map these to permissions on files, account passwords, Kerberos tickets, etc. SASL contains both an authentication part and an encryption component. To use SASL with **sendmail**, get a copy of Cyrus SASL from ftp.andrew.dmu.edu/pub/cyrus-mail.

TLS: Transport Layer Security

TLS, another encryption/authentication system, is specified in RFC3207. It is implemented in **sendmail** as an extension to SMTP called STARTTLS. You can even use both SASL and TLS.

TLS is a bit harder to set up and requires a certificate authority. You can pay VeriSign big bucks to issue you certificates (signed public keys identifying an entity), set up your own certificate authority, or go to OpenCA or equivalent. Strong authentication is used in place of a hostname or IP address as the authorization token for relaying mail or for accepting a connection from a host in the first place. An entry such as

```
TLS_Srv:secure.example.com      ENCR:112
TLS_Clt:laptop.example.com      PERM+VERIFY:112
```

in the access_db indicates that STARTTLS is in use and that email to the domain secure.example.com must be encrypted with at least 112-bit encryption keys. Email from a host in the laptop.example.com domain should be accepted only if the client has authenticated itself.

Greg Shapiro and Claus Assmann of Sendmail, Inc., have stashed some (slightly dated) extra documentation about security and **sendmail** on the web. It's available from sendmail.org/~gshapiro and sendmail.org/~ca. The **index** link in ~ca is especially useful.

20.12 SENDMAIL PERFORMANCE

sendmail has several configuration options that improve performance. Although we have scattered them throughout the chapter, we expand on the most important ones in this section. These are options and features you should consider if you run a high-volume mail system (in either direction). Actually, if you really need to send 1,000,000 mail messages an hour and you aren't a spammer, your best bet might be to use the commercial side of **sendmail**, Sendmail, Inc.

Delivery modes

sendmail has four basic delivery modes: background, interactive, queue, and defer. Each represents a tradeoff between latency and throughput. Background mode delivers the mail immediately but requires **sendmail** to fork a new process to do it. Interactive mode also delivers immediately, but delivery is done by the same process and makes the remote side wait for the results. Queue mode queues incoming mail for delivery by a queue runner at some later time. Defer mode is similar to queue mode, but it also defers all map, DNS, alias, and forwarding lookups. Interactive mode is rarely used. Background mode favors lower latency, and defer or queueing mode favors higher throughput. The delivery mode is set with the option confDELIVERY_MODE and defaults to background.

Queue groups and envelope splitting

Queue groups let you create multiple queues for outgoing mail and control the attributes of each queue group individually. Queue groups are used with an envelope-splitting feature that distributes an envelope with many recipients (such as a message sent to a mailing list) across multiple queue groups. Several configuration primitives are used with queue groups. See the O'Reilly *sendmail* book or the **cf/README** file for examples and details.

Queue runners

sendmail forks copies of itself to perform the actual transport of mail. You can control how many copies are running at any given time and even how many copies are attached to each queue group. By using this feature, you can balance the activities of **sendmail** and the operating system on your busy mail hub machines.

Three **sendmail** options control the number of queue runner daemons processing each queue:

- The MAX_DAEMON_CHILDREN option specifies the total number of copies of the **sendmail** daemon that are allowed to run at any one time, including those running queues and those accepting incoming mail.
- The MAX_QUEUE_CHILDREN option sets the maximum number of queue runners allowed at one time.

- The MAX_RUNNERS_PER_QUEUE option sets the default runner limit per queue if no explicit value is set with the Runners= (or R=) parameter in the queue group definition.

Load average controls

sendmail has always been able to refuse connections or queue messages instead of delivering them when the system load average goes too high. Unfortunately, the load average has only a one-minute granularity, so it's not a very finely honed tool for smoothing out the resources consumed by **sendmail**. The DELAY_LA primitive lets you set a value of the load average at which **sendmail** should slow down; it will sleep for one second between SMTP commands for current connections and before accepting new connections. The default value is 0, which turns the mechanism off.

Undeliverable messages in the queue

Undeliverable messages in the mail queue can really kill performance on a busy mail server. **sendmail** has several features that help with the issue of undeliverable messages. The most effective is the FALLBACK_MX option, which hands a message off to another machine if it cannot be delivered on the first attempt. Your primary machine cranks out the messages to good addresses and shunts the problem children to a secondary fallback machine. Another aid is the host status directory, which stores the status of remote hosts across queue runs.

The FALLBACK_MX option is a big performance win for a site with large mailing lists that invariably contain addresses that are temporarily or permanently undeliverable. To use it, you specify the host to handle the deferred mail. For example,

```
define(`confFALLBACK_MX', `mailbackup.atrust.com')
```

forwards messages that fail their first delivery attempt to mailbackup.atrust.com for further processing. There can be multiple fallback machines if the designated hosts have multiple MX records in DNS.

The TO_ICONNECT option sets a timeout on the initial attempt to connect and send a message. If you set it short, more work is shunted to the fallback MTA. However, it does let the main server whip through the first pass at a large mailing list in record time.

On the fallback machines, you can use the HOST_STATUS_DIRECTORY option to help with multiple failures. This option directs **sendmail** to maintain a status file for each host to which mail is sent and to use that status information to prioritize the hosts each time the queue is run. This status information effectively implements negative caching and allows information to be shared across queue runs. It's a performance win on servers that handle mailing lists with a lot of bad addresses, but it can be expensive in terms of file I/O.

Here is an example that uses the directory **/var/spool/mqueue/.hoststat**. (You must create the directory first.)

```
define(`confHOST_STATUS_DIRECTORY', `/var/spool/mqueue/.hoststat')
```

If the **.hoststat** directory is specified with a relative path, it is stored beneath the queue directory. **sendmail** creates its own internal hierarchy of subdirectories based on the destination hostname.

For example, if mail to evi@anchor.cs.colorado.edu were to fail, status information would go in the **/var/spool/mqueue/.hoststat/edu./colorado./cs.** directory in a file called **anchor**. That's because the host anchor has an MX record with itself as highest priority. If the DNS MX records had directed anchor's email to host foo, then the filename would have been **foo**, not **anchor**.

A third performance enhancement for busy machines involves setting a minimum queue age so that any message that cannot be delivered on the initial try stays in the queue for a minimum time between delivery attempts. This technique is usually coupled with command-line flags that run the queue more often (e.g., **-q5m**). If a queue runner hangs on a bad message, another one starts in 5 minutes, improving performance for the messages that can be delivered. The entire queue is run in batches determined by which messages have been there for the required minimum time. Running **sendmail** with the flags **-bd -q5m** and including

```
define(`confMIN-QUEUE_AGE', `27m')
```

in the config file could result in a more responsive system.

Kernel tuning

If you plan to use a UNIX or Linux box as a high-volume mail server, you should modify several of the kernel's networking configuration parameters. Table 20.16 shows the parameters to change under Linux on a high-volume mail server along with their suggested and default values. Similar parameters exist for UNIX, perhaps under slightly different names.

Table 20.16 Kernel parameters to change on high-volume mail servers

Variable (relative to /proc/sys)	Default	Suggested
net/ipv4/tcp_fin_timeout	180	30
net/ipv4/tcp_keepalive_time	7200	1800
net/core/netdev_max_backlog	300	1024
fs/file_max	4096	16384
fs/inode_max	16384	65536

To reset the parameters of the networking stack on a Linux box, use the shell's **echo** command redirected to the proper variable in the **/proc** filesystem. Chapter 14, *TCP/IP Networking*, contains a general description of this procedure starting on page 490. These changes can be made permanent with the **sysctl** command or by putting the appropriate **echo** commands in a shell script that runs at boot time.

For example, to change TCP's FIN timeout value, you could use the following command:

```
linux$ sudo sh -c "echo 30 > /proc/sys/net/ipv4/tcp_fin_timeout"15
```

Solaris and HP-UX use the **ndd** command to tune network parameters. The HP-UX implementation is well documented, and **ndd -h** (help) gives a clear description of each variable, its range of values, and the default value. Solaris's **ndd** understands a question mark to mean that you want documentation, but you must backslash it (**ndd \?**) to protect it from the shell. Unfortunately, Solaris's **ndd** just names the tunable variables instead of describing them.

For example, to change the FIN timeout value with **ndd** on HP-UX, run

```
hp-ux$ sudo ndd -set tcp_fin_wait_2_timeout 30000
```

The time unit for **ndd** is milliseconds, thus the 30,000 instead of 30. On Solaris, the variable is called **tcp_fin_wait_2_flush_interval**, with no units given in the man page…but Google knows! In fact, the units are milliseconds, with the default value being 675,000. **ndd** is described in more detail in Chapter 14, *TCP/IP Networking* on page 498 for Solaris and page 504 for HP-UX.

AIX uses the **no** command to tune network parameters. **sudo no -L** lists tunable variables with their min, max, and current values along with the units of these values. If you want a change to be permanent, use **no** with the **-p** flag—your change will then survive a reboot.

For example, to set the TCP FIN_WAIT parameter, use

```
aix$ sudo no -p -o tcp_finwait2=60
```

The units are half-seconds, so the value 60 achieves the 30 seconds recommended in the tuning table above. **no** is also discussed on page 507.

20.13 SENDMAIL TESTING AND DEBUGGING

m4-based configurations are to some extent pretested. You probably won't need to do low-level debugging if you use them. One thing the debugging flags cannot test is your design. While researching this chapter, we found errors in several of the configuration files and designs that we examined. The errors ranged from invoking a feature without the prerequisite macro (e.g., using masquerade_envelope without having turned on masquerading with MASQUERADE_AS) to total conflict between the design of the **sendmail** configuration and the firewall that controlled whether and under what conditions mail was allowed in.

15. If you try this command in the form **sudo echo 30 > /proc/sys/net/ipv4/tcp_fin_timeout**, you just generate a "permission denied" message—your shell attempts to open the output file before it runs **sudo**. You want the **sudo** to apply to both the **echo** command and the redirection. Ergo, you must create a root subshell in which to execute the entire command: **sudo sh -c "echo…"**

You cannot design a mail system in a vacuum. You must be synchronized with (or at least not be in conflict with) your DNS MX records and your firewall policy.

Queue monitoring

You can use the **mailq** command (which is equivalent to **sendmail -bp**) to view the status of queued messages. Messages are queued while they are being delivered or when delivery has been attempted but has failed.

mailq prints a human-readable summary of the files in **/var/spool/mqueue** at any given moment. The output is useful for determining why a message may have been delayed. If it appears that a mail backlog is developing, you can monitor the status of **sendmail**'s attempts to clear the jam.

There are two default queues: one for messages received on port 25 and another for messages received on port 587 (the client submission queue). You can invoke **mailq -Ac** to see the client queue.

Here is some typical output from **mailq**. This case shows three messages waiting to be delivered:

```
$ sudo mailq
/var/spool/mqueue (3 requests)
-----Q-ID-----      --Size-- -----Q-Time-----   ------------Sender/Recipient-----------
k623gYYk008732   23217   Sat Jul 1 21:42   MAILER-DAEMON
      8BITMIME   (Deferred: Connection refused by agribusinessonline.com.)
                                              <Nimtz@agribusinessonline.com>
k5ULkAHB032374   279     Fri Jun 30 15:46  <randy@atrust.com>
              (Deferred: Name server: k2wireless.com.: host name lookup fa)
                                              <relder@k2wireless.com>
k5UJDm72023576   2485    Fri Jun 30 13:13  MAILER-DAEMON
              (reply: read error from mx4.level3.com.)
                                              <lfinist@bbnplanet.com>
```

If you think you understand the situation better than **sendmail** or you just want **sendmail** to try to redeliver the queued messages immediately, you can force a queue run with **sendmail -q**. If you use **sendmail -q -v**, **sendmail** shows the play-by-play results of each delivery attempt, information that is often useful for debugging. Left to its own devices, **sendmail** retries delivery every queue run interval (typically every 30 minutes).

Logging

See Chapter 11 for more information about syslog.

sendmail uses syslog to log error and status messages with the syslog facility "mail" and levels "debug" through "crit"; messages are tagged with the string "sendmail." You can override the logging string "sendmail" with the **-L** command-line option; this capability is handy if you are debugging one copy of **sendmail** while other copies are doing regular email chores.

The confLOG_LEVEL option, specified on the command line or in the config file, determines the severity level that **sendmail** uses as a threshold for logging. High values of the log level imply low severity levels and cause more info to be logged.

Table 20.17 gives an approximate mapping between **sendmail** log levels and syslog severity levels.

Table 20.17 sendmail log levels vs. syslog levels

L	Syslog levels	L	Syslog levels
0	No logging	4	notice
1	alert or crit	5–11	info
2	crit	≥12	debug
3	err or warning		

Recall that a message logged to syslog at a particular level is reported to that level and all those above it. The **/etc/syslog.conf** file determines the eventual destination of each message. Table 20.18 shows their default locations:[16]

Table 20.18 Vendor's sendmail logging locations

System	Log file location
Ubuntu	**/var/log/mail.log**
SUSE	**/var/log/mail**
Red Hat	**/var/log/maillog**
Solaris	**/var/log/syslog** and **/var/adm/messages**
HP-UX	**/var/adm/syslog/mail.log**
AIX	**/var/log/mail**

Several programs can summarize **sendmail** log files, with the end products ranging from simple counts and text tables (**mreport**) to fancy web pages (Yasma). You might need to—or want to—limit access to this data or at least inform your users that you are collecting it. Yasma (Yet Another Sendmail Log Analyzer), for example, lets you hide the username part of email addresses in its reports.

20.14 Exim

The Exim mail transport and submission agent was written in 1995 by Philip Hazel of the University of Cambridge and is distributed under the GNU General Public License. The current release, Exim version 4.71, came out in late 2009.

16. Wouldn't it be nice if standardization efforts could sort out some of these random and apparently meaningless differences so our scripts could be more portable?

Tons of Exim documentation are available on-line, as are a couple of books by the author of the software.

Googling for Exim questions often seems to lead to old, undated, and sometimes inappropriate materials, so check the official documentation first. A 400+ page specification and configuration document (**doc/spec.txt**) is included in the distribution. This document is also available from exim.org as a PDF file. It's the definitive reference work for Exim and is updated religiously with each new release.

There are two cultures with respect to Exim configuration: Debian's and the rest of the world's. Debian runs its own set of mailing lists to support users; we do not cover the Debian-specific configuration extensions here.

Exim releases 4.70 and later have dropped support for DomainKeys (the precursor to DKIM) and now include internal DKIM support by default. Both systems can and do coexist in the real world, but DKIM is on the IETF standards track and will eventually replace DomainKeys.

Exim is like **sendmail** in that it is implemented as a single process that performs all the mail chores. However, it does not carry all of **sendmail**'s historical baggage (support for ancient address formats, needing to get mail to hosts not on the Internet, etc.). When compiled with content scanning, it interfaces with common spam and virus scanners such as SpamAssassin and ClamAV. Policy control is implemented through ACLs (access control lists) that can accept or reject messages or pass them to external scanning software. Per-user filters are available through a special type of entry in users' **.forward** files. Many aspects of Exim's behavior are specified at compile time, the chief examples being Exim's database and message store formats.

The workhorses in the Exim system are called routers and transports. Both are included in the general category of "drivers." Routers decide how messages should be delivered, and transports decide on the mechanics of making deliveries. Routers are an ordered list of things to try, whereas transports are an unordered set of delivery methods.

Exim installation

You can download the latest distribution from exim.org, or if yours is a Linux site, from your favorite package repository. Refer to the top-level **README** file and the file **src/EDITME**, where you must set installation locations, user IDs, and other parameters. **EDITME** is over 1,000 lines long, but it's mostly comments that lead you through the compilation process; required changes are well labeled. After your edits, save the file as **../Local/Makefile** or **../Local/Makefile**-*osname* (if you are building configurations for several different operating systems from the same distribution directory) before you run **make**.

Here are a few of the important variables (our opinion) and suggested values (Exim developers' opinion) from the **EDITME** file. The first five are required, and the rest are recommended.

```
BIN_DIRECTORY=/usr/exim/bin             # Where the exim binary should live
SPOOL_DIRECTORY=/var/spool/exim         # Mail spool directory
CONFIGURE_FILE=/usr/exim/configure      # Exim's configuration file
SYSTEM_ALIASES_FILE=/etc/aliases        # Location of aliases file
EXIM_USER=ref:exim                      # User to run as after rootly chores

ROUTER_ACCEPT=yes                       # Router drivers to include
ROUTER_DNSLOOKUP=yes
ROUTER_IPLITERAL=yes
ROUTER_MANUALROUTE=yes
ROUTER_QUERYPROGRAM=yes
ROUTER_REDIRECT=yes

TRANSPORT_APPENDFILE=yes                # Transport drivers to include
TRANSPORT_AUTOREPLY=yes
TRANSPORT_PIPE=yes
TRANSPORT_SMTP=yes

SUPPORT_MAILDIR=yes                     # Mailbox formats to understand
SUPPORT_MAILSTORE=yes
SUPPORT_MBX=yes

LOOKUP_DBM=yes                          # Database lookup methods to include
LOOKUP_LSEARCH=yes                      # Linear search lookup
LOOKUP_DNSDB=yes                        # Allow almost arbitrary DNS lookups
LOOKUP_CDB=yes                          # Dan Bernstein's constant DB lookups
USE_DB=yes                              # Use Berkeley DB (from README)
DBMLIB=-ldb                             # (from README)
WITH_CONTENT_SCAN=yes                   # Include content scanning via ACLs

EXPERIMENTAL_SPF=yes                    # Include SPF support, needs libspf2
CFLAGS  += -I/usr/local/include         # From www.libspf2.org
LDFLAGS += -lspf2

LOG_FILE_PATH=/var/log/exim_%slog       # Log files: file, syslog, or both
LOG_FILE_PATH=syslog
LOG_FILE_PATH=syslog:/var/log/exim_%slog
EXICYCLOG_MAX=10                        # Compress/cycle log files, keep 10
```

Routers and transports must be compiled into the code if you intend to use them. In these days of large memories, you might as well leave them all in. Some default paths are certainly nonstandard: for example, the binary in **/usr/exim/bin** and the PID file in **/var/spool/exim**. You might want to tweak these values to match your other installed software.

About ten database lookup methods are available, including MySQL, Oracle, CDB,[17] and LDAP. If you include LDAP, you must specify the LDAP_LIB_TYPE variable to tell Exim what LDAP library you are using (the options are Netscape, Solaris, and a couple of versions of OpenLDAP). You may also need to specify the path to LDAP include files and libraries.

17. CDB is Dan Bernstein's constant database system; it scales well.

The **EDITME** file does a good job of telling you about any dependencies your database choices may require. Any entries above that have "(from README)" in their comment line were not listed in **src/EDITME** but rather in the **README**.

EDITME has many additional security options that you might want to include, such as support for SMTP AUTH, TLS, SASL, PAM, and options for controlling file ownerships and permissions. You can disable certain Exim options at compile time to limit the damage a hacker might cause if the software is compromised.

It's advisable to read the entire **EDITME** file before you complete the installation. It will give you a good feel for what you can control at run time through the configuration file. The top-level **README** file has lots of detail about OS-specific quirks that you may need to add to the **EDITME** file as well.

Once you have modified **EDITME** and installed it as **Local/Makefile**, run **make** at the top of the distribution tree followed by **sudo make install**. The next step is to test your shiny new **exim** binary and see if it delivers mail as expected. The **doc/spec.txt** file contains good testing documentation.

Once you are satisfied that Exim is working properly, link **/usr/sbin/sendmail** to **exim** so that Exim can emulate the traditional command-line interface to the mail system used by many user agents. You must also arrange for **exim** to be started at boot time.

Exim startup

On a mail hub machine, **exim** typically starts at boot time in daemon mode and runs continuously, listening on port 25 and accepting messages through SMTP. See Chapter 3, *Booting and Shutting Down*, page 97, for startup details for your operating system.

Like **sendmail**, Exim can wear several hats, and if started with specific flags or alternative command names, it performs different functions. Exim's mode flags are similar to those understood by **sendmail** because **exim** works hard to maintain compatibility when called by user agents and other tools. Table 20.19 lists a few common flags.

Table 20.19 Common exim command-line flags

Flag	Meaning
-bd	Runs in daemon mode and listens for connections on port 25
-bf or **-bF**	Runs in user or system filter test mode
-bi	Rebuilds hashed aliases (same as **newaliases**)
-bp	Prints the mail queue (same as **mailq**)
-bt	Enters address test mode
-bV	Checks for syntax errors in the configuration file
-d+-*category*	Runs in debug mode, very flexible category-based configuration
-q	Starts a queue runner (same as **runq**)

Any errors in the config file that can be detected at parse time are caught by **exim -bV**, but some errors can only be caught at run time. Misplaced braces are a common mistake.

The **exim** man page gives lots of detail on all the nooks and crannies of **exim**'s command-line flags and options, including extensive debugging information.

Exim utilities

The Exim distribution includes a bunch of utilities to help you monitor, debug, and sanity-check your installation. Below is the current list along with a brief description of each. See the documentation from the distribution for more detail.

- **exiwhat** – lists what Exim processes are doing
- **exiqgrep** – searches the queue
- **exiqsumm** – summarizes the queue
- **exigrep** – searches the main log
- **exipick** – selects messages based on various criteria
- **exicyclog** – rotates log files
- **eximstats** – extracts statistics from the log
- **exim_checkaccess** – checks address acceptance from a given IP address
- **exim_dbmbuild** – builds a DBM file
- **exinext** – extracts retry information
- **exim_dumpdb** – dumps a hints database
- **exim_tidydb** – cleans up a hints database
- **exim_fixdb** – patches a hints database
- **exim_lock** – locks a mailbox file
- **exilog** – visualizes log files across multiple servers

Another utility that is part of the Exim suite is **eximon**, an X Windows application that displays Exim's state, the state of Exim's queue, and the tail of the log file. Like the main distribution, you build it by editing a well-commented **EDITME** file in the **exim_monitor** directory and running **make**. However, in the case of **eximon** the defaults are usually fine, so you should not have to do much configuration to build the application. Some configuration and queue management can be done from the **eximon** GUI as well.

Exim configuration language

The Exim configuration language (or more accurately, languages: one for filters, one for regular expressions, etc.) feels a bit like the ancient (1970s) language Forth.[18] When first reading an Exim configuration, you might find it hard to distinguish between keywords and option names that are fixed by Exim and variable names that sysadmins define with configuration statements. We have tried to preface all variable names with `my_` to help with this issue.

18. For CS wizards, it's Turing-complete; mere mortals can substitute "powerful and complicated."

Although Exim is advertised as being easy to configure and is extensively documented, there is quite a learning curve for new users. The section "How Exim receives and delivers mail" in the specification document is essential reading for newcomers. It gives a good feel for the underlying concepts of the system.

When assigned a value, the Exim language's predefined options sometimes cause an action to occur. There are also about 120 predefined variables whose values may change as a result of one of the actions. These variables can be included in conditional statements.

The language for evaluating if statements and the like may remind you of the reverse Polish notation used during the heyday of Hewlett-Packard calculators. Let's look at a simple example. In the line

```
acl_smtp_rcpt = ${if ={25}{$interface_port} \
        {acl_check_rcpt} {acl_check_rcpt_submit} }
```

the acl_smtp_rcpt option, when set, causes an ACL to be implemented for each recipient (SMTP RCPT command) in the SMTP exchange. The value assigned to this option is either acl_check_rcpt or acl_check_rcpt_submit, depending on whether or not the Exim variable $interface_port has value 25.

We do not detail the Exim configuration language further, but refer you to its extensive documentation. In particular, pay close attention to the string expansion section of the Exim specification.

Exim configuration file

Exim's run-time behavior is controlled by a single configuration file, usually called **/usr/exim/configure**. Its name is one of the required variables specified in the **EDITME** file and compiled into the binary.

The supplied default configuration file, **src/configure.default**, is well commented and a good starting place for sites just getting set up with Exim. In fact, we recommend that you don't stray far from it until you really understand the Exim paradigm and need to elaborate on the default configuration for a specific purpose. Exim works hard to support common situations and has sensible defaults.

It is also helpful to stick with the variable names used in the default config file because they are assumed by the folks on the exim-users mailing list who will be answering your configuration questions.

exim prints a message to stderr and exits if you have a syntax error in your configuration file. It doesn't catch all syntax errors immediately, however, because it does not expand variables until it needs to.

The order of entries in the configuration file is not quite arbitrary: the global configuration options section must be first and must exist. All other sections are optional and can appear in any order.

Possible sections include

- Global configuration options (mandatory)
- acl – access control lists that filter addresses and messages
- authenticators – for SMTP AUTH or TLS authentication
- routers – ordered sequence to determine where a message should go
- transports – definitions of the drivers that do the actual delivery
- retry – policy settings for dealing with problem messages
- rewrite – global address rewriting rules
- local_scan – a hook for fancy flexibility

Each section except the first starts with a begin *section-name* statement—for example, begin acl. There is no end *section-name* statement; the end is signaled by the next section's begin statement. Indentation to show subordination makes the config file easier to read for humans, but it is not meaningful to Exim.

Some configuration statements name objects that will later be used to control the flow of messages. Those names must begin with a letter and contain only letters, numbers, and the underscore character. If the first non-whitespace character on a line is #, the rest of the line is treated as a comment. Note that this means you cannot put a comment on the same line as a statement; it will not be recognized as a comment because the first character is not #.

Exim lets you include files anywhere in the configuration file. Two forms of include are used:

```
.include absolute-path
.include_if_exists absolute-path
```

The first form generates an error if the file does not exist. Although include files keep your config file tidy, they are read several times during the life of a message, so it might be best to just include their contents directly into your configuration.

Global options

Lots of stuff is specified in the global options section, including operating parameters (limits, sizes, timeouts, properties of the mail server on this host), list definitions (local hosts, local hosts to relay for, remote domains to relay for), and macros (hostname, contact, location, error messages, SMTP banner).

Options

Options are set with the basic syntax

```
option_name = value[s]
```

where the *values* can be Booleans, strings, integers, decimal numbers, or time intervals. Multivalued options are allowed, in which case the various values are separated by colons.

Using the colon as a value separator presents a problem when you express IPv6 addresses, which use colons as part of the address. You can escape the colons by doubling them, but the easiest and most readable fix is to redefine the separator character with the < character as you assign values to the option. For example, both of the following two lines set the value of the localhost_interfaces option, which contains the IPv4 and IPv6 localhost addresses:

```
local_interfaces = 127.0.0.1 : ::::1
local_interfaces = <; 127.0.0.1 ; ::1
```

The second form, in which the semicolon has been defined as the separator, is more readable and less fragile.

There are a zillion options—more than 500 in the options index of the documentation. And we said **sendmail** was complicated! Most options have sensible defaults, and all have descriptive names. It's handy to have a copy of the **doc/spec.txt** file from the distribution in your favorite text editor when you are researching a new option. We don't cover all the options, just the ones that occur in our example configuration bits.

Lists

Exim has four kinds of lists, introduced by the keywords hostlist, domainlist, addresslist, and localpartslist. Here are two examples using hostlist:

```
hostlist my_relay_list = 192.168.1.0/24 : myfriend.example.com
hostlist my_relay_list = /usr/local/exim/relay_hosts.txt
```

Members can be listed in-line or taken from a file. If in-line, they are separated by colons. There can be up to 16 named lists of each type. In the in-line example above, we included all machines on a local /24 network and a specific hostname.

The symbol @ can be a member of a list; it means the name of the local host and helps make it possible to write a single generic configuration file that works for most nonhub machines at your site. The notation @[] is also useful and means all IP addresses on which Exim is listening; that is, all the IP addresses of localhost.

To reference a list, just put + in front of its name to match members of the list or !+ to match nonmembers; for example, +my_relay_list. There must be no space between the + and the name of the list.

Lists can include references to other lists and the ! character to indicate negation. Lists that include references to variables (e.g., $variable_name) make processing slower because Exim cannot cache the results of evaluating the list, which it does by default.

Macros

You can use macros to define parameters, error messages, etc. The parsing is primitive, so you cannot define a macro whose name is a subset of another macro without unpredictable results.

The syntax is

MACRO_NAME = rest of the line

For example, the first of the following lines define a macro named ALIAS_QUERY that looks up a user's alias entry in a MySQL database. The second line shows the use of the macro to do an actual lookup, with the result being stored in the variable called data.

```
ALIAS_QUERY = \
    select mailbox from user where login = '${quote_mysql:$local_part}';
data = ${lookup mysql{ALIAS_QUERY}}
```

Macro names are not required to be all caps, but they must begin with a capital letter. However, the all-caps convention aids clarity. The configuration file can include ifdefs that evaluate a macro and use it to determine whether or not to include a portion of the config file. Every imaginable form of ifdef is supported; they all begin with a dot.

ACLs (access control lists)

Access control lists filter the addresses of incoming messages and either accept or deny them. Exim divides incoming addresses into a local part that represents the user and a domain part that is the recipient's domain.

ACLs can be applied at any of the various stages of an SMTP conversation: HELO, MAIL, RCPT, DATA, etc. Typically, an ACL enforces strict adherence to the SMTP protocol at the HELO stage, checks the sender and the sender's domain at the MAIL stage, checks the recipients at the RCPT stage, and scans the message content at the DATA stage.

A slew of options named acl_smtp_*command* specify which ACL should be applied after each *command* in the SMTP protocol. For example, the acl_smtp_rcpt option specifies the ACL to run on each address that is a recipient of the message. You can define ACLs in the acl section of the config file, in a file that is referenced by the acl_smtp_*command* option, or in-line when the option is defined.

A sample ACL called my_acl_check_rcpt is defined below. We would invoke it by assigning its name to the acl_smtp_rcpt option in the global options section of the config file. If this ACL denies an address at the RCPT command, the sending server should give up and not try the address again. Another common ACL to use is acl_smtp_data, which would run on the message after it has been received, for example, to scan content.

```
begin acl
    my_acl_check_rcpt:
        accept  hosts = :
                control = dkim_disable_verify

        deny    message = Restricted characters in address
                domains = +local_domains
                local_parts = ^[.] : ^.*[@%!/|]
```

```
deny      message = Restricted characters in address
          domains = !+local_domains
          local_parts = ^[./|] : ^.*[@%!] : ^.*/\\.\\./

accept    local_parts = postmaster
          domains = +local_domains

require   verify = sender

accept    hosts = +relay_from_hosts
          control = submission
          control = dkim_disable_verify

accept    authenticated = *
          control = submission
          control = dkim_disable_verify

require   message = Relay not permitted
          domains = +local_domains : +relay_to_domains

require   verify = recipient
accept
```

This ACL, adapted from examples in the Exim documentation, ends with a default accept; you might want to rethink your ACLs to deny by default, as firewalls typically do. The default name for this access control list is acl_check_rcpt; you probably should not change its name (as we did, to emphasize that the name is something you specify, not a predefined Exim configuration option).

The first accept line, containing just a colon, is an empty list. The empty list of remote hosts matches cases in which a local MUA submitted a message on the MTA's standard input. If the address being tested meets this condition, the ACL accepts the address and disables DKIM signature validation, which is turned on by default. If the address does not match this address clause, control drops through to the next clause in the ACL definition.

The first deny stanza is intended for messages coming into your local domains. It rejects any address whose local part (the username) starts with a dot or contains the special characters @, %, !, /, or |. The second deny applies to messages being sent out by your users. It, too, disallows certain special characters and sequences in the local parts of addresses, in case your users' machines have been infected with a virus or other malware. In the past, such addresses have been used by spammers to confuse ACLs or have been guilty of creating security problems.

In general, if you are intending to use $local_parts (supposedly, the recipient's username) in a directory path (to store mail or look for a vacation file, for example) be very careful that your ACLs have filtered out any special characters that could cause unwanted behavior. (This example looks for the sequence /../, which could be problematic if the username is inserted into a path.)

The next accept stanza guarantees that mail to postmaster will always get through if it's sent to a local domain; this can help with debugging.

The require line checks to see if a bounce message can be returned, but it checks only the sender's domain.[19] If the sender's username is forged, a bounce message could still fail (that is, the bounce itself could bounce). You can add more extensive checking here by calling another program, but some sites consider such callouts abusive and might add your mail server to a blacklist or bad-reputation list.

The next accept stanza checks for hosts that are allowed to relay through this host, namely, local hosts that are submitting mail into the system. The control line specifies that **exim** should act as a mail submission agent and fix up any header deficiencies as the message arrives from the user agent. The recipient's address is not checked because many user agents get confused by error returns. (This is appropriate only for local machines relaying to a smart host, not for external domains that you might be willing to relay for.) DKIM verification is disabled because these messages are outbound from your users or relay friends.

The last accept stanza deals with local hosts that authenticate through SMTP AUTH. Once again, these messages are treated as submissions from user agents.

We next check the destination domain to which the message is headed and require that it be either in our list of local_domains or in our list of domains to which we allow relaying, relay_to_domains. (These domain lists are defined elsewhere.) Any destinations not in one of those lists are refused with the specified error message.

Finally, given that all previous requirements have been met but that no more-specific accept or deny rule has been triggered, we verify the recipient and accept the message. Most Internet messages to local users will fall into this category.

We haven't included any blacklist scanning in the example above. To access a blacklist, use one of the examples in the default config file or something like this:

```
deny    condition = ${if isip4{$sender_host_address}}
        !authenticated = *
        !hosts = +my_whitelist_ips
        !dnslists = list.dnswl.org
        domains = +local_domains
        verify = recipient
        message = You are on RBL $dnslist_domain: $dnslist_text
        dnslists = zen.spamhaus.org
        logwrite = Blacklisted sender [$sender_host_address] \
              $dnslist_domain: $dnslist_text
```

Translated to English, this code specifies that if a message matches *all* of the following criteria, it is rejected with a custom error message and logged (also with a custom message).

19. require means "deny if not matched."

- It's from an IPv4 address (some lists don't handle IPv6 correctly).
- It's not associated with an authenticated SMTP session.
- It's from a sender not in the local whitelist.
- It's from a sender not in the global (Internet) whitelist.
- It's addressed to a valid local recipient.
- The sending host is on the zen.spamhaus.org blacklist.

The variables dnslist_text and dnslist_domain are set by the assignment to dnslists, which triggers the blacklist lookup. This deny clause could be placed right after your checks for unusual characters in addresses.

Here's another example ACL that rejects mail if the remote side does not say HELO properly:

```
acl_check_mail:
    deny  message = 503 Bad sequence of cmds - must send HELO/EHLO first
          condition = ${if !def:sender_helo_name}
    accept
```

Exim solves the early talker problem (a more specific case of "not saying HELO properly") with the smtp_enforce_sync option, which is turned on by default.

Content scanning at ACL time

Exim supports powerful content scanning at several points in a message's traversal of the mail system: at ACL time (after the SMTP DATA command), at delivery time through the transport_filter option, or with a local_scan function after all ACL checks have been completed. You must compile support for content scanning into Exim by setting the WITH_CONTENT_SCAN variable in the **EDITME** file; it is commented out by default. This option endows ACLs with extra power and flexibility and adds two new configuration options: spamd_address and av_scanner.

Scanning at ACL time allows a message to be rejected in-line with the MTA's conversation with the sending host. The message is never accepted for delivery, so it need not be bounced. This way of rejecting the message is nice because it avoids backscatter spam caused by bounce messages to forged sender addresses.

Scanning for viruses

To scan for viruses, first assign your scanner type and its parameters to the av_scanner variable in the global options section of the config file. Table 20.20 lists the scanners understood by the current version of Exim and their corresponding av_scanner specifications.

Once you've set av_scanner, you can use the malware condition in the ACL that checks things after the DATA command in the SMTP conversation. Here is an example from the Exim documentation:

```
deny  message = This message contains malware ($malware_name)
      demime = *
      malware = *
```

Table 20.20 Antivirus scanners known to Exim

Scanner specification	Daemon or service
aveserver:*path-to-socket*	Kaspersky scanner daemon version 5
clamd:*ip-address port* or *path-to-socket*	ClamAV through TCP or local socket
cmdline:*path found-regex name-regex*	Generic command-line interface
drweb:*ip-address port* or *path-to-socket*	DrWeb daemon scanner (sald.com)
fsecure:*path-to-.fsav-file*	F-Secure daemon scanner (f-secure.com)
kavdaemon:*path-to-socket*	Kaspersky scanner daemon version 4
sophie:*path-to-socket*	Sophie interface to Sophos[a]

a. See clanfield.info/sophie. This scanner is the default (with path **/var/run/sophie**).

The malware clause calls the virus scanner if the value passed to it is true (which is always the case in this example). If you turn on demime and a message contains a MIME-encoded attachment, **exim** will de-MIME it for the antivirus scanner. Most scanners can do this decoding for themselves, however. To avoid having both **exim** and the scanner try to perform this task, include the demime clause only if the virus scanner needs it. Duplication won't cause errors, but it wastes resources and slows mail processing.

Scanning for spam

Exim uses SpamAssassin for spam scanning. SpamAssassin usually accepts messages on TCP port 783, but it can also use a local domain socket. Set the connection parameters in **exim**'s config file by assigning a value to the spamd_address variable. It accepts either an IP address and port separated by a space, or the absolute path to a local domain socket. You can specify multiple address/port pairs—up to 32 of them—to use multiple copies of SpamAssassin.

From the ACL associated with the SMTP DATA command, call SpamAssassin by assigning a username to the spam variable. If you specify nobody as the user, SpamAssassin uses a generic scanning profile; otherwise, it uses the profile associated with the user you specify (if such a profile exists).[20] These lines

```
deny  message = This message was classified as spam
      spam = nobody
```

would use the system-wide default spam profile. Just putting a spam statement in the config file doesn't work; you must assign a value.

Since SpamAssassin scanning is slow and most spam messages are short, you might do a size check and only scan small messages. For example:

```
deny  message = This message was classified as spam
      condition = ${if < {$message_size}{10K}}
      spam = nobody
```

20. At first glance, the fact that you get to specify a username seems flexible and nice. But because the scanning is done after the DATA command instead of at the RCPT command, the message has already qualified its recipients, and if there are several recipients, whose spam profile should you use?

There are much fancier things you can do with SpamAssassin scanning; refer to the Exim specification for all the details.

Authenticators

Authenticators are drivers that interact with the SMTP AUTH command's challenge/response sequence and identify an authentication mechanism acceptable to both client and server. Exim supports four mechanisms:

- AUTH_CRAM_MD5 (RFC2195)
- AUTH_CYRUS_SASL for use with the Cyrus IMAP software
- AUTH_PLAINTEXT, which includes both PLAIN and LOGIN
- AUTH_SPA, which supports Microsoft's Secure Password Authentication

If **exim** is receiving email, it is acting as an SMTP AUTH server. If it is sending mail, it is a client. Options that appear in the definitions of authenticator instances are tagged with a prefix of either server_ or client_ to allow for different configurations depending on the role Exim is playing.

Authenticators are used in access control lists, as in the following clause in the ACL example on page 817:

```
accept authenticated = *
```

Below is an example that shows both the client-side and server-side LOGIN mechanisms. This simple example uses a fixed username and password, which is OK for small sites but probably inadvisable for larger installations.

```
begin authenticators

    my_client_fixed_login:
        driver = plaintext
        public_name = LOGIN
        client_send = : myusername : mypasswd

    my_server_fixed_login:
        driver = plaintext
        public_name = LOGIN
        server_advertise_condition = ${if def:tis_cipher}
        server_prompts = User Name : Password
        server_condition = ${if and {{eq{$auth1}{username}} \
            {eq{$auth2}{mypasswd}}}}
        server_set_id = $auth1
```

Authentication data can come from many sources: LDAP, PAM, **/etc/passwd**, etc. The server_advertise_condition clause above prevents mail clients from sending passwords in the clear by requiring TLS security (through STARTTLS or SSL) on connection. If you want the same behavior when **exim** acts as the client system, use the client_condition option in the client clause, too, again with tis_cipher.

Refer to the documentation for details of all the possible Exim authentication options and for examples.

Routers

Routers work on recipient email addresses, either by rewriting them or by assigning them to a transport and sending them on their way. A particular router can have multiple instances, each with different options.

You specify a sequence of routers. A message starts with the first router and progresses through the list until the message is either accepted or rejected. The accepting router typically hands the message to a transport driver. Routers handle both incoming and outgoing messages. They feel a bit like subroutines in a programming language.

A router can return any of the following dispositions for a message:

- accept – the router accepts the address and hands it to a transport driver
- pass – this router can't handle the address; go on to the next router
- decline – router chooses not to handle the address; next router, please!
- fail – the address is invalid; router queues it for a bounce message
- defer – leaves the message in the queue for later
- error – there is an error in the router specification; message is deferred

If a message receives a pass or decline from all the routers in the sequence, it is unroutable. Exim bounces or rejects such messages, depending on the context.

If a message meets the preconditions for a router and the router ends with a no_more statement, then that message will not be presented to any additional routers, regardless of its disposition by the current router. For example, if your remote SMTP router has the precondition domains = !+local_domains and has no_more set, then only messages to local users (that is, those that would fail the domains precondition) will continue to the next router in the sequence.

Routers have many possible options; some common examples are preconditions, acceptance or failure conditions, error messages to return, and transport drivers to use.

The next few sections detail the routers called accept, dnslookup, manualroute, and redirect. The example configuration snippets assume that **exim** is running on a local machine in the example.com domain. They're all pretty straightforward; refer to the documentation if you want to use some of the fancier routers.

The accept router

The accept router labels an address as OK and passes the associated message to a transport driver. Below are examples of accept router instances called localusers for delivering local mail and save_to_file for appending to an archive.

```
localusers:
    driver = accept
    domains = example.com
    check_local_user
    transport = my_local_delivery
```

```
save_to_file:
      driver = accept
      domains = dialup.example.com
      transport = batchsmtp_appendfile
```

The localusers router instance checks that the domain part of the destination address is example.com and that the local part of the address is the login name of a local user. If both conditions are met, the router hands the message to the transport driver instance called my_local_delivery, which is defined in the transports section. The save_to_file instance is designed for dial-up users; it appends the message to a file specified in the batchsmtp_appendfile transport definition.

The dnslookup router

The dnslookup router is typically used for outgoing messages. It looks up the MX record of the recipient's domain and hands the message to an SMTP transport driver for delivery. Here is an instance called remoteusers:

```
remoteusers:
      driver = dnslookup
      domains = !+example.com
      transport = my_remote_delivery
```

See page 462 for more information about RFC1918 private address spaces.

The dnslookup code looks up the MX records for the addressee. If there are none, it tries the A record. A common extension to this router instance is to prohibit delivery to certain IP addresses; a prime example is the RFC1918 private addresses that cannot be routed on the Internet. See the ignore_target_hosts option for more information.

The manualroute router

The flexible manualroute driver can pretty much route email in whatever way you want. The routing information can be a table of rules matching by recipient domain (route_list) or a single rule that applies to all domains (route_data).

Below are two examples of manualroute instances. The first example implements the "smart host" concept, in which all outgoing nonlocal mail is sent to a central ("smart") host for processing. This instance is called smarthost and applies to all recipients' domains that are not (the ! character) in the local_domains list.

```
smarthost:
      driver = manualroute
      domains = !+local_domains
      transport = remote_snmp
      route_data = smarthost.example.com
```

The router instance below, firewall, uses SMTP to send incoming messages to hosts inside the firewall (perhaps after scanning them for spam and viruses). It looks up the routing data for each recipient domain in a CDB database that contains the names of local hosts. (You must build Exim with the LOOKUP_CDB option to be able to use CDB.)

```
firewall:
    driver = manualroute
    transport = remote-smtp
    route_data = ${lookup{$domain} cdb {/internal/host/routes}}
```

The redirect router

The redirect driver does address rewriting, such as that called for in the system-wide **aliases** file or in a user's **~/.forward** file. It usually does not assign the rewritten address to a transport; that task is left to other routers in the chain.

The first instance shown below, system_aliases, looks up aliases with a linear search (lsearch) of the **/etc/aliases** file. That's fine for a small **aliases** file, but if yours is huge, replace that linear search with a database lookup. The second instance, forwardfile, first verifies that mail is addressed to a local user, then checks that user's **.forward** file.

```
system_aliases:
    driver = redirect
    data = ${lookup{$local_part} lsearch {/etc/aliases}}

user_forward:
    driver = redirect
    check_local_user
    file = $home/.forward
    no_verify
```

The check_local_user option ensures that the recipient is a valid local user. The no_verify says not to verify that the address to which the forward file redirects the message is valid; just ship it.

Per-user filtering via .forward files

Exim allows not only forwarding through **.forward** files, but also filtering based on the contents of a user's **.forward** file. It supports its own filtering as well as the Sieve filtering that is being standardized by the IETF. If the first line of a user's **.forward** file is

```
#Exim filter
```

or

```
#Sieve filter
```

then the subsequent filtering commands (there are about 15 of them) can be used to determine where the message should be delivered. Filtering does not actually deliver messages—it just meddles with the destination. For example:

```
#Exim filter
if   $header_subject: contains SAGE or $header_subject: contains sysadmin
then
    save $home/mail/sage-sysadmin
endif
```

Electronic Mail

Lots of options are available that control what users can and cannot do in their **.forward** files. The option names begin with forbid_ or allow_. They're important to prevent users from running shells, loading libraries into binaries, or using the embedded Perl interpreter when they shouldn't. Check for new forbid_* options when you upgrade to be sure your users can't get too fancy in their **.forward** files.

Transports

Routers decide where messages should go, and transports actually take them there. Local transports typically append to a file, pipe to a local program, or speak the LMTP protocol to IMAP servers. Remote transports speak SMTP to their counterparts across the Internet.

There are five Exim transports: appendfile, lmtp, smtp, autoreply, and pipe; we detail appendfile and smtp. The autoreply transport is typically used to send vacation messages, and the pipe transport hands messages as input to a command through a UNIX pipe. As with routers, you must define instances of transports, and it's fine to have multiple instances of the same type of transport. Order is significant for routers, but not for transports.

The appendfile transport

The appendfile driver stores messages in **mbox**, **mbx**, **Maildir**, or **mailstore** format in a specified file or directory. You must have included the appropriate mailbox formats when you compiled Exim; they are commented out of the **EDITME** file by default. The following example defines the my_local_delivery transport (an instance of the appendfile transport) referred to in the localusers router instance definition on page 821.

```
my_local_delivery:
    driver = appendfile
    file = /var/mail/$local_part
    delivery_date_add
    envelope_to_add
    return_path_add
    group = mail
    mode = 0660
```

The various *_add lines add headers to the message. The group and mode clauses ensure that the transport agent can write to the file.

The smtp transport

The smtp transport is the workhorse of any mail system. Here, we define two instances, one for the standard SMTP port (25) and one for the mail submission port (587).

```
my_remote_delivery:
    driver = smtp

my_remote_delivery_port587:
    driver = smtp
    port = 587
    headers_add = X-processed-by: MACRO_HEADER port 587
```

The second instance, my_remote_delivery_port587, specifies the port and also a header to be added to the message that includes an indication of the outgoing port. MACRO_HEADER would be defined elsewhere in the configuration file.

Retry configuration

The retry section of the configuration file must exist or Exim will never attempt redelivery of messages that could not be delivered on the first attempt. You can specify three time intervals, each less frequent than the previous one. After the last interval has expired, messages bounce back to the sender as undeliverable. retry statements understand the suffixes m, h, d, and w to indicate minutes, hours, days, and weeks. You can specify different intervals for different hosts or domains.

Here's what a retry section looks like:

```
begin retry
        *       *       F, 2h, 15m;    F, 24h, 1h;     F, 4d, 6h
```

This example means, "For any domain, an address that fails temporarily should be retried every 15 minutes for 2 hours, then every hour for the next 24 hours, then every 6 hours for 4 days, and finally, bounced as undeliverable."

Rewriting configuration

The rewriting section of the configuration file starts with begin rewrite. It's used to fix up addresses, not to reroute messages. For example, you could use it on your outgoing addresses

- To make mail appear to be from your domain, not from individual hosts
- To map usernames to a standard format such as First.Last

Rewriting should not be used on addresses in incoming mail.

Local scan function

If you want to further customize **exim**, for example, to filter for the latest and greatest virus, you can write a C function to do your scanning and install it in the local_scan section of the config file. Refer to the Exim documentation for details and examples that show how to do this.

amavisd and Exim connection

To configure **exim** to send all mail destined for your domain to **amavisd** for virus or spam scanning, make the first router in your config file something like this:

```
amavis:
    no_verify_recipient
    driver = manualroute
    condition = ${if or {eq {$interface_port} {10025} \
        {eq {$received_protocol} {scanned-ok} } } {0} {1} }
    domain = local_domains
    transport = amavis
    route_list = * localhost byname
    self = send
```

The condition line says not to forward messages originating from port 10,025 to **amavisd**. This is the port on which messages return from **amavisd** after scanning, so such messages cannot go back to **amavisd** without creating a loop. The amavis transport is configured as follows:

```
amavis:
    driver = smtp
    port = 10024
    allow_localhost
```

You must also add the line

```
local_interfaces = 0.0.0.0.25 : 127.0.0.1.10025
```

to the start of the configuration file where global options are set, to tell **exim** to accept messages from any address on port 25 and from localhost on port 10,025, the **amavisd** return port.

This configuration would cause all scanning to be done off-line, so the bounce messages generated in response to virus and spam detections might themselves become backscatter spam. Placing amavis later in the ordered list of routers and letting Exim's rich ACL language take care of the easiest and most lightweight message checks might be a better solution. Even better, use **exim**'s ${run...} construct to force **amavisd** checking to occur in-line. Overall, **exim**'s built-in scanning ability makes **amavisd** somewhat less compelling.

Logging

Exim by default writes three different log files: a main log, a reject log, and a panic log. Each log entry includes the time the message was written. You specify the location of the log files in the **EDITME** file (before building **exim**) or in the run-time config file in the value of the log_file_path option. By default, logs are kept in the **/var/spool/exim/log** directory.

The log_file_path option accepts up to two colon-separated values. Each value must be either the keyword syslog or an absolute path with a %s embedded where the names **main**, **reject**, and **panic** can be substituted. For example,

```
log_file_path = syslog : /var/log/exim_%s
```

would log both to syslog (with facility "mail") and to the files **exim_main**, **exim_reject**, and **exim_panic** in the **/var/log** directory. Exim submits the **main** log entries to syslog at priority info, the **reject** entries at priority notice, and the **panic** entries at priority alert.

The **main** log contains one line for the arrival and delivery of each message. It can be summarized by the Perl script **eximstats**, included in the Exim distribution.

The **reject** log records information on the messages that have been rejected for policy reasons: malware, spam, etc. It includes the summary line for the message from the **main** log and also the original headers of the message that was rejected. If you change your policies, check the **reject** log to make sure that all is still well.

The **panic** log is for serious errors in the software; **exim** writes here just before it gives up. The **panic** log should not exist in the absence of problems. Ask **cron** to check it for you and if it exists, fix the problem that caused the panic and then delete the file. **exim** will recreate it when the next panic-worthy situation arises.

When debugging, you can increase the amount and type of data logged with the log_selector option. For example:

```
log_selector = +smtp_connection +snmp_incomplete_transaction +...
```

The logging categories that can be included or excluded by the log_selector mechanism are listed in the Exim specification, in the section called "Log files" toward the end. There are about 35 possibilities, including +all, which will really fill your disks!

exim also keeps a temporary log for each message it handles. It is named with the message ID and lives in **/var/spool/exim/msglog**. If you are having trouble with a particular destination, you should check there.

Debugging

Exim has powerful debugging aids. You can configure the amount of information you want to see about each potential debugging topic. **exim -d** tells **exim** to go into debugging mode, in which it stays in the foreground and does not detach from the terminal. You can add specific debugging categories to **-d** with a + or - in front of them to verbosify or eliminate a category. For example, **-d+expand+acl** requests regular debugging output plus extra details regarding string expansions and ACL interpretation. (These two categories are common problem spots.) You can tune more than 30 categories of debugging information; see the man page for a list.

A common technique when debugging mail systems is to start the MTA on a non-standard port and then talk to it through **telnet**. For example, to start **exim** in daemon mode, listening on port 26, with debugging info turned on, use

```
$ sudo exim -d -oX 26 -bd
```

You can then **telnet** to port 26 and type SMTP commands in an attempt to reproduce the problem you are debugging.

Alternatively, you can have **swaks** do your SMTP talking for you. It's a Perl script that makes SMTP debugging faster and easier. **swaks --help** gets you some documentation, and jetmore.org/john/code/#swaks supplies complete details.

If your log files show timeouts of around 30 seconds, that's suggestive of a DNS issue. Timeouts of 5 seconds are more likely to be **identd** query timeouts. (**identd** was a daemon intended to identify the actual sender of a mail message, but since it's so easily fooled, no one uses it anymore.)

20.15 Postfix

Postfix is another popular alternative to **sendmail**. Wietse Venema started the Postfix project when he spent a sabbatical year at IBM's T. J. Watson Research Center in 1996, and he is still actively developing it. Postfix's design goals included not only security (first and foremost!), but also an open source distribution policy, speedy performance, robustness, and flexibility. All major Linux distributions include Postfix, and since version 10.3, Mac OS X has shipped Postfix instead of **sendmail** as the default mail system.

See page 48 for more information about regular expressions.

The most important things to know about Postfix are, first, that it works almost out of the box (the simplest config files are only a line or two long), and second, that it leverages regular expression maps to filter email effectively, especially in conjunction with the PCRE (Perl Compatible Regular Expression) library. Postfix is compatible with **sendmail** in the sense that Postfix's **aliases** and **.forward** files have the same format and semantics as those of **sendmail**.

Postfix speaks ESMTP. Virtual domains and spam filtering are both supported. For address rewriting, Postfix relies on table lookups from flat files, Berkeley DB, DBM, LDAP, NIS, NetInfo, or SQL databases. Postfix also supports **sendmail**'s milter protocol, so you can easily customize its behavior with a multitude of publicly available milters (external programs that take over specific tasks during an SMTP session; see page 767).

Postfix architecture

Postfix is composed of several small, cooperating programs that send network messages, receive messages, deliver email locally, etc. Communication among them is performed through local domain sockets or FIFOs. This architecture is quite different from that of **sendmail** and Exim, wherein a single large program does most of the work.

The **master** program starts and monitors all Postfix processes. Its configuration file, **master.cf**, lists the subsidiary programs along with information about how they should be started. The default values set in that file cover most needs; in general, no tweaking is necessary. One common change is to comment out a program, for example, **smtpd**, when a client should not listen on the SMTP port.

The most important server programs involved in the delivery of email are shown in Exhibit D.

Exhibit D Postfix server programs

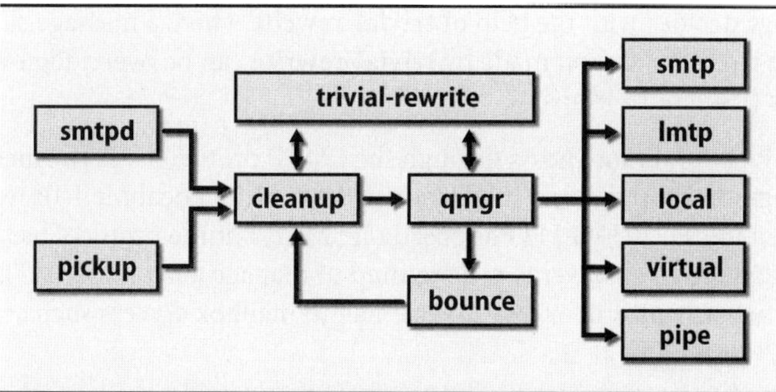

Receiving mail

smtpd receives mail entering the system through SMTP. It also verifies that the connecting clients are authorized to send the mail they are trying to deliver. When email is sent locally through the **/usr/lib/sendmail** compatibility program, a file is written to the **/var/spool/postfix/maildrop** directory. That directory is periodically scanned by the **pickup** program, which processes any new files it finds.

All incoming email passes through **cleanup**, which adds missing headers and rewrites addresses according to the canonical and virtual maps. Before inserting it in the incoming queue, **cleanup** gives the email to **trivial-rewrite**, which does minor fixing of the addresses, such as appending a mail domain to addresses that are not fully qualified.

Managing mail-waiting queues

qmgr manages five queues that contain mail waiting to be delivered:

- incoming – mail that is arriving
- active – mail that is being delivered
- deferred – mail for which delivery has failed in the past
- hold – mail blocked in the queue by the administrator
- corrupt – mail that can't be read or parsed

The queue manager generally selects the next message to process with a simple FIFO strategy, but it also supports a a complex preemption algorithm that prefers messages with few recipients over bulk mail.

In order not to overwhelm a receiving host, especially after it has been down, Postfix uses a slow-start algorithm to control how fast it tries to deliver email. Deferred messages are given a try-again time stamp that exponentially backs off so as not to waste resources on undeliverable messages. A status cache of unreachable destinations avoids unnecessary delivery attempts.

Sending mail

qmgr decides with the help of **trivial-rewrite** where a message should be sent. The routing decision made by **trivial-rewrite** can be overridden with lookup tables (transport_maps).

Delivery to remote hosts through the SMTP protocol is performed by the **smtp** program. **lmtp** delivers mail by using LMTP, the Local Mail Transfer Protocol defined in RFC2033. LMTP is based on SMTP, but the protocol has been modified so that the mail server is not required to manage a mail queue. This mailer is particularly useful for delivering email to mailbox servers such as the Cyrus IMAP suite.

local's job is to deliver email locally. It resolves addresses in the **aliases** table and follows instructions found in recipients' **.forward** files. Messages are forwarded to another address, passed to an external program for processing, or stored in users' mail folders.

The **virtual** program delivers email to "virtual mailboxes"; that is, mailboxes that are not related to a local Linux account but that still represent valid email destinations. Finally, **pipe** implements delivery through external programs.

Security

Postfix implements security at several levels. Most of the Postfix server programs can run in a **chroot**ed environment. They are separate programs with no parent/child relationship. None of them are setuid. The mail drop directory is group-writable by the postdrop group, to which the **postdrop** program is setgid.

Impressively, no remotely exploitable vulnerabilities have yet been identified in any version of Postfix.

Postfix commands and documentation

Several command-line utilities permit user interaction with the mail system:

- **sendmail**, **mailq**, **newaliases** – are **sendmail**-compatible replacements
- **postfix** – starts and stops the mail system (must be run as root)
- **postalias** – builds, modifies, and queries alias tables
- **postcat** – prints the contents of queue files
- **postconf** – displays and edits the main configuration file, **main.cf**
- **postmap** – builds, modifies, or queries lookup tables
- **postsuper** – manages the mail queues

The Postfix distribution includes a set of man pages that describe all the programs and their options. On-line documents at postfix.org explain how to configure and manage various aspects of Postfix. These documents are also included in the Postfix distribution in the **README_FILES** directory.

Postfix configuration

The **main.cf** file is Postfix's principal configuration file. The **master.cf** file configures the server programs. It also defines various lookup tables that are referenced from **main.cf** and that provide different types of service mappings.

The **postconf**(5) man page describes every parameter you can set in the **main.cf** file. There is also a **postconf** program, so if you just type **man postconf**, you'll get the man page for that instead of **postconf**(5). Use **man -s 5 postconf** to get the right version (**man 5 postconf** on HP-UX and AIX).

The Postfix configuration language looks a bit like a series of **sh** comments and assignment statements. Variables can be referenced in the definition of other variables by being prefixed with a $. Variable definitions are stored just as they appear in the config file; they are not expanded until they are used, and any substitutions occur at that time.

You can create new variables by assigning them values. Be careful to choose names that do not conflict with existing configuration variables.

All Postfix configuration files, including the lookup tables, consider lines starting with whitespace to be continuation lines. This convention results in very readable configuration files, but you must start new lines in column one.

What to put in main.cf

More than 500 parameters can be specified in the **main.cf** file. However, just a few of them need to be set at an average site. The author of Postfix strongly recommends that only parameters with nondefault values be included in your configuration. That way, if the default value of a parameter changes in the future, your configuration will automatically adopt the new value.

The sample **main.cf** file that comes with the distribution includes many commented-out example parameters, along with some brief documentation. The original version is best left alone as a reference. Start with an empty file for your own configuration so that your settings are not lost in a sea of comments.

Basic settings

Let's start with as simple a configuration as possible: an empty file. Surprisingly, this is a perfectly reasonable Postfix configuration. It results in a mail server that delivers email locally within the same domain as the local hostname and that sends any messages directed to nonlocal addresses directly to the appropriate remote servers.

Another simple configuration is a "null client"; that is, a system that doesn't deliver any email locally but rather forwards outbound mail to a designated central server. To implement this configuration, we define several parameters, starting with mydomain, which defines the domain part of the hostname, and myorigin, which is the mail domain appended to unqualified email addresses. If these two parameters are the same, we can write something like this:

```
mydomain = cs.colorado.edu
myorigin = $mydomain
```

Another parameter we should set is mydestination, which specifies the mail domains that are local. If the recipient address of a message has mydestination as its mail domain, the message is delivered through the **local** program to the corresponding user (assuming that no relevant alias or **.forward** file is found). If more than one mail domain is included in mydestination, these domains are all considered aliases for the same domain.

For a null client, we want no local delivery, so this parameter should be empty:

```
mydestination =
```

Finally, the relayhost parameter tells Postfix to send all nonlocal messages to a specified host instead of sending them directly to their apparent destinations:

```
relayhost = [mail.cs.colorado.edu]
```

The square brackets tell Postfix to treat the specified string as a hostname (DNS A record) instead of a mail domain name (DNS MX record).

Since null clients should not receive mail from other systems, the last thing to do in a null client configuration is to comment out the **smtpd** line in the **master.cf** file. This change prevents Postfix from running **smtpd** at all. With just these few lines, we've defined a fully functional null client!

For a "real" mail server, you'll need a few more configuration options as well as some mapping tables. We cover these in the next few sections.

Use of postconf

postconf is a handy tool that helps you configure Postfix. When run without arguments, it prints all the parameters as they are currently configured. If you name a specific parameter as an argument, **postconf** prints the value of that parameter. The **-d** option makes **postconf** print the defaults instead of the currently configured values. For example:

```
$ postconf mydestination
mydestination =
$ postconf -d mydestination
mydestination = $myhostname, localhost.$mydomain, localhost
```

Another useful option is **-n**, which makes **postconf** print only the parameters that differ from the default. If you ask for help on the Postfix mailing list, that's the configuration information you should put in your email.

Lookup tables

Many aspects of Postfix's behavior are shaped through the use of lookup tables, which can map keys to values or implement simple lists. For example, the default setting for the alias_maps table is

```
alias_maps = dbm:/etc/mail/aliases, nis:mail.aliases
```

Data sources are specified with the notation *type:path*. Note that this particular table actually uses two distinct sources of information simultaneously: a **dbm** database and an NIS map. Multiple values can be separated by commas, spaces, or both. Table 20.21 lists the available data sources; **postconf -m** shows this information as well.

Table 20.21 Information sources for Postfix lookup tables

Type	Description
dbm/sdbm	Traditional **dbm** or **gdbm** database file
cidr	Network addresses in CIDR form
hash/btree	Berkeley DB hash table or B-tree file (replaces **dbm**)
ldap	LDAP directory service
mysql	MySQL database
nis	NIS directory service
pcre	Perl-Compatible Regular Expressions
pgsql	PostgreSQL database
proxy	Access through **proxymap**, e.g., to escape a **chroot**
regexp	POSIX regular expressions
static	Returns the value specified as *path* regardless of the key
unix	The **/etc/passwd** and **/etc/group** files; uses NIS syntax[a]

a. unix:passwd.byname is the **passwd** file, and unix:group.byname is the **group** file.

Use the dbm and sdbm types only for compatibility with the traditional **sendmail** alias table. Berkeley DB (hash) is a more modern implementation; it's safer and faster. If compatibility is not a problem, use

```
alias_database = hash:/etc/mail/aliases
alias_maps = hash:/etc/mail/aliases
```

The alias_database specifies the table that is rebuilt by **newaliases** and should correspond to the table that you specify in alias_maps. The reason for having two parameters is that alias_maps might include non-DB sources such as mysql or nis that do not need to be rebuilt.

All DB-class tables (dbm, sdbm, hash, and btree) are based on a text file that is compiled to an efficiently searchable binary format. The syntax for these text files is similar to that of the configuration files with respect to comments and continuation lines. Entries are specified as simple key/value pairs separated by whitespace, except for alias tables, which use a colon after the key to retain **sendmail** compatibility. For example, the following lines are appropriate for an alias table:

```
postmaster:      david, tobias
webmaster:       evi
```

As another example, here's an access table for relaying mail from any client with a hostname ending in cs.colorado.edu.

```
.cs.colorado.edu   OK
```

Text files are compiled to their binary formats with the **postmap** command for normal tables and the **postalias** command for alias tables. The table specification (including the type) must be given as the first argument. For example:

```
$ sudo postmap hash:/etc/postfix/access
```

postmap can also query values in a lookup table (no match = no output):

```
$ postmap -q blabla hash:/etc/postfix/access
$ postmap -q .cs.colorado.edu hash:/etc/postfix/access
OK
```

Local delivery

The **local** program delivers mail to local recipients. It also handles local aliasing. For example, if mydestination is set to cs.colorado.edu and email arrives for evi@cs.colorado.edu, **local** first consults the alias_maps tables and then substitutes any matching entries recursively.

If no aliases match, **local** looks for a **.forward** file in user evi's home directory and follows the instructions in this file if it exists. (The syntax is the same as the right side of an alias map.) Finally, if no **.forward** file is found, the email is delivered to evi's local mailbox.

By default, **local** writes to standard **mbox**-format files under **/var/mail**. You can change that behavior with the parameters shown in Table 20.22.

Table 20.22 Parameters for local mailbox delivery (set in main.cf)

Parameter	Description
mail_spool_directory	Delivers mail to a central directory serving all users
home_mailbox	Delivers mail to ~*user* under the specified relative path
mailbox_command	Delivers mail with an external program, typically **procmail**
mailbox_transport	Delivers mail through a service as defined in **master.cf**[a]
recipient_delimiter	Allows extended usernames (see description below)

a. This option interfaces with mailbox servers such as the Cyrus **imapd**.

The mail_spool_directory and home_mailbox options normally generate **mbox**-format mailboxes, but they can also produce **Maildir** mailboxes. To request this behavior, add a slash to the end of the pathname.

If recipient_delimiter is +, mail addressed to evi+*whatever*@cs.colorado.edu is accepted for delivery to the evi account. With this facility, users can create special-purpose addresses and sort their mail by destination address. Postfix first attempts lookups on the full address, and only if that fails does it strip the extended components and fall back to the base address. Postfix also looks for a corresponding forwarding file, **.forward+***whatever*, for further aliasing.

Virtual domains

To host a mail domain on your Postfix mail server, you have three choices:

- List the domain in mydestination. Delivery is performed as described above: aliases are expanded and mail is delivered to the corresponding accounts.
- List the domain in the virtual_alias_domains parameter. This option gives the domain its own addressing namespace that is independent of the system's user accounts. All addresses within the domain must be resolvable (through mapping) to real addresses outside of it.
- List the domain in the virtual_mailbox_domains parameter. As with the virtual_alias_domains option, the domain has its own namespace. All mailboxes must live beneath a specified directory.

List the domain in only one of these three places. Choose carefully, because many configuration elements depend on that choice. We have already reviewed the handling of the mydestination method. The other options are discussed below.

Virtual alias domains

If a domain is listed as a value of the virtual_alias_domains parameter, mail to that domain is accepted by Postfix and must be forwarded to an actual recipient either on the local machine or elsewhere.

The forwarding for addresses in the virtual domain must be defined in a lookup table included in the virtual_alias_maps parameter. Entries in the table have the address in the virtual domain on the left side and the actual destination address on the right.

An unqualified name on the right is interpreted as a local username.

Consider the following example from **main.cf**:

```
myorigin = cs.colorado.edu
mydestination = cs.colorado.edu
virtual_alias_domains = admin.com
virtual_alias_maps = hash:/etc/mail/admin.com/virtual
```

In **/etc/mail/admin.com/virtual** we could then have the lines

```
postmaster@admin.com evi, david@admin.com
david@admin.com      david@schweikert.ch
evi@admin.com        evi
```

Mail for evi@admin.com would be redirected to evi@cs.colorado.edu (myorigin is appended) and would ultimately be delivered to the mailbox of user evi because cs.colorado.edu is included in mydestination.

Definitions can be recursive: the right hand side can contain addresses that are further defined on the left hand side. Note that the right hand side can only be a list of addresses. If you need to execute an external program or to use :include: files, then you need to redirect the email to an alias, which can then be expanded according to your needs.

To keep everything in one file, you can set virtual_alias_domains to the same lookup table as virtual_alias_maps and put a special entry in the table to mark it as a virtual alias domain. In **main.cf**:

```
virtual_alias_domains = $virtual_alias_maps
virtual_alias_maps = hash:/etc/mail/admin.com/virtual
```

In **/etc/mail/admin.com/virtual**:

```
admin.com            notused
postmaster@admin.com evi, david@admin.com
...
```

The right hand side of the entry for the mail domain (admin.com) is never actually used; admin.com's existence in the table as an independent entry is enough to make Postfix consider it a virtual alias domain.

Virtual mailbox domains

Domains listed under virtual_mailbox_domains are similar to local domains, but the list of users and their corresponding mailboxes must be managed independently of the system's user accounts.

The parameter virtual_mailbox_maps points to a table that lists all valid users in the domain. The map format is

```
user@domain        /path/to/mailbox
```

If the path ends with a slash, the mailboxes are stored in **Maildir** format. The value of virtual_mailbox_base is always prefixed to the specified paths.

You often want to alias some of the addresses in the virtual mailbox domain. Use a virtual_alias_map to do this. Here is a complete example. In **main.cf**:

```
virtual_mailbox_domains = admin.com
virtual_mailbox_base = /var/mail/virtual
virtual_mailbox_maps = hash:/etc/mail/admin.com/vmailboxes
virtual_alias_maps = hash:/etc/mail/admin.com/valiases
```

/etc/mail/admin.com/vmailboxes might contain entries like these:

```
evi@admin.com               nemeth/evi/
```

/etc/mail/admin.com/valiases might contain:

```
postmaster@admin.com evi@admin.com
```

You can use virtual alias maps even on addresses that are not virtual alias domains. Virtual alias maps let you redirect any address from any domain, independently of the type of the domain (canonical, virtual alias, or virtual mailbox). Since mailbox paths can only be put on the right hand side of the virtual mailbox map, use of this mechanism is the only way to set up aliases in that domain.

Access control

Mail servers should relay mail for third parties only on behalf of trusted clients. If a mail server forwards mail from unknown clients to other servers, it is a so-called open relay, which is bad. See *Relay control* on page 791 for more details.

Fortunately, Postfix doesn't act as an open relay by default. In fact, its defaults are quite restrictive; you are more likely to need to liberalize the permissions than to tighten them. Access control for SMTP transactions is configured in Postfix through "access restriction lists." The parameters shown in Table 20.23 control what should be checked during the different phases of an SMTP session.

Table 20.23 Postfix parameters for SMTP access restriction

Parameter	When applied
smtpd_client_restrictions	On connection request
smtpd_helo_restrictions	On HELO/EHLO command (start of the session)
smtpd_sender_restrictions	On MAIL FROM command (sender specification)
smtpd_recipient_restrictions	On RCPT TO command (recipient specification)
smtpd_data_restrictions	On DATA command (mail body)
smtpd_etrn_restrictions	On ETRN command[a]

a. This is a special command used for resending messages in the queue.

The most important parameter is smtpd_recipient_restrictions since access control is most easily performed when the recipient address is known and can be identified as being local or not. All the other parameters in Table 20.23 are empty in the default configuration. The default value is

```
smtpd_recipient_restrictions = permit_mynetworks, reject_unauth_destination
```

Each of the specified restrictions is tested in turn until a definitive decision about what to do with the mail is reached. Table 20.24 on the next page shows the common restrictions.

Table 20.24 Common Postfix access restrictions

Restriction	Function
check_client_access	Checks client host address by using a lookup table
check_recipient_access	Checks recipient mail address by using a lookup table
permit_mynetworks	Grants access to addresses listed in mynetworks
reject_unauth_destination	Rejects mail for nonlocal recipients; no relaying

Everything can be tested in these restrictions, not just specific information like the sender address in the smtpd_sender_restrictions. Therefore, for simplicity, you might want to put all the restrictions under a single parameter, which should be smtpd_recipient_restrictions since it is the only one that can test everything (except the DATA part).

smtpd_recipient_restriction is also where mail relaying is tested. You should keep the reject_unauth_destination restriction and carefully choose the "permit" restrictions before it.

Access tables

Each restriction returns one of the actions shown in Table 20.25. Access tables are used in restrictions such as check_client_access and check_recipient_access to select an action based on the client host address or recipient address, respectively.

Table 20.25 Actions for access tables

Action	Meaning
4*nn text*	Returns temporary error code 4*nn* and message *text*
5*nn text*	Returns permanent error code 5*nn* and message *text*
DEFER_IF_PERMIT	If restrictions result in PERMIT, changes it to a temp error
DEFER_IF_REJECT	If restrictions result in REJECT, changes it to a temp error
DISCARD	Accepts the message but silently discards it
DUNNO	Pretends the key was not found; tests further restrictions
FILTER *transport:dest*	Passes the mail through the filter *transport:dest*[a]
HOLD	Blocks the mail in the queue
OK	Accepts the mail
PREPEND *header*	Adds a header to the message
REDIRECT *addr*	Forwards this mail to a specified address
REJECT	Rejects the mail
WARN *message*	Enters the given warning *message* in the logs

a. See the section about spam and virus handling in Postfix starting on page 840.

As an example, suppose you wanted to allow relaying for all machines within the cs.colorado.edu domain and that you wanted to allow only trusted clients to post to the internal mailing list newsletter@cs.colorado.edu. You could implement these policies with the following lines in **main.cf**:

```
smtpd_recipient_restrictions =
          permit_mynetworks
          check_client_access hash:/etc/postfix/relaying_access
          reject_unauth_destination
          check_recipient_access hash:/etc/postfix/restricted_recipients
```

Note that commas are optional when the list of values for a parameter is specified.

In **/etc/postfix/relaying_access**:

```
.cs.colorado.edu    OK
```

In **/etc/postfix/restricted_recipients**:

```
newsletter@cs.colorado.edu   REJECT Internal list
```

The text after REJECT is an optional string that is sent to the client along with the error code. It tells the sender why the mail was rejected.

Authentication of clients and encryption

For users sending mail from home, it is usually easiest to route outgoing mail through the home ISP's mail server, regardless of the sender address that appears on that mail. Most ISPs trust their direct clients and allow relaying. If this configuration isn't possible or if you are using a system such as Sender ID or SPF, ensure that mobile users outside your network can be authorized to submit messages to your **smtpd**.

The solution to this problem is to use the SMTP AUTH mechanism to authenticate directly at the SMTP level. Postfix must be compiled with support for the SASL library to make this work. You can then configure the feature like this:

```
smtpd_sasl_auth_enable = yes
smtpd_recipient_restrictions =
          permit_mynetworks
          permit_sasl_authenticated
          ...
```

You also need to support encrypted connections to avoid sending passwords in clear text. Add lines like the following to **main.cf**:

```
smtpd_tls_security_level = may
smtpd_tls_auth_only = yes
smtpd_tls_loglevel = 1
smtpd_tls_received_header = yes
smtpd_tls_cert_file = /etc/certs/smtp.pem
smtpd_tls_key_file = $smtpd_tls_cert_file
smtpd_tls_protocols = !SSLv2
```

You will need to put a properly signed certificate in **/etc/certs/smtp.pem**. It's also a good idea to turn on encryption on outgoing SMTP connections:

```
smtp_tls_security_level = may
smtp_tls_loglevel = 1
```

Fighting spam and viruses

Postfix has many features that can help block suspicious email.

One class of protection features calls for strict implementation of the SMTP protocol. Legitimate mail servers should respect the protocol, but spam and virus senders often play fast and loose with it, thus giving themselves away. Unfortunately, broken mailers handling legitimate mail are still out there, so this technique isn't quite foolproof. Choose restrictions carefully, and monitor the log files.

Here are some of the main features in this category:

- reject_non_fqdn_* – rejects messages without a fully qualified sender domain (sender), recipient domain, (recipient) or HELO/EHLO hostname (hostname).
- reject_unauth_pipelining – aborts the session if the client doesn't wait to see the status of a command before proceeding.
- reject_unknown_sender_domain – rejects messages with an unresolvable sender domain. Postfix returns a temporary error message because the problem may result from a transient DNS glitch.
- reject_unknown_reverse_client_hostname – rejects messages from hosts that have no reverse DNS record.
- smtpd_helo_required – requires HELO/EHLO at the start of the conversation (parameter, either yes or no).
- strict_rfc821_envelopes – requires correct syntax for email addresses in the MAIL FROM and RCPT TO commands (parameter, yes or no).

The items above that are not marked as parameters are restrictions. You invoke them by including their names in smtpd_helo_restrictions (reject_non_fqdn_*) or smtpd_client_restrictions (the others). To test a restriction before putting it in production (always a good idea), insert the restriction warn_if_reject in front of it to convert the effect from outright rejection to warning log messages.

Blacklists

You can tell Postfix to check incoming email against a DNS-based blacklist; see *User or site blacklisting* on page 792 for more details. To enable this behavior, use the reject_rbl_client restriction followed by address of the DNS server to be consulted. A similar feature is reject_rhsbl_sender, which checks the domain name of the sender's address rather than the client's hostname.

Spam-fighting example

The following example represents a relatively complete spam-fighting configuration from the **main.cf** file:

```
strict_rfc821_envelopes = yes
smtpd_helo_required = yes
smtpd_recipient_restrictions =
    reject_unknown_sender_domain
    reject_non_fqdn_sender
    reject_non_fqdn_recipient
    permit_mynetworks
    permit_sasl_authenticated
    check_client_access hash:/etc/postfix/relaying_access
    reject_unauth_destination
    reject_unauth_pipelining
    reject_unknown_reverse_client_hostname
    reject_rbl_client zen.spamhaus.org
    permit
```

Note that we put some restrictions in front of permit_mynetworks. That tweak lets us verify that our own clients are sending out correctly formatted mail. This is an easy way to find out about configuration errors. The final permit action is the default but has been made explicit for clarity.

SpamAssassin and procmail

Postfix supports SpamAssassin and other filters of that ilk. See *Content scanning: spam and malware* on page 761 for general information about these tools.

procmail can be started from users' **.forward** files, but that's complicated and error prone. A better solution is to put the following line in **main.cf**:

```
mailbox_command = /usr/bin/procmail -a "$EXTENSION"
```

Postfix then uses **procmail** to deliver mail instead of writing messages directly to the mail spool. The arguments given to **procmail** pass the address extension (the portion after the +); it can then be accessed in **procmail** as $1.

Policy daemons

Postfix version 2.1 introduced a mechanism for delegating access control to external programs. These programs, called policy daemons, receive all the information that Postfix has about an email message and must return one of the disposition actions listed in Table 20.25 on page 838.

Greylisting is one of the more interesting features that can be implemented with a policy daemon. See page 765 for more information about greylisting and why you might want to employ it.

Content filtering

Postfix can use regular expressions to check the headers and bodies of email messages for contraband. It can also pass messages to other programs such as dedicated spam fighting tools or antivirus applications.

Header and body checks are performed in real time as messages are accepted through SMTP. Each regular expression that is checked invokes an action as specified in Table 20.25 on page 838 if the regex matches. For example, the line

```
header_checks = regexp:/etc/postfix/header_checks
```

in **main.cf** along with the following line in **/etc/postfix/header_checks**

```
/^Subject: reject-me/ REJECT You asked for it
```

would reject any message whose subject started with "reject-me". Though regular expression support is always nice, it comes with caveats in the context of email processing. In particular, this is not an effective method of spam or virus filtering.

Content filtering with amavisd

Industrial-strength virus filtering is usually implemented through **amavisd** (see page 769), a Perl program that interfaces mail server software with one or more antivirus applications. Such filters are configured with Postfix's content_filter parameter, which instructs Postfix to pass every incoming message once through the specified service. In addition to setting the content_filter parameter, you must modify some existing entries in the **master.cf** file and add some new ones.

Postfix and **amavisd** interact with each other by means of the standard SMTP and LMTP protocols. Postfix sends the mail to be analyzed to **amavisd** through LMTP. **amavisd** scans it and sends it back to Postfix through SMTP at an alternative port that's accessible only on the local machine and that has content-scanning disabled (thus avoiding a loop).

For mail coming in from the Internet, **amavisd** typically listens on port 10,024, and Postfix's back-door port is often 10,025. If we also process outgoing mail and want to differentiate it from incoming mail, we need a separate **amavisd** port for that—say, 10,026. The incoming mail can return to Postfix on the same return port as outgoing mail.

The configuration outlined below is a "post queue" setup that scans mail after it has been accepted into Postfix's queue. If you want to implement an in-line scanning setup, whereby the mail is scanned during the client's initial SMTP dialog, try the **amavisd-milter** helper tool, which lets you connect Postfix to **amavisd** as a milter.

On the **amavisd** side, make sure that **amavisd**'s configuration contains lines such as the following. (This configuration uses separate ports for inbound and outbound messages.)

```
$inet_socket_port = [10024,10026];
$notify_method  = 'smtp:[127.0.0.1]:10025';
$forward_method = 'smtp:[127.0.0.1]:10025';
$interface_policy{'10026'} = 'ORIGINATING';
$policy_bank{'ORIGINATING'} = {
    originating => 1,  # indicates client is ours
};
```

You now need to configure Postfix to send the mail to **amavisd**.

The **README.Postfix** file in the **amavisd-new** distribution includes about 20 lines of boilerplate configuration you can put into **/etc/postfix/master.cf** to make **amavisd** accessible and able to send mail back to Postfix. We don't duplicate it here; just cut and paste from the **README**.

To tell Postfix to send mail to **amavisd** for scanning, add this line to **main.cf**:

```
content_filter = amavisfeed:[127.0.0.1]:10024
```

For differentiating between incoming and outgoing mail, the configuration gets a bit more complicated. Instead of just the above directive, you need to modify smtpd_recipient_restrictions like this (changes in boldface):

```
smtpd_recipient_restrictions =
    reject_unknown_sender_domain
    reject_non_fqdn_sender
    reject_non_fqdn_recipient
    check_sender_access regexp:/etc/postfix/tag_as_originating.re
    permit_mynetworks
    permit_sasl_authenticated
    check_sender_access regexp:/etc/postfix/tag_as_foreign.re
    check_client_access hash:/etc/postfix/relaying_access
    reject_unauth_destination
    reject_unauth_pipelining
    reject_unknown_reverse_client_hostname
    reject_rbl_client zen.spamhaus.org
    permit
```

Then put the following line in the file **tag_as_originating.re**:

```
/^/  FILTER amavisfeed:[127.0.0.1]:10026
```

And in **tag_as_foreign.re**:

```
/^/  FILTER amavisfeed:[127.0.0.1]:10024
```

Mail from external hosts matches the tag_as_foreign.re restriction, which instructs Postfix to filter the mail by sending it to port 10,024. All mail matches the tag_as_originating.re restriction, but for external hosts it is replaced by the foreign restriction tag.

Electronic Mail

Debugging

When you have a problem with Postfix, first check the log files. The answers to your questions are most likely there; it's just a question of finding them. Every Postfix program normally issues a log entry for every message it processes. For example, the trail of an outbound message might look like this:

```
Aug 18 22:41:33 nova postfix/pickup: 0E4A93688: uid=506
    from=<dws@ee.ethz.ch>
Aug 18 22:41:33 nova postfix/cleanup: 0E4A93688: message-id=
    <20040818204132.GA11444@ee.ethz.ch>
Aug 18 22:41:33 nova postfix/qmgr: 0E4A93688: from=<dws@ee.ethz.ch>,
    size=577,nrcpt=1 (queue active)
Aug 18 22:41:33 nova postfix/smtp: 0E4A93688:
    to=<evi@ee.ethz.ch>,relay=tardis.ee.ethz.ch[129.132.2.217],delay=0,
    status=sent (250 Ok: queued as 154D4D930B)
Aug 18 22:41:33 nova postfix/qmgr: 0E4A93688: removed
```

As you can see, the interesting information is spread over many lines. Note that the identifier 0E4A93688 is common to every line: Postfix assigns a queue ID as soon as a message enters the mail system and never changes it. Therefore, when searching the logs for the history of a message, first concentrate on determining the message's queue ID. Once you know that, it's easy to **grep** the logs for all the relevant entries.

Postfix is good at logging helpful messages about problems that it notices. However, it's sometimes difficult to spot the important lines among the thousands of normal status messages. This is a good place to consider using some of the tools discussed in the section *Condensing log files to useful information*, which starts on page 358.

Looking at the queue

Another place to look for problems is the mail queue. As in the **sendmail** system, a **mailq** command prints the contents of a queue. You can use it to see if and why a message has become stuck.

Another helpful tool is the **qshape** script that's shipped with recent Postfix versions. It shows summary statistics about the contents of a queue. The output looks like this:

```
$ sudo qshape deferred
                 T   5 10 20 40 80 160 320 640 1280 1280+
        TOTAL 78   0  0  0  7  3   3   2  12    2    49
     expn.com 34   0  0  0  0  0   0   0   9    0    25
  chinabank.ph  5   0  0  0  1  1   1   2   0    0     0
prob-helper.biz  3   0  0  0  0  0   0   0   0    0     3
```

qshape summarizes the given queue (here, the deferred queue), sorted by recipient domain. The columns report the number of minutes the relevant messages have been in the queue. For example, you can see that 25 messages bound for expn.com have been in the queue longer than 1,280 minutes. All the destinations in this example are suggestive of messages having been sent from vacation scripts in response to spam.

qshape can also summarize by sender domain with the **-s** flag.

Soft-bouncing

If soft_bounce is set to yes, Postfix sends temporary error messages whenever it would normally send permanent error messages such as "user unknown" or "relaying denied." This is a great testing feature; it lets you monitor the disposition of messages after a configuration change without the risk of permanently losing legitimate email. Anything you reject will eventually come back for another try. Don't forget to turn off this feature when you are done testing or you will have to deal with every rejected message over and over again.

Testing access control

The easiest way to test access control restrictions is to try to send a message from an outside host and see what happens. This is a good basic test, but it doesn't cover special conditions such as mail from a domain where you have no login.

Postfix 2.1 introduced an extension to the SMTP protocol called XCLIENT that simulates submissions from another place. This feature is disabled by default, but with the following configuration line in **main.cf**, you can enable it for connections originating from localhost:

```
smtpd_authorized_xclient_hosts = localhost
```

A testing session might look something like this:

```
$ telnet localhost 25
Trying 127.0.0.1...
Connected to localhost.
Escape character is '^]'.
220 tardis.ee.ethz.ch ESMTP Postfix
XCLIENT NAME=mail.cs.colorado.edu ADDR=192.168.1.1
250 Ok
HELO mail.cs.colorado.edu
250 tardis.ee.ethz.ch
MAIL FROM: <evi@colorado.edu>
250 Ok
RCPT TO: <david@colorado.edu>
554 <david@colorado.edu>: Relay access denied
```

20.16 DKIM Configuration

Our DKIM coverage is a bit scattered. The introductory material is in the DNS chapter (on page 591) and on page 768 of this chapter. Here we concentrate on the email-related details of using DKIM through an external tool, **amavisd**, and directly, in conjunction with **sendmail**, Exim, and Postfix. **sendmail** and Postfix use milters to implement DKIM; Exim does it natively. The Exim implementation is new (late 2009) and still a bit rough around the edges.

DKIM: DomainKeys Identified Mail

DKIM is the new hope for positively identifying a sender's organization. If widely deployed, it would curb spammers' and phishers' ability to forge the sender's domain. Mail from your bank would really be from your bank—or at the very least, would not be categorized as phishing or spam.

DKIM replaces an earlier system called DomainKeys. DKIM uses public key cryptography (with keys stored in DNS) to let receivers verify both the origin and integrity of a message. These guarantees are becoming essential in our interconnected world, where so much business is done electronically. DKIM also prevents a sender from denying that he sent a message, a feature known as nonrepudiation.

A DKIM implementation has two halves: the part that signs outbound email as it leaves your site, and the part that verifies signatures on inbound email as it arrives. The first operation should be performed by your outgoing mail hub just before the mail leaves your site (after any internal rewriting and content scanning has been done). The second part, verification, should be done as soon as a message is received, before other scanning tools add to or change its headers.

sendmail.org has a couple of handy tools that are generic and can be used with any software that implements DKIM. The first is an ADSP wizard that accepts a domain name and generates the corresponding ADSP TXT records you must add to DNS to implement DKIM.[21] The second tool is a verifier that you can use to check your setup after it's all ready to go.

The details of DKIM and ADSP resource records are covered on page 591. They are currently still TXT records but may get their own DNS resource record types in the future. Both OpenSSL and **amavisd** include code to generate DKIM keys. Various DKIM milter packages also contain scripts that generate keys.

Once you have configured your MTA to generate DKIM signatures, you can send a message to sa-test@sendmail.net to verify that everything is working correctly. The server will email you back to tell you what security features it received.

If you have a Gmail account, another way to test is to send yourself a message there. Clicking on the "show details" link should reveal a signed-by field. You can also ask Gmail to "Show original" in the drop-down menu—this command shows you the raw message with all its headers, including the DKIM signature.

DKIM miltering

Software to implement DKIM was originally developed by Sendmail, Inc., for use as a milter to interface with the **sendmail** MTA. There are now two versions of

21. Don't publish your ADSP record until outbound message signing is set up and working properly, lest other sites start to reject your email.

this code: the original, DKIM-milter; and a code fork, OpenDKIM. Both packages are available as source code from sourceforge.net and in precompiled form from various package repositories. We illustrate use of the **sendmail** version, DKIM-milter v2.8.3.

The package contains **dkim-filter**, the milter that creates and verifies signatures, and several utilities to help debug and monitor DKIM usage. Here is a list:

- **dkim-filter** – generates and verifies DKIM signatures
- **dkim-genkey** – generates key pairs and required DNS records
- **dkim-stats** – summarizes statistics gathered by **dkim-filter**
- **dkim-testkey** – tests that keys are in the correct format and accessible
- **dkim-testssp** – tests the ADSP record (which used to be called SSP)

The first step in setting up the DKIM-milter package is to create a dedicated user account and group to own DKIM-related files. Use the name "dkim" for both. Make sure the account has a restricted shell such as **/bin/false**.

The **dkim-genkey** script generates a DKIM key pair. You specify the domain for which the key is intended with **-d** and the selector (key name, really) with **-s**. The defaults are example.com and "default". The **-r** flag restricts the key to use for email signing only, and **-t** indicates that you are testing DKIM. The keys are saved in separate files: *selector*.**private** for the private key and *selector*.**txt** for the DNS TXT record that contains the public key.

For example,

```
$ dkim-genkey -r -d example.com -s email
```

generates a key pair in the files **email.private** and **email.txt** in the current directory. Install the private key somewhere like **/etc/mail/dkim/keys**. Set the mode of the **/etc/mail/dkim** directory to 600 and **chown** it (recursively) to your dkim user and group. Add the DNS TXT record to the appropriate zone file, bump the serial number of the zone, and signal your name server. You can add an ADSP record once everything is tested and working, but don't do that just yet.

Run **dkim-testkey** to verify that your keys are OK. **dkim-testkey** produces no output if everything is fine, so silence is golden.

The next chore is the configuration of **dkim-filter** for use as a milter. Create a file **/etc/mail/dkim.conf** that's owned by your dkim user and group. Sample contents adapted from T. J. Nelson's on-line article *Setting up DKIM with Sendmail* follow:

```
Canonicalization simple
Domain mail.example.com
KeyFile /etc/mail/dkim/keys/email.key.pem
MTA MSA
PidFile /var/run/dkim-filter.pid
```

```
Selector email
Socket inet:8891@localhost
SignatureAlgorithm rsa-sha1
Syslog Yes
UserID dkim
X-Header Yes
Mode sv
InternalHosts /etc/mail/dkim-internal-hosts
```

The general format of entries in **dkim.conf** is

parameter value

A hash mark (#) introduces a comment. The distribution includes a well-commented sample configuration, **dkim-filter.conf.sample**, that includes a description of the variables and their default values. An even better description can be found in the **dkim-filter.conf** man page.

If you are configuring a central mail hub, the Domain line should be a comma-separated list of fully qualified domain names you will sign for, or a filename containing such a list.

The KeyFile parameter specifies the location of the private key used to sign messages. It is assumed that the first part of the filename is the selector (here, "email").

The MTA line lists the names of MTAs whose mail should always be signed rather than verified. It's analogous to the Name part of **sendmail**'s DAEMON_OPTIONS configuration parameter.

The Socket specification identifies the listening TCP socket; here, port 8,891 on localhost. The SignatureAlgorithm can be either rsa-sha1 or rsa-sha256; the latter is the default but is new enough that not all MTAs can use it. The X-Header parameter specifies that **dkim-filter** should add a header line to each scanned message. The Mode can be s for signing, v for verifying, or sv for both.

The InternalHosts parameter should point to a file that contains a list of the hosts whose outgoing mail should be signed. Hosts should be listed by fully qualified domain name.

Several configuration options can help with debugging. Check out MilterDebug, LogWhy, and SyslogSuccess. Some of these generate so much logging information that you should be sure to turn them off once you are satisfied with things.

Another series of options specifies what to do with messages whose signatures cannot be verified: On-Default, On-BadSignature, On-DNSError, On-Security, On-InternalError, and On-NoSignature. They each accept the values reject, tempfail, accept, and discard.

The system is highly configurable, and many more parameters (over 80) are described in the **dkim-filter.conf** man page.

DKIM configuration in amavisd-new

To use DKIM in **amavisd-new**, you must have the Perl module Mail::DKIM version 0.33 or later. If not, download it from CPAN. You must generate a key pair, turn on DKIM verification and signing, point to your private key file, and set some signing options.

amavisd itself can generate keys for DKIM:

```
$ amavisd genrsa /var/db/dkim/example.com-email.key.pem
```

The second argument to **amavisd** is the file in which to store the keys. Since it contains both the private and the public key, it's best to check the permissions and make sure that this file is not readable by the world or anyone you don't trust.

The following configuration snippet has been modified slightly from the section of the **amavisd-new** documentation called "bits and pieces." This example assumes that your site's domain is example.com and that you are using the selector "email" for your keys.

```
$enable_dkim_verification = 1;
$enable_dkim_signing = 1;
dkim_key('example.com', 'email', '/var/db/dkim/example.com-email.key.pem');
@dkim_signature_options_bysender_maps = (
    { '.' => { ttl => 21*24*3600, c => 'relaxed/simple' } } );
@mynetworks = qw(127.0.0.0/8 10.0.0.0/8 172.16.0.0/12 192.168.0.0/16);
```

The DKIM signature options line lets you override the default tags, which are stored in an associative array. Signatures can have 13 distinct tag values associated with them. Many, such as the d tag, which specifies the domain of the sender, are set automatically. An important tag is the s tag, which specifies the selector to use when DNS is queried for the public key to verify the signature. In this example, you override the default time-to-live (ttl) of 30 days with a value of 21 days. Some of the tags become important if mail is relayed (for example, through a mailing list) and you want signatures to survive the operation.

You can also specify the header fields to be included in the signature by assigning Boolean values to the associative array signed_header_fields. For example,

```
$signed_header_fields{'received'} = 0;
$signed_header_fields{'sender'} = 1;
$signed_header_fields{'to'} = 1;
$signed_header_fields{'cc'} = 1;
```

excludes the Received header but includes Sender, To, and Cc. The defaults are probably just fine for most sites.

You can use **amavisd showkeys** and **amavisd testkeys** to test your configuration. The **showkeys** command displays the public key that you should add to your DNS zone file for example.com. (Don't forget to change the zone's serial number and to signal your name server!) The **testkeys** command both tests the signing process and verifies that your key has been published in DNS.

DKIM in sendmail

You can implement DKIM for **sendmail** by using either milters (for in-line filtering; see page 767) or a dual-server setup in conjunction with **amavisd**. Here, we cover the use of DKIM-milter to sign and verify messages.

sendmail's configuration primitives masquerade_as and genericstable rewrite headers, so those primitives must be implemented before any DKIM signature is added; otherwise, the signature will not remain valid.

To support DKIM, **sendmail** must be built with milter support, have the OpenSSL and Berkeley DB libraries available, and have the DKIM-milter package installed (find it at sourceforge.net). Use OpenSSL to generate keys, and add them to your DNS zone as described on page 591, or use **dkim-genkey** as shown on page 846.

For this example, our domain is example.com. We chose the selector "email" and stored our private key in **email.private** and our public key in **email.key.pem**. We can test the keys with **dkim-testkey** as follows:

```
$ dkim-testkey -d example.com -k /var/db/dkim/email.key.pem -s ma
```

If all's well, **dkim-testkey** says nothing.

In your **sendmail** configuration file, **sendmail.mc**, add the line

```
INPUT_MAIL_FILTER(`dkim-filter', `S=inet:8891@localhost')
```

and rebuild the **sendmail.cf** file (**./Build sendmail.cf**; **sudo make install-cf**). Then restart **sendmail** and start the **dkim-filter** program.

DKIM in Exim

The Exim 4.70 release (late 2009) added native support for DKIM and dropped support for Yahoo!'s DomainKeys. Expect the feature set to continue to evolve as the Exim developers work out bugs and gain experience working with DKIM.

Exim's DKIM support is enabled by default. To turn it off, set DISABLE_DKIM=yes in **Local/Makefile** and rebuild and reinstall the package.

The Exim implementation signs outgoing messages in the SMTP transport configuration and verifies signatures on incoming messages through a new ACL, acl_smtp_dkim. Hub machines can disable the signature verification on messages they relay for local hosts by setting dkim_disable_verify for those messages.

Signing outgoing messages

The first DKIM implementation chore is to generate your cryptographic keys with OpenSSL as described on page 591 (in the DNS chapter). Several new Exim options must be defined for use by the SMTP transport. The options can include variables to be expanded when the transport is called. Table 20.26 contains a list of the DKIM-related signing options.

Table 20.26 DKIM signing options in Exim

Option	Type	Req'd	Contents
dkim_domain	String	Yes	Domain to sign with
dkim_selector	String	Yes	Key selector (name)
dkim_private_key	String	Yes	Private key or filename that contains it
dkim_canon	String	No	Canonicalization method: simple or relaxed
dkim_strict	String	No	If true, signing errors defer mail back to queue
dkim_sign_headers	String	No	Headers to include in signature

The first three "options" are required and must be configured; the rest are truly optional. By default, the canonicalization method (dkim_canon) is relaxed, messages that cause signing errors are sent without signatures (dkim_strict), and Exim uses the RFC4871 list of headers to sign (dkim_sign_headers). The mandatory options are straightforward, but if you have a complex site that hosts multiple real or virtual domains, you will have to be clever in defining them.

Verifying incoming signed messages

Incoming DKIM-signed mail messages are verified in the acl_smtp_dkim ACL. This ACL is called once for each signature and returns one of the following codes:

- none – message is not signed
- invalid – signature could not be verified (key unavailable or invalid)
- fail – signature failed verification for headers, body, or both
- pass – signature is valid

The status is returned in the $dkim_verify_status variable, with failure details in $dkim_verify_reason. There are lots of other $dkim_*variable* tags that give you access to the various fields of the signature and allow you to implement special policies (e.g., flagging messages from gmail.com that do not have signatures, or rejecting messages from paypal.com that do not verify).

A complete example

The following example is adapted from Phil Pennock's DKIM setup.[22] It includes definitions of acl_process_dkim to verify signatures and a router and a transport (dnslookup_signed and remote_dksign, respectively) to do the actual signing.

This configuration allows multiple domains to be signed and provides for multiple keys so that key rollover is possible. This file is stored in CDB format and maps keys such as "example.org" to values such as "d200912."

Key selectors are named d*yyyymm*, where d is just the letter "d" for date, *yyyy* is the year the key was generated, and *mm* is the month it was generated. Key files are named **rsa.private.***selector.domain* and are stored in a key directory defined

22. Phil is an active exim-users mailing list contributor.

with the macro DKKEY_DIR. Be sure this directory is readable by **exim** but not by the rest of the world.

```
######## macros to define the directories for databases and keys
CONFIG_DIR = path_to_config_dir
DKKEY_DIR = path_to_key_dir

######## main section: define the domains to sign and required DKIM acl
domainlist dksign_domains = cdb;CONFIG_DIR/dk.selector.cdb
acl_smtp_dkim = acl_process_dkim

######## ACL section: verify signature on incoming mail, add a header
acl_process_dkim:
    warn !dkim_status = none
        add_header = :at_start:X-DKIM-Report: $dkim_verify_status \
            ${if !eq{$dkim_verify_status}{pass}{$dkim_verify_reason }{}} \
            (Signer=$dkim_cur_signer) (Testing=$dkim_key_testing)

######## Router section: put just before "dnslookup" router, sign nonlocal
dnslookup_signed:
    driver = dnslookup
    domains = !+local_domains
    transport = remote_dksign
    condition = ${if match_domain{$sender_address_domain} \
        {+dksign_domains}}
    no_verify

######## Transport section: does the actual signing
remote_dksign:
    driver = smtp
    dkim_domain = $sender_address_domain
    dkim_selector = ${lookup {$dkim_domain} \
        cdb{CONFIG_DIR/dk.selector.cdb} {$value}fail}
    dkim_private_key = DKKEY_DIR/rsa.private.$dkim_selector.$dkim_domain
    dkim_strict = 1
```

These fragments result in outgoing messages being signed and incoming messages having their signatures verified and a DKIM report header added. Here's an example of that header:

```
X-DKIM-Report: pass (Signer=gmail.com) (Testing=0)
```

Further policy is needed if you are going to reject or punish messages whose signatures do not verify.

The no_verify line in the router section refers not to DKIM verification but rather to verifying the recipient's address; it is turned off in this router, but done in the dnslookup router that is next in line. No sense doing it twice.

DKIM in Postfix

DKIM is implemented in Postfix with the DKIM-milter software package described on page 846. Generate your key pair and test it with **dkim-testkey**; build a

dkim-filter.conf file from the sample in the distribution, and then teach Postfix to use **dkim-filter**. In **main.cf**, after any other milter options, add the lines

```
smtpd_milters = inet:localhost:8891
non_smtpd_milters = inet:localhost:8891
milter_protocol = 2
milter_default_action = accept
```

Now all you need to do is start **dkim-filter** and restart **postfix**.

20.17 Integrated email solutions

A host of integrated email solutions are available, ranging from free, open source products to pricey commercial offerings. All handle more than just electronic mail. Common groupware and conferencing features include

- Address book and shared contact list management
- Calendar and task management
- Mailing lists and bulletin boards
- Instant messaging
- SSL/TLS encryption
- Archiving and automatic backups
- Support for mobile devices (BlackBerry, iPhone, etc.)

Most of these megapackages include a configuration GUI that more or less replaces the need to read this humongous chapter. (Perhaps we should have put this section at the beginning of the chapter instead of the end.) Many are targeted as replacements for Microsoft Exchange.

Several products merit an explicit mention:

- Citadel (citadel.org) is an open source email and groupware package that has support contracts available.
- Zimbra (zimbra.com) straddles the divide between open source and proprietary systems. Its full-featured version is proprietary and costs money, but an only-slightly-hobbled version is open source and free.
- Kerio MailServer (kerio.com) is a proprietary system that, like Zimbra, is licensed on a per-user basis. For a large organization, these options can get pricey.
- Communigate Pro (communigate.com) folds voice and video into the usual email/groupware suite and offers either traditional unlimited licensing or use-based licensing.

You might also consider email appliances, hardware boxes that are usually built on hardened, stripped-down versions of FreeBSD UNIX or Linux. Three choices in this space are Cisco's IronPort Series and models from Sophos and Clearswift. These products typically perform antivirus and antispam filtering and then hand messages to Microsoft Exchange for delivery.

20.18 Recommended Reading

Rather than jumble together the references listed here, we've sorted them by MTA and topic.

General spam references

CLAYTON, RICHARD. "Good Practice for Combating Unsolicited Bulk Email." RIPE/Demon Internet. 2000, ripe.net/ripe/docs/ripe-206.html.

This document is aimed at ISPs. It has lots of policy information and some good links to technical subjects.

FIELD, JULIAN. *MailScanner: A User Guide and Training Manual.* University of Southampton Department of Electronics, 2007.

MCDONALD, ALISTAIR. *SpamAssassin: A Practical Guide to Configuration, Customization, and Integration.* Packt Publishing, 2004.

SCHWARTZ, ALAN. *SpamAssassin.* Sebastopol, CA: O'Reilly Media, 2004.

WOLFE, PAUL, CHARLIE SCOTT, AND MIKE ERWIN. *The Anti-Spam Tool Kit.* Emeryville, CA: Osborne, 2004.

sendmail references

COSTALES, BRYAN, CLAUS ASSMANN, GEORGE JANSEN, AND GREGORY NEIL SHAPIRO. *sendmail, 4th Edition.* Sebastopol, CA: O'Reilly Media, 2007.

This book is the definitive tome for **sendmail** configuration—1,300 pages' worth. It includes a sysadmin guide as well as a complete reference section. An electronic edition is available, too. The author mix includes two key **sendmail** developers (Claus and Greg) who enforce technical correctness and add insight to the mix.

Installation instructions and a good description of the configuration file are covered in the *Sendmail Installation and Operation Guide*, which can be found in the **doc/op** subdirectory of the **sendmail** distribution. This document is quite complete, and in conjunction with the **README** file in the **cf** directory, it gives a good nuts-and-bolts view of the **sendmail** system.

sendmail.org, sendmail.org/~ca, and sendmail.org/~gshapiro all contain documents, HOWTOs, and tutorials related to **sendmail**.

Exim references

HAZEL, PHILIP. *The Exim SMTP Mail Server: Official Guide for Release 4, 2nd Edition.* Cambridge, UK: User Interface Technologies, Ltd., 2007.

HAZEL, PHILIP. *Exim: The Mail Transfer Agent.* Sebastapol, CA: O'Reilly Media, 2001.

MEERS, JASON. *Getting started with EXIM.* exim-new-users.co.uk, 2007.

The Exim specification is the defining document for Exim configuration. It is very complete and is updated with each new distribution. A text version is included in the file **doc/spec.txt** in the distribution, and a PDF version is available from exim.org. There are also several how-to documents on the web site.

Postfix references

BLUM, RICHARD. *Postfix*. Sams Publishing, 2001.

DENT, KYLE D. *Postfix: The Definitive Guide*. Sebastopol, CA: O'Reilly Media, 2003.

HILDEBRANDT, RALF, AND PATRICK KOETTER. *The Book of Postfix: State of the Art Message Transport*. San Francisco, CA: No Starch Press, 2005.

This book is the best; it guides you through all the details of Postfix configuration, even for complex environments. The authors are active in the Postfix community and participate regularly on the postfix-users mailing list. The book is unfortunately out of print, but used copies are easily available.

postfix.org/SOHO_README.html is a guide to using Postfix at home or in a small office environment.

RFCs

RFCs 5321 and 5322 are the current versions of RFCs 821 and 822. They define the SMTP protocol and the formats of messages and addresses for Internet email. RFCs 5335 and 5336 cover extensions for internationalized email addresses. There are currently almost 90 email-related RFCs, too many to list here. See the general RFC search engine at rfc-editor.org for more.

20.19 EXERCISES

E20.1 Briefly explain the difference between a user agent (MUA), a delivery agent (DA), and an access agent (AA). Then explain the difference between a mail transport agent (MTA) and a mail submission agent (MSA).

E20.2 Inspect the mail queue on your local mail server. Is there cruft in the directory? Are there messages with no control files or control files with no messages? What is the oldest message in the queue? (Requires root access.)

E20.3 Explain what an MX record is. Why are MX records important for mail delivery? Give an example in which a misconfigured MX record might make mail undeliverable.

E20.4 Determine the design of mail service at your site and diagram it in the style of Exhibit B on page 754. Where is incoming mail scanned for spam or viruses? What about outgoing mail?

E20.5 Compare the use of **/etc/mail/aliases** with the use of an LDAP server or MySQL database to store mail aliases. What are the advantages and disadvantages of each?

★ E20.6 Write a brief description of the following email headers. What path did the email take? To whom was it addressed, and to whom was it delivered? How long did it spend in transit?

```
Delivered-To: sailingevi@gmail.com
Received: by 10.231.143.81 with SMTP id t17cs175323ibu;
   Mon, 28 Dec 2009 20:15:20 -0800 (PST)
Received: by 10.231.157.131 with SMTP id
   b3mr2134004ibx.19.1262060119841;
   Mon, 28 Dec 2009 20:15:19 -0800 (PST)
Return-Path: <garth@grsweb.us>
Received: from mail-relay.atrust.com (mail-relay.atrust.com
   [63.173.189.2]) by mx.google.com with ESMTP id
   12si19092249iwn.27.2009.12.28.20.15.19;
   Mon, 28 Dec 2009 20:15:19 -0800 (PST)
Received-SPF: neutral (google.com: 63.173.189.2 is neither permitted nor
   denied by best guess record for domain of garth@grsweb.us) client-
   ip=63.173.189.2;
Authentication-Results: mx.google.com; spf=neutral (google.com:
   63.173.189.2 is neither permitted nor denied by best guess record for
   domain of garth@grsweb.us) smtp.mail=garth@grsweb.us
Received: from mout.perfora.net (mout.perfora.net [74.208.4.194]) by
   mail-relay.atrust.com (8.12.11/8.12.11) with ESMTP id nBT4FI9r017821
   for <evi@atrust.com>; Mon, 28 Dec 2009 21:15:19 -0700
Received: from grsweb.us (wolverine.dreamhost.com [75.119.201.185]) by
   mrelay.perfora.net (node=mrus1) with ESMTP (Nemesis) id 0Ma0RD-
   1NgKS52KT9-00LeuN; Mon, 28 Dec 2009 23:15:17 -0500
Date: Mon, 28 Dec 2009 20:15:13 -0800
From: UNIX and Linux System Administration Handbook
   <garth@grsweb.us>
Reply-To: garth@grsweb.us
To: evi@atrust.com
Cc: garth@grsweb.us
Message-Id: <4b398251b11ab_e92383578b2d9b036f@wolverine.tmail>
Subject: New comments on Printing
Mime-Version: 1.0
Content-Type: text/html; charset=utf-8
X-Provags-ID:
   V01U2FsdGVkX18pouiYXif/bVfh+D9wFXMr24TahAzDNZqM+jA04iLR7S4
   olDXRpXlrbQMblNoZf5jO6edc+WIGC8Fi4hd5Ak15vBARASOFQYxNJWea9
   8SyQg==
X-Spam-Status: No, hits=-99.3 required=4.0 tests=BAYES_30,HTML_20_30,
   MIME_HTML_ONLY,USER_IN_WHITELIST version=2.55
X-Spam-Level:
X-Spam-Checker-Version: SpamAssassin 2.55 (1.174.2.19-2003-05-19-exp)
```

★ E20.7 What are the implications of being blacklisted at spamhaus.org or a similar service? What should you do if you find that your site has become blacklisted? Outline techniques you can use to stay off such lists in the first place.

★ E20.8 If your site allows **procmail** and if you have permission from your local sysadmin group, set up your personal **procmail** configuration file to illustrate how **procmail** can compromise security.

★★ E20.9 Explore the current MTA configuration at your site. What are some of the special features of the MTA that are in use? Can you find any problems with the configuration? In what ways could the configuration be made better?

★★ E20.10 Find a piece of spam in your mailbox and inspect the headers. Report any signs that the mail has been forged. Then run some of the tools mentioned in this chapter, such as SpamAssassin, and report their findings. How did you do at recognizing faked headers? Submit the spam and your conclusions about the sender, the validity of the listed hosts, and anything else that looks out of place.

sendmail-specific exercises

E20.11 What is **smrsh**, and why should you use it instead of **/bin/sh**? If **smrsh** is used at your site, what programs are allowed to run as the program mailer? Are any of them dangerously insecure?

E20.12 Write a small **/etc/mail/aliases** file that demonstrates three different types of aliases. Talk briefly about what each line does and why it could be useful.

★ E20.13 List the prefixes for files in the mail queue directory and explain what each one means. Why is it important to delete some queue files but very wrong to delete others? How can some of the prefixes be used to debug **sendmail** configuration mistakes?

★ E20.14 Explain the purpose of each of the following **m4** macros. If the macro includes a file, provide a short description of what the contents of the file should be.

a) VERSIONID
b) OSTYPE
c) DOMAIN
d) MAILER
e) FEATURE

★ E20.15 Explain how you would configure a **sendmail** server to accept email for both your own domain and a virtual domain. Allow the virtual domain to relay mail to an off-site mailbox.

Exim-specific exercises

E20.16 Take the ACL example for the SMTP RCPT command shown on page 815 and reverse its default behavior to deny, while letting the same addresses pass through.

★ E20.17 Version 4.70 and later removed the DomainKeys code in favor of DKIM. Simplify the example DKIM setup on page 851 to support only a single domain and single signing key. Then add some policy rules, such as logging unsigned mail from Gmail or Yahoo! or rejecting failed verifications from PayPal or your bank.

★ E20.18 Explain how you would configure an Exim server to accept mail for both your own domain and a virtual domain. Allow the virtual domain to relay mail to an off-site mailbox.

★ E20.19 Look through the configuration snippets in the **spec.txt** document in the Exim distribution and experiment with including some of them in your configuration. Turn on verbose logging for each thing you try and examine the log files to see if it has the desired behavior.

Postfix-specific exercises

E20.20 Try to set up a "null client"—that is, a mail system that only sends mail and can't receive it. Make sure that port 25 is closed.

E20.21 Configure Postfix to authenticate your site to your provider or company server (even Gmail!); use the following parameters:

```
smtp_sender_dependent_authentication
sender_dependent_relayhost_maps
smtp_sasl_auth_enable
smtp_sasl_password_maps
```

E20.22 Why do you think that Postfix supports so many map types?

E20.23 What would you use pcre maps for? Is value substitution something useful for mail systems? Do you need to use the **postmap** command to compile pcre maps?

E20.24 Look up the meaning of the recipient_delimiter parameter in the documentation (**postconf** man page). What could it be used for?

★ E20.25 Explain how you would configure Postfix to accept email for both your own domain and a virtual domain. Allow the virtual domain to relay mail to an off-site mailbox.

21 Network Management and Debugging

Net Mgmt

Because networks increase the number of interdependencies among machines, they tend to magnify problems. As the saying goes, "Networking is when you can't get any work done because of the failure of a machine you have never heard of."

Network management is the art and science of keeping a network healthy. It generally includes the following tasks:

- Fault detection for networks, gateways, and critical servers
- Schemes for notifying an administrator of problems
- General network monitoring, to balance load and plan expansion
- Documentation and visualization of the network
- Administration of network devices from a central site

On a single network segment, it is generally not worthwhile to establish formal procedures for network management. Just test the network thoroughly after installation and check it occasionally to be sure that its load is not excessive. When it breaks, fix it.

As your network grows, management procedures should become more automated. On a network consisting of several different subnets joined with switches or routers, you may want to start automating management tasks with shell scripts and simple programs. If you have a WAN or a complex local network, consider installing a dedicated network management station.

In many cases, your organization's reliability needs will dictate the sophistication of your network management system. A problem with the network can bring all work to a standstill. If your site cannot tolerate downtime, it may well be worthwhile to obtain and install a high-end enterprise network management system.

Unfortunately, even the best network management system cannot prevent all failures. It is critical to have a well-documented network and a high-quality staff available to handle the inevitable collapses.

21.1 Network troubleshooting

Several good tools are available for debugging a network at the TCP/IP layer. Most give low-level information, so you must understand the main ideas of TCP/IP and routing in order to use the debugging tools.

On the other hand, network issues can also stem from problems with higher-level protocols such as DNS, NFS, and HTTP. You might want to read through Chapter 14, *TCP/IP Networking*, and Chapter 15, *Routing*, before tackling this chapter.

In this section, we start with some general troubleshooting strategy. We then cover several essential tools, including **ping**, **traceroute**, **netstat**, **tcpdump**, and Wireshark. We don't discuss the **arp** command in this chapter, though it, too, is sometimes a useful debugging tool—see page 468 for more information.

Before you attack your network, consider these principles:

- Make one change at a time. Test each change to make sure that it had the effect you intended. Back out any changes that have an undesired effect.
- Document the situation as it was before you got involved, and document every change you make along the way.
- Problems may be transient, so begin by capturing relevant information with tools like **sar** and **nmon**. This information may come in handy as you are unraveling the problem.
- Start at one end of a system or network and work through the system's critical components until you reach the problem. For example, you might start by looking at the network configuration on a client, work your way up to the physical connections, investigate the network hardware, and finally, check the server's physical connections and software configuration.
- Communicate regularly. Most network problems affect lots of different people: users, ISPs, system administrators, telco engineers, network administrators, etc. Clear, consistent communication prevents you from hindering one another's efforts to solve the problem.

- Work as a team. Years of experience show that people make fewer stupid mistakes if they have a peer helping out. If the problem has any visibility, management will also want to be involved. Take advantage of managers' interest to get technical people from other groups on board and to cut through red tape where necessary.
- Use the layers of the network to negotiate the problem. Start at the "top" or "bottom" and work your way through the protocol stack.

This last point deserves a bit more discussion. As described on page 450, the architecture of TCP/IP defines several layers of abstraction at which components of the network can function. For example, HTTP depends on TCP, TCP depends on IP, IP depends on the Ethernet protocol, and the Ethernet protocol depends on the integrity of the network cable. You can dramatically reduce the amount of time spent debugging a problem if you first figure out which layer is misbehaving.

Ask yourself questions like these as you work up or down the stack:

- Do you have physical connectivity and a link light?
- Is your interface configured properly?
- Do your ARP tables show other hosts?
- Is there a firewall on your local machine?
- Is there a firewall anywhere between you and the destination?
- If firewalls are involved, do they pass ICMP ping packets and responses?
- Can you ping the localhost address (127.0.0.1)?
- Can you ping other local hosts by IP address?
- Is DNS working properly?[1]
- Can you ping other local hosts by hostname?
- Can you ping hosts on another network?
- Do high-level services such as web and SSH servers work?
- Did you really check the firewalls?

Once you've identified where the problem lies and have a fix in mind, take a step back to consider the effect that your subsequent tests and prospective fixes will have on other services and hosts.

21.2 PING: CHECK TO SEE IF A HOST IS ALIVE

The **ping** command is embarrassingly simple, but in many situations it is the only command you need for network debugging. It sends an ICMP ECHO_REQUEST packet to a target host and waits to see if the host answers back.

1. If a machine hangs at boot time, boots very slowly, or hangs on inbound SSH connections, DNS should be a prime suspect. Solaris and Linux use a sophisticated approach to name resolution that's configurable in **/etc/nsswitch.conf**. On these systems, the name service caching daemon (**nscd**) is of particular interest. If it crashes or is misconfigured, name lookups are affected. With the transition to IPv6 progressing, we find that many DSL routers provide DNS forwarding services that simply drop requests for IPv6 (AAAA) DNS records. This "optimization" causes long timeouts on all name resolution requests. Use the **getent** command to check whether your resolver and name servers are working properly (e.g., **getent hosts google.com**).

You can use **ping** to check the status of individual hosts and to test segments of the network. Routing tables, physical networks, and gateways are all involved in processing a ping, so the network must be more or less working for **ping** to succeed. If **ping** doesn't work, you can be pretty sure that nothing more sophisticated will work either.

However, this rule does not apply to networks that block ICMP echo requests with a firewall. Make sure that a firewall isn't interfering with your debugging before you conclude that the target host is ignoring a **ping**. You might consider disabling a meddlesome firewall for a short period of time to facilitate debugging.

If your network is in bad shape, chances are that DNS is not working. Simplify the situation by using numeric IP addresses when pinging, and use **ping**'s **-n** option to prevent **ping** from attempting to do reverse lookups on IP addresses—these lookups also trigger DNS requests.

Be aware of the firewall issue if you're using **ping** to check your Internet connectivity, too. Some well-known sites answer **ping** packets and others don't. We've found google.com to be a consistent responder.

Most versions of **ping** run in an infinite loop unless you supply a packet count argument. Under Solaris, **ping -s** provides the extended output that other versions use by default. Once you've had your fill of pinging, type the interrupt character (usually <Control-C>) to get out.

Here's an example:

```
linux$ ping beast
PING beast (10.1.1.46): 56 bytes of data.
64 bytes from beast (10.1.1.46): icmp_seq=0 ttl=54 time=48.3ms
64 bytes from beast (10.1.1.46): icmp_seq=1 ttl=54 time=46.4ms
64 bytes from beast (10.1.1.46): icmp_seq=2 ttl=54 time=88.7ms
^C
--- beast ping statistics ---
3 packets transmitted, 3 received, 0% packet loss, time 2026ms
rtt min/avg/max/mdev = 46.490/61.202/88.731/19.481 ms
```

The output for beast shows the host's IP address, the ICMP sequence number of each response packet, and the round trip travel time. The most obvious thing that the output above tells you is that the server beast is alive and connected to the network.

The ICMP sequence number is a particularly valuable piece of information. Discontinuities in the sequence indicate dropped packets. They're normally accompanied by a message for each missing packet.

Despite the fact that IP does not guarantee the delivery of packets, a healthy network should drop very few of them. Lost-packet problems are important to track down because they tend to be masked by higher-level protocols. The network may appear to function correctly, but it will be slower than it ought to be, not only because of the retransmitted packets but also because of the protocol overhead needed to detect and manage them.

To track down the cause of disappearing packets, first run **traceroute** (see the next section) to discover the route that packets are taking to the target host. Then ping the intermediate gateways in sequence to discover which link is dropping packets. To pin down the problem, you need to send a fair number of packets. The fault generally lies on the link between the last gateway you can ping without loss of packets and the gateway beyond that.

The round trip time reported by **ping** gives you insight into the overall performance of a path through a network. Moderate variations in round trip time do not usually indicate problems. Packets may occasionally be delayed by tens or hundreds of milliseconds for no apparent reason; that's just the way IP works. You should expect to see a fairly consistent round trip time for the majority of packets, with occasional lapses. Many of today's routers implement rate-limited or lower-priority responses to ICMP packets, which means that a router may delay responding to your ping if it is already dealing with a lot of other traffic.

The **ping** program can send echo request packets of any size, so by using a packet larger than the MTU of the network (1,500 bytes for Ethernet), you can force fragmentation. This practice helps you identify media errors or other low-level issues such as problems with a congested network or VPN.

On Linux systems, you specify the desired packet size in bytes with the **-s** flag.

```
$ ping -s 1500 cuinfo.cornell.edu
```

Under Solaris, HP-UX, and AIX, you simply add the desired packet size to the end of the **ping** command.

```
$ ping cuinfo.cornell.edu 1500
```

Note that even a simple command like **ping** can have dramatic effects. In 1998, the so-called Ping of Death attack crashed large numbers of UNIX and Windows systems. It was launched simply by transmission of an overly large ping packet. When the fragmented packet was reassembled, it filled the receiver's memory buffer and crashed the machine. The Ping of Death issue has long since been fixed, but several other caveats should be kept in mind regarding **ping**.

First, it is hard to distinguish the failure of a network from the failure of a server with only the **ping** command. In an environment where ping tests normally work, a failed ping just tells you that *something* is wrong.

Second, a successful ping does not guarantee much about the target machine's state. Echo request packets are handled within the IP protocol stack and do not require a server process to be running on the probed host. A response guarantees only that a machine is powered on and has not experienced a kernel panic. You'll need higher-level methods to verify the availability of individual services such as HTTP and DNS.

21.3 SmokePing: gather ping statistics over time

As mentioned earlier, even a healthy network occasionally drops a packet. On the other hand, networks should not drop packets regularly, even at a low rate, because the impact on users can be disproportionately severe. Because high-level protocols often function even in the presence of packet loss, you might never notice dropped packets unless you're actively monitoring for them.

For this purpose, you may want to check out SmokePing, an open source tool by Tobias Oetiker that keeps track of network latencies. SmokePing sends several ping packets to a target host at regular intervals. It shows the history of each monitored link through a web front end and can send alarms when things go amiss. You can get a copy from oss.oetiker.ch/smokeping.

Exhibit A shows a SmokePing graph. The vertical axis is the round trip time of pings, and the horizontal axis is time (weeks). The black line from which the gray spikes stick up indicates the median round trip time; the spikes themselves are the transit times of individual packets. Since the gray in this graph appears only above the median line, the great majority of packets must be traveling at close to the median speed, with just a few being delayed. This is a typical finding.

Exhibit A Sample SmokePing graph

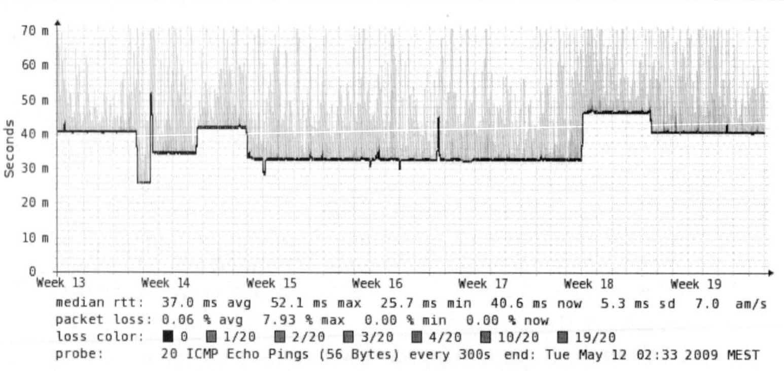

The stair-stepped shape of the median line indicates that the baseline transit time to this destination has changed several times during the monitoring period. The most likely hypotheses to explain this observation are either that the host is reachable by several routes or that it is actually a collection of several hosts that have the same DNS name but multiple IP addresses.

21.4 TRACEROUTE: TRACE IP PACKETS

traceroute, originally written by Van Jacobson, uncovers the sequence of gateways through which an IP packet travels to reach its destination. All modern operating systems come with some version of **traceroute**.[2] The syntax is simply

traceroute *hostname*

There are a variety of options, most of which are not important in daily use. As usual, the *hostname* can be specified as either a DNS name or an IP address. The output is simply a list of hosts, starting with the first gateway and ending at the destination. For example, a **traceroute** from our host jaguar to our host nubark produces the following output:

```
$ traceroute nubark
traceroute to nubark (192.168.2.10), 30 hops max, 38 byte packets
 1  lab-gw (172.16.8.254)  0.840 ms  0.693 ms  0.671 ms
 2  dmz-gw (192.168.1.254)  4.642 ms  4.582 ms  4.674 ms
 3  nubark (192.168.2.10)  7.959 ms  5.949 ms  5.908 ms
```

From this output we can tell that jaguar is three hops away from nubark, and we can see which gateways are involved in the connection. The round trip time for each gateway is also shown—three samples for each hop are measured and displayed. A typical **traceroute** between Internet hosts often includes more than 15 hops, even if the two sites are just across town.

traceroute works by setting the time-to-live field (TTL, actually "hop count to live") of an outbound packet to an artificially low number. As packets arrive at a gateway, their TTL is decreased. When a gateway decreases the TTL to 0, it discards the packet and sends an ICMP "time exceeded" message back to the originating host.

See page 582 for more information about reverse DNS lookups.

The first three **traceroute** packets have their TTL set to 1. The first gateway to see such a packet (lab-gw in this case) determines that the TTL has been exceeded and notifies jaguar of the dropped packet by sending back an ICMP message. The sender's IP address in the header of the error packet identifies the gateway, and **traceroute** looks up this address in DNS to find the gateway's hostname.

To identify the second-hop gateway, **traceroute** sends out a second round of packets with TTL fields set to 2. The first gateway routes the packets and decreases their TTL by 1. At the second gateway, the packets are then dropped and ICMP error messages are generated as before. This process continues until the TTL is equal to the number of hops to the destination host and the packets reach their destination successfully.

2. Even Windows has it, but the command is spelled **tracert** (extra history points if you can guess why).

Most routers send their ICMP messages from the interface "closest" to the destination. If you run **traceroute** backward from the destination host, you may see different IP addresses being used to identify the same set of routers. You might also discover that packets flowing in the reverse direction take a completely different path, a configuration known as asymmetric routing.

Since **traceroute** sends three packets for each value of the TTL field, you may sometimes observe an interesting artifact. If an intervening gateway multiplexes traffic across several routes, the packets might be returned by different hosts; in this case, **traceroute** simply prints them all.

Let's look at a more interesting example from a host in Switzerland to caida.org at the San Diego Supercomputer Center:[3]

```
linux$ traceroute caida.org
traceroute to caida.org (192.172.226.78), 30 hops max, 46 byte packets
 1  gw-oetiker.init7.net (213.144.138.193)  1.122 ms  0.182 ms  0.170 ms
 2  r1zur1.core.init7.net (77.109.128.209)  0.527 ms  0.204 ms  0.202 ms
 3  r1fra1.core.init7.net (77.109.128.250)  18.279 ms  6.992 ms  16.597 ms
 4  r1ams1.core.init7.net (77.109.128.154)  19.549 ms  21.855 ms  13.514 ms
 5  r1lon1.core.init7.net (77.109.128.150)  19.165 ms  21.157 ms  24.866 ms
 6  r1lax1.ce.init7.net (82.197.168.69)  158.232 ms  158.224 ms  158.271 ms
 7  cenic.laap.net (198.32.146.32)  158.349 ms  158.309 ms  158.248 ms
 8  dc-lax-core2--lax-peer1-ge.cenic.net (137.164.46.119)  158.60 ms * 158.71 ms
 9  dc-tus-agg1--lax-core2-10ge.cenic.net (137.164.46.7) 159 ms 159 ms 159 ms
10  dc-sdsc-sdsc2--tus-dc-ge.cenic.net (137.164.24.174) 161 ms 161 ms 161 ms
11  pinot.sdsc.edu (198.17.46.56)  161.559 ms  161.381 ms  161.439 ms
12  rommie.caida.org (192.172.226.78)  161.442 ms  161.445 ms  161.532 ms
```

This output shows that packets travel inside Init Seven's network for a long time. Sometimes we can guess the location of the gateways from their names. Init Seven's core stretches all the way from Zurich (zur) to Frankfurt (fra), Amsterdam (ams), London (lon), and finally, Los Angeles (lax). Here, the traffic transfers to cenic.net, which delivers the packets to the caida.org host within the network of the San Diego Supercomputer Center (sdsc) in La Jolla, CA.

At hop 8, we see a star in place of one of the round trip times. This notation means that no response (error packet) was received in response to the probe. In this case, the cause is probably congestion, but that is not the only possibility. **traceroute** relies on low-priority ICMP packets, which many routers are smart enough to drop in preference to "real" traffic. A few stars shouldn't send you into a panic.

If you see stars in all the time fields for a given gateway, no "time exceeded" messages are arriving from that machine. Perhaps the gateway is simply down. Sometimes, a gateway or firewall is configured to silently discard packets with expired TTLs. In this case, you can still see through the silent host to the gateways beyond. Another possibility is that the gateway's error packets are slow to return and that **traceroute** has stopped waiting for them by the time they arrive.

3. We removed a few fractions of milliseconds from the longer lines to keep them from folding.

Some firewalls block ICMP "time exceeded" messages entirely. If such a firewall lies along the path, you won't get information about any of the gateways beyond it. However, you can still determine the total number of hops to the destination because the probe packets eventually get all the way there.

Also, some firewalls may block the outbound UDP datagrams that **traceroute** sends to trigger the ICMP responses. This problem causes **traceroute** to report no useful information at all. If you find that your own firewall is preventing you from running **traceroute**, make sure the firewall has been configured to pass UDP ports 33434–33534 as well as ICMP ECHO (type 8) packets.

A slow link does not necessarily indicate a malfunction. Some physical networks have a naturally high latency; UMTS/EDGE/GPRS wireless networks are a good example. Sluggishness can also be a sign of high load on the receiving network. Inconsistent round trip times would support such a hypothesis.

Sometimes, you may see the notation !N instead of a star or round trip time. It indicates that the current gateway sent back a "network unreachable" error, meaning that it doesn't know how to route your packet. Other possibilities include !H for "host unreachable" and !P for "protocol unreachable." A gateway that returns any of these error messages is usually the last hop you can get to. That host usually has a routing problem (possibly caused by a broken network link): either its static routes are wrong, or dynamic protocols have failed to propagate a usable route to the destination.

If **traceroute** doesn't seem to be working for you or is working slowly, it may be timing out while trying to resolve the hostnames of gateways through DNS. If DNS is broken on the host you are tracing from, use **traceroute -n** to request numeric output. This option disables hostname lookups; it may be the only way to get **traceroute** to function on a crippled network.

traceroute needs root privileges to operate. To be available to normal users, it must be installed setuid root. Several Linux distributions include the **traceroute** command but leave off the setuid bit. Depending on your environment and needs, you can either turn the setuid bit back on or give interested users access to the command through **sudo**.

Recent years have seen the introduction of several new **traceroute**-like utilities that can bypass ICMP-blocking firewalls. See the PERTKB Wiki for an overview of these tools at tinyurl.com/y99qh6u. We especially like **mtr**, which has a **top**-like interface and shows a sort of live **traceroute**. Very neat!

When debugging routing issues, it can be helpful to take a look at your site from the perspective of the outside world. Several web-based route tracing services let you do this sort of inverse **traceroute** right from a browser window. Thomas Kernen maintains a list of these services at traceroute.org.

21.5 NETSTAT: GET NETWORK STATISTICS

netstat collects a wealth of information about the state of your computer's networking software, including interface statistics, routing information, and connection tables. There isn't really a unifying theme to the different sets of output, except that they all relate to the network. Think of **netstat** as the "kitchen sink" of network tools—it exposes a variety of network information that doesn't fit anywhere else. Here, we discuss the five most common uses of **netstat**:

- Inspecting interface configuration information
- Monitoring the status of network connections
- Identifying listening network services
- Examining the routing table
- Viewing operational statistics for various network protocols

Inspecting interface configuration information

netstat -i shows the configuration and state of each of the host's network interfaces along with the associated traffic counters. The output is generally tabular but the details vary by system:

```
solaris$ netstat -i
Name     Mtu  Net/Dest  Address   Ipkts      Ierrs Opkts     Oerrs Collis Queue
lo0      8232 loopback  localhost 319589661  0     319589661 0     0      0
e1000g1  1500 host-if1  host-if1  369842112  0     348557584 0     0      0
e1000g2  1500 host-if2  host-if2  93141891   0     121107161 0     0      0
```

```
hp-ux$ netstat -i
Name Mtu   Network      Address            Ipkts    Ierrs Opkts    Oerrs Coll
lan0 1500  192.168.10.0 hpux11             2611259  0     2609847  0     0
lo0  32808 loopback     hpux11.atrust.com
```

```
aix$ netstat -i
Name Mtu   Network      Address    ZoneID Ipkts   Ierrs Opkts   Oerrs Coll
en3  1500  link#2       0.11.25.39.e0.b6  41332   0     14173   3     0
en3  1500  192.168.10   IBM               41332   0     14173   3     0
lo0  16896 link#1                         1145121 0     1087387 0     0
lo0  16896 127          loopback          1145121 0     1087387 0     0
lo0  16896 ::1                          0 1145121 0     1087387 0     0
```

On Linux, you may want to use **ifconfig -a** instead of **netstat -i**. It prints similar information in a more detailed and more verbose format.

```
linux$ ifconfig -a
eth0      Link encap:EthernetHWaddr 00:15:17:4c:4d:00
          inet addr:192.168.0.203Bcast:192.168.0.255Mask:255.255.255.0
          inet6 addr: fe80::215:17ff:fe4c:4d00/64 Scope:Link
          UP BROADCAST RUNNING MULTICASTMTU:1500Metric:1
          RX packets:559543852 errors:0 dropped:62 overruns:0 frame:0
          TX packets:457050867 errors:0 dropped:0 overruns:0 carrier:0
```

```
        collisions:0 txqueuelen:1000
        RX bytes:478438325085 (478.4 GB)TX bytes:228502292340 (228.5 GB)
        Memory:b8820000-b8840000

eth1    Link encap:EthernetHWaddr 00:15:17:4c:4d:01
        BROADCAST MULTICASTMTU:1500Metric:1
        RX packets:0 errors:0 dropped:0 overruns:0 frame:0
        TX packets:0 errors:0 dropped:0 overruns:0 carrier:0
        collisions:0 txqueuelen:1000
        RX bytes:0 (0.0 B)TX bytes:0 (0.0 B)
        Memory:b8800000-b8820000

lo      Link encap:Local Loopback
        inet addr:127.0.0.1Mask:255.0.0.0
        inet6 addr: ::1/128 Scope:Host
        UP LOOPBACK RUNNINGMTU:16436Metric:1
        RX packets:1441988 errors:0 dropped:0 overruns:0 frame:0
        TX packets:1441988 errors:0 dropped:0 overruns:0 carrier:0
        collisions:0 txqueuelen:0
        RX bytes:327048609 (327.0 MB)TX bytes:327048609 (327.0 MB)
```

This host has two network interfaces: one for regular traffic, plus a second interface that is currently not in use (it has no IP address and is not marked UP). RX packets and TX packets report the number of packets that have been received and transmitted on each interface since the machine was booted. Many types of errors are counted in the error buckets, and it is normal for a few to show up.

Errors should be less than 1% of the associated packets. If your error rate is high, compare the rates of several neighboring machines. A large number of errors on a single machine suggests a problem with that machine's interface or connection. A high error rate everywhere most likely indicates a media or network problem. One of the most common causes of a high error rate is an Ethernet speed or duplex mismatch caused by a failure of autosensing or autonegotiation.

Although a collision is a type of error, it is counted separately by **netstat**. The field labeled Collisions reports the number of collisions that were experienced while packets were being sent. Use this number to calculate the percentage of output packets (TX packets) that resulted in collisions.

On a switched network with full duplex links—that is, on any modern variety of Ethernet—you should not see any collisions, even when the network is under heavy load. If you do see collisions, something is seriously wrong. You might also want to make sure that flow control is enabled on your switches and routers, especially if your network contains links of different speeds.

We have often traced network problems back to el cheapo pieces of desktop network equipment, such as a switch that has gone haywire and needs to be power-cycled or replaced.

Monitoring the status of network connections

With no arguments, **netstat** displays the status of active TCP and UDP ports. Inactive ("listening") servers that are waiting for connections are normally hidden, but you can see them with **netstat -a**.[4] The output looks like this:

```
linux$ netstat -a
Active Internet connections (servers and established)
Proto   Recv-Q  Send-Q  Local Address   ForeignAddress     State
tcp     0       0       *:ldap          *:*                LISTEN
tcp     0       0       *:mysql         *:*                LISTEN
tcp     0       0       *:imaps         *:*                LISTEN
tcp     0       0       bull:ssh        dhcp-32hw:4208     ESTABLISHED
tcp     0       0       bull:imaps      nubark:54195       ESTABLISHED
tcp     0       0       bull:http       dhcp-30hw:2563     ESTABLISHED
tcp     0       0       bull:imaps      dhcp-18hw:2851     ESTABLISHED
tcp     0       0       *:http          *:*                LISTEN
tcp     0       0       bull:37203      baikal:mysql       ESTABLISHED
tcp     0       0       *:ssh           *:*                LISTEN
...
```

This example is from the host otter, and it has been severely pruned; for example, UDP and UNIX socket connections are not displayed. The output above shows an inbound SSH connection, two inbound IMAPS connections, one inbound HTTP connection, an outbound MySQL connection, and a bunch of ports listening for other connections.

Addresses are shown as *hostname.service*, where the *service* is a port number. For well-known services, **netstat** shows the port symbolically, using the mapping defined in **/etc/services**. You can obtain numeric addresses and ports with the **-n** option to **netstat**. Like most network debugging tools, **netstat** is painful to use without the **-n** flag if your DNS is broken.

Send-Q and Recv-Q show the sizes of the local host's send and receive queues for the connection; the queue sizes on the other end of a TCP connection might be different. These numbers should tend toward 0 and at least not be consistently nonzero. (Of course, if you are running **netstat** over a network terminal, the send queue for your connection may never be 0.)

The connection state has meaning only for TCP; UDP is a connectionless protocol. The most common states you'll see are ESTABLISHED for currently active connections, LISTEN for servers waiting for connections (not normally shown without **-a**), and TIME_WAIT for connections in the process of closing.

netstat -a is primarily useful for debugging higher-level problems once you have determined that basic networking facilities are working correctly. It lets you verify that servers are set up correctly and facilitates the diagnosis of certain types of miscommunication, particularly with TCP. For example, a connection that stays

4. Connections for "UNIX domain sockets" are also shown, but since they aren't related to networking, we do not discuss them here.

in state SYN_SENT identifies a process that is trying to contact a nonexistent or inaccessible network server.

See Chapter 13 for more information about kernel tuning.

If **netstat** shows a lot of connections in the SYN_WAIT condition, your host probably cannot handle the number of connections being requested. This inadequacy may be due to kernel tuning limitations or even to malicious flooding.

Identifying listening network services

One common question in this security-conscious era is "What processes on this machine are listening on the network for incoming connections?" **netstat -a** shows all the ports that are actively listening (any TCP port in state LISTEN, and potentially any UDP port), but on a busy machine, those lines can get lost in the noise of established TCP connections.

On Linux, use **netstat -l** to see only the listening ports. The output format is the same as for **netstat -a**. You can also add the **-p** flag to make **netstat** identify the specific process associated with each listening port.[5] The sample output below shows three common services (**sshd**, **sendmail**, and **named**) followed by an unusual one:

```
linux$ netstat -lp
...
tcp    0    0    0.0.0.0:22     0.0.0.0:*   LISTEN   23858/sshd
tcp    0    0    0.0.0.0:25     0.0.0.0:*   LISTEN   10342/sendmail
udp    0    0    0.0.0.0:53     0.0.0.0:*            30016/named
udp    0    0    0.0.0.0:962    0.0.0.0:*            38221/mudd
...
```

mudd with PID 38221 is listening on UDP port 962. If you don't know what **mudd** is, you might want to follow up on this.

For security, it's also helpful to look at machines from an outsider's perspective by running a port scanner. **nmap** is very helpful for this; see page 914.

Examining the routing table

netstat -r displays the kernel's routing table. The following sample output is from a Red Hat machine with two network interfaces. (The output varies slightly among operating systems.)

```
redhat$ netstat -rn
Kernel IP routing table
Destination   Gateway        Genmask        Flags MSS Window  irtt Iface
192.168.1.0   0.0.0.0        255.255.255.0  U       0 0          0 eth0
10.2.5.0      0.0.0.0        255.255.255.0  U       0 0          0 eth1
127.0.0.0     0.0.0.0        255.0.0.0      U       0 0          0 lo
0.0.0.0       192.168.1.254  0.0.0.0        UG      0 0         40 eth0
...
```

5. On UNIX systems that don't support **netstat**'s **-p** flag, the **lsof** command can provide this information (and more). See page 145 for more about **lsof**.

Destinations and gateways can be displayed either as hostnames or as IP addresses; the **-n** flag requests numeric output.

See page 466 for more information about the routing table.

Flags characterize the route: U means up (active), G is a gateway, and H is a host route. U, G, and H together indicate a host route that passes through an intermediate gateway. The D flag (not shown) indicates a route resulting from an ICMP redirect. The remaining fields show TCP segment and window sizes along this route along with an initial round trip time estimate and the name of the interface.

Use this form of **netstat** to check the health of your system's routing table. It's particularly important to verify that the system has a default route and that this route is correct. The default route is represented by an all-0 destination address (0.0.0.0) or by the word default. It is possible not to have a default route entry, but such a configuration would be highly atypical on anything but a backbone router.

Viewing operational statistics for network protocols

netstat -s dumps the contents of counters that are scattered throughout the network code. The output has separate sections for IP, ICMP, TCP, and UDP. Below are pieces of **netstat -s** output from a typical server; they have been edited to show only the tastiest pieces of information.

```
Ip:
    671349985 total packets received
    0 forwarded
    345 incoming packets discarded
    667912993 incoming packets delivered
    589623972 requests sent out
    60 dropped because of missing route
    203 fragments dropped after timeout
```

Be sure to check that packets are not being dropped or discarded. It is acceptable for a few incoming packets to be discarded, but a quick rise in this metric usually indicates a memory shortage or some other resource problem.

```
Icmp:
    242023 ICMP messages received
    912 input ICMP message failed.
    ICMP input histogram:
        destination unreachable: 72120
        timeout in transit: 573
        echo requests: 17135
        echo replies: 152195
    66049 ICMP messages sent
    0 ICMP messages failed
    ICMP output histogram:
        destination unreachable: 48914
        echo replies: 17135
```

In this example, the number of echo requests in the input section matches the number of echo replies in the output section. Note that "destination unreachable" messages can still be generated even when all packets are apparently forwardable.

Bad packets eventually reach a gateway that rejects them, and error messages are then sent back along the gateway chain.

```
Tcp:
    4442780 active connections openings
    1023086 passive connection openings
    50399 failed connection attempts
    0 connection resets received
    44 connections established
    666674854 segments received
    585111784 segments send out
    107368 segments retransmited
    86 bad segments received.
    3047240 resets sent
Udp:
    4395827 packets received
    31586 packets to unknown port received.
    0 packet receive errors
    4289260 packets sent
```

It's a good idea to develop a feel for the normal ranges of these statistics so that you can recognize pathological states.

21.6 Inspection of live interface activity

One good way to identify network problems is to look at what's happening right now. How many packets were sent in the last five minutes on a given interface? How many bytes? Are collisions or other errors occurring? You can answer all these questions by watching network activity in real time. Different tools come into play depending on your OS.

On Solaris, you can append an interval in seconds and a count value to **netstat -i**:

```
solaris$ netstat -i 2 3
    input   e1000g    output       input    (Total)     output
packets errs packets errs colls packets errs  packets errs colls
17861    0    26208   0    0    17951    0     26298   0    0
4        0    2       0    0    4        0     2       0    0
1        0    1       0    0    1        0     1       0    0
...
```

HP-UX and AIX expect a single number that sets the interval (in seconds) at which statistics are to be printed.

```
$ netstat -i 2
   (lan0)-> input          output        (Total)-> input          output
           packets        packets                 packets         packets
           9053713        9052513                10115002        10113803
                 8              8                       8               8
                22             22                      22              22
                 9              9                       9               9
...
```

Linux's **netstat** has no interval option, so for Linux we recommend a completely different tool: **sar**. (We discuss **sar** from the perspective of general system monitoring on page 1129.) Most distributions don't install **sar** by default, but it's always available as an optional package. The example below requests reports every two seconds for a period of one minute (i.e., 30 reports). The **DEV** argument is a literal keyword, not a placeholder for a device or interface name.

```
redhat$ sar -n DEV 2 30
17:50:43  IFACE rxpck/s  txpck/s   rxbyt/s   txbyt/s  rxcmp/s  txcmp/s rxmcst/s
17:50:45     lo    3.61     3.61    263.40    263.40     0.00     0.00     0.00
17:50:45   eth0   18.56    11.86   1364.43   1494.33     0.00     0.00     0.52
17:50:45   eth1    0.00     0.00      0.00      0.00     0.00     0.00     0.00
```

This example is from a Red Hat machine with two network interfaces. The output includes instantaneous and average readings of interface utilization in units of both bytes and packets. The second interface (eth1) is clearly not in use.

The first two columns state the time at which the data was sampled and the names of the network interfaces. The next two columns show the number of packets received and transmitted, respectively.

The rxbyt/s and txbyt/s columns are probably the most useful since they show the actual bandwidth in use. The final three columns give statistics on compressed (rxcmp/s, txcmp/s) and multicast (rxmcst/s) packets.

sar -n DEV is especially useful for tracking down the source of errors. **ifconfig** can alert you to the existence of problems, but it can't tell you whether the errors came from a continuous, low-level problem or from a brief but catastrophic event. Observe the network over time and under a variety of load conditions to solidify your impression of what's going on. Try running **ping** with a large packet payload (size) while you watch the output of **sar -n DEV**.

21.7 Packet sniffers

tcpdump and Wireshark belong to a class of tools known as packet sniffers. They listen to network traffic and record or print packets that meet criteria of your choice. For example, you can inspect all packets sent to or from a particular host, or TCP packets related to one particular network connection.

Packet sniffers are useful both for solving problems that you know about and for discovering entirely new problems. It's a good idea to take an occasional sniff of your network to make sure the traffic is in order.

Packet sniffers need to be able to intercept traffic that the local machine would not normally receive (or at least, pay attention to), so the underlying network hardware must allow access to every packet. Broadcast technologies such as Ethernet work fine, as do most other modern local area networks.

See page 537 for more information about network switches.

Since packet sniffers need to see as much of the raw network traffic as possible, they can be thwarted by network switches, which by design try to limit the propagation of "unnecessary" packets. However, it can still be informative to try out a sniffer on a switched network. You may discover problems related to broadcast or multicast packets. Depending on your switch vendor, you may be surprised at how much traffic you can see.

In addition to having access to all network packets, the interface hardware must transport those packets up to the software layer. Packet addresses are normally checked in hardware, and only broadcast/multicast packets and those addressed to the local host are relayed to the kernel. In "promiscuous mode," an interface lets the kernel read all packets on the network, even the ones intended for other hosts.

Packet sniffers understand many of the packet formats used by standard network services, and they can print these packets in human-readable form. This capability makes it easier to track the flow of a conversation between two programs. Some sniffers print the ASCII contents of a packet in addition to the packet header and so are useful for investigating high-level protocols.

Since some protocols send information (and even passwords) across the network as cleartext, you must take care not to invade the privacy of your users. On the other hand, nothing quite dramatizes the need for cryptographic security like the sight of a plaintext password captured in a network packet.

Sniffers read data from a raw network device, so they must run as root. Although this root limitation serves to decrease the chance that normal users will listen in on your network traffic, it is really not much of a barrier. Some sites choose to remove sniffer programs from most hosts to reduce the chance of abuse. If nothing else, you should check your systems' interfaces to be sure they are not running in promiscuous mode without your knowledge or consent. On all systems, the output of **ifconfig** labels promiscuous interfaces with the flag PROMISC. On Linux systems, the fact that an interface has been switched to promiscuous mode is also recorded in the kernel log.

tcpdump: industry-standard packet sniffer

tcpdump, yet another amazing network tool by Van Jacobson, is available as a package for most Linux distributions and can be installed from source on our other example systems. **tcpdump** has long been the industry-standard sniffer, and most other network analysis tools read and write trace files in **tcpdump** format, also known as **libpcap** format.

By default, **tcpdump** tunes in on the first network interface it comes across. If it chooses the wrong interface, you can force an interface with the **-i** flag. If DNS is broken or you just don't want **tcpdump** doing name lookups, use the **-n** option. This option is important because slow DNS service can cause the filter to start dropping packets before they can be dealt with by **tcpdump**.

The -v flag increases the information you see about packets, and -vv gives you even more data. Finally, **tcpdump** can store packets to a file with the **-w** flag and can read them back in with the **-r** flag.

Note that **tcpdump -w** saves only packet headers by default. This default makes for small dumps, but the most helpful and relevant information may be missing. So, unless you are sure you need only headers, use the **-s** option with a value on the order of 1560 (actual values are MTU-dependent) to capture whole packets for later inspection.

As an example, the following truncated output comes from the machine named nubark. The filter specification **host bull** limits the display of packets to those that directly involve the machine bull, either as source or as destination.

```
$ sudo tcpdump host bull
12:35:23.519339 bull.41537 > nubark.domain:  A? atrust.com. (28) (DF)
12:35:23.519961 nubark.domain > bull.41537:  A 66.77.122.161 (112) (DF)
```

The first packet shows bull sending a DNS lookup request about atrust.com to nubark. The response is the IP address of the machine associated with that name, which is 66.77.122.161. Note the time stamp on the left and **tcpdump**'s understanding of the application-layer protocol (in this case, DNS). The port number on bull is arbitrary and is shown numerically (41537), but since the server port number (53) is well known, **tcpdump** shows its symbolic name, domain.

Packet sniffers can produce an overwhelming amount of information—overwhelming not only for you but also for the underlying operating system. To avoid this problem on busy networks, **tcpdump** lets you specify complex filters. For example, the following filter collects only incoming web traffic from one subnet:

```
$ sudo tcpdump src net 192.168.1.0/24 and dst port 80
```

The **tcpdump** man page contains several good examples of advanced filtering along with a complete listing of primitives.[6]

Solaris includes a sniffer in the base system that works much like **tcpdump**. It is called **snoop**. HP-UX, AIX, and most Linux distributions do not seem to include a packet sniffer in the base install.

```
solaris$ snoop
Using device /dev/e1000g0 (promiscuous mode)
nubark -> solaris TCP D=22 S=58689 Ack=2141650294 Seq=3569652094 Len=0
    Win=15008 Options=<nop,nop,tstamp 292567745 289381342>
nubark -> solaris TCP D=22 S=58689 Ack=2141650358 Seq=3569652094 Len=0
    Win=15008 Options=<nop,nop,tstamp 292567745 289381342>
? -> (multicast)  ETHER Type=023C (LLC/802.3), size = 53 bytes
...
```

6. If your filtering needs exceed **tcpdump**'s capabilities, consider **ngrep** (ngrep.sourceforge.net), which can filter packets according to their contents.

If you are using Solaris zones, note that **snoop** only works properly in the global zone, even when you are debugging a problem in a nonglobal zone.

Wireshark and TShark: tcpdump on steroids

tcpdump has been around since approximately the dawn of time, but a newer open source package called Wireshark (formerly known as Ethereal) has been gaining ground rapidly. Wireshark is under active development and incorporates more functionality than most commercial sniffing products. It's an incredibly powerful analysis tool and should be included in every networking expert's tool kit. It's also an invaluable learning aid.

Wireshark includes both a GUI interface (**wireshark**) and a command-line interface (**tshark**). Linux distributions make it a snap to install. UNIX administrators should check wireshark.org, which hosts the source code and a variety of precompiled binaries.

Wireshark can read and write trace files in the formats used by many other packet sniffers. Another handy feature is that you can click on any packet in a TCP conversation and ask Wireshark to reassemble (splice together) the payload data of all the packets in the stream. This feature is useful if you want to examine the data transferred during a complete TCP exchange, such as a connection used to transmit an email message across the network.

Wireshark's capture filters are functionally identical to **tcpdump**'s since Wireshark uses the same underlying **libpcap** library. Watch out, though—one important gotcha with Wireshark is the added feature of "display filters," which affect what you see rather than what's actually captured by the sniffer. The display filter syntax is more powerful than the **libpcap** syntax supported at capture time. The display filters do look somewhat similar, but they are not the same.

See page 274 for more information about SANs.

Wireshark has built-in dissectors for a wide variety of network protocols, including many used to implement SANs. It breaks packets into a structured tree of information in which every bit of the packet is described in plain English.

Exhibit B on the next page shows Wireshark's capture of a DNS query and response. The table near the top of the screen shows the two packets involved. The first packet is the request on its way to the DNS server, and the second packet is the answer coming back. The response packet is selected, so the middle panel shows its disassembly. The lower panel shows the packet in the form of raw bytes.

The expanded section of the tree shows the packet's DNS payload. The raw content can also be interesting to look at because it sometimes contains telltale text fragments that hint at what is going on. Scanning the text is especially handy when there is no built-in dissector for the current protocol. Wireshark's help menu provides many great examples to get you started. Experiment!

Exhibit B A pair of DNS packets in Wireshark

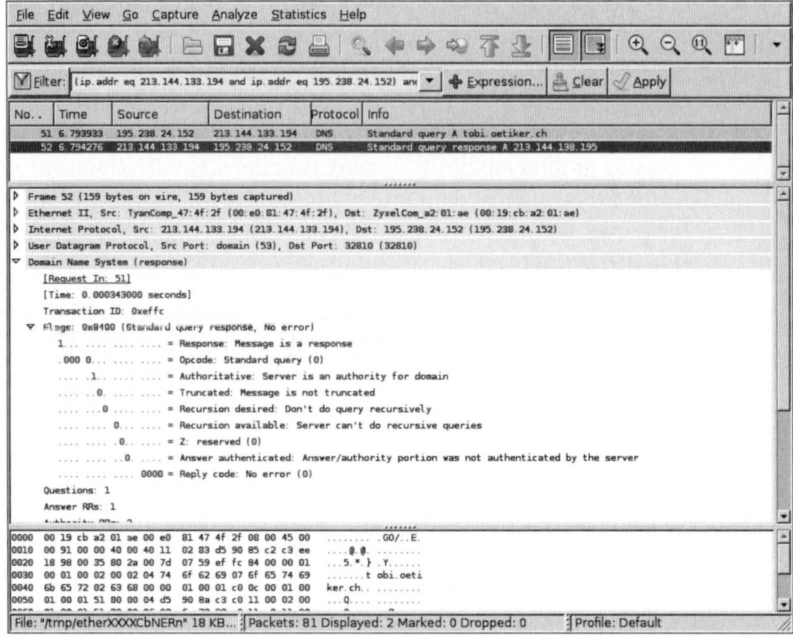

A note of caution regarding Wireshark: although it has lots of neat features, it has also required many security updates over the years. Run a current copy, and do not leave it running indefinitely on sensitive machines; it might be a potential route of attack.

21.8 The ICSI Netalyzr

We have looked at several tools for network debugging and for reviewing specific aspects of the network configuration. But even with your own best efforts at monitoring, it's useful to have someone else take a peek at your network from time to time. The Netalyzr is a service provided by the International Computer Science Institute at Berkeley that provides a useful "second opinion." To use it, just point your Java-enabled browser at netalyzr.icsi.berkeley.edu (note: missing 'e').

The Netalyzr tests your Internet connection in a variety of ways. It has the advantage of being able to access your network both from inside (through the Java program that runs in your browser) and from the perspective of ICSI's servers.

Exhibit C shows the Netalyzr report for a workstation on a private network that's attached to the outside world through a DSL link. The Netalyzr seems to be generally happy with the setup except for a few quibbles about the Apache web proxy that's in use. (Blocking malformed HTTP requests may actually be a useful feature, however.)

Exhibit C A Netalyzr report

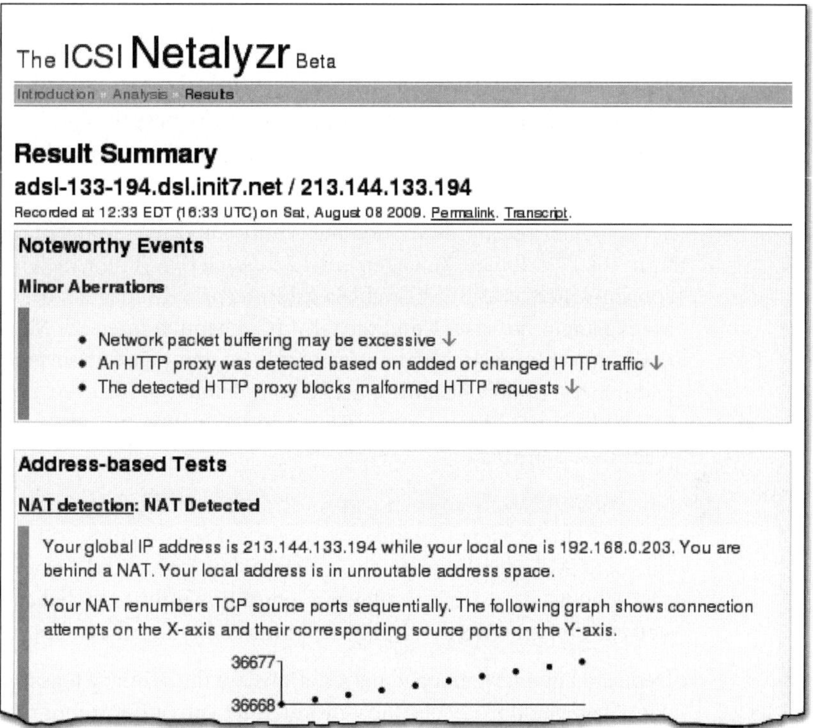

The full report contains sections that report on the environment's IP connectivity, bandwidth, latency, buffering, and handling of fragmented packets, among other topics. The tests for DNS and HTTP anomalies are particularly strong.

21.9 Network management protocols

Networks have grown rapidly in size and value over the last 20 years, and along with that growth has come the need for an efficient way to manage them. Commercial vendors and standards organizations have approached this challenge in many different ways. The most significant developments have been the introduction of several standard device-management protocols and a glut of high-level products that exploit those protocols.

Network management protocols standardize a way of probing a device to discover its configuration, health, and network connections. In addition, they allow some of this information to be modified so that network management can be standardized across different kinds of machinery and performed from a central location.

The most common protocol used with TCP/IP is the Simple Network Management Protocol, SNMP. Despite its name, SNMP is actually quite complex. It defines a hierarchical namespace of management data and a way to read and write the data at each node. It also defines a way for managed servers and devices ("agents") to send event notification messages ("traps") to management stations.

The protocol itself is simple; most of SNMP's complexity lies above the protocol layer in the conventions for constructing the namespace and in the unnecessarily baroque vocabulary that surrounds SNMP like a protective shell. As long as you don't think too hard about its internal mechanics, SNMP is easy to use.

Several other standards are floating around out there. Many of them originate from the Distributed Management Task Force (DMTF), which is responsible for concepts such as WBEM (Web-Based Enterprise Management), DMI (Desktop Management Interface), and the CIM (Conceptual Interface Model). Some of these concepts, particularly DMI, have been embraced by several major vendors and may eventually become a useful complement to (or even a replacement for) SNMP. For now, however, the vast majority of networking gear management takes place over SNMP.

Since SNMP is only an abstract protocol, you need both a server program ("agent") and a client ("manager") to use it. Perhaps counterintuitively, the server side of SNMP represents the thing being managed, and the client side is the manager. Clients range from simple command-line utilities to dedicated management stations that graphically display networks and faults in eye-popping color.

Dedicated network management stations are the primary reason for the existence of management protocols. Most products let you build a topographic model of the network as well as a logical model; the two are presented together on-screen, along with a continuous indication of the status of each component.

Just as a chart can reveal the hidden meaning in a page of numbers, a network management station can summarize the state of a large network in a way that's easily accepted by a human brain. This kind of executive summary is almost impossible to get in any other way.

A major advantage of network management by protocol is that it promotes all kinds of network hardware onto a level playing field. UNIX and Linux systems are all basically similar, but routers, switches, and other low-level components are not. With SNMP, they all speak a common language and can be probed, reset, and configured from a central location. It's nice to have one consistent interface to all the network's hardware.

21.10 SNMP: The Simple Network Management Protocol

When SNMP first became widely used in the early 1990s, it started a mini gold rush. Hundreds of companies came out with SNMP management packages. Most pieces of network hardware that are intended for production use (as opposed to household use) now incorporate an SNMP agent.

Before we dive into the gritty details of SNMP, we should note that the terminology associated with it is some of the most wretched technobabble to be found in the networking arena. The standard names for SNMP concepts and objects actively lead you away from an understanding of what's going on. The people responsible for this state of affairs should have their keyboards smashed.

SNMP organization

SNMP data is arranged in a standardized hierarchy. This enforced organization allows the data space to remain both universal and extensible, at least in theory. Large portions are set aside for future expansion, and vendor-specific additions are localized to prevent conflicts. The naming hierarchy is made up of "Management Information Bases" (MIBs), structured text files that describe the data accessible through SNMP. MIBs contain descriptions of specific data variables, which are referred to with names known as object identifiers, or OIDs.

Translated into English, this means that SNMP defines a hierarchical namespace of variables whose values are tied to "interesting" parameters of the system. An OID is just a fancy way of naming a specific managed piece of information.

The SNMP hierarchy is much like a filesystem. However, a dot is used as the separator character, and each node is given a number rather than a name. By convention, nodes are also given text names for ease of reference, but this naming is really just a high-level convenience and not a feature of the hierarchy. (It is similar in principle to the mapping of hostnames to IP addresses.)

For example, the OID that refers to the uptime of the system is 1.3.6.1.2.1.1.3. This OID is also known by the human-readable (though not necessarily "human-understandable without additional documentation") name

iso.org.dod.internet.mgmt.mib-2.system.sysUpTime

The top levels of the SNMP hierarchy are political artifacts and generally do not contain useful data. In fact, useful data can currently be found only beneath the OID iso.org.dod.internet.mgmt (numerically, 1.3.6.1.2).

The basic SNMP MIB for TCP/IP (MIB-I) defines access to common management data: information about the system, its interfaces, address translation, and protocol operations (IP, ICMP, TCP, UDP, and others). A later and more complete reworking of this MIB (called MIB-II) is defined in RFC1213. Most vendors that provide an SNMP server support MIB-II. Table 21.1 on the next page presents a sampling of nodes from the MIB-II namespace.

In addition to the basic MIB, there are MIBs for various kinds of hardware interfaces and protocols, MIBs for individual vendors, and MIBs for particular hardware products.

A MIB is only a schema for naming management data. To be useful, a MIB must be backed up with agent-side code that maps between the SNMP namespace and the device's actual state. SNMP agents that run on UNIX, Linux, or Windows

Table 21.1 Selected OIDs from MIB-II

OID[a]	Type	Contents
system.sysDescr	string	System info: vendor, model, OS type, etc.
system.sysLocation	string	Physical location of the machine
system.sysContact	string	Contact info for the machine's owner
system.sysName	string	System name, usually the full DNS name
interfaces.ifNumber	int	Number of network interfaces present
interfaces.ifTable	table	Table of infobits about each interface
ip.ipForwarding	int	1 if system is a gateway; otherwise, 2
ip.ipAddrTable	table	Table of IP addressing data (masks, etc.)
ip.ipRouteTable	table	The system's routing table
icmp.icmpInRedirects	int	Number of ICMP redirects received
icmp.icmpInEchos	int	Number of pings received
tcp.tcpConnTable	table	Table of current TCP connections
udp.udpTable	table	Table of UDP sockets with servers listening

a. Relative to iso.org.dod.internet.mgmt.mib-2.

come with built-in support for MIB-II. Most can be extended to support supplemental MIBs and to interface with scripts that do the actual work of fetching and storing these MIBs' associated data.

SNMP agents are complex beasts, and they have seen their share of security issues. Instead of relying on whatever agent your vendor happens to toss over the wall to you, it may be prudent to compile and install a current copy of NET-SNMP. See *The NET-SNMP agent*, opposite page, for details.

SNMP protocol operations

There are only four basic SNMP operations: get, get-next, set, and trap.

Get and set are the basic operations for reading and writing data to the node identified by a specific OID. Get-next steps through a MIB hierarchy and can read the contents of tables as well.

A trap is an unsolicited, asynchronous notification from server (agent) to client (manager) that reports the occurrence of an interesting event or condition. Several standard traps are defined, including "I've just come up" notifications, reports of failure or recovery of a network link, and announcements of various routing and authentication problems. Many other not-so-standard traps are in common use, including some that simply watch the values of other SNMP variables and fire off a message when a specified range has been exceeded. The mechanism by which the destinations of trap messages are specified depends on the implementation of the agent.

Since SNMP messages can potentially modify configuration information, some security mechanism is needed. The simplest version of SNMP security is based on the concept of an SNMP "community string," which is really just a horribly obfuscated way of saying "password." There's usually one community string for read-only access and another that allows writing.

Although many organizations still use the original community-string-based authentication, version 3 of the SNMP standard introduced access control methods with higher security. Although configuring this more advanced security requires a little extra work, the risk reduction is well worth the effort. If for some reason you can't use version 3 SNMP security, at least be sure you've selected a hard-to-guess community string.

RMON: remote monitoring MIB

The RMON MIB permits the collection of generic network performance data (that is, data not tied to any one particular device). Network sniffers or "probes" can be deployed around the network to gather information about utilization and performance. Once a useful amount of data has been collected, statistics and interesting information about the data can be shipped back to a central management station for analysis and presentation. Many probes have a packet capture buffer and can provide a sort of remote **tcpdump** facility.

RMON is defined in RFC1757, which became a draft standard in 1995. The MIB is broken up into nine "RMON groups." Each group contains a different set of network statistics. If you have a large network with many WAN connections, consider buying probes to reduce the SNMP traffic across your WAN links. Once you have access to statistical summaries from the RMON probes, there's usually no need to gather raw data remotely. Many switches and routers support RMON and store at least some network statistics.

21.11 The NET-SNMP agent

When SNMP was first standardized, Carnegie Mellon University and MIT both produced implementations. CMU's implementation was more complete and quickly became the de facto standard. When active development at CMU died down, researchers at UC Davis took over the software. After stabilizing the code, they rehomed it at the SourceForge repository. The package is now known as NET-SNMP, and it is the authoritative free SNMP implementation for UNIX and Linux. The latest version is available from net-snmp.sourceforge.net.

NET-SNMP includes an agent, some command-line tools, a server for receiving traps, and even a library for developing SNMP-aware applications. We discuss the agent in some detail here, and on page 885 we look at the command-line tools.

As in other implementations, the agent collects information about the local host and serves it to SNMP managers across the network. The default installation includes MIBs for network interfaces, memory, disk, processes, and CPU. The agent is easily extensible since it can execute an arbitrary command and return the command's output as an SNMP response. You can use this feature to monitor almost anything on your system with SNMP.

By default, the agent is installed as **/usr/sbin/snmpd**. It is usually started at boot time and reads its configuration information from files in the **/etc/snmp** directory. The most important of these files is **snmpd.conf**, which contains most of the configuration information and ships with a bunch of sample data collection methods enabled. Although the intention of the authors seems to have been for users to edit only the **snmpd.local.conf** file, you must edit **snmpd.conf** at least once to disable any default data collection methods that you don't plan to use.

The NET-SNMP **configure** script lets you specify a default log file and a couple of other local settings. You can use **snmpd -l** to specify an alternative log file or **-s** to direct log messages to syslog. Table 21.2 lists **snmpd**'s most important flags. We recommend that you always use the **-a** flag. For debugging, you should use the **-V**, **-d**, or **-D** flags, each of which gives progressively more information.

Table 21.2 Useful flags for NET-SNMP snmpd

Flag	Function
-l *logfile*	Logs information to *logfile*
-a	Logs the addresses of all SNMP connections
-d	Logs the contents of every SNMP packet
-V	Enables verbose logging
-D	Logs debugging information (lots of it)
-h	Displays all arguments to **snmpd**
-H	Displays all configuration file directives
-A	Appends to the log file instead of overwriting it
-s	Logs to syslog (uses the daemon facility)

It's worth mentioning that many useful SNMP-related Perl, Ruby, and Python modules are available from the respective module repositories.

21.12 Network management applications

We begin this section by exploring the simplest SNMP management tools: the commands provided with the NET-SNMP package. These commands can familiarize you with SNMP, and they're also great for one-off checks of specific OIDs. Next, we look at Cacti, a program that generates beautiful historical graphs of SNMP values, and Nagios, an event-based monitoring system. We conclude with some recommendations of what to look for when purchasing a commercial network monitoring system.

The NET-SNMP tools

Even if your system comes with its own SNMP server, you may still want to compile and install the client-side tools from the NET-SNMP package. Table 21.3 lists the most commonly used tools.

Table 21.3 Command-line tools in the NET-SNMP package

Command	Function
snmpdelta	Monitors changes in SNMP variables over time
snmpdf	Monitors disk space on a remote host via SNMP
snmpget	Gets the value of an SNMP variable from an agent
snmpgetnext	Gets the next variable in sequence
snmpset	Sets an SNMP variable on an agent
snmptable	Gets a table of SNMP variables
snmptranslate	Searches for and describes OIDs in the MIB hierarchy
snmptrap	Generates a trap alert
snmpwalk	Traverses a MIB starting at a particular OID

In addition to their value on the command line, these programs are tremendously handy in simple scripts. It is often helpful to have **snmpget** save interesting data values to a text file every few minutes. (Use **cron** to implement the scheduling; see Chapter 9, *Periodic Processes*.)

snmpwalk is another useful tool. Starting at a specified OID (or at the beginning of the MIB, by default), this command repeatedly makes "get next" calls to an agent. This behavior results in a complete list of available OIDs and their associated values. **snmpwalk** is particularly handy when you are trying to identify new OIDs to monitor from your fancy enterprise management tool.

Here's a truncated sample **snmpwalk** of the host tuva. The community string is "secret813community", and **-v1** specifies simple authentication.

```
$ snmpwalk -c secret813community -v1 tuva
SNMPv2-MIB::sysDescr.0 = STRING: Linux tuva.atrust.com 2.6.9-11.ELsmp #1
SNMPv2-MIB::sysUpTime.0 = Timeticks: (1442) 0:00:14.42
SNMPv2-MIB::sysName.0 = STRING: tuva.atrust.com
IF-MIB::ifDescr.1 = STRING: lo
IF-MIB::ifDescr.2 = STRING: eth0
IF-MIB::ifDescr.3 = STRING: eth1
IF-MIB::ifType.1 = INTEGER: softwareLoopback(24)
IF-MIB::ifType.2 = INTEGER: ethernetCsmacd(6)
IF-MIB::ifType.3 = INTEGER: ethernetCsmacd(6)
IF-MIB::ifPhysAddress.1 = STRING:
IF-MIB::ifPhysAddress.2 = STRING: 0:11:43:d9:1e:f5
IF-MIB::ifPhysAddress.3 = STRING: 0:11:43:d9:1e:f6
```

```
IF-MIB::ifInOctets.1 = Counter32: 2605613514
IF-MIB::ifInOctets.2 = Counter32: 1543105654
IF-MIB::ifInOctets.3 = Counter32: 46312345
IF-MIB::ifInUcastPkts.1 = Counter32: 389536156
IF-MIB::ifInUcastPkts.2 = Counter32: 892959265
IF-MIB::ifInUcastPkts.3 = Counter32: 7712325
...
```

In this example, we see some general information about the system, followed by statistics about the host's network interfaces: lo0, eth0, and eth1. Depending on the MIBs supported by the agent you are managing, a complete dump can run to hundreds of lines.

SNMP data collection and graphing

Network-related data is best appreciated in visual and historical context. It's important to have some way to track and graph performance metrics, but your exact choice of software for doing this is not critical.

One of the most popular early SNMP polling and graphing packages was MRTG, written by Tobi Oetiker. MRTG is written mostly in Perl, runs regularly out of **cron**, and can collect data from any SNMP source. Each time the program runs, new data is stored and new graph images are created.

Another useful tool in this area is RRDtool, also by Tobi Oetiker. It is an application tool kit for storing and graphing performance metrics. All the leading open source monitoring solutions are based on RRDtool, including our favorite, Cacti.

Cacti, available from cacti.net, offers several attractive features. Using RRDtool as its back end, it stores monitoring data in zero-maintenance, statically sized databases. Cacti stores only enough data to create the graphs you want. For example, Cacti could store one sample every minute for a day, one sample every hour for a week, and one sample every week for a year. This consolidation scheme lets you maintain important historical information without having to store unimportant details or consume your time with database administration.

Second, Cacti can record and graph any SNMP variable, as well as many other performance metrics. You're free to collect whatever data you want. When combined with the NET-SNMP agent, Cacti generates a historical perspective on almost any system or network resource.

Exhibit D shows some examples of the graphs created by Cacti. These graphs show the load average on a server over a period of multiple weeks along with a day's traffic on a network interface.

Cacti sports easy web-based configuration as well as all the other built-in benefits of RRDtool, such as low maintenance and beautiful graphing. See the RRDtool home page at rrdtool.org for links to the current versions of RRDtool and Cacti, as well as dozens of other monitoring tools.

Exhibit D Examples of Cacti graphs

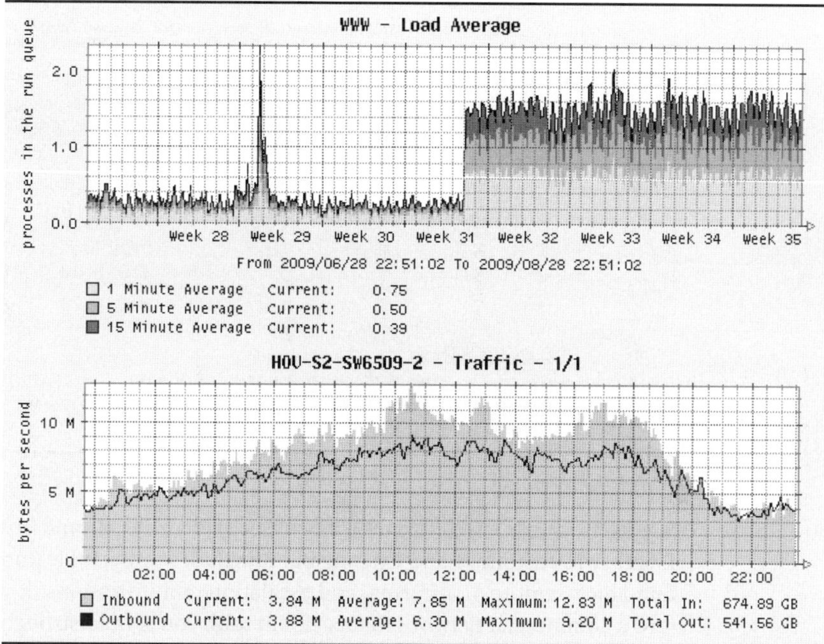

Nagios: event-based service monitoring

Nagios specializes in real-time reporting of error conditions. It includes scores of scripts for monitoring services of all shapes and sizes, along with extensive SNMP monitoring capabilities. Perhaps its greatest strength is its modular, heavily customizable configuration system that allows custom scripts to be written to monitor any conceivable metric. Although Nagios does not help you determine how much your bandwidth utilization has increased over the last month, it can page you when your web server goes down.

The Nagios distribution includes plug-ins that supervise a variety of common points of failure. You can whip up new monitors in Perl, or even in C if you are feeling ambitious. For notification methods, the distribution can send email, generate web reports, and use a dial-up modem to page you. As with the monitoring plug-ins, it's easy to roll your own.

In addition to sending real-time notifications of service outages, Nagios keeps a historical archive of this data. It provides several powerful reporting interfaces that track availability and performance trends. Many organizations use Nagios to measure compliance with service level agreements; Exhibit E on the next page shows the availability of a DNS server.

Exhibit E Server availability as shown by Nagios

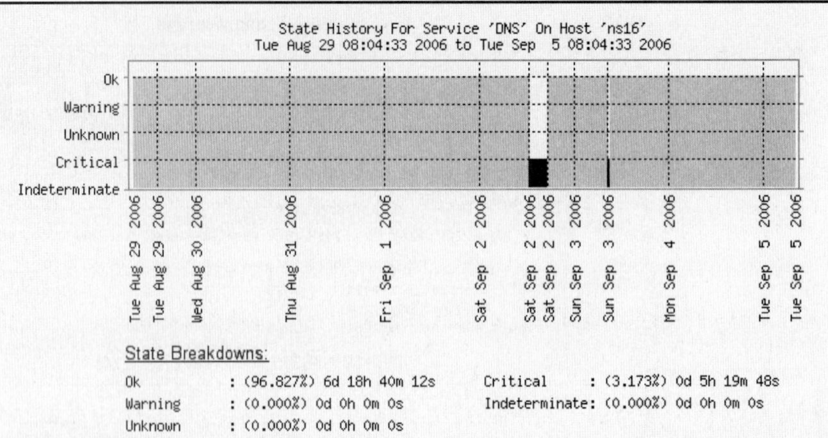

Nagios works very well for networks of fewer than a thousand hosts and devices. It is easy to customize and extend, and it includes powerful features such as redundancy, remote monitoring, and escalation of notifications. If you cannot afford a commercial network management tool, you should strongly consider Nagios. You can read more at nagios.org.

The ultimate network monitoring package: still searching

As we reviewed the state of network management packages for this edition of the book, we found the software landscape bustling with activity, just as it has been for most of the last decade. However, most packages are still using RRDtool somewhere in their guts to do their logging and graphing. No high-level standard akin to **vi** or **emacs** has yet arrived on the scene.

Two well-funded companies based on the "open source plus" model (GroundWork Open Source and Zenoss) have debuted network management packages backed by serious advertising dollars and polished interfaces. In the traditional free software arena, the packages Munin (munin.projects.linpro.no) and **collectd** (collectd.org) have gained quite a following.

Munin is especially popular in the Scandinavian countries. It's built on a clever architecture in which the data collection plug-ins not only provide data but also tell the system how the data should be presented.

collectd is written in C for performance and portability. It runs even on tiny systems without hampering performance or requiring any additional dependencies. At the time of this writing, **collectd** comes with over 70 data collection plug-ins.

Commercial management platforms

Hundreds of companies sell network management software, and new competitors enter the market every week. Instead of recommending the hottest products of the moment (which may no longer exist by the time this book is printed), we identify the features you should look for in a network management system.

Data-gathering flexibility: Management tools must be able to collect data from sources other than SNMP. Many packages include ways to gather data from almost any network service. For example, some packages can make SQL database queries, check DNS records, and connect to web servers.

User interface quality: Expensive systems often offer a custom GUI or a web interface. Most well-marketed packages today tout their ability to understand XML templates for data presentation. A UI is not just more marketing hype—you need an interface that relays information clearly, simply, and comprehensibly.

Value: Some management packages come at a stiff price. HP's OpenView is both one of the most expensive and one of the most widely adopted network management systems. Many corporations find definite value in being able to say that their site is managed by a high-end commercial system. If that isn't so important to your organization, you should look at the other end of the spectrum for free tools like Cacti and Nagios.

Automated discovery: Many systems offer the ability to "discover" your network. Through a combination of broadcast pings, SNMP requests, ARP table lookups, and DNS queries, they identify all your local hosts and devices. All the discovery implementations we have seen work pretty well, but none are very accurate on a complex (or heavily firewalled) network.

Reporting features: Many products can send alert email, activate pagers, and automatically generate tickets for popular trouble-tracking systems. Make sure that the platform you choose accommodates flexible reporting; who knows what electronic devices you will be dealing with in a few years?

Configuration management: Some solutions step far beyond monitoring and alerting. They enable you to manage actual host and device configurations. For example, a CiscoWorks interface lets you change a router's configuration in addition to monitoring its state with SNMP. Because device configuration information deepens the analysis of network problems, we predict that many packages will develop along these lines in the future.

21.13 NetFlow: connection-oriented monitoring

SNMP is widely known for its ability to report the amount of network traffic flowing through an interface. But if you want to know more about the exact type of traffic and its destinations, SNMP is not much help. On a UNIX box you could run a sniffer to unearth some additional details, but this option isn't available on a dedicated router.

In response, router vendors have come up with their own solutions to this problem. The most popular of these solutions is Cisco's NetFlow protocol.

NetFlow tracks every connection with seven keys: source and destination IP address, source and destination port number, protocol (TCP, UDP, etc.), type of service (ToS), and logical interface. This metadata, combined with additional information such as the number of packets and bytes involved, can be sent to any suitable collector.

The predominant NetFlow protocol versions are v5 and v7, which are usually lumped together because they're the same except that v7 adds an additional field (source router). v7 is used on Cisco Catalyst switches. Version 9 is gaining popularity. Its template-based nature makes it very flexible.

You can have your NetFlow router send a running account of its metadata to a suitable receiver such as CAIDA's **cflowd**. On a busy network link, this configuration generates a huge amount of data, so you may need to provision substantial disk space and look into analysis tools that are up to the task.

For the latter, one possibility is Dave Plonka's FlowScan package. It has unfortunately not been updated in some time, but it still works well. You can find it at net.doit.wisc.edu/~plonka/FlowScan.

Monitoring NetFlow data with nfdump and NfSen

Another pair of useful tools for collecting and analyzing NetFlow data are Peter Haag's **nfdump** (nfdump.sourceforge.net) and NfSen (nfsen.sourceforge.net). The collector (**nfcapd**) stores NetFlow data on disk for later processing by **nfdump**.

nfcapd and **nfdump** handle NetFlow protocol versions v5/v7 and v9. For IPv6 support, you'll have to use v9; versions 5 and 7 do not support it.

nfdump works a bit like **tcpdump** (see page 875). It has a similar filter syntax that has been adapted for NetFlow data. Flexible output formats let you customize the display of records. Built-in summarizers show you the top N talkers[7] on your network and other useful information.

The following (slightly condensed) **nfdump** output shows which IP addresses and networks exchange the most traffic, which ports are currently the most active, and

7. A "talker" is the NetFlow term for a device that creates network traffic.

more. The **-s ip/flows** option asks for information about any source or destination IP address, sorted by flows. **-n 10** limits the display to the top 10 items.

```
linux$ nfdump -M /data/nfsen/profiles-data/live/upstream
    -r 2009/07/28/12/nfcapd.200907281205 -n 10 -s ip/flows
Top 10    IP Addr ordered by flows:
Date first seen   Durat'n IP Addr         Flows Pkts  Bytes  pps bps   bpp
2009-07-28 12:02 467.596 192.168.96.92   27873 67420 3.8 M  144 67347 58
2009-07-28 12:02 462.700 192.168.96.107  18928 43878 4.7 M  94  85522 112
2009-07-28 12:02 464.443 192.168.96.198  17321 45454 3.5 M  97  63884 81
2009-07-28 12:02 454.299 172.16.152.40   11554 29093 1.3 M  64  23996 46
2009-07-28 12:02 362.586 192.168.97.203  6839  11104 1.2 M  30  28883 117
2009-07-28 12:02 393.600 172.16.220.139  4802  12883 618384 32 12568 48
2009-07-28 12:02 452.353 192.168.96.43   4477  5144  554709 11 9810  107
2009-07-28 12:02 456.306 192.168.96.88   3416  6642  697776 14 12233 105
2009-07-28 12:02 459.732 192.168.96.108  2544  25555 3.2 M  55  58478 131
2009-07-28 12:02 466.782 192.168.96.197  2143  24103 5.3 M  51  94988 229

Summary: total flows: 98290, total bytes: 311.6 M, total packets: 759205, avg
    bps: 5.3 M, avg pps: 1623, avg bpp: 430
Time window: 2009-07-28 12:02:12 - 2009-07-28 12:09:59
Total flows processed: 98290, skipped: 0, Bytes read: 5111164
Sys: 0.310s flows/second: 317064.5   Wall: 0.327s flows/second: 300366.1
```

Since the NetFlow data is stored on disk, you can analyze it repeatedly with different sets of filters. Another nice feature is **nfdump**'s ability to match incoming and outgoing flows into a single bidirectional flow.

NfSen is a web front end for NetFlow data that sits on top of **nfdump** and therefore combines graphing capabilities with all the features of **nfdump**. It displays the data in three different categories: flows, packets, and bytes. NfSen does more than just create static graphs, though—it lets you navigate through data, point to interesting peaks in the graphs, and drill down to the individual flows. You can also apply arbitrary **nfdump** filters to refine the display. The combination of easy GUI browsing with the underlying power of **nfdump** makes NfSen a powerful tool.

NfSen lets you save your filter and display settings together as a profile so that you can easily return to a specific type of analysis in the future. For example, you might define profiles that monitor traffic for your DMZ, your web server, or a client's network.

Profiles also make NfSen a valuable tool for security incident response teams because they make it easy to track specific types of incidents or network traffic. For example, Exhibit F on the next page shows a display that's customized for investigating "SYN flood" denial of service attacks.

Exhibit F A "SYN flood" profile for NfSen

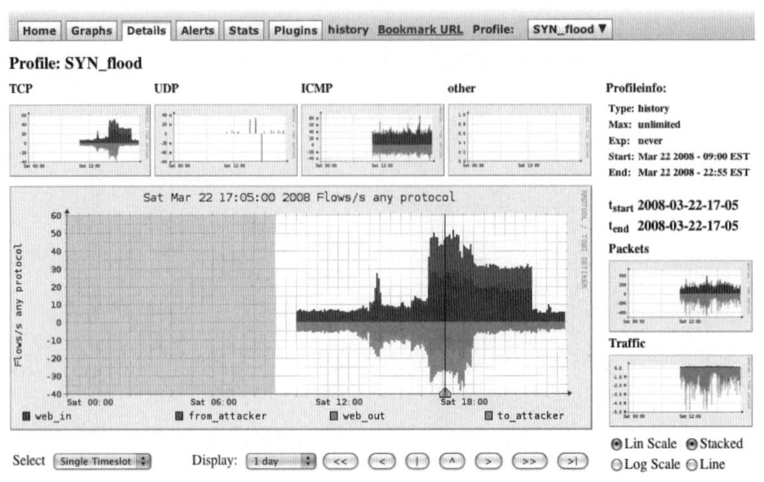

A security investigation usually happens hours or days after the incident that triggered it, but if you save NetFlow data as a matter of course, you can easily create an NfSen profile that looks back to an earlier time period. This retrospective view lets you identify the IP addresses involved in an attack and track down other hosts that may have been affected. You can also set up NfSen to watch your flows outside of office hours and to trigger alarms when certain conditions are met.

Setting up NetFlow on a Cisco router

To get started with NetFlow, you must first configure your network device to send NetFlow data to **nfcapd**. This section outlines the configuration of NetFlow on a Cisco router.

Export of NetFlow data is enabled per interface:

```
ios# interface fastethernet 0/0
ios# ip route-cache flow
```

To tell the router where to send the NetFlow data, enter the following command:

```
ios# ip flow-export nfcapd-hostname listen-port
```

The options below break up long-lived flows into 5-minute segments. You can choose any segment length between 1 and 60 minutes, but it should be equal to or less than **nfdump**'s file rotation period, which is 5 minutes by default.

```
ios# ip flow-export version 5
ios# ip flow-cache timeout active 5
```

On the Catalyst 6500/7600, you must enable NDE (NetFlow Data Export) in addition to normal NetFlow export.

Here's how:

```
ios# mls flow ip interface-full
ios# mls flow ipv6 interface-full
ios# mls nde sender version 5
```

On a busy router, consider aggressively timing out small flows:

```
ios# mls aging fast time 4 threshold 2
ios# mls aging normal 32
ios# mls aging long 900
```

You still need the traditional NetFlow configuration, including **ip flow ingress** or **ip route-cache flow** on every interface, so that you see "software switched" flows such as those that go to the router itself.

For NetFlow v9, the configuration may be even longer. Depending on your IOS version, you can also define your own template. With the introduction of Flexible NetFlow (FNF), the NetFlow environment has become even more complex.

21.14 Recommended Reading

Wikipedia includes a nice (though somewhat compressed) overview of SNMP with pointers to RFCs. It's a good starting point.

MAURO, DOUGLAS R., AND KEVIN J. SCHMIDT. *Essential SNMP (2nd Edition)*. Sebastopol, CA: O'Reilly Media, 2005.

SIMPLEWEB. *SNMP and Internet Management Site*. simpleweb.org.

You may find the following RFCs to be useful as well. We replaced the actual titles of the RFCs with a description of the RFC contents because some of the actual titles are an unhelpful jumble of buzzwords and SNMP jargon.

- RFC1155 – Characteristics of the SNMP data space (data types, etc.)
- RFC1156 – MIB-I definitions (description of the actual OIDs)
- RFC1157 – Simple Network Management Protocol
- RFC1213 – MIB-II definitions (OIDs)
- RFC3414 – User-based Security Model for SNMPv3
- RFC3415 – View-based Access Control Model for SNMPv3
- RFC3512 – Configuring devices with SNMP (best general overview)
- RFC3584 – Practical coexistence between different SNMP versions
- RFC3954 - Cisco Systems NetFlow Services Export Version 9

21.15 Exercises

E21.1 You are troubleshooting a network problem, and **netstat -rn** gives you the following output. What is the problem and what command would you use to fix it?

```
Destination    Gateway    Genmask         Flags MSS  Window irtt Iface
128.138.202.0  0.0.0.0    255.255.255.0   U       40 0         0 eth0
127.0.0.0      0.0.0.0    255.0.0.0       U       40 0         0 lo
```

★ E21.2 Write a script that monitors a given set of machines and notifies an administrator by email if a machine becomes unresponsive to pings for some set amount of time. Don't hard-code the list of machines, the notification email address, or the amount of time to determine unresponsive behavior.

★ E21.3 Experiment with changing the netmask on a machine on your local network. Does it still work? Can you reach everything at your site? Can other machines reach you? Do broadcasts work (e.g., ARP requests or DHCP discover packets)? Explain your findings. (Requires root access.)

★ E21.4 Use the **traceroute** command to discover routing paths on your network.

a) How many hops does it take to leave your facility?
b) Are there any routers between machines on which you have accounts?
c) Can you find any bottlenecks?
d) Is your site multihomed?

★★ E21.5 Design a MIB that includes all the variables you as a Linux sysadmin might want to query or set. Leave ways for the MIB to be extended to include that important new sysadmin variable you forgot.

★★ E21.6 Use **wireshark** or **tshark** to capture traffic that illustrates the following protocols. For TCP sessions, include and indicate the initial and final packets. Submit clean, well-formatted output. (Requires root.)

a) ARP
b) ICMP echo request and reply
c) SMTP
d) HTTP
e) DNS
f) Samba
g) SSH

★★ E21.7 Set up Cacti graphs that show the packets transmitted to and from a local router. This project requires an SNMP package to query the router, and you must know the router's read-only community string.

☆☆ E21.8 Write a script that uses RRDtool to track network traffic as reported by **netstat -i**, and create a web page with **rrdcgi** that shows the results. This exercise will probably take you several hours if you have never worked with RRDtool before. Dig in! It is well worth the effort, both because knowing how to whip up such scripts will come in handy and because familiarity with RRDtool will help you tweak and tune it when it's used as a component of network management packages.

22 Security

Despite Hollywood's best efforts, the maintenance of a secure computing environment remains unglamorous and largely unappreciated. It is a system administration discipline born of necessity; if UNIX and Linux systems are going to house sensitive data and control critical processes, we *must* protect them.

Such protection requires resources, both in terms of sysadmin time and in the hard currency of security-related equipment. Unfortunately, many organizations don't make the appropriate investments in this area until an incident has already occurred.

In November 1988, we experienced our first real taste of the security threat posed by a world-wide network as the Robert Morris, Jr., Internet worm was unleashed onto the Internet (see the Wikipedia article on "Morris worm"). Before that event, the Internet lived in an age of innocence. Security was a topic that administrators thought about mostly in the "what if" sense. A big security incident usually consisted of something like a user gaining administrative access to read another user's mail, often just to prove that he could.

The Morris worm wasted thousands of administrator hours but greatly increased security awareness on the Internet. Once again, we were painfully reminded that good fences make good neighbors. A number of excellent tools for use by system administrators (as well as a formal organization for handling incidents of this nature) came into being as a result.

Today, security breaches are commonplace. According to the 2008 CSI/FBI *Computer Crime and Security Survey,*[1] responding organizations reported an average annual loss ascribable to security breaches of $234,000. Most large organizations report having at least one significant security breach each year.

Addressing this problem isn't as easy as you might think. Security is not something that you can buy in a box or as a service from a third party. Commercial products and services can be part of a solution for your site, but they are not a panacea. Achieving an acceptable level of security requires an enormous amount of patience, vigilance, knowledge, and persistence—not just from you and other administrators, but from your entire user and management communities.

As the system administrator, you must personally ensure that your systems are secure, that they are vigilantly monitored, and that you and your users are properly educated. You should familiarize yourself with current security technology, actively monitor security mailing lists, and hire professional security experts to help with problems that exceed your knowledge.

22.1 Is UNIX secure?

Of course not. Neither UNIX nor Linux is secure, nor is any other operating system that communicates on a network. If you must have absolute, total, unbreachable security, then you need a measurable air gap[2] between your computer and any other device. Some people argue that you also need to enclose your computer in a special room that blocks electromagnetic radiation (Wikipedia: "Faraday cage"). How fun is that?

You can work to make your system somewhat more resistant to attack. Even so, several fundamental flaws in the UNIX model ensure that you will never reach security nirvana:

- UNIX is optimized for convenience and doesn't make security easy or natural. The system's overall philosophy stresses easy manipulation of data in a networked, multiuser environment.
- The software that runs on UNIX systems is developed by a large community of programmers. They range in experience level, attention to detail, and knowledge of the system and its interdependencies. As a result, even the most well-intended new features can introduce large security holes.

1. This survey is conducted yearly and can be found at gocsi.com.
2. Of course, wireless networking technology introduces a whole new set of problems. Air gap in this context means "no networking whatsoever."

- Most administrative functions are implemented outside the kernel, where they can be inspected and tampered with. Hackers have broad access to the system.

On the other hand, since some systems' source code (e.g., Linux, OpenSolaris) is available to everyone, thousands of people can (and do) scrutinize each line of code for possible security threats. This arrangement is widely believed to result in better security than that of closed operating systems, in which a limited number of people have the opportunity to examine the code for holes.

Many sites are a release or two behind, either because localization is too troublesome or because they do not subscribe to a software maintenance service. In any case, when security holes are patched, the window of opportunity for hackers often does not disappear overnight.

It might seem that security should gradually improve over time as security problems are discovered and corrected, but unfortunately this does not seem to be the case. System software is growing ever more complicated, hackers are becoming better and better organized, and computers are connecting more and more intimately on the Internet. Security is an ongoing battle that can never really be won.

Remember, too, that

$$\text{Security} = \frac{1}{(1.072)(\text{Convenience})}$$

The more secure your system, the more constrained you and your users will be. Implement the security measures suggested in this chapter only after carefully considering the implications for your users.

22.2 How security is compromised

This chapter discusses some common security problems and their standard countermeasures. But before we leap into the details, we should take a more general look at how real-world security problems tend to occur. Most security lapses fit into the following taxonomy.

Social engineering

The human users (and administrators) of a computer system are the weakest links in the chain of security. Even in today's world of heightened security awareness, unsuspecting users with good intentions are easily convinced to give away sensitive information. No amount of technology can protect against the user element—you must ensure that your user community has a high awareness of security threats so that they can be part of the defense.

This problem manifests itself in many forms. Attackers cold-call their victims and pose as legitimately confused users in an attempt to get help accessing the system. Administrators unintentionally post sensitive information on public forums when troubleshooting problems. Physical compromises occur when seemingly legitimate maintenance personnel rewire the phone closet.

The term "phishing" describes attempts to collect information from users through deceptive email, instant messages, or even SMS messages. Phishing can be especially hard to defend against because the communications often include victim-specific information that lends them the appearance of authenticity.

Social engineering continues to be a powerful hacking technique and is one of the most difficult threats to neutralize. Your site security policy should include training for new employees. Regular organization-wide communications are an effective way to provide information about telephone dos and don'ts, physical security, email phishing, and password selection.

To gauge your organization's resistance to social engineering, you might find it informative to attempt some social engineering attacks of your own. Be sure you have explicit permission to do this from your own managers, however. Such exploits look very suspicious if they are performed without a clear mandate. They're also a form of internal spying, so they have the potential to generate resentment if they're not handled in an aboveboard manner.

Many organizations find it useful to communicate to users that administrators will never request their passwords, whether by email, instant message, or telephone. Tell users to report any such password requests to the IT department immediately.

Software vulnerabilities

Over the years, countless security-sapping bugs have been discovered in computer software (including software from third parties, both commercial and free). By exploiting subtle programming errors or context dependencies, hackers have been able to manipulate systems into doing whatever they want.

Buffer overflows are a common programming error and one with complex implications. Developers often allocate a predetermined amount of temporary memory space, called a buffer, to store a particular piece of information. If the code isn't careful about checking the size of the data against the size of the container that's supposed to hold it, the memory adjacent to the allocated space is at risk of being overwritten. Crafty hackers can input carefully composed data that crashes the program or, in the worst case, executes arbitrary code.

Fortunately, the sheer number of buffer overflow exploits in recent years has raised the programming community's consciousness about this issue. Although buffer overflow problems are still occurring, they are often quickly discovered and corrected, especially in open source applications. Newer programming systems such as Java and .NET include mechanisms that automatically check data sizes and prevent buffer overflows. Sometimes.

Buffer overflows are a subcategory of a larger class of software security bugs known as input validation vulnerabilities. Nearly all programs accept some type of input from users (e.g., command-line arguments or HTML forms). If the code processes such data without rigorously checking it for appropriate format and content, bad things can happen. Consider the following simple example:

```
#!/usr/bin/perl
# Example user input validation error

open(HTMLFILE, "/var/www/html/$ARGV[0]") or die "trying\n";
while(<HTMLFILE>) { print; }
close HTMLFILE;
```

The intent of this code is probably to print the contents of some HTML file under **/var/www/html**, which is the default document root for the Apache web server on Red Hat servers. The code accepts a filename from the user and includes it as part of the argument to open. But if a malicious user entered **../../../etc/passwd** as the argument, the contents of **/etc/passwd** would be echoed!

What can you as an administrator do to prevent this type of attack? Very little, at least until a bug has been identified and addressed in a patch. Keeping up with patches and security bulletins is an important part of most administrators' jobs. Most Linux distributions include automated patching utilities, such as **yum** on Red Hat and **apt-get** on Ubuntu. OpenSolaris also has automated (and failsafe) updates implemented through **pkg image-update**. Take advantage of these utilities to keep your site safe from software vulnerabilities.

Configuration errors

Many pieces of software can be configured securely or not-so-securely. Unfortunately, because software is developed to be useful instead of annoying, not-so-securely is often the default. Hackers frequently gain access by exploiting software features that would be considered helpful and convenient in less treacherous circumstances: accounts without passwords, disks shared with the world, and unprotected databases, to name a few.

A typical example of a host configuration vulnerability is the standard practice of allowing Linux systems to boot without requiring a boot loader password. GRUB can be configured at install time to require a password, but administrators almost always decline the option. This omission leaves the system open to physical attack. However, it's also a perfect example of the need to balance security against usability. Requiring a password means that if the system were unintentionally rebooted (e.g., after a power outage), an administrator would have to be physically present to get the machine running again.

One of the most important steps in securing a system is simply making sure that you haven't inadvertently put out a welcome mat for hackers. Problems in this category are the easiest to find and fix, although there are potentially a lot of them and it's not always obvious what to check for. The port and vulnerability scanning tools covered later in this chapter can help a motivated administrator identify problems before they're exploited.

22.3 SECURITY TIPS AND PHILOSOPHY

This chapter discusses a wide variety of security concerns. Ideally, you should address all of them within your environment. Most administrators should probably digest the contents of this entire chapter more than once.

Most systems do not come secured out of the box. In addition, customizations made both during and after installation change the security profile for new systems. Administrators should take steps to harden new systems, integrate them into the local environment, and plan for their long-term security maintenance.

When the auditors come knocking, it's useful to be able to prove that you have followed a standard methodology, especially if that methodology conforms to external recommendations and best practices for your industry.

We use a localization checklist to secure new systems. A system administrator applies the standard hardening steps to the system, and a security administrator then confirms that the steps were followed correctly and keeps a log of newly secured systems.

Patches

Keeping the system updated with the latest patches is an administrator's highest-value security chore. Most systems are configured to point at the vendor's repository, which makes applying patches as simple as running a few commands. Larger environments can use a local repository that mirrors that of the vendor.

A reasonable approach to patching should include the following elements:

- A regular schedule for installing routine patches that is diligently followed. Consider the impact on users when designing this schedule. Monthly updates are usually sufficient; regularity is more important than immediacy. It is not acceptable to fix high-profile zero-day vulnerabilities but neglect other updates.

- A change plan that documents the impact of each set of patches, outlines appropriate postinstallation testing steps, and describes how to back out the changes in the event of problems. Communicate this change plan to all relevant parties.

- An understanding of what patches are relevant to the environment. Administrators should subscribe to vendor-specific security mailing lists and blogs, as well as to generalized security discussion forums such as Bugtraq. An accurate inventory of applications and operating systems used in your environment helps ensure complete coverage.

Unnecessary services

Most systems come with several services configured to run by default. Be sure to disable (and possibly remove) any that are unnecessary, especially if they are network daemons. One way to see which services are running is to use the **netstat** command. Here's partial output from a Solaris system:

```
solaris$ netstat -an | grep LISTEN
    *.111              *.*        0    0  49152    0  LISTEN
    *.32771            *.*        0    0  49152    0  LISTEN
    *.32772            *.*        0    0  49152    0  LISTEN
    *.22               *.*        0    0  49152    0  LISTEN
    *.4045             *.*        0    0  49152    0  LISTEN
```

A variety of techniques can identify the service that's using an unknown port. On most systems, **lsof** or **fuser** may be of help. Under Linux, either command can identify the PID of the process that's using a given port:

```
ubuntu$ sudo fuser 22/tcp
22/tcp:            2454  8387

ubuntu$ sudo lsof -i:22
COMMAND   PID  USER    FD   TYPE   DEVICE   SIZE  NODE  NAME
sshd      2454  root   3u   IPv4     5730          TCP  *:ssh(LISTEN)
sshd      2454  root   4u   IPv6     5732          TCP  *:ssh(LISTEN)
```

Once you have the PIDs, you can then use **ps** to identify specific processes. If the service is unneeded, stop it and make sure that it won't be restarted at boot time.

Unfortunately, the availability of **lsof** and **fuser** varies by system, and implementations differ widely. Many versions of both tools lack support for network sockets.

If **lsof** and **fuser** aren't available (or aren't useful), you can either look up "well known" service ports in the **/etc/services** file or run **netstat** without the **-n** option to let it do this lookup for you.

The security risks inherent in some network protocols render them unsafe in almost all circumstances. FTP, Telnet, and the BSD "r" programs (**rcp**, **rlogin**, and **rsh**) use insecure authentication and data transfer methods. They should be disabled on all systems in favor of more secure alternatives such as SSH.

Remote event logging

See Chapter 11 for more information about syslog.

The syslog facility forwards log information to files, lists of users, or other hosts on your network. Consider setting up a secure host to act as a central logging machine that parses forwarded events and takes appropriate action. A single centralized log aggregator can capture logs from a variety of devices and alert administrators whenever meaningful events occur. Remote logging also prevents hackers from covering their tracks by rewriting or erasing log files on systems that have been compromised.

Most systems come configured to use syslog by default, but you will need to customize the configuration to set up remote logging.

Backups

See Chapter 10 for more information about backups.

Regular system backups are an essential part of any site security plan. They fall into the "availability" bucket of the CIA triad discussed on page 944. Make sure that all partitions are regularly dumped and that you store some backups off-site. If a significant security incident occurs, you'll then have an uncontaminated checkpoint from which to restore.

Backups can also be a security hazard. A stolen collection of tapes can circumvent the rest of the system's security. When storing tapes off-site, use a fireproof safe to deter theft and consider using encryption. If you are thinking about using a contract storage facility, ask for a physical tour.

Viruses and worms

UNIX and Linux have been mostly immune from viruses. Only a handful exist (most of which are academic in nature), and none have done the costly damage that has become commonplace in the Windows world. Nonetheless, this fact hasn't stopped certain antivirus vendors from predicting the demise of the platform from malware—unless you purchase their antivirus product at a special introductory price, of course.

The exact reason for the lack of malicious software is unclear. Some claim that UNIX simply has less market share than its desktop competitors and is therefore not an interesting target for virus authors. Others insist that UNIX's access-controlled environment limits the damage from a self-propagating worm or virus.

The latter argument has some validity. Because UNIX restricts write access to system executables at the filesystem level, unprivileged user accounts cannot infect the rest of the environment. Unless the virus code is being run by root, the scope of infection is significantly limited. The moral, then, is not to use the root account for day-to-day activities.

See Chapter 20 for more information about email content scanning.

Perhaps counterintuitively, one valid reason to run antivirus software on UNIX servers is to protect your site's Windows systems from Windows-specific viruses. A mail server can scan incoming email attachments for viruses, and a file server can scan shared files for infection. However, this solution should supplement desktop antivirus protection rather than replace it.

ClamAV by Tomasz Kojm is a popular, free antivirus product for UNIX and Linux. This widely used GPL tool is a complete antivirus toolkit with signatures for thousands of viruses. You can download the latest version from clamav.net.

Trojan horses

Trojan horses are programs that aren't what they seem to be. An example of a Trojan horse is a program called **turkey** that was distributed on Usenet a long time ago. The program said it would draw a picture of a turkey on your terminal screen, but it actually deleted files from your home directory.

Trojan fragments appear in major software packages now and then. **sendmail**, **tcpdump**, OpenSSH, and InterBase have all issued advisories regarding malicious software in their products. These Trojans typically embed malicious code that allows attackers to access the victim's systems at will. Fortunately, most vendors fix the software and issue an advisory in a week or two. Be sure to watch the security mailing lists for any network software packages you run on your hosts.

Even given the number of security-related escapades the UNIX community has seen over the last few years, it is remarkable how few Trojan horse incidents have occurred. Credit for this state of affairs is due largely to the speed of Internet communication. Obvious security problems tend to be discovered quickly and widely discussed. Malicious packages don't stay available for very long on well-known Internet servers.

You can be certain that any software that has been discovered to be malicious will cause a big stink on the Internet. Google the name of a software package before installing it and make sure the first page of results doesn't look incriminating.

Rootkits

The craftiest hackers try to cover their tracks and avoid detection. Often, they hope to continue using your system to distribute software illegally, probe other networks, or launch attacks against other systems. They often use "rootkits" to help them remain undetected. Sony's Trojan horse employed rootkit-like capabilities to hide itself from the user.

Rootkits are programs and patches that hide important system information such as process, disk, or network activity. They come in many flavors and vary in sophistication from simple application replacements (such as hacked versions of **ls** and **ps**) to kernel modules that are nearly impossible to detect.

Host-based intrusion detection software such as OSSEC is an effective way to monitor systems for the presence of rootkits. There are also rootkit finder scripts (such as **chkrootkit**, chkrootkit.org) that scan the system for known rootkits.

Although programs are available to help administrators remove rootkits from a compromised system, the time it takes to perform a thorough cleaning would probably be better spent saving data, reformatting the disk, and starting from scratch. The most advanced rootkits are aware of common removal programs and try to subvert them.

Packet filtering

If you're connecting a system to a network that has Internet access, you *must* install a packet-filtering router or firewall between the system and the outside world. As an alternative, some systems let you implement packet filtering with software on the system itself, an option we discuss starting on page 935. Whatever the implementation, the packet filter should pass only traffic for services that you specifically want to provide or use from that system.

Passwords

We're simple people with simple rules. Here's one: every account must have a password, and it needs to be something that can't easily be guessed. It's never a good idea to send plaintext reusable passwords across the Internet. If you allow remote logins to your system, you must use SSH or some other secure remote access system (discussed starting on page 926).

Vigilance

To ensure the security of your system, you must monitor its health, network connections, process table, and overall status regularly (usually, daily). Perform regular self-assessments, using the power tools discussed later in this chapter. Security problems tend to start small and grow quickly, so the earlier you identify an anomaly, the better off you'll be.

General philosophy

Effective system security has its roots in common sense. Some rules of thumb:

- Don't put files on your system that are likely to be interesting to hackers or to nosy employees. Trade secrets, personnel files, payroll data, election results, etc., must be handled carefully if they're on-line. Securing such information cryptographically provides a far higher degree of security than simply trying to prevent unauthorized users from accessing the files that contain the juicy tidbits.
- Your site's security policy should specify how sensitive information is handled. See Chapter 32, *Management, Policy, and Politics*, and the security standards section in this chapter (page 945) for some suggestions.
- Don't provide places for hackers to build nests in your environment. Hackers often break into one system and then use it as a base of operations to get into other systems. Sometimes hackers may use your network to cover their tracks while they attack their real target. Publicly exposed services with vulnerabilities, world-writable anonymous FTP directories, shared accounts, and neglected systems all encourage nesting activity.
- Set traps to help detect intrusions and attempted intrusions. Tools such as OSSEC, Bro, Snort, and John the Ripper (described starting on page 916) keep you abreast of potential problems.
- Religiously monitor the reports generated by these security tools. A minor problem you ignore in one report may grow into a catastrophe by the time the next report is sent.

- Teach yourself about system security. Traditional know-how, user education, and common sense are the most important parts of a site security plan. Bring in outside experts to help fill in gaps, but only under your close supervision and approval.
- Prowl around looking for unusual activity. Investigate anything that seems unusual, such as odd log messages or changes in the activity of an account (more activity, activity at strange hours, or perhaps activity while the owner is on vacation).

22.4 Passwords and user accounts

*See page 176 for more information about the **passwd** file.*

Poor password management is a common security weakness. By default, the contents of the **/etc/passwd** and **/etc/shadow** files determine who can log in, so these files are the system's first line of defense against intruders. They must be scrupulously maintained and free of errors, security hazards, and historical baggage.

UNIX allows users to choose their own passwords, and although this is a great convenience, it leads to many security problems. When you give users their logins, you should also instruct them on how to choose a good password. Passwords should be at least eight characters long and should include numbers, punctuation, and changes in case. Nonsense words, combinations of simple words, or the first letters of words in a memorable phrase make the best passwords. (Of course, "memorable" is good but "traditional" is hacker bait; make up your own phrase.) The comments in the section *Choosing a root password* on page 111 are equally applicable to user passwords.

It is important to continually verify (preferably daily) that every login has a password. Entries in the **/etc/shadow** file that describe pseudo-users such as "daemon" who own files but never log in should have a star or an exclamation point in their encrypted password field. These do not match any password and thus prevent use of the account.

At sites that use a centralized authentication scheme such as LDAP or Active Directory, the same logic applies. Enforce password complexity requirements, and lock out accounts after a few failed login attempts.

Password aging

Most systems that have shadow passwords also allow you to compel users to change their passwords periodically, a facility known as password aging. This feature may seem appealing at first glance, but it has several problems. Users often resent having to change their passwords, and since they don't want to forget the new password, they choose something simple that is easy to type and remember. Many users switch between two passwords each time they are forced to change, or increment a digit in the password, defeating the purpose of password aging. PAM modules (see page 908) can help enforce strong passwords to avoid this pitfall.

On Linux systems, the **chage** program controls password aging. Using **chage**, administrators can enforce minimum and maximum times between password changes, password expiration dates, the number of days to warn users before their passwords expire, the number of days of inactivity that are permissible before accounts are automatically locked, and more. The following command sets the minimum number of days between password changes to 2, the maximum number to 90, the expiration date to July 31, 2010, and warns the user for 14 days that the expiration date is approaching:

```
$ sudo chage -m 2 -M 90 -E 2010-07-31 -W 14 ben
```

For more information about user account settings, see Chapter 7.

Other systems implement password aging differently, usually with less granularity. Under Solaris, you set password aging preferences in **/etc/default/password**. Password aging on HP-UX systems is controlled through the **smc** console, and in AIX it's configured in the file **/etc/security/user**.

Security

Group logins and shared logins

Any login that is used by more than one person is bad news. Group logins (e.g., "guest" or "demo") are sure terrain for hackers to homestead and are prohibited in many contexts by federal regulations such as HIPAA. Don't allow them at your site. However, technical controls can't prevent users from sharing passwords, so education is the best enforcement tactic.

User shells

In theory, you can set the shell for a user account to be just about any program, including a custom script. In practice, the use of shells other than standards such as **bash** and **tcsh** is a dangerous practice, and the risk is even greater for passwordless logins that have a script as their shell. If you find yourself tempted to create such a login, you might consider a passphrase-less SSH key pair instead.

Rootly entries

The only distinguishing feature of the root login is its UID of zero. Since there can be more than one entry in the **/etc/passwd** file that uses this UID, there can be more than one way to log in as root.

A common way for a hacker to install a back door after having obtained a root shell is to edit new root logins into **/etc/passwd**. Programs such as **who** and **w** refer to the name stored in **utmp** rather than the UID that owns the login shell, so they cannot expose hackers that appear to be innocent users but are really logged in as UID 0.

Don't allow root to log in remotely, even through the standard root account. Under OpenSSH, you can set the PermitRootLogin configuration option to No in the **/etc/ssh/sshd_config** file to enforce this restriction.

On Solaris, you can put CONSOLE=/dev/console in **/etc/default/login** to prohibit root logins from locations beside the console.

Because of **sudo** (see page 113), it's rare that you'll ever need to log in as root, even on the system console.

22.5 PAM: COOKING SPRAY OR AUTHENTICATION WONDER?

PAM stands for "pluggable authentication modules." The PAM system relieves programmers of the chore of implementing authentication systems and gives sysadmins flexible, modular control over the system's authentication methods. Both the concept and the term come from Sun Microsystems (now part of Oracle) and from a 1996 paper by Samar and Lai of SunSoft.

In the distant past, commands like **login** included hardwired authentication code that prompted the user for a password, tested the password against the encrypted version obtained from **/etc/shadow** (**/etc/passwd** at that time, really), and rendered a judgment as to whether the two passwords matched. Of course, other commands (e.g., **passwd**) contained similar code. It was impossible to change authentication methods without source code, and administrators had little or no control over details such as whether the system should accept "password" as a valid password. PAM changed all of that.

PAM puts the system's authentication routines into a shared library that **login** and other programs can call. By separating authentication functions into a discrete subsystem, PAM makes it easy to integrate new advances in authentication and encryption into the computing environment. For instance, multifactor authentication can be supported without changes to the source code of **login** and **passwd**.

For the sysadmin, setting the right level of security for authentication has become a simple configuration task. Programmers win, too: they no longer have to write tedious authentication code, and more importantly, their authentication systems are implemented correctly on the first try. PAM can authenticate all sorts of activities: user logins, other forms of system access, use of protected web sites—even the configuration of applications.

System support for PAM

All of our example systems support PAM. Configuration information goes in the **/etc/pam.d** directory (Linux) or in the **/etc/pam.conf** file (Solaris, HP-UX, and AIX). The formats of the configuration files are basically the same, but the UNIX systems put everything in one file and the Linux systems have a file for each service or command that uses PAM.

PAM support is nearly universal at this point, but if you're using some other variant of UNIX and want to check whether your system uses PAM, you can run **ldd /bin/login** to see if that binary links to PAM's shared library, **libpam**.

PAM configuration

PAM configuration files are a series of one-liners, each of which names a particular PAM module to be used on the system.

The general format is

```
[service] module-type control-flag module-path [arguments]
```

Fields are separated by whitespace.

Linux systems don't use a *service* field, or more accurately, they put each service in its own configuration file and let the filename assume the role of the UNIX *service* parameter. The *service* can name an authentication context to which the configuration line applies (e.g., login for vanilla user logins) or can contain the keyword other to set system defaults.

Here's an illustrative snippet from a Solaris system; all *module-path* fields are relative to the **/usr/lib/security** directory.

```
# login service

login   auth  requisite        pam_authtok_get.so.1
login   auth  required         pam_dhkeys.so.1
login   auth  required         pam_unix_cred.so.1
login   auth  required         pam_unix_auth.so.1
login   auth  required         pam_dial_auth.so.1
...
```

Individual PAM modules have finer granularity than just "authenticate the user," so there may be several lines in a PAM configuration file for any given service and module type. A series of lines for a given service and module type form a "stack."

The order in which modules appear in the PAM configuration file is important. For example, the module that prompts the user for a password must come before the module that checks that password for validity. One module can pass its output to the next by setting either environment variables or PAM variables.

The *module-type* parameter—auth, account, session, or password—determines what the module is expected to do. auth modules identify the user and grant group memberships. Modules that do account chores enforce restrictions such as limiting logins to particular times of day, limiting the number of simultaneous users, or limiting the ports on which logins can occur. (For example, you would use an account-type module to restrict root logins to the console.) session chores include tasks that are done before or after a user is granted access; for example, mounting the user's home directory. Finally, password modules change a user's password or passphrase.

The *control-flag* specifies how the modules in the stack should interact to produce an ultimate result for the stack. Table 22.1 on page 910 shows the common values.

If PAM could simply return a failure code as soon as the first individual module in a stack failed, the *control-flags* system would be simpler. Unfortunately, the system is designed so that most modules get a chance to run regardless of their sibling modules' success or failure, and this fact causes some subtleties in the flow of control. (The intent is to prevent an attacker from learning which module in the PAM stack caused the failure.)

Table 22.1 PAM control flags

Flag	Stop on failure?	Stop on success?	Comments
binding[a]	No	Yes	Like sufficient, but can't fail without failing the stack
include[a]	–	–	Includes another config file at this point in the stack
optional	No	No	Significant only if this is the lone module
required	No	No	Failure eventually causes the stack to fail
requisite	Yes	No	Same as required, but fails stack immediately
sufficient	No	Yes	The name is kind of a lie; see comments below

a. Linux and Solaris only for include, Solaris only for binding

required modules are required to succeed; a failure of any one of them guarantees that the stack as a whole will eventually fail. However, the failure of a module that is marked required doesn't immediately stop execution of the stack. If you want that behavior, you need to use the requisite control flag instead of required.

The success of a sufficient module aborts the stack immediately. However, the ultimate result of the stack isn't guaranteed to be success because sufficient modules can't override the failure of earlier required modules. If an earlier required module has already failed, a successful sufficient module aborts the stack *and* returns failure as the overall result. Solaris's binding flag acts like sufficient, but failure of the binding module ensures eventual failure of the stack. By contrast, failure of a sufficient module is treated like the failure of an optional module: it makes no difference to the final result unless it is the only module in the stack.

Clear as mud, hmm? To make things even more complicated, Linux has a parallel system of alternative control flags that you can theoretically use instead of these cross-system standards. Overall, the *control-flag* system would take another page or two to really explain in detail. We don't do that here, however, because PAM configurations tend to be relatively stereotyped; you're unlikely to be writing your own from scratch. We mention some of the details only to impress upon you that the control flags don't have the straightforward meanings their names might suggest. If you're going to modify your systems' security settings, make sure that you understand the system thoroughly and that you double-check the particulars. (You won't configure PAM every day. How long will you remember which version is requisite and which is required?)

For easy reference, here's another copy of that same Solaris **pam.conf** example:

```
# login service

login   auth  requisite        pam_authtok_get.so.1
login   auth  required         pam_dhkeys.so.1
login   auth  required         pam_unix_cred.so.1
login   auth  required         pam_unix_auth.so.1
login   auth  required         pam_dial_auth.so.1
...
```

Let's look at the specific modules.

The pam_authtok_get library routine prompts the user for a login name (if one has not already been set) and password and stores these values in the authentication token called PAM_AUTHTOK. The pam_dhkeys module is used for RPC (remote procedure call) authentication for NIS or NIS+ and is looking for Diffie-Hellman keys, hence the name.

The pam_unix_cred module sets the credentials for the authenticated user, and the pam_unix_auth module performs the actual authentication, checking that the value stored in PAM_AUTHTOK is the user's correct password. Finally, the module pam_dial_auth authenticates the user for dialup access according to the contents of **/etc/dialups** and **/etc/d_passwd**.

You may see the same code module referred to more than once in a configuration file, with different *module-type* values. That's fine; multiple type implementations are often collected into a single library if they share significant code.

A detailed Linux configuration example

Linux moves each set of PAM configuration lines that refer to the same *service* into a separate file named after that service. The format is otherwise the same except that the *service* field is no longer needed.

For example, the **/etc/pam.d/login** file from a SUSE system is reproduced below with the included files expanded to form a more coherent example.

```
auth       requisite   pam_nologin.so
auth       [user_unknown=ignore success=ok ignore=ignore auth_err=die
    default=bad] pam_securetty.so
auth       required    pam_env.so
auth       required    pam_unix2.so
account    required    pam_unix2.so
password   requisite   pam_pwcheck.so nullok cracklib
password   required    pam_unix2.so use_authtok nullok
session    required    pam_loginuid.so
session    required    pam_limits.so
session    required    pam_unix2.so
session    optional    pam_umask.so
session    required    pam_lastlog.so nowtmp
session    optional    pam_mail.so standard
session    optional    pam_ck_connector.so
```

The auth stack includes several modules. On the first line, the pam_nologin module checks for the existence of the **/etc/nologin** file. If it exists, the module aborts the login immediately unless the user is root. The pam_securetty module ensures that root can only log in on terminals listed in **/etc/securetty**. This line uses the alternative Linux syntax described in the **pam.conf** man page. In this case, the requested behavior is similar to that of the required control flag. pam_env sets environment variables from **/etc/security/pam_env.conf**, and finally, pam_unix2 checks the user's credentials by performing standard UNIX authentication. If any of these modules fail, the auth stack returns an error.

The account stack includes only the pam_unix2 module, which in this context assesses the validity of the account itself. It returns an error if, for example, the account has expired or the password must be changed. In the latter case, the module collects a new password from the user and passes it to the password modules.

The pam_pwcheck line checks the strength of proposed new passwords by calling the **cracklib** library. It returns an error if the new password does not meet the requirements. However, it also allows empty passwords because of the nullok flag. The pam_unix2 line updates the actual password.

Finally, the session modules perform several housekeeping chores. pam_loginuid sets the kernel's loginuid process attribute to the user's UID. pam_limits reads resource usage limits from **/etc/security/limits.conf** and sets the corresponding process parameters that enforce them. pam_unix2 logs the user's access to the system, and pam_umask sets an initial file creation mode. The pam_lastlog module displays the user's last login time as a security check, and the pam_mail module prints a note if the user has new mail. Finally, pam_ck_connector notifies the **ConsoleKit** daemon (a system-wide daemon that manages login sessions) of the new login.

At the end of the process, the user has been successfully authenticated and PAM returns control to **login**.

22.6 Setuid programs

Setuid programs (executables on which the setuid bit has been set) run as the user that owns the executable file. For example, the **passwd** program must run as root in order to modify the **/etc/shadow** file when users change their passwords. See *Setuid and setgid execution* on page 106 for basic information about this feature.

Programs that run setuid, especially ones that run setuid to root, are prone to security problems. The setuid commands distributed with the system are theoretically secure; however, security holes have been discovered in the past and will undoubtedly be discovered in the future.

The surest way to minimize the number of setuid *problems* is to minimize the number of setuid *programs*. Think twice before installing software that needs to run setuid, and avoid using the setuid facility in your own home-grown software. *Never* use setuid execution on programs that were not explicitly written with setuid execution in mind.

You can disable setuid and setgid execution on individual filesystems by specifying the **nosuid** option to **mount**. It's a good idea to use this option on filesystems that contain users' home directories or that are mounted from less trustworthy administrative domains.

It's useful to scan your disks periodically to look for new setuid programs. A hacker who has breached the security of your system sometimes creates a private setuid shell or utility to facilitate repeat visits. Some of the tools discussed starting on page 914 locate such files, but you can do just as well with **find**. For example, the one-liner script

```
/usr/bin/find / -user root -perm -4000 -print |
    /bin/mail -s "Setuid root files" netadmin
```

mails a list of all files that are setuid to root to the "netadmin" user. (In practice, you may need to be more specific about which filesystems to search.)

22.7 Effective use of chroot

The **chroot** system call confines a process to a specific directory. It disallows access to files outside or above that directory and thereby limits the damage the process can cause if it should be compromised by a hacker.

The **chroot** command is a simple wrapper around this system call. In addition, some security-sensitive daemons have **chroot** support built in and need only have this mode turned on in their configuration files.

Security experts sometimes frown upon use of **chroot** for security purposes because they believe that when it is poorly used or misunderstood, it can give administrators a false sense of security. They complain that some administrators use **chroot** to excuse themselves from other forms of security diligence such as regular software updates and close security monitoring.

These points are not inaccurate, but they're not the last word on **chroot**, either. Similar claims could be made regarding network firewalls, but few experts would recommend removing the packet filter from your network. Used correctly and as a supplemental layer of protection, **chroot** is a worthy addition to your security arsenal (even if that was not the feature's original design intent).

The following scenarios illustrate reasonable uses of **chroot**:

- You want to run a non-root daemon process such as Apache or BIND within a restricted filesystem subtree. If the daemon is compromised, the attacker will be restricted to the subtree as long as no privilege escalation vulnerabilities exist.
- You want to restrict remote users to a specific set of files and commands.

However, **chroot** can only protect you in these scenarios if all of the following conditions are met:

- All processes in the **chroot** jail run without root privileges. Processes that run as root always have the ability to break out of the **chroot** jail.
- You are not using setuid root execution within the jail.

- The **chroot** environment is up to date and minimal, in the sense that it contains only the executables, libraries, and configuration files that are needed to support the intended task.

In this era of shared libraries and interprocess dependencies, constructing a proper jail cell can be tricky. The JailKit (olivier.sessink.nl/jailkit) includes several scripts to help you create **chroot**ed environments.

22.8 Security Power Tools

Some of the time-consuming chores mentioned in the previous sections can be automated with freely available tools. Here are a few of the tools you'll want to look at.

Nmap: network port scanner

Nmap is a network port scanner. Its main function is to check a set of target hosts to see which TCP and UDP ports have servers listening on them.[3] Since most network services are associated with "well known" port numbers, this information tells you quite a lot about the software a machine is running.

Running Nmap is a great way to find out what a system looks like to someone on the outside who is trying to break in. For example, here's a report from a production Ubuntu system:

```
ubuntu$ nmap -sT ubuntu.booklab.atrust.com

Starting Nmap 4.20 ( http://insecure.org ) at 2009-11-01 12:31 MST
Interesting ports on ubuntu.booklab.atrust.com (192.168.20.25):
Not shown: 1691 closed ports
PORT     STATE   SERVICE
25/tcp   open    smtp
80/tcp   open    http
111/tcp  open    rpcbind
139/tcp  open    netbios-ssn
445/tcp  open    microsoft-ds
3306/tcp open    mysql

Nmap finished: 1 IP address (1 host up) scanned in 0.186 seconds
```

By default, **nmap** includes the **-sT** argument to try to connect to each TCP port on the target host in the normal way.[4] Once a connection has been established, **nmap** immediately disconnects, which is impolite but not harmful to a properly written network server.

3. As described in Chapter 14, a port is a numbered communication channel. An IP address identifies an entire machine, and an IP address + port number identifies a specific server or network conversation on that machine.

4. Actually, only the privileged ports (those with port numbers under 1,024) and the well-known ports are checked by default. Use the **-p** option to explicitly specify the range of ports to scan.

From the example above, we can see that the host ubuntu is running two services that are likely to be unused and that have historically been associated with security problems: **portmap** (rpcbind) and an email server (smtp). An attacker would most likely probe those ports for more information as a next step in the information-gathering process.

The STATE column in **nmap**'s output shows open for ports that have servers listening, closed for ports with no server, unfiltered for ports in an unknown state, and filtered for ports that cannot be probed because of an intervening packet filter. **nmap** does not classify ports as unfiltered unless it is running an ACK scan. Here are results from a more secure server, secure.booklab.atrust.com:

```
ubuntu$ nmap -sT secure.booklab.atrust.com

Starting Nmap 4.20 ( http://insecure.org ) at 2009-11-01 12:42 MST
Interesting ports on secure.booklab.atrust.com (192.168.20.35):
Not shown: 1691 closed ports
PORT     STATE SERVICE
25/tcp   open    smtp
80/tcp   open    http

Nmap finished: 1 IP address (1 host up) scanned in 0.143 seconds
```

In this case, it's clear that the host is set up to allow SMTP (email) and an HTTP server. A firewall blocks access to other ports.

In addition to straightforward TCP and UDP probes, **nmap** also has a repertoire of sneaky ways to probe ports without initiating an actual connection. In most cases, **nmap** probes with packets that look like they come from the middle of a TCP conversation (rather than the beginning) and waits for diagnostic packets to be sent back. These stealth probes may be effective at getting past a firewall or at avoiding detection by a network security monitor on the lookout for port scanners. If your site uses a firewall (see *Firewalls* on page 932), it's a good idea to probe it with these alternative scanning modes to see what they turn up.

nmap has the magical and useful ability to guess what operating system a remote system is running by looking at the particulars of its implementation of TCP/IP. It can sometimes even identify the software that's running on an open port. The **-O** and **-sV** options, respectively, turn on this behavior. For example:

```
ubuntu$ sudo nmap -sV -O secure.booklab.atrust.com

Starting Nmap 4.20 ( http://insecure.org ) at 2009-11-01 12:44 MST
Interesting ports on secure.booklab.atrust.com (192.168.20.35):
Not shown: 1691 closed ports
PORT     STATE    SERVICE   VERSION
25/tcp   open     smtp      Postfix smtpd
80/tcp   open     http      lighttpd 1.4.13
Device type: general purpose
Running: Linux 2.4.X|2.5.X|2.6.X
OS details: Linux 2.6.16 - 2.6.24
Nmap finished: 1 IP address (1 host up) scanned in 8.095 seconds
```

This feature can be very useful for taking an inventory of a local network. Unfortunately, it is also very useful to hackers, who can base their attacks on known weaknesses of the target OSes and servers.

Keep in mind that most administrators don't appreciate your efforts to scan their network and point out its vulnerabilities, however well intended your motive. Do not run **nmap** on someone else's network without permission from one of that network's administrators.

Nessus: next-generation network scanner

Nessus, originally released by Renaud Deraison in 1998, is a powerful and useful software vulnerability scanner. At this point, it uses more than 31,000 plug-ins to check for both local and remote security flaws. Although it is now a closed source, proprietary product, it is still freely available, and new plug-ins are released regularly. It is the most widely accepted and complete vulnerability scanner available.

Nessus prides itself on being the security scanner that takes nothing for granted. Instead of assuming that all web servers run on port 80, for instance, it scans for web servers running on any port and checks them for vulnerabilities. Instead of relying on the version numbers reported by the service it has connected to, Nessus attempts to exploit known vulnerabilities to see if the service is susceptible.

Although a substantial amount of setup time is required to get Nessus running (it requires several packages that aren't installed on a typical system), it's well worth the effort. The Nessus system includes a client and a server. The server acts as a database and the client handles the GUI presentation. Nessus servers and clients exist for both Windows and UNIX platforms.

One of the great advantages of Nessus is the system's modular design, which makes it easy for third parties to add new security checks. Thanks to an active user community, Nessus is likely to be a useful tool for years to come.

John the Ripper: finder of insecure passwords

One way to thwart poor password choices is to try to break the passwords yourself and to force users to change passwords that you have broken. John the Ripper is a sophisticated tool by Solar Designer that implements various password-cracking algorithms in a single tool. It replaces the tool **crack**, which was covered in previous editions of this book.

Even though most systems use a shadow password file to hide encrypted passwords from public view, it's still wise to verify that your users' passwords are crack resistant.[5] Knowing a user's password can be useful because people tend to use the same password over and over again. A single password might provide access to another system, decrypt files stored in a user's home directory, and allow access to

5. Especially the passwords of system administrators who have **sudo** privileges

financial accounts on the web. (Needless to say, it's not very security-smart to re-use a password this way. But nobody wants to remember ten passwords.)

Considering its internal complexity, John the Ripper is an extremely simple program to use. Direct **john** to the file to be cracked, most often **/etc/shadow**, and watch the magic happen:

```
$ sudo ./john /etc/shadow
Loaded 25 password hashes with 25 different salts (FreeBSD MD5 [32/32])
password  (jsmith)
badpass   (tjones)
```

In this example, 25 unique passwords were read from the shadow file. As passwords are cracked, John prints them to the screen and saves them to a file called **john.pot**. The output contains the password in the left column with the login in parentheses in the right column. To reprint passwords after **john** has completed, run the same command with the **-show** argument.

As of this writing, the most recent stable version of John the Ripper is 1.7.3.4. It's available from openwall.com/john. Since John the Ripper's output contains the passwords it has broken, you should carefully protect the output and delete it as soon as you are done checking to see which users' passwords are insecure.

As with most security monitoring techniques, it's important to obtain explicit management approval before cracking passwords with John the Ripper.

hosts_access: host access control

Network firewalls are a first line of defense against access by unauthorized hosts, but they shouldn't be the only barrier in place. Two files, **/etc/hosts.allow** and **/etc/hosts.deny**, also referred to as TCP wrappers, can restrict access to services according to the origin of network requests. The **hosts.allow** file lists the hosts that are allowed to connect to a specific service, and the **hosts.deny** file restricts access. However, these files control access only for services that are **hosts_access** aware, such as those managed by **inetd**, **xinetd**, **sshd**, and some configurations of **sendmail**.

In most cases it is wise to be restrictive and permit access only to essential services from designated hosts. We suggest denying access by default in the **hosts.deny** file with the single line

```
ALL:ALL
```

You can then permit access on a case-by-case basis in **hosts.allow**. The following configuration allows access to SSH from hosts on the 192.168/16 networks and to **sendmail** from anywhere.

```
sshd: 192.168.0.0/255.255.0.0
sendmail: ALL
```

The format of an entry in either file is *service: host* or *service: network*. Failed connection attempts are noted in syslog. Connections from hosts that are not permitted to access the service are immediately closed.

Most Linux distributions include **hosts.allow** and **hosts.deny** files by default, but they're usually empty. Our other example systems all offer TCP wrappers as an option after installation.

Bro: the programmable network intrusion detection system

Bro is an open source network intrusion detection system (NIDS) that monitors network traffic and looks for suspicious activity. It was originally written by Vern Paxson and is available from bro-ids.org.

Bro inspects all traffic flowing into and out of a network. It can operate in passive mode, in which it generates alerts for suspicious activity, or in active mode, in which it injects traffic to disrupt malicious activity. Both modes likely require modification of your site's network configuration.

Unlike other NIDSs, Bro monitors traffic flows rather than just matching patterns inside individual packets. This method of operation means that Bro can detect suspicious activity based on who talks to whom, even without matching any particular string or pattern. For example, Bro can

- Detect systems used as "stepping stones" by correlating inbound and outbound traffic
- Detect a server that has a back door installed by watching for unexpected outbound connections immediately after an inbound one
- Detect protocols running on nonstandard ports
- Report correctly guessed passwords (and ignore the incorrect guesses)

Some of these features require substantial system resources, but Bro includes clustering support to help you manage a group of sensor machines.

The configuration language for Bro is complex and requires significant coding experience to use. Unfortunately, there is no simple default configuration for a novice to install. Most sites require a moderate level of customization.

Bro is supported to some extent by the Networking Research Group of the International Computer Science Institute (ICSI), but mostly it's maintained by the community of Bro users. If you are looking for a turnkey commercial NIDS, you will probably be disappointed by Bro. However, Bro can do things that no commercial NIDS can do, and it can either supplement or replace a commercial solution in your network.

Snort: the popular network intrusion detection system

Snort (snort.org) is an open source network intrusion prevention and detection system originally written by Marty Roesch and now maintained by Sourcefire, a commercial entity. It has become the de facto standard for home-grown NIDS deployments and is also the basis of many commercial and "managed services" NIDS implementations.

Snort itself is distributed for free as an open source package. However, Sourcefire charges a subscription fee for access to the most recent set of detection rules.

A number of third-party platforms incorporate or extend Snort, and some of those projects are open source. One excellent example is Aanval (aanval.com), which aggregates data from multiple Snort sensors in a web-based console.

Snort captures raw packets off the network wire and compares them with a set of rules, aka signatures. When Snort detects an event that's been defined as interesting, it can alert a system administrator or contact a network device to block the undesired traffic, among other actions.

Although Bro is a much more powerful system, Snort is a lot simpler and easier to configure, attributes that make it a good choice as a "starter" NIDS platform.

OSSEC: host-based intrusion detection

Do you lie awake at night wondering if the security of your systems has been breached? Do you think a disgruntled coworker might be installing malicious programs on your systems? If you answered yes to either of these questions, you may want to consider installing a host-based intrusion detection system (HIDS) such as OSSEC.

OSSEC is free software and is available as source code under the GNU General Public License. Commercial support is available from Third Brigade (recently acquired by Trend Micro). OSSEC is available for Linux, Solaris, HP-UX, AIX, and Windows. It provides the following services:

- Rootkit detection
- Filesystem integrity checks
- Log file analysis
- Time-based alerting
- Active responses

OSSEC runs on the systems of interest and monitors their activity. It can send alerts or take action according to a set of rules that you configure. For example, OSSEC can monitor systems for the addition of unauthorized files and send email notifications like this one:

```
Subject: OSSEC Notification - courtesy - Alert level 7
Date: Fri, 15 Jan 2010 14:53:04 -0700
From: OSSEC HIDS <ossecm@courtesy.atrust.com>
To: <courtesy-admin@atrust.com>

OSSEC HIDS Notification.
2010 Jan 15 14:52:52
```

```
Received From: courtesy->syscheck
Rule: 554 fired (level 7) -> "File added to the system."
Portion of the log(s):

New file
'/courtesy/httpd/barkingseal.com/html/wp-content/uploads/2010/01/hbird.jpg'
added to the file system.

 --END OF NOTIFICATION
```

In this way, OSSEC acts as your 24/7 eyes and ears on the system. We recommend running OSSEC on every production system, in combination with a change management policy (discussed in Chapter 32, *Management, Policy, and Politics*, on page 1211).

OSSEC basic concepts

OSSEC has two primary components: the manager (server) and the agents (clients). You need one manager on your network, and you should install that component first. The manager stores the file-integrity-checking databases, logs, events, rules, decoders, major configuration options, and system auditing entries for the entire network. A manager can connect to any OSSEC agent, regardless of its operating system. The manager can also monitor certain devices that do not have a dedicated OSSEC agent.

Agents run on the systems you want to monitor and report back to the manager. By design, they have a small footprint and operate with a minimal set of privileges. Most of the agent's configuration is obtained from the manager. Communication between the server and the agent is encrypted and authenticated. You need to create an authentication key for each agent on the manager.

OSSEC classifies alerts by severity at levels 0 to 15; 15 is the highest severity.

OSSEC installation

OSSEC is not yet part of the major UNIX and Linux distributions, even as a fetchable package. Therefore, you will need to download the source code package with a web browser or a tool such as **wget** and then build the software:

```
$ wget http://ossec.net/files/ossec-hids-latest.tar.gz
$ tar -zxvf ossec-hids-latest.tar.gz
$ cd ossec-hids-*
$ sudo ./install.sh
```

The install script asks what language you prefer (use "en" for English), and then what type of installation you want to perform: server, agent, or local. If you are only installing OSSEC on a single, personally managed system, you may want to choose local. Otherwise, first do the server install on the system you want to be your OSSEC manager, and then install the agent on that and all other systems you want to monitor. The install script asks some additional questions, too, such as to what email address alerts should be sent and which monitoring modules should be enabled.

Once the installation has finished, start OSSEC with

```
server$ sudo /var/ossec/bin/ossec-control start
```

Next, register each agent with the manager. On the server, run

```
server$ sudo /var/ossec/bin/manage_agents
```

You'll see a menu that looks something like this:

```
****************************************
* OSSEC HIDS v2.3 Agent manager.
* The following options are available:
****************************************
   (A)dd an agent (A).
   (E)xtract key for an agent (E).
   (L)ist already added agents (L).
   (R)emove an agent (R).
   (Q)uit.
Choose your action: A,E,L,R or Q:
```

Select option **A** to add an agent, and then type in the name and IP address of the agent. Next, select option **E** to extract the agent's key. Here's what that looks like:

```
Available agents:
   ID: 001, Name: linuxclient1, IP: 192.168.74.3
Provide the ID of the agent to extract the key (or '\q' to quit): 001
Agent key information for '001' is:
MDAyIGxpbnV4Y2xpZW50MSAxOTIuMTY4LjcOLjMgZjk4YjMyYzlkMjg5MWJlMT
...
```

Finally, log in to the agent system and run **manage_agents** there:

```
agent$ sudo /var/ossec/bin/manage_agents
```

On the client, you will see that the menu has somewhat different options.

```
****************************************
* OSSEC HIDS v2.3 Agent manager.
* The following options are available:
****************************************
   (I)mport key from the server (I).
   (Q)uit.
Choose your action: I or Q:
```

Select option **I** and then cut and paste the key you extracted above. After you have added an agent, you must restart the OSSEC server. Repeat the process of key generation, extraction, and installation for each agent you want to connect.

OSSEC configuration

Once OSSEC is installed and running, you'll want to tweak it so that it gives you just enough information, but not too much. The majority of the configuration is stored on the server in the **/var/ossec/etc/ossec.conf** file. This XML-style file is well commented and fairly intuitive, but it contains dozens of options.

A common item you may want to configure is the list of files to ignore when doing file integrity (change) checking. For example, if you have a custom application that writes its log file to **/var/log/customapp.log**, you can add the following line to the <syscheck> section of the file:

```
<syscheck>
<ignore>/var/log/customapp.log</ignore>
</syscheck>
```

After you've made this change and restarted the OSSEC server, OSSEC will stop alerting you every time the log file changes. The many OSSEC configuration options are documented at ossec.net/main/manual/configuration-options.

It takes time and effort to get any HIDS system running and tuned. But after a few weeks, you'll have filtered out the noise and the system will start to provide valuable information about changing conditions in your environment.

22.9 Mandatory Access Control (MAC)

Mandatory Access Control is an alternative to the traditional UNIX access control system that vests control of all permissions in the hands of a security administrator. In contrast to the standard model (described in Chapter 4, *Access Control and Rootly Powers*, and to some extent in Chapter 6, *The Filesystem*), MAC does not allow users to modify any permissions, even on their own objects.

MAC security policies control access according to the perceived sensitivity of the resource being controlled. Users are assigned a security classification from a structured hierarchy. Users can read and write items at the same classification level or lower but cannot access items at a higher classification. For example, a user with "secret" access can read and write "secret" objects but cannot read objects that are classified as "top secret."

A well-implemented MAC policy relies on the principle of least privilege (allowing access only when necessary), much as a properly designed firewall allows only specifically recognized services and clients to pass. MAC can prevent software with code execution vulnerabilities (e.g., buffer overflows) from compromising the system by limiting the scope of the breach to the few specific resources required by that software.

Needless to say, kernel modifications are necessary to implement MAC on UNIX and Linux. Our example UNIX systems (Solaris, HP-UX, and AIX) all are available in MAC-enabled versions at additional cost. These versions are called Solaris Trusted Extensions (formerly Trusted Solaris), HP-UX Security Containment, and Trusted AIX, respectively.

Unless you're handling sensitive data for a government entity, it is unlikely that you will ever need or encounter these security-enhanced editions.

Security-enhanced Linux (SELinux)

SELinux implements MAC for Linux systems. Although it has gained a foothold in a few distributions, it is notoriously difficult to administer and troubleshoot. This unattributed quote from a former version of the SELinux Wikipedia page vents the frustration felt by many sysadmins:

> *"Intriguingly, although the stated raison d'être of SELinux is to facilitate the creation of individualized access control policies specifically attuned to organizational data custodianship practices and rules, the supportive software tools are so sparse and unfriendly that the vendors survive chiefly on 'consulting,' which typically takes the form of incremental modifications to boilerplate security policies."*

Despite the administrative complexity of SELinux, its adoption has been slowly growing, particularly in environments, such as government agencies, with strict security requirements. Of our example Linux distributions, Red Hat Enterprise Linux has the most mature SELinux model. SELinux is available as an optional package for Ubuntu and SUSE.

Policy development is a complicated topic. To protect a new daemon, for example, a policy must carefully enumerate all the files, directories, and other objects to which the process needs access. For complicated software like **sendmail** or the Apache **httpd**, this task can be quite complex. At least one company offers a 3-day class on policy development.

Fortunately, many general policies are available on-line, and most distributions come with reasonable defaults. These can easily be installed and configured for your particular environment. A full-blown policy editor that aims to ease policy application can be found at seedit.sourceforge.net.

SELinux has been present in Red Hat Enterprise Linux since version 4. A default installation of RHEL enables SELinux protection out of the box.

/etc/selinux/config controls the SELinux configuration. The interesting lines are

```
SELINUX=enforcing
SELINUXTYPE=targeted
```

The first line has three possible values: enforcing, permissive, or disabled. The enforcing setting ensures that the loaded policy is applied and prohibits violations. permissive allows violations to occur but logs them through syslog, which is valuable for debugging. disabled turns off SELinux entirely.

SELINUXTYPE refers to the type of policy to be applied. Red Hat has two policies: targeted, which defines additional security for daemons that Red Hat has protected,[6] and strict, which protects the entire system. Although the strict policy is available, it is not supported by Red Hat; the restrictions are so tight that the

6. The protected daemons are **httpd**, **dhcpd**, **mailman**, **named**, **portmap**, **nscd**, **ntpd**, **mysqld**, **postgres**, **squid**, **winbindd**, and **ypbind**.

system is difficult to use. The targeted policy offers protection for important network daemons without affecting general system use, at least in theory. But even the targeted policy isn't perfect. If you're having problems with newly installed software, check **/var/log/messages** for SELinux errors.

SUSE uses Novell's implementation of MAC, called AppArmor. However, as of version 11.1, SUSE also includes basic SELinux functionality.

Ubuntu ships with AppArmor by default. SELinux packages are maintained for Ubuntu by Russell Coker, the Red Hat bloke who generated the targeted and strict policies.

22.10 Cryptographic security tools

Many of the UNIX protocols in common use date from a time before the wide deployment of the Internet and modern cryptography. Security was simply not a factor in the design of many protocols; in others, security concerns were waved away with the transmission of a plaintext password or with a vague check to see if packets originated from a trusted host or port.

These protocols now find themselves operating in the shark-infested waters of large corporate LANs and the Internet, where, it must be assumed, all traffic is open to inspection. Not only that, but there is little to prevent anyone from actively interfering in network conversations. How can you be sure who you're really talking to?

Cryptography solves many of these problems. It has been possible for a long time to scramble messages so that an eavesdropper cannot decipher them, but this is just the beginning of the wonders of cryptography. Developments such as public key cryptography and secure hashing have promoted the design of cryptosystems that meet almost any conceivable need.

An excellent resource for those interested in cryptography is RSA Laboratories' *Frequently Asked Questions about Today's Cryptography*, available for free from rsa.com/rsalabs. Despite the name, it is a book-length treatise downloadable in PDF format. The document hasn't been updated since 2000, but most of the information remains valid. Additionally, Stephen Levy's book *Crypto* is a comprehensive guide to the history of cryptography.

Kerberos: a unified approach to network security

The Kerberos system, designed at MIT, attempts to address some of the issues of network security in a consistent and extensible way. Kerberos is an authentication system, a facility that "guarantees" that users and services are in fact who they claim to be. It does not provide any additional security or encryption beyond that.

Kerberos uses DES to construct nested sets of credentials called "tickets." Tickets are passed around the network to certify your identity and to give you access to network services. Each Kerberos site must maintain at least one physically secure machine (called the authentication server) to run the Kerberos daemon. This daemon issues tickets to users or services that present credentials, such as passwords, when they request authentication.

In essence, Kerberos improves upon traditional password security in only two ways: it never transmits unencrypted passwords on the network, and it relieves users from having to type passwords repeatedly, making password protection of network services somewhat more palatable.

The Kerberos community boasts one of the most lucid and enjoyable documents ever written about a cryptosystem, Bill Bryant's "Designing an Authentication System: a Dialogue in Four Scenes." It's required reading for anyone interested in cryptography and is available at

web.mit.edu/kerberos/www/dialogue.html

Kerberos offers a better network security model than the "ignoring network security entirely" model, but it is neither perfectly secure nor painless to install and run. It does not supersede the other security measures described in this chapter.

Unfortunately (and perhaps predictably), the Kerberos system distributed as part of Windows' Active Directory uses proprietary, undocumented extensions to the protocols. As a result, it does not interoperate well with distributions based on the MIT code. Fortunately, the **winbind** module lets UNIX and Linux systems interact with Active Directory's version of Kerberos. See *Configuring Kerberos for Active Directory integration* on page 1156 for more information.

Security

PGP: Pretty Good Privacy

See page 763 for more information about email privacy.

Phil Zimmermann's PGP package provides a tool chest of bread-and-butter cryptographic utilities focused primarily on email security. It can be used to encrypt data, to generate signatures, and to verify the origin of files and messages.

PGP has an interesting history that includes lawsuits, criminal prosecutions, and the privatization of portions of the original PGP suite. Currently, PGP's file formats and protocols are being standardized by the IETF under the name OpenPGP, and multiple implementations of the proposed standard exist. The GNU project provides an excellent, free, and widely used implementation known as GnuPG at gnupg.org. For clarity, we refer to the system collectively as PGP even though individual implementations have their own names.

PGP is perhaps the most popular cryptographic software in common use. Unfortunately, the UNIX/Linux version is nuts-and-bolts enough that you have to understand a fair amount of cryptographic background in order to use it. Although you may find PGP useful in your own work, we don't recommend that you support it for users because it has been known to spark many puzzled questions. We have found the Windows version to be considerably easier to use than the **gpg** command with its 52 different operating modes.

Software packages on the Internet are often distributed with a PGP signature file that purports to guarantee the origin and purity of the software. However, it is difficult for people who are not die-hard PGP users to validate these signatures—not because the process is complicated, but because true security can only come from having collected a personal library of public keys from people whose identities you have directly verified. Downloading a single public key along with a signature file and software distribution is approximately as secure as downloading the distribution alone.

Some email clients, such as Mozilla Thunderbird, have add-ons that provide a simple GUI for encrypted incoming and outgoing messages. Enigmail, the solution for Thunderbird, can even search on-line public key databases if the key for your recipient isn't already in your key ring. See enigmail.mozdev.org for details.

SSH: the secure shell

The SSH system, written by Tatu Ylönen, is a secure replacement for **rlogin**, **rcp**, and **telnet**. It uses cryptographic authentication to confirm a user's identity and encrypts all communications between the two hosts. The protocol used by SSH is designed to withstand a wide variety of potential attacks. The protocol is documented by RFCs 4250 through 4256 and is now a proposed IETF standard.

SSH has morphed from being a freely distributed open source project (SSH1) to being a commercial product that uses a slightly different (and more secure) protocol, SSH2. Fortunately, the open source community has responded by releasing the excellent OpenSSH package (maintained by OpenBSD), which now implements both protocols.

The main components of SSH are a server daemon, **sshd**, and a few user-level commands, notably **ssh** for remote logins and **sftp/scp** for copying files. Other components are an **ssh-keygen** command that generates public key pairs and a couple of utilities that help support secure X Windows.

sshd can authenticate user logins in several different ways. It's up to you as the administrator to decide which of these methods are acceptable:

- **Method A:** If the name of the remote host from which the user is logging in is listed in **~/.rhosts**, **~/.shosts**, **/etc/hosts.equiv**, or **/etc/shosts.equiv**, then **sshd** logs in the user automatically without a password check. This scheme mirrors that of the old **rlogin** daemon and in our opinion is *never* acceptable for normal use.
- **Method B:** As a refinement of method A, **sshd** can also use public key cryptography to verify the identity of the remote host. For that to happen, the remote host's public key (generated at install time) must be listed in the local host's **/etc/ssh_known_hosts** file or the user's **~/.ssh/known_hosts** file.

If the remote host can prove that it knows the corresponding private key (normally stored in **/etc/ssh_host_key**, a world-unreadable file), then **sshd** logs in the user without asking for a password.

Method B is more restrictive than method A, but we think it's still not quite secure enough. If the security of the originating host is compromised, the local site will be compromised as well.

- **Method C: sshd** can use public key cryptography to establish the user's identity. At login time, the user must have access to a copy of his or her private key file and must supply a password to decrypt it. The key can also be created without a password, which is a reasonable option for automating logins from remote systems.

  This method is the most secure, but it's annoying to set up. It also means that users cannot log in when traveling unless they bring along a copy of their private key file (perhaps on a USB key, hopefully encrypted).

  If you decide to use key pairs, make extensive use of **ssh -v** during the troubleshooting process.

- **Method D:** Finally, **sshd** can simply allow the user to enter his or her normal login password. This makes **ssh** behave very much like **telnet**, except that the password and session are both encrypted. The main drawbacks of this method are that system login passwords can be relatively weak if you have not beefed up their security, and that ready-made tools (such as John the Ripper) have been designed to break them. However, this method is probably the best choice for normal use.

Authentication policy is set in **/etc/sshd_config**. This file gets filled up with configuration rubbish for you as part of the installation process, but you can safely ignore most of it. The options relevant to authentication are shown in Table 22.2.

Table 22.2 Authentication-related options in /etc/sshd_config

Option	Meth[a]	Dflt	Meaning when turned on
RhostsAuthentication	A	No	Obeys **~/.shosts**, **/etc/shosts.equiv**, etc.
RhostsRSAAuthentication	B	Yes	Allows **~/.shosts** et al., but requires host key
IgnoreRhosts	A,B	No	Ignores the **~/.rhosts** and **hosts.equiv** files[b]
IgnoreRootRhosts	A,B	No[c]	Prevents **rhosts/shosts** authentication for root
RSAAuthentication	C	Yes	Allows per-user public key authentication
PasswordAuthentication	D	Yes	Allows use of normal login password

a. The authentication methods to which this variable is relevant
b. But continues to honor **~/.shosts** and **shosts.equiv**
c. Defaults to the value of IgnoreRhosts

Our suggested configuration, which allows methods C and D but not methods A or B, is as follows:

```
RhostsAuthentication no
RhostsRSAAuthentication no
RSAAuthentication yes
PasswordAuthentication yes
```

It is never wise to allow root to log in remotely. Superuser access should be achieved through the use of **sudo**. To encourage this behavior, use the option

```
PermitRootLogin no
```

The first time you connect to a new system through SSH, you are prompted to accept the remote host's public key (which is usually generated as part of the server's installation of OpenSSH, or soon thereafter). A truly paranoid user might manually verify it, but most of us blindly accept the key, which is then stored in the **~/.ssh/known_hosts** file for future use. SSH won't mention the server's key again unless it changes. Unfortunately, users' rubber-stamping the keys of new systems leaves you vulnerable to a man-in-the-middle attack if the host key was actually being presented by an attacker's system.

A DNS record known as SSHFP has been developed to address this vulnerability. The premise is that the server's key is stored as a DNS record. When a client connects to an unknown system, SSH looks up the SSHFP record to verify the server's key rather than asking the user to verify it.

The **sshfp** utility, available from xelerance.com/software/sshfp, generates SSHFP DNS resource records either by scanning a remote server or by parsing a previously accepted key from the **known_hosts** file. (Of course, either choice assumes that the source of the key is known to be correct.) Usage is quite simple: use the **-s** flag to generate a key from a network scan, or use **-k** to scan the **known_hosts** file (the default). For example, the following command generates a BIND-compatible SSHFP record for solaris.booklab.atrust.com:

```
solaris$ sshfp solaris.booklab.atrust.com
solaris.booklab.atrust.com   IN  SSHFP 1 1 94a26278ee713a37f6a78110f1ad9bd...
solaris.booklab.atrust.com   IN  SSHFP 2 1 7cf72d02e3d3fa947712bc56fd0e0a3i...
```

Add these records to the domain's zone file (be careful of the names and the $ORIGIN), reload the domain, and use **dig** to verify the key:

```
solaris$ dig solaris.booklab.atrust.com. IN SSHFP | grep SSHFP
; <<>> DiG 9.5.1-P2 <<>> solaris.booklab.atrust.com. IN SSHFP
; solaris.booklab.atrust.com. IN SSHFP
solaris.booklab.atrust.com.  38400  IN  SSHFP 1 1 94a26278ee713a37f6a78110f...
solaris.booklab.atrust.com.  38400  IN  SSHFP 2 1 7cf72d02e3d3fa947712bc56f...
```

ssh does not consult SSHFP records by default. Add the VerifyHostKeyDNS option to **/etc/ssh/ssh_config** to enable it. As with most SSH client options, you can also pass **-o "VerifyHostKeyDNS yes"** on the **ssh** command line when first accessing a new system.

SSH has a couple of ancillary functions that are useful for system administrators. One of these is the ability to tunnel TCP connections securely through an encrypted SSH channel, thereby allowing connectivity to insecure or firewalled services at remote sites. This functionality is ubiquitous among SSH clients and is simple to configure. Exhibit A shows a typical use of an SSH tunnel and should help clarify how it works.

Exhibit A An SSH tunnel for RDP

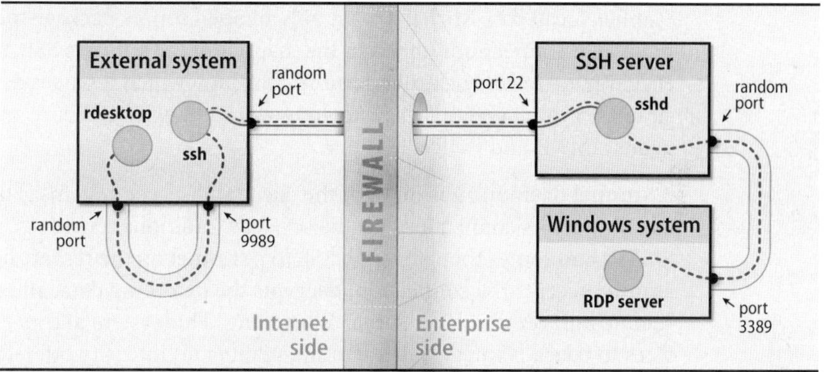

In this scenario, a remote user wants to establish an RDP (remote desktop) connection to a Windows system on the enterprise network. Access to that host or to port 3389 is blocked by the firewall, but since the user has SSH access, he can route his connection through the SSH server.

To set this up, the user logs in to the remote SSH server with **ssh**. On the **ssh** command line, he specifies an arbitrary (but specific; in this case, 9989) local port that **ssh** should forward through the secure tunnel to the remote Windows machine's port 3389. (For the standard OpenSSH implementation, the option to request this behavior is simply **-L** *localport*:*remotehost*:*remoteport.)* All source ports in this example are marked as random since programs choose an arbitrary port from which they initiate connections.

To access the Windows machine's desktop, the user then opens the remote desktop client (here, **rdesktop**) and enters localhost:9989 as the address of the server to connect to. The local **ssh** receives the connection on port 9989 and tunnels the traffic over the existing connection to the remote **sshd**. In turn, **sshd** forwards the connection to the Windows host.

Of course, tunnels such as these can be intentional or unintentional back doors as well. System administrators should use tunnels with caution and should also watch for unauthorized misuse of this facility by users.

In recent years, SSH has become the target of regular brute-force password attacks. Attackers perform repeated authentication attempts as common users, such as root, joe, or admin. Evidence of the attacks can be seen in the logs as hundreds or thousands of failed logins. Disabling password authentication is the best protection against these attacks. For now, attackers seem to be focusing only on port 22, so moving your SSH server to another port is an effective countermeasure. But history shows that this type of "security through obscurity" is rarely effective for long. Running password checks on your systems can reveal weak passwords that are likely to be broken by brute-force attacks.

Stunnel

Stunnel, created by Michal Trojnara, is an open source package that encrypts arbitrary TCP connections, much in the manner of SSH. It uses SSL, the Secure Sockets Layer, to create end-to-end tunnels through which it passes data to and from an unencrypted service. It is known to work well with insecure services such as Telnet, IMAP, and POP.

A **stunnel** daemon runs on both the client and server systems. The local **stunnel** usually accepts connections on the service's traditional port (e.g., port 25 for SMTP) and routes them through SSL to a **stunnel** on the remote host. The remote **stunnel** accepts the connection, decrypts the incoming data, and routes it to the remote port on which the server is listening. This system allows unencrypted services to take advantage of the confidentiality and integrity offered by encryption without requiring any software changes. Client software need only be configured to look for services on the local system rather than on the server that will ultimately provide them.

The Telnet protocol makes a good example because it consists of a simple daemon listening on a single port. To **stunnel**ify a Telnet link, you first create an SSL certificate. Stunnel is SSL library independent, so any standards-based implementation will do; we like OpenSSL. To generate the certificate:

```
server$ sudo openssl req -new -x509 -days 365 -nodes -out stunnel.pem
    -keyout stunnel.pem
Generating a 1024 bit RSA private key
.++++++
................................++++++
writing new private key to 'stunnel.pem'
-----
You are about to be asked to enter information that will be incorporated
into your certificate request.
What you are about to enter is what is called a Distinguished Name or a DN.
There are quite a few fields but you can leave some blank
For some fields there will be a default value,
If you enter '.', the field will be left blank.
Country Name (2 letter code) [GB]:US
State or Province Name (full name) [Berkshire]:Colorado
Locality Name (eg, city) [Newbury]:Boulder
```

```
Organization Name (eg, company) [My Company Ltd]:Booklab, Inc.
Organizational Unit Name (eg, section) []:
Common Name (eg, your name or server's hostname) []:server.example.com
Email Address []:
```

This command creates a self-signed, passphrase-less certificate. Although not using a passphrase is a convenience (a real human doesn't have to be present to type a passphrase each time **stunnel** restarts), it also introduces a security risk. Be careful to protect the certificate file with strong permissions.

Next, define the configuration for both the server and client **stunnel**s. The standard configuration file is **/etc/stunnel/stunnel.conf**, but you can create several configurations if you want to run more than one tunnel.

```
cert = /etc/stunnel/stunnel.pem
chroot = /var/run/stunnel/
pid = /stunnel.pid
setuid = nobody
setgid = nobody
debug = 7
output = /var/log/stunnel.log
client = no

[telnets]
accept = 992
connect = 23
```

There are a couple of important points to note about the server configuration. First, the chroot statement confines the **stunnel** process to the **/var/run/stunnel** directory. Paths for accessory files may need to be expressed in either the regular system namespace or the **chroot**ed namespace, depending on the point at which they are opened. Here, the **stunnel.pid** file is actually located in **/var/run/stunnel**.

The [telnets] section has two statements: accept tells **stunnel** to accept connections on port 992, and connect passes those connections through to port 23, the actual Telnet service.

The client configuration is similar:

```
cert = /etc/stunnel/stunnel.pem
chroot = /var/run/stunnel/
pid = /stunnel.pid
setuid = nobody
setgid = nobody
debug = 7
output = /var/log/stunnel.log
client = yes

[telnets]
accept = 23
connect = server.example.com:992
```

A couple of directives are reversed relative to the server configuration. The statement client = yes tells the program to initiate **stunnel** connections rather than accept them. The local **stunnel** listens for connections on port 23 and connects to the server on port 992. The hostname in the connect directive should match the entry specified when the certificate was created.

Both the client and the server **stunnel**s can be started with no command-line arguments. If you check with **netstat -an**, you should see the server **stunnel** waiting for connections on port 992 while the client **stunnel** waits on port 23.

To access the tunnel, a user simply **telnet**s to the local host:

```
client$ telnet localhost 23
Trying 127.0.0.1...
Connected to localhost (127.0.0.1).
Escape character is '^]'.
Red Hat Enterprise Linux WS release 4 (Nahant Update 2)
Kernel 2.6.9-5.EL on an i686
login:
```

The user can now safely log in without fear of password thievery. A vigilant administrator would be careful to use TCP wrappers to restrict connections on the client to only the local interface—the intent is not to allow the world to **telnet** securely to the server! **stunnel** is one of several programs that have built-in wrapper support and do not require the use of **tcpd** to restrict access. Visit stunnel.org for instructions.

22.11 Firewalls

In addition to protecting individual machines, you can also implement security precautions at the network level. The basic tool of network security is the firewall, a device or piece of software that prevents unwanted packets from accessing networks and systems. Firewalls are ubiquitous today and are found in devices ranging from desktop systems and servers to consumer routers and enterprise-grade network appliances.

Packet-filtering firewalls

A packet-filtering firewall limits the types of traffic that can pass through your Internet gateway (or through an internal gateway that separates domains within your organization) on the basis of information in the packet header. It's much like driving your car through a customs checkpoint at an international border crossing. You specify which destination addresses, port numbers, and protocol types are acceptable, and the gateway simply discards (and in some cases, logs) packets that don't meet the profile.

Packet-filtering software is included in Linux systems in the form of **iptables**, in Solaris and HP-UX as IPFilter, and in AIX as **genfilt**. See the details beginning on page 935 for more information.

Although these tools are capable of sophisticated filtering and bring a welcome extra dose of security, we generally discourage the use of UNIX and Linux systems as network routers and, most especially, as enterprise firewall routers. The complexity of general-purpose operating systems makes them inherently less secure and less reliable than task-specific devices. Dedicated firewall appliances such as those made by Check Point and Cisco are a better option for site-wide network protection.

How services are filtered

Most well-known services are associated with a network port in the **/etc/services** file or its vendor-specific equivalent. The daemons that provide these services bind to the appropriate ports and wait for connections from remote sites.[7] Most of the well-known service ports are "privileged," meaning that their port numbers are in the range 1 to 1023. These ports can only be used by a process running as root. Port numbers 1024 and higher are referred to as nonprivileged ports.

Service-specific filtering is based on the assumption that the client (the machine that initiates a TCP or UDP conversation) uses a nonprivileged port to contact a privileged port on the server. For example, if you wanted to allow only inbound SMTP connections to a machine with the address 192.108.21.200, you would install a filter that allowed TCP packets destined for port 25 at that address and that permitted outbound TCP packets from that address to anywhere.[8] The exact way that such a filter is installed depends on the kind of router or filtering system you are using.

*See page 977 for more information about setting up an **ftp** server.*

Some services, such as FTP, add a twist to the puzzle. The FTP protocol actually uses two TCP connections when transferring a file: one for commands and the other for data. The client initiates the command connection, and the server initiates the data connection[9]. Ergo, if you want to use FTP to retrieve files from the Internet, you must permit inbound access to all nonprivileged TCP ports since you have no idea what port might be used to form an incoming data connection.

This tweak largely defeats the purpose of packet filtering because some notoriously insecure services (for example, X11 at port 6000) naturally bind to nonprivileged ports. This configuration also creates an opportunity for curious users within your organization to start their own services (such as a **telnet** server at a nonstandard and nonprivileged port) that they or their friends can access from the Internet.

One common solution to the FTP problem is to use the SSH file transfer protocol. The protocol is currently an Internet draft but is widely used and mature. It is commonly used as a subcomponent of SSH, which provides its authentication and

7. In many cases, **inetd** or **xinetd** does the actual waiting on their behalf. See page 1188 for details.
8. Port 25 is the SMTP port as defined in **/etc/services**.
9. This summary describes traditional FTP, also known as "active FTP." Some systems support "passive FTP," in which the client initiates both connections.

encryption. Unlike FTP, SFTP uses only a single port for both commands and data, handily solving the packet-filtering paradox. A number of SFTP implementations exist. We've had great luck with the command-line SFTP client supplied by OpenSSH.

If you must use FTP, a reasonable approach is to allow FTP to the outside world only from a single, isolated host. Users can log in to the FTP machine when they need to perform network operations that are forbidden from the inner net. Since replicating all user accounts on the FTP "server" would defeat the goal of administrative separation, you may want to create FTP accounts by request only. Naturally, the FTP host should run a full complement of security-checking tools.

Modern security-conscious sites use a two-stage filtering scheme. In this scheme, one filter is a gateway to the Internet, and a second filter lies between the outer gateway and the rest of the local network. The idea is to terminate all inbound Internet connections on systems that lie in between these two filters. If these systems are administratively separate from the rest of the network, they can provide a variety of services to the Internet with reduced risk. The partially secured network is usually called the "demilitarized zone" or DMZ.

The most secure way to use a packet filter is to start with a configuration that allows no inbound connections. You can then liberalize the filter bit by bit as you discover useful things that don't work and, hopefully, move any Internet-accessible services onto systems in the DMZ.

Stateful inspection firewalls

The theory behind stateful inspection firewalls is that if you could carefully listen to and understand all the conversations (in all the languages) that were taking place in a crowded airport, you could make sure that someone wasn't planning to bomb a plane later that day. Stateful inspection firewalls are designed to inspect the traffic that flows through them and compare the actual network activity to what "should" be happening.

For example, if the packets exchanged in an FTP command sequence name a port to be used later for a data connection, the firewall should expect a data connection to occur only on that port. Attempts by the remote site to connect to other ports are presumably bogus and should be dropped.

So what are vendors really selling when they claim to provide stateful inspection? Their products either monitor a very limited number of connections or protocols or they search for a particular set of "bad" situations. Not that there's anything wrong with that; clearly, some benefit is derived from any technology that can detect traffic anomalies. In this particular case, however, it's important to remember that the claims are *mostly* marketing hype.

Firewalls: how safe are they?

A firewall should not be your primary (or only!) means of defense against intruders. It's only one component of what should be a carefully considered, multilayered security strategy. The use of firewalls often confers a false sense of security. If a firewall lulls you into relaxing other safeguards, it will have had a *negative* effect on the security of your site.

Every host within your organization should be individually patched, hardened, and regularly monitored with one or more tools such as Bro, Snort, Nmap, Nessus, and OSSEC. Likewise, your entire user community needs to be educated about basic security hygiene. Otherwise, you are simply building a structure that has a hard crunchy outside and a soft chewy center.

Ideally, local users should be able to connect to any Internet service they want, but machines on the Internet should only be able to connect to a limited set of local services hosted within your DMZ. For example, you may want to allow SFTP access to a local archive server and allow SMTP connections to a server that receives incoming email.

To maximize the value of your Internet connection, we recommend that you emphasize convenience and accessibility when deciding how to set up your network. At the end of the day, it's the system administrator's vigilance that makes a network secure, not a fancy piece of firewall hardware.

22.12 Linux firewall features

As stated earlier, we don't really recommended the use of Linux (or UNIX, or Windows) systems as firewalls because of the insecurity of running a full-fledged, general-purpose operating system.[10] However, a hardened Linux system is a workable substitute for organizations that don't have the budget for a high-dollar firewall appliance. Likewise, it's a fine option for a security-savvy home user with a penchant for tinkering. In any case, a local filter such as **iptables** can be an excellent supplemental security measure to consider when hardening a system.

If you are set on using a Linux machine as a firewall, make sure that it's up to date with respect to security configuration and patches. A firewall machine is an excellent place to put into practice all of this chapter's recommendations. (The section that starts on page 932 discusses packet-filtering firewalls in general. If you are not familiar with the basic concept of a firewall, it would probably be wise to read that section before continuing.)

Rules, chains, and tables

Version 2.4 of the Linux kernel introduced an all-new packet-handling engine, called Netfilter, along with a command-line tool, **iptables**, to manage it. **iptables**

10. That said, many consumer-oriented networking devices, such as Linksys's router products, use Linux and **iptables** at their core.

applies ordered "chains" of rules to network packets. Sets of chains make up "tables" and are used for handling specific kinds of traffic.

For example, the default **iptables** table is named "filter". Chains of rules in this table are used for packet-filtering network traffic. The filter table contains three default chains: FORWARD, INPUT, and OUTPUT. Each packet handled by the kernel is passed through exactly one of these chains.

Rules in the FORWARD chain are applied to all packets that arrive on one network interface and need to be forwarded to another. Rules in the INPUT and OUTPUT chains are applied to traffic addressed to or originating from the local host, respectively. These three standard chains are usually all you need for firewalling between two network interfaces. If necessary, you can define a custom configuration to support more complex accounting or routing scenarios.

In addition to the filter table, **iptables** includes the "nat" and "mangle" tables. The nat table contains chains of rules that control Network Address Translation (here, "nat" is the name of the **iptables** table and "NAT" is the name of the generic address translation scheme). The section *Private addresses and network address translation (NAT)* on page 462 discusses NAT, and an example of the nat table in action is shown on page 493. Later in this section, we use the nat table's PREROUTING chain for anti-spoofing packet filtering.

The mangle table contains chains that modify or alter the contents of network packets outside the context of NAT and packet filtering. Although the mangle table is handy for special packet handling, such as resetting IP time-to-live values, it is not typically used in most production environments. We discuss only the filter and nat tables in this section, leaving the mangle table to the adventurous.

Rule targets

Each rule that makes up a chain has a "target" clause that determines what to do with matching packets. When a packet matches a rule, its fate is in most cases sealed; no additional rules will be checked. Although many targets are defined internally to **iptables**, it is possible to specify another chain as a rule's target.

The targets available to rules in the filter table are ACCEPT, DROP, REJECT, LOG, MIRROR, QUEUE, REDIRECT, RETURN, and ULOG. When a rule results in an ACCEPT, matching packets are allowed to proceed on their way. DROP and REJECT both drop their packets; DROP is silent, and REJECT returns an ICMP error message. LOG gives you a simple way to track packets as they match rules, and ULOG expands logging.

See page 974 for more information about Squid.

REDIRECT shunts packets to a proxy instead of letting them go on their merry way. For example, you might use this feature to force all your site's web traffic to go through a web cache such as Squid. RETURN terminates user-defined chains and is analogous to the return statement in a subroutine call. The MIRROR target swaps the IP source and destination address before sending the packet. Finally, QUEUE hands packets to local user programs through a kernel module.

iptables firewall setup

Before you can use **iptables** as a firewall, you must enable IP forwarding and make sure that various **iptables** modules have been loaded into the kernel. For more information on enabling IP forwarding, see *Tuning Linux kernel parameters* on page 421 or *Security-related kernel variables* on page 492. Packages that install **iptables** generally include startup scripts to achieve this enabling and loading.

A Linux firewall is usually implemented as a series of **iptables** commands contained in an **rc** startup script. Individual **iptables** commands usually take one of the following forms:

```
iptables -F chain-name
iptables -P chain-name target
iptables -A chain-name -i interface -j target
```

The first form (**-F**) flushes all prior rules from the chain. The second form (**-P**) sets a default policy (aka target) for the chain. We recommend that you use DROP for the default chain target. The third form (**-A**) appends the current specification to the chain. Unless you specify a table with the **-t** argument, your commands apply to chains in the filter table. The **-i** parameter applies the rule to the named interface, and **-j** identifies the target. **iptables** accepts many other clauses, some of which are shown in Table 22.3.

Table 22.3 Command-line flags for iptables filters

Clause	Meaning or possible values
-p *proto*	Matches by protocol: **tcp**, **udp**, or **icmp**
-s *source-ip*	Matches host or network source IP address (CIDR notation is OK)
-d *dest-ip*	Matches host or network destination address
--sport *port#*	Matches by source port (note the double dashes)
--dport *port#*	Matches by destination port (note the double dashes)
--icmp-type *type*	Matches by ICMP type code (note the double dashes)
!	Negates a clause
-t *table*	Specifies the table to which a command applies (default is filter)

A complete example

Below we break apart a complete example. We assume that the eth1 interface goes to the Internet and that the eth0 interface goes to an internal network. The eth1 IP address is 128.138.101.4, the eth0 IP address is 10.1.1.1, and both interfaces have a netmask of 255.255.255.0. This example uses stateless packet filtering to protect the web server with IP address 10.1.1.2, which is the standard method of protecting Internet servers. Later in the example, we show how to use stateful filtering to protect desktop users.

Our first set of rules initializes the filter table. First, all chains in the table are flushed, then the INPUT and FORWARD chains' default target is set to DROP. As with any other network firewall, the most secure strategy is to drop any packets you have not explicitly allowed.

```
iptables -F
iptables -P INPUT DROP
iptables -P FORWARD DROP
```

Since rules are evaluated in order, we put our busiest rules at the front.[11] The first rule allows all connections through the firewall that originate from within the trusted net. The next three rules in the FORWARD chain allow connections through the firewall to network services on 10.1.1.2. Specifically, we allow SSH (port 22), HTTP (port 80), and HTTPS (port 443) through to our web server.

```
iptables -A FORWARD -i eth0 -p ANY -j ACCEPT
iptables -A FORWARD -d 10.1.1.2 -p tcp --dport 22 -j ACCEPT
iptables -A FORWARD -d 10.1.1.2 -p tcp --dport 80 -j ACCEPT
iptables -A FORWARD -d 10.1.1.2 -p tcp --dport 443 -j ACCEPT
```

The only TCP traffic we allow to our firewall host (10.1.1.1) is SSH, which is useful for managing the firewall itself. The second rule listed below allows loopback traffic, which stays local to the host. Administrators get nervous when they can't **ping** their default route, so the third rule here allows ICMP ECHO_REQUEST packets from internal IP addresses.

```
iptables -A INPUT -i eth0 -d 10.1.1.1 -p tcp --dport 22 -j ACCEPT
iptables -A INPUT -i lo -d 127.0.0.1 -p ANY -j ACCEPT
iptables -A INPUT -i eth0 -d 10.1.1.1 -p icmp --icmp-type 8 -j ACCEPT
```

For any IP host to work properly on the Internet, certain types of ICMP packets must be allowed through the firewall. The following eight rules allow a minimal set of ICMP packets to the firewall host, as well as to the network behind it.

```
iptables -A INPUT -p icmp --icmp-type 0 -j ACCEPT
iptables -A INPUT -p icmp --icmp-type 3 -j ACCEPT
iptables -A INPUT -p icmp --icmp-type 5 -j ACCEPT
iptables -A INPUT -p icmp --icmp-type 11 -j ACCEPT
iptables -A FORWARD -d 10.1.1.2 -p icmp --icmp-type 0 -j ACCEPT
iptables -A FORWARD -d 10.1.1.2 -p icmp --icmp-type 3 -j ACCEPT
iptables -A FORWARD -d 10.1.1.2 -p icmp --icmp-type 5 -j ACCEPT
iptables -A FORWARD -d 10.1.1.2 -p icmp --icmp-type 11 -j ACCEPT
```

See page 473 for more information about IP spoofing.

We next add rules to the PREROUTING chain in the nat table. Although the nat table is not intended for packet filtering, its PREROUTING chain is particularly useful for anti-spoofing filtering. If we put DROP entries in the PREROUTING chain, they need not be present in the INPUT and FORWARD chains, since the PREROUTING chain is applied to all packets that enter the firewall host. It's cleaner to put the entries in a single place rather than to duplicate them.

11. However, you must be careful that reordering the rules for performance doesn't modify functionality.

```
iptables -t nat -A PREROUTING -i eth1 -s 10.0.0.0/8 -j DROP
iptables -t nat -A PREROUTING -i eth1 -s 172.16.0.0/12 -j DROP
iptables -t nat -A PREROUTING -i eth1 -s 192.168.0.0/16 -j DROP
iptables -t nat -A PREROUTING -i eth1 -s 127.0.0.0/8 -j DROP
iptables -t nat -A PREROUTING -i eth1 -s 224.0.0.0/4 -j DROP
```

Finally, we end both the INPUT and FORWARD chains with a rule that forbids all packets not explicitly permitted. Although we already enforced this behavior with the **iptables -P** commands, the LOG target lets us see who is knocking on our door from the Internet.

```
iptables -A INPUT -i eth1 -j LOG
iptables -A FORWARD -i eth1 -j LOG
```

Optionally, we could set up IP NAT to disguise the private address space used on the internal network. See page 492 for more information about NAT.

One of the most powerful features that Netfilter brings to Linux firewalling is stateful packet filtering. Instead of allowing specific incoming services, a firewall for clients connecting to the Internet needs to allow incoming responses to the client's requests. The simple stateful FORWARD chain below allows all traffic to leave our network but only allows incoming traffic that's related to connections initiated by our hosts.

```
iptables -A FORWARD -i eth0 -p ANY -j ACCEPT
iptables -A FORWARD -m state --state ESTABLISHED,RELATED -j ACCEPT
```

Certain kernel modules must be loaded to enable **iptables** to track complex network sessions such as those of FTP and IRC. If these modules are not loaded, **iptables** simply disallows those connections. Although stateful packet filters can increase the security of your site, they also add to the complexity of the network. Be sure you need stateful functionality before implementing it in your firewall.

Perhaps the best way to debug your **iptables** rulesets is to use **iptables -L -v**. These options tell you how many times each rule in your chains has matched a packet. We often add temporary **iptables** rules with the LOG target when we want more information about the packets that get matched. You can often solve trickier problems by using a packet sniffer such as **tcpdump**.

22.13 IPFilter for UNIX systems

Most UNIX vendors don't have their own firewall software.[12] But it's easy enough to add: IPFilter, an open source package developed by Darren Reed, supplies NAT and stateful firewall services for UNIX systems. Solaris includes it by default, and it's also available as an add-on for HP-UX, AIX, and many other systems, including Linux. You can use IPFilter as a loadable kernel module (which is recommended by the developers) or include it statically in the kernel.

12. IBM is an exception. AIX does include a separate packet-filtering suite in its IP Security implementation, although the suite does not do stateful filtering. See the man pages for **genfilt** to get started.

IPFilter is mature and feature-complete. The package has an active user community and a history of continuous development. It is capable of stateful tracking even for stateless protocols such as UDP and ICMP.

IPFilter reads filtering rules from a configuration file (usually **/etc/ipf.conf** or **/etc/ipf/ipf.conf**) rather than making you run a series of commands as does **iptables**. An example of a simple rule that could appear in **ipf.conf** is

```
block in all
```

This rule blocks all inbound traffic (that is, network activity received by the system) on all network interfaces. Certainly secure, but not particularly useful!

Table 22.4 shows some of the possible conditions that can appear in an **ipf** rule.

Table 22.4 Commonly used ipf conditions

Condition	Meaning or possible values
on *interface*	Applies the rule to the specified interface
proto *protocol*	Selects packet according to protocol: tcp, udp, or icmp
from *source-ip*	Filters by source: host, network, or any
to *dest-ip*	Filters by destination: host, network, or any
port = *port#*	Filters by port name (from **/etc/services**) or number[a]
flags *flag-spec*	Filters according to TCP header flags bits
icmp-type *number*	Filters by ICMP type and code
keep state	Retains details about the flow of a session; see comments below

a. You can use any comparison operator: =, <, >, <=, >=, etc.

IPFilter evaluates rules in the sequence in which they are presented in the configuration file. The *last* match is binding. For example, inbound packets traversing the following filter will always pass:

```
block in all
pass in all
```

The block rule matches all packets, but so does the pass rule, and pass is the last match. To force a matching rule to apply immediately and make IPFilter skip subsequent rules, use the quick keyword:

```
block in quick all
pass in all
```

An industrial-strength firewall typically contains many rules, so liberal use of quick is important to maintain the performance of the firewall. Without it, every packet is evaluated against every rule, and this wastefulness is costly.

Perhaps the most common use of a firewall is to control access to and from a specific network or host, often with respect to a specific port. IPFilter has powerful syntax to control traffic at this level of granularity. In the following rules, inbound traffic is permitted to the 10.0.0.0/24 network on TCP ports 80 and 443 and on UDP port 53.

```
block out quick all
pass in quick proto tcp from any to 10.0.0.0/24 port = 80 keep state
pass in quick proto tcp from any to 10.0.0.0/24 port = 443 keep state
pass in quick proto udp from any to 10.0.0.0/24 port = 53 keep state
block in all
```

The keep state keywords deserve special attention. IPFilter can keep track of connections by noting the first packet of new sessions. For example, when a new packet arrives addressed to port 80 on 10.0.0.10, IPFilter makes an entry in the state table and allows the packet through. It also allows the reply from the web server even though the first rule explicitly blocks all outbound traffic.

keep state is also useful for devices that offer no services but that must initiate connections. The following ruleset permits all conversations that are initiated by 192.168.10.10. It blocks all inbound packets except those related to connections that have already been initiated.

```
block in quick all
pass out quick from 192.168.10.10/32 to any keep state
```

The keep state keywords work for UDP and ICMP packets, too, but since these protocols are stateless, the mechanics are slightly more ad hoc: IPFilter permits responses to a UDP or an ICMP packet for 60 seconds after the inbound packet is seen by the filter. For example, if a UDP packet from 10.0.0.10, port 32,000, is addressed to 192.168.10.10, port 53, a UDP reply from 192.168.10.10 will be permitted until 60 seconds have passed. Similarly, an ICMP echo reply (ping response) is permitted after an echo request has been entered in the state table.

See page 462 for more information about private addresses and NAT.

Network address translation (NAT) is another feature offered by IPFilter. NAT lets a large network that uses RFC1918 private IP addresses connect to the Internet through a small set of Internet-routable IP addresses. The NAT device maps traffic from the private network to one or more public addresses, sends requests across the Internet, and then intercepts the responses and rewrites them in terms of the local IP addresses.

IPFilter uses the map keyword (in place of pass and block) to provide NAT services. In the following rule, traffic from the 10.0.0.0/24 network is mapped to the current routable address on the e1000g0 interface.

```
map e1000g0 10.0.0.0/24 -> 0/32
```

The filter must be reloaded if the address of e1000g0 changes, as might happen if e1000g0 leases a dynamic IP address through DHCP. For this reason, IPFilter's NAT features are best used at sites that have a static IP address on the Internet-facing interface.

IPFilter rules are flexible and configurable. Advanced features such as macros can considerably simplify the rules files. For details on these advanced features, see the official IPFilter site at coombs.anu.edu.au/~avalon.

The IPFilter package includes several commands, listed in Table 22.5.

Table 22.5 IPFilter commands

Cmd	Function
ipf	Manages rules and filter lists
ipfstat	Obtains statistics about packet filtering
ipmon	Monitors logged filter information
ipnat	Manages NAT rules

Of the commands in Table 22.5, **ipf** is the most commonly used. **ipf** accepts a rule file as input and adds correctly parsed rules to the kernel's filter list. **ipf** adds rules to the end of the filter unless you use the **-Fa** argument, which flushes all existing rules. For example, to flush the kernel's existing set of filters and load the rules from **ipf.conf**, use the following syntax:

```
solaris$ sudo ipf -Fa -f /etc/ipf/ipf.conf
```

IPFilter relies on pseudo-device files in **/dev** for access control, and by default only root can edit the filter list. We recommend leaving the default permissions in place and using **sudo** to maintain the filter.

Use **ipf**'s **-v** flag when loading the rules file to debug syntax errors and other problems in the configuration.

IPFilter is preinstalled in the Solaris kernel, but you must enable it with

```
solaris$ sudo svcadm enable network/ipfilter
```

before you can use it.

22.14 Virtual private networks (VPNs)

In its simplest form, a VPN is a connection that makes a remote network appear as if it is directly connected, even if it is physically thousands of miles and many router hops away. For increased security, the connection is not only authenticated in some way (usually with a "shared secret" such as a password), but the end-to-end traffic is also encrypted. Such an arrangement is usually referred to as a "secure tunnel."

Here's a good example of the kind of situation in which a VPN is handy: Suppose that a company has offices in Chicago, Boulder, and Miami. If each office has a connection to a local ISP, the company can use VPNs to transparently (and, for the most part, securely) connect the offices across the untrusted Internet. The company could achieve a similar result by leasing dedicated lines to connect the three offices, but that would be considerably more expensive.

Another good example is a company whose employees telecommute from their homes. VPNs would allow those users to reap the benefits of their high-speed and inexpensive cable modem service while still making it appear that they are directly connected to the corporate network.

Because of the convenience and popularity of this functionality, everyone and his brother is offering some type of VPN solution. You can buy it from your router vendor as a plug-in for your operating system or even as a dedicated VPN device for your network. Depending on your budget and scalability needs, you may want to consider one of the many commercial VPN solutions.

If you're without a budget and looking for a quick fix, SSH can do secure tunneling for you. See the end of the SSH section on page 926.

IPsec tunnels

If you're a fan of IETF standards (or of saving money) and need a real VPN solution, take a look at IPsec (Internet Protocol security). IPsec was originally developed for IPv6, but it has also been widely implemented for IPv4. IPsec is an IETF-approved, end-to-end authentication and encryption system. Almost all serious VPN vendors ship a product that has at least an IPsec compatibility mode. Linux, Solaris, HP-UX, and AIX all include native kernel support for IPsec.

IPsec uses strong cryptography to provide both authentication and encryption services. Authentication ensures that packets are from the right sender and have not been altered in transit, and encryption prevents the unauthorized examination of packet contents.

In tunnel mode, IPsec encrypts the transport layer header, which includes the source and destination port numbers. Unfortunately, this scheme conflicts with the way in which most firewalls work. For this reason, most modern implementations default to using transport mode, in which only the payloads of packets (the data being transported) are encrypted.

There's a gotcha involving IPsec tunnels and MTU size. It's important to ensure that once a packet has been encrypted by IPsec, nothing fragments it along the path the tunnel traverses. To achieve this feat, you may have to lower the MTU on the devices in front of the tunnel (in the real world, 1,400 bytes usually works). See page 453 in the TCP chapter for more information about MTU size.

All I need is a VPN, right?

Sadly, there's a downside to VPNs. Although they do build a (mostly) secure tunnel across the untrusted network between the two endpoints, they don't usually address the security of the endpoints themselves. For example, if you set up a VPN between your corporate backbone and your CEO's home, you may be inadvertently creating a path for your CEO's 15-year-old daughter to have direct access to everything on your network.

Bottom line: you need to treat connections from VPN tunnels as external connections and grant them additional privileges only as necessary and after careful consideration. Consider adding a special section to your site security policy that covers the rules that apply to VPN connections.

22.15 CERTIFICATIONS AND STANDARDS

If the subject matter of this chapter seems daunting to you, don't fret. Computer security is a complicated and vast topic, as countless books, web sites, and magazines can attest. Fortunately, much has been done to help quantify and organize the available information. Dozens of standards and certifications exist, and mindful system administrators should consider their guidance.

One of the most basic philosophical principles in information security is informally referred to as the "CIA triad."

The acronym stands for

- Confidentiality
- Integrity
- Availability

Confidentiality concerns the privacy of data. Access to information should be limited to those who are authorized to have it. Authentication, access control, and encryption are a few of the subcomponents of confidentiality. If a hacker breaks into a system and steals a database containing customer contact information, a compromise of confidentiality has occurred.

Integrity relates to the authenticity of information. Data integrity technology ensures that information is valid and has not been altered in any unauthorized way. It also addresses the trustworthiness of information sources. When a secure web site presents a signed SSL certificate, it is proving to the user not only that the information it is sending is encrypted but also that a trusted certificate authority (such as VeriSign or Equifax) has verified the identity of the source. Technologies such as PGP and Kerberos also guarantee data integrity.

Availability expresses the idea that information must be accessible to authorized users when they need it or there is no purpose in having it. Outages not caused by intruders, such as those caused by administrative errors or power outages, also fall into the category of availability problems. Unfortunately, availability is often ignored until something goes wrong.

Consider the CIA principles as you design, implement, and maintain systems. As the old security adage goes, "security is a process."

Certifications

This crash course in CIA is just a brief introduction to the larger information security field. Large corporations often employ many full-time employees whose job is guarding information. To gain credibility in the field and keep their knowledge current, these professionals attend training courses and obtain certifications. Prepare yourself for acronym-fu as we work through a few of the most popular certifications.

One of the most widely recognized security certifications is the CISSP, or Certified Information Systems Security Professional. It is administered by (ISC)^2, the International Information Systems Security Certification Consortium (say *that* ten times fast!). One of the primary draws of the CISSP is (ISC)^2's notion of a "common body of knowledge" (CBK), essentially an industry-wide best practices guide for information security. The CBK covers law, cryptography, authentication, physical security, and much more. It's an incredible reference for security folks.

One criticism of the CISSP has been its concentration on breadth and consequent lack of depth. So many topics in the CBK, and so little time! To address this, (ISC)^2 has issued CISSP concentration programs that focus on architecture, engineering, and management. These specialized certifications add depth to the more general CISSP certification.

The System Administration, Networking, and Security (SANS) Institute created the Global Information Assurance Certification (GIAC) suite of certifications in 1999. Three dozen separate exams cover the realm of information security with tests divided into five categories. The certifications range in difficulty from the moderate two-exam GISF to the 23-hour, expert-level GSE. The GSE is notorious as one of the most difficult certifications in the industry. Many of the exams focus on technical specifics and require quite a bit of experience.

Finally, the Certified Information Systems Auditor (CISA) credential is an audit and process certification. It focuses on business continuity, procedures, monitoring, and other management content. Some consider the CISA an intermediate certification that is appropriate for an organization's security officer role. One of its most attractive aspects is that it involves only a single exam.

Although certifications are a personal endeavor, their application to business is undeniable. More and more companies now recognize certifications as the mark of an expert. Many businesses offer higher pay and promotions to certified employees. If you decide to pursue a certification, work closely with your organization to have it help pay for the associated costs.

Security standards

Because of the ever-increasing reliance on data systems, laws and regulations have been created to govern the management of sensitive, business-critical information. Major pieces of U.S. legislation such as HIPAA, FISMA, NERC CIP, and the

Sarbanes-Oxley Act (SOX) have all included sections on IT security. Although the requirements are sometimes expensive to implement, they have helped give the appropriate level of focus to a once-ignored aspect of technology.

For a broader discussions of industry and legal standards that affect IT environments, see page 1222.

Unfortunately, the regulations are filled with legalese and can be difficult to interpret. Most do not contain specifics on how to achieve their requirements. As a result, standards have been developed to help administrators reach the lofty legislative requirements. These standards are not regulation specific, but following them usually ensures compliance. It can be intimidating to confront the requirements of all the various standards at once, so it's usually best to first work through one standard in its entirety.

ISO 27002

The ISO/IEC 27002 (formerly ISO 17799) standard is probably the most widely accepted in the world. First introduced in 1995 as a British standard, it is 34 pages long and is divided into 11 sections that run the gamut from policy to physical security to access control. Objectives within each section define specific requirements, and controls under each objective describe the suggested "best practice" solutions. The document costs about $200.

The requirements are nontechnical and can be fulfilled by any organization in a way that best fits its needs. On the downside, the general wording of the standard leaves the reader with a sense of broad flexibility. Critics complain that the lack of specifics leaves organizations open to attack.

Nonetheless, this standard is one of the most valuable documents available to the information-security industry. It bridges an often tangible gap between management and engineering and helps focus both parties on minimizing risk.

PCI DSS

The Payment Card Industry Data Security Standard (PCI DSS) is a different beast entirely. It arose out of the perceived need to improve security in the credit card processing industry following a series of dramatic exposures. For example, in June 2005, CardSystems Services International revealed the "loss" of 40 million credit card numbers.

The U.S. Department of Homeland Security has estimated that $49.3 billion was lost to identity theft in 2009 alone. Not all of this can be linked directly to credit card exposure, of course, but increased vigilance by vendors would certainly have had a positive impact. The FBI has even connected credit card fraud to the funding of terrorist groups. Specific incidents include the bombings in Bali and the Madrid subway system.

The PCI DSS standard is the result of a joint effort between Visa and MasterCard, though it is currently maintained by Visa. Unlike ISO 27002, it is freely available for anyone to download. It focuses entirely on protecting cardholder data systems and has 12 sections that define requirements for protection.

Because PCI DSS is focused on card processors, it is not generally appropriate for businesses that don't deal with credit card data. However, for those that do, strict compliance is necessary to avoid hefty fines and possible criminal prosecution. You can find the document at pcisecuritystandards.org.

NIST 800 series

The fine folks at the National Institute of Standards and Technology (NIST) have created the Special Publication (SP) 800 series of documents to report on their research, guidelines, and outreach efforts in computer security. These documents are most often used in connection with measuring FISMA compliance for those organizations that handle data for the U.S. federal government. More generally, they are publicly available standards with excellent content and have been widely adopted by industry.

The SP 800 series includes more than 100 documents. All of them are available from csrc.nist.gov/publications/PubsSPs.html. Here are a few that you might want to consider starting with: NIST 800-12, *An Introduction to Computer Security: The NIST Handbook*; NIST 800-14, *Generally Accepted Principles and Practices for Securing Information Technology Systems*; NIST 800-34 R1, *Contingency Planning Guide for Information Technology Systems*; NIST 800-39, *Managing Risk from Information Systems: An Organizational Perspective*; NIST 800-53 R3, *Recommended Security Controls for Federal Information Systems and Organizations*; NIST 800-123, *Guide to General Server Security.*

Common Criteria

The Common Criteria for Information Technology Security Evaluation (commonly known as the "Common Criteria") is a standard against which to evaluate the security level of IT products. These guidelines have been established by an international committee of members from a variety of manufacturers and industries. See commoncriteriaportal.org to learn more about the standard and certified products.

OWASP

The Open Web Application Security Project (OWASP) is a not-for-profit worldwide organization focused on improving the security of application software. They are best known for their "top 10" list of web application security risks, which serves to remind all of us where to focus our energies when securing applications. Find the current list and a bunch of other great material at owasp.org.

22.16 Sources of security information

Half the battle of keeping your system secure consists of staying abreast of security-related developments in the world at large. If your site is broken into, the break-in probably won't be through the use of a novel technique. More likely, the chink in your armor is a known vulnerability that has been widely discussed in vendor knowledge bases, on security-related newsgroups, and on mailing lists.

CERT: a registered service mark of Carnegie Mellon University

In response to the uproar over the 1988 Robert Morris, Jr., Internet worm, the Defense Advanced Research Projects Agency (DARPA) formed an organization called CERT, the Computer Emergency Response Team, to act as a clearing house for computer security information. CERT is still the best-known point of contact for security information, although it seems to have grown rather sluggish and bureaucratic of late. CERT also now insists that the name CERT does not stand for anything and is merely "a registered service mark of Carnegie Mellon University."

In mid-2003, CERT partnered with the Department of Homeland Security's National Cyber Security Division, NCSD. For better or worse, the merger has altered the previous mailing list structure.

The combined organization, known as US-CERT, offers four announcement lists, the most useful of which is the "Technical Cyber Security Alerts." Subscribe to any of the four lists at forms.us-cert.gov/maillists.

SecurityFocus.com and the BugTraq mailing list

SecurityFocus.com specializes in security-related news and information. The news includes current articles on general issues and on specific problems; there's also an extensive technical library of useful papers, nicely sorted by topic.

SecurityFocus's archive of security tools includes software for a variety of operating systems, along with blurbs and user ratings. It is the most comprehensive and detailed source of tools that we are aware of.

The BugTraq list is a moderated forum for the discussion of security vulnerabilities and their fixes. To subscribe, visit securityfocus.com/archive. Traffic on this list can be fairly heavy, however, and the signal-to-noise ratio is poor. A database of BugTraq vulnerability reports is also available from the web site.

Schneier on Security

Bruce Schneier's blog is a valuable and sometimes entertaining source of information about computer security and cryptography. Schneier is the author of the well-respected books *Applied Cryptography* and *Secrets and Lies*, among others. Information from the blog is also captured in the form of a monthly newsletter known as the Crypto-Gram. Learn more at schneier.com/crypto-gram.html.

SANS: the System Administration, Networking, and Security Institute

SANS is a professional organization that sponsors security-related conferences and training programs, as well as publishing a variety of security information. Their web site, sans.org, is a useful resource that occupies something of a middle ground between SecurityFocus and CERT: neither as frenetic as the former nor as stodgy as the latter.

SANS offers several weekly and monthly email bulletins that you can sign up for on their web site. The weekly NewsBites are nourishing, but the monthly summaries seem to contain a lot of boilerplate. Neither is a great source of late-breaking security news.

Vendor-specific security resources

Because security problems have the potential to generate a lot of bad publicity, vendors are often eager to help customers keep their systems secure. Most large vendors have an official mailing list to which security-related bulletins are posted, and many maintain a web site about security issues as well. It's common for security-related software patches to be distributed for free, even by vendors that normally charge for software support.

Security portals on the web, such as SecurityFocus.com, contain vendor-specific information and links to the latest official vendor dogma.

Ubuntu maintains a security mailing list at

https://lists.ubuntu.com/mailman/listinfo/ubuntu-security-announce

You can find SUSE security advisories at

novell.com/linux/security/securitysupport.html

You can join the official SUSE security announcement mailing list by visiting

suse.com/en/private/support/online_help/mailinglists/index.html

Subscribe to the "Enterprise watch" list to get announcements about the security of Red Hat's product line at redhat.com/mailman/listinfo/enterprise-watch-list.

Despite Oracle's acquisition of Sun Microsystems, Sun's original security blog at blogs.sun.com/security/category/alerts continues to be updated. When the branding and location are updated, you can probably still find a pointer there.

You can access HP's various offerings through us-support.external.hp.com for the Americas and Asia, and europe-support.external.hp.com for Europe.

The security-related goodies have been carefully hidden. To find them, enter the maintenance/support area and select the option to search the technical knowledge base. A link in the filter options on that page takes you to the archive of security bulletins. (You will need to register if you have not already done so.) You can access security patches from that area as well.

To have security bulletins sent to you, return to the maintenance/support main page and choose the "Subscribe to proactive notifications and security bulletins" option. Unfortunately, there does not appear to be any way to subscribe directly by email.

Sign up for AIX security notifications through the "My notifications" link at ibm.com/systems/support.

Security information about Cisco products is distributed in the form of field notices, a list of which can be found at cisco.com/public/support/tac/fn_index.html along with a news aggregation feed. To subscribe to Cisco's security mailing list, email majordomo@cisco.com with the line "subscribe cust-security-announce" in the message body.

Other mailing lists and web sites

The contacts listed above are just a few of the many security resources available on the net. Given the volume of info that's now available and the rapidity with which resources come and go, we thought it would be most helpful to point you toward some meta-resources.

One good starting point is the linuxsecurity.com, which logs several posts every day on pertinent Linux security issues. It also keeps a running collection of Linux security advisories, upcoming events, and user groups.

(IN)SECURE magazine is a free bimonthly magazine containing current security trends, product announcements, and interviews with notable security professionals. Read some of the articles with a vial of salt nearby, and be sure to check the author at the end—he may be pimping his own products.

Linux Security (linuxsecurity.com) covers the latest news in Linux and open source security. Subscribe to the RSS feed for best results.

The Linux Weekly News is a tasty treat that includes regular updates on the kernel, security, distributions, and other topics. LWN's security section can be found at lwn.net/security.

22.17 What to do when your site has been attacked

The key to handling an attack is simple: don't panic. It's very likely that by the time you discover the intrusion, most of the damage has already been done. In fact, it has probably been going on for weeks or months. The chance that you've discovered a break-in that just happened an hour ago is slim to none.

In that light, the wise owl says to take a deep breath and begin developing a carefully thought out strategy for dealing with the break-in. You need to avoid tipping off the intruder by announcing the break-in or performing any other activity that would seem abnormal to someone who may have been watching your site's operations for many weeks. Hint: performing a system backup is usually a good idea at this point and (hopefully!) will appear to be a normal activity to the intruder.[13]

13. If system backups are not a "normal" activity at your site, you have much bigger problems than the security intrusion.

This is also a good time to remind yourself that some studies have shown that 60% of security incidents involve an insider. Be very careful with whom you discuss the incident until you're sure you have all the facts.

Here's a quick 9-step plan that may assist you in your time of crisis:

Step 1: Don't panic. In many cases, a problem isn't noticed until hours or days after it took place. Another few hours or days won't affect the outcome. The difference between a panicky response and a rational response will. Many recovery situations are exacerbated by the destruction of important log, state, and tracking information during an initial panic.

Step 2: Decide on an appropriate level of response. No one benefits from an over-hyped security incident. Proceed calmly. Identify the staff and resources that must participate and leave others to assist with the post-mortem after it's all over.

Step 3: Hoard all available tracking information. Check accounting files and logs. Try to determine where the original breach occurred. Back up all your systems. Make sure that you physically write-protect backup tapes if you put them in a drive to read them.

Step 4: Assess your degree of exposure. Determine what crucial information (if any) has "left" the company, and devise an appropriate mitigation strategy. Determine the level of future risk.

Step 5: Pull the plug. If necessary and appropriate, disconnect compromised machines from the network. Close known holes and stop the bleeding. CERT provides steps for analyzing an intrusion. The document can be found at

> cert.org/tech_tips/win-UNIX-system_compromise.html

Step 6: Devise a recovery plan. With a creative colleague, draw up a recovery plan on nearby whiteboard. This procedure is most effective when performed away from a keyboard. Focus on putting out the fire and minimizing the damage. Avoid assessing blame or creating excitement. In your plan, don't forget to address the psychological fallout your user community may experience. Users inherently trust others, and blatant violations of trust make many folks uneasy.

Step 7: Communicate the recovery plan. Educate users and management about the effects of the break-in, the potential for future problems, and your preliminary recovery strategy. Be open and honest. Security incidents are part of life in a modern networked environment. They are not a reflection on your ability as a system administrator or on anything else worth being embarrassed about. Openly admitting that you have a problem is 90% of the battle, as long as you can demonstrate that you have a plan to remedy the situation.

Step 8: Implement the recovery plan. You know your systems and networks better than anyone. Follow your plan and your instincts. Speak with a colleague at a similar institution (preferably one who knows you well) to keep yourself on the right track.

Step 9: Report the incident to authorities. If the incident involved outside parties, report the matter to CERT. They have a hotline at (412) 268-7090 and can be reached by email at cert@cert.org. Provide as much information as you can.

A standard form is available from cert.org to help jog your memory. Here are some of the more useful pieces of information you might provide:

- The names, hardware, and OS versions of the compromised machines
- The list of patches that had been applied at the time of the incident
- A list of accounts that are known to have been compromised
- The names and IP addresses of any remote hosts that were involved
- Contact information (if known) for the administrators of remote sites
- Relevant log entries or audit information

If you believe that a previously undocumented software problem may have been involved, you should report the incident to the software vendor as well.

22.18 Recommended reading

Barrett, Daniel J., Richard E. Silverman, and Robert G. Byrnes. *Linux Security Cookbook.* Sebastopol, CA: O'Reilly Media, 2003.

Bauer, Michael D. *Linux Server Security (2nd Edition).* Sebastopol, CA: O'Reilly Media, 2005.

Bryant, William. "Designing an Authentication System: a Dialogue in Four Scenes." 1988. web.mit.edu/kerberos/www/dialogue.html

Cheswick, William R., Steven M. Bellovin, and Aviel D Rubin. *Firewalls and Internet Security: Repelling the Wily Hacker (2nd Edition).* Reading, MA: Addison-Wesley, 2003.

Curtin, Matt, Marcus Ranum, and Paul D. Robinson. "Internet Firewalls: Frequently Asked Questions." 2004. interhack.net/pubs/fwfaq

Farrow, Rik, and Richard Power. *Network Defense article series.* 1998-2004. spirit.com/Network

Fraser, B., Editor. *RFC2196: Site Security Handbook.* 1997. rfc-editor.org

Garfinkel, Simson, Gene Spafford, and Alan Schwartz. *Practical UNIX and Internet Security (3rd Edition).* Sebastopol, CA: O'Reilly Media, 2003.

Kerby, Fred, et al. "SANS Intrusion Detection and Response FAQ." SANS. 2009. sans.org/resources/idfaq

Lyon, Gordon Fyodor. *Nmap Network Scanning: The Official Nmap Project Guide to Network Discovery and Security Scanning.* Nmap Project, 2009.

MANN, SCOTT, AND ELLEN L. MITCHELL. *Linux System Security: The Administrator's Guide to Open Source Security Tools (2nd Edition)*. Upper Saddle River, NJ: Prentice Hall PTR, 2002.

MORRIS, ROBERT, AND KEN THOMPSON. "Password Security: A Case History." *Communications of the ACM*, 22 (11): 594-597, November 1979. Reprinted in *UNIX System Manager's Manual*, 4.3 Berkeley Software Distribution. University of California, Berkeley, April 1986.

RITCHIE, DENNIS M. "On the Security of UNIX." May 1975. Reprinted in *UNIX System Manager's Manual*, 4.3 Berkeley Software Distribution. University of California, Berkeley, April 1986.

SCHNEIER, BRUCE. *Applied Cryptography: Protocols, Algorithms, and Source Code in C*. New York, NY: Wiley, 1995.

STEVES, KEVIN. "Building a Bastion Host Using HP-UX 11." HP Consulting. 2002. tinyurl.com/5sffy2

THOMPSON, KEN. "Reflections on Trusting Trust." in *ACM Turing Award Lectures: The First Twenty Years 1966-1985*. Reading, MA: ACM Press (Addison-Wesley), 1987.

Exercises begin on the next page.

22.19 Exercises

E22.1 Discuss the strength of SSH authentication when passwords are used versus when a passphrase and key pair are used. If one is clearly more secure than the other, should you automatically require the more secure authentication method?

★ E22.2 SSH tunneling is often the only way to tunnel traffic to a remote machine on which you don't have administrator access. Read the **ssh** man page and write a command line that tunnels traffic from localhost port 113 to mail.remotenetwork.org port 113. The forwarding point of your tunnel should also be the host mail.remotenetwork.org.

★ E22.3 Pick a recent security incident and research it. Find the best sources of information about the incident and find patches or workarounds that are appropriate for the systems in your lab. List your sources and the actions you propose for protecting your lab.

★ E22.4 With permission from your local sysadmin group, install John the Ripper, the program that searches for logins with weak passwords.

a) Modify the source code so that it outputs only the login names with which weak passwords are associated, not the passwords themselves.

b) Run John the Ripper on your local lab's password file (you need access to **/etc/shadow**) and see how many breakable passwords you can find.

c) Set your password to a dictionary word and give **john** just your own entry in **/etc/shadow**. How long does **john** take to find it?

d) Try other patterns (capital letter, number after dictionary word, single-letter password, etc.) to see exactly how smart **john** is.

★★ E22.5 In the computer lab, set up two machines: a target and a prober.

a) Install **nmap** and Nessus on the prober. Attack the target with these tools. How could you detect the attack on the target?

b) Set up a firewall on the target; use **iptables** to defend against the probes. Can you detect the attack now? If so, how? If not, why not?

c) What other defenses can be set up against the attacks?

(Requires root access.)

★★ E22.6 Using a common security mailing list or web site, identify an application that has recently encountered a vulnerability. Find a good source of information on the hole and discuss the issues and the best way to address them.

☆☆ E22.7 Setuid programs are sometimes a necessary evil. However, setuid shell scripts should be avoided. Why?

☆☆ E22.8 Use **tcpdump** to capture FTP traffic for both active and passive FTP sessions. How does the need to support an anonymous FTP server affect the site's firewall policy? What would the firewall rules need to allow? (Requires root access.)

☆☆ E22.9 What do the rules in the following **iptables** output allow and disallow? What would be some easy additions that would enhance security and privacy? (Hint: the OUTPUT and FORWARD chains could use some more rules.)

```
Chain INPUT (policy ACCEPT)
target   prot  opt  source     destination
block    all   --   anywhere   anywhere

Chain FORWARD (policy ACCEPT)
target   prot  opt  source     destination
         all   --   anywhere   anywhere

Chain OUTPUT (policy ACCEPT)
target   prot  opt  source     destination

Chain block (1 references)
target   prot  opt  source           destination
ACCEPT   all   --   anywhere         anywhere      state RELATED,ESTABLISHED
ACCEPT   tcp   --   anywhere         anywhere      state NEW tcp dpt:www
ACCEPT   tcp   --   anywhere         anywhere      state NEW tcp dpt:ssh
ACCEPT   tcp   --   128.138.0.0/16   anywhere      state NEW tcp dpt:kerberos
ACCEPT   icmp  --   anywhere         anywhere
DROP     all   --   anywhere         anywhere
```

☆☆ E22.10 Inspect a local firewall's rulesets. Discuss what you find in terms of policies. Are there any glaring security holes? (This exercise is likely to require the cooperation of the administrators responsible for your local site's security.)

☆☆☆☆☆ E22.11 Write a tool that determines whether any network interfaces at your site are in promiscuous mode. Run it periodically on your networks to try to quickly spot such an intrusion. How much load does the tool generate? Do you have to run it on each machine, or can you run it from afar? Can you design a sneaky packet that would tell you if an interface was in promiscuous mode, and if so, what does it look like? (Requires root access.)

23 Web Hosting

Today, UNIX and Linux systems are the predominant platform for serving web content and web applications. They are ideal systems for this task because they were designed from the ground up as preemptive, multitasking systems. They can handle a high volume of web requests, and they can do it efficiently, securely, and reliably.

In some respects, web-based applications have actually simplified sysadmins' jobs. "Web 2.0" features like AJAX (Asynchronous JavaScript and XML) and dynamic HTML bring users the functionality and responsiveness of locally installed applications but relieve sysadmins of a multitude of deployment headaches: the only software required on the client side is a web browser.

On the server side, the LAMP (Linux, Apache, MySQL, and PHP/Perl/Python)[1] stack is a common configuration that is also highly functional. For database-driven applications, Ruby on Rails is a popular open source web application framework built on the Ruby language. Both of these stacks are reasonable choices and are easy to support.

1. Non-Linux UNIX distributions refer to this collection simply as "AMP." Solaris folks call it "SAMP," and the Windows folks call it "WAMP." Go figure.

23.1 WEB HOSTING BASICS

Hosting a web site isn't substantially different from providing any other network service. A daemon listens for connections on TCP port 80 (the HTTP standard), accepts requests for documents, and transmits them to the requesting user's browser. Many of these documents are generated on the fly in conjunction with databases and application frameworks, but that's incidental to the underlying HTTP protocol.

Resource locations on the web

See page 448 for more information about the Internet Society.

Information on the Internet is organized into an architecture defined by the Internet Society (ISOC). This well-intended (albeit committee-minded) organization helps ensure consistency and interoperability throughout the Internet.

ISOC defines three primary ways to identify a resource: Uniform Resource Identifiers (URIs), Uniform Resource Locators (URLs), and Uniform Resource Names (URNs). URLs and URNs are really specialized types of URIs, as illustrated in Exhibit A.

Exhibit A Uniform resource taxonomy

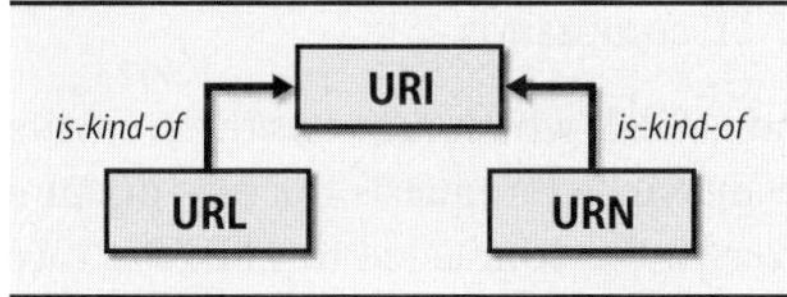

So what's the difference?

- URLs tell you how to locate a resource by describing its primary access mechanism (e.g., http://admin.com).
- URNs identify ("name") a resource without implying its location or telling you how to access it (e.g., urn:isbn:0-13-020601-6).

When do you call something a URI? If a resource is only accessible through the Internet, refer to it as a URL. If it could be accessed through the Internet or through other means, then you're using a URI.

Uniform resource locators

Most of the time, you'll be dealing with URLs, which describe how to access an object through five basic components:

- Protocol or application
- Hostname
- TCP/IP port (optional)
- Directory (optional)
- Filename (optional)

Table 23.1 shows some of the protocols that can be used in URLs.

Table 23.1 URL protocols

Proto	What it does	Example
file	Accesses a local file	file:///etc/syslog.conf
ftp	Accesses a remote file via FTP	ftp://ftp.admin.com/adduser.tar.gz
http	Accesses a remote file via HTTP	http://admin.com/index.html
https	Accesses a remote file via HTTP/SSL	https://admin.com/order.shtml
ldap	Accesses LDAP directory services	ldap://ldap.bigfoot.com:389/cn=Herb
mailto	Sends email to a designated address	mailto:linux@book.admin.com

How HTTP works

HTTP is a stateless client/server protocol. A client asks the server for the "contents" of a specific URL. The server responds either with a spurt of data or with some type of error message. The client can then go on to request another object.

Because HTTP is so simple, you can turn yourself into a crude web browser by running **telnet**. Just **telnet** to port 80 on your web server of choice. Once you're connected, you can issue HTTP commands.

The most common command is GET, which requests the contents of a document. Usually, GET / is what you want, since it requests the root document (usually, the home page) of whatever server you've connected to. HTTP is case sensitive, so make sure you type commands in capital letters.

```
$ telnet localhost 80
Trying 127.0.0.1...
Connected to localhost.atrust.com.
Escape character is '^]'.
GET /
<contents of your default file appear here>
Connection closed by foreign host.
```

A more "complete" HTTP request would include the HTTP protocol version, the host that the request is for (required to retrieve a file from a name-based virtual host), and other information. The response would then include informational headers as well as response data. For example:

```
$ telnet localhost 80
Trying 127.0.0.1...
Connected to localhost.atrust.com.
Escape character is '^]'.
GET / HTTP/1.1
Host: www.atrust.com

HTTP/1.1 200 OK
Date: Sat, 01 Aug 2009 17:43:10 GMT
Server: Apache/2.2.3 (CentOS)
```

```
Last-Modified: Sat, 01 Aug 2009 16:20:22 GMT
Content-Length: 7044
Content-Type: text/html

<contents of your default file appear here>
Connection closed by foreign host.
```

In this case, we told the server we were going to speak HTTP protocol version 1.1 and named the virtual host from which we were requesting information. The server returned a status code (HTTP/1.1 200 OK), its idea of the current date and time, the name and version of the server software it was running, the date that the requested file was last modified, the length of the requested file, and the requested file's content type. The header information is separated from the content by a single blank line.

Content generation on the fly

In addition to serving up static documents, an HTTP server can provide the user with content that has been created on the fly. For example, if you wanted to provide the current time and temperature to users visiting your web site, you might have the HTTP server execute a script to obtain this information. This amaze-the-natives trick is often accomplished with the Common Gateway Interface, or CGI.

CGI is not a programming language but rather a specification by which an HTTP server exchanges information with other programs. CGI scripts are most often written in Perl, Python, or PHP. But really, any programming language that can perform real-time I/O is acceptable.

Embedded interpreters

The CGI model provides complete flexibility in that the web developer is free to use any interpreter or scripting language. Unfortunately, starting a separate process for every script call can be a performance nightmare on busy web servers that serve a significant amount of dynamic content.

In addition to supporting external CGI scripts, many web servers define a plug-in architecture that allows script interpreters such as Perl and PHP to be embedded within the web server itself. This bundling significantly increases performance because the web server no longer needs to fork a separate process to deal with each script request. The architecture is largely invisible to script developers. Whenever the server sees a file ending in a specified extension (such as **.pl** or **.php**), it sends the contents of the file to the embedded interpreter to be executed. Table 23.2 on the next page lists some common embedded interpreters that run inside Apache.

FastCGI

Another trick you can use in some situations is FastCGI (fastcgi.com). This module improves the performance of scripts by starting them once and then leaving them running to service multiple requests. This arrangement amortizes the cost

Table 23.2 Embedded scripting modules for the Apache web server

Language	Name of embedded interpreter	Learn more
Perl	mod_perl	perl.apache.org
Python	mod_python	modpython.org
PHP	mod_php (traditional)	apache.org
	Zend server (commercial accelerator)	zend.com
Ruby on Rails	Phusion Passenger (aka mod_rails or mod_rack)	modrails.com

of starting the interpreter and parsing the script across multiple requests. It can be faster than running the interpreter inside Apache itself.

Unfortunately, scripts must be modified to understand and conform to this new way of interacting with the web server. The basic protocol is easy to implement, but FastCGI scripts cannot afford to be sloppy about memory management. Loose ends cause the script's memory footprint to grow over time. Another potential hazard is the persistence of data across requests; programmers must ensure that requests cannot interact. Web developers will need to weigh whether the performance improvement from FastCGI is worth the extra effort and risk.

Some administrators prefer FastCGI to embedded interpreters because individual scripts can be restarted without affecting the rest of the system when they go awry. With embedded interpreters, you may need to restart the entire web server if one interpreter starts acting up.

Script security

For the most part, CGI scripts and server plug-ins are the concern of web developers and programmers. Unfortunately, they collide with the job of the system administrator in one important area: security. Because CGI scripts and plug-ins have access to files, network connections, and other ways of moving data from one place to another, their execution can potentially affect the security of the machine on which the HTTP server is running. Ultimately, a CGI script or plug-in gives anyone in the world the ability to run a program (the script) on your server. Therefore, CGI scripts and the files processed by plug-ins must be just as secure as any other network-accessible program.

OWASP, the Open Web Application Security Project (owasp.org), publishes a variety of excellent materials about web security. For general information about system security, see Chapter 22.

Application servers

Complex enterprise applications may need more functionality than a basic HTTP server can provide. For example, modern-day Web 2.0 pages often contain a subcomponent that is tied to a dynamic data feed (e.g., a stock ticker). Although it's possible to implement this functionality with Apache through technologies such as AJAX and JavaScript Object Notation (JSON), some developers prefer a more fully featured language such as Java. The common way to interface Java applications to an enterprise's other data sources is with a "servlet."

Servlets are Java programs that run on the server on top of an application server platform. Application servers can work independently or in concert with Apache. Most application servers were designed by programmers for programmers and lack the concise debugging mechanisms expected by system administrators. Table 23.3 highlights some common UNIX/Linux application servers.

Table 23.3 Application servers

Server	Type	Web site
Tomcat	Open source	tomcat.apache.org
GlassFish	Open source	glassfish.dev.java.net
JBoss	Open source	jboss.org
OC4J	Commercial	oracle.com/technology/tech/java/oc4j
WebSphere	Commercial	ibm.com/websphere
WebLogic	Commercial	oracle.com/appserver/weblogic/weblogic-suite.html
Jetty	Open source	eclipse.org/jetty

If you are faced with supporting one of these application servers, seek product-specific documentation and training. Trust us; this is not a technology you can pick up "on the fly" like most UNIX and Linux applications. You've been warned.

Load balancing

It's difficult to predict how many hits (requests for objects, including images) or page views (requests for HTML pages) a server can handle per unit of time. A server's capacity depends on the system's hardware architecture (including subsystems), the operating system it is running, the extent and emphasis of any system tuning that has been performed, and perhaps most importantly, the construction of the sites being served. (Do they contain only static HTML pages, or must they make database calls and numeric calculations?)

Only direct benchmarking and measurement of your actual site running on your actual hardware can answer the "how many hits?" question. Sometimes, people who have built similar sites on similar hardware can give you information that is useful for planning. In no case should you believe the numbers quoted by system suppliers. Also remember that your bandwidth is a key consideration. A single machine serving static HTML files and images can easily serve enough data to saturate an OC3 (155 Mb/s) link.

That said, instead of single-server hit counts, a better parameter to focus on is scalability; a web server typically becomes CPU- or IO-bound before saturating its Ethernet interface. Make sure that you and your web design team plan to spread the load of a heavily trafficked site across multiple servers.

Load balancing adds both performance and redundancy. Several different load balancing approaches are available: round robin DNS, load balancing hardware, and software-based load balancers.

See Chapter 17 for more information about DNS and its behavior.

Round robin DNS is the simplest and most primitive form of load balancing. In this system, multiple IP addresses are assigned to a single hostname. When a request for the web site's IP address arrives at the name server, the client receives one of the IP addresses in response. Addresses are handed out one after another, in a repeating "round robin" sequence.

Round robin load balancing is extremely common. It is even used by Google. For example, if you query the DNS infrastructure for www.google.com, you might get something like the following records:

```
$ dig www.google.com a
...
;; QUESTION SECTION:
;www.google.com.            IN     A

;; ANSWER SECTION:
www.google.com.      0      IN     CNAME     www.l.google.com.
www.l.google.com.    65     IN     A         74.125.95.104
www.l.google.com.    65     IN     A         74.125.95.105
www.l.google.com.    65     IN     A         74.125.95.106
www.l.google.com.    65     IN     A         74.125.95.147
www.l.google.com.    65     IN     A         74.125.95.99
www.l.google.com.    65     IN     A         74.125.95.103
```

In this example, the name www.google.com is mapped to the canonical name www.l.google.com. Google adds this layer of indirection so that it can delegate responsibility for content delivery to a downstream provider such as Akamai (see *Content distribution networks* on page 978 for more context) without giving the CDN control of its root domain.

A DNS client can pick any one of the A records returned for www.l.google.com; it is supposed to do so randomly. Contrary to popular belief, the order in which the A records are returned has no significance. In particular, the first one is not "primary." Because clients select addresses randomly, the load for this site is distributed roughly evenly across these six servers.

The problem with round robin DNS is that if a server goes down, DNS data must be updated to reroute traffic away from it. Long timeouts on the A records can make this operation tricky and unreliable. On the other hand, short timeouts thwart caching and so make DNS lookups of your site slower and more resource intensive. See *Caching and efficiency* on page 556 for a discussion of this tradeoff.

In the example above, the A records can be cached for 65 seconds before they expire. That's a relatively short timeout. If you have a backup server available, you might prefer to use a longer timeout for the A records and to simply reassign a disabled server's IP address to the backup server.

Load balancing hardware is an easy alternative to round robin DNS, but one that requires some spare cash. Commercial third-party load balancing hardware includes the Big-IP Controller from F5 Networks, Nortel's Alteon web switching products, and Cisco's Content Services Switches. These products distribute incoming work according to a variety of configurable parameters and can take the current response times of individual servers into account.

Software-based load balancers don't require specialized hardware; they can run on a UNIX server. Both open source and commercial solutions are available. The open source category includes the Linux Virtual Server (linuxvirtualserver.org) and the proxy load balancing functionality (mod_proxy_balancer) introduced in Apache 2.2. An example of commercial offerings in this space are those sold by Zeus, zeus.com.

Google actually uses a combination of custom load-balancing DNS servers (with round robin records) and load balancing hardware. See the Wikipedia article for "Google platform" for more details.

Keep in mind that most sites these days are dynamically generated. This architecture puts a heavy load on database servers. If necessary, consult your database administrator to determine the best way to distribute load across multiple database servers.

23.2 HTTP SERVER INSTALLATION

Installing and maintaining a web server is easy. Web services rank far below email and DNS in complexity and difficulty of administration.

Choosing a server

Several HTTP servers are available, but you'll most likely want to start with the Apache server, which is well known in the industry for its flexibility and performance. As of January 2010, 54% of web servers on the Internet were running Apache (currently serving up content for over 111 million sites). Microsoft accounts for most of the remainder at 24% of servers. This market share split between Apache and Microsoft has been relatively stable for the last five years. More detailed market share statistics over time are available here:

news.netcraft.com/archives/web_server_survey.html

You can find a useful comparison of currently available HTTP servers at the site serverwatch.com/stypes (select "web" in the Server Type menu). Here are some of the factors you may want to consider in making your selection:

- Robustness
- Performance
- Timeliness of updates and bug fixes
- Availability of source code

- Level of commercial or community support
- Cost
- Access control and security
- Ability to act as a proxy
- Ability to handle encryption

The Apache HTTP server is "free to a good home," and full source code is available from the Apache Group site at apache.org. The less adventurous may want to install a prebuilt binary package; see the hints provided in the table below. Some vendors avoid the name "Apache," but that's the server you get nonetheless.

Table 23.4 Locations of Apache binaries

System	Directory	Recommended source of binaries
Linux	**/usr/sbin**	Installed as part of standard distribution
Solaris	**/usr/apache2**	Installed as part of standard distribution
HP-UX	**/opt/apache**	Install HP-UX 11i "Web Server Suite"
AIX	**/usr/IBMIHS**	Install IBM HTTPServer product

Installing Apache

If you do decide to download the Apache source code and compile it yourself, start by executing the **configure** script included with the distribution. This script automatically detects the system type and sets up the appropriate makefiles. Use the --**prefix** option to specify where in your directory tree the Apache server should live. For example:

```
$ ./configure --prefix=/etc/httpd/
```

If you don't specify a prefix, the default is **/usr/local/apache2**.

You can use **configure** --**help** to see the entire list of possible arguments, most of which consist of --**enable**-*module* and --**disable**-*module* options that include or exclude various functional components that live within the web server.

You can also compile modules into dynamically shared object files by specifying the option --**enable**-*module*=**shared** (or use --**enabled-mods-shared=all** to make all modules shared). That way, you can decide later which modules to include or exclude; only modules specified in your **httpd** configuration are loaded at run time. This is actually the default configuration for the binary-only Apache package—all the modules are compiled into shared objects and are dynamically loaded when Apache starts.

The only disadvantages to using shared libraries are a slightly longer startup time and a very slight degradation in performance (typically less than 5%). For most sites, the benefit of being able to add new modules on the fly and to turn existing modules off without having to recompile outweighs the slight performance hit.

For a complete list of standard modules, see httpd.apache.org/docs-2.2/mod.

Although the default set of modules is reasonable, you may also want to enable the modules shown in Table 23.5.

Table 23.5 Useful Apache modules that are not enabled by default

Module	Function
authn_dbm	Uses a DBM database to manage user/group access (recommended if you need per-user, password-based access to areas of your web site)
rewrite	Rewrites URLs with regular expressions
expires	Lets you attach expiration dates to documents
proxy	Uses Apache as a proxy server
mod_ssl	Enables support for the Secure Sockets Layer[a] for HTTPS

a. Also known as Transport Layer Security or TLS; see page 971.

Likewise, you may want to disable the modules listed in Table 23.6. For security and performance, it's a good idea to disable modules that you know you will not be using.

Table 23.6 Apache modules we suggest removing

Module	Function
asis	Allows designated file types to be sent without HTTP headers
autoindex	Displays the contents of directories that don't have a default HTML file
env	Lets you set special environment variables for CGI scripts
userdir	Allows users to have their own HTML directories

When **configure** has finished executing, run **make** and then **make install** to actually compile and install the appropriate files.

Compiling Apache on AIX is unfortunately not so straightforward. See the tips and tricks at people.apache.org/~trawick/apache-2-on-aix.html.

Configuring Apache

Once you've installed the server, configure it for your environment. The config files are kept in the **conf** subdirectory of the installation directory. Examine and customize the **httpd.conf** file, which is divided into three sections.

The first section deals with global settings such as the server pool, the TCP port on which the HTTP server listens for queries (usually port 80, although you can choose another—and yes, you can run multiple HTTP servers on different ports on a single machine), and the settings for dynamic module loading.

The second section configures the "default" server, the server that handles any requests that aren't answered by VirtualHost definitions (see page 971). Configuration parameters in this section include the user and group as whom the server will run (something other than root!) and the all-important DocumentRoot statement, which defines the root of the directory tree from which documents are served. This section also addresses issues such as the handling of "special" URLs like those that include the ~*user* syntax to access a user's home directory.

You manage global security concerns in the second section of the configuration file as well. Directives control access on a per-file basis (the <File> directive) or on a per-directory basis (the <Directory> directive). These permission settings prevent access to sensitive files through **httpd**. You should specify at least two access controls: one that covers the entire filesystem and one that applies to the main document folder. The defaults that come with Apache are sufficient, although we recommend that you remove the AllowSymLinks option to prevent **httpd** from following symbolic links in your document tree. (We wouldn't want someone to accidentally create a symbolic link to **/etc**, now would we?) For more Apache security tips, see

httpd.apache.org/docs-2.2/misc/security_tips.html

The third and final section of the config file sets up virtual hosts. We discuss this topic in more detail on page 971.

Once you have made your configuration changes, check the syntax of the configuration file by running **httpd -t**. If Apache reports "Syntax OK," then you're good to go. If not, check the **httpd.conf** file for typos.

Running Apache

You can start **httpd** by hand or from your system's startup scripts. The latter is preferable, since this configuration ensures that the web server restarts whenever the machine reboots. To start the server by hand, type something like:

```
$ apachectl start
```

See Chapter 3 for more information about startup scripts.

Analyzing log files

With your web site in production, you're likely to want to gather statistics about the use of the site, such as the number of requests per page, the average number of requests per day, the percentage of failed requests, and the amount of data transferred. Make sure you're using the "combined" log format (your CustomLog directives should have the word combined at the end instead of common). The combined log format includes each request's referrer (the page from which the URL was linked) and user agent (the client's browser and operating system).

Your access and error logs appear in Apache's **logs** directory. The files are human readable, but they contain so much information that you really need a separate analysis program to extract useful data from them. There are literally hundreds of different log analyzers, both free and commercial.

Two free analyzers worth taking a look at are Analog (analog.cx) and AWStats (awstats.sourceforge.net). These both provide fairly basic information.

If you're looking for information about traffic and usage patterns for a web site, check out Google Analytics at analytics.google.com. This service requires that you put a small stub on each web page you want to track, but it then provides all the data gathering and analysis infrastructure for free.[2]

Optimizing for high-performance hosting of static content

The hosting community has learned over the last few years that one of the easiest ways to create a high-performance hosting platform is to optimize some servers for hosting static content.

One way to address this need is through the use of an in-kernel web server or in-kernel web page cache. Because these systems do not copy data to or from user space before returning it to a requestor, they achieve some incremental performance gains. However, because the solutions operate in kernel space, they entail some additional security risk. We recommend using them with extreme caution.

A kernel-based web server called TUX that runs in conjunction with a traditional web server such as Apache is available for some Linux distributions. When possible, TUX serves up static pages without leaving kernel space, much as **rpc.nfsd** serves files. Although TUX was developed by Red Hat (Red Hat now calls it the Red Hat Content Accelerator), it's been released under the GPL and can be used with other Linux distributions. Unfortunately, configuring TUX can be something of a challenge. The system was popular in the early 2000s, but its popularity has since dwindled. For details, see redhat.com/docs/manuals/tux.

On the Solaris platform, Sun has released the Solaris Network Cache and Accelerator (NCA) to provide in-kernel content caching. NCA intercepts the traffic going to and from **httpd** and caches static pages. When subsequent requests arrive for the same content, they're served from cache without involving **httpd**.

23.3 Virtual interfaces

In the early days, a UNIX machine typically acted as the server for a single web site (e.g., acme.com). As the web's popularity grew, everybody wanted to have a web site, and overnight, thousands of companies became web hosting providers.

See Chapter 14 for more information on basic interface configuration.

Providers quickly realized that they could achieve significant economies of scale if they were able to host more than one site on a single server. This trick would allow acme.com, ajax.com, toadranch.com, and many other sites to be transparently

2. Of course, this arrangement also gives Google access to your traffic data, which may or may not be a good thing.

served by the same hardware. In response to this business need, virtual interfaces were born.

The idea is simple: a single machine responds on the network to more IP addresses than it has physical network interfaces. Each of the resulting "virtual" network interfaces can be associated with a corresponding domain name that users on the Internet might want to connect to. Thus, a single machine can serve literally hundreds of web sites.

Virtual interfaces allow a daemon to identify connections based not only on the destination port number (e.g., port 80 for HTTP) but also on the connection's destination IP address. Today, virtual interfaces are in widespread use and have proved to be useful for applications other than web hosting.

Using name-based virtual hosts

The HTTP 1.1 protocol also defines a form of virtual-interface-like functionality (officially called "name-based virtual hosts") that eliminates the need to assign unique IP addresses to web servers or to configure a special interface at the OS level. This approach conserves IP addresses and is useful for some sites, especially those (such as universities) at which a single server is home to hundreds or thousands of home pages.

Unfortunately, the scheme isn't very practical for commercial sites. It reduces scalability (you must change the IP address of the site to move it to a different server) and may also have a negative impact on security (if you filter access to a site at your firewall according to IP addresses). Additionally, name-based virtual hosts require browser support to use SSL.[3] Given these limitations of name-based virtual hosts, it appears that true virtual interfaces will be around for a while.

Configuring virtual interfaces

Setting up a virtual interface involves two steps. First, you must create the virtual interface at the TCP/IP level. The exact way you do this depends on your version of UNIX; the next few sections provide instructions for each of our example systems. Second, you must tell the Apache server about the virtual interfaces you have installed. We cover this second step starting on page 971.

Linux virtual interfaces

Linux virtual interfaces are named with the notation *interface:instance*. For example, if your Ethernet interface is eth0, then the virtual interfaces associated with it could be eth0:0, eth0:1, and so on. All interfaces are configured with the **ifconfig** command. For example, the command

```
$ sudo ifconfig eth0:0 128.138.243.150 netmask 255.255.255.192 up
```

configures eth0:0 and assigns it an address on the 128.138.243.128/26 network.

3. A relatively new feature called Server Name Indication (SNI) enables the use of SSL with virtual hosts, but older browsers do not support it.

To make virtual address assignments permanent on Red Hat, you create a separate file for each virtual interface in **/etc/sysconfig/network-scripts**. For example, the file **ifcfg-eth0:0** that corresponds to the **ifconfig** command shown above contains the following lines:

```
DEVICE=eth0:0
IPADDR=128.138.243.150
NETMASK=255.255.255.192
NETWORK=128.138.243.128
BROADCAST=128.138.243.191
ONBOOT=yes
```

Ubuntu's approach is similar to Red Hat's, but the interface definitions must appear in the file **/etc/network/interfaces**. The entries corresponding to the eth0:0 interface in our example above are

```
iface eth0:0 inet static
    address 128.138.243.150
    netmask 255.255.255.192
    broadcast 128.138.243.191
```

On SUSE systems, you can either create virtual interfaces ("aliases") with YaST or create the interface files manually. To do it with YaST, first select "Traditional method with **ifup**" on the Global Options tab of Network Settings.

Under SUSE, an interface's IP addresses are all configured within a single file. To configure these files manually, look in **/etc/sysconfig/network** for files whose names start with **ifcfg-***ifname*.

For example, add these lines to the config file to define two virtual interfaces:

```
IPADDR_1=128.138.243.149
NETMASK_1=255.255.255.192
STARTMODE_1="auto"
LABEL_1=0
IPADDR_2=128.138.243.150
NETMASK_2=255.255.255.192
STARTMODE_2="auto"
LABEL_2=1
```

The suffixes that follow IPADDR and NETMASK (here, _1 and _2) don't have to be numeric, but for consistency, this is a reasonable convention. Note that you'll also need to edit **/etc/sysconfig/network/config** and set NETWORKMANAGER="no" so that the virtual interfaces will be recognized.

Solaris virtual interfaces

Solaris supports virtual interfaces (aka "secondary interfaces") through the concept of a physical interface and a logical unit. For example, if hme0 were the name of a physical interface, then hme0:1, hme0:2, and so on would be the names of the corresponding virtual interfaces. By default, each physical interface can have up to

256 virtual identities attached to it. If you need to change this limit, use **ndd** to change the parameter ip_addrs_per_if (see page 498 for details on using **ndd**).

To configure a virtual interface, just run **ifconfig** on one of the virtual names. (The underlying physical interface must already have been "plumbed.") In most cases, you'll want to set up the system so that the **ifconfig**s for virtual interfaces happen automatically at boot time.

Here is an example in which a Solaris machine has an address in private address space on an internal virtual private network (VPN) and an external address for the Internet, both associated with the same physical interface, hme0. To have these interfaces configured automatically at boot time, the administrator has set up two hostname files: **/etc/hostname.hme0** and **/etc/hostname.hme0:1**.

```
$ ls -l /etc/host*
-rw-r--r--   1 root   10  Nov  4 10:19   /etc/hostname.hme0
-rw-r--r--   1 root   16  Dec 21 19:34   /etc/hostname.hme0:1
```

Hostname files can contain either hostnames from the **/etc/hosts** file or IP addresses. In this case, the administrator has used one of each:

```
$ cat /etc/hostname.hme0
overkill
$ cat /etc/hostname.hme0:1
206.0.1.133
$ grep overkill /etc/hosts
10.1.2.9    overkill overkill.domain
```

At boot time, both addresses are automatically configured (along with the loopback address, which we omitted from the output shown below):

```
$ ifconfig -a
hme0: flags=863<UP,BROADCAST,NOTRAILERS,RUNNING,MULTICAST> mtu
      1500 inet 10.1.2.9 netmask ffffff00 broadcast 10.1.2.255
hme0:1: flags=863<UP,BROADCAST,NOTRAILERS,RUNNING,MULTICAST> mtu
      1500 inet 206.0.1.133 netmask ffffff80 broadcast 206.0.1.255
```

HP-UX virtual interfaces

On HP-UX, you add virtual interfaces with the **ifconfig** command. The syntax is very similar to that of Solaris. For example, to add the first interface, you would execute the command

```
$ sudo ifconfig lan0:1 192.168.69.1 up
```

AIX virtual interfaces

On AIX, you create an "alias" to add additional IP addresses to an interface. For example, to add 192.168.1.3 as a virtual IP address for the en0 interface, you can use **ifconfig**:

```
$ sudo ifconfig en0 192.168.1.3 netmask 255.255.255.0 alias
```

However, this alias is only temporary. To create a permanent virtual IP, use the **chdev** command:

```
$ sudo chdev -l en0 -a alias4=192.168.1.3,255.255.255.0
```

Telling Apache about virtual interfaces

In addition to creating the virtual interfaces, you need to tell Apache what documents to serve when a client tries to connect to each interface (IP address). You do this with a VirtualHost clause in the **httpd.conf** file. There is one VirtualHost clause for each virtual interface that you've configured. Here's an example:

```
<VirtualHost 128.138.243.150>
    ServerName www.company.com
    ServerAdmin webmaster@www.company.com
    DocumentRoot /var/www/htdocs/company
    ErrorLog logs/www.company.com-error_log
    CustomLog logs/www.company.com-access_log combined
    ScriptAlias /cgi-bin/ /var/www/cgi-bin/company
</VirtualHost>
```

In this example, any client that connects to the virtual host 128.138.243.150 is served documents from **/var/www/htdocs/company**. Nearly any Apache directive can go into a VirtualHost clause to define settings specific to that virtual host. Relative directory paths, including those for the DocumentRoot, ErrorLog, and CustomLog directives, are interpreted in the context of the ServerRoot.

With name-based virtual hosts, multiple DNS names all point to the same IP address. The Apache configuration is similar, but you specify the primary IP address on which Apache should listen for incoming named virtual host requests and you omit the IP address in the VirtualHost clause:

```
NameVirtualHost 128.138.243.150

<VirtualHost *>
    ServerName www.company.com
    ServerAdmin webmaster@www.company.com
    DocumentRoot /var/www/htdocs/company
    ErrorLog logs/www.company.com-error_log
    CustomLog logs/www.company.com-access_log combined
    ScriptAlias /cgi-bin/ /var/www/cgi-bin/company
</VirtualHost>
```

In this configuration, Apache looks in the HTTP headers to determine the requested site. The server listens for requests for www.company.com on its main IP address, 128.138.243.150.

23.4 The Secure Sockets Layer (SSL)

The SSL protocol secures communications between a web site and a client browser. URLs that start with https:// use this technology. SSL uses cryptography to prevent eavesdropping, tampering, and message forgery.

The browser and server use a certificate-based authentication scheme to establish communications, after which they switch to a faster cipher-based encryption scheme to protect their actual conversation.

SSL runs as a separate layer underneath the HTTP application protocol. SSL simply supplies the security for the connection and does not involve itself in the HTTP transaction. Because of this hygienic architecture, SSL can secure not only HTTP but also protocols such as SMTP and FTP. For more details, see the Wikipedia entry for "Secure Sockets Layer." [4]

In the "early days" of SSL use, most symmetric encryption keys were a relatively weak 40 bits because of U.S. government restrictions on the export of cryptographic technology. After years of controversy and lawsuits, the government relaxed some aspects of the export restrictions, allowing SSL implementations to use 128-bit keys for symmetric key ciphers.

Generating a Certificate Signing Request

The owner of a web site that is to use SSL must generate a Certificate Signing Request (CSR), a digital file that contains a public key and a company name. The "certificate" must then be "signed" by a trusted source known as a Certificate Authority (CA). The signed certificate returned by the CA contains the site's public key and company name along with the CA's endorsement.

Web browsers have built-in lists of CAs whose signed certificates they will accept. A browser that knows of your site's CA can verify the signature on your certificate and obtain your public key, thus enabling it to send messages that only your site can decrypt. Although you can actually sign your own certificate, a certificate that does not come from a recognized CA prompts most browsers to notify the user that the certificate is potentially suspect. In a commercial setting, such behavior is obviously a problem. But if you want to set up your own certificate authority for internal use and testing, see

httpd.apache.org/docs/2.2/ssl/ssl_faq.html#aboutcerts.

You can obtain a certificate signature from any one of a number of certificate authorities. Enter "SSL certificate" into Google and take your pick. The only real differences among CAs are the amount of work they do to verify your identity, the warranties they offer, and the number of browsers that support them out of the box (most CAs are supported by the vast majority of browsers).

Creating a certificate to send to a CA is relatively straightforward. OpenSSL must be installed, which it is by default on most systems. Here is the procedure.

First, create a 1024-bit RSA private key for your Apache server:

```
$ openssl genrsa -des3 -out server.key 1024
```

4. Transport Layer Security (TLS) is the protocol that succeeds SSL and is implemented in all modern browsers. However, the web community still refers to the overall protocol and concept as SSL.

You are prompted to enter and confirm a passphrase to encrypt the server key. Back up the **server.key** file to a secure location (readable only by root), and be sure to remember the passphrase you entered. The curious can view the numeric details of the key with this command:

```
$ openssl rsa -noout -text -in server.key
```

Next, create a Certificate Signing Request (CSR) that incorporates the server key you just generated:

```
$ openssl req -new -key server.key -out server.csr
```

Enter the fully qualified domain name of the server when you are prompted to enter a "common name." For example, if your site's URL is https://company.com, enter "company.com" as your common name. Note that you need a separate certificate for each hostname—even to the point that "www.company.com" is different from "company.com." Companies typically register only one common name; they make sure any SSL-based links point to that hostname.

You can view the details of a generated CSR with the following command:

```
$ openssl req -noout -text -in server.csr
```

You can now send the **server.csr** file to the CA of your choice to be signed. It is not necessary to preserve your local copy. The signed CSR returned by the CA should have the extension **.crt**. Put the signed certificate in a directory with your **httpd** conf files, for example, **/usr/local/apache2/conf/ssl.crt**.

Configuring Apache to use SSL

HTTP requests come in on port 80, and HTTPS requests use port 443. Both HTTPS and HTTP traffic can be served by the same Apache process. However, SSL does not work with name-based virtual hosts; each virtual host must have a specific IP address. (This limitation is a consequence of SSL's design.)

To set up Apache for use with SSL, first make sure that the SSL module is enabled within **httpd.conf** by locating or adding the line

```
LoadModule ssl_module       libexec/mod_ssl.so
```

Then add a VirtualHost directive for the SSL port:

```
<VirtualHost 128.138.243.150:443>
    ServerName www.company.com
    ServerAdmin webmaster@www.company.com
    DocumentRoot /var/www/htdocs/company
    ErrorLog logs/www.company.com-ssl-error_log
    CustomLog logs/www.company.com-ssl-access_log combined
    ScriptAlias /cgi-bin/ /var/www/cgi-bin/company
    SSLEngine on
    SSLCertificateFile /usr/local/apache2/conf/ssl.crt/server.crt
    SSLCertificateKeyFile /usr/local/apache2/conf/ssl.key/server.key
</VirtualHost>
```

Note the :443 after the IP address and also the SSL directives that tell Apache where to find your private key and signed certificate.

When you restart Apache, you will be asked to enter the passphrase for your **server.key** file. Because of this interaction, **httpd** can no longer start up automatically when the machine is booted. If you want, you can remove the encryption from your private key to circumvent the need to enter a password:

```
$ cp server.key server.key.orig
$ openssl rsa -in server.key.orig -out server.key
$ chmod 400 server.key server.key.orig
```

Of course, anyone who obtains a copy of your unencrypted key can then impersonate your site.

For more information about SSL, see the following resources:

httpd.apache.org/docs-2.2/ssl/ssl_faq.html
httpd.apache.org/docs/2.2/mod/mod_ssl.html

23.5 Caching and proxy servers

The Internet and the information on it are still growing rapidly. Ergo, the bandwidth and computing resources required to support it are growing rapidly as well. How can this state of affairs continue?

The only way to deal with this growth is to use replication. Whether it's on a national, regional, or site level, Internet content needs to be more readily available from a closer source as the Internet grows. It just doesn't make sense to transmit the same popular web page from Australia across a very expensive link to North America millions of times each day. There should be a way to store this information once it's been sent across the link once.

Fortunately, there is—at least at the site level. A web proxy lets you cache and manage your site's outbound requests for web content.

Here's how it works. Client web browsers contact the proxy server to request an object from the Internet. The proxy server then makes a request on the client's behalf (or provides the object from its cache) and returns the result to the client. Proxy servers of this type are often used to enhance security or to filter content.

In a proxy-based system, only one machine needs direct access to the Internet through the organization's firewall. At organizations such as K–12 schools, a proxy server can also filter content so that inappropriate material doesn't fall into the wrong hands. Many commercial and freely available proxy servers are available today. Some of these systems are purely software based, and others are embodied in a hardware appliance. An extensive list of proxy server technologies can be found at web-caching.com/proxy-caches.html.

The next couple of sections describe the Squid Internet Object Cache,[5] a popular stand-alone cache. We also delve briefly into the proxy features of the mod_cache module for the Apache web server.

Using the Squid cache and proxy server

Squid is a caching and proxy server that supports several protocols, including HTTP, FTP, and SSL.

Proxy service is nice, but it's Squid's caching features that are really worth getting excited about. Squid not only caches information from local user requests but also allows construction of a hierarchy of Squid servers.[6] Groups of Squid servers use the Internet Cache Protocol (ICP) to communicate information about what's in their caches.

With this feature, administrators can build a system in which local users contact an on-site caching server to obtain content from the Internet. If another user at that site has already requested the same content, a copy can be returned at LAN speed (usually 100 Mb/s or greater). If the local Squid server doesn't have the object, perhaps the server contacts the regional caching server. As in the local case, if anyone in the region has requested the object, it is served immediately. If not, perhaps the caching server for the country or continent can be contacted, and so on. Users perceive a performance improvement, so they are happy.

For many, Squid offers economic benefits. Because users tend to share web discoveries, significant duplication of external web requests can occur at a reasonably sized site. One study has shown that running a caching server can reduce external bandwidth requirements by up to 40%.

To make effective use of Squid, you'll likely want to force your users to use the cache. Either configure a default proxy through Active Directory (in a Windows-based environment) or configure your router to redirect all web-based traffic to the Squid cache by using the Web Cache Communication Protocol, WCCP.

Setting up Squid

Squid is easy to install and configure. Since Squid needs space to store its cache, you should run it on a dedicated machine that has plenty of free memory and disk space. A configuration for a large cache would be a machine with 32GiB of RAM and 8TB of disk.

You may be able to find precompiled Squid binaries for your system, or you can download a fresh copy of Squid from squid-cache.org. If you choose to compile it yourself, run the **configure** script at the top of the source tree after you unpack the distribution. This script assumes that you want to install the package in

5. Why "Squid"? According to the FAQ, "all the good names were taken."
6. Unfortunately, some sites mark all their pages as being uncacheable, which prevents Squid from working its magic. In a similar vein, Squid isn't able to cache dynamically generated pages.

/usr/local/squid. If you prefer some other location, use the **--prefix**=*dir* option to **configure**. After **configure** has completed, run **make all** and then **make install**.

Once you've installed Squid, you must localize the **squid.conf** configuration file. See the **QUICKSTART** file in the distribution directory for a list of the changes you need to make to the sample **squid.conf** file.

You must also run **squid -z** by hand to build and zero out the directory structure in which cached web pages will be stored. Finally, you can start the server by hand with the **RunCache** script; it will normally be started by a script when the machine boots.

To test Squid, configure your desktop web browser to use the Squid server as a proxy. This option is usually found in the browser's preferences panel.

Reverse-proxying with Apache

For security or load balancing reasons, it's sometimes useful for web hosting sites to proxy *inbound* requests (that is, requests to your web servers that are coming in from browsers on the Internet). Since this is backward from the typical use of a web proxy (handling outbound requests from browsers at your site), such an installation is called a reverse proxy.

See Chapter 22 for more information about DMZ networks.

One popular configuration puts a reverse proxy on your site's DMZ network to accept Internet users' requests for services such as web-based email. The proxy then passes these requests along to the appropriate internal servers. This approach has several advantages:

- It eliminates the temptation to allow direct inbound connections to servers that are not in the DMZ.
- You need to configure only a single DMZ server, rather than one server for each externally accessible service.
- You can control the accessible URLs at a central choke point, providing some security benefit.
- You can log inbound requests for monitoring and analysis.

Configuring Apache to provide reverse proxy service is relatively straightforward. Inside a `VirtualHost` clause in Apache's **httpd.conf** file, you use the `ProxyPass` and `ProxyPassReverse` directives.

- `ProxyPass` maps a remote URL into the URL space of the local server, making that part of the local address space appear to be a mirror of the remote server. (In this scenario, the "local" server is the DMZ machine and the "remote" server is the server on your interior network.)
- `ProxyPassReverse` hides the real server by "touching up" outbound HTTP headers that transit the proxy.

Below is a snippet of the reverse proxy configuration needed to insert a UNIX DMZ system in front of a Microsoft Outlook Web Access (OWA) server that provides web-based email.

```
<Location /rpc>
    ProxyPass https://wm.monkeypaw.com/rpc
    ProxyPassReverse https://wm.monkeypaw.com/rpc
    SSLRequireSSL
</Location>

<Location /exchange>
    ProxyPass https://wm.monkeypaw.com/exchange
    ProxyPassReverse https://wm.monkeypaw.com/exchange
    SSLRequireSSL
</Location>

<Location /exchweb>
    ProxyPass https://wm.monkeypaw.com/exchweb
    ProxyPassReverse https://wm.monkeypaw.com/exchweb
    SSLRequireSSL
</Location>

<Location /public>
    ProxyPass https://wm.monkeypaw.com/public
    ProxyPassReverse https://wm.monkeypaw.com/public
    SSLRequireSSL
</Location>

<Location /oma>
    ProxyPass https://wm.monkeypaw.com/oma
    ProxyPassReverse https://wm.monkeypaw.com/oma
    SSLRequireSSL
</Location>

<Location /Microsoft-Server-ActiveSync>
    ProxyPass https://wm.monkeypaw.com/Microsoft-Server-ActiveSync
    ProxyPassReverse https://wm.monkeypaw.com/Microsoft-Server-ActiveSync
    SSLRequireSSL
</Location>
```

In this example, proxy services are provided for only a few top-level URLs: /rpc, /exchange, /exchweb, /public, /oma, and /Microsoft-Server-ActiveSync. For security reasons, it's a good idea to limit the requests allowed through the proxy.

23.6 Scaling beyond your limits

On the web, "overnight success" can be a system administrator's nightmare. Being mentioned on a popular blog or showing up on digg.com can increase your web traffic by several orders of magnitude. Even "real" popularity growth can rapidly outstrip your local servers' capacity or the bandwidth of your network connection. But fear not; these are good problems to have, and many possible solutions are available.

Cloud computing

See Chapter 24, Virtualization, for more information about cloud computing.

Cloud hosting gives you access to a virtualized instance of the operating system of your choice without the need to house the hardware at your site. In fact, the hardware and its maintenance are completely abstracted—you have only the most general idea of where your virtualized instance is actually running.

Many cloud hosting providers exist, but Amazon remains the trailblazer and market leader with their Amazon Web Services (AWS) offering (aws.amazon.com). In less than 5 minutes, you can start a new Linux or UNIX instance. You log in with **ssh** to administer it, just as you would with a system in your own data center. Best of all, the service is incredibly inexpensive (currently around 10 cents per instance-hour in the U.S. region for the lowest service tier).

Several services can be layered on top of the cloud to automatically bring servers on-line and off-line according to load or other conditions. Amazon's native facility is called Auto Scaling. RightScale (rightscale.com) is a third-party provider that sells a well-integrated scaling service.

Co-lo hosting

Co-location is another way of hosting your systems in a remote data center, but in the co-location scenario you typically own or rent the server hardware. This arrangement may be preferable to a cloud-based solution in cases where standards or regulatory requirements prohibit the use of a cloud data center (e.g., some cases involving PCI DSS) or where custom hardware is necessary. Some I/O intensive applications also perform better on dedicated hardware, although the virtualized world is quickly catching up.

See Chapter 27, for more information about data center tiers.

There are hundreds of co-location providers. Select one at a tier appropriate to your needs as defined by the Uptime Institute (uptimeinstitute.org). Commercial applications are usually housed in Tier 3 or Tier 4 data centers.

Content distribution networks

Most of the content on the Internet is static: images, documents, software downloads. By putting copies of these static components close to users (in network terms), you can reduce or eliminate the need to serve that data from the original source and haul it across the network backbone.

A system of computers that provides this service is called a content distribution network, or CDN. Intercontinental network links are often congested, so CDNs are particularly important when quick access to popular content on other continents is desired.

Most CDNs operate as for-profit endeavors funded by content providers that want to ensure the availability and responsiveness of their sites without scaling up their own infrastructure. Akamai Technologies (akamai.com) operates the most successful and well known CDN platform. Limelight (limelightnetworks.com) and Disney-owned EdgeCast (edgecast.com) are the biggest upstart contenders.

When implemented correctly, the use of a CDN is completely transparent to the end user. Some objects may come from a relatively local server or cache, while other objects may originate directly from the source. However, all this speed and transparency comes with a high price tag. You'll need a fat wallet to include CDN service in your hosting plans.

23.7 Exercises

E23.1 Configure a virtual interface on your workstation. Run **ifconfig** before and after to see what changed. Can you ping the virtual interface from another machine on the same subnet? From a different network? Why or why not? (Requires root access.)

E23.2 In your browser, visit a popular content-rich site such as abcnews.com and view the page source (View->Page Source in Firefox, Page->View source in IE). Use **dig** to look up the DNS entries for the hosts of individual object URLs. Can you determine which objects are hosted by a content delivery network?

☆ E23.3 With a packet sniffer (**tcpdump**), capture a two-way HTTP conversation that uploads information (e.g., filling out a form or a search field). Annotate the session to show how your browser conveyed information to the web server. (Requires root access.)

☆ E23.4 Use a packet sniffer to capture the traffic when you open a busy web page such as the home page for amazon.com or cnn.com. How many separate TCP connections are opened? Who initiates them? Could the system be made more efficient? (Requires root access.)

☆ E23.5 Locate log files from an Internet-accessible web server, perhaps the main server for your site. Examine the log files. What can you say about the access patterns over a period of a few hours? What errors showed up during that period? What privacy concerns are illustrated by the contents of the log files? (May require root access.)

☆☆ E23.6 Install Apache on your system and create a couple of content pages. From other machines, verify that your web server is operating. Find the Apache log files that let you see what browsers are hitting your server. Configure Apache to serve some of its content pages to the virtual interface created in E23.1. (Requires root access.)

SECTION THREE

BUNCH O' STUFF

24 Virtualization

As enterprise data centers continue to rack up servers to slake the insatiable information appetite of the modern business, system administrators struggle with a technical conundrum: how can existing systems be managed more efficiently to save power, space, and cooling costs while continuing to meet the needs of users?

Software vendors have historically discouraged administrators from running their applications with other software, citing potential incompatibilities and in some cases even threatening to discontinue support in cases of noncompliance. The result has been a flood of single-purpose servers. Recent estimates have pegged the utilization of an average sever at somewhere between 5% and 15%, and this number continues to drop as server performance rises.

One answer to this predicament is virtualization: allowing multiple, independent operating systems to run concurrently on the same physical hardware. Administrators can treat each virtual machine as a unique server, satisfying picky vendors (in most cases) while simultaneously reducing data center costs. A wide variety of hardware platforms support virtualization, and the development of virtualization-specific CPU instructions and the increasing prevalence of multicore processors have vastly improved performance. Virtual servers are easy to install and require less maintenance (per server) than physical machines.

Implementations of virtualization have changed dramatically over the years, but the core concepts are not new to the industry. Big Blue used virtual machines in early mainframes while researching time-sharing concepts in the 1960s, allowing users to share processing and storage resources through an abstraction layer. The same techniques developed by IBM were used throughout the mainframe heyday of the 1970s until the client-server boom of the 1980s. The technology lay dormant during the 1980s and 1990s until the cost and manageability problems of enormous server farms rekindled interest in virtualization for modern systems. VMware is widely credited with having started the current virtualization craze by creating a virtualization platform for the Intel x86 architecture in 1999.

Today, virtualization technology is a flourishing business, with many vendors twisting knobs and pushing buttons to create unique entries into the market. VMware remains a clear leader and offers products targeted at business of all sizes, along with management software to support highly virtualized organizations. The open source community has responded with a project known as Xen, which is supported commercially by a company called XenSource, now owned by Citrix. With the release of Solaris 10, Sun introduced some powerful technology known collectively as zones and containers that can run more than 8,000 virtual systems on a single Solaris deployment. These are just a few of the players in the market. There are dozens of competing products, each with a slightly different niche.

See page 206 for more information about storage area networks.

Although server virtualization is our primary focus in this chapter, the same concepts apply to many other areas of the IT infrastructure, including networks, storage, applications, and even desktops. For example, when storage area networks or network-attached storage are used, pools of disk space can be provisioned as a service, creating additional space on demand. Applying virtualization to the desktop can be useful for system administrators and users alike, allowing for custom-tailored application environments for each user.

The many virtualization options have created a struggle for hapless UNIX and Linux administrators. With dozens of platforms and configurations to choose from, identifying the right long-term approach can be a daunting prospect. In this chapter, we start by defining the terms used for virtualization technologies, continue with a discussion of the benefits of virtualization, proceed with tips for selecting the best solution for your needs, and finally, work through some hands-on implementation activities for some of the most commonly used virtualization software on our example operating systems.

24.1 Virtual vernacular

The virtualization market has its own set of confusing terms and concepts. Mastering the lingo is the first step toward sorting out the various options.

Operating systems assume they are in control of the system's hardware, so running two systems simultaneously causes resource conflicts. Server virtualization is an abstraction of computing resources that lets operating systems run without direct knowledge of the underlying physical hardware. The virtualization software parcels out the physical resources such as storage, memory, and CPU, dynamically allocating their use among several virtual machines.

UNIX administrators should understand three distinct paradigms: full virtualization, paravirtualization, and OS-level virtualization. Each model resolves the resource contention and hardware access issues in a slightly different manner, and each model has distinct benefits and drawbacks.

Full virtualization

Full virtualization is currently the most accepted paradigm in production use today. Under this model, the operating system is unaware that it is running on a virtualized platform. A "hypervisor," also known as a virtual machine monitor, is installed between the virtual machines ("guests") and the hardware.

Such hypervisors are also known as bare-metal hypervisors since they control the physical hardware. The hypervisor provides an emulation layer for all of the host's hardware devices. The guest operating system is not modified. Guests make direct requests to the virtualized hardware, and any privileged instructions that guest kernels attempt to run are intercepted by the hypervisor for appropriate handling.

Bare-metal virtualization is the most secure type of virtualization because guest operating systems are isolated from the underlying hardware. In addition, no kernel modifications are required, and guests are portable among differing underlying architectures. As long as the virtualization software is present, the guest can run on any processor architecture. (Translation of CPU instructions does, however, incur a modest performance penalty.)

VMware ESX is an example of a popular full virtualization technology. The general structure of these systems is depicted in Exhibit A.

Exhibit A Full virtualization architecture

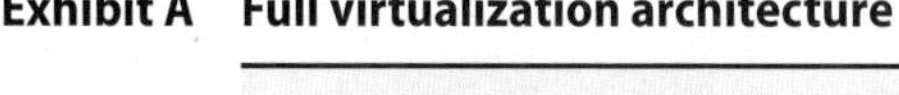

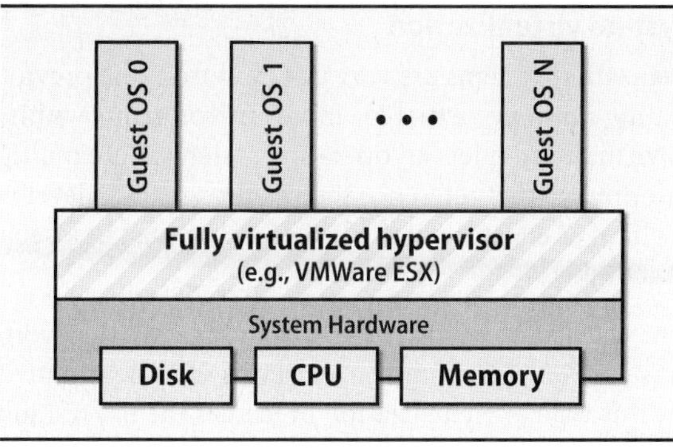

Paravirtualization

Paravirtualization is the technology used by Xen, the leading open source virtual platform. Like full virtualization, paravirtualization allows multiple operating systems to run in concert on one machine. However, each OS kernel must be modified to support "hypercalls," or translations of certain sensitive CPU instructions. User-space applications do not require modification and run natively on Xen machines. A hypervisor is used in paravirtualization just as in full virtualization.

The translation layer of a paravirtualized system has less overhead than that of a fully virtualized system, so paravirtualization does lead to nominal performance gains. However, the need to modify the guest operating system is a dramatic downside and is the primary reason why Xen paravirtualization has scant support outside of Linux and other open source kernels.

Exhibit B shows a paravirtualized environment. It looks similar to the fully virtualized system in Exhibit A, but the guest operating systems interface with the hypervisor through a defined interface, and the first guest is privileged.

Exhibit B Paravirtualization architecture

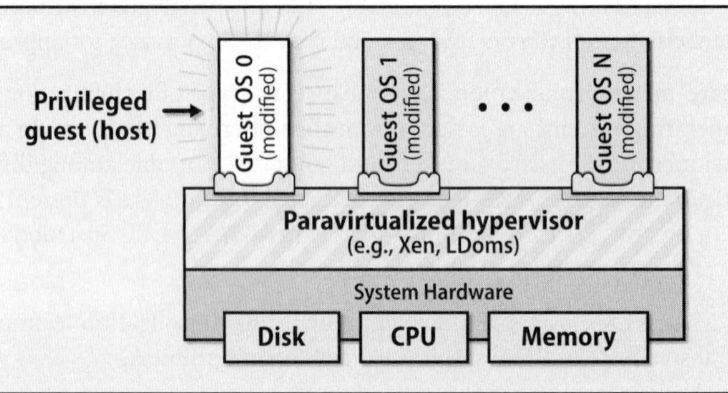

Operating system virtualization

OS-level virtualization systems are very different from the previous two models. Instead of creating multiple virtual machine environments within a physical system, OS-level virtualization lets an operating system create multiple, isolated application environments that reference the same kernel. OS-level virtualization is properly thought of as a feature of the kernel rather than as a separate layer of software abstraction.

Because no true translation or virtualization layer exists, the overhead of OS-level virtualization is very low. Most implementations offer near-native performance. Unfortunately, this type of virtualization precludes the use of multiple operating systems since a single kernel is shared by all guests (or "containers" as they are commonly known in this context).[1] AIX workload partitions and Solaris containers and zones are examples of OS-level virtualization.

OS-level virtualization is illustrated in Exhibit C.

Exhibit C OS-level virtualization architecture

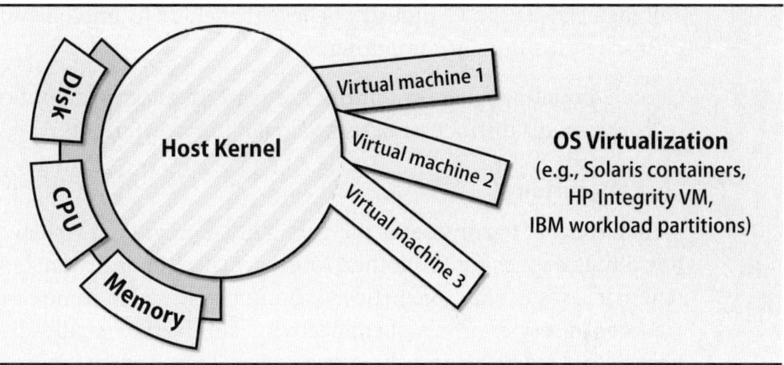

Native virtualization

In an attempt to distinguish their hardware offerings, the silicon heavyweights AMD and Intel are competing head to head to best support virtualization through hardware-assisted ("native") virtualization. Both companies offer CPUs that include virtualization instructions, eliminating the need for the translation layer used in full and paravirtualization. Today, all major virtualization players can take advantage of these processors' features.

Cloud computing

In addition to traditional virtualization, a relatively recent offering in the industry known informally (and, to some, begrudgingly) as cloud computing is an alternative to locally run server farms. Cloud computing offers computing power as a service, typically attractively priced on an hourly basis. The most obvious benefit is the conversion of server resources into a form of infrastructure analogous to power or plumbing. Administrators and developers never see the actual hardware they are using and need have no knowledge of its structure. The name comes from the traditional use of a cloud outline to denote the Internet in network diagrams.

As a system administration book, this one focuses on cloud computing at the server level, but applications are also being moved to the cloud (commonly known as software-as-a-service, or SAAS). Everything from email to business productivity suites to entire desktop environments can be outsourced and managed independently.

1. This is not entirely true. Solaris containers have a feature called "branded zones" that allows Linux binaries to run on a Solaris kernel.

Cloud services are commonly bundled with a control interface that adjusts capacity on demand and allows one-click provisioning of new systems. Amazon's Elastic Compute Cloud (EC2) is the most mature of the first-generation services of this type. It has been widely adopted by companies that offer next-generation web platforms. Love it or hate it, utility computing is gaining traction with bean counters as a cheaper alternative to data centers and localized server infrastructure. Talking heads in the IT industry believe that cloud technologies in their myriad forms are the future of computing.

Cloud computing relies on some of the same ideas as virtualization, but it should be considered a distinct set of technologies in its own right.

Live migration

A final concept to consider is the possibility of migrating virtual machines from one physical machine to another. Most virtualization software lets you move virtual machines in real time between running systems, in some cases without interruptions in service or loss of connectivity. This feature is called live migration. It's helpful for load balancing, disaster recovery, server maintenance, and general system flexibility.

Comparison of virtualization technologies

Although the various virtualization options are conceptually different, each technique offers similar results in the end. Administrators access virtual systems in the same way as they access any normal node on the network. The primary differences are that hardware problems may affect multiple systems at once (since they share hardware) and that resource contention issues must be debugged at the same level at which virtualization is implemented (e.g., in the hypervisor).

24.2 Benefits of virtualization

Given the many blessings of virtual computing, it's surprising that it took so many years to be developed and commercially accepted. Cost savings, reduced energy use, simplified business continuity, and greater technical agility are some of the main drivers of the adoption of virtual technologies.

Cost is a major factor in all new IT projects, and with virtualization, businesses realize immediate short-term cost savings because they purchase fewer servers. Instead of acquiring new servers for a new production application, administrators can spin up new virtual machines and save in up-front purchasing costs as well as ongoing support and maintenance fees. Cooling requirements are cut dramatically since virtual servers do not generate heat, resulting in additional savings. Data centers also become easier to support and less expensive to maintain. With some organizations consolidating up to 30 physical servers onto a single virtual host, a quick glance at the savings in rack space alone is sure to set data center managers blushing with pride.

A reduced ecological impact is an easy marketing win for businesses as well. Some estimates suggest that nearly one percent of the world's electricity is consumed by power-hungry data centers.[2] Modern multicore CPUs are used more efficiently when several virtual machines are running simultaneously.

Business continuity—that is, the ability of a company to survive physical and logical crises with minimal impact on business operations—is a vexing and expensive problem for system administrators. Complex approaches to disaster recovery are simplified when virtual servers can be migrated from one physical location to another with a single command. The migration technologies supported by most virtualization platforms allow applications to be location independent.

Because hypervisors can be accessed independently of the virtual servers they support, server management ceases to be grounded in physical reality and becomes fully scriptable. System administrators can respond quickly to customer requests for new systems and applications by making use of template-driven server provisioning. Scripts can automate and simplify common virtual system administration tasks. A virtual server's boot, shutdown, and migration chores can be automated by shell scripts and even scheduled through **cron**. Discontinued operating systems and applications can be moved off unsupported legacy hardware onto modern architectures.

Virtualization increases availability. Live migration allows physical servers to be taken down for maintenance without downtime or interruptions in service. Hardware upgrades do not impact the business, either. When it's time to replace an aging machine, the virtual system is immediately portable without a painful upgrade, installation, test, and cutover cycle.

Virtualization makes the rigorous separation of development, test, staging, and production environments a realistic prospect, even for smaller businesses. Historically, maintaining these separate environments has been too expensive for many businesses to bear, even though regulations and standards may have demanded it. The individual environments may also benefit; for example, quality assurance testers can easily restore a test environment to its baseline configuration.

In terms of immediate gratification, few technologies seem to offer as many possibilities as server virtualization. As we'll see in the next section, however, virtualization is not a panacea.

24.3 A PRACTICAL APPROACH

The transition to a virtualized environment must be carefully planned, managed, and implemented. An uncoordinated approach will lead to a motley assortment of unstable, unmanageable implementations that do more harm than good. Furthermore, the confidence of stakeholders is easily lost: early missteps can complicate

2. Estimated by Jonathan Koomey in his excellent study "Estimating total power consumption by servers in the U.S. and the world."

future attempts to move reluctant users to new platforms. Slow and steady wins the race.

It's important to choose the right systems to migrate since some applications are better suited to virtualization than others. Services that already have high utilization might be better left on a physical system, at least at the outset. Other services that are best left alone include these:

- Resource intensive backup servers or log hosts
- High-bandwidth applications, such as intrusion detection systems
- Busy I/O-bound database servers
- Proprietary applications with hardware-based copy protection
- Applications with specialized hardware needs, such as medical systems or certain scientific data gathering applications

Good candidates for virtualization include these:

- Internet-facing web servers that query middleware systems or databases
- Underused stand-alone application servers
- Developer systems, such as build or version control servers
- Quality assurance test hosts and staging environments
- Core infrastructure systems, such as LDAP directories, DHCP and DNS servers, time servers, and SSH gateways

Starting with a small number of less critical systems will help establish the organization's confidence and develop the expertise of administrators. New applications are obvious targets since they can be built for virtualization from the ground up. As the environment stabilizes, you can continue to migrate systems at regular intervals. Large organizations might find that 25 to 50 servers per year is a sustainable pace.

Plan for appropriate infrastructure support in the new environment. Storage and network resources should support the migrations plans. If several systems on the same physical host will reside on separate physical networks, plan to trunk the network interfaces. Include appropriate attachments for systems that will use space on a SAN. Make smart decisions about locating similar systems on the same physical hardware to simplify the infrastructure. Finally, make sure that every virtual machine has a secondary home to which it can migrate in the event of maintenance or hardware problems on the primary system.

Don't run all your mission-critical services on the same physical hardware, and don't overload systems with too many virtual machines.

Thanks to rapid improvements in server hardware, administrators have lots of good options for virtualization. Multicore, multiprocessor architectures are an obvious choice for virtual machines since they reduce the need for context switches and facilitate the allocation of CPU resources. New blade server products from major manufacturers are designed for virtual environments and offer high I/O and memory capacity. Solid state disk drives have inherent synergy with virtualization because of their fast access times and low power consumption.

24.4 Virtualization with Linux

Two major projects are vying for the title of Linux virtualization champion: Xen and KVM. In one corner, Xen is an established, well-documented platform with wide support from the distribution heavyweights. In the other corner, KVM has been accepted by Linus Torvalds into the mainstream Linux kernel. It enjoys a growing fan base, and both Ubuntu and Red Hat are supporting it.

In this section we'll stay out of the ring and stay focused on the pertinent system administration details for each technology.

Introduction to Xen

Initially developed by Ian Pratt as a research project at the University of Cambridge, the Linux-friendly Xen has grown to become a formidable virtualization platform, challenging even the commercial giants in terms of performance, security, and especially cost. As a paravirtual hypervisor, the Xen virtual machine monitor claims a mere 0.1%–3.5% overhead, far less than fully virtualized solutions. Because the Xen hypervisor is open source, a number of management tools exist with varying levels of feature support. The Xen source is available from xen.org, but many distributions already include native support.

Xen is a bare-metal hypervisor that runs directly on the physical hardware. A running virtual machine is called a domain. There is always at least one domain, referred to as domain zero (or dom0). Domain zero has full hardware access, manages the other domains, and runs all device drivers. Unprivileged domains are referred to as domU. All domains, including dom0, are controlled by the Xen hypervisor, which is responsible for CPU scheduling and memory management. A suite of daemons, tools, and libraries completes the Xen architecture and enables communication between domU, dom0, and the hypervisor.

Several management tools simplify common Xen administration tasks such as booting and shutting down, configuring, and creating guests. Xen Tools is a collection of Perl scripts that simplify domU creation. MLN, or Manage Large Networks, is another Perl script that creates complex virtual networks out of clean, easily understood configuration files. ConVirt is a shockingly advanced GUI tool for managing guests. It includes drag-and-drop live migration, agentless multi-server support, availability and configuration dashboards, and template-driven provisioning for new virtual machines. For hardened command-line junkies, the unapologetic built-in tool **xm** fits the bill.

Linux distributions vary in their support of Xen. Red Hat originally expended significant resources on including Xen in its distributions before ditching it for the competing KVM software. Xen is well supported in SUSE Linux, particularly in the Enterprise 11 release. Canonical, the company behind Ubuntu Linux, has taken an odd approach with Xen, wavering on support in most releases before finally dropping it in version 8.10 in favor of KVM (although Xen is still mentioned in documentation). Once installed, basic Xen usage differs little among distributions. In general, we recommend Red Hat or SUSE for a large Xen-based virtualization deployment.

Xen essentials

A Linux Xen server requires a number of daemons, scripts, configuration files, and tools. Table 24.1 lists the most interesting puzzle pieces.

Table 24.1 Xen components

Path	Purpose
/etc/xen	Primary configuration directory
xend-config.sxp	Top-level **xend** configuration file
auto	Guest OS config files to autostart at boot time
scripts	Utility scripts that create network interfaces, etc.
/var/log/xen	Xen log files
/usr/sbin/xend	Master Xen controller daemon
/usr/sbin/xm	Xen guest domain management tool

Each Xen guest domain configuration file in **/etc/xen** specifies the virtual resources available to a domU, such as disk devices, CPU, memory, and network interfaces. There is one configuration file per domU. The format is extremely flexible and gives administrators granular control over the constraints that will be applied to each guest. If a symbolic link to a domU configuration file is added to the **auto** subdirectory, that guest OS will be automatically started at boot time.

The **xend** daemon handles domU creation, migration, and other management tasks. It must always remain running and typically starts at boot time. Its configuration file, **/etc/xen/xend-config.sxp**, specifies the communication settings for the hypervisor and the resource constraints for dom0. It also configures facilities for live migration.

See the footnote on page 308 for more info about sparse files.

Guest domains' disks are normally stored in virtual block devices (VBDs) in dom0. The VBD can be connected to a dedicated resource such as a physical disk drive or logical volume. Or it can be a loopback file, also known as a file-backed VBD, created with **dd**. Performance is better with a dedicated disk or volume, but files are more flexible and can be managed with normal Linux commands (such as **mv** and **cp**) in domain zero. Backing files are sparse files that grow as needed. Unless the system is experiencing performance bottlenecks, a file-backed VBD is usually the better choice. It's a simple process to transfer a VBD onto a dedicated disk if you change your mind.

Similarly, virtual network interfaces (aka VIFs) can be set up in multiple ways. The default is to use bridged mode, in which each guest domain is a node on the same network as the host. Routed and NAT modes configure guest domains to be on a private network, accessible to each other and domain 0 but hidden from the rest of the network. Advanced configurations include bonded network interfaces and VLANs for guests on different networks. If none of these options fit the bill, Xen network scripts are customizable to meet almost any unique need.

Xen guest installation with virt-install

One tool for simple guest installation is **virt-install**, bundled as part of Red Hat's **virt-manager** application.[3] **virt-install** is a command-line OS provisioning tool. It accepts installation media from a variety of sources, such as an NFS mount, a physical CD or DVD, or an HTTP location.

For example, the installation of a guest domain might look like this:

```
redhat$ sudo virt-install -n chef -f /vm/chef.img -l http://example.com/myos
    -r 512 --nographics
```

This is a typical Xen guest domain with the name "chef," a disk VBD location of **/vm/chef.img**, and installation media obtained through HTTP. The instance has 512MiB of RAM and uses no X Windows-based graphics support during installation. **virt-install** downloads the files needed to start the installation and then kicks off the installer process.

You'll see the screen clear, and you'll go through a standard text-based Linux installation, including network configuration and package selection. After the installation completes, the guest domain reboots and is ready for use. To disconnect from the guest console and return to dom0, type <Control-]>.

See page 1138 for more details on VNC.

It's worth noting that although this incantation of **virt-install** provides a text-based installation, graphical support through Virtual Network Computing (VNC) is also available.

The domain's configuration is stored in **/etc/xen/chef**. Here's what it looks like:

```
name = "chef"
uuid = "a85e20f4-d11b-d4f7-1429-7339b1d0d051"
maxmem = 512
memory = 512
vcpus = 1
bootloader = "/usr/bin/pygrub"
on_poweroff = "destroy"
on_reboot = "restart"
on_crash = "restart"
vfb = [  ]
disk = [ "tap:aio:/vm/chef.dsk,xvda,w" ]
vif = [ "mac=00:16:3e:1e:57:79,bridge=xenbr0" ]
```

3. Install the **python-virtinst** package for **virt-install** support on Ubuntu.

You can see that the NIC defaults to bridged mode. In this case, the VBD is a "block tap" file that provides better performance than does a standard loopback file. The writable disk image file is presented to the guest as **/dev/xvda**. This particular disk device definition, tap:aio, is recommended by the Xen team for performance reasons.

The **xm** tool is convenient for day-to-day management of virtual machines, such as starting and stopping VMs, connecting to their consoles, and investigating current state. Below, we show the running guest domains, then connect to the console for chef. IDs are assigned in increasing order as guest domains are created, and they are reset when the host reboots.

```
redhat$ sudo xm list
Name                ID  Mem(MiB)  VCPUs  State   Time(s)
Domain-0             0      2502      2  r-----    397.2
chef                19       512      1  -b----     12.8
redhat$ sudo xm console 19
```

To effect any customization of a guest domain, such as attaching another disk or changing the network to NAT mode instead of bridged, you should edit the guest's configuration file in **/etc/xen** and reboot the guest. The **xmdomain.cfg** man page contains excellent detail on additional options for guest domains.

Xen live migration

A domain migration is the process of moving a domU from one physical host to another, and a live migration does so without any loss of service. Practically speaking, this is one of the handiest and most magical of virtualization tricks for system administrators. Open network connections are maintained, so any SSH sessions or active HTTP connections will not be lost. Hardware maintenance, operating system upgrades, and physical server reboots are all good opportunities to use migration magic.

One important requirement for implementing migrations is that storage must be shared. Any storage needed by the domU, such as the disk image files on which the virtual machine is kept, must be accessible to both host servers. File-backed virtual machines are simplest for live migration since they're usually contained in a single portable file. But a SAN, NAS, NFS share, or iSCSI unit are all acceptable methods of sharing files among systems. However the VBD is shared, be sure to run the domU on only one physical server at a time. Linux filesystems do not support direct, concurrent access by multiple hosts.

Additionally, because the IP and MAC addresses of a virtual machine follow it from one host to another, each server must be on the same layer 2 and IP subnets. Network hardware learns the new location of the MAC address once the virtual machine begins sending traffic over the network.

Once these basic requirements are met, all you need are a few configuration changes to the hypervisor configuration file, **/etc/xen/xend-config.sxp**, to enable migrations. Table 24.2 describes the pertinent options; they are all commented out in a default Xen installation. After making changes, restart **xend** by running **/etc/init.d/xend restart**.

Table 24.2 Live migration options in the xend configuration file

Option	Description
xend-relocation-server	Enables migration; set to yes
xend-relocation-port	Network port used for migration activities
xend-relocation-address	Interface to listen on for migration connections. If unspecified, Xen listens on all interfaces in dom0.
xend-relocation-hosts-allow	Hosts from which to allow connections[a]

a. This should never be blank; otherwise, connections will be allowed from all hosts.

In the process of migrating a virtual machine between hosts, the domU's memory image traverses the network in an unencrypted format. Administrators should keep security in mind if the guest has sensitive data in memory.

Before attempting a migration, the guest's configuration file must be in place on both the source and destination servers. If the location of the disk image files differs between hosts (e.g., if one server mounts the shared storage in **/xen** and the other in **/vm**), this difference should be reflected in the disk = parameter of the domain's configuration file.

The migration itself is simple:

```
redhat$ sudo xm migrate --live chef server2.example.com
```

Assuming that our guest domain chef is running, the command migrates it to another Xen host, **server2.example.com**. Omitting the **--live** flag pauses the domain prior to migration. We find it entertaining to run a **ping** against chef's IP address during the migration to watch for dropped packets.

KVM

KVM, the Kernel-based Virtual Machine, is a full virtualization tool that has been included in the mainline Linux kernel since version 2.6.20. It depends on the Intel VT and AMD-V virtualization extensions found on current CPUs.[4] It is the default virtualization technology in Ubuntu, and Red Hat has also changed gears from Xen to KVM after acquiring KVM's parent company, Qumranet.

Since KVM virtualization is supported by the CPU hardware, many guest operating systems are supported, including Windows. The software also depends on a modified version of the QEMU processor emulator.

4. Does your CPU have them? Try **egrep '(vmx|svm)' /proc/cpuinfo** to find out. If the command displays no output, the extensions are not present. On some systems, the extensions must be enabled in the system BIOS before they become visible.

Under KVM, the Linux kernel itself serves as the hypervisor; memory management and scheduling are handled through the host's kernel, and guest machines are normal Linux processes. Enormous benefits accompany this unique approach to virtualization. For example, the complexity introduced by multicore processors is handled by the kernel, and no hypervisor changes are required to support them. Linux commands such as **top**, **ps**, and **kill** show and control virtual machines, just as they would for other processes. The integration with Linux is seamless.

Administrators should be cautioned that KVM is a relatively young technology, and it should be heavily tested before being promoted to production use. The KVM site itself documents numerous incompatibilities when running guests of differing operating system flavors. Reports of live migrations breaking between different versions of KVM are common. Consider yourself forewarned.

KVM installation and usage

Although the technologies behind Xen and KVM are fundamentally different, the tools that install and manage guests operating systems are similar. As under Xen, you can use **virt-install** to create new KVM guests. Use the **virsh** command to manage them.[5] These utilities depend on Red Hat's **libvirt** library.

Before the installation is started, the host must be configured to support networking in the guests.[6] In most configurations, one physical interface is used to bridge network connectivity to each of the guests. Under Red Hat, the network device configuration files are in **/etc/sysconfig/network-scripts**. Two device files are required: one each for the bridge and the physical device.

In the examples below, **peth0** is the physical device and **eth0** is the bridge:

/etc/sysconfig/network-scripts/peth0

```
DEVICE=peth0
ONBOOT=yes
BRIDGE=eth0
HWADDR=XX:XX:XX:XX:XX:XX
```

/etc/sysconfig/network-scripts/eth0

```
DEVICE=eth0
BOOTPROTO=dhcp
ONBOOT=yes
TYPE=Bridge
```

Here, the eth0 device receives an IP address through DHCP.

The flags passed to **virt-install** vary slightly from those used for a Xen installation. To begin with, the --**hvm** flag indicates that the guest should be hardware virtualized, as opposed to paravirtualized. In addition, the --**connect** argument guarantees that the correct default hypervisor is chosen, since **virt-install** sup-

5. You can use **virsh** to manage Xen domUs as well, if you wish.
6. This is equally true with Xen, but **xend** does the heavy lifting, creating interfaces in the background.

ports more than one hypervisor. Finally, the use of **--accelerate** is recommended, to take advantage of the acceleration capabilities in KVM. Ergo, an example of a full command for installing an Ubuntu server guest from CD-ROM is

```
ubuntu$ sudo virt-install --connect qemu:///system -n UbuntuHardy
    -r 512 -f ~/ubuntu-hardy.img -s 12 -c /dev/dvd --os-type linux
    --accelerate --hvm --vnc
Would you like to enable graphics support? (yes or no)
```

Assuming that the Ubuntu installation DVD has been inserted, this command launches the installation and stores the guest in the file **~/ubuntu-hardy.img**, allowing it to grow to 12GB. Since we specified neither **--nographics** nor **--vnc**, **virt-install** asks whether to enable graphics.

The **virsh** utility spawns its own shell from which commands are run. To open the shell, type **virsh --connect qemu:///system**. The following series of commands demonstrates some of the core functionality of **virsh**. Type **help** in the shell to see a complete list, or see the man page for the nitty-gritty details.

```
ubuntu$ sudo virsh --connect qemu:///system
virsh # list --all
 Id  Name                 State
------------------------------------------
 3   UbuntuHardy          running
 7   Fedora               running
 -   Windows2003Server    shut off

virsh # start Windows2003Server
Domain WindowsServer started

virsh # shutdown FedoraExample
Domain FedoraExample is being shutdown

virsh # quit
```

Live migrations with KVM appear to be a work in progress; the implementation has changed dramatically between versions. Migrations between systems with differing CPU architectures may require special patches. We do not recommend depending on KVM live migrations in a production environment until some level of stability has been reached.

24.5 Solaris zones and containers

Sun brought OS-level virtualization to the system administration game earlier than most with the inclusion of zones and containers in Solaris 10 (circa 2005). Extensive on-line documentation and a community of active supporters have led to wide acceptance and adoption of this technology in the business community. Flexibility and a rich suite of management tools also help make Solaris virtualization an easy sell.

Zones and containers are not Solaris's only virtualization tools. The xVM project includes a Xen-based hypervisor called LDOM for virtual machines along with a powerful management tool for deploying and managing large numbers of guest systems. Sun's hardware technology (along with the systems from many other vendors) can physically partition hardware at the electrical layer, permitting more than one operating system to run concurrently on the same chassis. We don't discuss these additional technologies in this book, but they're worth looking into for sites with a lot of Sun hardware.

Zones and containers are distinct from other virtualization tools, so let's begin with a quick overview to help wrap some structure around the commands we examine later.

The terms "zone" and "container" are largely interchangeable. In the strictest sense, a zone is a protected execution environment and a container is a zone plus resource management. In practice, the terms are equivalent, and that's how we use them in this chapter.

All Solaris systems have a "global zone," which runs the kernel and all processes on the system, *including* those in other zones. A nonglobal zone is a virtual Solaris system that runs alongside the global zone. Network traffic and processes running in a nonglobal zone are not visible from other nonglobal zones, but all process activity is visible from the global zone. For security, it's important to limit access to the global zone to system administrators.

Two types of zones, whole-root and sparse, are available. A whole-root zone contains its own copy of the operating system files and independent filesystems but requires much more storage space. A sparse zone shares many of its filesystems with the global zone, mounting them read-only.

Resource pools are collections of system resources, such as processors, that can be allocated among zones. At least one resource pool, the default pool, exists on all systems, and it contains all the system's resources. All zones, including the global zone, must have at least one resource pool. You can create multiple resource pools to allocate the available system resources among running zones.

A resource pool consists of at least one resource set (which is currently limited to a division of CPU resources) and a scheduling algorithm. Multiple zones can share a single resource pool, in which case the scheduler will determine how the CPU usage is shared among the zones that use the resource pool.

Zones support a variety of different scheduling algorithms for use in different circumstances, but we focus on the most popular, "fair share scheduling," here.

Let's ground all this detail with a concrete example. Imagine a system running two physical CPUs. This particular system is going to run two virtual Solaris systems: one with a proprietary application that requires at least one full CPU, plus a lightweight web server that has no particular resource requirements. Exhibit D shows the Solaris implementation of this architecture.

Exhibit D Solaris containers example

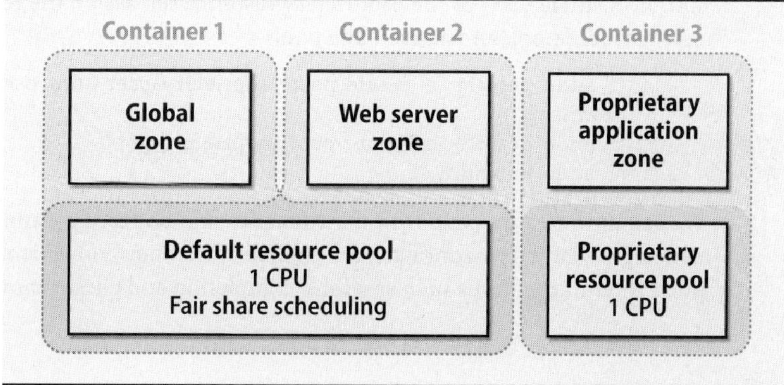

Exhibit D shows three containers, one each for the proprietary software, the web server, and the original (global) Solaris instance. In addition, there are three zones, one each for the proprietary application, the web server, and global. There are two resource pools, each with one CPU.

The web server and the global zone share the default resource pool, which contains one CPU and uses the fair share scheduling algorithm. Each of the zones has one share (not depicted), meaning that CPU resources will be divided evenly between the global and web server zones. The proprietary application uses a separate resource pool with a dedicated CPU.

Solaris provides several command-line tools for managing containers, zones, and resources. Most importantly, zones and resource pools each have a configuration tool and an administration tool: **zonecfg**, **zoneadm**, **poolcfg**, **pooladm**.

You must construct resource pools with **pooladm** before you can assign them to a zone. Enable pools with the **-e** flag, then run **pooladm** with no arguments to see the current status:

```
solaris$ sudo pooladm -e
solaris$ sudo pooladm

system default
        string      system.comment
        int         system.version 1
        boolean     system.bind-default true
        string      system.poold.objectives wt-load
...
```

We've truncated the lengthy output; the command continues to print the current resource pool information and available CPU status. The default pool is called pool_default, and it includes all available CPU resources.

The **poolcfg** command creates a new pool. In the series of commands below, we allocate a single CPU to the proprietary resource set, assign the resource set to a new resource pool, and activate the pool.

```
solaris$ sudo poolcfg -c 'create pset proprietary-pset (uint pset.min=1; uint
    pset.max=1)'
solaris$ sudo poolcfg -c 'create pool proprietary-pool'
solaris$ sudo pooladm -c
```

We can now create a zone with the **zoneadm** and **zonecfg** commands. Running **zonecfg** opens a new configuration shell for the zone. Conveniently, the tool supports shell-like features such as <Tab> completion and cursor movement hot keys.

At a minimum, the zone must be

- Created;
- Given a storage path for the zone files and filesystems;
- Given an independent IP address;
- Assigned to one of the system's active NICs;
- Assigned the resource pool we created above.

Here's how:

```
solaris$ sudo zonecfg -z proprietary-zone
zonecfg:proprietary-zone> create
zonecfg:proprietary-zone> set zonepath=/zones/proprietary-zone
zonecfg:proprietary-zone> set autoboot=true
zonecfg:proprietary-zone> add net
zonecfg:proprietary-zone:net> set address=192.168.10.123
zonecfg:proprietary-zone:net> set physical=e1000g0
zonecfg:proprietary-zone:net> end
zonecfg:proprietary-zone> set pool=proprietary-pool
zonecfg:proprietary-zone> verify
zonecfg:proprietary-zone> commit
zonecfg:proprietary-zone> exit
```

Note that the **zonecfg** prompt shows you the object you're currently working on.

At this point the zone has been configured, but it is not actually installed or ready to run. This is a full Solaris system, and it needs to have packages installed, just as a normal system would. The **zoneadm** utility installs, boots, and performs other operations on the zone.

```
solaris$ sudo zoneadm -z proprietary-zone install
Preparing to install zone <proprietary-zone>.
Creating list of files to copy from the global zone.
...
solaris$ sudo zoneadm -z proprietary-zone boot
solaris$ sudo zoneadm list
global
proprietary-zone
```

Now the zone is running, and an invocation of **zlogin -C proprietary-zone** will connect to its console. The boot process for a zone is much like that of a physical system, so connecting with **zlogin** before bootstrapping is complete displays output from the boot process. We must perform all the normal configuration for a new system, such as choosing language options and an authentication method.

The remaining task is to create a zone for our web server. Since the web server zone will share the default resource pool with the global zone, it isn't necessary to create a new pool. Instead, we would just create the zone with **zonecfg** as shown above, but with **set pool=pool_default**.

There is considerably more depth to zones and containers than we've shown here. Advanced features that administrators should be aware of include migration of zones between physical systems (although live migrations are not supported), ZFS resources for smaller whole-root zones, and "branded zones" that support running binaries from other platforms (e.g., Linux) on a Solaris kernel.

24.6 AIX WORKLOAD PARTITIONS

IBM has been in the virtualization game a long time. They pioneered the concept in the 1960s, but it wasn't until the release of AIX 6.1 in late 2007 that software virtualization was included in AIX. Any system capable of running AIX 6 supports workload partitions (WPARs). (This technology is distinct from IBM's various logical partition implementations found in versions as early as 4.3.)

WPARs run in an isolated execution environment. Processes can only communicate with peers in the same partition. Signals and events in the global environment do not affect the partition, and vice versa. WPARs can have their own dedicated network addresses.

WPARs are served in two delicious flavors: system and application.

- A system WPAR shares only the AIX kernel with the global environment (the host, essentially). An application running in a system WPAR believes it is running in an independent AIX installation with its own **inetd** daemon for networking autonomy.
- An application WPAR runs a single application in an isolated environment. It shares all filesystems with the global environment and cannot provide remote access capabilities. The application WPAR exits when the application completes.

IBM provides several tools for managing WPARs, continuing the AIX tradition of convenient administration. We discuss the command-line interface here, but administrators should be aware that in typical AIX fashion, there is a full SMIT interface as well as WPAR Manager, a web-based management interface for centralized management of multiple servers and their workload partitions.

You create a system WPAR with the **mkwpar** command. The only required argument is **-n** to name it. Thus, the command **mkwpar -n mario** creates a partition named "mario." **mkwpar** creates the relevant filesystems, installs the appropriate filesets, and prepares subsystems and services. This process takes only a short time; when it's finished, run **startwpar mario** to start the WPAR.

The **/wpars** directory in the global environment will contain the filesystems for mario. You can list the WPARs from the global environment with **lswpar**:

```
aix$ sudo lswpar
Name    State  Type  Hostname  Directory
---------------------------------------------------------
mario   A      S     mario     /wpars/mario
```

To attach as root to the console, use **clogin mario**. Could it be any easier?

This simple example leaves out a number of important considerations and customization opportunities. For one, new software cannot be installed in the mario WPAR because the **/usr** and **/opt** filesystems are by default mounted read-only to save space. No network interfaces are available. The simplified procedure above also ignores IBM's excellent resource management features, which facilitate administrative control over the WPAR's use of CPU, memory, virtual memory, and other resources.

To create a more usable instance, you can beef up your **mkwpar** command with some additional arguments. The version below creates a WPAR with the following attributes:

- The name of the WPAR is mario (**-n**).
- Name resolution settings are inherited from the global instance (**-r**).
- Private, writable **/opt** and **/usr** filesystems are created (**-l**).
- The WPAR uses the IP address 192.168.10.15 on the en0 interface from the global WPAR (**-N**).
- The CPU allocated to this WPAR will be a minimum of 5%, a soft maximum of 15%, and an absolute limit of 25% (**-R**).

```
aix$ sudo mkwpar -n mario -r -l -N interface=en3 address=192.168.10.15
    netmask=255.255.255.0 broadcast=192.168.10.255 -R active=yes
    CPU=5%-15%,25%
```

This invocation is a little chewier than a basic **mkwpar** and it takes longer to execute because of the duplication of **/usr** and **/opt**.

To modify a partition after it has been created, use the **chwpar** command. You can stop a partition with **stopwpar** and remove it for good with **rmwpar**.

Application WPARS are handled very similarly. Instead of **mkwpar**, application WPARs are created with **wparexec**. Parameters are generally identical to those of **mkwpar**, but rather than providing a name, you provide the application to execute as an argument. For example, to run Apache in its own application WPAR, simply use **wparexec /usr/local/sbin/httpd**.

24.7 Integrity Virtual Machines in HP-UX

If HP's goal is to confuse administrators with the most disorganized possible approach to virtualization, they have succeeded admirably. On a stand-alone, low-end server, the Integrity Virtual Machines software shares hardware resources among multiple guest operating systems. For larger systems with multiple cores, HP has a more powerful software partitioning technology called Virtual Partitions, aka vPars. Additionally, the hardware partitioning service known as nPartitions provides a true electrical-level separation between running servers. These technologies, along with HP's clustering software, are collectively referred to as the Virtual Server Environment.

In this section we cover only Integrity Virtual Machines. IVM is a full virtualization technology, and unmodified versions of Windows and Linux can run on an HP-UX host. Each guest is given a preconfigured proportion of CPU time. Memory and storage allocation is also tunable. An unlimited number of guests may be configured, but the number of running virtual machines is capped at 256.

Network connectivity for guest machines consists of three components:

- A physical network adapter in the host, also known as a pNIC
- A guest network adapter, referred to as a virtual NIC or vNIC
- A virtual switch, or vswitch, that creates a network between the host and one or more guests

The intricacies of the various network configurations offered in an Integrity installation are daunting, but we appreciate the flexibility the system offers. For purposes of this discussion, we'll create a single vswitch that maps to the same network the host lives on. This is the simplest configuration and is equivalent to the bridged networks discussed elsewhere in this chapter.

Much as in Xen, the host can supply storage to guests from physical disks, DVDs, tape changers, or files in the host operating system. Also eerily reminiscent of Xen, milking the best performance out of a storage device is something of an art.

Consult HP's *Installation, Configuration, and Administration Guide* for a thorough guide to complex network configurations and techniques for optimizing storage performance.

Creating and installing virtual machines

The commands that create, install, and manage virtual machines are powerful yet simple. Each command name starts with an **hpvm** prefix, with the rest of the command corresponding to the desired action. For example, to create a new virtual machine, the command is **hpvmcreate**.

Various arguments to each command control the configuration of the guest operating systems, and there are no static files for the administrator to manage. Changes to a guest are made with the **hpvmmodify** command.

Before you create a virtual machine, its storage and network resources must be available. In the example below, we first create a filesystem on one of the host's physical disks to store the guest, then create a vswitch to provide the guest's network connectivity. To summarize the virtual machine creation process:

- Create a storage resource for the guest's files.
- Create a virtual switch for network connectivity.
- Create the virtual machine.
- Start and install the virtual machine.

In the series of commands below, we use the **mkfs** command to create a filesystem on the physical device **disk3**, an arbitrary disk that happened to be available on our lab system. It will eventually store the guest's operating system, applications, and data. The file is mounted under **/vdev**, and finally the **hpvmdevmgmt** command (not to be confused with the **hpwndkwlvyfm** command) creates a usable storage entity called **disk1**.

```
hp-ux$ sudo mkfs -F vxfs -o largefiles /dev/disk/disk3
hp-ux$ sudo mount /dev/disk/disk3 /vdev/vm0disk/
hp-ux$ sudo hpvmdevmgmt -S 8G /vdev/vm0disk/disk1
```

The next step is to create a virtual switch for use by the guest. A single vswitch can be used by multiple guests.

```
hp-ux$ lanscan
Hardware Station        Crd Hdw   Net-Interface NM MAC   HP-DLPI DLPI
Path     Address        In# State NamePPA       ID Type  Support Mjr#
0/0/3/0  0x00306EEA9237 0   UP    lan0 snap0    1  ETHER Yes     119
0/1/2/0  0x00306EEA720D 1   UP    lan1 snap1    2  ETHER Yes     119
hp-ux$ sudo hpvmnet -c -S vm0switch -n 0
hp-ux$ sudo hpvmnet -b -S vm0switch
```

Here, the handy **lanscan** command finds all the system's network interfaces. We need the identifier for the network interface on the correct network; in this case it's the 0 in lan0. Using the **hpvmnet** command, we create the switch by using lan0, then start it in the next command with the **-b** argument.

Now that the necessary resources have been created, it's finally time to create the virtual machine itself.

```
hp-ux$ sudo hpvmcreate -P vm0 -O hpux -r 2G
    -a network:lan:vswitch:vm0switch -a disk:scsi::file:/vdev/vm0disk/disk1
hp-ux$ sudo hpvmstart -P vm0
```

This command creates a virtual machine called vm0, allocates 2GiB of memory to it, uses the virtual switch vm0switch, and selects the storage device we created above. The new virtual machine is then started with the **hpvmstart** command.

Installation of the virtual machine is identical to installing a physical machine from the console. Attach to the console with **hpvmconsole -P vm0** and disconnect with <Control-B>. To check the status of a guest, use **hpvmstatus -P vm0**.

24.8 VMware: an operating system in its own right

VMware is the biggest player in the bleeding edge virtualization industry and was the first vendor to develop techniques to virtualize the fractious x86 platform. VMware developed techniques for handling seventeen problematic instructions that previously prevented virtualization from becoming ubiquitous. The release of the VMware Workstation product in 1999 sparked a call to arms for more efficient computing—a call that is still reverberating today.

VMware is a third-party commercial product that is worthy of consideration when you are choosing a site-wide virtualization technology. The primary products of interest to UNIX and Linux administrators are ESX and ESXi, both of which are bare-metal hypervisors for the Intel x86 architecture. ESXi is free, but some useful functionality, such as console access, has been removed. ESX targets the enterprise with scriptable installations, features for monitoring through SNMP, and support for booting from a storage area network (SAN) device.

In addition to the ESX products, VMware offers some powerful, advanced products that facilitate centralized deployment and management of virtual machines. They also have the most mature live migration technology we've seen. Unfortunately, their client management interface runs only on Windows at this time. Collectively, VMware's products create a next generation IT environment, in-depth coverage of which is unfortunately beyond the scope of this chapter.

HP-UX and AIX cannot run as VMware virtual machines because those operating systems run on proprietary processor architectures that VMware does not emulate. Linux is of course well supported. Solaris can also run under VMware since its code base covers both the SPARC and x86 platforms.

24.9 Amazon Web Services

All the cool kids are getting into cloud computing, and Amazon Web Services (AWS) is leading the pack. Starting in early 2006, Amazon began to productize the infrastructure behind its amazon.com site by selling access to a suite of APIs and web services. These services have become an immensely powerful, scalable, and highly available computing and service platform for anyone that needs cheap, instantaneous computing power or storage.

The core suite of AWS offerings of interest to a UNIX administrator include

- EC2, the Elastic Compute Cloud – a platform for scalable computing. An EC2 "instance" is a server located on the Internet that runs an operating system of your choice and is under your complete control. You can add and remove instances at will. EC2 is based on Xen, and many different operating systems are supported.

- EBS, the Elastic Block Store – persistent, disk-like storage for EC2 instances. EBS is similar in concept to SAN storage. It lets EC2 instances preserve and share state across invocations.
- S3, Simple Storage Services – a highly available, long-term storage infrastructure. S3 differs from EBS in that it is not intended to be mounted as a filesystem but instead stores and retrieves objects through an API.

These services give administrators unprecedented flexibility and scalability, at the cost of losing some control over hardware and network configuration.

Administrators and developers alike must also consider the security implications of moving services to the cloud. Sensitive data should be left in a physical data center, especially when subject to regulations such as Sarbanes-Oxley or HIPAA (in the United States). Regulatory requirements may or may not preclude the use cloud computing, but until the courts work out the kinks, it's better to play it safe.

Where, then, does the AWS become useful? In terms of cost, availability, and dynamic scalability, it's difficult to compete with AWS as a web-hosting platform. The cost for on-demand EC2 instances currently ranges from $0.09 to $0.68 per hour, depending on the computing power of the instance. S3 storage is priced at $0.15 per GB per month. These pennies add up (the cheapest possible EC2 instance works out to about $379/year on a three-year plan), but with power, cooling, and maintenance included, the bottom line is generally more attractive than self-hosted servers when all costs are considered.

With limitless processing capacity, the cloud is also attractive as a distributed computing platform. In fact, AWS could be useful for hosting email, DNS, or other services that are normally provided in the data center.

AWS is at heart a set of SOAP APIs, but Amazon provides some simple command-line wrappers written in Java as well as a web-based GUI and a Firefox plug-in. AWS can run both Linux and Windows as guest operating systems.

The steps to get an instance up and running with persistent storage include

- Installing and configuring a Java run-time environment (make sure the JAVA_HOME environment variable points to the right place);
- Creating S3 and EC2 accounts with Amazon Web Services;
- Downloading and installing the EC2 tools;
- Creating an EC2 instance from an Amazon Machine Image (AMI), which is the disk image of a configured operating system, possibly with some extra software installed. There are many to choose from, or you can roll your own.
- Creating an EBS volume and attaching it to your instance.

The AWS web site contains the account signup pages and all the necessary downloads. To start using AWS, download the command-line tools and the access identifiers, which consist of a certificate and a private key.

Make a directory called **~/.ec2** and move the downloaded certificate file, key file, and extracted tools to that directory. All EC2 commands will reside in **~/.ec2/bin**, with library dependencies in **~/.ec2/lib**. To set up the environment for easy use, add the following to the shell's login script. (For bash, the file is **~/.bash_login** or **~/.bash_profile**.)

```
export EC2_HOME=~/.ec2
export PATH=$PATH:$EC2_HOME/bin
export EC2_PRIVATE_KEY=$EC2_HOME/pk-<long string value>.pem
export EC2_CERT=$EC2_HOME/cert-<long string value>.pem
export JAVA_HOME=/path/to/java
```

Finally, before choosing an image and starting it, create a key pair that you'll use to gain access to the image. The **ec2-add-keypair** command creates a new key pair. Any new images that are created will automatically be configured to use the new public key for SSH authentication on the root account.

```
ubuntu$ ec2-add-keypair my-keypair
KEYPAIR my-keypair b0:65:11:df:05:43:3b:f7:42:93:fb:0e:7f:63:22:13:ff:88:e5:ae
-----BEGIN RSA PRIVATE KEY-----
MIIEowIBAAKCAQEAoiJxHIHjuXOqeEoKae1uj8ny55INuWS5hOQVBxfuhEwG7kttz
    kiuF8B7U4C4
...
82827HZO/9cCok6FP8loOAR8GIJvDzvWozZ7hdRhc/i6isWBiMTDQQUItk79fI9atk7P
-----END RSA PRIVATE KEY-----
```

This key will be needed in the future, so save everything but the line beginning with KEYPAIR to a file in the **~/.ec2** directory and make sure the permissions are 600. Never share the private key file—it contains the keys to the cloud kingdom!

Now it's time to choose an AMI. There are an enormous number of AMIs to choose from, many created by Amazon and many contributed (or sold) by the community. It's also possible to build a custom AMI for private use, possibly configured with the particulars of your environment or preinstalled with all your needed applications.

After choosing an image, note its identifier. The command below lists the AMIs created by Amazon. Having added the tools directory to the PATH variable, you can execute EC2 commands anywhere.

```
ubuntu$ ec2-describe-images -o amazon
IMAGE    ami-ba4eaad3    /aws-quickstart/phpquickstart.manifest.xml
    amazon  available  public   i386   machine
IMAGE    ami-b44bafdd    /aws-quickstart/rubyquickstart.manifest.xml
    amazon  available  public   i386   machine  aki-a71cf9ce  ari-a51cf9cc
IMAGE    ami-1c54b075    /aws-quickstart/tomcatquickstart.manifest.xml
    amazon  available  public   i386   machine  aki-a71cf9ce  ari-a51cf9cc
...
```

Virtualization

The image name typically has a brief description to help you understand its purpose and configuration, but details are available in an on-line directory. To spin up the PHP quick start AMI from the list above, use the following command:

```
ubuntu$ ec2-run-instances  ami-ba4eaad3 -k my-keypair
ubuntu$ ec2-describe-instances
RESERVATION    r-56aa053f        default
INSTANCE    i-1343fb7a    ami-ba4eaad3          pending    my-keypair    0
    m1.small    2008-12-22T01:43:27+0000    us-east-1c
```

The **ec2-describe-instances** output reflects that the instance is still booting (status "pending") and that it's using the key pair set with the name **my-keypair**.

Importantly, the output shows that the instance is running in the us-east-1c availability zone. Amazon has segmented its systems into separate availability zones, so that a user who wants to guarantee that several instances will run in physically separate data centers can request this on the command line. This value will also be needed to attach an EBS volume.

Finally, the command shows that the instance type is m1.small. This code tells you the amount of resources available to the system. Amazon has defined several standard profiles; m1.small is the default and includes a single 32-bit EC2 CPU, 1.7GB memory, and 160GB of (nonpersistent) disk. Of course, the actual hardware your server runs on probably looks nothing like this; it's just a way of describing your allocation.

Once the instance is running, any network ports you need to access must be authorized through another EC2 command, **ec2-authorize**:

```
ubuntu$ ec2-authorize default -p 22
```

In this case, port 22 (for SSH) is authorized for all hosts in the default group. (Groups are a mechanism for managing collections of instances. New instances are provisioned in the default group unless otherwise specified.) After you've been authorized on port 22, you can finally connect to your new instance. To do so, first find the hostname, then SSH to it just as if it were another node on the Internet (because it is!).

```
ubuntu$ ec2-describe-instances
RESERVATION    r-56aa053f       default
INSTANCE    i-1343fb7a    ami-ba4eaad3    ec2-67-202-24-235.compute-
    1.amazonaws.com    domU-12-31-39-02-5E-55.compute-1.internal
    runninmy-keypair    0        m1.small    2008-12-22T01:43:27+0000
    us-east-1c
ubuntu$ ssh -i ~/.ec2/id_rsa-my-keypair
    root@ec2-67-202-24-235.compute-1.amazonaws.com
```

This command uses the key pair saved above to connect to the new instance's root account. For security reasons, we recommend disabling root SSH access.

The only remaining problem is that instances are not persistent. That is, when this instance terminates, any changes to its disk or memory state are not captured. EBS provisions storage volumes just as new instances are provisioned. Here, we create a volume and attach it to the running host.

```
ubuntu$ ec2-create-volume -s 1 -z us-east-1c
VOLUME    vol-5de80c34    1    us-east-1c    creating    2008-12-22T02:02:
    53+0000
ubuntu$ ec2-attach-volume vol-5de80c34 -i i-1343fb7a -d /dev/sdf
ATTACHMENT    vol-5de80c34    i-1343fb7a    /dev/sdf    attaching    2008-
    12-22T02:04:01+0000
ubuntu$ ec2-describe-volumes
VOLUME    vol-5de80c34    1    us-east-1c    in-use    2008-12-22T02:02:
    53+0000
ATTACHMENT    vol-5de80c34    i-1343fb7a    /dev/sdf    attached    2008-12-
    22T02:04:01+0000
```

See the Adding a Disk chapter for more information about creating filesystems.

These commands create a new EBS storage volume in the us-east-1c availability zone and attach it as the device **/dev/sdf** to the instance created above. To create a filesystem and begin using the volume, log in to the instance and proceed as if you were creating a filesystem on a physical disk.

Remember that AWS charges by the hour for instances, so unused instances and volumes should be cleaned up. Before terminating an unneeded instance, be sure to detach any EBS volumes and gracefully shut down the system, just as you would a physical host.

```
ubuntu$ ec2-detach-volume vol-5de80c34
ATTACHMENT    vol-5de80c34    i-1343fb7a    /dev/sdf    detaching    2008-
    12-22T02:04:01+0000
ubuntu$ ec2-terminate-instances  i-1343fb7a
INSTANCE    i-1343fb7a    running    shutting-down
ubuntu$ ec2-delete-volume vol-5de80c34
VOLUME    vol-5de80c34
```

In addition to the command-line interface, Amazon offers a web management interface that can initiate the same operations as the command-line tools, such as starting and stopping instances, attaching storage volumes, and allocating IP addresses. A Firefox web browser plug-in called ElasticFox provides similar functionality from within the browser itself.

Amazon regularly introduces new features and products to its web services product line. Auto-scaling of EC2 instances automatically spins up new servers to prevent outages when the load is high. The CloudWatch feature monitors metrics such as CPU usage and disk I/O for quick response to changing conditions. Keep an eye on the AWS blog at aws.typepad.com for feature enhancements and product announcements.

24.10 Recommended Reading

The web site virtualization.info is an excellent source of current news, trends, and gossip in the virtualization and cloud computing sectors.

Troy, Ryan. *VMware Cookbook: A Real-World Guide to Effective VMware Use.* Sebastopol, CA: O'Reilly Media, 2009.

Crawford, Luke. *The Book of Xen: A Practical Guide for the System Administrator.* San Francisco, CA: No Starch Press, 2009.

Hess, Kenneth. *Practical Virtualization Solutions: Virtualization from the Trenches.* Upper Saddle River, NJ: Prentice Hall PTR, 2009.

24.11 Exercises

E24.1 Briefly compare and contrast the different approaches to virtualization. In what category is KVM? Why is cloud computing a distinct technology from virtualization?

E24.2 Modern Intel and AMD processors include special instructions that improve virtualization support. What are these instructions, and what special functions do they accomplish? Given a running system and a knowledge of the processor model, describe at least two ways of determining whether the virtualization instructions are supported.

E24.3 What new features has Amazon Web Services started to support since this chapter was written? Are they enhancements to the existing infrastructure or entirely new services?

★ E24.4 Create an Amazon Web Services account and a public key pair. Set up a Java environment and create an EC2 instance. Can you access the console directly? What does this imply? Assuming that the instance was intended to contain sensitive data, what steps could you take to reassure a client that the data would be protected in the cloud?

★ E24.5 A large enterprise is planning the deployment of a new customer relationship management (CRM) solution that consists of redundant front end web servers, middleware servers, and a database server. Which of these CRM components should be virtualized? Explain.

25 The X Window System

The X Window System, also called X11 or simply X, is the foundation for most graphical user environments for UNIX and Linux. X is the natural successor to a window system called (believe it or not) W, which was developed as part of MIT's Project Athena in the early 1980s. Version 10 of the X Window System, released in 1985, was the first to achieve widespread deployment, and version 11 (X11) followed shortly thereafter. Thanks to the system's relatively liberal licensing terms, X spread quickly to other platforms, and multiple implementations emerged. Much as in the case of TCP/IP, X's elegant architecture and flexibility have positioned it as the world's predominant non-Windows GUI.

In 1988, the MIT X Consortium was founded to set the overall direction for the X protocol. Over the next decade, this group and its successors issued a stream of protocol updates. X11R7.5 is today's latest and greatest, with the trend apparently heading toward adding new numbers to the version designation instead of incrementing the existing ones.

XFree86 became the de facto X server implementation for most platforms until a licensing change in 2004 motivated many systems to switch to a fork of XFree86 that was unencumbered by the new licensing clause. That fork is maintained by the nonprofit X.Org Foundation and is the predominant implementation in use today. In addition, the X.Org server has been ported to Windows for use in the Cygwin Linux compatibility environment. (Several commercial X servers for Windows are also available; see page 1136 for more information.)

This chapter describes the X.Org version of X, which is used by all of our example systems except HP-UX. The implementations of X.Org and XFree86 have diverged architecturally, but most of the administrative details remain the same. It is often possible to substitute **xf86** for **xorg** in commands and filenames to guess at the appropriate XFree86 version.

Solaris systems through version 10 included both the X.Org server and Xsun, yet another implementation of X.[1] Xsun remains common on SPARC systems running Solaris 10, but x86 systems typically run X.Org. However, X.Org now supports SPARC, and the OpenSolaris project has stated that X.Org will be the only supported X platform in the future. Therefore, we do not discuss Xsun here.

By default, AIX does not include an X Window System environment. To install one, run **smitty easy-install**, select the **lpp** library source, and then choose either CDE (for the traditional IBM-blessed Motif platform) or KDE (for the more modern option).[2] What you get is a highly customized version of the X.Org environment that has been stripped down to look more like the older X systems of the Motif era. However, it supports X11R7.5 under the hood.

The X Window System can be broken down into a few key components. First, it provides a *display manager* whose main job is to authenticate users, log them in, and start up an initial environment from startup scripts. The display manager also starts the *X server*, which defines an abstract interface to the system's bitmapped displays and input devices (e.g., keyboard and mouse). The startup scripts also run a *window manager*, which allows the user to move, resize, minimize, and maximize windows, as well as to manage separate virtual desktops. Finally, at the lowest level, applications are linked to a *widget library* that implements high-level user interface mechanisms such as buttons and menus. Exhibit A illustrates the relationship between the display manager, the X server, and client applications.

The X server understands only a very basic set of drawing primitives over a network API; it does not define a programming interface to high-level entities such as buttons, text boxes, menus, and sliders. This design achieves two important goals. First, it allows the X server to run on a computer that is completely separate from that of the client application. Second, it allows the server to support a variety of different window managers and widget sets.

1. Xsun included support for Display PostScript, which once upon a time was thought to be the display language of the future.

2. It is possible, but not recommended, to have both environments installed simultaneously. See page 1028 for more information about desktop environments.

Exhibit A The X client/server model

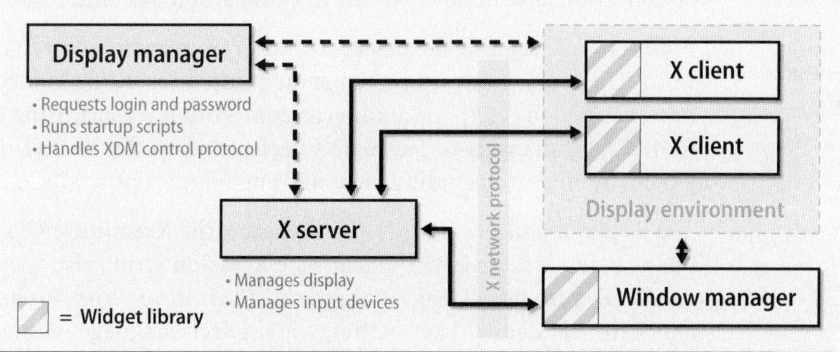

Application developers have their choice of several common widget libraries and user interface standards. Unfortunately, the choice often depends more on religious affiliation than on any real design considerations. Although freedom of choice is good, X's UI agnosticism and lack of design leadership did result in many years of poor user interfaces. Fortunately, the fit and finish of the mainstream X environments has improved markedly. Both the KDE and GNOME desktop environments sport modern web browsers, user-friendly file managers, and modern multimedia capabilities.

In this chapter, we explain how to run programs on a remote display and how to enable authentication. We then discuss how to configure the X.Org server and how to troubleshoot configuration errors. Finally, we touch briefly on some of the available window managers and desktop environments.

25.1 The Display Manager

The display manager presents the user with a (graphical) login screen and is usually the first thing a user sees when sitting down at the computer. It is not required; many users disable the display manager and start X from the text console or from their **.login** script by running **startx** (which itself is a wrapper for the **xinit** program, which starts the X server).

xdm (for X display manager) is the original display manager, but modern replacements such as **gdm** (the GNOME display manager) and **kdm** (the KDE display manager) deliver additional features and are more aesthetically pleasing. The display manager can manage remote logins to other X servers through the XDMCP protocol, and it can also handle display authentication (see *Client authentication* on page 1016).

Configuration files in the **xdm**, **gdm**, or **kdm** subdirectory of **/etc/X11** specify how the display manager will run. For example, you can edit the **Xservers** file to change the display number used for this server if multiple servers will be running on other virtual terminals. Or, you might alter the server layout with the **-layout** option if you have defined layouts to suit multiple systems.

See page 908 for more information about PAM.

In the typical scenario, the display manager prompts for a username and password. The user's password is then authenticated according to the PAM configuration specified in **/etc/pam.d/xdm** (or **gdm/kdm** if you are using the GNOME or KDE display managers). The login screen can also offer several alternative desktop environments, including the important failsafe option discussed below.

The display manager's final duty is to execute the **Xsession** shell script, which sets up the user's desktop environment. The **Xsession** script, also most often found in **/etc/X11/{xdm,gdm,kdm}**, is a system-wide startup script. It sets application defaults, installs standard key bindings, and selects language settings. The **Xsession** script then executes the user's own personal startup script, usually **~/.xsession**, to start up the window manager, task bar, helper applets, and possibly other programs. GNOME and KDE also have their own startup scripts that configure the user's desktop in accordance with GNOME's and KDE's configuration tools; this scheme is less error-prone than users' editing of their own startup scripts.

When the execution of **~/.xsession** completes, the user is logged out of the system and the display manager goes back to prompting for a username and password. Therefore, **~/.xsession** must start all programs in the background (by appending an **&** to the end of each command) *except for the last one,* which is normally the window manager. (If all commands in **~/.xsession** are run in the background, the script terminates right away and the user is logged out immediately after logging in.) With the window manager as the final, foreground process, the user is logged out only after the window manager exits.

The failsafe login option lets users log in to fix their broken startup scripts. This option can usually be selected from the display manager's login screen. It opens only a simple terminal window; once the window closes, the system logs the user out. Every system should allow the failsafe login option; it helps users fix their own messes rather than having to page you in the middle of the night.

Forgetting to leave a process in the foreground is the most common startup problem, but it's hardly the only possibility. If the cause of problems is not obvious, you may have to refer to the **~/.xsession-errors** file, which contains the output of the commands run from **~/.xsession**. Look for errors or other unexpected behavior. In a pinch, move the **~/.xsession** script aside and make sure you can log in without it. Then restore one or two lines at a time until you find the offending line.

25.2 Process for running an X application

The process required to run an X application may at first seem overly complex. However, you will soon discover the flexibility afforded by the client/server display model. Because display updates are transmitted over the network, an application (the client) can run on a completely separate computer from the one that displays its graphical user interface (the server). An X server can have connections from many different applications, all of which run on separate computers.

To make this model work, clients must be told what display to connect to and what screen to inhabit on that display. Once connected, clients must authenticate themselves to the X server to ensure that the person sitting in front of the display has authorized the connection.

See page 926 for more information about SSH.

Even with authentication, X's intrinsic security is weak. You can manage connections somewhat more securely by routing them through SSH (see *X connection forwarding with SSH* on page 1017). We strongly recommend the use of SSH for X connections over the Internet. It's not unreasonable for local traffic, either.

The DISPLAY environment variable

X applications consult the DISPLAY environment variable to find out where to display themselves. The variable contains the hostname or IP address of the server, the display number (identifying the particular instance of an X server to connect to), and an optional screen number (for displays with multiple monitors). When applications run on the same computer that displays their interfaces, you can omit most of these parameters.

The following example shows both the format of the display information and the **bash** syntax used to set the environment variable:

```
client$ DISPLAY=servername.domain.com:10.2; export DISPLAY
```

This setting points X applications at the machine servername.domain.com, display 10, screen 2. Applications establish a TCP connection to the server on port number 6000 plus the display number (in this example, port 6010), where the X server handling that display should be listening.

Keep in mind that every process has its own environment variables. When you set the DISPLAY variable for a shell, its value is inherited only by programs that you run from that shell. If you execute the commands above in one **xterm** and then try to run your favorite X application from another, the application won't have access to your carefully constructed DISPLAY variable.

Another point worth mentioning is that although X applications send their graphical displays to the designated X server, they still have local `stdout` and `stderr` channels. Some error output may still come to the terminal window from which an X application was run.

See page 561 for more information about DNS resolver configuration.

If the client and server are both part of your local organization, you can usually omit the server's full domain name from the DISPLAY variable, depending on how your name server's resolver has been configured. Also, since most systems run only a single X server, the display is usually 0. The screen number can be omitted, in which case screen 0 is assumed. Ergo, most of the time it's fine to set the value of DISPLAY to *servername*:0.

If the client application happens to be running on the same machine as the X server, you can simplify the DISPLAY variable even further by omitting the hostname. This feature is more than just cosmetic: with a null hostname, the client libraries use a UNIX domain socket instead of a network socket to contact the X server. In addition to being faster and more efficient, this connection method bypasses any firewall restrictions on the local system that are trying to keep out external X connections. The simplest possible value for the DISPLAY environment variable, then, is simply ":0".

Client authentication

Although the X environment is generally thought to be relatively insecure, every precaution helps prevent unauthorized access. In the days before security was such a pressing concern, it was common for X servers to welcome connections from any client running on a host that had been marked as safe with the **xhost** command. But since any user on that host could then connect to your display and wreak havoc (either intentionally or out of confusion), the **xhost** method of granting access to clients was eventually deprecated. We do not discuss it further.

The most prevalent alternative to host-based security is called magic cookie authentication. While the thought of magic cookies might inspire flashbacks in some of our readers, in this context they are used to authenticate X connections. The basic idea is that the X display manager generates a large random number, called a cookie, early in the login procedure. The cookie for the server is written to the **~/.Xauthority** file in the user's home directory. Any clients that know the cookie are allowed to connect. Users can run the **xauth** command to view existing cookies and to add new ones to this file.

The simplest way to show how this works is with an example. Suppose you have set your DISPLAY variable on the client system to display X applications on the machine at which you are sitting. However, when you run a program, you get an error that looks something like this:

```
client$ xprogram -display server:0
Xlib: connection to "server:0.0" refused by server
xprogram:  unable to open display 'server:0'
```

This message tells you that the client does not have the right cookie, so the remote server refused the connection. To get the right cookie, log in to the server (which you have probably already done if you are trying to display on it) and list the server's cookies by running **xauth list**:

```
server$ xauth list
server:0  MIT-MAGIC-COOKIE-1  f9d888df6077819ef4d788fab778dc9f
server/unix:0  MIT-MAGIC-COOKIE-1  f9d888df6077819ef4d788fab778dc9f
localhost:0  MIT-MAGIC-COOKIE-1  cb6cbf9e5c24128749feddd47f0e0779
```

Each network interface on the server has an entry. This example shows a cookie for the Ethernet, a cookie for the UNIX domain socket used for local connections, and a cookie for the localhost loopback network interface.

The easiest way to get the cookie onto the client (when not using SSH, which negotiates the cookie for you) is with good old cut-and-paste. Most terminal emulators (e.g., **xterm**[3]) let you select text with the mouse and paste it into another window, usually by pressing the middle mouse button. Conveniently, the **xauth add** command accepts as input the same format that **xauth list** displays. You can add the cookie to the client like this:

```
client$ xauth add server:0  MIT-MAGIC-COOKIE-1
    9d888df6077819ef4d788fab778dc9f
```

You should verify that the cookie was added properly by running **xauth list** on the client. With the DISPLAY environment variable set and the correct magic cookie added to the client, applications should now display correctly on the server.

If you are having trouble getting cookies to work, you can drop back temporarily to **xhost** authentication just to verify that there are no other problems (for example, firewalls or local network restrictions that are preventing the client from accessing the server). Always run **xhost -** (that is, **xhost** with a dash as its only argument) to disable **xhost** authentication once your test is complete.

X connection forwarding with SSH

Magic cookies increase security, but they're hardly foolproof. Any user who can obtain your display's cookie can connect to the display and run programs that monitor your activities. Even without your cookie, the X protocol transfers data over the network without encryption, allowing it to be sniffed by virtually anyone.

See page 926 for more information about SSH.

You can boost security with SSH, the secure shell protocol. SSH provides an authenticated and encrypted terminal service. However, SSH can also forward arbitrary network data, including X protocol data, over a secure channel. X forwarding is similar to generic SSH port forwarding, but because SSH is X-aware, you gain some additional features, including a pseudo-display on the remote machine and the negotiated transfer of magic cookies.

You typically **ssh** from the machine running the X server to the machine on which you want to run X programs. This arrangement can be confusing to read about because the SSH *client* is run on the same machine as the X *server*, and it connects to an SSH *server* that is on the same machine as the X *client* applications. To make it worse, the virtual display that SSH creates for your X server is local to the remote system. Exhibit B on the next page shows how X traffic flows through the SSH connection.

3. Or **aixterm** on AIX. Clever, hmm?

Exhibit B Using SSH with X

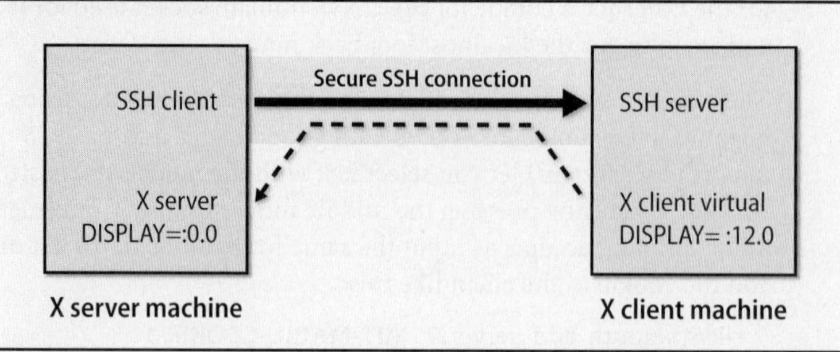

Your DISPLAY variable and authentication information are set up automatically by **ssh**. The display number starts at :10.0 and increments for each SSH connection that is forwarding X traffic.

An example might help show the sequence.

```
x-server$ ssh -v -X x-client.mydomain.com
SSH-2.0-OpenSSH_5.1
debug1: Reading configuration data /home/boggs/.ssh/config
debug1: Reading configuration data /etc/ssh/ssh_config
debug1: Applying options for *
debug1: Connecting to x-client.mydomain.com [192.168.15.9] port 22.
debug1: Connection established.
Enter passphrase for key '/home/boggs/.ssh/id_rsa':
debug1: read PEM private key done: type RSA
debug1: Authentication succeeded (publickey).
debug1: Entering interactive session.
debug1: Requesting X11 forwarding with authentication spoofing.
debug1: Requesting authentication agent forwarding.
x-client$
```

You can see from the last two lines that the client is requesting forwarding for X11 applications. X forwarding must be enabled on both the SSH server and the SSH client, and the client must still have the correct cookie for the X server. If things do not seem to be working right, try the **-X** and **-v** flags as shown above (for OpenSSH) to explicitly enable X forwarding and to request verbose output.[4] Also check the global SSH configuration files in **/etc/ssh** to make sure that X11 forwarding has not been administratively disabled. Once logged in, you can check your display and magic cookies:

```
x-client$ echo $DISPLAY
localhost:12.0
x-client$ xauth list
x-client/unix:12  MIT-MAGIC-COOKIE-1  a54b67121eb94c8a807f3ab0a67a51f2
```

4. Note that **ssh** also has a **-Y** flag that trusts all client connections. This feature may solve some forwarding problems, but use it only with extreme caution.

Notice that the DISPLAY points to a virtual display on the SSH server. Other SSH connections (both from you and from other users) are assigned different virtual display numbers. With the DISPLAY and cookie properly set, the client application can now be run.

```
x-client$ xeyes
debug1: client_input_channel_open: ctype x11 rchan 4 win 65536 max 16384
debug1: client_request_x11: request from 127.0.0.1 35411
debug1: channel 1: new [x11]
debug1: confirm x11
debug1: channel 1: FORCE input drain
```

With the debugging information enabled with **ssh -v**, you can see that **ssh** has received the X connection request and dutifully forwarded it to the X server. The forwarding can be a little slow on a distant link, but the application should eventually appear on your screen.

25.3 X SERVER CONFIGURATION

The X.Org server, **Xorg**, was once notorious for being difficult to configure for a given hardware environment. However, a tremendous amount of effort has been put into making **Xorg** ready to eat right out of the box, and many modern systems run it successfully without any configuration file. However, it is still possible to manually adapt the **Xorg** server to a wide array of graphics hardware, input devices, video modes, resolutions, and color depths.

X Windows

If your system is running fine without an **Xorg** configuration file, great! It may be using the KMS module, which is described later in this chapter. Otherwise, you have two options. Option one is to manually configure the **xorg.conf** file. The sections below describe manual configuration. Truth be told, this may be your only real option in some situations. Option two is to use the **xrandr** tool to configure your server; it's covered starting on page 1025.

The **Xorg** configuration file is normally located in **/etc/X11/xorg.conf**, but the X server searches a slew of directories to find it. The man page presents a complete list, but one point to note is that some of the paths **Xorg** searches contain the hostname and a global variable, making it easy for you to store configuration files for multiple systems in a central location.

AIX operates without an **xorg.conf** configuration file and instead tries to automatically recognize all AIX hardware display types. You can pass configuration hints as arguments to the X server.

Several programs can help you configure X (e.g., **xorgconfig**), but it's a good idea to understand how the configuration file is structured in case you need to view or edit the configuration directly. You can gather some useful starting information directly from the X server by running **Xorg -probeonly** and looking through the output to identify your video chipset and any other probed values. You can also run **Xorg -configure** to have the X server create an initial configuration file that is based on the probed values. It's a good place to start if you have nothing else.

The **xorg.conf** file has several sections, each of which starts with the Section keyword and ends with EndSection. Table 25.1 lists the most common section types.

Table 25.1 Sections of the xorg.conf file

Section	Description
ServerFlags	Lists general X server configuration parameters
Module	Specifies dynamically loadable extensions for accelerated graphics, font renderers, and the like
Device	Configures the video card, driver, and hardware information
Monitor	Describes physical monitor parameters, including timing and display resolutions
Screen	Associates a monitor with a video card (Device) and defines the resolutions and color depths available in that configuration
InputDevice	Specifies input devices such as keyboards and mice
ServerLayout	Bundles input devices with a set of screens and positions the screens relative to each other

It is often simplest to build a configuration file from the bottom up by first defining sections for the input and output devices and then combining them into various layouts. With this hierarchical approach, a single configuration file can be used for many X servers, each with different hardware. It's also a reasonable approach for a single system that has multiple video cards and monitors.

Exhibit C shows how some of these sections fit together into the X.Org configuration hierarchy. A physical display Monitor plus a video card Device combine to form a Screen. A set of Screens plus InputDevices form a ServerLayout. Multiple server layouts can be defined in a configuration file, though only one is active for a given instance of the **Xorg** process.

Exhibit C Relationship of xorg.conf configuration sections

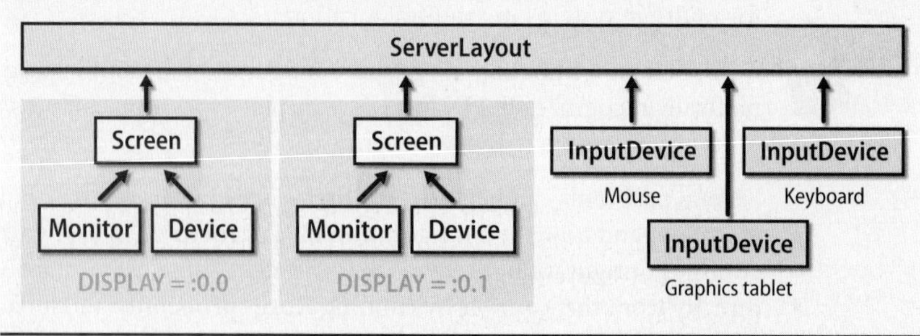

Some of the sections that make up the **xorg.conf** file are relatively fixed. The defaults can often be used straight from an existing or example configuration file. Others, such as the Device, Monitor, Screen, InputDevice, and ServerLayout sections, depend on the host's hardware setup. We discuss the most interesting of these sections in more detail in the following subsections.

Device sections

A Device section describes a particular video card. You must provide a string to identify the card and a driver appropriate for the device. The driver is loaded only if the device is referenced by a corresponding Screen section. A typical device section might look like this:

```
Section "Device"
    Identifier        "Videocard0"
    Driver            "radeon"
    option            value
    ...
EndSection
```

The manual page for the driver, radeon in this example, describes the hardware that's driven as well as the options the driver supports. If you are experiencing strange video artifacts, you might try setting options to turn off hardware acceleration (if supported), slowing down video memory access, or modifying interface parameters. It is generally a good idea to check the web to see if other people have experienced similar problems before you start randomly changing values.

Monitor sections

The Monitor section describes the displays attached to your computer. It can specify detailed timing values. The timing information is necessary for older hardware, but most modern monitors can be probed for it. Display specifications can usually be obtained from the manufacturer's web site, but nothing beats having the original manual that came with the monitor. Either way, you will want to know at least the horizontal sync and vertical refresh frequencies for your model.

A typical Monitor section looks like this:

```
Section "Monitor"
    Identifier   "ViewSonic"
    Option       "DPMS"
    HorizSync    30-65
    VertRefresh  50-120
EndSection
```

As with all of the sections, the Identifier line assigns a name by which you later refer to this monitor. Here we have turned on DPMS (Display Power Management Signaling) so that the X server can power down the monitor when we sneak away for a donut and some coffee.

The HorizSync and VertRefresh lines, which apply only to CRT monitors, should be filled in with values appropriate for your monitor. They may be specified as a frequency range (as above) or as discrete values separated by commas. The driver can theoretically probe for supported modes, but specifying the parameters keeps the driver from attempting to use unsupported frequencies.

Screen sections

A Screen section ties a device (video card) to a monitor at a specific color depth and set of display resolutions. Here's an example that uses the video card and monitor specified above.

```
Section "Screen"
    Identifier     "Screen0"
    Device         "Videocard0"
    Monitor        "ViewSonic"
    DefaultDepth 24
    Subsection "Display"
        Depth     8
        Modes     "640x400"
    EndSubsection
    Subsection "Display"
        Depth     16
        Modes     "640x400" "640x480" "800x600" "1024x768"
    EndSubsection
    Subsection "Display"
        Depth     24
        Modes     "1280x1024" "1024x768" "800x600" "640x400" "640x480"
    EndSubsection
EndSection
```

As you might expect, the screen is named with an Identifier, and the identifiers for the previously defined video device and monitor are mentioned. This is the first section we have introduced that has subsections. One subsection is defined for each color depth, with the default being specified by the DefaultDepth field.

A given instance of the X server can run at only one color depth. At startup, the server determines what resolutions are supported for that depth. The possible resolutions generally depend on the video card. *Special keyboard combinations for X* on page 1026 describes how to cycle through the resolutions that are defined here.

Any modern video card should be able to drive your monitor at its full resolution in 24-bit or 32-bit color. If you want to run old programs that require a server running in 8-bit color, run a second X server on a separate virtual console. Use the **-depth 8** flag on the **Xorg** command line to override the DefaultDepth option.

InputDevice sections

An InputDevice section describes a source of input events such as a keyboard or mouse. Each device gets its own InputDevice section, and as with other sections, each is named with an Identifier field. If you are sharing a single configuration file among machines with different hardware, you can define all the input devices; only those referenced in the ServerLayout section are used. Here is a typical keyboard definition:

```
Section "InputDevice"
    Identifier     "Generic Keyboard"
    Driver         "Keyboard"
    Option         "AutoRepeat" "500 30"
    Option         "XkbModel" "pc104"
    Option         "XkbLayout" "us"
EndSection
```

You can set options in the keyboard definition to express your particular religion's stance on the proper position of the Control and Caps Lock keys, among other things. In this example, the AutoRepeat option specifies how long a key needs to be held down before it starts repeating and how fast it repeats.

The mouse is configured in a separate InputDevice section:

```
Section "InputDevice"
    Identifier     "Generic Mouse"
    Driver         "mouse"
    Option         "CorePointer"
    Option         "Device" "/dev/input/mice"
    Option         "Protocol" "IMPS/2"
    Option         "Emulate3Buttons" "off"
    Option         "ZAxisMapping" "4 5"
EndSection
```

The CorePointer option designates this mouse as the system's primary pointing device. The device file associated with the mouse is specified as an Option; Table 25.2 lists the mouse device multiplexer files for our example systems.

Table 25.2 Common mouse device files

OS	Device file
Linux	**/dev/input/mice**
Solaris	**/dev/mouse**
HP-UX	**/dev/deviceFileSystem/mouseMux**
AIX	**/dev/mouse0**

The communication protocol depends on the particular brand of mouse, its features, and its interface. You can set it to auto to make the server try to figure out the protocol for you. If your mouse wheel doesn't work, try setting the protocol to IMPS/2. If you have more than a few buttons, try using the ExplorerPS/2 protocol. Some Solaris users report success with the VUID protocol.

The Emulate3Buttons option lets a two-button mouse emulate a three-button mouse by defining a click on both buttons to stand in for a middle-button click.

The ZAxisMapping option is sometimes needed to support a scroll wheel or joystick device. Most mice these days have at least three buttons, a scroll wheel, a built-in MP3 player, a foot massager, and a beer chiller.[5]

ServerLayout sections

The ServerLayout section is the top-level node of the configuration hierarchy. Each hardware configuration on which the server will be run should have its own instance of the ServerLayout section. The layout used by a particular X server is usually specified on the server's command line.

This section ties together all the other sections to represent an X display. It starts with the requisite Identifier, which names this particular layout. It then associates a set of screens with the layout.[6] If multiple monitors are attached to separate video cards, each screen is specified along with optional directions to indicate how they are physically arranged. In this example, screen one is on the left and screen two is on the right.

Here is an example of a complete ServerLayout section:

```
Section "ServerLayout"
    Identifier   "Simple Layout"
    Screen       "Screen 1" LeftOf "Screen 2"
    Screen       "Screen 2" RightOf "Screen 1"
    InputDevice  "Generic Mouse" "CorePointer"
    InputDevice  "Generic Keyboard" "CoreKeyboard"
    Option       "BlankTime"    "10"  # Blank the screen in 10 minutes
    Option       "StandbyTime"  "20"  # Turn off screen in 20 minutes (DPMS)
    Option       "SuspendTime"  "60"  # Full hibernation in 60 minutes (DPMS)
    Option       "OffTime"      "120"# Turn off DPMS monitor in 2 hours
EndSection
```

Some video cards can drive multiple monitors at once. In this case, only a single Screen is specified in the ServerLayout section. Following the screen list is the set of input devices to associate with the layout. The CorePointer and CoreKeyboard options are passed to the InputDevice section to indicate that the devices are to be active for the configuration. Those options can also be set directly in the corresponding InputDevice sections, but it's cleaner to set them in the ServerLayout.

The last few lines configure several layout-specific options. In the example above, these all relate to DPMS, which is the interface that tells Energy Star-compliant monitors when to power themselves down. The monitors must also have their DPMS options enabled in the corresponding Monitor sections.

5. Not all options are supported by **Xorg**. Some options sold separately.
6. Recall that screens identify a monitor/video card combination at a particular color depth.

xrandr: not your father's X server configurator

The X Resize and Rotate Extension (RandR) lets clients dynamically change the size, orientation, and reflection of their X server screens. **xrandr** is the command-line interface to this extension.

Of course, we would all love to spend a few days tediously crafting each line of the **xorg.conf** file to support that brand-new SUPERINATOR 3000 system with its four deluxe displays. But in many cases, you can have **xrandr** do the configuration for you and be done in time to grab a few beers. Run with no arguments, **xrandr** shows the available displays and their possible resolutions.

```
$ xrandr
VGA-0 connected 1024x768+0+0 (normal left inverted right x a...) 0mm x 0mm
   1024x768         61.0        60.0        59.9        59.9
   800x600          60.3        61.0        59.9        56.2        59.8
   640x480          59.9        61.0        59.4        59.5
DVI-0 connected 1024x768+0+0 (normal left inverted right x a...) 0mm x 0mm
   1024x768         60.0        60.0
   800x600          60.3        59.9
   640x480          59.9        59.4
```

You can specify the resolution to use for each display along with the display's placement relative to other displays.[7] For example:

```
$ xrandr --auto --output VGA-0 --mode 800x600 --right-of DVI-0
```

The **--auto** argument turns on all available monitors. The **--output** and **--mode** arguments set the VGA display to a resolution of 800 × 600, and the **--right-of** argument specifies that the VGA display is physically located to the right of the DVI display. (The latter option is needed to properly implement desktop continuity.) Run **xrandr --help** to see the many available options.

If you want **xrandr** to run automatically when you start the X server, you can put it in your **~/.xprofile** file, which is executed at server startup.

Kernel mode setting

To make the system's presentation more seamless and flicker free, responsibility for setting the initial mode of the graphics display is now being pushed into the Linux kernel through the "kernel mode setting" (KMS) module. As of kernel version 2.6.30-10.12, KMS defaults to initializing the video card very early in the kernel's boot sequence.

You enable or disable KMS through settings in the video driver configuration files in **/etc/modprobe.d**. For example, if you have an ATI Radeon video card, you can turn off KMS by adding the following line to **/etc/modprobe.d/radeon.conf**:

```
options radeon modeset=0
```

7. Before using **xrandr** for the first time, run **Xorg -configure** to reset the **xorg.conf** file to a known, clean state.

X Windows

The KMS module is still young and it does not currently support all video cards. If you're lucky enough to have a supported card, your best bet is to rename the **xorg.conf** file so that the X server tries to start without it and defaults to the KMS configuration.

25.4 X SERVER TROUBLESHOOTING AND DEBUGGING

X server configuration has come a long way over the last decade, but it can still be difficult to get things working just the way you would like. You may need to experiment with monitor frequencies, driver options, proprietary drivers, or extensions for 3D rendering. Ironically, it is the times when the display is not working correctly that you are most interested in seeing the debugging output on your screen. Fortunately, the X.Org server gives you all the information you need (and a lot that you don't) to track down the problem.

Special keyboard combinations for X

Because the X server takes over your keyboard, display, mouse, and social life, you can imagine that it might leave you with little recourse but to power the system down if things are not working. However, there are a few things to try before it comes to that.

If you hold down the Control and Alt keys and press a function key (F1–F6), the X server takes you to one of the text-based virtual terminals. From there you can log in and debug the problem. To get back to the X server running on, say, virtual terminal 7, press <Alt-F7>.[8] If you are on a network, you can also try logging in from another computer to kill the X server before resorting to the reset button.

For virtual console support on Solaris, enable the svc:/system/vtdaemon:default SMF service and the console-login:vt[2-6] services.

If the monitor is not in sync with the card's video signal, try changing the screen resolution. The available resolutions are specified on a Modes line from the Screen section of the configuration file. The exact Modes line that is active depends on the color depth; see *Screen sections* on page 1022 for details. The X server defaults to the first resolution shown on the active Modes line, but you can cycle through the different resolutions by holding down Control and Alt and pressing the plus (+) or minus (-) key on the numeric keypad.

Pressing <Control-Alt-Backspace> kills the X server immediately. If you ran the server from a console, you will find yourself back there when the server exits. If a display manager started the server, it usually respawns a new server and prompts again for a login and password. You have to kill the display manager (**xdm**, **gdm**, etc.) from a text console to stop it from respawning new X servers.

8. The X server requires the <Control> key to be held down along with the <Alt-Fn> key combination to switch virtual terminals, but the text console does not.

When X servers attack

Once you have regained control of the machine, you can begin to track down the problem. The simplest place to start is the output of the X server. This output is occasionally visible on virtual terminal 1 (<Control-Alt-F1>), which is where startup program output goes. Most often, the X server output goes to a log file such as **/var/log/Xorg.0.log** (**/var/X11/Xserver/logs/Xf86.0.log** on HP-UX).

As seen below, each line is preceded by a symbol that categorizes it. You can use these symbols to spot errors (EE) and warnings (WW), as well as to determine how the server found out each piece of information: through default settings (==), in a config file (**), detected automatically (--), or specified on the X server command line (++).

Let's examine the following snippet from an Ubuntu system:

```
X.Org X Server 1.6.0
Release Date: 2009-2-25
X Protocol Version 11, Revision 0
Build Operating System: Linux 2.6.24-23-server i686 Ubuntu
Current Operating System: Linux nutrient 2.6.28-11-generic #42-Ubuntu SMP
    Fri Apr 17 01:57:59 UTC 2009 i686
Build Date: 09 April 2009  02:10:02AM
xorg-server 2:1.6.0-0ubuntu14 (buildd@rothera.buildd)
    Before reporting problems, check http://wiki.x.org
    to make sure that you have the latest version.
Markers: (--) probed, (**) from config file, (==) default setting,
    (++) from command line, (!!) notice, (II) informational,
    (WW) warning, (EE) error, (NI) not implemented, (??) unknown.
(==) Log file: "/var/log/Xorg.0.log", Time: Sun May 10 22:11:47 2009
(==) Using config file: "/etc/X11/xorg.conf"
(==) ServerLayout "MainLayout"
(**) |-->Screen "Screen 0" (0)
(**) |   |-->Monitor "Monitor 0"
(**) |   |-->Device "Console"
(**) |-->Input Device "Mouse0"
(**) |-->Input Device "Keyboard0"
...
```

The first lines tell you the version number of the X server and the X11 protocol version it implements. Subsequent lines tell you that the server is using default values for the log file location, the configuration file location, and the active server layout. The display and input devices from the config file are echoed in schematic form.

One common problem that shows up in the logs is difficulty with certain screen resolutions, usually evidenced by those resolutions not working or the X server bailing out with an error such as "Unable to validate any modes; falling back to the default mode." If you have not specified a list of frequencies for your monitor, the X server probes for them by using Extended Display Identification Data (EDID). If your monitor does not support EDID or if your monitor is turned off when X is started, you need to put the frequency ranges for X to use in the Monitor section of the configuration file.

Rounding error in the results obtained from an EDID probe can cause some resolutions to be unavailable even though they should be supported by both your video card and monitor. Log entries such as "No valid modes for 1280x1024; removing" are evidence of this. The solution is to tell the X server to ignore EDID information and use the frequencies you have specified; the following lines in the Device section are what you need:

```
Option  "IgnoreEDID" "true"
Option  "UseEdidFreqs" "false"
```

As another example, suppose you forgot to define the mouse section properly. The error would show up like this in the output:

```
(==) Using config file: "/etc/X11/xorg.conf"
Data incomplete in file /etc/X11/xorg.conf
    Undefined InputDevice "Mouse0" referenced by ServerLayout "MainLayout".
(EE) Problem parsing the config file
(EE) Error parsing the config file
Fatal server error:
no screens found
```

Once X is up and running and you have logged in, you can run the **xdpyinfo** command to get more information about the X server's configuration.[9] **xdpyinfo**'s output again tells you the name of the display and the X server version information. It also tells you the color depths that are available, the extensions that have been loaded, and the screens that have been defined, along with their dimensions and color configurations.

xdpyinfo's output can be parsed by a script (such as your **~/.xsession** file) to determine the size of the active screen and to set up the desktop parameters appropriately. For debugging, **xdpyinfo** is most useful for determining that the X server is up and listening to network queries, that it has configured the correct screen and resolution, and that it is operating at the desired color bit depth. If this step works, you are ready to start running X applications.

25.5 A BRIEF NOTE ON DESKTOP ENVIRONMENTS

The flexibility of the X Window System client/server model has, over the years, led to an explosion of widget sets, window managers, file browsers, tool bar utilities, and utility programs. The first comprehensive environments, OpenLook and Motif, were elegant for their time but proprietary. Licensing fees for the development libraries and window manager made them inaccessible to the general public.

9. We don't recommend logging into X as root because this operation may create a bunch of default startup files in root's home directory, which is usually / or **/root**. It's also notably insecure. Instead, log in as a regular user and use **sudo**. Ubuntu enforces this discipline by default.

As applications became more advanced and demanded progressively more support from the underlying window system, it became clear that a comprehensive approach to advancing the platform was required. From this need were born the two big players in modern desktop environments: GNOME and KDE. Although some users have strong feelings regarding which is the One True Way, both are relatively complete desktop managers. In fact, just because you are running in one realm does not mean you cannot use applications from the other; just expect a different look and feel and a brief sense of discontinuity in the universe.

The freedesktop.org project is dedicated to creating an environment that will allow applications to be compatible with any desktop environment.

KDE

KDE, which stands for the K Desktop Environment, is written in C++ and built on the Qt tool kit library. It is often preferred by users who enjoy eye candy, such as transparent windows, shadows, and animated cursors. It looks nice, but it can be slow on anything but a high-end workstation. For users who spend a lot of time clicking around in the desktop rather than running applications, the tradeoff between efficiency and aesthetics may ultimately decide whether KDE is the appropriate choice.

KDE is often preferred by people transitioning from a Windows or Mac environment because of its pretty graphics. It's also a favorite of technophiles who love to be able to fully customize their environment. For others, KDE is simply too much to deal with and GNOME is the simpler choice.

Applications written for KDE almost always contain a K somewhere in the name, for example, Konqueror (the web/file browser), Konsole (the terminal emulator), or KWord (a word processor). The default window manager, KWin, supports the freedesktop.org Window Manager Specification standard, configurable skins for changing the overall look and feel, and many other features. The KOffice application suite contains word processing, spreadsheet, and presentation utilities. KDE sports a comprehensive set of development tools, including an integrated development environment (IDE).

GNOME

GNOME is written in C and is based on the GTK+ widget set. The name GNOME was originally an acronym for GNU Network Object Model Environment, but that derivation no longer really applies; these days, GNOME is just a name.

With the recent addition of support for Compiz (compiz.org), GNOME has acquired many of the eye candy features that it previously lacked. Overall, GNOME is still less glitzy than KDE, is not as configurable, and is slightly less consistent. However, it is noticeably cleaner, faster, simpler, and more elegant. Most Linux distributions use GNOME as the default desktop environment.

Like KDE, GNOME has a rich application set. GNOME applications are usually identifiable by the presence of a G in their names. One of the exceptions is the standard GNOME window manager, called Metacity (pronounced like "opacity"), which supplies basic windowing functions and skinning of the GNOME UI. Following the GNOME model, Metacity is designed to be lean and mean.

If you want some of the extra features you may be used to, such as smart window placement, you need the support of external applications such as **brightside** or **devilspie**. Unfortunately, bling is one area in which KDE still has a leg up.

Office applications include AbiWord for word processing, Gnumeric as a spreadsheet, and one of the more impressive projects to come out of GNOME, The GIMP for image processing. A file manager called Nautilus is also included. Like KDE, GNOME provides an extensive infrastructure for application developers. Altogether, GNOME offers a powerful architecture for application development in an easy-to-use desktop environment.

Which is better, GNOME or KDE?

Ask this question on any public forum and you will see the definition of "flame war." Because of the tendency for people to turn desktop preference into a personal crusade, the following paragraphs may be some of the least opinionated in this book.

The best answer is to try both desktops and decide for yourself which best meets your needs. Keep in mind that your friends, your users, and your manager may all have different preferences for a desktop environment, and that is OK.

Remember that your choice of desktop environment does not dictate which applications you can run. No matter which desktop you choose, you can select applications from the full complement of excellent software made available by both of these (and other) open source projects.

25.6 Recommended reading

The X.Org home page, x.org, includes information on upcoming releases as well as links to the X.Org wiki, mailing lists, and downloads.

The man pages for **Xserver** and **Xorg** (or just **X** on AIX) cover generic X server options and **Xorg**-specific command-line options. They also include a general overview of X server operation.

The **xorg.conf** man page covers the config file and describes its various sections in detail. This man page also lists video card drivers in its REFERENCES section. Look up your video card here to learn the name of the driver, then read the driver's own man page to learn about driver-specific options.

25.7 Exercises

E25.1 Use SSH to run an X program over the network. Use **ssh -v** to verify that X forwarding is set up correctly. What is the DISPLAY variable set to after you log in? List the cookies by running **xauth** and verify that magic cookie authentication is active for that display.

E25.2 Write a shell command line or script to parse the output of **xdpyinfo** and print the current screen resolution in the format XxY, e.g., 1024×768.

E25.3 Examine the **Xorg** log file (**/var/log/Xorg.0.log**) and determine as many of the following items as possible:

a) What type of video card is present and which driver does it use?
b) How much video memory does the card have?
c) Was EDID used to probe monitor settings? How do you know?
d) What modes (resolutions) are supported?
e) Is DPMS enabled?
f) What does the server think the physical screen dimensions are?
g) What device file is used for the mouse?

E25.4 What flag disables nonlocal TCP connections to the X server? Explain why this option is useful.

26 Printing

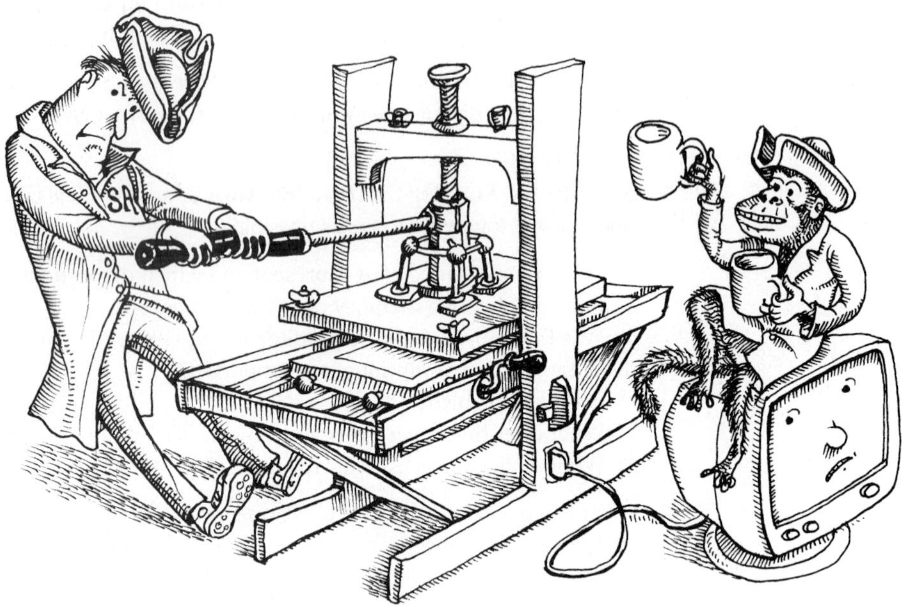

UNIX printing is a mess. Let us elaborate.

Linux printing is quite nice. So is Mac OS X printing. Both are built on the Common UNIX Printing System (CUPS), an up-to-date, sophisticated, network- and security-aware printing system. CUPS provides a modern, browser-based GUI as well as shell-level commands that allow printing and control of the printing system from scripts.

Just as newer mail transport systems supply a command called **sendmail** that lets older scripts (and older system administrators!) work as they always did back in **sendmail**'s glory days, CUPS supplies commands such as **lp** and **lpr** that are backward-compatible with traditional UNIX printing systems. So everyone is happy.

Given its name, you might guess that CUPS could be found on UNIX systems as well. Alas, you'd be wrong. None of our example UNIX platforms—Solaris, HP-UX, and AIX—use it. Even worse, a quick Google search reveals that attempts to install CUPS on these systems typically fail.

Instead, these systems offer variants of the creaky, decades-old System V and BSD printing systems. If it was good enough for a PDP-11, it should be good enough for you! The unfortunate fact is that Microsoft Windows and Mac OS dominate the document processing world, so UNIX vendors are not under much pressure to improve printing support. Until UNIX vendors adopt CUPS (or you adopt Linux or Mac OS), you'll have to learn the older printing systems, too.

We start this chapter with a general discussion of printing systems and printing terminology. We go on to describe the various UNIX and Linux printing systems and their architectures. We move on to the specifics of printer configuration and administration, then conclude with a brief guide to print-system debugging, a tour of optional printing-related software, and some general administration hints.

Before we start, though, here's a point worth making: system administrators often consider printing a lower priority than users do. Administrators are used to reading documents on-line, but users typically want hard copy, and they want the printing system to work 100% of the time.

26.1 Printing-System Architecture

Printing relies on a handful of pieces:

- A print "spooler" that collects and schedules jobs. The word "spool" originated as an acronym for Simultaneous Peripheral Operation On-Line. Now it's just a generic term.
- User-level utilities (a command-line interface and/or GUI) that talk to the spooler. These utilities send jobs to the spooler, query the system about jobs (both pending and complete), remove or reschedule jobs, and configure the other parts of the system.
- Back ends that talk to the printing devices themselves. (These are normally unseen and hidden under the floorboards.)
- A network protocol that lets spoolers communicate and transfer jobs.

A good way to approach printer administration is to figure out what parts of the system fulfill each of these roles. Unfortunately, it varies a lot.

Major printing systems

Each of the target systems covered in this book supplies a printing system from one of three families: System V, BSD, or CUPS. We'll talk about where these names came from by-and-by: they're historical, but useful. A system's printing software doesn't necessarily come from the same lineage as the OS itself. For example, AIX, which was originally built on System V.0 with some V.2 extensions, uses a BSD print system.

There are add-on printing systems you can install yourself (such as the ill-fated LPRng), but printing is often so enmeshed with other parts of the operating system that it's a long and uphill battle to make this work. Installing your own printing system is like installing your own shell: UNIX gives you the freedom to do it, and you might have good reason to, but you're on your own. In this book, we only cover the printing software that comes by default.

You can tell what kind of printing software your system has by looking for the spooler. CUPS has **cupsd**, BSD has **lpd**, and System V has **lpsched**, so the command **which cupsd lpd lpsched** tells you which one you have.

Print spoolers

Each system has a spooler: a piece of software that receives print jobs, stores them, prioritizes them, and sends them out sequentially to one or more printers. You'll sometimes see the spooler referred to as a print daemon or print server.

Some printers (usually high-end models) have their own internal spoolers. If telling your print daemon to discard all the jobs in its queue does not fix a problem right away, consider that there may still be jobs stored inside the printer. To discard those as well, you may need to shut off the printer and restart it.

The **lpd** (BSD) and **lpsched** (SysV) spoolers are stand-alone daemons that are specifically designed for printing. Applications on the system either talk to these servers or read and write spool or configuration files in "well known" locations such as **/var/spool** or **/etc**.

26.2 CUPS PRINTING

CUPS servers are also web servers, and CUPS clients are web clients. The clients can be commands such as the CUPS versions of **lpr** and **lpq**, or they can be applications with their own GUIs such as **kprinter**. Under the covers they're all web apps, even if they're only talking to the CUPS daemon on the local system. CUPS servers can also act as clients of other CUPS servers.

A CUPS server provides a web interface to its full functionality on port 631. For administrators, a web browser is usually the most convenient way to manage the system; just navigate to http://*printhost*:631. If you need secure communication with the daemon (and your system offers it) use https://*printhost*:433 instead. Scripts can use discrete commands to control the system, and users will probably access it through a GNOME or KDE interface. These routes are all equivalent.

HTTP is the underlying protocol for all interactions among CUPS servers and their clients. Actually, it's the Internet Printing Protocol, a souped-up version of HTTP. Clients submit jobs with the HTTP/IPP POST operation and request status with HTTP/IPP GET. The CUPS configuration files also look suspiciously similar to Apache configuration files.

Interfaces to the printing system

CUPS is modern enough that most CUPS printing is done from a GUI, and administration is often done through a web browser. As a sysadmin, though, you (and perhaps some of your hard-core terminal users) may want to use shell-level commands as well. CUPS provides work-alike commands for many of the basic, shell-level printing commands of both the classic BSD and System V printing systems. Unfortunately, CUPS doesn't necessarily emulate all the bells and whistles. Sometimes, it emulates the old interfaces entirely *too* well; instead of giving you a quick usage summary, **lpr --help** and **lp --help** just print error messages.

Still, many legacy scripts that use these commands work just fine with CUPS. Think of what's missing as an opportunity: if you want to contribute to world peace and Pareto optimality, there's still code left for you to write (or if you're using an older system, code left for you to port).

Here's how you might print the files **foo.pdf** and **/tmp/testprint.ps** to your default printer under CUPS:

```
$ lpr foo.pdf /tmp/testprint.ps
```

The **lpr** command transmits copies of the files to the CUPS server, **cupsd**, which stores them in the print queue. CUPS processes each file in turn as the printer becomes available.

When printing, CUPS examines both the document and the printer's PostScript Printer Description (PPD) file to see what needs to be done to get the document to print properly. (As we discuss in more detail on page 1072, PPD files are used even for non-PostScript printers.)

To prepare a job for printing on a specific printer, CUPS passes it through a series of filters. For example, one filter might reformat the job so that two reduced-size page images print on each physical page (aka "2-up printing"), and another might transform the job from PostScript to PCL. Filters can also perform printer-specific processing such as printer initialization. Some filters perform rasterization, turning abstract instructions such as "draw a line across the page" into a bitmap image. Such rasterizers are useful for printers that do not include their own rasterizers or that don't speak the language in which a job was originally submitted.

The final stage of the print pipeline is a back end that transmits the job from the host to the printer through an appropriate protocol such as Ethernet. The back end also communicates status information in the other direction, back to the CUPS server. To see your available back ends, try the command

```
$ locate backend | grep -i cups
```

After transmitting the print job, the CUPS daemon returns to processing its queues and handling requests from clients, and the printer goes off to print the job it was shipped.

The print queue

cupsd's centralized control of the printing system makes it easy to understand what the user-level commands are doing. For example, the **lpq** command requests job status information from the server and reformats it for display. Other CUPS clients ask the server to suspend, cancel, or reprioritize jobs. They can also move jobs from one queue to another.

Most changes require jobs be identified by their job number, which you can get from **lpq**. For example, to remove a print job, just run **lprm** *jobid*.

lpstat -t summarizes the print server's overall status.

Multiple printers and queues

The CUPS server maintains a separate queue for each printer. Command-line clients accept an option (typically **-P** *printer* or **-p** *printer*) to specify which queue you want to address. You can also set a default printer for yourself by setting the PRINTER environment variable

```
$ export PRINTER=printer_name
```

or by telling CUPS to use a particular default for your account.

```
$ lpoptions -dprinter_name
```

When run as root, **lpoptions** sets system-wide defaults in **/etc/cups/lpoptions**, but it's more typically used by individual, nonroot users. **lpoptions** lets each user define personal printer instances and defaults, which it stores in **~/.lpoptions**. **lpoptions -l** lists the current settings.

Printer instances

If you have only one printer but want to use it in several ways—say, both for quick drafts and for final production work—CUPS lets you set up different "printer instances" for these different uses.

For example, if you already have a printer named Phaser_6120, the command

```
$ lpoptions -p Phaser_6120/2up -o number-up=2 -o job-sheets=standard
```

creates an instance named Phaser_6120/2up that performs 2-up printing and adds banner pages. Once the instance has been created, the command

```
$ lpr -P Phaser_6120/2up biglisting.ps
```

prints the PostScript file **biglisting.ps** as a 2-up job with a banner page.

Network printing

From CUPS' perspective, a network of machines isn't very different from an isolated machine. Every computer runs a **cupsd**, and all the CUPS daemons talk to one another.

If you're working on the command line, you configure a CUPS daemon to accept print jobs from remote systems by editing the **/etc/cups/cupsd.conf** file (see *Network print server setup* on page 1039). By default, servers that are set up this way broadcast information every 30 seconds about the printers they serve. As a result, computers on the local network automatically learn about the printers that are available to them. You can effect the same configuration by clicking a check box in the CUPS GUI in your browser.

If someone has plugged in a new printer, if you've brought your laptop into work, or if you've just installed a new workstation, you can tell **cupsd** to look and see what's out there by clicking on the Find New Printers button in the Administration tab of the CUPS GUI.

Because broadcast packets do not cross subnet boundaries, it's a bit tricker to make printers available to multiple subnets. One solution is to designate a slave server on each subnet that polls the other subnets' servers for information and then relays that information to machines on the local subnet.

For example, suppose the print servers allie (192.168.1.5) and jj (192.168.2.14) live on different subnets and we want both of them to be accessible to users on a third subnet, 192.168.3. We designate a slave server (say, copeland, 192.168.3.10) and add these lines to its **cupsd.conf** file:

```
BrowsePoll allie
BrowsePoll jj
BrowseRelay 127.0.0.1 192.168.3.255
```

The first two lines tell the slave's **cupsd** to poll the **cupsd**s on allie and jj for information about the printers they serve. The third line tells copeland to relay the information it learns to its own subnet. Simple!

Need a more sophisticated setup? Multiple queues for one printer, each with different defaults? A single server that load-balances by parceling out jobs to several printers? Multiple servers that each handle interchangeable instances of the same kind of printer? **lpd** or Windows clients? There's too much variation to go through here, but CUPS handles all these situations, and the documentation can walk you through the details. (See the section on documentation, starting on page 1083.)

Printing

Filters

Rather than using a specialized printing tool for every printer, CUPS uses a chain of filters to convert each printed file into something the printer can understand.

The CUPS filter scheme is elegant. Given a document and a target printer, CUPS uses its **.types** files to figure out the document's MIME type. It consults the printer's PPD file to figure out what MIME types the printer can handle. It then uses the **.convs** files to deduce what filter chains could convert one format to the other, and what each prospective chain would cost. Finally, it picks a chain and passes the document through those filters. The final filter in the chain passes the printable format to a back end, which transmits the data to the printer through whatever hardware or protocol the printer understands.

Let's flesh out that process a bit. CUPS uses rules in **/etc/cups/mime.types** to suss out the incoming data type. For example, the rule

```
application/pdf pdf string (0,%PDF)
```

means "If the file has a **.pdf** extension or starts with the string %PDF, then its MIME type is application/pdf."

CUPS figures out how to convert one data type to another by looking up rules in the file **mime.convs** (usually in **/etc/cups** or **/usr/share/cups**). For example,

```
application/pdf application/postscript 33 pdftops
```

means "To convert an application/pdf file to an application/postscript file, run the filter **pdftops**." The number 33 is the cost of the conversion. When CUPS finds that several filter chains can convert a file from one type to another, it picks the chain with the lowest total cost. (Costs are chosen by whoever created the file—the distribution maintainers, perhaps. We have no idea how. If you want to spend time tuning them because you think you can do a better job, you may have too much free time.)

The last component in a CUPS pipeline is a filter that talks directly to the printer. In the PPD of a non-PostScript printer, you may see lines such as

```
*cupsFilter: "application/vnd.cups-postscript 0 foomatic-rip"
```

or even

```
*cupsFilter: "application/vnd.cups-postscript foomatic-rip"
```

The quoted string has the same format as a line in **mime.convs**, but there's only one MIME type instead of two. This line advertises that the **foomatic-rip** filter converts data of type application/vnd.cups-postscript to the printer's native data format. The cost is zero (or omitted) because there's only one way to do this step, so why pretend there's a cost? (Some PPDs for non-PostScript printers, like those from the Gutenprint project, are slightly different.)

To find the filters available on your system, try running **locate pstops**. **pstops** is a popular filter that massages PostScript jobs in various ways, such as adding a PostScript command to set the number of copies. Wherever you find **pstops**, the other filters won't be far away.

You can ask CUPS for a list of the available back ends by running **lpinfo -v**. If your system lacks a back end for the network protocol you need, it may be available from the web or from your Linux distributor.

CUPS server administration

cupsd starts at boot time and runs continuously. All of our example Linux distributions are set up this way by default.

The CUPS configuration file is called **cupsd.conf**; it's usually found in **/etc/cups**. The file format is similar to that of the Apache configuration file. If you're comfortable with one of these files, you'll be comfortable with the other. You can view and edit **cupsd.conf** with a text editor or, once again, from the CUPS web GUI.

The default config file is well commented. The comments and the **cupsd.conf** man page are good enough that we won't belabor the same information here.

CUPS reads its configuration file only at startup time. If you change the contents of **cupsd.conf**, you have to restart **cupsd** for changes to take effect. If you make changes through **cupsd**'s web GUI, it restarts automatically. To restart **cupsd** from the command line, just run **/etc/init.d/cups restart** or **/etc/initd.cupsys restart**, whichever is present.

You can also configure the system through desktop-specific GUI tools. For example, under KDE, you can use the KDE Print Manager, accessible through the KDE control center. We found some problems with the KDE Print Manager during our testing, however. For example, it complained about not understanding certain options found in some distributions' default **cupsd.conf** files. The browser GUI is safer and is certainly authoritative.

Network print server setup

If you're having trouble printing from the network, go into the browser-based CUPS GUI and make sure you've checked all the right boxes. Possible problem areas include an unpublished printer, a CUPS server that isn't broadcasting its printers to the network, or a CUPS server that won't accept network print jobs.

If you're editing the **cupsd.conf** file directly, you'll need to make a couple of changes. First, change

```
<Location />
Order Deny,Allow
Deny From All
Allow From 127.0.0.1
</Location>
```

to

```
<Location />
Order Deny,Allow
Deny From All
Allow From 127.0.0.1
Allow From netaddress
</Location>
```

Replace *netaddress* with the IP address of the network from which you want to accept jobs (e.g., 192.168.0.0). Then look for the `BrowseAddress` keyword and set it to the broadcast address on that network plus the CUPS port; for example,

```
BrowseAddress 192.168.0.255:631
```

These steps tell the server to accept requests from any machine on the designated subnet and to broadcast what it knows about the printers it's serving to every CUPS daemon on that network. That's it! Once you restart **cupsd**, it comes back as a server.

Printer autoconfiguration

You can use CUPS without a printer (for example, to convert files to PDF or fax format), but its typical role is to manage real printers. In this section we review the ways in which you can deal with the printers themselves.

In some cases, adding a printer is trivial. CUPS tries to autodetect USB printers when they're plugged into the system and figure out what to do with them.

Printer manufacturers typically supply installation software that does most of the setup work for you on Windows and even Mac OS X (which also uses CUPS). However, few vendors explicitly support Linux.

Even if you have to do some configuration work yourself, adding a printer is often no more painful than plugging in the hardware, connecting to the CUPS web interface at localhost:631/admin, and answering a few questions. KDE and GNOME come with their own printer configuration widgets, which you may prefer to the CUPS interface. (We like the CUPS GUI.)

If someone else adds a printer and one or more CUPS servers running on the network know about it, your CUPS server will learn of its existence. You don't have to explicitly add the printer to the local inventory or copy PPDs to your machine. It's magic.

Network printer configuration

Network printers—that is, printers whose primary hardware interface is an Ethernet jack—need some configuration of their own just to be proper citizens of the TCP/IP network. In particular, they need to know their own IP addresses and netmasks. That information is usually conveyed to them in one of two ways.

Modern printers can get this information across the network from a BOOTP or DHCP server, and this method works well in environments that have many such printers. See *DHCP: the Dynamic Host Configuration Protocol* on page 469 for more information about DHCP.

Alternatively, you can assign the printer a static IP address from its console, which usually consists of a set of buttons on the printer's front panel and a one-line display. Fumble around with the menus until you discover where to set the IP address. (If there is a menu option to print the menus, use it and put the printed version underneath the printer for future reference.)

A few printers give you access to a virtual console through a serial port. It's a nice idea, but the total amount of work is probably more than suffering through the front-panel interface. The principles are the same.

Once configured, network printers usually have a web console accessible from a browser. However, printers need to have an IP address and be up and running on the network before you can get to them this way, so this interface is unavailable just when you might want it most.

After your printer is on the network and you can ping it, make sure to secure it as described in the section *Secure your printers* on page 1081.

Printer configuration examples

Let's add the parallel printer groucho and the network printer fezmo from the command line.

```
$ sudo lpadmin -p groucho -E -v parallel:/dev/lp0 -m pxlcolor.ppd
$ sudo lpadmin -p fezmo -E -v socket://192.168.0.12 -m laserjet.ppd
```

Groucho is attached to port **/dev/lp0** and fezmo is at IP address 192.168.0.12. We specify each device in the form of a universal resource indicator (URI) and choose an appropriate PPD from the ones in **/usr/share/cups/model**.

As long as **cupsd** has been configured as a network server, it immediately makes the new printers available to other clients on the network. No restart is required.

CUPS accepts a wide variety of URIs for printers. Here are a few more examples:

- ipp://zoe.canary.com/ipp
- lpd://riley.canary.com/ps
- serial://dev/ttyS0?baud=9600+parity=even+bits=7
- socket://gillian.canary.com:9100
- usb://XEROX/Phaser%206120?serial=YGG210547

Some types take options (e.g., serial) and others don't. **lpinfo -v** lists the devices your system can see and the types of URIs that CUPS understands.

Printer class setup

A "class" is a set of printers that share a queue. Jobs in the queue print on whichever printer becomes available first. The commands below create the class haemer and adds three printers to it: riley, gilly, and zoe.

```
$ sudo lpadmin -p riley -c haemer
$ sudo lpadmin -p gilly -c haemer
$ sudo lpadmin -p zoe -c haemer
```

Note that there is no explicit step to create the class; the class exists as long as printers are assigned to it. In fact, CUPS is even smarter than that: if multiple printers on a network are all given the same name, CUPS treats them as an implicit class and load-shares jobs among them. Unless all the printers are located in the same room, this may not be the behavior you want.

Service shutoff

If you want to remove a printer or class, that's easily done with **lpadmin -x**.

```
$ sudo lpadmin -x fezmo
$ sudo lpadmin -x haemer
```

OK Mr. Smarty Pants, but what if you just want to disable a printer temporarily for service instead of removing it? You can block the print queue at either end. If you disable the tail (the exit or printer side) of the queue, users can still submit jobs, but the jobs will never print. If you disable the head (the entrance) of the queue, jobs that are already in the queue can still print, but the queue rejects attempts to submit new jobs.

The **cupsdisable** and **cupsenable** commands control the exit side of the queue, and the **reject** and **accept** commands control the submission side.[1] For example,

```
$ sudo cupsdisable groucho
$ sudo reject corbet
```

Which to use? It's a bad idea to accept print jobs that have no hope of being printed in the foreseeable future, so use **reject** for extended downtime. For brief interruptions that should be invisible to users (e.g., changing a toner cartridge), use **cupsdisable**.

Administrators occasionally ask for a mnemonic to help them remember which commands control which end of the queue. Consider: if CUPS "rejects" a job, that means you can't "inject" it. Another way to keep the commands straight is to remember that accepting and rejecting are things you can do to print *jobs*, whereas disabling and enabling are things you can do to *printers*. It doesn't make any sense to "accept" a printer or queue.

CUPS itself sometimes temporarily disables a printer that it's having trouble with (e.g., if someone has dislodged a cable). Once you fix the problem, remember to re-**cupsenable** the queue. If you forget, **lpstat** will tell you. (For a complete discussion of this issue and an alternative approach, see linuxprinting.org/beh.html.)

Other configuration tasks

Today's printers are infinitely configurable, and CUPS lets you tweak a wide variety of features through its web interface and through the **lpadmin** and **lpoptions** commands. As a rule of thumb, **lpadmin** is for system-wide tasks and **lpoptions** is for per-user tasks.

lpadmin can restrict access to printers and queues. For example, you can set up printing quotas and specify which users can print to which printers.

Table 26.1 lists the commands that come with CUPS and classifies them according to their origin.

1. Older versions of CUPS use **enable** and **disable** instead of **cupsenable** and **cupsdisable**. Unfortunately, **enable** is also a **bash** built-in command, so **bash** assumes you mean its own **enable** unless you specify the full pathname of the command. As it happens, **bash**'s version of **enable** enables and disables **bash** built-ins, so you can use it to disable itself with **enable -n enable**.

Table 26.1 CUPS's command-line utilities and their origins

	Command	Function
CUPS	**cups-config**[a]	Prints API, compiler, directory, and link information
	cupsdconf[a]	Configures CUPS through a KDE interface
	cupsdisable[b]	Stops printing on a printer or class
	cupsenable[b]	Restarts printing on a printer or class
	lpinfo	Shows available devices or drivers
	lpoptions	Displays or sets printer options and defaults
	lppasswd	Adds, changes, or deletes digest passwords
System V	**accept**, **reject**	Accepts or rejects queue submissions
	cancel	Cancels print jobs
	lp	Enqueues jobs for printing
	lpadmin	Configures printers and classes
	lpmove	Moves an existing print job to a new destination
	lpstat	Prints status information
BSD	**lpc**	Acts as a general printer-control program
	lpq	Displays print queues
	lpr	Enqueues jobs for printing
	lprm	Cancels print jobs

a. Don't confuse these tools. **cups-config** is a command-line tool that's included with CUPS, and **cupsdconf** is a GUI tool in KDEPrint.

b. These are actually just the **disable** and **enable** commands from System V, renamed.

26.3 Printing from desktop environments

We've mentioned already that we encourage the use of the native CUPS GUI for administration rather than the use of add-ons such as those designed for KDE. The native GUI is authoritative and also happens to be pretty good.

Another point to consider is portability. You may already be struggling with three different families of printing systems—why add to the confusion by struggling with several different administrative GUIs, too? If your CEO wants to print from his brand-new Macintosh, you may not know where to click to get to the latest Apple-designed GUI configuration widgets. But if you browse to localhost:631, you'll find yourself in familiar territory.

Still, if all your users are on a particular desktop environment, you may decide to use that desktop's GUI to support them. As an example, consider KDEPrint, the overarching framework for printing under KDE.

KDEPrint provides its own tools for adding printers, administering print jobs, restarting print servers, and so on. Like other KDE tools, it has a KDE look and feel, affording consistency for KDE users. (You've probably noticed that even KDE utility names have a distinctive look and feel. Someone once asked us if **ksh** was a KDE application.)

KDEPrint is not tied to CUPS. Although it can handle all of CUPS's features, it can be configured to work with everything from LPRng to a generic external program. If for some reason you can't run CUPS (or worse, you have to switch back and forth between print systems), you can still use KDEPrint to manage printing. Be forewarned that CUPS is more capable than other printing systems, so if you have to downshift to an alternative printing system, some of KDEPrint's functionality may disappear.

Here are the major components of KDEPrint that you should know about:

- **kprinter**, a GUI tool that submits print jobs
- The Add Printer wizard, which autodetects network printers (JetDirect, IPP, and SMB) and some locally connected printers. The Add Printer wizard also lets you add and configure printers that it doesn't autodetect.
- The Print Job Viewer, which moves and cancels print jobs and shows print job status information
- The *KDEPrint Handbook*, which documents the system. It's available through the KDE Help Center but can be annoyingly hard to find. An easier route is to invoke something like **kprinter** and click on Help. Another alternative is to use the KDE browser, **konqueror**, by running **konqueror help:/kdeprint**. KDEPrint documentation can also be found at printing.kde.org.
- The Print Manager, which is the main GUI management tool for the printing system. It, too, can be a bit hard to find. You can poke around in your main desktop menu, although the location in the menu tree varies from distribution to distribution. Another option is to run **kcmshell printmgr** or **konqueror print:/manager**.

The Add Printer wizard and the Print Job Manager are accessible through either **kprinter** or the KDE Print Manager, not to mention the URLs print:/manager and print:/printers in Konqueror.

Per-user information for KDEPrint is stored under **~/.kde**. The files are human readable but designed to be changed through the Print Manager. Tinker with them at your peril.

kprinter: print documents

kprinter is a GUI replacement for **lpr**. It can be used from the command line without a GUI. For example, the command

```
$ kprinter --nodialog -5 -P lj4600 riley.ps gillian.pdf zoe.prn
```

is equivalent to

```
$ lpr -5 -P lj4600 riley.ps gillian.pdf zoe.prn
```

Your users probably don't care; they want a GUI. Show them how to drag files from the file manager or desktop into the **kprinter** dialog, then print the entire batch. Replace **lpr** with **kprinter** in their browser's Print dialog, and they'll have a GUI print dialog. Teach them to click on their "Keep this dialog open after printing" check box, and they won't experience a restart delay every time they print.

Take note of the "Print system currently in use" menu, evidence of KDEPrint's system neutrality. Note also that **kprinter** offers print-to-PDF and print-to-fax functions even if your network has no actual printers. The advanced options are also worth a look; you can queue your résumé for printing and specify that it be printed after your boss goes home.

Konqueror and printing

Many web browsers recognize a set of special-purpose URIs that act as gateways to idiosyncratic functionality. You've probably at least tried about:config and about:mozilla in Firefox. Similarly, the print: family of URIs is Konqueror's secret gateway to the world of KDEPrint.

The print:/ URL shows you all the possibilities. print:/jobs monitors print jobs, and print:/manager starts the Print Manager inside of Konqueror.

Even though you're not dealing directly with CUPS here, what makes all this relatively easy is the underlying fact that CUPS is a web server. Browsers know how to talk to web servers, so it's relatively easy to tweak them to add CUPS-specific printing features.

26.4 SYSTEM V PRINTING

System V's printing software is the oldest and most primitive of the printing systems we cover—so old that it wasn't designed with network printing in mind. Most vendors that use it have made numerous changes. As usual with vendor-specific software maintenance, some modifications have added useful functionality while others seem gratuitous.

Among our example systems, Solaris and HP-UX use the System V software. Both have modified it significantly. Below, we discuss the standard system, but with many vendor-specific notes.

Overview

A user who wants to print something must either use the **lp** command or a command that invokes **lp** indirectly. **lp** puts data into the spool directory associated with its destination. The **lpsched** daemon determines when and where the data should be printed, then executes an interface program that formats the data and sends it to the correct printer. Table 26.2 on the next page lists the commands in the System V printing system.

Table 26.2 System V printing commands

	Cmd	Location	Function
General	**accept**	**/usr/sbin**	Turns on acceptance of jobs into a queue
	cancel	**/bin**	Removes print jobs from a queue
	disable	**/bin**	Disables printing of jobs from a queue
	enable	**/bin**	Enables printing of jobs from a queue
	lp	**/bin**	Queues jobs for printing
	lpadmin	**/usr/sbin**	Configures the printing system
	lpmove	**/usr/sbin**	Moves jobs between queues
	lpsched	**/usr/lib**	Schedules and prints jobs
	lpshut	**/usr/sbin**	Stops printing services
	lpstat	**/bin**	Reports the status of printing services
	reject	**/usr/sbin**	Stops acceptance of jobs into a queue
Solaris	**lpfilter**	**/usr/sbin**	Controls print filters
	lpforms	**/usr/sbin**	Controls the use of preprinted forms
	lpget	**/bin**	Reads configuration settings
	lpset	**/bin**	Modifies configuration settings
	lpusers	**/usr/sbin**	Controls queue priorities
HP-UX	**lpalt**	**/bin**	Modifies jobs in a queue
	lpana	**/usr/sbin**	Analyzes performance logs
	lpfence	**/usr/sbin**	Sets the minimum job priority for a printer
	lpr	**/bin**	Supports BSD printing

Destinations and classes

Each printing "destination" has a name that consists of up to 14 alphanumeric characters and underscores. A destination is usually a printer, but it doesn't have to be. For example, a destination could be a file to which many users may need to append text. Because printing systems are queuing systems, you could use **lp** to avoid a situation in which two people attempt to add to the file at the same time.

Every destination belongs to zero or more classes. A class is a group of destinations that all serve the same purpose in some way, For example, if a site has two printers in the same room, they might be combined into a class. Likewise, two printers with similar features (such as color, resolution, duplex, or speed) might be grouped into a class. **lpsched** would direct output submitted to that class to whichever printer became available first. Class names have the same restrictions as destination names.

For better or worse, you'll see "destination" used to mean "printer or class," and "printer" and "destination" used interchangeably. You should be able to tell from context which meaning is intended.

A brief description of lp

lp is a user-level command that enqueues data for printing. **lp** copies the submitted data (which can come either from named files or from **lp**'s standard input) into a file or set of files in the spool directory. Under HP-UX, the spool directory for a destination is **/var/spool/lp/request/***dest* where *dest* is the name by which **lp** knows the printer or class of printers. Solaris uses the gratuitously different, pluralized version, **/var/spool/lp/requests/***dest*.

Spool files are named *xxxn*, where *n* is a job identification number assigned by **lp** and *xxx* varies from system to system. This filename identifies the job both to the user and internally to the printing system. We refer to this name as the job identification, or jobid for short.

lp -d queues the input for output to a specific destination (either a printer or a class). Without the **-d** option, **lp** uses the contents of the LPDEST environment variable as the name of the output destination. If this environment variable is not set, **lp** queues the data for output to the default destination, which the system administrator can set with **lpadmin -d**.

In Solaris, if no default device has been specified with **lpadmin -d**, then **lp** searches the ~**/.printers** file, the **/etc/printers.conf** file, and finally, the Federated Naming Service for a default destination.

lpsched and lpshut: start and stop printing

The **lpsched** daemon sends files placed in the spool directory by **lp** to an appropriate device as soon as one is available. **lpsched** keeps a log of each file it processes and of any errors that occur.

In Solaris, the default log file is **/var/lp/logs/lpsched**. HP-UX keeps the log file in **/var/adm/lp/log**; when **lpsched** starts (normally at boot time), it moves the old log aside to **oldlog** and starts a new one.

A log file looks something like this:

```
***** LP LOG: Jul 6 12:05 *****
pr1-107    garth    pr1    Jul 6    12:10
pr-112     scott    pr1    Jul 6    12:22
pr-117     evi      pr2    Jul 6    12:22
pr1-118    garth    pr1    Jul 6    12:25
pr1-119    garth    pr1    Jul 6    13:38
pr-132     evi      pr1    Jul 6    13:42
```

The first column is the jobid of each job. The second column is the user who requested the job. The third column is the actual printer the job was sent to, and the last column is the time at which the job was queued.

The HP-UX system in this example lists two printers: pr1 and pr2, both of which are in the class pr. The user garth always specified the specific printer pr1, so that's where his jobs were always sent. The users scott and evi, on the other hand, specified the class pr, so their jobs were sent to the first available printer in that class.

To stop **lpsched** for any reason, run **lpshut** as root or as the user lp. When **lpsched** is not running, no jobs will actually be printed, although **lp** can still queue jobs for printing. Jobs that are being printed when the daemon is stopped will be reprinted in their entirety when the daemon is restarted.

lpsched creates the file **/var/spool/lp/SCHEDLOCK** to indicate that it is running. If you try to start another copy of **lpsched**, it notices that this file exists and refuses to run. If you stop **lpsched** by any means other than **lpshut**, you must remove the **SCHEDLOCK** file by hand before you can restart **lpsched**.

lpadmin: configure the printing environment

The **lpadmin** command tells the printing system about your printer configuration. It names printers, creates classes, and specifies the default printer. All the **lpadmin** command really does is create and modify a collection of text files that are found in the **/var/spool/lp** directory.

Despite the fact that you can read these configuration files, they are a good place to practice the old adage "look but don't touch"; the files are format-sensitive and break easily.

Solaris's **lpadmin** tries to use a BSD-like printer description file to make the system easier to configure. But in fact, it ends up just spreading the configuration information out into two additional locations: **/etc/printers.conf** and **/etc/lp**.

Solaris wants **lpsched** to be running during most administrative commands. On the other hand, most HP-UX **lpadmin** commands do not work when **lpsched** is running, so **lpsched** must be stopped with **lpshut** before you try to use **lpadmin**. (Perhaps these vendors are reluctant to move to CUPS because it would be the same on all systems and would deprive the world of richness and diversity?)

Before the printing system can send jobs to a particular printer, you must tell it that the printer exists. To add a new printer, execute

```
$ sudo lpadmin -pprinter -vdevice { -eprinter | -mmodel | -iinterface }
      [ -cclass - ] [ -l | -h ]
```

where *printer* is the name of the new printer (both internally in the queuing system and at the level of user commands) and *device* is the device file with which the printer is associated. The *device* is usually a special file underneath the **/dev** directory, but it can be any file.

The flags **-e**, **-m**, or **-i** tell the queuing system which printer interface program to use. The interface program is responsible for actually formatting jobs before they are sent to the printer. System V interface programs are analogous to CUPS filters. See the section *Filters* on page 1037 for more details.

A printer's interface program can be specified in three ways:

- -e*printer* – in this case, *printer* is the name of an existing printer. This method of specifying the interface program is useful if you're adding a printer that is exactly like an existing one. **lpadmin** makes a copy of the interface program under the new destination's name.
- -**m***model* – with this option, *model* is a type of device for which your system has a standard interface program. To determine which models your system supports, look in **/var/spool/lp/model**. When you use this form, **lpadmin** makes a copy of the file **/var/spool/lp/model/***model* to be used exclusively by the new destination.
- -**i***interface* – with the **-i** option, *interface* is the full pathname of a program to be used as the interface script. Most versions of **lpadmin** make a copy of the interface program, so if you want to change the program after you have run **lpadmin**, you must change the destination-specific copy and not your original.

HP-UX lets you specify programs that return status information and cancel printer jobs. These programs are specified like interface scripts, but different option prefixes are used (**-ocm** and **-osm** for cancel and status scripts, respectively).

lpadmin also accepts the following additional options:

- -**p***printer* tells **lpadmin** which printer or printers you are referring to. Combine this flag with other options to modify a printer.
- -**c***class* specifies the name of a *class* in which the printer should be included. Any number of classes can be specified for a given printer. If you specify a nonexistent class, it is created. The class name is limited to 14 characters.
- -**x***printer* removes printer from the print system. If *printer* is the only member of a class, then that class is also removed. Neither a printer nor a class can be removed if it has jobs queued for output. If queued jobs are keeping you from removing a printer, use the **reject** command to stop new jobs from being spooled and use the **lpmove** or **cancel** command to clear the existing jobs. If **lpadmin -x** still won't remove the printer, follow the advice on page 1053.
- -**r***class* removes a printer from *class*. The **-r** flag does not remove the printer; it just removes it from the class. If the specified printer is the only member of the class, the class itself is removed.

lp does not accept requests for a new printer until told to do so by **accept**.

System V printing commands often accept a quoted, comma-separated list of destinations in place of a single destination. For example, the command

```
$ sudo /usr/sbin/lpadmin -p"howler-lw,ralphie-lw" -ceng-printers
```

adds the printers howler-lw and ralphie-lw to the eng-printers class. Table 26.3 summarizes the flags understood by **lpadmin**.

Table 26.3 lpadmin flags

Flag	Function
-p*printer*	Specifies the printer to which other options apply
-d*dest*	Makes *dest* the system's default printing destination
-x*dest*	Removes *dest* from the printing system
-c*class*	Adds the printer to *class*
-r*class*	Removes the printer from *class*
-e*dest*	Copies another printer's interface program
-i*interface*	Makes *interface* the interface program for the printer
-m*model*	Makes the printer use the interface program for *model*
-h	Signifies that the printer is hardwired
-v*file*	Specifies the full path of the printer device file
-D"*desc*"	Sets the printer description string to *desc*
-L"*location*"	Sets a textual description of where a printer lives

lpadmin examples

The following examples show various uses of **lpadmin**.

```
$ sudo lpadmin -phowler-lw -v/dev/tty06 -mPostScript -cpr
```

This command tells the printing system that a printer to be called howler-lw is connected to **/dev/tty06**, that the printer should be in the class pr, and that the interface program for PostScript printers should be used. **lpadmin** takes care of creating the spool directory for you.

The command

```
$ sudo lpadmin -dpr
```

sets the system's default destination to class (or printer) pr, and the command

```
$ sudo lpadmin -phowler-lw -L"Conference room"
```

sets the description string for howler-lw.

```
$ sudo lpadmin -phowler-lw -rpr -cfast
```

removes howler-lw from class pr and adds it to class fast;

```
$ sudo lpadmin -xhowler-lw
```

removes howler-lw completely.

lpstat: get status information

lpstat shows the status of the printing system. If executed without any arguments, it gives the status of all jobs that belong to the user who executed it. With a **-p** flag, **lpstat** gives information about the status of a particular printer. For example,

```
$ lpstat -phowler-lw
howler-lw is now printing pr-125. enabled since Jul 4 12:25
```

shows the status of printer howler-lw. To determine the status of the **lpsched** daemon, run **lpstat -r**. For example,

```
$ lpstat -r
scheduler is running
```

shows that everything is OK. Table 26.4 lists the flags understood by **lpstat**.

Table 26.4 lpstat flags

Flag	Function
-r	Shows the status of the **lpsched** daemon
-d	Shows the default destination
-c*class*	Lists the members of *class*
-o*arg*	Shows the status of output requests for *arg*
-u*user*	Shows the status of jobs submitted by *user*
-p*printer*	Shows the status of *printer*
-v*printer*	Lists the output device associated with *printer*
-a*dest*	Shows the acceptance status of *dest*
-s	Shows a summary of status information
-t	Shows all status information

cancel: remove print jobs

cancel removes from the queue jobs that are queued or being printed. You can invoke **cancel** with either a job number (determined with **lpstat**) or with a printer name. If you specify a printer, then the job currently being printed is canceled.

See page 153 for more information about setuid execution.

The **cancel** command is usually owned by the pseudo-user lp with group bin and mode 6775 so that anyone can use it to cancel jobs that are obviously bogus. If someone who did not send a job cancels it, mail is sent to the job's owner. If users abuse this privilege, set the mode of the command so that it does not run setuid.

accept and reject: control spooling

If a printer will be unavailable for a long time (for example, because of a hardware failure), spooling to that device should be disabled so that users who are unaware of the situation do not fill the queue. Disable spooling with the **reject** command. For example, the following command makes **lp** reject requests on howler-lw:

```
$ sudo reject -r"howler-lw will be down until Tuesday" howler-lw
```

The **-r** flag is optional, but it is a nice way to tell users why the printer is rejecting requests. When someone tries to print a file, **lp** displays your message:

```
$ lp -dhowler-lw myfile
lp: cannot accept requests for destination "howler-lw"
  -- howler-lw will be down until Tuesday
```

accept *printer* tells **lp** to begin accepting requests for *printer*. You must run **accept** once for each new printer added with **lpadmin** because new printers are configured to reject requests by default. You can give **accept** and **reject** a class name instead of a printer name to enable or disable spooling for an entire class.

enable and disable: control printing

The **disable** command tells **lpsched** to stop sending jobs to a particular printer. Unlike **reject**, **disable** does not stop **lp** from queuing jobs for the printer. However, queued jobs will not be output until the printer is reenabled with **enable**. **disable** does not normally abort printing of the current job, but the **-c** option requests this behavior. Like **reject**, **disable** supports a **-r** flag that allows you to explain why a printer is disabled. For example, the command

```
$ sudo disable -r"Being cleaned, back in 5 minutes" howler-lw
```

disables printing on howler-lw. To restart printing, type:

```
$ sudo enable howler-lw
```

lpmove: transfer jobs

It's sometimes necessary to move jobs queued for one printer or class to another printer. You accomplish this feat with **lpmove**, which you run with a list of jobids and the name of a new printer. For example, the command

```
$ sudo lpmove howler-lw-324 howler-lw-325 anchor-lj
```

would move the jobs numbered 324 and 325 from the queue for howler-lw to the queue for anchor-lj. You can also give **lpmove** a printer or class as a source. For example, the command

```
$ sudo lpmove howler-lw anchor-lj
```

moves all jobs queued for howler-lw to the queue for anchor-lj. When **lpmove** is used in this way, it has the side effect of executing a **reject** on the printer of origin. In the preceding example, **lp** would no longer accept requests for howler-lw.

By design, the HP-UX version of **lpmove** cannot be used when **lpsched** is running. Run **lpshut** first.

Interface programs

An interface program takes information from a file that **lpsched** specifies, formats it, and sends the formatted data to its stdout. The interface program is also responsible for setting the correct modes on its output device and for generating headers and trailers if they are desired. Interface programs are usually shell scripts, but they can be executable binaries, too.

lpsched calls interface programs with the following arguments:

jobid user title copies options file …

where

- *jobid* is the job identification that is assigned by **lp**
- *user* is the user to whom the job belongs
- *title* is an optional title supplied by the user
- *copies* is the number of copies to print
- *options* are user-supplied options
- The *files* are full pathnames of files to be printed

All of the arguments are supplied each time the interface program is executed, but some of them may be null strings. The interface program gets its standard input from **/dev/null**, and both standard output and standard error are directed to the destination device as specified by **lpadmin -v**.

Unlike CUPS or the BSD printing system, which use different filters for different file formats, System V requires that interface programs handle all the kinds of data that the printer can accept. (They are also required to fail nicely if they receive unrecognizable input.) For this reason, interface programs are usually just shell scripts that process their arguments and call other programs to do the real work of formatting.

In essence, the interface script for a printer is responsible for the entire output stage of the printing system. Although the use of interface scripts makes customization easy, it also leads to different printers behaving in very different ways.

Interfaces are almost essential if you are planning on printing to anything other than a generic text or PostScript printer. Today, almost all printers use them. Inkjet printers absolutely require an interface to translate the print job to their format of choice.

An interface program should exit with a 0 on successful completion and with an integer in the range 1 to 127 if an error is encountered. If a job fails, the interface script should attempt to reprint it. If a serious error occurs, the interface program should **disable** (see page 1052) the printer. If you are having erratic printing problems, you can probably find the cause somewhere in the interface script.

What to do when the printing system is completely hosed

Sometimes, attempts to configure and unconfigure printers leave the system confused. The config files that hold printer information are complicated and neurotic—one stray character can leave a printer in an unusable state.

If you somehow create a printer that is confusing the system, the best solution is to remove the destination completely and start over. Sometimes, the system can be so confused that even removing the printer is hard.

The following brute-force technique will often rescue you from this sort of situation. Here, we try to remove the printer hoser. (Don't use this exact sequence unless your equivalent of hoser is a single printer and not a class.)

```
$ sudo lpshut
$ sudo lpadmin -xhoser
$ sudo find /usr/spool/lp -name hoser | xargs rm -rf    # remove queued jobs
$ sudo lpsched
$ sudo lpstat -t
```

The first two commands turn off the spooler and attempt to remove the printer according to the USDA-approved method. If the system is confused, **lpadmin -x** may fail. The **find** command removes all interface programs and spool directories for the printer. **lpsched** restarts the spooler, and **lpstat** should show you that there are no more references to hoser within the printing system.

26.5 BSD AND AIX PRINTING

We could have just called this section "AIX printing" because AIX is the only one of our example systems that still uses the BSD system. But we call the system by its traditional name because you may encounter it on other systems as well.

The BSD printing system was designed for use with old-fashioned line printers, but good design has let it scale to support many more modern printers and printer languages. The network portion of the BSD printing system also extends to large, heterogeneous networks and permits many computers to share printers. At one point, the BSD print spooler, **lpd**, became so widely accepted that it found its way into the firmware of some network printers.

An overview of the BSD printing architecture

Access to printers is controlled by the **lpd** daemon. **lpd** accepts print jobs from users or from other (remote) **lpd**s, processes them, and sends them on to an actual printer. To accomplish these steps, **lpd** reads printer configuration information from **/etc/printcap**, the system's printer information database.

Users invoke the **lpr** program to submit their print jobs to **lpd**. These two processes communicate through the UNIX domain socket **/dev/printer**.

To determine what printer to send a job to, **lpr** first looks at the command line. If you've supplied a **-P***printer* argument, *printer* becomes the destination. Otherwise, **lpr** checks the environment to see if the PRINTER variable is defined, and if so, **lpr** uses the variable's value. If all else fails, **lpr** submits the job to the system-wide default printer, which is the printer named "lp", or if there is no lp, to the first printer described in the **/etc/printcap** file. Almost all printing-related commands, including **lpq** and **lprm**, understand the PRINTER environment variable and the **-P** argument.

As soon as **lpr** knows where the current job is headed, it looks up the printer in **/etc/printcap**. The **printcap** file tells **lpr** where to put print jobs bound for that printer. This spool directory is often **/var/spool/lpd/***printername*.

lpr creates two files in the spool directory for each job. The first file's name consists of the letters **cf** (control file) followed by a number that identifies the job. This file contains reference and handling information for the job, such as the identity of the user who submitted it. The numeric portion of the filename allows space for only three digits, so the printing system becomes confused if more than 999 jobs are queued. The second file's name begins with **df** (data file) followed by the same number. This file contains the actual data to be printed. After the file has been spooled, **lpr** notifies the **lpd** daemon of the job's existence.

When **lpd** receives this notification, it consults the **printcap** file to determine whether the destination is local or remote. If the printer is connected locally, **lpd** checks to be sure a printing daemon is running on the appropriate printer's queue and creates one (by forking a copy of itself) if necessary.

If the requested printer is connected to a different machine, **lpd** opens a connection to the remote machine's **lpd** and transfers both the data and the control file. **lpd** then deletes the local copies of these files.

Scheduling for print jobs is done on a first-in, first-out basis, but the system administrator can modify the printing agenda by using **lpc** on individual jobs. Unfortunately, there is no way to permanently instruct the printing system to give preferential treatment to jobs spooled by a particular user or machine.

When the job is ready to print, **lpd** creates a series of UNIX pipes between the spool file and the printing hardware through which the data to be printed is transported. In the middle of this channel, **lpd** installs a filter process that can review and edit the contents of the data stream before it reaches the printer.

Filter processes can perform various transformations on the data or do nothing at all. Their chief purposes are to provide formatting and to support any device-specific protocols that may be required for dealing with a particular printer. A printer's default filter is specified in **/etc/printcap**, but the default filter can be overridden on the **lpr** command line.

Printing environment control

For day-to-day maintenance of the printing system, you need only three commands: **lpq**, **lprm**, and **lpc**. **lpq** shows you the queue of jobs waiting to be printed on a particular printer. **lprm** deletes jobs. Both of these commands are available to users, and both work across a network (if you're lucky), though only the superuser can remove someone else's job.

lpc lets you make a number of changes to the printing environment, such as disabling printers and reordering print queues. Although some of its functions are available to users, **lpc** is primarily an administrative tool. Table 26.5 summarizes the commands and daemons associated with the BSD printing system.

Table 26.5 BSD printing commands

Cmd	Location	Function
lpc	**/usr/sbin**	Controls a printer or queue
lpd	**/usr/sbin**	Schedules and prints jobs
lpq	**/usr/bin**	Shows print queue contents and status
lpr	**/usr/bin**	Queues jobs for printing
lprm	**/usr/bin**	Cancels a queued or printing job
lptest	**/usr/bin**	Generates an ASCII test pattern

lpd: spool print jobs

If you start **lpd** with the **-l** flag, it logs print requests through syslog under the "lpr" facility. Without the **-l** flag, **lpd** logs only errors.

Access control is at the granularity of hosts; the BSD printing system does not support access control for specific remote users. Only hosts whose names appear in the files **/etc/hosts.equiv** or **/etc/hosts.lpd** are allowed to spool print jobs. Because of security issues, the use of **hosts.equiv** is deprecated; use **hosts.lpd**.

lpr: submit print jobs

lpr is the only program on a BSD-style system that can queue files for printing. Other programs that cause files to be printed (for example, **enscript** or a browser) must do so by calling **lpr**.

The -#*num* flag prints *num* copies, and the **-h** flag suppresses the header page. For example, to print two copies of a file named **thesis** to a printer called howler-lw, just run

```
$ lpr -Phowler-lw -#2 thesis
```

lpq: view the printing queue

lpq is normally used with just a **-P** option to select a printer, although the **-l** flag is available to produce more detailed output. Output from **lpq** looks like this:

```
$ lpq
anchor-lj is ready and printing
Rank    Owner    Job   Files             Total Size
active  garth    314   domain.2x1.ps     298778 bytes
1st     kingery  286   standard input    17691 bytes
2nd     evi      12    appendices        828 bytes
...
```

The output lines are always in order, with the active job on top and the last job to be printed on the bottom. If the first job is listed as `1st` rather than `active`, no printing daemon is running on the printer, and you'll need to restart it.

The second column names the user who spooled each job, and the third column gives the job's identification number; this number is important to know if you intend to manipulate the job later with **lprm** or **lpc**. The fourth column shows the filenames that were listed on the **lpr** command line that spooled the job. If the data came in through a pipe, the entry in this column is `standard input`. The job size unfortunately gives no information about how many pages a job will produce or how long it will take to print.

lprm: remove print jobs

The most common form of **lprm** is **lprm** *jobid*, where *jobid* is the job identification number reported by **lpq**. **lprm** *user* removes all jobs belonging to *user*. **lprm** without arguments removes the active job. **lprm** - (that's a hyphen) removes all the jobs you submitted; if you are root, it removes every job in the queue. Ordinary users can't remove each other's jobs, but the superuser can remove any job.

Perversely, **lprm** fails silently but produces output on success. If you don't see output that looks like this

```
dfA621xinet dequeued
cfA621xinet dequeued
```

after running **lprm**, it means the command failed. Either **lprm** couldn't remove the job, or you invoked the command incorrectly.

The printing system records the host on which a job originated as well as the user who spooled it, and **lprm**'s matching process takes both pieces of data into account. Thus garth@sigi is not equivalent to garth@boulder, and neither can remove the other's jobs.

Trying to **lprm** the active job can cause problems on some printers. The filter process for the job may not be properly notified of the termination, with the result that the whole system comes to a grinding halt with the filter process holding an exclusive lock on the port and preventing other processes from using the printer.

The only way to fix this situation is to use **ps** to identify the filter processes and to kill them off by hand. **lpc** is useless in this situation. Rebooting the system always cures a hung printer, but this is a drastic measure. Before you resort to a reboot, kill and restart the master copy of **lpd** and manually remove jobs from the spool directory with the **rm** command.

lpc: make administrative changes

The **lpc** command can perform the following functions:

- Enable or disable queuing for a particular printer
- Enable or disable printing on a particular printer

- Remove all jobs from a printer's queue
- Move a job to the top of a printer's queue
- Start, stop, or restart the **lpd** daemon
- Get printer status information

When the printing system is running smoothly, **lpc** works just fine. But as soon as a filter gets stuck or some other minor problem appears, **lpc** tends to wig out completely. And it lies: it sometimes claims to have fixed everything when in reality, it has done nothing at all. You may have to fix things up by hand or even power-cycle your equipment when BSD printing gets badly snarled.

lpc cannot be used across a network, so you must log in to the machine that owns the printer you want to manipulate. **lpc** is normally used interactively, although you can also invoke it in a one-shot mode by putting one of the interactive commands on **lpc**'s command line. Once you have activated **lpc**, the various commands described below are available:

help [*command*]

help without arguments shows you a short list of all available **lpc** commands. With an argument, it shows a one-line description of a particular command.

enable *printer*
disable *printer*

These commands enable or disable spooling of jobs to the named printer. Users who attempt to queue files are politely informed that spooling has been disabled. Jobs that are already in the queue are not affected.

start *printer*
stop *printer*

start enables and **stop** disables printing on the named printer. Print jobs can still be spooled when a printer has been stopped, but they will not be printed until printing is restarted. **start** and **stop** operate by setting or clearing owner execute permission on **/var/spool/lpd/***printer***/lock**. They also start and kill the appropriate daemons for the printer. **stop** allows the active job to complete before disabling printing.

abort *printer*

abort is just like **stop**, but it doesn't allow the active job to complete. When printing is reenabled, the job will be reprinted.

down *printer message*
up *printer*

These commands affect both spooling and printing. Use them when a printer is really broken or has to be taken off-line for an extended period. The *message* parameter supplied to **down** can be as long as you like (on one line) and need not be quoted; it will be put in the printer's **/var/spool/lpd/***printer***/status** file and shown to users who run **lpq**. You'll normally want to use this feature to register a short explanation of why the printer is unavailable and when it will be back in service. The **up** command reverses the effect of a down.

clean *printer*

The **clean** command removes all queued jobs from the printer's queue but allows the current job to complete.

topq *printer jobid*
topq *printer username*

The first form of **topq** moves the specified job to the top of the printer's queue. The second form promotes all jobs belonging to *username.*

restart *printer*

The **restart** command restarts a printing daemon that has mysteriously died. You'll know that the daemon is dead when **lpq** tells you "no daemon present." Although you might think **restart** would have the same effect as a **stop** followed by a start, it does not; **restart** will not restart a printer that still has a filter running.

status *printer*

The **status** command shows you four things about a printer: whether spooling is enabled, whether printing is enabled, the number of entries in the queue, and the status of the daemon for that printer. If no entries are in the queue, you'll see something like this:

```
lpc> status cer
cer:
        queuing is enabled
        printing is enabled
        no entries
        no daemon present
```

The fact that no daemon is present is not a cause for concern; printer-specific daemons go away after the queue is empty and aren't restarted by the master copy of **lpd** until another job is spooled.

The /etc/printcap file

/etc/printcap is the BSD printing system's master database. It contains information necessary for printing to local and remote printers. A printer must be described in the **printcap** file before jobs can be submitted to it.

/etc/printcap uses the same format as **/etc/termcap** and **/etc/remote**. The first item in each entry is a list of names for the printer, separated by vertical bars. The names are followed by a number of configuration settings separated by colons. Configuration options are of the form *xx*, *xx=string*, or *xx#number*, where *xx* is the two-character name of a parameter and *string* and *number* are values to be assigned to it. When no value is assigned, the variable is Boolean and its presence indicates "true."

The null statement is acceptable, so you can place two colons side by side. It is helpful to begin and end each line with a colon to make subsequent modifications easier. Comments in **/etc/printcap** start with a pound sign (#). Entries can span several lines if intermediate lines are terminated with a backslash. Continuation lines are, by convention, indented.

The syntax of the **printcap** file is illustrated in the following example, which defines a remote printer attached to the machine anchor:

```
anchor-lj|cer|1-56|LaserJet 5M in lab:\
    :lp=/var/spool/lpd/anchor-lj/.null:\
    :sd=/var/spool/lpd/anchor-lj:\
    :lf=/var/adm/lpd-errs:\
    :rw:mx#0:rm=anchor:rp=anchor-lj:
```

From the first line, we can see that "anchor-lj", "cer", "1-56", and "LaserJet 5M in lab" are all equivalent names for the same printer. These names are the printer's given name, a well-known abbreviation, the room number of the printer's location, and a full description.

You can give your printers as many names as you like, but you should include at least three forms of the primary name:

- Full name – hostname and type of printer (e.g., "anchor-lj")
- Short name – three or four characters, easy to type (e.g., "cer")
- Descriptive name – other information (e.g., "LaserJet 5M in lab")

The next two lines in our example contain configuration settings for device name (lp), spool directory (sd), and error log file (lf). The last line specifies a read-write connection with the printer (rw), the maximum file size (mx, unlimited in this case), the remote machine name (rm), and the remote printer name (rp).

Jobs submitted to the printing system without a specific destination are routed to the first printer that has "lp" as one of its aliases. Don't use lp as a printer's primary name since that makes it difficult to change the default printer. If no printer has the name lp, the first printer in the **printcap** file is the system-wide default printer.

printcap variables

The flexibility of the **printcap** file is largely responsible for the BSD printing system's adaptability. The details are documented in the **printcap** man page, so we discuss only the most common variables here. They're shown in Table 26.6.

All **printcap** entries should include at least a specification of the spool directory (sd), the error log file (lf), and the printing device (lp). Modern printers should generally be opened for reading and writing (rw) so that the printer can send error and status messages back to the host.

Table 26.6 Commonly used printcap variables

Name	Type	Meaning	Example
sd	string	Spool directory	sd=/var/spool/lpd/howler-lw
lf	string	Error log file	lf=/var/log/lpr
lp	string	Device name	lp=/dev/lp0
rw	bool	Open device read/write	rw
af	string	Accounting file	af=/usr/adm/lpr.acct
mx	number	Maximum file size	mx#0
rm	string	Remote machine name	rm=beast.xor.com
rp	string	Remote printer name	rp=howler-lw
of	string	Output filter	of=/usr/libexec/lpr/lpf
if	string	Input filter	if=/usr/sbin/stylascii
sh	bool	Suppress headers	sh

sd: spool directory

Each printer should have its own spool directory. All spool directories should be in the same parent directory (usually **/var/spool/lpd**) and should have the same name as the full name of the printer they serve (anchor-lj in the preceding example). A spool directory is needed, even if the printer being described lives on a different machine, because spooled files are stored locally until they can be transmitted to the remote system for printing.

When you install a new printer, you must create its spool directory by hand. Permissions should be 775, with both owner and group daemon.

The spool directory for a printer also contains two status files: **status** and **lock**. The **status** file contains a one-line description of the printer's state. This information is maintained by **lpd** and viewed with the **lpq** command. The **lock** file prevents multiple invocations of **lpd** from becoming active on a single queue and holds information about the active job. The permissions on the **lock** file are manipulated by **lpc** to control spooling and printing on the printer.

lf: error log file

See Chapter 11 for more information about log files.

Errors generated by print filters are logged to the file named in this variable. One error log can be shared by all printers, and it can be placed anywhere you like. When a log entry is made, the name of the offending printer is included. Even remote printers should have log files, just in case of a communication problem with the remote machine.

Keep in mind that **lpd** sends error messages to syslog with facility lpr. Some filters send their error messages to syslog as well, leaving nothing in their **printcap**-specified log files. Check both of these locations when problems arise.

lp: device name

The device name for a printer must be specified if the printer is local. This name is usually the file in the **/dev** directory that represents the port to which the printer is attached.

lpd uses an advisory lock on the **lp** file to determine if the printer is in use. Even if the printer is really accessed through a network connection, you should provide a value for the lp variable. Specify a unique dummy file that was created for that purpose and that exists on a local disk.

rw: device open mode

If a printer can send status information back to the host through its device file, the Boolean variable rw should be specified to request that the device be opened for both reading and writing. Read-write mode is useful for accounting and status reporting, and some filters require it.

af: accounting file

You can enable accounting by simply specifying an accounting file on the machine to which the printer is physically connected. Accounting records are not written until a job is actually printed, so there is no point in specifying an accounting file in **printcap** entries for remote printers.

For a summary of accounting information, use the **pac** command. By convention, printer accounting data files are usually called **/var/adm/***printer***-acct**. They list the number of pages printed for each job (usually a lie), the hostnames on which the jobs originated, and the usernames of the jobs' owners.

It is the responsibility of the printer's input filter to generate accounting records. Unless the filter actually queries the printer for its page count before and after the job, the page counts are extremely suspect.

mx: file size limits

The mx variable limits the amount of data that can be spooled at one time. (If fed to the wrong language interpreter, PostScript or PCL files can print hundreds of pages of garbage.)

On some systems, mx defaults to some value other than 0 (no limit), and an explicit mx#0 entry is necessary to allow large jobs. Note that mx is a numeric field, so you need to say mx#0, not mx=0.

rm and rp: remote access information

In most situations, you will want to access a printer from more than one machine on the network. Even if the printer is a network device, you should pick a single machine to be responsible for communicating with it. All other machines should forward jobs to the designated handler. With this setup, you have **lpd** take care of queuing the jobs in order rather than having several machines constantly fighting over control of the printer. It also gives you a single place to look when printing is not working.

Remote machines (machines that are not directly connected to the printer) have a simple **printcap** entry that tells where to send the job, as in the example on page 1060. The rm variable specifies the machine to which jobs should be sent, and the rp variable gives the name of the printer on that machine.

The fact that **printcap** entries are different for local and remote printers necessitates a bit of subterfuge on the part of the system administrator if one printcap file is to be shared among several machines. The fix is to make the local and remote names for a printer distinct; for example, howler-lw-local and howler-lw. This configuration makes howler-lw a "remote" printer even on the machine where it actually lives, but that's perfectly OK. You must refer to howler-lw-local if you want to use the **lpc** command, however.

of, if: printing filters

Filters serve several purposes. The default printing filter (usually **/usr/lib/lpf**) fixes up various nonprinting sequences and writes out an accounting record if appropriate. Unfortunately, filters are not standardized. Any of several filter packages could do the same job, but each vendor tends to have unique filters.

If you have a laser or inkjet printer, or even an ancient typesetter or plotter, the necessary filters will usually have been provided with the printer's software. If you need to configure a printer for which you have no software, read through the details in the rest of this section. Otherwise, skip ahead; ignorance is bliss.

Filters are usually just shell scripts that call a series of translation programs. The filter program must accept the print job on standard input, translate the job to a format appropriate for the device, and send the result to standard output.

If the user does not specify a filter when executing **lpr**, either the if (input filter) or the of (output filter) is used. The names are deceptive—both actually send data to a printer.

If the **printcap** entry lists an input filter but does not specify an output filter, the device is opened once for each job. The filter is expected to send one job to the printer and then exit.

Conversely, if an output filter is specified without an input filter, **lpd** opens the device once and calls the filter program once, sending all the jobs in the queue in a big clump. This convention is OK for devices that take a long time to connect to; however, such devices are extremely rare.

If both an input filter and an output filter are specified, the banner page is sent to the output filter, and the output filter is called even if banners are turned off. The input filter is called to process the rest of the job. This combination of options is really too confusing for mere mortals. Avoid it.

If you have to write new filters, stick to using input filters, as they are easier to debug. Input filters are called with numerous arguments, which vary among implementations. The most interesting are the username, host of origin, and accounting file name. If you want to do accounting for the printer, the input filter must generate the accounting records and append them to the accounting file. If you want to restrict access to a printer (for example, to deny printing to the user "guest"), the input filter must also take care of that since **lpd** has no built-in way to prevent individual users from printing.

To clarify the uses of filters, let's look at a simple example of an input filter script. This example is for a PostScript printer connected to a local serial line.

```
#!/bin/bash
/usr/local/bin/textps $* | /usr/local/bin/psreverse
```

Because the printer is serially connected, **lpd** takes care of opening the device with the correct modes, as specified in the **printcap** file. The first program called is **textps**, which looks at the input and decides if it is PostScript (which our printer expects), and if not, converts it to PostScript. **textps** gets all the filter arguments that were passed (the $*) and is expected to generate accounting records from that information. The second program, **psreverse**, reverses the order of the pages so that they come out in a proper stack.

printcap variables for serial devices

Many **printcap** variables and features are involved in the handling of old-style serial printers. If you have to support one of these, one approach is to plan time for reviewing the manual pages and drinking heavily. If you don't drink, spend your department's alcohol budget on a new printer.

printcap extensions

A nice feature of the **lpr/lpd** system is that it does not mind if you supply values for nonstandard **printcap** variables. Often, when a particular printer needs more configuration information than the base system defines, you can put extra variables in **printcap** for the printer's filters to use.

For example, the output filter for a network printer might need to know the network name of the device. The printcap entry for the printer might contain an entry such as

```
:nn=laser.colorado.edu:\
```

The use of **printcap** extensions allows all of the configuration information for a printer to be stored in one convenient place. If you see variables in the **printcap** file that are not discussed in the **printcap** man page, check the documentation for the printer filters to determine the meanings of the variables.

Our site has taken advantage of this feature to document the physical location of each printer. Our printers have entries such as

```
:lo=Room 423, Engineering building:\
```

We have scripts that monitor paper and toner levels in the printers and send mail to support staff with instructions such as "Take more paper to room 423 in the Engineering building" when necessary.

26.6 WHAT A LONG, STRANGE TRIP IT'S BEEN

You can see from the previous sections how different the three major printing systems are from one another, why having vendors complete the migration from older systems to CUPS would be helpful, and why CUPS's decision to provide commands that mimic those of the older systems is a wise one.

How did things get this way? This section presents some historical background.

Printing history and the rise of print systems

Decades ago, the most common printers were ASCII line printers. Laser printers were expensive and rare. High-resolution output devices required custom driver software and formatting programs.

Today, instead of connecting to a single computer through a serial or parallel port, laser printers often connect to a TCP/IP network over an Ethernet, Wi-Fi, or Bluetooth link. Laser printers have lost the low-end market to inkjet printers. Color printers used to be a luxury, but like color photography and color monitors, they're now the norm. Finding a black-and-white printer will soon be as hard as finding a black-and-white television. Or any television, for that matter.

Special-purpose printers, scanners, copiers, and fax machines are being pushed aside by multifunction devices that do all these jobs. Some of these now read files directly from your digital camera's memory card.

Early printers were primitive, and so were their spoolers. The computer you were working on was assumed (correctly) to be connected directly to the printer. Printer configuration consisted of answering questions such as "Serial or parallel?" This was true for non-UNIX systems, too, though the non-UNIX systems were proprietary: IBM systems knew how to drive IBM printers, Apple computers knew how to drive Apple LaserWriters, and so on.

The earliest commercial UNIX application, sold by INTERACTIVE Systems Corporation, was a document production system for a law firm. The key pieces were a text editor, markup languages (**nroff/troff**), and printing software.

As the complexity of the world increased, several attempts were made to create unified standards for UNIX, but none of them succeeded. The printing protocols in use got older and creakier.

The BSD and System V printing systems were both developed for the line printers of yore. These systems, hacked and overloaded in an attempt to keep up with evolving technologies, were never really up to the job of supporting modern printers, and each new printer feature, such as duplexing (double-sided printing), required a lot of special-case hacks.

Why were there two competing printing systems, and was there any important difference between them? Stand up in the middle of a users' group meeting and yell, "Anyone who uses **vi** instead of **emacs** is an idiot!" Then come ask us again.

Network printing added another universe of complexity. Early network printing systems were idiosyncratic and used an assortment of protocols for printer-to-spooler communication, client-to-spooler communication, and network traffic negotiation.

HP's JetDirect printers often accepted raw data on port 9100, as did printers from other manufacturers that adopted HP's convention. Printers with internal **lpd** daemons (implementations of the BSD protocol) expected jobs on port 515.

Gritting its teeth, the IETF's Printer Working Group created the Internet Printing Protocol (IPP), which it built on top of HTTP. This choice structured interactions in terms of simple GET and POST requests and let printing take advantage of standard technologies for authentication, access control, and encryption.

Michael Sweet and Andrew Senft of Easy Software Products (ESP) brought IPP to UNIX in the form of the CUPS implementation. Apple adopted CUPS for Mac OS X (and, in 2007, bought the source code), and CUPS became the most complete implementation of IPP on the planet. CUPS is an open source project, fixes many older systems' problems, and is freely redistributable.

Printer diversity

In addition to diversity in print systems, administrators face diversity in the printers themselves.

Because printers can plug into computers, users tend to lump them in with peripherals such as mice and monitors. They're more complicated than that. They're really more like smartphones or routers, but with moving parts.

At one time, the most powerful computer Apple made was the Apple LaserWriter. Today, your desktop machine is probably more powerful than your printer, but the printer is still a computer. It has a CPU, memory, an operating system, and perhaps even a disk.

If it's a network printer, it has its own network stack and IP address. If you have a network printer around, enter its address (or DNS name) into your web browser. Chances are, the printer will serve up some web pages that let you administer the printer hardware: the printer is running its own web server.

(Since system administrators are security minded, you may already be thinking, "Does that mean a printer could be compromised or hit by a denial of service attack?" You bet. See the section on security that starts on page 1081.)

What operating system is your printer running? What?! You don't know? Not surprising. You probably can't find out, either, without some digging—and perhaps not even then. The operating system varies from vendor to vendor and sometimes even from model to model. Mid-range and higher-end printers may even run some derivative of UNIX or Linux.

Your printer may handle a variety of network protocols and accept jobs in any of several different printer-specific page-description and document-description languages. It may even understand and print common bitmap formats such as GIF, JPG, and TIFF.

Your printer may only print in black and white, or it may print in color. It may print pages at resolutions that range from 150 through 2400 dots per inch (dpi), or even at asymmetric resolutions such as 1200 x 600—1200dpi in one direction and 600 in the other.

If you're administering a larger facility, you may need to support several models of printers from several different manufacturers, each of which has different capabilities. This state of affairs means that the printing software on your computers must be prepared to communicate with diverse (and sometimes unknown) hardware through an array of protocols.

26.7 Common printing software

There's more to printing than just spooling and printing jobs. Even on a stock Ubuntu system (which uses CUPS), the command

```
$ man -k . | egrep -i 'ghostscript|cups|print(er|ing| *(job|queue|filter))'
```

lists well over a hundred printing-related man pages—and that's just a quick and dirty search. (Not everything you find will be printing-related. **apcupsd** is a daemon that talks to Universal Power Supplies made by APC, and even the **print** command has nothing to do with printing.) Several of these commands and tools are worth knowing about and work across all three of the printing systems covered in this book.

Both the BSD and System V print systems lack many of the format translation facilities that are needed to drive modern printers. So, most vendors that use these systems have at least one set of tools that sits on top of their printing system to provide the additional features. These tools are sometimes included in the OS, but more often they are extra-cost add-ons. Third-party and freely distributed packages are also in wide use.

pr is one of the oldest printing tools. It reformats text files for the printed page. It breaks its input into pagefuls of 66 lines, adds headers and footers, and can double-space text. It's perfect for minor massaging of text files on their way to the printer. (Why 66? Because that's how many lines fit on an old, green-and-white line printer page.)

Adobe's **enscript** command performs similar conversions with quite a few more bells and whistles. Its output is PostScript. GNU **enscript** is an open source version of this command that is backward compatible with Adobe's; however, GNU **enscript** offers a wealth of new features, including language-sensitive highlighting, support for various paper sizes, font downloading, and user-defined headers.

One of **enscript**'s main claims to fame was its implementation of 2-up printing. If you're not using CUPS, that feature can still be useful. If you *are* using CUPS, you don't need **enscript** for this; try **lpr -o number-up=2**.

At the high end of the complexity spectrum is Ghostscript, originally written by Exeter graduate L. Peter Deutsch so that he could print PostScript documents on inexpensive PCL printers. Today, Ghostscript interprets both PostScript and PDF. CUPS uses it as a filter, but Ghostscript can also create page images for the screen, either on its own or with help from front ends such as Evince, **gv**, GNOME Ghostview (**ggv**), or KDE's KGhostView.

Linux distributions all come with a free version of Ghostscript. If you need to install and build Ghostscript yourself, see ghostscript.com. A commercial version of Ghostscript with support is available from Artifex Software.

26.8 Printer languages

A print job is really a computer program written in a specialized programming language. These programming languages are known collectively as page description languages or PDLs. The language interpreters for these PDLs often run inside the printers themselves.

Pages encoded in a PDL can be much smaller and faster to transmit than the equivalent raw images. (Or, in some cases, bigger.) PDL descriptions can also be device independent and resolution independent.

PDLs you may encounter include PostScript, PCL5, PCL6 (also called PCL/XL or "pxl"), and PDF. Many printers can accept input in more than one language. We touch on each of these languages briefly in the sections below.

Printers have to interpret jobs written in these languages and transform them into some form of bitmap representation that makes sense to the actual imaging hardware. Therefore, printers contain language interpreters. Just as with C or Java, these languages exist in multiple versions, and the versions make a difference. Most PostScript printers understand PostScript Level 3, but if you send a Level 3 program to a printer that only understands Level 2, the printer may be confused.

Rasterizing a PDL description (or anything else, such as an image file) into a bitmap page image is called "raster image processing," and a program that performs such rasterization is called a RIP. "To rip" is sometimes used informally as a verb—this has nothing to do with CDs, DVDs, BitTorrent, or the DMCA.

It's possible to rip print jobs in your computer and view the images on your display. We discuss host-based interpreters that do this, such as Ghostscript, on page 1078. You could in theory use your computer to rip jobs for printing and ship the completed (and much larger) bitmaps off to be printed by a not-very-smart print device. In fact, this is the way that many Windows "GDI" printers work. The level of support for this mode of operation varies widely among systems.

PostScript

PostScript is still the most common PDL found on UNIX and Linux systems. It was invented at Adobe Systems, and many PostScript printers still use an interpreter licensed from Adobe. Almost all page layout programs can generate PostScript, and some work with PostScript exclusively.

PostScript is a full-fledged programming language. You can read most PostScript programs with a text editor or with **less**. The programs are full of parentheses, curly braces, and slashes, and often start with the characters `%!PS`. Although these starting characters are not required by the language itself, PostScript interpreters and other printing software often look for them when trying to recognize and classify print jobs.

PCL

PCL is Hewlett-Packard's Printer Control Language. It's understood by HP printers as well as many other brands; some printers speak only PCL. Unlike PostScript, which is a Turing-complete, generalized programming language, PCL just tells printers how to print pages. PCL jobs are binary, not human readable, and usually much shorter than the equivalent PostScript. Applications seldom generate PCL directly, but filters can convert PostScript to PCL.

PCL also varies more than PostScript. The differences are minor but annoying. Jobs that print correctly on a LaserJet 5si can print slightly wrong on a LaserJet 5500, and vice versa. It's not just this pair of models, either; every PCL printer has a custom PCL dialect with commands to exploit that printer's features.

For example, if you tell your computer you have a LaserJet 4500 when you actually have a LaserJet 4550, it may generate some PCL commands that the 4550 ignores or misinterprets. If you have a stored PCL print job—say, a blank purchase request form—and you replace the printer for which it was generated with something newer, you may have to regenerate the job.

Worse still, HP has defined two almost completely unrelated language families called PCL: PCL5 (PCL5C means color and PCL5E means black and white) and PCL6 (also called PCL/XL). Nowadays, it's normal for new HP printers to have language interpreters for both.

PDF

Adobe's Portable Document Format is produced by Adobe Acrobat and many other non-Adobe applications. OpenOffice, for example, prefers to export documents as PDF.

PDF documents are platform independent, and PDF is routinely used to exchange documents electronically for both on-line and off-line (printed) use. The final text of this book was delivered to the book printer as a PDF file.

PDF is a document description language, not just a page description language. It describes not only individual pages, but also the overall structure of a document: which pages belong to which chapters, which text columns flow to other text columns, and so on. It also accommodates a variety of multimedia, hypertext, and scripting features for on-screen use.

Some printers interpret PDF directly. If yours doesn't, a host of PDF viewers and translators (including Ghostview, **xpdf**, **kpdf**, Evince, and Acrobat Reader) can convert your PDF documents into something else (such as PostScript) that is more widely understood. Your print system may even hide the conversion requirement from you and automatically convert PDF documents before sending them to the printer.

XPS

Worth a mention, too, is Microsoft's XML Paper Specification, aka XPS, aka OpenXPS. XPS is not yet widely used even on Windows systems. UNIX and Linux support is currently scant, although Artifex already has an XPS interpreter. Linux distributions will undoubtedly start to support XPS if it becomes popular.

PJL

PJL, Hewlett-Packard's Printer Job Language, is not really a PDL. It's a metalanguage that describes printer jobs. We mention it here because you'll see it mentioned in printer descriptions. You'll also need to know about it if you're looking at the internals of print jobs to try to solve printing problems.

PJL is a job control language that specifies things such as a job's PDL, whether the job is duplex or simplex, what size paper to use, and so on. The PJL commands come at the start of the job, and the PJL statements all start with @PJL:

```
@PJL SET COPIES=3
@PJL COMMENT FOO BAR MUMBLE
@PJL SET DUPLEX=ON
@PJL SET PAGEPROTECT=OFF
@PJL ENTER LANGUAGE=PCL
```

Non-HP printers may understand (or deliberately ignore) PJL, but if you're having trouble printing something that contains PJL on a non-HP printer, try removing the PJL with a text editor and resubmitting the job.

Printer drivers and their handling of PDLs

What if a printer supports only a subset of the languages you need to process? If you download a PostScript file from the web and your printer only understands PCL5E, what do you do? If your printer doesn't interpret PDF directly, how do you print a PDF file?

One option is to convert the file by hand. Your boxes come with plenty of conversion utilities; there's almost always some way to turn what you have into something your printers can print. Browsers can transform HTML (or XHTML) pages into PostScript. OpenOffice can turn MS Word files into PDF. Ghostscript can turn PDF into PostScript and PostScript into almost anything, including PCL.

An easier approach is to let your printing system do the work for you. Some systems, such as CUPS, have some built-in knowledge about which conversions need to be done and can set up the conversions for you automatically.

If you need to determine what PDL a file uses and you can't tell from the filename (e.g., **foo.pdf**), the **file** command can tell you (unless the file starts with a chunk of PJL instructions, in which case **file** just says "HP Printer Job Language data").

Save a few print jobs to files instead of shipping them to a printer, and you can see what a program in one of these languages looks like. A minute or two perusing files of each of these types in your text editor will give you a good feel for how different they are. (Don't **cat** them directly to your screen, since only PostScript is ASCII. Random binary data tends to confuse terminal emulators.)

PostScript:

```
%!PS-Adobe-3.0
%%BoundingBox: 0 0 612 792
%%Pages: 1
% ...
% Draw a line around the polygons...
pop pop pop dup 0 setgray 0 0 moveto dup 0 lineto 0.707106781 mul dup
    lineto closepath stroke
PDF:
%PDF-1.3
%A?A?AA"
 81 0 obj
<<
/Linearized 1
/O 83
/H [ 915 494 ]
/T 125075
>>
endobj
 xref
81 24
0000000016 00000 n
 A^<8f>
```

Printing

```
^P^@A?A`<9e>
endstream
endobj
```

PCL5:

```
^[E^[&l1o0o1t0l6D^[&l1X^[*r0F^[*v0n1O^[*p4300X^[%1BDT~,1TR0TD1SP1FT10,50
CF3,1LB.~;^[%1A^[*c100G^[*v2T^[&a0P^[*p0X^[*p0Y^[(10U^[(s1p12vsb4148T^[&l0
E^[*p0Y^[*ct7920Y^[(10U^[(s1p12vsb4101T^[&a0P^[&l0o66f0E^[9^[&a0P^[*p0X^[*
p0Y^[*p474Y^[*p141X^[(10U^[(10U^[(s1p12vsb4101T^[*p402Y^[*p186X^[*v0O^[*c9
00a4b100g2P^[*v1O^[*p250Y^[*v0O^[*c900a4b100g2P^[*v1O^[*v0O^[*c4a156b100g2
P^[*v1O^[*p251Y^[*p187X^[*v0O^[*c899a154b10g2P^[*v1O^[*p346Y^[*p256X
```

PCL/XL:

```
A`X^BX^BA?<89>A^@A?<86>A^CA?<8f>AA^@A?<88>A^AA?<82>HA^@A?(A^@A?
%AA?cA^A^P^@TimesNewRmnBdA?A?A?UUA?BA?A?Au^BA?A?o<85>A"A>^CA^
BA?LkAf^@^@A?A!dA^A:^@
```

26.9 PPD FILES

When you invoke **lpr** to print **book.ps** on the color printer Pollux, **lpr** may come back and ask you what size paper you want to print on. But wait—how does the system know to tell its client, **lpr**, that Pollux can print on A4 paper? How does it know Pollux can handle PostScript, and what should it do if it can't? Where does it find the information that Pollux is a color printer?

If you're using CUPS, all this information is kept in PostScript Printer Description (PPD) files that describe the attributes and capabilities of your printers. The CUPS daemon reads the PPDs for its printers and passes information about them to clients and filters as needed.

PPDs were first developed for the Mac world, but they were quickly adopted by Windows as well. Mac and Windows printer drivers use the PPD file to figure out how to send PostScript jobs to the printer. For example, it makes no sense to ask a single-sided, black-and-white printer sold in America to print a duplex, color document on European B4-sized paper.

Every PostScript printer has its own PPD file created by the vendor, although the file is not always easy to find. Check the installation disk and the vendor's web site.

PPD files are just text files. Take a look at one in a text editor to see the type of information it contains. On a network, PPDs can even be remote—CUPS clients can get all the PPD information they need from the relevant CUPS server.

CUPS also uses PPDs to describe printers that lack a PostScript interpreter. An extra field does the trick. Look:

```
$ grep cupsFilter /usr/share/ppd/ghostscript/model/pxlmono.ppd
*cupsFilter:     "application/vnd.cups-postscript 100 pstopxl"
*cupsFilter:     "application/vnd.cups-pdf 0 pstopxl"
```

You can **diff** a couple of related PPDs (try **pxlmono.ppd** and **pxlcolor.ppd**) to see exactly how two printers differ.

If you need a PPD file and your printer vendor doesn't supply one—say, because the printer doesn't have a PostScript interpreter and the vendor doesn't care about anything but Windows—go to linuxprinting.org and hunt through the Foomatic database for more information. Your printer may also be supported by the Gutenprint project (gutenprint.sourceforge.net). If you have a choice of PPDs from these sources and your users want every last drop of quality, the ones marked "foomatic+gutenprint" are often quite good. However, you'll still have to experiment with the printer configuration to find out what options give the best output.

If a PPD file is nowhere to be found:

- You should have consulted linuxprinting.org before you acquired the printer. Even if you got the printer out of a dumpster, "free" doesn't always mean "inexpensive."
- There may well be a PPD file that will let you print something, even if it doesn't take advantage of all your printer's features. For example, we've had good luck using generic HP drivers on non-HP printers.

Though CUPS depends on PPDs, older printing systems make no use of them. For the BSD or System V printing systems, you can either massage your PostScript or you can live with what you get by default.

26.10 Paper sizes

Users want output on physical sheets of paper. Paper comes in sizes and shapes. To make your users happy, you should know the basic facts about paper sizes.

In the United States and Canada, the most common paper size is called letter and is 8.5 × 11 inches. Some Linux distributions (e.g., Knoppix and SUSE) are produced in Europe, where they don't even know what inches are, or in England, where they do know but don't use them to measure paper. In these places, and in Japan, the common paper type is called A4, and printers all come with A4 trays. Ergo, some distributions' printing utilities produce A4 page images by default.

A4 paper makes sense because it's irrational—mathematically speaking, that is. The ratio of length to width of A4 paper is $\sqrt{2}$. If you slice a piece of A4 paper in half horizontally, you get two half-size pieces of paper that have the same length-to-width ratio: $\sqrt{2}$. This paper size is called A5. Cut A5 in half and you get two sheets of A6. In the other direction, A3 is twice the area of A4, but the same shape, and so on.

In other words, you can manufacture A0 paper, which has an area of one square meter, and use a paper cutter to create the other sizes you need. The only common U.S. paper size you can play this kind of game with is ledger (11 × 17 inches, also known as tabloid), which you can slice in half to get two sheets of letter.

There are also an ISO B series and C series that preserve the $\sqrt{2}$ aspect ratio but have different base areas. B0 paper is one meter tall, and C0 paper has an area of two square meters. Engineers will see immediately that the sides of B*n* paper are the geometric means of A*n* – 1 and A*n* sides, while C*n* paper sides are the geometric means of A*n* and B*n*.

What does all this mean? B*n* has the same look as A*n* but is bigger, and C*n* is intermediate between the two. A report on A4 paper fits beautifully in a C4 manila folder. Folding an A4 letter down the middle to make it A5 lets it slide into a C5 envelope. Fold it again and it slides just as nicely into a C6 envelope.

To confuse things slightly, Japan has its own B series that's similar but different. Although it has the same aspect ratio as the ISO papers, the size of Japanese B4 paper is the arithmetic mean of A3 and A4, which (engineers will also see immediately) makes it slightly larger than ISO B4 paper. There is no Japanese C series.

Just as the ISO system makes it easy to copy two pages of a B5 textbook onto a single B4 handout, it makes all types of n-up printing (printing several reduced-sized page images on the same page) trivial. European copiers often have buttons that reduce or expand by a factor of $\sqrt{2}$.

If you have a CUPS system with the **paperconf** command, you can use it to print the dimensions of various named papers in inches, centimeters, or printer's points (72^{nds} of an inch). For the Americans, Table 26.7 lists some typical uses for common sizes to give a sense of their scale.

Table 26.7 Common uses for ISO paper sizes

Sizes	Common uses
A0, A1	Posters
A3, B4	Newspapers
A4	Generic "pieces of paper"
A5	Note pads (roughly 5 × 8 inches)
B5, B6	Books, postcards, German toilet paper
A7	"3 × 5" index cards
B7	Passports (even U.S. passports are B7)
A8	Business cards
B8	Playing cards

Unfortunately, A4 paper is slightly thinner and longer (8.3 × 11.7 inches) than American letter paper. Printing an A4 document on letter paper typically cuts off vital slivers such as headers, footers, and page numbers. Conversely, if you're in Europe or Japan and try to print American pages on A4 paper, you may have the sides of your documents chopped off, though the problem is less severe.

Individual software packages may have their own defaults regarding paper size. For example, GNU **enscript** is maintained in Finland by Markku Rossi and defaults to A4 paper. If you're American and your distribution hasn't compiled in a different default, one option is to grab the source code for **enscript** and reconfigure it. Typically, however, it's easier to set the paper type on the command line or in a GUI configuration file. If your documents come out with the ends or sides cut off, paper size conflicts are a likely explanation.

You may also be able to adjust the default paper size for many printing tasks with the **paperconfig** command, the PAPERSIZE environment variable, or the contents of the **/etc/papersize** file. (Note: **paperconfig** != **paperconf**.)

Admittedly, not all output is on paper. If you take a color picture to the bakery department of a large supermarket, they can probably make you a cake that has a copy of that picture on top of it. These pictures are printed by specialized bitmap printers that use edible inks. Large, rectangular cakes are known as sheet cakes, and they come in standard sizes, too. Unfortunately, we'll have to limit our discussion of sheet sizes to paper. You can't talk about everything...

26.11 Printer practicalities

Printers can bring troubles and frustrations. Here are some general guidelines to help limit those. When all else fails, just be glad you're not still using a dot-matrix printer connected via an RS-232 serial port. (Unless, of course, you are.)

Printer selection

If you're using CUPS, before you buy a printer or accept a "free" printer that someone else is throwing away, go to the Foomatic database at linuxprinting.org (funded and run by the Linux Foundation) and check to see how well the printer is supported. The database classifies printers into four categories ranging from Paperweight to Perfectly; you want Perfectly.

Everyone likes printers with embedded PostScript interpreters. Configuration of these printers is invariably easy.

Non-PostScript printers tend to be less well supported. To print to these, you need software that converts print jobs into the printer's preferred PDL or data format. Chances are, this software is available either from your Linux/UNIX vendor or from one of the other locations mentioned in this chapter. Still, CUPS handles most of these printers pretty well, too.

If you're not using CUPS and you have a PostScript printer, you're probably still in good shape. If you have a non-PostScript printer, try using Ghostscript to turn PostScript and PDF documents into something your printer can accept.

GDI printers

Windows still holds an advantage in a couple of areas, one of which is its support for very low-end printers. The el cheapo printers used on Windows systems are known collectively as GDI printers or WinPrinters. These printers have very little built-in intelligence and lack interpreters for any real PDL. They expect rasterization to be performed by the host computer.

Some of the information needed to communicate with GDI printers is hidden in proprietary, Windows-specific code. Such secrecy hinders efforts to develop support for these devices, but the open source community has demonstrated a remarkable aptitude for reverse engineering. CUPS supports many WinPrinters.

A second area of strength for Windows is its support for brand-new printers. Just as with new video and audio cards, new printers are first released with Windows drivers that fully support all the model's documented and undocumented features. Even CUPS support generally lags. If you buy a fancy, just-released printer because you need its advanced features, you may have to resign yourself to driving it from Windows for a while.

Legacy UNIX systems, which typically don't run CUPS, have an even tougher time with these printers. If you want to use a WinPrinter but only have legacy UNIX systems, consider buying an inexpensive Mac, Linux, or Windows box to run the printer. You can always share the printer over the network.

Double-sided printing

A duplexer is a hardware component that lets a printer print on both sides of the page. Some printers include them by default, and others support them as an optional add-on. We like them; they save both paper and filing space.

If you don't have access to (or can't afford) a printer that duplexes, you can run paper through a printer once to print the odd pages, then flip the paper over and run it a second time for the even pages. Experiment with a two-page document to find out which way to flip the paper, then tape instructions to the printer.

A variety of printing software can help with this process. For example, Ghostview (**gv**) has icons that let you mark odd or even pages, and an option to print only marked pages. The CUPS versions of **lp** and **lpr** handle this task with the options **-o page-set=odd** and **-o page-set=even**. You can even enshrine these options in a printer instance if you use them frequently; see page 1036.

Some printers, particularly inexpensive laser printers, are not designed with double-sided printing in mind. Their manufacturers often warn of the irreparable damage that is sure to attend printing on both sides of the page. We have never actually seen a case of such damage, but surely printer manufacturers wouldn't steer you wrong just to sell more expensive printers. Would they?

Other printer accessories

In addition to duplexers, many printers let you add memory, extra paper trays, hard disks, and other accessories. These upgrades can allow the printer to handle jobs that would otherwise be indigestible, or at the very least, they can let jobs print more efficiently. If you have problems getting jobs to print, review the error logs to see if more printer memory might help resolve the problem. See, for example, the comments regarding CUPS logging on page 1082.

Serial and parallel printers

If your printer is directly attached to your computer with a cable, it's using some form of serial or parallel connection.

Although the parallel standard has not aged gracefully, it does provide us with ports that require relatively little tinkering. If you have a parallel printer, it will probably be easy to set up—that is, if you can find a computer with a parallel port to hook it to.

A serial connection on older Mac hardware could be FireWire, but serial connections on newer computers are usually USB. For Linux, check the database of supported USB devices at linuxprinting.org to see the status of your hardware.

You almost certainly do not have an old-fashioned RS-232 serial printer. If you do, it's going to require a mess of extra configuration. The spooler software has to know the appropriate values for the baud rate and other serial options so that it can communicate properly with the printer. Even CUPS lets you handle these, by specifying options in the URI for the device (see the on-line CUPS *Software Administrators Manual* for details). However, our suggestion is to not bother; it's faster and cheaper to buy a modern printer than to figure out the exact combination of serial magic needed to get things working.

Network printers

Many printers contain full-fledged network interfaces that allow them to sit directly on a network and accept jobs through one or more network or printing protocols. Data can be sent to network-attached printers much faster than to printers connected to serial or parallel ports.

Laser printers are likely to be network printers. Inkjet printers, less so, but networked inkjets do exist. If you want to know whether you have a network printer, look for an Ethernet port or a wireless antenna on its back panel.

Other printer advice

Some administrative issues related to printing transcend the details of your printing system. For the most part, these issues arise because printers are temperamental mechanical devices that cost money every time they are used.

Use banner pages only if you have to

Your system can usually print header and trailer pages for each job that show the title of the job and the user who submitted it. These banner pages are sometimes useful for separating jobs on printers used by many different people, but in most cases they're a waste of time, toner, and paper.

On BSD systems, suppress them by setting the Boolean printcap variable sh. On System V systems, don't have your interface script generate them.

With CUPS, you can globally disable banner pages in your GUI or by running **lpadmin**, then turn them on for any individual jobs that might benefit from them:

```
$ lpr -o job-sheets=confidential gilly.ps
```

CUPS lets you turn on banners for individual users by using **lpoptions**. You can also create a printer instance that adds banner pages to jobs (see *Printer instances* on page 1036). CUPS also lets you create a custom banner page by copying an existing one from **/usr/share/cups/banners** and modifying it. Put the new page in with the others under a new name.

Fan your paper

Printers are supposed to pull one page at a time from the paper tray. Sometimes, though, blank pages stick together and your printer will try to feed two or more pages at a time. You can minimize the frequency of this problem just by fanning paper before you load it. Hold one side of the ream, bend the paper, and run your thumb down the opposite edge as you would riffle through a deck of cards. It's low-tech, it's free, and it works.

Some inkjet paper cares which side is up. Its packaging should indicate the preferred orientation.

Provide recycling bins

All kinds of computer paper are recyclable. You can use the boxes that paper comes in as recycling bins; the paper fits in them perfectly. Post a sign asking that no foreign material (such as staples, paper clips, or newspaper) be discarded there.

Use previewers

Users often print a document, find a small error in the formatting, fix it, and then reprint the job. This waste of paper and time can easily be avoided with software that lets users see, on-screen, what the printed output will look like.

Having previewers isn't enough; your users have to know how to use them. They're sometimes happy to learn. One use of accounting records is to check for cases in which the same document has been printed repeatedly. It can point you to a user who doesn't know about previewers.

Previewing is built into many modern WYSIWYG editors, browsers, and print-job aggregators. For other types of documents, your options vary. Tools such as

Ghostview (**gv**) preview random PostScript and PDF documents. For **roff**, pipe the output of **groff** into Ghostview; for TeX output, try **xdvi**, **kdvi**, or Evince.

Buy cheap printers

Printer hardware technology is mature. You don't need to spend a lot of money for good output and reliable mechanics.

Don't splurge on an expensive "workgroup" printer just because you have a workgroup. If you're only printing text, an inexpensive "personal" printer can produce good-quality output, be nearly as fast and reliable, and weigh tens of pounds less. One 10-page-a-minute printer can serve about five full-time writers. You may be better off buying five $150 printers for a group of 25 writers than one $750 printer.

Even if you stick to mainstream brands, no individual manufacturer is a universally safe bet. We have had excellent experiences with HP laser printers. They are solid products, and HP has been very aggressive in supporting both Linux and CUPS. Even so, some of HP's printers have been complete disasters. Look for reviews on the Internet before buying. Here, too, cheap is an advantage: a $150 mistake is easier to cover up than a $750 mistake.

Keep extra toner cartridges on hand

Faded or blank areas on a laser-printed page are hints that the printer is running out of toner. Buy replacement cartridges before you need them. In a pinch, remove the cartridge from the printer and gently rock it to redistribute the remaining toner particles. You can often get another few hundred pages out of a cartridge this way.

Streaks and spots probably mean you should clean your printer. Look on the printer to see if there is a "clean" cycle. If not, or if the cleaning cycle doesn't help, read the manufacturer's cleaning instructions. Most toner cartridges include an imaging drum, so try swapping toner cartridges to verify that the problem is really the printer and not the cartridge. If none of these procedures resolve the streaks, pay to have the printer serviced.

Printer manufacturers hate the use of recycled and aftermarket cartridges, and they go to great lengths to try to prevent it. Many devices use "keyed" consumables whose identities are detected (either electronically or physically) by the printer. Even if two printers look identical, such as the Xerox Phaser 6120 and the Konica-Minolta Magicolor 2450, it doesn't necessarily mean that you can use the same cartridges in both.

Sometimes you can do surgery to convert one vendor's cartridges to another's printer, but it helps to know what you're doing. Usually, you just make a mess. If you spill toner, vacuum up as much of the material as possible and wipe up the remainder with cold water. Contrary to common belief, laser printer toner is not toxic, but as with all fine powders, you should not inhale the toner dust.

When you replace a cartridge, save the box and baggie the new cartridge came in to use when recycling the spent one. Then find a company to take the old cartridge off your hands.

Keyed consumables spurred the growth of companies ("punch and pours") that refill old cartridges for a fraction of the new-cartridge price. Cartridge recyclers are usually also punch-and-pours, so you can recycle your old cartridges and get replacements at the same time.

Opinions on the quality and life span of recycled cartridges vary. One punch-and-pour we know won't refill color toner cartridges or sell remanufactured ones because they believe the savings are less than the increased maintenance costs for the printers that use them.

Pay attention to the cost per page

Most inexpensive printers are sold at close to their manufacturing cost. The manufacturers make their money on the consumables, which are disproportionately expensive. As of this writing, a quick check reveals that Amazon is selling for $80 a laser printer that takes toner cartridges costing $65. You can buy a cheap inkjet printer for less than $50 at Wal-Mart, but it won't be long before you need to buy a set of replacement ink cartridges that cost more than the printer.[2] You can feign outrage over this, but printer companies have to make their money on something. Cheaper cartridges would just mean pricier printers.

A good rule of thumb is that inkjet printers are cheap as long as you don't print with them. Laser printers have a higher initial cost, but the consumables are cheaper and last longer. A full-color page from an inkjet printer can cost 20–50 times as much as an analogous print from a laser printer. It also requires special paper and prints more slowly. Inkjet cartridges empty quickly and frequently plug up or go bad. The ink usually runs when wet, so don't use an inkjet to print a recipe book for use in the kitchen. On the other hand, you can now get photo prints from an inkjet that look as good as prints from a photo lab. Color laser photos? Nice enough, but no comparison.

All printers have failure-prone mechanical parts. Cheap printers break faster.

In other words, it's all tradeoffs. For low-volume, personal use—printing a web page or two a day, or printing a couple of rolls of film per month—a low-cost, general purpose inkjet is an excellent choice.

Next time you go printer shopping, estimate how long you want to keep your printer, how much printing you do, and what kind of printing you need before you buy. Assess quantitatively the long-term cost per page for each candidate printer. Ask your local punch-and-pour whether they remanufacture cartridges for the printer, and at what price.

2. Keep in mind, though, that many inexpensive printers come with "starter" cartridges that include less ink or toner than a standard replacement.

Consider printer accounting

Printer accounting can give you a good feel for how your printing resources are being consumed. At medium-to-large installations, consider using it just to keep tabs on what's going on. The per-job overhead is unimportant, and you get to see who is using the printer. Demographic information about the sources of print jobs is valuable when you are planning the deployment of new printers.

Secure your printers

Network printers typically support remote management. Even if you don't have CUPS and IPP, you can configure and monitor them from a web browser with HTTP, and perhaps with SNMP. Through the remote interface, you can set parameters such as the printer's IP address, default gateway, syslog server, SNMP community name, protocol options, and administrative password.

By default, most remotely administrable printers are unprotected and must have a password (or perhaps an SNMP "community string") assigned as part of the installation process. The installation manuals from your printer manufacturer should explain how to do this on any particular printer.

GUI administration tools, such as the CUPS browser interface, are increasingly able to hide vendor variations from you. Expect this trend to continue.

26.12 Troubleshooting tips

Printers combine all the foibles of a mechanical device with the communication eccentricities of a foreign operating system. They (and the software that drives them) delight in creating problems for you and your users. Here are some general tips for dealing with printer adversity.

Restarting a print daemon

Always remember to restart daemons after changing a configuration file.

You can restart **cupsd** in whatever way your system normally restarts daemons: **/etc/init.d/cups restart**, or something similar. In theory, you can also send **cupsd** a HUP signal. Unfortunately, this seems to just kill the daemon on SUSE systems.

Alternatively, you can use the CUPS GUI or another GUI interface such as the KDE Print Manager application to restart **cupsd**.

Other systems have their own specialized methods for resetting the print system; often, they are vendor specific. For example, AIX uses the following sequence:

```
$ sudo stopsrc -s lpd
$ sudo startsrc -s lpd
```

Just what you would have guessed, right?

Logging

CUPS maintains three logs: a page log, an access log, and an error log. The page log lists the pages that CUPS has printed. The other two logs are just like the access log and error log for Apache, which should not be surprising since the CUPS server is a web server.

The **cupsd.conf** file specifies the logging level and the locations of the log files. They're all typically kept underneath **/var/log**.

Here's an excerpt from a log file that corresponds to a single print job:

```
I [26/Jul/2009:18:59:08 -0600] Adding start banner page "none" to job 24.
I [26/Jul/2009:18:59:08 -0600] Adding end banner page "none" to job 24.
I [26/Jul/2009:18:59:08 -0600] Job 24 queued on 'Phaser_6120' by 'jsh'.
I [26/Jul/2009:18:59:08 -0600] Started filter /usr/libexec/cups/filter/pstops (PID
    19985) for job 24.
I [26/Jul/2009:18:59:08 -0600] Started backend /usr/libexec/cups/backend/usb
    (PID 19986) for job 24.
```

Problems with direct printing

Under CUPS, to verify the physical connection to a local printer, you can directly run the printer's back end. For example, here's what we get when we execute the back end for a USB-connected printer:

```
$ /usr/lib/cups/backend/usb
direct usb "Unknown" "USB Printer (usb)"
direct usb://XEROX/Phaser%206120?serial=YGG210547 "XEROX Phaser 6120"
    "Phaser 6120"
```

When the USB cable for the Phaser 6120 is disconnected, that printer drops out of the back end's output:

```
$ /usr/lib/cups/backend/usb
direct usb "Unknown" "USB Printer (usb)"
```

Network printing problems

Before you start tracking down a network printing problem, make sure you can print from the machine that actually hosts the printer. Your "network printing problem" may just be a "printing problem." Also make sure that the network is up.

Next, try connecting to the printer daemon. You can connect to **cupsd** with a web browser (*hostname*:631) or the **telnet** command (**telnet** *hostname* **631**).

Network **lpd** print jobs are delivered on TCP port 515. Unless you want to be printing jobs for strangers, your firewall should block all traffic to this port from the Internet. To test your connectivity to a remote **lpd** server, **telnet** to port 515 of the server. If you can establish a connection, you can at least verify that the network is working and that **lpd** is running on the server.

If you have problems debugging a network printer connection, keep in mind that there must be a queue for the job on some machine, a way to decide where to send the job, and a method of sending the job to the machine that hosts the print queue. On the print server, there must be a place to queue the job, sufficient permissions to allow the job to be printed, and a way to output to the device.

Any and all of these will, at some point, go wrong, so be prepared to hunt in many places, including these:

- System log files on the sending machine, for name resolution and permission problems
- System log files on the print server, for permission problems
- Log files on the sending machine, for missing filters, unknown printers, missing directories, etc.
- The print daemon's log files on the print server's machine, for messages about bad device names, incorrect formats, etc.
- The printer log file on the printing machine, for errors in transmitting the job (as specified by the lf variable in the **/etc/printcap** file on BSD printing systems)
- The printer log file on the sending machine, for errors about preprocessing or queuing the job

Consult your system's documentation to determine which of these log files are available and where the files are located. The system's log files are usually specified in syslog's configuration file, **/etc/syslog.conf**. The locations of CUPS log files are specified in **/etc/cups/cupsd.conf**.

Distribution-specific problems

Every program has bugs.[3] On Ubuntu systems, for example, there seem to be CUPS updates every month or so. Some problems are worse than others, and some have security implications.

On some older versions of Red Hat Enterprise Linux, CUPS was badly broken. The right solution for those systems is an OS upgrade, but if you can't install a newer release, try installing the current release of CUPS.

26.13 Recommended reading

Each vendor and GUI supplies its own, idiosyncratic printing-system-specific documentation. KDE includes man pages for the KDEPrint commands, plus the *KDEPrint Handbook*. You can find additional information at printing.kde.org. All of these sources contain useful references to other documentation. (Actually, the KDE documentation is a great introduction to CUPS even if you don't use KDE.)

3. And every program can be shortened. Therefore, as the saying goes, any program can be reduced to a single line that doesn't work.

CUPS comes with a lot of documentation in HTML format. An excellent way to access it is to connect to a CUPS server and click the link for on-line help. Of course, this isn't any help if you're consulting the documentation to figure out why you can't connect to the CUPS server. On your computer, the documents should be installed in **/usr/share/doc/cups** in both HTML and PDF formats. If they aren't there, ask your distribution's package manager or look on cups.org.

The cups.org forums are a good place to ask questions, but do your homework first and ask politely.

If you're running Linux, try linuxprinting.org. It's a vast collection of Linux printing resources and a good place to start when answering questions. The site also has a nice CUPS tutorial that includes a troubleshooting section.

Wikipedia and SUSE both supply good CUPS overviews. You can find SUSE's at en.opensuse.org/SDB:CUPS_in_a_Nutshell.

If you want a printed CUPS reference manual, we recommend the following one. This is the CUPS bible, right from the horse's mouth.

SWEET, MICHAEL R., *CUPS: Common UNIX Printing System*. Indianapolis, Indiana: Sams Publishing, 2001.

26.14 EXERCISES

E26.1 Find someone who isn't computer literate (an art student, your mother, or perhaps a Microsoft Certified Professional) and teach that person how to print a PDF document on your system. Did your subject find any of the steps confusing? How could you make the process easier for other users?

E26.2 Using a web browser, visit a printer on your network. If you have CUPS, visit a CUPS server on your system with the same browser. What prevents you from making administrative changes to that server's printers?

E26.3 Visit a real or virtual big-box store such as Sam's Club or Amazon.com and pick three color laser printers you can buy for under $400. If you had to purchase one of these printers for your organization tomorrow, which one would it be and why? Make sure you've checked the database at linuxprinting.org.

E26.4 You have been asked to design the system software to run inside a laser printer aimed at the corporate workgroup market. What distribution will you start with? What additional software will you need to add? Will you have to write all of it? How will you accommodate Windows and Mac OS clients? (Hint: Check out Linux distributions designed for "embedded systems.")

27 Data Center Basics

A service is only as reliable as the data center that houses it. For those with hands-on experience, that's just common sense. But for upper management, the data center can seem like a faraway and almost imaginary land.

With the rise of desktop workstations and the move away from big-iron computing, it once appeared that the days of the central data center might be numbered. In reality, the need for properly designed data centers is higher today than ever before. These facilities house the mission-critical servers (often running UNIX or Linux) that feed the world's hunger for on-line data and applications.

Certain aspects of data centers—such as their physical layout, power, and cooling—were traditionally designed and maintained by "facilities" or "physical plant" staff. However, the fast-moving pace of IT technology and the increasingly low tolerance for downtime have forced a shotgun marriage of IT and facilities staff as partners in the planning and operation of data centers. As a sysadmin, you get to play the role of "subject matter expert" for the facilities folks.[1]

1. At least, if you want to sleep at night…

A data center is composed of:

- A physically safe and secure space
- Racks that hold computer, network, and storage devices
- Electric power sufficient to operate the installed devices
- Cooling, to keep the devices within their operating temperature ranges
- Network connectivity throughout the data center, and to places beyond (enterprise network, partners, vendors, Internet)

27.1 Data Center Reliability Tiers

Several aspects of a data center's design contribute to the overall availability it can provide, including

- **Uninterruptible power supplies (UPSs)** – UPSs provide power when the normal long-term power source (e.g., the commercial power grid) becomes unavailable. Depending on size and capacity, they can provide anywhere from a few minutes to a couple of hours of power. UPSs alone cannot support a site in the event of a long-term outage.

- **On-site power generation** – If the commercial grid is unavailable, on-site standby generators can provide long-term power. Generators are usually fueled by diesel, LP gas, or natural gas and can support the site as long as fuel is available. It is customary to store at least 72 hours of fuel on-site and to arrange to buy fuel from multiple providers.

  Generator-backed facilities still need UPSs to cover the short time (usually less than 60 seconds) required to start the generators and transfer from grid to generator power.

- **Redundant power feeds** – In some locations, it may be possible to obtain more than one power feed from the commercial power grid (possibly from different power generators).

- **Mechanical systems** – These are also known as HVAC systems, but in the context of a data center, only cooling is really relevant—no heat necessary! A plethora of available technologies provide both primary and standby cooling.

The Uptime Institute is an industry group that researches and guides data centers. They have developed a four-tier system for classifying the reliability of data centers, which we summarize in Table 27.1. In this table, N means that you have just enough of something (UPSs, generators) to meet normal needs. N+1 means that you have one spare; 2N means that each device has its own spare.

Centers in the highest tier must be "compartmentalized," which means that groups of systems are powered and cooled in such a way that the failure of one group has no effect on other groups.

Table 27.1 Uptime Institute availability classification system

Tier	Generators	UPSs	Power feeds	HVAC	Availability
1	None	N	Single	N	99.671%
2	N	N+1[a]	Single	N+1	99.741%
3	N+1	N+1[a]	Dual, switchable	N+1	99.982%
4	2N	2N	Dual, simultaneous	2N	99.995%

a. With redundant components

Even 99.671% availability may sound pretty good at first glance, but it works out to nearly 29 hours of downtime per year. 99.995% availability corresponds to 26 minutes of downtime per year.

Exhibit A Courtesy of xkcd.com

Of course, no amount of redundant power or cooling is going to keep an application available if it's administered poorly or is improperly architected. The data center is a foundational building block, necessary but not sufficient to ensure overall availability from the end user's perspective.

You can learn more about the Uptime Institute's availability standards from their web site, uptimeinstitute.org.

27.2 Cooling

Just like humans, computers work better and live longer if they're happy in their environment. Maintenance of a safe operating temperature is a prerequisite for this happiness.

See Chapter 28, Green IT, for a discussion of data center energy savings.

The American Society of Heating, Refrigerating and Air-conditioning Engineers (ASHRAE) traditionally recommended data center temperatures (measured at server inlets) in the range of 68° to 77°F (20° to 25°C). In an effort to support organizations' attempts to reduce energy consumption, ASHRAE released

Data Center

updated guidance in 2008 that enlarged the recommended temperature range to 64.4° to 80.6°F (18° to 27°C).

Temperature maintenance starts with an accurate estimate of your cooling load. Traditional textbook models for data center cooling (even those from the 1990s) may be up to an order of magnitude off from the realities of today's high-density blade server chassis. Hence, we have found that it's a good idea to double-check the cooling load estimates produced by your HVAC folks.

You'll definitely need an HVAC engineer to help you calculate the cooling load that your roof, walls, and windows (don't forget solar load) contribute to your environment. HVAC engineers usually have a lot of experience with those components and should be able to give you a good estimate. The part you need to check up on is the internal heat load for your data center.

You need to determine the heat load contributed by the following components:

- Roof, walls, and windows (from your HVAC engineer)
- Electronic gear
- Light fixtures
- Operators (people)

Electronic gear

You can estimate the heat load produced by your servers (and other electronic gear) by determining the servers' power consumption. Direct measurement of power use is by far the best way to obtain this information. Your friendly neighborhood electrician can help, or you can purchase an inexpensive meter and do it yourself.[2] Most equipment is labeled with its maximum power consumption in watts, but typical consumption tends to be significantly less than the maximum.

You can convert power consumption to the standard heat unit, BTUH, by multiplying by 3.413 BTUH/watt. For example, if you wanted to build a data center that would house 25 servers rated at 450 watts each, the calculation would be

$$\left(25 \text{ servers}\right)\left(\frac{450 \text{ watts}}{\text{server}}\right)\left(\frac{3.412 \text{ BTUH}}{\text{watt}}\right) = 38{,}385 \text{ BTUH}$$

Light fixtures

As with electronic gear, you can estimate light fixture heat load based on power consumption. Typical office light fixtures contain four 40-watt fluorescent tubes. If your new data center had six of these fixtures, the calculation would be

$$\left(6 \text{ fixtures}\right)\left(\frac{160 \text{ watts}}{\text{fixture}}\right)\left(\frac{3.412 \text{ BTUH}}{\text{watt}}\right) = 3{,}276 \text{ BTUH}$$

2. The Kill A Watt meter made by P3 is a popular choice at around $20.

Operators

At one time or another, humans will need to enter the data center to service something. Allow 300 BTUH for each occupant. To allow for four humans in the data center at the same time:

$$\left(4 \text{ humans}\right)\left(\frac{300 \text{ BTUH}}{\text{human}}\right) = 1{,}200 \text{ BTUH}$$

Total heat load

Once you have calculated the heat load for each component, sum the results to determine your total heat load. For our example, we assume that our HVAC engineer estimated the load from the roof, walls, and windows to be 20,000 BTUH.

20,000	BTUH for roof, walls, and windows
38,385	BTUH for servers and other electronic gear
3,276	BTUH for light fixtures
1,200	BTUH for operators
62,861	BTUH total

Cooling system capacity is typically expressed in tons. You can convert BTUH to tons by dividing by 12,000 BTUH/ton. You should also allow at least a 50% slop factor to account for errors and future growth.

$$\left(62{,}681 \text{ BTUH}\right)\left(\frac{1 \text{ ton}}{12{,}000 \text{ BTUH}}\right)\left(1.5\right) = 7.86 \text{ tons of cooling required}$$

See how your estimate matches up with the one from your HVAC folks.

Hot aisles and cold aisles

You can dramatically reduce your data center's cooling difficulties by putting some thought into its physical layout. The most common and effective strategy is to alternate hot and cold aisles.

Facilities that have a raised floor and are cooled by a traditional CRAC (computer room air conditioner) unit are often set up so that cool air enters the space under the floor, rises up through holes in the perforated floor tiles, cools the equipment, and then rises to the top of the room as warm air, where it is sucked into return air ducts. Traditionally, racks and perforated tiles have been placed "randomly" about the data center, a configuration that results in relatively even temperature distribution. The result is an environment that is comfortable for humans but not really optimized for computers.

A better strategy is to lay out alternating hot and cold aisles between racks. Cold aisles have perforated cooling tiles and hot aisles do not. Racks are arranged so that equipment draws in air from a cold aisle and exhausts it to a hot aisle; the exhaust sides of two adjacent racks are therefore back to back. See Exhibit B on the next page for an illustration of this basic concept.

Exhibit B Hot and cold aisles, raised floor

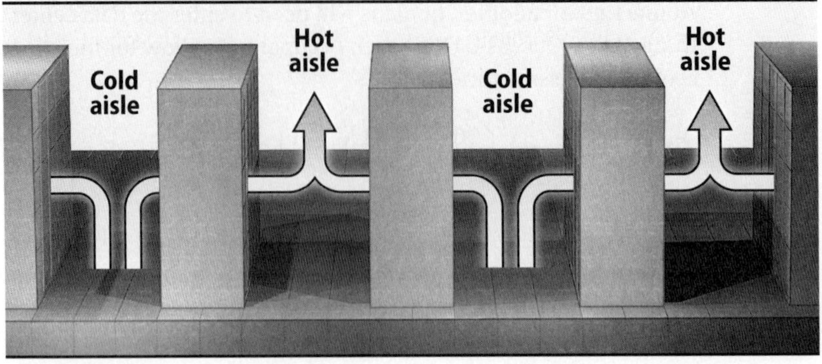

This arrangement optimizes the flow of cooling so that air inlets always breathe cool air rather than another server's hot exhaust. Properly implemented, the alternating row strategy results in aisles that are noticeably cold and hot. You can measure your cooling success with an infrared thermometer, which is an indispensable tool of the modern system administrator. This point-and-shoot $100 device (such as the Fluke 62) instantly measures the temperature of anything you aim it at, up to six feet away. Don't take it out to the bars.

If you *must* run cabling under the floor (see *Racks* on page 1094 for a discussion of this), run power under cold aisles and network cabling under hot aisles.

Facilities without a raised floor can use in-row cooling units such as those manufactured by APC (www.apcc.com). These units are skinny and sit between racks. Exhibit C shows how this system works.

Exhibit C Hot and cold aisles with in-row cooling (bird's-eye view)

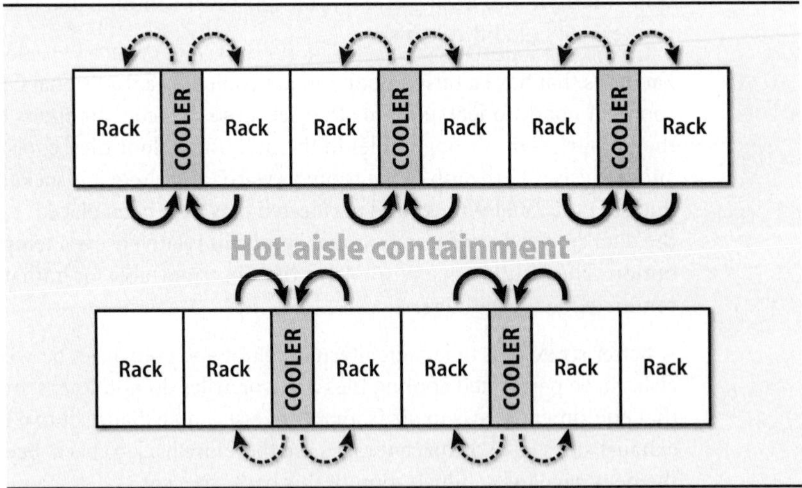

Both CRAC and in-row cooling units need a way to dissipate heat outside the data center. This requirement is typically satisfied with a loop of liquid refrigerant (such as chilled water, Puron/R410A, or R22) that carries the heat outdoors. We omitted the refrigerant loops from Exhibits B and C for simplicity, but most installations will require them. See Chapter 28, *Green IT*, for some comments on using cool outdoor air as an alternative to mechanical refrigeration.

Humidity

According to the 2008 ASHRAE guidelines, data center humidity should be kept between 30% and 55%. If the humidity is too low, static electricity becomes a problem. If it is too high, condensation can form on circuit boards and cause short circuits and oxidation. Depending on your geographic location, you may need either humidification or dehumidification equipment to maintain a proper level of humidity.

Environmental monitoring

If you are supporting a mission-critical computing environment, it's a good idea to monitor the temperature (and other environmental factors, such as noise and power) in the data center even when you are not there. It can be very disappointing to arrive on Monday morning and find a pool of melted plastic on your data center floor.

Fortunately, automated data center monitors can watch the goods while you are away. We use and recommend the Sensaphone (sensaphone.com) product family. These inexpensive boxes monitor environmental variables such as temperature, noise, and power, and they phone or page you when they detect a problem. You can reach Sensaphone in Aston, Pennsylvania, at (610) 558-2700.

27.3 Power

Computer hardware requires clean, stable power. In a data center, this means at the very least a power conditioner that filters out spikes and produces the correct voltage levels and phases.

See page 100 for more information about shutdown procedures.

Servers and network infrastructure equipment should be put on uninterruptible power supplies. Good UPSes have an RS-232, Ethernet, or USB interface that can be attached either to the machine to which they supply power or to a centralized monitoring infrastructure that can elicit a higher-level response. Such connections let the UPS warn computers or operators that power has failed and that a clean shutdown should be performed before the batteries run out.

UPSs are available in various sizes and capacities, but even the largest ones cannot provide long-term backup power. If your facility must operate on standby power for longer than a UPS can handle, you need a local generator in addition to a UPS.

A large selection of standby power generators are available, ranging in capacity from 5 kW to more than 2,500 kW. The gold standard is the family of generators made by Cummins Onan (onan.com). Most organizations select diesel as their fuel type. If you're in a cold climate, make sure you fill the tank with "winter mix diesel" or substitute Jet A-1 aircraft fuel to prevent gelling. Diesel is chemically stable but can grow algae, so consider adding an algicide to diesel you will store for an extended period.

Generators and the infrastructure to support them are expensive, but they can save money in some ways, too. If you install a standby generator, your UPSs need only be large enough to cover the short gap between the power going out and your generator coming on-line.

If UPSs or generators are part of your power strategy, it is extremely important to have a periodic test plan in place. We recommend that you test all components of your standby power system at least every 6 months. In addition, you (or your vendor) should perform preventative maintenance on standby power components at least annually.

Rack power requirements

Planning the power for a data center is one of the most difficult challenges you may face. Typically, the opportunity to build a new data center or to significantly remodel an existing one comes up only every decade or so, so it's important to look far down the road when it comes to power.

Most architects have a bias toward calculating the amount of power needed in a data center by multiplying the center's square footage by a magic number. This approach proves to be ineffective in most real-world cases because the size of the data center alone tells you very little about the types of equipment it might eventually house. Our recommendation is to use a per-rack power consumption model and to ignore the amount of floor space.

Historically, data centers have been designed to provide between 1.5 kW and 3 kW to each rack. But now that server manufacturers have started squeezing servers into 1U of rack space and building blade server chassis that hold 20 or more blades, the power needed to support a full rack of modern gear has skyrocketed.

One approach to solving the power density problem is to put only a handful of 1U servers in each rack, leaving the rest of the rack empty. Although this technique eliminates the need to provide more power to the rack, it's a prodigious waste of space. A better strategy is to develop a realistic projection of the power that might be needed by each rack and to provision power accordingly.

Equipment varies in its power requirements, and it's hard to predict exactly what the future will hold. A good approach is to create a system of power consumption tiers that allocates the same amount of power to all racks in a particular tier. This scheme is useful not only for meeting current equipment needs but also for planning future use. Table 27.2 outlines some basic starting points for tier definitions.

Table 27.2 Power-tier model for racks in a data center

Power tier	Watts/rack
Ultra-high density[a]	25 kW
Very high density (e.g. blade servers)[b]	20 kW
High density (e.g., 1U servers)	16 kW
Storage equipment	12 kW
Network switching equipment	8 kW
Normal density	6 kW

a. Projected top tier in 2015
b. Current top tier in 2010

The power allocations for the upper tiers in Table 27.2 may seem generous, but they are not so hard to reach, even with today's equipment. APC measured the power consumption of a chassis containing 14 IBM BladeCenter HS20s at 4,050 watts.[3] Six of those chassis in a rack consume 24.3 kW. Without cooling, that's enough power to reduce 50 pounds of steel, aluminum, or silicon to a liquid puddle within 15 minutes. Needless to say, you'll need special cooling arrangements and multiple power supplies for these configurations.

Once you've defined your power tiers, estimate your need for racks in each tier. On the floor plan, put racks from the same tier together. Such zoning concentrates the high-power racks and lets you plan cooling resources accordingly.

kVA vs. kW

One of the many common disconnects between IT folks, facilities folks, and UPS engineers is that each of these groups uses different units for power. The amount of power a UPS can provide is typically labeled in kVA (kilovolt-amperes). But computer equipment and the electrical engineers that support your data center usually express power in watts (W) or kilowatts (kW). You might remember from fourth grade science class that watts = volts × amps. Unfortunately, your fourth grade teacher failed to mention that watts is a vector value, which for AC power includes a "power factor" (pf) in addition to volts and amps.

If you are designing a bottle-filling line at a brewery that involves lots of large motors and other heavy equipment, ignore this section and hire a qualified engineer to determine the correct power factor to use in your calculations. For modern-day computer equipment, you can cheat and use a constant. The equations you can use for a "probably good enough" conversion between kVA and kW are

kVA = kW / .85
kW = kVA * .85

3. See the white paper "Power and Cooling for Ultra-High Density Racks and Blade Servers" at apc.com.

A final point to note on this topic is that when estimating the amount of power you need in a data center (or to size a UPS), you should measure devices' power consumption with a clamp-on ammeter (aka current clamp) such as the Fluke 902 rather than relying on the manufacturer's stated values as shown on the label (which typically represent maximum consumption values).

Remote control

You may occasionally find yourself in a situation in which you need to regularly power-cycle a server because of a kernel or hardware glitch. Or, perhaps you have non-UNIX servers in your data center that are more prone to this type of problem. In either case, you may want to consider installing a system that lets you power-cycle problem servers by remote control.

A reasonable solution is manufactured by American Power Conversion (APC). Their MasterSwitch product is similar to a power strip, except that it can be controlled by a web browser through its built-in Ethernet port. You can reach APC at (401) 789-0204 or on the web at apc.com.

27.4 Racks

The days of the traditional raised-floor data center—in which power, cooling, network connections, and phone lines are all hidden underneath the floor—are over. Have you ever tried to trace a cable that runs under the floor of one of these labyrinths? Our experience is that while it looks nice through glass, a "classic" raised-floor room is a hidden rat's nest. Today, you should use a raised floor to hide electrical power feeds, to distribute cooled air, and for *nothing else*. Network cabling (both copper and fiber) should be routed through overhead raceways designed specifically for this purpose.

In a dedicated data center, storing equipment in racks (as opposed to, say, setting it on tables or on the floor) is the only maintainable, professional choice. The best storage schemes use racks that are interconnected with an overhead track system for routing cables. This approach confers that irresistible high-tech feel without sacrificing organization or maintainability.

The best overhead track system is manufactured by Chatsworth Products (Chatsworth, CA, (818) 882-8595; chatsworth.com). Using standard 19" single-rail telco racks, you can construct homes for both shelf-mounted and rack-mounted servers. Two back-to-back 19" telco racks make a high-tech-looking "traditional" rack (for cases in which you need to attach rack hardware both in front of and in back of equipment). Chatsworth provides the racks, cable races, and cable management doodads, as well as all the hardware necessary to mount them in your building. Since the cables lie in visible tracks, they are easy to trace and you will naturally be motivated to keep them tidy.

27.5 Tools

A well-outfitted sysadmin is an effective sysadmin. Having a dedicated tool box is an important key to minimizing downtime in an emergency. Table 27.3 lists some items to keep in your tool box, or at least within easy reach.

Table 27.3 A system administrator's tool box

General tools	
Hex (Allen) wrench kit	Ball-peen hammer, 4 oz.
Scissors	Electrician's knife or Swiss army knife
Small LED flashlight	Phillips-head screwdrivers: #0, #1, and #2
Socket wrench kit	Pliers, both flat-needlenose and regular
Stud finder	Ridgid SeeSnake micro inspection camera
Tape measure	Slot-head screwdrivers: 1/8", 3/16", and 5/16"
Torx wrench kit	Teensy tiny jeweler's screwdrivers
Tweezers	
Computer-related specialty items	
Digital multimeter (DMM)	Cable ties (and their Velcro cousins)
Infrared thermometer	PC screw kit (such as those from crazypc.com)
RJ-45 end crimper	Portable network analyzer/laptop
SCSI terminators	Spare Category 5 and 6A RJ-45 crossover cables
Spare power cord	Spare RJ-45 connectors (solid core and stranded)
Static grounding strap	Wire stripper (with an integrated wire cutter)
Miscellaneous	
Can of compressed air	Dentist's mirror (possibly a telescoping one)
Cellular telephone	First-aid kit, including ibuprofen and acetaminophen
Electrical tape	Home phone and pager #s of on-call support staff
Q-Tips	List of emergency maintenance contacts[a]
	Six-pack of good microbrew beer (suggested minimum)

a. And maintenance contract numbers if applicable

27.6 Recommended reading

Telecommunications Infrastructure Standard for Data Centers. ANSI/TIA/EIA 942.

ASHRAE Inc. *ASHRAE 2008 Environmental Guidelines for Datacom Equipment.* Atlanta, GA: ASHRAE, Inc., 2008.

Eubank, Huston, Joel Swisher, Cameron Burns, Jen Seal, and Ben Emerson. *Design Recommendations for High Performance Data Centers.* Snowmass, CO: Rocky Mountain Institute, 2003.

27.7 Exercises

E27.1 Why would you want to mount your computers in a rack?

★ E27.2 Environmental factors affect both people and machines. Augment the factors listed in this book with some of your own (e.g., dust, noise, light, clutter, etc.). Pick four factors and evaluate the suitability of your lab for man and machine.

★ E27.3 A workstation draws 0.8 A, and its monitor draws 0.7 A @ 120 V.

a) How much power does this system consume in watts?

b) With electricity going for about $0.12/kWh, what does it cost to leave this system on year-round?

c) How much money can you save annually by turning off the monitor for an average of 16 hours a day (either manually or with Energy Star features such as DPMS)?

d) What is the annual cost of cooling this system? (State your assumptions regarding cooling costs and show your calculations.)

★★ E27.4 Design a new computing lab for your site. State your assumptions regarding space, numbers of machines, and type and power load of each machine. Then compute the power and cooling requirements for the lab. Include both servers and client workstations. Include the layout of the room, the lighting, and the expected human load as well.

28 Green IT

You might think that a book about system administration would be the last place to find a chapter on environmental and social consciousness. But now that large IT installations have become commonplace, the environmental impact and resource consumption of the equipment we oversee have started to attract attention. Green IT is the art and science of reducing these hidden and not-so-hidden costs.

Although each of us can make a difference through small changes in our choices and behavior, most improvement comes from centrally driven efforts to effect change. For example, no amount of "Choose unleaded gasoline! It's a whole lot better!" would have equalled the impact of the federal mandate to stop producing cars that required lead. Guess who can set similar mandates for your IT organization? You can!

But why bother? Bragging rights and the satisfaction of doing the right thing for the planet may be reason enough for some. But there are practical reasons to convince decision-makers in your organization to consider a green IT effort as well:

- **Lower initial costs** – by minimizing the equipment that your organization buys and uses, you reduce capital expenditures. By minimizing the size of the data center required, you can reduce real estate costs.

- **Lower operating costs** – power, management, and maintenance for equipment cost money over time. Efficient use of fewer pieces of equipment means that your organization spends less on the direct costs of operations.
- **Indirect cost savings** – you pay for electricity twice: once to power your equipment, and then again to cool down the equipment after it has converted that expensive power into heat.[1] Less equipment means less cooling, less square footage for IT projects, and fewer people dedicated to IT operations. Fewer people means less spent on rent, office cooling, wages, benefits, and support.

This chapter focuses on some basic concepts you can use to reduce your IT organization's energy and resource consumption. We've targeted organizations that have from 1 to 500 servers in their data centers. If your environment is larger, you should consider hiring an expert in green data-center construction to achieve the most dramatic results.

28.1 Green IT Initiation

What exactly does it mean to be "green"? We define it as

- Lower power consumption
- Smaller physical plant requirements
- Lower consumption of consumables
- Recyclable outputs

There is no silver bullet or single path to a green IT environment. Despite some vendors' claims, you cannot purchase one product that makes all the greenness in the world shower down upon you. Specifically, green IT is a lot more than just server virtualization. And, like so many aspects of system administration, green IT is more a journey than a destination. You must first visualize where you want to go, map out a plan to get there, and chart your progress along the way. Ongoing measurement and monitoring must be key elements of your overall plan.

Start your green IT journey by assessing the eco-friendliness of your current environment. Take a comprehensive view of all IT within your organization, not only to maximize the project's impact but also to ensure that you don't ultimately end up playing the "squeeze the balloon" game. For example, it might seem eco-wonderful to remove *all* the servers from your environment until you discover that eliminating your 50 managed servers has resulted in users purchasing and deploying 600 rogue server-class systems in their cubicles as part of a "personal server deprivation revolt."

1. The informational work done by IT equipment is not significant in a thermodynamic sense. Computers are essentially 100% efficient at converting electricity into heat.

Here is some information to gather as you start your green IT assessment:

- **Equipment survey** – everything, including servers, laptops, workstations, monitors, printers, storage devices, network gear, backup devices, UPSs, and cooling units. Capture the location, model number, "size" (in units appropriate to the specific equipment), and age of each item.

  It's helpful to have power consumption data for each item as well. Rated power consumption can be misleading—better to measure a device's actual energy use with a Kill A Watt meter, which costs around $20.[2] For devices that have both active and sleep states (e.g., printers), you may want to record average energy use over a one-day or one-week period.

- **Accounting of consumables** – paper, toner, storage media

- **Organizational metrics** – including gross revenue, number of employees, number of physical locations, total facility energy consumption, IT equipment energy consumption (in data centers), data center cooling energy consumption, total IT capital cost, total IT operations cost, and total facilities costs for data centers.

Once you've collected this baseline data, identify one to three targets for optimization. These targets should be tied to your organization's overall strategy for success and growth, and if achieved, they should also demonstrate progress toward becoming a greener IT shop. We can't tell you what targets will work best for your environment, but here are some appropriate examples:

- Data center energy consumption per dollar of gross revenue
- Number of employees per physical server
- Sheets of paper used per employee per month
- Average energy consumption of an employee's workspace equipment
- Average life of a laptop computer
- Data center energy use as a proportion of total facility use[3]

Plan to reassess your green IT status at least yearly, but review energy consumption monthly.

28.2 The Green IT Eco-Pyramid

It's easy to see how eco-unfriendly your organization is. The hard part is making (and monitoring) progress toward the goal of being green. To help you navigate the sea of choices presented in this chapter, we map green IT strategies into three divisions, as shown in Exhibit A on the next page.

2. This product is designed for the North American market, but similar products exist for other markets. A version made for the UK can be found at reuk.co.uk/Buy-UK-Power-Meter.htm.
3. This metric multiplied by 100 yields the percentage of facility power delivered to IT equipment and is known in the industry as "DCiE." It is a standard metric that can be used to compare organizations. Power usage effectiveness (PUE) is the reciprocal of DCiE and is a common benchmark for very large data centers.

Exhibit A Approaches to green IT

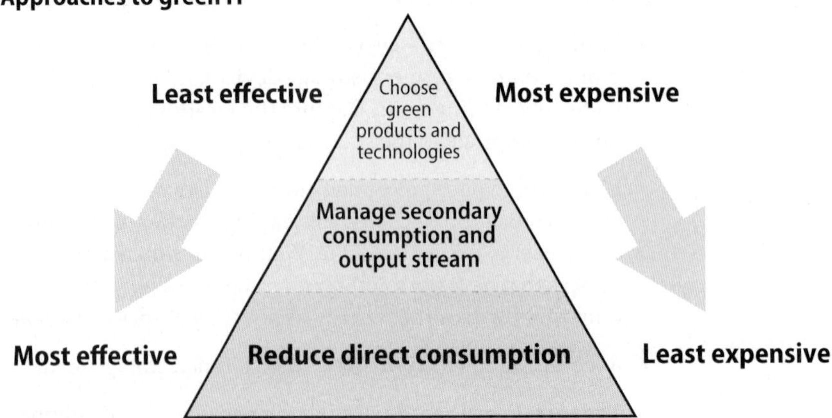

We show these categories in the form of a pyramid because the strategies at the bottom have the most significant impact and are most likely to provide secondary benefits. As you go up the pyramid, the strategies involve more cost and effort and tend to be less effective.

Reducing direct consumption should always be your first-choice strategy; less is more. If you can achieve your mission with less effort and fewer resources, that eliminates both capital and operational costs.

Mitigation of secondary consumption is the next best strategy. For example, the cooling needed to support a server counts as secondary consumption since it only occurs because the server exists in the first place. Optimizing the HVAC system to minimize cooling expenses saves money, but it doesn't save as much as eliminating the server entirely.

Perhaps somewhat nonintuitively, choosing products and technologies that have been designed to be "green" is our lowest-value strategy. Think of it this way: we first reduce the number of cars on the road as much as possible, and only then do we replace the remaining cars with fuel efficient models.

28.3 Green IT strategies: data center

Data centers are excellent targets for green IT initiatives because they typically operate 7 × 24 × 365 and are under the direct control of the IT group. A study by Lawrence Berkeley Laboratories showed that data centers can be as many as 40 times more energy-intensive than conventional office space.[4]

At this level of consumption, special strategies are required. As shown in Exhibit B, the strategies to reduce direct consumption at the bottom of the pyramid are

4. See eetd.lbl.gov/emills/PUBS/PDF/ACEEE-datacenters.pdf for lots of gory details.

the most effective approaches. You don't need to use every strategy in a given environment, but every little bit counts.

Exhibit B Green IT strategies for data centers

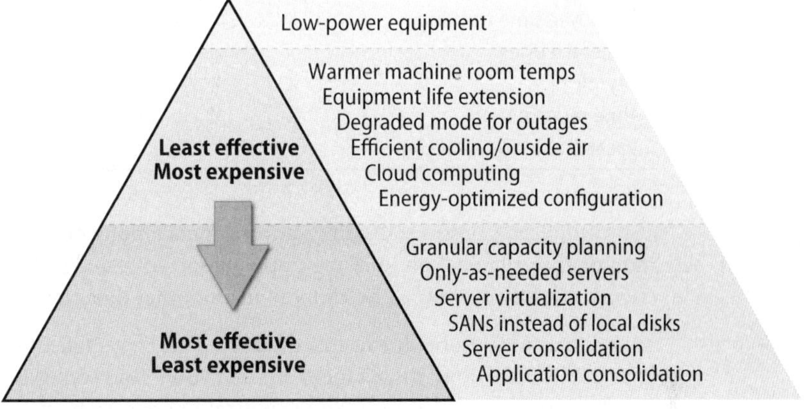

Application consolidation

Over time, organizations and IT departments tend to accumulate applications. New applications come onboard to support specific business initiatives and the CEO's pet projects, but old applications rarely die. More commonly, they linger "on the road to retirement" for a decade with no one being willing to take the risk of pulling the plug. Whatever the reason, the number one opportunity for progress in an established organization is to consolidate applications to the minimum set that meets current business needs.

Let's consider an example organization that has three applications: EmployeeLinq, AccountAwesome, and ElectricClockster. Although this is a simplified example, it's loosely based on real-world applications used by one organization that we examined. Each of the applications had a back-end database server, an application server, and a web front-end server. That's a total of nine servers to support these three applications.

The first step toward consolidation is to map out the functions provided by each application. Table 28.1 on the next page shows the features of our example apps. As you can see, there's quite a bit of overlap.

This organization had three systems that could be (and were!) used to track time, two systems that could do payroll (though only one was currently in use), and many other overlapping functions.

This situation came to pass because three different departments—Finance, Human Resources, and Operations—had each chosen their own application. Not only does this lack of coordination waste energy and computing resources, but it

Table 28.1 Functional breakdown of three applications

Function	EL	AA	EC
Accounts payable/receivable		X	
Benefits management	X	X	
Employee time tracking	X	X	X
General ledger		X	
Payroll	X	X	
Time reporting	X	X	X
Vacation/sick day tracking		X	X

also complicates or forestalls integration of data among departments. In this case, moving the organization to a single application trimmed software, hardware, and energy costs by over 60% and resulted in smoother data flow within the company.

Your situation is probably not this dramatic, but if you take the time to map out your application domains, chances are that you'll find some significant overlap. The business case for consolidating applications is easy to make because the projected results can (at least in part) be expressed in dollars saved. Data integration and operational improvements are just icing on the cake.

Server consolidation

Most organizations have at least a few "single purpose" servers that operate at 10% utilization or less. For example, we've seen many organizations that have dedicated NTP (network time protocol) servers. NTP is a low-overhead protocol that requires very little computational effort. Reserving a server for NTP is like flying a Boeing 767 cross-country with only one passenger.

Server consolidation is a close cousin of application consolidation and is equally effective. Instead of bundling multiple functions into one application, you bundle multiple services onto one server machine.

Unlike Windows, UNIX and Linux excel at preemptive multitasking. A good solution in the NTP case is to run the NTP daemon on the same servers that provide common infrastructural services such as DNS and Kerberos.[5]

Another common opportunity for server consolidation is presented by database servers that are dedicated to a single application. If you have competent sysadmins and DBAs (and good monitoring), a single database server should be able to host the databases for many applications. Once again, this consolidation reduces license fees, capital costs, and energy consumption.

5. NTP is a special case in that its response latency must be kept low. However, that doesn't mean you can't run other services on the same machine. NTP server daemons are commonly **nice**d to give them ready access to the CPU whenever they want it (see page 129). You can achieve similar ends—perhaps even a bit more reliably—through server virtualization.

In some cases, you may be able to reduce the number of servers you need by replacing old, less powerful servers with a smaller number of new, more powerful, and more energy-efficient servers.

SAN storage

One common indicator of IT gluttony is a fleet of servers that are loaded up with hard disks. For example, imagine a data center that has 100 servers, each with six 1TB disks. That's 600 disks that must be manufactured, maintained, powered, and eventually scrubbed and disposed of. The likelihood that these drives' average utilization exceeds 50% is virtually nil.

This approach results in excessive waste because it chops the storage into discrete chunks that cannot be efficiently managed to make "just the right amount" of storage available to each server or application. Some servers may have less than 1TB of actual data in play while others are underprovisioned at 6TB and unable to benefit from the idle drives in their neighbor's chassis. The reality is that it's hard to push much above 30% storage utilization in a typical data center that has discrete storage for each server.

A good alternative to this approach is a storage area network or SAN; see page 274 for more details. SAN technology provides highly reliable storage that is also eco-friendly because sysadmins can allocate the centralized storage space efficiently. Many organizations exceed 90% utilization on their SANs. That's triple the efficiency of discrete storage. Now that SANs can run on Ethernet, there is no longer any major hardware hurdle to deploying this wonderful tool.

Server virtualization

Server virtualization seems to be everyone's favorite topic in the green IT arena, although some of the current buzz is probably fueled by the marketing dollars of the companies selling virtualization platforms.

Server virtualization (covered in detail in Chapter 24) is in fact a fantastic tool. Its eco-impact is similar to that of server consolidation. In both approaches, several applications or services end up running on a single computer. Virtualization reduces energy consumption by reducing the number of chassis in production and achieving higher utilization of the remaining units.

Virtualization offers some additional features that are not provided by consolidation, such as the ability to easily scale out identical systems, the ability to reserve a portion of the hardware's capacity for a given server, and the ability to migrate virtual servers among physical chassis. Those aspects of virtualization are a win.

Virtualization also has a dark side. Applications that are I/O intensive typically do not virtualize well and tend to be more sluggish in a virtualized environment. The virtualization process itself consumes resources, so virtualized systems have overhead that physical systems do not. The additional layers of abstraction introduced by virtualization require constant vigilance on the part of system administrators, both because the virtualization itself must be actively managed and because virtualization may affect the operation of the hosted systems.

Virtualization is best employed in environments that have adequate IT staff and mature processes. At this point, we don't really recommend server virtualization for beginning sysadmins. However, the technology is rapidly becoming more reliable and easier to use. Soon, it will be inescapable.

Only-as-needed servers

Only-as-needed servers are powered down when not in use. This approach works best in cases where the demand for computing power is predictably cyclical; for example, when the server is linked to the accounting cycle or to work that is only done in the wee hours of the morning. This isn't a common technique, but every once in a while there's a green IT savings opportunity so special that only this trick fits.

You can roll your own implementation with some scripts and Ethernet-connected (managed) power strips. Platforms such as RightScale (rightscale.com) extend the concept into demand-based territory. Using systems such as this, you can set thresholds at which additional servers are automatically spun up (or spun down) according to metrics such as CPU load or transaction volume.

Granular utilization and capacity planning

In green IT, as in other areas, you can only manage what you can measure. Careful data collection is an essential tool for optimizing your environment.

If you track your site's use of resources such as CPU and memory (see Chapter 29, *Performance Analysis*), you can plan your hardware deployments so that you don't have to buy overprovisioned servers "just to make sure" your capacity is sufficient. Monitoring and analysis take time, but they're an excellent basis for "lean and mean" data center management.

Buy only what you need; use only what you must.

Energy-optimized server configuration

Some systems give you the opportunity to save energy by altering the behavior of the system itself.

Power-saving options for Linux

CPUs and CPU cores can be idled to reduce their power consumption. To achieve the lowest possible power consumption, you pack as many threads as possible onto one core or CPU and do not activate additional cores or CPUs until they are needed. Conversely, to achieve the best possible performance, you distribute threads as widely as possible among cores and CPUs to minimize the time-costs of context switching and cache contention. In theory, you must trade away some performance to reduce power consumption.

In practice, the opportunity to idle parts of the CPU only arises when the system isn't busy. In those circumstances, the additional overhead of packing threads onto one core may have no detectable effect. Experiment to see if you can discern any difference with your specific workload.

The process scheduler's power management system consults two control variables, both of which are set through files in the **/sys/devices/system/cpu** directory. The **sched_mc_power_savings** variable controls whether all cores on a CPU are used before activating another CPU, and the **sched_smt_power_savings** variable controls whether all thread slots on a core are used before activating another core. In both cases, a value of 0 turns power saving off and a 1 turns it on.

For example, to turn on both power-saving modes, you could use the commands

```
$ sudo sh -c 'echo 1 > /sys/devices/system/cpu/sched_mc_power_savings'
$ sudo sh -c 'echo 1 > /sys/devices/system/cpu/sched_smt_power_savings'
```

To make these changes persistent across reboots, check out the **sysctl** command or add the lines to a startup script such as **/etc/init.d/local** on Ubuntu or SUSE (create it if necessary) or **/etc/rc.local** on Red Hat.

A computer's CPU is one of its most profligate consumers of energy (just look at those heat sinks!), so aggressive power management can significantly reduce the system's power use.

Filesystem power savings

You can save power and increase performance by preventing filesystems from maintaining a "last access" time (st_atime) for every file. This information isn't very useful, and it theoretically adds a tax of one seek and one write to every file operation. (The real-world impact is harder to quantify because of block caching.)

Zedlewski et al. analyzed hard disk power consumption in a 2003 paper and concluded that seeks cost about 4 millijoules each on an IBM Microdrive; the cost is probably at least double that for a standard drive with its larger armature. Combining the cost of seeks with the cost of writes, we calculate the benefit of disabling last access times to be up to several kWh per drive per year. Not a huge savings, but probably worthwhile for the performance benefits alone; the energy savings are just gravy.

On most filesystems, you can turn off maintenance of the last access time with the **noatime** option to **mount**:

```
$ sudo mount -o remount,noatime /
```

Some Linux systems also support the **relatime** mount option, which provides hybrid functionality. Under this option, last access time is only updated if the previous value is earlier than the file's modification time. This mode allows tools such as mail readers to correctly identify cases in which an interesting file has been changed but not yet read.

Cloud computing

See page 987 for more information about cloud computing.

Take a deep breath, and think outside the box—outside the box of your data center, that is. The recent availability of "cloud computing" has brought many benefits, but one worth mentioning here is energy efficiency. In their quest to provide low-cost, high-reliability services, providers like Amazon have constructed ultra-high-efficiency data centers and utilization management processes. These cloud providers can supply compute cycles that are more eco-friendly than you could ever achieve in your own data center.

If you have applications (especially web applications) that don't absolutely have to live under your own roof, consider outsourcing their infrastructure to a cloud data center. You still have complete administrative control of the virtual systems that run in this environment. You just never get to physically "hug" them.

Free cooling

Nothing is more disturbing on a cold winter's day than to walk outside a data center and see the compressor pad whirling away at full speed. It's 10 degrees outside, but the HVAC engineer apparently designed a system that uses mechanical cooling (and an amazing amount of energy) to pull heat out of the data center regardless of the ambient temperature.

Fortunately, some modern HVAC engineers specialize in data centers and have a better solution to this problem: use outside air for cooling when the temperature is low enough.

Of course, this solution isn't available everywhere or in every season. The Green Grid, a consortium of technology companies dedicated to advancing energy efficiency in data centers, now produces "free cooling" maps for North America and Europe that illustrate how many hours a year a center can be cooled by outside air in a given area. A more detailed on-line cooling calculator is also available—check it out at thegreengrid.org.

Efficient data center cooling

Various tricks of data center design can be used to reduce the amount of energy used for cooling. For example, the hot aisle/cold aisle layout described on page 1089 concentrates cooling where it is most needed and allows other parts of the data center to operate at higher temperatures.

See Chapter 27, *Data Center Basics*, for a broader discussion of some of these tips.

Degraded mode for outages

Many organizations are obsessed with availability (aka uptime). What often aren't considered are the additional energy and resources used to ensure a particular level of availability.

Internal customers are accustomed to thinking of services as being either up or down. Consider offering *degraded* service as an additional choice for fault management, and ask whether that might meet the customers' availability needs.

For example, instead of running a fully redundant set of equipment for every production environment, you could use server virtualization to deploy several applications to a single chassis in the event of an outage. This configuration might supply all the standard functionality, but at slower speed than normal. In some cases, this tradeoff can reduce the organization's capital costs by 50% or more.

Equipment life extension

Electronics manufacturing consumes energy and generates toxic waste, so purchases of new equipment entail an environmental cost that isn't necessarily reflected in the price tag. Unfortunately, the technology industry has become so accustomed to rapid innovation and product development that manufacturers often discontinue support for equipment after just a few years.

If your current equipment meets your business needs and is reasonably energy efficient, you may want to consider a life extension strategy.[6] Such a scheme typically involves scouring eBay and other sources of salvage equipment for similar systems you can acquire cheaply and bring to your site as a source of vintage spare parts. This approach typically extends system life by two to three years, though in at least one case we have kept a system running eight extra years this way.

If older equipment is not meeting performance requirements or cannot be supplemented by on-site spares, another option is to buy new equipment for the production environment and reassign the current equipment to a development environment, where performance and reliability are not as important. This approach doesn't avoid new purchases entirely, but it may delay purchases for the development environment for a year or two.

If equipment simply must be retired, make sure that you turn it over to a legitimate computer recycler who will break it down into component pieces and recycle each piece appropriately. Make sure the recycler has a certified data destruction program so that your data doesn't later show up in someone else's hands.

Computers contain a surprising amount of toxic waste. Whatever you do, don't just throw old equipment into the dumpster—that waste typically goes to a landfill not designed to handle electronics.

Some regions have organizations that provide computer recycling services for free. In the Portland, Oregon, area, freegeek.org is a model recycling program.

6. If your current equipment is not energy efficient, you may be better off replacing it immediately to achieve operational energy savings, even when disposal and replacement costs are considered.

Warmer temperature in the data center

Approximately one-third of the energy consumed in a traditional data center goes to support cooling. Historically, data centers have maintained temperatures in the range of 68–77 degrees Fahrenheit. These values are now seen as conservative.

In early 2009, the American Society of Heating, Refrigerating and Air-Conditioning Engineers (ASHRAE) issued guidance that an expanded range of 64.4–80.6 degrees Fahrenheit is acceptable for data centers. Raising the data center temperature by three degrees typically saves an estimated 12% in cooling costs.

See Chapter 27, *Data Center Basics*, for additional cooling tips.

Low-power equipment

When procuring new equipment, take the time to select products that have minimal environmental impact.

The IEEE has standardized the criteria for environmental assessment of electronics in IEEE publication 1680. One evaluation system based on IEEE P1680, the Electronic Products Environmental Assessment Tool (EPEAT), considers a wide range of potential impacts that might be involved in a product's manufacture. It can help you compare products uniformly. The system currently covers desktop and laptop computers, thin clients, workstations, and computer monitors. It is required for U.S. federal government purchases. Visit EPEAT at epeat.net.

Note that EPEAT compliance requires conformance to Energy Star standards (in version 5.0 as of July 1, 2009) for energy consumption during use.

Some server manufacturers (including Dell, Sun, IBM, and HP) offer environmentally focused product families. But even eco-friendly servers have an environmental impact and consume power. The existence of these product lines should not be viewed as a license to add equipment in the name of being green. Focus *first* on reducing the number of servers that you need, *then* pick the most eco-friendly option for meeting that need.

28.4 Green IT strategies: user workspace

Staff work areas present another set of opportunities to green up your operations. Exhibit C summarizes some improvements to consider.

Below are listed workspace arenas in which green IT can be a player. Most of the accompanying suggestions are straightforward, and you'll find many of them familiar from other sources. (Chances are that you're already doing some of them.)

- **User education** – encourage users to power off equipment that's not needed, to think before they print documents, and to let desktop equipment go into a power-saving mode instead of running a screen saver (or, better yet, turn it off).

Exhibit C Green IT strategies for the workspace

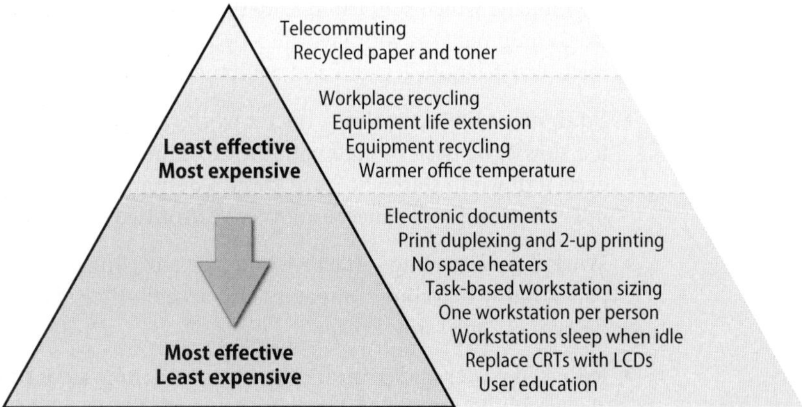

- **Monitors** – replace CRTs with LCD monitors. They use significantly less power and contain fewer toxic elements.
- **Workstation idle** – centrally configure workstations to "sleep" or power-off when idle for a given period (e.g., 30 minutes).
- **Workstation count** – limit desktop workstations to one per user. Users who claim to need more than one workstation should be encouraged to use a desktop virtualization client.
- **Task-based sizing** – don't buy "one size fits all" workstations. Have three or four tiers of workstation specifications so that users have the appropriate configuration for their task mix.
- **Personal heaters** – this is not really an IT topic per se, but it's a pet peeve of ours, and the IT department is usually the one to notice. Do not allow the use of personal space heaters in users' offices or cubicles. Explain to users that such heaters feed a vicious cycle in which the office HVAC and the heater fight in an effort to enforce different temperature targets. If the user's work area is truly the wrong temperature, escalate the issue with the appropriate HVAC support team. (Maybe you can offer them some VIP IT support in exchange for their assistance.)
- **Print duplexing** – configure printers to default to double-sided, two-up printing. This works fine for most routine printing, and users can always select something other than the default for special cases.
- **eDocument campaign** – launch a campaign or contest within your organization to find ways to eliminate the use of printed documents.
- **Office temperature** – since office computing equipment is designed to work at much higher temperatures than humans are, raise that office cooling setting to 78°F or higher.

- **Equipment recycling** – once or twice a year, hold equipment recycling days during which staff can pile up their unwanted, unused, or underutilized equipment for your favorite recycling company to haul off. If you're really eco-friendly, let staff add equipment from home to the pile.
- **Equipment life extension** – once a workstation has become too old or too slow to be used by staff with the most intense computing demands, cycle it down to staff who have lower requirements. They'll see it as an upgrade, and you'll squeeze another year or two of life out of it.
- **Workplace recycling** – start a workplace recycling program for used paper. Many recycling companies also accept office plastics (soda bottles, etc.) in the same stream.
- **Recycled paper and printer cartridges** – become a consumer of recycled goods. Purchase 100% recycled paper for your printers and copiers, and buy recycled toner cartridges as well. We've had outstanding luck with Boise Aspen 100 as general-purpose recycled printer paper that's inexpensive and has outstanding ecological characteristics.
- **Telecommuting** – encourage staff to telecommute one or more days per week by installing and supporting technologies that facilitate remote access, such as VPNs, VOIP service at home, and web-available applications. In addition to the benefits for the staff involved, telecommuting reduces the use of transportation and office support services. Make sure, though, that telecommuters turn off their equipment at whichever site they're not occupying on a given day. Otherwise, this policy can backfire, at least from an energy conservation perspective.

28.5 Green IT friends

If you're looking to do even more in the green IT space, you can find both camaraderie and guidance from a variety of organizations and resources. Table 28.2 lists some of the groups that we're familiar with and recommend.

Table 28.2 The green mafia

Organization	Web site	Description
Energy Star	energystar.gov	Consumer product standards
EPEAT	epeat.net	Green electronics manufacturing
French Green IT	greenit.fr	French Green IT blog
Green IT Observatory	greenit.bf.rmit.edu.au	Australian green IT research
Green IT Promo Council	greenit-pc.jp	Green IT for Japan and Asia
Green Standards Trust	greenstandards.org	Office equipment recycling
IT Industry Council	itic.org	General best practices for IT
Less Watts	lesswatts.org	Saving power with Linux
The Green Grid	thegreengrid.org	Data center focus

In addition to stockpiling green ideas, many of these organizations have their own sets of benchmark data that you can use to find out how your organization compares with others of similar size and activity.

28.6 Exercises

E28.1 Use a Kill A Watt meter to measure the power consumption of your desktop workstation under various load conditions, including sleep mode or power-save mode. How much power would be saved if you turned your workstation off every night?

E28.2 Write a script that emails the system administrator when CPU load indicates that a new server should be spun up.

E28.3 Make a list of the main applications that your organization uses today. Which ones have overlapping functionality?

E28.4 Visit thegreengrid.org and determine if your location could benefit by using outside air for cooling.

☆ E28.5 Organizations such as TerraPass and Carbonfund.org sell CO_2 "offsets" through which organizations can compensate for their carbon emissions. For example, one common strategy used by offsetters is to subsidize the development of carbon-neutral energy sources (e.g., solar and wind power), with the goal of reducing future emissions.

These programs have proved controversial. Some observers doubt the reality of the claimed emission reductions, while others question the programs on philosophical grounds.[7]

Select a specific carbon offset provider and assess the plausibility of the strategies it is pursuing. Are the programs sufficiently well documented that you could make your own evaluation of their quality? Has any impartial group evaluated this provider, and if so, what were their conclusions?

7. WordPress developer Mark Jaquith wrote, "It's like killing a person, and then convincing a murderer to kill one less person. You didn't negate your murder. You still killed the person. Convincing someone else to reduce their emissions doesn't make up for your emissions." We don't necessarily endorse this view, but it is representative the anti-offset perspective.

29 Performance Analysis

Performance analysis and tuning are often likened to system administration witchcraft. They're not really witchcraft, but they do qualify as both science and art. The "science" part involves making careful quantitative measurements and applying the scientific method. The "art" part relates to the need to balance resources in a practical, level-headed way, since optimizing for one application or user may result in other applications or users suffering. As with so many things in life, you may find that it's impossible to make everyone happy.

A sentiment widespread in the blogosphere has it that today's performance problems are somehow wildly different from those of previous decades. That claim is inaccurate. It's true that systems have become more complex, but the baseline determinants of performance and the high-level abstractions used to measure and manage it remain the same as always. Unfortunately, improvements in baseline system performance correlate strongly with the community's ability to create new applications that suck up all available resources.

This chapter focuses on the performance of systems that are used as servers. Desktop systems typically do not experience the same types of performance issues that servers do, and the answer to the question of how to improve performance on a desktop machine is almost always “Upgrade the hardware.” Users like this answer because it means they get fancy new systems on their desks more often.

One of the ways in which UNIX and Linux differ from other mainstream operating systems is in the amount of data that is available to characterize their inner workings. Detailed information is available for every level of the system, and administrators control a variety of tunable parameters. If you still have trouble identifying the cause of a performance problem despite the available instrumentation, source code is often available for review. For these reasons, UNIX and Linux are typically the operating systems of choice for performance-conscious consumers.

Even so, performance tuning isn’t easy. Users and administrators alike often think that if they only knew the right “magic,” their systems would be twice as fast. One common fantasy involves tweaking the kernel variables that control the paging system and the buffer pools. These days, kernels are pretuned to achieve reasonable (though admittedly, not optimal) performance under a variety of load conditions. If you try to optimize the system on the basis of one particular measure of performance (e.g., buffer utilization), the chances are high that you will distort the system’s behavior relative to other performance metrics and load conditions.

The most serious performance issues often lie within applications and have little to do with the underlying operating system. This chapter discusses system-level performance tuning and mostly leaves application-level tuning to others. As a system administrator, you need to be mindful that application developers are people too. (How many times have you said, or thought, that “it must be a network problem”?) Given the complexity of modern applications, some problems can only be resolved through collaboration among application developers, system administrators, server engineers, DBAs, storage administrators, and network architects. In this chapter, we help you determine what data and information to take back to these other folks to help them solve a performance problem—if, indeed, the problem lies in their area. This approach is far more productive than just saying, “Everything looks fine; it’s not my problem.”

In all cases, take everything you read on the web with a ~~tablespoon~~ cup of salt. In the area of system performance, you will see superficially convincing arguments on all sorts of topics. However, most of the proponents of these theories do not have the knowledge, discipline, and time required to design valid experiments. Popular support means very little; for every hare-brained proposal, you can expect to see a Greek chorus of “I increased the size of my buffer cache by a factor of ten just like Joe said, and my system feels *much, much* faster!!!” Right.

Here are some rules to keep in mind:

- Collect and review *historical* information about your system. If the system was performing fine a week ago, an examination of the aspects of the system that have changed may lead you to a smoking gun. Keep baselines and trends in your hip pocket to pull out in an emergency. As a first step, review log files to see if a hardware problem has developed.

Chapter 21, *Network Management and Debugging*, discusses some trend analysis tools that are also applicable to performance monitoring. The **sar** utility discussed on page 1129 can also be used as a poor man's trend analysis tool.

- Tune your system in a way that lets you compare the current results to the system's previous baseline.
- Always make sure you have a rollback plan in case your magic fix actually makes things worse.
- Don't intentionally overload your systems or your network. The kernel gives each process the illusion of infinite resources. But once 100% of the system's resources are in use, the kernel has to work hard to maintain that illusion, delaying processes and often consuming a sizable fraction of the resources itself.
- As in particle physics, the more information you collect with system monitoring utilities, the more you affect the system you are observing. It is best to rely on something simple and lightweight that runs in the background (e.g., **sar** or **vmstat**) for routine observation. If those feelers show something significant, you can investigate further with other tools.

29.1 What you can do to improve performance

Here are some specific things you can do to improve performance:

- Ensure that the system has enough memory. As we see in the next section, memory size has a major influence on performance. Memory is so inexpensive these days that you can usually afford to load every performance-sensitive machine to the gills.
- If you are using UNIX or Linux as a web server or as some other type of network application server, you may want to spread traffic among several systems with a commercial load balancing appliance such as Cisco's Content Services Switch (cisco.com), Nortel's Alteon Application Switch (nortel.com), or Brocade's ServerIron (brocade.com). These boxes make several physical servers appear to be one logical server to the outside world. They balance the load according to one of several user-selectable algorithms such as "most responsive server" or "round robin."

  These load balancers also provide useful redundancy should a server go down. They're really quite necessary if your site must handle unexpected traffic spikes.
- Double-check the configuration of the system and of individual applications. Many applications can be tuned to yield tremendous performance improvements (e.g., by spreading data across disks, by not performing DNS lookups on the fly, or by running multiple instances of a server).

- Correct problems of usage, both those caused by "real work" (too many servers run at once, inefficient programming practices, batch jobs run at excessive priority, and large jobs run at inappropriate times of day) and those caused by the system (such as unwanted daemons).
- Eliminate storage resources' dependence on mechanical operations where possible. Solid state disk drives (SSDs) are widely available and can provide quick performance boosts because they don't require the physical movement of a disk or armature to read bits. SSDs are easily installed in place of existing old-school disk drives.[1]
- Organize hard disks and filesystems so that load is evenly balanced, maximizing I/O throughput. For specific applications such as databases, you can use a fancy multidisk technology such as striped RAID to optimize data transfers. Consult your database vendor for recommendations. For Linux systems, ensure that you've selected the appropriate Linux I/O scheduler for your disk (see page 1130 for details).
- It's important to note that different types of applications and databases respond differently to being spread across multiple disks. RAID comes in many forms; take time to determine which form (if any) is appropriate for your particular application.
- Monitor your network to be sure that it is not saturated with traffic and that the error rate is low. A wealth of network information is available through the **netstat** command, described on page 868. See also Chapter 21, *Network Management and Debugging*.
- Identify situations in which the system is fundamentally inadequate to satisfy the demands being made of it. You cannot tune your way out of these situations.

These steps are listed in rough order of effectiveness. Adding memory and balancing traffic across multiple servers can often make a huge difference in performance. The effectiveness of the other measures ranges from noticeable to none.

Analysis and optimization of software data structures and algorithms almost always lead to significant performance gains. But unless you have a substantial base of local software, this level of design is usually out of your control.

29.2 Factors that affect performance

Perceived performance is determined by the basic capabilities of the system's resources and by the efficiency with which those resources are allocated and shared.

1. Current SSDs have two main weaknesses. First, they are an order of magnitude more expensive per gigabyte than traditional hard disks. Second, they may be rewritten only a limited number of times before wearing out. Their rewrite capacity is high enough to be immaterial for desktop machines (tens of thousands of writes per block), but it's a potential stumbling block for a high-traffic server. See page 212 for more information about SSDs.

The exact definition of a "resource" is rather vague. It can include such items as cached contexts on the CPU chip and entries in the address table of the memory controller. However, to a first approximation, only the following four resources have much effect on performance:

- CPU utilization
- Memory
- Storage I/O
- Network I/O

If resources are still left after active processes have taken what they want, the system's performance is about as good as it can be.

If there are not enough resources to go around, processes must take turns. A process that does not have immediate access to the resources it needs must wait around doing nothing. The amount of time spent waiting is one of the basic measures of performance degradation.

CPU utilization is one of the easiest resources to measure. A constant amount of processing power is always available. In theory, that amount is 100% of the CPU cycles, but overhead and various inefficiencies make the real-life number more like 95%. A process that's using more than 90% of the CPU is entirely CPU bound and is consuming essentially all of the system's available computing power.

Many people assume that the speed of the CPU is the most important factor affecting a system's overall performance. Given infinite amounts of all other resources or certain types of applications (e.g., numerical simulations), a faster CPU *does* make a dramatic difference. But in the everyday world, CPU speed is relatively unimportant.

Disk bandwidth is a common performance bottleneck. Because traditional hard disks are mechanical systems, it takes many milliseconds to locate a disk block, fetch its contents, and wake up the process that's waiting for it. Delays of this magnitude overshadow every other source of performance degradation. Each disk access causes a stall worth millions of CPU instructions. Solid state drives are one tool you can use to address this problem; they are significantly faster than drives with moving parts.

Because of virtual memory, disk bandwidth and memory can be directly related if the demand for physical memory is greater than the supply. Situations in which physical memory becomes scarce often result in memory pages being written to disk so they can be reclaimed and reused for another purpose. In these situations, using memory is just as expensive as using the disk. Avoid this trap when performance is important; ensure that every system has adequate physical memory.

Network bandwidth resembles disk bandwidth in many ways because of the latencies involved in network communication. However, networks are atypical in that they involve entire communities rather than individual computers. They are also particularly susceptible to hardware problems and overloaded servers.

29.3 How to analyze performance problems

It can be difficult to isolate performance problems in a complex system. As a sysadmin, you often receive anecdotal problem reports that suggest a particular cause or fix (e.g., "The web server has gotten painfully sluggish because of all those damn AJAX calls…"). Take note of this information, but don't assume that it's accurate or reliable; do your own investigation.

A rigorous, transparent, scientific methodology helps you reach conclusions that you and others in your organization can rely on. Such an approach lets others evaluate your results, increases your credibility, and raises the likelihood that your suggested changes will actually fix the problem.

"Being scientific" doesn't mean that you have to gather all the relevant data yourself. External information is usually very helpful. Don't spend hours looking into issues that can just as easily be looked up in a FAQ.

We suggest the following five steps:

Step 1: Formulate the question.

Pose a specific question in a defined functional area, or state a tentative conclusion or recommendation that you are considering. Be specific about the type of technology, the components involved, the alternatives you are considering, and the outcomes of interest.

Step 2: Gather and classify evidence.

Conduct a systematic search of documentation, knowledge bases, known issues, blogs, white papers, discussions, and other resources to locate external evidence related to your question. On your own systems, capture telemetry data and, where necessary or possible, instrument specific system and application areas of interest.

Step 3: Critically appraise the data.

Review each data source for relevance and critique it for validity. Abstract key information and note the quality of the sources.

Step 4: Summarize the evidence both narratively and graphically.

Combine findings from multiple sources into a narrative précis and, if possible, a graphic representation. Data that seems equivocal in numeric form can become decisive once charted.

Step 5: Develop a conclusion statement.

Arrive at a concise statement of your conclusions (i.e., the answer to your question). Assign a grade to indicate the overall strength or weakness of the evidence that supports your conclusions.

29.4 System performance checkup

Enough generalities—let's look at some specific tools and areas of interest. Before you take measurements, you need to know what you're looking at.

Taking stock of your hardware

Start your inquiry with an inventory of your hardware, especially CPU and memory resources. This inventory can help you interpret the information presented by other tools and can help you set realistic expectations regarding the upper bounds on performance.

On Linux systems, the **/proc** filesystem is the place to look to find an overview of what hardware your operating system thinks you have (more detailed hardware information can be found in **/sys**; see page 438). Table 29.1 shows some of the key files. See page 421 for general information about **/proc**.

Table 29.1 Sources of hardware information on Linux

File	Contents
/proc/cpuinfo	CPU type and description
/proc/meminfo	Memory size and usage
/proc/diskstats	Disk devices and usage statistics

Four lines in **/proc/cpuinfo** help you identify the system's exact CPU: vendor_id, cpu family, model, and model name. Some of the values are cryptic; it's best to look them up on-line.

The exact info contained in **/proc/cpuinfo** varies by system and processor, but here's a representative example:

```
suse$ cat /proc/cpuinfo
processor       : 0
vendor_id       : GenuineIntel
cpu family      : 6
model           : 15
model name      : Intel(R) Xeon(R) CPUE5310@ 1.60GHz
stepping        : 11
cpu MHz         : 1600.003
cache size      : 4096 KB
physical id     : 0
cpu cores       : 2
siblings        : 2
...
```

The file contains one entry for each processor core seen by the OS. The data varies slightly by kernel version. The processor value uniquely identifies each core. physical id values are unique per physical socket on the circuit board, and core id values are unique per core within a physical socket. Cores that support hyper-threading (duplication of CPU contexts without duplication of other processing features) are identified by an ht in the flags field. If hyperthreading is actually in use, the siblings field for each core shows how many contexts are available on a given core.

Another command to run for information on PC hardware is **dmidecode**. It dumps the system's Desktop Management Interface (DMI, aka SMBIOS) data. The most useful option is **-t** *type*; Table 29.2 shows the valid *types*.

Table 29.2 Type values for dmidecode -t

Value	Description
1	System information
2	Base board Information
3	Chassis information
4	Processor information
7	Cache information
8	Port connector information
9	System slot information
11	OEM strings
12	System configuration options
13	BIOS language information
16	Physical memory array
17	Memory device
19	Memory array mapped address
32	System boot information
38	IPMI device information

The example below shows typical information:

```
suse$ sudo dmidecode -t 4
# dmidecode 2.7
SMBIOS 2.2 present.

Handle 0x0004, DMI type 4, 32 bytes.
Processor Information
        Socket Designation: PGA 370
        Type: Central Processor
        Family: Celeron
        Manufacturer: GenuineIntel
        ID: 65 06 00 00 FF F9 83 01
        Signature: Type 0, Family 6, Model 6, Stepping 5
...
```

Bits of network configuration information are scattered about the system. **ifconfig -a** is the best source of IP and MAC information for each configured interface.

On Solaris systems, the **psrinfo -v** and **prtconf** commands are the best sources of information about CPU and memory resources, respectively. Example output for these commands is shown below.

```
solaris$ psrinfo -v
Status of virtual processor 0 as of: 01/31/2010 21:22:00
  on-line since 07/13/2009 15:55:48.
  The sparcv9 processor operates at 1200 MHz,
      and has a sparcv9 floating point processor.
Status of virtual processor 1 as of: 01/31/2010 21:22:00
  on-line since 07/13/2009 15:55:49.
  The sparcv9 processor operates at 1200 MHz,
      and has a sparcv9 floating point processor.
```

```
solaris$ prtconf
System Configuration:  Sun Microsystems  sun4v
Memory size: 32640 Megabytes
System Peripherals (Software Nodes):

SUNW,Sun-Fire-T200
...
```

Under HP-UX, **machinfo** is an all-in-one command you can use to investigate a machine's hardware configuration. Here's some typical output:

```
hp-ux$ sudo machinfo
CPU info:
  1 Intel(R) Itanium 2 processor (1.5 GHz, 6 MB)
      400 MT/s bus, CPU version B1

Memory: 4084 MB (3.99 GB)

Firmware info:
  Firmware revision:  02.21
  FP SWA driver revision: 1.18
  BMC firmware revision: 1.50

Platform info:
  Model:            "ia64 hp server rx2600"
OS info:
  Nodename:  hpux11
  Release:   HP-UX B.11.31
Machine:     ia64
```

It takes a bit of work to find CPU and memory information under AIX. First, use the **lscfg** command to find the names of the installed processors.

```
aix$ lscfg | grep Processor
+ proc0                                   Processor
+ proc2                                   Processor
```

You can then use **lsattr** to extract a description of each processor:

```
aix$ lsattr -E -l proc0
frequency     1898100000      Processor Speed          False
smt_enabled   true            Processor SMT enabled    False
smt_threads   2               Processor SMT threads    False
state         enable          Processor state          False
type          PowerPC_POWER5  Processor type           False
```

lsattr can also tell you the amount of physical memory in the system:

```
aix$ lsattr -E -l sys0 -a realmem
realmem    4014080      Amount of usable physical memory in Kbytes
```

Gathering performance data

Most performance analysis tools tell you what's going on at a particular point in time. However, the number and character of loads probably changes throughout the day. Be sure to gather a cross-section of data before taking action. The best information on system performance often becomes clear only after a long period (a month or more) of data collection. It is particularly important to collect data during periods of peak use. Resource limitations and system misconfigurations are often only visible when the machine is under heavy load.

Analyzing CPU usage

You will probably want to gather three kinds of CPU data: overall utilization, load averages, and per-process CPU consumption. Overall utilization can help identify systems on which the CPU's speed is itself the bottleneck. Load averages give you an impression of overall system performance. Per-process CPU consumption data can identify specific processes that are hogging resources.

You can obtain summary information with the **vmstat** command. **vmstat** takes two arguments: the number of seconds to monitor the system for each line of output and the number of reports to provide. If you don't specify the number of reports, **vmstat** runs until you press <Control-C>.

The first line of data returned by **vmstat** reports averages since the system was booted. The subsequent lines are averages within the previous sample period, which defaults to five seconds. For example:

```
$ vmstat 5 5
procs      -----------memory---------- ---swap-------io---- --system-- ----cpu----
 r  b  swpd     free   buff     cache  si so   bi  bo    in    cs us sy id wa
 1  0   820 2606356 428776 487092   0  0 4741  65  1063 4857 25  1 73  0
 1  0   820 2570324 428812 510196   0  0 4613  11  1054 4732 25  1 74  0
 1  0   820 2539028 428852 535636   0  0 5099  13  1057 5219 90  1  9  0
 1  0   820 2472340 428920 581588   0  0 4536  10  1056 4686 87  3 10  0
 3  0   820 2440276 428960 605728   0  0 4818  21  1060 4943 20  3 77  0
```

Although exact columns may vary among systems, CPU utilization stats are fairly consistent across platforms. User time, system (kernel) time, idle time, and time

Performance

waiting for I/O are shown in the us, sy, id, and wa columns on the far right. CPU numbers that are heavy on user time generally indicate computation, and high system numbers indicate that processes are making a lot of system calls or are performing lots of I/O.

A rule of thumb for general-purpose compute servers that has served us well over the years is that the system should spend approximately 50% of its nonidle time in user space and 50% in system space; the overall idle percentage should be nonzero. If you are dedicating a server to a single CPU-intensive application, the majority of time should be spent in user space.

The cs column shows context switches per interval (that is, the number of times that the kernel changed which process was running). The number of interrupts per interval (usually generated by hardware devices or components of the kernel) is shown in the in column. Extremely high cs or in values typically indicate a misbehaving or misconfigured hardware device. The other columns are useful for memory and disk analysis, which we discuss later in this chapter.

Long-term averages of the CPU statistics let you determine whether there is fundamentally enough CPU power to go around. If the CPU usually spends part of its time in the idle state, there are cycles to spare. Upgrading to a faster CPU won't do much to improve the overall throughput of the system, though it may speed up individual operations.

As you can see from this example, the CPU generally flip-flops back and forth between heavy use and idleness. Therefore, it's important to observe these numbers as an average over time. The smaller the monitoring interval, the less consistent the results.

On multiprocessor machines, most tools present an average of processor statistics across all processors. On Linux, Solaris, and AIX, the **mpstat** command generates **vmstat**-like output for each individual processor. The **-P** flag lets you specify a specific processor to report on. **mpstat** is useful for debugging software that supports symmetric multiprocessing—it's also enlightening to see how (in)efficiently your system uses multiple processors. Here's an example that shows the status of each of four processors:

```
linux$ mpstat -P ALL
08:13:38 PM  CPU %user  %nice  %sys  %iowait  %irq  %soft  %idle   intr/s
08:13:38 PM    0  1.02   0.00  0.49     1.29  0.04   0.38  96.79   473.93
08:13:38 PM    1  0.28   0.00  0.22     0.71  0.00   0.01  98.76   232.86
08:13:38 PM    2  0.42   0.00  0.36     1.32  0.00   0.05  97.84   293.85
08:13:38 PM    3  0.38   0.00  0.30     0.94  0.01   0.05  98.32   295.02
```

On a workstation with only one user, the CPU generally spends most of its time idle. Then when you render a web page or switch windows, the CPU is used heavily for a short period. In this situation, information about long-term average CPU usage is not meaningful.

The second CPU statistic that's useful for characterizing the burden on your system is the "load average," which represents the average number of runnable processes. It gives you a good idea of how many pieces the CPU pie is being divided into. The load average is obtained with the **uptime** command:

```
$ uptime
11:10am  up 34 days, 18:42, 5 users, load average: 0.95, 0.38, 0.31
```

Three values are given, corresponding to the 5, 10, and 15-minute averages. In general, the higher the load average, the more important the system's aggregate performance becomes. If there is only one runnable process, that process is usually bound by a single resource (commonly disk bandwidth or CPU). The peak demand for that one resource becomes the determining factor in performance.

When more processes share the system, loads may or may not be more evenly distributed. If the processes on the system all consume a mixture of CPU, disk, and memory, the performance of the system is less likely to be dominated by constraints on a single resource. In this situation, it becomes most important to look at average measures of consumption, such as total CPU utilization.

See page 123 for more information about priorities.

Modern single-processor systems are typically busy with a load average of 3 and do not deal well with load averages over about 8. A load average of this magnitude is a hint that you should start to look for ways to spread the load artificially, such as by using **nice** to set process priorities.

The system load average is an excellent metric to track as part of a system baseline. If you know your system's load average on a normal day and it is in that same range on a bad day, this is a hint that you should look elsewhere (such as the network) for performance problems. A load average above the expected norm suggests that you should look at the processes running on the system itself.

Another way to view CPU usage is to run the **ps** command with arguments that show you how much of the CPU each process is using (**-aux** for Linux and AIX, **-elf** for HP-UX and Solaris). On a busy system, at least 70% of the CPU is often consumed by just one or two processes. Deferring the execution of the CPU hogs or reducing their priority makes the CPU more available to other processes.

*See page 133 for more information about **top**.*

An excellent alternative to **ps** is a program called **top**. It presents about the same information as **ps**, but in a live, regularly updated format that shows the status of the system over time.[2] AIX's **topas** command is even nicer.

On virtualized systems, **ps**, **top**, and other commands that display CPU utilization data may be misleading. A virtual machine that is not using all of its virtual CPU cycles allows other virtual machines to use (steal) those cycles. Any measurement that is relative to the operating system, such as clock ticks per second, should be examined carefully to be sure you understand what is really being reported. See

2. Refreshing **top**'s output too rapidly can itself be quite a CPU hog, so be judicious in your use of **top**.

Chapter 24, *Virtualization*, for additional information about various virtualization technologies and their implications.

How the system manages memory

The kernel manages memory in units called pages that are usually 4KiB or larger. It allocates virtual pages to processes as they request memory. Each virtual page is mapped to real storage, either to RAM or to "backing store" on disk. (Backing store is usually space in the swap area, but for pages that contain executable program text, the backing store is the original executable file. Likewise, the backing store for some data files may be the files themselves.) The kernel uses a "page table" to keep track of the mappings between these made-up virtual pages and real pages of memory.

The kernel can effectively allocate as much memory as processes ask for by augmenting real RAM with swap space. Since processes expect their virtual pages to map to real memory, the kernel may have to constantly shuffle pages between RAM and swap as different pages are accessed. This activity is known as paging.[3]

The kernel tries to manage the system's memory so that pages that have been recently accessed are kept in memory and less active pages are paged out to disk. This scheme is known as an LRU system since the least recently used pages are the ones that get shunted to disk.

It would be inefficient for the kernel to keep track of all memory references, so it uses a cache-like algorithm to decide which pages to keep in memory. The exact algorithm varies by system, but the concept is similar across platforms. This system is cheaper than a true LRU system and produces comparable results.

When memory is low, the kernel tries to guess which pages on the inactive list were least recently used. If those pages have been modified by a process, they are considered "dirty" and must be paged out to disk before the memory can be reused. Pages that have been laundered in this fashion (or that were never dirty to begin with) are "clean" and can be recycled for use elsewhere.

When a process refers to a page on the inactive list, the kernel returns the page's memory mapping to the page table, resets the page's age, and transfers it from the inactive list to the active list. Pages that have been written to disk must be paged in before they can be reactivated if the page in memory has been remapped. A "soft fault" occurs when a process references an in-memory inactive page, and a "hard fault" results from a reference to a nonresident (paged-out) page. In other words, a hard fault requires a page to be read from disk and a soft fault does not.

The kernel tries to stay ahead of the system's demand for memory, so there is not necessarily a one-to-one correspondence between page-out events and page allocations by running processes. The goal of the system is to keep enough free

3. Ages ago, a second process known as "swapping" could occur by which all pages for a process were pushed out to disk at the same time. Today, demand paging is used in all cases.

memory handy that processes don't have to actually wait for a page-out each time they make a new allocation. If paging increases dramatically when the system is busy, it would probably benefit from more RAM.

Linux is still evolving rapidly, and its virtual memory system has not quite finished going through puberty—it's a little bit jumpy and a little bit awkward. You can tune the kernel's "swappiness" parameter (**/proc/sys/vm/swappiness**) to give the kernel a hint about how quickly it should make physical pages eligible to be reclaimed from a process in the event of a memory shortage. By default, this parameter has a value of 60. If you set it to 0, the kernel resorts to reclaiming pages that have been assigned to a process only when it has exhausted all other possibilities. If you set the parameter higher than 60 (the maximum value is 100), the kernel is more likely to reclaim pages. (If you find yourself tempted to modify this parameter, it's probably time to buy more RAM for the system.)

If the kernel fills up both RAM and swap, all VM has been exhausted. Linux uses an "out-of-memory killer" to handle this condition. This function selects and kills a process to free up memory. Although the kernel attempts to kill off the least important process on your system, running out of memory is always something to avoid. In this situation, it's likely that a substantial portion of the system's resources are being devoted to memory housekeeping rather than to useful work.

Analyzing memory usage

Two numbers summarize memory activity: the total amount of active virtual memory and the current paging rate. The first number tells you the total demand for memory, and the second suggests the proportion of that memory that is actively used. Your goal is to reduce activity or increase memory until paging remains at an acceptable level. Occasional paging is inevitable; don't try to eliminate it completely.

You can determine the amount of paging (swap) space that's currently in use. Run **swapon -s** on Linux, **swap -l** under Solaris and AIX, and **swapinfo** under HP-UX.

```
linux$ swapon -s
Filename     Type        Size      Used  Priority
/dev/hdb1    partition   4096532   0     -1
/dev/hda2    partition   4096564   0     -2

solaris$ swap -l
swapfile             dev   swapl   blocks  free
/dev/dsk/c0t0d0s1    32,1     16   164400  162960

hp-ux$ swapinfo
             Kb      Kb        Kb    PCT   START/          Kb
TYPE      AVAIL    USED      FREE   USED    LIMIT    RESERVE   PRI   NAME
dev     8388608       0   8388608     0%        0          -     1   /dev/vg00/lvol
```

swapinfo and **swapon** report usage in kilobytes, and **swap -l** uses 512-byte disk blocks. The sizes quoted by these programs do not include the contents of core memory, so you must compute the total amount of virtual memory yourself.

Performance

```
VM = size of real memory + amount of swap space used
```

On UNIX systems, paging statistics obtained with **vmstat** look similar to this output from Solaris:

```
solaris$ vmstat 5 5
procs     memory            page              disk          faults
r b w   swap   free  re mf pi po fr de sr  s0 s6 s4 --  in  sy  cs
0 0 0  338216 10384  0  3  1  0  0  0  0   0  0  0  0  132 101 58
0 0 0  341784 11064  0 26  1  1  1  0  0   0  0  1  0  150 215 100
0 0 0  351752 12968  1 69  0  9  9  0  0   0  0  2  0  173 358 156
0 0 0  360240 14520  0 30  6  0  0  0  0   0  0  1  0  138 176 71
1 0 0  366648 15712  0 73  0  8  4  0  0   0  0 36  0  390 474 237
```

CPU information has been removed from this example. Under the procs heading is shown the number of processes that are immediately runnable, blocked on I/O, and runnable but swapped. If the value in the w column is ever nonzero, it is likely that the system's memory is pitifully inadequate relative to the current load.

The columns under the page heading give information about paging activity. All columns represent average values per second. Table 29.3 shows their meanings.

Table 29.3 Decoding guide for vmstat paging statistics

Column	Meaning
re	Number of pages reclaimed (rescued from the free list)
mf	Number of minor faults (minor meaning "small number of pages")
pi	Number of kilobytes paged in
po	Number of kilobytes paged out
fr	Number of kilobytes placed on the free list
de	Number of kilobytes of "predicted short-term memory shortfall"
sr	Number of pages scanned by the clock algorithm

The de column is the best indicator of serious memory problems. If it often jumps above 100, the machine is starved for memory. Unfortunately, some versions of **vmstat** don't show this number.

On Linux systems, paging statistics obtained with **vmstat** look like this:

```
linux$ vmstat 5 5
procs -----------memory---------- -swap- ---io--- --system-- -------cpu-------
 r b  swpd  free   buff   cache   si so  bi bo     in   cs us sy id wa st
 5 0     0 66488 40328 597972    0  0 252 45   1042  278  3  4 93  1  0
 0 0     0 66364 40336 597972    0  0   0 37   1009  264  0  1 98  0  0
 0 0     0 66364 40344 597972    0  0   0  5   1011  252  1  1 98  0  0
 0 0     0 66364 40352 597972    0  0   0  3   1020  311  1  1 98  0  0
 0 0     0 66364 40360 597972    0  0   0 21   1067  507  1  3 96  0  0
```

As in the UNIX output, the number of processes that are immediately runnable and that are blocked on I/O are shown under the procs heading. Paging statistics are condensed to two columns, si and so, which represent pages swapped in and out, respectively.

Any apparent inconsistencies among the memory-related columns are for the most part illusory. Some columns count pages and others count kilobytes. All values are rounded averages. Furthermore, some are averages of scalar quantities and others are average deltas.

Use the si and so fields to evaluate the system's paging behavior. A page-in (si) does not necessarily represent a page being recovered from the swap area. It could be executable code being paged in from a filesystem or a copy-on-write page being duplicated, both of which are normal occurrences that do not necessarily indicate a shortage of memory. On the other hand, page-outs (so) always represent data written to disk after being forcibly ejected by the kernel.

If your system has a constant stream of page-outs, it's likely that you would benefit from more physical memory. But if paging happens only occasionally and does not produce annoying hiccups or user complaints, you can ignore it. If your system falls somewhere in the middle, further analysis should depend on whether you are trying to optimize for interactive performance (e.g., a workstation) or to configure a machine with many simultaneous users (e.g., a compute server).

On a traditional hard disk, you can figure that every 100 page-outs cause about one second of latency.[4] If 150 page-outs must occur to let you scroll a window, you will wait for about 1.5 seconds. A rule of thumb used by interface researchers is that an average user perceives the system to be "slow" when response times are longer than seven-tenths of a second.

Analyzing disk I/O

You can monitor disk performance with the **iostat** command. Like **vmstat**, it accepts optional arguments to specify an interval in seconds and a repetition count, and its first line of output is a summary since boot. Like **vmstat**, it also tells you how the CPU's time is being spent. Here is an example from Solaris:

```
solaris$ iostat 5 5
     tty         sd0              sd1              nfs1           cpu
tin tout   kps tps serv   kps  tps  serv   kps  tps serv    us sy  wt id
 0    1     5   1   18    14    2    20     0    0    0     0  0   0  99
 0   39     0   0    0     2    0    14     0    0    0     0  0   0 100
 2   26     3   0   13     8    1    21     0    0    0     0  0   0 100
 3  119     0   0    0    19    2    13     0    0    0     0  1   1  98
 1   16     5   1   19     0    0     0     0    0    0     0  0   0 100
```

4. We assume that about half of disk operations are page-outs.

Columns are divided into topics (in this case, five: tty, sd0, sd1, nfs1, and cpu), with the data for each topic presented in the fields beneath it. **iostat** output tends to be somewhat different on every system.

The tty topic presents data concerning terminals and pseudo-terminals. This information is basically uninteresting, although it might be useful for characterizing the throughput of a modem. The tin and tout columns give the average total number of characters input and output per second by all of the system's terminals.

Each hard disk has columns kps, tps, and serv, indicating kilobytes transferred per second, total transfers per second, and average "service times" (seek times, essentially) in milliseconds. One transfer request can include several sectors, so the ratio between kps and tps tells you whether there are a few large transfers or lots of small ones. Large transfers are more efficient. Calculation of seek times seems to work only on specific drives and sometimes gives bizarre values (the values in this example are reasonable).

iostat output on Linux, HP-UX, and AIX looks more like this:

```
aix$ iostat
...
Device:    tps   Blk_read/s   Blk_wrtn/s   Blk_read    Blk_wrtn
hdisk0    0.54         0.59         2.39     304483     1228123
hdisk1    0.34         0.27         0.42     140912      216218
hdisk2    0.01         0.02         0.05       5794       15320
hdisk3    0.00         0.00         0.00          0           0
```

Each hard disk has the columns tps, Blk_read/s, Blk_wrtn/s, Blk_read, and Blk_wrtn, indicating I/O transfers per second, blocks read per second, blocks written per second, total blocks read, and total blocks written.

Disk blocks are typically 1KiB in size, so you can readily determine the actual disk throughput in KiB/s. Transfers, on the other hand, are nebulously defined. One transfer request can include several logical I/O requests over several sectors, so this data is also mostly useful for identifying trends or irregular behavior.

The cost of seeking is the most important factor affecting disk drive performance. To a first approximation, the rotational speed of the disk and the speed of the bus to which the disk is connected to have relatively little impact. Modern disks can transfer hundreds of megabytes of data per second if they are read from contiguous sectors, but they can only perform about 100 to 300 seeks per second. If you transfer one sector per seek, you can easily realize less than 5% of the drive's peak throughput.

Seeks are more expensive when they make the heads travel a long distance. If you have a disk with several filesystem partitions and files are read from each partition in a random order, the heads must travel back and forth a long way to switch between partitions. On the other hand, files within a partition are relatively local to one another. When partitioning a new disk, consider the performance implications and put files that are accessed together in the same filesystem.

To really achieve maximum disk performance, you should put filesystems that are used together on different disks. Although the bus architecture and device drivers influence efficiency, most computers can manage multiple disks independently, thereby dramatically increasing throughput. For example, it is often worthwhile to split frequently accessed web server data and logs among multiple disks.

It's especially important to split the paging (swap) area among several disks if possible, since paging tends to slow down the entire system. Many systems can use both dedicated swap partitions and swap files on a formatted filesystem.

Some systems also let you set up multiple "memory-based filesystems," which are essentially the same thing as PC RAM disks. A special driver poses as a disk but actually stores data in high-speed memory. Many sites use a RAM disk for their **/tmp** filesystem or for other busy files such as web server logs or email spools. Using a RAM disk reduces the memory available for general use, but it makes the reading and writing of temporary files blindingly fast. It's generally a good deal.

*See page 144 for more information about **lsof** and **fuser**.*

The **lsof** command, which lists open files, and the **fuser** command, which shows the processes that are using a filesystem, can be helpful for isolating disk I/O performance issues. These commands show interactions between processes and filesystems, some of which may be unintended. For example, if an application is writing its log to the same device used for database logs, a disk bottleneck may result.

xdd: analyze disk subsystem performance

Modern storage systems can involve network or SAN-attached elements, RAID arrays, and other layers of abstraction. Consider the **xdd** tool for measuring and optimizing these complex systems. **xdd** is available under the GPL and runs on all of our example systems (not to mention Windows).

xdd measures subsystem I/O on single systems and on clusters of systems. It is well documented and yields accurate and reproducible performance measurements. You can read more about it at ioperformance.com.

sar: collect and report statistics over time

The **sar** command is a performance monitoring tool that has lingered through multiple UNIX and Linux epochs despite its somewhat obtuse command-line syntax. The original command has its roots in early AT&T UNIX.

At first glance, **sar** seems to display much the same information as **vmstat** and **iostat**. However, there's one important difference: **sar** can report on historical as well as current data.

*The Linux package that contains **sar** is called sysstat.*

Without options, the **sar** command reports CPU utilization for the day at 10-minute intervals since midnight, as shown below. This historical data collection is made possible by the **sal** script, which is part of the **sar** toolset and must be set up to run from **cron** at periodic intervals. **sar** stores the data it collects underneath the **/var/log** directory in a binary format.

```
linux$ sar
Linux 2.6.18-92.ELsmp (bajafur.atrust.com)  01/16/2010

12:00:01 AM       CPU   %user   %nice   %system   %iowait    %idle
12:10:01 AM       all    0.10    0.00      0.04      0.06    99.81
12:20:01 AM       all    0.04    0.00      0.03      0.05    99.88
12:30:01 AM       all    0.04    0.00      0.03      0.04    99.89
12:40:01 AM       all    0.09    0.00      0.03      0.05    99.83
12:50:01 AM       all    0.04    0.00      0.03      0.04    99.88
01:00:01 AM       all    0.05    0.00      0.03      0.04    99.88
```

In addition to CPU information, **sar** can also report on metrics such as disk and network activity. Use **sar -d** for a summary of this day's disk activity or **sar -n DEV** for network interface statistics. **sar -A** reports all available information.

sar has some limitations, but it's a good bet for quick-and-dirty historical information. If you're serious about making a long-term commitment to performance monitoring, we suggest that you set up a data collection and graphing platform such as Cacti. Cacti comes to us from the network management world, but it can actually graph arbitrary system metrics such as CPU and memory information. See page 886 for some additional comments on Cacti and an example of the graphs that it's capable of producing.

nmon and nmon_analyser: monitor in AIX

On AIX systems, **nmon** is the monitoring tool of choice. It is similar to **sar** in many ways.

Stephen Atkins of IBM developed a super-spreadsheet called **nmon_analyser** that processes the data collected by **nmon**. It's great for producing cleaned-up data as well as for creating presentation graphs. It analyzes data with more sophistication than does **sar**. For example, it can calculate weighted averages for hot-spot analysis and can integrate IBM and EMC disk performance information. Although **nmon_analyser** is not officially supported by IBM, you can find it at

ibm.com/developerworks/aix/library/au-nmon_analyser

Choosing a Linux I/O scheduler

Linux systems use an I/O scheduling algorithm to mediate between processes competing to perform disk I/O. The I/O scheduler massages the order and timing of disk requests to provide the best possible overall I/O performance for a given application or situation.

Four different scheduling algorithms are available in the Linux 2.6 kernel. You can take your pick. Unfortunately, the scheduling algorithm is set at boot time (with the **elevator=***algorithm* kernel argument), so it's not easy to change. The system's scheduling algorithm is usually specified in the GRUB boot loader's configuration file, **grub.conf**.

The available algorithms are

- Completely Fair Queuing (**elevator=cfq**): This is the default algorithm and is usually the best choice for general-purpose servers. It tries to evenly distribute access to I/O bandwidth. (If nothing else, the algorithm surely deserves an award for marketing: who could ever say no to a completely fair scheduler?)
- Deadline (**elevator=deadline**): This algorithm tries to minimize the latency for each request. It reorders requests to increase performance.
- NOOP (**elevator=noop**): This algorithm implements a simple FIFO queue. It assumes that I/O requests have already been optimized or reordered by the driver or will be optimized or reordered by the device (as might be done by an intelligent controller). This option may be the best choice in some SAN environments and is the best choice for SSD drives.

By determining which scheduling algorithm is most appropriate for your environment (you may need to run trials with each scheduler) you may be able to improve I/O performance.

oprofile: profile Linux systems in detail

oprofile is an incredibly powerful integrated system profiler for Linux systems running the 2.6 kernel or later. All components of a Linux system can be profiled: hardware and software interrupt handlers, kernel modules, the kernel itself, shared libraries, and applications.

If you have a lot of extra time on your hands and want to know exactly how your system resources are being used (down to the smallest level of detail), consider running **oprofile**. This tool is particularly useful if you are developing your own in-house applications or kernel code.

Both a kernel module and a set of user-level tools are included in the **oprofile** distribution, which is available for download at oprofile.sourceforge.net.

As of early 2010, a new system for tracing performance is on the horizon. Known as the performance events ("perf events") subsystem, it provides a level of instrumentation never before seen in the Linux kernel. This is likely to be the future of Linux performance profiling and is slated to eventually replace **oprofile**.

29.5 Help! My system just got really slow!

In previous sections, we've talked mostly about issues that relate to the average performance of a system. Solutions to these long-term concerns generally take the form of configuration adjustments or upgrades.

However, you will find that even properly configured systems are sometimes more sluggish than usual. Luckily, transient problems are often easy to diagnose. Most of the time, they are caused by a greedy process that is simply consuming so much CPU power, disk, or network bandwidth that other processes are affected. On occasion, malicious processes hog available resources to intentionally slow a system or network, a scheme known as a "denial of service" or DOS attack.

You can often tell which resource is being hogged without even running a diagnostic command. If the system feels "sticky" or you hear the disk going crazy, the problem is most likely a disk bandwidth or memory shortfall.[5] If the system feels "sluggish" (everything takes a long time, and applications can't be "warmed up"), the problem may lie with the CPU load.

The first step in diagnosis is to run **ps auxww** (**ps -elf** on Solaris and HP-UX) or **top** to look for obvious runaway processes. Any process that's using more than 50% of the CPU is likely to be at fault. If no single process is getting an inordinate share of the CPU, check to see how many processes are getting at least 10%. If you snag more than two or three (don't count **ps** itself), the load average is likely to be quite high. This is, in itself, a cause of poor performance. Check the load average with **uptime**, and use **vmstat** or **top** to check whether the CPU is ever idle.

If no CPU contention is evident, run **vmstat** to see how much paging is going on. All disk activity is interesting: a lot of page-outs may indicate contention for memory, and disk traffic in the absence of paging may mean that a process is monopolizing the disk by constantly reading or writing files.

There's no direct way to tie disk operations to processes, but **ps** can narrow down the possible suspects for you. Any process that is generating disk traffic must be using some amount of CPU time. You can usually make an educated guess about which of the active processes is the true culprit.[6] Use **kill -STOP** to suspend the process and test your theory.

Suppose you do find that a particular process is at fault—what should you do? Usually, nothing. Some operations just require a lot of resources and are bound to slow down the system. It doesn't necessarily mean that they're illegitimate. It is sometimes useful to **renice** an obtrusive process that is CPU-bound, however.

Sometimes, application tuning can dramatically reduce a program's demand for CPU resources; this effect is especially visible with custom network server software such as web applications.

Processes that are disk or memory hogs can't be dealt with so easily. **renice** generally does not help. You do have the option of killing or stopping the process, but we recommend against this if the situation does not constitute an emergency. As with CPU pigs, you can use the low-tech solution of asking the owner to run the process later.

5. That is, it takes a long time to switch between applications, but performance is acceptable when an application is repeating a simple task.
6. A large virtual address space or resident set used to be a suspicious sign, but shared libraries have made these numbers less useful. **ps** is not very smart about separating system-wide shared library overhead from the address spaces of individual processes. Many processes wrongly appear to have tens of megabytes of active memory.

The kernel allows a process to restrict its own use of physical memory by calling the **setrlimit** system call.[7] This facility is also available in the C shell through the built-in **limit** command. For example, the command

```
% limit memoryuse 32m
```

causes all subsequent commands that the user runs to have their use of physical memory limited to 32MiB (Solaris uses **memorysize** rather than **memoryuse**). This feature is roughly equivalent to **renice** for memory-bound processes.

If a runaway process doesn't seem to be the source of poor performance, investigate two other possible causes. The first is an overloaded network. Many programs are so intimately bound up with the network that it's hard to tell where system performance ends and network performance begins. See Chapter 21 for more information about the tools used to monitor networks.

Some network overloading problems are hard to diagnose because they come and go very quickly. For example, if every machine on the network runs a network-related program out of **cron** at a particular time each day, there will often be a brief but dramatic glitch. Every machine on the net will hang for five seconds, and then the problem will disappear as quickly as it came.

Server-related delays are another possible cause of performance crises. UNIX and Linux systems are constantly consulting remote servers for NFS, Kerberos, DNS, and any of a dozen other facilities. If a server is dead or some other problem makes the server expensive to communicate with, the effects ripple back through client systems.

For example, on a busy system, some process may use the **gethostent** library routine every few seconds or so. If a DNS glitch makes this routine take two seconds to complete, you will likely perceive a difference in overall performance. DNS forward and reverse lookup configuration problems are responsible for a surprising number of server performance issues.

29.6 Recommended reading

Cockcroft, Adrian, and Bill Walker. *Capacity Planning for Internet Services.* Upper Saddle River, NJ: Prentice Hall. 2001.

Drepper, Ulrich. *What Every Programmer Should Know about Memory.* lwn.net/Articles/250967.

Ezolt, Phillip G. *Optimizing Linux Performance.* Upper Saddle River, NJ: Prentice Hall PTR, 2005.

Johnson, S., et al. *Performance Tuning for Linux Servers.* Indianapolis, IN: IBM Press, 2005.

7. More granular resource management can be achieved through the Class-based Kernel Resource Management functionality; see ckrm.sourceforge.net.

LOUKIDES, MIKE, AND GIAN-PAOLO D. MUSUMECI. *System Performance Tuning (2nd Edition).* Sebastopol, CA: O'Reilly & Associates, 2002.

TUFTE, EDWARD R. *The Visual Display of Quantitative Information (2nd Edition).* Cheshire, CT: Graphics Press, 2001.

29.7 EXERCISES

E29.1 Make an educated guess as to what the problem might be in each of the following scenarios:

a) When switching between applications, the disk thrashes and there is a noticeable lag.

b) A numerical simulation program takes more time than normal, but system memory is mostly free.

c) Users on a busy LAN complain of slow NFS access, but the load average on the server is very low.

d) Running a command (any command) often produces the error message "out of memory."

★ E29.2 Load balancing can dramatically impact server performance as seen from the outside world. Discuss several load balancing mechanisms.

★ E29.3 List the four main resources that can affect performance. For each resource, give an example of an application that could easily lead to the exhaustion of that resource. Discuss ways to alleviate some of the stress associated with each scenario.

★ E29.4 Write three simple programs or scripts. The first should drive the CPU's %system time high. The second should drive the CPU's %user time high. The third should affect neither of these measures but should have a high elapsed time. Use your programs in conjunction with the commands described in the *Analyzing CPU usage* section (starting on page 1121) to see what happens when you stress the system in various ways.

★ E29.5 Write two simple programs or scripts. The first should be read-intensive and the second write-intensive. Use your programs with the commands in the *Analyzing disk I/O* section (starting on page 1127) to see what happens when you stress the system in various ways. (For bonus points, give each of your programs the option to use either a random or a sequential access pattern.)

★★ E29.6 Choose two programs that use a noticeable amount of system resources. Use **vmstat** and the other tools mentioned in this chapter to profile both applications. Make a claim as to what each program does that makes it a resource hog. Back up your claims with data.

30 Cooperating with Windows

Chances are high that your environment includes both Microsoft Windows and UNIX systems. If so, these operating systems can assist each other in many ways. Among other feats, Windows applications can run from a UNIX desktop or access a UNIX server's printers and files. UNIX applications can display their user interfaces on a Windows desktop.

Both platforms have their strengths, and they can be made to work together. Windows is a popular and featureful desktop platform, capable of bridging the gap between the user and the network cable. UNIX, on the other hand, is a reliable and scalable infrastructure platform. So let's not fight, OK?

30.1 Logging in to a UNIX system from Windows

See page 926 for more information about SSH.

Users may often find themselves wanting to head for the snow-covered slopes of a good **bash** session without abandoning the Windows box on their desk. The best remote access tool for UNIX and Linux systems is the secure shell protocol, SSH.

Several SSH client implementations are available for Windows. Our current favorite, the open source PuTTY, is simple and effective. It supports many of the features you have come to expect from a native terminal application such as **xterm**.

SSH also supports file transfer, and PuTTY includes two command-line clients for this purpose: **psftp** and **pscp**. Hard-core "never touch a command line" Windows users might prefer the graphical WinSCP client from winscp.net.

Another good option is to install the more general UNIX-on-Windows Cygwin package and to run its SSH utilities from **rxvt**. There's more information about Cygwin starting on page 1140.

A nifty zero-footprint Java implementation of SSH called MindTerm is available from AppGate (appgate.com). It's free for personal use. It runs on any system that supports Java and can be configured in a variety of ways.

Of the commercial SSH client implementations, our favorite is VanDyke Software's SecureCRT, available for purchase from vandyke.com. SecureCRT supports all our favorite terminal features, and VanDyke offers excellent customer service and an open-minded attitude toward feature requests from customers. Like PuTTY, SecureCRT features built-in SFTP file transfer software.

An interesting feature of SSH is its ability to forward TCP ports between client and server. For example, this feature allows you to set up on the client a local port that forwards incoming connections to a different port on a machine that is only reachable from the server. Although this feature opens a world of new possibilities, it is also potentially dangerous and is something you must be aware of when granting SSH access to your server. Fortunately, the port-forwarding feature can be disabled on the server side to limit SSH to terminal access and file transfer.

30.2 Accessing remote desktops

Graphical desktops on UNIX are tied to the free X Window System, which is in no way related to Microsoft Windows. X was developed at MIT in the mid-1980s and has been adopted as a standard by all UNIX workstation manufacturers and Linux distributions. It has been through several major updates, but a stable base was finally reached with version 11, first published in the early 1990s. The version number of the protocol was appended to X to form X11, the name by which it is most commonly known. (The name "Windows" by itself always refers to Microsoft Windows, both in this chapter and in the real world.)

X11 is a client/server system. The X server is responsible for displaying data on the user's screen and for acquiring input from the user's mouse and keyboard. It communicates with client applications over the network. The server and clients need not be running on the same machine.

A more detailed discussion of the X Windows architecture can be found in Chapter 25, *The X Window System*, which starts on page 1011.

X server running on a Windows computer

X11 is a rich protocol that has incorporated many extensions over the years. The implementation of an X server is, therefore, rather complex. Nevertheless, X server implementations now exist for almost every operating system. X itself is OS agnostic, so X11 clients running on a UNIX box can display on an X server running under Microsoft Windows and still be controlled as if the user were sitting at the system console.

Unfortunately, the original designers of the X protocols did not devote much thought to security. Every program that connects to your X server can read everything you type on the keyboard and see everything displayed on your screen. To make matters worse, remote programs need not even display a window when accessing your X server; they can simply lurk silently in the background.

Several methods of securing X11 have been proposed over time, but they have all tended to be somewhat complex. The bottom line is that you are best off preventing all remote connections to your X server unless you are absolutely sure of what you are doing. Most X servers are configured to refuse remote connections by default, so you should be safe as long as you do not run the **xhost** program (or its equivalent) to grant remote access.

See page 926 for more information about SSH.

Unfortunately, granting remote access is exactly what you need to do when you seek to run programs on UNIX and display their interfaces on Windows. So, how to run a remote application without granting remote access to the X server? The most common method is to use a feature of the SSH protocol that is specifically designed to support X11. This scheme creates a secure tunnel between X clients running on the remote host and the local X server. Programs started on the remote host display automatically on the local machine, but through the magic of SSH, the local X server perceives them as having originated locally.

Note that X forwarding only works if the X forwarding features have been enabled on both the SSH server and the SSH client. If you use the PuTTY SSH client on Windows, simply activate the X11 forwarding feature in its setup screen. On the SSH server side (that is, the X11 client side; the UNIX machine), make sure that the **/etc/ssh/sshd_config** file contains the line

```
X11Forwarding yes
```

If you modify the SSH server configuration, make sure you restart the **sshd** process to activate the new configuration. The `X11Forwarding` option is enabled by default on most UNIX systems that ship OpenSSH.

As our technical reviewer Dan Foster notes, forwarding X connections over SSH "can be excruciatingly slow, even on a LAN, and it is even worse if there is any network latency." VNC, discussed below, is an alternative.

Although Apple provides a free X server for Mac OS X, Microsoft unfortunately offers no corresponding feature. A free X server for Windows is available from the Cygwin project (cygwin.com), and it works very well once you've configured it. The Xming server for Windows is an excellent alternative that's much easier to configure. Commercial X servers for Windows include Exceed and X-Win32. These offer much simpler configuration at a rather steep price.

VNC: Virtual Network Computing

In the late 1990s, a few people at AT&T Labs in Cambridge, UK, developed a system for remote desktop access called VNC. Their idea was to marry the simplicity of a dumb terminal with the modern world of window systems. In contrast to X11, the VNC protocol does not deal with individual applications. Instead, it creates a complete virtual desktop (or provides remote access to an existing desktop) as a unit.

AT&T published the VNC software under a liberal source license. This openness allowed other folks to hop on the bandwagon and create additional server and viewer implementations, as well as protocol improvements that reduced the consumption of network bandwidth. Today, VNC viewers are available for most devices that provide some means for graphical display. VNC servers for UNIX, Linux, and Windows are widely available. VNC implementations exist even for most smartphones.

The UNIX VNC server implementation is essentially a graphics adapter emulator that plugs into the X.Org X Windows server. Running a **vncserver** from your UNIX account creates a new virtual desktop that runs in the self-contained world of the UNIX machine. You can then use a VNC viewer to access that desktop remotely. We recommend taking advantage of the **vncpasswd** command before starting the server for the first time to establish a connection password.

The VNC protocol is stateless and bitmap based. Therefore, viewers can freely connect and disconnect. Moreover, several viewers can access the same server at the same time. This last feature is especially useful for remote support and for training setups. It also facilitates shared console access for system administration.

VNC servers in the Windows world do not normally create an extra desktop; they simply export the standard Windows desktop as it is displayed on screen. The main application for this technology is remote support.

These days, the original authors of the VNC protocol are running their own company, RealVNC (realvnc.com). The UltraVNC project (uvnc.com) is concentrating on the Windows domain with a very fast and feature-rich Windows-based VNC server implementation, and TightVNC (tightvnc.com) is working on improved compression ratios. These groups do talk with each other, so features tend to cross-pollinate among the various implementations.

The VNC protocol has been designed with extensibility in mind. All combinations of viewers and servers can work together; they pick the best protocol variant that both sides understand. Implementation-specific features (such as file transfer) can only be accessed by a server and client running from the same project.

Windows RDP: Remote Desktop Protocol

Ever since Windows 2000 Server, every Windows box has the technical ability to provide graphical remote access to several users at the same time. The remote access component is called Remote Desktop, and it uses a protocol called the Remote Desktop Protocol (RDP) to communicate between client and server. RDP clients for UNIX let administrators manage Windows systems from a UNIX desktop. They are an indispensable tool for UNIX administrators who have Windows systems in their environments.

To take advantage of RDP, you must enable it on the server (Windows) side and set up a client to access it. On Windows 7, go to the System control panel, click Remote settings, and select an option in the Remote Desktop box. Older versions of Windows might require you to manually enable the Terminal Server service.

On the UNIX side, install the open source **rdesktop** program (www.rdesktop.org) to display Windows desktops on your UNIX workstation. Clients exist for most other operating systems, too, including mobile devices.

RDP can also map the server's printers and disks onto the client.

30.3 Running Windows and Windows-like applications

As discussed in Chapter 24, the free but proprietary product VMware Server from vmware.com lets you run multiple operating systems simultaneously on PC hardware. VMware emulates entire virtual "guest machines" on top of a host operating system, which must be either Linux or Windows. Regardless of the host OS, you can install most Intel-compatible operating systems into one of VMware's virtual machines. From the guest machine's perspective, the operating system runs exactly as it would on dedicated hardware, and applications install normally. Other virtualization offerings such as KVM and VirtualBox can also run Windows and should be candidates for running Windows applications.

A different approach is taken by the Wine system from winehq.org. Wine implements the Windows programming API in the UNIX environment, allowing you to run Windows applications directly on top of X. This free software translates native Windows API calls to their UNIX counterparts and can do so without using any Microsoft code. Wine supports TCP/IP networking, serial devices, and sound output. It runs on Linux, BSD, Mac OS, and Solaris systems.

A large number of Windows applications run in Wine without problems, and others can be made to work with a few tricks; see the web site for details. Unfortunately, getting an application to run under Wine is often not so simple. The talented folks at codeweavers.com have written a commercial installer system that can make some of the balkier Windows apps work correctly.

If your tool of choice is supported by CodeWeavers, great. But even if it is not, give the application a try—you might be pleasantly surprised. If an application does not work on its own and you cannot find any prewritten hints, be prepared to spend some serious spare time whipping it into shape if you are determined to do it on your own. If you have the budget, you can consider contracting CodeWeavers to help you.

Win4Lin is a commercial alternative to Wine from NeTraverse. Win4Lin claims to be more stable than Wine and to support a few more Microsoft applications. However, it requires kernel modifications, which Wine does not. Win4Lin is available from win4lin.com.

Dual booting, or why you shouldn't

If you've ever installed Linux on a computer that had a former life as a Windows machine, you have doubtless been offered the option to set up a dual boot configuration. Such configurations function pretty much as promised. It is even possible to mount Windows partitions under Linux and to access Linux filesystems under Windows. Read all about setting up a dual boot configuration on page 85.

But wait! If you are doing real work and need access to both Windows and UNIX, be very skeptical of dual booting as a possible solution in the context of a production system. Dual boot setups represent Murphy's Law at its worst: they always seem to be booted into the wrong OS, and the slightest chore usually requires multiple reboots. With the advent of widespread virtualization and cheap computing hardware, there's usually no reason to put yourself through this torture.

Microsoft Office alternatives

A few years ago, Sun released an open source version of StarOffice, its Microsoft Office-like application suite, under the name OpenOffice.org. OpenOffice.org includes a spreadsheet, a word processor, a presentation package, a drawing application, and a database application similar to Microsoft Access. These tools can read and write files generated by their Microsoft analogs. You can download the suite from openoffice.org.

OpenOffice.org is available on all major platforms, including Windows, Linux, Solaris, Mac OS X, and most other versions of UNIX. If you're looking for a package with a commercial support contract, you can also buy Sun's StarOffice, which is essentially OpenOffice.org in a box with support and better spell-checking.

Google competes on the application front with its Google Apps offering. In addition to its powerful Gmail and Google Calendar offerings, Google also includes basic word processing and spreadsheets. These free products include collaboration features that let multiple users edit documents simultaneously from several locations. Since all of Google's apps run in a web browser, they can be used on virtually any operating system. You can export and import content in various formats, including those of Microsoft Office.

30.4 Using command-line tools with Windows

What many UNIX people miss most when working on Windows systems is their beloved command-line terminal. Not just any old terminal application or the abomination known as the DOS box, but a proper **xterm** with support for window resizing, colors, mouse control, and all the fancy **xterm** escape sequences.

Although Windows has no stand-alone (i.e., without X) native port of **xterm**, a neat little program called **rxvt** comes awfully close. It is part of the Cygwin system, downloadable from cygwin.com. If you install Cygwin's X server, you can use the real **xterm**.

Cygwin is distributed under the GNU General Public License and contains an extensive complement of common UNIX commands as well as a porting library that implements the POSIX APIs under Windows. Cygwin's reconciliation of the UNIX and Windows command-line and filesystem conventions is well thought out and manages to bring many of the creature comforts of a UNIX shell to native Windows commands. In addition to making UNIX users feel at home, Cygwin makes it easy to get UNIX software running under Windows. See cygwin.com for more details.

The MKS Toolkit is a commercial alternative to Cygwin. See MKS's web site at mkssoftware.com for more information.

A growing list of UNIX software now also runs natively on Windows, including Apache, Perl, BIND, PHP, MySQL, Vim, Emacs, Gimp, Wireshark, and Python. Before attempting to force an application to work on Windows with something like Cygwin, find out if a native implementation is available.

30.5 Windows compliance with email and web standards

In an ideal world, everybody would use open standards to communicate and happiness would abound. But this is not an ideal world, and many have accused Windows of being a mess of proprietary protocols and broken implementations of Internet standards. Partially true, perhaps, but Windows can play along nicely in some parts of the standards world. Two of these areas are email and web service.

In the wild history of the web, a number of corporations have tried to embrace and extend the web in ways that would allow them to lock out competition and give their own business a mighty boost. Microsoft is still engaged in this battle at the browser level with its numerous extensions peculiar to Internet Explorer. At the underlying level of the HTTP protocol, however, Windows and Windows browsers are relatively platform agnostic.

Microsoft provides its own web server, IIS, but the adoption of IIS has historically lagged that of Apache running on Linux by a significant margin. Unless you are locked in to a server-side technology such as ASP, or your vendor's product requires IIS, there's no compelling reason to use Windows machines as web servers.

For email, Microsoft touts its Exchange Server product as the preferred server-side technology. Truth be told, Exchange Server's capabilities do outshine those of Internet-standard mail systems, particularly when the mail clients consist of Windows boxes running Microsoft Outlook. But fear not: Exchange Server can also speak SMTP for inbound and outbound mail, and it can serve up mail to UNIX clients through the standard IMAP and POP protocols.

On the client side, both Outlook and its free younger sibling Windows Mail can connect to UNIX IMAP and POP servers (as can most other third-party email user agents for Windows). Mix and match in any combination you like. More information about POP and IMAP can be found starting on page 756.

30.6 Sharing files with Samba and CIFS

In the early 1980s, IBM designed an API that let computers on the same network subnet talk to one another using names instead of cryptic numeric addresses. The result was called the Network Basic/Input Output System, or NetBIOS. The combination of NetBIOS and its original underlying network transport protocol was called the NetBIOS Extended User Interface, or NetBEUI. The NetBIOS API became quite popular, and it was adapted for use on top of a variety of different network protocols such as IPX, DECNet, and TCP/IP.

Microsoft and Intel developed a file-sharing protocol on top of NetBIOS and called it "the core protocol." Later, it was renamed the Server Message Block protocol, or SMB for short. A later evolution of the SMB protocol known as the Common Internet File System (CIFS) is essentially a version of SMB that has been cleaned up and tuned for operation over wide area networks. CIFS is the current lingua franca of Windows file sharing.

In the Windows world, a filesystem or directory made available over the network is known as a "share." It sounds a bit strange to UNIX ears, but we follow this convention when referring to CIFS filesystems.

Samba: CIFS server for UNIX

Samba is an enormously popular software package, available under the GNU Public License, that implements the server side of CIFS on UNIX and Linux hosts. It was originally created by Andrew Tridgell, who first reverse-engineered the SMB protocol and published the resulting code in 1992. Here, we focus on Samba version 3.

Today, Samba is well supported and under active development to expand its functionality. It provides a stable, industrial-strength mechanism for integrating Windows machines into a UNIX network. The real beauty of Samba is that you only need to install one package on the server; no special software is needed on the Windows side.

CIFS provides five basic services:

- File sharing
- Network printing
- Authentication and authorization
- Name resolution
- Service announcement (file server and printer "browsing")

Samba not only serves files through CIFS, but it can also perform the basic functions of a Windows Active Directory controller. As a domain controller, Samba supports advanced features such as Windows domain logins, roaming Windows user profiles, and CIFS print spooling.

Most of Samba's functionality is implemented by two daemons, **smbd** and **nmbd**. **smbd** implements file and print services, as well as authentication and authorization. **nmbd** provides the other major CIFS components: name resolution and service announcement.

Unlike NFS, which requires kernel-level support, Samba requires no drivers or kernel modifications and runs entirely as a user process. It binds to the sockets used for CIFS requests and waits for a client to request access to a resource. Once a request has been authenticated, **smbd** forks an instance of itself that runs as the user who is making the requests. As a result, all normal file-access permissions (including group permissions) are obeyed. The only special functionality that **smbd** adds on top of this is a file-locking service that gives client PCs the locking semantics to which they are accustomed.

Samba installation

Samba is known to work with all of our example systems.[1] Linux distributions package it as a matter of course. Patches, documentation, and other goodies are available from samba.org. Make sure you are using the most current Samba packages available for your system since many updates fix security vulnerabilities.

On all systems, you'll need to edit the **smb.conf** file (which is to be found in either **/etc/samba/smb.conf** or **/etc/smb.conf**) to tell Samba how it should behave. In this file, you specify the directories and printers that should be shared, their access rights, and Samba's general operational parameters. The Samba package comes with a well-commented sample **smb.conf** file that is a good starting place for new configurations. Note that once Samba is running, it checks its configuration file every few seconds and loads any changes you make.

It's important to be aware of the security implications of sharing files and other resources over a network. For a typical site, you need to do two things to ensure a basic level of security:

- Explicitly specify which clients can access the resources shared by Samba. This part of the configuration is controlled by the `hosts allow` clause in the **smb.conf** file. Make sure that it contains only the IP addresses (or address ranges) that it should.
- Block access to the server from outside your organization. Samba uses encryption only for password authentication. It does not use encryption for its data transport. In almost all cases, you should block access from

1. HP also offers a Samba derivative called the HP CIFS Server, which is available for download from the HP software depot.

outside your organization to prevent your users from accidentally downloading files in the clear across the Internet. Blocking is typically implemented at the network firewall level; Samba uses UDP ports 137 through 139 and TCP ports 137, 139, and 445.

Since the release of Samba version 3, excellent documentation has been available on-line from samba.org.

Samba comes with sensible defaults for its configuration options, and most sites will need only a small configuration file. Use the command **testparm -v** to get a listing of all the Samba configuration options and the values to which they are currently set. This listing includes your settings from the **smb.conf** file as well as any default values you have not overridden.

Avoid setting options in the **smb.conf** file unless they are different from the default values and you have a clear idea of why you want to lock them down. The advantage of this approach is that your configuration automatically adapts to the settings recommended by the Samba authors when you upgrade to a newer version of Samba.

That having been said, do make sure that password encryption is turned on:

```
encrypt passwords = true
```

This option encrypts the password exchange between Windows clients and the Samba server. It's currently the default, and there's no conceivable situation in which you would want to turn it off.

The encryption feature requires the Samba server to store a special Windows password hash for every user. Windows passwords work in a fundamentally different way from UNIX passwords, and therefore it is not possible to use the passwords from **/etc/shadow**.[2]

Samba provides a special tool, **smbpasswd**, for setting up these passwords. For example, let's add the user tobi and set a password for him:

```
$ sudo smbpasswd -a tobi
New SMB password: password
Retype new SMB password: password
```

Users can change their own Samba passwords with **smbpasswd** as well:

```
$ smbpasswd -r smbserver -U tobi
New SMB password: password
Retype new SMB password: password
```

This example changes the Samba password of user tobi on the server smbserver.

2. Windows passes the current user's credentials to the Samba server when establishing a connection. For this reason, users' Samba passwords are usually set to match their Windows passwords.

Filename encoding

Starting with version 3.0, Samba encodes all filenames in UTF-8. If your server runs with a UTF-8 locale, this a great match.[3] If you are in Europe and you are still using one of the ISO 8859 locales on the server, you will find that filenames with special characters such as ä, ö, ü, é, or è look rather odd when you type **ls** in a directory in which such files have been created with Samba and UTF-8. The solution is to tell Samba to use the same character encoding as your server:

```
unix charset = ISO8859-15
display charset = ISO8859-15
```

Make sure that the filename encoding is correct right from the start. Otherwise, files with oddly encoded names will accumulate. Fixing them can be quite a complex task later on.

User authentication

In the Windows authentication systems, the client does not trust the server; the user's password never travels across the net as plaintext. Instead, Windows uses a Kerberos-based challenge/response method for authentication. A Windows client can authenticate to a Samba server by using Kerberos as well.

Windows saves your login username and password and tries to use these credentials to authenticate you to network services whenever it is presented with an authentication request. So, if a user has the same username and password combination on your Windows box as on your Samba server, Samba grants seemingly passwordless access to the appropriate Samba shares. All the authentication happens transparently in the background.

The downside of the challenge/response approach is that the server has to store plaintext-equivalent passwords. In actual fact, the server's copies of the passwords are locally encrypted, but this is primarily a precaution against casual browsing. An intruder who gains access to the encrypted passwords can use them to access the associated accounts without the need for further password cracking. Samba passwords must be protected even more vigorously than the **/etc/shadow** file.

In complex environments with multiple Samba servers, it makes sense to operate a centralized directory service that makes sure the same password is active on all servers. Samba supports LDAP and Windows authentication services. LDAP is discussed in Chapter 19, *Sharing System Files*.

To merge the authentication systems of Windows and UNIX, you have two basic options. First, you can configure a Samba server to act as a Windows Active Directory controller. (See *Active Directory authentication* starting on page 1154 for more information about how to implement this option.) Alternatively, you can install the pGina software (sourceforge.net/projects/pgina) on your Windows clients. This clever application replaces the standard Windows login system with a

3. Type **echo $LANG** to see if your system is running in UTF-8 mode.

framework that supports all sorts of standard authentication services, including LDAP and NIS.

Basic file sharing

If each user has a home directory, the homes can be "bulk shared":

```
[homes]
comment = Home Directories
browseable = no
valid users = %S
writeable = yes
guest ok = no
```

This configuration allows the user oetiker (for example) to access his home directory through the path *sambaserver*\oetiker from any Windows system.

At some sites, the default permissions on home directories allow people to browse one another's files. Because Samba relies on UNIX file permissions to implement access restrictions, Windows users coming in through CIFS can read one another's home directories as well. However, experience shows that this behavior tends to confuse Windows users and make them feel exposed. The valid users line in the configuration fragment above tells Samba to prevent connections to other people's home directories. Leave it out if this is not what you want.

Samba uses its magic [homes] section as a last resort. If there is an explicitly defined share in the configuration for a particular user's home directory, the parameters set there override the values set through [homes].

Group shares

Samba can map Windows access control lists (ACLs) to either file permissions or ACLs (if the underlying filesystem supports them). In practice, we find that the concept of ACLs tends to be too complex for most users. Therefore, we normally just set up a special share for each group of users that requires one and configure Samba to take care of setting the appropriate permissions. Whenever a user tries to mount this share, Samba checks to make sure the applicant is in the appropriate UNIX group and then switches its effective UID to the designated owner of the group share (a pseudo-user created for this purpose). For example:

```
[eng]
comment = Group Share for engineering
; Everybody who is in the eng group may access this share.
; People will have to log in using their Samba account.
valid users = @eng
; We have created a special user account called "eng". All files
; written in this directory will belong to this account as
; well as to the eng group.
force user = eng
force group = eng
path = /home/eng
```

```
; Disable NT Acls as we do not use them here.
nt acl support = no

; Make sure that all files have sensible permissions.
create mask = 0660
force create mask = 0660
security mask = 0000
dirctory mask = 2770
force directory mask = 2770
directory security mask = 0000

; Normal share parameters
browseable = no
writeable = yes
guest ok = no
```

A similar effect can be achieved through Samba's inherit permissions option. If that option is enabled on a share, all new files and directories inherit their settings from their parent directory:

```
[eng]
comment = Group Share for engineering
path = /home/eng
nt acl support = no
browseable = no
writeable = yes
inherit permissions = yes
```

Because Samba will now propagate settings from the parent directory, it's important to set the permissions on the root of the share appropriately:

```
$ sudo chmod u=rw,g=rws,o= /home/eng
$ sudo chgrp eng /home/eng
$ sudo chown eng /home/eng
```

Note that this configuration still requires you to create an eng pseudo-user to act as the owner of the shared directory.

Transparent redirection with MS DFS

Microsoft's Distributed File System (MS DFS) lets directories within a share trigger clients to transparently automount other shares as soon as they are accessed. For habitués of UNIX and Linux this does not sound like a big deal, but for Windows the whole concept is quite revolutionary and unexpected.

Here is an example:

```
[global]
; Enable MS DFS support for this Samba server.
host msdfs = yes
...
[mydfs]
; This line tells Samba that it has to look out for
```

```
; DFS symlinks in the directory of this share.
msdfs root = yes
path = /home/dfs/mydfs
```

You create symbolic links in **/home/dfs/mydfs** to set up the actual automounts. For example, the following command makes the **jump** "directory" a link to one of two directories on other servers. (Note the single quotes. They are required for protection of the backslashes.)

```
$ sudo ln -s 'msdfs:serverX\shareX,serverY\shareY' jump
```

If more than one source is provided (as here), Windows will fail over between them. Users who access **\\server\mydfs\jump** will now actually be reading files from shareX on serverX or shareY on serverY, depending on availability. If the filesystems are exported read/write, you must make sure you have some mechanism in place to synchronize the files. **rsync** can be helpful for this.

With Samba, you can also redirect all clients that access a particular share to a different server. This is something a Windows server cannot do.

```
[myredirect]
msdfs root = yes
msdfs proxy = \\serverZ\shareZ
```

Note that DFS only works for users who have the same username and password on all the servers involved.

smbclient: a simple CIFS client

In addition to its many server-side features, the Samba package includes a simple command-line file transfer program called **smbclient**. You can use this program to access any Windows or Samba server. For example:

```
$ smbclient //phobos/c\$ -U BOULDER\\ben
Password: password
Domain=[BOULDER] OS=[Windows Vista (TM) Business 6001 Service Pack 1]
    Server=[Windows Vista (TM) Business 6.0]
smb: \>
```

Once you have successfully logged in to the file server, you use standard **ftp**-style commands (such as **get**, **put**, **cd**, **lcd**, and **dir**) to navigate and transfer files. Type **?** to see a full list of the available commands.

Linux client-side support for CIFS

Linux includes direct client-side support for the SMB/CIFS filesystem. You can mount a CIFS share into your filesystem tree much as you can with any other filesystem that is directly understood by the kernel. For example:

```
$ sudo mount -t cifs -o username=joe //redmond/joes /home/joe/mnt
```

Although this feature is useful, keep in mind that Windows conceptualizes network mounts as being established by a particular user (hence the **username=joe** option above), whereas UNIX regards them as more typically belonging to the system as a whole. Windows servers generally cannot deal with the concept that several different people might be accessing a mounted Windows share.

From the perspective of the UNIX client, all files in the mounted directory appear to belong to the user who mounted it. If you mount the share as root, then all files belong to root, and garden-variety users might not be able to write files on the Windows server.

The mount options **uid**, **gid**, **fmask**, and **dmask** let you tweak these settings so that ownership and permission bits are more in tune with the intended access policy for that share. Check the **mount.cifs** manual page for more information about this behavior.

To allow users to mount a Windows share on their own, you can add a line in the following format to your **/etc/fstab** file:

```
//redmond/joes /home/joe/mnt cifs
     username=joe,fmask=600,dmask=700,user,noauto 0 0
```

Because of the user option specified here, users can now mount the filesystem just by running the command

```
$ mount /home/joe/mnt
```

mount prompts the user to supply a password before mounting the share.

See Chapter 18 for more information about NFS.

Although NFS is the UNIX standard for network file service, in some situations it may make more sense to use Samba and CIFS to share files among UNIX and Linux computers. For example, in some versions of NFS, it is dangerous to allow users to perform mounts of corporate filesystems from their personal laptops.[4] However, you can safely use CIFS to give these laptops access to their owner's home directories.

30.7 SHARING PRINTERS WITH SAMBA

The simple approach to printer sharing is to add a [printers] section to the **smb.conf** file; this makes Samba share all local printers. Samba uses the system printing commands to do its work, but since UNIX printing is not very standardized, you may have to tell Samba which particular printing system is in use on your server. To do that, set the printing option to an appropriate value; check the **smb.conf** man page for the list of printing systems that are currently supported.

```
[printers]
; Where to store print files before passing them to the printing system?
path = /var/tmp
```

4. NFSv3 security is based on the idea that the user has no root access on the client and that UIDs match on the client and server. This is not normally the case for self-managed machines. NFSv4 does better UID mapping than NFSv3 and is dramatically more secure.

```
; Everybody can use the printers.
guest ok = yes
; Let Samba know this share is a printer.
printable = yes
; Show the printers to everyone looking.
browseable = yes
; Tell samba what flavor of printing system the system is using.
printing = cups
```

See Chapter 26 for more information about printing.

Windows clients can now use these printers as network printers, just as if they were hosted by a Windows server. There is one small problem, though. The Windows client will want know what kind of printer it is using, and it will ask the user to select an appropriate printer driver. This leads to quite a lot of support requests from users who do not know how to proceed in this situation. If the particular printer in question requires a driver that is not included with Windows, the situation becomes even more support-intensive.

Fortunately, you can configure Samba to furnish the necessary Windows printer drivers to the Windows clients. But to make this work, you must do some preparation. First, to make sure that Samba behaves like a print server, add appropriate entries to the [global] section of the **smb.conf** file:

```
[global]
; Who is our printer admin
printer admin = printadm
; The following have the right value by default.
disable spoolss = no
; Don't bother showing it; you cannot add printers anyway
show add printer wizard = no
; Assuming you want everybody to be able to print
guest ok = yes
browseable = no
```

Now Samba knows that it is a print server, and it will accept the user printadm as its printer administrator.

If you are going to provide printer drivers for your Windows clients, there has to be a place to store the drivers. This is done through a special share called [print$].

```
[print$]
comment = Printer Driver Area
; Place to store the printer drivers
path = /var/lib/samba/printers
browseable = yes
guest ok = yes
read only = yes
; Who can administer the printer driver repository
write list = printadm
```

Before you can start to upload printer drivers to the new print server, you must take care of a few more details at the system level. Make sure the printadm account exists and has permission to access Samba.

```
$ sudo useradd printadm
$ sudo smbpasswd -a printadm
```

Samba can store printer drivers only if the appropriate directory structure exists and is owned by printadm (as defined in the write list option):

```
$ sudo mkdir -p /var/lib/samba/printers
$ sudo cd /var/lib/samba/printers
$ sudo mkdir W32X86 WIN40 x64
$ sudo chown -R printadm .
```

At this point there are two options: you can either walk to a Windows box and upload the printer drivers from there, or you can use Samba tools to do it all from the command line. Unfortunately, there is no simple way of knowing what exactly has to be installed for a particular driver, so we recommend the first approach in most circumstances. Only if you are faced with repeatedly installing a driver on multiple servers is it worthwhile to examine the installation and learn to replicate it with command-line tools.

Installing a printer driver from Windows

To install drivers from a Windows client, open a connection to the Samba server by typing *sambaserver* in the Start -> Run dialog box. Windows will ask you to log in to the Samba server. Log in as the user printadm. If all goes well, a window pops up with a list of shares provided by the server.

Within the Printers subfolder you should see all the printers you have shared from your server. Right-click in the blank space around the printer icons to activate the Server Properties dialog, then add your favorite printer drivers by making use of the Drivers tab.

The uploaded drivers end up in the directory specified for the [print$] share. At this point, you might want to take a quick peek at the properties of the driver you just uploaded. This list of files is what you will have to provide to the Samba command-line tool if ever you want to automate the uploading of the driver.

Once the proper drivers have been uploaded, you can now associate them with specific printers. Bring up the Properties panel of each printer in turn (by right-clicking and selecting Properties) and select the appropriate drivers in the Advanced tab. Then open the Printing Defaults dialog and modify the settings. Even if you are happy with the default settings, make at least one small change to force Windows to store the configuration data structures on the Samba server. Samba then provides that data to clients that access the printer. If you miss this last step, you may end up with clients crashing because no valid default configuration can be found when they try to use the printer.

Installing a printer driver from the command line

As you may have guessed already, some of these steps are hard to replicate without Windows, especially the setting of printer defaults. But if you want to set up hundreds of printers on a Samba server, you may want to try to do it from the command line all the same. Command-line configuration works particularly well for PostScript printers because the Windows PostScript printer driver works correctly without default configuration information.

If you made a note of the files required by a particular driver, you can install the driver from the command line. First, copy the required files to the [print$] share:

```
$ cd ~/mydriver
$ smbclient -U printadm '//samba-server/print$' -c 'mput *.*'
```

Next, assign the driver to a particular printer. Let's assume you have a simple PostScript printer with a custom PPD file:

```
$ rpcclient -U printadm -c "\
adddriver \"Windows NT x86\" \"Our Custom PS:\
PSCRIPT5.DLL:CUSTOM.PPD:PS5UI.DLL:PSCIPT.HLP:NULL:NULL:PSCRIPT.NTF\"" \
samba-server
```

The backslashes at the ends of lines allow the command to be split onto multiple lines for clarity; you can omit these and enter the command on one line if you prefer. The backslashes before double quotes distinguish the nested sets of quotes.

The long string in the example above contains the information listed in the property dialog of the printer driver that is seen when the printer driver is being installed from Windows:

- Long printer name
- Driver filename
- Data filename
- Configuration filename
- Help filename
- Language monitor name (set this to NULL if you have none)
- Default data type (set this to NULL if there is none)
- Comma-separated list of additional files

To configure a printer to use one of the uploaded drivers, run

```
$ rpcclient -U printadm -c "\
set driver \"myprinter\" \"Our Custom PS\"" samba-server
```

30.8 Debugging Samba

Samba usually runs without requiring much attention. However, if you do have a problem, you can consult two primary sources of debugging information: the log files for each client and the **smbstatus** command. Make sure you have appropriate log file settings in your configuration file.

```
[global]
; The %m causes a separate file to be written for each client.
log file = /var/log/samba.log.%m
max log size = 1000
; How much info to log. You can also specify log levels for components
; of the system (here, 3 generally, but level 10 for authentication).
log level = 3 auth:10
```

Higher log levels produce more information. Logging takes time, so don't ask for too much detail unless you are debugging. Operation can be slowed considerably.

The following example shows the log entries generated by an unsuccessful connect attempt followed by a successful one.

```
[2009/09/05 16:29:45, 2] auth/auth.c:check_ntlm_password(312)
  check_ntlm_password:  Authentication for user [oetiker] -> [oetiker] FAILED
     with error NT_STATUS_WRONG_PASSWORD
[2009/09/05 16:29:45, 2] smbd/server.c:exit_server(571)
  Closing connections
[2009/09/05 16:29:57, 2] auth/auth.c:check_ntlm_password(305)
  check_ntlm_password:  authentication for user [oetiker] -> [oetiker] ->
     [oetiker] succeeded
[2009/09/05 16:29:57, 1] smbd/service.c:make_connection_snum(648)
  etsuko (127.0.0.1) connect to service oetiker initially as user oetiker
     (uid=1000, gid=1000) (pid 20492)
[2009/09/05 16:29:58, 1] smbd/service.c:close_cnum(837)
  etsuko (127.0.0.1) closed connection to service oetiker
[2009/09/05 16:29:58, 2] smbd/server.c:exit_server(571)
  Closing connections
```

The **smbcontrol** command is handy for altering the debug level on a running Samba server without altering the **smb.conf** file. For example,

```
$ sudo smbcontrol smbd debug "4 auth:10"
```

The example above would set the global debug level to 4 and set the debug level for authentication-related matters to 10. The **smbd** argument specifies that all **smbd** daemons on the system will have their debug levels set. To debug a specific established connection, you can use the **smbstatus** command to figure out which **smbd** daemon handles the connection and then pass its PID to **smbcontrol** to debug just this one connection. At log levels over 100 you will start to see (encrypted) passwords in the logs.

smbstatus shows currently active connections and locked files. This information is especially useful when you are tracking down locking problems (e.g., "Which user has file **xyz** open read/write exclusive?"). The first section of output lists the resources that a user has connected to. The last section lists any active file locks.

```
$ sudo smbstatus          # Some output lines condensed for clarity
Samba version 3.4.1
  PID     Username  Group     Machine
-------------------------------------------------------------------
 10612    trent     atrust    tanq           (192.168.20.6)
  5283    ned       atrust    ithaca         (192.168.20.1)
  1037    paul      atrust    pauldesk2      (192.168.20.48)
  8137    trent     atrust    atlantic       (192.168.1.3)
  1173    jim       jim       jim-desktop    (192.168.20.7)
 11563    mgetty    mgetty    mgetty         (192.168.20.5)
  6125    brian     brian     brian-desktop  (192.168.20.16)

Service    pid     machine        Connected at
-------------------------------------------------------------------
swdepot2   18335   john-desktop   Fri Sep 18 13:21:40 2009
swdepot2   1173    jim-desktop    Thu Sep 3 15:47:58 2009
goldmine   1173    jim-desktop    Thu Sep 3 15:38:44 2009
swdepot2   1037    pauldesk2      Tue Sep 8 10:59:28 2009
admin      1037    pauldesk2      Tue Sep 8 10:59:28 2009

Locked files:
Pid   DenyMode    Access   R/W     Oplock               Name
---------------------------------------------------------
1037  DENY_WRITE  0x20089  RDONLY  EXCLUSIVE+BATCH  /home/paul/smsi...
6125  DENY_WRITE  0x2019f  RDWR    NONE             /home/trent/rdx...
1037  DENY_WRITE  0x2019f  RDWR    NONE             /home/ben/samp...
18335 DENY_WRITE  0x2019f  RDWR    NONE             /home/ben/exa...
```

If you kill the **smbd** associated with a certain user, all its locks disappear. Some applications handle this gracefully and reacquire any locks they need. Others, such as MS Access, freeze and die a horrible death with much clicking required on the Windows side just to be able to close the unhappy application. As dramatic as this may sound, we have yet to see any file corruption resulting from such a procedure. In any event, be careful when Windows claims that files have been locked by another application. Often Windows is right and you should fix the problem on the client side by closing the offending application instead of brute-forcing the locks on the server.

30.9 Active Directory authentication

The Windows desktops lurking on your network most likely use Microsoft's Active Directory system for authentication, directory services, and other network services. Active Directory (AD) collects users, groups, computers, and operating system polices under a single umbrella, centralizing and simplifying system administration. It is also one of the primary reasons why Windows has gained a permanent foothold in many enterprises. UNIX has assembled some of the pieces of this puzzle, but none of the UNIX solutions are as polished or as widely implemented as Active Directory.

See page 908 for more information about PAM.

Ever devious, the Samba project folks have made great strides toward providing Active Directory support for UNIX and Linux environments. With the help of Samba, Linux systems can join an Active Directory domain and allow access to the system by accounts defined in AD that have no entries in the **/etc/passwd** file. Linux UIDs are derived from their analogous Windows user identifiers, known as security identifiers or SIDs. By leveraging PAM, a home directory can automatically be created for a user who doesn't already have one. The integration system even allows the **passwd** command to change a user's AD password. All of this Windows integration magic is handled by a component of Samba called **winbind**.

Active Directory embraces and extends several standard protocols, notably LDAP and Kerberos. In an attempt to achieve IT system management nirvana, Microsoft has unfortunately sacrificed compliance with the original protocols, creating an intoxicating web of proprietary RPC dependencies.

See page 739 for more information about the name service switch.

To emulate the behavior of an Active Directory client, **winbind** hooks into PAM, NSS, and Kerberos. It converts authentication and system information requests into the appropriate Microsoft-specific formats. From the standpoint of UNIX, Active Directory is just another source of LDAP directory information and Kerberos authentication data.

You must complete the following configuration chores before your Linux system can enter Active Directory paradise:

- Install Samba with support for Active Directory and identity conversion.
- Configure the name service switch, **nsswitch.conf**, to use **winbind** as a source of user, group, and password information.
- Configure PAM to service authentication requests through **winbind**.
- Configure Active Directory as a Kerberos realm.

See Chapter 17 for more information about DNS.

UNIX and Linux AD clients should also use AD controllers to service their DNS requests and to set their clocks with NTP. Ensure as well that the system's fully qualified domain name is listed in **/etc/hosts**. In some cases, it's necessary to add the domain controller's IP address to **/etc/hosts**, too. However, we discourage this if you're using Active Directory for DNS service.

winbind is an excellent option for Linux systems, but UNIX has largely been left out in the cold. We have heard reports of UNIX sites successfully deploying the same general scheme described here, but each system has a few caveats, and the integration tends to be not as clean as on Linux. For UNIX systems, we suggest using one of the alternatives described on page 1160.

Getting ready for Active Directory integration

Samba is included by default on most Linux distributions, but some distributions do not include the identity mapping services needed for a full AD client implementation. Those components can be fiddly to set up correctly if you're compiling from source code, so we recommend installing binary packages if they're available for your distribution.

The Samba components, on the other hand, should be as fresh as possible. Active Directory integration is one of Samba's newer features, so downloading the most recent source code from samba.org can eliminate frustrating bugs.

If you build Samba from source, configure it with the **idmap_ad** and **idmap_rid** shared modules. The appropriate argument to the **./configure** script is

--with-shared-modules=idmap_ad,idmap_rid

Build and install Samba with the familiar **make**, **sudo make install** sequence. When installed correctly, the **winbind** library is deposited in **/lib**:

```
ubuntu$ ls -l /lib/libnss_winbind.so.2
-rw-r--r-- 1 root root 21884 2009-10-08 00:28 /lib/libnss_winbind.so.2
```

The **winbind** daemon is stopped and started through normal operating system procedures. It should be restarted after changes to **nsswitch.conf**, **smb.conf**, or the Kerberos configuration file, **krb5.conf**. There is no need to start it until these other services have been configured.

Configuring Kerberos for Active Directory integration

Kerberos is infamous for complex configuration, particularly on the server side. Fortunately, you only need to set up the client side of Kerberos, which is a much easier task. The configuration file is **/etc/krb5.conf**.

First, double-check that the system's fully qualified domain name has been included in **/etc/hosts** and that NTP is using an Active Directory server as a time reference. Then, edit **krb5.conf** to add the realm as shown in the following example. Substitute your site's AD domain for ULSAH.COM.

```
[logging]
    default = FILE:/var/log/krb5.log
[libdefaults]
    clockskew = 300
    default_realm = ULSAH.COM
    kdc_timesync = 1
    ccache_type = 4
    forwardable = true
    proxiable = true
[realms]
    ULSAH.COM = {
        kdc = dc.ulsah.com
        admin_server = dc.ulsah.com
        default_domain = ULSAH
    }
[domain_realm]
    .ulsah.com = ULSAH.COM
    ulsah.com = ULSAH.COM
```

Several values are of interest in the above example. A 5-minute clock skew is allowed even though the time is set through NTP. This gives some slack in the event of an NTP problem. The default realm is set to the AD domain, and the key distribution center, or KDC, is configured as an AD domain controller. **krb5.log** might come in handy for debugging.

Request a ticket from the Active Directory controller by running the **kinit** command. Specify a valid domain user account. "administrator" is usually a good test, but any account will do. When prompted, type the domain password.

```
ubuntu$ kinit administrator@ULSAH.COM
Password for administrator@ULSAH.COM: <password>
```

Use **klist** to show the Kerberos ticket:

```
ubuntu$ klist
Ticket cache: FILE:/tmp/krb5cc_1000
Default principal: administrator@ULSAH.COM

Valid starting     Expires            Service principal
10/11/09 13:40:19  10/11/09 23:40:21  krbtgt/ULSAH.COM@ULSAH.COM
renew until 10/12/09 13:40:19

Kerberos 4 ticket cache: /tmp/tkt1000
klist: You have no tickets cached
```

If a ticket is displayed, authentication was successful and you configured Kerberos correctly. In this case, the ticket is valid for 10 hours and can be renewed for 24 hours. (You can use the **kdestroy** command to invalidate the ticket.)

See the man page for **krb5.conf** for additional configuration options.

Samba as an Active Directory domain member

Like other Samba components, **winbind** is configured in the **smb.conf** file. Configure Samba as an AD domain member with the security = ads option.

A working configuration is reproduced below. We set our Kerberos realm and pointed Samba authentication at the domain controller. We also set up the user identity mapping with **smb.conf**'s idmap options. Note that the configuration of individual shares in **smb.conf** is separate from the configuration of AD authentication services; only domain authentication is shown here.

```
[global]
    security = ads
    realm = ULSAH.COM
    password server = 192.168.7.120
    workgroup = ULSAH
    winbind separator = +
    idmap uid = 10000-20000
    idmap gid = 10000-20000
    winbind enum users = yes
    winbind enum groups = yes
    template homedir = /home/%D/%U
    template shell = /bin/bash
```

```
client use spnego = yes
client ntlmv2 auth = yes
encrypt passwords = yes
winbind use default domain = yes
restrict anonymous = 2
```

Most of the options here are straightforward, but see **man smb.conf** for details.

Of particular note is the winbind use default domain option. If you're using multiple AD domains, this value should be no. If you're using only one domain, however, setting this value to yes lets you omit the domain during authentication (you can use "ben" as opposed to "ULSAH\ben", for example). Additionally, the winbind separator value specifies an alternative to the backslash when usernames are typed. The workgroup value should be the short name of the domain. A domain such as linux.ulsah.com would use LINUX as the workgroup value.

After configuring Samba, restart the Samba and **winbind** services to make these new settings take effect.

It's finally time to join the system to the domain; use the Samba-provided **net** tool, which borrows its syntax from the Windows command of the same name. **net** accepts several protocols for communicating with Windows. We use the **ads** option to target Active Directory.

Ensure that a ticket exists by running **klist** (and request one with **kinit** if it does not), then use the following command to join the domain:

```
ubuntu$ sudo net ads join -S DC.ULSAH.COM  -U administrator
Enter administrator's password: <password>
Using short domain name -- ULSAH
Joined 'UBUNTU' to realm 'ulsah.com'
```

We specified an AD server, dc.ulsah.com, on the command line (not strictly necessary) and the administrator account. By default, AD adds the new system to the Computer organizational unit of the domain hierarchy. If the system appears in the Computers OU within Windows' AD Users and Computers tool, the domain join operation was successful. You can also examine the system state with the **net ads status** command. See the **net** man page for additional options, including LDAP search operations.

Name service switch configuration is simple. The system's **passwd** and **group** files should always be consulted first, but you can then punt to Active Directory by way of **winbind**. These entries in **nsswitch.conf** do the trick:

```
passwd:    compat winbind
group:     compat winbind
shadow:    compat winbind
```

Once NSS has been configured, you can test AD user and group resolution with the **wbinfo** command. Use **wbinfo -u** to see a list of the domain's users and

wbinfo -g to see groups. The command **getent passwd** shows the user accounts defined in all sources, in **/etc/passwd** format:

```
ubuntu$ getent passwd
root:x:0:0:root:/root:/bin/bash
daemon:x:1:1:daemon:/usr/sbin:/bin/sh
...
bwhaley:x:10006:10018::/home/bwhaley:/bin/sh
guest:*:10001:10001:Guest:/home/ULSAH/guest:/bin/bash
ben:*:10002:10000:Ben Whaley:/home/ULSAH/ben:/bin/bash
krbtgt:*:10003:10000:krbtgt:/home/ULSAH/krbtgt:/bin/bash
```

The only way to distinguish local users from domain accounts is by user ID and by the ULSAH path in the home directory, apparent in the last three entries above. If your site has multiple domains or if the winbind use default domain option is not set, the short domain name is prepended to domain accounts (for instance, ULSAH\ben).

PAM configuration

See page 908 for general information about PAM.

At this point the system has been configured to communicate with Active Directory through Samba, but authentication has not been configured. Setting up PAM to do authentication through Active Directory is a bit tricky, mostly because the specifics differ widely among Linux distributions.

The general idea is to configure **winbind** as an authentication module for all the services that should have Active Directory support. Some distributions, such as Red Hat, conveniently set up all services in a single file. Others, such as Ubuntu, rely on several files. Table 30.1 lists the appropriate files for each of our example Linux distributions.

Table 30.1 PAM configuration files for winbind support

System	Authentication	Session
Ubuntu	**common-account**, **common-auth**, **sudo**	**common-session**
SUSE	**common-auth**, **common-password**, **common-account**	**common-session**
Red Hat	**system-auth**	**system-auth**

To enable **winbind** authentication, add

```
auth sufficient pam_winbind.so
```

at the beginning of each file. An exception is SUSE's **common-password** file, in which you must replace the auth keyword with password:

```
password sufficient pam_winbind.so
```

PAM can create home directories automatically if they don't exist when a new (to the system) user logs in. Since Active Directory users aren't added by the standard **useradd** command, which is normally responsible for creating home directories, this feature is quite helpful. Add the following line to PAM's session configuration file as indicated in Table 30.1:

```
session required pam_mkhomedir.so umask=0022 skel=/etc/skel
```

With this configuration, PAM creates home directories with octal permissions 755 and with account profiles copied from **/etc/skel**.

You may also want to restrict access to the local system to users who are in a particular Active Directory group. To do that, add the following line to PAM's session configuration file:

```
session required /lib/security/$ISA/pam_winbind.so use_first_pass
    require_membership_of=unix_users
```

Here, only users in the AD group unix_users can log in.

Alternatives to winbind

Although the "free as in beer" route to Active Directory clienthood outlined above works well enough, it is error prone and riddled with complexity. Alternatives exist for administrators who want a relatively painless installation and troubleshooting support from a knowledgeable third party.

Products from Likewise Software automate **winbind**, name service switch, PAM, and identity mapping configuration for more than 100 Linux distributions and UNIX variants, including all the example systems referenced in this book. Likewise also includes a group policy object agent, which permits some centralized configuration for AD-enabled UNIX systems. Several GUI plug-ins, including a management console and an Active Directory snap-in, simplify installation and configuration. A limited version is available for free, or you can pay for support and complete functionality. Find details at likewise.com.

Another option that skirts **winbind** entirely is a tool kit called Quest Authentication Services. It offers many of the same features as Likewise's tools, but adds additional group policy management features. Be prepared to open your wallet, as Quest's tools do not come cheap. See quest.com/authentication-services for the full scoop.

30.10 Recommended reading

TERPSTRA, JOHN H. *Samba-3 by Example: Practical Exercises to Successful Deployment (2nd Edition)*. Upper Saddle River, NJ: Prentice Hall PTR, 2006. (An on-line version of this book is available at samba.org.)

TERPSTRA, JOHN H., JELMER R. VERNOOIJ. *The Official Samba-3 HOWTO and Reference Guide (2nd Edition)*. Upper Saddle River, NJ: Prentice Hall PTR, 2006. (An on-line version of this book is available at samba.org.)

30.11 Exercises

E30.1 Why would you want to block Internet access to ports 137–139 and 445 on a Samba server?

E30.2 Install the Cygwin software on a Windows machine and use **ssh** in **rxvt** to connect to a UNIX machine. What differences from PuTTY do you find?

★ E30.3 In the lab, compare the performance of a client that accesses files through Samba with one that accesses files from a native CIFS server (i.e., a Windows machine). If your two test servers have different hardware, devise a way to adjust for the hardware variation so that the comparison is more indicative of the performance of the server software. (May require root access.)

★★ E30.4 In the lab, use a packet sniffer such as **tcpdump** or Wireshark to monitor a **telnet** session between Windows and a UNIX server. Obtain and install the PuTTY software and repeat the monitoring. In each case, what can you see with the packet sniffer? (Requires root access.)

★★ E30.5 Set up a Samba print server that provides Windows printer drivers for all the printers it shares. Make sure the printers come with a sensible default configuration.

★★ E30.6 Configure the system of your choice to authenticate to an Active Directory environment. Make sure that password changes work and that home directories are automatically created at login for new users.

31 Serial Devices and Terminals

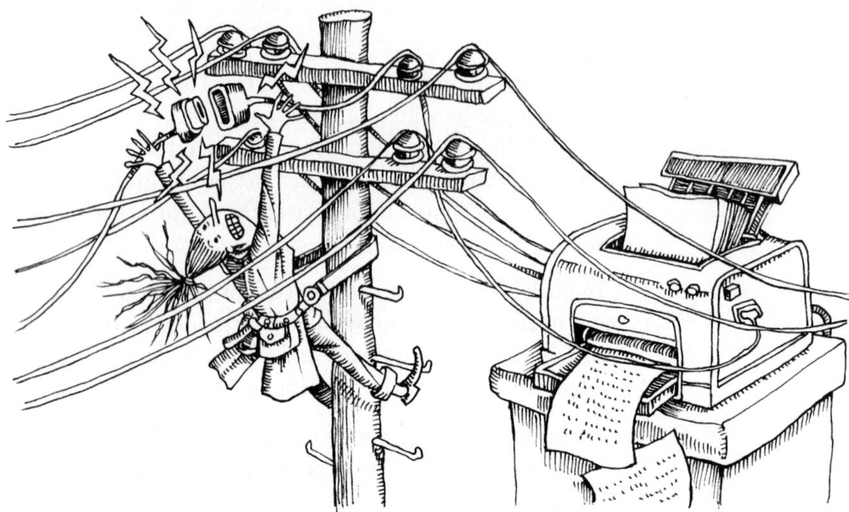

An operating system with over 40 years of history is sure to be dragging some cruft along with it. Some would put support for serial devices into this category, arguing that it's a technology from a bygone era that is best forgotten. Compared to today's multi-megabit serial interfaces such as USB, traditional serial ports may indeed seem too slow and twiddly to be useful.

In fact, an understanding of serial interfaces is an essential component of any system administrator's tool box. For better or worse, the UNIX command-line interface is based on the ancient concept of a serial terminal and the associated commands and control structures remain in use today. Even if you have never been within 50 paces of a hardwired terminal, you're still using the same basic OS facilities that supported it. For example, the console window on your UNIX or Linux desktop is really a pseudo-terminal, as is the device to which you appear to be connected when you log in through the network.

Actual RS-232C serial ports are still around, too. They're no longer the general facility they used to be, but they remain important in several situations. They're the common denominator for bootstrapping all types of hardware devices, from lights-out enterprise-class server managers to embedded systems the size of a thumbnail, including custom hardware projects. They're a medium you can use to communicate with legacy systems. There are even cases in which you might run into an actual hardwired terminal, such as on a manufacturing floor.

This chapter describes how to connect and use RS-232-based serial devices in the modern world. The first few sections address serial hardware and cabling considerations. Then, starting on page 1171, we talk about the software infrastructure that supports both hardwired terminals and the pseudo-terminals that emulate them. Finally, we cover the use of a UNIX or Linux system to communicate with the serial consoles of other devices.

31.1 The RS-232C standard

Most slow-speed serial ports conform to some variant of the RS-232C standard. This standard specifies the electrical characteristics and meaning of each signal wire, as well as the pin assignments on the traditional 25-pin (DB-25p) serial connector shown in Exhibit A.

Exhibit A A male DB-25 connector

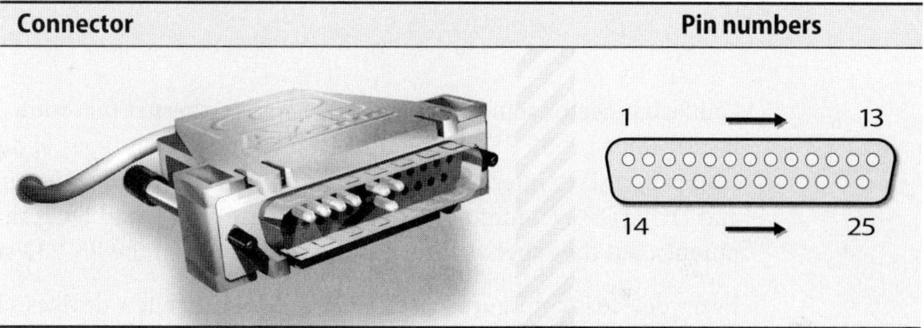

Full RS-232C[1] is never used in real-world situations since it defines numerous signals that are unnecessary for basic communication. DB-25 connectors are also inconveniently large. As a result, 9-pin DB-9 connectors are now commonly used instead of the original 25-pin flavor. In cases where structured cabling is used, RJ-45 connectors are also a convenient alternative. Both of these connectors are described in the section titled *Alternative connectors* starting on page 1165.

Exhibit A shows a male DB-25. As with all serial connectors, the pin numbers on a female connector are a mirror image of those on a male connector so that like-numbered pins mate. The diagram is drawn from the orientation shown, as if you were facing the end of the cable, about to plug the connector into your forehead.

Note that in Exhibit A, only seven pins are actually installed, which is typical. The RS-232 signals and their pin assignments on a full-size DB-25 connector are

Serial Devices

1. To be technically correct, this standard should now be referred to as EIA-232-E. However, no one will have the slightest idea what you are talking about.

shown in Table 31.1. Only the shaded signals are ever used in practice (at least on computer systems); all others can be ignored.

Table 31.1 RS-232 signals and pin assignments on a DB-25

Pin	Name	Function	Pin	Name	Function
1	FG	Frame ground	14	STD	Secondary TD
2	TD	Transmitted data	15	TC	Transmit clock
3	RD	Received data	16	SRD	Secondary RD
4	RTS	Request to send	17	RC	Receive clock
5	CTS	Clear to send	18	–	Not assigned
6	DSR	Data set ready	19	SRTS	Secondary RTS
7	SG	Signal ground	20	DTR	Data terminal ready
8	DCD	Data carrier detect	21	SQ	Signal quality detector
9	–	Positive voltage	22	RI	Ring indicator
10	–	Negative voltage	23	DRS	Data rate selector
11	–	Not assigned	24	SCTE	Clock transmit external
12	SDCD	Secondary DCD	25	BUSY	Busy
13	SCTS	Secondary CTS			

Unlike connector standards such as USB and Ethernet that were designed to be mostly idiot-proof, RS-232 requires you to know what types of devices you are connecting. Two interface configurations exist: DTE (Data Terminal Equipment) and DCE (Data Communications Equipment). DTE and DCE share the same pinouts, but they specify different interpretations of the RS-232 signals.

Every device is configured as either DTE or DCE; a few devices support both, but not simultaneously. Computers, terminals, and printers are generally DTE, and most modems are DCE. DTE and DCE serial ports can communicate with each other in any combination, but different combinations require different cabling.

There is no sensible reason for both DTE and DCE to exist; all equipment could use the same wiring scheme. The existence of two conventions is merely one of the many pointless historical legacies of RS-232.

DTE and DCE can be confusing if you let yourself think about the implications too much. When that happens, just take a deep breath and reread these points:

- The RS-232 pinout for a given connector type is always the same, regardless of whether the connector is male or female (matching pin numbers always mate) and regardless of whether the connector is on a cable, a DTE device, or a DCE device.

- All RS-232 terminology is based on the model of a straight-through connection from a DTE device to a DCE device. By "straight through," we mean that TD on the DTE end is connected to TD on the DCE end, and so on. Each pin connects to the same-numbered pin on the other end.

- Signals are named relative to the perspective of the DTE device. For example, the name TD (transmitted data) really means "data transmitted from DTE to DCE." Despite the name, the TD pin is an *input* on a DCE device. Similarly, RD is an input for DTE and an output for DCE.
- When you wire DTE equipment to DTE equipment (computer-to-terminal or computer-to-computer), you must trick each device into thinking the other is DCE. For example, both DTE devices expect to transmit on TD and receive on RD. You must cross-connect the wires so that one device's transmit pin goes to the other's receive pin, and vice versa.
- Three sets of signals must be crossed in this fashion for DTE-to-DTE communication (if you choose to connect them at all). TD and RD must be crossed. RTS and CTS must be crossed. And each side's DTR pin must be connected to both the DCD and DSR pins of the peer.
- To add to the confusion, a cable crossed for DTE-to-DTE communication is often called a "null modem" cable. You might be tempted to use a null modem cable to hook up a modem, but since modems are DCE, that won't work! A cable for a modem is called a "modem cable" or a "straight cable."

Exhibit B shows pin assignments and connections for both null-modem and straight-through cables. Only signals used in the real world are shown.

Exhibit B Pin assignments and connections for DB-25 cables

Legend		Straight		Null modem	
Frame ground	FG	1	1	1	1
Transmitted data	TD	2	2	2	2
Received data	RD	3	3	3	3
Request to send	RTS	4	4	4	4
Clear to send	CTS	5	5	5	5
Data set ready	DSR	6	6	6	6
Signal ground	SG	7	7	7	7
Data carrier detect	DCD	8	8	8	8
Data terminal ready	DTR	20	20	20	20

31.2 Alternative connectors

The following sections describe the most common modern connector systems, DB-9 and RJ-45. Despite their physical differences, these connectors provide access to the same electrical signals as a DB-25. Devices that use different connectors are always compatible if the right kind of converter cable is used.

The DB-9 variant

The DB-9 is the most common modern-day embodiment of RS-232. It's a 9-pin connector that looks like a "DB-25 junior" and supplies the eight most commonly used signals. Pin 9 is left unconnected.

Exhibit C A male DB-9 connector

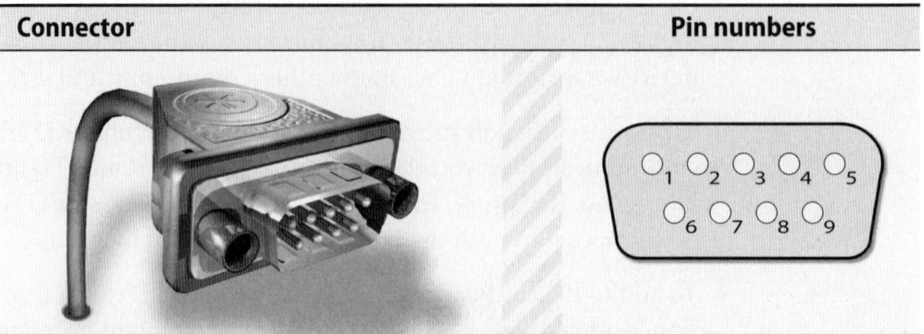

Table 31.2 DB-9 Pinout

DB-9	Signal	Function
1	DCD	Data carrier detect
2	RD	Received data
3	TD	Transmitted data
4	DTR	Data terminal ready
5	SG	Signal ground
6	DSR	Data set ready
7	RTS	Request to send
8	CTS	Clear to send

The RJ-45 variant

An RJ-45 is an 8-wire modular telephone connector. The use of RJ-45s makes it easy to run serial communications through your building's existing wiring if the wiring plant was installed with twisted-pair Ethernet in mind.

RJ-45 jacks for serial connections are usually not found on computers or on garden-variety serial equipment, but they are often used as intermediate connectors for routing serial lines through patch panels. RJ-45s are compact, self-securing, cheap, and easy to crimp onto the ends of custom-cut cables. An inexpensive crimping tool is required.

Several systems map the pins on an RJ-45 connector to those on a DB-25. Table 31.3 shows the official RS-232D standard, which is used only haphazardly.

Exhibit D A male RJ-45 connector

Connector	Pin numbers

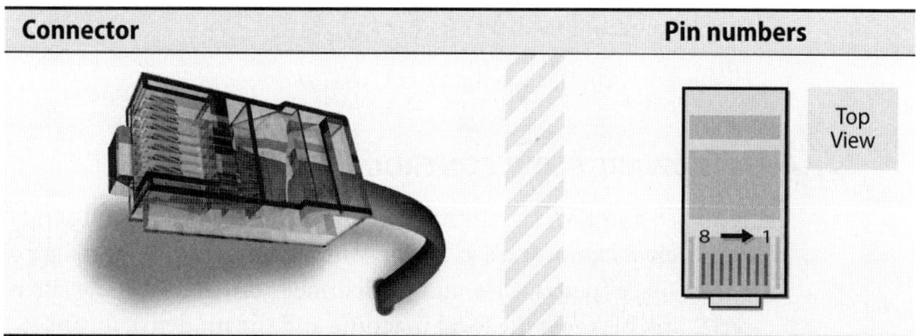

Table 31.3 Pins for an RJ-45 to DB-25 straight cable

RJ-45	DB-25	Signal	Function
1	6	DSR	Data set ready
2	8	DCD	Data carrier detect
3	20	DTR	Data terminal ready
4	7	SG	Signal ground
5	3	RD	Received data
6	2	TD	Transmitted data
7	5	CTS	Clear to send
8	4	RTS	Request to send

A well-thought-out standard for RJ-45 to DB-25 wiring was created by Dave Yost. If you're planning to use a significant amount of serial cabling, be sure to check it out at yost.com/computers/RJ45-serial.

31.3 Hard and soft carrier

UNIX expects to see the DCD signal, carrier detect, go high (positive voltage) when a serial device is attached and turned on. If your serial cable has a DCD line and your computer really pays attention to it, you are using what is known as hard carrier. Most systems also allow soft carrier; that is, the computer pretends that DCD is always asserted.

For certain devices (such as traditional hardwired terminals), soft carrier is a great blessing. You can get away with using only three wires for each serial connection: transmit, receive, and signal ground. However, modem connections really need the DCD signal. If a terminal is connected through a modem and the carrier signal is lost, the modem should hang up (especially on a long distance call!).

You can specify soft carrier for a serial port in the configuration file for whatever client software you use in conjunction with the port (e.g., **gettydefs** or **inittab** for a login terminal or **printcap** for a printer). You can also use **stty -clocal** to enable soft carrier on the fly.

For example,

```
suse$ sudo stty -clocal < /dev/ttyS1
```

enables soft carrier for the port **ttyS1**.

31.4 Hardware flow control

The CTS and RTS signals make sure that a device does not send data faster than the receiver can process it. For example, if a modem is in danger of running out of buffer space (perhaps because the connection to the remote site is slower than the serial link between the local machine and the modem), it can tell the computer to shut up until more room becomes available in the buffer.

Flow control is essential for high-speed modems and is also very useful for serial printers. On systems that do not support hardware flow control (either because the serial ports do not understand it or because the serial cable leaves CTS and RTS disconnected), flow control can sometimes be simulated in software with the ASCII characters XON and XOFF. However, software flow control must be explicitly supported by high-level software, and even then it does not work very well.

XON and XOFF are <Control-Q> and <Control-S>, respectively. This is a problem for **emacs** users because <Control-S> is the default key binding for the **emacs** search command. To fix the problem, bind the search command to another key or use **stty start** and **stty stop** to change the terminal driver's idea of XON and XOFF.

Most terminals ignore the CTS and RTS signals. By jumpering pins 4 and 5 together at the terminal end of the cable, you can fool the few terminals that require a handshake across these pins before they will communicate. When the terminal sends out a signal on pin 4 saying "I'm ready," it gets the same signal back on pin 5 saying "Go ahead." You can also jumper the DTR/DSR/DCD handshake like this.

As with soft carrier, hardware flow control can be set through configuration files or with the **stty** command.

On Sun hardware, flow control for built-in serial ports must be set up with the **eeprom** command.

On some HP platforms, you may need to set flow control for built-in serial ports with the Guardian Service Processor (GSP).

31.5 Serial device files

Serial ports are represented by device files in or under **/dev**. Even today, many computers have one or two serial ports built in, mainly as a communication mechanism of last resort. In the past, such ports were usually known by names such as **/dev/ttya** and **/dev/ttyb**, but naming conventions have diverged over time, and those ports are now often named **/dev/ttyS0** or**/dev/tty1**.

Sometimes, more than one device file refers to the same serial port. For example, **/dev/cua/a** on a Solaris system refers to the same port as **/dev/term/a**. However, the minor device number for **/dev/cua/a** is different:

```
solaris$ ls -lL /dev/term/a /dev/cua/a
crw-------   1 uucp   uucp   37, 131072   Jan 11 16:35 /dev/cua/a
crw-rw-rw-   1 root   sys    37, 0        Jan 11 16:35 /dev/term/a
```

As always, the names of the device files do not really matter. Device mapping is determined by the major and minor device numbers, and the names of device files are merely a convenience for human users.

Multiple device files are primarily used to support modems that handle both incoming and outgoing calls. In the Solaris scheme, the driver allows **/dev/term/a** to be opened only when DCD has been asserted by the modem, indicating the presence of an active (inbound) connection (assuming that soft carrier is not enabled on the port). **/dev/cua/a** can be opened regardless of the state of DCD; it's used when connecting to the modem to instruct it to place a call. Access to each device file is blocked while the other is in use.

On HP-UX, serial device files are not always created automatically. You can use the **ioscan** command to force the system to look for them, something like

```
hp-ux$ sudo ioscan -C tty -fn
```

You can then create the device files with

```
hp-ux$ sudo mksf -H port-from-ioscan-output -d asio0 -a0 -i -v
```

AIX appears to be moving away from supporting serial interfaces entirely. In particular, if you have a system with multiple LPARs (see Chapter 24), serial interfaces are not available by default. You may have to purchase special hardware to obtain serial connectivity in this case.

31.6 SETSERIAL: SET SERIAL PORT PARAMETERS UNDER LINUX

The serial ports on a PC can appear at several different I/O port addresses and interrupt levels (IRQs). These settings might be configured through the system's BIOS, or they might be set automatically through plug and play (PnP) code at boot time. On rare occasions, you may need to change a serial port's address and IRQ settings to accommodate some cranky piece of hardware that is finicky about its own settings and only works correctly when it has co-opted the settings normally used by a serial port. Unfortunately, the serial driver may not be able to detect such configuration changes without your help.

The traditional UNIX response to such diversity is to allow the serial port parameters to be specified when the kernel is compiled. Fortunately, Linux lets you skip this tedious step and change the parameters on the fly with the **setserial** command. **setserial -g** shows the current settings.

```
ubuntu$ setserial -g /dev/ttyS0
/dev/ttyS0, UART: 16550A, Port: 0x03f8, IRQ: 4
```

To set the parameters, you specify the device file and then a series of parameters and values. For example, the command

```
ubuntu$ sudo setserial /dev/ttyS1 port 0x02f8 irq 3
```

sets the I/O port address and IRQ for **ttyS1**. It's important to keep in mind that this command does not change the hardware configuration in any way; it simply informs the Linux serial driver of the configuration. To change the actual settings of the hardware, consult your system's BIOS.

setserial changes only the current configuration, and the settings do not persist across reboots. Unfortunately, there isn't a standard way to make the changes permanent; each of our example distributions does it differently.

The **/etc/init.d/setserial** script on Ubuntu systems is used for serial port initialization. It reads parameters for each port from **/var/lib/setserial/autoserial.conf**.

SUSE's **/etc/init.d/serial** script handles serial port initialization. Unfortunately, this script has no configuration file; you must edit it directly to reflect the commands you want to run. Bad SUSE! The script uses its own little metalanguage to construct the **setserial** command lines, but fortunately there are plenty of commented-out example lines to choose from.

Red Hat's **/etc/rc.d/rc.sysinit** script checks for the existence of **/etc/rc.serial** and executes it at startup time if it exists. No example file is provided, so you must create the file yourself if you want to make use of this feature. Just list the **setserial** commands you want to run, one per line. For completeness, it's probably a good idea to make the file executable and to put **#!/bin/sh** on the first line; however, these *touches d'élégance* aren't strictly required.

31.7 Pseudo-terminals

Hardwired CRT terminals may be nothing more than museum fodder these days, but their spirit lives on in the form of pseudo-terminals. These pairs of device files emulate a text terminal interface on behalf of services such as virtual consoles, virtual terminals (e.g., **xterm**), and network login services like **telnet** and **ssh**.

Here's how it works. Each of the of the paired device files accesses the same device driver inside the kernel. The slave device is named something like **/dev/ttyp1**. A process that would normally interact with a physical terminal, such as a shell, uses the slave device in place of a physical device such as **/dev/ttyS0**. A host process such as **sshd** or **telnetd** opens the corresponding master device—in this example, **/dev/ptyp1**. The pseudo-terminal device driver shuttles keystrokes and text output between the two devices, hiding the fact that no physical terminal exists.

Although pseudo-terminals don't need a baud rate or flow control strategy, most of the other terminal attributes and settings covered in this chapter apply to them.

The **expect** scripting language uses a pseudo-terminal to control a process (such as **ftp** or **parted**) that expects to interact with a human user. It is quite useful for automating certain types of sysadmin tasks.

31.8 Configuration of terminals

Cheap computers have replaced ASCII terminals. However, even the "terminal" windows on a graphical display (such as **xterm**) use the same drivers and configuration files as real terminals, so system administrators still benefit by understanding how this archaic technology works.

Terminal configuration involves two main tasks: making sure that a process is attached to a terminal to accept logins, and making sure that information about the terminal is available once a user has logged in. Before we dive into the details of these tasks, however, let's look at the entire login process.

The login process

See page 88 for more information about the ***init*** *daemon.*

The login process involves several different programs, the most important of which is the **init** daemon. One of **init**'s jobs is to spawn a process, known generically as a **getty** (but not on Solaris, which calls it a **ttymon**), on each terminal port that is turned on in the **/etc/ttys** or **/etc/inittab** file. The **getty** sets the port's initial characteristics (such as speed and parity) and prints a login prompt.

The actual name of the **getty** program varies among Linux distributions, and some distributions include multiple implementations. Red Hat and SUSE use a simplified version called **mingetty** to handle logins on virtual consoles. To manage terminals and dial-in modems, they provide Gert Doering's **mgetty** implementation. Ubuntu uses a single **getty** written by Wietse Venema et al.; this version is also available on SUSE systems under the name **agetty**. An older implementation called **uugetty** has largely been superseded by **mgetty**. Finally, HylaFAX (hylafax.org), a popular open source fax server, has its own version of **getty** called **faxgetty**.

To distinguish among this plenitude of **getty**s, think of them in order of complexity. **mingetty** is the simplest and is essentially just a placeholder for a **getty**. It can only handle logins on Linux virtual consoles. **agetty** is a bit more well-rounded and handles both serial ports and modems. **mgetty** is the current king of the hill. It handles incoming faxes as well as logins and does proper locking and coordination so that the same modem can be used as both a dial-in and a dial-out line.

The sequence of events in a complete login is as follows:

- **getty** prints a login prompt (along with the contents of the **/etc/issue** file on Linux systems).
- A user enters a login name at **getty**'s prompt.
- **getty** runs the **login** program with the specified name as an argument.
- **login** requests a password and validates the account against **/etc/shadow** or an administrative database system such as NIS or LDAP.

- **login** prints the message of the day from **/etc/motd** and runs a shell.
- The shell executes the appropriate startup files.[2]
- The shell prints a prompt and waits for input.

When the user logs out, control returns to **init**, which wakes up and spawns a new **getty** on the terminal port.

Files in **/etc** control the characteristics associated with each terminal port. These characteristics include the presence of a login prompt and **getty** process on the port, the baud rate to expect, and the type of terminal that is assumed to be connected to the port.

Unfortunately, terminal configuration is one area where there is little agreement among vendors. Table 31.4 lists the files used by each system.

Table 31.4 Terminal configuration files

System	On/off	Terminal type	Parameters	Monitor
Ubuntu[a]	**/etc/event.d/***tty*[b]	**/etc/ttytype**	**/etc/gettydefs**	**getty**
SUSE	**/etc/inittab**	**/etc/ttytype**	**/etc/gettydefs**	**getty**
Red Hat	**/etc/inittab**	**/etc/ttytype**	**/etc/gettydefs**	**getty**
Solaris[c]	**_sactab**	**_sactab**	**zsmon/_pmtab**	**ttymon**
HP-UX	**/etc/inittab**	**/etc/ttytype**	**/etc/gettydefs**	**getty**
AIX[d]	**/etc/inittab**	**/etc/security/login.cfg**	ODM database	**getty**

a. Ubuntu has moved from **init** to **upstart** for TTY/**getty** management; see page 1175.
b. Virtual consoles are defined in **/etc/default/console-setup**.
c. Solaris configuration files are in **/etc/saf** and should be managed with **sacadm**.
d. To ensure consistency, use SMIT to modify TTY parameters on AIX.

The /etc/ttytype file

On many systems, terminal type information is kept in a file called **/etc/ttytype**. The format of an entry in **ttytype** is

```
termtype device
```

where *device* is the short name of the device file representing the port and the *termtype* names an entry in the **termcap** or **terminfo** database. When you log in, the TERM environment variable is set to the value of this field.

Here is a sample **ttytype** file:

```
wyse     console
dialup   ttyi0
dialup   ttyi1
vt320    ttyi2
h19      ttyi3
dialout  ttyi4
```

2. **.profile** for **sh** and **ksh**; **.bash_profile** and **.bashrc** for **bash**; **.cshrc** and **.login** for **csh/tcsh**.

The /etc/gettytab file

The **gettytab** file associates symbolic names such as std.9600 with port configuration profiles that include parameters such as speed, parity, and login prompt. Here is a sample:

```
# The default entry, used to set defaults for other entries, and in cases
# where getty is called with no specific entry name.

default:\
    :ap:lm=\r\n%h login\72 :sp#9600:

# Fixed-speed entries

2|std.9600|9600-baud:\
    :sp#9600:
h|std.38400|38400-baud:\
    :sp#38400:
```

The format is the same as that of **printcap** or **termcap**. The lines with names separated by a vertical bar (|) list the names by which each configuration is known. The other fields in an entry set the options to be used with the serial port.

The /etc/gettydefs file

Like **gettytab**, **gettydefs** defines port configurations used by **getty**. A given system will usually have one or the other, never both. The **gettydefs** file looks like this:

```
console# B9600 HUPCL # B9600 SANE IXANY #login: #console
19200# B19200 HUPCL # B19200 SANE IXANY #login: #9600
9600# B9600 HUPCL # B9600 SANE IXANY HUPCL #login: #4800
4800# B4800 HUPCL # B4800 SANE IXANY HUPCL #login: #2400
2400# B2400 HUPCL # B2400 SANE IXANY HUPCL #login: #1200
1200# B1200 HUPCL # B1200 SANE IXANY HUPCL #login: #300
300# B300 HUPCL # B300 SANE IXANY TAB3 HUPCL #login: #9600
```

The format of an entry is

label# initflags # finalflags # prompt #next

getty tries to match its second argument with a *label* entry. If it is called without a second argument, the first entry in the file is used. The *initflags* field lists **ioctl**(2) flags that should be set on a port until **login** is executed. The *finalflags* field sets flags that should be used thereafter.

There must be an entry that sets the speed of the connection in both the *initflags* and the *finalflags*. The flags that are available vary by system; check the **gettydefs** or **mgettydefs** man page for authoritative information.

The *prompt* field defines the login prompt, which may include tabs and newlines in backslash notation. The *next* field gives the label of an **inittab** entry that should be substituted for the current one if a break is received. This was useful decades ago when modems didn't negotiate a speed automatically and you had to match speeds by hand with a series of breaks. Today, it's an anachronism. For a hardwired terminal, *next* should refer to the label of the current entry.

Each time you change the **gettydefs** file, you should run **getty -c gettydefs**, which checks the syntax of the file to make sure that all entries are valid.

The /etc/inittab file

See page 88 for more information about the role of ***init****.*

init supports various "run levels" that determine which system resources are enabled. There are seven run levels, numbered 0 to 6, with "s" recognized as a synonym for level 1 (single-user operation). When you leave single-user mode, **init** prompts you to enter a run level unless an initdefault field exists in **/etc/inittab** as described below. **init** then scans the **inittab** file for all lines that match the specified run level.

Run levels are usually set up so that you have one level in which only the console is enabled and another level in which all **getty**s are enabled. You can define the run levels in whatever way is appropriate for your system; however, we recommend that you not stray too far from the defaults.

Entries in **inittab** are of the form

id:run-levels:action:process

Here are some simple examples of **inittab** entries:

```
# Trap CTRL-ALT-DELETE
ca::ctrlaltdel:/sbin/shutdown -t3 -r now

# Run gettys in standard runlevels
1:2345:respawn:/sbin/mingetty tty1
2:2345:respawn:/sbin/mingetty tty2
```

In this format, *id* is a one- or two-character string that identifies the entry; it can be null. For terminal entries, it is customary to use the terminal number as the *id*.

run-levels enumerates the run levels to which the entry pertains. If no levels are specified (as in the first line), then the entry is valid for all run levels. *action* tells how to handle the *process* field; Table 31.5 lists some of the commonly used values.

If one of the *run-levels* matches the current run level and the *action* field indicates that the entry is relevant, **init** uses **sh** to execute (or terminate) the command specified in the *process* field. The Wait? column in Table 31.5 tells whether **init** waits for the command to complete before continuing.

In the example **inittab** lines above, the last two lines spawn **mingetty** processes on the first two virtual consoles (accessed with <Alt-F1> and <Alt-F2>). If you add hardwired terminals or dial-in modems, the appropriate **inittab** lines look similar to these. However, you must use **mgetty** or **getty** (**agetty** on SUSE) with such devices because **mingetty** is not sophisticated enough to handle them correctly. In general, respawn is the correct action and 2345 is an appropriate set of levels.

Table 31.5 Common values for the /etc/inittab *action* field

Value	Wait?	Meaning
initdefault	–	Sets the initial run level
boot	No	Runs when **inittab** is read for the first time
bootwait	Yes	Runs when **inittab** is read for the first time
ctrlaltdel	No	Runs in response to a keyboard <Control-Alt-Delete>[a]
once	No	Starts the process once
wait	Yes	Starts the process once
respawn	No	Always keeps the process running
powerfail	No	Runs when **init** receives a power-fail signal
powerwait	Yes	Runs when **init** receives a power-fail signal
sysinit	Yes	Runs before accessing the console
off	–	Terminates the process if it is running, on some systems

a. Linux systems only.

The command **telinit -q** makes **init** reread the **inittab** file.

getty configuration for Linux

Different **getty**s require different configuration procedures. The **getty/agetty** version found on SUSE and Ubuntu is generally a bit cleaner than the **mgetty** version because it accepts all of its configuration information on the command line (in **/etc/inittab**).

The general model is

/sbin/getty *port speed termtype*

where *port* is the device file of the serial port relative to **/dev**, *speed* is the baud rate (e.g., 38400), and *termtype* identifies the default terminal type for the port. The *termtype* refers to an entry in the **terminfo** database. Most emulators simulate a DEC VT100, denoted **vt100**. Most of the many other minor options relate to the handling of dial-in modems.

mgetty is a bit more sophisticated than **agetty** in its handling of modems and integrates both incoming and outgoing fax capability. Unfortunately, its configuration is a bit more diffuse. In addition to other command-line flags, **mgetty** can accept an optional reference to an entry in **/etc/gettydefs** that specifies configuration details for the serial driver. Unless you're setting up a sophisticated modem configuration, you can usually get away without a **gettydefs** entry.

Use **man mgettydefs** to find the man page for the **gettydefs** file. It's named this way to avoid conflict with an older **gettydefs** man page that no longer exists on any Linux system.

A simple **mgetty** command line for a hardwired terminal looks like this:

/sbin/mgetty -rs *speed device*

speed is the baud rate (e.g., 38400), and *device* is the device file for the serial port (use the full pathname).

If you want to specify a default terminal type for a port when using **mgetty**, you must specify it in a separate file, **/etc/ttytype**, and not on the **mgetty** command line. The format of an entry in **ttytype** is described on page 1172.

Ubuntu Upstart

Ubuntu has replaced its **init** with a rearchitected version called Upstart that starts and stops services in response to events. The executable file for Upstart is still known as **/sbin/init**, however.

Upstart uses one file for each active terminal in **/etc/event.d**. For example, if we wanted a **getty** to run on ttyS0, **/etc/event.d/ttyS0** might look like this:

```
# ttyS0 - getty

# This service maintains a getty on ttyS0 from the point when
# the system is started until it is shut down again.

start on runlevel 2
start on runlevel 3
start on runlevel 4
start on runlevel 5

stop on runlevel 0
stop on runlevel 1
stop on runlevel 6 respawn
exec /sbin/getty 38400 ttyS0
```

See page 94 for some additional comments on Upstart.

Solaris and sacadm

Rather than traditional UNIX **getty**s that watch each port for activity and provide a login prompt, Solaris has a convoluted hierarchy called the Service Access Facility that controls TTY monitors, port monitors, and many other things that provide a lot of complexity but little added functionality.

To set up a serial port to provide a login prompt, you must first configure a "monitor" that watches the status of the port (**ttymon**). You then configure a port monitor that watches the TTY monitor. For example, to set up a 9,600 baud monitor on **ttyb** to print a login prompt with terminal type VT100, you would use the following commands.

```
solaris$ sudo sacadm -a -p myttymon -t ttymon -c /usr/lib/saf/ttymon -v 1
solaris$ sudo pmadm -a -p myttymon -s b -i root -fu -v 1 -m "`ttyadm -d
    /dev/term/b -l 9600 -T vt100 -s /usr/bin/login`"
```

The **/etc/ttydefs** file is used much like **gettydefs** on other systems to set speed and parity parameters.

See the manual pages for **saf**, **sacadm**, **pmadm**, **ttyadm**, and **ttymon** as well as the terminals chapter in the Solaris AnswerBook for more information about setting up these monitors. Have fun.

31.9 Special characters and the terminal driver

The terminal driver supports several special functions that you access by typing particular keys (usually control keys) on the keyboard. The exact binding of functions to keys can be set with the **tset** and **stty** commands. Table 31.6 lists some of these functions, along with their default key bindings.

Table 31.6 Special characters for the terminal driver

Name	Default	Function
erase	<Control-?>	Erases one character of input
werase	<Control-W>	Erases one word of input
kill	<Control-U>	Erases the entire line of input
eof	<Control-D>	Sends an "end of file" indication
intr	<Control-C>	Interrupts the currently running process
quit	<Control-\>	Kills the current process with a core dump
stop	<Control-S>	Stops output to the screen
start	<Control-Q>	Restarts output to the screen
susp	<Control-Z>	Suspends the current process
lnext	<Control-V>	Interprets the next character literally

Depending on what a vendor's keyboards look like, the default for ERASE might be either <Control-H> or the delete character. (The actual keyboard key may be labeled "backspace" or "delete," or it may show only a backarrow graphic.) Unfortunately, the existence of two different standards for this function creates a multitude of problems.

You can use **stty erase** (see the next section) to tell the terminal driver which key code your setup is actually generating. However, some programs (such as text editors and shells with command-editing features) have their own idea of what the backspace character should be, and they don't always pay attention to the terminal driver's setting. In a helpful but confusing twist, some programs obey both the backspace and delete characters. You may also find that systems you log in to through the network make different assumptions from those of your local system.

Solving these annoying little conflicts can be a Sunday project in itself. In general, there is no simple, universal solution. Each piece of software must be individually beaten into submission. Two useful resources to help with this task are the *Linux Backspace/Delete mini-HOWTO* from tldp.org and a nifty article by Anne Baretta at ibb.net/~anne/keyboard.html. These notes are both written from a Linux perspective, but the problem (and solutions) are not limited to Linux.

31.10 STTY: SET TERMINAL OPTIONS

stty lets you directly change and query the various settings of the terminal driver. There are about a zillion options, but most can be safely ignored. **stty** generally uses the same names for driver options as the **termios** man page does, but occasional discrepancies pop up.

A good combination of options to use for a plain-vanilla terminal is

```
solaris$ stty intr ^C kill ^U erase ^H -tabs
```

Here, **-tabs** prevents the terminal driver from taking advantage of the terminal's built-in tabulation mechanism, a useful practice because many emulators are not very smart about tabs. The other options set the interrupt, kill, and erase characters to <Control-C>, <Control-U>, and <Control-H> (backspace), respectively.

You can use **stty** to examine the current modes of the terminal driver as well as to set them. **stty** with no arguments produces output like this:

```
solaris$ stty
speed 38400 baud;
erase = ^H; eol = M-^?; eol2 = M-^?; swtch = <undef>;
ixany
tab3
```

For a more verbose status report, use the **-a** option:

```
solaris$ stty -a
speed 38400 baud; rows 24; columns 80;
intr = ^C; quit = ^\; erase = ^H; kill = ^U; eof = ^D; eol = M-^?; eol2 = M-^?;
swtch = <undef>; start = ^Q; stop = ^S; susp = ^Z; dsusp = ^Y; rprnt = ^R;
werase = ^W; lnext = ^V; flush = ^O;
-parenb -parodd cs8 hupcl -cstopb cread -clocal -crtscts
-ignbrk brkint -ignpar -parmrk -inpck -istrip -inlcr -igncr icrnl ixon -ixoff
-iuclc ixany imaxbel
opost -olcuc -ocrnl onlcr -onocr -onlret -ofill -ofdel nl0 cr0 tab3 bs0 vt0 ff0
isig icanon iexten echo echoe echok -echonl -noflsh -xcase -tostop -echoprt
echoctl echoke
```

The format of the output is similar but lists more information. The meaning of the output should be intuitively obvious if you've written a terminal driver recently.

stty operates on the file descriptor of its standard input, so you can set and query the modes of a terminal other than the current one by using the shell's input redirection character (<). You must be the superuser to change the modes on someone else's terminal.

31.11 TSET: SET OPTIONS AUTOMATICALLY

tset initializes the terminal driver to a mode appropriate for a given terminal type. The type can be specified on the command line; if the type is omitted, **tset** uses the value of the TERM environment variable.

tset supports a syntax for mapping certain values of the TERM environment variable into other values. This feature is useful if you often log in through a modem or data switch and would like to have the terminal driver configured correctly for the terminal you are really using on the other end of the connection rather than something generic and unhelpful such as "dialup."

For example, suppose that you use **xterm** at home and that the system you are dialing in to is configured to think that the terminal type of a modem is "dialup." Putting the command

```
tset -m dialup:xterm
```

in your **.login** or **.profile** file sets the terminal driver appropriately for **xterm** whenever you dial in.

Unfortunately, the **tset** command is not really as simple as it pretends to be. To have **tset** adjust your environment variables in addition to setting your terminal modes, you need lines something like this:

```
set noglob
eval `tset -s -Q -m dialup:xterm`
unset noglob
```

This incantation suppresses the messages that **tset** normally prints (the **-Q** flag), and asks that shell commands to set the environment be output instead (the **-s** flag). The shell commands printed by **tset** are captured by the backquotes and fed to the shell as input with the built-in command **eval**, causing the commands to have the same effect as if they had been typed by the user.

set noglob prevents the shell from expanding any metacharacters such as * and ? that are included in **tset**'s output. This command is not needed by **sh/ksh** users (nor is the **unset noglob** to undo it), since these shells do not normally expand special characters within backquotes. The **tset** command itself is the same no matter what shell you use; **tset** looks at the environment variable SHELL to determine what flavor of commands to print.

31.12 Terminal unwedging

Some programs (e.g., **vi**) make drastic changes to the state of the terminal driver while they are running. This meddling is normally invisible to the user, since the terminal state is restored when the program exits or is suspended. However, a program can crash or be killed without performing this housekeeping step. When this happens, the terminal may behave very strangely: it might fail to handle newlines correctly, to echo typed characters, or to execute commands properly.

Another common way to confuse a terminal is to accidentally run **cat** or **more** on a binary file. Most binaries contain a mix of 8-bit characters that is guaranteed to send some of the less-robust emulators into outer space.

To fix this situation, use **reset** or **stty sane**. **reset** is actually just a link to **tset** on many systems, and it can accept most of **tset**'s arguments. However, it is usually run without arguments. Both **reset** and **stty sane** restore the default state of the terminal driver and send out an appropriate reset code from **termcap/terminfo** if one is available.

In many cases for which a **reset** is appropriate, the terminal has been left in a mode in which no processing is done on the characters you type. Most terminals generate carriage returns rather than newlines when the Return or Enter key is pressed. Without input processing, this key generates <Control-M> characters instead of sending off the current command to be executed. To enter newlines directly, use <Control-J> or the line feed key (if there is one) instead of Return.

31.13 Debugging a serial line

Debugging serial lines is not difficult. Here are some typical errors:

- Forgetting to tell **init** to reread its configuration files
- Forgetting to set soft carrier when using three-wire cables
- Using a cable with the wrong nullness
- Soldering or crimping connectors upside down
- Connecting to the wrong wire because of bad or nonexistent wire maps
- Setting the terminal options (including speed) incorrectly

A breakout box is an indispensable tool for debugging serial cabling problems. It is patched into the serial line and shows the signals on each pin as they pass through the cable. The better breakout boxes have both male and female connectors on each side and so are flexible in their positioning. LEDs associated with each "interesting" pin show when the pin is active.

Some breakout boxes are read-only and just let you monitor the signals; others let you rewire the connection and assert a voltage on a particular pin. For example, if you suspect that a cable needs to be nulled (crossed), you can use the breakout box to override the actual cable wiring.

31.14 Connecting to serial device consoles

Perhaps the most common and useful application of RS-232 today is to connect to the serial "console" of another device. The device could be anything from a manageable UPS or network switch to an embedded Linux system such as the TiVo box under your TV. For example, you might connect a serial line to the UPS that powers your equipment rack in a remote data center so that you can shut off power remotely in an emergency.

The basic steps for connecting to a serial console are as follows:

- Attach a cable between the serial port on your UNIX system and the device you want to talk to. See the discussion earlier in this chapter about the various connector types and pinouts that might be necessary. You'll most likely need a null modem cable. These are available at your nearest computer store.
- Install or identify the terminal communication software you will use on your UNIX or Linux system. Decades ago, the standard command for this was **cu** or **tip**. You can still use these in a pinch, but modern-day alternatives such as **minicom** and **picocom** are better. Linux distributions normally include one of these; on other systems, you may need to install the software yourself (see freshmeat.net/projects/minicom or freshmeat.net/projects/picocom, respectively).
- Configure your communication software to open the correct device file (see the discussion earlier in this chapter). Usually, names like **/dev/ttya**, **/dev/tty1**, **/dev/ttyS0**, or **/dev/S0** are good first guesses.
- Set the baud rate, stop bits, and flow control to match the defaults used on the target device. These parameters are usually outlined in the manual for the device, but you can also try all possible combinations. If you don't know the correct baud rate, an "old dog" trick is to connect and type a few characters. If you have to type multiple characters to get a single character of garbage, you've set the baud rate too high. If typing one or two characters produces many characters of garbage, you've set the baud rate too low. Shhhh… don't tell anyone!
- Once you've successfully connected, you should be able to enter commands on the remote console. If you find that the device suddenly hangs on long output, you have probably misconfigured the flow control; typing <Control-Q> will sometimes get you by.

If you have trouble connecting, the first debugging step should be to remove the crossover in the cable, or to add one if you didn't start with one. Don't forget that if you're connecting to a remote UNIX box, you'll need to set up a **getty** on the far end to listen for your connection and present a login prompt.

Exercises begin on the next page.

31.15 Exercises

E31.1 What is a null modem cable? How is it used to connect DCE and DTE serial devices?

E31.2 Can you use a three-wire serial cable for a serial modem connection? For a serial printer? Why or why not?

E31.3 How does traditional serial hardware flow control work? What can be done if a system does not understand hardware flow control?

E31.4 What is a pseudo-terminal? What programs use pseudo-terminals?

E31.5 Devise **inittab** entries that

a) Run a program called **server-fallback**, wait for it to finish, and then immediately halt the system if the power fails.

b) Respawn a server called **unstable-srv** if it crashes.

c) Run a script called **clean-temp** that removes all temporary files each time the system is rebooted.

★ E31.6 A friend of yours carelessly left himself logged in overnight in the computing lab and is now experiencing strange problems when he runs shell applications. Programs quit or suspend, and previous input disappears when certain commands and input are given; however, some things seem to work normally. What could an unfriendly user have done to cause such behavior? Explain how you could test your answer. How could the problem be fixed? Who would do such a mean thing?

32 Management, Policy, and Politics

You may run the smartest team of administrators ever, but if your technical management is inadequate, you will be miserable and so will your users. In this chapter we discuss the nontechnical aspects of running a successful information technology (IT) support organization, along with a few technical tidbits that help shore up the managerial end of system administration.

Most of the topics and ideas presented in this chapter are not specific to a particular environment. They apply equally to a part-time system administrator and to a large group of full-time professionals in charge of a major IT installation. Like green vegetables, they're good for you no matter what size meal you're preparing.

Good sysadmins have both technical skills and "soft skills." The ability to organize a group of administrators and make sure they meet the organization's needs can be the difference between an OK administrator and a great one.

In addition to management hints, this chapter also includes sections on topics such as IT policy, best practices, and standards compliance.

32.1 The purpose of IT

An IT organization is more than a group of technical folks who fix printers and computers when there are problems. From a strategic perspective, IT is a collection of people and roles that serve the needs of the organization by supporting users and systems. Never forget the golden rule of system administration: enterprise needs drive IT activities, not the other way around.

The IT group needs to cooperate with other groups within the organization to make sure it is providing the best possible value. A few of the areas that require such cross-functional negotiation are spending, policy, management, and service level agreements (SLAs).

In many organizations—especially in small companies and in small divisions within large companies—the system administrator wears many hats, possibly including that of a group leader or manager. Understanding some of the key areas in which IT interfaces with the rest of the organization will help make that relationship smoother and more effective.

At a bare minimum, an IT organization must

- Maintain a list of open tasks
- Prioritize its task list and allocate resources
- Communicate task status to users and the enterprise
- Work with the enterprise to ensure its needs are met
- Monitor the computing environment, including security monitoring
- Track emerging technologies
- Develop skills in its staff
- Assist with regulatory compliance
- Document and follow repeatable processes
- Measure progress toward negotiated goals and report status
- Plan for and be ready for disasters
- Be flexible enough to keep users happy while being disciplined enough to keep administrators happy

Budgeting and spending

IT spending should be aligned with the goals of the larger organization. The IT budget has a dramatic impact on the extent and quality of IT services the rest of the organization can expect to receive, so it's critically important that the IT staff help everyone understand this connection and make appropriate tradeoffs.

IT spending as a percentage of the organization's total budget varies quite a bit, but it's generally a nontrivial component. The average organization spends between 2% and 9%. The percentage varies among industries, with the mean being approximately 4% to 5%.

This total budget is further subdivided into capital and operating expenses. Capital expenses generally go toward equipment purchases. Operating costs include labor and services such as WAN connectivity. Various feats of legerdemain are available to convert one type of expense into another. For example, equipment leases turn capital expenses into operating expenses, and prepaid maintenance contracts on new equipment allow service expenses to be capitalized. You probably don't care about the distinction between these expense types, but your accountants do, so it's your issue as well.

System administrators need to understand the budget because their ability to plan for the year ahead depends on it. For example, if an administrator would like to implement both a centralized logging system and a security monitoring solution, the budget is a relevant constraint. If the budget allocates only enough money for one server, the administrator will either have to prioritize the projects or come up with a solution that lets both systems run on the same server. (Virtualization is a great option in this example, but there are other situations in which sharing is not so easy or cost effective.) If the administrator can contribute to the budget planning process, he or she might lobby for more money if the expenses can be reasonably predicted to increase the business's satisfaction with its IT infrastructure.

IT policy

IT policies affect everyone in the organization, so they are important components of the organization's overall strategy. System administrators are major contributors to the development and maintenance of good policies. Administrators are sometimes directly responsible for developing policy; in other cases, administrators may be asked to review policies developed by other members of the organization. Either way, the system administrators provide valuable input. Many organizations have one set of policies that end users are expected to follow and another set of policies for administrators. Administrators should be familiar with both sets of policies and should develop organizational procedures that support them.

Documentation, policy's kissing cousin, can sometimes be ignored or deprioritized relative to "real work." Most sysadmins don't like writing documentation, but it's important to the smooth functioning of the IT system. Set up a wiki or use other tools that make it easy for administrators to jot down short notes and make it easy for others to locate relevant information for later review or use.

A couple of good choices for this role are MediaWiki and Confluence. MediaWiki, the software behind Wikipedia, is a free package written in PHP (mediawiki.org). Confluence is an enterprise solution that is not free and is designed for medium- and large-sized organizations. You can install it on your own server or purchase a hosted solution if you'd rather not manage it locally (atlassian.com). The "list of wiki software" Wikipedia page catalogs many other options, and wikimatrix.org is helpful for making detailed comparisons.

Specific policies, and the way that these policies play a role in compliance, are discussed later in this chapter (see page 1215).

Service level agreements

System administration is a service, and both people and computers are the recipients of that service. For the IT organization to successfully provide this service, keep users happy, and meet the needs of the enterprise, the exact details of the service being provided must be negotiated, agreed upon, and documented in "service level agreements" or SLAs. A good SLA sets appropriate expectations and serves as a reference when questions arise. (But remember, IT provides solutions, not roadblocks!)

Users are happy when

- Their computers are up and running and they can log in
- Their other resources such as printers and file servers are available
- Their data files stay as they left them
- Their application software is installed and works as it's supposed to
- Friendly, knowledgeable help is available when needed

Users want these things 24 hours a day, 7 days a week. Preferably for free. Users are miserable when

- They experience downtime, whether scheduled or unscheduled
- Upgrades introduce sudden, incompatible changes
- They receive incomprehensible messages from the system or sysadmins
- They receive long explanations of why things aren't working

When something is broken, users want to know when it's going to be fixed. That's it. They don't really care which hard disk or generator broke, or why; leave that information for your managerial reports.

From a user's perspective, no news is good news. The system either works or it doesn't, and if the latter, it doesn't matter why. Our customers are happiest when they don't even notice that we exist! Sad, but true.

It's equally important to keep your staff happy. Good administrators are hard to find, and their needs must be considered when your site's administrative systems are designed. System administrators and other technical staff are happy when

- Their computers and support systems are up and running
- They have the resources needed to do their jobs (dual monitors!)
- They have the latest and greatest software and hardware tools
- Their work is challenging, or at least interesting (minimal drudgery)
- They can work without being constantly interrupted
- They can be creative without the boss meddling and micromanaging
- Their work hours and stress levels are within reason

Technical people need more than just a paycheck at the end of the month to keep them going. They need to feel that they have a degree of creative control over their work and that they are appreciated by their peers, their boss, and their users.

The requirements for happy customers and happy IT staff have some factors in common. However, a few things seem to be orthogonal or even in direct conflict. The boss must make sure that all these differing expectations can be made compatible and attainable.

An SLA helps align end users and support staff. A well-written SLA addresses each of the issues discussed in the following sections.

Scope and descriptions of services

This section is the foundation of the SLA because it describes what the organization can expect from IT. It should be written in terms that can be understood by nontechnical staff. Some example services might be

- Email
- Internet and web access
- File servers
- Business applications
- Printing

The standards that IT will adhere to when providing these services must also be defined. For example, an availability section would define the hours of operation, the agreed-upon maintenance windows, and the expectations regarding the times at which IT staff will be available to provide live support. One organization might decide that regular support should be available from 8:00 a.m. to 6:00 p.m. on weekdays but that emergency support must be available 24/7. Another organization might decide that it needs standard live support available at all times.

Here is a list of issues to consider when documenting your standards:

- Response time
- Service (and response times) during weekends and off-hours
- House calls (support for machines at home)
- Weird (unique or proprietary) hardware
- Upgrade policy (ancient hardware, software, etc.)
- Supported operating systems
- Standard configurations
- Expiration of backup tapes
- Special-purpose software
- Janitorial chores (cleaning screens and keyboards, vacuuming grilles)

When considering service standards, keep in mind that many users will want to customize their environments (or even their systems) if the software is not nailed down to prevent this. The stereotypical IT response is to forbid all user modifications, but although this policy makes things easier for IT, it isn't necessarily the best policy for the organization.

Address this issue in your SLAs, and try to standardize on a few specific configurations. Otherwise, your goals of easy maintenance and scaling to grow with the organization will meet some serious impediments. Encourage your creative, OS-hacking employees to suggest modifications that they need for their work, and be diligent and generous in incorporating these suggestions into your standard configurations. If you don't, your users will work hard to subvert your rules.

Queue management policies

In addition to knowing what services are provided, users must also know about the priority scheme used to manage the work queue. Priority schemes always have wiggle room, but try to design one that covers most situations with few or no exceptions. Some priority-related variables are listed below:

- The importance of the service to the overall organization
- The security impact of the situation (has there been a breach?)
- The service level the customer has paid or contracted for
- The number of users affected
- The importance of any relevant deadline
- The loudness of the affected users (squeaky wheels)
- The importance of the affected users (this is a tricky one, but let's be honest: some people in your organization have more pull than others)

Although all these factors will influence your rankings, we recommend a simple set of rules together with some common sense to deal with the exceptions. Basically, we use the following priorities:

- Many people cannot work
- One person cannot work
- Requests for improvements

If two or more requests have top priority and the requests cannot be worked on in parallel, we base our decision regarding which problem to tackle first on the severity of the issues (e.g., email not working makes almost everybody unhappy, whereas the temporary unavailability of a web service might hinder only a few people). Queues at lower priorities are usually handled in a FIFO manner.

Users generally assume that all their important data is stored on backup tapes that will be archived forever. But backup media don't last indefinitely; magnetic media in particular have a finite lifetime after which reading data becomes difficult. (You must periodically rewrite your data, possibly to newer media, if you want to keep it for a long time.) Backup tapes can also be subpoenaed, so your organization may not *want* old data to be available forever. It's best to work with the people in charge of such decisions to draw up a written agreement that specifies how long backups must be kept, whether multiple copies are to be made (required? permissible? never?), and where those copies must be stored.

These decisions should be made in the context of an organization-wide data retention policy. This type of policy is covered later in this chapter, but in general, you need to classify your data and develop a retention schedule for each class.

Make your backup and retention policies available to users. This measure promotes realistic expectations regarding both backups and recoveries. It also puts users on notice that they must take precautions of their own if they feel they need better data protection than is provided for in their SLA.

In particular, users should understand whether or not the files on their local workstations will be backed up. Many organizations back up their centralized file servers but do not back up individual workstations. Usually, the workstations are cloned from system images and are considered disposable. Users need to know this so they can store critical information appropriately.

Roles and responsibilities

You must document who is responsible for what. Organizations that do not divide duties become inefficient and ineffective. Problems fall through the cracks because it's not clear who owns which problem domains. Problems can also fall prey to groupthink, where it takes two or three administrators to take care of a single task. Some examples of defined roles are the following:

- Backup administrator
- Storage area network (SAN) and file service maven
- Application wrangler
- Patching and security czar
- Guy who nobody is quite sure what he does[1]

Or, you might map out roles and responsibilities according to the descriptions of services you have already defined. This approach may imply that you have to delineate responsibilities from an administration perspective rather than from the user's point of view.

Don't forget to include "understudy" responsibilities in your taxonomy. Staff members won't be in the office every day, and you need to know who to go to when a domain's primary administrator is away.

Conformance measurements

An SLA needs to define how the organization will measure your success at fulfilling the terms of the agreement. Targets and goals allow the staff to work toward a common outcome and can lay the groundwork for cooperation throughout the organization. Of course, you must make sure you have tools in place to measure the agreed-upon metrics.

At a minimum, you should track the following metrics for your IT infrastructure:

- Percentage or number of projects completed on time and on budget
- Percentage or number of SLA elements fulfilled
- Uptime percentage by system (e.g., email 99.92% available through Q1)
- Percentage or number of tickets that were satisfactorily resolved

1. OK, maybe you don't need this role in *your* IT group. But it is an industry standard.

- Average time to ticket resolution
- Percentage or number of security incidents handled according to the documented incident handling process

32.2 The structure of an IT organization

Now that we have addressed the overall function of an IT organization, we can peek inside its structure. As a support organization grows, it becomes clear that not everybody in the group can or should know everything about the infrastructure. Instead, you must find a balance between efficiency and separation of duties.

Role separation adds a layer of checks and balances to the IT organization. Over time, this feature is becoming more and more important as standards and regulations creep into even the smallest of organizations.

Take, for example, a 20-person U.S. company that has developed a hosted application for medical facilities. If this application stores any protected health information (PHI), then the organization's systems must all comply with the dreaded Health Insurance Portability and Accountability Act (HIPAA). Among other things, this legislation requires you to define roles to protect access to sensitive data. For example, the tasks of determining what access a user should have and of actually provisioning that access must be executed by two different people.

A typical structure for an IT organization centers on a ticketing system and includes a help desk, an enterprise architecture group, an operations group, and a management layer. As shown in Exhibit A, every part of the IT organization interacts with the ticketing system.

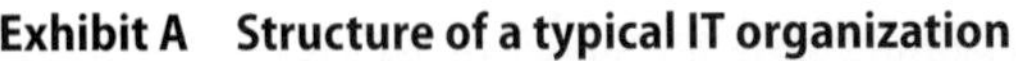

Exhibit A Structure of a typical IT organization

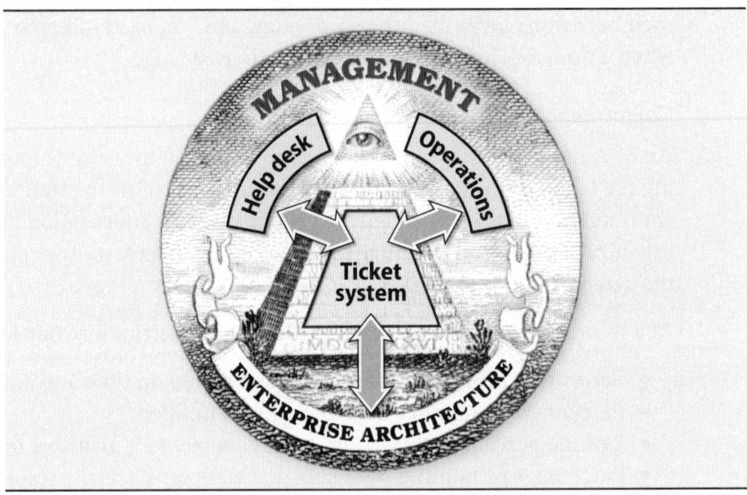

The foundation: the ticketing and task management system

A ticketing and task management system lies at the heart of every functioning IT group. Having a good system in place will help your staff avoid two of the most common workflow pitfalls:

- Tasks falling through the cracks because everyone thinks they are being taken care of by someone else
- Resources wasted through duplication of effort when multiple people or groups work on the same problem without coordination

Common functions of ticketing systems

A trouble ticket system accepts requests through various interfaces (email, web forms, and command lines being the most common) and tracks them from submission to solution. Managers can assign tickets to staff groups or to individual staff members. Staff can query the system to see the queue of pending tickets and perhaps resolve some of them. Users can find out the status of a request and see who is working on it. Managers can extract high-level information such as

- The number of open tickets
- The average time to close a ticket
- The productivity of sysadmins
- The percentage of unresolved (rotting) tickets
- Workload distribution by time to solution

The request history stored in the ticket system becomes a history of the problems with your IT infrastructure and the solutions to those problems. If that history is easily searchable, it becomes an invaluable resource for the sysadmin staff.

Resolved trouble messages can be sent to novice sysadmins and trainees, inserted into a FAQ system, or just logged. New staff members can benefit from receiving copies of closed tickets because those tickets include not only technical information but also examples of the tone and communication style that are appropriate for use with customers.

Like all documents, your ticketing system's historical data can potentially be used against your organization in court. Follow the document retention guidelines set up by your legal department.

Most request-tracking systems automatically confirm new requests and assign them a tracking number that submitters can use to follow up or inquire about the request's status. The automated response message should clearly state that it is just a confirmation. It should be followed promptly by a message from a real person that explains the plan for dealing with the problem or request.

Ticket ownership

Work can be shared, but in our experience, responsibility is less amenable to distribution. Every task should have a single, well-defined owner. That person need not be a supervisor or manager, just someone willing to act as a coordinator—someone willing to say, "I take responsibility for making sure this task gets done."

An important side effect of this approach is that it is implicitly clear who implemented what or who made what changes. This transparency becomes important if you want to figure out why something was done in a certain way or why something is suddenly working differently or not working anymore.

Being "responsible" for a task should not equate to being a scapegoat if problems arise. If your organization defines responsibility as blameworthiness, you may find that the number of available project owners quickly dwindles. Your goal in assigning ownership is simply to remove ambiguity about who should be addressing each problem. Don't punish staff members for requesting help.

From a customer's point of view, a good assignment system is one that routes problems to a person who is knowledgeable and can solve the problems quickly and completely. But from a managerial perspective, assignments need to occasionally be challenging to the assignee so that the staff continue to grow and learn in the course of their jobs. Your job is to balance the need to play to employee's strengths with the need to keep employees challenged, all while keeping both customers and employees happy.

Larger tasks can be anything up to and including full-blown software engineering projects. These tasks may require the use of formal project management and software engineering tools. We don't describe these tools here; nevertheless, they're important and should not be overlooked.

Sometimes sysadmins know that a particular task needs to be done, but they don't do it because the task is unpleasant. A sysadmin who points out a neglected, unassigned, or unpopular task is likely to receive that task as an assignment. This situation creates a conflict of interest because it motivates sysadmins to remain silent regarding such situations. Don't let that happen at your site; give your sysadmins an avenue for pointing out problems. You can allow them to open up tickets without assigning an owner or associating themselves to the issue, or you can create an email alias to which issues can be sent.

User acceptance of ticketing systems

Receiving a prompt response from a real person is a critical determinant of customer satisfaction, even if the personal response contains no more information than the automated response. For most problems, it is far more important to let the submitter know that the ticket has been reviewed by a real person than it is to fix the problem immediately. Users understand that administrators receive many requests, and they're willing to wait a fair and reasonable time for your attention. But they're not willing to be ignored.

The mechanism through which users submit tickets affects their perception of the system. Make sure you understand your organization's culture and your users' preferences. Do they want a web interface? A custom application? An email alias? Maybe they're only willing to make phone calls!

It's also important that administrators take the time to make sure they understand what users are actually requesting. This point sounds obvious, but think back to the last five times you emailed a customer service or tech support alias. We'd bet there were at least a couple of cases in which the response seemed to have nothing to do with the question—not because those companies were especially incompetent, but because accurately parsing trouble tickets is harder than it looks.

Once you've read enough of a ticket to develop an impression of what the customer is asking about, the rest of the ticket starts to look like "blah blah blah." Fight this! Clients hate waiting for a ticket to find its way to a human, only to learn that the request has been misinterpreted and must be resubmitted or restated. Back to square one.

Tickets are often vague or inaccurate because the submitter does not have the technical background needed to describe the problem in the way that a sysadmin would. That doesn't stop users from making their own guesses as to what's wrong, however. Sometimes these guesses are perfectly correct. Other times you must first decode the ticket to determine what the user *thinks* the problem is, then trace back along the user's train of thought to intuit the underlying problem.

Sample ticketing systems

Tables 32.1 and 32.2 below summarize the characteristics of several well-known trouble ticketing systems. Table 32.1 shows open source systems, and Table 32.2 shows commercial systems.

Table 32.1 Open source trouble ticket systems

Name	Input[a]	Lang	Back[b]	Web site
Double Choco Latte	W	PHP	PM	dcl.sourceforge.net
Mantis	WE	PHP	M	mantisbt.org
OTRS	WE	Perl	PMOD	otrs.org
RT: Request Tracker	WE	Perl	M	bestpractical.com
Scarab	W	Java	M	scarab.tigris.org
Trouble Ticket Express	WE[c]	Perl	FM[c]	troubleticketexpress.com

a. Input types: W = web, E = email
b. Back end: M = MySQL, P = PostgreSQL, O = Oracle, D = DB2, F = flat files
c. Email and MySQL options require the purchase of an add-on module (but they're cheap).

We like Mantis a lot. It was originally developed to track bugs in the software for a video game. It runs on Linux, Solaris, Windows, Mac OS, and even OS/2. Mantis is lightweight, simple, easily modifiable, and customizable. It requires MySQL, PHP, and a web server. But its most important feature is good documentation!

Another nice system is OTRS, the Open Ticket Request System. OTRS features web interfaces for both customers and sysadmins, as well as an email interface. OTRS is highly customizable (e.g., greeting messages configurable by queue) and can even log the time spent on a ticket.

Table 32.2 shows some of the commercial alternatives for request management. Since the web sites for commercial offerings are mostly marketing hype, details such as the implementation language and back end are not listed.

Table 32.2 Commercial trouble ticket systems

Name	Scale	Web site
EMC Ionix (Infra)	Huge	infra-corp.com/solutions
HEAT	Medium	frontrange.com
Remedy (now BMC)	Huge	remedy.com
ServiceDesk	Huge	ca.com/us/service-desk.aspx
Track-It!	Medium	numarasoftware.com

Some of the commercial offerings are so complex that they need a person or two dedicated to maintaining, configuring, and keeping them running (you know who you are, Remedy and ServiceDesk). These systems are appropriate for a site with a huge IT staff but are a waste for the typical small, overworked IT staff.

Ticket dispatching

In a large group, even one with an awesome ticketing system, one problem still remains to be solved: it is inefficient for several people to divide their attention between the task they are working on right now and the request queue, especially if requests come in by email to a personal mailbox. We have experimented with two solutions to this problem.

Our first try was to assign half-day shifts of trouble queue duty to staff members in our sysadmin group. The person on duty would try to answer as many of the incoming queries as possible during a shift. The problem with this approach was that not everybody had the skills to answer all questions and fix all problems. Answers were sometimes inappropriate because the person on duty was new and was not really familiar with the customers, their environments, or the specific support contracts they were covered by. The result was that the more senior people had to keep an eye on things and so were not really able to concentrate on their own work. In the end, the quality of service was worse and nothing was really gained.

After this experience, we created a “dispatcher” role that rotates monthly among a group of senior administrators. The dispatcher is responsible for checking the ticketing system for new entries and for farming tasks out to specific staff members. If necessary, the dispatcher contacts users to extract any additional information that is necessary to prioritize requests. The dispatcher uses a home-grown staff-skills database to decide who on the support team has the appropriate skills and time to address a given ticket. The dispatcher also makes sure that requests are resolved in a timely manner.

Skill sets within IT

The ticketing system keeps track of work, but you must still make sure you have the right staff skills needed to perform that work. This requirement includes the help desk! Nothing is more annoying to an experienced user than a support contact who asks, "Have you plugged in the power cable?" while frantically searching a customer service database in the background. On the other hand, it's a waste of resources to have your most experienced administrator explain to a novice user how to find the delete key in some word processing system.

In general, a staff member with many entries in the skill list is more "valuable." However, there is nothing wrong with having staff with fewer skills, as long as you have enough work for them to do.

An accurate skill list helps you verify that you have sufficient skill-specific manpower to deal with vacations and illnesses. You can build the skill list as problems arise and are solved by members of the staff. Include the task, the staff member's name, and the demonstrated level of expertise.

Skills should be defined at an appropriate level of abstraction, neither too specific nor too general. The following list of sample skills demonstrates an appropriate level of granularity:

- Create users, remove users, set passwords, change quotas
- Create CVS or SVN accounts
- Manage backups and restores
- Integrate new drivers into Windows Remote Installation Service (RIS)
- Package a Windows application in MSI format
- Create and install software application packages on Linux
- Install new hardware
- Analyze log files
- Debug mail server issues
- Debug printing problems
- Debug general hardware problems
- Create DNS entries
- Manage software licenses
- Manage security, especially antivirus software, patches, and upgrades
- Resolve Samba-related requests
- Configure DHCP
- Configure an LDAP server
- Add or remove web sites (configure Apache)

Time management

System administration involves more context switches in a day than many jobs have in a year, and user support personnel bear the brunt of this chaos. Every administrator needs good time-management skills. Without them, you won't be able to keep up with your day-to-day responsibilities and you will become frustrated and depressed. (Or, if already frustrated and depressed, you will become more so.)

Sysadmin burnout is rampant. Most administrators last only a few years. No one wants to be constantly on call and continually yelled at. Finding ways to manage your time efficiently and keep your customers happy is a win/win situation.

32.3 The help desk

The help desk is a major component of the IT group structure shown in Exhibit A (page 1190). The task of the help desk is to deal with the human beings who use and depend on the computer systems you maintain.

Scope of services

Help desk staff fulfill the portions of the IT SLA that define what kinds of direct assistance an individual within the organization can expect to receive. Issues addressed by the help desk include desktop support, application support, and first-tier sysadmin issues such as server outages, network problems, and file restores.

In addition to offering the usual ticket-based or hotline support, this division can also offer ancillary services such as training seminars. These measures help increase customers' self-sufficiency and reduce the number of support requests.

It's also important to document an escalation policy. Employees need to know what to do when their needs are not being met—or when they want to express their gratitude for a job well done.

Help desk availability

Good IT support means that qualified staff are available to help whenever a customer needs them.

Most problems are minor and can safely enter a service queue. Others are work-stoppers that merit immediate attention. Automated responses from a request-tracking system and recorded telephone messages announcing regular office hours just cause annoyance. Make sure that users can always access a path of last resort if the need arises. A cell phone that rotates among sysadmin staff outside business hours is usually sufficient.

Help desk addiction

Unfortunately, excellent support sometimes breeds dependence. It's easy for users to get in the habit of consulting the help desk even when that isn't appropriate. If you recognize that someone is using the support system for answers they could get just as easily from the man pages or from Google, you might try answering their questions by quoting the relevant man page or URL. Be careful, though: this tactic can really anger users when not presented with the utmost respect.

32.4 The enterprise architects

The second IT subgroup in Exhibit A, the enterprise architects, consists of the admins who hold the overall technical vision for the organization. This role almost always includes some number of UNIX or Linux administrators. These individuals consider both the immediate and long-term impacts of new systems on the overall infrastructure. They understand how the organization will evolve in coming years and how the requirements of today will feed the requirements of tomorrow.

The enterprise architects are also responsible for understanding how systems interact. For example, in an organization that stores sensitive information about customers, the architects must understand how enabling database encryption will impact end users and determine whether this impact is acceptable.

The following sections present a selection of architectural best practices to consider when planning your site's IT design. These principles are particularly important when the configuration you will be supporting is new or unusual since these situations can be difficult to benchmark against real-world peers. Well-designed processes incorporate or foster adherence to these principles.

Make processes reproducible

System administration is not one of the performing arts. Whatever is done should be done consistently and repeatably. Usually, this means that the lowest level of changes should be made by scripts or by configuration programs rather than by system administrators. Variations in configuration should be captured in config files for your administrative software.

For example, a script that sets up a new machine should not be asking questions about IP numbers and packages to install. Instead, it should check a system configuration directory to determine what to do. It can present this information for confirmation, but the choices should be preordained. The less user interaction, the smaller the chance for human error.

But let us be clear: we are not describing a site at which high-level administrative priests make policy decisions to be carried out by mindless drones. Reproducibility is just as relevant if you are the only administrator at your site. It's not a good idea to make off-the-cuff configuration decisions that leave no audit trail. If a parameter needs to be changed, modify the central configuration information and propagate outward from there.

Leave a trail of bread crumbs

Who did what, and for what purpose? If there are problems with your system, fixing is much quicker when you can go back to the last working state, or at least figure out what has changed since then. Apart from the "what," it is also important to know the "who" and "why." Speaking with the person who implemented a troublesome change often leads to important insight. You may be able to quickly undo the change, but sometimes the change was made for a good reason and undoing it will only make things worse.

More details about revision control systems can be found starting on page 397.

Revision control systems provide one useful way to keep track of changes. They provide both a historical record of the actual data over time and information about which sysadmin performed the change. If used correctly, each modification is accompanied by a comment that explains the reasoning behind it. Automated tools can check in the config files they modify and identify themselves in the comment. That way, it's easy to identify a malfunctioning script and back out the changes it made.

If your organization uses a ticketing system, that is another place to keep track of changes. You can create a ticket for every change, and that ticket can include the who, what, when, where, and why. Possibly just as important, the ticket can also include a backout plan. That way, if something goes wrong at two in the morning, the on-call administrator does not have to wake up other sysadmins.

You and your staff must be disciplined about opening a ticket for each change. Tracking systems only provide their full benefit if they are used by every administrator for every change.

Recognize the criticality of documentation

Documentation is so important to a scalable infrastructure that we have made it a major section of its own, starting on page 1200.

Customize and write code

The use of existing tools is a virtue, and you should exploit those tools whenever you can. But no site in the world is exactly like yours, and your organization is certain to have some unique requirements. An IT infrastructure that precisely fills the organization's needs provides a competitive edge and increases everyone's productivity.

With its excellent scriptability and cornucopia of open source tools, UNIX is the ideal basis for a well-tuned infrastructure. In our view, a system administration group without a software development function is hobbled.

Keep the system clean

System management is not just about installing and adding and configuring; it's also about knowing what to keep, what to throw out, and what to refurbish. We call this concept "sustainable management." It's wonderful to be able to add a new computer to your environment in 5 minutes, and it's great to be able to create a new user account in 10 seconds. But if you look ahead, it's equally important to be able to find and remove old accounts and computers in an organized way. Sustainability in system management means that you have the tools and concepts needed to run your operation over the long haul in an organized fashion.

32.5 The operations group

The final role we discuss in this chapter is that of operations. In business terms, operations means "doing the day-to-day schlock that constitutes the business's essential purpose." In an IT sense, ops is where many of the tasks that are normally referred to as "system administration" live. Some examples are backups, monitoring, patching, upgrading, installing new software, and debugging.

The operations division is responsible for the installation and maintenance of the IT infrastructure. As a rule of thumb, the enterprise architecture and operations groups deal with computers and wires, whereas the help desk deals with people.

Operations focuses on creating a stable and dependable environment for customers. Availability and reliability are its key concerns. Operations staff should not perform experiments or make quick fixes or improvements on a Friday afternoon. The chance of failure (and of nobody but customers noticing the problems over the weekend) is just too high.

Aim for minimal downtime

Many people depend on the computing infrastructure we provide. An internal department can probably live for a while without its web site, but an Internet mail order company such as Amazon.com cannot. Some folks won't notice if your print server is down, but an employee with a hard deadline for completing a document or proposal will be very unhappy indeed. In most organizations, losing access to email usually makes everybody crabby. Central file servers are another potential source of disaster.

At some sites you will need to provide emergency service. In some types of organizations that operate around the clock—such as hospitals—this might mean 24/7 on-site coverage by experienced sysadmin staff.

Even if you don't have the budget or need to explicitly provide 24/7 coverage, you should be prepared to take advantage of any administrators that happen to be around late at night or on weekends. A rotating cell phone or on-line notification system can often provide "good enough" emergency coverage. Make sure that users can access this coverage in some easy and well-known way. For example, an email alias might relay an SMS message to a floating cell phone.

Document dependencies

To make accurate claims regarding availability or uptime, you must know not only your own strengths and weaknesses (including the reliability of the hardware you deploy) but also the dependencies of the IT systems on other hardware, software, and personnel. For example:

- **Power:** independent power sources and circuits, surge and short protection, backup power systems such as generators and UPSes, building power wiring, maps of power supplied to specific pieces of equipment
- **Network:** building wiring, backup lines, customer service numbers for ISPs, network topology, contact information for other groups within the organization that have their own network management function
- **Hardware:** high-availability systems and procedures for using them, hot/cold standbys, spare parts, hardware maintenance contracts

Repurpose or eliminate older hardware

To maintain your infrastructure, you must buy new machines, repurpose older ones, and throw out ancient ones. We cover procurement later in the purchasing section, but getting rid of old favorites is just as important.

Because users and management can be reluctant to upgrade obsolete equipment, you sometimes have to take the initiative. Financial information is the most persuasive evidence. If you can demonstrate on paper that the cost of maintaining old equipment exceeds the cost of replacement, you can remove many of the intellectual objections to upgrading. Sometimes it's also useful to replace heterogeneous hardware just to save the time and effort needed to keep all the different OS and software versions up to date.

Inexpensive Intel/PC hardware is the standard architecture base on the desktop, especially now that Apple ships on Intel hardware. The prevalence of PCs has over the years shifted the expense of computing from the hardware side to the software and support sides.

The best way to maintain a dependable, well-performing infrastructure is to be proactive. Develop a policy that anticipates and describes the expected lifetimes of your various systems. For example, you might keep laptops for three years, desktops for four years, and servers for five. These numbers may also vary by vendor and maintenance contract.

Planning the replacement of old hardware saves time and pain in the long run. If you have a policy of replacing laptops every three years, you are much less likely to get paged at midnight when a traveling executive suddenly cannot get to his or her email because the laptop has crashed.

Maintain local documentation

Just as most people accept the health benefits of exercise and leafy green vegetables, everyone appreciates good documentation and has a vague idea that it's important. Unfortunately, that doesn't necessarily mean that they'll write or update documentation without prodding.

Why should we care, really?

- Documentation reduces the likelihood of a single point of failure. It's wonderful to have tools that deploy workstations in no time and distribute patches with a single command, but these tools are nearly worthless if no documentation exists and the expert is on vacation or has quit.
- Documentation aids reproducibility. When practices and procedures aren't stored in institutional memory, they are unlikely to be followed consistently. When administrators can't find information about how to do something, they have to wing it.
- Documentation saves time. It doesn't feel like you're saving time as you write it, but after spending a few days re-solving a problem that has been tackled before but whose solution has been forgotten, most administrators are convinced that the time is well spent.
- Finally, and most importantly, documentation enhances the intelligibility of the system and allows subsequent modifications to be made in a manner that's consistent with the way the system is supposed to work. When modifications are made on the basis of only partial understanding, they often don't quite conform to the architecture. Entropy increases over time, and even the administrators that work on the system come to see it as a disorderly collection of hacks. The end result is often the desire to scrap everything and start again from scratch.

Local documentation serves many purposes. Have you ever walked into a machine room needing to reboot one server, only to face racks and racks of hardware, all alike and all unlabeled? Or had to install a piece of hardware that you've handled before, but all you can remember about the chore was that it was hard to figure out?

Local documentation should be kept in a well-defined spot. Depending on the size of your operation, this might be a directory on a file server that is mounted on all your machines, a wiki, or perhaps even in the home directory of a special system user account.

Once you have convinced your administrators to document configurations and administration practices, it's important to protect this documentation as well. A malicious user can do a lot of damage by changing your organization's documentation. Make sure that people who need the documentation can find it and read it (make it searchable), and that everyone who maintains the documentation can change it. But balance accessibility with the need for protection.

Wiki-type documentation is particularly nice in that you can easily undo any malicious changes. Other systems can be protected in a similar way by a revision control system.

Standardized documentation

Our experience suggests that the easiest and most effective way to maintain documentation is to standardize on short, lightweight documents. Instead of writing a system management handbook for your organization, write many one-page documents, each of which covers a single topic. Start with the big picture and then break it down into pieces that contain additional information. If you have to go into more detail somewhere, write an additional one-page document that focuses on steps that are particularly difficult or complicated.

This approach has several advantages:

- Your boss is probably only interested in the general setup of your environment. That is all that's needed to answer questions from above or to conduct a managerial discussion. Don't pour on too many details or you will just tempt your boss to interfere in them.
- The same holds true for customers.
- A new employee or someone taking on new duties within your organization needs an overview of the infrastructure to become productive. It's not helpful to bury such people in information.
- It's more efficient to use the right document than to browse through a large document.
- You can index pages to make them easy to find. The less time administrators have to spend looking for information, the better.
- It's easier to keep documentation current when you can do that by updating a single page.

This last point is particularly important. Keeping documentation up to date is a huge challenge; documentation is often is the first thing to be dropped when time is short. We have found that a couple of specific approaches keep the documentation flowing.

First, set the expectation that documentation be concise, relevant, and unpolished. Cut to the chase; the important thing is to get the information down. Nothing makes the documentation sphincter snap shut faster than the prospect of writing a dissertation on design theory. Ask for too much documentation and you may not get any. Consider developing a simple form or template for your sysadmins to use. A standard structure helps to avoid blank-page anxiety and guides sysadmins to record pertinent information rather than fluff.

Second, integrate documentation into processes. Comments in configuration files are some of the best documentation of all. They're always right where you need them, and maintaining them takes virtually no time at all. Most standard configuration files allow comments, and even those that aren't particularly comment friendly can often have some extra information sneaked into them.

Locally built tools can require documentation as part of their standard configuration information. For example, a tool that sets up a new computer can require information about the computer's owner, location, support status, and billing information even if these facts aren't directly relevant to the machine's software configuration.

Documentation should not create information redundancies. For example, if you maintain a site-wide master configuration file that lists machines and their IP addresses, there should be no other place where this information is updated by hand. Not only is it a waste of your time to make updates in multiple locations, but inconsistencies are also certain to creep in over time. When this information is required in other contexts and configuration files, write a script that obtains it from (or updates) the master configuration. If you cannot completely eliminate redundancies, at least be clear about which source is authoritative. And write tools to catch inconsistencies, perhaps run regularly from **cron**.

The advent of tools such as wikis, blogs, and other simple knowledge management systems has made it much easier to keep track of IT documentation. Set up a single location where all your documents can be found and updated. Don't forget to keep it organized, however. One wiki page with 200 child pages all in one list is cumbersome and difficult to use. Be sure to include a search function to get the most out of your system.

Hardware labeling

Some documentation is most appropriate when written out on a piece of paper or taped to a piece of hardware. For example, emergency procedures for a complete system or network failure are not particularly useful if they are stored on a dead or unreachable machine.

Every computer should be identifiable without someone's switching it on and logging in, because those activities will not always be possible. Uniquely label each workstation, server, printer, tape drive, and piece of network equipment. Labels should include the item's name and IP address (if it has one). Labels for peripherals should identify the host on which they live and the device files through which the device is accessed.

In a server room it is useful to have these labels on both the front and the back of the machines (especially in cramped racks) so that you can easily find the switch of the machine you want to power-cycle.

If your environment includes many different types of systems, it may be useful to add additional information such as architecture, boot instructions, special key sequences, pointers to additional documentation, the vendor's hotline, or the phone number of the person in charge. Recording key sequences may seem a bit silly, but servers are often connected to a console server rather than a dedicated monitor, and administrators need to know how to get to the correct system.

Be sure your central records and inventory data contain a copy of the information included on all these little sticky labels. This data is handy if you manage your machines through a TCP/IP connection to your console server instead of spending your work day in a noisy machine room.

In cases with extensive machine-specific data, you might consider deploying a bar coding system that lets you pull up all the relevant details for a device on a mobile laptop. (Of course, that mobile system shouldn't itself depend on a properly functioning network or database server.)

Network documentation

Network wiring must be scrupulously documented. Label all cables, identify patch panels and wall outlets, and mark network devices. Always make it easy for your wiring technicians to keep the documentation up to date; keep a pencil and forms hanging on the wall of wiring closets so that it's painless to note that a cable moved from one device to another. You can transfer this data to on-line storage at regular intervals.

Most network devices (e.g., routers and switches) can be reconfigured over the network. Although you can now move machines among subnets from your cozy office, documentation becomes even more important. Be careful, because you can now screw up a much bigger part of your infrastructure more quickly and more thoroughly.

You might consider using a software package such as Rancid to help you keep track of your device configurations. These tools also catch accidental and forgotten changes, which can drastically reduce unplanned downtime.

User documentation

Prepare a short document that you can give to new users. It should document local customs, procedures for reporting problems, the names and locations of printers, your backup and downtime schedules, and so on. This type of document can save an enormous amount of sysadmin or user services time. You should also make the information available on the web. A printed document is more likely to be read by new users, but a web page is easier to refer to at the time questions arise. Do both and keep them updated regularly. Outdated on-line documentation or FAQs are worse than useless.

In addition to documenting your local computing environment, you may want to prepare some introductory material about UNIX for your power users. We provide printed one-page crib sheets that list the commands and applications commonly needed by our user community.

Keep environments separate

Organizations that write and deploy their own software need separate development, test, and production environments so that releases can be staged into general use through a structured process. Separate, that is, but identical; make sure that when development systems are updated, the changes propagate to the test and production environments as well. Of course, the configuration updates themselves should be subject to the same kind of structured release control as the code. "Configuration changes" include everything from OS patches to application updates and administrative changes.

It is critical to protect your production environment by enforcing role separation throughout the promotion process. For example, the developers who have administrative privileges in the development environment should not be the same people who have administrative and promotion privileges in other environments. A disgruntled developer with code promotion permissions could conceivably insert malicious code at the development stage and then promote it through to production. By distributing approval and promotion duties to other people, you require multiple people to collude or make mistakes before problems can find their way into production systems.

Document your code promotion process and follow it religiously. Don't make exceptions. If you find that the regular process is not efficient enough for emergency changes, document an emergency change process and then make sure it is followed. You should also audit the code promotion process and go back and make retroactive adjustments where necessary.

Developers are sometimes frustrated by the level of documentation required in this type of system. Consider holding some lunch-and-learn sessions to help them understand the motivations for your requirements. Developers who are bought in as co-conspirators are more likely to follow the standard procedures.

Automate, automate, automate

Your site-wide management system should contain the following major elements:

- **Automated setup of new machines:** This is not just OS installation; it also includes all the additional software and local configuration necessary to allow a machine to enter production use. It's inevitable that your site will need to support more than one type of configuration, so include multiple machine types in your plans from the beginning.
- **Systematic patching and updating of existing machines:** When you identify a problem with your setup, you need a standardized and easy way to deploy updates to all affected machines. Note that because computers are not turned on all the time (even if they are supposed to be), your update scheme must correctly handle machines that are not on-line when the update is initiated. You can check for updates at boot time or update on a regular schedule; see Chapter 12 for more information.
- **A monitoring system:** Your users should not have to call you to tell you that the server is down. Not only is it unprofessional, but you have no idea how long the system has been down. The first person to call you is

probably not the first person to have experienced problems. You need some kind of monitoring system that raises an alarm as soon as problems are evident. But alarms are tricky. If there are too many, sysadmins start to ignore them; if too few, important problems go unnoticed.

- **A communication system:** Keep in touch with the needs of your users; supporting them is the ultimate goal of everything you do as a system administrator. A request-tracking system is a necessity (see page 1191). A central location where users can find system status and contact information (typically on the web) is also helpful.

32.6 Management

The role of IT management is to define the IT group's overall strategy and to oversee the IT organization. Many responsibilities fall on the managers' shoulders:

- Leading the group, bringing vision, and providing necessary resources
- Hiring, firing, staff assessment, and skill development
- Assigning tasks to the staff and tracking progress
- Ensuring and measuring compliance with SLAs
- Negotiating changes and updates to SLAs
- Communicating with the managers of the overall organization
- Handling problems: staff conflicts, rogue users, ancient hardware, etc.
- Acting as a "higher authority" to whom users can escalate problems
- Overseeing the development of a scalable infrastructure
- Planning for disasters and emergencies
- Extracting documentation from squirrelly sysadmins' heads
- Facilitating security through policy development (both for users and for administrators) and enforcement

It might seem that the task of interfacing with customers is missing from this list. However, we believe that this role is actually best filled by members of the technical staff. Managers frequently do not have the technical background to evaluate the difficulty and feasibility of customers' requests. There are likely to be fewer surprises on both sides of the table when those doing the actual work have input into the deliverables and schedules that are promised to customers.

Leadership

Leadership is hard to describe. But when lacking or poorly executed, its absence is all too readily apparent. In a way, leadership is the "system administration" of organizations: it sets the direction, makes sure the components work together, and keeps the whole system running with as few error messages as possible.

Unfortunately, the technical prowess that makes someone a great system administrator doesn't necessarily translate to the leadership role, which requires a more people-centered skill set. People are a lot harder to master than Perl.

For new managers with strong technical backgrounds, it can be particularly hard to focus on the job of management and avoid the temptation to do engineering work. It's sometimes more comfortable and more fun to dive into solving a technical problem than to have a long-overdue conversation with a "difficult" staff member. But which is more valuable to the organization?

A simple (and perhaps eye-opening) check on your level of leadership is the following. Make a list of the tasks your organization is working on. Use one color to mark the areas in which you are steering the boat, and a different color to mark the areas in which you are rowing or pulling the boat. Which color is dominant?

Personnel management

Personnel management can be particularly challenging. As part of your oversight function, you deal both with your employees' technical and personal sides. Technically brilliant sysadmins can sometimes be poor communicators. As their manager, you need to keep them on the growth curve in both dimensions.

Technical growth is relatively easy to promote and quantify, but personal growth is just as important. Below are some important questions to ask when assessing an employee's user interface:

- Is this person's behavior suitable for our work environment?
- How does this person interact with authorities, customers, suppliers?
- Does this person get along with other members of the team?
- Does this person have leadership skills that should be developed?
- How does this person respond to criticism and technical disputes?
- Does this person actively work to address gaps in his or her knowledge?
- How are this person's communication skills?
- Can this person plan, implement, and demonstrate a customer's project?
- Does this person demonstrate ownership of his or her tasks?
- Does this person tend to find solutions, or roadblocks?

Hiring

It's important to make these assessments for potential new hires as well as for existing employees. The personal qualities of job applicants are often overlooked or underweighted. Don't take shortcuts in this area—you'll surely regret it later!

There are two approaches to building a staff of system administrators:

- Hire experienced people.
- Grow your own.

Experienced people may come up to speed faster, but you sometimes want them to unlearn certain things or change old habits. Conversely, inexperienced administrators may require fairly extensive technical training. Regardless of which option you choose, it's helpful to have documented, comprehensive policies and procedures. If your existing IT staff have clear direction and understand your policies and procedures, they can be leaders in their own right and help to acclimate newcomers to your organization's way of doing things.

Some of the qualities of a good system administrator are contradictory. A sysadmin must be brash enough to try innovative solutions when stuck on a problem but must also be careful enough not to try anything truly destructive. Interpersonal skills and problem-solving skills are both important, but they often seem to lie on orthogonal axes. While all of your sysadmins don't need to be stellar communicators, a few personable sysadmins will go a long way toward promoting customer satisfaction.

When hiring sysadmins, you will have to decide which characteristics are the most important for a particular role. For example, if you are hiring a server administrator who will be focused on back-end systems and have little interaction with customers, you might rank communication skills somewhat lower than technical skills. But since this person will be part of a larger team, you can't ignore interpersonal skills entirely.

To assess technical expertise, you might try drafting a set of pertinent technical questions you can pose to interviewees. You might even try sticking a bogus question in among the real ones to measure the BS factor in an applicant's answers.

We believe that in-person interviews are important. You will learn more about an applicant in the first 15 minutes of an in-person interview than you can in a longer phone conversation.

We also believe strongly in checking references. During the reference check, we like to ask open-ended questions that give the respondent a chance to send subtle messages about the applicant. Listen carefully! People generally do not like to say negative things during a reference check, but they may give you subtle hints if you are paying close attention.

Some of the questions to ask will emerge from your interview with the candidate. For example, if the interview raises concern about whether an applicant pays close attention to details, you might ask a reference something like "Would you consider the applicant more of a detail-oriented person or a big-picture thinker?"

Firing

If you make a hiring mistake, fire early. You may miss a few late bloomers, but keeping people who are not pulling their own weight can alienate your other staff members as they take up the slack and clean up the duds' messes. Your customers will also realize that certain individuals don't get things done and start demanding a particular system administrator for their jobs. You don't want your customers interfering with management decisions in your daily business.

In many organizations it is very hard to fire someone, especially after the initial evaluation period is over. Make sure that initial evaluations are taken seriously.

Later, you may have to collect data showing incompetence, give formal warnings, set performance goals, and so on.

Mechanics of personnel management

There is more to integrating a new employee into your infrastructure than just writing an offer letter. You must be aware of and honor your organization's rules regarding advertising for positions, trial periods, reviews, and so on.

Another set of chores define the mechanics of getting a new person settled with a desk, computer, keys, accounts, and **sudo** access. Your processes should ensure that a system administrator hired to administer a particular set of servers is not given carte blanche to administer any system in the company.

Just as important are the policies and procedures to follow when a sysadmin leaves the organization. You need a checklist to ensure you don't forget anything. Your checklist should include things such as

- Removing the user's domain account (LDAP or Active Directory)
- Removing the user's UNIX and Linux accounts
- Removing the user from all the site's **sudoers** files
- Collecting keys and access cards (document all keys and cards collected)
- Collecting a company cell phone

Some organizations can print a definitive list of access rights and hardware that have been given to each employee. This is a great way to make sure you haven't forgotten anything.

In the United States, it's common for employees to give two weeks' notice before quitting. Some sites forego the two-week period and walk the employee to the door, immediately revoking all physical and network access. Smart!

Quality control

Managers set the tone for quality control. Each task should have clear criteria for completion. In addition to the work inherent in each task, completion criteria might include

- Testing the solution
- Updating local documentation
- Propagating the solution to all affected machines
- Completing the trouble ticket with details of the actions taken
- Getting the ticket initiator to sign off on the resolution as satisfactory

Even a simple task, such as creating a **cron** job to help with a daily administrative chore, should include a testing phase to ensure that the change works as intended. More complex tasks should include a documented test plan.

Ideally, your IT group would have a culture in which sysadmins take it upon themselves to ensure that each job is done well and completely. But to achieve that steady state, you may have to do some close monitoring; this is a good situation in which to apply the maxim that you should "inspect what you expect."

Management without meddling

As a technically competent manager, you will frequently be tempted to advise employees on how to do their jobs. But be careful. There are situations where this is appropriate, but there are also situations where you need to let your employees grow and become fully responsible for their work.

We think of employee development as being a little bit like parenting. If a staff member is about to make a mistake that will give IT a black eye, cause serious damage, or otherwise cause a problem that is difficult to recover from, it's time to investigate. Ask the staff member to explain the game plan, and make sure he or she understands the likely consequences of the plan. If the staff member still seems to be on the wrong path, you will probably need to step in.

On the other hand, if someone is about to make a mistake that could serve as a good learning opportunity without causing undue harm, it might be a good time to step back. Lessons learned through direct experience are retained better than those communicated by word of mouth.

Of course, pitfalls lie in both directions. You don't want to be perceived as a micromanager, but you also don't want to be seen as withholding information from your staff or as someone who lets staff fail when they could be succeeding. Support your staff even when they've made mistakes and help them learn. Never allow mistakes to become an ongoing source of embarrassment.

Community relations

System administration is a funny business. If you do your job well, users take your seamless computing environment for granted and nobody notices what you do. But in today's world of viruses, spam, bloated applications, and total dependence on the Internet, the IT staff is an indispensable part of the organization.

Your satisfied customers are your best marketing device. However, there are other ways to gain visibility within your organization and within the broader community. Based on our experience with tooting our own horn, we suggest the following methods as being particularly effective.

- Hold town hall meetings where users can express their concerns and ask questions about the computing infrastructure. You might prepare for such a meeting by analyzing users' support requests and open the meeting with a short presentation on the most troublesome topics you've identified. Provide refreshments to ensure a good turnout.

- Leave plenty of time for questions and make sure you have knowledgeable staff available to answer them. Don't try to bluff your way out of unexpected questions, though. If you don't know the answer off-hand, it's best to admit this and follow up later.

- Design a seminar series directed at end users within your organization. Schedule meetings at two- or three-month intervals and publish the topics to be presented well in advance.
- Attend conferences on system administration and give talks or write papers about the tools you develop. Such presentations not only give you feedback from your peers but they also show your customers (and your boss) that you do your job well.

System administration is ultimately about dealing with people and their needs. Personal relationships are as important as they are in any business. Talk to your customers and colleagues, and make time for personal discussions and exchanges.

If you support multiple groups of people, consider assigning a specific staff member to act as an account manager for each group. This liaison should take on responsibility for the general happiness of the customer and should speak regularly with end users. Channel news and information about changes in the computing environment through the liaison to create additional opportunities for contact.

Management of upper management

To effectively discharge your management duties (particularly those in the "leadership" arena), you need the respect and support of your own management. You need the ability to define your group's structure and staffing, including decision authority over hiring and firing. You need control over task assignments, including the authority to decide when goals have been achieved and staff can be reassigned. Finally, you need to be responsible for representing your group both within the larger organization and to the world at large.

Upper management sometimes has no idea what system administrators do. Use your trouble ticketing system to provide this information; it can help when you or your boss needs to campaign for additional staff or equipment. Also make sure that management understands the different roles of the help desk and the operations team. They need to know that the person who answers the phone when they dial the help desk is not the same person who configures the routers and servers. This clarity will go a long way toward keeping expectations in line.

It may be wise to keep good records even in the absence of a particular goal. Managers, especially nontechnical managers, are often way off in their estimates of the difficulty of a task or the amount of time it will take to complete. This inaccuracy is especially noticeable for troubleshooting tasks.

Try to set expectations realistically. If you don't have much experience in planning your work, double or triple your time estimates for large or crucial tasks. If an upgrade is done in two days instead of three, most users will thank you instead of cursing you as they might have if your estimate had been one day.

When it comes to making changes to production systems, you need to follow a documented change management process. This process should include approval from a change advisory board. Having management participate in the approval process will tend to decrease the number of user complaints. Users who see that the CEO is on-board with moving to a new email system are less likely to call you up insisting that you consider their favorite alternative.

Security is a common problem area. Tightening security typically means inconveniencing users, and the users often outweigh you both in number and whining ability. Increased security may reduce users' productivity; before implementing a proposed security change, do a risk analysis to be sure both management and users understand why it is a good idea.

Make sure that any security change that impacts users (e.g., converting from passwords to RSA/DSA keys for remote logins) is announced well in advance, is well documented, and is well supported at changeover time. You might even consider holding workshops at which users can learn about the change and maybe even bring in a laptop so that the first time they use the new system there is someone there to help them. Documentation should be easy to understand and should provide cookbook-type recipes for dealing with the new system. Allow for extra staffing hours when you first cut over to the new system so you can deal with frustrated, panicked users.

Purchasing

In many organizations, the group of people that make purchasing decisions does not include system administrators. This is, of course, fine for many decisions, but when the purchasing team is acquiring IT-related items, system administrators should have an opportunity to express their opinions and possibly even make a case for why one system should be chosen over another.

Sysadmins can provide good information about compatibility with the local environment, the competence of vendors (especially third-party resellers), and the reliability of certain types of equipment. Reliability information is particularly important when ordering systems that affect the organization's overall ability to function.

Another important piece of information that sysadmins can contribute is the impact that a new system will have on the organization's IT security and regulatory compliance. A good example might be a hospital in which a clinical department orders new imaging systems without consulting the system administration group. Unfortunately, when the hardware arrives and the sysadmins are called in to configure it, they realize that it does not interact with the hospital's authentication system. In fact, it does not require user login at all! Now the hospital has spent thousands of dollars on a system that is not HIPAA-compliant, and they will either need to purchase a new system or work with the vendor to get individual authentication capabilities incorporated. Neither of these is a good option, and the hospital would have been better off if the system administrators had been called in to foresee these problems and recommend a different vendor.

Sysadmins need to know about any new system (hardware or software) that's being ordered so that they can determine how to integrate it into the current infrastructure and predict what projects and resources will be needed to support it.

Keep in mind that although system administrators can offer recommendations, the organization will make the ultimate purchasing decision. If the organization purchases something the system administrators think is a bad choice, that item still needs to be supported—ignoring systems you don't like is not an option.

In organizations that must channel purchases to the lowest bidder, document evaluation criteria in addition to cost. Clauses such as "must be compatible with existing environment," or "must be able to run XYZ package well" are relatively open ended and let you consider factors other than just the price when making purchasing decisions.

The incremental impact and cost of a piece of hardware is not constant. Is it the 60th of that architecture or the first? Does it have enough local disk space for the system files? Does it have enough memory to run today's bloated applications? Is there a spare network port to plug it into? Is it a completely new OS? Is it compliant with relevant regulations? How does it fit into the organization's long-range plans? Has the system been considered and approved by the enterprise architects?

Conflict resolution

Several chores that fall on the manager's plate have the general flavor of getting along with people (usually customers, staff, or management) in sticky situations. We first look at the general approach and then talk about the special case of dealing with "rogue" customers, sometimes known as cowboys.

Conflicts in the system administration world often occur between system administrators and their customers, colleagues, or suppliers. For example, a customer is not happy with the services rendered, a vendor didn't deliver promised materials or services on time, a colleague didn't do what was expected, or an engineering department insists that it needs control over the configurations of its desktops.

Mediation

Most people don't like to talk about conflicts or even admit that they exist. When emotions flare, it's generally because the conflict has been addressed much too late, after an unsatisfactory situation has been endured for a long time. During the festering phase, the parties build up resentment and ruminate on each other's villainous motives.

A face-to-face meeting with a neutral mediator in attendance can sometimes defuse the situation. Try to constrain the session to a single topic and limit the time to no more than one hour. These measures can lower the chance of the meeting degenerating into an endless gripe session.

The goal of a mediation session is to find a win/win solution for both parties. Formal mediation training can be obtained through multiple organizations, but here are some basic principles:

- Give each party a chance to express its desired outcome. Record these points in a neutral fashion on a whiteboard that both parties can see.
- As mediator, your goal is to highlight areas of agreement and to find commonality between both sets of desired outcomes.
- You may not reach agreement in one meeting. But if you can make progress toward finding common ground, consider the meeting a success.
- Build on any common ground you've identified in subsequent sessions. After just a couple meetings, you may develop enough common ground that both parties can be satisfied with the outcome.

Rogue users and departments

The introduction of closely managed systems and processes often causes conflict. Technically inclined users (and sometimes entire departments) may feel that centralized system administration cannot adequately accommodate their configuration needs or their need for autonomous control over the computers they use.

Your first impulse may be to try and strong-arm such rogue users into accepting standard configurations in order to minimize the cost and time required to support them. However, this iron-fisted approach usually ends up creating both unhappy users and unhappy sysadmins. Keep in mind that rogue users' desires are often perfectly legitimate and that it is the sysadmins' job to support them or, at least, to refrain from making their lives more difficult.

The most desirable solution is to identify the underlying reasons for the users' reluctance to accept managed systems. In many cases, you can address their needs and bring them back into the fold.

An alternative to the integration strategy is to trade support for autonomy. You might allow rogue users or groups to do what they want, with the explicit understanding that they must also take on responsibility for keeping the customized systems running. If you do this, be sure to protect your other resources. Install a firewall between the systems you manage and the systems managed by the outlaws. This precaution will help thwart break-ins and viruses emanating from the segregated network.

Have the residents of the segregated network sign a policy document that sets security guidelines. For example, if their systems interfere with the rest of the organization, their network connection can be turned off until they are no longer impacting the rest of the organization. The fix for such an issue might include requiring them to patch critical vulnerabilities or to install antivirus software.

All organizations have their "bleeding edgers," users who are hooked on getting the latest stuff immediately. Such users are prepared to live with the inconvenience of beta versions and unstable prereleases as long as their software is up to date. Find ways to deal with these people as useful resources rather than as thorns in your side. They are ideal candidates to test new software and are often willing to feed bug reports back to you so that problems can be fixed.

Creative system administration is also needed to deal with the increasing number of mobile devices being brought to work. You must find ways of providing service for these (generally untrusted) devices without endangering the integrity of your systems. A separate network might be a good idea. Another option is to have the laptops run through a VPN that enforces "posture assessment."

Posture assessment ensures that the laptops adhere to your most important security policies. For example, you might require all machines connecting through the VPN to have a set of critical patches installed. For Windows laptops, you might also require antivirus software.

32.7 Policies and procedures

Comprehensive IT policies and procedures serve as the groundwork for a modern IT organization. Policies set standards for users and administrators and foster consistency for everyone involved. More and more, policies require acknowledgement in the form of a signature or other proof that the user has agreed to abide by their contents. Although this may seem excessive to some, it is actually a great way to protect administrators in the long run.

The ISO/IEC 27001 standard is a good basis for constructing your policy set. It weaves general IT policies with other important elements such as IT security and the role of the Human Resources department. In the next few sections, we discuss the ISO/IEC 27001 framework and highlight some of its most important and useful elements.

The difference between policies and procedures

Policies and procedures are two distinct things, but they are often confused, and the words are sometimes even used interchangeably. This sloppiness creates confusion, however. To be safe, think of them this way:

- Policies are documents that define requirements or rules. The requirements are usually specified at a relatively high level. An example of a policy might be that incremental backups must be performed daily, with level 0 backups being completed each week.
- Procedures are documents that describe how a requirement or rule will be met. So, the procedure associated with the policy above might say something like "Incremental backups are performed using Backup Exec software, which is installed on the server backups01…"

This distinction is important because your policies should not change very often. You might review them annually and maybe change one or two pieces. Procedures, on the other hand, evolve continuously as you change your architecture, systems, and configurations.

Some policy decisions are dictated by the software you are running or by the policies of external groups, such as ISPs. Some policies are mandatory if the privacy of your users' data is to be protected. We call these topics "nonnegotiable policy."

In particular, we believe that IP addresses, hostnames, UIDs, GIDs, and usernames should all be managed site-wide. Some sites (multinational corporations, for example) are clearly too large to implement this policy, but if you can swing it, site-wide management makes things a lot simpler. We know of a company that enforces site-wide management for 35,000 users and 100,000 machines, so the threshold at which an organization becomes too big for site-wide management must be pretty high.

Other important issues have a larger scope than just your local sysadmin group:

- Handling of security break-ins
- Filesystem export controls
- Password selection criteria
- Removal of logins for cause
- Copyrighted material (e.g., MP3s and DVDs)
- Software piracy

Policy best practices

Several policy frameworks are available, and they generally cover roughly the same territory. The following topics are examples of those that are typically included in an IT policy set.

- Information security policy
- External party connectivity agreements
- Asset management policy
- Information classification system
- Human Resources security policy
- Physical security policy
- Access control policies
- Security standards for development, maintenance, and new systems
- Incident management policy
- Business continuity management (disaster recovery)
- Regulatory compliance policy

Procedures

Procedures in the form of checklists or recipes can codify existing practice. They are useful both for new sysadmins and for old hands. Better yet are procedures that include executable scripts.

Several benefits accrue from standard procedures:

- Chores are always done in the same way.
- Checklists reduce the likelihood of errors or forgotten steps.
- It's faster for the sysadmin to work from a recipe.
- Changes are self-documenting.
- Written procedures provide a measurable standard of correctness.

Here are some common tasks for which you might want to set up procedures:

- Adding a host
- Adding a user
- Localizing a machine
- Setting up backups for a new machine
- Securing a new machine
- Removing an old machine
- Restarting a complicated piece of software
- Reviving a web site that is not responding or not serving data
- Upgrading the operating system
- Patching software
- Installing a software package
- Upgrading critical software (**sendmail**, **gcc**, **named**, OpenSSL, etc.)
- Backing up and restoring files
- Expiring backup tapes
- Performing emergency shutdowns

Many issues sit squarely between policy and procedure. For example:

- Who can have an account?
- What happens when they leave?

The resolutions of such issues need to be written down so that you can stay consistent and avoid falling prey to the well-known, four-year-old's ploy of "Mommy said no, let's go ask Daddy!"

32.8 Disaster recovery

Your organization depends on a working IT environment. Not only are you responsible for day-to-day operations, but you must also have plans in place to deal with any reasonably foreseeable eventuality. Preparation for such large-scale problems influences both your overall game plan and the way that you define daily operations. In this section, we look at various kinds of disasters, the data you need to gracefully recover, and the important elements of a disaster plan.

Risk assessment

Before a disaster recovery plan is completed, it's a good idea to pull together a risk assessment to help you understand what assets you have, what risks they face, and what mitigation steps you already have in place. The NIST 800-30 special publication details an extensive risk assessment process. You can download it here:

http://csrc.nist.gov/publications/nistpubs/800-30/sp800-30.pdf

Part of the risk assessment process is to make an explicit, written catalog of the potential disasters you want to protect against. Disasters are not all the same, and you may need several different plans to cover the full range of possibilities. For example, some common threat categories are

- Floods
- Fires
- Earthquakes
- Hurricanes and tornadoes
- Electrical storms and power spikes
- Power failures, both short and long term
- Extreme heat or failure of cooling equipment
- Device hardware failures (dead servers, fried hard disks)
- Network device failures (routers, switches, cables)
- Malicious users, both external and internal[2]
- Accidental user errors (deleted or damaged files and databases, lost configuration information, lost passwords, etc.)

For each potential threat, consider and write down all the possible implications of that event.

Once you understand the threats, you need to prioritize the services within your IT environment. Build a table that lists your IT services and assigns a priority to each. For example, a "software as a service" company might rate its external web site as a top-priority service, while an office with a simple, informational external web site might not worry about the site's fate during a disaster.

Disaster management

More and more, organizations are designing their critical systems to automatically fail over to secondary servers in the case of problems. This is a great idea if you have little or no tolerance for services being down. However, don't fall prey to the belief that because you are mirroring your data, you do not need off-line backups. Even if your data centers are miles apart, it is certainly possible that you could lose both of them. Make sure you include data backups in your disaster planning.

Read more about cloud computing starting on page 987.

Cloud computing is another disaster-planning resource that is gaining traction. Through services such as Amazon's EC2, you can get a remote site set up and functioning within minutes, without having to pay for dedicated hardware. You pay only for what you use, when you use it. This is a great and inexpensive alternative to a dedicated warm-backup site, albeit one that requires considerable technical planning.

2. As of 2005, about half of security breaches originated with insiders.

A disaster recovery plan should include the following sections (based on the NIST disaster recovery standard, 800-34):

- **Introduction** – purpose and scope of the document
- **Concept of operations** – system description, recovery objectives, information classification, line of succession, responsibilities
- **Notification and activation** – notification procedures, damage assessment procedures, plan activation
- **Recovery** – the sequence of events and procedures required for recovery of lost systems
- **Return to normal operations** – concurrent processing, reconstituted system testing, return to normal operations, plan deactivation

We are accustomed to using the network to communicate and to access documents. However, these facilities may be unavailable or compromised after an incident. Store all relevant contacts and procedures off-line. Know where to get recent dump tapes and how to make use of them without reference to on-line data.

In all disaster scenarios, you will need access to both on-line and off-line copies of essential information. The on-line copies should, if possible, be kept on a self-sufficient machine: one that has a rich complement of tools, has key sysadmins' environments, runs its own name server, has a complete local **/etc/hosts** file, has no file-sharing dependencies, has a printer attached, and so on. Don't use an old junker that's no good for anything else; the disaster recovery storage machine should be fast and should have plenty of memory and scratch disk space you can use for restores and compares during recovery. The machine needs a complete development environment so that it can patch and recompile any compromised software. It helps if the machine also has interfaces for all the types of disk drives used at your site (IDE, SATA, SCSI, FC-AL, etc.).

Here's a list of handy data to keep on the backup machine and in the form of a printed booklet or optical disc:

- An outline of the recovery procedure: who to call, what to say
- Service contract phone numbers and customer numbers
- Key local phone numbers: police, fire, staff, boss
- Inventory of backup tapes and the backup schedule that produced them
- Network maps
- Software serial numbers, licensing data, and passwords
- Copies of software installation media (can be kept as ISO files)
- A copy of your systems' service manuals
- Vendor contact info for that emergency disk you need immediately
- Administrative passwords

- Data on hardware and software configurations: OS versions, patch levels, partition tables, PC hardware settings, IRQs, DMAs, and the like
- Startup instructions for systems that need to be brought back on-line in a particular order

Staff for a disaster

Your disaster recovery plan should document who will be in charge in the event of a catastrophic incident. Set up a chain of command and keep the names and phone numbers of the principals off-line. We keep a little laminated card with important names and phone numbers printed in microscopic type. Very handy—and it fits in your wallet.

It may be that the best person to put in charge is a sysadmin from the trenches, not the IT director (who is usually a poor choice for this role).

The person in charge must be someone who has the authority and decisiveness to make tough decisions based on minimal information (e.g., a decision to disconnect an entire department from the network). The ability to make such decisions, communicate them in a sensible way, and lead the staff through the crisis are probably more important than having theoretical insight into system and network management.

An important but sometimes unspoken assumption made in most disaster plans is that sysadmin staff will be available to deal with the situation. Unfortunately, people get sick, go on vacation, leave for other jobs, and in stressful times may even turn hostile. Consider what you'd do if you needed extra emergency help. (Not having enough sysadmins around can sometimes constitute an emergency in its own right if your systems are fragile or your users unsophisticated.)

You might try forming a sort of NATO pact with a local consulting company that has sharable system administration talent. Of course, you must be willing to share back when your buddies have a problem. Most importantly, don't operate close to the wire in your daily routine. Hire enough system administrators and don't expect them to work 12-hour days.

Power and HVAC

Test your disaster recovery plan before you need to use it. An untested plan is no plan at all! Test and update the plan annually.

See page 1091 for more information about standby power options.

Test your generators and UPSes on a monthly or quarterly schedule, depending on how much risk your management is willing to accept. Verify that everything you care about is plugged into a UPS, that the UPS batteries are healthy, and that the failover mechanism works. To test an individual UPS, just unplug it from the wall. To make sure that all critical equipment is properly UPSified, you may have to throw the circuit breakers. Know your power system's dependencies and points of failure.

UPSes need maintenance, too. This function is probably outside the scope of your sysadmin duties, but you are responsible for ensuring that it is performed.

If you have a generator, contract with a local company that can deliver fuel for the generator when you need it. Keep enough fuel on hand to power your systems during an extended outage, but remember that fuel eventually goes bad. Gasoline starts to turn in as little as one month. Even when treated with a stabilizer additive, gasoline should not be stored for more than a year. Diesel is more chemically stable than gasoline but can support the growth of algae, so consider an algicidal additive for diesel that will be held for an extended period.

Most power outages are of short duration, but plan for two hours of battery life so that you have time to shut down machines properly in the event of a longer interruption. Most UPSes have a USB port or Ethernet interface that you can use to initiate a graceful shutdown of noncritical machines after a defined period without power.

Take advantage of power outages to do any five-minute upgrades that you have already tested but have not yet deployed. You're down anyway, so people expect to be inconvenienced. In some shops, an extra five minutes during a power outage is easier to accept than a scheduled downtime with a week's notice. If you have old machines that you suspect are not in use anymore, leave them turned off until someone complains. It might not be until weeks later—or never—that the "missing" machine is noticed.

See Chapter 28 for more information about environmental issues.

Cooling systems often have a notification system that can call you if the temperature gets too high. Tune the value of "too high" so that you have time to get in before machines start to fry after the cooling system pages you; we use 76 degrees instead of 90, but some of us live in the mountains 45 minutes away (in summer, indeterminate in winter). Keep a couple of mechanical or battery-operated thermometers in the machine room—losing power means that you lose all those nifty electronic indicators that normally tell you the temperature.

If you co-locate equipment at a remote site, ask to see the hosting site's backup power facilities before you sign a contract. Verify that the generator is real and is tested regularly. Ask to be present at the next generator test; whether or not you get to see an actual test, you're likely to get useful information.

Internet connection redundancy

ISPs are occasionally swallowed as part of a merger. Such mergers have demolished many companies' carefully laid plans for maintaining redundant connections to the Internet. A post-merger ISP often consolidates circuits that belonged to the independent companies. Customers that formerly had independent paths to the Internet may then have both connections running through a single conduit and once again be at the mercy of a single backhoe fiber cut.

ISPs have also been known to advertise "redundant circuits" or "backup connections" of questionable value. On closer inspection you may find that yes, there are two fibers but both are in the same conduit, or it may be that the backup connection transits an already saturated ATM cloud. Hold a yearly review with your ISPs to verify that you still have genuine redundancy.

Security incidents

System security is covered in detail in Chapter 22, *Security*. However, it's worth mentioning here as well because security considerations impact the vast majority of administrative tasks. There is no aspect of your site's management strategy that can be designed without due regard for security. For the most part, Chapter 22 concentrates on ways of preventing security incidents from occurring. However, thinking about how you might recover from a security-related incident is an equally important part of security planning.

Having your web site hijacked is a particularly embarrassing type of break-in. For the sysadmin at a web hosting company, a hijacking can be a calamitous event, especially when it involves sites that handle credit card data. Phone calls stream in from customers, from the media, from the company VIPs who just saw the news of the hijacking on CNN. Who will take the calls? What should that person say? Who is in charge? What role does each person play? If you are in a high-visibility business, it's definitely worth thinking through this type of scenario, coming up with some preplanned answers, and perhaps even having a practice session to work out the details.

Sites that accept credit card data have legal requirements to deal with after a hijacking. Make sure your organization's legal department is involved in security incident planning, and make sure you have relevant contact names and phone numbers to call in a time of crisis.

When CNN or Slashdot announces that your web site is down, the same effect that makes highway traffic slow down to look at an accident on the side of the road causes your Internet traffic to increase enormously, often to the point of breaking whatever it was that you just fixed. If your web site cannot handle an increase in traffic of 25% or more, consider having your load balancing device route excess connections to a server that presents a page that simply says "Sorry, we are too busy to handle your request right now."

Develop a complete incident handling guide to take the guesswork out of managing security problems. See page 950 for more details on incident management.

32.9 Compliance: Regulations and Standards

IT auditing and governance are big issues today. Regulations and quasi-standards for specifying, measuring, and certifying compliance have spawned myriad acronyms: SOX, ITIL, COBIT, and ISO 27002, just to name a few. Unfortunately, this alphabet soup is leaving something of a bad taste in system administrators' mouths, and software to implement all the controls deemed necessary by recent legislation is currently lacking.

Some of the major advisory standards, guidelines, industry frameworks, and legal requirements that may apply to system administrators are listed below. The legislative requirements are largely specific to the United States. However, the standards do contain some good advice even for organizations that are not required to adhere to them. It might be worth breezing through a few of them just to see if there are any best practices you might want to adopt. (The standards are listed in alphabetical order.)

- The **CJIS (Criminal Justice Information Systems)** standard applies to organizations that track criminal information and integrate that information with the FBI's databases. Its requirements can be found on-line at fbi.gov/hq/cjisd/cjis.htm.

- **COBIT** is a voluntary framework for information management based on industry best practices. It is developed jointly by the Information Systems Audit and Control Association (ISACA) and the IT Governance Institute (ITGI); see isaca.org for details. COBIT's mission is "to research, develop, publicize, and promote an authoritative, up-to-date, international set of generally accepted information technology control objectives for day-to-day use by business managers and auditors."

  The first edition of the framework was published in 1996, and we are now at version 4.0, published in 2005. This latest iteration was strongly influenced by the requirements of the Sarbanes-Oxley Act. It includes 34 high-level objectives that cover 215 "control objectives" categorized into four domains: Plan and Organize, Acquire and Implement, Deliver and Support, and Monitor and Evaluate.

- **COPPA, the Children's Online Privacy Protection Act**, regulates organizations that collect or store information about children under age 13. Parental permission is required to gather certain information; see coppa.org for details.

- **FERPA, the Family Educational Rights and Privacy Act**, applies to all institutions that are recipients of federal aid administered by the Secretary of Education. This regulation protects student information and accords students specific rights with respect to their data. For details, see ed.gov/policy/gen/guid/fpco/ferpa/index.html.

- **FISMA, the Federal Information Security Management Act**, applies to all government agencies and contractors to government agencies. It's a large and rather vague set of requirements that seek to enforce compliance with a variety of IT security publications from NIST, the National Institute of Standards and Technology. Whether or not your organization falls under the mandate of FISMA, the NIST documents are worth reviewing. See csrc.nist.gov/publications/PubsTC.html.

- The **FTC's Safe Harbor framework** bridges the gap between the U.S. and E.U. approaches to privacy legislation and defines a way for U.S. organizations that interface with European companies to demonstrate their data security. See export.gov/safeharbor/eg_main_018236.asp.
- The **Gramm-Leach-Bliley Act (GLBA)** regulates financial institutions' use of consumers' private information. If you've been wondering why the world's banks, credit card issuers, brokerages, and insurers have been pelting you with privacy notices, that's the Gramm-Leach-Bliley Act at work. See ftc.gov/privacy/privacyinitiatives/glbact.html.
- **HIPAA, the Health Insurance Portability and Accountability Act**, applies to organizations that transmit or store protected health information (aka PHI). It is a broad standard that was originally intended to combat waste, fraud, and abuse in health care delivery and health insurance, but it is now used to measure and improve the security of health information as well. See hhs.gov/ocr/privacy/index.html.
- **ISO 27001** and **ISO 27002** are a voluntary (and informative) collection of security-related best practices for IT organizations. See iso.org.
- **ITIL** is the **IT Infrastructure Library**, a collection of manuals originally developed by the British government that outline a framework for the management of IT services. It is voluntary but has become widely used. See itil.org and the ITIL section at the end of this list for details.
- **CIP (Critical Infrastructure Protection)** is a family of standards from the North American Electric Reliability Corporation (NERC) that promote the hardening of infrastructural systems such as power, telephone, and financial grids against risks from natural disasters and terrorism.

  In a textbook demonstration of the Nietzschean concept of organizational "will to power," it turns out that most of the economy falls into one of NERC's 17 "critical infrastructure and key resource" (CI/KR) sectors and is therefore richly in need of CIP guidance. Organizations within these sectors should be evaluating their systems and protecting them as appropriate. See cip.gmu.edu/cip.
- The **Payment Card Industry Data Security Standard (PCI DSS)** was created by a consortium of payment brands including American Express, Discover, MasterCard, and Visa. It covers the management of payment card data and is relevant for any organization that accepts credit card payments. The standard comes in two flavors: a self-assessment for smaller organizations and a third-party audit for organizations that process more transactions. See pcisecuritystandards.org.
- The **FTC's Red Flag Rules** require anyone who extends credit to consumers (i.e., any organization that sends out bills) to implement a formal program to prevent and detect identity theft. The rules require credit

issuers to develop heuristics for identifying suspicious account activity; hence, "red flag." Search for "red flag" at ftc.gov for details.

- Last but certainly not least, the **IT general controls (ITGC)** portion of the **Sarbanes-Oxley Act (SOX)** applies to all public companies and is designed to protect shareholders from accounting errors and fraudulent practices. See sec.gov/rules/final/33-8124.htm.

ITIL: the Information Technology Infrastructure Library

Among these standards, the Information Technology Infrastructure Library (ITIL) has become a de facto standard for organizations seeking a comprehensive IT service management solution. ITIL processes are divided into six groups:

- **Help desk** – IT services for clients and for submitting problem reports and requests; also includes provisions for tracking and escalating issues
- **Incident management** – a reactive process whose goal is to restore service after an incident has caused a disruption
- **Problem management** – identifies the causes of incidents to prevent future service disruptions
- **Configuration management** – encapsulates information about the components of an infrastructure and their interdependencies
- **Change management** – processes for managing changes within the infrastructure
- **Release management** – similar to change management, but used for large-scale changes within the organization

Large organizations may have a formal ITIL program complete with a ticketing system that closely mirrors ITIL concepts and definitions. But even a small organization that uses an open source ticketing system can adopt policies that encourage sensible change management. All changes should require the submission of a change request, approval by a change board, and tracking through a change ticket. All incidents should be required to follow a documented process of incident handling that includes post-incident analysis to determine whether the problem was handled in the best possible way.

More generally, it's fine to interpret voluntary standards in light of your site's specific needs and constraints. The main goal is to understand the concepts embodied in the standards and to absorb some of their philosophy. Some of the standards listed above are hundreds of pages long, so they can be difficult to even approach; feel free to make use of summaries and condensed versions.

NIST: the National Institute for Standards and Technology

NIST publishes a host of standards that are useful to administrators and technologists. Some of the most commonly used ones are mentioned below, but if you are ever bored and looking for standards, you might check out their web site. You will not be disappointed.

NIST 800-53, *Recommended Security Controls for Federal Information Systems and Organizations,* describes how to assess the security of information systems. If your organization has developed an in-house application that holds sensitive information, NIST 800-53 can help you make sure you have really secured it. Beware, however: embarking on a NIST 800-53 compliance journey is not for the faint of heart. You are likely to end up with a document that is close to 100 pages long and that includes excruciating details.[3]

NIST 800-34, *Contingency Planning Guide for Information Technology Systems*, is NIST's disaster recovery bible. It is directed at government agencies, but any organization can benefit from it. Following the NIST 800-34 planning process takes time, but it forces you to answer important questions such as, "Which systems are the most critical?", "How long can we survive without these systems?", and "How are we going to recover if our primary data center is lost?"

32.10 Legal issues

The U.S. federal government and several states have laws regarding computer crime. At the federal level, there are two pieces of legislation from the early 1990s and two more recent ones:

- The Federal Communications Privacy Act
- The Computer Fraud and Abuse Act
- The No Electronic Theft Act
- The Digital Millennium Copyright Act

Some big issues in the legal arena are the liability of sysadmins, network operators, and web hosting sites; peer-to-peer file-sharing networks; copyright issues; and privacy issues. The topics in this section comment on these issues and a variety of other legal debacles related to system administration.

Privacy

Privacy has always been difficult to safeguard, but with the rise of the Internet, it is in more danger than ever. Medical records have been repeatedly disclosed by poorly protected systems, stolen laptops, and misplaced backup tapes. Databases full of credit card numbers have been compromised. Web sites purporting to offer antivirus software actually install spyware when used. Fake email arrives almost daily, appearing to be from your bank and alleging that problems with your account require you to verify your account data. Usually, a close inspection of the email reveals that the data would go to a hacker in eastern Europe or Asia and not to your bank. This type of attack is called "phishing."

3. If you plan to do business with a U.S. government agency, you may be required to complete a NIST 800-53 assessment whether you want to or not...

Technical measures can never protect against these attacks because they target your site's most vulnerable weakness: its users. Your best defense is a well-educated user base. To a first approximation, no legitimate email or web site will ever

- Suggest that you have won a prize
- Request that you "verify" account information or passwords
- Ask you to forward a piece of email
- Ask you to install software you have not explicitly searched for
- Inform you of a virus or other security problem

Users who have a basic understanding of these dangers are more likely to make sensible choices when a pop-up window claims they have won a free MacBook.

Policy enforcement

Log files may prove to you beyond a shadow of a doubt that person X did bad thing Y, but to a court it is all just hearsay evidence. Protect yourself with written policies. Log files sometimes include time stamps, which are useful but not necessarily admissible as evidence unless your computer is running the Network Time Protocol (NTP) to keep its clock synced to a reference standard.

You may need a security policy in order to prosecute someone for misuse. It should include a statement such as this: "Unauthorized use of computing systems may involve not only transgression of organizational policy but also a violation of state and federal laws. Unauthorized use is a crime and may involve criminal and civil penalties; it will be prosecuted to the full extent of the law."

We advise you to display a splash screen that advises users of your snooping policy. You might say something like: "Activity may be monitored in the event of a real or suspected security incident."

You may want to ensure that users see the notification at least once by including it in the startup files you give to new users. If you require the use of SSH to log in (and you should), you can configure **/etc/ssh/sshd_config** so that SSH always shows the splash screen.

Be sure to specify that by the act of using their accounts, users acknowledge your written policy. Explain where users can get additional copies of policy documents and post key documents on an appropriate web page. Also include the specific penalty for noncompliance (deletion of the account, etc.). It is more important that you demonstrate a good faith effort to notify users of their responsibilities than that you get the notifications precisely correct in a legal sense.

In addition to the splash screen approach, it's a good idea to have users sign a policy agreement before they are given access to your systems. This acceptable use agreement should be crafted in conjunction with your legal department. If you don't have signed agreements from current employees, make a sweep to collect them, then make signing the agreement a standard part of the induction process for new hires.

You might also consider offering periodic information security training sessions. This is a great opportunity to educate users about important issues such as phishing scams, when it's OK to install software and when it's not, password security, and any other points that are relevant to your environment.

Control = liability

ISPs typically have an appropriate use policy (AUP) dictated by their upstream providers and required of their downstream customers. This "flow down" of liability assigns responsibility for users' actions to the users themselves, not to the ISP or the ISP's upstream provider. Such policies have been used to attempt to control spam and to protect ISPs in cases where customers have stored illegal or copyrighted material in their accounts. Check the laws in your area; your mileage may vary.

Your policies should explicitly state that users are not to use company resources for illegal activities. However, that's not really enough—you also need to discipline users if you find out they are doing naughty things. Organizations that know about naughty things but do not act on them are complicit and can be prosecuted. Unenforced or inconsistent policies are worse than none, from both a practical and legal point of view.

Because of the risk of being found complicit in user misbehavior, some sites limit the data that they log, the length of time for which log files are kept, and the amount of log file history kept on backup tapes. Some software packages help with the implementation of this policy by including levels of logging that help the sysadmin debug problems but that do not violate users' privacy. However, always be aware of what kind of logging might be required by local laws or by any regulatory standards that apply to you.

Software licenses

Many sites have paid for K copies of a software package and have N copies in daily use, where K < N. Getting caught in this situation could be damaging to the company, probably more damaging than the cost of those N-minus-K other licenses. Other sites have received a demo copy of an expensive software package and hacked it (reset the date on the machine, found the license key, etc.) to make it continue working after the expiration of the demo period. How do you as a sysadmin deal with requests to violate license agreements and make copies of software on unlicensed machines? What do you do when you find that machines for which you are responsible are running pirated software?

It's a very tough call. Management will often not back you up in your requests that unlicensed copies of software be either removed or paid for. Often, it is a sysadmin who signs the agreement to remove the demo copies after a certain date, but a manager who makes the decision not to remove them.

We are aware of several cases in which a sysadmin's immediate manager would not deal with the situation and told the sysadmin not to rock the boat. The admin then wrote a memo to the boss asking to correct the situation and documenting the number of copies of the software that were licensed and the number that were in use. The admin quoted a few phrases from the license agreement and carbon copied the president of the company and his boss's managers. In one case, this procedure worked and the sysadmin's manager was let go. In another case, the sysadmin quit when even higher management refused to do the right thing. No matter what you do in such a situation, get things in writing. Ask for a written reply, or if all you get is spoken words, write a short memo documenting your understanding of your instructions and send it to the person in charge.

32.11 Organizations, conferences, and other resources

Many UNIX and Linux support groups—both general and vendor specific—help you network with other people who are using the same software. Table 32.3 presents a brief list of organizations, but plenty of other national and regional groups are not listed in this table.

Table 32.3 UNIX and Linux organizations of interest to system administrators

Name	URL	What it is
FSF	fsf.org	Free Software Foundation, sponsor of GNU
USENIX	usenix.org	UNIX users group, quite technical
SAGE	sage.org	The System Administrators Guild associated with USENIX; holds the yearly LISA conference
LOPSA	lopsa.org	League of Professional System Administrators, a spinoff from USENIX/SAGE
SANS	sans.org	Runs sysadmin and security conferences; less technical than SAGE, with a focus on tutorials
The Linux Foundation	linuxfoundation.org	A nonprofit consortium dedicated to fostering the growth of Linux
AUUG	auug.org.au	Australian UNIX Users Group, covers both technical and managerial aspects of computing
SAGE-AU	sage-au.org.au	Australian SAGE, holds yearly conferences in Oz
SANE	sane.nl	System Administration and Network Engineering group, has yearly conferences in Europe

FSF, the Free Software Foundation, sponsors of the GNU project ("GNU's Not Unix," a recursive acronym). The "free" in the FSF's name is the "free" of free speech and not that of free beer. The FSF is also the origin of the GNU Public License, which is now in its third version and covers many of the free software packages used on UNIX and Linux systems.

USENIX, an organization of users of Linux, UNIX, and other open source operating systems, holds one general conference and several specialized (smaller) conferences or workshops each year. The general conference has a parallel track devoted to open systems that features ongoing OS development in the Linux and BSD communities.

The big event for sysadmins is the USENIX LISA (Large Installation System Administration) conference held in late fall. Trade shows are often associated with these conferences.

As a service to the Linux community, the Linux Foundation operates a USENIX workshop dedicated to Linux kernel development. Access to this two-day event is by invitation only.

SAGE, USENIX's System Administrators Guild, is the first international organization for system administrators. It promotes administration as a profession by sponsoring conferences and informal programs. See sage.org for the details.

SAGE, together with USENIX, its parent organization, puts on system and network administration conferences offering tutorials and technical sessions, invited talks, and help sessions. Occasionally, one-day workshops on special topics run in parallel. For information, see usenix.org.

The USENIX and SAGE newsletter—;login:—is produced by both organizations; it contains administrative news, tips, reviews, and announcements of interest to sysadmins. SAGE has a list of resources for sysadmins. See sage.org for current information.

In 2005, a falling out between USENIX and SAGE left the future of SAGE in doubt. The result was that some of the old-timers in the SAGE organization formed a separate organization called LOPSA, the League of Professional System Administrators, lopsa.org. As of early 2010, LOPSA doesn't yet hold conferences, but they do have some training sessions scheduled. SAGE gave up its sysadmin certification program; let's hope that LOPSA will pick it up.

SANS offers many courses and seminars in the security space and runs a certification program. The exam format is multiple choice, open book, with a time limit. Applicants can take two practice exams before the real thing. Individual certificates focus on narrow topics; applicants can also earn a general security (GSEC) certification. Certification is valid for only 2–3 years, so you must keep up with recent developments and recertify (for an added fee) to stay current. See giac.org for details.

Many local areas have regional UNIX, Linux, or open systems user groups. Some of these are affiliated with USENIX and some are not. The local groups usually have regular meetings, workshops with local or visiting speakers, and, often, dinner together before or after the meetings. They're a good way to network with other sysadmins in your area.

The premier trade show for the networking industry is Interop; its tutorial series is also of high quality. Interop used to be an annual event that was eagerly awaited by techies and vendors alike. Interops now happens several times a year—a traveling network circus, so to speak. The salaries of tutorial speakers have been cut in half, but the quality of the tutorials seems to have survived.

32.12 Recommended Reading

LIMONCELLI, THOMAS A. *Time Management for System Administrators.* Sebastopol, CA: O'Reilly Media, 2005.

MACHIAVELLI, NICCOLÒ. *The Prince.* 1513.
Available on-line from gutenberg.org/etext/1232

BROOKS, FREDERICK P., JR. *The Mythical Man-Month: Essays on Software Engineering.* Reading, MA: Addison-Wesley, 1995.

SENFT, SANDRA, AND FREDERICK GALLEGOS. *Information Technology Control and Audit (3rd Edition).* Boca Raton, FL: Auerbach Publications, 2008.

The site itil-toolkit.com is a good place to start if you seek to understand the mountains of jargon and management-speak associated with ITIL processes and standards.

The site itl.nist.gov is the landing page for the NIST Information Technology Laboratory. Lots of information about standards. Go to the publications page.

The web site of the Electronic Frontier Foundation, eff.org, is a great place to find commentary on the latest issues in privacy, cryptography, and legislation. Always interesting reading.

sans.org/resources/policies hosts the SANS security policy project. Several good sample IT policies are available from this site.

Lots of great resources for system administrators are also available on the SAGE site: sage.org/field/field.html.

32.13 Exercises

E32.1 What are your organization's recurring procedures? Which are infrequently performed and reinvented each time? Which are risky?

E32.2 What are your dependencies on external providers? Do you need and have a plan B? Explain why or why not. Describe plan B if it exists.

E32.3 Briefly interview several internal customers to determine their expectations with respect to the availability of the computing infrastructure. Are the expectations consistent? Are they reasonable? Are they consistent with the system administration group's stated goals?

E32.4 What organized infrastructure for system management is already established at your site? Identify the pieces that are still missing.

E32.5 One of your co-workers is going to leave for lunch tomorrow and never return, but you don't yet know which one. (No, you don't get to pick.) What critical procedures might be affected, and how prepared is your organization to cover for the missing staff member? What documentation would have to exist in order to avoid a service disruption?

E32.6 What would happen if *you* didn't come in for the next three months? How much would your colleagues hate you when you finally came back, and why? What can you do in the next two weeks to reduce the trauma of such an event?

☆ E32.7 Your boss orders you to cut the system administration budget by 30% by the end of the current year. Can you quantify the consequences of this cut? Present a summary that will allow the boss to make an informed decision regarding which services to reduce or discontinue.

☆ E32.8 Who are some of the current major corporate supporters of Linux? What are their interests and motivations? What sort of contributions are they making?

☆ E32.9 You are cleaning up after a disk crash and notice files in the **lost+found** directory. When you investigate further, you find that some of the files are mail messages that were sent between two students who are setting up a back door around the department firewall to archive MP3 files on a remote file server. What should you do? Are there policies or regulations in place that cover such incidents?

☆☆ E32.10 Evaluate your site's local documentation for new users, sysadmins, standard procedures, and emergencies.

☆☆ E32.11 Forecast the future of the various commercial and free UNIX and Linux variants over the next five years. How will the current development and distribution models hold up over time? What will be the long-term impact of the adoption of Linux by hardware vendors? Differentiate between the server and desktop markets.

Index

We have alphabetized files under their last components. And in most cases, *only* the last component is listed. For example, to find index entries relating to the **/etc/mail/aliases** file, look under **aliases**. Our friendly vendors have forced our hand by hiding standard files in new and inventive directories on each system.

Numbers

A

B

D

E

G

H

I

J

M

N

O

Q

R

S

V

W

X

Y

Z

A Brief History of System Administration

From the desk of Dr. Peter H. Salus, technology historian

In the modern age, most folks have at least a vague idea what system administrators do: work tirelessly to meet the needs of their users and organizations, plan and implement a robust computing environment, and pull proverbial rabbits out of many different hats. Although sysadmins are often viewed as underpaid and underappreciated, most users can at least identify their friendly local sysadmin—in many cases, more quickly than they can name their boss's boss.

It wasn't always this way. Over the last 40 years (and the 20-year history of this book), the role of the system administrator has evolved hand-in-hand with UNIX and Linux. A full understanding of system administration requires an understanding of how we got here and of some of the historical influences that have shaped our landscape. Join us as we reflect on the many wonderful years.

The Dawn of Computing: System Operators (1952–1960)

The first commercial computer, the IBM 701, was completed in 1952. Prior to the 701, all computers had been one-offs. In 1954, a redesigned version of the 701 was announced as the IBM 704. It had 4,096 words of magnetic core memory and three index registers. It used 36-bit words (as opposed to the 701's 18-bit words) and did floating-point arithmetic. It executed 40,000 instructions every second.

But the 704 was more than just an update: it was incompatible with the 701. Although deliveries were not to begin until late 1955, the operators of the eighteen 701s in existence (the predecessors of modern system administrators) were already fretful. How would they survive this "upgrade," and what pitfalls lay ahead?

IBM itself had no solution to the upgrade and compatibility problem. It had hosted a "training class" for customers of the 701 in August 1952, but there were no textbooks. Several people who had attended the training class continued to meet informally and discuss their experiences with the system. IBM encouraged the operators to meet, to discuss their problems, and to share their solutions. IBM funded the meetings and made available to the members a library of 300 computer programs. This group, known as SHARE, is still the place (50+ years later) where IBM customers meet to exchange information.[1]

From single-purpose to time sharing (1961–1969)

Early computing hardware was physically large and extraordinarily expensive. These facts encouraged buyers to think of their computer systems as tools dedicated to some single, specific mission: whatever mission was large enough and concrete enough to justify the expense and inconvenience of the computer.

If a computer was a single-purpose tool—let's say, a saw—then the staff that maintained that computer were the operators of the saw. Early system operators were viewed more as "folks that cut lumber" than as "folks that provide what's necessary to build a house." The transition from system operator to system administrator did not start until computers began to be seen as multipurpose tools. The advent of time sharing was a major reason for this change in viewpoint.

John McCarthy had begun thinking about time sharing in the mid-1950s. But it was only at MIT (in 1961–62) that he, Jack Dennis, and Fernando Corbato talked seriously about permitting "each user of a computer to behave as though he were in sole control of a computer."

In 1964, MIT, General Electric, and Bell Labs embarked on a project to build an ambitious time-sharing system called Multics, the Multiplexed Information and Computing Service. Five years later, Multics was over budget and far behind schedule. Bell Labs pulled out of the project.

UNIX is born (1969–1973)

Bell Labs' abandonment of the Multics project left several researchers in Murray Hill, NJ, with nothing to work on. Three of them—Ken Thompson, Rudd Canaday, and Dennis Ritchie—had liked certain aspects of Multics but hadn't been happy with the size and the complexity of the system. They would gather in front of a whiteboard to discuss design philosophy. The Labs had Multics running on

1. Although SHARE was originally a vendor-sponsored organization, today it is independent.

its GE-645, and Thompson continued to work on it "just for fun." Doug McIlroy, the manager of the group, said, "When Multics began to work, the very first place it worked was here. Three people could overload it."

In the summer of 1969, Thompson became a temporary bachelor for a month when his wife, Bonnie, took their year-old son to meet his relatives on the west coast. Thompson recalled, "I allocated a week each to the operating system, the shell, the editor, and the assembler...it was totally rewritten in a form that looked like an operating system, with tools that were sort of known; you know, assembler, editor, shell—if not maintaining itself, right on the verge of maintaining itself, to totally sever the GECOS[2] connection...essentially one person for a month."

Steve Bourne, who joined Bell Labs the next year, described the cast-off PDP-7 used by Ritchie and Thompson: "The PDP-7 provided only an assembler and a loader. One user at a time could use the computer...The environment was crude, and parts of a single-user UNIX system were soon forthcoming...[The] assembler and rudimentary operating system kernel were written and cross-assembled for the PDP-7 on GECOS. The term UNICS was apparently coined by Peter Neumann, an inveterate punster, in 1970." The original UNIX was a single-user system, obviously an "emasculated Multics." But although there were aspects of UNICS/UNIX that were influenced by Multics, there were also, as Dennis Ritchie said, "profound differences."

"We were a bit oppressed by the big system mentality," he said. "Ken wanted to do something simple. Presumably, as important as anything was the fact that our means were much smaller. We could get only small machines with none of the fancy Multics hardware. So, UNIX wasn't quite a reaction against Multics...Multics wasn't there for us anymore, but we liked the feel of interactive computing that it offered. Ken had some ideas about how to do a system that he had to work out...Multics colored the UNIX approach, but it didn't dominate it."

Ken and Dennis's "toy" system didn't stay simple for long. By 1971, user commands included **as** (the assembler), **cal** (a simple calendar tool), **cat** (catenate and print), **chdir** (change working directory), **chmod** (change mode), **chown** (change owner), **cmp** (compare two files), **cp** (copy file), **date**, **dc** (desk calculator), **du** (summarize disk usage), **ed** (editor), and over two dozen others. Most of these commands are still in use.

By February 1973, there were 16 UNIX installations. Two big innovations had occurred. The first was a "new" programming language, C, based on B, which was itself a "cut-down" version of Martin Richards' BCPL (Basic Combined Programming Language). The other innovation was the idea of a pipe.

A pipe is a simple concept: a standardized way of connecting the output of one program to the input of another. The Dartmouth Time-Sharing System had communication files, which anticipated pipes, but their use was far more specific. The

2. GECOS was the General Electric Comprehensive Operating System.

notion of pipes as a general facility was Doug McIlroy's. The implementation was Ken Thompson's, at McIlroy's insistence. ("It was one of the only places where I very nearly exerted managerial control over UNIX," Doug said.)

"It's easy to say '**cat** into **grep** into…' or '**who** into **cat** into **grep**' and so on," McIlroy remarked. "It's easy to say and it was clear from the start that it would be something you'd like to say. But there are all these side parameters… And from time to time I'd say 'How about making something like this?' And one day I came up with a syntax for the shell that went along with piping, and Ken said 'I'm going to do it!'"

In an a orgy of rewriting, Thompson updated all the UNIX programs in one night. The next morning there were one-liners. This was the real beginning of the power of UNIX—not from the individual programs, but from the relationships among them. UNIX now had a language of its own as well as a philosophy:

- Write programs that do one thing and do it well.
- Write programs to work together.
- Write programs that handle text streams as a universal interface.

A general-purpose time-sharing OS had been born, but it was trapped inside Bell Labs. UNIX offered the promise of easily and seamlessly sharing computing resources among projects, groups, and organizations. But before this multipurpose tool could be used by the world, it had to escape and multiply. Katy bar the door!

UNIX HITS THE BIG TIME (1974–1990)

In October 1973, the ACM held its Symposium on Operating Systems Principles (SOSP) in the auditorium at IBM's new T.J. Watson Research Center in Yorktown Heights, NY. Ken and Dennis submitted a paper, and on a beautiful autumn day, drove up the Hudson Valley to deliver it. (Thompson made the actual presentation.) About 200 people were in the audience, and the talk was a smash hit.

Over the next six months, the number of UNIX installations tripled. When the paper was published in the July 1974 issue of the *Communications of the ACM*, the response was overwhelming. Research labs and universities saw shared UNIX systems as a potential solution to their growing need for computing resources.

According to the terms of a 1958 antitrust settlement, the activities of AT&T (parent of Bell Labs) were restricted to running the national telephone system and to special projects undertaken on behalf of the federal government. Thus, AT&T could not sell UNIX as a product and Bell Labs had to license its technology to others. In response to requests, Ken Thompson began shipping copies of the UNIX source code. According to legend, each package included a personal note signed "love, ken."

One person who received a tape from Ken was Professor Robert Fabry of the University of California at Berkeley. By January 1974, the seed of Berkeley UNIX had been planted.

Other computer scientists around the world also took an interest in UNIX. In 1976, John Lions (on the faculty of the University of New South Wales in Australia) published a detailed commentary on a version of the kernel called V6. This effort became the first serious documentation of the UNIX system and helped others to understand and expand upon Ken and Dennis's work.

Students at Berkeley enhanced the version of UNIX they had received from Bell Labs to meet their needs. The first Berkeley tape (1BSD, short for 1st Berkeley Software Distribution) included a Pascal system and the **vi** editor for the PDP-11. The student behind the release was a grad student named Bill Joy. 2BSD came the next year, and 3BSD, the first Berkeley release for the DEC VAX, was distributed in late 1979.

In 1980, Professor Fabry struck a deal with the Defense Advanced Research Project Agency (DARPA) to continue the development of UNIX. This arrangement led to the formation of the Computer Systems Research Group (CSRG) at Berkeley. Late the next year, 4BSD was released. It became quite popular, largely because it was the only version of UNIX that ran on the DEC VAX 11/750, the commodity computing platform of the time. Another big advancement of 4BSD was the introduction of TCP/IP sockets, the generalized networking abstraction that spawned the Internet and is now used by most modern operating systems. By the mid-1980s, most major universities and research institutions were running at least one UNIX system.

In 1982, Bill Joy took the 4.2BSD tape with him to start Sun Microsystems (now part of Oracle America) and the SunOS operating system. In 1983, the court-ordered divestiture of AT&T began. One unanticipated side effect of the divestiture was that AT&T was now free to begin selling UNIX as a product. They released AT&T UNIX System V, a well-recognized albeit somewhat awkward commercial implementation of UNIX.

Now that Berkeley, AT&T, Sun, and other UNIX distributions were available to a wide variety of organizations, the foundation was laid for a general computing infrastructure built on UNIX technology. The same system that was used by the astronomy department to calculate star distances could be used by the applied math department to calculate Mandelbrot sets. And that same system was simultaneously providing email to the entire university.

The rise of system administrators

The management of general-purpose computing systems demanded a different set of skills than those required just two decades earlier. Gone were the days of the system operator who focused on getting a single computer system to perform a specialized task. System administrators came into their own in the early 1980s as people who ran UNIX systems to meet the needs of a broad array of applications and users.

Because UNIX was popular at universities, and because those environments included lots of students who were eager to learn the latest technology, universities were early leaders in the development of organized system administration groups. Universities such as Purdue, the University of Utah, the University of Colorado, the University of Maryland, and the State University of New York (SUNY) Buffalo became hotbeds of system administration.

System administrators also developed an array of their own processes, standards, best practices, and tools (such as **sudo**). Most of these products were built out of necessity; without them, unstable systems and unhappy users were the result.

Evi Nemeth became known as the "mother of system administration" by recruiting undergraduates to work as system administrators to support the Engineering College at the University of Colorado. Her close ties with folks at Berkeley, the University of Utah, and SUNY Buffalo created a system administration community that shared tips and tools. Her crew, often called the "munchkins" or "Evi slaves" attended USENIX and other conferences and worked as on-site staff in exchange for the opportunity to absorb information at the conference.

It was clear early on that system administrators had to be rabid jacks of all trades. A system administrator might start a typical day in the 1980s by using a wire-wrap tool to fix an interrupt jumper on a VAX backplane. Mid-morning tasks might include sucking spilled toner out of a malfunctioning first-generation laser printer. Lunch hour could be spent helping a grad student debug a new kernel driver, and the afternoon might consist of writing backup tapes and hassling users to clean up their home directories to make space in the filesystem. A system administrator was, and is, a fix-everything, take-no-prisoners guardian angel.

The 1980s were also a time of unreliable hardware. Rather than living on a single silicon chip, the CPUs of the 1980s were made up of several hundred chips, all of them prone to failure. It was the system administrator's job to isolate failed hardware and get it replaced, quickly. Unfortunately, these were also the days before it was common to FedEx parts on a whim, so finding the right part from a local source was often a challenge.

In one case, our beloved VAX 11/780 was down, leaving the entire campus without email. We knew there was a business down the street that packaged VAXes to be shipped to the (then cold-war) Soviet Union "for research purposes." Desperate, we showed up at their warehouse with a huge wad of cash in our pocket, and after about an hour of negotiation, we escaped with the necessary board. At the time, someone remarked that it felt more comfortable to buy drugs than VAX parts in Boulder.

System administration documentation and training

As more individuals began to identify themselves as system administrators—and as it became clear that one might make a decent living as a sysadmin—requests for documentation and training became more common. In response, folks like Tim O'Reilly and his team (then called O'Reilly and Associates, now O'Reilly Media) began to publish UNIX documentation that was based on hands-on experience and written in a straightforward way.

See Chapter 32, Management, Policy, and Politics, for more pointers to sysadmin resources.

As a vehicle for in-person interaction, the USENIX Association held its first conference focused on system administration in 1987. This Large Installation System Administration (LISA) conference catered mostly to a west coast crowd. Three years later, the SANS (SysAdmin, Audit, Network, Security) Institute was established to meet the needs of the east coast. Today, both the LISA and SANS conferences serve the entire U.S. region, and both are still going strong.

In 1989, we published the first edition of this book, then titled *UNIX System Administration Handbook*. It was quickly embraced by the community, perhaps because of the lack of alternatives. At the time, UNIX was so unfamiliar to our publisher that their production department replaced all instances of the string "etc" with "and so on," resulting in filenames such as **/and so on/passwd**. We took advantage of the situation to seize total control of the bits from cover to cover, but the publisher is admittedly much more UNIX savvy today. Our 20-year relationship with this same publisher has yielded a few other good stories, but we'll omit them out of fear of souring our otherwise amicable relationship.

UNIX hugged to near death, Linux is born (1991–1995)

By late 1990, it seemed that UNIX was well on its way to world domination. It was unquestionably the operating system of choice for research and scientific computing, and it had been adopted by mainstream businesses such as Taco Bell and McDonald's. Berkeley's CSRG group, then consisting of Kirk McKusick, Mike Karels, Keith Bostic, and many others, had just released 4.3BSD-Reno, a pun on an earlier 4.3 release that added support for the CCI Power 6/32 (code named "Tahoe") processor.

Commercial releases of UNIX such as SunOS were also thriving, their success driven in part by the advent of the Internet and the first glimmers of e-commerce. PC hardware had become a commodity. It was reasonably reliable, inexpensive, and relatively high-performance. Although versions of UNIX that ran on PCs did exist, all the good options were commercial and closed source. The field was ripe for an open source PC UNIX.

In 1991, a group of developers that had worked together on the BSD releases (Donn Seeley, Mike Karels, Bill Jolitz, and Trent R. Hein), together with a few other BSD advocates, founded Berkeley Software Design, Inc. (BSDI). Under the leadership of Rob Kolstad, BSDI provided binaries and source code for a fully functional commercial version of BSD UNIX on the PC platform. Among other things, this project proved that inexpensive PC hardware could be used for production computing. BSDI fueled explosive growth in the early Internet as it became the operating system of choice for early Internet service providers (ISPs).

In an effort to recapture the genie that had escaped from its bottle in 1973, AT&T filed a lawsuit against BSDI and the Regents of the University of California in 1992, alleging code copying and theft of trade secrets. It took AT&T's lawyers over two years to identify the offending code. When all was said and done, the lawsuit was settled and three files (out of more than 18,000) were removed from the BSD code base.

Unfortunately, this two-year period of uncertainty had a devastating effect on the entire UNIX world, BSD and non-BSD versions alike. Many companies jumped ship to Microsoft Windows, fearful that they would end up at the mercy of AT&T as it hugged its child to near-death. By the time the dust cleared, BSDI and the CSRG were both mortally wounded. The BSD era was coming to an end.

Meanwhile, Linus Torvalds, a Helsinki college student, had been playing with Minix and began writing his own UNIX clone.[3] By 1992, a variety of Linux distributions (including SuSE and Yggdrasil Linux) had emerged. 1994 saw the establishment of Red Hat and Linux Pro.

Multiple factors have contributed to the phenomenal success of Linux. The strong community support enjoyed by the system and its vast catalog of software from the GNU archive make Linux quite a powerhouse. It works well in production environments, and some folks argue that you can build a more reliable and performant system on top of Linux than you can on top of any other operating system. It's also interesting to consider that part of Linux's success may relate to the golden opportunity created for it by AT&T's action against BSDI and Berkeley. That ill-timed lawsuit struck fear into the hearts of UNIX advocates right at the dawn of e-commerce and the start of the Internet bubble.

But who cares, right? What remained constant through all these crazy changes was the need for system administrators. A UNIX system administrator's skill set is directly applicable to Linux, and most system administrators guided their users gracefully through the turbulent seas of the 1990s. That's another important characteristic of a good system administrator: calm during a storm.

A world of Windows (1996–1999)

Microsoft first released Windows NT in 1993. The release of a "server" version of Windows, which had a popular user interface, generated considerable excitement just as AT&T was busy convincing the world that it might be out to fleece everyone for license fees. As a result, many organizations adopted Windows as their

3. Minix is a PC-based UNIX clone developed by Andrew S. Tanenbaum, a professor at the Free University in Amsterdam.

preferred platform for shared computing during the late 1990s. Without question, the Microsoft platform has come a long way, and for some organizations it *is* the best option.

Unfortunately, UNIX, Linux, and Windows administrators initially approached this marketplace competition in an adversarial stance. "Less filling" vs. "tastes great" arguments erupted in organizations around the world.[4] Many UNIX and Linux system administrators started learning Windows, convinced they'd be put out to pasture if they didn't. After all, Windows 2000 was on the horizon. By the close of the millennium, the future of UNIX looked grim.

UNIX and Linux thrive (2000–present)

As the Internet bubble burst, everyone scrambled to identify what was real and what had been only a venture-capital-fueled mirage. As the smoke drifted away, it became clear that many organizations with successful technology strategies were using UNIX or Linux *along with* Windows rather than one or the other. It wasn't a war anymore.

UNIX and Linux system administrators who had augmented their skills with Windows became even more valuable. They were able to bridge the gap between the two worlds and leverage both for the benefit of the organization. A number of evaluations showed that the total cost of ownership (TCO) of a Linux server was significantly lower than that of a Windows server, a metric that matters in rough economic times.

Today, UNIX and Linux are thriving. Commercial variants of UNIX, including AIX, Solaris, and HP-UX, have continued to meet the needs of their respective markets. Linux and PC-based UNIX variants have continued to expand their market share, with Linux being the only operating system whose market share on servers is growing at the time of this writing (spring 2010). Not to be left out, Apple's current operating system, Mac OS X, is also based on UNIX.[5]

Much of the recent growth in UNIX and Linux has occurred in the domain of virtualized and cloud computing. (See Chapter 24, *Virtualization*, for more information about these technologies.) Once again, these environments all share one thing in common: systems administrators. Your skills as a system administrator apply whether the box is physical or virtual!

UNIX and Linux tomorrow

No matter what developments await UNIX and Linux over the next few years, one thing is certain: UNIX and Linux need you! System administrators hold the

4. Just for the record, Windows is indeed less filling.
5. Even Apple's iPhone runs a stripped-down cousin of UNIX, and Google's Android operating system includes abstractions from the Linux kernel.

world's computing infrastructure together, solve the hairy problems of efficiency and scalability, and provide expert technology advice to users and managers alike.

We are system administrators. Hear us roar!

Recommended reading

McKusick, Marshall Kirk, Keith Bostic, Michael J. Karels, and John S. Quarterman. *The Design and Implementation of the 4.4BSD Operating System (2nd Edition).* Reading, MA: Addison-Wesley, 1996.

Salus, Peter H. *A Quarter Century of UNIX.* Reading, MA: Addison-Wesley, 1994.

Salus, Peter H. *Casting the Net: From ARPANET to Internet and Beyond.* Reading, MA: Addison-Wesley, 1995.

Salus, Peter H. *The Daemon, the Gnu, and the Penguin.* Marysville, WA: Reed Media Services, 2008. This book was also serialized at www.groklaw.net.

In Defense of AIX

A dialog with Dan Foster

AIX has been around since the 1980s, but this edition is the first to include it as an example system. We considered adding AIX to several previous editions, but always judged it to be too different from other versions of UNIX—and perhaps a bit too peculiar—to fit comfortably alongside them.

We wanted to welcome AIX with open arms. Nevertheless, careful readers may notice a certain consistency of tone regarding AIX, a tone that is not altogether laudatory. Like an unhousebroken puppy, AIX always seems to be doing something wrong and never quite understanding why everyone seems so upset.

We feel bad; who likes to yell at a puppy? To help balance the scales, we asked Dan Foster, one of our technical reviewers from the AIX world, to weigh in on AIX's good side. Herewith, our indictment against AIX, and Dan's response.

Our wild accusations

AIX is an IBM mainframe operating system of the 1970s that is cruelly trapped in the body of a UNIX system. Although the UNIX plumbing keeps the system running, AIX has no particular interest in being UNIX or in following UNIX conventions. It employs a variety of hairpieces, corsets, and makeup kits to project an image more consistent with IBM's taste. It's an open, modular system that longs to be closed and monolithic.

Those who approach AIX as UNIX will discover a series of impediments. AIX does not really trust administrators to understand what they are doing or to directly modify the system. Instead of simplicity, modularity, and flexibility, AIX offers structure. Considerable engineering effort has been spent to catalog administrative operations and to collect them into the System Management Interface Tool (SMIT). If what you need isn't in the catalog...well, don't you worry your pretty little head about that.

Unfortunately, SMIT isn't AIX's only added layer of indirection. SMIT operations map to shell commands, so every SMIT operation requires a dedicated command that implements it in one step. Hence, the rich profusion of command families (such as **crfs/chfs/rmfs**) that implement predefined recipes. These commands add complexity and overhead without creating much value; other UNIX systems do just fine without them.

Because administrative operations are mediated through software, AIX sees no need to store information in text files. Instead, it's squirreled away in a variety of binary formats and logs, most notably the Object Data Manager. Sysadmins can use generic ODM commands to inspect and modify this data, but that's something of a black art, and it's generally discouraged. Overall, the ODM is a dark and mysterious continent with many backwaters, much like the Windows registry.

If one persists in cutting away at AIX's carapace, one does eventually discover a sad little UNIX homunculus lying contorted therein. But it's not a healthy creature; it's wrinkled with age, its skin pale from lack of exposure to the outside world and to the last few decades of UNIX advancements. Clearly, IBM considers the real action to be somewhere other than the UNIX mainstream.

Dan Foster's case for the defense

Ouch! You don't paint a very charitable picture. However, I think it's fair to characterize many of your objections as "not invented here" syndrome; in other words, as resistance to anything that doesn't toe the standard UNIX line.

There's some validity to your general point that AIX aspires to be more than just another UNIX clone. That's not necessarily bad. AIX is not for cowboys. It's designed to facilitate reliability, consistency, and ease of administration. It has different goals from other UNIX systems, so it looks and feels a bit different, too.

AIX draws a variety of useful tools from IBM's mainframe and AS/400 systems. For example, it uses a centralized error logging facility that applications can easily hook into through an API. That system facilitates error reporting, administrator notification, and problem diagnosis. Syslog tries to implement some of these features for UNIX generally, but as this book's many sections on logging show, it's not consistently used. (Years later, Sun adopted a similar approach with the fault management daemon, **fmd**, in Solaris 10.)

Another case in point is hardware management. AIX gives you centralized diagnostic tools for just about any supported device. It even logs repair actions (which, in some cases, can disable fault LEDs and generate issue-resolution notifications), thus providing an audit trail. The system is easy to extend through callback hooks, but it doesn't leave you on your own as most versions of UNIX do.

To address one of your specific complaints, task-specific commands are a feature, not a bug! They benefit administrators in several ways.

- As even your own example shows, AIX command sets are named clearly and consistently. That can't be said of UNIX generally. **mk*** commands create entities, **rm*** commands remove them, **ch*** commands modify them, and **ls*** commands show you the current state. These structured command families yield predictable results and reduce the time needed for training. They make it less likely that you'll use the wrong command during a 2:00 a.m. emergency while you're bleary-eyed and new to AIX. (SMIT menus help here too, of course.)

- Commands can validate their arguments; configuration files cannot. A wrapper command can ensure that a proposed change won't break the system. If it would, the command can complain or refuse to make the change. That's much nicer than discovering problems the hard way when things break randomly after a configuration file change.
- Task-specific commands facilitate scripting. Not only do they combine functions and validate arguments, but they also relieve scripts of the need to parse and manage complex configuration files. That makes scripts shorter, more reliable, and easier to maintain (and teach!). Think of these commands as a high-level administration library that's built into the operating system and that works with every scripting language.
- The provision of a defined administrative interface reduces dependencies on particular file formats or implementations. It frees IBM to change its back ends and to introduce new technologies without breaking legacy scripts. For example, the ODM currently stores its data in Berkeley DB files. However, IBM could easily change the ODM to use LDAP or some other future technology while keeping the ODM commands and user interface the same.

And don't be a SMIT-hater! SMIT is a flexible system that implements a variety of interfaces (X11, web page, command-line client). That flexibility means you can use the same general interface whether you're sitting at a desktop machine or working from home late at night.

SMIT simplifies complex procedures and gets novice administrators up to speed quickly. It's been used and maintained for many years and has undergone a variety of user interface studies aimed at improving it. It's easy to use regardless of your familiarity with UNIX in general or AIX in particular. And it's a great learning tool, even for experienced administrators. You can fill out a SMIT form with your desired values and have SMIT show you the exact command it would run to implement your request. There's nothing like this on any other system, and it's great.

As for AIX not "really" being UNIX, that simply isn't true. AIX was originally based on BSD, and some vestiges of that era (such as AIX's use of mbufs in its networking stack) remain even in today's systems. Later editions were refocused on the System V base. AIX has been certified as conforming to the Single Unix Specification (SUS), X/Open, and POSIX standards. IBM has also exploited UNIX's legendary portability to bring AIX to systems ranging from PS/2 PCs to mainframes. The Deep Blue system (an IBM HPC supercomputing cluster) that beat chess grand master and world champion Garry Kasparov in widely publicized human-vs.-computer chess matches in 1996 and 1997 ran AIX!

Colophon

This book was for the most part written and produced on Windows systems. We used Adobe FrameMaker for layout and a variety of other Adobe applications for illustrations and production. Some contributors ran FrameMaker under Wine on Linux systems (see page 1139). One author ran FrameMaker on a virtualized Windows system under Mac OS X. (See tinyurl.com/vmwrite for details.) These virtualized environments worked well.

Lisa Haney drew the interior cartoons with a 0.05mm Staedtler pigment liner, then scanned them and converted them to 1200dpi bitmaps. The cover artwork was executed on black Ampersand Clayboard (a scratchboard) with Dr. Martin's Dyes for color. After scanning, the cover art was color-corrected in Photoshop and the layout completed in Adobe Illustrator.

The body text is Minion Pro, designed by Robert Slimbach. Headings, tables, and illustrations are set in Myriad Pro SemiCondensed by Robert Slimbach and Carol Twombly, with Fred Brady and Christopher Slye.

For "code" samples, we have long sought a fixed-width font that looks similar to Courier but that lacks Courier's many typesetting problems. Our search remains fruitless. In this book, we use Peter Matthias Noordzij's proportional-width PMN Caecilia and line up columns manually with tabs. Unfortunately, Caecilia is missing some characters needed for technical typesetting, and its italic version is noticeably slimmer than its roman.

This edition marks the first time that the authors have all worked on a shared tree of source files. In the past, the sticking point has been FrameMaker's binary file format, which makes it impossible to merge multiple sets of revisions. For this edition, we used an unholy combination of Subversion (page 399), TortoiseSVN (page 401), Miramo's free DZbatcher utility (datazone.com), and home-grown Perl scripts to keep the authoritative documents in FrameMaker's second-class MIF format, an XML-like alternative. This scheme sort of works, but it requires that everyone use the same version of FrameMaker and that at least one team member have a working knowledge of MIF.

About the Contributors

Terry Morreale is a senior engineer and director of client services at Applied Trust. She holds a degree in Computer Science from the University of Colorado as well as the following industry certifications: CISSP, GIAC Gold Certified Incident Handler, and ITILv3 Foundations. When she's not working, Terry can be found reading, running, hanging with her two kids, or enjoying a glass of red wine.

Ned McClain is co-founder and CTO of Applied Trust, where he helps clients of all sizes with architecture and operations. His work focuses on performance, availability, and security, but a special place in his heart is reserved for system administration. Ned has a degree in Computer Science from Cornell University's College of Engineering and carries CISSP, MCP, and ITIL certifications. Ned blogs regularly at barkingseal.com.

Ron Jachim received an MS from Wayne State University in Detroit, Michigan, where he now serves as an adjunct professor. He leverages his 20 years of real-world UNIX experience both while teaching and at his position with Ford Motor Company. He combines management skills with technical passion to architect resilient infrastructure solutions involving thousands of servers and to improve the performance of global applications.

David Schweikert is a product manager at Open Systems AG, a managed security services provider in Switzerland. His team is responsible for the configuration management and monitoring of more than 1,500 UNIX servers in over 100 countries. David is the developer of Mailgraph (a tool that plots mail statistics) and Postgrey (a greylisting implementation for Postfix). See david.schweikert.ch.

Tobi Oetiker is an engineer by education and a system administrator by vocation. For ten years he worked for the Swiss Federal Institute of Technology, where he spoiled students and staff with a deluxe UNIX environment. Since 2006, he has worked for his own company, OETIKER+PARTNER AG, where he manages UNIX servers for industry customers, improves his pet open source projects (MRTG™, RRDtool, and SmokePing) and applies these tools to solve customers' problems. In November 2006, Tobi received the prestigious SAGE Outstanding Achievement Award for his work on MRTG and RRDtool. See tobi.oetiker.ch.

About the Authors

For general comments and bug reports, please contact ulsah@book.admin.com. Because of the volume of email that this alias receives, we regret that we are unable to answer technical questions.

Evi Nemeth (sailingevi@gmail.com) has retired from the Computer Science faculty at the University of Colorado. She is currently exploring the Pacific on her 40-foot sailboat named *Wonderland*. This is her *last* edition—it's impossible to keep up with the latest sysadmin toys when anchored in paradise with a 30 baud packet radio email connection.

Garth Snyder (garth@garthsnyder.com) has worked at NeXT and Sun and holds a BS in Engineering from Swarthmore College and an MD and an MBA from the University of Rochester.

Trent R. Hein (trent@atrust.com) is the co-founder of Applied Trust, a company that provides IT infrastructure consulting services. Trent holds a BS in Computer Science from the University of Colorado.

Ben Whaley (ben@atrust.com) is the Director of Enterprise Architecture at Applied Trust, an IT consulting company based in Boulder, Colorado. Ben earned a BS in Computer Science from the University of Colorado in 2004.

About the Authors

SERVER INFORMATION

Cut out and tape to individual server machines. See admin.com for a PDF version of this form.

Basics

FQDN ....

Owner ....

Owner contact info ....

Primary function ....

Critical services ....

Hardware

Hardware model ....

Memory ....

CPU type ....

Local disk configuration ....

Purchase date ....

End-of-life date ....

Inventory control ID ....

Software

Operating system ....

Build image ....

Update schedule / strategy ....

Major add-on packages ....

Disaster recovery

Root password location ....

Backup system / server ....

Nagios coverage ....

SERVER INFORMATION

Cut out and tape to individual server machines. See admin.com for a PDF version of this form.

Basics

FQDN ____________

Owner ____________

Owner contact info ____________

Primary function ____________

Critical services ____________

Hardware

Hardware model ____________

Memory ____________

CPU type ____________

Local disk configuration ____________

Purchase date ____________

End-of-life date ____________

Inventory control ID ____________

Software

Operating system ____________

Build image ____________

Update schedule / strategy ____________

Major add-on packages ____________

Disaster recovery

Root password location ____________

Backup system / server ____________

Nagios coverage ____________

SERVER INFORMATION

Cut out and tape to individual server machines. See admin.com for a PDF version of this form.

Basics

FQDN	
Owner	
Owner contact info	
Primary function	
Critical services	

Hardware

Hardware model	
Memory	
CPU type	
Local disk configuration	
Purchase date	
End-of-life date	
Inventory control ID	

Software

Operating system	
Build image	
Update schedule / strategy	
Major add-on packages	

Disaster recovery

Root password location	
Backup system / server	
Nagios coverage	

SERVER INFORMATION

Cut out and tape to individual server machines. See admin.com for a PDF version of this form.

Basics

FQDN ....

Owner ....

Owner contact info ....

Primary function ....

Critical services ....

Hardware

Hardware model ....

Memory ....

CPU type ....

Local disk configuration ....

Purchase date ....

End-of-life date ....

Inventory control ID ....

Software

Operating system ....

Build image ....

Update schedule / strategy ....

Major add-on packages ....

Disaster recovery

Root password location ....

Backup system / server ....

Nagios coverage ....

SERVER INFORMATION

Cut out and tape to individual server machines. See admin.com for a PDF version of this form.

Basics

FQDN ....

Owner ....

Owner contact info ....

Primary function ....

Critical services ....

Hardware

Hardware model ....

Memory ....

CPU type ....

Local disk configuration ....

Purchase date ....

End-of-life date ....

Inventory control ID ....

Software

Operating system ....

Build image ....

Update schedule / strategy ....

Major add-on packages ....

Disaster recovery

Root password location ....

Backup system / server ....

Nagios coverage ....

Notes

Notes